PRINCIPLES OF
POLITICAL SCIENCE

Dr. ANUP CHAND KAPUR
M.A., Ph.D.

S. CHAND
PUBLISHING

S Chand And Company Limited
(ISO 9001 Certified Company)

S Chand And Company Limited
(ISO 9001 Certified Company)
Head Office: D-92, Sector–2, Noida – 201301, U.P. (India), Ph. 91-120-4682700
Registered Office: A-27, 2nd Floor, Mohan Co-operative Industrial Estate, New Delhi – 110 044, Phone: 011-49731800
www.**schandpublishing.com**; e-mail: **info@schandpublishing.com**

Marketing Offices:

Chennai : Ph: 23632120; chennai@schandpublishing.com
Guwahati : Ph: 2738811, 2735640; guwahati@schandpublishing.com
Hyderabad : Ph: 40186018; hyderabad@schandpublishing.com
Jalandhar : Ph: 4645630; jalandhar@schandpublishing.com
Kolkata : Ph: 23357458, 23353914; kolkata@schandpublishing.com
Lucknow : Ph: 4003633; lucknow@schandpublishing.com
Mumbai : Ph: 25000297; mumbai@schandpublishing.com
Patna : Ph: 4011400; patna@schandpublishing.com

First Edition 1950
Twentieth Edition 1996
Subsequent Editions and Reprints 1997, 99, 2000, 2001, 2002, 2003, 2004, 2005, 2006 (Twice), 2007, 2008, 2009
Revised and Enlarged Edition 2010; Reprints 2018, 2019, 2020, 2021 (Thrice)

Low Priced Students' Paperback Edition (LPSPE), 2022
Reprint 2022 (Thrice), 2025 (Twice)
Reprint 2026

ISBN: 978-93-550-1051-3 **Product Code:** H5POL41PLSC10ENAA21L

PRINTED IN INDIA
By Shri Shyamlal Printing Press Private Limited, Plot 20/4, Site-IV, Industrial Area Sahibabad, Ghaziabad – 201 010 and Published by S Chand And Company Limited, A-27, 2nd Floor, Mohan Co-operative Industrial Estate, New Delhi – 110 044.

PREFACE TO THE 21ST REVISED EDITION

The Twenty-first Edition of this book received as wide reception and within a short span of just about two years there was a rapid succession of reprints which necessitated to bring out a fresh edition consolidating the entire text and give it a logical shape.

I am grateful to the learned teachers, at all levels, for their wide patronage in recommending the book to their students. I am equally grateful to my Publishers for their cooperation.

GOKAL NIWAS **Dr. Anup Chand Kapur**
Turner Road, Clement Town
Dehradun-248002

PREFACE TO THE FIRST EDITION

There are some admirable textbooks on Political Science, yet I have ventured to bring out another volume on the subject. India having become a Sovereign and Independent Republic, the Independent Republic, the study of Political Science has acquired an added importance for all of us, particularly for students. Our students must be familiar with the complexity of the national and international problems, and must also cultivate a scientific and unbiased approach to all such problems. Students of today are the statement and administrators of tomorrow and they will have to use their best talents for making India a great nation.

In writing this book I do not claim any originality. My aim throughout has been to give students an easily intelligible exposition of the origin of the State and forms and types of government, and I have taken special pains to present impartially the different aspects of every question. I have illustrated the text, wherever necessary, with the actual working of the political institutions in different countries of the world, with special emphasis on Indian Administration—past and present—embracing, too, the provisions of the Draft Constitution of India. While doing so I have not been oblivious of the fact that the book is primarily intended to cater to the needs of the students offering Political Science as one of their electrify subjects for the degree examination of Indian universities. The course covered, however, is substantially that prescribed by the Punjab University from 1950.

I have tried to consult the best available sources of information in respect of the various subjects dealt within the book. I take this opportunity to acknowledge my indebtedness to the great masters from whom I have borrowed so profusely. I also express my respectful feelings of gratitude to my teachers, Principal G.D. Sondhi, I.E.S. (Retd.), Dr. C.J. Chacko, now Principal, Saint Andrew's College, Gorakhpur, Dr. J.N. Khosala, sometime Head of the Department of Political Science, Punjab University, now a member of the Indian Foreign Service, and Principal Sri Ram Sharma, D.A.V. College, Shoplapur, who inspired me with zeal for the study of Political Science, and always gave me their unflinching support, guidance and encouragement. My grateful thanks are due to Professor Dinanath Kak of my college for his indefatigable and ungrudging assistance in reading the manuscript of the book and for offering many valuable suggestions. In fact, the book owes many improvements in expression to him.

My wife, as in case of almost everything which I have ever published, has helped me in reading the proofs.

KAPURTHALA **Author**

April 15, 1950

CONTENTS

PART–I
THE NATURE AND ORIGIN OF THE STATE

PART–II
THE ORGANISATION OF THE STATE

PART–III

THE FUNCTIONS OF THE STATE

PART-I

The Nature and Origin of the State

1 CHAPTER

Nature and Scope of Political Science

Nature of Political Science. Aristotle tells us a simple truth when he says, "He who is unable to live in society, or who has no need because he is sufficient for himself, must be either a beast or god." It means that man is a social animal. He is born in society and lives in society. This is obviously for two reasons. Man is a very gregarious animal. He is easily affected by sympathy and the desire for sympathy. He prefers company to solitude. He admires and imitates others, and he likes to be admired and imitated. These social impulses aside, necessity also compels man to live a social life. No man is self-sufficient, and nature has not created one. His needs are many and purposes numerous. For the satisfaction of his diverse needs and the fulfilment of his various purposes, he must associate with his fellows and seek their cooperation. Such is the testimony of history. Here and there an individual or a family has subsisted apart from the rest of the human race, but that is an exception rather than a rule. The general rule is that men live, and always have lived, in social groups.

If man is social by nature, he is selfish and quarrelsome too. This aspect of the nature of man, and the instinct of living together and cooperating with one another require adjustment of behaviour according to some accepted rules. These rules prescribe a course of conduct based upon men's need for one another. The first and the most important rule of social conduct is: "To do unto others as you would have others do unto you." It means, that I should provide for others the same conditions of life as I wish for myself. If I wish to grow and prosper, I owe it to others that they, too, should have the same conditions of life as I wish for myself. When I allow others what I wish for myself, I recognise my obligations to others, while establishing my claims on others. Realization of this fact is a way of regulating human conduct. But all conduct in society must conform to certain set rules of common behaviour. The rules governing a society may be few or many. They can range from a few primitive traditions, handed down orally, from one generation to another, or to the whole complex set of constitutional and governmental regulations which we associate with the modern State.

A prerequisite of such a society is that it must be properly organised. An unorganised society is more a mob than a society and the mob is subject to no restraint. An organised society must also be territorially settled. People do not develop a community of interests unless they live a settled life occupying a definite territory distinct from other communities similarly organised. Mutual adjustment and cooperation, a life to share common weal and woe, is the *sine qua non* of a common life on a common land. Then, an organised society requires the presence of some individuals to enforce rules of universal application for uniform behaviour and ensure their observance. In the absence of such an agency, there is neither cohesion nor unity of purposes for which men had organised themselves and settled down territorially.

The society, thus organised, is called the *State*, rules which determine social conduct are the *laws* of the *State* and the individuals who enforce the laws and see that they are equally observed by all constitute its *government*. The subject that deals with man in relation to the State and its government is called *Political Science*. Political Science may be defined, in its simplest form, as the study of man in the process of governing himself.

Is man a political animal ? An elementary starting point for all political theory, therefore, is the existential fact that members of the human species live together, whatever may be the elements of instinct, habit, necessity or choice that induce people to form societies. If man is a social animal, is he then necessarily a political animal? Aristotle said he is, and it has remained a generally accepted truth until recently. But opinion now veers round the belief that man is neither instinctively nor by learning necessarily a political animal. Adherents of this point of view, who are now many, particularly in the United States of America, admit that few people ever live outside the State. They also admit that the advantages of living together far outweigh the disadvantages. "Nonetheless, though human beings must and do live in political systems and share the benefits of political life, they do not necessarily participate in political life; they are not necessarily interested in politics, nor do they always care what happens in politics; nor know much about political events, or share in making decisions."[1] In fact, in most States "the political stratum is a minority of the adult population. Moreover, those who are highly interested, concerned, informed, and active are an even smaller minority, within the political stratum."[2] Political systems, they argue, are developed simply because human beings are social and as they cannot live together without entering into relationships of influence, consequently, "Whenever these relationships become stable and repetitive, political systems exist."[3]

But this is exactly not so. The practice of politics is necessarily as old as society itself. It is born when men began to speculate about the rules of conduct by which they should be governed and matured with the succeeding generations when they began to ask whether these rules by which their ancestors were governed ought to be accepted, or ought to have been accepted in the past, why some societies choose different rules from others, whether it is possible to discover general rules of conduct which could or should be applicable to all societies. In answering these questions they go into the basic questions of purposes for which human societies exist and their relation to the purposes of human life itself. It is obviously a quest for a just and happy life for men assembled together in a territorially integrated society and, as such, the best form of relationship manifested in their governance that can ensure such a life. This quest has been incessantly going on

1. Dahl, Robert A., *Modern Political Analysis*, pp. 59-60.
2. *Ibid*, p. 60.
3. *Ibid*, p. 56.

for centuries together without reaching agreed conclusions. Nor is there any likelihood that men will ever do so, for human civilisations are forever changing and so do change their values. What seems true, and even self-evident for one generation or one civilisation is frequently rejected by the succeeding generations. "Each generation," explains Dorothy Pickles, "as it becomes adult is faced with the responsibility of deciding whether to accept the rules made or accepted by earlier generations, or whether to challenge their validity and try to replace them by others."[4]

It does not, however, mean that all men are equally concerned with the political life of society to which they belong. Some peoples are indifferent to politics, others deplore them. But quite a many play the game of politics. Even the ordinary citizen, making up his mind whether to vote for A or B, may be invisibly trying to answer a sort of question which Plato and Aristotle had tried to answer over 2,000 years ago, namely, what is the best form of government? He may not be thinking in terms of vital issues involved in such a question. He may be simply trying to decide whether A or B is more likely to further his personal or professional interests. Even so, he is one of thousands of his fellow citizens who is incessantly helping to formulate an answer of some kind to the question: what is the best form of government for me ? And the multitude of different answers given by him and his fellow citizens go to form the way in which government in a particular country develops. It is the wisdom of generations that goes to make the political apparatus of a country and its culture.

The impact which one individual citizen makes on his own or the succeeding generations may be very small, but some critics of the existing social order "have so touched the minds or hearts of their fellow citizens or citizens of other times or other countries that they have helped to bring about great changes in the organisation of government".[5] Plato and Aristotle still exercise profound influences on the thought of Western Europe and Rousseau and Marx are the *beau ideal* of millions of people beyond the frontiers of their own countries. Locke's teachings had a deep impact on the Americans and the French, the former seeking to justify their struggle for independence and freedom from foreign rule and the latter seeking to justify man's right to revolt against the arbitrary rule, which had plagued these countries for centuries together. Gandhi dedicated himself to uplift man and society simultaneously. He was out to moralise man and society and in his attempt to realise a better ordering of society, he devised a new moral strategy; the method of regulating along non-violent lines group life in its political, economic and international aspects. By his twin principles of truth and non-violence, Gandhi revolutionised the course of politics and the present-day world standing on the brink of an abysmal cataclysm does find solace in the Gandhian outlook and his peaceful techinque. Gandhi's teachings are more relevant today than they were in his lifetime and this fact has been universally admitted.

Scope of Political Science. There is no general agreement on the nature and scope of Political Science, "the master science" as Aristotle described it, since there is no generally accepted definition of the discipline, and its organising concept the State. The

4. Pickles, Dorothy M., *Introduction to Politics*, pp. 15-16.
5. *Ibid.*

definitions of both Political Science and the State, the latter in particular, reveal the bias of the thinkers, for example, the metaphysical (Hegel), the juridical (Austin), the sociological (MacIver), the descriptive (Garner) and many others with their own distinctive labels. In fact, there are as many definitions as there are writers on the subject and all these definitions give to the entity — the State — different meanings and conflicting roles. This tendency continues even now though in a slightly different form. "The recent definitions of politics (as a study)," writes Frank Thakurdas, "are not so much cast in the discipline of the thinker (easily detectable) but in the conceptual framework that he has worked out in advance (as it were) the basic presupposition of his personal manner of interpreting the complete phenomenon of politics. But also including the 'purpose' that the studies involve in terms of the practical ends they subserve."[6]

Some writers restrict the scope of Political Science to the study of the State alone, for example, Bluntschli. All such writers exclude the study of government from the scope of Political Science, for the State for them obviously includes the study of government. There are others who hold that Political Science deals only with government. Karl W. Deutsch says, "Because Politics, the making of decisions by public means, it is primarily concerned with government, that is, with the direction and self-direction of large communities of the people."[7] According to Robson, "The purpose of political science is to throw light on political ideas and political action so that the government of man may be improved." Harold Laski takes a more realistic view and emphasises that the scope of Political Science embraces the study of both the State and government, although he maintains that the State in reality means the government.

Government is the helmsman[8] of the ship of the State. There can be no State without government. The State is a people organised for law within a definite territory. This entity, the soveriegn political unity of life, orders and compels obedience by punishing those who violate its commands. But no State acts by itself. There must be present in every State some men or body of men competent to issue orders on its behalf and to see that they are actually obeyed. That is the government. This is, however, the conventional field of functions of the government. The modern government has emerged as an active and positive agent in the direction of affairs of all communities. In the older democracies, and still more in the newer developing States as well as in the Communist countries, government is looked on as a major, or even the dominant, organising power in society. A description of the State must, therefore, include the study of the structure and functions of government, its forms and institutions, modes of representation, interaction of political parties, interest groups, mass media of communication, relationships involving rule, authority and power and most important of all, the problems connected with the emergence of a big and active government both in the national and international fields.

---

6. "The Expanding Frontier of Political Science", *The Indian Journal of Political Science,* October-December 1973, p. 404.
7. Deutsch, Karl W., *Politics and Government*, p. 5.
8. Webster's Third International Dictionary notes that the word "govern" comes from the old French word *governer* which is from the Latin *gubernare* (to steer, pilot, govern), which in turn is from the Greek *kybernam.* The Greek word for the steersman or the helmsman of a ship is *keybernetes.*

The State, all the same, remains the central subject of the study of Political Science as the whole mechanism of government emerges from and revolves around this entity. The need for government arises because there had been and there is need for the State. The need for the State is deeply embedded in the compelling necessities of human life and the advantages accruing from dwelling together on a defined territory and sharing the benefits of political life. Without the State, life itself cannot be sustained. But this is not the only object of the political life. The State comes into existence, as Aristotle said, "originating in the bare needs of the life of man and continuing in existence for the sake of good life". Whether man is a political animal or not, it remains an unchallengeable fact that man cannot be what he desires to be without the State. It is premature to accept the recent system theory, domestic and international, with all its innovations. So long as the State remains a matter of reality in practical politics and its citizens are required to preserve its sovereignty and integrity, and the unquestioned respect for the symbols of its distinctness, like the national flag and the national anthem, is instilled in them from their very childhood, it is an indispensable institution for the existence of its nationals and their development.

When the State plays such a vital role in the lite of man, it becomes all the more important to know it in all its aspects: what the State has been, what it is, and what it ought to be. The State, as it is, refers to its existing structure and the analysis of the principles and practices of modern governments. But what the State is can only be understood by knowing what it had been. As we have seen, the way in which government in a country develops is the wisdom of generations. This involves the study of the origin of the State, its evolution, and the development of the mechanism through which it functions.

But knowledge of the past and the present of the State does not exhaust the scope of Political Science. We must also try to gather how far the existing structure of the State and its institutions respond to the needs of man and determine his well-being. This had been the unceasing quest of generations all through these centuries and it continues to exist with a never-ending zeal. This quest reinforces the need for a deep knowledge of the past and its comparison with the present. The process involved makes us wiser for the future as it sharpens our intellect to reform the existing institutions so that they may adequately cater to the aspirations of the generations to come. It means to discover the principles that should be adhered to in operating the machinery of the State, to criticise what is bad or inefficient and to suggest improvements so that the State may serve its purpose meaningfully. It is the dream for the ideal for the fulfilment of which all people have always yearned and striven, though what an ideal life is and how it can be achieved is a subject of controversy. All this relates to the study of the State as it ought to be. Here Political Science enters the realm of political ethics and studies the moral problems of mankind in order to establish the principles of collective morality. We consider and evaluate the purposes and ends of the State and the fundamental topics involved in such a study are: the ethical foundations of authority; the nature and limits of political obligation; the rights and freedoms of the individuals, groups and nations; and an examination of the entire body-politic from the point of view of the ultimate ends of human life. The approach may be speculative or analytical, or in the case of Plato, a combination of both.

In the last four decades or so there has been an upheaval, "intellectual revolution" as it is described, in the thoughts and ideas of American political scientists and the innovations they have introduced have greatly influenced the nature and subject matter of our study. The approach to the traditional theory of Political Science, as they call it, is criticised on grounds of parochialism and formalism. The focus of study in the past, it is explained, tended to be primarily on institutions and their legal norms, rules and regulations, or on political ideas and ideologies rather than on performance, interaction and behaviour. The modern political analysis, guided by sociological, anthropological and psychological methods and theories, rests upon four basic principles: (1) the search for more comprehensive scope; (2) the search for realism; (3) the search for precision: and (4) the search for intellectual order. The object is to free the discipline of Political Science from the value judgments or quasi-ethical or philosophical judgments.

These modern political scientists seek to develop a kind of empirically oriented and value-free Political Science and bring it at par with natural sciences. Values are thought to be subjective preferences about which science has nothing to do. Traditionally, the study of political values—of what, for example, ought to be the political structure and what political goals ought to be sought—has been the field of political philosophers. A main concern of the modern political philosophers is the study of great thinkers of the past—Plato, Aristotle, Machiavelli, Hobbes, Locke, Rousseau among others. In the process he will analyse such value words as 'justice', 'rights', 'freedom'. This activity is currently supplemented by the study of values as political facts. To take a specific example, while the students of Political Science remain interested in the historical formulations of the argument that we ought to obey the law because we have consented to it by participating in the choice of government, and spend time in analysing the nature of 'consent' in all its variety, there are now investigations to discover to what extent 'consent', as defined, is in fact a value subscribed to in a particular society and what consequences for political behaviour follow from the acceptance of the value. That is, there is increasing importance attached to the political setting—the political values and attitudes which together make the political culture.[9]

Separated, rather than divorced, from the study of political values is the study of political institutions. For a long period the study essentially centred around the legislatures, executives and judiciaries, the three institutions for making, carrying out and interpreting the law. As the study developed and knowledge advanced, the area extended to include political parties, bureaucracies, interest groups and other groups engaged in politics which have a continuous existence. At a later stage, it was further supplemented by how political communications work through press, radio, television, discussions or meetings and how demands emerge and are formulated through interest groups and political parties and their impact on government's policies. The emphasis is on procedures and institutions through which authoritative decisions are made and the outcome of such decision-making in the form of rule-making, rule-application and rule-adjudication, to use terms broader and more meaningful than the traditional legislative, executive and judicial functions.

9. Rowe, Eric, *Modern Politics*, p. 7.

The keynote is on facts and as a consequence, political institutions are themselves evaluated to see to what extent theory and practice diverge; the values of the present and the past in varying degrees.

Recently, emphasis has been placed on the study of what is called 'political behaviour'. This approach, which is not restricted to declared behaviouralists, concentrates on the behaviour of the individuals and groups within political institutions. The aim is to get behind the formal structure and to study the actual processes of politics in order to uncover the "inside story" and has led to a new or revived interest in the impact of social factors in the political life. This branch of political studies owes a great deal to other social sciences, particularly sociology. "It is always the focus of interest," says MacIver, "that distinguishes one social science from another. We should not think of the social sciences as dividing between them physical separate areas of reality. What distinguishes each from each is the selective interests."[10] A student of Political Science must see the problems of the State and the processes involved therein against a background of general knowledge, either existing or to be acquired, as a basis for comment and assessment.

Political Science, thus, enters into various fields and touches many horizons. The process of specialisation on the various aspects of the discipline, orientation of methodology, importantly behavioural, and the interdisciplinary explanations have together brought about a radical change in the scope of the discipline. Political decisions are not made in a vacuum or due only to the personal idiosyncrasies of political actors. Economic factors, the social structure, the class, status and stratification systems influence both the content and mode of making political decisions. Nor can one remain oblivious of 'political orientations' of the members of society—how citizens 'see' the political system itself, how they react to it emotionally, how they evaluate it morally. Equally important is the 'political socialisation' process—how members' general attitudes have been influenced by family, churches, work-groups, etc. The political system is an aspect of the social system and political activity and its study is a special category of social study and activity. Politics is, therefore, not isolated from other human activities. Students of Political Science must take due consideration of the environments in which the political system is set, particularly the social setting, otherwise their study is devoid of realities and consequently barren.

Despite the advances made in the recent political analysis, there is no unified theory of Political Science to present. Almond and Powell admit that the new developments are trends only and not as completed accomplishments. The most important work, both empirical and theoretical, is still to be done. Yet, there is no denying the fact that the analytical-cum-empirical method "has definitely enlarged the field of our inquiry as it has cleared up the rust in which many helpful distinctions within the framework of political studies lay obscured. It is not that the traditional boundaries have been obliterated; they may merely have been extended and given a sharpness and depth hitherto unknown."[11]

---

10. MacIver, R.M., and Page, C.H., *Society; An Introductory Analysis,* p.V.
11. Frank Thakurdas, "The Expanding Frontier of Political Science," *The Indian Journal of Political Science*, October-December 1973, pp. 405-06.

TERMINOLOGICAL DISTINCTIONS

It is rather unfortunate that there is no commonly accepted name for the subject of our study. Some call it Politics, others name it Political Theory and many designate it as Political Philosophy. The absence of a commonly accepted title causes a good deal of confusion in understanding what it concerns the State and government and the problems related thereto. It is, accordingly, necessary to know precisely what all these terms signify and then give the discipline a proper name.

Politics. The term Politics was first used by Aristotle and he called it "the master science". The word Politics is derived from the Greek word *polis* meaning a city. To the Greeks the city was the *State* and the subject that dealt with the City-State and its problems was designated Politics. In our times, some eminent political scientists, as Harold Laski,[12] R. H. Solatu[13], Karl Deutsch and many others[14] prefer the term Politics for the subject matter of our study.

But ordinary usage equates *Politics* with party politics and politicians with party politicians. As a result, it emphasises disagreement, which is so prominent in party politics. In this context politics of one country differs from the politics of another country and within the same country politics of one party differs from the politics of another party, as each party offers its own solution of the problems which concern the country. For example, politics of the Indian National Congress, though split into four hostile wings, differs from the politics of the Janata Dal or the Communist Party of India, itself divided into two warring camps.

It follows that a politician is a person who interests himself in the politics of his country and that of a particular party which conforms to his political views. He is not a student of Political Science. He is only concerned with the present problems that confront the country and their solution as his party suggests. Politics is, accordingly, an art rather than a science. But Political Science is a scientific study of the State—its nature, conditions, origin and developments—and government, their functions and purposes and the institutions they foster in order to make the task of "good life" possible. A student of Political Science will know something of society whose political system is involved, its history and traditions, its physical and human environments in order to assess to what extent the existing institutions fulfil the aspirations of the people and help in achieving the goal of "good life". A politician may have nothing to do with all this.

But the term Politics has acquired a new meaning in the context of advancements of late made in the discipline of Political Science. It hinges upon the political activity carried on in human environment, in time and space, and thus a product of economy, the society, history and geography. Political activity is based on agreement and whenever there is freedom a great deal of politics is likely to be found. This follows because men

12. Harold Laski gave to his famous book the title: *A Grammar of Politics.* The title of his other book is: *An Introduction to Politics.*
13. R.H. Solatu's book also carries the title: *An Introduction to Politics.*
14. Karl W. Deutsch, Professor of Government, Harvard University, names his book: *Politics and Government* and G.M, Carter and J.H. Herz wrote, in 1961, an informative book *Government and Politics* in the *Twentieth Century.*

have diverse views, interests and characteristics. Disagreement, though a necessary condition of politics, is not enough in itself. Order is also required if politics is not to disappear into chaos or civil war. An organised society is a restraint on disagreement, that is, the recognised limits to disagreement and the measure of agreement necessary to maintain order. That is the way of social bebaviour and political life. The extent of agreement may be much greater than the necessary minimum, but if that minimum is absent politics is no more. Conversely, if members are forced to behave as if there were virtually no disagreement then politics is seriously curtailed; if not destroyed.[15]

Politics may be found in a variety of associations and groups, whether the group be a trade union, a country or an international organisation. At all levels the same forces and identical urges operate. All associations or groups where men are banded together must agree to ensure order and consequent continuity, and where they have disagreements which are subsequently resolved, in policy which is applied on behalf of the group, then politics exists in that collection of men and women. Robert Dahl is of the opinion that every human association has a political aspect and it is in this context that he defines a political system. A political system, he says, "is any persistent pattern of human relationship that involves, to a significant extent, power, rule, or authority".[16] He would, accordingly, include in his definition of a political system all sorts of human associations, as private clubs, business firms, religious organizations, civil groups, primitive tribes, clans, "perhaps even families". All these associations have to provide for their internal 'government', and all these 'governments' operate in response to forces that it seems natural to call 'political'; the same striving for power and exercise of influence in policy-making. Politics is, thus, a struggle for power on all the three levels it can be looked at—State, intra-State and inter-State—and it is of the same specie. The role of leadership as well as the struggle for leadership is inherent in the game of politics. Bertrand de Jouvenal explains that political activity is the urge in the human person to control and dominate and direct the wills of other individuals, which may assume many forms, but is manifest, wherever men enter into group life, as they must. That it does not manifest in all persons equally, is perhaps nature's obscure blessings."[17]

It follows then that every society or group requires that some people have power over other people which is recognised by a sufficiently large number of people as legitimate; acceptable to them. In the primitive society the urge to dominate was sheer naked force. Advancement of civilisation made possible the gradual transformation of brute force exercised and today there is competition for power and for influence over the holders of power and it is duly regularised or institutionalised. Politics, as such, is striving to share power, or to influence its distribution as well as the actual exercise of such power. Lasswell and Kaplan, accordingly, define Politics "as an empirical discipline, (as) the study of the shaping and sharing of power"[18] and "a political act (as) one performed in power perspectives"[19] in every phase of the society.

---

15. Rowe, Eric, *Modern Politics,* pp. 2-3.
16. Dahl, Robert A, *Modern Political Analysis*, p. 6.
17. Jouvenal Bertrand de, *Pure Theory of Politics*, Chs. 1 and 3, pp. 14-40.
18. Lasswell, Harald D., and Kaplan, Abraham, *Power and Society,* p. xiv.
19. *Ibid,* p. 240.

But this analysis does not reveal the whole content and scope of Political Science. It has preference for particular and limited scale of studies of a strictly empirical character; a zeal for precision and objectivity. It is the study of the political systems in their relation to social structure, which altogether ignores how the State, the pivotal entity of the discipline, and its institutions did actually emerge and the process of their development. Unless the student of Political Science knows about the origin of the State, though the term has been discarded by the modern American political scientists, yet it is the only entity still universally recognised both in national and international politics and is familiar with its institutional framework and the manner in which it has worked over the years, his study remains lop-sided, if not barren, and the search for realism and precision becomes a futile effort. Loss of grasp of internal coherence and independent influence of political institutions do not render it a wholesome study and, accordingly, the term Politics does not explain the real significance and scope of the discipline.

Political Theory. Political theory has been variously described. While some make it synonymous with Political Philosophy, as if both the terms are interchangeable[20], there are others who contend that Political Theory is inseparable from Political Thought.[21] Andrew Hacker[22] and S.S. Wolin[23] point out the necessity of separating it from Political Philosophy and Political Ideology. David Smith suggests that Political Theory is "the most encompassing of intellectual activity" and classifies Philosophy, Thought and Ideology as specific forms of Political Theory.[24]

Ernest Barker made a succinct distinction, in his article on "Greek Political Thought and Theory in the Fourth Century BC", which he reaffirmed in his inaugural at Cambridge University in 1928. He suggested that Political Thought is general and is the thinking of the whole community at a particular historical stage and is reflected in the writings of poets, statesmen, publicists, etc., whereas Political Theory is a "highly personal vision of an individual" of the political reality for which his theory seeks to offer an explanation.[25] This distinction is emphasised by Leo Strauss in his article: "*What is Political Philosophy*?" and while elaborating it he stressed the differing forms in which the two find expression. "Political Theory through a formal 'treatise', Political Thought, because of its general character, is diffused and is a conglomeration of current political ideas that govern the life of a society at a particular stage of its history, and is reflected through all the known means of communication including poetry, literature and art."

Three ingredients of Political Thought distinguish it from Political Theory. Firstly, Political Thought is the thought .of the community relating to political life at a particular period of history. Secondly, it is most general, for it is the sum of political opinions or beliefs expressed either in defence or repudiation of a policy or programme or a political

20. Voegelin, Eric, *The New Science of Politics: An Introduction*, p. 1.
21. Meehan, Eugene J., *Contemporary Political Thought: A Critical Study*, p. 3.
22. Hacker, Andrew, *Political Theory; Philosophy, Ideology, Science*, pp. 2–5.
23. Wolin, S.S., *Politics and Vision.*
24. Smith, David G., "Political Science and Political Theory", *American Political Science Review*, September 1957, pp. 734-46.
25. Barker, Ernest, *Cambridge Ancient History*, Vol. V, p. 505.

order. Thirdly, The contents of the affirmation or repudiation are directly inspired or determined by the historical context. "While its primary thrust is in relation to 'specific events', its form is far from fixed, and in this collective participation not only politicians..., Publicist (the political commentator of leading newspapers and semi-popular weekly), the angry or committed poet, the philosopher who infrequently is tempted to comment (Marx did it all the time) or the letters to the editor, etc., each in his particular mode, contributes to the general fund of this 'Thought', which then reflects the spirit of a decade or an 'age'."[26] Political Thought, as Leo Strauss explained, is time-bound; rooted and conditioned by the historical context. It is commonly said that a thinker is the "Child of his age", though it may not be neatly so.

The Thought may be Utopian. Some thinker, a Campenella, Harrington or Owen, deeply touched by the suffering and strife which plague the society may set an ideal model of a social order for man to live in. Such a model is the product of romantic idealization and is the thinking of an individual inspired by circumstances then prevailing no doubt, but a utopia all the same; an imaginary state of ideal perfection. The ideal social order is conceived as a panacea for all human ills and is acclaimed an idyllic state of justice—happiness and contentment all-round and no grievance to ventilate. It is a bliss to live in such a society.

Some writers regard Plato's Republic as Utopia "of a timeless and spaceless dimension—a world of dream which cannot even act as a sedative to troublous times." But these writers overlook the intensely realistic concern of Plato. Even Karl Popper, Plato's bitterest critic of the twentieth century, concedes that he was the first social scientist and an ardent reformer.

The sharp rise in the ideological thinking between the two World Wars—Communism in Russia, Fascism in Italy and Naziism in Germany—and the aggressive dogmatism with which these ideologies were preached and practised, brought into focus the need to clearly distinguish Political Ideology from the Political Theory. The necessity of such a distinction was deemed all the more important in the light of Karl Marx's challenge that all thinking is ideological.

Political Ideology means a system of ideas about life, society and government, which through long and intensive processes of propaganda and usage, tend to become the characteristic belief or dogma of a particular group, party or nationality. "It is a theory of social life," says Roucek, "which approaches social realities from the point of view of a political ideal and interprets them consciously or unconsciously to prove the correctness of the analysis and to justify the ideal."[27] It is intended to justify a particular system of power in society in order to realise a good and blissful life. The ideologist is committed to the ideology he professes and proclaims it vigorously urging others to accept it unquestionably. He tolerates neither criticism nor opposition and demands from others, too, total commitment to the ideology and the values it sustains. Ideological politics, as Frank Thakurdas says, is "doctrinaire, didactic, dogmatic, transitory, prescriptive, polemical

26. Thakurdas, Frank, "The Expanding Frontier of Political Science", *The Indian Journal of Political Science*, October-December, 1973, pp. 412–13.
27. Roucek, Joseph, *Introduction to Political Science*, p. 1.

and propagandist, partisan, combative and destructive; whose appeal is in the nature of a religious belief, which would not suffer either doubt or criticism."[28] Ideology, unlike Political Philosophy, is not a search for truth and for knowledge based on truth. The test of a political ideology lies in its application. Preston King writes, "Political Philosophy evokes reflection and understanding while ideology is more likely to imply *commitment* and *action*." He further contends that ideology is used "to convey both the notions of intended and actual application".[29] Ideology, therefore, must possess a political character, a guide to direct political action and getting things done in a predetermined direction.

The meaning of Political Theory now becomes sufficiently clear. It may embrace the entire system or so partial as to deal with only one or a few empirical generalisations. It is a self-conscious, systematic attempt of a single mind, which seeks to offer an analytical explanation of the phenomenon of politics. In contrast with Political Thought, which reflects mere opinion or belief, Political Theory is largely an attempt to seek the truth as the thinker sees it. A political theorist shall have no personal interest in the political system of any one country or class or party. "His vision of reality and his image of good, ideally speaking, will not be clouded, nor his theory will be special pleading."[30]

Political theory has three ingredients which have been classified into three groups. The first is, its factual and descriptive component in the same manner as History has a purely chronological and descriptive component. Secondly, it is made up of the generalizations which reduce to order the huge mass of political data and the complications of policy-making. "Such empirically based generalizations aspire to the neutrality, if not the precision of science and are sometimes called rules or principles. It is these generalizations and hypotheses which seek to explain a political system by discovering its operating principles." And, the third component is the moral component. As a rule, the older the theory the more broadly ethical it is, and the more subordinate is the purely descriptive and neutral.[31]

In order to clearly understand the writings of a theorist, it is necessary to consider and weigh the general context of ideas within which he was working and also see them as a response to more immediate circumstances. "It might well be said," remarks Derek Crabtree, "that political theory only arises in times of political crisis; when all is well within the body-politic then the incentive to theorise is lacking."[32] Both Aristotle and Plato wrote at a time when the *polis*, institutionally, was on the brink of decline, and the political theory of both these writers can be seen as essentially aiming at a means of preventing the decay which they already sensed. Hobbes' Leviathan was a response to the crisis of the English society at the time of the civil war and the *Federalist Papers*, of Hamilton, Madison and Jay, were based on the need to secure the adoption of the new American federal constitution. But it does not mean that all these theorists were concerned

28. Thakurdas, Frank, "The Expanding Frontier of Political Science", *The Indian Journal of Political Science*, October-December 1973, p. 416.
29. King, P., and Parekh, B. (ed.), *Politics and Experience*, pp. 350-351.
30. Refer to Andrew Hacker, *Political Theory*, p. 5.
31. Haridwar Rai, "Political Theory: New Viewpoints in Meaning and Method", *The Indian Journal of Political Science*, October-December 1969, p. 534.
32. Derek Crabtree, *"Political Theory"*, Wiseman, Victor H. (ed.), *Political Science*, p. 158.

in solving the contemporary problems and that their writings had no significance once those problems had been resolved. The important fact is that in each case, "while advocating solutions or policies appropriate to the situation of their day, they sought to secure the acceptance of those recommendations by appealing to a general view of politics. If only we will accept the analysis of politics which they offer us we shall be led to accept the practical advice they offer."[33] Taking the example of Madison, the analysis of American society and government that he offered in his contribution to the *Federalist Papers* still eminently merits the detailed and critical scrutiny which Robert Dahl has given it in his *Preface to Democratic Theory*, for it represents a cogent analysis of the nature of limited government in a plural society, and not merely a piece of special pleading for the adoption of a particular decision in 1787.

The two broad varieties of Political Theory are the classical and the contemporary. The former by tradition refers to the writings of Plato, Aristotle, Rousseau, Kant, Hegel or even Laski which deal with politics from a broadly moral point of view. Plato examined a number of points which have continued to exercise philosophers to the present time: what is the nature of the good or goodness at which man should aim ? How can it be known ? Given that we know the good, what is the political order that embodies it ? What are the right relations between the man and the State ? and, lastly, why ought men to obey the State ? Plato dealt with these questions via the literary form of the dialogue, whereas his celebrated pupil Aristotle treated them in much more formal systematic manner and his *Nichomachean Ethics* and *Politics* set the pattern of political speculation for many centuries. The history of Political Theory is the history of varying answers to these questions which have been given by subsequent philosophers and thinkers.

Up until the twentieth century Political Theory was a normative "enterprise" and its focus of attention was the moral criterion of political conduct and it sought to answer questions, such as, the nature of the State and what was the end or the good at which it should aim, or sought to demonstrate that one set of institutional arrangements or form of government was the ideal which ought to be implemented, as embodying the true end. Such Political Theory is "heavily and curiously culture-bound"[34] and its task is "to pass moral judgments."[35] Assuming a moral ideal for all human institutions and the State being the greatest of such institutions, all political thinkers concentrated on "ideal models" rather than on "process models" and interpreted the State in terms of ethics and sought to determine its relation to the moral constitution and development of man.[36] Its central idea was the "moral evaluation of the political power"[37], employing logical analysis and deductive reasoning in deriving conclusions.

But discontentment against the classical theory, in which ethical content was "writ large", began simmering in the twenties of the present century and in the post-1945 period not only the ranks of its critics swelled, but they also vehemently challenged the legitimacy of the theoretical enterprise and some even proclaimed its "demise." Prominent

33. *Ibid.*
34. Guild, Nelson P., and Palmer, Kenneth T., *Introduction to Politics,* p. 3.
35. Field, G.C., *Political Theory,* p. xvi.
36. Barker, Ernest, *Political Thought in England* 1848-1914, p. 5.
37. Gewirth, Alan, *Political Philosophy*, p. 3.

among those who ushered in this "intellectual revolution" were Herbert Simon, David B. Truman, V.O. Key Jr., Robert A. Dahl, David Easton, Heinz Eulau, Charles Hyneman, Carl Friedrich, and Harold Lasswell. Their analysis of the discipline of Political Science even penetrated the Oxford University which had till then been recognised the "home" of Political Theory or Philosophy among the English-speaking countries.

The term Political Theory as used in the contemporary sense may mean the scientific theory, the positivist theory or the behavioural theory. It is a quest for realism, precision, comprehensiveness, and detachment in order to obtain "neat and tidy" results to explain and generalise political phenomena. This search for actuality has led to reorienting political theory to empirical research, strategies and techniques. The contemporary political scientists, accordingly, seek to stress "direct observation, objective measurement, systematic data collection, the operationalizing of concepts, quantification, a deliberate search for regularities and variations, and systematic comparison across groups and cultures in an effort to ascertain the limits of generalisations."[38] They believe that a political scientist, like a physical scientist, should observe his data as a disinterested person and must not import his own point of view in his observations. His approach should be objective and in terms of the "observed and observable" and, consequently, value free. They outright reject the assumption that theory is knowledge, and contend that it is only a tool on the road to knowledge. Viewed in this way, political theory is neither prescriptive nor oriented towards action. "Rather it is explanatory and oriented towards understanding. It is, in itself, the tool of the seeker rather than the doer. It does not imply a set of values, nor a set of facts; but is a process by which sense is made out of facts by relating and ordering them."[39]

Four peculiarities of this approach, as R.L. Rathore points out, may be noted: "(i) the unit firstly is subjected to a theoretical and empirical analysis rather than to a simple study of structures, institutions and ideologies; (ii) this approach is carried on within the framework of other disciplines, namely, psychology, sociology and cultural anthropology; (iii) this approach is concerned with formulating hypotheses and definitions which can be verified; and (iv) it stresses the mutual inter-dependence of theory and research."[40] In brief, political behaviour theories are nothing more than the application of precise scientific methods to the study of politics, sans metaphysical assumptions but with the insistence that all induction must rest on observation of facts.

The result is "a radical transformation", as Easton calls it, "in conceptions of the tasks and functions of theory."[41] It has developed its own language and new concepts have been invented to make the study wholesome, matter of fact and meaningful. The concept of the "State" has been discarded and in its place "political system" is used, as the former is limited by its legal and institutional meanings; instead of "powers", which is again a legal concept in its connotation, the term "functions" is used; and instead of

38. Rathore, R.L., "In Defence of Political Theory", *The Indian Journal of Political Science*, October-December 1975, p. 331.

39. As cited in Haridwar Rai, *"Political Theory: New Viewpoints in Meaning and Method"*, *Ibid*., October-December 1969, p. 353.

40. Rathore, R.L., "The Nature of Political Theory." *Ibid*, April-June, 1976, p. 52.

41. Easton, David; *A System Analysis of Political Life*, p. 3.

"offices" (legal again) the concept of "role" is preferred. Similarly, instead of "institutions", which is a formal norm, "structure" is used and instead of "public opinion" and "citizenship training", which are formal in meaning, "political culture" and "political socialisation" are used. The inter-connection among all these terms rests on the "action" or a "behavioural" base, one term suggests another and correlates the other components of the social process. The advocates of the innovations claim, "we are not simply adding terms to new vocabulary, but rather are in the process of developing or adapting a new one...; this is not only a matter of conceptual vocabulary; it is an intimation of a major step in the nature of political science as science."[42] Some of these concepts flow from the disciplines of Sociology and Anthropology in the study of political phenomenon removing the traditional barriers in the various sub-fields. The importance of interdisciplinary approach, especially the influence of Psychology, Sociology, Anthropology and Statistics, as an aid to a complete knowledge of complex phenomenon of man's organised political life can hardly be underestimated, though we may not entirely agree with the nature of Political Theory as enunciated by contemporary political scientists.

Political Philosophy. Political Philosophy and Political Theory are not synonymous, though former is a component part of the latter. When in the nineteenth century a distinction was made between "Theoretical Politics" and "Applied Politics", many writers preferred to name "Theoretical Politics" as Political Philosophy and they assigned many reasons for it. Some British political thinkers argued that the study of the phenomenon of the State constituted a part of the study of the universe with which philosophy proper was concerned and as philosophy was the unifier of knowledge, the study relating to the State should be regarded as one of its sub-divisions. Others maintained that as Politics was concerned primarily with constructing, on the basis of certain psychological premises, the system of relations which ought to be established among the persons governing and between them and the governed in a society, the State, its structure, its nature and its purposes depended upon our conception of right and wrong, and, as such, the subject relating to the principles underlying political institutions should appropriately be called Political Philosophy.

This is not a correct appraisal of the nature of Political Philosophy. Political Philosophy, as distinct from Political Theory and Political Ideology, has a wider purpose and deeper concern about man's political life, for the purpose of political life cannot be separated from the purpose of life itself. It seeks to explain this aspect of man's life and activity in its multidimensional aspects and, accordingly, Political Philosophy deals with the nature and purpose of the State, the rights and duties of the people, the place of the individual in relation to the State and the ideal which it ought to achieve. The political philosopher, like a political theorist, seeks an explanation or offers one for the complex phenomenon of the State, but, unlike the latter, his focus of attention is the enduring elements of political life and he endeavours to suggest how best the purpose of political life ought to be realised. He is a seeker after truth and for knoweldge based on truth. He is not concerned with a particular issue or problems that confront the State and require immediate solution. His quest is for enduring solution of the complexities of man's

42. Almond, Gabriel A., and Coleman, James S. (eds.), *The Politics of the Developing Areas*, p. 4.

political life and he travels beyond the frontiers of a particular country or region and may encompass the whole mankind. His recommendations are for all people and for all climes and, consequently, may command universal significance transcending the immediate historical context which influenced his philosophy.

But the philosophy of all great masters is their personal vision of the complexities of political life and in their search for an ideal society of their way of thinking, they delve deep into the realm of imagination and create the web of an ideal model, completely oblivious of the realities of life. Contemporary political scientists are now engaged in an intensive quest for the real and they have adopted scientific methods to arrive at the actuality. Their emphasis, as said before, is to study the phenomena of political life starting with carefully refined hypotheses, using rigorous methods of observation, measuring, counting and using mathematical tools wherever possible and ending with cautious, modest conclusions. They denounce classical theory as it is value-laden. But no political theory, classical or contemporary, can develop in the absence of values and reason. If the scientific method gives precision, it must also take account of the ideal conditions for which man has ever yearned. Political theory cannot advance without considering what is better than present. Political Science is an empirical study of the dynamic man. Circumstances change and so do man's environments and habits. Some of the conclusions have persisted for centuries, others have been rejected, others again are accepted today and may be rejected by future generations. Idealism is as much a part of human life as realism and both need to be so blended that their interaction produces results conforming to the reality of life itself, for the State is ultimately a "fellowship of men" aiming at the "enrichment of the common life".[43] No political theory, therefore, can subserve its purpose without consideration of the "ends of action" and "the discussion of values". Without them it is barren.

Political Science. Political Science is the scientific designation of the subject of our study, and this name has been accepted by the political scientists drawn from various countries who assembled in a meeting under the auspices of the UNESCO. It covers the whole range of knowledge regarding the political governance of man. According to Paul Janet, Political Science "is that part of social science which treats the foundations of the State and the principles of government." The foundations of the State and principles of government have their roots in the past and their branches swing towards the future. It is a systematic study which goes deep into the political problems of yesterday for the benefit of today and utilises the wisdom gained therefrom for the aspirations of better tomorrow.

With the interaction of the new forces during recent times necessitating new approaches to the study of Political Science, it has been suggested that Political Science should no longer be defined in terms of objects such as the State. It should be defined only in terms of activity and, accordingly, Catlin defines Political Science as the study of "the act of human and social control" or the "study of control relationship of wills".[44] There are others who would hardly make it distinguishable from the subject matter of Sociology.

43. Laski, Harold J., *A Grammar of Politics,* p. 37.

44. Catlin, George, E.G., *A Study of Principle of Politics,* pp. 69, 75-76.

German writers regard it as the study concerning "the problem of power and social control".[45] Whatever be the merits of such definitions. they have not so far taken any tangible shape and the well-accepted ideas about Political Science continue to hold good. Contemporary political scientists discard the over-rationalistic account of institutions and clothe the old tools used in the governance of man with new terms and concepts derived from sociological and anthropological theories wholesome.

So far we have treated the subject of our study as a science. Aristotle regarded 'Politics' as the master or supreme science. Distinguished scholars, like Bodin, Hobbes, Sidgwick, and Bryce, had held the same view. But some earlier writers denied this claim of Political Science. They maintained that there could be no such thing as a scientific study of the phenomena of the State and government. They agreed with Burke that there was no science of politics any more than there was a science of aesthetics, "for the lines of politics are not like the lines of mathematics. They are broad and deep as well as long. They admit of exceptions; they demand modifications. No lines can be laid down for civil or political wisdom. They are a matter incapable of exact definition." Even Maitland said, "When I see a good set of examination questions headed by the word 'Political Science', I regret not the questions but the title."[46] Sir Frederick Pollock, on the other hand, asserted that "there is a science of politics in the same sense, and to the same, or about the same extent, as there is a science of morals".[47]

But whether Political Science is really a science or not depends upon what we regard as the test of a science.[48] Does a science involve merely systematic reasoning, or must the reasoning be exact and the conclusions clearly defined and subject to no exceptions as in the case of natural or physical sciences ? Moreover, does the claim of Political Science to be a science involve the power to predict the political future ?

Political Science is neither an exact science nor can it claim to predict the future with certainty. The results in physical sciences, like Physics and Chemistry, are definite and remain true under given conditions for all men and in different climes. If there is any variation, it can be tested and explained. But it is not possible to place men in a laboratory as if they were guinea pigs, nor is it possible to impose precise laboratory conditions on the political sphere in real life. Political Science deals with men and it is a living subject matter which can be explained in terms of living human activity. It cannot be expressed in fixed or static formulae. Man is dynamic and so must his institutions be. They must adjust themselves with the changing demands of man and his manifold needs. No institution is today what it was yesterday and what it will be tomorrow, anymore than I am myself the same on two consecutive days. It is the human element or the livingness of the subject which makes Political Science inexact and indefinite.[49]

45. Robson, W.A., *The University Teaching of Social Sciences: Political Science* (Unesco), p. 19.
46. Maitland, F.W., *Collected Papers,* Vol. III, p. 302.
47. Pollock, F., *An Introduction to the History of the Science of Politics,* p. 2.
48. The obstacles in the scientific study of Political Science have been cogently discussed by W.G. Runciman in his *Social Science and Political Theory.*
49. Burke observed, "However widely and carefully the materials may be gathered, their character makes it impossible that Politics should even become a Science in the sense which mechanics or chemistry is a Science."

Then, in the subject-matter of Political Science is involved the problem of values, though contemporary political scientists have attempted to make the subject value free. All political issues can best be explained in terms of moral and ethical standards. or, to put it more precisely, they should be based on justice. From the times of Plato and Aristotle men's ideas of what is just do not agree and the riddle of social justice remains unresolved. The endeavour in search of justice will continue in future too and, yet, without any definite agreement thereon. Consequently, it is impossible for Political Science to attain the same degree of exactness and universal application of its laws as in the physical or even biological sciences. "There are two words in medicine," a Professor of Medicine said to his pupils, "that you never use. They are 'Always' and 'Never' "— and the same applies to Political Science.

Nevil Johnson suggests five distinct aspects in which Political Science appears to differ from the physical and the natural sciences.[50] Firstly, in physical and natural sciences the evidence is objective, usually measured and expressed quantitatively whereas in Political Science we assess the significance of evidence and personal judgments are involved. Secondly, experiments can be repeated in the physical and the natural sciences, but in politics the problems are unique. Then, in politics there are too many uncertainties in the materials and evidence for prediction; we aim rather at "informed and critical estimates." Fourthly, in politics, also, our revised conclusions do not always rest upon fresh evidence but sometimes upon reinterpretations, new points of view and insight; 'old' works are not necessarily worthless Finally, when we ask political questions we at the same time begin to shape the answers we shall give; such answers spring from imagination and insight. In general, our methods of enquiry have much in common with those in the natural sciences: the manner in which we work out causal explanations and test them owe much to their example. But we cannot produce a blueprint for action or make statements with the same degree of accuracy as the natural sciences.

If by 'science' is meant a systematised body of knowledge the facts of which have been accurately and impartially collected, arranged and classified, through the use of various scientific methods of observation, comparison and analysis, with cautious statements of findings, then, Political Science can claim to be a science. It is true that we cannot experiment with man and political phenomena lack continuity of development. It is also true that students of Political Science differ materially on their methods, principles and conclusions. And when political problems in the last analysis depend upon our conceptions of right and wrong, there has always been and presumably always will be fundamental disagreement over its first principles. But "we can become," as Herman Finer remarks, "the prophets of the probable if not the seers of the certain." Prediction and absolute certainty are not the goal of Social Sciences. Even Physical Sciences cannot claim to achieve to that extent. The sweeping changes which have taken place in Physics and Chemistry during the past century show how tentative are formulations even in natural sciences. It might, on the other hand, be argued that some of the political theories expounded by Aristotle, or John Stuart Mill, or the authors of *The Federalist Papers* "have stood the test of time better than contemporary doctrines of chemistry, for example."[51]

50. Wiseman, H. Victor (ed.), *Political Science,* pp. 22-23.

51. Brown, Bernard E., *New Directions in Contemporary Politics,* p. 5.

Let it, however, be conceded that hypotheses concerning political behaviour can never be fully verified because of the complex, shifting and ever changing nature of the political universe. Yet, the political scientist endeavours to read the present in the light of the past in order to become wiser for the future. He tries to systematise his facts, analyses clearly cause and effect, and tries to unfold principles and detect general tendencies. The mass of historical facts and the contemporary data of the actual working of political institutions and the behaviour of the operators of these institutions are sufficient to enable him to observe, collect and classify general facts. "If the situations are not identical, they are not completely different: there are recognisable similarities." The phenomena of the State, thus, exhibit a certain order, regularity and connection in their sequences. They are the result of the operation of certain fixed laws universal in application. The aim of science is the discovery of universal laws and the laws of science are based on experience and they are verifiable in experience. J.A. Thomson has cogently said that "the aim of science is to describe the impersonal facts of experience in verifiable terms as exactly as possible, as completely as possible."[52] Science tries to understand clearly and completely "what commonsense understands only dimly and partially." In fact, all serious study must be 'scientific' in the sense that "all conclusions must be based on ascertainable facts, and research carried out with the minimum prejudice and emotion and with the maximum of rational enquiry." The scientist must have a passion for facts, and his mind must not be coloured by personal bias, that is, he conducts his enquiry in a spirit of scientific detachment.

If this is the aim of science, it is sufficient to justify the claim of Political Science to be ranked as a science, though it is the most inexact of all the sciences belonging to the family of social sciences. James Bryce compared it to an inexact natural science, like Meteorology, as Alfred Marshall compared Economics with the science of tides. The aim of Political Science, however, is not only to formulate scientific laws of the political governance of man, but also to establish a way of life which, according to Aristotle, is the way that leads to good life. A good life is the art of living together in a spirit of togetherness; a rational conduct of human life, first, as the citizens of the State to which men belong and, then, as members of the common humanity. Peoples of all the States have yet to learn the art of good life in all its aspects and once this art is mastered, there will really be a happier and just life. And art is not antithesis to science. It can be based on science.

METHODOLOGY

Political Science is, thus, an organised body of knowledge the facts of which have been scientifically and systematically observed, collected and classified, and from these facts are formulated and proved a series of propositions or principles which form the basis of the science. These principles are used as a groundwork for further investigation. It was not until the nineteenth century that the phenomena of the State came to be regarded as a proper field for scientific investigation and since then many methods and approaches have been suggested and employed. Auguste Comte suggested three principal methods of

52. Thomson, J.A., *Introduction to Sciences*, p. 57.

investigation, viz., observation; experiment; and comparison. Bluntschli considered philosophical and historical as the only two methods, which need be used for investigation and correct conclusions. John Stuart Mill recognised four methods: (1) the chemical or experimental; (2) the geometrical or abstract; (3) the physical or concrete deductive; and (4) the historical method. Mill held the first two methods false and placed emphasis on the deductive and the historical methods only. James Bryce held that observational; experimental; historical; and comparative methods were the only correct and proper methods to give conclusive results. Deslandres, a French scholar, recognises six methods: the sociological; the comparative; the dogmatic; the juridical; the method of good sense; and the historical method.

Some recent writers have emphasised the importance of sociological, biological, psychological and statistical methods of investigation. Contemporary political scientists significantly recognise and practise the psychological method with close ties to Economics. Great importance is also given to comparative and statistical methods, the latter especially in the study of public opinion. In United Kingdom seven different methods are in use: historical, juridical, philosophical, institutional, analytical, observational and sociological. The sociological method endeavours to relate the political system of a country to the social structure, habits, ideas, psychology and customs of the community. Robson advocates the analytical method. The Marxist dialectical method is followed in Communist countries. According to Schaff and Eurlich, the basic principles of Marxist dialectical method lies in postulating the examination of problems in their integrity, that is, in examining phenomena in their interdependence and mutual relations. They observe that in order "to attain knowledge of political reality, the Marxist dialectical method makes use of sociology which is built on a consistent material basis, and resorts, in turn, to an analysis of the social process in terms of the property relations which exist in any given society."[53]

There is, therefore, no single method which can come to the rescue of a political scientist and help him to unfold the phenomena of the State and government with some degree of precision. The generally accepted methods of political investigation are: (1) the Observational Method. (2) the Experimental Method, (3) the Historical Method, (4) the Comparative Method, (5) the Method of Analogy, and (6) the Philosophical Method. To these may be added the Statistical or Quantitative Method.

The Observational Method. The older generation of political scientists discounted the observational method and based their theories on *a priori* assumptions, that is, the drawing of specific conclusions from premises pre-assumed to be infallible. This was the method of deductive logic and political thinkers grounded their theories upon premises taken from the Holy Scriptures, from the works of Aristotle or from other authorities who were supposed to be eminent.

It was only during the Renaissance, and particularly as a result of new discoveries, that the search for reality motivated political thinkers to observe, collect and analyse facts about the actual workings of governments and their institutions. Observational method is one of the ways of empirical studies and James Bryce was its great advocate. He attached great importance to the study of the problems and institutions on the spot, to investigate

53. *Contemporary Political Science* (Unesco), pp. 17-18.

their operations and form conclusions therefrom. He visited the United States of America, Canada, France, Switzerland, Australia and New Zealand, studied the people and their countries, closely observed the workings of their institutions and formed his own conclusions. He wrote: "The best way to get a genuine and exact first-hand knowledge of the data is to mix in practical politics. In such a country as France or the United States a capable man can, in a dozen years, acquire a comprehension of the realities of popular government ampler and more definite than any which books supply."[54] The political investigator, James Bryce asserted, must not confine his observations to one single country. His field of investigation should be so wide as to include the political phenomena of all countries, for the fundamentals of human nature are the same everywhere, except for the differences in their political habits and temperaments. "The first desideratum for a political scientist," he said, "is to get the fact and then make sure of it. Get it perfectly clear. Polish it till it sparkles and shines like a gem. Then connect it with other facts. Examine it in its relation to them, for in that lies its worth and its significance. It is of little use alone. So make it a diamond in the necklace, a stone, perhaps a cornerstone in your building."[55] Bryce's two famous books, *The American Commonwealth* and *Modern Democracies* (two volumes), are the result of his labours in pursuit of the observational method.

The observational method is based on direct observation and reflection. It is practical and its utility is obvious. It helps in arriving at certain political principles in the light of the observations made and information obtained. But as Sait has said, "A science of Politics can be developed only through observation, which is more laborious and far more open to error than experiment." Authentication of the facts observed is a long and arduous process and what appears to be a fact may not be so or it may be partially borne by facts. Laski has correctly remarked that the processes of government "are very like an iceberg; what appears on the stirface may be but a small part of the reality beneath." Next the human factor intervenes. The facts analysed may smack, and they very often do, of the prejudices of the investigator. Whether he ackowledges the fact or not, he will look on some people and policies as good and on others as evil.[56] Moreover, what we observe is a comparison of contemporary political institutions. It gives no clue to the past and provides no wisdom for the future unless other methods of investigation are coupled with it. It must, however, be noted that increasing use is now being made of this method, particularly in India.

The Experimental Method. The experimental method is at its best where a given phenomenon can be studied under conditions favourable to the investigation by excluding disturbing agencies. It is observation under conditions arranged by ourselves. But such scientific experimentation is not possible in Political Science, for it deals with man and his political institutions. "We cannot do in Politics," says Lewis, "what the experimenter does in Chemistry. ... We cannot take a portion of the community in our hand as the King of Brobdigang took Gulliver, view it in different aspects and place it in different positions

54. Bryce, J., *Modern Democracies,* Vol. I, p. 10.
55. Presidential Address, *American Political Science Review,* Vol. III, p. 10.
56. Bryce, too, emphasised that observation must be factual and not superficial and should be free from objective distortions.

in order to solve social problems and satisfy our speculative curiosity."[57] Experiments in Physical Sciences can be tried over and over again till the final and required result is obtained. Experiments in Political Science, on the other hand, can never be repeated. No ingenuity of man can reproduce identical conditions. Bryce has aptly said that "conditions can never be exactly reproduced as Heraclitus says that one cannot step twice into the same river."[58] Moreover, political institutions in every country are the logic of its own people and their requirements. We cannot transplant them in other lands. For example, we cannot have a replica of British institutions in India. Even if we have them, their success cannot be guaranteed. Analysing the causes of success of direct legislation in Switzerland, James Bryce said the institution is "racy of the soil". There are institutions "which, like plants, flourish only on their hillside and under their own sunshine."[59]

There is, however, some truth in the oft-quoted saying that man is wiser after experience. We may not experiment in Political Science as we do in a Physical Science, but practical experiments in political institutions are being constantly made, consciously or unconsciously. Every government makes experiments when it adopts a new policy or enacts a new law. Governmental policy changes and laws are amended or repealed if their public utility is not abundantly proved. All this amounts to experiments for the purpose of testing and improving. Dyarchy, for example, was experimented within the Provinces of India under the Government of India Act, 1919, but its working soon disclosed the inhercnt defects in the system and it was discarded in the Provinces under the Government of India Act, 1935. The Constitution of India is committed to prohibition and some State Governments experimented with it, total or partial. The Government of India appointed Tek Chand Committee to recommend a uniform policy based upon a rational evaluation of such an experiment. The Government of India enacted the Gold Control Order, which now stands more or less repealed, because the experiment did not fulfil the desired purpose underlying it. Various States adopted the scheme of separation of executive and judicial functions. The experiment proved a success and the two wings of government are now separated in almost all the States. Munro describes the British Constitution "as the mother of constitutions and Parliament as the mother of parliaments."[60] It means that other countries borrowed from Britain parliamentary institutions what she was the first to experiment with.

By experimental method is, thus, implied that it is based on observation and experience. Its 'laboratory' consists of sovereign and independent States into which the world is divided. For the political researcher every change in the governmental structure, law or policy, has significance as it is the result of experiment. When South Korea was invaded in June, 1950, politicians and political commentators urged that the mistake made in 1938 should not be repeated. But while doing so, they were not drawing exact parallels, nor claiming any infallibility in their predictions. They were simply pointing out the existence of certain facts which seemed to them to warrant the assumption that the pattern of 1938 might be repeated, and warned of the consequences if their analysis was correct. "We

57. Lewis, George C., *Methods of Observation and Reasoning in Politics,* Vol. I, pp. 164–65.
58. Bryce, J., *Modern Democracies,* Vol. I, p. 14.
59. *Ibid.,* pp. 453–54.
60. Munro, W.B., *The Governments of Europe*, p. 1.

deal with tendencies," says Harold Laski, "we can predict on the basis of experience. But our predictions are limited by the necessity of recognising that the facts are not within our control. We can influence and attempt and hope; the certainty and precision of the chemist, or even the physiologist, can never be ours."

The Historical Method. The historical method supplements the experimental method. Gilchrist remarks, "The source of experiments of Political Science is history; they rest on observation and experience. Every change in the form of government, every law passed, every war fought is an experiment in Political Science." The study of Political Science, according to Laski, "must be an effort to codify the results of experience in the history of states."[61] Political institutions grow instead of being made. They are the product of history and to know them as they really are, we must grasp the evolution of all those forces which have moulded and shaped them in their present form. Our conclusions remain uncertain, if they are not built upon historical analysis. Nor can we become wiser for the future. It is only by knowing the past and the present that we can plan for the ideal institutions of tomorrow. Laski has succinctly said, "What it is and why it is, it is by reason of its history. Its becoming is the clue of its being and it is from that being that we must wrest its secret."[62] In brief, our traditions and institutions are determined for us by our past. We are the consequences of these traditions and institutions which we did not make and which we can only partially alter. Appeal to history, therefore, is an invaluable aid to students of Political Science.

Montesquieu, Savigny, Seeley, Maine, Freeman and Laski are some of the eminent exponents of the historical method. Karl Marx found it an exclusive method. He explained the origin of the capitalist society in history and gave it the name of Materialistic Conception of History. But Sidgwick and other followers of the Philosophical School give to the historical method a secondary place for two reasons. First, they maintain, that the historical method serves no useful purpose in solving our present and future needs as it refers only to the experience of what the political institutions had been. Every age, it is argued, has its own problems and every problem requires a solution relative to the time in which it occurs. Secondly, history is a mere narration of events and it is not concerned with the goodness or badness of such events. Goodness or badness is only determined by ethical or philosophical standards and, accordingly, the philosophical method must precede the historical method.

Sidgwick's arguments are quite convincing. In the historical method superficial resemblances, usually fascinating, but generally misleading, are very often made much of. In the opinion of James Bryce, the historical investigator is more susceptible to emotional influences and he very often confuses "the personal or accidental factor with the general cause at work." Ernest Barker, too, criticised the historical method and said, "... the State is ... concerned less with the historical processes than with the fundamental

61. Laski, Harold J., *The Danger of Being a Gentleman and Other Essays,* p. 36.

62. *Ibid.* Refer to what Sir Frederick Pollock says: "The historical method seeks an explanation of what institutions are and are tending to be, more in the knowledge of what they have been and how they came to be what they are, than in the analysis of them as they stand." *An Introduction to the History of the Science of Politics,* p. 11.

realities—essence, purposes and value—which transcend the category of time."[63] In spite of these well reasoned objections the utility of the historical method cannot be discounted. History has now become much more objective. It also justifies goodness and badness of political actions, provided the investigator proceeds with an impartial mind free from prejudices and presuppositions, correlating economic, geographical or other scientific approaches. Seeley has rightly said, "We must think, reason, generalize, define, and distinguish; we must also collect, authenticate, and investigate. If we neglect the first process, we shall accumulate facts to little purpose, because we shall have no test by which to distinguish facts which are important from those which are unimportant; and, of course, if we neglect the second process, our reasoning will be baseless and we shall but weave scholastic cobwebs."

The Comparative Method. The comparative method of investigation is as old as Aristotle. He is said to have studied as many as 158 constitutions and after analysing and comparing them, he arrived at certain definite conclusions. In modern times the comparative method has been used by Montesquieu, De Tocqueville, Bryce, and many others. Recently, the method of comparison has come under intensified discussion. A report by a research panel in Comparative Government was published in 1944. The UNESCO project, and the handbook it published, *Contemporary Political Science*, at least touched on the question. It was discussed to a considerable extent at the round table on the teaching of Political Science organized by the International Political Science Association in 1952 and in the subsequent report by W.A. Robson.[64] The interest shown on this occasion encouraged the International Political Science Association to devote a particular round table on the study of "Comparative Government," which was held in Florence from April 5-10, 1954, followed by a report of Professor Gunnar Heckscher.[65] There was agreement amongst the forty participants in the round table on the importance of studying the Comparative Governments and the reasons for which such a study was regarded as profitable. Professor Gunnar Heckscher writes in his report : "Comparative studies are the core of any study of 'foreign' governments. They are of pedagogical importance, especially if we are to gain a reasonably realistic and relativistic view of our own government. Because of the growth of international contacts, scientific, political or economic comparisons between different countries, as well as a knowledge of foreign institutions; are of great political value." Then, he beautifully sums up the contribution of the comparative method to the development of Political Science itself. He says, "If we regard our field of study as mainly descriptive, comparisons are required to help us refine our tools of description. If we have hopes of establishing a general theory on an inductive basis, we can do so only through comparison. If we attempt to test specific hypotheses, this is possible only if we bring in a sufficient number of examples, to be investigated by the comparative method."[66]

The comparative method aims at the study of existing political institutions or those which have existed in the past, to assemble a definite body of material from which the

63. Barker, Ernest, *The Study of Political Science and its Relation to Cognate Studies*, p. 18.
64. *The University Teaching of Political Science* (Unesco).
65. *The Study of Comparative Government and Politics,* p.15.
66. *Ibid.*

investigator, by selection, comparison, and elimination, may discover the ideal types and progressive forces of political history. By comparison, we accumulate material, arrange and classify it, and by the process of co-ordination and elimination deduce certain results therefrom. It enables us to determine common causes and effects by making a comparative study of the past and the existing political institutions. Bryce compared the working of democracy in different countries and, then, accounted for its merits and defects as a form of government. The Indian Constituent Assembly amply benefited from this method.

But the use of the comparative method needs great care. Comparative analysis does not have as its guiding principle the assumption that there is one best way of government, which, when discovered, is to be adopted everywhere. There is limited practicability of transferring the fruits of political ingenuity from one country to another. When we compare political institutions with a view to finding out general principles underlying them, we must take into account the differences in the social, moral, intellectual, temperamental, political and economic conditions of the countries concerned or the communities compared. Comparison is most advantageous between countries and peoples with more or less similar conditions, as, for example, India and Pakistan. It is now generally believed that the parliamentary system of government, as obtainable in Britain, cannot work in India and Pakistan on the same lines and with the same ease and facility. This is primarily due to the differences in the temperament and genius of the people belonging to both the countries, their economic and social conditions, their moral and legal standards, and their political training and experience in administration. The comparative study succeeds only when due prominence is given to the human element; their manners, customs, habits and environments. It, then, lessens the dangers of meaningless comparison of "empty form and ossified rituals." Merriam correctly said that like all social sciences, Political Science "can be truly scientific only to the degree in which it contributes to the creation of a science of man." It is also necessary to stress the enormously growing importance of sociological study to the study of the comparative method. One of great contributions of contemporary Political Science is "that it is proving ...., the extent to which cooperation with sociology is possible as well as indispensable to political science in general and especially to comparative studies."[67]

As a result of the work of D. Easton, G.A. Almond and D. Apter, the discipline of comparative politics has virtually been re-oriented by the influence of structure-function analysis. In an article published in 1957, *An approach to the Analysis of Political Systems*, Easton suggested that a solution to the problem of comparing governments could be found by examining political life in terms of a system receiving certain *inputs* from the society and converting them into *outputs* affecting the society. He said that all governments processed *inputs* and transformed them into *outputs*. General comparisons, therefore, could be made and they would amount to a detailed examination of the content of both sides of the operation. Taking Easton's analysis as a starting point, Gabriel Almond looked for the functions which could be included among the *inputs* and *outputs* of all political systems. Looking at the conversion process which takes place within the political system, he showed that six such functions could be separated. First, on the *input* side,

67. *Ibid.*, p. 23.

demands are (1) formulated (or articulated) and (2) combined (or aggregated). Second, on the *output* side, rules are (3) formulated (rule-making), (4) applied (rule-application) and (5) adjudicated in individual cases (rule-adjudication). These various activities are (6) communicated within the system and outside. Almond also showed that, "apart from converting *inputs* into *outputs*, the system has also to be defined in terms of its ability to maintain and adapt itself (through a process of political socialisation) and in terms of the character of its achievements (capability)."[68]

Almond's analysis is known as structural-functionalism. The yardstick with which political systems are measured consists of the functions which are performed by the political system and the units which are being compared are the various structures which compose individual political systems. Once the functions of a political system are defined operationally and the structures categorised with precision, it will become, Almond asserts, possible to write an equation of each political system which will show how much of each function is fulfilled by a particular structure. This Almond describes as the 'probabilistic theory of the polity'.

Whatever be the merits of structural-functionalism and the possibilities of major advances likely to emerge from this analysis, there is no denying the fact that the study of comparative government has grown during recent years and has, indeed, become a major branch of study with scholars working on detailed problems and theorists attempting grand syntheses. It may not achieve a great deal "but this should not be allowed to obscure its potentiality. The student may find it one of the most rewarding and stimulating parts of Political Science".[69]

The Method of Analogy. Prof. Gilchrist suggests one more inductive method, that of analogy. This method has been made use of by Herbert Spencer. He says that both the State and an organism possess the sustaining, distributary and the regulating systems and both exhibit the same process of development. From this analogy, he concludes that the State is an organism. The method of analogy is, no doubt, good and it serves a useful purpose. But analogy is not proof. What analogy leads to is merely a hypothesis. It gives probability and not certainty and the farther the analogy is carried the more misleading it becomes. The difficulty of its application in Political Science is all the more marked because of the vast number of circumstances surrounding any given instance.

The Statistical or the Quantitative Method. Another method which has recently become increasingly important and is being widely used in the study of political phenomena is the Statistical or Quantitative method. It attempts to describe and measure in quantitative terms and is especially applied to the study of political parties and public opinion. The statistical technique has also been extended to the study of comparative government and international relations. David Thomson is of the opinion that "until some such statistical and sociological technique is applied to international relations, the science of studying international relations will make little further progress in method."[70]

The analysis of public opinion is as old as Plato, but as a field of scientific investigation

68. Almond, G.A., and Powell, G.B., *Comparative Politics, A Developmental Approach,* pp. 74-79.
69. Blondel, J. (ed.), *Comparative Government,* p. xii.
70. *Contemporary Political Science* (Unesco), p. 593.

with the aid of statistical tools it is only a generation old. In the immediate background are such writers as Tonnies, Tarde, Le Bon, Wallas and Bryce. But two books, Lawrence Lowell's *Public Opinion and Popular Government*, and Walter Lipmann's *Public Opinion* "did much to delineate the field in terms meaningful to American political science."[71] Especially following Lipmann's work, public opinion has become a field of specialization in American Universities. The application of statistical techniques to the analysis of various types of political and governmental data has been advanced by Stuart Rice, Louis Bean, Harold F. Gosnell and others. H. Dewey Anderson and Percy E. Davidson have applied the statistical technique to such widely varied fields as voting motivation, occupational mobility as it affects state-governmental operations, occupational trends upon a national and local basis, and concentration of economic power and its effect on political power. In some of the Western countries "public opinion polls" or "Gallup polls" are held. If skilfully framed and conducted, such polls have shown themselves, in Britain as in America, to be capable of a high degree of accuracy.

It is, however, necessary to exercise great care in the collection and use of the statistics. Lowell has aptly said that "statistics, like real pies, are good if you know the person who made them, and are sure of the ingredients" as "by themselves they are strangely likely to mislead, because unless the subject is understood in all its bearings, some element can easily be left out of account which wholly falsifies the result."[72] To put it rather bluntly, there are three kinds of lies, the white, black and statistics, and it is the last kind which is so difficult to nail or counteract. Statistics are manipulated to suit the party purposes and explained to distort the facts for electoral gains and political manoeuvring. It cannot, however, be denied that a knowledge of statistical principles and sampling method is often useful to the political scientists.

The Philosophical Method. The methods of investigation so far considered are inductive methods. These methods start with certain facts which are either historical in their character or are the result of experiment, comparison or observation and, then, certain conclusions regarding the political phenomena are arrived at. The philosophical method, on the other hand, is deductive or *a priori* and its prominent exponents are Plato, Rousseau, Hegel, Bradley, Kant, Bosanquet, and Sidgwick. The deductive method implies reasoning from or developing particular conclusions from a number of general principles or propositions which are admitted or assumed to be true. The philosophical or *a priori* method is, thus, reasoning from cause to effect, from a general principle to its consequences. In Political Science this method of investigation starts from some abstract original idea about human nature and draws deduction from that idea as to the nature of the State, its aims, its fractions and its future. It then attempts to harmonise its theories with the actual facts of history.

Attempts have recently been made to differentiate between a political scientist and a political philosopher. It is maintained that not all students of Political Science confine themselves to the quest of factual knowledge of the discipline. Some are mainly concerned with the search for moral knowledge. These political philosophers are interested not so

71. Dwight Waldo, *Political Science in the United States of America* (Unesco), p. 73.

72. Lowell, A.L., *The Philosophy of Politics, American Political Science Review,* Vol. IV, p. 10.

much in how people and governments behave as they are in how they ought to behave. If the political scientist studies reality and tries to explain various political phenomena and the working of the institutions, the political philosopher essentially studies ideas and tries to discover which have the greatest validity.[73] The works of Plato, Aristotle, St. Thomas Aquinas, Niccolo Machiavelli, Thomas Hobbes, John Locke, Jean Jacques Rousseau, Edmund Burke, Jeremy Bentham, G.W.F. Hegel, Karl Marx, and John Stuart Mill all deal with the perennial questions of justice, equality, freedom, why should a citizen obey the State ?, is man good or evil by nature ?, is the society or the individual prior ? and a host of other similar questions. These are moral questions and there is more than one answer to each of them. Rousseau says that men are equal, and Burke would deny that proposition. Hegel asserts that society is more important than the individual, and Mill replies that the individual is prior to society. We read the works of all these political thinkers because they provide the best starting point for the study of the moral aspects of political life.

Ronald Pennock and David Smith maintain that political scientists often debate the relative merits of various political values, such as liberty and order, and in doing so, "they are philosophizing rather than practising." Accordingly, it is asserted, that their field of study should properly be denominated "Government" or "Politics" rather than by the more restricted term "Political Science." As it is, Pennock and Smith conclude, "We must recognize that we have scientific political scientists and philosophical political scientists. There is an important place in the profession for those who leave questions of political ethics to others and who strive for the greatest possible detachment in judging trends and seeking to determine cause and effect in political matters."[74] In other words, some "division of labour" is desirable "between those who consider what goals should be pursued and those who concentrate on discovering the best ways of attaining particular goals, or who merely try to chart the course we are following and predict whither we are bound."[75]

According to Talcott Parsons,[76] the basic functions of every social system are four: it must maintain its own basic patterns, particularly those of its own governing and control; it must adapt itself to changing conditions in both its physical environment in nature and its human environment in terms of other systems; it must integrate its different tasks and functions; and if it has specific goals beyond mere adaptation, integration and the maintenance of its patterns, it must move to attain its goals. From Parson's approach, Karl W. Deutsch derives a way of looking at "Politics" and the sub-systems of society in the context of these basic functions. Referring to the *integrative* sub-system of every society, he says that it consists mainly in its "culture or cultural sector, including education, religion, philosophy and art." Religion and philosophy, like education, teach the people "the long-run nature of the universe, the long-run values of mankind, and, perhaps the

73. Andrew Hacker, *The Study of Politics: The Western Traditional and American Origins*, pp. 8–9.
74. J. Ronald Pennock and David G. Smith, *Political Science: An Introduction,* p. 22.
75. *Ibid.* Also refer to H. Victor Wiseman (ed.), *Political Science.* Mark the title of the book: *Political Science: An Outline for the Intending Student of Government, Politics and Political Science.*
76. Talcott Parsons, *The Social System.*

long-run purpose for which mankind still exists."[77] The Government, or "more generally, the political sector," according to Deutsch, is the typical goal-attaining sub-system. "It is the government that organizes the society for the pursuit of whatever goals the society may have chosen. Pursuing a goal involves forming an image of it, which we may call an *intention,* and then finding the means to implement the intention, or a course toward the goal."[78]

In any political activity where means and ends are involved *ought to be* cannot be altogether ruled out, no matter how we look at the subject of our study. Ethical considerations, therefore, become imperative and some precepts of political conduct are necessarily to be prescribed. Philosophy, then, intervenes, in the study of Political Science. But the pitfall to be avoided in applying the philosophical method is that of attempting to defend one's own personal opinion. The Philosophical method, like other methods in the study of Political Science, demands a detached and objective point of view. Though none can be completely objective, it is the desideratum and we must strive for as best as we can.

Then, the goal to be attained must not be utopian. Philosophers, swayed by their idealism, create conditions of their imagination and weave a web of ideas which is devoid of facts and realities of life. Sir Thomas More, in his *Utopia,* conceived of 'that ideal State which is contrary to the facts of history and human nature. Such a philosophy degenerates into a mere ideology with dangerous results. Karl Popper says that the speculative or utopian method ``which chooses an ideal state of society as the aim, which all our political actions should serve, is likely to produce violence" and that ``the utopian engineers who design and execute the utopian blueprint" must ``become omniscient as well as omnipotent. They become gods."[79] Even Oakshott does not spare those who seek ``to turn a private dream into a public and compulsory manner of living."[80] Political Philosophy must rise above all ideology. *Ought to be* must, as far as possible, coincide with *what it can be.*

Conclusion. The real method of Political Science is an evaluative analysis: uniting description with theory. People do not stop with analysis. They also pass judgment on the political process in terms of abstract ideals many of which have an ethical content. For example, if a political scientist studies an institution like the British Parliament, he will, of course, collect all pertinent factual data about that body—about its historical growth, its functions, membership, organisation, relations with other branches of government, and so on—and he will present his information in a systematic form. But this much does not exhaust his task. He may have to give answers to a host of additional questions connected with his inquiry. Are the functions of Parliament clear-cut and appropriate ? Does Parliament find sufficient time to do its job efficiently and satisfactorily ? Are the members as competent as their responsibilities demand ? Are the members well informed and do they adequately perform their duties ? Do they place special interests before the public

77. Deutsch, Karl W., *Politics and Government,* p. 134.
78. *Ibid.*, p. 133.
79. Popper, Karl, *Conjectures and Refutations,* pp. 357-63.
80. Oakshott Michael, *Rationalism in Politics,* pp. 184-88.

good ? What is the position of the private members ? Such questions cannot be avoided in the analysis of Parliament and they cannot be adequately answered without reference to certain ideal objectives and criteria. The attempt at answering them is an evaluation and here analytical method combines with the philosophical method.

Similarly, a political philosopher does not and cannot altogether exclude a concern for institutions, however ethereal his end and however celestial his aspiration. "Since political achievement is for men and through men," says Herman Finer, "political achievement is through institutions, which are nothing but men acting more or less deliberately in a fairly durable concert for the attaiment of a considered complex of ends." The political philosopher begins with an end and then finds ways and means, that is, institutions. Plato started with his ideal of justice and established a systematic philosophy of social relationships ordered by government. Hobbes was mortally afraid of strife, disorder and death and he believed that monarchy was the most stable and orderly kind of government which could ensure peace and order and he used the doctrine of Social Contract as a weapon of defence for absolute government and as a justification of Stuart despotism. John Locke proceeded from the pursuit of happiness and tolerance and justified the need of government by consent. "The happiness and the security of the individual," explains Dunning, "figure (in Locke's Thesis) not as essential to the perpetuity of a government, but as the end for which alone government is ever called into existence."

The study of Political Science, therefore, springs from both inductive and deductive methods. Induction and deduction are not incompatible methods; they supplement each other. Realism must be blended with idealism. If realism does not partake of idealism, we cannot march towards the goal of an ideal political organisation. The experiences and phenomena of political life should illumine the light of ideas.

It must, however, be remembered that no methodology of Political Science can lead to true conclusions, unless we take human nature into account. After all the State exists for man and it endeavours to cater to his needs in order to make his life happy. Man is the central subject of our study and we must go to his psychology to find out the really correct solution of his problems. Hitherto political thinkers had regarded man as a rational being and accepted this nature of man as a dogmatic truth and consequently the starting point of their investigations. Recently, Graham Wallas, in his book *Human Nature in Politics*, has revolted against this traditional assumption of human nature. Man, according to Graham Wallas, is hardly rational in his behaviour. "If, indeed, a man were followed," he writes, "through one ordinary day, without his knowing it, by a cinematographic camera and photographer and if all his acts and saying were produced before him next day, he would be astonished to find how few of them were the result of a deliberate search for the means attaining ends."[81] Whether we agree with Graham Wallas or not, the importance of psychology as a clue to political behaviour cannot be denied. Nor must the institutions of government be regarded as eternal or petrified. "Institutions are," as Finer says, "nothing but useful or useless habits: they were acquired for a purpose, and purpose changes. The world of political reality is not the printed world of books, or of

81. Graham Wallas, *Human Nature in Politics*, p. 126.

statutes, or of administrative rules and orders. The cut and dried is not political."[82] Institutions are really how they are worked and their actual working is subject to the political behaviour of man, that is, what men really do when faced with situations rather than what their alleged opinions or feelings are.

RELATION WITH OTHER SOCIAL SCIENCES

Sidgwick says that it is always useful for the proper understanding of any subject of inquiry to establish its relationship with other sciences and to see clearly what elements of its reasonings it has to take from them and what in its turn it may claim to give them. Political Science is deeply related to all other social sciences, because knowledge that is gained about any phase of human behaviour and attitudes, about the institutions that men build, or the ideas to which they respond in the mass, cannot fail to be of use in similar fields of inquiry. Each social science—sociology, anthropology, history economics, ethics, psychology, jurisprudence, geography and political science—supplements and fortifies the rest. If we divide them into different sciences, they are distinctions within a unity as all aim at the study of man in society. All are inter-dependent and inter-related. Each contributes importantly to the advancement of the other. Gunnar Heckscher succinctly says, "We cannot think of economics, sociology, political science, cultural anthropology, any more than of chemistry, mechanics, biology, etc., as a group of self-contained units, each clearly defined and independent of the others. We must rather think of science as a field of study which for practical purposes we have to divide between us, but which in principle is a whole, not a group of separate parts."[83] During recent times there has been an appreciable extension of the dimensions of Political Science, due to increase in interdisciplinary approach, as an aid to complete knowledge of an astonishing complex phenomenon—man's organized political life.

Sociology. The terms 'Sociology' and 'Political Science' are closely related. They both lack clearly defined meaning. The origin of the term 'Political Science' is rather old, as it is associated with the Greek word *polis* whereas the term 'Sociology' was coined by Auguste Comte in 1839 to designate the science of society. Comte had earlier used the term 'Social Physics' in the same sense, but later replaced it with 'Sociology' and since then, the use of the term has changed little.

Sociology is the parent science of all the social sciences. It is the science of society viewed as an aggregate of individuals or "it is the science of men in their associated process." It deals with social development in general and analysis and describes social life in all its phases and complexities through all ages and climes. Sociology may, thus, be defined as the science of the origin and development, structure and functions, of social groups, their forms, laws, customs, institutions, modes of life, thought and action and their contribution to human culture and civilisation. It seeks to discover the general principles underlying all social phenomena and social relationships and to establish the laws of change and growth in society.

Political Science and Sociology are so intimately connected that the "political is

82. Herman Finer, *Theory and Practice of Government*, p. 5.
83. Gunnar Heckscher, *The Study of Government and Politics,* p. 5.

embedded in the social and if Political Science remains distinct from Sociology, it will be because the breadth of the field calls for the specialist, and not because there are any well-defined boundaries marking it off from Sociology."[84] They are mutually contributory. Political Science gives to Sociology facts about the organisation and functions of the State, and obtains from it knowledge of the origin of political authority and laws which controlled society. The State in its early stages was more of a social than a political institution, and Giddings is of the opinion that "to teach the theory of the State to men who have not learned the first principles of sociology, is like teaching astronomy or thermodynamics to men who have not learned the Newtonian law of motion."[85] A political scientist must be a sociologist and a sociologist ought to be a political scientist. For example, the institution of marriage by itself is an element in the social life of man and is the concern of Sociology. But if a code of marriage, like the Hindu Marriage Act, is enacted to regulate it in a particular way, it at once falls within the domain of Political Science as it comes within the scope of organised control and obedience. The Hindu, the Sikh, the Muslim and the Christian communities by themselves are the subjects of Sociology, being parts of the Indian society, but when they quarrel among themselves and their quarrel flares up into communal riots, it not only represents the pathological side of Indian social life but also a problem of deep political concern to prevent their recurrence and to remove the causes of conflict in order to weld them into a patriotic nation. Likewise, if we study revolutions, we must take into account their social as well as their political causes as appearing in different environments. The analysis of political parties cannot be divorced from their relationship to social classes, and the sociology of the electorate—behaviour of man in the associated process—solves the difficulties emerging from the basic democratic mechanism.

In spite of this close affinity between Sociology and Political Science, the study of both the sciences is distinct and their problems are by no means the same. Giddings has said that the province of Political Science is not co-extensive with "the investigations of society but that the lines of demarcation can be drawn."[86] Sociology deals with man in all his varied social relations and in all forms of human associations. Its study is not confined to one aspect of man alone. Political Science, on the other hand, is a study of the political governance of man and it is a specialised branch of Sociology. It has a narrower and more restricted field to cover than Sociology. Secondly, the political life of man begins much later than his social life. Sociology is prior to Political Science. Thirdly, Sociology embraces the study of organised and unorganised communities and the conscious and unconscious activities of man. The province of Political Science is the politically organised society and conscious political activities of man. Finally, Political Science aims at the past, present and future determination of the political organisation of mankind whereas Sociology is the study of various social institutions that exist or have hitherto existed. It does not and cannot predict about the future of society and social relationships. Its study is empirical and has no philosophical trend to follow. The distinction between Political Science and Sociology has been aptly described by Ernest Barker. He says,

84. Garner, J.W., *Political Science and Government*, p. 29.
85. Giddings, *Principles of Sociology*, p. 37.
86. *Ibid.*, p. 35.

"Political theory only deals with political associations, united by a constitution and living under a government; sociology deals with all associations. Political theory assumes as a datum that man is a political being, it does not explain, as sociology seeks to do, how he came to be a political being."[87]

Political Sociology. During the past two decades or so collaboration between Political Science and Sociology has been increasingly emphasised and the sociological foundation of politics stressed. As pointed out earlier, the revolution in the study of American politics is the consequence of the penetration of sociological, anthropological and psychological methods and theories. There is the social and cultural matrix of politics. Explaining it, Pennock and Smith say, "Some politically relevant patterns of behaviour are imposed on man by the conditions of social life itself and certain psychological traits are brought out by society which in turn determine the social milieu."[88] The result is a new branch of study. Political Sociology explains the sociological interpretations of political phenomena and quite a sizable literature on the subject has been made available. Lipset, whose contribution is well-recognised, explains, "No Sociologist can conceive of a study of society that does not recognise the political system as a major part of the analysis. And many political scientists, particularly in recent years, have argued, sometimes with others in their own field, that it is impossible to study political processes except as special cases of more general sociological and psychological relationships."[89]

Political Sociology takes the concept of political system, first developed by David Easton, and seeks to examine it in sociological terms, on the basic assumption that political system of a country is "integrally related to its social system." A system, therefore, implies interdependence of parts. By interdependence is meant that when the properties of one component in a system change, all the other components and the system as a whole are affected. For example, when the rings of an automobile wear away, the motor car burns oil, the functioning of the other parts of the machine or system deteriorates, and the power of the vehicle declines. In the political system the emergence of mass political parties, or of media of mass communications, like the press, the radio and the television, have changed the performance of structures of the system and the general capabilities (that is, the way it performs as a unit in its environment) of the system in its domestic and foreign environments. To quote Almond and Powell, "... when one variable in a system changes in magnitude or in quality, others are subjected to strains and are transformed; the system changes its pattern of performance, or the unruly component is disciplined by regulatory mechanism."[90]

The sociological approach to politics bas been precisely summed up by Sartori. He says, "Political sociology is only born when the sociological and political approaches are combined at the point of intersection. If the sociology of politics deals with non-political reasons, while the people act the way they do in political life, then political sociology should include also the political reasons why people act the way they do. A real political

87. Sir Ernest Barker, *Political Thought in England* (1848–1914), p. 138.

88. Pennock, J. Ronald, and Smith, David G., *Political Science*, Chap. 3.

89. Lipset, S. H., *Political Man,* p. 92.

90. Almond, G.A., and Powell, G.B. Jr., *The Comparative Politics: A Developmental Approach,* pp. 17–18.

sociology is then a cross-disciplinary breakthrough, seeking enlarged models which reintroduced as variables the 'givens' of each component source."[91] Talking in concrete terms, Political Sociology is a connecting bridge between Sociology and Political Science. It believes in a two-way relationship between Sociology and Political Science, giving equal emphasis to social and political variables. Take for example the party system. Here Political Sociology does not explain the working of the party system only in terms of its response to and reflection of the socio-economic scene, but also investigates how the society is as much conditioned by the party system. India offers an apt and familiar illustration to explain the point. While Sociology of politics analyses Indian politics in terms of its caste-ridden society, Political Sociology adds to that enquiry how politics in India has affected the Indian caste system, giving rise to what is called 'politicalisation of caste'. The distinction between the sociology of politics and Political Sociology would help us in understanding the meaning of Political Sociology on which the specialists have so far disagreed.

Anthropology. Anthropology deals with racial divisions of man, his physical character, his geographic division. his environmental and social relations, and his cultural development. It is a science which studies mankind in relation to physical, social, and cultural development. The contribution of Anthropology to Political Science is considerable, and modern researches in the racial division, habits, customs, and organisations of primitive man help us to know the real origin of the State and the development of various political institutions. The political behaviour of man is greatly influenced by his racial origin and the environments in which he lives. Two common sayings illustrate the point: there is something run in the blood of man, and, man is the shuttlecock of his environments. The theory of nationalism as preached by Hitler and his dogma of superiority of the Aryan race solve many a knotty problem of recent political thought. Finally, race unity is one of the strongest bonds of nationality, and geographic unity is another important factor which fosters the sentiment of nationality.

We seek the help of Anthropology to prove that early society was communal in character, that is, its basis was the group rather than the individual, whom we now accept as the unit of our society. Anthropology also tells us that in early stages of the development of society, temporary marriage was the rule rather than the exception. But such a condition of society could not last for long and the need for regulating marriage was felt. With the regulation of marriage, civilisation advanced and people permanently settled down as territorial units paving the way for the emergence of the State. Thus, Anthropology greatly helps the study of Political Science. Without a good knowledge of early societies, their laws, customs, manners and modes of government, we cannot understand accurately the modern institutions and the political behaviour of the people.

Hitherto Anthropology was regarded as applying wholly or mainly to primitive society. But its scope is now widening and includes all types of society. "A knowledge of social anthropology," says Robson, "is essential for the study or practice of colonial administration; and it is necessary also for several other special topics of political science,

91. Sartori, G., "From the Sociology of Politics to Political Sociology; Lipset, S.M. (ed.), *Politics and the Social Sciences,* pp. 92–99.

such as area studies, colour and racial conflicts, international organisations for assisting underdeveloped countries, immigration and emigration."[92] Harold D. Lasswell approvingly cites C.D. Lerner[93] and says that the links between students of folk society—the distinctive subject-matter of social anthropology—and Political Science have been closer in recent years "as whirlwind modernization added to the turbulence of politics in Asia, Africa, South America, and many heretofore-isolated island communities."[94] He is of the opinion that in future years, "the data of anthropology will be highly pertinent to the consideration of various problems that are likely to grow into large dimensions."[95]

Anthropology has an inexhaustible source of data on every sphere of man and his culture and Political Science, as Robson says, "will draw on various parts of this repository as problems gain in their urgency."[96] During the last two decades voluminous literature has been published on the process of modernization of traditional societies of Asia and intricate tribal communities of Africa. Almost all those countries which became sovereign States after World War II started their careers with democratic institutions, generally of the parliamentary type, but barring a few, all of them succumbed to some or other form of authoritarian regime or dictatorial rule, military or totalitarian. Political Anthropology, which is now recognised as a fairly independent discipline, helps to solve the riddle of the failure of Western model of democratic institutions in these countries. The traditional elements, attitudes, values, patterns of behaviour and leadership weigh very heavily in the developing countries as compared with the more rationalised developed nations of the West and, consequently, the operational aspects of the democratic institutions can scarcely be understood in terms and manner familiar to the Western States. Bryce has aptly said that there are institutions which "like plants flourish only on their hillside and under their own sunshine."

Political Science and History. The relationship between Political Science and History is very close and intimate. John Seeley expressed this relationship in the following couplet—

"History without Political Science has no fruit,
Political Science without History has no root."

Seeley's emphasis seems to be rather exaggerated, yet no one can discount the dependence of the two disciplines on one another. The State and its political institutions grow instead of being made. They are the product of history and in order to understand them fully one must necessarily know the process of their evolution: how they have become what they are, and to what extent they have responded to their original purposes. All our political institutions have a historical basis as they depict the wisdom of generations. History furnishes sufficient material for comparison and induction, enabling us to build an ideal political structure of our aspirations. In the absence of historical data, the study of Political Science is sure to become entirely speculative or *a priori*. And *a priori*

92. Robson, W.A., *The University Teaching of Social Sciences : Political Science* (Unesco), p. 59.
93. *The Passing of Traditional Society.*
94. Lasswell, H.D., *The Future of Political Science*, p. 224.
95. *Ibid*, p. 225.
96. Robson, W.A., *The University Teaching of Social Science; Political Science* (Unesco), p. 57.

Political Science, as Laski observes, "is bound to break down simply because we never start with the clean slate." The writings of historians, in brief, form a vast reservoir of material which a student of Political Science can analyse into meaningful patterns and guide him in understanding the present and outlining the future. Moreover, with its chronological treatment, history offers a sense of growth and development thereby providing a base or an insight into the social changes.

Robson is of the opinion that some knowledge of History is clearly indispensable for Political Science and cites the explanation offered by Professor R. Solatu at the Cambridge Conference (from 6 to 10 April, 1952). Professor Solatu said, "that he had been baffled all through his teaching career, especially during the 20 years he had spent in the Middle East, about how to teach the history of political philosophy to students whose historical background is usually inadequate, and often limited to purely political theory since the French Revolution." Where Political Science is not approached through History, he remarked, "the student may easily get a confused outline, in which most historical allusions are lost on him, supplemented by a slight acquaintance with a few classical texts of political philosophy, the background of which he scarcely understands." Moreover, a knowledge of History is particularly necessary in the sphere of Comparative Government.

History, in its turn, has much to borrow from Political Science. Our knowledge of history is meaningless, if the political bearings of events and movements are not adequately evaluated. The history of the nineteenth-century Europe, for example, is an incomplete narration of facts unless full significance of the movements, like nationalism, imperialism, individualism, socialism, etc., are brought out. Similarly, the history of India's independence is devoid of all logic, if we do not sufficiently explain the political result of the rise of the Indian National Congress; the Muslim demand for separate electorates; the benevolent despotism of the Government of India Act, 1909; Montagu's August 1917 Declaration; the Reforms of 1919 and the experiment with Dyarchy; the recommendations of the Simon Commission; the deliberations of the Round Table Conferences; the Communal Award; the Government of India Act, 1935; the implications of the Atlantic Charter; the 1942 Quit India Movement; Cripps Proposal; Simla Conference; declarations of Lord Wavell and Pethick-Lawrence; the Cabinet Mission Plan; the June 3, 1947, Announcement; and the Independence Act, 1947. "Political Science," says Bryce, "stands midway between history and politics, between the past and the present. It has drawn its materials from the one, it has to apply them to the other."

Both Political Science and History are contributory and complementary. So intimate is the affinity between the two that Seeley maintained: "Politics is vulgar when not liberalised by History, and History fades into mere literature when it loses sight of its relation to Politics." Separate them, says Burgess, and the one becomes a cripple, if not a corpse, the other a will-o'-the-wisp.

It does not, however, mean that Political Science is a beggar at the door of History. Nor does it mean, as Freeman says, that history "is past politics or that politics is present history." Political Science is, undoubtedly, dependent on History for its material, but it supplies only a part of the material. History is a chronological narration of events including wars, revolutions, military campaigns, economic upheavals, religious and social movements, and the rest. A good part of this material is not required by Political Science. The main concern of a political scientist is to study the evolution of the political institutions and the facts which bear, directly or indirectly, on the State and government, and its socio-economic problems. Political Science selects facts out of History. We are not so much concerned with the causes of the Revolution of 1688 in Britain as we are concerned with the advent of limited monarchy in that country and the beginning of the responsible form of government. Likewise, we are not interested on the causes of World War II and the strategy of the fighting powers. Our interest is to study and evaluate whether World War II was in reality a war of Democracy vs. Dictatorship, and whether it fulfilled the purpose for which it was fought. We are also interested in the shape of things that came over in the post-war political structure of the world as a result of this war.

History deals with concrete and matter of fact things. It presents to us not only facts, but the causal connection between the facts. Political Science is speculative as well, since it deals with what the State ought to be. This speculative character of the subject necessitates the consideration of abstract types of political institutions and laws. History has hardly anything to do with this aspect of Political Science. Finally, the historian's task is not to pass moral judgments, but the political scientist is bound to do so. It is here that Political Science joins hands with Ethics and parts company with Sociology, History and Economics.

The conclusion is obvious. Political Science and History are two distinct disciplines with separate problems, yet they have a common subject in the phenomena of the State, and, as such, their spheres touch at many points and overlap at others. Leacock succinctly remarks that some of History "is part of Political Science, the circle of their contents overlapping an area enclosed by each."

Economics. Till recently, Economics was regarded as a branch of Political Science. The Greeks called Economics by the name of Political Economy. Aristotle, in classifying the States, declared that the key fact is whether the State is ruled by the rich or the poor. He also observed that the way the bulk of the people earn their living, whether they are farmers, herdsmen, mechanics, shopkeepers, or day-labourers, will have much to do determining the nature of the State and its government. His discussion on revolution is also based on the proposition that the struggle between the rich and the poor is the underlying cause of most revolutions.[97] Locke's *Second Treatise of Civil Government* discusses topics that nowadays would be considered the province of Economics. Adam Smith, the English classical economist, in his famous book, *An Inquiry into the Nature and Causes of the Wealth of Nations*, refers to two important objects of Political Economy: to provide sufficient revenue for the people, and to supply the State, or what he calls commonwealth, with a revenue sufficient for the public administration. Without clinching the matter, he summed up that political economy "proposes to enrich the people and the sovereign."

Modern economists do not agree with the older point of view. They regard Economics as a separate discipline, which seeks to inquire how man gets his income and how he uses it. Alfred Marshall, the celebrated economist, considers it "on the one side the study of the wealth and on the other and more important side a part of the study of man." Its scope

97. Refer to the *Politics of Aristotle,* translated by Sir Ernest Barker, especially Books III and V.

is the study of human welfare and includes a discussion on Consumption, Production, Exchange, and Distribution—the four pillars on which the edifice of Economics is built.

In spite of its treatment as a separate discipline, there is now no difference of opinion that Political Science and Economics are auxiliary to one another. Man in society is a common factor in the study of both these sciences and it is the welfare of man and society for which each strives. The study of both Political Science and Economics is directed to the same common end. The welfare of man can only be obtained under conditions of an orderly society, because both are inseparable. It is the function of the State to secure these conditions so that every individual gets an opportunity for pursuing his activities, economic activities, of course, preceding the rest.

But no State can remain content merely to provide conditions of peace and order. The purpose of the State is to create that atmosphere which may be conducive to the good life of man and to give all an equal opportunity for growth and development. The State performs certain functions in order to achieve its purpose. It is one of the important functions of the State to see what its citizens consume. Every State is vitally concerned with the health of its people, as the people are the health of the State. The weak, the infirm, and the destitute cannot be good citizens, and a State inhabited by such people is socially, economically, and politically a cripple. It is the duty of the State to see that its nationals get sufficient and wholesome food to eat. It must also see that the people are adequately provided for, especially during times of crisis and emergency, with the requisite necessaries of life and that, too, at a reasonable level of prices. At the same time, the State may, for reasons of health of the people, either prohibit or restrict the use of certain commodities like liquor and other intoxicants.

It also becomes necessary for the State to see how commodities are produced and the nature and conditions of their production. For example, the Government of India is now making ceaseless efforts for growing and producing more, as the existing scale of production does not keep pace with the total demand of the country with its explosive growth of population and agriculture, the mainstay of the people, is a gamble in rains. It is the duty of the government to maintain sufficient reserves of food to cope with the vagaries of nature and other natural calamities. When demand exceeds supply, conditions of scarcity are created and prices rise. Rising prices cause distress for the masses and throw out of gear the orderly conditions of society. It is the primary duty of the government to remove conditions of distress and alleviate the sufferings of the people. But no country produces only for its internal needs. Some goods it cannot produce and imports from other countries. Others it produces advantageously and in abundance. It is for the State to determine its import and export policy and such a policy influences the scale of production.

The producer of one commodity is the consumer of another commodity. No man produces everything for himself. He must rely upon others and exchange with them his surplus goods. But goods are not exchanged for goods. A system of barter is highly inconvenient and money economy has taken its place. Money is now the medium of exchange and the measure of value. It is the function of the State to coin money and regulate it. The total amount of money in the hands of the people affects prices. Stable prices are the need of every State. The government carefully watches fluctuations in prices and determines whether more or less money should circulate. Similarly, banks, too, play an important role in controlling the price level by regulating credit. The paper currency of a modern State is issued by its Central or Reserve Bank. The Central Bank may either be a State-owned bank or the result of private enterprise. But whatever it is, a Central Bank must necessarily be the creation of a special Act of the legislature. Moreover, economic prosperity of every country depends upon the soundness of its banking organisation. It is within the jurisdiction of the State to regulate the functions of banks by necessary laws or even to nationalise them, if necessary.

The most baffling problem which confronts every country is that of distribution. In Economics, under the heading distribution, we study how the landlord, the worker, the capitalist, and the organiser are paid for the work each does in the field of production. The capitalist society, with its system of production and distribution, has brought about an uneven distribution of wealth. The theory of Socialism aims at bringing about that political structure of society where the national wealth of a country is most evenly distributed and one section of society does not thrive at the cost of the rest. The theories of Individualism and Socialism, with its different varieties, illustrate better than any other the interaction of Political Science and Economics.

Political and economic conditions act and react on one another. As a matter of fact, the solution of many of the economic problems must come through political agencies and the major problems of every State are economic in character. World War II was characterised as a war of democracy against dictatorship. But the causes of the War were really economic. The rise of Nazi-ism was also due to the economic crippling of Germany by the victorious powers after World War I. The failure of the League of Nations may be ascribed to the policy of economic aloofness and economic self-sufficiency to which every member-State steadfastly clung after World War I. Britain's political policy in India, and her reluctance to grant independence to Indians was more an economic expediency than a political advantage. The burning questions of present-day politics, viz., government control of industries, the relations of the State to industries, its attitude towards labour and capital, and a multitude of other similar problems, are all economic questions intertwined in the political issues. The cry that economic democracy should precede political democracy has revolutionised the political structure of every State. One may even say that the theory of government administration is largely economic in its approach when seeking to interpret matters concerning the Welfare State, public financial policies and relationships between government and private enterprise. When government itself undertakes production, it performs purely an economic function.

A good government, in brief, judiciously plans for plenty and it is judged in terms of specific economic achievements, that is, by the harsh realities of administrative performance; by the production of food and arrangements for its distribution at a reasonable price, by the growing production and equitable distribution of essential commodities, by the growth of employment opportunities, by the timely and efficient completion of development projects and by the judgment of their priorities.

Till recently, contemporary political theory heavily relied upon Sociology in explaining the process and impact of politics. But of late, it has more tilted towards Economics and noted economists, such as Downs, Buchanan, Tullock, Rothenburg, Olson and quite a few more, now define the basic issues of new political analysis in terms of economics and are constructing new concepts, findings and theories. "The New Political Economy", the name given by William C. Mitchell[98], to this analysis has not taken any tangible shape so far, but a convincing beginning has been made in "Welfare Economics" and in the development of such tools as "Cost benefit analysis", "System Theory", "Program-budgeting." and "Economic Theory" more generally. The tools it adopts are descriptive and statistical, but "mathematics and deductive model-building."

Ethics. Ethics deals with morality and formulates rules which should influence the behaviour of man while living in society. It investigates the rightness or wrongness of man's conduct and prescribes ideals to which he would direct his efforts. The line of demarcation between Political Science and Ethics is quite distinct. Though both Political Science and Ethics aim at the noble and righteous life of man, yet the former is primarily concerned with the political governance of man whereas the latter refers to man's conduct and morality; that is, whereas Political Science deals with political order, Ethics deals with moral order. Ethics also judges man's conduct and in the last resort touches on what the conduct ought to be. Political Science has nothing to do with it. The laws of the State prescribe only the way of life and are concerned with the external actions of man. Moral laws prescribe absolute standards of right and wrong, justice and injustice, but the laws of the State follow standard of expediency. What a law prohibits may not be an immoral act. Finally, Political Science is concerned with man as a citizen. Ethics is concerned with man as a man and, as such, it is prior to Political Science.

But a political idea cannot be divorced from an ehtical idea. Man can only pursue his moral ends while living in the State. Aristotle rightly said that a good citizen is possible in a good State and that a bad State makes bad citizens. He further maintained that while the State comes into existence for the sake of life, it continues to exist for the sake of good life. Good life is the end of the State and all political problems revolve around it. What is morally wrong cannot be politically right, because there cannot be a good State where wrong ethical ideals prevail.

So close is the relation between Political Science and Ethics that Plato and Aristotle hardly distinguished between the two. The Greek philosophers, in fact, laid more stress on the moral side of the State. Plato's *Republic* is as much a study in Ethics as it is in Political Science. Machiavelli was the first to distinguish between the two and he made Political Science independent of Ethics. He also differentiated between public morality and private morality. Hobbes, an English philosopher, followed Machiavelli in his arguments and reasonings. Kant, on the other hand, said, "True politics cannot take a single step forward unless it has first done homage to morals."

The modern view is rather conflicting. The concept of Scientific Relativism, which has a Germanic origin[99] and has now taken firm roots in the United States, has created complete dichotomy between Political Science and Ethics. It is asserted that introduction of value-judgments in political analysis impedes scientific objectivity and makes the

98. Refer to Mitchell, William C., "The Shape of New Political Theory to Come: From Political Sociology to Political Economy", Lipset, S.M. (ed.), *Politics and the Social Sciences,* pp. 101–32.
99. Brecht, Arnold, *Political Theory,* pp. 207–08.

discipline and any inquiry into its processes speculative. Stuart Rice, in his *Quantitative Methods in Politics*, blamed social scientists for having set their task as "the creation of a science of moral ends" which involved a contradiction in terms. He called for a clear distinction between science and philosophy. Karl Llewellyn made an explicit statement when he emphasised the separation of the realms of *Is* and *Ought* and the inability of science to teach us where to go. Of values, he said, "As we move into these value-judgments we desert entirely the solid sphere of objective observation, of possible agreement among all normal trained observers and enter into the airy sphere of individual ideals and subjectivity." He added that in order to prove a value one must refer to another, more general value and that, in the last analysis, "the end which is sought must be posited or assumed. It cannot be arrived at by scientific procedure."[100]

R.M. MacIver supports Stuart Rice and says, "Science itself tells us nothing, just nothing about the way we *should* act, and the ends we *should* seek."[101] At the round-table "Beyond Relativism in Political Theory," held at the annual meeting of the American Political Science Association, December, 1946, "general agreement on the logical separation of *Is* and *Ought* was expressed at the outset."[102] In 1936, Harold D. Lasswell brought out his *Politics*: *Who Gets, What, When and How* ! which was a thesis on Scientific Method and Value Relativism. In a later book, he made Political Science "a value-free Science" and defined it "as an empirical discipline, (as) the study of the shaping and sharing of power"[103] and "a political act (as) one performed in power perspectives."[104] Power, rule, authority or political influence, thus, became the central organising idea of the subject of Political Science and its scope was riveted upon it.

But not all the twentieth century thinkers subscribe to this point of view. There are some who believe that Scientific Method can deal with values as precisely as with facts. According to Alfred Weber, all scientific activity is "entirely tied to values." The French philosopher, Jacques Maritan, calls for a reinclusion of metaphysics in the realm of Political Science. Metaphysics, he maintains, wrongly ousted from science by the Scientific Method is science in the ampler sense. Likewise, Eric Voegelin, in his book, *The New Science of Politics*, severely refutes the argument that "Science" can only apply to Scientific Method. He calls for a "restoration" of Political Science, or for its "retheorization", by reviving the attempts made by the Greek philosophers and the medieval Christian scholars to provide an ontological description of the order of values, "The theoretical orientation of man in his world, the great instrument for man's understanding of his own position in the universe."[105]

In a paper submitted to 'the UNESCO project "Methods in Political Science", Thomas I. Cook observed, "I urge, finally, that the most glaring need of the social sciences today is to relate ethical concepts, in their general outline long discovered and scientifically verified, at once to the methods and results of modern sociological investigation, to

100. Rice, Stuart, *Quantitative Methods in Politics,* p. 15.
101. MacIver, Robert M, *The Pursuit of Happiness, A Philosophy for Modern Living*, p. 173.
102. Brecht, Arnold, *Political Theory,* p. 214.
103. Lasswell, H.D., and Abraham Kaplan, *Power and Society*, p. xiv.
104. *Ibid.,* p. 240.
105. As cited in Arnold Brecht's *Political Theory,* p. 273.

determine the proper sphere of the methods; to winnow and relate in systems, the results. I add here that in political science this need is specially obvious." This approach seemed to him the only one which promised an effectively unified system of Social Sciences, "within which political science may receive a definable place, fulfil an intelligent role, possess clear scope and function, and consequently develop appropriate methods and relevant special techniques."[106] When the end of the State is to create that atmosphere in which man can reach the full stature of his personality, the proper sphere of the functions of the State cannot be determined without moral considerations. The doctrine of International legal values or International ethics cements the principles of International Law and their binding nature. Professor Ivor Brown says, "Politics is but ethics writ large. Ethical theory is incomplete without political theory, because man is an associated creature and cannot live fully in isolation; political theory is idle without ethical theory because its study and its results depend fundamentally on our scheme of moral values, our conceptions of right and wrong." Moreover, Political Science is concerned with what the State ought to be. ``The great question'', in the words of Lord Acton, "is to discover, not what governments prescribe, but what they ought to prescribe."

A lasting contribution to Political Science is M.K Gandhi's plea for spiritualising politics. "There are no politics," said Gandhi, "devoid of religion", and Gandhi's religion consisted in truth and love. Wherever there was truth and love, there was non-violence, non-attachment and, thus, even-mindedness, i.e., action without the desire for results. Gandhi, in brief, desired to moralise man and society. He, then, emphasised that moral means must be adopted to achieve desirable results. As the seed, so is the tree, Gandhi declared.

The justification of what the State does is to be sought in the moral values it helps us to realise and it ought to provide for attaining the ideal end; the highest goal of man's life. It means that Political Science is conditioned by Ethics. But the main body of material with which the two disciplines deal is distinct.

Psychology. Psychology deals with the behaviour of man and elucidates what he actually does. It enquires into the mind of man and his behaviour, both as an individual and in groups, and explains the motives of human action. It seeks to determine how far human conduct is rational or instinctive or traditional. Political Science, which deals with the political relationship of human beings, cannot ignore the psychological effects. The State and its political institutions are the products of the human mind and can best be understood in terms of the mind. Theories about political conduct that are not grounded in an adequate psychology are apt to be defective. This has been well shown in some of the contributions that modern social psychology has made to Political Science. Barker says, "The application of the psychological clue to the riddles of human activity has indeed become the fashion of the day. If our forefathers thought biologically, we think psychologically."

The affinity between Political Science and Psychology has been greatly emphasised during recent times. Gabriel Tarde, Le Bon, MacDougall, Graham Wallas, and Baldwin are the prominent writers who have given psychological explanations of almost all the

106. *Contemporary Political Science,* (Unesco), p. 76.

political problems. They ascribe the unity of the State to psychological factors and the form of government and its laws are in conformity to the temperamental habits of the people. Political traditions and institutions, they assert, are what the human mind has made them. Bagehot, in his *Physics and Politics*, explains the successful working of the constitutional system of government in Great Britain in terms of the psychology and the genius of the people of that country. Government to be stable and really popular must reflect and express the mental ideas and moral sentiments of those who are subject to its authority; in short, it must be in harmony with what Le Bon calls the mental constitution of the race. In the democratic processes the part played by social psychology is, thus, subtle. Modern psychologists study men in groups as well as individual behaviour. The study of social psychology often has more direct relevance for the political scientist than does individual psychology.

There can be little doubt that the psychological approach to problems of Political Science is very valuable. Political Science has hitherto been much under the influence of philosophy and, consequently, oblivious of the realities of life. Thinkers assumed certain facts about human nature and dogmatically accepted them as self-evident truths. The result was an inaccurate analysis of the political institutions and the political behaviour of man. The advocates of physiological approach, therefore, say that we need "to reinvigorate our minds from the wells of direct observation" and the study of Political Science shall be futile unless we exactly know the way in which human beings behave as individuals and members of society under different influences.

It does not, however, mean that all political problems have a psychological explanation to offer. The areas of study in Political Science differ significantly in the extent to which they have thus far been subjected to the behaviourist approach. Its penetration is uneven. The area which has been subjected to the greatest influence is probably that of public opinion, voting and elections, political parties and pressure groups, international relations and public administration. It has also been applied to the general concepts, such as 'power' and 'influence', and of definitions of Political Science, such as that which sees it as a study of *Who Gets, What, When and How* !. Foreign and comparative government probably stand in the middle while its effect is the least in public law, jurisprudence, and judicial affairs. Moreover, Psychology does not concern itself with moral values. It does not say anything about what the State and its institutions ought to be. Furthermore, the psychologist seeks to explain life in terms of savage instinct, and social psychology leads us to explain the higher by the lower. This does not seem to be the correct evolutionary method. The right procedure is to explain the lower by the higher. "Man explains the monkey, and not monkey the man." It is not logical to explain civilised life by the conditions of primitive times. It is a bad argument that the thing is final, because it is primitive.

MacDougall and other psychologists explain the origin of instincts that operate in society. They do not, however, explain how and why these instincts arise in society. Finally, according to Catlin, Psychology is concerned with mental acts which must be considered in relation to the observable individual mind. But Political Science is concerned with "the impulsive or willed" relations of social beings.

Jurisprudence. No less close and no less ancient is the connection between Political Science and Jurisprudence, the science of law. The former is the study of the State and government whereas the latter is the study of law. If human beings are to live a life of togetherness and safeguard the existence of the community itself, they must accept certain rules of conduct. The rules governing society may be few or many. They can range from a few primitive traditions, handed down orally from one generation to another, to the whole complex set of constitutional and governmental regulations which are associated with the modern State. The regulations of the State are called laws and these are formulated, administered and enforced by the government. Every State, no matter what its form of government, develops its own constitutional law. Similarly, every political philosophy embraces or implies a jurisprudence. From a social point of view, laws must be influenced by their environments. As is the structure of society, so is the content of laws. In a community of large land-owners the laws will not be the same as in a country of peasant farmers. Similarly, the laws governing private property and the conditions of labour will be different under a capitalistic pattern of society and a socialistic one. The constitutional law of a democratic government basically differs from that in a dictatorship.

Strictly speaking, Jurisprudence is a sub-division of Political Science, as it is the State that creates and maintains the conditions of law. But it is now treated as a separate study because of the vastness of its scope and its specialised study of law. Moreover, law is concerned with classes of persons and classes of situations in general, and often hypothetical terms. Similarly, law may establish fictions that are convenient as working formulae, though they may have no bearing on actual life. A lawyer's approach is normative whereas the approach of a student of Political Science is both normative and descriptive. This is how the political scientist relates the subject-matter of his study to the realities of life and thereby corrects the distortions of legalism.

Public Administration. Public Administration deals with the administrative activities of government and Pfiffner defines it "as the co-ordination of collective efforts to implement public policy." It covers everything the civil agencies of government do, or could do, to help the body-politic attain its purpose. Public administration is really a part of Political Science, though it is now regarded and accepted as a separate subject of study. This dichotomy arose because of the two senses in which the term public administration was used in the nineteenth century. In a broader sense, public administration referred to the work involved in the actual conduct of the affairs of government, regardless of the particular branch concerned. In a narrow sense, it referred to the operations of the administrative branch only, with defined functions of enforcing the policy as distinct from the policy determining function. The policy determining function was deemed to be the political branch of government whereas the policy enforcing function its administrative branch. This distinction between the two branches of government led public administration to be regarded as a separate subject of study. Goodnow asserted, "The fact is ... that there is a large part of administration which is unconnected with politics, which should be relieved very largely, if not altogether, from the control of political bodies. It is unconnected with politics because it embraces fields of semi-scientific, quasi-judicial and quasi-business or commercial activities—work which has little, if any, influence on the expression of the true State will."

But that is not exactly so. Administration is only a means to the attainment of the objectives of the State. While discussing the purpose and scope of Public Administration, Leonard D. White says, "The immediate objective of the art of public administration is the most efficient utilization of resources at the disposal of officials and employees. In their broader context, the ends of administration are the ultimate objects of the State itself—the maintenance of peace and order, the progressive achievement of justice, the instruction of the young, protection against disease and insecurity, the adjustment and compromise of conflicting groups and interests—in short, the attainment of the good life:"[107] This similarity in the ends of Public Administration and Political Science, particularly in the context of a democratic government and a Welfare State, made possible, in the thirties of the present century, an evaluation of the relationship between the two. It is now generally agreed that the attempt to demarcate clear-cut functions of government is impossible. Government is a continuous process. It is true that the process contains phases. Legislation is one phase, administration another. But these are merged together and at certain points become indistinguishable. The distinction between policy determining functions and administrative functions is too hazy, for, as Herbert Simon says, the whole process of government and administration is one of "decision-making." Homer Durham goes to the extent of accepting the concept of "Administrative Politics."

This is, again, an extreme view. Yet, it is incorrect to assert that Political Science and Public Administration are separate and autonomous structures or processes. "To argue," as White says, "that they should be separate and independent is hardly defensible, given the nature of democratic government." Even the traditional concept of civil service neutrality is undergoing a radical change. "The concept," writes S. Lall, is "being rapidly transformed, without a conscious realisation, from a negative doctrine of political sterilization and neutrality to a positive, non-partisan participation in the management of the country's affairs."[108] Administration today is no longer just the execution of policy; it reacts upon policy and actively participates in its making.

Geography. It is maintained by certain writers that geographical and physical conditions greatly influence the character, the national life of the people, and their political institutions. Aristotle was of the opinion that without geography neither political nor strategical wisdom can go far. Bodin was the first modern writer who dwelt upon the relationship between Political Science and Geography. Rousseau tried to establish a relationship between climatic conditions and forms of government. He argued that warm climates are conducive to despotism, cold climates to barbarism and moderate climates to a good polity. Montesquieu, another French scholar, also emphasised the influence of physical environments on the forms of government and liberty of the people. But Buckle excels all. In his *History of Civilisation*, he maintained that "the actions of men, and therefore of societies, are determined by reciprocal interaction between the mind and external phenomena." He asserted that the actions of the individual and societies are influenced by the physical environments, particularly climate, food, soil, and the "general aspects of nature." In short, Buckle repudiates the generally accepted idea that the free will of man determines the action of the individual and society.

107. White, L.D., *Introduction to the Study of Public Administration*, p. 3.
108. *The Indian Journal of Public Administration*, January-March, 1958, p. 1.

It is axiomatically true that geographical location is an important factor in moulding the destiny of every State, and it greatly influences its national and international policies, and political institutions. And to fathom the actual impact of geographical factors on the political life of a nation, particularly in relation to its foreign policy, a new discipline of Geopolitics has developed. Thus, an island nation may readily become a moral power whereas a nation with rich natural resources may become more powerful in world politics. The nation controlling the Suez canal or the Panama canal becomes by that very fact extremely important to other nations. The geographical position of Germany, located as she is in the centre of Europe and without natural boundaries, is a compelling reason for her to remain a great military power. "Our historico-political destiny," wrote Professor Hintze, "lies in our geographical position."

It is really no exaggeration to say that geographical conditions always influence in considerable measure the determination of national policies and to some extent the character of the political institutions. Bryce has aptly said that "in any country physical conditions and inherited institutions so affect the political institutions of a nation as to give its government distinctive character." The obvious reference is to Great Britain and Switzerland.

Biology. Biology deals with animal life and its evolution. Some eminent writers sought to convert Political Science by treating the State as "a phase of development from associations formed among animals of a species included in the subject matter of natural history." Herbert Spencer is the most prominent exponent of the biological conception of the State, although the theory is as old as Plato Spencer's explanation, in brief, is that the State is like a biological organism in all its essentials. It is the product of evolution and is subject to the laws of birth, growth and decay. Just as in the case of an organism there is mutual dependence of the parts, so are the individuals who constitute the State. Spencer also tried to establish that like the three parts of an organism—the sustaining, the distributary and the regulating systems—the State, too, has three systems.

There are two views on the relationship between Political Science and Biology. Some writers argue that the State is an organism; others maintain that the State is like an organism. One may reject the assertion that the State is an organism, but it must be admitted that the State in its unity is like an organism; it has a collective life. The analogy, however, should not be extended beyond this, lest, in the words of Lord Acton, we may come to grief to which analogies, metaphors and parallelisms generally lead to.

Statistics. With the advance in the statistical theory and method and the recent tendency toward quantitative measurements in social situations, the relationship between Political Science and Statistics has become close and deep. The quantitative evaluation of political and administrative phenomena is regarded by political scientists as an indispensable instrument of knowledge. The statistical approach is usually employed in conjunction with other methods. Beatrice Webb records in her autobiography, "I had learnt the relation between personal observation and statistics ..., though, I never acquired the statistical instrument because I had not the requisite arithmetic. I became aware that every conclusion derived from observation or experiment had to be qualified as well as verified by the relevant statistics."[109]

109. Beatrice Webb, *My Apprenticeship*, pp. 339–40.

There is now a school of opinion which describes statistics as a branch of Political Science. But this is not correct. Statistics is a separate field of investigation in itself, requiring experts to make applications of the method. Yet, it cannot be ignored that the operation of cause and effect is made convincingly concrete and definite in many instances by the use of statistics, when the ordinary methods of observation and speculation fail to give the true reality involved therein. As Wilson observes, "While a statistical result does not provide an ethic or a norm to be embodied in policy, once the policy has been supported by rational conclusions as to what men desire of political society, statistics is invaluable in attaining the result." Modern governments essentially depend upon the statistical material and the data it provides in solving very many political riddles. With a Welfare State throwing its full weight on planning, statistics and its extensive use has become indispensable and every department of government keeps its own statistical cell and the administration is centred around the statistical results. Legislation aimed at public welfare must be guided by statistics and the various aspects of the welfare of the people, for example, taxation and expenditure policy, trade, natural resources, employment, social conditions in general as vice, crime, illiteracy, population, etc., have a statistical interpretation. Whatever be the utility of statistics and its importance in most forms of political investigation, it must be remembered that statistics may show the failure of a given political or legislative project, but it does not establish the futility of the policy.

SUGGESTED READINGS

Abraham Kaplan: *Power and Society.*

Almond, G.A., and Coleman, J.S. (eds.): *The Politics of Developing Areas: Introduction.*

Almond, G.A., and Powell, G.B.: *Comparative Politics: A Developmental Approach.*

Andrew Hacker: *Political Theory, Ideology, Science.*

Andrew Hacker: *The Study of Politics.*

Appadorai, A.: *The Substance of Politics.*

Arnold Brecht: *Political Theory: The Foundations of Political Thought.*

Arent Hannah: *Between Past and Future, Six Lectures in Political Thought.*

Asirvatham, E.: *Political Theory.*

Barker, E.: *The Study of Political Science and its Relation to Cognate Studies.*

Bentham, J.: *An Introduction to the Principles of Morals*

Bernard, E. Brown: *New Directions in Comparative Politics.*

Blondel, J.: *Comparative Government.*

Carritt, E.F.: *Morals and Politics.*

Catlin, G.E.G.: *A Study of Principles of Politics.*

Catlin, G.E.G.: *The Science and Methods of Politics.*

Crossman, R.H.S.: *Government and the Governed.*

Curtis, M.: *Comparative Government and Politics*

Dahl, R.A.: *Modern Political Analysis.*

Darte Germino: *Beyond Ideology, The Revival of Political Theory.*

Deutsch, Karl W.: *Politics and Government.*

Easton, D.: *The Political System.*

Field, G.C.: *Political Theory.*

Freeman, E.A.: *Comparative Politics.*

Garner, J.W.: *Introduction to Political Science.*

Garner, J.W.: *Political Science and Government.*
Gilchrist, R.N.: *Principles of Political Science.*
Gurnar Heckscher: *The Study of Comparative Government and Politics.*
Hyneman, C.S.: *The Study of Politics.*
James C. Charlesworth: *Contemporary Political Analysis.*
Laski, H.J.: *An Introduction of Politics.*
Laski, H.J.: *The Danger of Being a Gentleman and other Essays.*
Lasswell, H.D.: *The Future of Political Science.*
Lasswell, H.D. and Kaplan, A.: *Power and Society.*
Lerner, D., and Lasswell, H.D. (eds.): *The Policy Sciences.*
Lipson, L.: *The Great Issues of Politics.*
Lord, A.R.: *The Principles of Politics.*
Miller, J.D.B. : *The Nature of Politics.*
OakShott, M.: *Social and Political Doctrine of Contemporary Europe.*
Pennock, J. R., and Smith, D.G.: *Political Science, An Introduction.*
Pickles. Dorothy, M.: *Introduction to Politics,* Chap. 1.
Pollock. Sir, F.: *Introduction to the History of the Science of Politics,* Chap. I.
Robson. W.A.: *The University Teaching of Social Sciences: Political Science* (Unesco).
Rodee, C.C.: *Introduction to Political Science.*
Selley, J. R.: *Introduction to Political Science,* Lecture 1.
Sidgwick. H.: *Elements of Politics,* Chap. 1.
Thomas Aspragens, Jr.: *The Dilemma of Contemporary Political Theory.*
Unesco: *Contemporary Political Science.*
Waldo, Dwight: *Political Science in the United States of America* (Unesco).
Wallas, G.: *Human Nature in Politics,* Part I.
Wilson, F.G.: *Elements of Modern Politics.*
Wiseman, H.V. (Ed.): *Political Science.*

2

CHAPTER

Modern Politics

We discussed in the preceding Chapter the main ingredients of the modern politics. It has been said that there had been something of an intellectual revolution in the United States of America, and out of it has emerged a trend to master the new complexities both in developed and developing countries, by breaking out of "parochialism." This trend to create a new intellectual order may be summarised, as Almond and Powell do, under four headings: "(1) The search for comprehensiveness; (2) The search for realism; (3) The search for precision; and (4) The search for theoretical order."

But the modern innovations are not accomplished facts and do not present a unified theory. There is a sharp divergence of approach and technique amongst the innovators themselves and no one can say with certainty what shape Political Science may take ultimately. The most important work both empirical and theoretical is still to be done and during most recent times a swing is witnessed towards what it has been discarded earlier and that, too, vehemently. Yet no student of Political Science can remain oblivious of the main directions of innovators. A wise bird uses both wings to fly and we have emphasised the new trends and the various concepts used therein in the context of what an innovator would call the 'parochialism of a traditionalist.'

New ways of saying and doing things have always tempted some and horrified others. In Political Science particularly, methods of study and objectives of inquiry are subject to deep controversy. New approaches and objectives are likely to arouse, and actually they have, passions. Nor should the innovators frown on the 'traditionalists'. A dynamic study, as the discipline of Political Science is, must offer empirical solution also to the problems which confront the 'Age of the New Nation', the name that historians certainly will not fail to give our century. All this renders the subject exceedingly complex and its expanded dimensions.

New Dimensions. 'New Dimensions' is a new term meaning more or less the same as the old one 'scope'. Any discussion about scope or dimensions will inevitably involve a discussion about subject-matter, objectives and methodological assumptions. All the three have undergone a sea-change in the last six decades or so. The changes undergone by them are, no doubt, important but more important and relevant, as A.B. Mathur says, "are the causes responsible for these changes."[1] A commonplace argument is that these

1. Mathur, A.B., "The New Dimensions of Political Science ", *The Indian Journal of Political Science*, January-March 1986, p. 18.

changes have been brought about by the vast sociological, economic, scientific and technological revolution sweeping across the world, changing man's outlook in life and the world and transforming his concept of society, power, legitimacy, freedom and authority, rights and duties. State as an instrument of power, as an agent of social welfare and a bulwark against authoritarianism too has undergone a total change. "The expanded dimensions of Political Science, therefore, present a vast mosaic which can be understood partly historically and partly analytically."[2]

As said earlier, the warp and woof of the history of political thought is constituted by the writings of Plato, Aristotle, Augustine, Bodin, Locke, Rousseau, Mill, Burke and Marx. For centuries the study of Political Science was rivetted upon the seminal ideas of these illustrious masters who were not academics, but men of practical or public life. They went deep into the basic questions of purposes for which human societies exist and their relations to the purposes of human life.Theirs was a quest for just and happy life for which men assembled together in a territorially integrated society. They had no vested interests in accelerating or impeding the progress of Political Science as a discipline. They were all liberal thinkers and the last in the line of this glorious intellectual tradition was perhaps John Stuart Mill (1806–1873).

The end of the liberal tradition marked the phenomenal expansion of the university system and, consequently, the beginning of the new phase in the development of Political Science. Political scholars occupying prestigious university chairs, departing from the traditional approach, emphasised the need to develop a scientific approach to natural and social affairs. This they did by "expounding the virtues of a scholarly way of analysing politics, whereupon, by comparison, any more traditional sort of speculation about public affairs appeared to be less incisive or plainly mistaken." As years rolled by, great quantity of scholarly work accumulated and the new expertise of academicians as a class became so highly regarded that "for political scientists at least, it seemed reasonable to honour the old tradition for its historical stature" than for any relevance to the contemporary society.

The most amazing consequence of it all is that a "large number of American citizens have come to learn about public life from a particular aggregation of academic specialists rather than, as in the past, from a tradition based upon the works of great men in many walks of life." Knowledge was, thus, compartmentalised in the tighter moulds of rigidity. The conditions of work in the universities, prejudices, ideologies, processes of thinking deliberately generated by powerful social and economic interests, in short, the "contemporary socio-economic milieu, more than dispassionate comprehension of public affairs, have tended to determine the outlook of specialists and experts in all social sciences including Political Science." As a result, political scientists, as a group, tend to endorse "certain views of the polity as opposed to others."

Just before the Second World War there was a comprehensive view of American Society "which seemed suitable for remaining loyal to science, and at the same time, for assimilating the results of its exercise." But John Dewey and Karl Popper, neither of them a political scientist, "reflected a new and tough-minded version of liberalism which

2. *Ibid.*

worked its way into the discipline of Political Studies." Karl Popper provided the new philosophy of science, in terms much more specific than those of Dewey. The most authentic statement of his philosophy, linking it directly to democratic politics, appeared in *The Open Society and Its Enemies* (1945). All statements of science, said Popper, are scientific to the extent that it is possible to associate them with unambigous evidence. That is a belief is entitled to be called "scientific if it is expressed in terms that can be clearly proved or disproved, as distinguished from moral.and religious statements couched in terms of values that cannot be supported or contradicted." But it is very difficult to prove what we believe about humanity, society or nature. Science, in short, is a matter of methods and not results. Indeed a scientist's work may produce very few of the latter. But if he faithfully employs the proper methods, his findings will be "maximally reliable". Popper, in short, suggested how social research might be conducted and justified within a liberal society.

In the wake of the Second World War and deep into the 1960s, all the noted political scientists, sociologists. commentators on public affairs were of the opinion that ideologies "were, or ought to be, considered properly defunct." The crux of their argument was that any belief in ideology precludes scientific social research and "leads only to political disaster." Thus, the transition from dispassionate contemplation of public affairs to a study of politics according to rules laid down by the scientific community marked the first phase in the acquisition of new dimensions. The old subject matter, that is, the study of society as a moral organism and the objectives of the study as to how far the state helped to live a moral and, therefore, a happy life were abandoned. A new concept of society or state emerged stripped of all moral precepts and considerations..

But it was in the field of methodological assumptions that the study of politics underwent a revolutionary change. The knowledge of the nature of man, of nature and its relation with man, intuition, historical perspective and the external varieties social life as discovered by great thinkers were deemed totally obsolete and "unserviceable tools" with which a society could be studied, much less understood. Scientific tools of enquiry free from the constricting influence of moral values or values of any kind came to be accepted as the means of exploring the new dimensions of Political Science. The one school which made "a big splash was behavioural school which tried to give to the study of Political Science a new orientation, a new image and a new meaning."

Behaviouralism. The new scientific outlook, as a result of fact-value dichotomy, helped in a great measure to the growth of 'science of politics' movement geared to sophisticated scientific methodology. "It is not saying too much," remarked Arnold Brecht, "that ours has become the methodological century in the social sciences."[3] The scientific study of Political Science is popularly known as political behaviouralism. It is, however, important to note that most of the scholars who subscribe to this approach constitute a heterogeneous group united only by dissatisfaction with the traditional Political Science.[4] But we are here essentially concerned with those behaviouralists who subscribe to its scientific credo and obviously the fundamental assumptions that underlie it. For example,

3. Brechet, Arnold, *Political Theory : The Foundations of Twentieth Century Political Thought;* chap. VI.
4. Kirkpatrick, Evron M., "The Impact of Behavioural Approach, Traditional Political Science" in Austin Ranny (ed,), *Essays on the Behavioural Study of Politics*, p. 11.

David Truman, David Easton and many others of their like. Truman contends that the new approach deals with the verified principles of human behaviour "through the use of methods similar to those of natural sciences." Similarly, David Easton observed that despite shifts in emphasis, the underlying assumption of the behaviouralists is the same to build "a science of politics modeled after the methodological assumptions ol the natural sciences".[5]

Under the impact of 'behavioural' or 'scientific' approach vigorous attempts have been made to render Political Science of the order of Physics and Chemistry. There has been significant increase in the use of empirical and quantitative methods and attempts to evolve conceptual frameworks, models, theories, meta theories, and paradigms. Consequently, Political Science appears to have drifted away from the reality of the World and is lost in facts and data. "Political scientists, especially the behaviouralists, like the heroes of Turgeneev's *Fathers and Sons* believe that science would solve all problems and cure all ills."[6] Thus, the scientific movement which had arrived to take Political Science "away" from "dogma" — from religious dogma as well as from dogmas of national tradition or of personal conviction—and on to reality"[7] was lost in the dogma of science and the "ideology of no ideology." The new group of social scientists "favouring a non-ideological" science of society whom Alfred Weber called the "socially unattached intellectuals"[8] and Karl Manneheim named "free floating" "classless aggregation" failed to fulfil the aim of carrying forward the tradition of science.

Post-behaviouralism. It was soon realised that the development of a pure science of Politics was a cry for the moon. Micro studies, as formed the basis of their research, did not measure up to the ideal as the level of generality was sure to be low. Leo Strauss charged political scientists with the error of absolutizing the relative.[9] It was also pointed out, and quite relevantly, that their researches lacked objectivity. Even in the selection of research problems reflected bias. And as for the interpretation of data, personal preferences importantly played their role. It is very difficult for a researcher "to mark off his two different roles: as a scientist concerned with a dispassionate analysis of facts and as a citizen clinging to his preferences while participating in political activities. He is, however, charged with what is called "existential schizophrenia."[10]

Political Science, thus, pushed out of reality became merely an academic discipline "disengaged from facts."[11] It was then abundantly apparent that behavioural approach is similar to the philosophical irrelevance. In 1969, David Easton declared the end of the behavioural revolution and the beginning of a new era in the study of Politics; an era

5. Easton, David, *A Framework of Political Analysis*, p. 8.
6. Bhola Prasad Singh, "The Problem of Value in the Post-behavioural Era", *The Indian Journal of Political Science,* July-September, 1986, p. 356.
7. Brecht, *op. cit.*, p. 5.
8. Quoted in Mannheim, Karl, *Ideology and Utopia : An Introduction, to the Sociology of Knowledge*, p. 155. Mannheim borrowed this concept from Max Weber.
9. Leo Strauss, "An Epilogue" in Herbert J. Strong (ed.), *Essays on the Scientific Study of Politics,* p. 320.
10. Richard J. Bern Stein, *The Restructuring of Social and Political Theory,* p. 174.
11. Cobban, A., "Ethics and the Decline of Political Theory" in Gould and Thurssby (eds.) *Contemporary Political Thought: Issues in Scope, Value and Directions,* p. 298.

popularly called Post-behaviouralism. Its main thesis is "relevance" and "action."[12] This approach renewed the interest in and appreciation of the classics of Political Philosophy. For example, in reply to the statement that political scientists should give ethics to the philosophers and concern primarily with the description and analysis of political behaviour, behaviouralists of the rank of Almond replied that leaving ethics to philosophers was not desirable. "Practical judgment of 'good' and 'evil' in the area of public policy is the special responsibility of social scientists."[13] The behaviouralists had realised that hitherto they had failed to comprehend that facts and values are closely intertwined with each other and that, in Political Science, one cannot separate them except in very trivial circumstances and instances. This realization led them to the Post-behavioural era.

In fact, the very concept of value-free scientific inquiry is "a farce and is misleading." Certain values and norms are always present in any social research.[14] H.R.G. Greaves argues that a value-free Political Science is a myth and that "it has been insufficiently understood how far description in this field is independent for significance upon analysis and explanation into which values enter."[15] A social scientist who claims to engage himself in the kinds of value-free research practised by the chemist or biologist only befools himself and his readers for as Leo Strauss points out: "The value judgments which are forbidden to enter through the front door of Political Science ... enter ... through the back door."[16]

To sum up, the post-behaviouralist movement in Political Science has reopened the issue of fact-value separation. According to this school of thought, political scientists need not abdicate the spirit of their discipline at the altar of science or any other empiricism. "Moderate empiricism, sound analytical techniques, carefully chosen terminology, self-conscious attention to logical inferences, quantification, and the use of scientific data, are useful. But too much obsession with science would kill the spirit of the discipline." It is, accordingly, not prudent to abandon science, but to simply put it to better way and use. Kaplan rightly believes that "if a man fails to consider moral and political questions seriously, he may reduce himself and his progeny to an ugly and distasteful, if not brutal, animality."[17] Thus, values must be studied as values, not scientifically and yet scientifically."[18]

Politics. The modern political scientists introduce the reader to the study of politics and accept it as the hub of political activity. Ordinary use equates politics with party politics and politicians with party politicians, engaged in the politics of their respective parties born out of disagreement on the policies and programmes each party owns and propagates and, therefore, they conflict on the issues. As a result, politics emphasises

12. Easton, David, *"The New Revolution in Political Science, op cit.* p. 105.
13. "Political Science and Ethics" in Gould and Thurssby, *op. cit.*, p. 287.
14. Markovic, Mihails, "Ethics of a critical social science", reprinted in ICSSR *News Letter,* October 1976 — March 1977.
15. Greaves, H.R. G., "Political Theory Today" in McCoy, Charles and Playford J. (eds.) *Apolitical Politics: a Critique of Behaviouralism,* p. 285.
16. Strauss, L, *What is Political Philosophy*, p. 21.
17. Kaplan, Morton A., *Dissent and The State in Peace and War, p. XIV.*
18. *Ibid.,* p. 269.

disagreement and here is the rub. Disagreement, which is so prominent in party politics, correctly identifies a basic quality of politics in its wider sense. It, then, follows that men have diverse views, interests and characteristics, they differ in their views on the nature of man and his role in the world, have conflicting interests as young and old, employer and employee, rich and poor, and also differ psychologically being cautious; or impetuous, timid and brave and so on. This variety of human kind, in so far as it is reflected in disagreement, provides the basis for politics.

Disagreement, though a necessary condition for politics, is not a sufficient condition, order is also required. If politics is not to disappear into chaos or civil war, there needs to be both recognised limits to disagreement and the measure of agreement necessary to maintain order. The existence of this order is reflected in that collection of institutions and behaviour patterns which together make up the political community.

Political situations arise out of disagreement within an ordered community. The resolution of the conflicts which emerge will depend upon the distribution of influence within the community and the efficiency with which those with influence use their resources. Time and again the advocates of incompatible policies will confront each other. There will be influence clashes. The influence employed may involve the use of rewards or punishments. But whatever form it takes, the relative influence of the groups and the response to the conflict by other groups, including the government, will decide the outcome—will decide *Who gets What, When and How*. The passage from disagreement to policy is determined by the influence exerted. The importance of influence in the policy-making process accounts for descriptions of politics as the shaping and sharing of such influence.

Political activity, then, is the activity which occurs in an ordered community and by which disagreements are resolved and translated into policy. Such authoritative decisions reflect divergences of beliefs, interests and influence within the community. The student of politics is concerned with the activity which leads to those decisions; with the institutions within which the activity is carried on and the goals towards the attainment of which the decisions are directed.

Politics may be found in a variety of associations or groups. Where men are banded together because there is agreement and, therefore, order and consequent continuity, and where they have disagreements which are subsequently resolved into policy which is applied on behalf of the group, then, politics exists in that collection of men and women. This is so whether the group be a club, a trades union, a country or an international organization. To express it in proper terminology, politics can be looked at as on three levels—State, intra-State and inter-State. We are all to some extent involved at some level, many of us at more than one, and the importance of the levels varies for the individual. The State level of politics has traditionally been given pride of place, as it has the monopoly of regulating the use of legitimate force within the territory, and some students of Political Science consider it as the only level. State politics includes the activities of general and local State organisations so that State politics in India includes what is called national and regional governments including local governments in their respective territorial limits.

Study of Politics. Political activities in any particular time and place reflect the values, beliefs and attitudes which are currently held in that society. Traditionally the study of political values rivets on what ought to be the political structure and what goals ought to be sought and it has been the customary field of all political philosophers. A modern political philosopher will concern himself, no doubt, with the study of the great thinkers of the past but in this process he will minutely examine and analyse such value words as 'justice', 'rights', 'freedom' and supplement them by the study of values as political facts. His field is, therefore, comprehensive as he examines simultaneously the empirical aspect of such values and their validity in the present context. To express it in concrete terms, while students of politics remain interested in the historical formulations of arguments that we ought to obey laws because we have consented to it by participating in the choice of the government, and analyse the nature of 'consent' in all its aspects, an endeavour is also made to discover now to what extent 'consent' as defined is in fact a value subscribed to in a particular society and what consequences of political behaviour follow from the acceptance of the value. That is, there is increasing importance attached to the "political setting"—the political values and attitudes which together make political culture.

Separated, rather than divorced, from the study of political values is the study of political institutions. Till very recently, the study of Political Science primarily centred around the legislatures, the executives and judiciaries, the institutions for making, carrying and interpreting law. As the study of Political Science developed, other areas—political parties, interest and other permanent groups and the media of communication—were included in the scope of the subject. All this entailed the study of facts and their actual performance. For example, what is the procedure followed when a bill becomes law and what is the system by which the rulers are chosen and how judges are appointed ? Such a study includes consideration of values for the political institutions reflect, in varying degree, the values of the present and the past. As a consequence, the political institutions are themselves evaluated to see to what extent theory and practice diverge.

Recently, emphasis has been placed on the study of what is called 'political behaviour'. This approach, which is not restricted to declared behaviouralists, concentrates on the behaviour of individuals and groups within political institutions. The intention is to get behind the formal structures in order to know how actually the actors behave in the realm of politics. It is the study of the 'inside story' in the actual processes of politics. This branch of political studies relating to the behaviour of man owes a great deal to students of other social sciences, especially Sociology, who brought with them not only a difference of approach, and new ideas, but also propagated a more scientific study of politics.

Though the distinction has been made here between three types of political inquiry, they are interrelated. No single approach by itself can solve the riddles of politics. Political activities reflect values and other qualities of the political culture; another concept of modern innovation. They occur in institutions which reflect values and behaviour of the past and provide the arena for current activities which are the behaviour of individuals within institutions.

Political System. We have mentioned in the preceding paragraph the danger of viewing politics as isolated from other human activities and on the corresponding need for cooperation from the students of many fields towards increasing man's knowledge of political systems in general. A political system is an aspect of the social system, and political activity and study is a special category of social activity and study. The boundary of politics is often not clear, so that, for example, actions of trades union leaders may sometimes be induded in politics and sometimes not. The same is true of activities in areas more often thought of as economic, cultural and so on. For the purpose of analysis, the political system may be separated from economic and other systems but in practice the study of one system remains lopsided if not aided by other areas of the social system. When a 'traditionalist' attempts to establish relationship of Political Science with other social sciences and concludes that the knowledge gained by any phase of human behaviour and attitudes about the institutions that men build, or the ideas to which they respond in the mass, cannot fail to be of use in similar fields of inquiry, he is really emphasising the relevance of the social system in which each social science supplements and fortifies the rest. Friedrich gives a simple but matter-of-fact definition of a system. He says, "When several parts that are distinct and different from each other compose a whole leaving a defined functional relation to each other which establishes a mutual dependence of these parts upon each other so that the destruction of one entails the destruction of the whole, then such a constellation is called a system."

Hitherto the study of Political Science had primarily hinged upon the State, government and the institutional framework. The analysis was, thus, limited by legal and institutional meanings and the realities of politics were not taken cognisance of. The concept of a political system is a new way of looking at the political phenomena and its analysis in all aspects. Its study includes "all the interactions which affect the use of or threat of use of legitimate physical coercion. The political system includes not only governmental institutions such as legislative, court and administrative agencies, but all structures such as kinship ties and caste groupings; and anomic phenomena such as associations, riots and demonstrations as well as formal organisations like parties and media of communication." Robert Dahl's definition is succinct. He says, "A political system is a persistent pattern of human relationships, that involves to a significant extent power, rule or authority." A political system, as such, embraces interactions between formal and informal socio-political and legal institutions in a given society having its multi-dimensional impact including the environment. The student of Political Science must, therefore, be aware of the environment in which the political system is set, particularly the social setting.

The basic assumption of a political system is that it is a variety of the social system and the study of one system .cannot yield meaningful results without reference to other areas of the social system. It means that the various systems constituting the social system are interdependent. By interdependence is meant that when the properties of one component in a social system change, there is a chain reaction and all other components and the system as a whole are affected. To repeat a familiar example, when the rings of an automobile wear away, the motor car burns oil, the functioning of the other parts of the machine or system deteriorates, and the power of the vehicle declines. To put it in the words of Almond and Powell, "... when one variable in a system changes in magnitude and quality, others are subjected to strains and are transformed, the system changes its pattern of performance, or the unruly component is disciplined by regulatory mechanism." The emergence of political parties with their network of separate organisation and the mass media of communication, like the press, the radio and the television, significantly changed the performance of the structures of a political system and the capabilities (that is, the way it performs as a unit in its environment) of the system in its domestic and foreign environments.

Three characteristics of a political system will be thus obvious. The first is comprehensiveness, meaning thereby that a political system does not only consist of the legal structure (legislative, executive and judiciary) or even political parties, pressure and interest groups and the media of communication, but it also includes all the social structures as kinship, lineage, religion, caste and status groups as well as the economic phenomena, revolutions, riots and terrorism, a new phenomenon with its national and internatioal ramifications.

The second characteristic is interdependence, and it obviously flows from the first. As said earlier, if one component of the whole system changes, it has its impact on other components of the system and, as such, on the system as a whole, though the extent may not be the same in proportion on all the components of the system.

The third is the independent boundaries of all the component parts of the social system. Almond and Powell explain that the boundaries of a political system are subject to large fluctuations in different environments. During the war-time the boundaries become extended as the entire social structure is to be geared up to meet the exigencies of war and to win it too. The Punjab crisis and the activities of the terrorists during the first six years necessitated arming the executive with unprecedented powers to contain terrorism and restore conditions of normalcy. The disturbed conditions had also paralysed the economy of the state, and created conditions of uncertainty for one particular religious community resulting into some families of that community to migrate to other parts of the country disturbing the social structure of the Punjab and its cultural values. Similarly, of course, not to the same extent, the boundaries again are changed on the day of elections, general or mid-term, as the voters become politicians for a day. With the return of normal conditions the boundaries of a political system contract.

Political Culture. Any given political process takes place in a unique environment. A given political unit has a physical location. It will be of a particular size as determined by its territorial boundaries and with a given terrain and climate. All such characteristics will affect the political activity that occurs there. The political importance of the physical setting is uncertain, "but some consequence there will be if only by affecting the size of the population and the ease of communication and thereby the relative strength and co-ordination of that population compared to other political units."

The politics of a particular community is also affected by its economy, which may be basically agricultural or industrial or, more generally, a mixture of the two. The economy may provide a mere subsistence or plenty even verging on superfluity. India has a mixed economy, though 70 per cent of the population is dependent, directly or indirectly, on agriculture. The total wealth of the country is most unevenly distributed and 37 per cent of the total population live under poverty line. In Switzerland, there is no poor and in Canada there is superfluity. A particular economy will create particular possibilities. In a country with basically agricultural economy the population will be predominantly rural leading a corporate life with family as the pivot of loyalty. On the other hand, in a highly industrialised and urbanized economy it would just be the reverse. Because of the development in the means of transport and communication men of diverse customs, habits, beliefs and languages would come together in larger units, become accustomed to close proximity and thereby develop wider allegiances.

The social relations which develop in a particular place and which are related to the methods of producing goods and services, provide a social setting for political activity. A society may be one in which all the members, may be of the same race, subscribe to similar religious beliefs and in which disparities of wealth and social status are small. Another society may be multi-racial, have many religious groups, and show marked caste, class and social distinctions; India being such a society. In the former, decision-taking may be simple whereas in the latter the conflict potential is much greater and its politics may, consequently, be more acrimonious and decision-taking result from the interaction of numerous clearly defined groups. Whatever the social environment, the relationships existing in non-political spheres may be expected to carry over into the political. There is, thus, a continuous interaction between the physical, social and political. The physical setting both affects and is affected by the social, as the social and political also affect both each other and the physical situation.

The individuals who make up a society in which a political system is set may be categorised according to race, wealth, economic ideology and even religion, but really there is more to the setting than what is often termed the social structure. In the social system there exists also the culture of the society. The individual members of the society will have certain values, beliefs and emotional attitudes which make up the culture the community of which political attitudes are a part. Such social behaviour has its basis in the culture of a society and, similarly, political behaviour has its basis in the political culture.

A political culture is a pattern of individual values, beliefs and emotional attitudes. Individual notions of what is right or wrong, good and bad in political affairs, together make up the value pattern—the pattern of norms, of what it is considered *ought* to be. Closely linked with such values will be the beliefs about what it really is, that is, of what exists in the world of politics. The values and beliefs of an individual are such that his emotions are aroused in the realm of politics. Such political emotions sustain values and beliefs and are evoked by symbols.

If a political culture were merely the individual writ large, then one might speak of a completely homogeneous culture. However, it is more; it is a unique pattern of values and beliefs and emotional attitudes of a collection of individuals. In the modern world, while in some countries the degree of cultural differences is relatively small, differences will, no doubt, be found. Such heterogeneity of a political culture rests in differences between the political culture of groups and in differences between individuals. Where the differences between a group and the whole are substantial, there is a political sub-culture.

In some countries the military form just such a group, in others the political culture of the bureaucracy, the parliamentarians, an extremist party, a particular race, caste, class or religion may provide a political sub-culture. In any individual case one, few or many sub-cultures may exist. India is a notable example of many sub-cultures and her unity is born out of this diversity. A political sub-culture most likely to be found is that of rulers and the governed. Within the group of rulers there may be many who retain important elements of the political culture of the mass, but those who exercise vast influence are found, in general, to vary from the many in their orientation to politics. To take the example of India, again, there exists in common parlance the congress culture.

The important political values and beliefs of a society are those which concern the political arrangements as a whole; particular institutions and policies of how they are produced and the place of the individual within the political process. At the general level the value placed by members on the total political unit—the nation in a nation-State—is especially significant. The value placed on the overall political unit and other units, such as the tribe, the region, even the village is reflected in a hierarchy of loyalties and depending on the placing of units in the hierarchy, nationalism or particularism will predominate. In modern industrial communities individuals now commonly identify with the nation. Nevertheless, strong intra-national loyalties are to be found even in developed countries, as, for example, in Belgium and Canada. They are more intense in India. After independence of the country in 1947, regionalism reasserted itself more vigorously and today particularism is the norm, universalism is the exception. Recently, it has been coupled with fundamentalism which is really a disturbing phenomenon.

Political beliefs are symbolised in every society. Certain of these symbols and symbolic activities are obvious enough. The flag, singing of national anthem, Republic and Independence Day celebrations and martyrdom of Gandhi, father of the Indian nation, draw attention to national identity and reinforce it. In long established nation-States the function of such symbols, for example, the public display of the constitutional document and recitation of its contents by schoolchildren in the United States or the opening of the British Parliament by the Monarch, is to sustain the commitment to the nation. In newly independent countries such symbols may need to be created and manipulated to produce allegiance or strengthen it where it is weak. There is no difficulty in providing examples of symbols appropriate for all levels of political values and beliefs. Their number is evidence of their importance and their ability to survive.

Political culture is not static. Its characteristics may change as a result of the import of alien ideas, industrialization, the impact of new leaders, population changes and many other factors. The continuity of the culture, even in the face of such occurrences, is a sign of the effectiveness of the process by which political culture is passed from generation to generation—the process of political socialization.

Political Socialisation. Political socialisation is the process by which the values, beliefs and emotions of a political culture are passed on to succeeding generations. The process starts at an early age and continues throughout life. The institutions of family, school, church, work-groups, political party and so on being its agencies and they together go to cement the cultural heritage. Of these, the family is the first in order of time, and in order of importance, in directing the outcome.

The family is the most natural and the least formal institution. It constitutes the earliest environment of man and exercises a great formative influence on him. While offering to its members a natural and comfortable shelter within the available means, it introduces them very easily to the wider aspects of social life. It is in the family that the child learns attitudes towards others, including those in authority, both inside and outside the family. He learns to differentiate between himself and others and to value certain actions and persons more highly than others. The contribution of the family in the whole process of socialisation of the individual will depend, among other things, on the extent to which the family differentiates itself from others, for example, a black family in a white community, the degree of mobility in that society and the valuation of family by loyalty within the culture.

Next to the family is the school which sharpens the intellect to understand the implications of the values and beliefs. But the outcome of the early schooling also varies. It will clearly differ according to whether or not the school system is governmental, denominational or public, highly centralised and uniform and the extent to which educators encourage a questioning attitude to the knowledge transferred. In denominational institutions and in societies as in Pakistan and other Islamic countries where religion and politics are inseparable, political soialisation moves in one direction and it is highly indoctrinated and, therefore, not conducive for the value of direct citizenship or 'civics education.'

The outcome of the process will reflect the impact upon the individual of his peer group; a friendly group more or less of the same age-group sharing similar problems. Under pressures within this group and as a result of higher education and/or employment he will come to have more or less standard expectations of how he and others will behave in political situations. He may be of a group which is traditionally expected to 'go into' politics as others might be expected to follow the family trade or profession. Alternatively, he may be of a group which traditionally 'keeps out' of politics. From whichever group he comes he will have political expectations which will include a level of participation, an attitude to political change and an attitude towards the influence structure. In developed countries, like the United States and Sweden, remarks James S. Coleman, "The socializing influence of parents and teachers begins to decrease in early adolescence and from their Peer groups exercise increasingly important influences on political attitudes and behaviour." And as a person still grows older, other influences as necessitated by circumstances and prevailing conditions and environment create their impact which is more enduring.

Two other important agencies that contribute to the process of political socialisation are the political party and the mass media. A political party is a free association of men, organised for promoting by their collective effort particular set of principles and policies calculated to further the interest of the nation. The party has become a vital instrument of moulding and shaping public opinion, whose tone is largely determined by the character, intelligence and integrity of the party leaders. A party holds together and thrives by such psychological forces as those of sympathy, imitation, competition and pugnacity. The parties keep the political issues alive; each party explaining its own point of view through various channels of communication at its command. By their discussion and propaganda they mobilize political action and offer a choice to the electors to select their rulers and their programme. Trust is the key word in political culture and the response to particular programme will reflect the amount of trust that exists for a party within the political realm. Disagreement about values is an obvious source of political conflict and sides are readily taken on all such issues. As a consequence of ordering of competing men and measures the political parties create and open lines of communication between governors and governed, through which government may govern more effectively, oppositions oppose and the many react.

Free discussion of public affairs from the platform, the press and other media, which are numerous in complex societies whether pluralistic or totalitarian, is a vital process in the mobilization of political socialisation, for it is through these agencies that issues are presented, discussed in their various aspects and public opinion is formed. A free press is a fearless press and Lippmann attached so much importance to the daily press that he called it the "bible of democracy", an epitome of citizenship. Similarly, the radio, the television and the cinema are effective media of educating the people in public affairs and, thereby stirring their sense of political socialization, provided the opinion they shape is not manufactured. Where the mass media are a monopoly controlled by the State, public opinion is largely what it is made to be. Such conditions are not conducive to the development of political socialisation.

INFLUENCE, AUTHORITY AND POWER

Influence. 'Influence', 'authority' and 'power' are among the most common key words in politics. They are present at all levels in a political system, but they are differently presented, though certain ground is common that a human relationship exists and that the assessment of one or other of the parties affects the behaviour of the other. "The effect is consciously sought, for to have contributed to a state of affairs by accident is normally not considered evidence of the exercise of influence (power, authority)." Eric Rowe considers influence to embrace both authority and power, though he admits that there are important differences between the terms. He, however, feels the need of an "umbrella word" to encompass the three and since no really satisfactory one springs to his mind, he prefers the use of the term 'influence' and in this usage authority and power become special cases of "influence."

The dictionary meaning of the word 'influence' is "power of producing effect, especially unobtrusively: effect of power exerted." It implies relationship between 'influence' and 'power', for example, those who exercise power they exert influence and, as such, they can make others, individuals or groups, to act as they direct or wish them to do. But the influence so exerted is not accompanied by sanctions which is the *sine qua non* of power. Power is a command and, therefore, an imperative and its disobedience means exercise of coercion. Influence, on the other hand, is sans coercion. It is the response to the influence that matters, though it may affect the policy-making. The interest and pressure groups as well as the consultative bodies exert influence on the policy-making process, though all such agencies have no power to compel compliance in preferred directions. So do other organised groups engaged in politics which include trade unions, employers' organisations, the professional groups, as teachers, doctors, lawyers and so on. The strategy of the organised groups may be to exert influence on the agencies of government directly or indirectly. Most groups will operate both ways and the emphasis will depend largely on the political system, how far it is responsive to the public in a pluralistic society and on the ability of the group to obtain access and influence the policy of the government. In democratic politics participation in politics is widespread, political competition without violence is the norm and the politically influential in a competitive polity are limited both by the existing and potential competition. In a totalitarian polity there is an official ideology and the ideology is totalitarian in that the totality of social life is considered a legitimate matter for political control. In other totalitarian systems, which are the modern phenomenon and the traditional distinction is drawn between democracies and despotisms, there is absence of sophisticated ideology in which political is equated with the social. In political systems so described the ruler is supreme and all institutions are his agencies. In such politics influence is highly concentrated, competition is weak, nominal or nonexistent and rule is often arbitrary.

Authority and Legitimacy. Merriam uses 'authority' as an all-embracing term as Eric Rowe did for 'influence'. He writes that there must be "a concentration of recognised authority for common good and power of common action; a final authority capable of commanding the loyalty of the greatness of citizen." It implies that there must be a concentration of recognised authority; it should be capable of commanding the loyalty of the bulk of society; it is the final authority to command as it is legitimate. An authority which is not legitimate has little chance of surviving. But authority in practical politics, like influence, is not synonymous with power, although authority and power usually go together. When we refer to persons in 'authority' or to the 'authorities', the implication is that such persons or groups of persons have a right to be specially important in forming our political decisions and affecting our political behaviour. This acknowledged right is not afforded because the decisions or acts are approved by us or others, but because the advice or command emanates from the 'authorities'. This rightness rests in the source. The source is considered legitimate.

Max Weber gives the classical statement of different types of authority, the most universal and primitive case being that "resting on an established belief in the sanctity of immemorial traditions and the legitimacy of the status of those exercising authority under them." There is also a claim to legitimacy which rests on the "belief in the legality of patterns of normative rules and the rights of those elevated to authority under such rules to issue commands." In the third type, legitimacy is based on "devotion to the specific and exceptional sanctity, heroism, or exemplary character of an individual person", and of normative patterns or order revealed or ordained by him.

In the traditional and legal forms of authority the emphasis is on rules and in the other, called by Weber, 'charismatic', the accent is on the personal qualities. In practice, political authority is not of a pure type but a mixture. Much authority is based on traditions and is important as it is in Britain. So deeprooted have the conventions of the Constitution, as Dicey has named them, been found in the habits of Englishmen, and so firmly the mechanism of government is created on their foundation that without them the political system of the country becomes maimed if not absolutely unworkable. The United States has a written constitution and utmost importance is attached to legality, but some Presidents, as Woodrow Wilson and Franklin Roosevelt, have exercised significant charismatic authority. Similarly, in Cuba where Castro exercised largely charismatic authority legal authority is also present. The charismatic authority of Jawaharlal Nehru was proverbial coupled with the legal authority the Constitution conferred on the office of the Prime Minister.

To sum up, authority is often described as power exercised with general approval, that is, as legitimate power or the approved use of force. This view both restricts the notion of authority and gives it the wrong emphasis. The essence of authority is not that it is power (or force); it is that those who possess it may affect the judgment or actions of others without use of force because those who are to be affected acknowledge the right of the others so to affect them. The authority may, of course, be backed up "by the largest arsenal of coercion in the society, but authority, as such, is effective without coercion: Acceptance of authority is the recognition of a moral right."

Power. Power, like authority, is a means of favourably affecting the behaviour of another, but by might not right. Those who possess and exercise power use force to impose their will. But the essence of authority is not power, although authority and power are normally found together. Even widely acclaimed rulers cannot rule by authority alone. They must, from time to time, coerce. If, however, the coercion is widespread, indiscriminate and regular and there is much resentment against its use, it means there is "loss of authority", a phrase which underlines the key distinction suggesting a heavy reliance on power to be a sign that authority is on the wane. Mrs. Indira Gandhi's authority waned after 1973 and this swing could be attributed to diverse factors coupled with Jayaprakash Narayan's movement in Bihar for her removal from the office of the Prime Minister of India. To legitimise her authority she proclaimed, without the approval of her cabinet, a state of internal emergency. What the emergency wrought is a matter of history. The Congress (I), the party she headed, was dislodged from power in the parliamentary elections in January 1977. Mrs. Gandhi was also defeated in her own constituency which she had nursed so fondly for about a decade. Despite the unbounded power that President Ershad had commanded and exercised for nearly nine years over Bangaladesh, his authority totally collapsed and he had to demit his office on the unrelenting demand of the combined Opposition and upon refusal of the Army Commanders to support his authority any longer.

Authority and power may pass gradually or dramatically from one individual or group to another and be either dispersed or concentrated. In the Parliamentary and presidential patterns of government there is alteration in government and the periodic elections, after regularly specified intervals, and the right to govern flows from the electorate. This is a gradual and constitutional process of transfer of power from one group or individual to another. The dramatic change may occur under unusual circumstances as in the case of General Zia-ul-Haq's *coup* in Pakistan and General Ershad's in Bangladesh. But it was the people's power that swept Mrs. Corazon Aquino to the helm in the Philippines replacing President Ferdinand Marcos' dictatorial rule in February 1986. The change of government in France in 1958 came about abruptly with a marked element of melodrama at the final stage which brought General De Gaulle to power ushering the era of the fifth Republic. After the Watergate scandal the authority of the United States President, Richard Nixon, was completely eclipsed. The credibility of the Republican Government became suspect in the international community and Nixon resigned from his office.

In a society like the United States of America where there is separation between the executive and legislative branches and levels of government, and where individuals and groups technically outside of government are acknowledged to have the right and might to participate in policy-making, there is a diffusion of authority and power. In the U.S.S.R. by contrast both authority and power were, before Perestrokia, concentrated. Technically, authority and power are concentrated in the Cabinet in the Parliamentary system of government. The Cabinet is a wheel within a wheel. Its outside ring consists of a party that has a majority in the representative chamber; the next ring being the Ministry, which contains men who are most active within the party; and the smallest of all being the Cabinet, containing the real leaders or chiefs. By this means is secured that unity of party action which depends upon placing the directing power in the hands of a body small enough to agree and influential enough to control. The Cabinet, in brief, is the driving and the steering force.

The exercise of power may involve the allocation of rewards or the dispensation of penalties or both. These may include the granting or withholding of direct or indirect financial benefits, such as income tax rebates or preferential higher education, and also a less obviously material benefit such as a symbol of rank or status, for example, a knighthood. Such rewards and penalties are often sufficient for the purpose without recourse to coercion, such as imprisonment or death. It is in this context that Herbert Goldhammer and Edwards Shill define power as "the ability to influence the behaviour of others in accordance with one's own ends."

Our conclusion is now obvious. Wherever we find politics we discover conflict and the ways in which human beings cope with conflict. Indeed, when human beings live together in associations and create rules, authorities, or governments to deal with these conflicts, the very attempts to rule also help to generate conflicts. Which comes first, power or conflict, need not detain us; we find both conflict and power wherever human beings live together. This phenomenon exists everywhere, therefore, politics is everywhere. But not all associations have equal powers. The State is the association that has the greatest power within particular territory. Contemporary political scientists discard the use of the term State, but practical politics still recognises this universal entity to lay down the framework within which all other exercises of power must function. The State gives the directions and it also enforces them; if necessary by employing armed forces. The State is the only association within the national frontiers which can use the nation's armed forces to compel obedience to its orders. How essential that control is to the State's effective power is one of the clearest lessons of history.

This definition of the State in terms of power may be formally satisfactory, in that it explains where power resides while it is unchallenged. It explains the nature of the relationship between government and the governed as long as the latter do in actual fact approve of, or acquiesce in, the decisions of the former. But it does not tell us what causes subjects to decide to cease to accept the rule of one government and replace it by another. Governments change, sometimes peacefully, sometimes as a result of revolution. When that happens, the new government is supreme, as was its predecessor, but something of importance to the citizens has happened. The power of the new government may be used for quite different ends from those which the previous government pursued. A definition in terms of power, therefore, is unsatisfactory in that it does not tell us something about the ends.

All governments may be alike in being formally supreme, but, in actual practice, governments vary widely in the way they use their power. An absolute monarch is not bound to take any account of the wishes of the subjects. In a dictatorship, too, the government is not responsible to the nation for the way in which it uses its power, though it usually retains some of the democratic vocabulary and the formal framework of democratic institutions. In a parliamentary democracy, the nation itself, through the medium of its electorate and its parliament, decides in greater or less detail the way in which a government will use its power. Both government and people agree to bind themselves, the one to act in accordance with the wishes of the electorate and to accept the latter's verdict on its performance, the other to change a government which does not meet with its approval only in accordance with a procedure laid down in advance. The form of government varies. There may be a written constitution, or written laws, supplemented to a greater or less extent by unwritten laws, conventions, traditions and customs but the principle remains the same: the last word remains with the people.

The power of the people as an *ultima ratio* is a confusing term in the midst of complexities of the social conditions prevailing in the modern world. It is, however, useful in that it reminds us that we are dealing with the power, not of inanimate machine, but of human beings over their fellowmen. It is not possible to define in quantitative terms how much exercise of power by the rulers the governed will stand without revolution, because the amount will vary with historical, geographical and ideological conditions. But we know from history that, however absolute the right to exercise power may be, there is a limit in practice. Human beings will stand just so much. Among the real and intangible factors which help the rulers to know when it is danger of overstepping the mark are the common and social traditions which, as Dicey said, have formed the outlook of both the governors and the governed. There are certain things which, quite literally, cannot be done at a particular time and in a particular place. It is this incalculable reserve power possessed by the governed which makes it difficult to decide where, in a State, ultimate power really resides.

Political Elites. The concept of political elites was first brought into the realm of politics by H.D. Lasswell. Since then much has been written on political elites and the cases argued in detail and with sophistication, but the common theme is that in any and every polity there is a distinct and identifiable group of persons which constitutes the political elites. This elite may change without revolution and one ruling group be replaced by another. For example, landowning elites have been superseded peacefully by commercial and industrial elites. Elite theorists acknowledge that there is supersession of elites, circulation of elites and internal competition, but maintain that an identifiable political elite or class is always to be found. The main argument hinges upon the fact that in every society there exists a minority of population which takes the majority decisions of the society. According to Lasswell, "Elites are the power holders of a body-politic."

The theory of elites is not an innovation of the contemporary political scientists. Its origin goes back to the ancient Greeks. Plato's concept of 'Philosopher kings' epitomised the essentials of the elite theory clothed in the virtuous qualities which the rulers were sought to possess. Aristotle, Plato's disciple, distinguished between the 'normal' and 'perverted' forms of government and aristocracy for him was the government of the talented and the best and the rulers directed their energies for the good of the people. Oligarchy was for Aristotle the perverted and, therefore, degenerated form of government, though we do not distinguish now between aristocracy and oligarchy. Even the cabinet in a parliamentary system is really a group of elites who are collectively the magnet of policy and the Prime Minister, who heads it, is the tallest of all, the keystone of the cabinet arch.

All democracies have become mass democracies; they all have plebiscitary elements, that is, they also give room to personal leadership—the personality of the leader. People vote for policies or against them. But they essentially vote for or against a man who leads the party contesting to secure the mandate. It is a contest between elites and the popularity of a given leader can be assessed only in an open contest provided both by the parliamentary and presidential systems. When the electorate vote for a party leader they also vote for the party he heads so that his party may govern. If elected, the leader selects his own team consisting of the real leaders who are the elites in the party politics and are deemed to be the best to rule. The rule is, therefore, by the political elites. Maurice Duverger maintains that a government of the people and by the people, as a classical explanation of democracy, "must be replaced by another formula—government by an elite sprung from the people." But it does not mean that the theory of elites contradicts the liberal democratic State. In democratic polities decisions result from competition and often cooperation between groups or leadership of groups. As we said earlier, the elite may change without revolution and one ruling group may be replaced by another. The elites of the ruling group, therefore, cannot act arbitrarily. In a competitive polity the ruling group is limited both by the existing and the potential competition. Such competition is dependent upon continued freedom to publicize, to criticize, to associate with others of like mind—and to survive after doing so because the day of reckoning (elections) is always in sight.

POLITICAL CHANGE, DEVELOPMENT AND STABILITY

Political Change. Change is a natural phenomenon and in all ages change occurs, but the modern world is distinguished by the rapidity and extent of change. Change in the methods of communication, in economic, social and political life. What happens in New York, Cairo or Sydney can be witnessed instantaneously in London or New Delhi, or read about in newspapers in a matter of hours or of minutes. Change is all around us and its quality and quantity produces increasingly unanticipated future.

Even in the physical environment, where a certain stability might be expected, the speed of the process has increased. True, the landmass remains constant or changes little, but changes that occur in the physical environment generally are largely the result of changes in population, in the economy and in the technology and these are rapid. A population explosion will affect the need man has to change his environment by affecting the life of the road surfaces, the speed at which houses degenerate into slums and many other matters. Adaptation to these needs may lead to changes in the methods of production and distribution, leading to further changes in the physical environment, with additional effects on the economic and other social arrangements and leading to the formulation of new ideas about what social organisation is or ought to be.

All these factors give rise to political change, for the process by which public policy is arrived at, and the policy itself, is essentially affected by physical and social alterations and politicians, political institutions and political ideas interact on the world around them. As with other types of change, the political may differ in extent, direction and speed. All these notions must be taken care of while considering distinctions between reform and revolution.

Reform and Revolution. In a polity where there is an inadequate adjustment to the forces of change political tension increases and dissatisfied groups take strong anti-government action, which may develop into unconstitutional activity. Such action may aim merely at attracting attention and publicizing particular grievances. Demonstrations against nuclear weapons, for example, have a limited goal—to change a policy—and if this is reached politics returns to normal. Whether such policy protests are allowed by a regime will depend upon on how firmly based it is in public esteem and the extent to which its existence is endangered by the demonstrations. Policy protests of this kind mentioned may develop into revolutions as the aims are extended or the techniques changed, but initially they seek reform.

Opposition on a mass scale is a very different matter. The massive, passive resistance or the civil disobedience movement in India launched by M.K. Gandhi before Independence was not directed against particular policies of the British Government but against the whole notion of the colonial rule. The aim was political independence of the country from the alien government and rule by Indians themselves according to their own genius. Where, as in this case, the aim pursued entails or implies the overthrow of the prevalent regime, or a radical change in a whole range of policies, there is a revolutionary situation.

The distinction between reform and revolution in terms of the extent or importance of the proposed changes is clearly significant, but account must also be taken of the weapons used and the speed of change. A change, even in a matter of major importance, say, the radical extension of the franchise, is in the nature of reform if it is achieved by methods such as peaceful demonstrations and petitioning. Such reforms have often been hastened by the threat of revolution and occasionally inability to obtain it has resulted in the threat becoming a reality. It might still be called a reform if the weapons actually used were those of non-violent persuasion, and continue to be so even if violence actually occurred but was sporadic and the consequence of "excessive zeal rather than intent." The Hungarian uprising and the troubles in Ireland were revolutions and not reformist movements because violence was accepted and not accidental and because the aim was primarily to win and not to seek concessions.

In ordinary language the word revolution is often used to describe both the method of inducing change and scope of the changes. In this wider sense, it means, as MacIver has said, "to embrace decisive changes in the character of Government, even though they do not involve the violent overthrow of an established order." The revolution of 1688 in Britain, for example, was a peaceful revolution. In the narrower sense, the word revolution refers exclusively to the methods used to bring about particular changes in'the system of government. It leaves out of account what the revolution is about, who are the revolutionaries, and how far they are successful in achieving their ends. The emphasis is on the use of violence, or extra-constitutional means, involving a temporary breakdown of the system which is being challenged and its replacement by another system or constitution.

Revolution and reform are not the monopoly of declared revolutionaries or reformers. Innovators are not aware ot the consequences which may follow from their acts. To the extent that the future is uncertain, in theory any person or group may accidentally trigger a revolution or reform if the present circumstances are propitious. Luther is a clear example of a reformer who started a revolution. The question then arises as to what determines the present circumstances. This is not the place to enter into the "free-will/ determinist controversy, but if we agree that after an action one may reasonably say that 'He could have acted otherwise' we accept that the future is not given. Revolutions or reforms, then, may be planned or unplanned by the men or the social forces who light the fuse."

Political change is more likely to be generated by the few than the many. Normally revolutions are the consequence of activity by a small number who, by skill in the use of violence, or political manipulation, carry the day. In modern times, particularly in Africa and South America, the military has been the prominent as revolutionaries. Pakistan and Bangladesh also come in this category. This is understandable in such politics for the military is often the only disciplined group and also the only possessor of higher education, technical skill and modern weapons of destruction. Those responsible for reform are much less easy to identify, particularly in complex political systems. Often individuals and groups, both in and out of government, are involved and share responsibility.

Whatever be the genesis of change, the outcome will depend on the relative strength of the parties in conflict. In the case of revolutions there are but two sides (revolutionaries and government) who fight while the many observe, and in the end one group is victorious. In the case of reform, the government is often a third party to a conflict between those outside government who favour reform and those who do not. Here the government may perform the function customary in pluralistic societies of 'holding the ring' and subsequently declaring the "winner or dividing the prize." The government may wait before it intervenes to bring the two sides together, may arbitrate at the request of the parties, declare a truce or refer the matter to a body to inquire into the situation. Reform, then, is a contest with a referee and rules; a revolution is a free-for-all.

Development and Stability. Currently, consideration of change is centred on the process of modernization. Interest of academics, administrators, politicians and others in the newly developed countries of the post-war period has spread to other underdeveloped territories and the interest has been sustained by the concern of modernized countries to provide aid, from altruistic or other motives. To modernize such places means exploiting natural resources, altering flora and fauna, eliminating or at least decreasing disease, increasing electrification, both in the rural and urban areas, improving administration and so on. But the difficulty involved in the process is where best to start, on how wide a front and what are the likely consequences in one field of activity in another. More mechanised and efficient farming may involve discouraging small units which may even entail their elimination and, thus, villages being superseded by estate housing and changed attitudes to authority and self-help. If education is held back, the subsequeut teachers and admmistrators come from outside, introducing new sub-cultures which in turn will have economic and other consequences. If education advances speedily it will aid communication internally and externally, increase political activity and increase aspirations, making for instability and endangering progress in other sectors. The maintenance of political stability is essential if modernization is to take place and in many territories going through the process the stability has been won at the price of free institutions.

Authoritarianism in developing countries may prove a passing phase, disappearing when modernization has reached a stage which allows freedom with stability. In many economically developed countries there are stable political systems embodying free institutions. It, however, "remains to be seen whether these are the outcome of a unique combination of circumstances, or whether the social and political consequences of development, by their nature, tend in that direction."

SUGGESTED READINGS

Almond, G.A. and Coleman, J.S. (Eds.) : The *Politics of Developing Areas.*

Almond, G. A. and Verba, S : *The Civic Culture.*

Apter, D.E. : *The Politics of Modernization.*

Bottomore, T.B. : *Elites and Society.*

Crick, B. : In *Defence of Politics.*

Dahl, R.A. : *Modern Political Analysis.*

Hacker, A. : *Political Theory.*

Hyman, H. : *Political Socialization.*

Lasswell, H. : *Politics : Who Gets What, When, How.*

Lasswell, H. D., Kaplan, A. : *Power and Society.*

Lerner, D. and Schramm. : *Communication and Change in Developing Countries.*

Lipset, S.M. : *Political Man.*

Pye, L.W. and Verba, S. (Eds.) : *Political Culture and Political Development*

Russell, B. : *Power : A New Social Analysis.*

Weldon, T.D. : The *Vocabulary of Politics.*

Wiseman, H.V. : *Political Systems.*

Wiseman, H.V. : *Political Science.*

3

CHAPTER

The Nature of the State

Meaning of the State. The term "State", which is the central subject of our study, has a scientific meaning. We do not use it with the same vagueness and ambiguity as it is used by a man in the street. It is often, but erroneously, used as a synonym for "nation", "society", "government", etc. But all these terms have definite meanings of their own in Political Science and should be clearly distinguished one from the other. The term State is also very commonly used to express the collective action of the community, through the agency of the government, as distinguished from individual action. For instance, when we talk about "State management", "State regulation", "State aid", etc., we actually use the word State for government. Similarly. when we talk about the twenty-six units of the Indian Republic or the fifty states which make the United States of America, we do not give the word its scientific meaning. None of them is really a State. In Political Science the term State has a more specific and definite meaning which has little in common with most of its various ordinary meanings.

As used in Political Science, the term State means an assemblage of people occupying a definite territory under an organised government and subject to no outside control. One hundred and eighty-five (185) manifestations of it are members of the United Nations. There are many more which are not members of the organization. All of them share common characteristics. They are groups of people living on, and exercising control over, a definite territory. They are divided into government and subjects; the rulers and the ruled. Some sort of system or order is represented by each. Rules of law are established and in some measure maintained, and compulsion is exercised, and the right to it is recognized both by the members of the group and by the outside world.

There can be no community without the people to form one, and no common life without some definite piece of territory to live in. When people live a collective life, they fulfil the meaning of Aristotle's famous phrase, "Man is a social animal", and when they live a settled life on a definite territory to realize the purpose of collective living, they fulfil the meaning of Aristotle's second famous phrase : "Man is a political animal." But man is not so good as we want to believe that he is. There are all kinds of men and even good men exhibit selfish behaviour because they live in society. Pride, ambition, avarice, revenge, lust, hyprocrisy and other traits of disorderly appetites race with the goodness of man and people are usually concerned with their own welfare first and foremost. This is the evidence of history. "Society", Burke says, "requires not only that the passions of individuals should be subjected, but that even in the mass and body, as well as in the individuals, the inclinations of men should frequently be thwarted, their will controlled, and their passions brought into subjection."[1] The best that can be done is to control the worst manifestations of human perversity by means of political authority. The people are bound by rules of common behaviour and their violation is accompanied by punishment. That is the State. Society meets man's companionship, the State solves the problems created by such companionship. The State is, thus, some form of association with some special characteristics, particularly that of its territorial connection and of its use of force. It is charged with the duty to maintain those conditions of life for which the State came into existence and for which it continues to exist.

The State is a natural, a necessary, and a universal institution. It is natural because it is rooted in the reality of human nature. It is necessary, because, as Aristotle said, "The State comes into existence originating in the bare needs of life and continuing in existence for the sake of good life." Man needs the State to satisfy his diverse needs and to be what he desires to be. Without the State he cannot rise to the full stature of his personality. In fact, in the absence of such a controlling and regulating authority, society cannot be held together and there will be disorder and chaos. What food means to the human body the State means to man. Both are indispensable for his existence and development. The State is, accordingly, a universal institution. It has existed whenever and wherever man has lived in an organised society, although the term State is the product of the sixteenth century and Machiavelli was the first to give it a scientific meaning. He observed, "All the powers which have had and have authority over man are states (state) and are either monarchies or republics."[2] The structure of the state had been subject to a great evolution. The general process was from the similar and simple mechanism of the past to a highly dissimilar and complex mechanism of today.

Definition of the State. Though the State is a necessary and a universal institution, no two writers agree on its definition. There have been many different views about the nature of the State and hence its incompatible definitions. It may well seem curious, says R.M. MacIver, that so great and obvious a fact as the State should be the object of quite conflicting definitions. "Some writers define the State as essentially a class structure... others regard it as the one organisation that transcends class and stands for the whole community. Some interpret it as a power system, others as a welfare system....Some view it entirely as a legal construction, either in the old Austinion sense which made it a relationship of governors and governed, or, in the language of modern jurisprudence, as a community 'organised for action under legal rules.' Some identify it with the nation, others regard nationality as incidental or unnecessary or even as a falsifying element which inhibits the State in its natural functions. Some regard it as a mutual insurance society, others as the very texture of all our life. To some it is a necessary evil, and to a very few an evil that is or will be unnecessary someday, while to others it is 'the word the spirit has made for itself'. Some class the State as one in the order of 'corporations' and others think of it as indistinguishable from society itself." Gabriel Almond prefers to use the term "Political System" for the State, as the latter is limited by legal and

1. Edmund Burke, *Reflections on the Revolution in France,* p. 57.
2. Machiavelli, N., *The Prince, I.*

institutional meanings.[3] This disagreement is primarily due to the fact that every writer has defined it from his own point of view. If the author is a sociologist, like Oppenheimer or a philosopher like Hegel, or an economist, or a behaviourist, or a lawyer, his peculiar prepossessions may lead him either to distort the reality by emphasising some actual characteristics of the State and ignoring the rest, or to free himself altogether from reality and picture the State as he thinks it ought to be.

Out of this maze of confusion we select a few definitions which fairly represent the weight of authority, and by comparing them try to know what is common in them. Holland defines the State as "a numerous assemblage of human beings, generally occupying a certain territory, amongst whom the will of the majority, or of an ascertainable class of persons, is by the strength of such a majority: or class, made to prevail against any of their number who oppose it." Hall says, "The marks of an independent State are that the community constituting it is permanently established for a political end, that it possesses a defined territory and that it is independent of external control," and a State exists, according to Oppenheimer, "when a people is settled in a country under its own sovereign government." Bluntschli says, "The State is the politically organised people of a definite territory," and, according to Woodrow Wilson, it "is the people organised for law within a definite territory." MacIver defines it as "an association which, acting through law as promulgated by a government endowed to this end with coercive power, maintains within a community territorially demarcated the universal external conditions of social order." Harold Laski defines the State as "a territorial society divided into Government and subjects claiming, within its allotted physical area, a supremacy over all other institutions." Gabriel Almond says that the Political System, the term he uses for the State, "is that system of interactions to be found in all independent societies which perform the functions of integration and adaptation[4] (both internally and vis-a-vis other societies) by means of the employment, or threat of employment, of more or less legitimate physical compulsion." The Political System, he explains, "is the legitimate, order-maintaining or transforming system in the society."[5] Pennock and Smith define the State as a political system comprising all the people in a defined territory and possessing an organization (government) with the power and authority to enforce its will upon its members, by resort, if necessary, to physical sanctions, and not subject in the like manner to the power and authority of another polity."[6] Robert Dahl says, "The political system made up of the residents of the territorial area and Government of the area is a 'State'."[7]

Notwithstanding the disagreement amongst these writers, all agree in ascribing to the State the three elements: people, territory and government. Disagreement again becomes prominent in respect of the fourth element of sovereignty. Those who deny to the State

3. Gabriel, A. Almond and James, S. Coleman, *The Politics of Developing Areas,* p. 4.
4. In explaining the functions of integration and adaptation, Almond says, "It is of course true that political systems typically perform the functions of maintaining the integration of a society, adapting and changing elements of the kinship, religious and economic systems, protecting the integrity of political systems from outside threats, or expanding into and attacking other societies." *Ibid.,* p. 5.
5. *Ibid.,* p. 7.
6. J. Ronald Pennock and David G. Smith, *Political Science*, p. 126.
7. Robert A. Dahl, *Modern Political Analysis,* p. 12.

the element of sovereignty, attribute a special quality to government. It is habitually obeyed, says Sidgwick; it is superior to individual wishes, says Esmien; it claims unlimited authority, says Zimmern; it is endowed with coercive power, says MacIver; it is sovereign, says Oppenheimer. When government is accorded superior quality, it is really the quality of the State. The essence of the State, according to Finer, is in its monopoly of coercive power. "This, then, is the State; and its supreme power and monopoly of coercion (which it can devolve in many ways on its own terms) is sovereignty."[8] The sovereign is "legally supreme over any individual or group",[9] says Laski, and the sovereign possesses "supreme coercive power." The State and government are by no means the same thing. Government is merely an essential instrument or contrivance of the State through which its authority is manifested and purpose realized. Taking cognisance of all such considerations, Garner gives a matter-of-fact definition of the State. He defines the State as "a community of persons, more or less numerous, permanently occupying a definite portion of territory, independent, or nearly so, of external control, and possessing an organized government to which the great body of inhabitants render habitual obedience."[10]

ELEMENTS OF THE STATE

The State must, therefore, possess the elements of—

1. Population;
2. Territory;
3. Government;
4. Sovereignty.

1. **Population.** Two conclusions flow from the discussion on the meaning and nature of the state: (1) that the State is a human institution; the product of man's gregarious nature and the result of necessitites of human life, and (2) population and land are the starting point of any study of man in his organised groups. It is the people who make the State, without them there can be none. But population must be large enough to make a State and sustain it. The members of one single family do not make a State; there should be a series of families. No limit, however, can be placed on the number of the people constituting the State. Differences in population, other things remaining the same, do not make any difference in the nature of the State, although opinions as to its size have varied from time to time.

Plato and Aristotle put definite limitations on the population of the State. Their ideal was the Greek City-State, like Athens and Sparta. Plato fixed the number at 5,040 citizens. Aristotle held that neither ten nor a hundred thousand could make a good State, both these numbers were extremes. He laid down the general principle that the number should be neither too large nor too small. It should be large enough to be self-sufficing and small enough to be well governed. Rousseau, the high priest of direct democracy, determined 10,000 to be an ideal number for a State.

8. Finer, Herman, *The State in Theory and Practice,* p. 9.
9. Harold J. Laski, *The Theory and Practice of Modern Government* p. 10.
10. Garner, J.W., *Political Science and Government,* p. 52.

The modern tendency is in favour of States with huge population. It is believed that manpower of the State must swell as population is the sinews of war and power. Hitler's and Mussolini's governments gave bounties to couples producing children above a given minimum. Issueless and unmarried persons were taxed. The erstwhile Soviet Union encouraged the growth of her population. The 1936[11] Constitution guaranteed State aid and honours bestowed on members of large families and unmarried mothers. In India, the problem is to check the ever growing population due to the wide disequilibrium between the population and the available means of production. China has a system of incentives and disincentives to observe a one-child family norm.

But the size of the population is no criterion of the State. Monaco and China are entities with equal status of statehood, although the disparity in the population of both these States is significantly marked. Similarly, increase or loss in population makes no difference in its Statehood. Though no limit, either theoretical or practical, can be placed on the population of a State, yet the population must be sufficient to maintain a State organisation, and it should not be more than what the territorial resources of the State are capable of supporting. But behind all these quantitative factors lie qualitative elements in evaluating the problem of the population of a State. Population cannot be reckoned in mathematical terms; the kind of people they are matters no less than their numbers. Aristotle rightly said that a good citizen makes a good State and a bad citizen a bad State. A good citizen must be intelligent, disciplined, and healthy. Healthy citizens are the health of the State, for disease diminishes intelligence, capacity for work, energy and vitality; it makes for poor production, laziness and lethargy. Similarly, good citizens will not allow religious or political differences to destroy the State's unity and security. The people of india have yet to learn the requisites of good citizenship, though in numbers they stand in the front row.

2. Territory. Some writers ignore territory as an element of the State. Leon Duguit says, "The word State designates the rulers... or else the society itself in which the differentiation between rulers and ruled exists and in which, for that very reason, a public power exists."[12] Duguit is chiefly interested in the differentiation between rulers and ruled which takes place "in almost all human societies, large or small, primitive or civilised," and then, he tersely says that "territory is not an indispensable element in the formation of a State." Sir John Seeley, too, does not regard territory as an essential attribute of the State."[13] If a society is held together, he maintains, by the principle of government, it constitutes a State, and Political Science should not concern itself only with the so called civilised society. Why should we not say that States are found in deserts of Arabia and in other regions where the soil is unfruitful and discourages fixed settlement and agriculture ? W.W. Willoughby says, "The State itself then is neither the people, the Government, the Magistracy, nor the Constitution. Nor is it indeed the territory over which its authority extends. It is the given community of given individuals, viewed in a certain aspect, namely, as a political unity."

11. Article 122 of the 1936 *Constitution of USSR.*
12. As quoted in E.M. Sait's *Political Institutions—A Preface,* p. 92.
13. Seeley, J., *Introduction to Political Science* pp. 31-37.

But such views are rarely encountered now. They have been rejected, not on theoretical grounds, but because of certain practical considerations. Even Duguit admits that in practice there can be no State without a fixed territory. Just as every person belongs to a State, so does every square yard of earth. There is no State without its proper territory, large or small, and no territory that is not part of some State, large or small.[14] And as far as we personally are concerned, it is our connection with a particular territory that normally creates our membership of a State. I am a citizen of India, because I was born there, or because my father was born there. My fellow citizens are my fellow-residents, and it is this sharing of the same territory that creates most of our common interests. Living together on a common land welds the people in a community of interests and it is a powerful incentive to fellow-feeling. Love for the territory inculcates the spirit of patriotism, which has been described in all ages and stages as a supreme virtue of man. Some reverentially call their country 'fatherland' while others call it "motherland" and they all invoke his or her blessings and vow to safeguard its territorial integrity. Territorial integrity of the State is the most cherished sentiment of oneness and the object of patriotism and both together for its permanent existence.

Moreover, the conduct of international relations would be seriously impeded without the requirement of a defined territory. All authorities on International Law are now agreed that a fixed territory must be a condition of Statehood. People and government are not enough. The occupation of a fixed territory is also essential, otherwise the State could not be readily identified and held to account if one attempts to conquer or violate the integrity of another.

Land, water and airspace within the defined territorial area comprise the territory of the State. It embraces the geographical limits of the State, its rivers and lakes. the natural resources it has, and the airspace above. Generally, the 'territorial limits of a State extend to a distance of three miles (4.4 Kilometres) of the sea from the coast, though in practice the maritime jurisdiction is sought to be extended further by the States. As a result of the extensive developments in aviation, radio-communication and space-flights, the importance of the territorial sovereignty of the States over airspace has, during recent times, assumed a vital role.

There are at present 185 States which are members of the United Nations and alongside of such giants as China, India and the United States there are such pigmies as Monaco, Renitria and Luxemberg[15] as independent States. No limit, like population, can be put on the territory of the State, although opinion has differed on the political utility of a small and a big State. Plato drew a close analogy between the stature of a well-formed man and the size of a normal State. Aristotle was also favourably inclined toward the State of a moderate size. Rousseau took his cue from Plato's analogy and set definite limits to the size of a well-governed State. He maintained that in general "a small State is proportionately stronger than a large one." Montesquieu said that there is a necessary relation between the size of the State and the form of government best adapted to it.

Popular government, it is claimed, can be applied only to a small State. In a small

14. Except the tribal belt on the North-West Frontier of Pakistan inhabited by
15. Luxemberg has a poplation of 33,000.

State the population is limited and the people have the best opportunity to assemble together and express their opinions. They can exercise vigilance, which is the price of democracy, far more effectively when the State is small. De Tocqueville said, "The history of the world offers no instance of a great nation retaining the form of a republican government for a long series of years. It may be advanced with confidence that the existence of a great republic will always be exposed to far greater dangers than that of a small one....All the passions which are most fatal to republican institutions spread with an increasing territory, while the virtues which maintain their dignity do not augment in the same proportion."[16] Direct democracy can only flourish in a small State and Switzerland is cited as a living example. A small State, it is further argued, evinces more unity and greater patriotism. It is a compact class of people who live a corporate life. Each stands for all and all stand for each, concentrating their energies collectively in promoting common welfare.

Small States, on the other hand, are relatively less secure. They fall an easy prey to bigger States which are usually aggressive, and history is full of examples of many a naked aggression. Hitler in no time trampled Poland and other Central European countries. Japan did the same in the Far East. Recent opinion is invariably in favour of bigger States. Trietschke, the German philosopher, in his work on "Politics" (*Politik*), published a little before World War I, declared that "the State is power," and it is a sin for the State to be small. He said that even the idea of a small State "is ridiculous on account of its weakness, which in itself is reprehensible because it masquerades as strength."

Economic resources cannot be left out of account while evaluating the utility of small States. The modern tendency is towards planning and self-sufficiency, and it can only be realised when the terntory of the State is large enough to abound in a variety of natural resources. The scale of production determines the mode of production. Large-scale production is always accompanied by rationalization of industry in order to advantageously compete in the international market, besides commanding an extensive and stable domestic market. After all, the economic conditions of a State determine the political stature of its people. In this competing world a large number of small States endanger international peace.

The improved political devices run down the argument that small States are best suited for democracy. The representative system, growing familiar to Europe from the twelfth and thirteenth centuries and now taking roots in Asia and Africa, has vastly extended the scope of democratic institutions. Federalism has also proved its value. Federalism has reconciled local autonomy with national unity, diversity with uniformity, and it has enabled local communities to retain much of their individual character and yet they cooperate for certain purposes in a single State.

Big States, according to Trietschke, "are more adapted than small ones to promote the development of intellectual culture." The resources which a big State possesses, the talent it can command, and the greater genius it can produce immensely help the cultural advancement of a nation and consequently its civilisation. Lord Acton, a great admirer

16. De Tocqueville, A., *Democracy in America* (translated by Reeves), Vol. I, p. 170.

of big States, while summing up the defects of small States, says that they "isolate and shut off their inhabitants, to narrow the horizon of their views; and to dwarf in some degree the proportion of their ideas. Public opinion cannot maintain its liberty and purity in small dimensions, and the currents that come from large communities sweep over a contracted territory... . These States, like the minuter communities of the Middle Ages, serve a purpose, by constituting partitions and securities of self-government in the larger States but they are impediments to the progress of society, which depends on the mixture of races under the same government."[17]

The principles of representation and federalism, operating in the transformed mechanical environment, have invalidated some of the political premises of the past and public opinion today veers round big States. Yet, large and small States continue to be discussed. But as long as power remains the primary factor in international politics, States must either be large or make no attempt to play an important political role. It must, however, be emphasised that there should be some proportion between the population and territory of the State. If there is a disproportionate disparity between the two, the State must suffer from all those economic and political disabilities which are natural to such a situation. The State, in brief, must be viable or capable of maintaining a separate independent existence. This can be possible only if it has adequate area and resources to support the increasing population and to adequately meet the needs of defence and an efficient administration. The modern demands for an efficient and up-to-date defence and administration are ever-growing and consume a pretty big slice of the resources of all States.

3. **Government.** The purpose for which people live together cannot be realized unless they are properly organised and accept certain rules of conduct. The agency created to enforce such rules of conduct and to ensure obedience is called government. Government is the focus of the common purpose of the people occupying a definite territory and it is through this medium that common policies are determined, common affairs are regulated and common interests promoted. Without government the people will be just a babel of tongues with no cohesion and means of collective action. They would divide themselves into groups, parties and even warring associations and thus creating conditions of utter chaos and even civil war. It is, therefore, imperative that there should be a common authority and a consequent order wherever people live. It is the prerequisite of human life and, as such, government is an essential element of the State. The State cannot and does not exist without a government, no matter what form a government may assume.

4. **Sovereignty.** Sovereignty of the State is its most essential and distinguishable feature. A people inhabiting a definite portion of territory and having a government do not constitute a State. They must be internally supreme and free from external control. Sovereignty of the State has two aspects, internal sovereignty and external sovereignty. Internal sovereignty is the State's monopoly of authority inside its boundaries. This authority cannot be shared with any other State and none of its members within its territory can owe obedience to any other State. If the State admits no rival within its own

17. Acton, Lord, *History of Freedom and Other Essays,* p. 295.

territory, it logically follows that it has no authority outside its own territory. Each State is independent of other States. Its will is its own, unaffected by the will of any other external authority. This clarifies the meaning of external sovereignty. We shall return to the discussion on Sovereignty in a later Chapter.[18]

Every State, therefore, must have its population, a definite territory, a duly established government, and sovereignty. Absence of any of these elements denies to it the status of Statehood. Accordingly, the term "State" generally used for the twenty-five units of the Indian Republic or for any one of the fiffy States, which make the United States of America, is a misnomer. None of them is sovereign. They possess the elements of population, territory and government and are autonomous in their own spheres of jurisdiction. But autonomy is not sovereignty and lack of sovereignty does not entitle them to be ranked as States.

STATE AND GOVERNMENT

State and Government. In everyday language, the two terms, the State and Government, are often used interchangeably as if there is no difference between them. The Stuarts in England did not differentiate between the two with a view to justifying their absolute authority. Louis XIV of France used to say, "I am the State." Some Political philosophers, too, like Hobbes, used the terms State and government as if they were identical in meaning. But the State and government are by no means the same thing. They are not synonymous, for it is perfectly possible to conceive of communities, primitive nomadic tribes, for example, which are not 'States' in the sense in which India, Pakistan, Britain, and the United States of America are, but which have governments in thc sense of accepted rules of conduct, by which law and order are maintained. Indeed, it could be argued, says MacIver, that "where the family exists and it exists everywhere in human society government already exists." If this is so, governmeat can exist independently of the State. But no State can exist without government. Without a government the "population would be an incoherent, unorganized, anarchic mass with no means of collective action."[19]

Government is the agency or the machinery through which common policies are determined and by which common affairs are regulated and common interests promoted. It is the manifestation of the State and it consists of all those persons, institutions and agencies by which the will and policy of the State is expressed and carried out. It is a misnomer to equate government, as in current speech we sometimes do, with its controlling element, as, for instance, a Ministry in Great Britain and India, and the President and his 'cabinet' in the United States. When we refer to 'a change of government' in any of these countries, it really means change in the controlling elements of the government and not a change in the government itself. It is true that a change in the controlling element of government in a State has an important impact on the government, but ministers or a President do not make the whole government. Even emperors and kings abdicate, as did Edward VIII of Britain and King Farouk of Egypt, but with these changes the whole

18. See Chapter 8.

19. Garner. J.W., *Political Science and Government,* p. 101.

political and administrative structure is not altered. Government includes "the whole network of local institutions, elected bodies and appointed officials, the whole civil service in all its ramifications, down to the lowest official charged with the carrying out of policy,"[20]

"The State", declared the United States Supreme Court, "itself is an ideal person, intangible, invisible, immutable. Government is an agent, within the sphere of its agency of perfect representative, but outside of that it is a lawless usurpation." Elaborating the point Woodrow Wilson remarked that the State "is juristically wholly organized in its government and can only speak through the government." Two results flow from it. Government is the organization of the State; its working machinery. The State has authority inherent in itself whereas government has no inherent powers. The authority, of which it is the "bearer," as Germans express it, is exercised by the government as its agent. It can only do those things and perform such functions as government is specifically authorized to do in accordance with the provisions and limitations set forth in its charter or constitution. MacIver says, "When we speak of the State, we mean the organization of which government is the administrative organ." A State has a constitution, a code of laws, a way of setting up its government, a body of its citizens. When we think of this whole structure we think of the State." "It is, then, clear that being an agent of the State the government has only a lease of authority, revocable by the sovereign. The State, in brief, is the principal, the master, to which authority the government must ultimately bow. The master in possession of original and plenary authority can take back the powers it has delegated to its agent, diminish them or even expand them at will.

Secondly, the State possesses the character of permanence and continuity. The controlling elements of government change after the expiry of stated period or sometimes even earlier and replaced by others, but the State is not subject to this order of change and replacement. It would, however, not be quite accurate to say so on the analogy of Tennyson's famous poem "The Brook" that 'Governments' come and go, but States go on for ever. States are not eternal. Sovereignty is the essence of the State and as long as a State retains its sovereign character, it remains the State. With the disappearance of sovereignty, it loses its character of Statehood. States come to an end, usually by forceful annexation, but rarely by the voluntary union of one another.[21] The State also loses its identity when there is a total extinction of its population. But 'governments' can and do change, without the permanency of the State being disturbed. France had many forms of government between 1789 and today[22] and every change brought in more or less an entirely new set-up in the political organization of the State, but France remained France. Italy remained Italy when it moved from constitutional to fascist monarchy and then on to a republic. So did Russia of the Tsars after the revolution of 1917. There is no change in the Statehood of Pakistan with the secession of East Bengal, now Bangladesh, except for a sizeable diminution in its territory.

20. Roger, H. Soltau, *An Introduction to Politics,* p. 107.
21. For instance, the merging of Scotland into Great Britain by the Act of Union of 1707.
22. The form of Government in France changed in 1790, 1792, 1795, 1799, 1815 (twice), 1830, 1848, 1852, 1870, 1940, 1944 and 1958.

Despite these obvious differences, the State and government are identified as if they are one. The State is an abstraction whereas government is emphatically concrete. It is the working machinery of the State and it wields on its behalf that legal authority which is the inherent power of the State. In daily life,. it is not so much with the abstract State as with the government that an ordinary man comes into contact. "For those who seek concreteness rather than abstraction," says Croce, "the State is nothing but government, and assumes complete reality only in the government". Laski is correct when he says that for the purposes of practical administration, the State is nothing but government.[23] G.D.H. Cole is also of the same opinion. For him, the State is "nothing more or less than the political machinery of government in a community."[24] It is, indeed, a fact that at a given time and in a given territory, the government tends to incarnate the State as its sole agent and representative, and power is its monopoly. Moreover, it is the type of government in power that gives any State its distinctive political form. Rome was first a republic, then an empire. France from 1814 to 1870 was in turn a monarchy, a republic, an empire, and again a republic. Britain is now a constitutional monarchy, which she was not until 1688. Pakistan was an Islamic Republic till October 8, 1958, when the Constitution was abrogated and Martial Law imposed. It twice became a military dictatorship in between 1958 and 1972 and once again in 1977. All this means that the governments of these States are, or were, of that particular form. Government and State, thus, become practically identical.

But the difference between the two still remains distinct. The characteristics of territoriality and all-inclusiveness point to the basic distinguishing characteristic of the State. The State is both a sociological and a legal entity. I am an Indian, because I belong to the State of India and when I pledge allegiance to the national flag, the State is the entity for which the symbol stands. I do not pledge allegiance to the government whose controlling element, Ministry, is subject to periodical change. Nor do I pledge allegiance to the unorganised mass of people. My only pledge is to this political entity, the State, whose sovereignty and integrity all Indians are pledged to maintain, no matter at what sacrifice. The State is a people organised for law within a definite territory. Government is its organization to which is delegated the power to enforce its will on its members by resort, if necessary, to physical sanctions. The Constitution of the State provides for the organization of government and it prescribes what it should and what it should not do. If it oversteps the limits so prescribed, actions of the government become unconstitutional and, accordingly, void. Finally, sovereign and independent States are international entities and the subject matter of international law. Government of a State is only its dealing agency.

STATE AND SOCIETY

State and Society. We must also clearly distinguish between the State and Society, because "to identify the social with the political is to be guilty of the grossest of all confusions, which completely bars any understanding of either society or State." To equate the State with society is to justify State interference in all aspects of human life,

23. Harold Laski, *A Grammar of Politics,* p. 131.
24. G.D.H. Cole, *Self-Government in Industry,* p. 119.

thereby significantly affecting individual liberty. Aristotle's State was an omnicompetent State as he saw no difference between the State and society. A dictator, too, will pay scant attention to this distinction. There is no sphere of life which a dictator's State will not cover. For Hitler and Mussolini there was nothing above the State, nothing beyond it, nothing besides it.

Society is the product of man's instinctive desire for association which finds expression in the aggregation of people having common interests and united together by what may be called "consciousness of the kind." The people who live together think alike, associate with one another, and make common efforts for a common purpose or plan. They establish, what Sociologists call, "functional" institutions for the realisation of that common purposes which associated men together. It may be a club, a debating society, a religious, economic or political association. All combined together make the social structure and aim to serve the various purposes for which the society came into existence. "Social relations are threads of life" and social institutions "form the loom on which the threads are woven into a cloth or garment." Society stands for the whole scheme of life and it is interwoven by different associations which serve different purposes to complete the whole purpose of life. Political purpose is one of those purposes and it is performed by the State. The State is, therefore, one of these "functional" institutions, the creation of man's will and reason. It is organised in a special way to secure certain results. It emerges and exists within society, but "is not", as MacIver says, "even the form of society." The geographical areas of the State and society may be the same and their membership may also be identical, but they are distinct in origins, aims and functions. The State exists for one single purpose and its functions are relative to that purpose. Society exists for a number of purposes, "some great and some small, but all in their aggregate deep as well as broad."[25] The organisation of the State "is not all social organisation," as MacIver puts it, "the ends for which the State stands are not all the ends which humanity seeks, and quite obviously the ways in which the State pursues its object are only some of the ways in which within society, men strive for the objects of their desire."

Since society is natural and instinctive and the State is the creation of will and reason, society is prior to the State and it embraces all communities organised and unorganised. Organisation is not the essential characteristic of society. But the State must necessarily be organised. The Pathans of the Tribal Area, on the North-West Frontier of Pakistan, do not form a State, though every tribe is a distinct social unit. Similarly, certain groups of Eskimos have no recognisable political organisation.

The State is definitely a territorial organisation. Society recognises no territorial limitations. Its branches may be spread in other parts of the universe too. Then, society embraces the whole life of man and all those social ties, like the family, the caste, the church, the club, etc., which bind men together. The State is concerned only with those social relationships that express themselves through government. It has no jurisdiction over others. MacIver has beautifully expressed this difference. He says that "there are social forms, like the family or the church or the club, which owe neither their origin nor their inspiration to the State; and social forces, like custom or competition, which the

25. Barker, E., *Principles of Social and Political Theory,* p. 42.

State may protect or modify, but certainly does not create; and social motives, like friendship or jealousy, which establish relationships too intimate and personal to be controlled by the great engine of the State."[26]

The State is sovereign and it lays down a system of imperatives. If one disobeys the imperatives of the State, which take the form of laws, one can be punished. But society does not possess coercive power. That is the monopoly of the State. Society, no doubt, has its own rules which regulate social behaviour, but they are not imperatives. They are simply rules of conduct, which the members of society are desired to observe. It has no authority to force obedience. Nor can it physically punish those who disobey its rules. Society ensures the observance of its rules by persuasion, and appeal to the good will of its members. Barker rightly says, "The area of society is voluntary cooperation, its energy is good will and its method is elasticity, while the area of the State is mechanical action, its energy is force and its method is rigidity."

While the State is not identical with society, yet it provides the framework of the social order. According to Laski, the State is a way of regulating human conduct. "Any analysis of its character reveals it as a method of imposing principles of behaviour by which men must regulate their lives."[27] The conditions in which we are born, grow up, are educated, work, enjoy our leisure; own property, marry, have children and die, are all laid down by the State, and the government can compel us to comply with them. All births must be registered otherwise all kinds of complications can arise. Similarly, parents are obliged to send their children to school for a certain number of years. They are obliged to notify the authorities if they suffer from certain infectious diseases. Citizens must pay taxes to the State, whether they approve of the use to which the money is put or not. They must clothe themselves decently, behave with propriety in the streets, avoid making themselves a nuisance to their neighbours, and they must respect the persons and property of other people. There is, in fact, hardly a single human activity which is not in some way regulated by the State. All conduct in society must conform to the way of life prescribed by the laws of the State, as the State makes and maintains its laws not for the sake of laws, but for what they do to individual lives. The State, thus, represents the highest form of social organisation and it exists to regulate and cement social relations. It binds people together and enjoins upon them to observe certain uniform rules of behaviour, without which we cannot think of a well-ordered social life.

It may, however, again be emphasised that "the State is a structure not co-eval and co-extensive with society, but built within it as a determinate order for the attainment of a specific end."[28] The end of the State is to provide those conditions of togetherness without which the happiness of man cannot be secured. But the State can serve its purpose best when it performs it own functions efficiently and refrains from trespassing into others. If it does, then the State stands equated with society embracing the whole life of man. This will make the State omnicompetent and omnicompetence really means incompetence. It may mean even something more. The happiness of the individual may

26. MacIver, R.M., *The Modern State,* p. 5.
27. Laski, H., *An Introduction to Politics,* p. 15.
28. MacIver, R M., *The Modern State,* p. 40.

be sacrificed in the name of the glory and prosperity of the State. In this way, all social activities, which constitute the social order, will ultimately be at the mercy of the government, for "the State is", as Laski says, "for the purpose of practical administration, the government." The government may prescribe anything which it may like and as it likes. But this is neither the way of the State nor that of the government. The State is the creation and agent of society and, therefore, its subordinate. Both society and the State strive to achieve the common objective: the free development of man's personality; his happiness. This is possible only when the distinction and collaboration between the two is properly recognised. Following is the summary to clarify the points involved in the discussion:

1. Society is instinctive to man and is spontaneous in its growth and development. MacIver says, "Wherever living beings enter into, or maintain, willed relations with one another, there society exists." The State is one of the associations contained within society, the creation of man's will and reason to maintain and cement the various aspects of social life. Two results, then, follow:
   (*i*) society is both prior to and wider than the State; and
   (*ii*) society is a complex of all such associations as economic, educational, religious, political and cultural.

   Society precedes the State just as it precedes the family, the church, the corporation, the political party. It unites all these as a tree unites its branches. The State is one of these associations, and it has become the most prominent of all because it controls and coordinates the various aspects of social life.
2. The purposes of society are many and diverse whereas the purpose of the State is only one; its political organization and its end is related to its purpose to which it must confine itself.
3. The State is definitely territorial, society is not. Loyalty to the State does not exhaust all the social obligations of man.
4. The structure of society is elastic and it is based upon the voluntary cooperation of its members; it appeals and persuades. The State is compact, its actions are mechanical, its methods are rigid and its power is force.
5. The State issues orders and their disobedience is accompanied by physical punishment. Society acts upon its members through customs. conventions and moral rules. It exercises social pressures but not force.
6. In spite of these differences between society and the State, they are connected and inter-dependent. Social conduct must conform to the way of life prescribed by the laws of the State. But the State must not trespass into the sphere not assigned to its jurisdiction.

STATE AND ASSOCIATIONS

State and Association. Society, as said before, is not a mere aggregate of individuals, but a collection of groups composed of individuals. These groups are voluntarily formed by man for the satisfaction of his various and diversified needs, such as, social, religious, cultural, economic, educational, recreational, and many others. All these groups express and develop the sociability of man. In the beginning man's social wants were few and the groups were limited in number. But in the complex life of our times social wants have multiplied enormously and today society is a veritable network of such associations. Barker says, "We see society less as a number of individuals leading a common life, we see it more as an association of individuals already united in various groups, each with its common file, in a further and higher group for a further and higher common purpose."

An association is defined as "a group of persons or members who are associated and organised into a unity of will for a common end."[29] Cole defines it: "Any group of persons pursuing a common purpose or system or aggregation of purposes by a course of cooperative action extending beyond a single act, and for this purpose agreeing together upon certain methods of procedure and laying down, in however rudimentary a form, rules for common action."[30] An association, therefore, embraces a group of people having a common purpose or purposes for which they associated and organised themselves. A mere group of men do not form an association. Every association must have, in the first place, some specific purpose or purposes to fulfil. Secondly, individuals so associated should be duly organised. Without organisation it becomes just a collection of individuals or a crowd. A crowd has no method of doing things and achieving its purpose, as there is no common bond of cohesion between them. And there must be some man or body of men to see that the rules of the association are duly obeyed to realise its purpose. Every association necessarily has its constitution, a code of rules and a way of setting up its government; churches, political parties, and trade unions, for example.

The State, too, is a group of human beings. It comes into existence, like other groups, to satisfy human needs through concerted action. While each group has its distinctive character and problems, yet all pursue their activities to secure a happy and good life. In spite of this close resemblance between the State and other associations, there are some fundamental differences which distinguish the State from any other association.

1. The State is a territorially integrated association and its territory is most distinctly demarcated. The jurisdiction of each State lapses beyond its territorial limits. But voluntary associations are not restricted to a definite territory. Many of them are international in scope, spread all the world over, and include in their membership citizens of many States, as the Rotary Club, the Lions Club, the Red Cross Society, and the Boy Scouts and Girl Guides. The membership of each State is distinct. I am a citizen of India while John is a citizen of, say, United States of America.

2. Membership of the State is compulsory. One must be a member of one State or another;[31] there is no other option for him. But membership of other associations, except the family, is voluntary and optional. It is for each individual to decide whether he should be a member of one association or many associations at the same time; it is his own option and choice. He is also free to withdraw from any association whenever he elects to do so; it is his own decision.

29. MacIver, R.M., *The Modern State,* p. 6.

30. Cole, G.D.H., *Social Theory,* p. 37.

31. Occasionally, there may be a case of double citizenship, but it is exceptional and for a temporary period.

3. The State is a permanent and enduring association unless it is conquered and annexed or its units disintegrate and secede as in the erstwhile Soviet Union. Governments may come or go, the sovereignty may shift from one centre to another; the State continues. But many associations have only a temporary existence. An association may cease to exist as soon as the purpose for which it came into existence had been realised. Some associations disappear, because of internal dissensions. Even violent internal commotions and changes do no affect the existence of the State; they may simply lead to a change in the government.

4. Each association is promoted for a specific object or objects and its activities are limited to the pursuit of those interests. In other words, the sphere of activity of every voluntary association is well defined. The province of the State, on the other hand, is much wider and its activities are manifold. It is charged with the care of general rather than particular interests. MacIver says that the State "is essentially an order-creating organisation. It exists to establish order, not, of course, merely for the sake of order, but for the sake of all the potentialities of the life which require that basis of order."

5. The State is sovereign and it possesses the power to enforce its decisions. Voluntary associations do not possess the legal power of coercion. If the members of an association disobey its rules and regulations, they cannot be physically punished. It has no means to command and enforce obedience. It can only morally condemn the wrong-doer, though it may be admitted that in some cases moral condemnation is worse than physical punishment.

6. The State possesses the power to control the activities of all voluntary associations. It can even ban the existence of an association if it is deemed to have acted or is likely to act so as to disturb public peace and security. As a matter of fact, no State would permit the formation, or continued existence within its territorial limits, of an association for criminal or immoral purposes, or one whose objects are avowedly hostile to the public policy of the State. Examples when associations have been declared unlawful or have been dissolved by the command of the State are too numerous to quote. The Government of India in 1962 declared the Rashtriya Swayam Sevak Sangh (RSS) an unlawfull association and banned its activities. The ban was lifted afterwards. Internal Emergency declared in June 1975 again banned it. It was banned on December 9, 1992 for the third time along with the Vishwa Hindu Parishad (VHP). The Bajrang Dal, and the Islamic Sewak Sanghy. Till March 31, 1993, "associations and groups, including the four mentioned above, stood banned under the provisions of the Unlawful Activities (Prevention) Act, 1967. The Pakistan Government, during General Ayub Khan's military regime, prohibited the organisation of private military formations and then liquidated political parties. General Zia-ul-Haq repeated it in 1977 after his military coup and the ban on political parties continued till 1987.

7. Finally, the State can create many associations and prescribe their functions. The universities in every country are established by the laws of the State and their functions are clearly defined therein. Similarly, it may create corporations or other kinds of associations for certain specific purposes.

COMMUNITY AND INSTITUTIONS

Community. Community and institution are two terms which are frequently used in Political Science and yet without a definite meaning attached to them. We defined society as a group of people living interdependently, attempting to solve their problems through common action. There are large societies and small. Local societies are usually referred to as communities. Indeed, society itself may be defined as a gregarious community. "By community", says MacIver, "I mean an area of common life, village or town, or district, or country, or even wider area."[32] Common life and common consciousness are the two distinctive features of a community, whatever be the extent of area they refer to. The men who live together on a common land "develop in some kind or degree distinctive common characteristics, manners, traditions, mode of speech and so on."[33] Once this distinctiveness from others is realized, they constitute a community. There are in a community suggestions of common values and a homogeneous culture. It is evident that the smaller a community is, the more common and firm are its social values. Conversely, the larger the community, the less agreement there will be upon social values, whether they may be ideological, religious, political, cultural, etc. India is a huge country inhabited by different religious communities as the Hindus, the Muslims, the Sikhs, the Christians and many others. Then, the people of India speak different languages and constitute linguistic communities. Communities based on the conception of language, as Maharashtrians, Bengalis, Punjabis, Haryanvis, embrace all people living in their respective areas and professing different religions. There may also be a commercial community and a community of intellectuals. In both these cases neither the bonds of religion nor the bonds of language intervene. They constitute a community of interest. Every country and every nation presents such crossing and recrossing currents of common life. "The conception of a community may thus be a conception of a machinery of wheels within wheels, or it may be a conception of a geometrical problem in which the lines bisect and trisect from several directions."[34]

A community may, thus, be a part of the wider community, and, in fact, "all community is a question of degree." The whole world makes a community and it is the largest of all. Family is a community of blood and it is the smallest of all. Nation is also a community. A nation is a real feeling of unity which defies all other apparent diversities, like religion and language. Small communities exist within the great communities and this process is the natural outcome of civilization. But the object of a small or great community is the same. It is a group of people tied by common affinities, and aiming at a common good life. It is a circle within a circle and we need the smaller as well as the larger circles of community. The great community brings us opportunity, stability; economy, the constant stimulus of a richer, more varied culture. But by living in the smaller community we find the nearer, more intimate satisfactions. The larger community provides peace and protection, patriotism and sometimes war, automobiles and radio. The smaller provides friends and friendship, gossip and face-to-face rivalry, local pride and abode. Both are essential to the full life process."[35]

32. MacIver, R.M., *Community,* p. 22.

33. *Ibid.,* pp. 22-23.

34. Ilyas Ahmed, *The First Principles of Politics,* p. 21.

35. MacIver and Page, *Society: An Introductory Analysis,* p. 11.

Two points mark the difference between a community and an association. A community comprises all the people in a given area bound together by ties arising out of neighbourhood. It suggests strong ties of recognized interest, but no organization. An association must be organized. When a group provides itself with an organization for the achievement of its stated purpose, it becomes an association. An association is not bound by limits of neighbourhood and ties arising therefrom. It may have world-wide roots combining together diverse people who engage themselves in the pursuit of a common purpose and its fulfilment.

Institutions. Society is a honeycomb of associations, but no association can function without an institution. An institution is the form, the structure or the framework of an association. It is a means by which the purpose of an association is realized; the instrument "through which common interests are realized, the mechanism on which is based the success or failure of an association." Or to put it in a simple way, institution is a group of people working towards a common aim. A university is an association and its common aim is realized through the agencies of its various teaching departments, colleges affiliated to it and the administrative office working under the control of the Registrar. Similarly, government is the institution of a political association, the State. It is through the mechanism of government that the State fulfils its purpose.

An institution is not always a mere framework. It is as living as an association and a smaller institution is by itself an institution of a large association. Thus, a political party, a judicial tribunal, a legislative body, an administrative bureau, all are institutions as government itself is the institution of an association, the State. The people who comprise them may come and go as time passes, but the institutions once established, endure, though they may be moulded and shaped by the people who comprise them according to the changing needs of the time. Monarchy in Britain is an institution, but it is not the same today as it was during the times of the Tudors or Stuarts or even during the Victorian era. Similarly, British Parliament is an institution and it took more than eight centuries to transform it into its present position and stature. The leaders of a political party will rise or fall over a period of years, but.the party continues as an institution, unless it disintegrates.

Moreover, the common aim that an institution pursues can be a very general one. The members of a legislative body, for example, will not always agree on bills which should be passed or in what form. Nor will the judges of a judicial tribunal always hand down unanimous decisions. But they do agree on when to meet, on how to handle their business, and on what it is they are supposed to be doing. Thus, all members of Parliament in India know that they assemble in New Delhi on appointed dates to pass laws; all Justices of the Supreme Court know that it is their job to decide cases. The President of India knows his job and performs his functions in accordance with the provisions of the Constitution. An institution, thus, consists of individuals, general goals, and rules for reaching those goals.

There can be a one-man institution as the Presidency in India, America and France or Monarchy in England. It may consist of a score of them as the cabinet, or hundreds of them as Parliament or a Congress, or it may be a multimillion-member institution as a political party. Some institutions have limited goals whereas others have more comprehensive. In some the members of an institution are strong in their loyalty to its aim while in others they are apathetic or even obstructive. Parliament in India and various Assemblies of her State legislatures stand as a clear testimony of obstruction. To sum up, "politics cannot function without institutions, and an understanding of politics requires an awareness of how they operate."[36]

NATURE OF THE STATE

There are many speculations regarding the nature of the State and the relation between the State and the individual. Six important theories deserve special mention. The first is the *monistic* theory. The advocates of the monistic theory argue that individuals who compose the State have no independent existence "but are mere automatic units in the whole mass, each dependent on the other and upon the whole for its continued existence."[37] They have no independent individuality of their own and all that they are, they owe it to the society of which they are a part. This is really the Idealist or the Absolutist theory of the State and we discuss it at a later stage. Sharply opposed to the monistic theory is the *monadnistic* or purely individualistic theory which conceives society as a mere aggregation of individuals "each in large measure living in isolation and independent of his associates, capable of surviving and even flourishing without the aid of the State beyond a mere minimum of collective restraint for the protection of the weak against the aggression of the strong."[38] Every individual is, thus, a self-contained unit and there is no interdependence of one on the other. He can survive and even flourish without the aid of the State. The necessity of the State is found in giving protection to the weak against the aggression of the strong. The State is, accordingly, a police State and it exists to protect and restrain, not to foster and promote.

Then, there is the dualistic theory; a compromise between the monistic theory and the monadnistic theory. According to this theory every individual leads a life of his own, but each is, in a way, dependent upon others for his welfare. His existence is neither merged in that of the whole, nor is he entirely isolated from and independent of his social surroundings. Fourthly, we have the organic theory which considers the State as a unity similar to that which characterises a biological organism. The Juristic theory and the Marxist theory are the other two.

THE ORGANIC NATURE OF THE STATE

Organic theory explained. The union of individuals forming the State has been described as similar to the union between the several parts of an animal body, wherein all parts are functionally related and none can exist in isolation from the rest. Just as the body has a naturat unity, so has a social group. An arm lives and moves only as a part of an organic whole. Amputated from the body, it dies. The Organic Theory is a biological conception which describes the State in terms of "natural science, views the individuals which

36. Andrew Packer, *The Study of Politics*, p. 10.
37. Garner, J.W.. *Political Science and Government.* p. 211.
38. *Ibid.*, p. 212.

compose it as analogous to the cells of a plant or animal, and postulates a relation of interdependence between them and society such as exists between the organs and parts of a biological organism and the whole structure." In other words, as the animal body is composed of cells, so is the State composed of several individuals, and as is the "relation of the hand to the body, or the leaf to the tree, so is the relation of man to society. He exists in it and it in him."[39] The State is an organic unity—"a living spiritual being."

History of the Theory. The Organic Theory is as old as political thought itself. Plato compared the State to a man of great stature, and conceived a resemblance in their functions. He said that "the best ordered commonwealth was one whose structural organisation resembled most nearly in principle to that of the individual." Cicero, too relied, upon the same analogy and likened the head of the State to the spirit which rules the human body. Among writers of the Middle Ages and early modern times, the theory was supported notably by John of Salisbury, Marsiglio Althusius and many others. It, also, found favour with Hobbes and Rousseau, although the analogies and comparisons which they made were superficial.

With the decline of the Social Contract Theory, in the early part of the nineteenth century, the theory of the organic nature of the State found a new and vigorous expression. The ancient and medieval writers had merely drawn an analogy between the State and an organism. They held that the State resembled an organism. But writers of the nineteenth century regarded the State as an organism. Even fanciful and very often vain elaborations of the organic conception, attributing, for instance, to the State an alimentary system, a nervous system, a circulatory system, etc., became the theme of the time. Indeed, the "fascination of the theory with its biological analogies and parallelisms became so widespread that political science, for a time, seemed in danger of being swallowed up by natural science."[40]

The new theory, that the State is an organism, took root in German soil and there it found its most notable advocates. But the culmination of the theory was reached in the writings of Bluntschli. The State, he asserted, is the very "image of human organism." As "an oil painting," he said, "is something more than a mere aggregation of drops of oil, as a statue is something more than a combination of marble particles, as a man is something more than a mere quantity of cells and blood corpuscles, so the nation is something more than a mere aggregation of citizens, and the State something more than a mere collection of external regulations." He stretched his biological analogy to the extreme and endowed the State with the quality of sex, describing it as having a male personality.

Theory as expanded by Spencer. The theory that the State is an organism received a most scientific treatment at the hands of Herbert Spencer, the English philosopher. Spencer believed that social life is a part of an ever-evolving nature and starting from the idea of a universal evolution, he afterwards included biological evolution in his analysis. He asserted that society is an organism and it differs in no essential principle from other biological organisms. The attributes of an organism and society, he maintained, are similar and the

39. Leacock, S., *Elements of Political Science*, p. 75.

40. Garner, J.W., *Political Science and Government*, p. 212.

permanent relations existing between their various parts are also the same. Both exhibit the same process of development. The animal and social bodies, Spencer affirmed, begin as germs, all similar and simple in structure. As they grow and develop, they become unlike and complex in structure. Their process of development is the same; both moving from similarity and simplicity to dissimilarity and complexity. "As the lowest type of animal is all stomach, respiratory surface or limb, so primitive society is all warrior, all hunter, all builder, or all tool-maker. As society grows in complexity, division of labour follows, i.e., new organs with different functions appear, corresponding to the differentiation of functions in the animal, in which fundamental trait they become entirely alike."

In either case there is a mutual dependence of parts. Just as the hand depends on the arm and the arm on the body and head, so do the parts of the social organism depend on each other. Every organism depends for its life and full performance of its functions on the proper coordination and interrelation of the units. As the diseased condition of one organ affects the health and proper functioning of other organs, similarly, individuals who form the society are inseparably connected with one another for the realisation of their best self. There is so much dependence of one on the other that the distress of one paralyses the rest of the society. "If the iron worker in the social organism stops work, or the miner or the food producer, or the distributor fails to discharge his natural functions in the economy of the society, the whole suffers injury just as the animal organism suffers from the failure of its members to perform their functions." Society and organism, it is further pointed out, are both subject to wear and tear and then replacement. Just as cell tissues and blood corpuscles in the animal organism wear out and are replaced by new ones, in nthe same manner, old, infirm, and diseased persons die, giving place to newly born persons.

Spencer, then, gives some structural analogies between society and organism. He says, society, too, has three systems corresponding to the sustaining system, the distributary system and the regulating system in an organism. The sustaining system in an organism consists of mouth, gullet, stomach and intestines it is by means of this' system that food is disgested and the whole organic machine is sustained. Society has its own sustaining system and it is the productive system comprising the manufacturing districts and agricultural areas. The distributary system in an organism consists of the blood vessels, heart, arteries and veins and they carry blood to all parts of the body. Means of communication and transport in the social struccture correspond to the distributary system in an organism. What the arteries and veins mean to the human body roads, railways, post and telegraph services mean to society.[41] Finally, the regulating system is the nerve-motor mechanism which regulates the whole body. Government in the body politic, regulates and controls the activities of the individuals, and it is analogous to the regulating system.

From these points of agreement, Spencer concludes that the State is an organism. But he himself admits that the identity between the two is not complete. There is one "extreme unlikeness" in the structure of the body-politic and that of the animal organism. The animal organism is *concrete* in structure, that is, its units are bound together in close contact and they form a concrete whole. The social body, on the other hand, is *discrete*.

41. Spencer published an essay in *Westminster Review,* in 1860, in which he drew "a parallel' between the up and down lines of a railway which furnishes the circulation of commodities in the social organism, and the arteries and veins of an animal, money being the blood corpuscles and the telegraph wires the nerves.

Its parts are separate and distinct, or, to quote Spencer, the units of the social body are free and "more or less widely dispersed."

Spencer also points out another difference between an organism and a social body. This difference, he admits, is very important because it "greatly affects our notion of the ends to be achieved by social organisation." He says that there is no "nerve sensorium" in the social body. That is to say, there is no single centre of consciousness in society as is found in the living body. In an organism, consciousness is concentrated in one definite part of the whole, the cerebrum or brain. In society, it is diffused or spread over the whole. Every individual member in a society has his own conscience and he acts for himself independently of others.

But even these "fundamental" points of difference in the structure of the body-politic and that of the animal organism did not deter Spencer from his thesis that the State is an organism. As a matter of fact, he built on those differences his theory of Individualism. He concluded that the State should leave the individual alone to pursue his own welfare, for "society exists for the benefit of its members, not its members for the benefit of society." Herbert Spencer did not, however, realise that his conclusion was the very negation of the organic nature of the State.

Other Advocates of the Theory. The organic theory lost its prestige after Albert Schaffle, the Austrian publicist, who emphasised at great length the anatomical, physiological, biological and psychological resemblances between society and the animal body. He asserted that society is an organism "whose protoplasm or unit is man, the State or government in the one corresponding to the brain in the other." Among others who have emphatically defended the organic theory are the French writers, notably, August Comte, Fouille and Rene Worms. Comte described human society as the highest stage in organic evolution, "embodying the completest development of that natural harmony or organisation and action...."[42] Rene Worms says that "the anatomy, physiology, and pathology of society possess striking similarities to the structure, function and pathology of living beings." But the attempts to draw "literal" analogies between society and living organisms have now been abandoned. Today, the organic conception of the State "has survived (with insignificant exceptions) only in the older Hegelian form; the State an end in itself; its evolution controlled by its own laws; its functionally different parts, interdependent and inseparable, all existing for and dependent upon a vigorous life of the corporate national life."[43]

Evaluation of the Theory. There are two points of view about the organic nature of the State. Barker says, "The State is not an organism; but it is like an organism."[44] The organic analogy has a useful purpose to serve as it emphasises the unity of the State. The State is not a mere aggregation of people. It is a social unity. Man cannot lead a life of isolation. Dependence is his very psychology and individuals depend on one another and on the State as a whole. The welfare of each is involved in the welfare of all. He cannot be separated from society, just as a hand or a leg, without losing its utility cannot be separated from the body. The State has a collective life like an organism. The attainment

42. Coker, F.W., *Recent Political Thought*, p. 410.
43. *Ibid.*, p. 411.
44. Ernest Barker, *Political Thought in England* (1848-1914), p. 91.

of the common purpose depends upon the proper performance by every individual of his functions or duties. Every citizen has social obligations to himself, to his family, to his neighbours, and to the society of which he is a unit. Hobhouse rightly sums up, "... the life of society and the life of an individual do resemble one another in certain respects, and the term 'organic' is as justly applicable to the one as to the other for an organism is a whole, consisting of interdependent parts. Each part lives and functions and grows by subserving the life of the whole. It sustains the rest and is sustained by them and through their mutual support comes a common development."[45]

So far we agree and accept the proposition that the State is like an organism. But the farther these analogies are carried, the more misleading they become. The user of analogy tends to forget that the resemblances he notices hold good only within the limits where they overlap. The objects compared are plainly not identical, as to compare identicals is useless, but possess, besides their common features, other traits that distinguish them.

At many points the comparison between society and an organism is exceedingly superficial. There is no similarity between the cells of an organism and the individuals who compose society. The cells have no independent life of their own. They are mechanical pieces of matter. Each is fixed in its place, having no power of thought or will, and existing solely to support and perpetuate the life of the whole. The individuals, on the other hand, are independent, intellectual and moral human beings. They do not act like a machine. Each individual has a physical life independent of the whole and each strives to make his own destiny. It is true that man cannot be the best of himself independently of society, but he can live, if he so wishes, an independent life of his own. This is not possible in an organism. If parts are cut off from their parent body, they die. Chop off a branch from a tree, a limb from a human body, and both perish.

It is, again, true that the State has grown from similarity and simplicity to dissimilarity and complexity. But even common reason does not believe that it is subject to the same process of birth, growth and decay as an organism. An animal organism comes into existence by the union of two organisms. This is not the method of the birth of the State. The process of its growth is also not similar. Organisms grow from within and through internal adaptation. They grow "unconsciously independent of volition, entirely dependent on its environment and the natural laws of the biological world."[46] The machinery of the State and its laws, on the other hand, change to adjust themselves to the altered needs and requirements of the people. And all this change is brought about as a result of volition and conscious efforts of its members. "Its growth, if such it may be called, is largely the result of the conscious action of its individual members and is to a great extent self-directed."[47] Then, an organism dies. The State is not liable to death. It is permanent; it endures. To sum up, in the words of Jellinek, "Growth, decline and death are not necessary processes of State life though they are inseparable from the life of the organism. The State does not originate or renew itself as a plant or as an animal does."

45. Hobhouse, L.T., *Social Evolution and Political Theory,* p. 87.

46. Gettell, R.G., *Introduction to Political Science,* p. 88.

47. Garner, J. W., *Political Science and Government,* p. 220.

The Organic Theory does not help us in answering the baffling, but practical question of what the State should do. In fact, the Organic Theory has been used to support views on the province of the State ranging from Individualism to Socialism. Herbert Spencer uses it as a basis for the theory of *laissez faire* and limits the functions of the State only to the prevention of violence and fraud.The State should, accordingly, limit its activities to those particular functions for which it arose. From the "discrete" nature of the social body, he concluded that every individual exists for his own good only and not for the happiness of the whole. In close contrast to Spencer's theory of Individualism are the supporters of extreme socialism and absolutism of the State. Relying upon the organic nature of the State, the German writers maintained that "the State, as the highest organism, is the important unit, and collective activity is the ideal of social progress".

Herbert Spencer's conclusion that the individual should otherwise be left alone is a forced one. The Organic Theory, with all its analogies, in the form in which it is usually stated, is pregnant with dangerous results. "Some of these biological comparisons are ingenious and well stated; to many writers they have proved fascinating and seductive; to others they have constituted the basis of an argument for a theory of the State which would sacrifice individual to society." The central idea of the theory is to merge the individual in the social group and consequently regard him as a vulgar fraction. To repeat the words of Leacock, "As is the relation of the hand to the body, or the leaf to the tree, so is the relation of man to society. He exists in it, and it in him." What this relationship actually means, the world witnessed in Hitler's Germany and Mussolini's Italy. Communist countries, like Soviet Russia and China, also amplify it. Jellinek has rightly said, "We had better reject the theory in toto lest the danger from the larger amount of falsity in the analogy should outweigh the good in the little truth it contains".

Juristic Theory. The Juristic Theory of the State embodies the point of view of the jurists who seek to explain the nature of the State in terms of legal concepts. They endow the State with a fictitious legal personality as they look upon the State as a legal "person" possessing, like a natural physical person, an individuality, self-consciousness and a will of its own. They view the State as an organ for the creation, interpretation and enforcement of law, and for the protection of all legal rights.

Not all jurists agree amongst themselves. There are some who regard the State as the sole and exclusive creator of law while others reject this opinion and maintain that a large body of law in the past was never enacted or created by the State. It essentially, the latter claim, consisted of customs and usages which no legal sovereign could afford to ignore. A jurist like Duguit would go to the length of asserting that law may exist anterior to the creation of the State, and therefore is independent of its will, and that the State is bound by this law and has no right to override or disregard its prescriptions.

But German jurists, like F.J. Stahl, Lorenz Von Stein, Otto Gierke, and H.G. Trietschke, vest the State with a real, as opposed to a fictitious, personality having a legal will of its own distinct from the sum of the wills of the individuals composing the State, and a capacity for expressing its will in words and acts, and as the creator and possessor of rights.

Thus, jurists themselves look differently on the nature of the State. As long as the conception of the State being a person means "nothing more than that it is a sovereign corporation, that is, an 'artificial' person, as the law regards all corporations, and as such possesses a collective will, a legal capacity, and power of collective action, apart from the will, the capacity and the power of action of the numerous individuals who compose it, just as a private corporation has a continued existence and possesses rights and obligations which are distinct from those of the shareholders," the juristic analysis is good and useful and may be accepted. But the conception of the real personality of the State, as asserted by some eminent German jurists, is pregnant with pernicious results. One may accept the proposition that the State, like other corporations, has a legal personality and it can sue and be sued. It may own property, and States do, direct and undertake economic enterprises and perform other functions as the custodian of the interests of the present and future generations. Citizens of the State suffer from telescopic defects: they discount the future and put premium on the present. Moreover, individual interests change and shift. The State is a permanent legal entity and it suffers from no telescopic defects. It endures and represents the collective will and collective interests of all the citizens rather than individual interests represented by individual will. But to say that the State has a real personality apart from that of the citizens is to vest that entity with absolute powers which may prove antagonistic to the interests of a citizen and may dwarf his individuality, if not altogether suppress it. The Juristic Theory of the State is, therefore, to be accepted only to the extent of attributing to the State a fictitious legal personality for certain specified purposes. For example, International Law characterises the State as a "person" and it is nothing more than "the juridical personification of the nation."

Marxian Theory of the State. The Marxian or Communist theory of the State[48] finds its full expression in the philosophy of Karl Marx. The basis of his doctrine is a philosophy of history, supplemented by a theory of the State and a body of economic theory. Briefly stated, the State, according to this theory, is a "super-structure." Its form is determined by the exigencies of class struggle and the demands of the underlying material situation. Defined as an instrument of exploitation and coercion, the State is regarded as the product and manifestation of the irreconcilable class antagonism. At every stage of its development, a single class is dominant and this dominant class controls the State and uses its machinery to further its exploitation of the exploited class, which is the non-possessing class. Under capitalism, the State is in essence a committee of the bourgeoisie for the oppression and exploitation of the working class, the proletariat.

The Marxian theory rejects the very basis of the State, namely, that it is a natural and necessary institution. The State is an artificial vehicle of coercion; and is a product of society at a certain stage of its economic development. The State, Frederick Engels wrote, "has not existed from all eternity. There have been societies that did without it, that had no conception of the state and state power. At a certain stage of economic development, which was necessarily bound up with the cleavage of society into classes, the state became a necessity owing to cleavage."[49] The State has, therefore, no moral stature and useful purpose to serve. It is an organ of class rule, "an organ for the oppression of one class by another, it creates 'order' which legalises and perpetuates this

48. For a critical analysis of Marxism refer to Chaps. 29 and 30.
49. Frederick Engels, The *Origin of the Family, Private Property and the State,* p. 285.

oppression by moderating the collision between the classes."[50] The ancient and the feudal States were organs for the exploitation of the slaves and the serfs and "the contemporary representative state is an instrument of exploitation of wage-labour by capital."[51] The revolution of the past was that of the slaves and serfs against feudalism and it found its expression in the French Revolution. The one in the future, Marx predicted, will be the revolution of the wage-earners against the bourgeoisie in their bid to establish the Socialist Commonwealth.

When the revolution comes, the capitalist class will disappear and a classless society headed by the Dictatorship of the Proletariat takes its place. "In order to break down the resistance of the bourgeois," says Marx, "the workers invest the State with a revolutionary spirit." A few remaining elements of capitalism must be swept away and the minds of men purged of the remnants of capitalist mentality with which they were infected. The Dictatorship of the Proletariat will continue with the State, but it will be a revolutionary State invested with oppressive and autocratic powers. The proletarian dictatorship takes up the work of both construction and destruction; construction of Socialism and complete destruction of Capitalism. Once the *bourgeoisie* has been completely suppressed and the remnants of the Capitalist system are removed, the necessity of the State will cease to exist. The State will "wither away" and the emerging society will be classless and Stateless.

The Marxian Theory of the State ignores human nature altogether and the development of historical events and processes. The entire historical-economic thesis of Marx is untenable. The influence of non-economic interests, such as religious and historical, cannot be brushed aside with contempt. Both these influences, *inter alia*, have played a significant role in the historical growth of society and the State. Then, the State is not the result of exploitation pure and simple, as the Marxist theory claims. Exploitation may have played a vital role in the formation of the State, but it cannot be the only cause of the origin of the State. MacIver has rightly said, "Significant as that motive was, it did not work alone. The authority of the elders over the younger kin was not exploitation, but it played a part in the making of the State. The tribal sense of justice evoked agencies of jurisdiction, and they too were conditions of the emerging State. And many factors contributed to create the kind of political loyalty without which the State would have never grown to maturity."[52]

Marx's entire emphasis on the origin and development of the State is on force. He considers the State as a vehicle of oppression and maintains that the capitalist class has arisen to power, has consolidated its position and authority and retains its pre-eminence through the use of force. He concludes that power can be wrested from this class only through the use of force, no matter how ruthless it may have to be. The Communists will, therefore, capture the capitalist State by force and consolidate the Dictatorship of the Proletariat by force. Force is the essence of the Proletarian State. Two questions mark the discussion here. Will the use of force come to an end when the State 'withers away"?

50. *Lenin, Selected Works,* Vol. II (Moscow: Foreign Languages Publishing House), p. 44.
51. *Ibid,* p. 148.
52. MacIver and Page, Society, p. 590.

Secondly, will the State at all 'wither away'? There was no trace of it under the former Soviet Russia. Nor is there any in China and other Communist countries that exist. Both these vital instruments of Communist ideology constitute the whole of development of a Communist Society.

SUGGESTED READINGS

Barker, E.: *Political Thought in England: Spencer to Present Day,* pp. 175–83.

Barker, E.: *Principles of Social and Political Theory,* pp. 42-77.

Follet, M.P.: *The New State, Chaps. I-IV.*

Garner, J.W.: *Introduction to Political* Science, Chaps. III-IV.

Garner, J.W.: *Political Science and Government,* Chaps. IV-VII.

Gettel, R.G.: *Introduction to Political Science,* Chap. II.

Gilchrist, R.N.: *Principles of Political Science,* Chap. II.

Karl, W. Deutsch: *Politics and Government: How People Decide Their Fate,* Chap. 1.

Laski, H.J.: Grammar of Politics, Chap. VI.

Iaski, *H.J.: The State in Theory and Practice,* Chap. II.

Leacock, S.: *Elements of Political Science,* Chap. I.

MacIver, R.M.: *The Modern State, Introduction.*

MacIver, R.M. and Page, C.H.: *Society: An Introductory Analysis.*

MacIver, R.M.: *The Web of Government.*

Mill, J.S.: *Representative Government.*

Robson, W.A.: *The University Teaching of Political Science,* Chaps. I, III.

Sidgwick, H.: The *Elements of Politics,* Chap. XIV.

Unesco : *Contemporary Political Science.*

Wilson, W.: *The State,* pp. 27-30.

4

CHAPTER

Origin of the State

Introductory. While introducing the State, in the first Chapter, we said that it originated in the bare needs of life and continues in existence for the good life of man. But it is shrouded in mystery when and how the State came into existence. The recent researches in the sciences of Anthropology, Ethnology, and Comparative Philology throw some light on the subject, but all this is not sufficient to offer a matter-of-fact explanation of the origin of the State. Speculation is, then, the only alternative and we examine a number of theories that have been advanced from time to time, varying with the credulity of the age. The most important of these theories are:

1. The Theory of Divine Origin.
2. The Theory of Force.
3. The Theory of Social Contract.
4. The Patriarchal and Matriarchal Theories.
5. The Historical or Evolutionary Theory.

The Historical or Evolutionary Theory is now accepted as the correct theory of the origin of the State. The Patriarchal and Matriarchal Theories, which seek to explain that family is the nucleus of the State and either father or mother had really been the head of the family in ancient times, are not separate theories of the origin of the State. They form part of the accepted Historical or Evolutionary Theory, although we have treated them separately for clarity and proper understanding. The theories of Divine Origin, Force and Social Contract are speculative and stand rejected. But it does not mean that they have no practical utility. Each one of these theories contains some element of truth and aids us in penetrating the realm of the past and helps to find out how and why the State came into existence. To examine and reject a speculative theory is a means of arriving at the truth. It is only by groping in the dark that we hope to reach the light. Leacock has rightly said that the "rejection of what is false in the speculative theories of the past will aid in establishing more valid conclusions on the residual basis of what is true." What exists is never new. It is a monument of human effort, the result of prolongcd activity. We cannot understand any contemporary institution without some knowledge of its genetic background. Speculative theories exhibit the spirit of the time in which they flourished and are, consequently, the index of the people, their thoughts, and their environments and describe the forces that moulded and shaped the practices of the State. Finally, speculative theories led to the development of political thought. Men of merit thought and considered, discussed and criticised the various theories enunciated from time to time and it paved the way for further developments in political thinking. The Social Contract theory replaced the theory of Divine Origin and the former was replaced by the Historical or Evolutionary theory.

THE THEORY OF DIVINE ORIGIN

The Theory Explained. The theory of Divine Origin, though one of the earliest, has a simple explanation to offer. It is a theory of political authority and not a theory of the origin of the State. The State, its advocates maintain, was created by God and governed by His deputy or Viceregent. It was His will that men should live in the world in a state of political society and He sent His deputy to rule over them. The ruler was a divinely appointed agent and he was responsible for his actions to God alone. As the ruler was the deputy of God, obedience to him was held to be a religious duty and resistance a sin. The advocates of the Divine Origin Theory, in this way, placed the ruler above the people as well as law. Nothing on earth could limit his will and restrict his power. His word was law and his actions were always just and benevolent. To complain against the authority of the ruler and to characterise his actions as unjust was a sin for which there was divine punishment.

The theory of the Divine Origin of the State is as old as Political Science itself. There is sufficient evidence to prove now that early States were based on this conception and all political authority was connected with certain unseen powers. The earliest ruler was a combination of priest and king or the magic man and king. The authority and reverence which a ruler commanded depended upon his position as a priest or a magic man. Religion and politics were so inextricably mixed up in the primitive society that not a hazy line of demarcation could be drawn between the two.

Even today, the State of Pakistan does not seem to draw a distinction between religion and politics. Sir Mohammad Zafarullah Khan, the then Pakistan Foreign Minister, while speaking on the Objective Resolution in the Pakistan Constituent Assembly in 1949, said: "Those who sought to draw a distinction between the spheres of religion and politics as being mutually exclusive put too narrow a construction upon the functions of religion."[1] The abrogated Constitutions declared Pakistan an Islamic Republic to be governed with the Islamic principles. President Zia-ul-Haq significantly modified the 1973 Constitution to bring it in conformity to the injunctions of Islam. In addition to Islamic Arab States, the Islamic Republic of Iran, the Islamic Republic State of Bangladesh and the Islamic State of Afghanistan are the most recent examples of theocratic States.

The theory that the State and its authority has a Divine Origin and sanction finds unequivocal support in the scriptures of almost all religions in the world. In the *Mahabharata*, it is recounted that the people approached God and requested him to grant them a ruler who should save them from the anarchy and chaos prevailing in the state of nature. "Without a Chief, O Lord", they prayed, "we are perishing. Give us a Chief whom we shall worship in concert and who will protect us."[2] The theory of Divine

1. *The Statesman*, Northern India Edition, New Delhi, March 14, 1949.
2. Refer to U. Ghoshal's *A History of Indian Political Theories,* p, 175.

Origin, however, received a new impetus with the advent of Christianity. "Render unto Caesar the things that are Caesar's," said Jesus Christ, and Paul amplified this in his Epistle to the Romans, which has been quoted by writers time and again in support of the theory of Divine Origin. We are, thus, told, "Let every soul be subject unto the higher powers. For there is no power but of God: the powers that be are ordained of God. Whosoever, therefore, resisteth the power, resisteth the ordinance of God: and they that resist shall receive themselves damnation...."[3]

The theory of Divine Origin so enunciated, believed in and accepted, thus, implied:—

1. that God deliberately created the State and this specific act of His grace was to save mankind from destruction;
2. that God sent his Deputy or Viceregent to rule over mankind. The ruler was a divinely appointed agent and he was responsible for his actions to God alone whose Deputy the ruler was. All were ordained to submit to his authority and disobedience to his command was a sin for which there was divine punishment.

The Divine Right of Kings. There were direct and precise instructions to the faithful. Although the Roman Empire was a pagan empire, Paul had ordered Christians to accept its authority as derived from God and thereby admitted that the State, whatever the personal morality of the monarch, was divinely ordained. During the Middle Ages in Europe the theory of the Divine Origin of the State was transformed into the doctrine of the Divine Right of Kings. The temporal authority, having emerged victorious over the spiritual authority, claimed that it was a divine favour to the Viceregents of divine authority. Even today the Queen of Great Britain is a Queen "by the Grace of God".

The Stuarts in England found refuge in the doctrine of the Divine Right of Kings and its leading exponent was James I. Sir Robert Filmer was its enthusiastic supporter. Bousset advocated it in France and supported the despotism of Louis XIV. It was claimed that Kings ruled by divine right and the subjects had no recourse against them. "Kings", wrote James I, "are breathing images of God upon earth" and disobedience to their commands was disobedience to God. "As it is atheism and blasphemy to dispute what God can do, so it is presumption and high contempt in a subject to dispute what a King can do, or to say that a King cannot do this or that." Even rebellion in the cause of religion was deemed a sacrilege because, "the State of monarchy is the supremest thing upon earth; for Kings are not only God's lieutenants upon earth, and sit upon God's throne, but even by God himself they are called Gods." As men are children of God, so are men children of the King and they owe him an equal obedience, Without a King there could be no civil society, as the people were a mere "heedless multitude" incapable of making laws. All law proceeded from the King as the divinely instituted law-giver of his people. The only choice for the people was submission to the authority of the King or complete anarchy. The King could not be held answerable for his actions to human judgment. He was responsible to God alone. "A bad King will be judged by God but he must not be judged by his subjects or by any human agency for enforcing the law, such as the estates or the courts." The law resided ultimately "in the breast of the King."

3. Romans, xiii, 1-7.

The main points in the doctrine of the Divine Right of Kings may, thus, be summed up:—

1. Monarchy is divinely ordained and the King draws his authority from God;
2. Monarchy is hereditary and it is the divine right of a King that it should pass from father to son;
3. The King is answerable to God alone; and
4. Resistance to the lawful authority of a King is a sin.

The theory of the Divine Right of Kings, originally used in the Middle Ages to serve as a bulwark against the claims of the Church Fathers, was later used by Kings and their supporters to defend their existence against the political consciousness of the people—when the people claimed that ultimately power and sovereign authority rested with them.

Evaluation of the Theory. That the State is divinely created does not find any place in the present political thought. The State is essentially a human institution, and it comes into existence when a number of people occupying a definite territory organise themselves politically for achieving common ends. The laws of the State are made by men and enforced by them. The State, therefore, originated in the bare needs of the life of man and continues in existence for the satisfaction of those needs and aspirations for a good life. To accept it as the creation of God is to defy nature itself and to exalt the State to a position above criticism and change. The Divine Origin theory is dangerous as it justifies the arbitrary exercise of royal authority by holding that authority has a religious sanction and origin, and Kings are the vicars of God. When the ruler is made responsible for his actions to God alone and law is held to reside ultimately "in the breast of the King", it is tantamount to preaching absolutism and making the King a despot. Even if it be conceded that the King is the viceregent or deputy of God, then, how can the existence of a bad King be justified ? History abounds in examples of bad and vicious Kings. God personifies virtue, grace and benevolence and so should be His deputy. It is, accordingly, bad logic to accept the dogma of James I that "Kings are breathing images of God upon earth." Even in the scriptures the theory does not find unequivocal support. The Bible tells us, "Render unto Caesar the things that are Caesar's and unto God the things that are God's." This saying of Christ does not justify the Divine Origin of the State. Finally, the theory does not consider any other form of government except monarchy and that, too, absolute monarchy. Such a form of government is antagonistic to the democratic ideal which accepts consent as the basis of the State.

The Divine Origin theory is dismissed as an explanation of the origin of the State. At the same time, the theory has a certain value. We cannot ignore the part which religion played in the development of the State. The early rulers combined unto themselves the authority and functions of a king and a priest. Law had a religious sanction and "divine" or religious law appealed to primitive man more than human law. Obedience to the State was deemed a religious duty and religious worship was supported by government. Belief in a common religion was, thus, a great combining factor which welded the people in the pursuit of common ends. "It taught men to obey" when they were "not yet ready to govern themselves."[4] Finally, the theory of Divine Origin adds a moral tone to the functions of the State. "To regard the State as the work of God is to give it a high moral

4. Gettel, R.G., *Introduction to Political Science,* p. 81.

status, to make it something which the citizen may revere and support, something which he may regard as the perfection of human life."[5] The Divine Origin Theory and with that the Divine Right of Kings was discredited in the seventeenth and eighteenth centuries in the West and was replaced by the Social Contract Theory and Rousseau's concept of popular sovereignty. Thus, the 'Voice of God' gave place to 'the voice of the people.'

THE THEORY OF FORCE

The Statement of the Theory. The theory of Force is another fallacious theory, but historically important, which is offered as an explanation of the origin and meaning of the State. There is an old saying that 'war beget the king,' and true to this maxim, the theory of Force emphasises the origin of the State in the subordination of the weak to the strong. The advocates of the theory argue that man, apart from being a social animal, is bellicose by nature. There is also a lust for power in him. Both these desires prompt him to exhibit his strength and in the early stages of the development of mankind a person physically stronger than the rest captured and enslaved the weak. He collected in this way a band of followers, fought with others, and subjugated the weak. Having increased the number of his followers, over whom he exercised undisputed authority, he became a tribal chief. A clan fought against a clan and a tribe against a tribe. The powerful conquered the weak and this process of conquest and domination continued till the victorious tribe secured control over a definite territory of a considerable size under the sway of its tribal chief, who proclaimed himself the King. Leacock gives a matter-of-fact explanation of the Force Theory when he says that "historically it means that government is the outcome of human aggression, that the beginnings of the State are to be sought in the capture and enslavement of man by man, in the conquest and subjugation of feebler tribes, and generally speaking in the self-seeking domination acquired by superior physical force. The progressive growth from tribe to kingdom, and from kingdom to empire is but a continuation of the same process."[6] The theory, in fine, tells us that the State is primarily the result of forcible subjugation through long continued warfare among primitive groups and "historically speaking," as Jenks says, "there is not the slightest difficulty in proving that all political communities of the modern type owe their existence to successful warfare."[7]

Once the State had been established, force, which had hitherto been utilised for subjugating others. was used as an instrument for maintaining internal order and making it secure from any kind of external aggression. But this alone was not sufficient. Force was used as the sinews of war and power and in a bid for superiority, one State fought against another, eliminating the weaker and only those survived which either could not be conquered, or no venture was made to conquer them as they were comparatively powerful. The theory of Force, therefore, traces the origin and development of the State to conquest and "justifies its authority by the proposition that might is right."[8] The theory

5. Gilchrist, R.N., *Principles of Political Science,* p. 74.
6. Leacock, E., *Elements of Political Science,* p. 32.
7. Jenks, E., *A Short History of Politics,* p. 71.
8. Gettell, R.G., *Introduction to Political Science,* p. 79.

has, thus, four implications. First, force is not only a historical factor, but is the present essential feature of the State; secondly, that the States were born of force only; thirdly, that power is their justification and *raison d'etre*; and, finally, that the maintenance and extension of power within and without is the sole aim of the State

Theory used in support of diverse purposes. The theory of Force has been advanced by different thinkers and writers for advocating their own point of view. It was first used by the Church Fathers in the medieval period to discredit the State, and to establish the supremacy of the Church. They claimed that the Church was divinely created whereas the State was the outcome of brute force. Gregory VII wrote in 1080: "Which of us is ignorant that kings and lords have had their origin in those who, ignorant of God, by arrogance, rapine, perfidy, slaughter, by every crime which the devil agitating as the prince of the world, have continued to rule over their fellowmen with blind cupidity and intolerable presumption."

In modern times the Individualists owned the theory to protect individual liberty against government encroachment. They characterised the State as a necessary evil and argued that the State should leave the individual alone, *laissez faire*, and should not interfere in what he does, except for the maintenance of internal peace and external security. The Individualists base their arguments on the principle of survival of the fittest and try to prove that it is only the strong who survive and the weak go to the wall. The Socialists, on the other hand, hold that the State is the outcome of the process of aggressive exploitation on the weaker by the stronger; the latter constituting the propertied class who had ever manned administration and directed the machinery of the government to their own benefit. The existing system of industrial organisation, it is maintained, hinges upon force because "a part of the community has succeeded in defrauding their fellows of the just reward of their labour." They further argue that force is the origin of civil society and government represents merely the coercive organisation which tends to curb and exploit the working class in order to maintain the privileged position of the propertied class. The theory of Socialism is a revolt against the State, as it is the product of force and power is its justification and *raison d'etre*. Karl Marx, accordingly, concluded that the State must ultimately 'wither away'.

During recent times the theory of Force was a favourite theme of political philosophy with German writers. Imbued with the desire to make their country a Greater Germany, and at the peak of its glory, they lavished praise on force and considered its indiscriminate use as the most important factor for the solidarity of the nation. Treitschke said that "the State is the public power of offence and defence, the first task of which is the making of war and the administration of justice." War, he said, consolidates a people, reveals to each individual his relative unimportance, causes factional hostilities to disappear, and intensifies patriotism and national idealism. "The grandeur of history," he further maintained, "lies in the perpetual conflict of nations" and "the appeal to arms will be valid until the end of history." General Von Bernhardt held might as "the supreme right, and the dispute as to what is right is decided by the arbitrament of war. War gives a biologically just decision, since the decision rests on the very nature of things." Nietzsche preached the doctrine of the will to power and the superman. The individual who can command the highest admiration, according to this doctrine, is the strong man who compels other men to act in fulfilment of his will. Nietzsche, while glorifying the "masterly" virtues of man, says that a truly moral person "has no place for the vulgar and slavish virtue of humility, self-sacrifice, pity, gentleness." Hitler and Mussolini put into real practice the doctrines of these writers. They regarded force as the normal means for maintaining a nation's prestige, cultural influence, commercial supremacy in the world, and for holding the allegiance of citizens at home. This general doctrine of political authoritarianism, both with Hitler and Mussolini, became "a creed of dominance by intimidation—militancy in international relations and forcible suppression of political dissent in domestic government."[9] Hitler and Mussolini pushed mankind into another World War, causing unprecedented misery, havoc and destruction. The United Nations Organization was established after the War to save the succeeding generations from the scourge of war. Yet there is no end to war. There is a show of might everywhere and a never-ending race between all powers, big and small, to invent and manufacture deadly weapons of warfare, some to defend, others to offend.

Criticism of the Theory. Force, indeed, has played an important part in the origin and development of the State. Some of the greatest empires of today have been established through 'blood and iron.' We may see even more of this 'blood and iron' in the days to come. Force is an essential element of the State. Internally, the State requires force to ensure obedience to its commands. Externally, it is necessary to repel aggression and to preserve the integrity of the State. Without force no State can exist and sovereignty of the State always rests ultimately on force. Kant said, "Even a population of devils would find it to their advantage to establish a coercive State by general consent."

But, all this does not sufficiently explain the origin of the State. Force is, no doubt, one of the factors which contributed to the evolution of the State. It is, however, not the only one, nor the most important factor, and the theory of force "errs in magnifying what has been only one factor in the evolution of society into the sole controlling force."[10] Force is, also, not the only basis of the State. Something other than force is necessary in binding the people together. It is will, not force, which is the real basis of the State. Sheer force can hold nothing together because "force always disrupts—unless it is made subservient to common will."[11] Force we do need in maintaining the State, but its indiscriminate use cannot be permitted. It must be used as a medicine and not a daily diet as force is the criterion of the State and not its essence. If it becomes the essence of the State, the State will last so long as force can last. Indiscriminate use of force has always been the forerunner of revolutions, overthrowing governments which rest on force. Since the State is a permanent institution, only moral force can be its permanent foundation. T.H. Green has aptly said that "it is not coercive power as such but coercive power exercised according to law, written or unwritten, for maintenance of the existing rights from external or internal invasions, that makes a State." Might with rights is as lasting as human minds on which it depends.

Moreover, the Theory of Force unduly emphasises the principle of the survival of the

9. Coker, F.W., *Recent Political Thought,* p. 439.

10. Leacock, S., *Elements of Political Science,* p. 33.

11. MacIver, R.M., *The Modern State*, p. 222.

fittest. It means that might is right and those who are physically weak should go to the wall. It is dangerous to employ such a principle in the internal existence of the State. Might without right is antagonistic to individual liberty. The State is duly bound to protect equally the weak and the strong and create equal opportunities for all. Externally, if might is the supreme right, and the dispute as to what is right is decided by the arbitrament of war, there can be no international peace. Every State will be at perpetual war with the rest. This is a condition of chaos, pure and simple, endangering the peace and security of the world. The attention and efforts of every State will be directed towards war-preparedness and to win the war, if it comes. War, which is an *alias* for murder, glorifies brute force, suppressing the moral forces. This is the mean self of man and not his real sell. Is this the end for which the State exists?

THE THEORY OF SOCIAL CONTRACT

The Theory Explained. Foremost in historical importance is the Theory of Social Contract. It postulates a *state of nature* as the original condition of mankind and a *social contract,* deliberately and voluntarily made, as the means of escape therefrom. Some political thinkers who advocated the theory of Social Contract were of the opinion that the state of nature was *pre-social*; whereas others regarded it as *pre-political*. But whatever it was, the state of nature was antecedent to the institution of government, that is, prior to the establishment of government. The state of nature was not an organized society. Each man living therein led a life of his own, uncontrolled by any laws of human imposition. Nor was there any human authority to regulate his relations with others. Men living in the state of nature were subject only to such regulations as nature was supposed to prescribe for them. This code of regulations was given the name of the *law of nature* or *natural law.*

No two thinkers on the Social Contract Theory are at one as to the conditions that prevailed in the state of nature. Some described it as a state of "ideal innocence and bliss". Others gave a gloomy and dismal picture and characterised it as a state of "wild savagery", where might was right. Some others considered it as a state of "insecurity", though not of savagery, accompanied by some tangible inconveniences. But whatever it was, all thinkers were agreed that those who lived in the state of nature were ultimately compelled, for one reason or another, to abandon it and substitute the state of nature by a *civil society* or a body-politic where each man led a life of union with his other fellowmen. The law of nature, which regulated the conduct of the individuals who lived in the state of nature, was replaced by man-made laws.

Thus emerged civil society and it was the result of a mutual *consent* or *contract*; man taking upon himself the duty of observing and obeying all those laws which assured the safety and protection of all other members of the newly organised community or body-politic. These laws were prescribed by the mutually agreed authority. Human law was substituted for the natural law and in return for *natural rights* every man found "himself clothed with *social rights*." These rights were maintained and guaranteed by the mutually established authority.

All this process of development was the result of a *contract* or "bargain dictated by the individual's own interest, an exchange of obligations in return for privileges." What were the terms of the contract, who were the parties to the contract, and what was the extent of the powers of the authority mutually appointed to enforce the laws of the body-politic? There were sharp differences of opinion on all those points as each thinker had sought to establish different conclusions and vindicate different principles. All advocates of the Theory of Social Contract were, however, unanimous on the essential idea that the State was a deliberate human creation, the result of consent or contract.

There are three essential elements in the Theory of Social Contract. First is the state of nature wherein man had not *organised* himself in bonds of political cohesion and, therefore, in a political society. He was independent and free and subject to no obligations and man-made laws. He simply obeyed the law of nature. What the law of nature precisely meant, was his own interpretation and determination. Such a condition in the state of nature created conditions of uncertainty for all as none felt secure both in his person and property. No man could for ever endure such conditions of life and ultimately decided to quit the state of nature. This he did by common consent or agreement or contract or covenant with his fellowmen who lived with him in the state of nature. This is the second element in the Theory of Social Contract. The third is that as a result of common consent or contract or covenant a civil society was established where laws of the State and civil rights prevailed in place of natural law and natural rights. The final element is the process by which one way of life was given up for another way of life.

History of the Theory. The Theory of Social Contract is as old as political thought itself and it had found adequate support both in the East and West. Kautilya, the Minister of Chandragupta Maurya, elaborated it in his *Arthasastra*. He wrote, "People suffering from anarchy, as illustrated by the proverbial tendency of a large fish swallowing a small one, first elected Manu to be their King, and allotted one-sixth of the grains grown and one-tenth of their merchandise as sovereign's dues. Supported by this payment Kings took upon themselves the responsibility of maintaining the safety and security of their subjects."[12] The Greek philosopher Plato dealt with the Contract Theory in his works, the *Crito* and the *Republic*. Aristotle, on the other hand, repudiated the theory when he said that the State was a natural institution. Roman Law, which exercised so powerful an influence from the twelfth century onwards, made it clear that most of the positive rules obeyed by men were created by contract. The feudal relationship between the lord and the vassal was essentially a contractual relationship. The Church Fathers, in their early writings, gave some support to the theory, although they abandoned it eventually. It was only during and after the Middle Ages that the idea of Social Contract found a significant place in the discussions of political thinkers. Manegold of Lautenbach maintained that the King could be deposed if "he violates the agreement according to which he was chosen ...."[13]

In the sixteenth and seventeenth centuries the supporters of the Social Contract Theory multiplied and there was more or less universal acceptance of the doctrine. Hooker was the first scientific writer who gave a logical exposition of the Theory of

12. *Arthasastra*, Bk. I, Ch. XIII.
13. As quoted in Sabine, G H., *A History of Political Theory*, p. 241.

Social Contract,[14] though he used it to defend the Established Church against the attacks of its enemies. The theory also received impetus from the writings of Hugo Grotius, the Dutch jurist. But it found real support at the hands of Hobbes, Locke and Rousseau. In our discussions of the theory of Social Contract we are primarily concerned with the political philosophy of these three writers, collectively known as the 'contractualists'.

THOMAS HOBBES (1588–1679)

Thomas Hobbes, sometime tutor to Charles II of England, published his book, the *Leviathan*, in 1651. In this book, he gave a striking exposition of the theory of Social Contract. Hobbes had no mind to give the theory of the origin of the State. He wrote, while the memory of the Civil War of 1642, and the King's (Charles I) execution was still vivid, to justify the rule of the Stuarts and believed, that England could be saved only by absolute monarchy. His object was to defend the absolute power of the monarch and he used the doctrine of the Social Contract to support it.

Some critics of Hobbes have stigmatised him as a "pensioner" of the Stuarts. This is an exaggeration. Yet, it remains true that Hobbes supported and defended Stuart despotism when there was an irresistible opposition against such a power. He was convinced that nothing could be too high a price to pay for the preservation of order and that the best security for this was to be found in the unlimited authority of the King.[15]

The State of Nature. Hobbes began his thesis with the state of nature, which he characterised as the *pre-social* phase of human nature. The state of nature, as Hobbes described it, was a condition of unmitigated selfishness and rapacity. Men had no sense of right and wrong and they fell upon each other with savage ferocity. There was a perpetual and restless desire with them to satisfy their appetites and desires with a craving for gain and glory which came to an end only with their death. Natural rights which men enjoyed in the state of nature were nothing short of might and natural liberty was nothing more than "the liberty that each man hath to use his own power for the preservation of his own nature." They did not know pity and compassion and if ever anyone did a good act it was the result of his "love of power and delight in the exercise of it."

From this analysis of the state of nature, Hobbes concluded that man was not at all social; indeed he found "nothing but grief in the company of his fellows"—all being almost equally selfish, self-seeking, cunning, egoistic, brutal, covetous and aggressive. The state of nature was, thus, a condition of perpetual war "where every man is enemy to every man" and where the rule of life was "only that to be every man's that he can get; and for so long as he can keep it." When men in the state of nature were like hungry wolves, each ready to devour the other, their lives were "solitary, poor, nasty, brutish and short."

14. Refer to Richard Hooker's *Laws of Ecclesiastical Polity.*

15. "His (Hobbes') principles were at least as contrary to the pretensions of the Stuarts whom he meant to support as to those of the revolutionists whom he meant to refute and more contrary to both than eitber royalist or parliamentarian was to the other. The friend of the king might well feel that Hobbes' friendship was as dangerous as Cromwell's enmity." Sabine, G.H., *A History, of Political Theory,* p. 456.

The Contract. These conditions were really intolerable and could not be left to continue indefinitely. Men yearned for peace and security of life and property and in a bid to escape from the misery and horrors of their natural condition, they covenanted among themselves to form a civil society or "Commonwealth" which would give to each individual person security of life and property. They, accordingly, agreed to surrender their natural rights into the hands of a common superior and to obey his commands. The covenant was of each with all and of all with each. Each man said to every man:

"I authorise and give up my right of governing myself to this man, or to this assembly of men, on this condition, that thou give up thy right to him, and authorise all his actions in like manner.... This is the generation of that great Leviathan, or rather (to speak more reverently) of that Mortal God, to which we owe under the immortal God, our peace and defence."

In this way, individuals *surrendered* their natural rights to some particular man or assembly of men. The person or assembly of persons to whom they surrendered their natural rights became sovereign and the covenanting individuals who agreed to submit to the authority of the sovereign became his *subjects*. The sovereign was not a party to the contract. Others had made a covenant to obey him; he had made no covenant to obey them. Consequently, the sovereign did not subject himself to conditions. Hobbes maintained that only a contract binding each and all to unquestioning obedience to a sovereign could really establish a stable commonwealth. Any introduction of 'condition,' in his opinion, was likely to create uncertainty and indefiniteness leading, again, to disputes incapable of a decisive settlement, and so to anarchy. The sovereign, thus, profited from the contract without being a party to it. For the future, however arbitrary that rule might be, the people retained no ultimate right to rise against the sovereign authority. The authority of the sovereign was final and irrevocable.

Here are the highlights of Hobbes' Social Contract:

1. It is a *social* contract and *not* a governmental contract. The sovereign is not a party to the contract, as he is the creation of the contract or, as Dunning puts it, "A superior, or sovereign, exists only by virtue of the pact, not prior to it." Individuals living in the state of nature, all equal, agreed with one another to give up their natural rights of doing anything that pleased them, and to possess anything that they could take and hold, to a common authority, and this common authority became by that fact their superior.

2. As the sovereign is not a party to the contract, he did not subject himself to any conditions; his authority is absolute and unlimited. All his subjects must obey him, otherwise there would be conflict, war, and a return to the wretchedness of the state of nature. "The only way," Hobbes said, "to erect such a common power...is to confer all their power and strength upon one man or upon one assembly of men, that may reduce all their wills by plurality of voice, unto one will."

3. The contract becomes irrevocably binding on the whole community as a perpetual social bond, for the individuals keep no rights to themselves, except the right to self-preservation. If the sovereign lost his power and conquered by another and he submitted to his authority, the subjects become the subjects of the conqueror. "But, if he be held prisoner or have not the liberty of his body, he is not understood to have given away the

right of sovereignty; and therefore his subjects are obliged to yield obedience to the magistrates formerly placed, governing not in their own name, but in his."[16]

4. Hobbes denied to the people the right to revolt against the authority of the sovereign. There can happen no breach to the covenant, even if his authority becomes arbitrary and despotic. In fact, the sovereign can never be wrong and his actions cannot be unjust. He cannot be justly accused by the subjects and "Whatsoever the sovereign doth is unpunishable by the subject."

5. Law is command of the sovereign and he is the sole source of law. "Civil, law is to every subject those rules which the commonwealth hath commanded him by word, writing or other sufficient sign of the will to make use for the distinction of right and wrong." The laws of the sovereign can never be unjust or immoral, "for the law is all the right reason we have, and...is the infallible rule of moral goodness."

6. Liberty is the gift of the sovereign in whom the will of the whole community is unified. The sovereign has "the whole power of prescribing the rules, whereby every man may know, what goods he may enjoy, and what actions he may do, without being molested by any of his fellow-subjects." In short, the liberty of the subjects can properly be thought of only in relation to the laws of the commonwealth. Liberty, according to Hobbes, consisted in:

(*i*) whatever the sovereign has not forbidden; and

(*ii*) what could not, by the nature of the original pact, be given up, that is, the right of self-preservation, which cannot be surrendered. "Without injustice, therefore, the individual may, in disobedience to the sovereign's command, refuse to kill himself, resist assault, refuse to accuse himself of an offence that would jeopardise his life, and with certain qualifications refuse to serve in the army."[17]

The liberty of the subjects, thus, consisted in: (*i*) what the sovereign permitted; and (*ii*) right of self-preservation which is retained by the people.

This is how Hobbes gave to his sovereign absolute, inalienable, indivisible and unlimited authority.[18] Hobbes' sovereign, so defined, need not necessarily be one man. Sovereignty may be located in an individual man and his successors (monarchy), or a group of men (aristocracy or democracy, according to the size of the group). But his preference for monarchy is an admitted fact. Monarchy, in the opinion of Hobbes, is not the legitimate form of government, but it is the best form. As a man, the king will be selfish like all men, but the self-indulgence of one is cheaper, he claimed, than the self-indulgence of many. "In a monarchy the private interest was the same with the public." A king cannot be rich, glorious or secure, if his people are poor, comtemptible or weak. Since he had got at the top, all his ambition lay in strengthening the State whereas members of a democratic or aristocratic assembly are liable to be swayed by ambition to intrigue against the State in the hope of seizing power. Their designs are a source of great danger to the community. Hobbes' conclusion was that, "other governments were

16. *Leviathan,* Part I, Chapter XXI.
17. Dunning, W.A., *A History of Political Theories from Luther to Montesquieu,* p. 288.
18. The Sovereign's power is limited only by the individual's right to self-preservation.

compacted by the artifice of men out of the ashes of monarchy after it had been ruined by seditions."

Evaluation of the Theory. Hobbes was the first Englishman to present a logical system of political philosophy. So skilfully did he blend the current political thought in his system of political administration and adapt it to his ends that he at once came into the front rank of political thinkers and "his theory became from the moment of its appearance the centre of animated controversy and enormous influence throughout Western Europe." Hobbes has been criticised vehemently. His ideas of what constituted a sound scientific method were those of his time and are now long out of date. Yet, his philosophy illustrates Bacon's saying that, "Truth emerges more easily from error than from confusion."

Nothing like the state of nature ever existed and there is absolutely no evidence in history to show the State to have emerged by mutual and deliberate agreement. The Social Contract is impossible, for the history of primitive societies has shown conclusively that men move from status to contract. Hobbes' claim is just the other way, namely, that men move from contract to status. Nor is man so inherently selfish, self-seeking and aggressive as Hobbes has described him. Man is a rational and social being, though his irrationality cannot be ignored altogether.[19] Hobbes' dogma that man is by nature unsocial and an "enemy of his kind" is diametrically opposed to the Aristotelian dogma, that man is a social animal. Society exists by nature and necessity and it has existed since man made his first appearance on this planet. As man is social, he cannot lead an isolated life and his sociability makes him a rational being, cooperative and sympathetic towards his fellowmen. Hobbes' ethical and political philosophy is based wholly on egoism and hedonism.

Hobbes described the state of nature as pre-social and pre-political. At the same time, he said that man enjoyed in the state of nature natural rights. Rights always arise in a society. If there is no society, as Hobbes' state of nature was, how could there exist any rights? Every right has a corresponding obligation. But Hobbes' man in the state of nature had no obligations; he did anything that pleased him, and possessed anything that he could take and hold against all others. Again, according to Hobbes, there was a surrender of rights. But it is against commonsense to believe that man would ever surrender all his rights. Hobbes himself becomes inconsistent when he says that man retained to himself the right of self-preservation.[20] There cannot be complete surrender and then reservation of a right.

A contract is always between two parties; it cannot be unilateral or one-sided. Hobbes makes the sovereign the beneficiary of the contract, but not a party to it. And the contract is perpetual and irrevocable. This transaction hardly appeals to human reason. Hobbes also fails to distinguish between the State and government. He confounds the legal

19. Rousseau writes, "That men are actually wicked, a sad and continued experience of them proves beyond doubt. But all the same, I think, I have shown that man is naturally good." Jean Jacques Rousseau, "A Discourse on the Origin of Inequality," *in the Social Contract and Discourses* (translated by G.D.H. Cole), p. 222.

20. "In case anarchy does actually come upon a society, and the sovereign no longer possesses the power to give the subjects that protection which is for the sole end of the social pact, their obligation to the sovereign *ipso facto* ceases." Dunning, W.A., *History of Political Theories from Luther to Montesquieu,* p. 289.

absolutism of the State with governmental absolutism, and he does not see that changes in the forms of government do not imply the dissolution of the State.

But when all this is said, Hobbes' *Leviathan* is of the very geatest importance. It is, in the words of Professor Oakeshott, "the greatest, perhaps the sole, masterpiece of political philosophy written in the English language." This is an exaggeration, yet, in spite of the fury of his critics, Hobbes continues to be widely read and makes a powerful appeal. The *Leviathan* is the first statement of complete sovereignty in the history of political thought. Hobbes contradicted the old concept of justice and maintained that Justice is created by law and that law is not the reflection of justice. Hobbes is also an Individualist in the sense that for him the world is and must always be made up of individuals. He does not believe in the people, common will or general will or common good.

JOHN LOCKE (1632–1704)

If Hobbes championed the absolute sovereignty of the monarch, John Locke, another English political philosopher, espoused the cause of limited monarchy in England. His theory was a justification of the Revolution of 1688, and the deposition of James II. The theory of John Locke is found in his two *Treatises on Civil Government* published anonymously in 1690, wherein he defended the ultimate right of the people to depose the monarch from his authority if he ever deprived them of their "liberties and properties."[21] Locke, in reality, sought, as he himself admitted, to "establish the throne of our great Restorer, our present King William, and make good his title in the consent of the people." Mark the words 'in the consent of the people' for this forms the keynote of Locke's theory. Civil power, according to Locke, is based upon consent.

The State of Nature. Locke, too, started with the state of nature. But his state of nature was *pre-political* and not *pre-social* and, as such, it did not present to him such a dismal state of affairs as it had done to Hobbes. Locke's man in the state of nature was neither selfish, nor self-seeking, nor aggressive. He was social and sympathetic towards others, because the law of nature, which was the law of *reason*, directed him to be so. Under the law of nature, as Dunning says, "of which reason is the interpreter, equality is the fundamental fact in men's relations to one another." But equality, for Locke, was not what it was for Hobbes. In Locke's state of nature men were equal and free to act as they thought fit, but "within the bounds of the law of nature." And the "bounds of the law of nature" enjoined upon them not to harm another in his life, health, liberty, or possessions. Locke's state of nature was "a state of peace, goodwill, mutual assistance and preservation," as he himself put it, in contrast to "a state of enmity, malice, violence and mutual destruction," as he described Hobbes' state of nature.

From the law of nature, as it prevailed in the state of nature, flowed, according to Locke, certain natural rights: rights to life, liberty and property. The right to liberty, he

21. "The community perpetually retains a supreme power of saving themselves from the attempts and designs of anybody, even of their legislators whenever they shall be so foolish or so wicked as to lay and carry on designs against the liberties and properties of the subject." *Treatises on Civil Government,* II, Sec. 149.

said, was man's right to do whatever he wanted to do so long as that was not incompatible with the law of nature. The right to property was man's right to anything with which he had mixed his labour, provided he made good use of it since "nothing was made by God for man to spoil or destroy." But the law of nature did not create rights alone. It imposed corresponding obligations as well, because rights had "a law to govern which obliges everyone; and reason which is that law teaches all mankind who will but consult it, that, being all equal and independent, no one ought to harm another in his life, health, liberty and possessions." That is, everyone in the state of nature, while valuing his own life, liberty and property, must also value and respect the life, liberty and property of others as a matter of duty. Such a state of nature in which men enjoyed rights and acknowledged their duties was both moral and social.

Need for Civil Society. But unfortunately peace was not secure in the state of nature. It was constantly upset by the "corruption and viciousness of degenerate men." This "ill condition," Locke said, was due to three important wants which remained unsatisfied in the state of nature : (1) the want of an established, settled, known law; (2) the want of a known and indifferent judge; and (3) the want of an executing power to enforce just decisions. Such an "ill condition," Locke asserted, was "full of fears and continual dangers", and in order to escape from all this and to gain certainty and security men made a contract to enter into civil society or the State. This contract was of *all with all* and Locke named it a social contract. The social contract put an end to the state of nature and substituted it by a civil society or the State. Each individual contracted with each to *give up* some of the rights he possessed in the state of nature. All he agreed to was to "give up everyone his single power of punishing to be exercised by such (authority) alone as shall be appointed to it amongst them, and by such rules as the community, or those authorised by them, to that purpose shall agree on." The social contract was, accordingly, no more than a transfer of certain rights and powers so that man's remaining rights would be protected and preserved. Secondly, the contract was for limited and specific purposes, and what was given up was transferred to the community as a whole and not to a man or to an assembly of men, as Hobbes had held. In this way, Locke recognised and established the sovereignty of the people, and that the State existed for the people who formed it: they did not exist for it.

Two Contracts. If men were objects for which the social contract was necessitated, that is, to create positive law, establish a known judge, and to create an authority to enforce just decisions, the society in its corporate capacity established the government and authorised it to make positive laws consistent with the law of nature, appoint impartial judges to decide disputes, and to enforce their decisions. There were, thus, two contracts according to Locke, though he did not say so explicitly. The first was a Social Contract which brought into being the civil society or the State. The second was a governmental contract when society in its corporate capacity established a government and selected a ruler to remove the inconveniences or "ill condition" which necessitated the formation of the civil society or the State. The second contract or governmental contract was subordinate to the first in as much as government was "only a fiduciary power" to act for certain ends, and its authority was confined to securing those ends. It was limited, moreover, to the condition that it was to be used in the exercise of "established known laws." If the government failed to secure the ends for which it was created and to which it had agreed, or did not exercise its authority according to the "established known laws," the community might dismiss it and appoint another government in its place. Here Locke establishes the inherent right of the people to revolt against the authority of the monarch, if he ever abused the terms of the contract to which he is a party, and ruled arbitrarily, ignoring the "established known laws" made by the representatives of the people.

The purpose of Locke is served. By making monarch a party to the contract he limits authority and subordinates it to Parliament, "the supreme power of the commonwealth." Three conclusions flow from it: (1) that the government exists for the good of the people; (2) that it should depend on their consent; and (3) that it should be limited and constitutional in its authority. If it is not for the good of the people, if it does not depend upon their consent, if it is not constitutional and exceeds the authority vested in it, the government can be legitimately overthrown. Locke, thus, justified the Revolution of 1688, and the deposition of James II, and'the accession of William and Mary to the throne of England.

Locke recognised the existence of three powers in the civil society or the State. There is first of all the legislative, which he called "the supreme power of the commonwealth." Legislature, he held, was the instrument through which the will of the community was expressed. Since the expression of that will preceded and determined its execution, that department of government which carried out the laws must be subordinate to the department that made them. Although, for Locke, the legislature was unquestionably the superior power, yet it was not sovereign. The idea of absolute, unlimited, and inalienable sovereign power in any human hands found no place in Locke's theory of Social Contract. Behind the "supreme" legislature stand the people, the final embodiment of power. "The community," said Locke, "perpetually retains a supreme power of saving themselves from the attempts and designs of anybody, even of their legislators, whenever they shall be so foolish or so wicked as to lay and carry on designs against the liberties and properties of the subject."

Secondly, there was the executive which, according to Locke, included the judicial power. The legislature need not always be in session, but the executive must be. Hence, he concluded, they "come often to be separated." There should be separation between the legislature and the executive, "because it may be too great a temptation to human frailty, apt to grasp at power, for the same persons who have the power of making laws to have also in their hands the power to execute them." This is how Locke enunciates the doctrine of the Separation of Powers which is enshrined in the American Constitution, though he is Montesquieu, not Locke, who is the author of the famous classification of powers into executive, legislative and judicial.

The third power that Locke recognised is what he called the federative—the power that made treaties. Locke has not more to tell us about the federative power, except that it is much less capable of being directed by positive laws and so must necessarily be left to the prudence and wisdom of those who are entrusted to manage it for public good.

To sum up, the following important points may be noted in Locke's doctrine of the Social Contract:—

1. Locke's state of nature is *pre-political* rather than *pre-social.*

2. His state of nature is not that of perpetual warfare as it is with Hobbes. It is a state in which men are equal and free to act as they thought fit within the bounds of the law of nature. The law of nature is the law of reason and the law of reason established certain natural rights and recognised certain duties. This state of nature in which men have rights and acknowleged duties, is moral and social in character.

3. But certain inconveniences are experienced in the state of nature. These inconveniences are three in number: uncertainty in the application of the law of reason; absence of a common judge to decide disputes according to the established law; and, no proper authority to execute those decisions. To escape from these inconveniences and the continued danger of fights, wars and confusions accompanying them, men through *voluntary* compacts formed political communities and the communities instituted governments.

4. According to Locke there are two contracts: *social contract* and *governmental contract*. The first put an end to the state of nature and substituted for it a civil society or the State. The second is made with a view to forming the government and selecting a ruler. But the second contract is subordinate to the first. Since the creation of government by a community followed the prior organisation of the community itself, the community can change the government without dissolving itself.

5. The ruler is a party to the contract.

6. There is not a surrender of rights as with Hobbes. It is only the transfer of a few given rights.

7. Law is not the command of the sovereign as Hobbes had said. According to Locke law must be the expression of the will of the people and it should be consistent with the law of reason.

8. Locke makes *consent* of the people the source of all governmental authority.

9. Locke concedes to the people the right to revolution and, thus, the ruler can be deprived of his authority, if ever he fails to fulfil the terms of his contract.

Evaluation of Locke's Theory. The most distinctive contribution of Locke to political theory is his doctrine of natural rights. Life, liberty, and property, he holds as inalienable rights of every individual. The end for which civil or political society is constituted is to secure these natural rights, and the attainment of these rights is made possible through the agency of the government. Locke, accordingly, makes a clear distinction between the State and government and introduces the theory of consent, which, in the words of Laski, now occupies a permanent place in English politics. According to Locke, government holds power on condition of, and derives its authority from, the consent of the people whom he ultimately holds sovereign. He emphasizes that "the sovereignty of the State is not the sovereignty of a ruler," and "the will of the State may limit the will and actions of a ruler." Government, for Locke is a trust and the authority of government must be exercised for fulfilling the needs which necessitated the formation of the civil society. If the government fails to function properly and in accordance with the wishes of the people, then, the community has the power to dissolve it and substitute another government in its place. "The happiness and the security of the individual figure, not as essential to the perpetuity of a government, but as the end for which alone government is ever called into existence."[22]

The main defect in Locke's theory is that he altogether ignores the concept of legal sovereignty. In the words of Gilchrist, "To use our terminology, Hobbes gives a theory of legal sovereignty without recognising the existence and power of political sovereignty; Locke recognises the force of political sovereignty, but does not give adequate recognition to legal sovereignty."[23] Nor is he sure where sovereignty really resides. He speaks of the supreme power of the people at one time and at another he talks of the supreme power of the legislative assembly. Similarly, his views on the state of nature, and that the people inhabiting it made two contracts are incredible. Locke's contribution to the theory of natural rights has also been subjected to severe criticism. For example, Bentham remarks that the concept of natural rights prevailing in the state of nature "is simple nonsense, rhetorical nonsense and nonsense on stilts." All the same, Locke is considered the ideological father of the American Revolution.

JEAN JAQUES ROUSSEAU (1712–1778)

Jean Jacques Rousseau, the great French writer of the eighteenth century, elaborated his theory in his famous work : *The Social Contract* published in 1762. Rousseau, unlike his English predecessors, Hobbes and Locke, had no purpose to serve, and no definite cause to uphold, although his teachings inspired the French Revolution of 1789. His object was "to find a form of association which will defend and protect with the whole common force the person and goods of each associate, and in which each, while uniting himself with all, may still obey himself alone, and remain free as before." Rousseau wanted to offer a logical explanation of the nature of civil society, though his logic is lost in the epigram and paradox in which he indulges too frequently. This was natural, because Rousseau was a man with abnormally intense feelings and emotions, a vivid imagination, and warm sympathies. He stated many of his ideas abstractly.

The State of Nature. The starting point in Rousseau's theory was the traditional state of nature. What the state of nature actually meant to him, Rousseau himself was neither clear nor consistent about it. He had thought and talked about it "because all world was thinking and talking about it,"[24] and Rousseau used it practically in all the various senses that had been attached to it. But "throughout the fluctuations of his usage, one idea alone appeared unmistakable, namely, that the natural state of man was vastly preferable to the social or civil state, and must furnish the norm by which to test and correct it."[25] Back to nature was his call. He had a romantic belief in the excellence of primitive simplicity and denounced the artificiality of "so-called civilised existence." He maintained that the progress of science and the arts had tended to degrade the morals of man. Return to natural simplicity, he held, was the only cure against all the corruption and degradation rampant in civil society. But it did not mean that Rousseau wanted to destroy civil

22. Dunning, *op. cit.* pp. 364-65.
23. Gilchrist, R.N., *Principles of Political Science,* p. 61.
24. Morley's *Rousseau,* Vol. I, p. 155.
25. Dunning, W.A., *History of Political Theories from Rousseau to Spencer,* pp. 12-13.

society. What he precisely meant by "return to nature" was that "nature must be the rule for men in society."[26] It would deliver mankind from the corrupt and artificial existence and that could be accomplished only by the creation of natural social conditions.

Rousseau's man in the state of nature was a "noble savage" who led a life of primitive simplicity and idyllic happiness. He was independent, contented, self-sufficient, healthy, fearless and "without need of his fellows or desire to harm them." It was only the primitive instinct and sympathy which united him with others. He knew neither right nor wrong and was away from all notions of virtue and voice.[27] It was, thus, a pure, simple and innocent life of perfect freedom and equality which Rousseau's men enjoyed in the state of nature. They were as yet free from the spiritless influence of civilisation and they sought their own happiness untrammelled by social laws and institutions.

But these conditions could not last for long. Two things emerged to corrupt this perfect scene. One was increase in population and the other was dawn of reason. With the increase in population, economic progress moved apace. The primitive life of simplicity and idyllic happiness disappeared. Fixed homes established the family, and the institution of property followed, sounding the knell of human equality. Man began to think in terms of *mine* and *thine*. "By nature man scarcely thinks," held Rousseau, "and, the man who reflects is a corrupt creature."[28] When man began to think in terms of *mine* and *thine*, there emerged the institution of private property. "The first man who, after enclosing a piece of ground, bethought himself to say 'this is mine,' and found people simple enough to believe him, was the real founder of civil society." The whole process of development may best be described in the words of Dunning: "The arts of agriculture and metallurgy were discovered; and in the application of them men had need of one another's aid. Cooperation revealed and emphasized the diversity of men's talents and prepared thus the inevitable result. The stronger man did the greater amount of work; the craftier got more of the product. Thus appeared the difference of rich and poor—the prolific source of all other sources of inequality."[29]

Emergence of Civil Society. The equality and happiness of the early state was lost. Mankind went rapidly into a state of war resembling Hobbes' state of nature. War, murder, wretchedness, and horror that had been unknown in the savage state became universal. The rich and the poor were ranged against each other in unrelenting hostility. That was a disquieting state of affairs and every individual became anxious to get rid of it. The escape was found in the formation of a civil society. Natural freedom gave place to civil freedom by a social contract of each with all and all with each. As a result of this contract a multitude of individuals became a collective unity—a society. The contract placed every individual in complete dependence on others—complete though mutual and

26. *Ibid.*, p. 13.
27. Rousseau said, "Original man had not the least notion of mine and thine, no true idea of justice....no vice, no virtues....unless we use these terms in the sense of qualities conducive to his own conservation."
28. If Rousseau's arguments are to be summarised, it means "intelligence is dangerous because it undermines reverence; science is destructive because it takes away faith; reason is bad because it sets prudence against moral intention. Without reverence, faith and moral intention there is neither character nor society." Sabine, G.H., *A History of Political Theory,* p. 578.
29. Dunning, W.A., *History of Political Theories from Rousseau to Spencer*, p. 10.

equal. The individual, in Rousseau's political system, "puts his person and all his power in common under the supreme direction of the general will and in our corporate capacity we receive each member as an indivisible part of the whole."

General Will. There was only one contract according to Rousseau, which was at once social and political. The individual surrendered himself completely and unconditionally to the will of the body of which he became a member. The body so created was a moral and collective body and Rousseau called it the *General Will.* The unique feature of the General Will was that it represented collective good as distinguished from the private interests of its members. It was the will of all the citizens when they were willing not their own private but the general good; it was the voice of all for the good of all. Rousseau went further and said that my will which willed the best interests of the State was my best will and it was, indeed, more real than my will which willed my private interests. All actions were the result of the will, but my will for the good of the State was morally superior to any other will, private or associational, which might, from time to time, determine my conduct. The General Will being the compound of the best wills of all citizens willing the best interests of the community and its lasting welfare, it must be sovereign. Since it was my will, my own real will, I ought always to follow it. If I did not, because some private and selfish interests induced me not to follow it, then the General Will could legitimately compel me to obey it. Indeed, it was the only authority that could legitimately coerce me, for it was my own will coming back to me even though I did not always recognise it as such. And in following it, I was fulfilling myself and was, thus, finding true freedom. Whoever refused to obey the General Will would be compelled to do so by the whole body. "This means nothing less than that he will be forced to be free; for this is the condition which secures him against all personal dependence."

The General Will, though by definition it could only deal with matters of public not private interest, was alone the judge of what constituted public or private interest. The General Will, moreover, could not allow anything to stand between it and the complete loyalty of its citizens. It was better, Rousseau believed, that other associations than the State should not exist, but if they did, they must always be subordinate, and if any conflict of loyalties should ever occur, citizens must always obey the State, because it was infallible and the custodian of the real interests of all.

The General Will must also, Rousseau said, "be inalienable and indivisible." Hence it could not be represented in parliamentary institutions. "As soon as a nation appoints representatives," he said, "it is no longer free, it no longer exists." England, he declared, was only free during elections, after which it "is enslaved and counts for nothing." Nor could the General Will be delegated in any manner whatever. Any attempt to delegate it would mean its end. "The moment there is a master, there is no longer a sovereign." Here is Rousseau, the apostle of popular sovereignty.

Rousseau made a clear distinction between government and the sovereign people. He said that General Will could not be an executive will. The people, who were sovereign, ought not to be responsible for the details of government. Those who made the law should not carry it out, for it was the characteristic of the sovereign General Will that it must be impersonal, and the decrees of government might frequently be particular and personal. Rousseau meant by government only the executive power. Law making was not a function of government but that of the sovereign. The people entrusted their executive power to their agent, the government. Government was, thus, only a subordinate authority; the result of the decree of the sovereign and not the creation of the contract. "There is only one contract in the State," emphasised Rousseau, "and this excludes every other."

Two consequencess follow from this. First, that the power of government can be limited, modified or taken away by the people, the master, whenever they choose so. Secondly, as government is subordinate to the sovereign, the actual form of government is a matter of secondary importance to Rousseau. So long as General Will is sovereign it matters not what form of government it may be, though he was convinced that the States should be small so that, when necessary, all citizens could get together and make laws. "The larger the State the less the liberty." By "liberty" Rousseau obviously means not freedom from political control but freedom for political control; freedom to determine the course of legislation. Such a direct democracy is the only legitimate form of government, because only in such a constitution does each man "obey himself alone and remain as free as before." Rousseau regarded representative government as a specious form of slavery.

For Rousseau, law is not the will of a class, but the will of the whole nation. "This will," he said, "is to be discovered simply by asking the nation to meet together and declare it. Only when I actively assist in legislation am I really a citizen and genuinely free; and, since the fewer the citizens are the more weight my voice has amongst them." Rousseau believed in direct government by citizens, who should themselves, in public meetings, make the laws; without being betrayed by elected representatives. His choice of direct democracy among the forms of government was largely based upon the Swiss Cantons, which he knew, and the ancient City-States, of which he had read.

Law is, accordingly, an expression of the General Will, which is the will of the society for the common good. It, therefore, demands my respect. But the common good is also my good; and so, finally, in obeying the law I am pursuing my own best interests and achieving what I really will. "It is to law alone that men owe justice and liberty....It is the celestial voice which dictates to each citizen the precepts of public reason, and teaches him to act according to the rules of his own judgment, and not to behave inconsistently with himself."

Another important result of the contract is that life and liberty of each member of the community is secured and founded on the General Will of the society as a whole. Equality and liberty, Rousseau said, are ensured, because each individual makes a complete surrender of himself and all his rights to the community. While doing so, he receives his person and rights back again as indivisible part of the sovereign community. Rousseau said, "Since each gives himself up to all, he gives himself up to none; and as there is acquired over every associate the same right that is given up by himself, there is gained the equivalent of what is lost, with greater power to preserve what is left." Each individual, thus, has a dual capacity. He is both a member of the sovereign body, and a subject.[30]

30. "Each individual contracting, so to speak, with himself, finds himself engaged under a double relation, namely, as a member of the sovereign towards the individuals, and as a member of the State towards the sovereign."

He is sovereign, as he himself is an integral unit of the community. He is subject, because he must obey the General Will and the General Will stands for public interest.

No individual can, therefore, justifiably disobey the General Will. The General Will, adds Rousseau, is infallible; it is always right and conducive to the public advantage. Moreover, by obeying the General Will the individual simply obeys himself as he himself is the creator of the General Will. Nor can the individual complain of any coercion. Real coercion, Rousseau says, never occurs in society. Even a criminal wills his own punishment. "In order then that the social compact may not be an empty formula, it tacitly includes the undertaking....that whoever refuses to obey the general will shall be compelled to do so by the whole body. This means nothing less than that he will be forced to be free....This alone legitimises civil undertakings, which, without it, would be absurd, tyrannical, and liable to the most frightful abuses." No act of the sovereign can, thus, be coercive. And how can it be coercive when the General Will is the repository of the interests and welfare of all. An individual can act capriciously when he wants something different from what the interests of the community demand. He does not, then, rightly know his own good or his own desires. Only the General Will can know it. Therefore, Rousseau repeatedly said that the General Will is always right. It cannot be wrong, because the General Will stands for the social good, which is itself the standard of right. "What is not right is merely not the General Will." In this way, Rousseau brought about a thorough submergence of the individual in the State. His emphasis throughout is that the real interest of the whole community must always be the real interest of each of us, even though it may not be our interest as we ourselves see it. This is what Rousseau means by complete surrender and he tried to prove, though not very successfully, that in making this complete surrender each of us is securing for himself the only true liberty. The State, to Rousseau, is a collective person, and "I obey it because only in so doing am I really myself, am I truly free." Freedom, in brief, is obedience to self-imposed laws. The law of the General Will is the highest law.

We now know a good deal about the General Will. It is the result of all men willing their best wills for the good of the State. It is sovereign, inalienable, indivisible, unlimited and one which cannot err. Yet we do not know how it is to be found and Rousseau himself can never tell us how we can be sure of finding the General Will. At times, he seems to suggest that the General Will is to be sought only when all unanimously agree, though he holds that the will of *All* is something very different from the General Will. The "will of all," he says, "is a mere total of selfish and casually coincident wills." At times, he implies that it is the majority will, though at other places he tells us that this can only be so "if all the characteristics of the General Will are still in the majority." At times, it appears that the residue left after cancelling out the differences expressed by all the citizens is to be regarded as the General Will. Rousseau is, thus, very vague in what he tells us about the General Will. "So much vagueness about something as important as the finding of the General Will," observes Wayper, "is to be regretted. Rousseau, who has told us so much about the General Will, has still not told us enough; indeed he has left us in such a position that nobody can be sure what the General Will is on any particular point."

Rousseau compared with Hobbes and Locke. Rousseau had drawn something from

Hobbes and something from Locke. In fact, he began with the method of Locke and ended with those of Hobbes. Both Rousseau and Locke agreed that man in the state of nature was free and happy. The need for a civil society was felt with emergence of certain disquieting affairs in the state of nature. For Locke these were the inconveniences as a result of uncertainty in the application of the law of reason, absence of a common judge to decide disputes arising therefrom, and absence of a common authority to enforce the decision. With Rousseau, increase in population and dawn of reason upon man were responsible for conflict of interests and strife in the state of nature. Formation of a civil society by means of a contract was deemed the only way out. Both Locke and Rousseau agreed that the fundamental social compact ought to have for its end and object the better preservation of the person and goods of every individual, that is, life, liberty, and property. Rousseau was also near Locke when he said that individuals surrendered their rights to the community; making people ultimately sovereign and a source of political authority. Both Locke and Rousseau made the distinction between the State and government, though Rousseau maintained that the institution of government was not the result of contract. Both believed that the contract did not remove the supreme power from the people.

Rousseau's "voice is the voice of Locke, but the hands are those of Hobbes." The influence of Hobbes upon Rousseau is, indeed, marked and singular. With Rousseau, as with Hobbes, the natural man in the state of nature was absolutely independent of others. The only difference between the two was that with Rousseau he was not at war with others, although eventually, when equality and happiness of the early state of nature was lost, Rousseau's mankind, too, went into a state of ceaseless warfare. Again, that there was only one contract by which each individual surrendered all his rights, and the authority of the sovereign to whom rights had been surrendered were strongly reminiscent of Hobbes. For Rousseau, it was the General Will which was sovereign; for Hobbes it was the King. But once Rousseau established the sovereign power in the General Will, he endowed it with as much absolute, unlimited, all-embracing, inalienable and indivisible powers as Hobbes had given to his sovereign monarch. Similarly, General Will, according to Rousseau, could neither be wrong nor unjust. It could even force the individual will to its own point of view. Are these conclusions not similar to those of Hobbes? The only difference is that in the case of Hobbes these are the attributes of a King, whereas with Rousseau they belong to the General Will and what this General Will precisely is, Rousseau remained throughout vague and indefinite about it. In any case, both Hobbes and Rousseau make man the plaything of the sovereign, no matter who the sovereign is, a King or the Generanl Will.

Evaluation of Rousseau's Theory. Rousseau was the apostle of popular sovereignty and the secret of his political philosophy is found in the substitution for "a sovereign" of "the sovereign."[31] He justified revolutions against arbitrary rule and was the pioneer to preach the ideals of democracy. Sidgwick says that the characteristic of Rousseau's revolutionary doctrine of popular sovereignty is that it rests on three very simple principles: "(1) That men are by nature free and equal; (2) that the rights of government must be based on some compact freely entered into by these equal and independent individuals;

31. MacIver, R.M., *The Modern State*, p. 442.

and (3) that the only contract at once just to the individuals becomes an indivisible part of a body that retains an inalienable right of determining its own internal constitution and legislation—a sovereign people."[32] Rousseau brings into prominence the idea of consent and establishes once for all that will, not force, is the basis of the State. He also champions the cause of direct democracy by vesting the legislative power in the people. Rousseau's political teachings had a profound appeal for the fathers of the Constitutions of the United States of America and France. To quote Dunning, Rousseau's spirit and "dogmas, however disguised and transformed, are seen everywhere both in the speculative system and in the governmental organisations of the stirring era that followed his death."[33] Rousseau died in 1778.

But the main defect in Rousseau's philosophy is in his explanation of the General Will. He places no limit on the absolute power of the whole over its members. Rousseau, indeed, gives no option to the individual will against the General Will, which can neither be wrong nor unjust. Similarly, individuals cannot protest against the authority of the General Will. Law, according to Rousseau, is the expression of the General Will. If the individual suffers from punishment, say the death penalty, he is really a consenting party to his own execution as he is a part of that sovereign will which made the law under which he is condemned. Rousseau really tried to explain how government can be justified—how men can submit to it and yet remain free men and not slaves, and he thought he could do that by showing that government is a natural development in as much as it is only in the State that men fully realize their capacities. Here he was preaching something which is fundamentally true and important. But unfortunately Rousseau is often obscure, not always consistent, and there is a vein of mysticism running through his doctrine. He wrapped up the lesson he was trying to teach in a language that paved the way for totalitarianism. And totalitarianism is a hateful doctrine, whether the individual is asked to make complete surrender to a mystical entity called the General Will or to a personal leader like Hitler or Mussolini. Then, Rousseau does not differentiate between the State and society and fusion of the two is a handy weapon with Rousseau's admirers in totalitarian States to suppress the individual, his aspirations and his personality. Finally, Rousseau's advocacy of small States, with limited population, and his categorical condemnation of representative institutions present practical difficulties, a direct democracy offers no solution for the political ills from which a nation-State is believed to suffer.

CRITICISM OF THE SOCIAL CONTRACT THEORY

The doctrine that the State originated in a contract was a favourite theme of political speculation during the seventeenth and eighteenth centuries. But in the nineteenth century it was subjected to a searching criticism. Even before the publication of Rousseau's *Social Contract,* Hume, the English philosopher, declared that contract as the basis of relations between the governors and the governed was incompatible with the facts of history. Jeremy Bentham said, "I bid adieu to the original contract, and I leave it to those

32. Sidgwick, H., *The Development of European Polity,* p. 390.

33. Dunning, W.A., *History of Political Theories from Rousseau to Spencer,* p. 39.

to amuse themselves with the rattle who could think they need it." Bluntschli characterised it "in the highest degree dangerous, since it makes the State and its institutions the product of individual caprice." Sir Henry Maine maintained that nothing could be "more worthless" than such an account of the origin of society and government as given by Hobbes.

As an explanation of the origin of the State the theory is now entirely discredited. The following points of criticism may be noted:—

Historically, the theory is a mere fiction. There is nothing in the whole range of history to show that the State has ever been deliberately created as a result of voluntary agreement. Nor can we suppose that man could ever think of governing himself when he lived under conditions of extreme simplicity, ignorance and even brutality by which the state of nature is characterized. The fact of the matter is that man can live only if he lives in society, and that he can live in society only if he accepts certain restraints on his freedom of action. These restraints are government in the germ. Society and State are natural institutions. It is man's social need which gives them existence and they continue to exist because of this need.

The example of the *Mayflower* compact of 1620 is very often cited in support of the theory of Social Contract. The Puritan emigrants to America, while they were still on board the ship *Mayflower*, drew up and signed a document which declared: "We....do, by these presents, solemnly and mutually, in the presence of God and one another, covenant and combine ourselves together into a civil body-politic, for our better ordering and preservation." But this is not a correct example; nor can any other similar example be cited to hold a parallel to the formation of the State by men living in the state of nature. The Puritans emigrating to new lands were not ignorant of political institutions. They were born and had lived in the State and when they went out of it they were fully familiar with the nature of their political governance, and the rights and duties of a citizen in a politically organised society. What the *Mayflower* compact really meant was "merely the transplanting to new lands of political institutions by men already subjected to political authority." And the covenant they concluded did not mark the origin of a new State. They remained subjects of England even after setting up their body-politic. When the United States of America came into being by virtue of a solemn compact (the Articles of Confederation), the State had been familiar to them both as an idea as well as a fact.

The theory of Social Contract is, indeed, remote from actualities and completely oblivious of facts. Nothing like the state of nature had ever existed and even Hobbes himself, after discussing the state of nature, admitted that "it was never generally so." The most primitive peoples that the Anthropologists have described, lived under a regulative system of some sort and conformed to rigid customary modes of behaviour. It is quite unhistorical to suppose that such men would resort to a contract. The very idea of a contract belongs to a later stage of social development than the hypothesis demands. Primitive man did not possess that maturity of outlook which the making of a social contract presupposes. Moreover, the conditions of a contract also presuppose a system of law to support it.

The advocates of the Contract Theory hold individuals as making a contract for their personal safety and the security of property. But history tells us just the other way. Early law was more communal than individual and the unit of society was not the individual but the family. "The family was the unit, property was held in common. Custom formed law and each man was born into his status in society.[34] Society has thus moved from *status* to *contract* and not from *contract* to *status,* as it has been maintained by the Contractualists. Contract is not the beginning, according to Sir Henry Maine, but the end of society.[35] In the primitive society birth determined the position of every man; it was not a matter of choice or voluntary arrangement. "He who is born a slave, let him remain a slave; the artisan, an artisan; the priest, a priest."[36] This is the command of status and we cannot imagine a slave having free choice to contract. If he has a free choice to contract, then he no longer remains a slave.

Even if it be granted that the State is the result of contract, commonsense will tell us that there are always two parties to the contract. There cannot be a one-sided contract, as was conceived by Hobbes. Moreover, every contract lapses after the death of one of the contracting parties. It cannot be made legally binding on the descendants of the original parties to the contract. Bentham remarks, "I am bound to obey not because my great-grandfather may be regarded as having made a bargain which he did not really make with the great-grandfather of George III, but simply because rebellion does more harm than good."

It is assumed by the Contractualists that men are equal in the state of nature. This assumption is incorrect. If status determined the position of man in the primitive society, then the natural inference is that inequality, rather than equality, existed in the state of nature. Nor can we accept human nature as it has been portrayed by the exponents of the Contract theory. The life of man may justly be described as a life lived in groups. And while living with others he is neither as bad as Hobbes, thinks, nor is he so good as Rousseau considers him to be. Both Hobbes and Rousseau have allowed their intellect to be carried away by their imaginations.

The conception of natural rights and natural liberty, as is said to have existed in the state of nature, is illogical and fallacious. Liberty cannot exist in the state of nature. Law is the condition of liberty. Without restraint liberty is nothing short of licence and a condition of licence is anarchy, pure and simple. The state of nature being pre-political and even pre-social, it was subject to no civil law. Rights, too, arise in a society and every right is accompanied by a corresponding obligation. If there is no society, we cannot think of rights. No rights existed before the State arose.[37] Finally, there can be no rights without a consciousness of common interest on the part of the members of a society and common consciousness was conspicuous by its absence in the state of nature. "Without common consciousness," writes Green, "there might be certain powers on the part of individuals, but no recognition of these powers by others as powers of which they allow

34. Gettell, R.G., *Introduction to Political Science,* p. 86.

35. Maine, Henry, *Ancient Law,* pp. 108-10.

36. Appadorai, A., *The Substance of Politics,* p. 36.

37. Green, T. H., *Lectures on Principles of Political Obligation,* with an introduction by A. D. Lindsay, p-48. "Natural right, as right in a state of nature which is not a state of society, is a contradiction." Also refer to p. 66.

the exercise nor any claim to such recognition; and without this recognition or claim to recognition there can be no right."[38]

Even on a rational analysis, the theory of Social Contract can no longer be upheld. The relationship between the individual and the State is not voluntary. Each one of us must compulsorily belong to a State and the ties which bind men together are permanent. Each of us is born into the State; we are part of the State; and the State is part of us. Burke has aptly said that the State "ought not be considered as nothing better than a partnership agreement on a trade of pepper and coffee, calico or tobacco or some other such low concern, to be taken up for a little temporary interest and to be dissolved by the fancy of the parties....It is to be looked on with reverence....It is a partnership in all science, a partnership in all art, a partnership in every virtue and in all-perfection. As the end of such a partnership cannot be obtained in many generations, it becomes a partnership not only between those who are living but between those who are dead and those who are to be born."

If the theory of Social Contract is accepted as the true origin of the State, it will make the State purely the handiwork of man, an artificial contrivance. But the State is neither the handiwork of man, nor the creation of God; nor the result of force. It is the product of growth and evolution and many factors enter into the process of its development.

Finally, the authors of the Contract Theory had no mind to trace the origin of the State. Their primary object was to establish the basis of political authority. Determined to prove certain results, they wove a web of their own and in a manner which suited their purpose and, thus, a contradictory theory has been presented as the origin of the State.

Value of the Theory. We reject, therefore, the doctrine that the State originated in a contract. At the same time, we cannot discount the practical value of the theory. It has the advantage of giving us perhaps the only sound assumption on which to build and maintain any system of political relationships. It insists upon the fundamental truth that no stable State can exist without the consent of its members, that it is they, and they alone, who make the State. It further emphasises that there is no State either before or without the people and that the State has no authority except that given to it by the people. The relationship of government to the governed is essentially one of contract or bargain as obedience is conditional on the government fulfilling its own part and doing that it is entitled to do by its Charter or Constitution and no more. The principle of consent, thus, became an important factor in the development of political thought and consequently it eclipsed the much talked of and, till then, widely accepted doctrine of the Divine Origin of the State. As Gilchrist points out, "the chief enemy to the Divine Theory was the Contract Theory." Both Locke and Rousseau declared in most unequivocal terms that the monarch derived his authority not from God but'from the people and he could continue to remain in office only on the condition of good government. The Contract Theory, therefore, served a useful purpose in its time by combating the claims of irresponsible rulers and class privilege.

The Contract Theory has also helped in the development of the modern concept of sovereignty. Hobbes paved the way for Austin, the exponent of legal sovereignty; Locke

---

38. *Ibid.,* p. 48.

was the champion of political sovereignty; and Rousseau was the high priest of popular sovereignty. Rousseau also brought into prominence the ideal of direct democracy. Indirect or representative democracy lost much of its appeal after the end of World War I. New devices of popular participation in the work of government began to be advocated, and the referendum is merely a modified form of Rousseau's conception of inalienable sovereignty of the people. Furthermore, the modern theory of a clear separation between the State and government has really come to us from Locke. Finally, the Contract Theory raises the common man on the pedestal of political glory. The modern cry of equal right of voting for all citizens is the legacy of Rousseau's ideal of equal political rights.

SUGGESTED READINGS

Barker, E.: *Social Contract.*

Cole, G.D.H. (Introduction by): *The Social Contract.*

Crossman, R.H.S.: *Government and the Governed,* Chaps. III-V.

Dunning, W.A.: *Political Theories from Rousseau to Spencer,* Chap. I.

Dunning, W.A.: *Political Theories from Luther to Montesquieu,* Chaps. VIII, X, XI.

Dunning, W.A.: *Encyclopaedia of Social Sciences,* Vol. 14

Garner, J.W.: *Political Science and Government,* Chap. X.

Gettel, R.G.: *Introduction to Political Science,* Chap. VI.

Gettel, R.G.: *History of Political Thought,* Chaps. XII, XV.

Greaves, H.R.G.: *The Foundations of Political Theory,* Chaps. I, II, III.

Haines, C.G., and Haines, B.N.: *Principles and Problems of Government.*

Hobbes, T.: *Leviathan,* Chaps. XIII, XIV, XVII, XVIII.

Laski, H.J.: *A Grammar of Politics.*

Laski, H.J.: *Political Thought in England from Locke to Bentham.*

Leacock, S.: *Elements of Political Science,* Chaps. II, III.

Locke, J.: *On Civil Government, Two Treatises.*

Lord, A.R.: *Principles of Politics,* Chap. II (1921).

Mabbot, J.D.: *The State and the Citizens,* Chaps. II- IV.

MacIver, R.M.: *The Web of Government,* Chap. II.

Maine, H.S.: *The Ancient Law,* pp. 108-10.

Rousseau, J.J.: *The Social Contract.*

Sabine, G.H.: *A History of Political Theory,* Chaps. XXIII, XXVI.

Sait, E.C.: *Political Institutions.*

Soltau, R.H.: *An Introduction to Politics.*

Wayper, C.L.: *Political Thought,* pp. 42, 82, 130-52.

Willoughby, W.W.: *The Nature of the State.*

5

CHAPTER

Origin of the State (Contd.)

PATRIARCHAL AND MATRIARCHAL THEORIES

Probable Origin in Family. "The question of exact political origin is unanswerable in the present state of knowledge", says Professor F. H. Hankins,[1] and anything that is advanced is largely, if not entirely, the result of speculation. It seems, however, safe to hazard that the State is the product of history and the family being the most primitive of all human groups, it must have had the starting point in this primary and earliest social unit. "In the family, the primary social unit," says MacIver, "there are always present the curbs and controls that constitute the essence of government... which is the continuation by the more inclusive society of a process of regulation that is highly developed with the family. The same necessities that create the family create also regulation....Here is the government in miniature, and already government of a quite elaborate character." It begins with marriage and inheritance, controls the simple economy, carries on the family worship, organises defence, arranges hunting and pasture, looks alter the upkeep of shelter, of supplies. Thus, a family is held to be the simplest and earliest link in the evolution of the State and the control exercised by a father over the members of his family is supposed to represent the origin of human government. There are, however, some political thinkers who believe that the State is simply an enlargement of the family. But all differ among themselves on the essential question whether the primary unit in the prehistoric times was the family or the tribe, and from whom descent was traced.

The Patriarchal Theory. The foremost among such theories is the Patriarchal Theory which seeks to explain that the State is an enlargement of the family. Originally, the family consisted of a man, his wife and children. The father was thc head of the family and his control and authority was complete in all respects over all its members. When his children married there was expansion in the original family and it led to the establishment of new families. But the authority of the father and head of the original family remained unabated as before, and it was duly acknowledged by all his descendants. This constituted a patriarchal family. In due course of time the patriarchal family expanded and developed into a clan. The members of a clan were bound to one another by ties of blood relationship, and all lived and functioned under the recognised authority of the senior living male member of the original family. A clan by its own expansion grew into

1. Quoted by Maxey in the introduction to his *Political Philosophies.*

a tribe. With the lapse of time many members withdrew from the parent tribe and settled in new lands in search of their living. This resulted, by virtue of the same process of development, in the founding of many new tribes. The tribes united by ties of blood relationship acted together for common purposes, particularly in defending themselves against the aggression of other tribes. This involved the recognition of some common authority under whose influence they could rally round. This is how the State has developed. Leacock, giving the process of this development, says, "First a household, then a patriarchal family, then a tribe of persons of kindred descent and finally nation—so emerges the social series erected on this basis."[2]

Aristotle believed that the State took form as a natural expansion of the family. A society of many families, he observes, "is called a village, and a village is most naturally composed of the descendants of one family, the children and the children's children, for which reason States were originally governed by kings, as the barbarian States now are, which are composed of those who had before submitted to kingly government; for every family is governed by the elder, as are the branches thereof, on account of their relation thereunto....And when many villages so entirely join themselves together as in every respect to form but one society, that society is a State, and contains, in itself, if I may so speak, the end and perfection of government."[3] According to Aristotle, the State makes its appearance as a kinship group an outgrowth of the family; and the authority of the earlier kings is derived from the authority of the head of the family.

Sir Henry Maine's Patriarchal Theory. The chief exponent of the Patriarchal Theory is Sir Henry Maine, at one time Law member of the Governor General's Executive Council in India. He elaborated his theory in his *Ancient Law* (1861) and *The Early History of Institutions* (1874). Maine went deep into history and derived his evidence regarding "the rudiments of the social State" from three sources—from "accounts by contemporary observers of civilisations less advanced than their own," from "the records which particular races have preserved concerning their primitive history," and from "ancient law."[4]

Maine maintained that society in primitive times was "in fact, and in the view of the men that composed it... an aggregation of families," and not a collection of individuals. The unit was the family and the ancient law was so framed as to recognise the patriarchal or family groups as perpetual and inextinguishable entities.[5] The eldest male parent—the eldest ascendant—was absolutely supreme in his household and his domination extended "to life and death, and is as unqualified over his children and their houses as over his slaves."[6] Over them he possessed despotic authority. He was not only absolute owner of property, including even what his children had acquired, but he could chastise and even kill, could sell or transfer by adoption, could marry or divorce any of his children at will. With the breaking up of the single families more families emerged, but all were held

2. Leacock. S., *Elements of Political Science*, p. 38.
3. *Politics*, pp. 1-2.
4. *Ancient Law*, p. 120.
5. *Ibid.*
6. *Ibid*, pp. 123-24.

together under the authority of the head of the first family. This was the beginning of the tribe. Many members of a tribe withdrew and settled in new places. Such withdrawals led to the growth of new tribes.[7] These tribes, still united by kinship, acted together for common purposes and ultimately formed a State. Maine, thus, outlines this process of development: "The elementary group is the family, connected by common subjection to the highest male ascendant. The aggregation of families forms the Gens or Houses. The aggregation of Houses makes the tribe. The aggregation of tribes constitutes the commonwealth."[8]

The following important points may be noted in Maine's theory:—

1. In the patriarchal family the element of paternity was the chief fact.
2. Descent was traced only through males and from the same ancestor. None of the descendants of a female was included in the primitive notion of family relationship. Kinship was, accordingly, purely agnatic.[9]
3. Permanent marriage was the rule, whether monogamy or polygamy.
4. The head of the family was the basis of all authority, and his power was unqualified over his children and their houses and other relations of all descendants, howsoever numerous.
5. He controlled not only the business affairs of the group which he headed, but its religion and its conduct.

The family was the primal unit of political society, "the seedbed of all larger growths of government," as Woodrow Wilson calls it.[10] Over the family the patriarch ruled with autocratic power. By virtue of the *patria potestas*, the flocks and herds of his sons belonged to him, and his domination extended to life and death, being as unqualified over his children and their dependents as over his slaves. But with the birth of new generations, a change occurred. The family shell was broken, because there was no longer any living male ancestor, a grandfather or great-grandfather, who could claim patriarchal authority over the whole group and maintain family cohesion. The single family had developed into several families; yet all of them were fully conscious of their ultimate kinship. Bound together by ties of common blood, and worship of the common ancestors, they associated in a wider common fellowship group, the *gens*, owing allegiance to some elected elder—perhaps the oldest living ascendant or the most capable. Similarly, the *gens* broadened into the tribe. The pastoral pursuits gave way to agriculture and settled life on a definite land became a matter of necessity; tribes united to form the State.

In support of his statement, Sir Henry Maine cited the Patriarchs of the Old Testament, "families" and "brotherhoods" of Athens, the *patria potestas* in Rome, and the Hindu joint-family system in India. To this may be added particularly the tribal system of the North-West Frontier of Pakistan. The Patriarchal Theory, thus, adopting the family as the unit and supposing "the headship bequeathed from one chief to another, by easy stages transforms the father into the chief or the king, and the family into a civil community." The Patriarchal Theory has during recent times received the unequivocal support of

7. *Ibid.* p. 138.
8. *Ibid,* p. 128.
9. *Ibid,* pp. 145-48.
10. *The State,* p. 15.

Duguit, another jurist, but a French national. Duguit maintains that the father "is the natural chief, the governor of the little state of which the members of the family are the governed. The ancient city was merely a union of families in which political power belonged to the father."

Criticism of the Theory. In the decade that followed the publication of Sir Henry Maine's *Ancient Law*, the Patriarchal Theory was subjected to severe attacks. McLennan and others denied Maine's claim that the patriarchal family was the earliest and original unit. There was no group in the primitive past, they urged, with a male at its head. The Matriarchal system was prior to the patriarchal system and tribe rather than family was the earliest unit of society. There was no permanent institution of marriage, they argued. A woman married more than one husband and because of the uncertainty of male parentage kinship was reckoned through women, that is, from mother to daughters. The patriarchal family developed in the later phase of human civilisation.

The early forms of social organisation, it has been maintained, were not so simple as the Patriarchal Theory tries to establish. Sir J. G. Frazer, in his classic work: The Golden Bough, warns that "he who investigates the history of institutions should constantly bear in mind the extreme complexity of the causes which have built up the fabric of human society, and should be on his guard against a subtle danger incidental to all science—the tendency to simplify unduly the infinite variety of the phenomena by fixing our attention on a few of them to the exclusion of the rest...."

It is, also, suggested that the theory does not offer an adequate explanation of the origin of the State. It is, in fact, just a speculation into the beginnings of the early society, particularly the family. Gilchrist says, "The patriarchal theory is one of the simplest explanations of the origin of the State, but one of its chief weaknesses is this very simplicity...."

The Matriarchal Theory. McLennan, Morgan and Jenks are the notable exponents of the Matriarchal Theory. They reject outright the proposition that the patriarchal family was the earliest form of society. Their thesis is that in primitive society there was no common male head. Kinship could only be traced through mother, *matriarch*, and the way of life was a horde or totem group.

The advocates of the Matriarchal Theory maintain that patriarchal family is possible where either the monogamous or the polygamous institution of marriage exists. Such an institution of marriage did not exist in the beginning of society. The earliest form of marriage was polyandry, one wife having several husbands. Wherever such an institution of marriage is present, the usual relations of husband and wife do not exist. Instead of a family composed of a man, his wife, and children there is a large and loosely connected group called a "horde" or "pack" organised for matrimonial purposes. In such a condition of society promiscuity of sexual relations prevails and kinship is traced through females and not males. McLennan shares with Morgan "the credit of having discovered the clan, a maternally organised, hereditary and unilateral unit, unilateral because children trader this system belonged to the clan of their mother, without regard to the clan of the fathcr."[11] The father belonged to a clan different from his wife's, owing to the existence

11. Merriam, C.E., and Barnes, H.E. (*Eds.*), *A History of Political Theories, Recent Times*, p. 435.

of the custom of exogamy—the practice of marrying only outside one's own clan or tribe. Jenks illustrated his proposition from the conditions existing among the natives of Australia and the Malaya Archipelago. He says, "It is the custom to speak of Australian and other savages as living in tribes;... it would really be better to call it the 'pack' for it more resembles a hunting than a social organisation. All its members are entitled to share in the proceeds of the day's chase, and, quite naturally, they camp and live together... but the real social unit of the Australians is not the 'tribe' but the *totem group*... The *totem group* is primarily a body of persons distinguished by the sign of some natural object, such as an animal or a tree, who may not intermarry with one another. 'Snake may not marry snake. Emu may not marry Emu.' This is the first rule of savage social organisation....The other side of the rule is equally startling. The savage may not marry within his totem, but he must marry into another totem specially fixed for him. More than this, he not only marries into the specified totem, but he marries the whole of the women of that totem in his own generation...."

The fundamental features of this society are:—

1. transient marriage relationships;
2. kinship is traced through females;
3. maternal authority is an established fact; and
4. only females succeed to property and power.

J.J. Bachofen, a Swiss writer, who is mainly responsible for tracing the origin of the Matriarchal Theory, held that in primitive society not only descent was traced through mother and property passed in the female line, but women also "played a conspicuous, in fact, dominant, role in body-politic."[12] His first stage of social evolution was one of chaos and sexual promiscuity, then followed the matriarchate, women having grown weary of lawlessness and with the help of religious superstition, having imposed their rule; but in time men found the matriarchal authority unendurable and, asserting their superior physical strength, introduced the patriarchate. Jenks contradicted Sir Henry Maine's statement that family expanded into houses and houses into a tribe. He affirmed that the process of development was just the other way. The Matriarchal Theory, thus, "derives the smaller from the larger group, not the larger from the smaller."[13] The following is the process of development of matriarchal society:—

1. First there is a tribe and it is the oldest and primary social group.
2. In time a tribe breaks into clans.
3. Clans in their turn give place to households.
4. At last, comes the modern family.

It is needless to go into details of the stages in this evolution. The individual family, however, came into existence when men began to lead a pastoral life. Pastoral occupations necessitated keeping of domestic animals. Women, it came to be realized, were the best to tend sheep and cattle while men employed themselves in more arduous tasks. This led to the growth of permanent houses and permanent marriages, either monogamous or polygamous. It is in this way that family came into existence. The patriarchal family,

12. *Ibid.* p. 434.
13. Maine, H., *Early Law and Custom.* p. 220.

emerged only when men adopted settled pastoral and agricultural habits in place of the wandering or hunting life of a primitive man.

Criticism of the Matriarchal Theory. That such a system of tribal relationship existed in the past and exists today is beyond doubt. Even Sir Henry Maine, in a later treatise, admitted the importance of a good deal of McLennan's evidence and he restated his theory in view of this evidence. Polyandry persists even today in some parts of the world including India.[14] But there is no adequate proof in support of the matriarchal system as the universal and necessary beginnng of society. Moreover, woman is the instrument of transmission. Nature has not made her to play an active part and being physically weak she must be dominated by the sex which is physically superior to her.[15] The Matriarchal Theory, therefore, cannot replace the Patriarchal Theory. The truth seems to be that history provides parallel examples of both the patriarchal and matriarchal systems and we can only conclude by agreeing with Stephen Leacock that "here the matriarchal relationship, and there a patriarchal regime, is found to have been the rule—either of which may perhaps be displaced by the other." Nonetheless, both the theories sufficiently establish that family is the original link in the evolution of the State.

Patriarchal and Matriarchal Theories are in essence sociological rather than political theories, seeking really to explain the beginning of human society and the process of its development. Even the point from which their authors start may not be a starting point. It is probable that centuries might have intervened between the actual beginning of mankind and the most archaic society about which we are told by the advocates of the Patriarchal and Matriarchal theories. Then, the nature of the family and the State are different; in their organization, functions and purpose. Willoughby says, "It would not be true to say that the State has developed out of this small unit (family). The two institutions are different in essence. In the family the location of authority is natural. In the state it is one of choice. Subordination is the principle of the family; equality that of the state. Furthermore, the functions or aims of the state are essentially different from, and even contradictory to, those of the family."[16] According to Willoughby, the Patriarchal and Matriarchal theories are "social rather than political hypotheses." One may not agree with this point of view, yet it is not sufficient to say that the State is the enlargement of the family despite the fact that the germ of government may be found in the family discipline.

THE HISTORICAL OR EVOLUTIONARY THEORY

We have so far discussed five theories in explanation of the origin of the State, but no single theory offers an adequate explanation. The State is, as Garner said, "neither the

14. According to information available from official sources in India, polyandry is prevalent in the districts of Kangra, Lahaul, Spiti, Kinnaur and Renuka tehsils in Sirmur district in Himachal Pradesh, in Tehri-Garhwal and Uttar Kashi districts in Uttar Pradesh. It is also practised by the Jaunsaris in Dehra Dun district, Maravas, Harijans and Dhobis in Tiruchirapalli; Oddars Bayans, Arundadiars and Uppiliars in Salem district in Tamil Nadu (formerly Madras), and by Muslims in Chandernagore, West Bengal. Recent investigation revealed that it still exists in the Bhurthala Mandav village, in Sangrur district in Punjab.
15. Refer to R.M. MacIver, *The Modern State,* p. 29.
16. Willoughby, W.W., *The Nature of the State,* p. 20.

handiwork of God, nor the result of superior physical force, nor the creation of resolution or convention, nor a mere expansion of the family." It is an institution of natural growth which originated in the bare needs of the life of man and continues in existence for the sake of good life. The theory which explains, and is now accepted as a convincing origin of the State, is the Historical or Evolutionary Theory. It explains that the State is the product of growth, a slow and steady evolution extending over a long period of time and ultimately shaping itself into the complex structure of a modern State. Burgess has aptly said that the State is a "continuous development of human society out of a grossly imperfect beginning through crude but improving forms of manifestation towards a perfect and universal organisation of mankind."

It is difficult to say how and when the State came into existence. Like all other social institutions, it must have emerged imperceptibly, supported by various influences and conditions. Apart from the influences of physical environment and geographical conditions, there are five important factors which made men to aggregate at different places and separated one group from another, thereby paving the way for the rise and growth of the State. These important factors are:

1. Kinship;
2. Religion;
3. Property and defence;
4. Force;
5. Political consciousness.

It must, however, be remembered that not any one of these influences has worked in isolation from others in the process of State building. They operated in various combinations, each playing its part in creating that unity and organisation that the State requires.

1. **Kinship.** The earliest form of social organisation was based upon blood relationship and kinship was the first and the strongest bond of unity. What bound people together and made them cohere into a group was the belief in common descent and the earliest and closest unit of kinship was the family. It is, of course, a disputed point whether tribe, group or family came first, yet it cannot be denied that family constituted the first link in the process of the evolution of the State, and government must have begun in a clearly defined family discipline; command and obedience. Even the advocates of the Matriarchal Theory ultimately veer round to the family and recognise the authority of the patriarch.

With the expansion of the family arose new families and the multiplication of families led to the formation of clans and tribes. Throughout the process of this evolution sanction of kinship was the only factor which bound the people together. Persons unconnected by ties of blood, unless admitted into the tribe by adoption, were deemed strangers and treated as enemies. The name of the common ancestor was the symbol of kinship. The "magic of names," as MacIver sums up, "reinforced the sense of kinship, as the course of generations enlarged the group. The blood bond of sonship changed imperceptibly into the social bond of the wider brotherhood. The authority of the father passed into the power of the chief. Once more under the aegis of kinship new forms arose which transcended it. Kinship created society and society at length created the state."[17] The origin of the political activity of man is, therefore, embedded in Aristotle's cogent remark that man is a social and political animal.

It is, then, clear that the germs of government must have begun in clearly defined family discipline and the patriarch evoked respect and obedience to authority. The authority of the father of the family over its members was complete, absolute and undisputed. The patriarch, who afterwards became the tribal chieftain, combined unto himself religious, administrative, judicial and military powers. This is the evidence of history.

2. Religion. Closely connected with kinship, as a factor in State-building, is religion. Kinship and religion in the primitive society were two aspects of the same thing and both acted simultaneously in welding together families and tribes. "Religion was the sign and seal of common blood, the expression of its oneness, its sanctity, its obligation."[18] When the bonds of kinship steadily weakened with the expansion of the family into the gens, the clans and the tribes, a common form of worship reinforced the sense of unity and respect for authority.

The primitive religion evolved from animism to ancestor-worship. The early man was surrounded by natural phenomena which he could not understand. He looked towards natural forces, such as storms, thunder and lightning, clouds and wind, the sun, moon and stars with awe and reverence. The changing seasons and the birth and death of vegetation made him stand aghast. To his innocent mind and uncultivated intellect the mystery of death and other psychological problems, like sleep, dreams and insanity, were insoluble. He interpreted all such phenomena as manifestation of some supernatural power. What he could not understand, he began to worship. He "saw God in clouds and heard him in the wind." Under such conditions emerged two forms of religion, worship of nature, and worship of ancestors. The hallowed ceremonies of ancestor worship were conducted at the family altar. There the living came into the presence of their great dead, the spirits of the departed, who exercised power to evil as well as to good and who must be appeased by the meticulous performance of sacred rites. In this way, came to be established a family of deities around which abundant traditions and myths came to be formed.

Ancestor-worship, thus, strengthened the bonds of family union which eventually contributed to the solidarity of the tribe. But these bonds were only local in character. When tribes expanded by incorporation or conquest, kinship and ancestor-worship proved weak ties of union among the diverse people spread over extended territory. Common belief in gods and deities, or worship of nature became the cementing bond of affinity and comradeship among such people, although remnants of the old family worship and legends of tribal heroes still formed a common national religion that served as a sanction of government and law. The sanction of law in primitive society was religion and, as it was the terrible aspect of religion that appealed to primitive minds, the breaking of law was followed by terrible punishment. This is how the relation of command and obedience, which was natural in family relations, was definitely established by religion.

17. MacIver, R.M., *The Modern State*, p. 35.
18. Woodrow Wilson, *The State*, p. 15.

Side by side grew up superstitions and magical customs. In primitive communities magical rites and incantations were practised both privately and publicly. Anyone who could propitiate the spirits, began to acquire commanding importance and unique influence. He was looked upon with awe and reverence and all bowed to his authority, since none could dare incur the wrath of the magic-man. The sorcerer became the leader and it is here that we witness the emergence of magician-kings. From magician the step to chief or king was simple. Magicians gave way to priests, when people had lost faith in the spirits and the power of magic. The priests, too, came into eminence in the same way as the magicians. The evidence available sufficiently shows that early kings were priest-kings, combining the duties of ceremonial observances and secular rule. The rise of the magician and of his kingly successor has been the special thesis of Sir James G. Frazer. According to Frazer's theory, the first form of tribal government was the gerontocracy or council of old men, representing the various families constituting the tribe. Their control over the tribe was perfect and complete as they alone were deemed to be familiar with the secret mysteries of the tribal religion, and they alone were considered eminently competent to know all that could be known about the spiritual world. Out of the council of elders emerged the magician, "a resolute and ambitious man, a clever and unscrupulous man, who pretended to extraordinary powers of divination and sorcery. The fertility of the soil, rain or drought, the success or failure of crops seemed to depend more upon his incantations and rituals than upon human effort. His influence, especially among an agricultural people, assumed enormous proportions. The magician eventually made himself priest-king."

Briefly, the value of religion in the evolution of the State can hardly be denied. In primitive society religion and politics were inextricably mixed up. Religion not only helped the unification of political communities, but it was religion alone which was responsible for subordinating barbaric anarchy and for teaching reverence and obedience. The importance of religion, as a force in the evolution of the State, was not limited to the earliest States alone. In Afghanistan religion has, even now much to do with politics. Islamic law is a force behind Pakistan, the Islamic Republic. Twenty-three Muslim theologists of Pakistan jointly pronounced a verdict (*fatwa*) against the election of a woman as the President or Khalifa of an Islamic State,[19] when Miss Fatima Jinnah[20] declared her intention to oppose President Ayub Khan in the Presidential election in 1964. Although a secular State, yet in India, too, religion still plays an important part in the political life of the country. India's political life is demarcated more on religion than on political issues. The legacy of religion in the political life of the country is found even in Britain as in the religious coronation of Kings or Queens and "the still-half-consciously lingering view of law and of State commands as something sacred." The tradition of the divine origin of political power dies hard.

3. **Property and Defence.** In order to understand the origin of the State and government we must observe how the kinship group earned its living. "The basic factor in any given society," says Laski, "is the way it earns its living all social relations are built upon

19. *The Statesman,* New Delhi, Sept. 30, 1964.

20. Sister of M.A. Jinnah, the architect of Pakistan.

provision for those primary material appetites without satisfying which life cannot endure. And an analysis of society will always reveal the close connection between its institutions and culture and the methods of satisfying material appetites. As these methods change, so also will the institutions and culture of the society change .... Changes in the methods of economic production appear to be the most vital factor in the making of changes in all other social patterns we know. For changes in those methods determine the changes of social relationships; and these, in their turn, are subtly interwoven with all the cultural habits of men."[21] The key to social behaviour must, therefore, be sought in the economic system.

Among primitive peoples there were successive economic stages that marked the growing importance of property and that brought about corresponding changes in social organisation. The three economic stages are the huntsman stage, the herdsman or pastoral stage and the husbandman or agricultural stage. They are universal stages in the sense that groups generally passed from the one to the other, from lower to higher.

The huntsman led a miserable existence, moving about in quest of game and of wild berries or roots. He had no property except the crude weapons and tools. It was a condition of primeval savagery and escape came through the domestication of wild animals. The domestic animals, originally kept as pets, proved a good way to provide against future periods of scarcity. Still later, it became apparent that the animals were useful for other purposes besides supplying meat in times of privation. The horse provided rapid means of movement, the cow provided milk and the sheep wool. He had also come to know that his flocks and herds could be vastly increased by systematic breeding. A huntsman became a herdsman and flocks and herds became his wealth. Simultaneously, other forms of property, for example, improved clothing, weapons, and domestic utensils, appeared.

Whatever may have been the earlier form of the family, pastoral life, which is marked with substantial property interests, increased the social dominance of the male.[22] It strengthened, if it did not create, the patriarchate. The patriarch exercised absolute control over the family, and over all its property. When the family expanded into the gens and the tribe, the patriarchal discipline prepared the way for tribal government. Poperty introduced all sorts of complications. There must reside sufficient power with the tribal authorities to settle property disputes between different families, and to regulate and safeguard the rights of ownership. Thus, the gradual increase of property entailed a corresponding intensification of social control. Tribesmen, who were accustomed to giving unquestioning obedience to their respective family heads, accepted the authority of the Council of Elders and of the chieftain who rose out of the Council.

At the same time, organised force was needed to repel the plundering raids of adjacent tribes. Concerted action for common defence against the hostile designs of others strengthened the solidarity of the tribe and increased the authority of the tribal organisation.

21. Laski, H.J., *The State in Theory and Practice,* p. 91.

22. Refer to R.M. MacIver, *The Modern State,* p. 31. According to him, the relatively settled pastoral life "accorded with, and in a sense, made necessary, the patriarchal family." He believes, as some others do, that the matrilineal family preceded the patrilineal. Property brought about the change.

The saying "war begat the king" is, according to Gettell, "at least a half truth, since military activity was a powerful force, both in creating the need for authority and law, and in replacing family organisations by system purely political." These conditions called for individual leadership. Some member of the Council of Elders or patriarchs, whose personal qualities, such as, military prowess, knowledge of human nature, oratorical capacity, with or without the assistance of religious superstitions, pushed his way to the front and raised himself far above his peers in prestige and influence. Tribesmen rallied round him and he was recognised as the chieftain. Since the qualities of leadership were likely to be inherited, the office of the chieftain became attached to a particular family and was transmitted like other forms of property. Generally, it passed on to the eldest member of the family, though, in times of unusual stress, when war or domestic violence threatened, the office went not to the eldest, but to the most competent of the chiefly lineage.

The institution of private property and its systematic development, thus, brought the nomadic herdsman to the threshold of the State. The State must possess the element of territoriality. Although the pastoral tribes confined their wanderings within roughly determined geographical limits, they were still nomads. The State came into existence when the people became permanently territorially settled.

The territorial State did not appear until population began to press upon subsistence. The herdsman needed much more land than the husbandman. As the pastoral tribe grew in numbers and flocks and herds multiplied, one of the two courses became imminent to follow: either new land might be acquired by migration or the old land put to more productive use. Fertile pastures, when brought under cultivation, could support a bigger population, and the tribesmen had long been experimenting with agriculture, with as crude methods as their tools. Rather than leave the region to which they had become attached, they supplemented their prevailing pastoral economy with the rudiments of agriculture. Gradually the herdsman became husbandman. The transition took place slowly, as, "by trial and error of by the imitation of some neighbouring agriculturists the methods of tillage are improved and their potentialities realised." When a pastoral kinship group settled on the land, the State began. The group had already set up a government; it acquired territoriality as well. The three elements of the State are: people; government and territory. When three had been attained, search for the fourth, sovereignty, followed.

Along with the new system of production, that is, agriculture, came great social changes. The first was, sharpening of class distinctions with the unequal distribution of wealth. The rise of social classes occurred in pastoral society and they were perpetuated in agricultural society. Besides nobles and commoners, there were slaves. When one tribe attacked the other, the captives were no longer killed and perhaps eaten. The pastoralist had plenty to eat, but felt the need of supplementing the labour resources of the family to care for the expanding herd and to protect it from beasts of prey and human marauders. He invented slavery as a substitute for cannibalism.[23] It was a beneficent invention and in the agricultural society systematic resort was made to slavery.

4. **Force.** The new system also placed a great emphasis upon military life, first for

23. Oppenheimer, R., *The State,* p. 37.

defence, then for conquest. It is often contended that the State began in conquest when the herdsmen conquered the husbandmen or peasants. The conquest theory is favourably received by the Sociologists. Oppenheimer, the most prominent advocate of this theory, maintains that "the cause of the genesis of all States is the contact between peasants and herdsmen, between labourers and robbers, between bottom lands and prairies."[24] The conquest theory does not explain the origin of the State. But the part played by warfare in moulding political institutions at any stage of human development cannot be discounted, more so in a primitive society. Private property, in the form of flocks and herds, afforded a strong incentive to looting, which in turn had to be checked by systematic defence and punitive expeditions against hostile tribes. Concerted action for common defence and chastisement of the warring tribes created the dire need for military leadership which was an important factor in creating the chieftainship and strengthening its powers. The office of the chieftain became hereditary and consequently it led to the establishment of the monarchy. Yet, the emergence of the State, as MacIver says, and he is supported by the weight of evidence, "is not due to force, although in the process of expansion force undoubtedly played a part."[25]

5. Political Consciousness. The last is political consciousness arising from the fundamental needs of life for protection and order. When the people settle down on a definite territory in pursuit of their subsistence and a desire to secure it from encroachment by others, the need for regulating things and persons is felt imminently and this is the essence of political consciousness. It is doubtful whether there was ever a conscious expression for such a need. But there is no denying the fact that the institution of private property and the requirements of self-defence, both from within and without the tribe, and consequently the emergence of military leadership was probably the first distinctive political authority to which the people ungrudgingly submitted. This military leader commanded the confidence of his people and he established some sort of political organisation, i.e., government, to meet the needs of protection and order. In some such way the State arose. People, territory, government and independence from others or sovereignty, as we describe it now, had come in.

Much of this, which we present as a regular process, was, of course, very slow and confused. The course of events must have also varied with the character and circumstances of each people. All the same, the spirit of organisation, as Woodrow Wilson says, "is natural twin born with man and the family." In its simple and rudimentary form germs of governmental organisation were found in the family discipline. Religion reinforced family discipline and gradually created the wider discipline necessary for the existence of the State. Custom was the first law and there was a religious sanction behind every custom and the magicians who controlled religious sanctions were more powerful than any agent of political authority. When human wants, economic, social and political, increased through the combination of diverse circumstances and conditions, the State, territorially established and forming a distinct group of people independent of others,

24. *Ibid,* p. 45.

25. *The Modern State,* p. 222. Similarly, Sir John Seeley considers conquest as the means, not of originating the State, but producing a new and abnormal type of State, which he calls "inorganic"—*Introduction to Political Science,* pp. 73-75.

became more complex in form, more universal in its range of activities, more indispensable to the needs of mankind. The distinction we now make so carefully between the State and society is of comparatively recent origin. In fact, a double process had been at work through all these centuries: one by which the State takes over powers hitherto enjoyed by society, and the other by which it abandons to society powers it no longer needs.

SUGGESTED READINGS

Barker, E.: *The Study of Political Science and its Relations to the Cognate Sciences.*

Dunning, W.A.: *History of Political Theories: Ancient and Medieval.*

Frazer, J.W.: *The Golden Bough.*

Garner, J.W.: *Introduction to Political Science,* Chap. IV.

Gettell, R.G.: *Introduction to Political Science,* Chap. VI.

Gilchrist, R.N.: *Principles of Political Science,* Chaps. III, IV.

Jenks, E.: *A Short History of Politics.*

Leacock, S.: *Elements of Political Science,* Chaps. II, III.

MacIver, R.M.: *The Web of Government,* Chap. II.

MacIver, R.M.: *Society : Its Structure and Changes.*

Maine, H.S.: *Ancient Law,* Chap. V.

Maine, H.S.: *Early History of Institutions.*

Oppenheimer, R. (Trans. by J.M. Gitterman): *The State.*

Selley, J.R.: *Introduction to Political Science,* Lecture III.

Soltau, R.H.: *Development of European Polity,* Lecture III.

Soltau, R.H.: *An introduction to Politics,* Chap. IV.

Willoughby, W.W.: *The Nature of the State,* Chaps. III-VI.

Wilson, W.: *The State,* Chap. I.

6

CHAPTER

The Evolution of the State

Evolution of the State. We discussed, in the last two Chapters, theories regarding the origin of the State and remarked that no single theory offers an adequate explanation. The State is neither the result of an artificial creation nor can it be said to have originated at a particular period of time. It is, on the other hand, the product of growth, a slow and steady evolution extending over a long period of time and embracing many elements in its development, prominent among which are kinship, religion, property and the need for self-defence from within and without. The starting point, however, is the family and the germs of governmental organisation are found in the family discipline. The transition from the family to the State must have been long and chequered. The first distinctively political unit was the tribe. In the days of nomadic habit the organisation of the tribe was sufficient to satisfy its needs. But when their travelling days were over, a settled life created new needs of organisation. Once the population was territorially integrated with fixed abodes, their common interests developed and the original kinship tie gave way to a new territorial tie. The original kinship, in fact, never disappeared. What actually occurred was a fusion of the two principles, kinship and common interests emerging out of the life of togetherness in the shape of territorial kinship on a common land.

But the process of the evolution of the State has not been uniform. Natural, environmental and temperamental differences of the people spread over different areas of the universe presented different conditions under which the State emerged at different times and places. As a result of these differences, very different types of States, with various forms and patterns, have co-existed and co-exist even now. It is, however, instructive to mark the following stages through which the State has evolved.

The Oriental Empire. Roaming tribes generally settled down in regions where nature was bountiful and responsive to the needs of man. The early nomadic tribes in search of pasture lands made the fertile valleys of the Ganges, the Nile, the Euphrates, the Tigris, the Yellow River, and the Yang Tse their homelands and, as a result of conquest and enslavement of the weaker tribes, established the earliest of States known to history. It was in these valleys that civilisation took its birth and kingdoms and empires flourished. These States were manned by hereditary monarchs who combined in themselves political and religious power. Law was what religion sanctioned and the king permitted. The subjects knew nothing about their rights and liberty. They were only recipients of orders and respectful submission to orders was their first and last duty. Gettell says that the Oriental States "represented to their people only the slave driver and the tax collector."

The earliest States were essentially power and property States, built on wealth and military force. They attracted the jealousy of the nomadic tribes beyond or of each other, and had little stability, the conqueror being conquered in his turn. Sometimes, the break-up came from within through the revolt of some subordinate official, who either made his province into an independent State or actually overthrew and replaced his sovereign lord. "Expansion by annexation, then disruption and reconstitution, either from within or by conquest from the outside," remarks Solatu, "were the normal process that marked those early empires."[1]

It must not, of course, be assumed that those States were primitive and barbarous. Most people know about the scientific knowledge of the Babylonians and Egyptians, their division of time, and their mathematical calculations. The code of Hammurabi regulated every aspect of life and revealed the existence of a highly organised, prosperous society, with a carefully worked out hierarchy of functions. The Sumerians are said to have established the systems of rotation of office, annual appointments and election by secret ballot. The Aryans were familiar with the institutions of constitutional monarchy, bicameralism, the office of the Speaker and various other devices necessary for a representative form of government.

Greek City-State. The next type of State development was the Greek City-State arising in Greece after 1000 B.C. In fact, the study of Political Science may be said to begin with the Greek City-States. The Greek City-States were the first communities to have given conscious thought to "politics." Although the Greek political institutions were probably not unique, yet they presented the most fully developed instance of a way of life and government of which records have come to us.

When the Greeks settled in Europe, they were divided into local communities organised on the primitive model according to clans and tribes. Each clan and tribe occupied distinct valleys and islands into which Greece was broken up by sea and hills. These valleys and islands, over the lapse of time, became centres of political life sharply different from the Oriental Empires. From the history of the Greek City-States, and especially from the history of Athens, we can trace how the tribal administration gradually gave place to the local principle in government, and how the local community was developed into the City–a new political type of governance. The Greek City was a true State in the modern sense of the term in which the political, economic, intellectual, and moral life of the people was focussed on the central city.

With the Greek City-State two ideas were integral. Each City was a politically organised State independent of others and proud of its independence. The Greeks never thought, and perhaps it was foreign to their nature, to merge their identity in any other City and to make a large unit of political administration. Secondly, the Greek City-State was deliberately limited in size and population. According to Greek political philosophy, the concentration of political, social and intellectual life at one central city was possible only

1. Roger H. Soltau, *An Introduction to Politics*, p. 60.

when the State was small. Aristotle put definite limitations on the population and size of the State. He held that neither ten nor a hundred thousand could make a good State, because both these numbers were extremes. He laid down the general principle that the number should be neither too large nor too small. It should be large enough to be self-sufficing and small enough to be well governed.

The Greek City-State developed to the stage of a conscious effort directed to the realisation of liberty and equal laws. It was a great experiment not only in the art of self-government, but also in quest of virtue. To be a citizen of the State did not merely imply, in the Greek view, the payment of taxes and the casting of a vote. It implied a direct and active cooperation in all the functions of civil and military life. A citizen was normally a soldier, a judge and a member of the governing assembly; and all his public duties he performed not through a deputy but in person; the gods of the city were his gods, and he must attend festivals. The State was, thus, identified with society. The Greek City was at once a State, church and school and it embraced the whole life of man. Since the object of the State was to secure a good life for all citizens, all forms of State control calculated to secure that end were considered proper and justified, and no line was drawn between matters political, moral, religious and economic. Burke's description of the State as "a partnership in all science, a partnersltip in all art, a partnership in every virtue and in all perfection" was the real life of the Greek City-State, and Athens at the height of her fame may be regarded as the embodiment of all that was most advanced in Greek political ideas.

The City-States of Greece were typical examples of direct democracy in the modern sense of the term. All citizens were directly associated with the governance of the State and it really meant the power of the people. But forms of government, according to Greek philosophers, were subject to cyclic changes. Monarchy was the first and in time it gave way to aristocracy. Aristocracy was succeeded by oligrachy. Then came polity and, finally, democracy. Democracy was held to be rule by the mob, an intolerable confusion which was succeeded, again, by monarchy and, thus, ran the course of cyclical political changes.

The Greek City-States fundamentally differed from the Oriental Empires. But there were snags, too, in the Greek political life. Their love of independence verging on separatism ultimately resulted in their collapse, when a powerful State arose in the north under Philip of Macedon. They were also wanting in what may be called the submissive virtues—patience, self-denial, and the spirit of compromise and tolerance. Their self-will and lack of disciplined life embittered the faction fight in their Cities between the rich and the poor, nobles and commons, friends of Athens and friends of Sparta. The works of the Greek historians and political thinkers clearly show that the Greek society of their time was not in a sound state. The philosophers were constantly returning to the question, what was virtue, and how it might be taught. And they looked on this question as one of immediate and even urgent importance to society. They felt that their countrymen were thinking too much of liberty, and far too little of discipline. And they foresaw that a people in this state of mind must fall before that power whose people were better disciplined than the Greeks. The Macedonians, and after them the Romans, proved the truth of this forecast.

The Greeks were also wanting in humanity. They made liberty the exclusive right of superior people and denied to others what they valued for themselves the most. Even the wisest of the Greeks regarded slavery as a natural institution and they never dreamt that civilised life was possible without slavery. Athens, for example, had only about 20,000 citizens who obtained leisure for their public duties by turning over all the rough work to a much larger body of slaves. Slavery is incompatible with civilisation and, as such, with democracy. A democratic society is one in which all enjoy equal rights and privileges without any barriers of class distinction. The brotherhood of man is its basis and all its members stand equal in the common fraternity. This means faith in man as a man and his personality.

The Greek City-State was an all-inclusive partnership in every aspect of human existence. But this broad inclusiveness made the Greeks neglect one of the most essential of political problems, that of clearly defining the functions of the State and separating it from various other associations which composed. society. "The failure to distinguish the State from the community," says MacIver, "left Athenian liberty itself a monument broken and defaced. The all-inclusive State, whether its dimensions are those of the city or nation, cannot draw the line between law and custom, between enforcement and spontaneity, between the conditions of order and those of culture. So long as the theory is accepted that the State is omnicompetent, there will be confusion and suppression....Under such a theory no form of life is safe, no religion, no opinion, unless its adherents control the government. So the very diversity which enriches a civilisation when recognised as existing of right, creates under the principle of the 'universal partnership' those violent and factious oppositions which on the contrary destroy it."

The Roman Empire. Rome was originally just one of the numerous little States which had been born in Italy, in much the same way and for the same geographical reasons as Greece. But after 500 B.C. the Italian City-States were united with Rome at the head. As there were fewer geographical barriers in Italy than in Greece, unification was more easily attained.

There are three definite periods which mark the growth of the Roman State. First, there was the monarchic City-State. The royal period lasted from the foundation of Rome about 753 B.C. to 510 B.C. At the head of the State was the king who was at once the hereditary and patriarchal chief of the people, the chief priest of the community, and the elected ruler of the State. On the death of the King, the sovereignty of the State reverted to the Council of Elders. The Elders appointed a temporary King for five days who, in his turn, nominated another Elder. This Elder actually named the new King subject to the approval of the assembled people. "The vote of the people was ratified by the approval of the gods, as given in the ceremony of inauguration." The powers of the King were described as "imperium" and were technically unlimited, both in times of peace and war. But there were two customary limitations to these powers. First, the King was expected to consult the Council of Elders and to follow their advice. Secondly, all cases involving capital punishment were submitted to the people for their final decision.

During the monarchical period only the nobility, called the patricians, had a share in political authority. The landless, propertyless common people, known as the plebians, had no share in the governance of the country and they enjoyed no political rights. But later on they acquired some privileges.

Monarchy in Rome came to an end in 510 B.C. in the same way as when the Greeks expelled their "tyrants." It was substituted by a Republic. Civil and military powers were vested in two officers called the Consuls, elected annually. But it did not mean equal political rights for all citizens. The plebians were subject to political, economic and social disabilities. They could not hold any public office. The patricians had entire control of the administration of law. The public land and pastures were allotted only to them. The plebians were also legally prohibited from marrying among the patricians. The former struggled for the removal of their disabilities and they eventually succeeded in getting all the three disabilities removed one by one. The constitution of the Republican Rome rested on four principles: divided authority; a short tenure of office for magistrates; the people were the final authority on all important matters; and the military authority of all magistrates was limited. But by the middle of the second century these principles were very often violated and the Republic came into disrepute. Division of authority disappeared and despotism began to reign. By this time Rome had extended her dominions over vast and distant lands. The Republic gave way to an Empire and the form of government adapted to a City-State was found incongruous with the administrative needs of the time.

The Roman Empire at one stage extended over England, France, Germany, Spain, Austria, the Balkans, Grece, Asia Minor, the whole of the Mediterranean coast and its hinterland. The governors sent to rule the distant parts of the Empire enjoyed wide discretionary powers and were practically independent of the Home Government. The only check on their authority was the possibility of impeachment at home on retirement. But it was just a nominal check.

In Rome itself a despotism of the extreme type was established. The Emperor became all-powerful and his word was law. The popular assemblies ceased to function and the old political maxim that the ruler received his power from the people gave place to the Divine Origin Theory. The authority of the Emperor was interpreted to have divinely originated and for a time he was worshipped as God. When Christianity was accepted as State religion, the Divine Origin Theory was explained to mean that the Emperor was the deputy of God on earth and unflinching obedience to his authority was obedience to God. In this way, the Republican Roman City-State became the centralised autocratic world-empire, thereby shifting the emphasis from the Greek ideals of liberty, democracy, and local independence to the Romans' ideals of unity, order, universal law, and cosmopolitanism.

The World Roman Empire at the height of its political glory made some very important contributions to political institutions. The Romans were not a brilliant people. They did but little work in art and philosophy, but they possessed in full measure the practical qualities in which the Greeks were deficient. They were patient, methodical, skilful in arranging compromises and in devising legal forms. The Greeks pursued their ideal of "liberty and equal laws" disregarding authority and discipline. The Romans held fast to authority, in the family and in the State. At the same time, they were ready to concede rights to all kinds of subject persons by extending to them the right of full Roman citizenship. While they were reducing one country after another to subjection and order, they were also developing their law on rational principles. The Romans studied the institutions and customs of the heterogeneous people over whom their authority extended and found a common element of equity and convenience for all. This Law of Nations, as they called it, was a great step forward, which widened the notions of lawyers and statesmen. They also applied the Greek notion of the Law of Nature to their legal system.

But the Roman Empire could not endure long. Among the causes which led to her decline and downfall "were the sacrifice of individual liberty for the sake of securing unity, the soulless efficiency which characterised her administration, the moral depravity of the upper classes, devastating pestilence, the unsound economic basis of the empire, failure to make rules for the succession of emperors, religious disintegration, and the invasion of barbarian hordes." In a word, the weakness of the Roman Imperial system was that "it remained too Roman, too centralised, too much dominated by the desires and interests of Rome, too dependent on the personality of the emperor of the day." Though Rome fell, yet she gave to the world the first well-organised and well-governed State. She also contributed importantly to many systems of law and her influence may be seen in the development of international law and world organization like the United Nations. Colonial administration is another contribution of the Roman Empire.

The Feudal State. It was on the ruins of the Roman Empire that the so-called feudal type of society came to be established. The tottering imperial rule gave rise to the growth of new principalities headed by the landed aristocracy. There was another factor which gave a fillip to this tendency. The Teutonic barbarians who overran the Roman Empire were wedded to the ideals of individualism, liberty and local self-government. The Roman ideals of administration, on the other hand, were concentration of authority, uniformity of law, and a centralised administration. Feudalism was an admixture of two opposite forces.

Feudalism is the name given to the form of society and government which prevailed in Europe from 476-1500 A.D. According to the feudal theory, the Kings were the vassals of the Emperor who, in his turn, was the vassal of God. They received their dominions as fiefs to be held on condition of loyalty to their lord. Each King, then, divided his dominions into sufficiently large parts and granted each part to a noble called the tenant-in-chief, on the condition of loyalty and service to the King. He continued to hold the land so long as he fulfilled his obligations. After his death the rights and duties of vassalage passed on to the heirs of the lord. The tenants-in-chief divided their respective lands into smaller units and gave them to their vassals on similar conditions. This process of division and transference continued to many stages. At all stages the vassal owed his lord fidelity which was promised by him at the ceremony of homage: "The vassal came before his lord, bare-headed and unarmed, and declared on his knees that he became his 'man'. The lord, then, kissed him and raised him from his knees. Then the vassal swore fidelity (fealty) to his lord."

The essential characteristics of feudalism may be summarised as :

1. the grant of land by a lord to a vassal who held it so long as he fulfilled his obligations of loyalty and service;
2. the existence of close personal ties between the lord and the vassal; and
3. the lord of an estate exercised the full or partial rights of sovereignty over all inhabitants living thereon.

The estate of the lord, big or small, was called a fief or feud, and, as such, the term feudalism.

The obligations of the vassal to his lord were military service normally limited to forty days in a year; payment of rent to the lord for his land and house: work at the lord's fields for a certain number of days in a year; payment to be made on occasions like knighting of the lord's eldest son, the marriage of his daughter, the ransoming of his person if the lord was made a prisoner of war; relief or payment made when a new heir succeeded to the fief; payment of flues when the vassal alienated the land to another party; lodging and hospitality to the lord and his followers on his journeys or hunting expeditions; and attendance at the lord's court.

The duties of the lord were to protect his vassal and to avenge his wrongs; defend his rights; and to secure him justice in all matters.

The chief characteristic of feudalism was the dispersal of governing power among hundreds of petty authorities both lay and ecclesiastical, all confined to small areas. But the feudal State was not a State in the real sense of the term. There was neither common citizenship nor common law. There was no central authority in the State and the loyalty of the people was divided at every step. The individual owed his allegiance to his immediate landlord and only through him to the King. The feudal system, in short, "was confusion rough organised." Out of this confusion emerged the superior authority of the Church, resulting in a deep and continuous conflict between the Spiritual and Temporal authorities. Absence of central authority, division of the loyalty of the people at every step, their religious infatuation, and the inconceivably vast property under the possession of the Church made it possible for the Pope to claim superiority over all the Princes. The Church had, in fact, taken over some function which legitimately belonged to the State. A separate system of law and courts developed for the clergy. Figgis has aptly observed, "In the Middle Ages the Church was not a State, it was the State; the State or rather the civil authority... was merely the police department of the Church."

The Nation-State. Feudalism was only "a temporary scaffolding or framework of order." It gave to the people of Europe some order, but a true national life could not grow on such a system. Many factors contributed to its decline. The general course of events had been that powerful lords subdued less powerful ones, and small kingdoms emerged by successful conquest or lucky marriage, and by the consolidation of an authority that was generally welcomed by the masses, if not by the more important lords, whose powers were gradually limited by the new monarchs. The Renaissance and the Reformation accelerated the pace of this change. The Tudors in England took advantage of the situation and demonstrated to the European countries how the people could unite and progress under a strong and centralised authority. The ties of unity were further fostered by the sentiments of nationality. Britain's insular position helped the British in attaining the full stature of an organised and conscious nationhood. The attempt of the English, in the early fifteenth century, to dominate France roused the national spirit in that country too. A similar awakening, due to various causes, had come in Spain and Portugal. The sixteenth century saw the Danish and Swedish peoples also similarly organised.

A new type of State, thus, emerged. The old concept of the State was replaced by the

State based on bonds of nationality strengthened by natural boundaries. A national State, with a distinct and separate territory of its own, gave rise to the modern theories of sovereignty and equality of States. The nation-State also helped the growth of international law.

The nation-States began their careers as absolute monarchies. When Papal authority was set aside, and feudal rights were giving way, it was natural for the people to cling to the central institution in which their political life was embodied. The growing national consciousness of the people had made them realise the need for consolidation. But consolidation demanded concentration of authority. Protestantism, too, while limiting the authority to a territorial State, placed the spiritual and civil authority in the hands of the King. The political thought of this period also supported absolutism. Machiavelli freed the ruler even from the limitations imposed by public morality. The theory of Divine Right of Kings championed the cause of absolute monarchy.

But the absolute authority of the Kings could not remain unchallenged for long. The next stage in the development of nation-State was the conflict between the King and the people. The people demanded their rights and privileges. They began to realise that power was ultimately theirs, if they wished to wield it. It was the rise of democracy and the aspirations for a representative system of government. Democracy brought with it three main principles; equality, popular sovereignty and nationality. The manifestation of the first principle was found in the Declaration of the Rights of Man drawn up by the French Revolutionaries in 1789. Ever since 1789, this principle "has been at work emancipating and elevating the hitherto unfree and downtrodden orders of society, and removing civil, religious and race disabilities from disqualified classes in the State." The Declaration of the Rights of Man also embraced the concept of popular sovereignty. It means, in simple words, that the people are the source of all authority, and law is the expression of their will. Finally, the principle of nationality requires that the people, who feel they are one, are free to choose their own form of government and to manage their affairs in their own way. Here, again, it may be stated that the French Revolution was primarily responsible for the revival of the national sentiment.

The advance of democracy wrecked absolutism and brought about a great improvement in the political customs of the civilised nations. The selfishness of the ruling families was checked and methods of government became milder and fairer. Laws were made with due consideration of the interests of the people, and opinions were freely brought to the test of discussion. Another characteristic of the democratic State had been the pursuit of the policy of *laissez faire* in the field of industry, trade and commerce. This policy "to let people alone" had certain obvious results. First, there had been a great expansion in enterprise and invention. Secondly, there had been a movement of diffusion owing to economic freedom. Finally, there had been a marked tendency in concentration both of capital and land.

The modern State is a nation-State and it has become the basic pattern throughout the world. It actualizes the principle of self-determination, or the right of each nation to govern itself. Loyalty in the nation-State is expressed to the nation, or, in other words, to the people. A nation-State, accordingly, places emphasis on the ethnic, if possible, and geographic unity of the people. It adopts all means at its disposal to preserve the integrity of its natural frontiers and tries to maintain a homogeneous and united people. This has been the course of the development of the State during the past five centuries.

Colonial Empires. Despite the emergence of democratic States in Europe and their emphasis on ethnic unity and natural boundaries, there had been a marked tendency towards the development of overseas empires. It is estimated that about half of the population of the world spread over more than half of the surface of the earth had been under the suzerainty of the imperial powers either as colonies, or protectorates, or spheres of influence. Imperialism may be described as the most impressive achievement and the most momentous world problem of our age. Competition for these colonial lands was one of the potent factors for the conflicts and wars among States, which characterised the first half of the twentieth century.

Subjugation of independent peoples to the great powers is incompatible with the theory of democracy and self-determination of peoples. Subject peoples, dispossessed of their political privileges and authority and subjected to economic disabilities, made insistent demands for their self-determination and independence. Within the last five decades the British Empire has become a "Commonwealth of Nations." Most of the rich Dutch Colonial Empire was lost when Indonesia became independent and a Republic. The events in Africa especially have proved to be the last phase in the history of the Colonial Empires.

Future of the State. The process of the evolution of the State is not yet complete. With the liquidation of the Colonial Empires, the former narrow ideas of nationalism are also breaking down and are now being replaced by the idea of internationalism. Developments in the means of communication and transport, expansion of international trade and establishment of various international organisations have further given a stimulus to the movement for internationalism. One may even say that if our fathers thought nationally, we think internationally. Suggestions have also been made for a world-State on the basis of a world federation. The late Professor Laski was a devoted champion of World Federation. He said that the nation-State was not the final unit of social organisation and that the pressure of world forces had already made the sovereignty of the State obsolete for any creative purpose. In his recent book, *Union Now*, C.A. Streit visualised a federal union of the various democratic nation-States. Like Laski, Streit, too, outlines the scheme and method of a world government of the federal type.

Federation may be the solution of the present world politics. It is a device which satisfies the claims of nationalities. As a form of government, it is likely to solve the problems of both nationalism and internationalism. But a World federal union is an impossible ideal unless the States change their political and economic attitudes and the tottering imperial powers voluntarily relinquish their imperial authority. The Anarchists and the Communists, too, shall have to change their attitude towards the State, as both aim to establish a stateless society. The future of the State, under the circumstances, is difficult to predict and time alone will reveal the shape of things to come.

Evolution in State Activity. We have travelled far from the oriental despotic empires to the democratic modern State. We have also ventured to speculate on the future of the State and concluded that the process of evolution is not yet complete. But the change in the forms and patterns of States has not been confined to outward forms, or to the principles on which they are based. It is no less marked in the functions the State performs, and the nature of its problems. If we just glance through the work of the government of any modern State, we find that the majority of items in its programme, for example, the education and protection of children, guarantees for workers in industry, cultural activities and elaborate national economic policies, would have been inconceivable to be within the province of mediaeval governments. The new concept of the Welfare State and the mechanism of planning demolish the old theories and narrow the fine distinction made between the State and society. The functions of the State now embrace the entire life of the nation and inevitably demand from its members greater rectitude and sacrifice for future prosperity and happiness. The modern State, therefore, depends far more on the sense of individual responsibility of all its members. We, of course, take for granted the neutrality of the State in matters of religion and expression of opinion. The recent rise of communal fundamentalism is., however, a sad development in the process of the evolution of the State as it is antithesis of secularism which is, generally speaking, the hallmark of the modern State which is plural in character.

SUGGESTED READINGS

Cassier, E.: *The Myth of the State.*

De Grazia, S.: *The Political Community.*

Derley, J.A.: *The Development of the State,* Chap. II.

Fowler, W.W.: *The City-State of the Greeks and Romans,* Chaps. IV-VI.

Gettell, R.G.: *Introduction to Political Science,* Chap. VI.

Jenks, E.: *History of Politics,* Chaps. VIII-XII.

MacIver, R.M.: *The Modern State,* Chaps. I-IV.

Marx, M.: *Foreign Governments,* Chaps. XXXIII, XXIV.

Sidgwick, H.: *The Development of European Polity.*

Soltau, R.H.: *An Introduction to Politics,* Chap. IV.

Streit, C.A.: *Union Now.*

7 CHAPTER

Nationalism

The modern State is a nation-State and it has become the basic pattern throughout the world. It actualises the principle of self-determination, or the right of every nationality to govern itself Loyalty to the nation-State is expressed through the nation or in other words to the people who "recognise their likeness, and emphasise their differences from other men. Their social heritage becomes distinctly their own as a man lends his own peculiar character to his home"[1] This sense of kinship, which binds them together and separates them from others, is essentially a sociological and secondarily a political phenomenon and it may be the result of many or some of the forces like common race and language, common religion, common residence in a contiguous area, common history of traditions and culture, and common aspirations. When the people, inspired of this special sense of unity, determine their political destiny and establish their own independent State, they become a nation and the State so formed is a nation-State. It adopts all possible means at its disposal to preserve the integrity of its frontiers and inculcates a spirit of homogeneity and a united people. This has been the course of the development of the State during the past five centuries.

The nation-State replaced the old concept of the State by the State based on bonds of nationality strengthened by natural frontiers. This process of evolution of the State brings into focus the concepts of nationality, nation and the State. All the three concepts need to be clearly identified as the vagueness with which they have been used is the source of much confusion, and misunderstanding of the import of each.

Nationality. Till recently, the terms nationality and nation were used interchangeably. Now they are used as two distinct terms, but even those have distinguished between them, have by no means been in agreement as to the difference. This is obviously due to the fact that both nation and nationality have to share the same adjectival form 'national' and they have the same root *natu* which connotes the idea of birth or race. But nation has now definitely become political in meaning as a consequence of the universal acceptance of the principle of 'one nation, one State.' It means a political unity—a body of people distinct from others having their own distinct and separate political identity. Nationality has no reference to political unity. It serves to indicate the totality of the natural qualities that characterise the nation, without the idea of legal status which is

---

1. Laski, H.J., *A Grammar of Politics*, p. 220.

connected with the term nation. Nationality emphasises its root meaning of common birth, real or fictitious. It is in this context that James Bryce defines nationality. He says, "A nationality is a population held together by certain ties, as for example, language and literature, ideas, customs and traditions, in such a way as to feel itself a coherent unity distinct from other populations similarly held together by like ties of their own." Whereas a nation is a nationality "which has organised itself into a political body either independent or desiring to be independent." John Stuart Mill's conception of nationality is materially similar to that of James Bryce. He says, "A portion of mankind may be said to constitute a nationality if they are united among themselves by common sympathies which do not exist between them and any others—which make them cooperate with each other more willingly, than with other people, desire to be under the same government and desire that it should be government by themselves or a portion of themselves exclusively."[2]

Nationality, thus, indicates a common spiritual or psychological sentiment among the people having some common affinities or a "socio-cultural complex," as MacIver puts it. Barnes says that nationality "is the collective name given to that complex of psychological and cultural factors which furnish the cohesive principle uniting a nation." It is, like religion, a matter of feelings thinking and living in pursuit of such a conviction. If any group of people begin to think themselves distinct from others, which distinction they are keen to maintain, they constitute a nationality.

The feelings of nationality are subjective and there is no measurable factor universal in application to which it can be traced.[3] It is a sentiment of unity, a common mass consciousness that may be the result of many factors, like common race and language, common history of victories won and sufferings endured, common traditions and customs giving birth to a common culture and common political aspirations. When all or some of these elements are present among the peoples, there is a feeling of kinship and their uniqueness that distinguishes them from others. All these factors have considerably contributed, at one stage or another, to the development of that sense of unity which marks off those who share it from the rest of mankind. All the same, none of these factors is indispensable, although the presence of as many of them as possible helps the growth of a psychological sentiment of unity and oneness.

Community of Race. Racial unity is one of the stronger bonds of cohesion. Writers, like Zimmern, put emphasis on racial purity and consider it as a vital factor helping in the formation and strengthening the idea of nationality. But racial unity is not a necessary element of nationality, for no race can claim its purity. Anthropology and history have shown that there is no pure race anywhere on earth. From the historic and prehistoric processes of development and amalgamation mankind found themselves split into a number of broad divisions mainly on geographical lines. Almost every section "hedged itself with pride and prejudice" and believed itself a pure and superior race.

By the community of race we may then mean a belief in a common origin, fictitious or legendary. Every nationality, as a matter of fact, has legendary tales of its non-historic origin which make the people to forget the diversity of their origins. Whenever a body

2. Mill, J.S., *Representative Government,* Ch. 16.
3. Laski, H.J., *A Grammar of Politics,* p. 220.

of people believe that they belong to one race, they become a group of common *consciousness* and interests. One of the subtle ways of satisfying this group *consciousness* is to judge one's own group by its best specimens and others by their worst. This group pride is a propelling force to the development of nationalism.

Community of Language. No less is the influence of language in binding the people together and developing in them the sentiment of likemindedness. It is very often assumed that language and race go hand in hand because the colour and quality of language determine the colour and quality of those who use it. The racialist theories of the Germans are largely based upon these fallacious assumptions. It cannot, however, be denied that there is nothing more which readily gives unity to people conscious of their divergent origins as the unity of the tongue. Language is the medium through which people express themselves, maintain mutual intercourse, share common thoughts and participate in their weal and woe in the same idioms. Common language helps the growth of feelings and traditions, at first through folk songs and folk tales and later through a written or printed literature. "There is nothing," says Ramsay Muir, "that will give unity to divergent races as the use of a common tongue, and in very many cases unity of language and community ideas which it brings, have proved the main binding force in a nation." Bohen explains that the concept of a mother-tongue has made language the source from which springs all intellectual and spiritual existence. Earnest Barker finds the closest affinities between nationality and language. "Each word is charged with associations that touch feelings and evoke thoughts. You cannot share their feelings and thoughts unless you can unlock their associations by having the key of language. You cannot enter the heart nor the mind of nation unless you know its speech. Conversely, once you have learned the speech you find that with it and by it you imbibe a deep and pervasive spiritual force."

The general view is that diversity in language greatly weakens national sentiments. The most recent example is the revolt of Bengalis in the erstwhile Eastern Wing of Pakistan and their secession from its Western Wing to form the sovereign State of Bangladesh. But if diversity of language weakens the national spirit, linguistic unity does not always bring national unity. It has not united the Irish with the British, nor the Austrians with the Germans. Spanish Americans show no disposition to join the Spaniards or even to consolidate in South America. The Swiss are a nation, though they are divided linguistically and four languages and a number of local dialects are far more generally spoken than the official languages. Paradoxical as it may seem, nothing whatever is done officially or privately, to lessen the linguistic differences. Nevertheless, language is important, not exclusive, as a factor in welding the people together in common ties.

Community of Religion. Religion had been at all stages of mankind's development and played an important role in binding the people in oneness of purpose and community of interests. If religion and kinship welded the ancients, it is a potential joining and separating force even today. There were several reasons for Belgium to break away in 1830 from the imposed union with Holland, but not the least was the diversity of religion. The partition of India in 1947 into two separate States, India and Pakistan, was essentially the result of Mohammed Ali Jinnah's two-nation theory based upon religious differences between the Hindus and the Muslims. But common religion did not deter the Bengali Muslims to secede from Pakistan and form a State of their own.

Religion, no doubt, was and is a great cementing force, but now writers are little inclined to lay stress on religion as a contemporary factor. "Sameness of religion" says Burgess, "was once a most potent factor in national development, but the modern principle of religious freedom has greatly modified its influence." If Burgess should have combined with the modern principle of religious freedom the modern decline in the religious faith, his explanation would have been more apt. In developed countries religion has since long been separated from politics and the cases are at least as numerous in which deep-rooted religious differences have formed no obstacle to national unification. Apart from religion, there are other factors which are a strong incentive to cohesion. The rise of fundamentalism during recent years is, however, alarming.

Garner appropriately sums up the importance of religion as a factor in the development of nationality. He says, "While community of religion has in some cases been a powerful factor in the development of nationality and in the strengthening of the bonds of national unity, and while in other cases the absence of it has contributed to the disruption of the State, it is no longer, thanks to the modern spirit of toleration, an essential or important element of determining nationality." Freedom of religious belief and the spirit of toleration at least take away the sting of fanaticism and create a sense of amity and neighbourly relations in societies containing diverse religious groups.

Geographic Unity. Geographic unity is another factor that fosters sentiments of unity. It is desirable that people constituting a nationality should occupy a fixed territory, the parts of which are contiguous, which they may proudly call their own, sweet home–country. A fixed and contiguous territory produces a community of interests and feelings of cooperation and sympathy. People living in contiguous areas form their own distinct habits, customs, traditions, culture, common experiences and interests that distinguish them from others. It develops national character of the people and affects their institutions.

But geographic unity is not an indispensable factor. Examples of nationalities spread over different lands are many, Jews being the most notable. They were scattered all the world over before the creation of their national home in Palestine and yet they constituted a nationality.

Common Historical Traditions. Common historical traditions are regarded by Ramsay Muir as an "indispensable factor" in cementing the bonds of nationality. John Stuart Mill has given them the first place of precedence and Hayes places them second only to language. Such traditions, Ramsay Muir says, involve a memory of sufferings endured and victories won in common, expressed in song and legend, in the dear name of great personalities that seem to embody in themselves the character and ideals of the nation, in the names of the sacred places wherein the national memory is enshrined. "Here is the source of that paradox of nationality, that it is only intensified by sufferings, and, like the giant Antueus in the Greek fable, rises with redoubled strength every time it is beaten down into the bosom of its mother earth. Heroic achievements, agonies heroically endured, these are the sublime food by which the spirit of nationhood is nourished; from these are born the sacred and imperishable traditions that make the soul of nations." The possession of national history, says Mill, and the consequent "community of recollections, collective pride and humiliation, pleasure and regret, connected with the same incidents in the past" are the most powerful factors to generate the sense of identity and sentiment of fellow-feelings.

Common Government. A people, howsoever heterogeneous in their outlook and sentiments, develop national feelings of oneness if they live for long under the same government. The process of unity is accelerated if the government is alien. People become unified in their resolve to free themselves from the shackles of foreign domination and exploitation. Two hostile classes come into existence; those struggling against the oppression and exploitation of the alien rulers and those who make all-out efforts to perpetuate their hold and suppress the aspirations of the subject people. Misgovernment is a prolific source of national awakening as the malcontents of today are the revolutionaries of tomorrow.

There is other side of the same problem also. When diverse people live for a long time under one government and the government is tolerant in its policy towards all such diverse elements, with the passage of time they merge into a single unified nationality. Their children become political half-castes, and the third and fourth generations lose their parental prejudices. The peoples of the original thirteen Colonies, which comprised the United States of America after the Declaration of Independence, were in their first generation either Englishmen, Germans, Poles or Czechs. Their political aspirations to get rid of foreign domination welded them in bonds of unity and all the different nationalities were fused together in one American nation. Common government is the instrumentality through which much of the common historical heritage of a people takes form.

Common Interests. Common interests, like economic and defensive, act as a fillip in strengthening the ties of unity. Economic and defensive problems are vital in the formation of federations. Economic interests reconciled Scotland to a union with England. The Zollverein bringing Germans with a customs union laid the foundation of the confederation in 1867. No one will, at the same time, deny that economic interests may intensify national consciousness.

Hayes says, "A nationality by acquiring unity and sovereign independence becomes a nation." Take the example of the Jews who have now established the Israel State in Palestine. Hitherto the Jews were a nationality; now they are a nation. A nationality may, accordingly, be defined as a nation in the making. Almost every nationality either had its own State (as the Scots), or aspires to form a State, whether it may be a new State or the rehabilitation of a previously existing State (as the Poles or Czechs before the Great War). There may still be a nationality even if it does not wish to become a nation. The Hindus, the Muslims, the Sikhs, and many others are nationalities within the Indian nation. The Welsh and the Scots are two distinct nationalities within the British nation. When a nation consists of distinct socio-economic groups, each of these groups may be called a nationality. But nationalities in India are divided fundamentally on religion and language. Both the Muslims and the Sikhs have unequivocally declared that politics for them is inseparable from their religions and their political behaviour is determined by the dictates of their religions. This stark reality that India is a multinational State is denied by almost all Indians, except a handful of them, like K.M. Pannikar and Professor Gadgil.

Professor Zimmern makes the following distinction between nationality and statehood:[4]

4. Zimmern, A.E., *Nationality and Government,* p. 51.

"While Nationality is subjective, Statehood is objective;

While Nationality is psychological, Statehood is Political;

While Nationality is a condition of mind, Statehood is a condition in law;

While Nationality is a spiritual possession, Statehood is an enforceable obligation.

While nationality is a way of feeling, Statehood is a condition inseparable from all civilised ways of living."

Nation. The word nation is derived from the Latin word *natio* which means born. This gives the term a racial or ethnical meaning. Etymologically, a nation is a people descended from a common stock. When used in this sense, a nation means a people welded together in a society by ties of blood relationship. Burgess and Leacock define a nation in a racial sense, though the former does not seem to consider common descent as an essential element. To him, nation is a "population of ethnic unity inhabiting a territory of a geographic unity." By ethnic unity he means a population having a common language and literature, a common tradition and history, a common custom and a common consciousness of rights and wrongs. Calvo, in his work, *International Law*, emphasises that the idea of nation is associated with origin of birth, community of race, community of language, etc. Leacock unequivocally says that the term nation, "though often loosely used, is properly to be thought of as having a racial or ethnographical significance."[5] It is a body of people united by common descent and a common language.

But race and nationality are two entirely distinct terms. As said earlier, there is no pure race anywhere on earth. The myth of purity of race is nothing else but pride and predjudice of those who believe that they represent a pure and superior race. Sidgwick has correctly said that some of the leading modern nations are "notoriously of very mixed race."[6] Nation, as such, has no racial significance. What makes a group of people a nation is not necessarily a community of race, language or religion, but a sentiment of common mass-consciousness or likemindedness. It is true that language and religion are important factors in knitting the people in common bonds of affinity and togetherness, but it seems clear that the community of religion and language, and community of national sentiment are not necessarily connected. Take the Swiss people. They do not speak a common language, nor do they profess a common religion, yet they constitute a nation and they are as patriotic and as conscious of their common membership of a nation as any other people. Both France and Spain have a Basque population, speaking a language of common origin and not spoken anywhere else in the world, but the Basques do not form a nation. Nor do Welsh and Breton Celts, though there is a common legendary racial and linguistic inheritance. A common religious belief has been, no doubt, a powerful nation-making force and powerful to disintegrate nations also; Pakistan and Bangladesh are two clear examples of this type. But they are two rare examples. Generally speaking, that stage in the history of civilisation seems to be nearly passed.

Barker gives a more realistic definition and analysis of a nation. A nation, he says, is a body of persons inhabiting a definite territory and thus united together by the primary

5. Leacock, S., *Elements of Political Science,* p. 15.
6. Sidgwick, H., *The Elements of Politics,* p. 223.

fact of living together on a common land. They were drawn from a number of races and they came from different breeds. But their wanderings brought them into this territory and they settled down here because it appealed them to settle down here. While living together for a sufficiently long time, they developed two forms of mental sympathy. The first was a common "capital of thoughts and feelings acquired and transmitted in the course of a common history : a common capital, of tradition; which includes as a rule a common language, a common religion (which may, however, assume a number of different forms), and a common culture variously expressed in art and architecture, in literature, in social habits and otherwise." The second was the common will to live together for the future freely and independently, thus, having common thoughts, feelings and aspirations and thereby exercising their right of political self-determination.[7]

When the mark of the State is stamped on the "territorial nation,"[8] as Barker calls it, it becomes a national community and the State so formed a national State. There must be a general social cohesion which should serve as a cementing material before the seal of the State can be effectively imposed on a population. If the seal of the State is stamped on a population which is not held together by the cementing bonds of a common tradition and sentiment, there is likely to be "cracking and splitting" as happened in Austria-Hungary and the Eastern Wing of Pakistan, now Bangladesh. It does not, however, mean that a single cohesive society is alwavs necessary for the State. There are still a good number of heterogeneous States that exist. But a single cohesive society is the basis of a harmonious and viable State.

The ties that bind the people to make them a nation are psychological and spiritual as they are in a nationality. They are common feelings of an ardent desire to live together and to serve or suffer for the cause of their Motherland or Fatherland, cemented by the memories of a common history; a memory of sufferings endured and victories won in common and the dear names of those great personalities who lifted them above and embodied unto themselves the character and ideals of the nation. These feelings make the people a community of patriotic sentiments and they transmit their common heritage to posterity to keep aglow the light and zest of patriotism in the deep recesses of their hearts so that they may ever remain dedicated custodians of the honour and integrity of the nation. A nation is, thus, the expression of the people's consciouness of unity and once this consciousness pricks through, it makes the people a nation. It is in the minds of the people that a nation is formed and created. A nation, according to Garner, "is a culturally homogeneous social group which is at once conscious and tenacious of its unity of psychic life and possession." Zimmern defines it as "a body of people united by a corporate sentiment of peculiar intensity, intimacy and dignity, related to a definite home-country." He succinctly says, "If a people feels itself to be a nation, it is a nation."

The nation, to sum up, is a human group, inhabiting a given territory, where its members may, but not necessarily, claim one origin, a certain indefinable community of culture, traditions, memories, aspirations and interests and above all a collective will to live together and make a common and concerted *modus vivendi* to live together for ever with honour and dignity. It must also be added that the term nation now implies, for the

7. Barker, E., *Principles of Social and Political Theory*, p. 53.
8. *Ibid.*, p. 55.

majority of writers, a further political and legal element. This community possesses common institutions and common laws and forms an independent political entity.

Nation and State. The theory of one nation, one State had its supporters in the past too, but it became the practical politics after World War I in 1918, when new nations were created in pursuance of the principle of self-determination. Since then there has been a tendency to equate nation with the State, which really they are not. For example, the constitution of the Republic of Argentina bears the title of the "Argentine Nation." Similarly, the name "United Nations" is a misnomer, for it is an international organisation of sovereign States and not nations. The State is a people organised for law within a definite territory and it is sovereign both internally as well as externally whereas a nation is a people psychologically bound together, with a common will to live together for ever and share the common weal and woe.

Certainly, the modern State is limited by national frontiers. We are members of the State within whose frontiers we are born and we can change our State allegiance or nationality only with the specific permission of the State to which we wish to belong. Still, the State is not synonymous with the nation: both are distinct in meaning and connotation. The Scots and the Welsh would claim to be members of a nation, but they are members not of a Scottish or Welsh State, but of the British State. In the course of history, States have annexed nations. Alsace and Lorraine were, from 1870 to 1914, part of the German State. From 1918 to 1940, they formed part of France and from 1940 to 1945, they again formed part of Germany. Today, they are once more part of France. If you ask an Alsatian whether he is French or German, he will reply that he is Alsatian and he may add that he is also French as he is a citizen of the State of France.

A mere organisation of the people under one government does not make them a nation. Austria-Hungary, before World War I, was a State, but not a nation. Inhabited by heterogeneous people, there was nothing other than political bonds which could knit them together in ties of oneness. Then, sovereignty is the most essential feature of the State whereas the people may continue to be a nation even if they do not retain their sovereign character, either as a result of conquest or annexation of their country. Germany and Japan no longer remained States, after World War II in 1945, though the Germans and the Japanese were still nations. Poland and Finland, before World War I, were nations, though not States. The term nation signifies the consciousness of'unity reinforced by psychological and spiritual feelings. Nationhood is, therefore, subjective while Statehood is objective and political.

Emergence of the nation-State. Nationality, as said earlier, is essentially ethnic and cultural and it is an urge to freedom of expression. It has been stimulated to intensity by clash with other groups and has upheld the dogma of independence. As such, it appeared in England about the fourteenth or fifteenth century, in France in the fifteenth, in Spain, Holland and Sweden in the sixteenth century, largely as a result of clash with foreigners. After the Reformation the theological fervour in many parts of Europe diminished, nationality fostered the sentiinents of unity of the peoples and it seemed to be an ideal worth dying for.[9] The partition of Poland towards the close of the eighteenth century

9. Hayes, C., *Essays on Nationalism,* pp. 50–51.

gave it a new impetus and endowed it with fresh sanctity. "Thenceforward," says Acton. "there was a nation demanding to be united in a State, a soul, as it were wandering in search of a body in which to begin life over again."[10] The French Revolution and Napoleon brought the people in the forefront in several European countries who reacted to their impact by developing a consciousness of nationalism.

The new type of State, thus, emerged. The old concept of the State was replaced by the State based on bonds of nationality strengthened by national boundaries. The nation-States began their careers as absolute monarchies. But the people soon began to challenge the absolute authority of Kings. They demanded their rights and privileges and claimed that power ultimately belonged to them. The French Revolution gave a fillip to their aspirations and reinforced their struggle for wresting power from Kings who had proclaimed themselves as the viceregents of God in defence of their right to rule and justify the exercise of their unlimited authority.

The Rights of Man drawn up by the French Revolutionaries in 1789 heralded the dawn of democracy as it rested on the two pillars of equality and popular sovereignty joining them with nationality. Ever since 1789 these principles had been at work emancipating and elevating the hitherto unfree and downtrodden orders of society and removing civil, religious and race disabilities from the disqualified people of the State. These principles not only made the people the ultimate source of authority, but inspired them to claim their right, if they felt that they were one and distinct from others, freedom to choose their own government and manage their own affairs in their own way.

Nationalism. Self-government and nationalism are twin-born. The French Revolution was primarily responsible for revival of national sentiment. Cohesion in the society was sought on the basis of kinship and sentiment of oneness aided by the natural boundaries that helped the formation and strengthening of such feelings. Since the cardinal principles of the Rights of Man were equality, and popular sovereignty joining them with nationality, loyalty and allegiance of the people were to rest with the nation alone and for that matter with the State integrity of which they were committed to preserve. This is the second stage in the development of the nation-State. Hans Kohn, accordingly, maintained that the French Revolution inherited and continued the centralising tendencies of the kings, but at the same time it filled the central organisation with a new spirit and gave it a power of cohesion unknown before. Nationalism was unthinkable before the emergence of the modern State in the period from the sixteenth to the eighteenth century. "Nationalism accepted the form, but changed it animating it with a new feeling of life and with a new religious fervour".[11] Kings gave way to the people and their aspirations.

Thenceforward nationalism became a dogma and dominated the human mind over a large part of the globe. Enthused with this new spirit and attitude of mind and a pattern of attention and desires, poets, historians, journalists and politicians roused the sentiments of nationalism in Central Europe and in the Balkans. Elsewhere in the Near East and far away in India, China and Japan "it began to cast a spell by promising relief from actual or threatened domination."[12] Meanwhile, the Industrial Revolution was made a means to

10. Acton, Lord, *History of Freedom and Other Essays,* pp. 275–76.
11. Hans Kohn, *The Idea of Nationalism,* p. 4.
12. Beni Prasad, *The Democratic Process,* p. 141.

promote national purposes and interests rather than to gain benefits for all communities and States. The Revolution had a national content and national purposes as its home was a national State and it spread chiefly to national States imbued with the traditions of mercantilism. "Even the enormous transit of ideas and news", Hayes says, "which the Industrial Revolution made possible, assumed for linguistic reasons, a complexion predominantly national."[13] The free trade movement was restricted to a few regions and derived its force mere chiefly from its temporary coincidence with national interests.

Nationalism came into its own in the early nineteenth century. Since then it has gradually spread throughout the world. Within the last six decades it flared up to new heights of militancy in Nazi Germany. It transformed an international movement in Soviet Russia into a strongly nationalistic movement. It even changed the complexion of the movement in China. It stirred passions to fever pitch in the Middle East, leading nations to take actions contrary to their economic interests, as in the case of Iran and probably Egypt, and it sparked powerful desire for self-government in majority of the colonial areas of the world. Once these colonies attained independence, it was attuned to the extreme type of nationalism in order to retain their newly won independence, placed as they were in the midst of power-hungry nations, and, at the same time, to accelerate the pace of economic growth to usher an era of just and happy life for the people hitherto trodden under the heels of the alien rulers.

Rightly understood, says Asirvatham, "nationalism stands for the historical process by which nationalities are transferred into political units and for the legitimate right of a people who form a distinct and vigorous nation or nationality to a place in the sun"[14] To put it straight, when a national group either aspires to become self-governing or when having achieved self-government, this fact becomes part of the complex of national sentiment, we speak of nationalism.

Nationalism is almost one idea for which masses of men live and die. It combines love of country and suspiciousness of foreigners. Love of country comes from shared values, and suspiciousness of foreigners comes from the belief that foreigners do not share such values in the same strength. "The first shared value is the love of familiar places—the neighbourhood, the land, the homes, the valleys, and the mountains, all of the surroundings that one loves because they have been a part of oneself from infancy."[15] This is the logical corollary of the eternal truth of man's nature that he is a social animal and his instinct of living together and cooperating with others among whom he lives—creates perpetual bonds of affinity and goodwill and a love for the land—home country—which provides them with the wherewithal of life. But nationalism, as it emerged with the nation-State, assumed the form of ancient group principle pride in one's group and resentment of injury to a member of one's group as it was an attack on the solidarity and the honour of the whole. Pride in one's group usually led to an imaginative abasement of all others. "Pain economy," says Beni Prasad, "set a high value on group solidarity and encouraged an exclusiveness which inspite of some contrary influences of a political and

13. Hayes, C.,*Essays on Nationalism,* pp. 50–51.
14. Asirvatham, E., *Political Theory*, p. 563.
15. Alfred De-Grazia, *The Elements of Political Science, Political Behaviour,* p. 290.

ethical character, sanctified group prejudices."[16] With the enlargement of human groups and their frequent contact, prejudice has crystallised round race and nation.

A Nationalist wants his people and his country to command all the respect and deference from others, his people to have all the power, all the wealth, and all the well-being. He tends to claim all the rectitude and virtue for it, as well as all enlightenment and skill; and he gives it a monopoly of his affection. In sum, he totally identifies himself with his nation. Devotion to the nation transcends all his loyalties, like the family, the village, the caste, religion and other associational loyalties. Hans Kohn defines nationalism in this context and says, it "is a state of mind permeating the large majority of the people and claiming to permeate all its members; it recognises the nation-State as the ideal form of political organization and the nationality as the source of all creative cultural energy and economic well-being. The supreme loyalty of man is therefore due to his nationality, as his own life is supposedly rooted in and made possible by its welfare."[17]

Nationalism has shown the vital quality of elasticity and stood for some regions the attainment of political unification; elsewhere for winning independence from alien rulers; with some States for the cultural assimilation of dissident groups; and with others for economic aggrandisement. In the last two cases it develops into cultural or economic imperialism. We shall discuss this aspect of nationalism later in the Chapter.

RIGHT OF SELF-DETERMINATION

Principle of Self-Determination. The modern theory is that each nationality should form a separate State and each State should comprise a single nation. The principle of mono-national State has lent support to the revolt of nations hitherto held in subjugation and the right of every nationality to become a nation. It stands for President Woodrow Wilson's right of self-determination of nations and nationalities enunciated by him in January 1918 and embodied in his famous Fourteen Points. He declared that an evident principle runs through all the programmes "I have outlined. It is the principle of justice to all peoples and nationalities and their right to live on equal terms of liberty and safety with one another, whether they may be strong or weak." In an address to the United States Congress, he elaborated the point and said, "Peoples and provinces are not to be bartered about from sovereignty to sovereighty as if they were mere chattels and pawns in the game. Peoples may now be dominated and governed only by their own consent. Self-determination is not a mere phrase. It is an imperative principle of action, which statesmen will henceforth ignore at their peril."[18]

President Franklin Roosevelt and Prime Minister Winston Churchill in a meeting on August 14, 1941, somewhere on the Atlantic, issued an Eight Point Joint Declaration (popularly known the Atlantic Charter) embodying the objectives for which the Allies were fighting against Germany and explained the principles that would serve as the basis of the future peace of the world. The United States and Britain solemnly pledged themselves

16. Beni Prasad, *A Democratic Process,* p. 132.
17. Hans Kohn, *The Idea of Nationalism,* p. 16.
18. As cited by F.L. Schuman in *International Politics,* p. 324.

not only to uphold the Rights of Man within their own territorial limits, but to enforce the same throughout the world. It was explicitly stated that neither the United States nor Britain sought territorial or other aggrandisement anywhere in the world and that both the countries would respect the rights of the peoples to choose their own forms of government. But British Prime Minister's nebulous note added to his subsequent statement in Parliament confined its application "to the States and nations of Europe now under Nazi yoke..."[19]

This doctrine of national self-rule was accepted and incorporated in the Charter of the United Nations. Chapter XI of the Charter on the Non-Self-Governing Territories fixed the principle of international accountability for the administering powers of these territories would be the progressive development of institutions of self-government

The principle of self-determination had earlier been advocated by some eminent thinkers and statesmen. John Stuart Mill maintained that "wherever the sentimemt of nationality exists in any force, there is a *prima facie* case for uniting all the members of the nationality under the same government, and a government to themselves apart." He regarded it as only a logical application of the right of self-determination and expressed the opinion that free institutions are next to impossible in a country made up of different nationalities. He explained that it is in general "necessary condition of free institutions that the boundaries of government should coincide in the main with those of nationalities".[20] James Bryce considered that the right of self-determination symbolised the struggle of the nationalities for the realisation of liberalism and democracy. MacIver held that the right of self-determination "has prepared the way for our modern democracies since the demand for self-government expands into the demand that the nation really govern itself."[21]

Appraisal of the Doctrine. The advocates of a mono-national State, who are numerous, claim that a single-nation State is the monument of common history and culture, common traditions and customs and common symbols and myths and such a homogeneity of the people fosters fellowship, cooperation, mutual trust and internal harmony. A cohesive society ensures promotion and preservation of social heritage, rapid material advancement and growth of civilisation. Hegel expounded the idea of the State as containing all the worth which the human being possessed. It was the guardian of the whole moral world, because organised moral life was to be found only within the State. To Bosanquet, who was profoundly influenced by Hegel, the State appeared as a complete idea of the realisation of the human capacity. Such a State could only be a mono-national State; the epitome of moral self-sufficiency, it is claimed. History provides innumerable examples of small independent States that have preciously contributed to the advancement of civilisation. The Greek City-State developed to the stage of a conscious effort directed to the realization of liberty and equal laws. It was a great experiment not only in the art of self-government, but also in quest of virtue. The Constitution of the Republican Rome rested on four principles: divided authority; a short tenure of office for magistrates; the final authority of the people on all important matters; and the military authority of all magistrates was limited. The relevance of these principles is as important now as it was then.

19. *The Indian National Register* (*1941.*), Vol..II, p. 324.
20. Mill, J.S., *'Representative Government,* Ch. 16.
21. MacIver, R.M., *Society: Its Structure and Changes,* p. 69.

A mono-national State is a homogeneous and viable State and the possibilities of "cracking and splitting," a normal feature of a multinational State, are remote, if not non-existent. There is a common centre of loyalty and allegiance and that is the nation. The mass consciousness of oneness divides the people on economic and political issues and not both horizontally and vertically. A single unified party or a group of parties, agreeing on basic fundamentals, man the government and pursue its policies and programmes vigorously with the electoral mandate at their back. But if the population, as Mill argued, is composed of various nationalities, the government may resort to the policy of 'divide and rule', an old maxim of statecraft to ensure its stability and the handy weapon to carry out its policies and programmes. If one single nationality happens to command a brute majority, it may even be ruthless in its policies and attitude towards nationalities in minority. Mill also argued that the security of a multinational State is always precarious as soldiers drawn from different nationalities lack the common incentive of oneness of interests and purposes.

The right of self-determination and to decide about one's own political future has a democratic basis, international recognition, and collective commitment of nations. It sparked the national-consciousness of the peoples yoked to the shackles of the foreign rulers. From the time of the declaration of Woodrow Wilson's Fourteen Points there had been an upsurge first in Europe and then in Asia, Africa and Latin America resulting into the ultimate liquidation of the Colonial Empires. Within the last five decades the British Empire has become a Commonwealth of Nations. Most of the rich Dutch Colonial Empire was lost when Indonesia became independent and a republic. The events in Africa proved a last phase in the history of the Colonial Empires. Today, there are just a few stray colonies that exist and the fate of their rulers is as precarious as it was of their predecessors or sin in the network of the defunct Colonial Empire.

The critics of the right of self-determination, though not many, are equally articulate and their criticism is rather trenchant. They assert that it is historically unsound and sociologically untenable. There are even now many States in which the population is composite and in all such States there is maximum freedom for all and all nationalities are equal participants in the affairs of the State. The notable examples of multinational States are the United States of America, Switzerland and India. The Swiss people are not a homogeneous whole. They sharply differ in race, language, religion and even to a certain extent in civilisation. Yet in this diversity is to be found unity in the Swiss nation and Switzerland presents to the world the most striking example of not only a united people, but one of the most united, and certainly the most patriotic among the peoples of Europe. The United States of America and India are two other examples of unity in diversity. When the people of a composite State stand on a footing of equality and the government is just to all, they forget their differences that divide them and with the lapse of time they become integral parts of a cohesive society.

Nor is it entirely true that liberty and free institutions can exist and flourish in a mono-national State alone. To cite, again, the example of Switzerland, one feels inclined to agree with Hans Kohn that Switzerland has "developed a democratic nationalism, similar to the one known in England and the United States, a nationalism made secure and strong by its insistence on individual liberty and on respect for diversity"[22] Switzerland was the first country in the world to establish republican institutions, and the only one State in Europe which has always been a republic. When the United States of America was born as an independent nation, Switzerland had behind it a republican tradition of some five hundred years. The impact of Swiss republican institutions had been profound on the United States of America, particularly, and other countries adopting the democratic way of life.

The United States of America itself originally consisted of thirteen Colonies of immigrants drawn from nearly all countries of Europe. By the gradual process of intermingling of different cultures, a new culture, a blend of English and Continental characteristics, conditioned by the environments of the New World, was produced. Together the new Americans fought their War of Independence and in the Declaration of Independence adopted on July 4, 1776, announced the birth of a new nation. There were in the words of Bluntschli, the conjunctioh of various peoples who gave to the new State of Americans "breadth and variety" that served "as an alloy to give strength and currency to the nobler metal".[23] The delegates of the thirteen original States, assembled at Philadelphia Convention in May 1787, to revise the Constitution of the Confederation, adopted entirely a new Constitution, which, according to Gladstone, was "the most wonderful work ever struck off at a given time by the brain and purpose of man." The new American system of government was based, as James Madison said, "on that honourable determination which animates every votary of freedom to rest our political experiments on the capacity of mankind for self-government." A publication of the United Sates Information Service gives a matter-of-fact summing-up: "The United States is a country of great diversity.... Geographically, there is a variety too . . . And at the core of this varied land are the people—the most varied of all, for they stem from countries and social levels throughout the world. But in spite of many differences, certain traditions—freedom, equality, individual rights—are common to all and are taught in the home, in the church, and in the schools."[24]

Lord Acton was a relentless critic of the mono-national State and the right of self-determination. He believed that a multinational State embodied the genius of all the nationalities and consequently it is the amalgam of vigour, promise and advancement. "The combination of different nations in one State," he argued, "is as necessary a condition of civilised life as the combination of men in society. Inferior races are raised by living in political union with races intellectually superior. Exhausted and decaying nations are revived by the contact of a younger vitality... . This fertilising and regenerating process can only be obtained by living under one government. It is in the cauldron of the State that the fusion takes place by which the vigour, knowledge and the capacity of one portion of mankind may be communicated to another."[25] He believed that a mono-national State is "more absurd and more criminal than the theory of Socialism," for when political and national boundaries coincide, society ceases to advance.

22. Hans Kohn, *Nationalism and Liberty,* p. 8.
23. Bluntschli', J.K., *Theory of the State,* p. 105.
24. *Facts About the United States* (1956), p. 4.
25. Acton, Lord, *History and Freedom and Other Essays*, p. 290.

Acton deprecated the whole doctrine of nationality at the time of its almost unquestioned ascendancy and uttered a solemn warning against the dangers which lurked in it. "By making the State and the nation commensurate with each other in theory," he wrote in 1862, "this principle reduces practically to a subject condition all other nationalities that may be within the State's boundary. It cannot admit them to an equality with the ruling nation which constitutes the State, because the State would then cease to be national, which would be a contradiction of the principle of its existence. According, therefore, to the degree of humanity and civilisation in that dominant body which claims all the rights of the community, the inferior race are exterminated, or reduced to servitude, or outlawed, or put in a condition of dependence."[26]

Presence of too many nation-States adds to international complications and helps to mount mutual rivalries and conflicts resulting ultimately into a conflagration involving in it even the major States. Lord Curzon remarked at the Lausanne Conference that the right of self-determination "is like a two-edged sword and can be admitted only with reservations." The right of self-determination fragmented many existing States, immediately after World War I, redrawing the political map of Europe, and gave a fillip to the struggle for freedom in subject countries in Asia and Africa. During the last four decades, it became a powerful instrument as well as an argument for liberation from their colonial masters. Today, there are 184 member-states of the United Nations.

Disintegration of Soviet Russia in 1991 brought into existence fifteen independent and sovereign states based on ethnicity and it is the most recent connotation of the right of self-determination. But the United States of America and many other countries, including India, are against the division of multi-ethnic states in the name of the right of self-determination and minority rights. Addressing a 53-nation commission on Human Rights in Geneva in February 1993, Morris Abraham, the United States Ambassador, explained that self-determination "should not be confused with ethnic isolationism." But ironically in today's world "Self-determination has become the world cry of groups which, for ethnic or religious reasons, are bent on dividing nations." Self-determination, he added, was intended for colonial people as self-determination meant the right to be free from imperialist power, often ruling from across an ocean. "In today's version, self-determination often is asserted against neighbours within the same territory". The controversy boils down to this fundamental question of what defines a nation and he himself answered,"If it is common culture, a common language and historical claims to territory, there could be thousands of nations instead of less than two hundred." The right of self-determination, "in the sense of right to break away from one's own nation, does not necessarily attach to a group simply because its individual members share ethnic, religious or cultural history", he emphasised.

But the birth of so many sovereign States has created an international disequilibrium. Most of these newly-born States are not viable units to firmly stand on their own legs in order to ensure a political and an economic poise. With their jittering political stability and precarious economic resources they have to perforce lean heavily on some big power, neighbouring or distant, who can come to their rescue and steer them through their

26. *Ibid.*, p. 289.

predicaments. This has two results. In the first place, it disturbs the balance of power in the international sphere, and, secondly, it creates an atmosphere of suspicion and distrust with the logical implication of a mad race for armaments. Every State, big or small, old or new, pursues a vigorous policy of arming itself against any future contingency and, thus, begins the hysteria of war-preparedness. That had been the course of history since the Treaty of Versailles. Laski has correctly said that nation-States enter into "a competition in the armament of power which acts so as to jeopardise the maintenance of peace, to provoke an atmosphere of nervous hostility, and to induce the smaller States into alliance with powerful neighbours that may win security by that multiplied strength. So organised, the distribution of nation-States resembles nothing so much as a powder magazine which, as in 1914, a single chance spark may suffice to provoke into conflagration."[27]

Two other disquieting legacies of the right of self-determination are: the hunger for new markets and the craze for economic self-sufficiency, especially with the newly-born States. Economic self-sufficiency is an *alias* for economic nationalism and it has more dangerous effects than political nationalism, though in the final analysis they are the two sides of the same coin. Economic self-sufficiency suffocates the normal channels of trade and commerce and worst of all is unethical restrictions on immigration and fanning of race-hatred. This tug-of-war between the nation-States is another major addition to the already existing vicious circle of international distrust and intrigue.

Whatever be the extent and substance in the criticism of the right of self-determination, it had been and still is the beau ideal of nationalities who aspire for nationhood and statehood. The urge for freedom and independence cannot be suppressed indefinitely by sheer naked force. It becomes impossible to contain it once it takes the shape of an upsurge. But a workable substitute that can lessen the ill-effects of too many nation-States and, at the same time, solves the problems of nationalities, differing in language, customs, history and their level of cultures, is the mechanism of a federal polity. It is a device to unify nationalities into a cohesive society and, simultaneously, provides them an opportunity to preserve their separate individuality through the process of adequate and abiding constitutional safeguards. The enlightened public opinion is strongly veering round to this point of view and some even suggest the feasibility of a world federation.

NATIONALISM AND INTERNATIONALISM

Inadequacy of nationalism. The emergence of the nation-State was hailed as a landmark in the evolution of the State as it provided a structure for the emotionally integrated people to live together in a cohesive society with shared values of common interests and purposes and the psychological satisfaction of common feelings which make them a community of patriotic sentiments. Many regarded the nation-State as "the ultimate unit in human organisation." But the nation-State soon after the start of its career degenerated and landed itself in the narrow alley of nationalism which excessively favoured an attitude of separatism, arrogance, and economic aggrandizement. Even race vanity and its

27. Laski, H.J., *A Grammar of Politics,* pp. 224–25.

counterpart, race contempt, was intensified by conflict of cultural and economic differences and in this display naked pride and political prestige surmounted the rest.

Fichte was responsible for a scheme of an international league to enforce peace, and nationhood was to him "a manifestation of the primordial, the divine, the eternal—the absolute." Yet he felt that a nation could not dispense with arrogance. Even Mazzini attacked the cosmopolitans on the ground that it was impossible to love all without distinction of nationality. Some statesmen bluntly stated the extreme implications of nationalism. While defending his Polish Policy, Von Bulow declared that "in the struggle between nationalities, one nation is the hammer and other the anvil; one is the victor and the other the vanquished. It is a law of life and development that when two civilizations meet they fight for supremacy."[28] When the nation is glorified and the State idolized, the characteristic of such a State is vigour and force. Tensions and conflicts mount and disputes between States, real or imaginary, are decided by the arbitrament of war. There had been a regular succession of wars, major and minor, since the birth of the nation-State and there seems no end to such wars. In fact, mankind is scared by past wars and is scared of new ones. In the nuclear age of our times, no country can afford to wait for defence to ward off the probabilities of war and to win it, if it actually comes. It is a contagion that ruthlessly spreads with disastrous results.

The nation-State is an exclusive State and it has two aspects. In the first place it means race superiority and its supremacy. The race problem becomes aggravated in proportion to the conjecture of physiological and cultural differences with economic conditions and political clash. On the economic side, the ideal of economic self-sufficiency combines with the exigencies of modern industry—its ever present needs of raw supplies and markets and sometimes cheap labour—to prompt the annexation or control of territories inhabited by weaker peoples. There is an old maxim that flag follows the trade and economic nationalism has its countcrpart in economic imperialism. Big industry and high finance manipulate the patriotic sentiments and enthusiasms and equate nationalism with imperialism. At this point nationalism merges itself into the wider questions of race, especially of colour, and we come to the "sliding scale of diplomatic language, hinterland, sphere of interest, sphere of influence, paramountcy, in protectorate, veiled or open... lease, rectification of frontier concession, etc."[29]

The eighteenth and nineteenth centuries saw many wars between the imperial powers. It was estimated that about half the population of the world spread over more than half the surface of the earth had been under the suzerainty of the imperial powers. This phase in the history of the Colonial powers is more or less over now, but colonialism has taken a new form. There is a regular race between the "big" powers to establish and extend their spheres of influence and the obvious victims are the underdeveloped and strategically important States. The most recent example of this political manoeuvring are Afghanistan and Kuwait.

Internationalism. The rationale of the nation-State was democratic as it joined nationality with the twin principles of self-government and equality. But nationality

28. As cited by Beni Prasad, *A Democratic Process,* p. 149.

29. Hobson, J.A., *Imperialism : A Study,* p. 10.

became, in the words of Tagore, "one of the most powerful anaesthetics" that the ingenuity of man has ever invented. Education often inculcates the type of patriotism which sanctifies an attitude of "my nation, right or wrong". The feelings of patriotism so drummed into us from the earliest childhood that it is "only by a considerable intellectual effort that any of us can liberate themselves from these forms of thought, to which we have been moulded."[30] Such a patriotic fervour to which nationals of all States had been taught and trained did not usher an era of peace, cordiality, mutual trust, goodwill and cooperation in the family of nations. On the other hand, the nation-State system is a dismal chronicle of national arrogance, aggression, chauvinism, expansionism and all the worst that human nature can display. Hayes, accordingly, comes to the conclusion that it is highly doubtful if "the recasting of political geography on national lines has actually promoted either humanity or justice and whether nationalism is a reliable harbinger of a quieter and better world in the immediate future."[31]

But the old ideas in the relations of races and nations have become anachronistic and the former notions of nationalism are breaking down in the atmosphere of contemporary civilisation. Laski says that "the scale of modern civilisation has made the national and sovereign State an institutional expedient of which the political unwisdom and moral danger are both manifest."[32] He categorically affirms that the notion of a sovereign independent State, on the international side, is "fatal to the well-being of humanity. The way in which a State should live in relation to other States is clearly not a matter to which the State is entitled to be the sole judge. The common life of States is a matter of common agreement between States." So strong is the contemporary opinion in favour of internationalism that one may even say that if our forefathers thought nationally, we think internationally. Suggestions have also been made for a World State on the basis of a world federation.

It is not implied that the tangles of centuries can be resolved so immediately. It is not given to any generation of men to write on a clean slate. The logic of history rules out the sudden dawn of internationalism. But much leeway has been made during the past seven decades or so. The rapid technological advancement in every country and the consequent economic growth and economy of plenty have removed the root causes of the conflict which made nations so exclusive in spirit and aim. The new means of transport and communication, the new industry and the new commerce have made the world a single economic unit and produced a new economic homogeneity in the economic interests of all the nations. In the seventeenth century an English writer vigorously propounded the doctrine that commercially a country could progress only at the expense of another.[33] That is no longer true and with general economic improvement it "will become the exact antithesis of the truth." Easy and frequent travel in all the countries has not only broken the barriers of distance, but has produced a better appreciation of the peoples, increased mutual understanding and removed crude notions so far held by the Western nations particularly about the Asiatics and the Africans.

30. Wells., H.G., *Commonsense of World Peace,* pp. 28–29.
31. Hayes., C., *Essays on Nationalism,* p. 137.
32. Laski, H.J., *A Grammar of Politics,* p. 225.
33. As cited in Beni Prasad, *A Democratic Process,* p. 153.

Internationalism is a way of life and pattern of behaviour and its prerequisite is to master the art of living together. Its rationale is the well-known dictum of Kant; "So act as to treat humanity whether in your person or that of another, in any case as an end, and never merely as a means." If nations follow the voice of reason and eschew emotions, parochial loyalties and narrow considerations *ipso facto* disappear and an atmosphere of fellow-feelings prevails that knows no territorial limits. The brotherhood of man is the basis of internationalism. It rouses no passions and does not blur man's vision to distort his notions. Reason is the just steward of man's mind. Internationalism presupposes the existence of sovereign national States and the voice of reason enjoins to reconcile national interests with the larger interests of mankind with a just mind in an atmosphere of mutual trust and goodwill. Interdependence is the natural necessity of nations and all are integral parts of one single human society and their weal and woe is inseparably intertwined. Laski has succinctly said that there are "no longer lotus-fields where men may linger careless of life about them. The world is one and indivisible in a sense so compelling that the only question before us is the method by which we represent this unity."[34]

The method of this unity and international solidarity is reflected in a vast network of inter-governmental bodies and in a series of international organisations and voluntary international organisations that have been established during the course of the present century. Any problem which affects or is likely to affect the peace, security and well-being of mankind is a matter of common concern and it is obligatory on all States to accept the decisions arrived at in the inter-governmental bodies and international conferences. The scope and subject matter that the international conferences and agencies deal with have expanded so tremendously that there is virtually no topic excluded from international treatment. For example, discussions on values of national currencies are frequent and a matter of vital common concern as the rise or fall in the value of the currency of one State has an impact on the economy of other States, if not to the same extent at least to a disturbing level of disequilibrium. Similarly, it is true of self-employment policies, health measures, educational policies, labour problems, population, protection of human rights and multitude of such other problems.

A sovereign nation-State, however, remain the basic foundation of all international activity. Laski and many other eminent thinkers have assailed the moral validity of the doctrine that attributes sovereignty to the State and emphatically maintain that it "will pass, as the divine right of the kings had its day." But it seems highly doubtful to happen in the foreseeable future. Sovereignty remains sovereignty and no State is prepared to surrender it, not even the communist countries whose ideological base is a stateless society. Even the subject matter of International Law are the sovereign States and membership of the United Nations is open for them alone. It is, accordingly, within the framework of the national State that sovereignty is to be interpreted restrictively in order to broaden the scope and obligatory nature of the decisions arrived at the international conferences. Obligatory character of the decisions by majority votes in various organs of the United Nations go counter to the principle of sovereignty and its orthodox attributes.

The modern nation-State, to sum up, is a sovereign State and it is within the four

34. Laski, H.J., *A Grammar of Politics*, p. 287.

walls of this framework that nationalism is to be reconciled to internationalism. A revision of present-day political arrangements is the *sine qua non* of the emergence of nationalism free from the taints of intolerance and aggression. It has two dimensions. Nationalism and internationalism are not antagonistic and exclusive, provided nationalism, as Laski says, is equated with right. The right of every nation to be equal to others, to preserve and promote its individuality and ensure its security with the corresponding obligation of recognising the same right of other nations and States. Thus, harmonising and balancing of diverse national interests in a spirit of mutual trust, cooperation and goodwill. Secondly, the spirit of exclusiveness and aggrandizement, which has long characterised human relationships and which the educational machinery in every nation-State has been used to inculcate, is out of tune with the present trends. It must give way to that of political equality and cooperation among all the peoples of the world. If this can happen, it may be safely said with Zimmern that "the road to internationalism lies through nationalism."[35]

WORLD GOVERNMENT

Concept and Prospects. It is now widely agreed that the real solution of international tensions, conflicts and wars can be found in a world authority which should be capable of asserting itself and effectievly compel obedience to its directions and authority. Laski was the most ardent advocate of such a world authority organised on a federal basis. He argued that the nation-State was not the final unit of social organisation and the ultimate unit in human allegiance, and that the pressnre of world forces had rendered the sovereignty of the State obsolete for any creative purpose. Albert Einstein outright rejected the idea of continuing with the nation-State even within the ambit of restricted exercise of its sovereign power and expressed the opinion "that the only step towards world government is world government itself"[36] and regretted that no real progress had been made in this area in the past so many years. Jawaharlal Nehru agreed with Einstein and affirmed that the world government "must and will come, for there is no other remedy for the world's sickness".[37] Kingsley Martin wrote in 1959 that war "is always likely until there is an international authority which is strong and universally accepted."[38] Robert Hutchins is of the opinion that war can be abolished only by a world authority, the imperative need is to start working for such a government. He argued that any effort to secure international control of atomic energy without discarding the existence of sovereign States is bound to fail and maintained that any "proposal for a world atomic authority is a proposal for world government."[39] M.K. Gandhi subscribed to the ideal of a world federation or, more accurately, a world confederation. He favourably reacted to Arthur Moore's idea and said that it was "entirely novel" and considered it as "the true ideal."[40] There are many more

35. Zimmern, A.E., *Nationality and Government,* p. 61.
36. Otto Nathan and Heinz Norden, *Einstein in Peace,* p. 443.
37. As cited in Iris Claude, Jr., *Power and lnternational Relations.* p. 213.
38. Kingsley Martin, *History and Human Nature,* p. 38.
39. Hutchins, R.M., *"Constitutional Foundations for World Order",* in Mendolvitz, n. 6, p. 64.
40. Refer to Arthur Moore's *"World Government"* in Kshitis Roy (ed), Gandhi Memorial Peace Number (Santniketan 1949), pp. 200–01.

who consider that a world government is the only way to provide collective security for the States.[41]

But no one has so far explained how the world government can be brought into existence and what precisely shall be its structure and the mechanism to work it. There has been an active movement in favour of a world State on a federal pattern, spearheaded by the United World Federalists with its base in the United States. The programme of the movement rests upon two propositions—"wars between groups of men forming social units take place when those units exercise unrestricted sovereign power... wars cease the moment sovereign power is transferred from them to a larger or higher unit."[42] Analogy of the original thirteen States of the United States of America is cited and it is argued that realising the "wisdom" of this experience a world government will be set up and once it is done world peace will prevail and wars disappear.

But is it possible to realize the ideal of world government in the near future ? There is no definite answer to this question. Some argue that gradualism defeats the purpose of the ideal as the nation States shall continue to exist, with the inter-State system of collective security, without eliminating the exigencies of conflicts and wars. As long as suspicion of aggression continues to exist, the States shall, as ever before, indulge in piling up armaments and a chance spark somewhere may endanger the peace of the world. Morgenthau, on the other hand, holds the view that people of the world are not willing to accept the world government, that they are not willing and able to do even what a world State might require of them in fulfilling its purposes. His conclusion is that international peace cannot be "permanent without a world State... that a world State cannot be established under the present moral, social and political condition of the world.... in no period of modern history was civilization more in need of permanent peace, and hence of a world state, and that in no period of modern history, were the moral, social and political conditions of the world less favourable for the establishment of a world State... as there can be no world State without a world community willing and able to support it."[43] The chances of the sense of a world community to grow under the existing conditions seem to be remote, if not altogether absent. Loyalty to the nation is overwhelmingly predominant over loyalty to the world community. It is true that progress in science and technology and interaction of various economic forces have brought the people of the world nearer to one another, but it is too much to believe that "there is a growing integration of the world community."[44] G. Parthasarathy has correctly said that in the developing countries of Asia, Africa and Latin America the most pressing problem is the poverty of large masses of the people. "Rapid economic development is not only a must for releasing the masses from the grinding poverty of which they are now conscious, but a precondition of any effective international economic integration. No doubt, tremendous advance in technology has been made, but the effects of the advance, as regards international economic integration, are by and large restricted to the developed countries." The task is, therefore, "first to accelerate the pace of economic development

---

41. Schuman, F.L., *The Commonwealth of Man.*
42. Harold Sprout and Margret Sprout, *Fouundation of International Politic,* pp. 228–29.
43. Hans J. Morgenthau, *Politics among Nations,* pp. 509–13.
44. Deshpande, *N.R., "Methods of Achieving World Order",* Harnam Singh (ed), *Studies in World Order,* p. 415.

in the developing countries to the point where a more unified world system can be built."[45] The developed countries are in the least interested in this vital aspect of the world order. In all the international conferences that have so far been held to devise ways and means to extend aid to the developing countries, the affluent States have done a precious little. There is no unanimity among them even on a minor issue, such as, the quantum of aid. A mere lip service to the poor nations does not fill in the gap and as long as the yawning disparities in the fortunes of the developed and developing countries remain, even the idea of a world federation shall be a nightmare, for equality the basis of a federal organisation and, more so, if the tone of nationalism is to be changed.

There may be a greater recognition for a world State among some peoples of the world, but political evolution varies from one people to another. Some older States, and developed too, which wield immense power and influence in the family of nations are averse to the sacrifice of their sovereignty with a view to creating a world State. There are many, if not all, among the newly independent States who would even dislike the idea of compromising their national sovereignty for the cause of world State, howsoever convincing the idea may be to them. No one can, indeed, think of a world State unless all, or almost all, the States, big and small, developed and underdeveloped, abandon sovereignty and spontaneously agree to the authority of the World Government in the sphere of international relations.

Then it involves the role of power in the organisation of the World State. Its advocates envisage a monopoly of the power vested in the World Government, as the success or failure of the World State shall depend upon its total effective power. Einstein stands for the "military monopoly of a super national organisation" and asserts that "military power should be completely and solely in the hands of the world federation."[46] This he deems essential if its laws are to be enforced effectively, the power to make war a virtual impossibility and to make futile all acts of aggression. Norman Cousins would equip the world organisation with force "adequate to deter aggression, adequate to carry out inspections as part of workable control over nuclear arms, adequate to keep the peace itself."[47] But is it feasible or even desirable to concentrate total military power at one single centre of authority ? As in the case of a nation-State force is not its basis, in the same token it cannot be the only criterion of the world State. No State, national or world, can alone he a power system. Even those who consider "power" as the central organising idea of the State admit that no State can enforce its laws by sheer force, if they violate the moral consensus of the society. A State that may attempt it shall invite "disintegration of its own fabric in anarchy or civil war and the frequency and destructiveness of civil war demostrate "that the existence of the State does not assure the preservation of the domestic peace."[48] Nicholas J. Spykman, another supporter of power politics, says, "Preserving order within the State is a question of making daily decisions that will adjust human frictions, balance social forces and compromise political conflicts."[49]

---

45. Parthasarathy, G., "World Economic Order", *Ibid.*, p. 148.
46. Otto Nathan and Hans Nordan, *Einstein on Peace,* pp. 409–432, 415, 477.
47. Norman Cousins, *In Place of Folly,* p. 109.
48. Hans J. Moregenthau as cited in L. Claude, Jr., *Power and International Relations, n.* 24.
49. Nicholas J. Spykman, *America's Strategy in World Politics,* p. 465.

Besides, realisation of the scheme of World State necessitates prior agreement among the States forming the World federation relating to organisation of its structure, and procedures. There must be full, free and firm agreement between the world government on the one side and its constituents on the other side with regard to the nature and extent of division of powers, for the success of a federal polity depends upon this basic principle. Defining the powers of the world government and ensuring uniform exercise of authority over the constituents is a task surrounded by insurmountable difficulties and complications. Then, how the different branches of governments, at both the levels, are to be organised and what should be the nature of representation of the federating States, big and small, on the World legislative body ? A federal polity stands for equality of representation for all the federating units in the upper chamber of the legislature. And the most knotty problem shall be the revenues of the world federation. What shall be its source of income—contributions by the States, and, if so, on what basis?

The ideal of world government if not utopian, is at least unrealizable in the near future. "It may come at the end of a long historical process if those interested in bringing it about continue to make persistent effort in that direction."[50] The establishment of a world government, if at all it comes, may well be accepted as the last stage in the evolution of mankind towards international amity and peace. The need of the day is the management and control of power. It cannot be eliminated altogether, but it can be managed effectively if there is determination and will of all nations, big and small, to do it.

SUGGESTED READINGS

Acton, Lord : *History of Freedom and Other Essays*

Beni Prasad : *A Democratic Process. Chs. XI, XII*

Elie, Kedourie : *Nationalism*

Gooch, G.P.: *Nationalism*

Harnam Singh (ed.) : *Studies in World Order*

Hayes C.J.H. : *Essays on Nationalism*

Hobson, J.A. . *Imperialism*

Jenks, E. : *The State and the Nation*

Kohn, Hans : *The Ideal of Nationalism*

Kohn, Hans : *Nationalism and Liberty*

Laski, H.J. : *A Grammar of Politics*

MacIver, R.M. : *Community*

Miller, Linda, B.: *World Order and Local Disorder*

Muir, R. : *Nationalism and Internationalism*

Shafer, Boyd, C.: *Nationalism, Myth and Reality*

Woolf, L. : *Imperialism and Civilisation*

Zimmern, A.E. : *Nationality and Government*

50. Verma, S.P., *"Struggle for Power"*, Harnam Singh(ed) *Studies in World Order,* p. 121.

8 CHAPTER

Sovereignty

We have said that what differentiates membership of the State from that of other associations is its compulsory nature and the fact that all other organizations and activities within the frontiers of the State are, in the last resort, subordinate to it. The State issues directions and it also enforces them, if necessary, by employing armed force. "The modern State," says Laski, "is a territorial society, divided into Government and subjects, claiming within its allotted physical area, supremacy over all other institutions." Sovereignty is the most important constituent element of the State and there can be no State without a Sovereign power. "The basis of State sovereignty," to quote Laski again, "is the contingent power to use the armed forces of the State to compel obedience to its will....And it is the possession of this legal right to resort to coercion which distinguishes the government of the State from the government of all other associations." How essential that control is to the State's effective power is one of the clearest lessons of history.

There are two aspects of sovereignty: internal sovereignty and external sovereignty. Internal sovereignty refers to the presence in every independent State of some person, assembly or group which has the final legal power to command and enforce obedience to its authority. This supreme authority is absolute over all individuals or associations of individuals within the State. It issues orders to all men and all associations within that area but it receives orders from none of them.[1] Its will is absolute and it is subject to no legal limitation. "What it proposes is right by the mere announcement of intention."[2]

By external sovereignty we mean that the State is subject to no other authority and, consequently, is independent of any compulsion or interference on the part of other States. If its authority is subject to the provisions of any treaty, or if it is limited by the rules of international law, the sovereign status of the State is not destroyed in any way. These are auto-limitations and are obeyed at the will of the State. There is no other authority which can coerce it into obedience. Each State is independent of other States. Its will is its own, unaffected by the will of any external power.

It follows that the sovereignty of the State is unlimited internally as well as externally.

1. Laski, H.J., *A Grammar of Politics,* p. 44.
2. *Ibid.*

It is original and absolute power and it cannot be divided. Division of sovereignty means destruction of sovereignty. Sovereignty represents the unity of the State, and the sovereign State is one which is externally free and internally supreme. The authority exercised by various organs of the State, that is, government, is delegated. Gettell has aptly said: "If Sovereignty is not absolute, no State exists, if sovereignty is divided, more than one State exist. There can be no legal power at the back of the sovereignty of the State and no legal check on its scope."[3]

Definitions of Sovereignty. Definitions of sovereignty, like definitions of the State, are many and varied. Bodin defined it as the "supreme power over citizens and subjects, unrestrained by law." Hugo Grotius defined it as "the supreme political power vested in him whose acts are not subject to any other and whose will cannot be overridden." Duguit says that sovereignty is the "commanding power of the State; it is the will of the nation organised in the State; it is the right to give unconditional orders to all individuals in the territory of the State." Burgess characterised it as "original, absolute, unlimited power over the individual subject and over all associations of subjects." He further says that sovereignty is "the underived and independent power to command and compel obedience." The sovereign is "legally supreme over any individual or group," says Laski, he possesses "supreme coercive power." Sovereignty, according to Jenks, is "an authority which, in the last resort, controls absolutely and beyond appeal the actions of every individual member of the community."

TERM SOVEREIGNTY AND ITS DEVELOPMENT

Origin of the Term. The term sovereignty is derived from the Latin word "superanus" which means supreme. The notion of sovereignty, as suggesting the supreme power in a territory, is modern and its emergence is connected with the rise of the modern nation-State. But it does not mean that the ancient and medieval ages had no idea of such a notion. For the ancients it simply meant "statement of the fact that there must be an ultimate control, someone with the last word in any case of dispute, able to make final adjustments in the sharing of responsibility and power; and that the State, and no other social force, must exercise this final authority." Creon says in Sophocles's tragedy Antigone, "Whatever the State appoints must be obeyed in everything, both small and great, just and unjust." Plato and Aristotle recognised the presence of the "supreme power" in the State and emphasised the respect for State authority; the finality of law. Aristotle claimed for the State a natural priority to the family and the individual. The Roman lawyers and the medieval writers spoke of "fulness of the power of the State."

The Middle Ages knew nothing about the doctrine and practice of concerted final authority. The political form, then, was feudalism, based on personal dependence and allegiance within many small groups. Feudalism was the antithesis of unified authority. There was open conflict between the Spiritual and Temporal authorities and if anybody, under the circumstances, could claim final authority, it was the Church and not the State.

3. Gettell, R. G., *Introduction to Political Science,* p. 95.

Moreover, peoples' firm belief in the laws of nature or God and the sanctity which was attached to such laws over man-made laws retarded the growth of the modern idea of sovereignty. Summing up the nature of sovereignty in the Middle Ages, Ward says, "The authority of Feudalism and the belief in the law of God or nature superior to the human law made impossible the modern idea of the unlimited and indivisible sovereignty of the State over all citizens."

The religious wars of the sixteenth century destroyed the unity of the Church and on the ruins of this destruction was built the modern State. The triumphant monarch either gradually destroyed or absorbed all possible rival intermediaries between himself and his subjects, including the Church. Sovereignty came to be regarded as one of the essential attributes of the State, incarnate in the king, the head of the State. His authority was final to define and pronounce the law. The emergence of the modern State, thus, gave a new meaning to the term sovereignty. The struggle which gave rise to the conception of sovereignty was undertaken and sustained by the monarch himself in order to establish his personal independence. To the victor belonged the spoils of war.

Bodin and Hobbes. The new reality of sovereignty of the State was given its philosophical justification by a Frenchman, Jean Bodin, and an Englishman, Thomas Hobbes, each writing during the full agony of the civil and religious wars of his country, the former at the beginning and the latter in the middle of the seventeenth century. Both Bodin and Hobbes defended the need for one single unified authority, which should be accepted by all and against which no group or individual could raise the objection of any earlier rights to independence or resistance. Rights were what the State granted, compatible with the unity of the State and keeping of peace and order within it. There could be only one power within the community, they urged, which could not be limited, or divided and shared. Bodin's sovereign was, however, subject to four limitations. Firstly, as the king did not possess supermundane sovereignty, God was above him. Secondly, the supreme power of the king over his subjects was "subordinated" to "the law of God and nature," that is, to the requirements of the moral order. Thirdly, the French King could not modify the succession or any part of public domain, and, finally, the king could not touch private property. But these limitations, Bodin maintained, did not limit the power of the king over the body-politic. His assertion that the Prince was the image of God meant that he was a sovereign living person and his authority transcended the whole political community just as God transcended the cosmos. He said either sovereignty meant nothing or it meant supreme power ruling over the entire body-politic. He thus defined sovereignty as "a power supreme over citizens and subjects, itself not bound by the laws." It gave orders and received orders from none.

In this way, the concept of sovereignty took a definite form at the moment when absolute monarchy was beginning to make its appearance in Europe. With Thomas Hobbes it reached its perfection when the sovereign power of the king was held to be natural and inalienable. His whole idea was to establish that the king possessed a natural and inalienable right to rule over his subjects. Once the people had agreed upon the fundamental law of the kingdom, and given the king and his descendants power over them, they were deprived of any right to govern themselves, and the full natural right to rule the body-politic resided in the person of the king whose authority was absolute and indivisible.

Sovereignty and the Modern Democratic State. Later, people began to realise that the king was a part of the governmental machine and, accordingly, an agent rather than a master, and, as such, he possessed subordinate and delegated authority, which could be revoked at the will of the master, the people. It was a protest against absolute monarchy. It began with John Locke, an English political philosopher, who justified the Glorious Revolution (1688), and found its fullest expression in the French Revolution. The French Revolution made the people sovereign, "and not only transferred to it," as Soltau remarks, "all the attributes of the old monarchy of divine right but removed all limitations, on the ground that the people, when governing itself, had no need to restrict its authority."[4] The State, in its corporate capacity, was, thus, endowed with all the attributes of sovereignty which the monarch previously possessed. Two factors reinforced the absolutism of the new democratic State. One was nationalism which added the claims of the nation to those of the sovereign people. The national State claimed not only unlimited authority at home over its members, but also the right to expand abroad at the expense of others. The second factor was the enormous increase in the province of the State following the Industrial Revolution. The activities of the State were not only limited to protection, administration and dispensation of justice, but it became "an organiser of economic life, an educator, an agent in practically every aspect of the collective existence." This meant an ever-increasing "mass of legislation and a great increase in the importance of the State as supreme law-maker, thus reinforcing the dogma of sovereignty, by giving it a much wider field of application."[5]

Rousseau. The concept of popular sovereignty and the identification of the people with the State was actually the result of the teachings of Rousseau, which he had propagated thirty years before the French Revolution. Rousseau made popular sovereignty the doctrine of individual freedom, but the myth of the General Will, which was "always right," made of it a vindication of much more comprehensive State power than any previous political thinker had offered since Plato. Rousseau injected into the nascent modern democracies a notion of sovereignty which was destructive of democracy and pointed towards the totalitarian State. People and the State having become one, the personality of the individual is merged in the social whole, for it is only the power of the State which makes the freedom of its members. Rousseau asserted that the will of the State is the will of the individual in so far as he has accepted this identification of himself with the community. His real self, his real will becomes part of the common or General Will for the common good. If he does not agree what the General Will consents for him, he pursues selfish ends and the General Will can compel him to agree and by doing so he is forced to be free. Thus, the mystical operations of the General Will create conditions of unheard absolutism. Rousseau's State was the Leviathan of Hobbes, crowned with the General Will instead of the crown of absolute monarchs who were described as tyrants.

4. Roger H. Soltau, *An Introduction to Politics,* p. 96.
5. *Ibid,* p. 98.

Hegel. The theory of sovereignty, as initiated by Rousseau, was given its complete and coherent form by Hegel, the German political thinker, who made it more definitely philosophical and metaphysical. "The State," he said, "is 'perfected rationality', the eternal and necessary essence of spirit, the rational in itself and for itself, an absolute fixed end in itself." In this way, Hegel completely identifies the State with society and asserts that only in and through the State does the individual receive what makes life worth living, without it he is nothing. Consequently, the rights of the State are unlimited, legally as a matter of fact and morally as a matter of right, and the individual lives in order to make his contribution to the common life of the State. He must be prepared to enjoy and sacrifice what the good of the common life of the State either grants him or demands from him. The State being not the agent of society, it does not exist for the performance of some specific purposes and with clearly defined functions. The State, for Hegel, is the supreme community and organised moral life is only possible within the State. It is the source of morality and of all civilised existence.

Austin and the Pluralists. The legal theory of sovereignty received its logical analysis at the hands of John Austin, an English jurist. Austin's conclusions formed the basis of the prevailing systems of jurisprudence and they exercised immense influence on political thought in England and the United States of America. Till recently, sovereignty has been viewed as absolute internal sovereignty and complete external independence. The Pluralists, the recent school of thought, reject outright the concept of absolute authority of the State and plead for division of sovereignty between the State and various other associations present within its territorial limits. They regard the State as an association like various other associations with a specific purpose to perform. The functions of the State are well-defined and it has no rightful claim to eminence. The Pluralists, in brief, maintain that sovereignty is divisible and the State is not supreme and unlimited in its authority.

KINDS OF SOVEREIGNTY

Present-day Confusion. It will be evident that the whole subject of sovereignty is a hopeless confusion of a number of different issues and viewpoints. This is essentially due to the confusion, in the past as well as in our own times, between what is and what some people would like the State to be. Extreme idealistic sovereignty is German in origin and tends to justify State absolutism which had been the traditional policy of Prussia and the gospel of Hegel, who was a Prussian. This theory found its echoes later in the totalitarianism of the Nazis and the Fascists. Then, some of the thinkers were exploring the abstract nature of sovereignty and have, as Bryce remarks, been engaged in barren discussions dragging us through "a dusty desert of words rather than of substance." Others have frequently done so, as MacIver says, with an ulterior motive "to get a speculative basis for a practical propaganda."

There is a second confusion between legal theory and political practice. The legal theory of sovereignty vests ultimate legal power in some definite person or body of persons. The authority of the sovereign is supreme and it possesses the power to enforce obedience to its will. But where is that ultimate authority to be found? There is not one single answer to this question. Not only does it vary from country to country, but it will not be always the same in the same country. In Britain, Parliament is sovereign and what it enacts is law. An Act of Parliament cannot be called into question in any court of law. Nor can it be declared invalid, for no law exists in Britain higher than that made by Parliament. But a recent Act of Parliament takes a precedence over a less recent one and supersedes any earlier statutory provisions inconsistent with it. In the United States, Congress is not sovereign. It is a delegated agency and its acts can be pronounced unconstitutional by the Supreme Court. It is the Constitution which is supreme there and the sovereign power is exercised by the constitution-amending authority. In a totalitarian State sovereignty will belong to the executive, since both legislative and judicial powers are subservient to it. Hitler retained the Reichstag as a subservient organ whose function was merely to record a formal approval of Nazi policy. And no Court in Germany could question the legality of the policy endorsed by the Reichstag.

The legal sovereign, in all democracies, must ultimately bow to the political sovereign. But what is this political sovereignty and where is such a sovereign? The problem of the real location of political sovereignty has not yet been solved. Finally, there is the confusion between the actual authority and its source. "It is one thing to say," writes Soltau, "that all authority comes from the people and another to say that the people actually govern." This they obviously cannot do; government is the action of the few. And when Rousseau said that the people actually govern, he introduced in their governance that mystic element of General Will which made it possible for his disciples to justify the omnicompetent and omnipotent State where sovereignty rested in the hands of a small number of men who make up the government. Because of these confusions and the unreality of the elaborate justification of the omnicompetent and omnipotent State, Laski and others have suggested that the theory of sovereignty should be kept out of political discussions. But dropping of sovereignty itself does not simplify matters. It is impossible to drop it, because it exists and since it exists we cannot avoid controversy. Indeed, one of the most effective means of getting to know the character of any system of government is to find out where sovereignty can actually be located and how it is really exercised. To know it is to know the different forms in which sovereignty is expressed.

Titular Sovereignty. Since the term sovereignty is used in different contexts, *titular* sovereignty is one of them. The origin of *titular* sovereignty goes back to the seventeenth century, immediately after the emergence of the nation-State. The nation-States were headed by absolute monarchies and the kings personified the sovereignty of the State. There was soon a conflict between the kings and their people. The people challenged the absolute and unlimited authority of the kings and demanded their own rights and privileges. They claimed that power was ultimately theirs and that the kings exercised limited authority delegated to them on their behalf. The kings, on their own part, found refuge in the Divine Origin Theory and Divine Right of Kings, and claimed divine privileges, freeing themselves from all human limitations. The people ultimately triumphed and democracy, with its representative institutions, came to be established in one form or another. The powers of the king were limited and defined by law or as prescribed by conventions. He was retained in his position as head of the State, but in all matters of administration he was compelled to seek the advice and consent of the representatives of the people. The representatives guided him in choosing and dismissing his ministers, in raising his revenues, and in almost every act of his government. This was the advent of constitutional government. The king remained only a symbol of authority, a legacy of the past. He personified the sovereignty of the State and in terms of law all authority belonged to him. But actual sovereignty rested somewhere else and the monarch simply exercised personal influence in the exercise of that authority. Influence is not authority and can be least sovereignty.

By *titular* sovereignty we mean sovereignty by the title only. It is another way of saying sovereignty in name or nominal sovereignty. It refers to the sovereign powers of the king or monarch who has ceased to exercise any real authority. In theory, he may still possess all the sovereign powers which were once enjoyed by him, but in actual practice there is some other man or body of men who act on behalf of the sovereign and exercise supreme authority. The best example of titular sovereignty is the British King who is even today "our sovereign lord the king." Legally, the powers of the king are supreme. He is the source of all authority, the acts of the government are his acts, and the officers of the State—civil and military—are his servants appointed and dismissed at his pleasure. He is also the fountain of justice and law. But in real practice all this is not true. The sovereignty of the king is now a legacy of the past. There is no action of government which is the result of his initiative. The actual power and direction of government rests with the king's duly constituted ministers. Lowell has beautifully summed up the whole position. He says, "According to the early theory of the constitution the ministers were the counsellors of the king. It was for them to advise and for him to decide. Now the parts are almost reversed. The king is consulted, but the ministers decide." The king has now ceased to exercise any real authority; it is titular.

An absolute monarch is all powerful. He is a real sovereign, the source of all commands and the final authority in all business of the State. But such a sovereign is difficult to find today. Even King Zahir Shah of Afghanistan could not claim to be a real sovereign. At the same time, he was neither titular. He had discretion and exercised some form of personal authority. The position of the Shah of Iran was more or less identical to that of the King of Afghanistan. Islamic Law determines the extent of authority of the Kings in the Middle East countries and they dare not violate the commands of the Quran and the Shariat, though they seen to be exercising unlimited authority. Where rudiments of democratic elements have entered the body-politic of a country, they are defended to be in conformity to and in accordance with the prescription of Islam.

Legal Sovereignty. The sovereignty of the State may further be looked at from two points of view: legal and political. Legal sovereignty is the conception of sovereignty in terms of law, and it refers to that person or body of persons who, by law, have the power to issue final commands. In every State there must be some authority which is determinate and visible in the sense that it should command all and the people may appeal to it as the final authority. Such an authority is known as the legal sovereign and the authority of the legal sovereign is supreme and final over all individuals and associations. No individual or group of individuals has the legal right to act contrary to the decisions of the sovereign power, even if such decisions override the prescriptions of divine law,[6] the principles of morality, or the mandates of public opinion. The courts recognise and apply only that law which emanates from the legal sovereign and disobedience to such a law is accompanied by punishment.

The authority of the legal sovereign is absolute and its will is illimitable, indivisible and inalienable. Law is simply the will of the sovereign. There is no one to question its validity. Within the sphere of law, there is, as Hobbes bluntly said, no such thing as an unjust command. The authority of the sovereign being unlimited, he has the legal right to will whatever he may happen to desire. All rights enjoyed by citizens are granted and enforced by the legal sovereign and there can be no rights against him. This implies that if the legal sovereign can grant rights, he can take them back or even annul them. In Britain, King-in-Parliament is the legal sovereign. In the United States the legal sovereign consists of the combination of authorities that have the power to amend the Constitution—Conventions, or two-thirds majority in each House of Congress which may propose amendments, and State Legislatures or State Conventions which may ratify them. It is, thus, the interaction of specified individuals and institutions according to specified rules of procedure.

This analysis is the lawyer's view of sovereignty. A lawyer is not concerned with the content of law, that is, its welfare content or the value component of law. He is only concerned with the legal source from which it emanates. According to Ritchie, "The legal sovereign is the lawyer's sovereign *qua* lawyer, the sovereign beyond which lawyers and courts refuse to look." But behind the legal sovereign there is another power which is unknown to law. It is the political sovereign, unorganised and incapable of expressing the will of the State in the form of legal command, but to whom the legal sovereign must ultimately bow.

The following characteristics of legal sovereignty may be noted:

1. The legal sovereign is always definite and determinate.
2. Legal sovereignty may reside either in the person of a monarch as in an absolute monarchy, or it may be vested in a body of persons as in a democracy; King or Queen and Parliament in Britain.
3. It is definitely organised, precise and known to law.
4. It alone has the power to declare in legal terms the will of the State.
5. Disobedience to the imperatives of the legal sovereign means physical punishment.
6. All rights emanate from the legal sovereign and it can take them back or even annul them.
7. The authority of the legal sovereign is absolute, illimitable and supreme. It is subject to no control within and without the State.

Political Sovereignty. But absolute and unlimited authority of the legal sovereign does not exist anywhere. Not even a despot can act independently and exclusively. His will is actually shaped by the many and varied influences which are unknown to law. All

6. Except in the Islamic countries where Islamic Law is supreme and unquestionable.

these influences are the real power behind the legal sovereign. As Dicey puts it, "Behind the sovereign which the lawyer recognises, there is another sovereign to whom the legal sovereign must bow."[7] This is called the political sovereign, and, according to Professor Gilchrist, the political sovereign is the sum total of the influences in a State which lie behind the law.[8]

As the political sovereign is not known to law, it is unorganised, indeterminate, and not even precise. In modern representative democracies the political sovereign is very often identified with either the whole mass of the people, or with the electorate or with public opinion. But the political sovereign is neither the electorate nor is it identical with the whole mass of the people, nor can it be identified with the public opinion. Taking first the electorate, no one can doubt its political power in a representative system of government. The legislature dare not disregard the will of the electorate. It may even command the legislature to do its bidding. If it does not, the members of the legislature may be punished at the next election for failure to obey the will of the electorate. Every few years, the electorate creates a new representative chamber, and in doing so it largely determines the nature of parliamentary commands. But on closer examination, it will be found that the electors have no independent opinion of their own. They are influenced by party politics and while casting their votes, they vote for the party rather than for the candidates. The decision of the electorate is also influenced by religious and caste considerations, particularly in India, and the role of press, publicity and propaganda in a democratic State is significant. Thus, so many influences, visible and hidden, affect the decisions of the electorate that it becomes difficult to say where sovereignty precisely lies.

In certain States and at certain times, the electoral sovereign may not exist. It does not exist in a monarchy when the king succeeds to the throne by hereditary right and exercises absolute power. It did not exist in Mussolini's Italy and Hitler's Germany. It did not also axist in the erstwhile Soviet Russia and other communist countries. In Italy and Germany the *de facto* Sovereign controlled both the legal Sovereign and the electoral Soveriegn. In the former Soviet Russia and other communist countries it was the communist party of that country and its politburo. The electoral Sovereign did not exist in Pakistan during the regimes of its chief Martial Law Administrators, General Ayub Khan, Yahya Khan and Zia-ul-Huq.

Nor can we take political sovereignty synonymous with the mass of the people. Quite a sizable number of the people are usually apathetic about politics. They do not want to govern themselves and would not know how to do so even if they wanted to. Then, all the people do not enjoy the right to vote. Those who do not enjoy this right can neither participate in the election of their representatives nor have they any constitutional means at their disposal to effectively influence the decisions of the legal sovereign. It is also possible that the masses may be under the influence of either the priestly class or landed aristocracy, or the militarists. Even if it is not, in the best of democracies, where the people believe that they govern themselves, it can still be suggested that real power

7. Dicey, A.V., *The Law of the Constitution* (1915), Introduction, pp. xviii-xix.
8. Gilchrist, R.N., *Principles of Political Science,* p. 93.

gravitates (or ascends) to a small elite. It is, therefore, not the mass of the people which constitute the political sovereign. It really rests in that class of people under whose influence they actually are.[9]

Similarly, political sovereignty cannot be equated to public opinion. Public opinion is of a highly fluctuating nature and it is susceptible to varied influences. Then, public opinion must have two characteristics. It should be, in the first place, an opinion of a public nature, and secondly, it should be as widely held by the public as possible. But one cannot always be sure that the Opinion actually held is of a public nature. Perhaps the demagogue might have made the decision for them, or the religious or caste appeal had influenced it. Finally, in a representative government, legislature is said to be the barometer of public opinion. Here public opinion is identified with the political sovereign and it may coincide with the legal sovereign, as the British Parliament is.

Political sovereignty, thus, proves to be vague and indeterminate. At many stages it becomes confusing and "the more one searches for this final authority the more it seems to elude one's grasp."[10] Yet, we cannot ignore its existence. Even Dicey, the nineteenth century constitutional lawyer, could not ignore it. He made the distinction between legal and political sovereignty. In Britain, he said, while Parliament was, from a legal point of view, the sovereign legislative power in the State, it was, from a political point of view, subject to two practical limitations. It could not enforce its will if the governed refused to obey and, since it was itself made up of individuals whose outlook was formed by the same social climate as that of their constituents, there were things that it would not, in practice, dream of trying to do, howsoever extensive its legal competence might be. "If a legislature decided that all blue-eyed babies should be murdered," said Leslie Stephen, "the preservation of blue-eyed babies would be illegal, but legislators must go mad before they could pass such a law and subjects be idiotic before they could submit to it."[11]

Political sovereignty may, then, mean the electoral plus all other vehicles and influences that mould and shape public opinion. Garner gives it a much wider scope when he says, "In a narrow sense the electorate constitutes the political sovereign, yet in a wide sense it may be said to be the whole mass of the population, including every person who

9. Sidgwick takes certain hypothetical cases and tries to illustrate the nature of political sovereignty. "Suppose that a monarch habitually obeys a priest, not for fear of extra-mundane penalties threatened by the latter, but from fear of finding it difficult to obtain obedience from his subjects if they believe him to be a special object of God's anger—we shall agree that he no longer completely possesses supreme political power. And if the influence of the priesthood over the monarch's subjects were so strong that the bulk of them unquestionably obey a direction of the chief priest to cease obeying the monarch, and if, therefore, the chief priest's directions were habitually obeyed by the monarch,—it would hardly be denied that the priest had become really, if not nominally, the political superior of the *monarch...."— The Elements of Politics,* pp. 627–28. Leacock sums up: "Following upon this line of argument we might well expect to find that the legal and political sovereign would but rarely coincide. In one State the priesthood, in another the military or landed classes, in another the personal entourage of the king or the predominant influence of the metropolis, might supply the real motive power that controls the public administration." — *Elements of Political Science,* p. 60.

10. Leacock, S., *Elements of Political Science*, p. 60.

11. Leslie Stephen, *Science of Ethics*, p. 143.

contributes to the moulding of public opinion whether he is a voter or not."[12] But this definition robs political sovereignty of its connotation as it is widely understood.

Relation between Political and Legal Sovereignty. The problem of good government, says Ritchie, is largely the problem of the proper relation between the legal and the ultimate sovereign. In a system of direct democracy legal and political sovereigns practically coincide, because the people are directly concerned in making laws. Their expressed will is not a mere opinion, but a law itself. They also elect and remove their rulers, In an indirect democracy representatives of the people make laws. They constitute the legal sovereign and the people who elect their representatives may roughly be called the political sovereign. Law ought to conform to the wishes of the electorate and the legislators must obey their mandate. If they do not, the electorate and the legislature are not in harmony with one another and disharmony between the two tends to create political friction. Really, legal and political sovereign are not two separate entities. They are two aspects of the sovereignty of the State, though expressed through different channels. When there is friction between the two it is highly detrimental to good government. Law must be the manifestation of the will of the people and if the legal sovereign cannot accept the verdict of the political sovereign, the representatives of the people should be re-elected and the legislature reorganised and reconstituted so as to become the mirror of their opinion. Laski has rightly said that "individual is, ultimately, the supreme arbiter of his behaviour" and "if the State is to be a moral entity, it must be built upon the organised acquiescence of the members."[13] The last word remains with the ultimate sovereign, the electorate. Indeed, in some democratic States there often seems to be, says Laski, "a larger degree of obedience from the sovereign Parliament to its constituents than there is the other way round; a series of by-elections, for instance, produce with amazing rapidity a change in the will and temper of the sovereign."

The legal sovereign, therefore, cannot act against the will of the political sovereign. If it does, a legal truth may become a political untruth. A legislature, which legislates in a manner contrary to the will of the people, will be replaced by one more faithful to the popular will. "In other words, the political sovereign lies behind and conditions and, thus, limits the legal sovereign, though, legally speaking, the legal sovereign is omnipotent."[14] The distinction between the legal and political aspects is necessary and useful in that it reminds us that we are dealing with the power, not of an inanimate machine, but of human beings over their fellowmen. We know from History that, however absolute the legal right to exercise power may be, there is a limit in practice. Human beings will stand just so much.

Popular Sovereignty. The doctrine. of popular sovereignty is the product of the sixteenth and seventeenth centuries. It emerged as an expression of resentment of the people against the despotic authority of the kings and their reliance on the theory of Divine Right. Popular Sovereignty attributes ultimate sovereignty to the people. This theory, first hinted by John Locke, was later expounded by Rousseau and it became the slogan of the French Revolution. According to Rousseau, the State came into existence

12. Garner, J.W., *Political Science and Government*, p. 160.
13. Laski, H.J., *Grammar of Politics*, pp. 62-63.
14. Gilchrist, R.N., *Principles of Political Science*, p. 94.

by explicit or tacit agreement. Explicitly, people said, "We want to be a State, a community." For Rousseau the State and the people were one. Having created the State, the people ought to control it and change it as they pleased, for whenever an individual decided that be belonged to a people, he already had decided that his people should be sovereign and that, being sovereign, they should run their own affairs. This is the doctrine of popular sovereignty.

The doctrine of popular sovereignty was propounded by Jefferson in the American Declaration of Independence and was incorporated in the Preamble of the Constitution by asserting that government derived its authority from the consent of the governed. An echo of it is found in Abraham Lincoln's First Inaugural Address: "This country, with its institutions, belongs to the people who inhabit it. Whenever they shall grow weary of the existing government, they can exercise their constitutional right of amending it, or their revolutionary right to dismember or overthrow it." This is Rousseau's theory of popular sovereignty in radical form. Since then popular sovereignty has become, as Bryce says, "the basis and watchword of democracy."[15]

In spite of our unflinching democratic faith in the dogma of popular sovereignty, it must be admitted that it is highly vague and indeterminate. We fail to determine and definitely say who these sovereign people are. Do we mean the entire unorganised mass of people living in the State, including women, children, idiots, insolvents and criminals? If so, then the sovereignty of the masses has no meaning in practical politics. The mass of the people cannot be organised and without organisation they constitute a mob, a babel of tongues, who can act neither actively nor effectively. Organisation is the foundation of sovereignty. But if people become organised and follow their leaders, where is their sovereignty? Sovereignty of the people, Gettell says, by the very definition of the State, is a contradiction in terms. If by the State we mean a people organised for law within a definite territory, "some organisation and method of government is the legal one, otherwise no State exists."[16]

It has been suggested that popular sovereignty refers to the sovereignty of the electorate. But sovereignty of the electorate has no legal basis unless it is expressed through channels prescribed by the constitution. The voters, in a representative form of government, do not themselves exercise actual sovereign power. They elect their representatives and it is through them, as members of the legislature, that the sovereign power is expressed. It, therefore, embraces manhood suffrage and the control of the legislature by the representatives of the people. But as a matter of reality, the control of the legislature rests in the parliamentary majority party which is determined by the majority of the voters who had elected them. Out of this majority party, too, emerges a ruling coterie who wield actual power. "The sovereignty of the people, therefore, can mean nothing more than the power of the majority of the electorate in a country where a system of approximate universal suffrage prevails, acting through legally established channels, to express their will and make it prevail."[17] Opinion, otherwise expressed by voters, however powerful that opinion may be, is not valid unless clothed in legal form.

15. Bryce, *Modern Democracies,* Vol. I, p. 143.
16. Gettell, R.G., *Introduction to Political Science,* p. 100.
17. Garner, J.W., *Introduction to Political Science,* p. 165.

The exercise of suffrage is not a true indication of popular sovereignty. In a modern democratic State not all the people are entitled to vote, and many who are entitled to vote are disinterested in the political process. They remain inarticulate. Therefore, the actual electors form a much smaller portion of the entire population. According to Gettell, not more than one-fifth of the population in any modern State are voters and within that number a majority would be but little more than one-tenth of the citizens.[18] Even these one-tenth of the citizens are not legally sovereign. Popular sovereignty cannot be equated with sovereignty of the electorate.

The idea of popular sovereignty is, indeed, highly confusing. At the same time, we cannot ignore the popular appeal it has. Ritchie, and other political thinkers[19] have tried to establish that the ultimate repository of political power is always found in the mass of the people. The State exists for the people and the mechanism of the State, that is, government, should function in accordance with the wishes of the people. While sovereignty in the legal sense may not be placed in the people, yet they are potentially a check on the legal sovereign. No legal sovereign can for long brush aside the will of the people. If it does, there are possibilities of revolution. In fact, the tendency with every modern State is to make legal sovereignty responsive to the popular demand as quickly as possible. We cannot, under the circumstances, ignore the force of "popular sovereignty." Gilchrist, however, suggests that "popular control" better indicates the idea underlying popular sovereignty.[20] This is a correct analysis and the modern democratic States have developed certain institutional devices, as referendum and initiative, to manifest the will of the people. Also, there are consultative councils and advisory bodies which surround every department of government in a democratic State and all matters pertaining to a department are referred to the relevant advisory body for its opinion and advice.

'De jure' and 'de facto' Sovereignty. Distinction must also be made between *de jure* and *de facto* sovereignty. *De jure* sovereignty is the legal sovereignty and it has its foundation in law. Its attribute is the right to govern and command obedience. But it may so happen that the *de jure* sovereign may not be able to command obedience while someone else, whose identity may or may not be recognised by law, is actually obeyed. That person or body of persons who actually exercises power, and who, for the time being, is able to enforce obedience, or to whose commands voluntary obedience is given by the bulk of the people, is called the *de facto* sovereign. The *de facto* sovereign may not be a legal sovereign. The criterion of sovereignty is actual obedience to command. Bryce says that "the person or body of persons who can make his or their will prevail whether according to the law or against the law: he, or they, are the *de facto* ruler, the person to whom obedience is actually paid." The *de facto* sovereign may be a usurping king, or a dictator, or a priest or a prophet, "in either case the sovereignty rests upon physical power or spiritual influence rather than legal right." Let us take a familiar example. On October 28, 1922, when Mussolini's Black Shirts marched on Rome, the legal sovereign was Parliament. Mussolini became Prime Minister in the prescribed manner. Immediately

---

18. Gettel, R.G., *Introduction to Political Science,* p. 100.
19. Refer to Sidgwick, H., *The Elements of Politics,* p. 630.
20. Gilchrist R.N., *Principles of Political Science,* p. 95.

after his appointment, he ruled Parliament and the country through Parliament. Parliament still remained the legal sovereign, but the actual or *de facto* sovereign was Mussolini. The commands which Parliament issued came from Mussolini and they were enforced by him as the leader of the Fascist Party. The legal sovereign did what it was told to do. Hitler, too, occupied a similar position in Germany. He controlled the legal sovereign—Reichstag—and he was the actual or *de facto* sovereign, or, to use Bryce's term, the practical sovereign. The Reichstag was a subservient organ to record formal approval of Nazi policy. Stalin, who in his lifetime was transformed into a superman possessing supernatural characteristics, was really the actual sovereign in the USSR for about three decades. He controlled the Government and the Party both. Collective leadership at any of these levels was just a myth.

History abounds in examples of *de facto* sovereignty. Many instances can be cited when legally constituted sovereign power was displaced in consequence of revolution or explusion by a usurper. The Bolshevik regime in Russia, following the Revolution of 1917, is the most familiar example, in recent times, of *de facto* sovereignty. Likewise Bachha Saka usurped the throne of Afghanistan after the flight of King Amanullah and became the *de facto* sovereign in that country. Italy's conquest of Abyssinia and General Franco's usurpation of power in Spain are other illustrations of *de facto* sovereignty. General Naguib's *coup d'etat* in Egypt and the abdication of King Farouk is also illustrative of *de facto* sovereignty. Nasser succeeded Naguib. The events in Iraq, Pakistan, Sudan, Burma, Bangladesh, Afghanistan, and in many other countries, particularly in Africa, tell the same story.

The *de facto* sovereign is, thus, the strongest active force in the State and capable of making its will prevail. But the *de jure* and *de facto* sovereignty should ultimately coincide, otherwise there is a danger of conflict between them. Garner says, "The sovereign who succeeds in maintaining his power usually becomes in the course of time the legal sovereign, through the acquiescence of the people or the reorganisation of the State, somewhat as actual possession in private law ripens into legal ownership through prescription."[21] New laws are made in order to give a definite status to the *de facto* in order to expedite the extinction of the previously existing *de jure* sovereign. The *de facto* sovereign himself, too, will not like to continue his authority based exclusively upon physical force for an indefinite period of time. There is, as Bryce has said, "a natural and instinctive opposition to submission to power which rests only on force."[22] The new sovereign will, therefore, endeavour to make his *de facto* claim converted into a legal right, because sovereignty established and exercised on a legal basis makes obedience spontaneous and enduring.

The *de facto* sovereignty will, thus, eventually procure *de jure* sovereignty. The principal criteria of *de jure* sovereignty within the State are success, the passage of time, and the establishment of a tradition. There is also another very important form of external recognition, the willingness of other States to exchange ambassadors and establish diplomatic relations. The most recent examnple is recognition of the Baltic States which

21. Garner, J.W., *Introduction to Political Science,* p. 168.
22. *Studies in History and Jurisprudence,* Vol. II, p. 516.

had seceded from the erstwhile Soviet Union and declared themselves independent and Sovereign states. Withholding of recognition by a great power may contribute to the fall of a *de facto* Sovereign power. Woodrow Wilson practically doomed the regime of Victoriana Huerta in Mexico in 1913 by refusing recognition. Customarily, recognition is granted to any regime indicating capacity to rule, as in the case of Bangladesh and Afghanistan. India was the first country to recognise both the new regimes. Occasionally, however, there may be opposition to a regime for the manner it captured power as in the case of Hureta, or for the philosophy underlying the new government as in the case of the Soviet Russia and the People's Republic of China.

The jurists of the Analytical School, however, outright reject the distinction between *de jure* and *de facto* sovereignty. They do not accept sovereignty in any other form or context except legal sovereignty, that is, what can be expressed in terms of law and sustained by law, "An unlawful sovereignty is a contradiction in terms", they assert. Austin has, accordingly, suggested that it would be more appropriate to use the terms, *de jure* and *de facto*, in respect of government rather than sovereignty.

AUSTIN'S THEORY OF SOVEREIGNTY

The Juristic analysis of sovereignty has a history stretching back to the Roman empire. The Roman jurists worked out a theory of *Imperium* and found the source of law in the will of the prince. In modern times the development of the theory of sovereignty coincided roughly with the growth of the State in power, functions and prestige. From Bodin, through Hobbes and Bentham, this juristic idea reached its climax in John Austin as contained in his lectures on Jurisprudence, published in 1832. Austin endeavoured to build up an exact juristic terminology and to present a clear outline of the organisation of a government's legal power.[23]

The theory of sovereignty, as enunciated by Austin, depends mainly upon his view of the nature of law. Law, according to Austin, is a "command given by a superior to an inferior.[24] From this definition of law he develops his theory of sovereignty in the following words:—

"If a *determinate* human superior, not in the habit of obedience to a like superior, receives *habitual* obedience, from the *bulk* of a given society, that determinate human superior is sovereign in that society, and that society (including the superior) is a society political and independent."[25]

Austin's doctrine of 'sovereign' may be reduced to the following propositions:—

(*i*) That there is, in every political and independent community, some person or body

23. Sabine, G.H., *A History of Political Thought,* p. 654. 24.
24. Austin says, "Every positive law, or every law, simply and strictly so called, is set by a sovcreign person or a sovereign body of persons to a member or members of the independent political society wherein that person or body of persons is sovereign or supreme."
25. Austin then proceeds: "To that determinate superior the other members of the society arc dependent. The position of its other members towards that determinate superior is a state of subjection or a state of dependence. The mutual relation which subsists between that superior and them may be styled the relation of sovereign and subject, or the relation of sovereignty and subjectivity."

of persons who exercise sovereign power. Sovereign power is as essential in every political society "as the centre of gravity in a mass of matter."[26]

(*ii*) That the sovereign is a determinate person or body of persons. "He is not necessarily a single person: in the modern western world he is very rarely so; but he must have so much of the attributes of a single person as to be determinate."[27] The State for Austin is a legal order in which there is a determinate authority acting as the ultimate source of power. Sovereignty, therefore, neither resides in the general will as Rousseau conceived, nor in the mass of the people, nor in the electorate, as none of them is a determinate body. Nor has the sovereignty of God or gods any significance in the business of the State. It is concerned with man and every State must have a determinate human superior who can issue commands and create laws. Hence human laws, and not divine laws, are the proper subject of State activity.

(*iii*) That such a determinate human superior must not himself obey any other higher authority. His will is supreme over all individuals and associations and he is subject to no control, direct or indirect. The determinate human superior may act unwisely, or dishonestly, or in an ethical sense, unjustly, but for the purpose of the legal theory the character of his action is unimportant. So long as laws emanate from the legal sovereign, they are commands which must be obeyed.

(*iv*) That the sovereign receives habitual obedience from the bulk of the community. That is to say, obedience must be a matter of habit and not merely occasional. Obedience rendered to an authority for a short time does not make it a sovereign. Austin's thesis is that obedience to the sovereign authority must be continuous, regular, undisturbed and uninterrupted. Moreover, obedience rendered to the sovereign must not necessarily be from the whole of the society. It is enough for purposes of the sovereign power if it comes from the bulk of the society—its large majority. Where habitual obedience from the bulk of the society is not forthcoming there is no sovereign power. Thus, sovereignty involves not only the submission of the many but also its permanence.

(*v*) That command is the essence of law. Whatever the sovereign commands is law, and law prescribes to do certain things and not to do others. Failure to obey laws, as commanded, is visited by a penalty.

(*vi*) That the sovereign power is indivisible. It is a unity and is incapable of division. Division of sovereignty means destruction of sovereignty.

In brief, Austin's analysis of sovereignty embraces the existence of the supreme power which is determinate, absolute, illimitable, inalienable, indivisible, all-comprehensive and permanent. It is subject to no limitation or command by any other superior person.

But Austin's theory is a lawyer's view of sovereignty and it has been subjected to a searching criticism, particularly by Sir Henry Maine and other historical jurists.[28] Sovereignty, according to Maine, does not reside in a determinate human superior. "A despot with a disturbed brain," he says, "is the sole conceivable example of such

26. Maine, H., *The Early History of Institutions,* p. 339.
27. *Ibid.,* p. 351.
28. Refer to Sidgwick, H., *Elements of Politics,* Appendix (A), p. 651.

sovereignty."[29] Maine emphasizes the existence of "vast mass of influences, which we may call for shortness moral, that perpetually shapes, limits, or forbids the actual direction of the forces by its sovereign."[30] He cites the example of Ranjit Singh, ruler of Punjab, whom Maine characterised as an absolute despot apparently possessing qualities of Austin's conception of the sovereign power. Ranjit Singh, Maine says, "could have commanded anything; the smallest.disobedience to his commands would have been followed by death or mutilation."[31] Yet, Ranjit Singh never "once in all his life" issued a command which Austin could call a law. "The rule which regulated the life of his subjects were derived from their immemorial usages, and these rules were administered by domestic tribunals, in families or village communities."[32] Even a despot like Ranjit Singh, Maine concludes, dare not issue a command which would compel an unwilling people to change their deep-rooted habits and customs. If he does it, he will confront the risk of revolution. Ranjit Singh's laws were primarily derived from customs, usages, and religious injunctions and they were administered by the village *panchayats* (councils). But it is not only in regard to "oriental society" that Maine finds Austin's analysis inadequate. In the "world of western civilisation," he says, no sovereign, however despotic, could disregard "the entire history of the community, the mass of its historic antecedents, which in each community determines how the sovereign shall exercise or forbear from exercising, his irresistible coercive power." Austin's conception of a determinate sovereign is also inconsistent with the well-accepted ideas of political and popular sovereignty. It ignores the power of public opinion and does not take into consideration the existence of political sovereignty, which is now believed as the ultimate sovereign power in a State. Sir Henry Maine, accordingly, concludes that it is a historical fact that the sovereign has never been determinate.

The Federal State presents another difficulty about vesting sovereignty in a determinate person or body. Sovereignty is indivisible and the sovereign body which has the power to amend the Constitution cannot be described as a determinate body. In the United States, for example, the constitutional powers of government are divided between the federal government and governments of the 'states' as the constituent units are named there. No change can be made in the Constitution without amending it. The Constitution amending body is Conventions or two-thirds majority of each House of Congress which may propose an amendment, and State legislatures or State Conventions which ratify them by a prescribed majority. In India, too, powers between the Central Government and the State Governments are divided and changes therein can be brought about by the process specified in the Constitution for amending it. The Constitution amending authority is sovereign, but this sovereign authority is diffused. There are three methods of amending the Indian Constitution. In some cases it is a simple majority of both the Houses of Parliament, in others, which are specified in the Constitution, it is the two-thirds majority of the members present and voting in each House of Parliament plus a majority of the total membership in each House, and ratified by the legislatures of one half of 'States,'

29. Maine, H., The *Early History of Institutions,* p. 359.
30. *Ibid.*
31. *Ibid.*, p. 380.
32. *Ibid.*, pp. 380-81.

constituent units, and for the rest it is a majority of the total membership in each House of Parliament and a majority of not less than two-thirds of the members present and voting in each House of Parliament. But the Constitution may itself limit the Constitution amending authority. Carl J. Friedrich maintains that where the constitution amending power is vested in the Legislature, "limitations are usually imposed upon it."[33] In France, an amendment of 1884 provided that the republican form of government should never be made the subject of proposed revision. Article V of the United States Constitution prescribes that no State, without its consent, can be deprived of its equal representation in the Senate.

Austin's definition of law that it is a "command given by a superior to an inferior," which forms the basis of his theory of sovereignty, cannot be accepted as a simple truth. Laski says that to think of law as simply a command is even for the jurist "to strain definition to the verge of decency."[34] No sovereign can ignore the existence of customary law which has grown through usage in every country. Customary law is not the fiat of a determinate superior, and in earlier stages of society laws were seldom, if ever, positive commands of a sovereign. Ranjit Singh, to again quote Maine, "never issued a command which Austin would call a law. He never made a law and never did or could have dreamed of changing the civil rules under which his subjects lived."[35] Even a sovereign legislative assembly, like the British Parliament, dare not pass a law which aims to violate the established customs and traditions of the country. MacIver has aptly said that "State has little power to make custom, and perhaps less to destroy it, although indirectly it influences customs by changing the conditions out of which they spring."[36] Custom is not a deliberate statute; it is the outcome of ages and even an autocrat must be the guardian and servant of customs, if he desires to obviate the possibilities of a revolution.[37] For, custom, "when attacked, attacks law in turn, attacks not only the particular law which opposes it, but what is more vital, the spirit of law-abidingness."[38] Austin himself was fully conscious of the force behind customs and maintained, "whatever the sovereign permits, he commands." Austin argued that customs, unless enforced by courts of justice, are merely "positive morality"; rules enforced by opinions. But as soon as courts of justice enforce them, they become commands of the sovereign, conveyed through the judges who are his delegates or deputies.

The concept of law, prior to the Analytical School, conveyed the notion of order first and then the notion of force. The Analytical Jurists, on the other hand, lay down unhesitatingly that the notion of force has priority over the notion of order. Austin lays too much emphasis on force and prescribes that disobedience of law is visited by a penalty. It means, in the words of the Analytical School, that people obey laws for fear of punishment. The modern view is that we obey laws not because their disobedience is accompanied by punishment; we obey them because there is in us the spirit of law-

33. Carl J. Friedrich, *Constitutional Government and Democracy,* p. 143.
34. Laski, *H., A Grammar of Politics,* p. 51.
35. Maine, H., *The Early History of Institutions,* p. 382.
36. MacIver, R.M., The *Modern State,* p. 160.
37. Gilchrist, R.N., *The Principles of Political Science,* p. 114.
38. MacIver, R. M., *The Modern State,* p. 161.

abidingness. Laski says, "The notion of command" in law "is contingent and indirect and the idea of penalty is, again, save in the most circuitous way, notably absent".[39] He holds that the individual conscience is the only true source of law. Austin's conception is also out of tune with a Welfare State. In a Welfare or Social-service State the content of law is of great importance than the source of law. We obey it, because it promotes social solidarity, as Leon Duguit says. He carries his argument to the extent that laws are not created by the State, but it is the laws that create the State. Krabbe discovers the spring of law in the community's sense of justice.

Austin's theory is further criticised on the ground that it invests the sovereign with absolute and illimitable powers. The Pluralists maintain that the State is an association like various other associations and, therefore, the sovereign authority cannot be invested with unique sovereign powers. They oppose the Austinian doctrine of a single and unified sovereignty, and emphasize the importance of associations, which are, for their purposes, as sovereign as the State is for its purpose. Sovereignty, accordingly, is neither unity nor absolute. It is diffused and hedged all around within and without the State. Externally, Austin's sovereign power is limited by the prescription of International Law, and the concept of internationalism has made it still more incompatible. Austin's theory of sovereignty, therefore, is now regarded not only a legal fiction, but a baneful and dangerous dogma which should be expunged from the literature on international relations. Laski is even of the opinion that the notion of an independent sovereign State is, on the international side, fatal to the well-being of humanity. It is a bold, but realistic statement which Laski makes and the developments since World War I (1914-18) testify it. Today, the States constitute an international society and it is commonly realised that the increasingly vast problems which concern the well-being of humanity are not local but international. The problems of food, health, education, and population are in essence local problems, but their solutions are found in the deliberations of international organisations like the W.F.O., the W.H.O., the UNESCO, etc.—all agencies of the United Nations. Even the restoration of order and establishment of lawful government within the country has become an international concern.

It is, impossible, under the circumstances, to accept the legal theory of sovereignty as valid for political philosophy, as it postulates for the sovereign such powers as cannot in fact be exercised. Moreover, it narrows down "the meaning of vital terms to a content which, if maintained, would be fatal to the existence of society."[40] We cannot accept law, which is an important factor in the life of the State, from the purely legal point of view. Law must be built upon general social environments. To separate it from all these forces and influences is to defeat the very purpose of law. It should, however, be admitted that as an analysis of strictly legal nature of sovereignty, Austin's is clear, and logical.

PLURALISM

The growth of associations, discharging various functions, in modern times provoked a revolt against the monistic theory of sovereignty and led to the political pluralism which

39. Laski, H., *A Grammar of Politics,* p. 62.
40. Hsiao Kung Chuan, *Political Pluralism*, p. 8.

constitutes one of the most remarkable movements in recent political theory. The monistic theory endows the State with a unitary sovereign power, either as the source of political authority as such or as the source of legal authority. It is the source from which law emanates which is supreme over all individuals and associations within its territorial limits, and is extremely independent of others. Monism regards all other associations as the creation of the State and dependent for their continued existence upon the will of the sovereign power. The functions which these associations perform are those that are conceded to them by the sovereign power.

The pluralists, on the other hand, declare that if a political theory is to be "philosophically true, scientifically sound, morally righteous, legally implicit in codes and decisions, and practically convenient," it must recognise the personality of a corporation as a real and spontaneous entity, with an inherent life and activity of its own. Social life is organised and finds expression through numerous associations which do not derive their existence or rights from the State. The State is, therefore, a federation, "an interlocking union of groups, assisting the discovery of self by each man with his diversified nature."

The pluralists regard the monistic theory of sovereignty as a pernicious and futile doctrine. The pluralistic State is simply a State in which there exists no single source of authority that is all-competent and comprehensive. There is no unified system of law, no centralised organ of administration and no generalisation of political will. "On the contrary, it is a multiplicity in its essence and manifestation, it is divisible into parts and should be divided." Pluralism, in brief, undertakes to transform the State. It criticises and "discredits" the State as it is, and seeks to reduce it from its place of "honour to servitude."[41] Lindsay, for example, says, "If we look at the facts it is clear enough that the theory of sovereign State has broken down." Laski, who was the most vehement critic of the monistic theory, said, "It is impossible to make legal theory of sovereignty valid for political philosophy." He was of the definite opinion that "it would be a lasting benefit to political science if the whole concept of sovereignty were surrendered,"[42] or, as Krabbe puts it, "the notion of sovereignty must be expunged from political theory."

Pluralistic Theory Explained. Laski says that sovereignty is neither absolute nor a unity. It is pluralistic, constitutional and responsible. He asserts that man's social nature finds expression in numerous associations or groups pursuing various ends—religious, social, economic, professional, political and recreational. The State is one of these groups and no one of these groups is superior, normally or practically, to others. All associations, which enter into the life of man, arise naturally and spontaneously and all act, within the sphere of their respective activities, independently of State control. Though the State is a primary and most important association, yet it can only claim to be *primus inter pares,* or first among equals. Being only one among many associations, the State has no rightful claim to eminence and it cannot be the sole repository of power or focus of loyalty. If it is sovereign, so are other associations within their spheres of activity, and man's loyalty

41. G.D.H. Cole, who is one of the central figures in advocating Pluralism, writes. "But as man has made the State, man can destroy it; and as man has made it great, man can restrict it. Moreover, as man has made the State, man can make something greater, something more fitted to exercise a final sovereignty, or at least to provide a final court of appeal." As quoted in Hsiao's *Political Pluralism,* p. 35.

42. Laski, H.J., *Grammar of Politics,* p. 55.

to them is as abiding as it is to the State. It is also possible that his loyalty to some group or organization of which he is a member, may receive priority over his loyalty to the State. There are Communists whose loyalty to their Party is stronger than their loyalty to their country. Members of the Society of Friends have a conscientious objection to being conscripted into the army, because they consider it morally wrong to fight for one's country. The State, accordingly, cannot in any important sense be said to be sovereign in its relations to other associations which come into existence independently of the State and function exclusively by themselves.[43] Each association has its own laws and government and it exacts obedience to those laws independently of the State.

The pluralists reject the distinction, which is so neatly made, between the State and government. They insist on a realistic Political Science and consider the distinction between the two as an artificial product of legal reasoning and logical refinement. Duguit is the foremost in this respect. He asserts that juristic entities, being legal fictions, have no place in realistic as distinguished from metaphysical discussion. We only know the government as a matter of reality and as it functions actually. The immediate power belongs to the government and the State and government are in fact the same. Laski also speaks of the State as the government and he rejects, likewise, the legalistic theory of the personality of the State. American political scientists substitute the State by a political system which in itself is a unit of the social system. Robert Dahl says that almost every human association has a political system and he even includes families in his definition of a political system.

The pluralistic theory, thus, finds its practical explanation in the bewildering variety of associations and groups which exist to promote the social, industrial, political and other varied interests of man. All these groups, as Laski says, determine, "quite largely, his choice of friends, of opportunities, of a career."[44] They plan his activities and provide him with opportunities for the expression of his desires. "They seek to give him mastery of the event, to enable him, in concert with like-minded men, to control the environment to a destiny he wants."[45] Society, in fine, far from consisting of a mass of isolated individuals, is actually a web of associations and groups that link men and women with one another. The old concept that society is an association of individuals in a common life does not hold good any longer. It is a "nation of joiners." Pluralism is, thus, a natural accompaniment of the "atomistic" view of society and human freedom. To put it in the words of Ernest Barker, the State is more an association of individuals, already united in various groups "for a further and more embracing common purpose."[46] It means that the State is only one among many other forms of human associations, and, as compared with other associations, it has no more superior claims to the individual's allegiance. The State and the associations and groups, as Maitland says, are the species of the same genus.

43. Coker, R.W., *Recent Political Thought,* p. 504; also refer to *A History of Political Theories. Recent Times,* Edited by C.E. Merriam and H.E. Barnes, pp. 89–98.
44. Laski, *Grammar of Politics,* p. 256.
45. *Ibid.* p. 257.
46. Ernest Barker, *Political Thought in England from Herbert Spencer to the Present Day,* pp.175–83.

The fact that society contains many associations has a number of consequences. First, it takes individuals out of a state of isolation and gives them a change to participate in the common endeavour, that is, the good of man and society. Secondly, it permits citizens to have a variety of loyalties and allegiances, thereby preventing the possibility that they might live under a single source of authority. Finally, "a network of voluntary associations stands as a 'buffer' between the relatively powerless individual and the potentially powerful state."[47] The pluralists, thus, consider the State as essential in the life of the individual as other associations composing society are. They are not against the State, but would discard the sovereign State with its absolute and indivisible power. They denounce coercive government and dispute its right, and even its power to compel obedience. They believe that the various associations and groups fulfil the many and diverse wants of the individual and help to make his life whole and rich, and, accordingly, assert that any interference on the part of the State, and for that matter of the government, in the independent existence and fuctioning of these associations is not only undesirable but defeats the purpose for which the State came into existence and continues to exist. Greaves says that the State is a system of order and, as such, it requires a body of rules "to provide in their certainty and predictability a foundation for order." It needs organs to make these rules and to interpret them. Clearly it is also necessary that the State should have at its command the use of physical force to ensure obedience to its rules. But "Order is merely a prerequisite for the achievement of ends which the members of the association have in common and in realization of which the state may be an instrument for realizing."[48] The State is not merely a system of order. It is a cooperative organization for the promotion of the well-being and development of the personalities of its members.

The central idea of Pluralism has been summed up by Gettell. He says, "The Pluralists deny that the State is a unique organisation; they hold that other associations are equally important and natural; they argue that such associations for their purpose are as sovereign as the State is for its purpose. They emphasize the inability of the State to enforce its will in practice against the opposition of certain groups within it. They deny that the possession of force by the State gives it any superior right. They insist on the equal rights of all groups that command thc allegiance of their members and that perform valuable functions in society. Hence sovereignty is possessed by many associations. It is not an indivisible unit; the State is not supreme or unlimited." All this may be reduced to the following bare analysis:—

1. The parts of the State are as real as the whole. The State is, therefore, distributive, not collective.
2. The distinction between the State and government is not real. Both are the same. The State does not command, it serves and is a public or social service organization.
3. The State is one among other groups which man needs to fulfil the purposes of his life. His allegiance is, accordingly, not unified. It is divided and diffused. His allegiance to the State may conflict with his allegiance to other associations, and may even take priority over his loyalty to the State.

---

47. Andrew Hacker, *The Study of Politics, The Western Tradition and American Origins.* p. 25.
48. Greaves, H.R.G., *The Foundations of Political Theory,* p. 14.

4. The State is not in any way a mysterious formation with supernatural or metaphysical characteristics. Omnipotent sovereignty is not true to facts. It is not unitary, but federal.
5. The State can serve its purpose by and through goodwill alone. It cannot destroy associations and groups, as it cannot create them. Nor can it enforce its will against the opposition of associations and groups within it. Since the State expresses the will or purpose of the human beings within it, it "does not enjoy any necessary pre-eminence for its demands," as Laski puts it. As the State is only one of the many associations to which the individual happens to belong, "politically there is no such thing as sovereignty at all", he concludes.

Development of the Theory. The theory of pluralism originated in the writings of Otto V. Gierke and F.W. Maitland in the last quarter of the nineteenth century, although earlier political thinkers, too, had recognised the part associations played in the life of man. The doctrine of Gierke and Maitland is that various associations, which exist within any society, are instinctive to man. They are not hypothetical, fictitious or created from without. Each association has a real personality and a collective consciousness and will. Each is independent of the State and may be even prior to it. According to Gierke, all such associations have their own rights, duties and functions. He argues that "the State should accept the common point of view that permanent associations have rights and duties as groups, whether or not the State has accepted them as corporations."[49]

Various Sociologists have also criticised the traditional structure of society. They regard the political side of the life of man as only one part of human activity and, accordingly, would seek to concentrate on group life in its various manifestations. Emile Durkheim argues for the restoration of the ancient occupational groups as a definitely recognised public organisation. "We have at present," he maintained, "no clear principles and no clear juridical sanctions through which to determine relations between employers or employees and the public."[50] The activities of any profession could be regulated only by a group embracing its functions and needs, such as a guild or a trade union. The professional groups must, therefore, be established for securing the economic regulation of all such professions and for purposes of political representation. Geographical representation, it is asserted, had lost its political, economic and social utility and, as such, geographical divisions should be replaced by vocational divisions which will reflect more accurately the various social interests.

There are other writers who have emphasized the autonomous rights of particular groups or who support some special type of social organisation. They protest against the omnicompetence of the State. Figgis criticises the efforts of the modern political leaders, "to invade the proper spheres of such essential social groups as churches, trade unions, local communities, and the family." The State, he says, did not create the family nor did it create the churches; nor even in any real sense can it be said to have created the clubs or trade unions, nor in the middle ages, the guild or the religious order, hardly even the universities or the colleges within the universities; they have all arisen out of the natural

49. As quoted in R.W. Cokers *Recent Political Thought,* p. 504.
50. *Ibid.,* p. 506.

associative instincts of mankind, and should all be treated by the supreme authority as having a life original and guaranteed to be controlled and directed like persons, but not regarded in their corporate capacity as mere names."[51] Figgis gives to the State a superior right over all other associations, but this superior right is only for coordination and adjustment.

Laski recognises complete automony for all associations. He emphasises that the parts of the State are as real as the whole. "We do not proceed," he says, "from the State to the parts of the State on the ground that the State is more fundamentally unified than its parts, but we, on the contrary, admit that parts are as real and as self-sufficient as the whole."[52] The essence of his arguments may be stated in his own words. He says, "But because society is federal, authority must be federal, also."[53] Laski assails the moral validity of the doctrine that attributes sovereignty to the State. The State, in his opinion, has no right to the allegiance of an individual except in so far as his conscience assents to. "The claim of authority upon myself is....legitimate proportionately to the moral urgency of its appeal."[54] He further said, "The only State to which I owe allegiance is the State in which I discover moral adequacy; and if a given State fails to satisfy that condition, I must, to be consistent with my own moral nature, attempt experiment....Our first duty is to be true to our conscience."[55] He tersely summed up, "We give to this particular group (the State) no particular merit."[56]

Laski would, thus, deny to the State any superior claim over other associations. He would even condition obedience to its authority. His general view is that the "sovereignty of the State will pass, as the divine right of the kings had its day." The State will continue only to coordinate the functions of various other associations without any right to assume omnipotence. Powers, in this way, will become coordinate instead of being hierarchical, and authority federal.

There are many other contemporary political writers who have advocated Pluralism—MacIver, Lindsay, Barker, G.D.H. Cole, Miss Follet and others. MacIver, for example, accepts the State as an association like various others within the community, although it exercises functions of a unique character. He gives the State an essential character of a corporation possessing "definite limits, definite powers and responsibilities." The business of the State, in his opinion, is merely to give "a form of unity to the whole system of social relationship." Barker does not accept the conception of the "real personality" of groups, but he admits that permanent groups within society existed prior to the State, and each of them has a corporate character and functions of its own. The State to him is a group of groups or a community of communities.

Evaluation of the Pluralistic Theory. What the Pluralists assert is true to a great

51. Figgs, J.N., *Churches in the Modern* State, p. 47.
52. Laski, H., *The Problem of Sovereignty*, p. 9.
53. Laski, H., *A Grammar of Politics*, p. 271.
54. *Ibid.*, p. 349.
55. *Ibid.*, p. 289.
56. Laski, H., "The Personality of Associations," *Harvard Law Review* xxxix (1915-16), p. 426, and as quoted in R.W. Coker's *Recent Political Thought*, p. 508.

extent. Our life is a group life and modern society is honeycombed with such organisations. No one can deny that voluntary groups and associations play an important role in the local and national life of the people. Man is not merely a citizen. He has his duty to the family, to the community and to himself. He owes allegiance to all such associations as make his life full and contribute to his well-being. A healthy society is one in which the individual has an abundance of opportunities for pursuing his own particular interests in collaboration with others. Accordingly, in general, the greater the number and variety of associations, the better will be his opportunities.

The Pluralist theory is a protest against the elevation of the State to mystical heights. Hegel viewed it as "God on earth" and invested it with not only supreme legal, but also supreme moral authority. Pluralism demarcates and limits the functions of the State and defines its authority. It accepts the State at par with other associations and demolishes the edifice of its glorification which Hegel built. Miss Follett in her book, *The New State*, sums up the merits of pluralism as follows:

1. The Pluralists "prick the bubble of present State's right to supremacy. They see that the State which has been slowly forming since the Middle Ages with its pretences and unfulfilled claims has not won either our regard or respect."
2. "They recognise the value of the group and they see that the variety of our group life today has a significance which must be immediately reckoned within political life." They also repudiate the notion that the groups are given authority by the State.
3. "They plead for a revivification of local life." The pluralists, thus, aim at decentralising authority and feel that the most imminent of our needs "is the awakening and invigorating, the educating and organising of the local unit."
4. "The Pluralists see that the interest of the State is not now always identical with the interests of its parts."
5. Pluralism is "the beginning of the disappearance of the crowd."
6. Finally, pluralism "contains the prophecy of the future because it had with keenest insight seized upon the problem of identity of association, of federalism."

But it may be noted that these associations can exist, grow, and achieve their objects only within the framework of the State, and that we cannot abandon the doctrine of the sovereignty of the State. Without sovereignty there can be no State and without the State we cannot have variety of associations, because for the collective life of man there must be some political organisation. If the State is to be abolished and replaced by autonomous associations, it is "not far removed from a condition of theoretical anarchy, in which each individual's conscience is the arbiter of his action."[57] Figgis described the State as the Society of "Societies" and assigned to it "a distinctive function and a superior authority" as an agency of coordination and adjustment. He asserted that one of the chief values in the several smaller groups consists in the fact that they foster loyalty to the State. To quote Figgis again, "It is largely to regulate such groups and to ensure that they do not outstep the bounds of justice that the coercive force of the State exists."[58]

The pluralists, in fact, have not attempted to make these groups independent of the

57. Gilchrist, R.N., *Principles of Political Science,* p. 104.
58. As quoted in Coker, R.W, *Recent Political Thought,* p. 513.

State. The State, Gierke says, "is distinguished from other social bodies by its position above them; for the State alone there is no limit through a higher collective existence; its will is the sovereign general will, the State is the highest *Machtverband*.[59] Paul Bancour regards the State as the sole representative of general interests and national solidarity. He would assign to the State the duty of preventing any group from acting aggressively towards other groups and its own members. Lindsay recognises the State as the "organisation of organisations." Miss Follett criticises the pluralists' conception of the State as "competing" for the citizen's loyalty. Even Laski did not propose to get rid of the State altogether. He recognised the distinction between the State and an association and defined the State as "the association to protect the interests of men as citizens." He agreed that "to satisfy the common needs, it must control other associations to the degree that secures for them the service such needs require." He also accepted the need of the "ultimate reserve power of the State." Laski finally conceded: "And however much we may reduce the direct administrative capacity of the political State, the fact remains that once it is charged with the provision of services which men stand in common need, it has their interests in trust to a degree with which no other body can, at least in a temporal sense, compete. Even if we abstract from the modern State the final control of international affairs, the civic area of internal matters that is left seems, at any casual glance, overwhelming."[60]

We may, then, conclude that in spite of their convincing arguments, the pluralists fail to "expunge" the notion of sovereignty from political theory as they claim. There is yet another interesting and perhaps somewhat surprising fact to note. "While most Pluralists have *sought* to drive sovereignty out of the front door of their new society, they quietly *smuggle* it again through back door, more or less disguised, but nevertheless a sovereignty." Such, indeed, is the case with Krabbe's "legal community" ruled by the sense of right, Duguit's monistic principle of "social solidarity", and Cole's "democratic supreme court of functional equity." The pluralists attempt to abolish sovereignty, but are finally compelled to restore it. There is always some ultimate authority in society, whether we find it in "natural law", "in reason", in "social solidarity", or in the individual's "sense of right." As soon as we admit the existence of an ultimate power, we must provide a channel for its expression, that is, a "determinate person", as the jurists say, "through whom the voice of the common good is heard." The pluralists may refuse to call this channel the sovereign person, but the fact is that with whatever name we may designate it, sovereignty is still sovereignty. It does not lose the quality of supremacy, no matter by whoin and in which manner it is exercised. In fact, the pluralists are not out to destroy sovereignty, but to recognise it so that the political power shall become the true expression of the community. "To destroy sovereignty", as Hsiao says, "is as dangerous as it is futile."[61]

The possession of power does not mean its perpetual exercise whenever the sovereign's command is opposed. If the opposition is resolute and determined, common sense and good judgment may suggest it to the sovereign to give way. If he does not, perhaps the

59. *Ibid.*, p. 512.

60. Laski, H., *The Problems of Sovereignty,* p. 75.

61. *Political Pluralism,* p. 140.

cost would be too great, disproportionate to the satisfaction of vindicating the law. Would it have been wiser to meet the Indian demand for *Swaraj* (independence) and Egyptian nationalism with wholesale military repression instead of granting independence to both the countries? The sovereign will always hesitate in taking drastic action. It is easy to recall many occasions on which the sovereign has given way before group pressure. The behaviour of the legal sovereign can best be explained by his dependence on the political sovereign. If the political sovereign has not been reduced to impotence as the mere tool of a dictator, he hangs over the head of the legal sovereign like a sword of Damocles. Even a dictator is afraid of his future and will hesitate to take an action which is likely to jeopardise his existence. MacIver appropriately says that "all governments depend simply upon a margin of strength, represented by the balance of opinion in their favour" and "an act which reduces the margin weakens its authority entirely out of proportion to the turn over of opinion.[62] If the legal sovereign flouts public opinion, when the voters finally act, they will entrust legal sovereignty to a different set of men and so reverse the unpopular policy of repressive actions.

But it does not mean that the entire pluralistic criticism of the monistic State is a vain attempt. The pluralists have done a useful service by emphasizing individual freedom and introducing the group into political thought. They have pointed out the way to a more concrete method of social organization than that hitherto generally employed. Sovereignty, they insist, must not be too narrowly political or legal. It must be representative of the diversity of social purposes—economic, religious, cultural, and other interests as well. In this way, sovereignty becomes the real and living manifestation of social purposes. The authority of such a sovereign is vastly more extended and ultimate than any sovereign power conceived by monistic lawyers who always take a narrow and abstract view of it. Such a conception of sovereignty retards the forces of absolutism set into motion by Hegel and his followers.

CHARACTERISTICS OF SOVEREIGNTY

The traditional distinctive attributes or characteristics of sovereignty are: permanence, exclusiveness, all-comprehensiveness, inalienability, indivisibility, and absoluteness.

Permanence. Sovereignty is permanent and it continues uninterrupted as long as the State exists. Changes in government do not mean cessation of sovereignty. Bearers of the authority of government may change, but the State endures and so does sovereignty. It does not cease with the "death or temporary dispossession of a particular bearer or the reorganisation of the State, but shifts immediately to a new bearer as the centre of gravity shifts from one part of a physical body to another when it undergoes external change."[63]

Exclusiveness. The sovereign power is exclusive and there is none to compete with it. There can be only one sovereign power in a State which can legally command the obedience of its inhabitants. To hold otherwise would be to deny the principle of the unity of the State and "to admit the possibility of an *imperium in imperio*."

62. MacIver, R.M., *The Modern State,* p. 292.
63. Garner, J.W., *Political Science and Government,* p. 170.

All-comprehensiveness. Sovereignty is universal in character and it extends to all persons and associations within its territorial limits. It is co-extensive in its operation with the jurisdiction of the State and comprehends within its scope all persons and things in the territory of the State. The modern State does not recognise the existence of any rival within its jurisdiction. There can be neither any person, nor any organisation, however universal, which can affect the sovereignty of the State.

The only exception to the universality of sovereignty is the extra-territorial jurisdiction allowed to embassies. An embassy is subject to the law of the State of which it flies the flag and the ambassador and his staff are amenable, within the premises of the embassy, to the law of their own country. The law of the State in which the embassy is located does not apply to it. It must, however, be remembered that the extra-territorial sovereignty is only a matter of international courtesy and is, under no circumstances, a limitation on the sovereignty of the State. If any State wishes, it can deny this privilege and history provides many such examples.

Inalienability. The sovereignty of the State cannot be alienated. Liber has said that "sovereignty can no more be alienated than a tree can alienate its right to sprout or a man can transfer his life and personality without self-destruction." The State and sovereignty are essential to each other. But when the State cedes a part of its territory, it does not mean that the State has lost its sovereignty. It is, on the other hand, "an excellent example of the working of the sovereignty of the State. All that happens is that, whereas formerly there was one State, now, with such cession, there are two States."[64]

Closely connected with inalienability is the attribute of the imprescriptibility of sovereignty. This means that sovereign power cannot be lost with the lapse of time by the non-exercise of such power. "Sovereignty cannot be lost," says Garner, "by mere lapse of time, as property in land may be lost by prescription at private law."

Indivisibility. The pluralists believe in the duality of sovereignty. The legal sovereignty aims at its unity. It is asserted that sovereignty is indivisible and division of sovereignty means destruction of sovereignty. Jellinek has remarked that the notion of a "divided, fragmented, diminished, limited, relative sovereignty" is the negation of sovereignty. If we accept the pluralist point of view and concede sovereignty to all associations and groups, it is simply to paralyse the existence of the State. The existence of several supreme wills, each equally capable of issuing commands and exacting obedience, would obviously result in conflicts, disintegration of the State, and ultimately in its extinction. Wherever it may reside, sovereignty "is an entire thing: to divide it is to destroy it. It is the supreme power in a State, and we might just as well speak of half a triangle as of half a sovereignty."[65]

But all do not subscribe to the view that sovereignty is unity. The question of divided sovereignty was brought into prominence when the United States of America emerged as a Federation. A federation is normally the result of a union between hitherto sovereign States. It is one of the essential features of a federation that while agreeing to a union, the federating units must preserve their individuality. The subjects of administration are,

64. Gilchrist, R.N., *Principles of Political Science,* p. 110.
65. As quoted in J.W. Garner's *Political Science and Government,* p. 173.

accordingly, divided between the newly created central government and the federating units. At the time of adopting the Constitution, it was generally held by the publicists in the United States that both the central government and the units of a federation remain sovereign within their own respective jurisdiction and sovereignty, as such, was divisible. This theory was strongly supported by Hamilton and Madison. It was endorsed by the Supreme Court in *Chisholm* v. *Georgia* (1792) wherein, it was held that "the United States are sovereign as to all the powers of government actually surrendered by the States while each State in the union is sovereign as to all the powers reserved." This theory of dual sovereignty received the approval of such eminent constitutional lawyers as Judges Cooley and Story and political writers as De Tocqueville, Hurd and many others. "There is no question," says Hurd, "that the statesmen of all sections who made the constitution of the United States understood that political sovereignty was capable of division according to its subjects and powers."

This is not a correct estimate of sovereignty in a federation. A federal union does not envisage two States. It makes only one State and, therefore, one sovereignty. The units of a federation are not really States. It is a misnomer if they are named so. They are subordinate lawmaking bodies with guaranteed powers. They are not sovereign, but autonomous within their sphere of powers as the national government is within its own sphere of jurisdiction. What is divided in a federation, between the centre and units, are the powers of government, and not sovereignty. Those who believe in the division of sovereignty confuse the State and government. Calhoun says, "There is no difficulty in understanding how powers appertaining to sovereignty may be divided and the exercise of one portion be delegated to one set of agents and another portion to another, or how sovereignty may be vested in one man, in a few or in many. But how sovereignty itself, the supreme power, can be divided ... it is impossible to conceive."

Where, then, do we discover sovereignty in a federation? The jurisdiction and powers of legislatures at the centre and in the units, called states both in the United States and India but Provinces in Canada, composing a federation are limited. They derive their authority from the Constitution and each gives legal expression to its will within prescribed limits. If they attempt to go beyond the powers therein enumerated, the courts are likely to hold such an act invalid. The legal sovereign in a federation is the body which can amend the Constitution and by doing so, gives commands to every other organ of government. The amending body is supreme; legislatures are subordinates. It is, however, important to note that in a federation the Constitution amending power is indeterminate. There is no single point or body in which such authority can be said to reside. Laski has said, "The discovery of sovereignty in a federal State is, practically, an impossible adventure."[66] It may, therefore, be concluded that sovereignty is a quality of the State. Like the honesty of a man or the beauty of a flower, it does not need to be located.

Absoluteness. The sovereignty of the State is absolute and unlimited. It is subject to no legal limitations, either internally or externally. Without sovereignty there can be no State. It is the supreme characteristic of Statehood. Sovereignty, therefore, implies absence of any restraint on its authority, either from within or without. To hold otherwise is to

66. Laski, H.J., *A Grammar of Politics,* p. 63.

create some higher power by which the sovereign authority is limited. Absoluteness of sovereignty also implies its universality, permanence and indivisibility.

All this is true in terms of law, but there is no such thing on earth as absolute sovereignty. It is through human agency that the sovereign power is expressed and exercised. Man can never be perfect and independent. Dependence is his very nature. How can he be absolutely sovereign then? Even the most despotic ruler is limited by his natural limitations. Sovereign power is, also, limited by what Gilchrist calls "human endurance." He says that the religion, education, character and environments of the sovereign must colour his actions.[67] There are, accordingly, limits of individuality, expediency and commonsense. Moreover, some writers hold the view that man possesses certain natural and inherent rights. These rights exist independently of the State and no sovereign can supersede them. Bluntschli says that even the State as a whole is not almighty, for it is limited externally by the rights of other States and internally by its own nature and by the rights of its individual members.

The doctrine that the State is absolutely supreme is fallacious and even dangerous. We have already discussed the nature of political sovereignty and the vast mass of influences which perpetually shape, limit or forbid the actual direction of the forces of society by the sovereign. There are some who even maintain that sovereignty is limited by the prescriptions of divine law. Sir Henry Maine tried to establish that the sovereign can, under no circumstances, act contrary to the immemorial customs and long-established traditions. No autocrat, to repeat, be he Ranjit Singh, or Galeazzo Visconi, can compel an unwilling people to change their deep-rooted habits and customs. He is always confronted with the risk of revolution. Nor has any State so far devised a machinery for controlling thoughts. In fact, none has gone as far as this, though the devise of brain-washing is there. Finally, there are limitations imposed by the rules of International Law and by the constitution of the State. The State may bind itself by treaty not to exercise its powers in certain ways. For instance, it might bind itself not to change its tariffs or the value of its currency without the consent of other States. Governments in constitutional States are set within legal orders which determine their bounds and may limit their activities. In the United States no government may pass an *ex post facto* law. Even the State, as it operates through the amending power, is subject to limitations. It may strive to enact law that runs so counter to the convictions of large number of its people that it fails to be obeyed and to receive the requisite "acceptance." Such was the case with prohibition in the United States.

What Sovereignty Means Today? We have dealt with so many conflicting issues involved in the concept of sovereignty. These conflicting issues are essentially the creation of nineteenth century jurists and political theorists who created such a maze that it becomes difficult to extricate oneself therefrom. The modern State is sovereign and it is now universally admitted that without sovereignty there can be no State. The sovereignty of the State is recognised, first, in a legal sovereign, which has *de jure*, that is, from the standpoint of law, the final word of command and whose authority, so far as law is concerned, is unlimited, absolute and supreme. With the establishment of the representative

67. Gilchrist, R.N., *Principles of Political Science,* p. 107.

system of government, a second sovereign makes its appearance and is called the political sovereign. Although the political sovereign is not known to law and remains indeterminate, yet the legal sovereign cannot brush aside what the political sovereign wills or desires to will. It is the *ultima ratio* and to its authority the legal sovereign must ultimately bow; otherwise it endangers its own existence. In a period of *political transition* or stress, some person or group in the community may become the centre of real or effective power, the actual or *de facto* sovereign. This sovereign may either destroy the other sovereigns, as General Ayub and Zia-ul-Haq did in Pakistan or General Daud, and his two successors in Afghanistan, or else, preserving them, as Hitler and Mussolini did bind them to his will. If the *de facto* sovereign establishes his stability, his *de facto* sovereignty will become *de jure* sovereignty. Whatever be the nature of sovereignty, we use the term with reservations.

The reservations are obvious and they hinge upon two important facts. First, the State is not society nor is it regarded as *sui generis*, one of its kind. It is one like many other associations which compose society no doubt, and it is the result of human endeavours and aspirations. Its purpose is to uplift man and men. This gives to the State an independent status and an eminent position in order to enable it to perform efficiently its functions of social regulation and adjustment. The authority of the State is, therefore, accepted and respected by all individuals and associations within it for what it does, that is, its services. Once this truth is realized, the second fact flows from it. Since the State is not the engine of power but service, the laws it makes are regulatory in nature rather than imperative in character. If the State continues to exist for the good life of man, naturally, it follows that "the test of a good law is whether it subserves the social purpose or not and whether it commands the willing allegiance of those whose interests it is made to promote." The Sociological jurists even believe that law is anterior and superior to the State. This belief directly challenges the assertion that the State makes law or law is what the sovereign wills. They uphold the sovereignty of law.

If we accept these two facts about the State and the nature of law, the term sovereignty assumes the role of authority and influence. All recent schools of thought concede that much to the State. And it is more appropriate to recognise it, if collective security and international peace are to be secured. The ultimate good of man and men cannot be cramped into the exclusiveness of States. It must transcend their boundaries. But will the States as a matter of reality, whatever be the extent of its logic and conviction, drop the use of the term sovereignty ? It is highly problematic in the context of the state of affairs in which we live, and sovereignty still remains sovereignty, as reminder of its orthodox characteristics.

When all is said, it cannot be denied that the recent political thought and a sharp swing towards internationalism have made a big dent on the traditional theory of sovereignty. No State can remain oblivious of public opinion for long, no matter whether it is national or international. If the welfare of the individuals and their happiness have any meaning, they must find full expression in what the State does within its territories and in relation to other States. If the State does not do so, it develops a split personality. Conflicting moral standards produce contradictions and maladjustments that cause violence, revolution, aggression and war. Laski has aptly said that "The notion of an independent sovereign State is, on the international side, fatal to the well-being of humanity. The way in which a State should live in relation to other States is clearly not a matter in which that State is entitled to be the sole judge. The common life of States is a matter of common agreement between States." The growth of a sense of international solidarity has been marked during the course of the present century by the establishment, not merely of a vast network of inter-governmental bodies, but also of a series of international functional organizations and of a large number of voluntary international associations. International conferences on International Language, and World Government have become accepted and normal events. In fact, any problem which affects or is likely to affect the peace and security of the world is a matter of common concern and it is obligatory on all the States to accept the decisions emerging therefrom. Events in relation to North Korea, Iran, Cuba and the Suez adequately illustrate it and the external aspect of the sovereignty of the State must now be examined in this context.

Moreover, the scope of subject matter that international conferences and agencies deal with has expanded tremendously. There is virtually no topic excluded from international treatment. For example, the discussion of values of national currencies has become common place. The same is true of self-employment policies, health measures, educational policies, the protection of human rights and so on. While sovereignty remains the foundation of all international activity, it tends to be interpreted restrictively in favour of broadening the bailiwick of international discussion. Decisions by majority votes in various organs of the United Nations and other organizations go counter to the principle of sovereignty.

It may, however, be noted that the United Nations is merely an external and organizational device designed to solve international problems. "Organizations succeed only," as Acharya J.B. Kriplani said, "when the mind behind them is reformed." In international affairs, too, reformation of the mind follows the most important rule of social conduct: do unto others as you would have others do unto you. If the nations adopt this simple rule of behaviour in their international transactions, sovereignty of the State in its legal manifestations stands modified. But statesmen do not always listen to the voice of reason in their international behaviour. Narrow loyalties and parochial considerations guide their decisions. Powerful States exploit their superior position by exercising undue influence in international politics and dominance over others. The United States assumed the role of World leadership after the successful end of the Gulf War and dismemberment of Soviet Russia. United States Secretary of State Warren Shristopher said, "We are undertaking the role of the World's most prominent power". The weaker States are, under the circumstances, left with no choice but to aggressively stir the sense of patriotism of their citizens and vigorously propagate to preserve the sovereignity and integrity of their motherland. They even symbolise the fatherland/motherland with some deity and publicly worship it and play with their emotions.

Despite all this, the United Nations itself is redefining the traditinal concept of Sovereignty. The U.N. Secretary-General Boutros Boutros-Ghali suggested that the centuries-old doctrine of absolute and exclusive sovereignty should be abandoned if the States are to remain and function within the comity of nations and from which there is no escape. Arguing that international cooperation is unavoidable and indispensable, he claimed "a pre-eminent status" for the United Nations. In his opinion the effectiveness of the United Nations had been undermined during the Cold War period because of conflicts and controversies between two super powers. An opporunity has now come to keep the United Nations "active and useful."

Similar arguments were proffered by Professor Lincoln Bloomfield, who suggested a revision of the U.N. Chapter of 1945 prohibiting United Nations interference in matters... essentially within the domestic jurisdiction of any State.[68] A revised definition of collective security, he said, would entail "an advance commitment by the community of nations... preferably as a whole ... to enforce agreed community norms against military aggression and other morally intolerable state behaviour... with force if necessary". He argued for the creation of United States Marshal type United Nations "peace officers" ready to untertake "armed humanitarian intervention" even against "threats created by technology".

What is noteworthy in the scheme envisaged by Dr. Boutros Boutros-Ghali and Professor Lincoln Bloomfield—the former a citizen of an African-Arab country that had supported the United States-United Nations action in the Persian Gulf, and the latter an American citizen and erstwhile United Nations expert in U.S. State Department and now representating a conservative academic "Think-tank" that it underscores a process of collective action resting "in both a broad international consensus and a deeply rooted American commitment." What Dr. Ghali and Professor Bloomfield have said in "tempered language", General Colin Powell, Chairman of the United States Joint Chief of Staff, has said in the plain language of a soldier. General Powell said, "No other nation on earth has the power we possess... we are obligated to lead... The last best hope of earth has no other choice. We must lead."

The practices of the United Nations clearly establish the fact that this association of sovereign democratic States in which a minority of elite members retain the privilege to make vital decisions, the United States unquestionally exercises the decisive role. As Indonesia's U.N. Ambassador has apply observed, "If you look at the Council (Security Council) in reality you will see that only one or two are making the decision." Therefore, "the merits of intervention anywhere in the world might be determined according to criteria preferred by the strongest member of the Security Council." Unless nations reach a consensus on giving up some sovereignty to achieve collective security, they will find themselves increasingly embattled by challenges to their ecconomic viability, their cultural integrity and indeed their sovereignty as well.

Sovereignty and Authority. The conclusion is now obvious. Even the Pluralists, with the exception of Laski, and possibly Lindsay, and Barker, in some of his writings, can be properly considered as having expunged the concept of State sovereignty from their theory. They all have assigned to the State a position, in this manifold organized society, not essentially different from that claimed by the traditional theorists. Nor is there anything in our experience so far to indicate that the internally sovereign State either is or will be an institution unnecessary for the further development of international cooperation and control. As Ernest Barker says, "A true internationalism... must recognize

68. Article 2, paragraph 7.

the existence of the State in all its fulness, and it must seek to comprehend States in its fold without any derogation from the fulness of their being."[69]

The most fundamental attack that can be made on the traditional doctrine of sovereignty is on the legal omnipotence which the term has acquired. But legal omnipotence has never existed. No sovereign authority has ever been omnipotent. Apart from various other limitations, the facts of nature and human behaviour limit the illimitable exercise of sovereign authority. If the term sovereignty is something really pernicious, we, then, need a term to express the fact that there must be, as Merriam puts it, "a concentration of recognized authority for the common good and of power of common action; a final authority capable of commanding the loyalty of the great mass of citizens."[70] The concomitant of political authority is its legitimacy. An authority is not legitimate if it cannot claim acceptance by and the loyalty of the bulk of the population. Authority which is not legitimate has little chance of surviving.

Thus, all individuals and political systems "need some sense of authority."[71] But authority must not be accepted blindly, uncritically or without limits. A legitimate authority, as Deutsch says, "has also an objective character. It implies that its commands will remain compatible with other values which we personally hold, and with the needs of the persons and communities which we hold dear."[72] Its test is performance, for authority is both the product of a political system and a condition for its future. Its effectiveness can be measured by the frequency and dependability with which it is obeyed in the absence of coercion. Absence of coercion implies consent and, therefore, loyalty. An authority which can evoke loyalty must be limited. It is limited in practice, says Solatu, "by many forces, moral, religious, scientific, by numerous social sanctions that both check and complete State action." There are hundreds of forces, he concludes, determining the sovereign will; how exactly they work is perhaps largely an academic question.[73]

SUGGESTED READINGS

Asirvatham., A.: *Political Theory,* Chap. X.

Austin, J.: *Lectures on Jurisprudence,* Vol. 1, Lecture VI.

Barker, E.: *Political Thought in England from Spencer to The Present Day,* pp. 175-83.

Bryce, J.: *Studies in History and Jurisprudence,* Vol. II.

Burgess, J.W.: *Political Science and Comparative Constitutional Law.*

Cohen, H.E.: *The Recent Theories of Sovereignty.*

Coker, R.W.: *Recent Political Thought,* Chap. VIII.

Deacy, J.Q.: *The State and Government.*

Elliot, W.Y.: *The Pragmatic Politics of H.J. Laski.*

Follett, M.P.: *The New State.*

Garner, J.W.: *Political Science and Government,* Chaps, VIII-IX.

69. Ernest Barker, *Political Thought in England from Herbert Spencer to the Present Day,* p. 246.
70. As cited by Roger H. Solatu in *An Introduction to Politics,* p. 104.
71. Karl W. Deutsch, *Politics and Government, How People Decide Their Fate,* p. 209.
72. *Ibid.*
73. Roger H. Solatu, *An Introduction to Politics,* p. 104.

Jouvenal, B. de,: *Sovereignty,* trans. J.F. Hunlington.

Gilchrist, R.N.: *Principles of Political Science,* Chap. V.

Hsiao, Kung Chuan : *Political Pluralism.*

Laski, H.J.: *Authority in the Modern State.*

Laski, H.J.: *Grammar of Politics,* Chap. II.

Laski, H.J.: *The Problem of Sovereignty.*

Lasswell, H.D. and Kaplan, A.: *Power and Society.*

MacIver, R.M.: *The Modern State,* Chaps. VI, VII, XV, XVI.

Magid. H.M.: *English Political Pluralism.*

Maine, H.S.: *Lectures on the Early History of Institutions.*

Maritain, J.: *Man and the State,* Chap. II.

Mattern, J.: *Concepts of State, Sovereignty and International Law.*

Merriam, C.E.: *History of the Theory of Sovereignty Since Rousseau.*

Merriam, C.E.: and Barnes, H.E. (Eds.): *A History of Political Theories, Recent Times,* Chap. III.

Rockow, L.: *Contemporary Political Thought in England,* Chaps. VI-VIII.

Ward, P.W.: *Sovereignty.*

9

CHAPTER

Relation between the Individual and the State

RIGHTS AND DUTIES

Meaning of Rights. The history of political thought points to a persistent belief among men that States ought to guarantee to individuals the enjoyment of a certain number of basic human rights, which constitute the essential conditions of "the good life." Rights are those conditions of social life without which man cannot be at his best or give of his best, what is needful to the adequate development and expression of his personality. Looked at negatively, rights are those opportunities the absence of which deprives man of something essential. A man without rights, absolutely dependent on the daily caprice of a superior authority, is a slave. All doctrines of freedom, therefore, assume the existence of rights and Laski has aptly said that every "State is known by the rights that it maintains."

There are certain bare necessaries without which man cannot live a life of his own. They are known as primary wants of life, and the higher needs of social life, for example, the need to have a family, the need to work in order to earn his living, the desire to live with his fellowmen, to express his opinion, and to share one another's weal and woe. Nature has, no doubt, given to man certain powers of action to satisfy his wants, but these powers are not devoid of reason. Power without discrimination and reason is another name for force. The basis of force is physical might, and might does not recognise rights. Use of might is not the way of common life, and a common life means a common good. The life of togetherness aiming at a common good demands that each man should exercise rationally his powers of satisfying his wants. He recognises that if he possesses the power to do a thing, so do others possess a similar power. He, accordingly, allows to others what he wishes for himself. Rights are, therefore, as Hobhouse puts it, "what we may expect from others, and others from us, and all genuine rights are conditions of social welfare. Thus, the rights anyone may claim are partly those which are essential to every man in order to be a rational human person, and partly those which are necessary for the fulfilment of the function that society expects from him. They are conditioned by, and correlative to, his social responsibilities."

Life, according to Aristotle, is not merely living but living well. If good life is the aim of man's life, then, its pursuit and achievement involves the fulfilment of certain conditions. It implies that every individual should be conscious of his own good and develop his powers of action to realise it. Secondly, he must be conscious of the good of others and help in creating conditions which lead to the development of their powers of action. Consciousness of this fact, namely, that individual good can be realised in common with the good of others, is the essence of rights. It is in this context that Laski defines rights as "those conditions of social life withotit which no man can seek, in general, to be himself at his best."[1] A right thus understood is an essential condition of the individual's self-development, as it is also a condition of social welfare. In the words of Bosanquet, "We have a right to the means that are necessary to the development of our lives in the direction of the highest good of the community of which we are a part." This right is recognised and sanctioned by society.

No Rights Outside Society. Two conclusions emerge from what has been said above. Firstly, rights are meaningless outside the organised society, because apart from communal life they are hopeless abstractions. If there is no society, there can be no rights. Robinson Crusoe had no rights on his lonely island. He was the master of all that he surveyed. There could be no limit to his freedom or activities. Limit to freedom arises only when there are others to exercise similar freedom. It is only in society that man recognises the freedom of others while exercising his own freedom. Recognition of this fact is the basis of rights, for our rights are the duties of others towards us and their rights are our duties towards them. In the words of Hobhouse, "Rights and duties, then, are conditions of social welfare, or as we define such welfare, of a life of harmony to this welfare; every member of the community stands in a double relation. He has his share in it. That is the sum of his rights. He has to contribute his share. That is the sum of his duty."[2] It follows that rights must be compatible with the common good expressed in "a complex of rights and duties linking men to each other."

Another way of saying this is that every right has a corresponding obligation or duty. If I have a right to work and earn my living, it is my duty to recognise the same right in others and concede to them their right to work and earn their living. I can enjoy my rights only if I respect the rights of others. "He that will not perform functions cannot enjoy rights any more than he who will not work ought to enjoy work."[3] My claim to rights arises from the fact that I share with others the pursuit of a common end and the common end is the good life of man and men. If I fail to perform my duty, it is for the State to see that I act as a moral unit of society. The State exists to maintain and coordinate the various claims of individuals.

Rights are, thus, claims that are socially recognised to make life happy, contented, harmonious, and, therefore, worth living. They are prior to the State as they fulfil the basic conditions of social life. The State does not create them. It only recognises, maintains and coordinates them so that all may realise the benefits of such rights and, in case of violation, may protect them. It is the primary function of the State to ensure that all equally enjoy their rights and create those conditions without which man cannot develop the powers inherent in him. It involves equal opportunities for all. Rights are a special kind of freedom, because they must be accorded to all men equally. If some people are

1. Laski., H., *A Grammar of Politics,* p. 91.
2. Hobhouse, L.T., *The Elements of Social Justice,* p. 34.
3. Laski, H., *A Grammar of Politics,* p. 95.

allowed to own property and others not, then property ownership is a privilege and not a right. Since the chief characteristic of rights is their equalitarian basis, it is necessary to define the basic rights and make them definite. When rights are formulated, neither the State nor the individuals may venture to trespass them. They command sanctity and, accordingly, are obeyed and enforced.

All we have said above about rights may be summed up as follows: —

1. Rights arise in society. They are the result of the social nature of man. Without society there can be no rights.
2. Every right has a corresponding obligation. My right is your duty and your right is my duty. Rights and duties are the same thing looked at from different points of view. They are two sides of a coin; they are correlative and can never be separated. This has been beautifully expressed by one of the writers. He says, "Rights without duties are like men without shadows: they only exist in fairy tales."
3. A right is not a claim. A claim is selfish in nature, as it affects the interests of a person or a number of persons. A right, on the other hand, is socially recognised aiming at the good of all and it has a social and moral end to serve. When I assert my rights, I do a public duty, because I guarantee to others what I claim for myself.
4. It follows that rights must be compatible with the common good. Society recognises only those rights which, in the last resort, are relative to some common good or moral good.
5. The State does not create rights. It simply maintains and coordinates those rights which are socially recognised. By giving such rights a legal sanction, the State ensures to every one the enjoyment of his rights, as rights have an equalitarian basis.
6. Rights must be definite and precise, hence, the necessity to define them. Rights do not remain rights when every individual has his own separate claims.
7. Rights have a tendency to grow. They must be consistent with the needs of man and the needs of man always change; they expand and so do rights. The dynamic nature of rights is manifested in their changing content.

CLASSIFICATION OF RIGHTS

Moral Rights. Rights are broadly divided into moral and legal rights. A moral right is that which is based on the ethical code of morality of the people, that is, what we think ought to be our rights. It extends "over the field of conduct and refers to all those actions and forbearances which it is our moral duty to perform." But a moral right is not supported by the laws of the State. Its sanction is the moral opinion of the community. If there is a breach of moral rights there is nothing legally to punish the recalcitrant. A *claim* is called a *right* not because it is just, but because it has been recognised by the State and can be enforced by any legal process or through the courts. Whenever we talk of moral rights we mean claims which can be converted into rights only when they have been recognised by the State. Moral claims even when designated as moral rights still lack the force to be enforced. It is my moral duty to help the poor, the needy, and the sick, because as a moral agent of society I must try to create conditions which may contribute to the social good. But if I fail in my moral duty, laws of the State do not take cognisance of it. It must, however, be remembered that a moral right has a moral reference with it. It is recognised and sanctioned by society. What is recognised and sanctioned by society must be sanctioned by laws of the State. No State, if it really does serve its purpose, can long afford to ignore things which are sanctioned by society. If it does, the citizens have a moral right to revolt against the authority of the State. History tells us that great reformers and leaders of the community had to battle against unjust laws and traditions in order to lift men to a higher moral level. Gandhi's mission in life was to moralise man and society and throughout his political career, first in Africa and then in India, he stood arrayed against tyranny of any kind, whether that tyranny was that of the State or of the individual.

Legal Rights. A legal right, on the other hand, is recognised and maintained by the laws of the State and is enforceable by a citizen in the court of law both against the government and other citizens. In simple words, legal rights are, what, in fact, are our rights. These rights are distinguishable from moral rights. Secondly, legal rights are uniform and open to all, irrespective of their caste, creed or colour. It must, however, be again emphasised that in a democratic State the government is sensitive to the pressure of public opinion and the legal and moral rights tend to harmonize and coalesce.

Legal rights are divided into (i) Civil Rights and (ii) Political Rights.

(i) **Civil Rights.** Civil rights provide for the fulfilment of the elementary conditions of social life, that is, rights which relate to the protection and enjoyment of life and property by individuals. Without them civilised life is not possible and they are regarded as essential to the free and progressive life of man. Their enjoyment is uuiversally guaranteed, because opportunities to all alike is the principle determining civil rights. Civil rights include the right to life and freedom from arbitrary arrest, freedom to acquire and hold property, to speak and write for publication, to meet publicly, to form associations for peaceful ends, to make contracts, etc. A well-organised State must protect the civil rights of its people against encroachments by both the individuals or associations of individuals, and by the State itself.

(ii) **Political Rights.** Political rights are not enjoyed by the individual in his personal or private capacity, but in his capacity as a citizen and they entitle him in the legal expression and administration of the sovereign power of the State. Political rights are the means by which an adult citizen is entitled, by the constitution and laws of the State, to participate in the affairs of the government of his country. They consist in the right to vote and elect, the right to be elected, the right to hold public offices, and so on. It is through the exercise of political rights that democracy operates and functions, and, it is only a democratic constitution which confers in absolute terms these rights on the people.

But the classification between the civil and political rights is not strictly adhered to, as there are certain rights which fall in both categories. For example, it is now generally recognised that the right to vote should belong to all adults, men and women. Then, certain rights, such as freedom of speech and assembly, are often regarded as being at once civil and political rights. Both civil and political rights aim to provide equal opportunities to all and, hence, the distinction between the two becomes hazy. Yet, this two-fold division has an important historical significance. Civil rights have existed and can exist even in those countries where political rights have been denied to the people. Political rights are the gifts of democracy and prerogative of the citizens of a democratic State.

Democracy is of two kinds, direct and indirect. Where direct democracy is operative, all the people enjoying political rights themselves participate in proposing laws and deciding on laws, in appointing the officers of the government and ratifying their policies and actions. But direct democracy is not obtainable now except in some of the *Cantons* of Switzerland. It can only exist in small States with limited areas and populations. Large States with huge populations have a system of indirect or representative democracy where citizens in possession of political rights elect their representatives and delegate to them the work of making laws, and out of them those who can command their confidence and have the ability to lead others, are entrusted with the work of the government. Some States having the apparatus of representative democracy have introduced some institutions of direct democracy, such as, the *referendum*, the *initiative* and the *recall*. The essence of a democratic government is that as many citizens as possible should share in the exercise of political rights, that there should be an equal opportunity for all citizens to be appointed to the highest offices in the government, and that the laws of the State should represent the will of the majority of the people. The majority which controls the government must respect and defend minority rights.

Each State decides what persons shall possess political rights and the extent of such rights. Aliens are everywhere debarred from the exercise of political rights. Similarly, all States exclude minors, criminals, and lunatics from the right to vote. Some States deny it to women. The age of the adults enjoying political rights also varies from State to State. Obviously, equal political rights for all are not possible. The State must organize its practical operations through the agency of its government efficiently and successfully and, accordingly, the right to participate in its affairs is given only to those citizens who possess the requisite mental and moral qualifications and unequivocally manifest, both in words and deeds, their loyalty and allegiance to the State of which they are citizens. The problem of the State, therefore, "in creating political rights is to secure an organization in which legal sovereignty will coincide as nearly as possible with political sovereignty, in which as many persons as possible may possess political rights as nearly equal as possible without destroying the efficiency of government, and, in general public opinion, may be made into law without tyrannizing over those who hold different opinions."[4] It means political rights must be exercised wisely, discreetfully and in a devoted service to the Society and the state of whcih they are citizens.

The Concept of Citizenship. The concept of citizenship goes back to the ancient Greek City-State of Athens where the population was divided into two distinct classes, the citizens and the slaves. The citizens, who just comprised 20,000 of the entire population, enjoyed both civil and political rights and they directly and actively cooperated in all the functions of the civil and military life of their State. A citizen was normally a soldier, a judge and a member of the governing assembly and all his public duties he performed not through a deputy but in person. The slaves, whose number was far in excess of the

4. Gettell, R.G., *Introduction to Political Science,* p. 154.

citizens, had no such rights and they suffered from all kinds of political and economic disabilities. Even the wisest of the Greeks regarded slavery as a natural institution and Aristotle considered it essential for citizenship and human progress. The slaves, in brief, were not entitled to the privilege of a citizen.

Much the same position continued in ancient Rome or in the European medieval free-cities, except that in the latter serfs took the place of the slaves. The rise of dynastic States in Western Europe around 1500 A.D again made the State the focus of sovereign powers, but the individual was still a subject, a recipient of orders and not a participant in the public affairs. The Glorious Revolution in Britain and the French Revolution reversed the scales and brought about a phenomenal change in the concept of citizenship. The theory of limited and free government recognised the brotherhood of man and claimed equality for all in the common fraternity. This view was powerfully supported by the sentiment of nationalism, which encouraged men to assume participation in the affairs of government as their right. The modern concept of citizenship is, therefore, the product of a limited government and of a sovereign State. It concerns the rights and privileges of the citizens of a State, as distinct from aliens.

A citizen may be defined as a full member of the State, enjoying, if properly qualified by age, residence, and other lesser requirements as necesitated by law, the fullest extent of rights and privileges in that State. As every right has a corresponding obligation, a citizen owes a duty to the State to provide the general well-being of his fellow citizens. He may even be called upon to sacrifice all that he has and all that he can claim to possess, including his life, to maintain the integrity and sovereignty of the State to which he belongs and owes allegiance. For the proper exercise of his rights and discharge of his duties, a citizen, to put it in the words of Laski, must make "contribution of one's instructed judgment to public good." To express it in another way, a citizen enjoys rights and owes duties to the State, which, *inter alia,* include defence of the State, maintenance of its unity and integrity, and provision of the general well-being and progress of the people with whom he shares his weal and woe.

Aliens and Citizens. An alien is not a citizen of the State in which he resides. He merely lives in another State or travels through it and owes allegiance to the State of which he is a citizen. In other words, an alien who owes allegiance to another State and whose loyalty and sympathy belong to a foreign country, is denied the enjoyment of political rights, and the laws of the State in which he temporarily resides do not permit him to participate in the politics of that country. Logically, it follows that if an alien has no rights, he owes no duties to the State in which he resides. He enjoys civil rights or most of them, obeys the laws of the State and pays all the taxes which the State may impose under law, but he owes no duties to that State. Some States, like the former Union of South Africa, subject aliens to various kinds of disabilities and may even debar them from owning property. In the United States, Canada and Australia, their Immigration Laws regulate the entry of the people of Asiatic origin. Though not quite similar, Britain, too, has recently regulated by law the entry of Indians and the people of some other countries and the rules made thereunder are unethical and humiliating. In Pakistan, the Ordinance promulgated in 1984 declared the Ahamediya sect of Muslims as "Non-Muslims" and they were denied even the basic rights including the right to ownership of property, the right to worship in Muslim mosques and use of Muslim epithets, the right to recruitment in Government services as also the right to exercise franchise and stand for elections. The Ahmediyas in Pakistan challenged the various provisions of the Ordinance, first in the High Court and later in the Supreme Court. The Supreme Court upheld the validity of the Ordinance in June 1993 and ruled that Ahmediyas are "not Muslims for the purpose of (the) constitution and law" in Pakistan. It means they are aliens and there are more than 50 lakh (5 million) Ahmediyas in Pakistan. When a country is at war, restrictions on aliens become pretty stringent, particularly on the citizens of the belligerent countries, who are called "enemy aliens" as distinguished from "friendly aliens", that is, citizens of States that are not at war.

Kinds of Citizenship. Citizenship is of two kinds, natural and naturalised. Natural citizenship is governed by the principles of *Jus Sanguinis* and *Jus Soli* or *Jus Loci*. According to the principle of *Jus Sanguinis* blood or descent determines citizenship. A child follows the nationality of his parents or one of them, regardless of the place of birth. But all States do not follow the principle of *Jus Sanguinis*. Some follow the principle of *Jus Soli* or the law of the soil. A child born in the State, where this principle is followed, becomes the natural citizen of that State, regardless of the citizenship of the parents. It is the place of birth alone which determines citizenship. The principle of *Jus Sanguinis* is older than the principle of *Jus Soli*. It was incorporated into the Roman Law. The principle of *Jus Soli* appeared at a later stage in response to the feudal theory of territorial sovereignty.

Majority of the States follow the principle of *Jus Sanguinis* as the basis of natural citizenship. There are, however, some States, for instance, India, Britain and the United States of America, which follow both the principles of *Jus Sanguinis* and *Jus Soli*. In these countries children born of citizen-parents become natural citizens whether born within the State or abroad. If born within the State, they are governed by the principle of *Jus Soli,* and if born in some other State the principle of *Jus Sanguinis* is the basis to determine their natural citizenship. Since there is no uniform principle followed by the States in determining natural citizenship, very often children acquire double citizenship at the same time. For instance, a child born of Indian parents on a visit to Britain acquires the natural citizenship of the country in which he is born in accordance with the principle of *Jus Soli* as well as that of India according to the principle of *Jus Sanguinis*. But on attaining the age of majority, he is free to retain the citizenship of the State of his choice and relinquish that of the other. One cannot be a citizen of two States at the same time.

Acquisition and Loss of Citizenship. Citizenship can also be acquired by an alien and it is called naturalised citizenship. Modern States differ widely in their attitude toward admitting aliens to citizenship by formal grant of naturalization. Citizenship conferred by this process "is gratuitous concession" on the part of the State to which naturalization is sought and it may be granted under prescribed conditions or may be refused for any reason which the State considers sufficient. In some States, the process is made easy and resident aliens are encouraged to acquire citizenship, in others the process is so difficult as to discourage the admission of new citizens. There are, however, some rules which are in usual practice.

The first is the rule of residence. All States prescribe a minimum period of an alien's residence in the State. In Britain and the United States it is five years whereas in France the period is ten years. In Japan the requirement of the minimum period of residence is waived if an alien married to a Japanese woman applies for naturalization. Secondly, an alien desiring naturalization is required to make a declaration on the prescribed form, of his intention to that effect. Thirdly, he must renounce his previous citizenship and take an oath of allegiance to the State of which he intends to become a naturalized citizen. Some States insist on the testimony of his good moral character, and that he should be solvent and financially sound to support himself. Some States require that the applicant should possess a working knowledge of the national language of the State.[5] Some States have imposed definite restrictions on the admission of persons of Asiatic origin or of certain races. Naturalisation may either be complete or partial. If a naturalised citizen stands at par with a natural citizen of the State in the enjoyment of his rights and privileges and there is no discrimination of any kind, naturalisation is complete. If discrimination is made between a natural citizen and a naturalised citizen in the enjoyment of rights and privileges, it is partial citizenship. For example, the Constitution of the United States of America does not permit a naturalised citizen to become the President of the State. Only natural citizens can occupy that august office.

With the acquisition of naturalization the citizenship of the parent State is lost. When a woman marries an alien, she generally loses the citizenship of her own State and acquires the citizenship of her husband's State. A person who enters into the service of another State and takes the oath of his office and allegiance to that State, he loses the citizenship of his original State. The laws of some States prescribe loss of citizenship of persons found guilty of heinous crimes, as treason and desertion from the army. The Constitution of India specifically prohibits the acceptance of a title awarded by a foreign government. If any Indian citizen accepts one, he violates the Constitution and forfeits his right to be a citizen of India until he relinquishes the title and reaffirms his allegiance to the country, and the government accepts such reaffirmation. But the common cause of loss of citizenship is expatriation, that is, relinquishment of citizenship. If a person naturalised in a State decides to again acquire the citizenship of his parent State and regains it, it is called repatriation. Repatriation may be voluntary or forced. If the State compulsorily repatriates a person from the State of his naturalization, it is forced repatriation. If it is of one's own accord, it is volunatry.

THEORIES OF RIGHTS

Various explanations of rights have been offered from time to time, but we consider only the following important theories:

1. The Theory of Natural Rights.
2. The Legal Theory of Rights.
3. The Historical Theory of Rights.
4. The Idealistic Theory of Rights.

5. In India an adequate knowledge of one of the Indian languages mentioned in Schedule VIII of the Constitution is required.

5. The Social Welfare Theory of Rights.
6. The Economic Theory of Rights.

The Theory of Natural Rights. The doctrine of Natural Rights is simple in explanation. It aims to emphasise that certain rights are so essential to any real personal life that they should be called "Natural". This idea rests on a belief in "Nature", as the original creating force which gave to every man the power of finding by reason the right principles on which to organise his life. These principles, it is claimed, are based upon the universal law, the law of nature, and are common to all people in all countries. They are the product of human nature, that is, all men are born with certain rights and these rights are inalienable.

The concept of Natural Rights originated in ancient Rome and came from the discovery that men of all races and countries living under Roman rule seemed to have some common rules of life, some objective standards of right and wrong given to them by the mere fact of their being men with human nature. This body of principles common to all men, the Romans called "Natural Law" and they based on it a considerable part of their legislation. Their principle of Natural Law finds its best explanation in the words of Cicero and therefrom flows the doctrine of Natural Rights. He said, "The existence of a universal and world-wide law, which is one with reason both in nature and human nature, and which accordingly knits together in a common social bond every being that possesses reason, whether God or man, the principle of natural law becomes recognition of intrinsic worth in human personality, with the necessary implication of equality and universal brotherhood." The Natural Law is, as such, the law of reason and is of universal application. It binds the people together in a common social bond by recognising the intrinsic worth in human personality. For the real personal life, equality and universal brotherhood are the two prerequisites.

In the Middle Ages, Natural Law was identified with the Law of God and of the Church and it no longer remained the assertion of the rights of man till it was revived in the seventeenth and eighteenth centuries. Locke was the first to restate it in purely philosophical terms, and he made it the source of political obligation. He assumed that certain rights were "natural" and, indeed, believed that the rights which the social contract was designed to protect were both natural to man and approved by God. "The Law of Nature", he said, "stands as an eternal rule to all men, legislators as well as others. The rules that they make for other men's actions must, as well as their own and other men's actions, be conformable to the Law of Nature, i.e., to the will of God, of which that is a declaration, and the fundamental law, of nature being the preservation of mankind, no human sanction can be good or valid against it." He also held that "the state of nature has a law of nature to govern it, and reason, which is that law, teaches all mankind who will but consult it, that being all equal and independent no one harm another in his life, health, liberty or possessions." The need for a civil society was felt, according to Locke, because of the presence of certain inconveniences in the state of nature and men agreed to transfer some of the rights in order to safeguard the remaining natural rights; life, liberty and property.

Locke's teachings had a profound effect on the Americans and the French, the former seeking to justify their struggle for independence and freedom from foreign control, and the latter seeking to justify revolt against arbitrary rule. The American Declaration of the Rights of Man stated: "We hold these truths to be well-evident that all men are created equal, that they are endowed by their creator with certain inalienable rights; that among these are life, liberty and the pursuit of happiness. That to secure these rights, governments are instituted among men, deriving their just powers from the consent of the governed; that whenever any form of government becomes destructive of those ends, it is the right of the people to alter or abolish it." Thirteen years later, these words of Jefferson echoed in the French National Assembly when it was declared that "the ignorance, the oblivion, the contempt of the rights of man were the only causes of public misfortunes and of the corruption of governments." The Assembly resolved "to state in a solemn declaration the natural, inalienable and sacred rights of man", which were equality in rights, liberty, property, security and resistance to oppression, together with the fact that sovereignty resides in the people.

These declarations gave a new emphasis to the doctrine of Natural Rights. While recognising the natural equality of men, they based consent as the only just basis for political obligation and set a norm for a free society wherein the happiness of man and his value of life would be universally revered. They also extended a promise to mankind, as Abraham Lincoln put it, "that in due time the weight shall be lifted from the shoulders of men, and that all should be given an equal chance" to determine their destiny. The later statements of Natural Rights drew their inspiration from these historic declarations of the Rights of Man.

The Sociological School, during recent times, has given a new meaning to the theory of natural rights. They reject completely the notion that natural rights are those which belonged to man in primitive society and that he brought them with him when the State was established. Natural rights, they maintain, are those immunities and freedoms of man which are conducive to the most effective functioning and rapid development of the social organism. What is natural must be in harmony with the essential conditions of existence and development of man. Natural rights, as Professor Giddings says, "are socially necessary forms of right, enforced by natural selection in the sphere of social relations; and in the long run there can be neither legal nor moral rights that are not grounded in natural rights as thus defined."

The doctrine of natural rights has been subjected to severe criticism. The term 'natural' has been given a variety of meanings and the concept of natural rights has, accordingly, varied with these interpretations. Since the term 'natural' is used without any precise meaning, there is no common list of natural rights, which may be acceptable to all the advocates of the theory; men have disagreed about rights, as they have disagreed about everything under the sun. For example, there is no unanimity of opinion, even in our own times, whether men and women are by nature equal. A British writer has claimed that six months scrutiny of a correspondence column revealed "a natural right to a living wage, a right to work, a right to trial by jury, a right to buy cigarettes after eight p.m., a right to camp in a caravan by the roadside, and a right to walk on the grouse moors of Scotland during the close season."[6] Then, rights cannot be independent of society and unless they

6. As quoted by J.D. Mabbott. *The State and the Citizen,* p. 58.

are recognised and upheld by the State there is no substance in them. The theory of the Contractualists that rights are pre-social or pre-political is untenable. Complete freedom for everyone is a political impossibility. Nature gives to individuals certain powers. These powers are not rights. They become rights when opportunity is given for their proper development and the State provides all such opportunities. Finally, there can be no inherent natural rights that are absolute under all conditions. Rights change with time and place and they do so according to the prevailing belief as to what is right and just. Some rights which were considered natural in the past, such as the right of revenge or the right to own slaves or large estates of land, have turned out not to be rights at all in other times and places, and societies function fairly well without these.

If by natural rights we mean those rights which are inherently for the good of man and which tend to create conditions necessary to lead a happy and full life and ensure the realisation of his potentialities as a human being, we agree with it and citizens must be guaranteed such freedoms. The State which does not guarantee these basic freedoms, denies to its citizens the very end for which it exists. Laski has aptly said, "Every State is known by the rights it maintains. Our method of judging its character lies, above all, in the contribution that it makes to the substance of man." Karl Deutsch ascribes to the concept of natural rights "an operational meaning."[7] He explains that natural behaviour is probable behaviour. It is "likely to occur whenever it is not prevented by artificial" obstacles, that is, by obstacles which are less probable and which can be maintained only by special efforts or arrangements." He defines natural rights as rights "which people are likely to claim whenever not specifically restrained from doing so, and likely to claim again as soon as the restraint ceases." Whether a particular right is a natural right in this sense — one that is claimed spontaneously at many times and places — is a question of fact and it is the task of Political Scientists to look at the facts "and to see whether and to what extent this is the case." Natural rights accepted as such "cannot be sold or signed away. By definition people will automatically claim it again as soon as no one stops them; and they will claim it anyway if they are strong enough." They are "imprescriptible" and "inalienable."

That there are certain basic rights, universal in nature, has been recognised by the Charter of the United Nations. The Charter has so much faith in the existence and reality of such rights that the clause about the promotion and encouragement of human rights and fundamental freedoms occurs five times in it. The Universal Declaration of Human Rights, passed and proclaimed by the United Nations Assembly on December 10, 1948, lays down a minimum standard of human rights based on the "inherent dignity" and the "equal and inalienable rights of all members of the human family." It affirms that all human beings ought to be treated as equals, and as having a fundamental right to individual liberty.

But if we examine the practice of a number of States which approved the Declaration, it would appear that they have interpreted very differently their common undertaking "to strive by teaching and education to promote respect for these rights and freedoms and, by progressive measures, national and international, to secure their universal and effective

7. Karl W. Deutsch, *Politics and Government; How People Decide Their Fate,* pp. 210–11.

recognition and observance." Soviet Russia refused to sign it, obviously for the reason that she did not believe in the principles of individual liberty as the majority of the members of the United Nations understood them. There are differences of practice, however, among the signatories too. "Americans would no doubt consider that the class distinctions which exist in Great Britain infringed the principle of equality, whereas the British and Americans could both be charged with infringements of the principle of equality between races."[8] General Ayub's Martial Law regime in Pakistan suspended all basic freedoms set forth in the Declaration and a complaint to this effect was made in a communication by the Chairman of the International League for the Rights of Man to the Secretary General of the United Nations.[9]

The World Conference on Human Rights, representing 160 countries that met at Vienna in June 1993, issued a declaration on the conclusion of its deliberations embodying its recommendations. It urged the United Nations and its relevant organisations to proclaim a "U.N. decade for human rights" to promote and protect these rights and create conditions for their full enjoyment by the people of the world.

It recommended that the U.N. General Assembly, when examining the report of this conference, expedite the proposal to establish the post of a High Commissioner for Human Rights. The incumbent of this office should be a senior official enjoying the full confidence and support of the Secretary General with the stature and resources necessary to give effect to new and important programmes outlined in the Vienna Declaration.

The conference called upon the International community to take necessary and effective steps to enhance cooperation to combat terrorism and its linkage in some countries to drug trafficking which aim at destruction of human rights, democracy, territorial integrity of States and destabilising of legitimately constituted governments. It pointed out that the countinuing acts of violence also aimed at undermining the quest for peaceful dismantling of apartheid.

The conference emphasised that democracy, development and respect for human rights and fundamental freedoms are interdependent and mutually reinforcing. It affirmed that the right to development is an inalienable, universal and integrated right. The conference expressed its dismay on "ethnic cleansing" and systematic rape of women in war situations creating mass exodus.

The Vienna conference was described as a kind of second universal declaration of human rights. L.M. Singhvi, the deputy leader of the Indian delegation, said, "This is the stuff of a new revolution. It is not as elegant, as precise, as terse, not as well put together as the earlier declaration of 1948, but it encompasses a whole range of developments which have taken place in the last 45 years, a whole range of concessions which have come to the threshold of human consciousness and whole lot of controversies which could not have been foreseen in 1948."

The Vienna conference was held at the appropriate time when human rights movement was beginning to consolidate and no proper stocktaking had been done since the last

8. Pickles, Dorothy, M., *Introduction to Politics,* p. 155.
9. *The Sunday Tribune.* Ambala Cantt., December 14, 1958, p. 1.

international conference held in the late 1950s. The final document that emerged from the 1993 conference is significant as it inspires all to go ahead with human rights as best as they can. But the most important aspect of this declaration is the acceptance that the right to self-determination does not mean the right to dismember another country.

The Legal Theory of Rights. According to the Legal Theory of Rights there are no rights which inhere in man; they are created and maintained by the State. Neither they are prior nor anterior to the State. The State formulates or defines rights, restricts their scope and provides guarantees for their enjoyment. Since the State is the source of all rights, there can be no rights without or against the State. To have rights against the State is tantamount to saying that the individual has no rights at all.

Such a theory of rights is not acceptable to pluralists and many others. Laski says that the State does not create rights, but only recognises them. Nor is it true, he says, that an individual has no rights against the State. The State must observe the rights of man and "it must give him those conditions without which he cannot be that best self that he may be."[10] It is not merely as a member of the State that the individual has rights. The State is one like various other associations of which he is a member, and all collectively create opportunities for him and contribute to his welfare. "Wherever men are banded together to perform a task that is part of the common welfare, that body so formed has rights as real, and as compelling, as the rights of the State."[11] To limit the rights of man because of his membership of the State alone "is to destroy his personality and not to preserve it."[12] A system of rights derived purely from law cannot be permanent. It implies that law is not the only source of rights. The real source of rights is our conception of right and wrong. "Rights," according to Plamenatz, "must have a foundation of right as against wrong." There is no security or civilised life if rights depend on the whims of the State and, for that matter, on the government. Laski even says that in the interest of the common good, it sometimes becomes the duty of the citizen to resist the State if it attempts to frustrate his rights. Any system of rights, as he puts it, must harmonise the three aspects of life. It must take into consideration the ideal claims of the individual for the common good; it must take cognisance of the reality of the claims of the association; and it must not be oblivious of the claims of the community on its constituent elements.[13]

The arguments referred to above are quite convincing. The Legal Theory does not give us a satisfactory explanation of rights. But all that the advocates of the legal theory say cannot be brushed aside. Rights which are not supported by the laws of the State remain only claims. Barker has correctly said that the State is the immediate source of rights. No State can for long overlook the claims which are deemed essential for the moral development of man. Once these claims are recognized, they become rights. Thomas Paine, a devoted champion of natural rights, maintained that every civil right grows out of a natural right, and natural rights, he defined, "are those which appertain to man in right of his existence. Of this kind are all the intellectual rights, or rights of the mind,

10. Laski, H., *A Grammar of Politics,* p. 93.
11. *Ibid.,* p. 92.
12. *Ibid.*
13. *Ibid.,* p. 141.

and also all those rights of acting as an individual for his own comfort and happiness, which are not injurious to the natural rights of others."[14] The essence of Paine's observation is that the representatives of the people should endeavour to win legal recognition for all our rights which have a moral basis. It is in this context that Laski made his classic statement that "Every State is known by the rights that it maintains." A right has, thus, both a moral and legal reference. "A typical right", as Bosanquet affirmed, "unites the two sides. It both is and ought to be, capable of being enforced at law."

The Historical Theory of Rights. The Historical Theory of Rights emphasizes that rights are the product of history. They have their origin in customs which once possessed practical social utility and passed on from one generation to another, ultimately having been recognised as inherent claims or rights. Ritchie says that "those rights which people think they ought to have are just those rights which they have been accustomed to have, or which they have a tradition (whether true or false) of having once possessed. Custom is primitive law." In explaining natural rights, advocates of the historical theory maintain that custom is their sanction. They are considered fundamental to the development of man, because they have been maintained by a long unbroken custom and the generations have habitually followed them: Habits are 'natural' as they grow. They are neither instituted nor are they invented.

Burke maintains that the French Revolution was based on the abstract rights of man, whereas the English Revolution was based on the customary rights of the people of that country. There is much truth in what Burke says. The French Revolution itself was the result of the conditions that prevailed in the country, but its slogan was liberty, equality and fraternity, the three abstract principles of universal application. The Glorious Revolution, on the other hand, was simply a reassertion of the historic liberties of Englishmen, which had been their heritage since the days of the Anglo-Saxons, and had found due expression in the *Magna Carta*, the Petition of Rights, and various other documents of constitutional importance.

There is much truth in the Historical Theory of Rights and many of our rights really find their origin in primitive customs. It does not, however, mean that the origin of all rights can be traced to customs and traditions. When rights are rigidly tied to customs alone, we altogether ignore the dynamic nature of society and the changing contents of rights. Rights change with the facts of time and place. History, as such, is not the only basis of rights and customs do not provide an absolute right or standard.

The Idealistic Theory of Rights. The Idealistic Theory of Rights is also known as the Personality Theory. According to this theory, rights are the external conditions essential to man's internal and real development. Krause describes the system of rights as "the organic whole of the outward conditions necessary to the rational life." Similarly, Henrici defines a right as "that which is really necessary to the maintenance of material conditions essential to the existence and perfection of human personality." In brief, the Idealistic Theory emphasises the creation of those conditions which help man to reach the fullest stature of his personality. Perfection of human personality is the end to which all rights are directed and subordinated. In other words, right to personality is man's fundamental

14. Thomas Paine, *Rights of Man,* pp. 32-34.

right and all other rights are derived from it. For example, the right to life, the right to liberty, the right to property, and all other similarly important rights are to be judged by their contribution towards the development of human personality. If I abuse any of these rights and retard my self-development, society is within its competence to deprive me of that right.

This explanation of rights discloses three important facts to which a reference has been made in the earlier part of this Chapter. The first is, that rights arise in society. As they arise in society they are inherent in the nature of man, and the inherent nature of man is to will his own good. To will his own good implies the good of others since isolated good of the individual is not possible. Secondly, every right has a corresponding obligation, that is, my right to self-development should not interfere with the right of development of others. Finally, individual rights are subordinated to the fundamental right of man's perfection. Society should see that the enjoyment of my rights helps me to attain the perfection of my personality. If any one of these rights does not help me towards reaching that end, society can deprive me of the enjoyment of that right. To sum up, my right of self-development is a similar right of self-development for others with whom I live an associated life. Personality is itself an element in the common good. Personality stands for "the fulfilment of man's vocation as a moral being" and rights are the means for the personal development or self-realisation. It is in this context that Laski says, "rights, in fact, are those conditions of social life without which no man can seek, in general, to be himself at his best." The system of rights is an organic whole which is moral in nature and helps to uplift the stature of man and society simultaneously.

Gandhi dedicated himself to the uplift of man and society simultaneously. He was out to moralise man and society. True morality, said Gandhi, must manifest itself in every action of the individual and also as a member of society. Both act and react upon each other. The Gandhian outlook may be reduced to a simple formula: "If you have to reform yourself you must do so while reforming society." This is also the essence of the Idealistic Theory of Rights.

The Idealistic Theory of Rights appeals to the moral and democratic mind of man, as it relates rights to morality rather than legality. Secondly, it does not subordinate the self-development of man to the social whole. Both act and react upon each other. The theory believes with Kant that no man is to be treated as a means to another's end; "it calls upon everybody to treat humanity in his own person and in the persons of others always as an end and never merely as a means." But the real difficulty arises in fixing the standards of moral freedom. What should be the conditions necessary for each individual for his fullest self-development? According to Gandhi it is the pursuit of truth and non-violence. But are these conditions of universal acceptance? Mankind has still to do much about it. Then, how are individual good and social good to be reconciled in case there is conflict between the two?

The Social Welfare Theory of Rights. The advocates of the Social Welfare Theory hold that rights are conditions of social welfare. They are the creation of society, and law, customs, traditions and the natural rights "should all yield to what is socially useful or socially desirable." What is socially useful should have for its test the greatest happiness of the greatest number. Take, for example, the right to speech. It is not an absolute right.

It is limited by the social needs of a coordinate body. Similarly, the right to property does not mean the right of the few to prosper at the cost of the many.

The Utilitarians, Bentham and Mill, are the real exponents of the Social Welfare Theory of Rights. They set up the principle of the greatest happiness of the greatest number and made it the criterion of utility. But utility, they believed, should be determined by considerations of reason and experience. Laski, too, accepts utility as the basis of rights, though he gave to the term a meaning which is consistent with the modified conditions of his times. He holds that the test of a right is utility, and the utility of a right is its value to all the members of the State.[15] The claims, he says, which the State must recognise "are those which, in the light of history, involve disaster when they are unfulfilled." Rights are not independent of society, but inherent in it. "We have them....for its protection as well as our own....Rights, therefore, are correlative with functions." We have rights so that we may contribute to the common good. My rights are built upon my contribution to the well-being of society. "I cannot have rights against the public welfare, for that, ultimately, is to give me rights against a welfare which is intimately and inseparably associated with my own."[16] Rights, as such, are built upon their utility to the individual and the community.

The Social Welfare Theory of Rights has much to commend. But one cannot say what social welfare actually means. Does it mean the greatest happiness of the greatest number, majority interest, or what is today understood to be the common good? In fact, much political wrong has been done during recent times to the individuality of man in the name of social good. The individuality of man and his rights have very often been sacrificed in order to extol social good in the name of social expediency. A social system which discounts individual personality and glorifies the common interest of society cannot continue for long. It is sure to provoke opposition from that section of society whose personality is crushed and rights frustrated.

The Economic Theory of Rights. Of recent origin is the Economic Theory of Rights and it finds its inspiration in the teaching of Karl Marx. It rejects the concept of natural and inalienable rights as also various other theories enunciated from time to time as an explanation of the nature of rights. Marx's thesis is simple and to a certain extent convincing too. He regards the State as a coercive agency to uphold the particular type of social organisation and law is a tool of the State that perpetuates and safeguards the interests of the dominant group in the society. Marx explained that political, social, religious and other institutions of any given historical era are determined by economic factors, which is essentially the mode of production. To each stage of production in the development of society corresponds as appropriate political form and an appropriate class structure and every system of production has given rise to two opposing classes, the exploiters and the exploited, the owners and the toilers — free man and slave, patrician and plebian, baron and serf, guildmaster and journeyman As in the ancient world the interests of the slave owners were opposed to that of the slaves, and in the Mediaeval Europe the interests of the feudal lords were opposed to that of the serfs, so in our times

15. Laski, H.J., *A Grammar of Politics*, p. 92.
16. *Ibid.*, p. 96.

the two opposing classes confronting one another are the employers and the workers, the exploiters and the exploited, and there is an uninterrupted warfare between the two, "now open, now concealed", as Marx has said.

Laski, too, mainly agrees with Marx's thesis and maintains that the way the economic power is distributed at any given time and place will shape the character of legal imperatives which are imposed on that time and place.[17] The economically dominant group in society controls and regulates the machinery of government and occupies all the key positions of power, authority and influence. The laws are so made and the policies of the governing class are so devised and formulated that they protect and further the interests of this group alone. It is a society of vested interests and relentless exploitation of the masses is its *raison d'etre.* Consequently, the dogmas of equality before the law and other fundamental rights of the people are only a cloak of inequality, in fact, slavery.

Rights are, as such, neither the product of human nature nor their origin can be traced to the hoary customs, or in their inherent utility, nor are rights the result of external conditions essential to man's internal and real development. The economic structure of society at a given period of time is the foundation on which the political system of a country is built and its legal framework formulated. In a capitalist society, the aim and nature of rights is to promote and foster the interests and privileges of the dominant economic group that owns productive forces, but is in a miscroscopic minority. For the masses rights are the instruments of their thraldom. Karl Marx finaly believes that rights can exist and flourish only in a classless society where all are equal and no one is an exploiter. He dismissed all talk of rights in a capitalist society and regarded fundamental rights, the pillars of democracy, the fetish of bourgeois jurisprudence.

There is much truth in what Karl Marx says and evidence of history is strong enough to support him. He opens a new vista of the nature and content of rights. But all that Karl Marx says is not correct. The laws of the State are the product of multiple sources and not alone the handiwork of the dominant economic class. It is an inescapable truth that rights can exist and flourish in a democratic setup which presupposes a society of equals and such a society is plural. It has been universally recognised now that economic democracy must precede political democracy and even the traditionally capitalist States have made determined efforts to make their political systems progressive, adaptable and flexible to meet the growing aspirations of the masses and provide all those amenities of life which can make a just and happy life for all. A just and happy life is the sum total of a complex of social forces in which equalising opportunity plays a vital role and brute economic disparities, that have plagued the society so far, are wiped out.

The concept of Economic Rights, as enunciated by Karl Marx, was faithfully reflected in the Constitutions of all the Communist countries, particularly in that of former Soviet Russia. But civil rights were subordinated to economic rights as they were to be in conformity to the interests of the working class and emphasised that the interests of the individuals and that of society were not incompatible. This is not the essence of rights. Laski says that rights are those conditions of social life without which man cannot be at his best or give of his best, what is needful to the adequate development and expression

17. Laski, H.J., *An Introduction to Politics,* p. 17.

of his personality. If inequality is iniquitous, economic equality alone and that, too, to strengthen a particular ideological system defeats the purpose of rights which aim to ensure all-round development of man and his personality. The true essence of rights is the creation of that atmosphere which is congenial for chiselling of man to be the best of himself. To rely exclusively on an economic factor and subordinating civil rights to economic rights is a lopsided effort that dwarfs man's personality.

Conclusion. There is not one single theory which can adequately explain the origin and nature of rights. Each theory is the product of its own time and in conformity to the genius of the people with whom the propounders of the theory were associated. There is some element of truth in all such theories. But there is one eternal truth that cannot be ignored. Individual good and social good go together. Society is an organic unity and welfare of the community is built upon the welfare of the individual; Both go hand in hand. This is the essence of rights. Welfare is all-embracing and well-feeding is one of its ingredients.

FUNDAMENTAL RIGHTS

The Bill of Rights. Rights, as we said before, are relative. They are limited by the rights of others and by considerations of social good. They also change with time and place. But there are certain basic rights which the civilised communities guarantee in normal times, because they are deemed fundamental to the existence and growth of man, and together with him of society. Without them life is sordid and meaningless. The tendency in a modern democratic State is to incorporate such basic rights in its Constitution so as to ensure their full enjoyment by all citizens without discrimination of any kind. A democratic government is representative, but the representative government is a government by the majority party, and it is possible that either as a result of political rivalry or by yielding to passion, it may curtail the cherished rights of the minority party or parties. In order to withdraw fundamental rights from the pitch of political controversy and to place them beyond the reach of majorities and officials they are embodied in the Constitution and given special sanctity. Their inclusion in the Constitution is a declaration of the fact that certain elementary rights of the individual are inviolable under all conditions and the shifting majorities in the legislature of the country should not be able to tamper with them. If they do, redress can be sought in courts of law. Courts become the custodian of fundamental rights.

A Bill of Rights, therefore, is a declaration of fundamental rights. It is a mechanism for the safeguarding of basic freedoms and may be defined as a series of rules generally embodied in a written Constitution setting forth the fundamental civil and political rights of the citizens and imposing certain limitations on the powers of the ordinary government, as a means of securing the enjoyment of those rights. They are enshrined in the Constitution to give them sanctity and special force. They cannot be invaded arbitrarily either by the legislature or the executive or any other authority. If it happens it is the duty of the courts to intervene and ensure the due observance of fundamental rights. In *Hurtado v. People of California*, Justice Mathews, of the United States Supreme Court, declared: "The limitations imposed by constitutional law upon the actions of Government, both state and national, are essential to the preservation of public and private rights notwithstanding the representative character of our political institutions. The enforcement of these limitations by judicial process is the device of self-governing communities to protect the rights of individuals and minorities as well against the power of numbers, as against the violence of public agents transcending the limits of public authority, even when acting in the name and wielding the force of government." Constitution is, thus, a check upon encroachment by any authority, especially the majority party in office, and the individuals. Judiciary is the unfailing guardian of the sanctity of the Constitution and it is its duty to uphold it. President Taft, of the United States of America, observed that constitutional safeguards "are the self-imposed restraints of a whole people upon a majority of them to secure sober action and a respect of the rights of the minority....In order to maintain the rights of the minority, and the individual and to preserve our constitutional balance, we have judges with courage to decide against the majority when justice and law require."

But in actual practice, the safeguards offered by a written Constitution for securing fundamental rights are not so straightforward as they might appear. Many of the rights accepted as fundamental at one time may become obsolete after some time. The obsolete rights continue to exist, because they are enshrined in the Constitution and constitutional changes are not easy to make, however great the need for such changes may be. Then, the Constitution requires interpretation. The American and Indian systems of judicial review disclose that it is a frail safeguard. The judges, while giving decisions, and in whatever legal dress such decisions are clothed, render political decisions and that, too, with a five to four majority in the United States and six to five in India as in the famous Golak Nath case.

All the same, no one can discount the political utility of the declaration of fundamental rights. It is true that fundamental safeguards alone do not ensure to a people the enjoyment of their basic liberties. But the guarantees for the fundamental rights, as embodied in the Constitution, are a visible expression of the nation's faith in the worth and value of man. They create a free atmosphere for the individual to rise to the full height of his stature. It is also an attempt to circumscribe the powers so that human freedom may not be subordinated to governmental functions. The powers and functions of government are so reconciled with the freedom of man that each may have the large freedom consistent with the demand of the social order. The Bill of Rights withdraws certain subjects from the vicissitudes of political controversy and defends minority rights. Laski says, "Bills of rights are quite undoubtedly a check upon a possible excess of the government of the day. They warn us that certain popular powers have had to be fought for, or may have to be fought for again....It (Bill of Rights) acts as a rallying point in the State for all who care deeply for the ideal of freedom:..." The Constitution of India contains a carefully chosen code of fundamental rights. There are, in this country, a score of minorities, and minorities of different kinds, both horizontally and vertically divided. The Chapter on Fundamental Rights is intended to forge unity out of the diversity by constitutionally securing the rights of the minorities rather than leave them to the whims of the shifting political majorities. Free societies must defend minority rights. Finally, a declaration of rights serves as an instrument of education. It provides a constant background for the political life of the people.

Negative and Positive Character of Rights. Many of the early lists of human rights are negative in character. They simply state what the government may not do to the individual. For example, the government may not imprison or kill him without due legal process or deny him equal protection of law. It may not stifle his freedom of speech or stop him from worship according to his conscience, or force him to worship against his conscience. Now the demand is for positive human rights. The right to life now includes the right to food and shelter and even medical aid. Freedom of speech implies the right to knowledge and education. It is argued that the absence of restraint is futile without the presence of opportunity and the knowledge and capacity to act.

Franklin D. Roosevelt expressed this perception of freedom in 1941, when he spoke of the "Four Freedoms", freedom of religion, freedom of speech, freedom from want and freedom from fear, which were to be established in all the countries of the world. Freedom of religion and freedom of speech are essentially negative in character whereas freedom from want and freedom from fear are significantly positive. Freedom from want requires a positive effort on the part of governments in the direction of production and distribution to eliminate hunger, squalor and disease. Freedom from fear requires the most complex action and it embraces the abolition of war and to end tyranny and persecution of any kind.

Roosevelt gave a more detailed list of positive human rights in his message to Congress in January, 1945, and called for a "Second Bill of Rights" for the American people. It has not been accomplished so far, but full employment legislation and President Nixon's proposal for a guaranteed minimum income are steps in this direction. The Constitutions of the erstwhile U.S.S.R. and other defunct Communist countries carried an impressive list of positive rights, for example, right to work and equal payment for equal work, right to leisure and against unemployment and exploitation of any kind.

SOME IMPORTANT CIVIL RIGHTS

All civilised States do not maintain an identical list of rights, although the tendency in modern times is to make the extent of these rights as comprehensive as possible. In addition to the usual basic rights, many countries offer guarantees against economic insecurity and exploitation, opportunities for free education and many other social facilities. The kind of rights recognised and maintained by each State is one of the ways by which States are recognised and differentiated.

Here are some of the important Civil Rights:

Right of Life and Security of Person. Rights arise because of man and his social nature. Without man there can neither be the State nor rights. Human life would be nowhere if the sacredness of this claim is not accepted. The right to life is, therefore, the most fundamental of all rights, as it is the very core of humanity. It means a claim to so live that the existence of one does not jeopardise the existence of others. It also means the right to defend oneself against attack. If any one makes an attack upon my life, it is my right to defend myself and even to use force for self-preservation. Use of force, however, is permitted only as an extreme measure.

Every State, however primitive its political organisation, must adequately provide for the personal safety of its citizens. In early societies the power to punish was private. The blood relations of the deceased avenged his death. The system of private revenge led to blood feuds. But now every State takes away from individuals their right of vengeance and substitutes in its place punishment as provided in its laws. The right to life is, thus, safeguarded by law. Punishment is held the logical consequence of the anti-social acts of those who violate law. Criminals are adequately punished as their acts disturb the moral order of society. According to Kant and Hegel, punishment is the negative reward for crime. It is that the criminal deserves and the State simply gives him his due. The advocates of this point of view plead that punishment for a murder should be death.

The modern idea of punishment is entirely different. It is argued that punishment should be neither retributive nor deterrent in character. It should be reformative. The reformative theory aims at reforming the psychology of the criminal. Instead of the murderer being hanged, modern penal law tends to regard him as one who must be removed from society for some time in order that he may reform and ultimately resume his place in society to contribute towards the welfare of society like all well-behaved citizens. Given necessary conditions, it is maintained, a Saul may become a Paul. Capital punishment, it is accordingly maintained, should be abolished and the system of jails should be substituted by reformatories.

The right to life also demands punishment of those who attempt to commit suicide. The reason is obvious. Every individual is an integral unit of society. If suicide is permitted, we deprive society of valuable lives who may contribute to its moral enrichment. Security to person cannot be claimed if the individual is allowed to murder himself. Suicide is an attempt to disintegrate society and inflict on it a social injury. It must, therefore, be punished, as it cuts at the very root of human life.

But to punish and imprison people for having attempted to commit suicide is now considered by many as barbaric and antediluvian. Societies for Right to Die with Dignity exist in most of the advanced countries. Euthanasia is the process advocated by these societies to end suffering of persons dying of incurable painful diseases. But no country has agreed to this process so far.[18]

The right to life is not absolute. If the State guarantees to its citizens the security to life, the citizens, too, owe a duty to the State to maintain its unity and integrity. During times of war or any other national emergency, it is the duty of all citizens to protect and uphold the sovereignty of the State even if they have to sacrifice their lives. Then, the right to life depends on obedience to laws. If laws are wilfully disobeyed there is neither certainty nor security. This means conditions of chaos and disorder and both life and property cannot be assured under these conditions.

Right to Liberty and Free Movement. If the right to life is the basis of society, the right to liberty is the essence of human existence. Man has not simply to live, but to live well and living well means living a moral, virtuous and happy life. Man has a moral vocation to perform or do his duty in the social life. This he can do only when he has

18. The Supreme Court of India has ruled that perpetually suffering individuals have the right to end their misery and possess the right to commit suicide, but there is no case on record so far.

complete freedom to exercise his faculties and to determine the general conditions of his life. It also implies that the movements of the individual should not be restricted by any arbitrary exercise of authority either by other individuals or by the government. Mere life without movement would be meaningless and without the exercise of human faculties it would not rise above the levels of animals. Since the right to liberty and free movement arises from the fact that every man contributes something to the good of society, slavery, in any form, is the antithesis of liberty.

But unrestrained freedom is the negation of freedom as it means freedom for no one. True freedom is really limited by freedom, that is, my freedom is limited by the freedom of others so that all may equally use their potentialities for their own good as well as for the common good. Liberty, as such, involves certain 'fundamentals' which must be guaranteed to each individual, and personal liberty is the foremost of all. The right to personal freedom means that no one may be wrongfully arrested or detained or coerced in any manner not prescribed by the laws of the State. Physical restraint is wrong, unless the individual is accused of an offence and is tried in a court of law, or when after trial he is convicted. If the personal freedom of a citizen is arbitrarily restricted by a government, which allows to its citizen the right to free movement, then, there are two alternatives before him. He may, in the first place, apply to a court for a writ of *Habeas Corpus*. When the writ is issued, the prisoner is produced before a court which enquires into the causes of his arrest or detention and orders him to be set free if his arrest is held illegal. In the second place, the accused person can seek redress for his arrest. Redress for arrest means that a person who has been wrongly arrested may sue the wrong-doer for damages or get him punished by a court of law.

The right to liberty and free movement is, however, not unlimited. A government may impose many restrictions on freedom of movement of the citizens during a period of war or at a time of national emergency.[19] War and other national emergencies demand that government should possess wide discretionary powers. These are, nevertheless, extraordinary powers to be exercised for extraordinary purposes and a resort to them should not be made in times of peace.

Right to Work. The right to work is implicit in the right to life, because in a rationally organised society man must live on the reward of his labour. It is, accordingly, necessary that society should provide him with facilities to perform his functions, and earn his living in order to maintain his life. If the State fails to provide such an opportunity, it deprives him of all those means which make possible the realisation of his personality. A struggling and starving man is a social decrepit. It is now being increasingly recognised that the modern State must guarantee the right to work to its citizens. But it does not mean the right to some particular work. If I become unemployed, I have not the right to

19. The Constitution of United States does not specifically provide for any kind of emergency. In Britain there is no prerogative of the Crown to make a proclamation of emergency. Emergency powers are given to the executive by Parliament. In India the determination of emergency rests with the President of the Republic on the advice of the Cabinet. The Constitution empowers the President to suspend the operation of Fundamental Rights including the right to enforce them (Article 32), as specified in the Presidential order. The Constitution (forty-fourth) Amendment Act now provides that the power to suspend the enforcement of Fundamental Rights shall not extend to the rights of life and liberty.

be provided with an identical work. "The right to work can mean no more than the right to be occupied in some share of those goods and services" which society needs.[20]

The right to work, also, implies that the worker must be paid adequate wages for his labour. He should be able to get enough of food, clothing, and shelter, including some comforts. If his wages are just sufficient to procure the bare necessaries of life, he is liable to become a physical wreck. Human machinery requires proper greasing and oiling if it is to work effectively and efficiently. Comforts not only lubricate human machinery, but make life something more than a mean satisfaction of ugly wants. Then, the worker must work only for reasonable hours. Human labour is subject to physiological and psychological limitations. Long hours of work mean frustration of personality as the worker has no leisure for creative work. The thing that makes a man a citizen is thought. If he has no time to think he loses the quality of a citizen. A good citizen means a good State. There is, accordingly, a "civic limit" to the energy "the State can, for its own sake, permit him to expend."[21]

Few States outside the former Soveit Russia have legally recognised the right to work. But no State can any longer afford to ignore it. There are two alternatives before the State. It should either provide work for every citizen, or make some provision for his maintenance so long as he remains unemployed. Unemployment insurance is a solution for the second alternative. Similarly, the State should intervene and see that the workers get adequate wages consistent with a decent standard of living and they are employed for reasonable hours of work, giving them ample leisure to develop their minds.

Right to Education. The right to education means that the State should make adequate provision for educating its citizens. Education sharpens intellect, equips individuals with the capacity to work and trains them in the art of citizenship. Citizenship has been defined "as the contribution of one's instructed judgment to the public good." Education is an indispensable condition to free individual development and makes man fit for the tasks of citizenship. Laski says, "In the long run, power belongs to those who can formulate and grasp ideas."[22] An uneducated individual can neither understand politics nor can he become vigilant about his interests and consequently his actual participation in the affairs of the State is generally negligible. Such a citizen is bound to be the slave of others. He will not have the opportunity to rise to the full stature of his personality. "He will go through life a stunted being whose impulses have never been ordered by reason into creative experiment."[23] This means the failure of democracy, for the people who are ultimate masters will not be able to exercise their franchise intelligently or perform their other civic duties satisfactorily. Hence, the democratic slogan is: "Educate the masters." Apparently, the right to education is a civil right, but really, it is a political right as it safeguards them.

Right to education does not, however, mean an identical intellectual training for all citizens. It only means provision for that type of education which should give an equal

20. Laski, H., *A Grammar of Politics,* p. 106.
21. *Ibid.,* p. 111.
22. *Ibid.,* p. 113.
23. *Ibid.,* p. 114.

opportunity to all citizens in that branch of knowledge for which they have an aptitude. Then, there should be a compulsory minimum level of education below which no one may fall, if he is to conform to the standard of a good citizen. Every citizen should have at least as much education as may enable him to weigh, judge, choose, and decide for himself. "He must be made to feel that this is a world in which he can by the use of his mind and will shape at once outline and substance."

Right to Property. For life to be worth living and an incentive for work, it is argued, every man should be free to use and enjoy his possessions, both movable and immovable. The right to property involves the right to the exclusive use of one's property, the right to alienate it by gift or exchange during life, and the right to bequeath.

The right to property is being widely questioned in recent times. Various arguments are advanced for its abolition or retention. Those who favour its retention urge that property has an ethical basis and it is essential for the realisation of the moral end of man. It is the reward for ability and, accordingly, it is necessary in some form for the existence of man, his growth and the development. Locke held that "the supreme power cannot take from any man any part of his property without his own consent. For the preservation of property being the end of government, and that for which men enter into society, it necessarily supposes and requires that the people should have property...."[24] It is also maintained that since the man of property is protected from fear of starvation, he can find adequate leisure to become an intellectual explorer and, thus, create those conditions which contribute to the progress of mankind. Finally, property nurses the virtues of patriotism, love of one's family, generosity, inventiveness, and energy — all so essential for the progressive development of society.

But the scramble for wealth and the traditions that grew out of it led to disproportionate accumulation with groups, classes and associations, and families. There have grown up corresponding systems of inheritance to perpetuate the possessions in the same social circles. The result is economic inequalities of a grave character which widen the social breaches and give the few power to control the conditions of the life of many. There results an "ethical dualism" which is reinforced by "temptations of egotistical and sensual gratification on the one hand and by servility and sychophancy on the other. Reputability and respectability adjust themselves to economic circumstances and tend to ally themselves with the principles of capricious waste, contrary to the true social interests. The system is materialistic in that it often divorces reward from responsibility and enjoyment of wealth from social function.[25] Such a system of acquisition and possession is highly iniquitous and is widely deprecated now. Some even argue for its total abolition and maintain that equality is not possible if the right to property is allowed to continue in its present form. Inequality, they maintain, is the cause of all our social, economic, and political ills. Such writers, who oppose the institution of private property as current, however, justify its retention to the extent needed for the development of human personality. For example, Laski is not altogether in favour of its abolition.[26] But he does not concede

24. John Locke, *Second Treatise,* p. 138.
25. Tawney, R.H., *The Acquisitive Society.*
26. Laski, H., *A Grammar of Politics,* Ch. V.

the right to property which is not the result of one's own labour, or the possession of which is against the social good, or which is not necessary to one's function in society. He makes a clear distinction between owning and earning and holds: "Those whose property is the result of other man's efforts are parasitic upon society."[27]

Almost every State outside erstwhile Soviet Russia recognises and guarantees the ownership of private property. In Soviet Russia it was only the right to personal property of citizens which was recognised and guaranteed and it included their income from work and their savings, their dwelling houses and subsidiary household economy, their household furniture and utensils and articles of personal use and convenience. But the attitude to property in all countries, including Communist countries that still exist, has now changed with the increasing emphasis on social rights. It is limited by the considerations of social justice and public welfare. If society does not create sufficient wealth to enable it to foot the bill of its expanding services, then it is obliged to take more of the income of the wealthy, in the form of taxes. The government may even resort to the policy of nationalisation on the ground that social claims must supersede individual claims. Otherwise too, the right to property, like other civil rights, is not absolute. It is subject to limitations. The laws of every State regulate the ownership and transfer of private property. The government may requisition houses, buildings, sites and factories for public purposes, and even fix ceilings on their holdings and ownership.

It will, thus, be clear that the right to property, *though all countries*, would uphold, but on conditions which differ considerably today from those that were considered normal even a couple of generations ago. Today, there are many conservatives in Britain, too, who support their belief in the right to property on the grounds put forward in 1912 by Lord Hugh Cecil. "The simple consideration," he wrote, "that it is wrong to inflict an injury upon any man suffices to constitute a right to property where such property already exists."

Right to Contract. The right to contract means that every citizen may work, live and freely contract on a basis of equality with others and with the same opportunities as his fellows. Contract is the essential basis of society. It cements business and social organisation. The State which does not secure to its citizens the right to contract cannot claim to be civilized and progressive. The Constitution of the United States of America prescribes that no State shall pass "any law impairing the obligation of contracts." A similar provision is made in the Constitution of India.

But there are certain kinds of contracts which the States do not recognise. No State recognises a contract concluded to deal in slaves or a contract involving bribes. Similarly, all contracts which are against the public good, for example, contracts made for illegal purposes, immoral traffic, or contracts which endanger the safety of the State, are regarded as void. Article 23(1) of the Constitution of India prohibits traffic in human beings. Article 24 provides that no child below the age of fourteen years shall be employed to work in any factory or mine or engaged in any other hazardous employment. The State can, thus, support only those contracts which are consistent with the end for which it exists.

27. *Ibid.*, p. 184.

Right to Speech and Express. The right to speech is an elementary necessity of man. There can be no society unless its members are free to express their opinions and exchange views without restraint. It is only through the medium of speech that we benefit from the opinions and experiences of others. Society becomes stagnated without free expression of opinion. Speech is, also, a means of self-protection. When we are free to express our opinion, we can protest against the tyranny and injustice of others, whether it is the tyranny of government or of any individual person. The right to speech, therefore, means freedom to express one's view on general subjects. It means that every individual is free to think and express his opinion in public without any interference by government. It implies that every individual should be free to criticise the policy pursued by the government. The freedom to think as you will, and to speak as you think, are indispensable means to the discovery and spread of political truth.

But truth alone is no index for freedom of speech, and, as such, the right to speech is also not absolute. The interests of social order and respect for the rights of others require restraints on liberty of expression. The laws of the State penalise utterances which tend to corrupt public morals, or defame individuals, incite people to crime, or which spread sedition and endanger the foundations of government established by law. Such restrictions on the right of speech are not intended to curtail individual liberty. They are imposed to ensure the liberty of others and safeguard the stability of the State. There is some difference of opinion as to the right of speech during war. But it is generally admitted that every citizen must subject himself to greater restraints during national emergency. Many things that might be said in time of peace may act as a hindrance to war effort and tend to jeopardize the independence and sovereignty of the State. Utterances prejudicial to the safety of the State cannot, accordingly, be permitted so long as the emergency lasts. Laski, however, does not concede to government the authority to restrict speech even during war. He allows the people the right to express their opinions about the war policy of the government. "No executive," he says, "has a right to move on its own way, whatever the opinion of its citizens. Those opinions must be made known in order to affect its activities. To penalise them at a time when it is, above all, urgent to perform the task of citizenship is fatal to the moral foundation of the State."

Freedom of speech is a valuable right. Apart from its contribution as a means to the development of social progress, the success of democracy depends upon the right to speech. Democracy is a government by criticism; clash of ideas and conflict of opinions. Out of this clash and conflict emerges the truth. Criticism of government policy creates an enlightened public opinion. It is, thus, a potent factor for the redress of public grievances.

> "This is true liberty, when free-born men
> Having to advise the public, may speak free."
>
> — Euripides.

When freedom of speech is allowed, government, too, possesses the means to benefit from the expression of the views of the public. It is a barometer of public opinion and the government which stifles public opinion prepares for its own destruction. Laski has aptly summed up this point. He says, "To allow a man to say what he thinks is to give his personality the only ultimate channel of full expression and his citizenship the only means of moral adequacy. To act otherwise is to favour those who support the *status quo,* and thus either drive the activities of men underground and, therefore, into a dangerous channel, or to suppress experience not less entitled than any other to interpret publicly its meaning."[28] But Laski also urges that the citizen has the right "to preach the complete inadequacy of the social order. He may demand its overthrow by armed revolution." He does not accept the argument of "reasons of State" and that the preaching of overthrowing the government by armed revolution would mean anarchy in the State. He says, "It is no answer to this view to urge that it is coronation of disorder. If views which imply violence have a sufficient hold upon the State to disturb its foundations, there is something radically wrong with the habits of the State."[29] It might be anarchy and, in fact, it is, but, he argues, it does not matter, for the peace in which injustice and tyranny go unquestioned is unworthy of existence. This is an extreme view which no State can permit, not even an advanced democracy, and everywhere "reasonable restrictions" are imposed on the right to speech.

The right to press means the right to publish what a man can lawfully speak. This right flows, *ipso facto*, from the right to speech. It implies publication of news, ideas, opinions and criticisms subject to the limitations which are imposed on the freedom of speech. The press plays a very important part in disseminating news and views and, thus, helps to create an enlightened public opinion. Milton has cogently said, "Give me the liberty to know, to utter and to argue freely, according to conscience above all liberties." A free press is fearless and it is a very powerful and effective vehicle to ventilate popular grievances, to criticise the policies of government and the actions of its officials and, as such, a mighty check on the tendency of the government to interfere with the rights of citizens. But the press does not serve as a valuable instrument of democracy when it is owned and controlled by the rich and is commercialized. "Democracy is a government by talk, but when 'money talks' democracy degenerates into plutocracy." It is, accordingly, essential for the success of democracy that free discussion and free criticism should flow from free press to help in shaping a genuine and responsible public opinion.

Right to Assembly and Association. The right to assembly and to form associations is implied in the right to speeeh. This right, too, is an elementary right of man. Associations, according to Gierke and Maitland, are instinctive to man. The pluralists even regard the State as an association. There is no doubt that the individual can impress his views only by acting with his fellows, and there are so many objectives which he cannot achieve singly but only in association with others. It is, accordingly, necessary that citizens should be free to form asociations and assemble very often to discuss and propagate their views. In all matters of public interest and policy they should be free to publicly discuss and express honest opinion. It also includes the right of petition and protest.

But the right to association is limited by the necessities of the State. So long as States preserve their sovereign national character, we cannot accept the proposition that the-State is an association. It is a sovereign State and it must ensure its continued existence. If the object of any association is to overthrow the State, it cannot be allowed to exist. The State may declare an association or a public meeting unlawful, if a breach of peace

28. Laski, H., *A Grammar of Politics,* pp. 118-19.
29. *Ibid.*

or the security of the government established by law is apprehended. The State may, also, prohibit an association which has become so powerful an engine of political strength as to endanger its existence.

Right to Religion and Conscience. The Constitution of India states: "Subject to public order, morality and health....all persons are equally entitled to freedom of conscience and the right freely to profess, practise and propagate religion."[30] But the Constitution subjects the right to religion and conscience to two limitations. First, the right to religion and conscience does not preclude the State from making any law regulating or restricting any economic, financial, political or other secular activity which may be associated with religious practice, and secondly, for social welfare and reform or for throwing open Hindu religious institutions of a public character to any class or section of Hindus.

The right to religion and conscience gives every citizen the liberty of belief and worship. It means that everyone is free to profess and follow any religion and perform the necessary rites connected with his religious practices. The State should have nothing to do with the religion of its citizens. It should be the private sanctuary of every individual. The State which recognises this principle is called a secular State. The Constitution declares India a secular democratic Republic which secures to all its citizens liberty of thought, expression, belief, faith and worship. The desecration and demolition of Babri Masjid on December 6, 1992, by the volunteers of the Bharatiya Janata Party, its associates the Bajrang Dal and Shiv Sena was condemned by both the Houses of Parliament and was described as an "attack on Secularism."[31]

But the right to religious faith is not admitted by all the States. Some States permit only a certain type of religious faith, others do not permit unrestricted worship. Pakistan does not allow idol worship and Pakistan Government's conception of idolatry is so narrow that it refused permission to India's High Commissioner to place a wreath on Mahatma Gandhi's statue in Karachi on his first death anniversary. The modern State, however, accepts the principle of religious tolerations. Nevertheless, no State permits worship which involves immorality. Nor can it allow any religious sect which endangers the existence of the State.

Right to Family. We have discussed importance of the family in the evolution of the State. In the continuance of the State family is its hope and the cradle of civilisation. The right to family is the most elementary right and it implies the right to marriage, the right against others in maintaining the purity of marriage relations, the right to the custody and control of children, and the right of inheritance. But the right of marriage and other family rights are to be exercised with due regard to the good of the community. As Gilchrist says, "The family state is a condition of the good life, but whereas in property the right is exercised in a thing, in the family state it is exercised over a person or persons, which implies that the individual exercising family right must recognize that the good of others is permanently and indefeasibly bound up with his own good."[32] The State may, therefore, restrict the right to family, if it is being used in a manner which is opposed to

30. Article 25(1), 13.
31. As reported in *The Hindu*, New Delhi, December 17, 1992.
32. Gilchrist, R.N., *Principles of Political Science,* p. 150.

general good. The Hindu Code Law regulates marriage and divorce and enforces certain obligations in the relations of husband and wife and of parents and children. No State recognizes temporary marriage. Many may prohibit polygamy. The minor in every State has no legal status. A fixed age of majority is recognised by every State, though it varies from State to State.

Right to Equality. Right to equality means the absence of legal discrimination against any one individual, group, class or race. In earlier times certain classes possessed special privileges or were judged by special law. The modern tendency is to enforce the same law over all persons in the State and to give all persons equal rights and privileges in the protection of their civil liberties. Democracy can only exist and flourish in a society of equals. The Constitution of India makes social and civil equality the bedrock of Indian polity. It guarantees equality of all persons before the law,[33] prohibits discrimination on grounds of religion, race, caste, sex or place of birth as between citizens,[34] and abolishes untouchability[35] on the one hand and titles on the other.[36]

The concept of equality of all persons before the law has a significant bearing and it is one of the ingredients of what Dicey calls the Rule of Law. The Rule of Law means three things with Dicey. It means, in the first place, the absolute supremacy of law. There should be nothing which may be characterised as an arbitrary power and every action of government must be authorised by law. Then, there should be the supremacy of law and no one may be punished except for definite breach of law which must be proved in a duly constituted court of law. Thirdly, it means equality before the law, that is, every citizen is subject to the ordinary law of the land and has to stand trial in the same law courts whatever his status or position in society. The Rule of Law is no respecter of persons. It is not 'a rule of men', but a measure of liberty enjoyed by the people. Law should neither be arbitrary nor should it guarantee privilege or take account of privilege. Rich and poor, high and low must be equal before the law. But the judiciary must be independent and impartial if the Rule of Law can mean anything real.

POLITICAL RIGHTS

Political rights are possessed by those persons whom the State permits to share in the legal expression and administration of its sovereign power. They give an equal opportunity to the individual, if he is worthy of it, to take part in the political affairs of his community and influence the policy of his government. Political rights consist in: (1) the right to vote; (2) the right to be elected and to represent the people; (3) the right to hold public offices; (4) the right to petition for redress of grievances; and (5) the right of criticising the government.

Right to Vote. By the right to vote we mean that every adult citizen has the right to express his opinion by casting a vote at the time of election what persons he desires

33. Article 94.
34. Article 15.
35. Article 17.
36. Article 18.

should undertake the task of government. The right to vote is the product of democracy. But even a democratic government does not grant this right to every citizen. Aliens, bankrupts, paupers, certain category of criminals and minors are often denied the right to vote. Some States deprive their female population of this right. But neither sex nor property, neither race nor creed, neither religion nor education should be the criterion for the grant of the right to vote. "Whenever," Laski says, "the body of voters is limited, the welfare realised excludes that of the persons excluded."[37] To allow owners of property alone to possess the right to franchise is undemocratic and it has proved disastrous to the interests of those who do not own property. Similarly, limiting the right to vote to a certain caste, creed, colour or sex has meant creation of special privileges for that class alone. Even Mill's argument that education should be the criterion of the right to vote has no popular appeal. The right to education, as said before, is now regarded as one of the important basic rights and all democratic countries have either made, or are endeavouring to make, at least primary education free and compulsory. It is contended that the right to vote should be as wide as possible and one man, one vote ought to be the maxim of a democratic government. "Popular control means that all adults share the political power; to say people are in law politically equal means at least that each adult has the vote. The suffrage is thus one criterion of democracy; to the extent that the suffrage is less than universal, to that extent the system is less democratic, less under popular control."[38]

Right to be Elected. The right to be elected or to represent the people is another important political right. In fact, the right to vote and the right to be elected as a representative are twin-born and essential for a democratic government. The responsibilities of representatives are enormous and difficult, because they make laws, control and determine the national expenditure and revenues, and in a parliamentary democracy control the executive and the national policy. It is, accordingly, necessary that the representatives should be chosen with due regard to their experience of public affairs and renowned for their honesty, integrity, broad outlook, and selfless patriotism. Every State now prescribes certain minimum qualifications which legislators ought to possess. "Absence of limitation," in the opinion of Laski, "may give us a Younger Pitt, but gives us a large number of members who go to the legislative assembly merely for the prestige which membership confers." This frustrates the ideal of democracy and representation. Laski suggests that a representative must possess previous experience and adequate knowledge of the working of a local body.

Right to Public Office. The Constitution of India provides equality of opportunity to all citizens in matters of employment under the State.[39] No citizen, the Constitution prescribes, shall on grounds of religion, race, caste or sex, descent, place of birth or any of them be ineligible for any office under the State.[40] This is the gift of democracy which gives equal right to all citizens. The poorest citizen is as eligible for the highest office

37. Laski, H., *A Grammar of Politics,* p. 115.
38. Mayo, Henry B., *Introduction to Democratic Theory,* (Sterling Publishers, Delhi, 1-967), p. 167.
39. Article 16(1).
40. Article 18 (2).

in the State as the richest. This shows that even the will of an average citizen has channels of direct access to the sources of authority spreading over all public offices, executive, legislative and judicial. To entrust the power to the mass of people means a more close and stringent scrutiny of public administration. But the 1973 Constitution of Pakistan, as well as its predecessor, denied the right to non-Muslims to stand and contest for the office of the President of the Islamic Republic. In the United States of America, a naturalised citizen is debarred to become a President. Such a denial debars a section of the community from access to a public office and is an undemocratic process.

It does not, however, mean that academic, professional and other like qualifications suited and appropriate to the office to be held cannot and should not be prescribed and enforced. What it really means is that whatever qualifications are prescribed and whatever mode of appointment is adopted, should be applicable to all alike and citizens should not be discriminated against on grounds of birth, religion, race, caste or sex. It is, indeed, imperative to prescribe appropriate and specific qualifications to ensure an honest, efficient and sound administration. Merit alone should be the sole criterion for all appointments. In India, due to historical reasons an exception has been made in the case of Scheduled Castes and Backward Classes and Tribes by fixing a certain percentage of representation for them. Intrinsically, this exception violates the basic principle of democracy. But the object of such an exception is to safeguard the interests of such castes and tribes, as they had been all through victims of the social highhandedness of the 'classes and castes' who regarded them as 'untouchables' and denied to them even the elementary requirements of life.

Right to Petition. The right to petition entitles every citizen to send petitions, either individually or collectively, to the competent authority, executive or legislative, for the redress of grievances. In democracy, the rulers cannot ignore the legitimate grievances of the people, because they are the ultimate sovereign. The government must feel the pulse of the people and promptly respond to their needs, otherwise it hazards its own existence. No democratic government can afford to forget that tomorrow is the day of election.

The right to send petitions for the redress of grievances is an old right and the people had been practising it in all the countries. The classical example is the Grand Remonstrance, well-known in the Constitutional History of England. Now the Rules of Business of the Legislative Assemblies in almost all countries provide for the submission of such petitions. The Question Hour itself is essentially for the ventilation of grievances of the people through their representatives. In Switzerland the right of petition takes the form of Initiative and a specified number of voters, through a signed petition, can initiate legislation either for the removal of certain evils in the existing law or providing for a new law the need for which is felt urgently.

Right to Criticising the Government. "A society that is able to discuss," says Laski, "does not need to fight, and the greater the capacity to maintain interest in discussion, the less danger there is of an inability to effect the compromises that maintain social peace." The government which provides adequate opportunities to criticise matters of its administration and policies is really a democratic government. Democracy is a government by criticism, for truth only comes out through the clash of opinion with opinion and every citizen has something of value to contribute and he must not be hindered in bringing it forward. "Democracy," according to Sir Stafford Cripps, "is a system of government in which every adult citizen is equally free to express his views and desires upon all subjects in whatever way he wishes, and to influence the majority of his fellow-citizens to decide according to those views, and to influence those desires." The right of criticising and assailing its policies is beneficial for the government, too, for it provides the government an opportunity to defend its intentions and practices and to acquaint the political sovereign with what exactly its aims are.

When John Stuart Mill made his historic statement that vigilance is the price of democracy, his emphasis was on free and frank criticism of the policies of the government and its administration. This is tantamount to controlling the government so that it may not act irresponsibly. Such control is more urgent today, for the functions of the government are so much more extensive and touch the very bones of individual lives. But the right to criticise the government is possible only in free and democratic States. It cannot be obtained in countries governed by dictators or those under foreign rule.

Right to Resist. It is often claimed that a citizen has the right to resist authority of the State, if he is genuinely convinced that a particular law or governmental action is against his moral sense of justice. But resistance to such laws of the State or governmental actions is only a moral right and not a legal right, for no State can permit an action which amounts to a defiance of its authority and may jeopardise even its own existence. On the side of morality and justice, it may, however, be conceded that if the majority of citizens really feel and believe that the laws of the State or the actions of the government are tyrannical and are against the true interest of the people and obedience thereto may have demoralizing and degenerating effects on them, they may resist against such laws and authority and may even revolt. We shall revert to this aspect of the problem in the concluding part of this Chapter.

Enforcement of Rights. Finally, every citizen must possess the right to enforce his rights. In the absence of such a right civil and political rights are meaningless. Article 32 of the Constitution of India guarantees to every citizen the right to move the Supreme Court for the enforcement of Fundamental Rights. And for that purpose the Supreme Court has been given the general power to safeguard the Fundamental Rights as well as the power to issue directions or orders or writs, including writs in the nature of *habeas corpus,*[41] *mandamus,*[42] *prohibition,*[43] *quo warranto*[44] and *certiorari*[45] which may be appropriate for any of the Fundamental Rights. In Britain, individual rights are safeguarded, although there is no declaration of Fundamental Rights, by means of the "prerogative writs" which have been called by Dicey "the bulwark of English Constitution." In the Constitution of the United States of America there is no specific provision empowering

41. *Habeas Corpus* is intended to protect the citizen from an unlawful arrest and detention, particularly at the order of the Executive.
42. *Mandamus* is used to enforce the performance of a public duty by an official. It is not available if there is any other adequate remedy.
43. *Writs of Prohibition and certiorari* are appropriate to complaints of excess of jurisdiction. Prohibition is intended to prevent an inferior court or tribunal from dealing with a matter over which it has no jurisdiction.
44. *Quo warranto* is issued for the purpose of determining the right of a person in office to hold on that office.
45. *Certiorart* is available when a tribunal acts without jurisdiction as well as when it exceeds jurisdiction.

the Supreme Court to issue writs. The framers of the Constitution had assumed that the common law writs would be available to the citizens, and, accordingly, they specifically prohibited against the suspension of *habeas corpus*.[46]

But in India while a Proclamation of Emergency is in operation, Fundamental Rights relating to the six freedoms can be suspended.[47] The President may also suspend the right to move Courts for the enforcement of any other fundamental right, except the right to life and liberty, but such an order must be passed by the Parliament.[48] It is, therefore, only a temporary measure.

THE CHANGING CONTENT OF RIGHTS

As said earlier, all States do not recognize and maintain an identical list of rights. They vary from State to State. Nor do we accept them dogmatically for all times and for all purposes. Rights are of changing content and they must vary with the wants of man and the conditions under which he lives. Things that appear fundamental to one may appear unnecessary to another. Our standards of values change and so do our methods of realization. Take, for example, the right to property. Our interpretation of this right is exactly not the same as was put upon it in the nineteenth century. Even in countries like Britain and the United States all political parties would uphold the right of the individual to possess property, but on conditions which differ considerably today from those that were considered normal, even a couple of generations ago. The right of social welfare has modified our conception of the existing rights and some of them may be actually incompatible with them.

If we compare the broad-based rights contained in the Universal Declaration of Rights with those of earlier declarations that have been mentioned earlier, it shall be clear that there are a number of rights which, today, are held to be natural, but were not thought near about two centuries ago. In the eighteenth century rights were thought of in almost exclusively political terms. The battle of economic equality had hardly begun. But most of the recent Constitutions, which became operative after the middle of the present century, have given due importance to the social and economic rights, as well as their political implications. As rights are of a changing content they cannot be catalogued tightly. The concept of natural rights, which are held fundamental for the life of man, has always been and must remain subjective. Rights are 'self evident' only, says Dorothy Pickles, "in their own time and place and, even then, only if expressed in vague and general terms that, in practice, mean different things to different men."

We cannot, therefore, have a rigid system of rights. Our theory of rights should be consistent with and in conformity to our individual, group and social needs. Any theory of rights which touches only one aspect of the problem is sure to create friction. The old

---

46. Article 1, Sec. 9 (2). It can, of course, be suspended when the public safety is endangered by rebellion or invasion.
47. As contained in Article 19. (1) Freedom of speech and expression, (2) freedom of assembly, (3) freedom of association, (4) freedom of movement, (5) freedom of residence and settlement, and (6) freedom of profession, occupation, trade or business.
48. Articles 358 and 359.

theory of Individualism is a political anachronism now, as it touches the individual alone. The good of man is not an isolated object to be realized. It embraces the interests of the individual, interests of the group to which he belongs, the interests of the community which embraces all those groups and the humanity at large.

The system of rights, as such, must be considered as a whole. Moreover, Political Science deals with operative ideals. These ideals are to be worked by man for the social good. Social good can best be secured if there is proper adjustment between the ideals of man and his institutions. In case of disequilibrium, there can be no moral development of man or realisation of his ideals. Rights, we may, then, conclude, are of a changing nature and they change in their content according to the needs of the individual and society. As for the present time, it is obvious that human reason has now become aware not only of the rights of man as a human being and a civic person, but also of his rights as a social person engaged in the process of production and consumption, and especially his rights as a working person knitted in close ties with the humanity at large.

DUTIES

What is Duty ? A duty is an obligation. A man is said to have a duty in any matter when he is under an obligation to do or not to do something. It is something we owe to others as social beings. When we live together we must let others live with us. This implies certain do's and don'ts. My right of living involves my duty to my fellowmen to allow them the same condition of life. What is a right in regard to one's self is a duty in regard to others. They are two aspects of the same thing or two sides of the same coin. If one looks at them from one's own point, they are rights. If oue looks at them from the standpoint of others, they are duties.

Correlation of Rights and Duties. It follows, then, that every right has a corresponding obligation or duty. Without duties there can be no rights. A valid claim is both a right and a duty. If society provides an individual with opportunities to feel happy and be prosperous, it also imposes an obligation upon him that he should allow others the same opportunities of happiness and prosperity. If I have a right to work and earn my living, it is my duty to recognize the same right in others and concede to them those conditions in which they can also enjoy their right to work and earn their living. This is a simple, but the primary rule of social conduct: do unto others as you wish to be done by. I can enjoy my rights only if I respect the rights of others. "A right," says Hobhouse, "is, no doubt, a species of claim. What distinguishes it from other claims is that it is one that it is the duty of everyone to respect, and unless the distinction is admitted there is no reason for the use of the term."[49] Without corresponding obligations the whole concept of rights becomes meaningless.

Since my claim to rights comes from the fact that I live with others and share with them the pursuit of a common end — social good — it is the duty of the State to see that I be a moral unit of society. As the State acting through the government maintains and coordinates rights and helps to create that atmosphere in which man can seek to

49. Hobhouse, L.T., *The Elements of Social Justice,* p. 36.

himself at his best, it is the duty of every citizen to help the government in realizing the purpose for which the State came into existence and continues to exist. This means that a citizen owes a duty to the State as organized in government.

Before the advent of democratic government emphasis was only laid on the "rights of man" as a condition precedent for social progress and welfare. Even today, in countries, which are despotically governed, the popular demand remains the same. But in countries with popular governments the emphasis is on the duties of a citizen and not merely on his rights. Such duties the citizen owes not to the State alone, but also to his family, neighhours, fellow-citizens and to society at large. The success of democracy will, in practice, be determined by the extent to which citizens are prepared to perform conscientiously the duties required of them. India amended her Constitution in December 1976 to incorporate a separate chapter (IV A) containing Fundamental Duties. These duties are unique inasmuch as they make a sharp departure from the normal duties which a citizen owes to the State. For example, to cherish the noble ideals "which inspired our national struggle for freedom; to promote harmony and the spirit of common brotherhood amongst all the people of India transcending religious, linguistic and regional or sectional diversities; to renounce practices derogatory to the dignity of women; to value and preserve the rich heritage of our composite culture; to protect and improve the natural environment including forests, lakes, rivers and wild life, and to have compassion for living creatures; to develop scientific temper, humanism and the spirit of inquiry and reform."

Duties : Moral and Legal. Duties, like rights, are of two kinds: moral and legal. A moral duty is that which is enjoined upon the people on moral grounds. It is true that moral duties form the basis of legal duties, but a moral duty may not be supported by the laws of the State. Its sanction is the moral opinion of the community. If there is a breach of moral duties there is nothing legally to punish the wrongdoer, though it may entail social condemnation. It is my moral duty to help the poor, the needy and the sick, because as a moral agent of society I must try to create those conditions which contribute to the social good. Similarly, I owe a duty to my parents to be obedient and respectful towards them. But, if I do not do my duty, the laws of the State cannot punish me for that. It is only a moral duty. Nevertheless, moral duties ought to be performed in view of their effect on public welfare.

Those duties, which are enjoined on citizens by the laws of the State and are enforceable in courts, are known as legal duties. Failure to perform legal duties is punishable. It is my duty to obey the laws of the State, if I do not, I can be punished accordingly.

Positive and Negative Duties. Duties may further be divided into positive and negative. When a citizen exercises his rights in such a way as to maximise social progress and welfare, he performs a positive duty. Examples of a positive duty are: obedience to the laws of the State, defence of the country, helping the State in maintaining law and order, paying taxes and local rates, to honestly exercise one's vote, to perform one's duties when elected to representative assemblies, etc. Positive duties aim at cooperation with government in realising the end of the State.

When a citizen does not do a thing which the law prohibits, he performs a negative duty. The law directs every citizen not to prevent others from exercising their rights and when he obeys the law, as such, he performs a negative duty. A negative duty implies obedience to don'ts as prescribed by law. But compulsion cannot go a long way towards making the citizen perform his duties. There must be spontaneity on his part and the will to do them fairly and honestly. It is, under the circumstances, necessary that laws must be the expression of the will of the people so that they may obey them willingly and not for fear of punishment.

Important Duties of a Citizen. Following are the most important among the citizen's duties to the State :

1. **Allegiance to the State.** Every citizen owes allegiance to the State to which he belongs. This implies the duty of defending the State in case of war, and service and loyalty to the State to maintain its integrity. It is the duty of every citizen to defend the State against all enemies and dangers and to assist in the maintenance of peace and order. The State can call upon any citizen to take up arms in its defence. In short, every citizen should be prepared, if necessary, to lay down his life in defending the State and to discharge the duties involved in his allegiance to the State. The Constitution of the former U.S.S.R. prescribed universal military service and regarded it as an honourable duty of the citizens. If military service is an honourable duty of the citizens of the U.S.S.R., the defence of the country is their sacred duty.

2. **To Obey Laws.** The first commandment to the Soviet citizen was to faithfully abide by the Constitution and the Soviet laws. In every State it is the supreme duty of citizens to obey its laws, respect its institutions, obey the orders and directions of the government and assist in creating that atmosphere wherein should flourish the spirit of law-abidingness. Good citizenship consists more in obedience to laws than in any other thing. Laws are made for the social good and those who respect and obey laws have the good of the community at heart. Disobedience of laws, violation of the rule of law, wilful defiance of authority and transgression of the directions of government retard the progress of the community and are the symptoms of a diseased State. It is an axiomatic truth coming down from Aristotle that a good citizen makes a good State. But should a citizen resist the laws of the State if they are unjust in his considered judgment? Laski is of the opinion that he has the right to resist. Barker too holds the same opinion, although he says that the mischief of obedience against the mischief of resistance should be properly weighed: We shall discuss this aspect of the problem later in the Chapter.

3. **Payment of Taxes.** For performing functions which the State undertakes, it has to spend huge sums of money. It is the duty of every citizen to pay taxes, national and local, punctually and regularly. If the State has no money, it cannot spend. Without money the State has not the wherewithal for working the machinery of government and for running it successfully, particularly when the sphere of the State is ever-expanding. Taxes have been held in all countries to be a compulsory contribution and it becomes a legal duty of citizens to pay them. There is no *quid pro quo* in a tax.

4. **Honest Exercise of Franchise and Holding a Public Office.** In a democratic State all adult citizens, subject to certain qualifications, enjoy the right to vote, to elect their representatives, and to offer themselves for election. Voting is a fundamental and

essential part of a citizen's duty to the government of his country. But this is not enough. A democratic form of government is a party government. A voter has to choose between one party and another. The vote should, therefore, be exercised with judgement, discretion, and rectitude. There can be no good government unless electors regard their votes as a sacred trust. Similarly, those who are elected should occupy the public offices in a spirit of service and justify the trust the electorate has reposed in them.

5. **Assistance in the Maintenance of Law and Order.** It is the duty of citizens to help the administration in the maintenance of law and order; the primary function of the State. The law imposes on citizens the obligation to inform the authorities if an offence has been committed or is likely to be committed and to render all possible assistance in the detection of crime. The State can call upon its citizens to render service in times of emergency and assist the government in maintaining peace and order, and ensure the safety of the State.

6. **Other Duties.** Similarly, it is the duty of citizens to serve as jurymen or to act as assessors, whenever called upon to do so. Citizens, also, owe a duty to the State to render service as members of public committees, organizations, local bodies, representative assemblies, etc., when required. Finally, every citizen should develop the 'social conscience' and 'public spirit'. He should place public good above private interests and render social service, whenever the occasion arises, as a willing worker. Citizenship is active and a good citizen is well-informed on all matters of public importance and he endeavours to arrive at a balanced judgment on them. That is why democracy is perpetually faced with the problem of deciding how to achieve a proper balance between rights and duties. The duties of citizen are many and arduous and the State, as a matter of reality, is what its citizens make it.

THE PROBLEM OF POLITICAL OBEDIENCE

Rights, we discussed, are inseparable from duties and duties we divided into negative and positive. When a citizen exercises his rights in such a way as to maximise social progress and welfare, he performs positive duties, which, *inter alia*, consist in allegiance to the State, its defence in case of war, service and loyalty to maintain the integrity of the State, obedience to its laws, and helping the administration in maintaining law and order. The positive duties, in fine, aim at active cooperation of the citizens with the government for realising the end of the State. The end of the State and how it can be secured has ever been the baffling problem of all times and with it has varied our conception of political authority and obedience to the State. The problem has assumed new dimensions now for two obvious reasons and both are the indirect results of the industrial evolution which is now near the point of culmination. The technological age or "Urban Civilisation," as Wilson calls it, has rendered the homogeneity of standards of life and conduct impossible and the breakdown of the traditional authority has tended to disrupt those types of social control that have been invaluable to political authority in the past. Secondly, the activities of the modern government have become so numerous and complex that they embrace every aspect of the citizen's life and at every step he is confronted with the authority of the State. Paradoxical as it is, while our ideas of individual and social welfare throw us more in the laps of the State, we have, at the same time, adopted a more critical attitude towards political authority.

Accordingly, the problem of obedience as a matter of duty for the citizen does not remain so simple. Old ideas do not solve the modern problem and yet they do help us to look at the question and solve it. The coercive authority at the disposal of the State to make us obey its laws has ever remained the most important answer to the question of political obedience and, with the breakdown of the long-established authorities, it has in modern times received an added importance. Force is, undoubtedly, an important element in the origin of the State and its maintenance, but it has not been the only or the most significant element in holding the State together. As MacIver says, "Men have often acquired dominance with the aid of force, but none has kept the position thus acquired by sole reliance on this means." Force is a crude weapon to apply to the mass of citizens to ensure obedience and a clumsy tool of political progress. T.H. Green has succinctly remarked that will,. not force, is the basis of the State. The State which lives and thrives upon force can never last long. Nor can it command the respect for its authority and spontaneity in obedience to its laws.

Another, but familiar, theory of obedience is the belief in the fact that the State provides a system of order, and people obey the State to ensure security to life and property. Hobbes, for example, thought that the guarantee of order by a ruler constituted in itself a sufficient claim on the citizen's obedience to his authority. But this is not exactly correct. Though order is an essential requirement of civilised life, yet there may be many people who would prefer to risk their lives to obtain different conditions rather than to live them out in a so-called peace which made life for them not worth living. The real essence of order, which the State is charged to maintain, is to create and sustain that atmosphere in which every man should get an opportunity for the development of his faculties so that all grow and expand to the best of their capacity and ability. It is, therefore, not order for the sake of order that evokes obedience. There is something higher and nobler with which the State is charged and that is the cue to the problem of obedience.

Religious belief and prejudices have also played their part in determining people's attitude to the problem of obedience. In the earlier stages of the development of the State, it was the "higher law" which enjoined that God had commanded men through Revelation to obey "the powers that be." In the seventeenth century many people held that it was part of man's duty to God to obey the State. In Britain, for instance, Sir Robert Filmer argued that, since it was natural for mankind to be ruled by Kings, it must have been so ordered by God. God, he said, had entrusted the right to govern to Adam and his descendants. Charles I had, therefore, a divine right to govern by virtue of his direct descent from Adam. Here was the theory of Divine Right of Kings which made obedience to the commands of the King a religious duty. The Kings regarded themselves as the breathing images of God on earth. The Theory of Divine Right of Kings also made succession to the throne hereditary. But when Kings regarded themselves answerable to God alone for their actions and the subjects had no right to question their authority, the virtuous qualities of obedience as a matter of filial duty were lost. The people revolted against the despotism of the rulers. Today, the theory of "higher law" does not find any adequacy as a matter of political belief. It must, however, be admitted that Islamic law still exercises a dominant influence in matters of obedience in the Muslim States and it is a great rallying force for political authority.

Out of the theory of "disobedience and nullification"[50] emerged the early democratic answer that men should obey the State because it was founded on contract. Hobbes was the first to give it a matter-of-fact analysis, but by excluding the King from the contract, he established that the authority of the sovereign was absolute and subject to no conditions. All subjects must obey him as disobedience to his authority meant conflict and war, the conditions which had made life "short, nasty and brutish" in the State of nature. John Locke, on the other hand, upheld the Revolution of 1688 and justified the reasons for which Charles I had been beheaded. He tried to analyse the reasons why men should obey the commands of the King, who had clearly been chosen not by God, but by the people through the medium of a democratically elected Parliament. His reference was to William and Mary who became the occupants of the British throne alter the Revolution of 1688.

Hume did not accept the theory of consent as the basis of obedience. He wrote, "Obedience or subjection becomes so familiar that most men never make an enquiry about its origin or cause, more than about the principle of gravity." He argued that even if it were true that government must ultimately rest on the consent of the people, it "usually means little more than the acquiescence of inertia." His conclusion was that people obey the State as a matter of habit. Similarly, Dr. Johnson believed that obedience to authority was not merely necessary to maintain order, but something natural to mankind. "Every man," he said, "is born consenting to some system of government." Edmund Burke was of the opinion that men ought to obey the State as they knew it, because it represented the accumulated wisdom of generations, and the accumulated wisdom of the society must be presumed to be sounder than the reasoning of an individual. The contribution of customs and traditions was also emphasised both by John Austin and Sir Henry Maine. They saw obedience to the State as something customary and traditional, "defined and crystallized—almost hallowed—by law."

But customs and traditions representing the accumulated wisdom of generations will only be obeyed so long as we are convinced that they are good customs and traditions which must be obeyed. If they represent the follies of the generations, then the legitimacy of obedience to them disappears. Karl Marx advanced his own arguments about the idea of habitual obedience. He held that the people obeyed the State as a matter of habit, though a bad habit. The Capitalist State, he maintained, was a conspiracy of the few against the exploited masses. It was tyranny "established by force and perpetuated by guile." The exploited and oppressed masses obeyed the State only so long as they were powerless to resist, "or because they were tricked by propaganda into believing that they ought not to resist. But once they realised the facts of their oppression and exploitation, they would unite to throw off their chains." Thus, begins an epoch of social revolution. Marx's analysis was the most famous of all revolutionary theories which explains social and political upheaval by bringing forth the economic and technological elements in human relationships.

50. Wilson, *The Elements of Modern Politics*, p. 173.

Most of the theories of obedience we have discussed above, have one common feature. They determined the relation between the individual and the State over which the former had little or no control. Obedience to the State was the result of either compulsion or duty or habit. But none provided an opportunity to the individual to decide when he should or should not obey. From the sixteenth to the eighteenth century European political thought filled in the gap and provided the answer that the basis for obedience was consent. At this stage of political development consent was postulated to be the condition of the contract, though the circumstances leading to the contract and its terms differed from one thinker to another. Nevertheless, one important result of the Social Contract Theory was that the individual himself decided his political destiny. Obedience was not divinely ordained, but was the result of man's own choice and determination and he agreed to obey for certain specific guarantees. As long as terms of the contract and conditions it prescribed were fulfilled, it was a "breach of faith", for either of the contracting parties, rulers and subjects, to deviate from it.

But the "breach of faith" theory was still no answer to the problem of political obedience. The idea of contract helped men to make the transition. "It was a bridge between the notion of an absolute ruler, responsible primarily, if not exclusively, to God, and the conception, which was to be developed in the nineteenth century, that Government ought to be responsible to the people through the medium of a democratically elected Parliament."[51] Rousseau gave a new meaning to the Contract Theory when he said, "The Government exists by grace of the sovereign and its power can be resumed or divided at will by the sovereign."[52] For Rousseau, the sovereign was the people, the sum of individuals acting as a community. The individual was himself an integral part of the community and he had the same extent of control over the activities of the community as the rest of his fellow citizens. The contract, according to Rousseau, was between two aspects of the individual, "Each giving himself to all, gives himself to nobody." Men were at one and the same "a passive body of subjects and an active body of sovereigns." Then, Rousseau introduced the concept of the General Will. Unlike Locke, he put no faith in the will of the majority. The General Will was the real will which was also the will of the individual, and by obeying the General Will he obeyed himself.

The eighteenth and early nineteenth centuries saw the emergence of two new ideas in the body-politic and they gave a new meaning to the problem of obedience. The first was the belief in human equality as enunciated by the constitution-makers of both the American and French Revolutions. The American Declaration of Independence in 1776 declared, "We hold these truths to be self-evident that all men are created equal." In 1789, the French Declaration of the Rights of Man affirmed that "Men are born and remain free and equal." The American Declaration also included the second idea. Among men's fundamental and inalienable rights was included the right to the pursuit of happiness. Once men began to believe that they were all equal and they had an equal right to conditions which made life worth living, they came to the conclusion that they were equal participants in the affairs of the State and they ought to have an equal right to

51. Pickles. Dorothy M., *Introduction to Politics,* p. 68.

52. *The Social Contract, Preface* by Ernest Barker, p. xlvi.

determine what made them happy. But one man's honey may be vinegar for another and, consequently, the happiness of some may be secured at the cost of the unhappiness of others. If so, who is to decide which shall have priority, happiness of some or unhappiness of others ? Then, what makes happiness for some may be considered morally wrong by others. How could this tangle be solved ? The first difficulty was solved by relying upon the concept of natural law. It was contended that operation of the natural law could produce universal happiness. Adam Smith, whose ideas dominated the nineteenth-century thought, maintained that the economic system in which individuals were all pursuing their own and often conflicting interests, would still produce, "by some beneficent law of God or nature, a happy and harmonious community." Another solution of the difficulty was offered by suggesting the creation of some political machinery which would decide what made happy people.

This is in line with the teachings of Rousseau, although traces of it are found in the Greek political thought too. The organic theories, as they are called, regarded the State as a universal aspect of the individual's will and it was, therefore, man's rational and moral duty to obey the State. The Greek philosophers tell us that it was in the perfect State that the perfect life of the individual could be found. Since the perfect life was a rational and moral life, the rational man would never think of disobeying the State. In fact, he would consider it his moral duty to accept political authority to enable him to attain perfect life. This view, which had come down the course of history, was expanded in the writings of Hegel. Hegel, the nineteenth-century German philosopher, assumed that the evolution of society was one of progress towards the good, and postulated the ultimate attainment of an ideal system in which the rational man would be free, because he would be in complete harmony with the will expressed by the laws and conventions of an ideal State. There would, then, be no problem of disobedience, for in the ideal State the government would always represent the real will of the community. Hegel's aim was to emphasise that State and citizens are inseparable and each moulds and shapes the other until they reach full development in harmony.

T.H. Green, another nineteenth-century philosopher, gave it a democratic interpretation when he said that if the State did not succeed in winning the allegiance of the citizen, the fault lay in all probability with the State. "It is a sign," he said, "that it is not a true State; that it is not fulfilling its primary function of maintaining law equally in the interest of all, but is being administered in the interest of classes." The essential point of difference between Hegel and Green was that with the former if the citizen did not freely obey, the citizen was not a true citizen whereas Green concluded that the State was not a true State if the eventuality of disobedience was to arise. Hegel, thus, glorified the State and regarded it as the "perfected rationality" to command and guide the individual. Even Trietschke, who regarded the State as power, did not hesitate to purify it with moral purposes, and argued that all morally minded persons must obey the State and accept its commands to guide their daily lives.

Organic theories, whether their intention was democratic or autocratic, had the common belief that a society possessed a personality of its own, that was different in some way from that of the individuals comprising it. They believed that, as Lindsay put it, "there is something which can be called a general will because there is something which can be called a common mind....When men who are working together pool their experiences and share their difficulties, there can and often does come out of their discussions a decision which is really the decision of the society, which no individual could have come to of himself, and which each yet recognises as more completely carrying out the purposes of society than his own original suggestion."[53]

The majority of the nineteenth-century political thinkers, in Britain at any rate, did not believe in the concept of the general will. Jeremy Bentham elaborated a theory of obligation which assumed, not only that human desires did conflict, but that, as far as we knew, they always would do so. He believed that the purpose of the government was to make men happy. He also believed that all men were equal and that they had an equal right to decide for themselves the kind of government which would bring them happiness. Since individuals differed in their views, they would not all be able to have what they wanted. But if all the individual wisdom, each man counting for one, were added, then the opinion expressed by the majority would represent the maximum happiness attainable in the circumstances. The purpose of the State, according to Bentham, was to bring the maximum happiness or social utility and we obeyed the State because it was in our interest to obey. Utility, thus, became the rationale of political happiness within the idea of majority rule.

Bentham's conclusions fulfilled both the conditions, the principle of equality and the right to happiness, necessary for political obedience. But Bentham's criterion of happiness was numerical. It did not take into consideration the qualitative aspect of happiness and, therefore, failed to answer what really constituted the best interests of the individuals and who should really govern them and how. John Stuart Mill could not accept the idea that happiness comprised things that could be added up in the number of votes like quantities of merchandise. "It is better," he said, "to be a human being dissatisfied than a pig satisfied; better to be Socrates dissatisfied than a fool satisfied."[54]

John Stuart Mill was right, but how could qualitative happiness be obtained? The answer was that the State could work only through institutions and human ingenuity had not so far devised any institution which was capable of measuring qualitative standards. And until we had found a way of translating the qualitative differences into institutional terms, they must remain irrelevant for political purposes. The only practical way so far discovered was that each man counts for one and all stood on a footing of equality and, therefore, had equal opportunities to make the best of themselves. My voice counted in the same way and with equal force as that of my neighbour and all of us had equal access to the facts which ought to influence our choice in electing our rulers and approving their policy.

But it cannot be denied that the majority rule and the theory of obedience to its authority had been the harbinger of all kinds of social, economic and political ills. The cult of majority rule has often stimulated intolerance to the extent that the minority or minorities bluntly question the rational justification of the majority to demand obedience to its unbridled authority. The pluralists even urge that the ordinary citizen has the duty

53. As quoted in Carritt's *Morals and Politics,* p. 204.

54. John Stuart Mill, *Utilitarianism, Liberty and Representative Government*, p. 9.

to ask:"Why should I obey the State?" Laski is of the opinion that those who have the moral sense must be allowed the right to judge the actions of the State and determine their attitude to political authority.

The psychological approach has its own explanation to offer in solving the knotty problem of obedience. James Bryce dealt with the problem comprehensively and sought to explain that "inertia, deference, sympathy, fear and reason were the outstanding motivations of obedience."[55] Though the psychological approach is valuable in explaining the issue of obedience, it does not explain why people should obey if the commands of the State do not find their approval and fail to coincide with their moral judgment? To put it in clear terms, should not the individual strive for the abolition of those laws which are arbitrary and have been imposed upon him by the tyrannical political authority, or are unjust or are opposed to the interests of the community as a whole? The tyranny of the majority is worse than the tyranny of an individual and it is a serious challenge to parliamentary democracy.

Here again, we come to the same question with which we began this discussion on political obedience. Has the citizen, besides purely as a legal duty, to obey the State? The answer involves broader ethical considerations and it can be treated logically with the end of the State. The end of the State, we said earlier, is to secure equity and justice for all citizens in order to realise the highest national well-being. This we cannot do by dwarfing man and frustrating his individuality. Man and society march together and both are inseparable. A moral man can make a moral society and for that matter a moral State and since the State is not an end, it is the moral judgment of man which should judge the actions of the State and determine whether it adequately fulfils its purpose. If the individual finds that his moral values do not coincide with the actions of the State, should he defy the political authority and disobey the laws which he considers oppressive and encroaching?

Laski is of the opinion that the State is to be judged by the moral test of adequacy and "if I hold that its power is being exercised, not for the ends implied in its nature, but for the ends incompatible therewith, the civic outcome of such perception is the duty of resistance." In the beginning, it is the moral duty of all right-thinking citizens that they should protest against all such unjust and oppressive laws or actions of the State, which do not provide for the reasonable satisfaction of their impulses, and adopt all legal and constitutional means to get them repealed. If their protest bears no fruit, they have the right to take the extreme step of even resisting the government by breaking those laws. "Nobody need challenge the right to resist," observes Srinivasan Sastri, "because resistance to the State may sometimes become a right and that very moment it becomes a duty as well. No one who cares for citizenship and for the public welfare can question the right of each citizen to judge for himself in the last extremity. When he has fought his fight and failed to undo a public wrong and he feels in his conscience that he cannot acquiesce in it, nothing ought to keep him from resistance if he thinks he ought to resist."[56] Resistance to laws and the authority of the State is, accordingly, a conflict between a

55. Bryce, J., *Studies in History and Jurisprudence,* Essay IX.

56. Sastri, V.S. Srinivasan, *The Rights and Duties of Indian Citizens*, pp. 97-98.

citizen's legal duties and his conscience, and the latter is the most cherished quality of a citizen. He is an active participant in the affairs of the State and ever vigilant about his rights and duties.

M.K. Gandhi, too, favoured resistance. His mission in life was to moralise man and society. A moral man and a moral society could only be obtained when truth stood arrayed against tyranny whether that tyranny was of the State or of the individual. Gandhi evolved a way of resisting evil through the organisation of truth and non-violence, *satyagraha*, holding on to the truth. The technique of *satyagraha* is Gandhi's unique contribution to the technique of resistance. Being a practical man, he ceaselessly fought all through his life against evils of all kinds first in South Africa and later in India and at both places he admirably won his non-violent battle.

But disobedience to the laws of the State should not be wanton. The decision to resist must be taken after a deep consideration and due caution with the conviction that the law to be resisted is immoral and socially harmful. Those who resort to resistance must also be sure of success in their venture. It is, in the opinion of MaCunn, "counsel not of cowardice but of prudence that resistance without a reasonable prospect of success, though it may speak of much personal heroism, is a political mistake and a public calamity." Gandhi's technique of *satyagraha* was the weapon of the strongest and the bravest, the true man of God who sought to conquer evil by truth and to resist physical force by taking suffering on himself instead of inflicting suffering upon the opponent.

Disobedience to the laws of the State shakes the very foundation of an ordered government and when the authority of government is shaken, there reigns nothing except confusion and chaos. It is tantamount to rebellion against the duly constituted authority of the State. Laski says, "I ought not to resist if I am convinced that the State is seeking, as best as it may, to play its part, and for most that perception will result from what enquiry they undertake. I ought not further to resist unless I have reasonable grounds for the belief that the changes I advocate are likely to result in the end I have in view." The duty of resistance, as such, is not merely a question of caution, but one of supreme political wisdom. It goes without saying that it is the duty of a citizen to protest against the unjust and oppressive laws of the State, but the form of protest, in the first instance, must be constitutional and legal. If the government deliberately brushes aside the devices of constitutional protests or frustrates them and continues heedlessly its capricious policy, then, resort to resistance is the only but the extreme course left. Resistance, however, should be the medicine and not a daily bread, or, as Laski puts it, "the right to disobedience is of course to be exercised at the margins of political conduct. No community could hope to fulfil its purpose if rebellion became a settled habit of the population." And one is not sure of the outcome of a rebellion. Even if it is successful and the revolting forces are able to overthrow the oppressive government and capture power, will the good which is likely to result outweigh the harm which the revolution has brought in? History can provide us with innumerable examples of the fact that nothing is more unpredictable than the course of a revolution. The aftermath of revolution is usually marked by the rise of a new autocracy. In sum, revolutions seldom, if ever, fulfil their promises. Old tyrants are replaced by new and the freedom won by some is paid for by the injustice visited on others.

It is, therefore, the duty of citizens to obey the laws of the State and respect the duly constituted authority, provided its laws and functions are in accord with the general opinion in the State and are based upon "justice", as Barker says, or "moral adequacy" as Laski suggests. The State must rise with the people and their aspirations. The people, too, must give a fair chance to the policies of the State to prove their worth to the citizen body. If the actions of the government are unjust or iniquitous and encroach upon the rights of the minorities, it is the duty of citizens to protest against the high-handedness of the majority and tap all constitutional means to get them remedied. Since democracy provides adequate means to seek redress, the spirit of resistance is of less value than in a government unresponsive to the will of the people. But if the majority uses heedless coercion rather than a rational appeal, to obey and agree to its policies, the duty to resist assumes a practical importance, irrespective of the considerations of order. It is both a moral and a political sin to keep on obeying when there is reason to disobey. Oppression and exploitation, according to Gandhi, are made possible by cooperation, willing or forced, of the oppressed in their own exploitation or oppression through cupidity, ignorance or fear. Eternal vigilance is the prime need to ensure liberty, and that is the essence of obedience. "Even the most despotic government," Gandhi maintained, "cannot stand except for the consent of the governed, which consent is often forcibly procured by the despot. Immediately the subject ceases to fear the despotic force his power is gone," Laski held the view that the danger today is not in disobedience but in obedience to the laws of government that are tyrannical and spell unbounded evil. But what about wilful disobedience, violent demonstrations, protests verging on sabotage, *bandhs* even government sponsored and *gheros* which now plague the political life in India? Do they fulfil the canons of Gandhi's disobedience or Laski's obedience?

SUGGESTED READINGS

Allen, G.K.: *Democracy and the Individual.*

Barker, E.: *Principles of Social and Political Theory,* pp. 136-72; 226-44.

Barker, E.: *Reflections on Government.*

Bosanquet, B.: *The Philosophical Theory of the State,* Chap. VIII.

Burns, C.D.: *Political Ideas,* Chap. VII.

Catlin, *G.E.G.: A Study of the Principles of Politics,* Chap. IV.

Cranston, Maurice: *Human Rights Today.*

Fellman, D.: *The Limits of Freedom.*

Gilchrist, R.N.: *Principles of Political Science,* Chap. VI.

Green, T.H.: *Lectures on Principles of Political Obligation,* Section A.

Hobhouse, L.T.: *The Elements of Social Justice.*

Hocking, W.E.: *Law and Rights*

Joad, C.E.M.: *Liberty Today.*

Laski, H.J.: *A Grammar of Politics,* Chap. III.

Laski, H.J.,: *Liberty in the Modern State.*

Lord, A.R.: *The Principles of Politics,* Chaps. VIII.

Mallwain, C.H.: *Constitutionalism : Ancient and Modern.*

Mill, J.S.: *On Liberty.*

Pickles, Dorothy M.: *Introduction to Politics,* Chaps. III, IV, VIII.

Pound, R.: *The Development of Constitutional Guarantees of Liberty.*

Ritchie, D.G.: *Natural Rights,* Chaps. XIV, XVI.

Russell, Bertrand: *Authority, and the Individual.*

Sidgwick, H.: *Elements of Politics,* Chaps. IV, VIII.

10

CHAPTER

Liberty and Equality

What is Liberty ? Liberty is derived from the Latin word *liber* which means free. It is a word of negative meaning denoting absence of restraint. Its primary significance is to do what one likes, regardless of all consequences. But this is obviously an impossibility. Liberty in the sense of a complete absence of restraint cannot exist. We cannot live together without common rules. The presence of common rules of behaviour is the consequence of our gregariousness. If I choose to do all that I wish, regardless of the interests of others among whom I live, there is likely to be perpetual strife and conflict in society; conditions of chaos and anarchy. Such a society does not provide freedom for me or for others. "Historic experience," as Laski has said, "has evolved for us rules of convenience which promote right living; and to compel obedience to them is a justifiable limitation of freedom."[1] By liberty, therefore we mean freedom to do everything provided it does not injure the freedom of others. It implies necessary restraint on all in order to ensure the greatest possible amount of liberty for each. Liberty, in this sense, can be maximised only when there is mutual respect and goodwill and all follow a simple rule of social behaviour: "Do unto others as you would have others do unto you." This simple rule of man's sociability tends to harmonise his liberty with that of his fellows and it entails such restraints as are reasonable and necessary to promote and ensure greatest possible extent of liberty to all. Reasonable restrictions do not destroy liberty; it is destroyed only when such restraints are arbitrary and unjust. "If restrictions embody an experience I can follow and accept," my liberty is not endangered. It is really enhanced. If I am not allowed to rob another person, or commit murder or suicide, or drive on the wrong side and recklessly, or park my vehicle in the middle of the road, or prove to be a public nuisance by my actions, my creative impulses do not suffer a frustration. Law is, accordingly, the condition of liberty provided the prohibitions it imposes are "built on the wills whom they affect"[2] and are not arbitrary and capricious.

But liberty is not a mere negative condition. It has a positive aspect, too, which is, indeed, significant and important. Liberty can exist only when the State maintains those conditions which help the citizen to rise to the full stature of his personality. It involves the opportunity for many-sided cumulative growth which consists in capacity to act, availability of an effective range of choices and spontaneity, that is, the ability to act in

1. Laski, H., *A Grammar of Politics,* p. 143.
2. *Ibid.*

accordance with one's own personality, "without having to make a great effort at self-denial or self-control and without being subjected to external constraints."[3] According to Laski, liberty is "the eager maintenance of that atmosphere in which men have the opportunity to be their best selves." It constitutes the enjoyment of those rights and the creation of such opportunities as help man to grow to be the best of himself, to develop his faculties, and to plan his life as he deems best. The true test of liberty lies in the laws of the State and extent to which they help a citizen to develop all that is good in him. Liberty is, thus, a product of rights. It thrives best where rights are guaranteed to all without any distinction of sex, creed, caste, colour or status in society.

Liberty and Sovereignty. The Individualists, the Anarchists, the Syndicalists and many other schools of thought regard liberty and sovereignty as opposed to each other and offer their own explanations. The Individualists assert that sovereignty of the State embraces every phase of human life and at every step the individual is required to obey its laws. Laws restrict liberty and frustrate initiative as they are of the nature of commands and prescribe a certain way of life. They hold that the State is a necessary evil and its functions are negatively regulative or protective. It should only maintain peace and order and leave the individual alone, *laissez faire*, to manage his own affairs and develop freely according to his own ability and capacity. The Anarchists are out to destroy the State and establish in its place a stateless society where liberty will be supreme. They regard political authority, in any of its forms, as unnecessary and undesirable. "Liberty of man," according to Bakunin, founder of scientific Anarchism, "consists soley in this, that he (individual) obeys the laws of Nature, because he has himself recognised them as such, and not because they have been imposed upon him externally by any foreign will whatever, human or divine, collective or individual." The Syndicalists are similarly hostile to the State as its laws and authority perpetuate the interests of the capitalist class of society. The Socialists, on the other hand, stand for maximization of the functions of the State and justify its interference in order to promote social good.

Apparently, there seems to be a fundamental contradiction between the sovereignty of the State and the liberty of the individual as the more there is of the one, the less there is of the other. But really it is not so. The purpose of the rights is to enable men to live, to enjoy life and to develop to the full potentialities of their individual personalities. Rights are means to an end and the State provides conditions to the realization of that end. That end, though it may differ in many ways for different individuals, may be summed up in one word, *liberty*, and it is the attainment of men's ambition to be free to live their own lives in their own way. But it means moral freedom and not absence of restraints on their freedom of action. Clearly, men who live in society cannot be free from restraints. If they are, the result will be, not liberty, but licence, anarchy and chaos. Restraints are necessary in the interest of order and of the harmonization, in so far as that is possible of our different conceptions of liberty. As Hobhouse has put it, "The liberty of each... must, on the principle of the common good, be limited by the rights of all,... in general, my rights are my liberties; and in protecting my rights, the community secures my liberties."

3. Karl W. Deutsch, *Politics and Government: How People Decide Their Fate,* pp. 36-37.

The system of rights is the system of harmonized liberties, because my rights are your duties and duties are nothing but restraints on unrestricted liberty. Laws are, accordingly, the condition of liberty. Laws do not curtail liberty, they maintain and enhance it. They create a condition in which every individual enjoys the maximum freedom to do as he pleases, compatible with the right of others to the same extent of freedom. If the murderer is arrested and convicted, it is the realization of liberty, for the law, which punishes the murderer, protects and defines the rights of men. Reasonable restraints on freedom of action actually add to happiness. Certain laws of the State add to the creative faculties of man. Laws limiting the hours of work are restraints on workers just as much as on employers. Originally, the workers bitterly opposed all such restraints. But these restraints save the workers from the temptation of injuring their health by excessive labour and consequently add to their well-being. The same is true of legislation forbidding child labour and establishing compulsory education. All such laws were fiercely resisted by parents who did not want to lose money the child might earn, if not forbidden to work or compulsorily sent to school. They were also condemned by well-meaning and sincere people as an interference with freedom. And so they were. But these interferences aimed to secure a fuller life for the children, and ultimately for the parents themselves. It is also true of numerous other measures. The order established by sensible laws and conventions opens up a number of possibilities which would not have existed otherwise. T.H. Green has justly said, "Much modern legislation interferes with freedom of contract, in order to maintain the conditions without which a free exercise of the human faculties is impossible."

The laws of the State, in sum, are not a negation of liberty. They are the medium of liberty. It is, however, wrong to claim that every prohibition issued by the State is justified and adds to the liberty of the people. If the prohibition goes beyond what is necessary and frustrates the life of spiritual enrichment, it is an invasion on the liberty of man. "What each of us desires in life is room for our personal initiative in the things that add to our moral stature. What is destructive of our freedom is a system of prohibitions which limits the initiative therein implied."[4] Man is really not free, if he feels that he has no means to express his opinion and impress his point of view upon those who exercise authority. Free expression of opinion is allowed in a country with a democratic machinery of government. There is no liberty where the individual is subordinated to the will of the whole community to merge his identity in it, or in an authoritarian State which will leave its citizens free for certain things, but not for expression of opinion in any way. To enjoy true liberty neither freedom nor authority can be absolute and complete. "Freedom unrestrained by responsibility becomes mere licence," says Dewey, "responsibility unchecked by freedom becomes mere arbitrary power. The question, then, is not whether freedom and responsibility shall be united, but how they can be united and reconciled to the best advantage. This is indeed the central problem of all political philosophy and practice." Freedom is, thus, all a matter of adjustment. Sovereignty carried to the extreme becomes tyranny and destroys liberty, and liberty carried to the extreme becomes anarchy and destroys sovereignty.

4. Laski, H., *A Grammar of Politics*, p. 143.

But the extent of liberty varies greatly from time to time and place to place. Conditions may be favourable to it or they may be most unfavourable. The role of the State in providing liberty also varies greatly. Nowadays, it is widely felt that negative liberty is not enough — that the State must do more than prevent intrusions upon liberty but that it must also take positive action to enable people to utilise their liberty effectively. Devices that extend liberty or make it effective also come under the head welfare and welfare embraces the entire life of man. It also means planning for the future to enhance the individual's all-rounded personality and ensure the unbounded advancement of the society to which he belongs. The problem of liberty has, accordingly, become more difficult than ever before. The enjoyment of liberty necessitates government with increased functions and also increased powers. As a result, the old problem of restraining authority itself, and of the prevention of arbitrariness and corruption of power becomes more serious now than ever before. In short, the constitutional democratic society must create and utilise authority with a view to the welfare of all individuals in society, yet it must prevent that authority from "becoming a new master which, under the guise of ensuring both security and greater well-being, destroys the hard-won freedoms of men."

KINDS OF LIBERTY

The term "liberty" has been used in a variety of senses and with a great latitude of connotation. Montesquieu said that "there is no word that admits of more various significations, and has made more different impressions on the human mind than that of liberty." For a clear understanding of what liberty stands for, we distinguish between the various meanings given to the term.

Natural Liberty. First, we have the concept of natural liberty. It is generally used to identify it with the unlimited right of man to do whatever he likes. Natural liberty is supposed to have been enjoyed by man independently of, and antecedent to, the existence of the State. With the emergence of the State absolute freedom of doing whatever one liked to do disappeared. While analysing his theory of Social Contract, Rousseau said, "What a man loses by the social contract is his natural liberty and an unlimited right to anything that tempts him, which he can obtain." But, as explained earlier, such a condition of liberty is impossible. It is licence rather than liberty, as natural and unlimited liberty of one encroaches upon the natural rights of others. True liberty can only be realised in the State and not without it. The liberty of one is not a contravention of the liberty of another. It is, according to Herbert Spencer, freedom for every man "to do that which he wills provided he infringes not the equal freedom of any other man."

The doctrine of natural liberty, though earlier in origin, is closely connected with the idea of the law of nature. According to the Romans, Natural Law or Law of Nature was the law of reason which bound together men in social bonds under common rules of life. The theologically-minded Middle Ages identified this Natural Law with the Law of God and of the Church. In the seventeenth and eighteenth centuries it became a dogma of political obligation. Locke, in particular, emphasized the connection between Natural Law and freedom, and his ideas were embodied in the American Declaration of Independence in which the equality and freedom of man are postulated. It received a still more vigorous treatment at the hands of Rousseau and provided a basis for the French

Revolution. Rousseau's political standard was the state of nature in which all men were equal. Natural equality, thus, became the essential principle of Natural Law and it conferred upon man certain inalienable rights. The eighteenth century *Encyclopedia* stated, "Natural equality is that which exists between all men by the very constitution of their nature. It is founded upon the human nature which is common to all men who are born, grow, live and die in the same way." Therefore, each must treat all others as equal to himself. The consequence of this is : first, that all men are naturally free; secondly, that we are to treat our inferiors as by nature our equals; thirdly, no one may claim any particular right above the rights of others unless he has acquired it. This is the true meaning of equality and if natural liberty confers such basic rights, which we may call natural rights, it is beyond doubt acceptable. But it is wrong to hold that natural rights confer the right to absolute freedom. Rights, as previously said, carry with them corresponding obligations.

Civil Liberty. Civil liberty, as opposed to natural liberty, refers to the liberty enjoyed by man in society. Freedom in isolation is meaningless. Freedom, to be real, involves the capacity to do or enjoy things in common with others, and no individual can permanently separate his own good from the common good. "We move in and out of the herd," it has been aptly said, and the truly free individual is the man who knows when to stress his need for freedom and when to realise the full advantage of social life, with all the restrictions it implies. "Man thinks alone and acts with others," said a poet, and this is the essence and method of social life. Civil liberty is the personal liberty of individuals, either by themselves or in association with one another, to choose and pursue objects which they deem good, provided that all enjoy that liberty equally. It is both positive and negative in character and includes individual's right to free action and immunity from interference provided it does not interfere with the identical liberty of others. This means that all those essential rights, we discussed earlier, must be clearly guaranteed and protected from arbitrary interference, both from other citizens and from government officials.

The civil liberty of individuals is protected against encroachment on the part of other individuals or association of individuals by the laws of the State, enforced by the organs of government, specially the police and courts. If my liberty is infringed by the action of another, the laws of the State come to my rescue and help me in the realization of my liberty. It means an adjustment of the relations of the individual through the laws of the State. The adjustment of man's relation to his fellowmen was one of the chief purposes for which the State came into being. With the lapse of time, there was further refinement and the State recognised the basic rights of man, made them definite and equally enjoyable by all classes in the State, and assured to all protection against encroachments. Thus, "Definite law, sure enforcement and equality before the law," as Gettell says, "marked the advance of civil liberty of man to man."

Protection of civil liberty against the interference of government is of comparatively recent origin. In the earlier stages of the development of the State the ruler personified its sovereignty and he exercised full control on the lives of his subjects. There could be no liberty under these circumstances. If the rulers sometimes agreed to respect certain liberties it was done under the stress of circumstances, and as soon as the stress was over unlimited and absolute exercise of authority would be the rule. With the advent of democracy a definite distinction was made between the State and government and checks were placed on the manner and extent of governmental action. The principles that defined and regulated the conduct of government, set a limit to its actions against the individual, and protected the rights and privileges of the individual, constituted the fundamental law of the State.

Every democratic State must now have its fundamental law. It may be written or unwritten. When the fundamental law is written and is embodied in a written document, called the constitution, it clearly prescribes how government is organised, the scope of its powers, the manner in which those powers are exercised, and the general guarantees of civil liberties. The Bill of Rights, which written constitutions usually contain, defines the sphere of civil liberties and prescribes remedies in case of their infringement. In a country, where the fundamental law is unwritten, as in Britain, the organisation of the government, the scope of its powers, the manner of their exercise and the guarantees of civil liberties are primarily the result of traditions, customs, usages and precedents or, to be brief, conventions of the Constitution, as Dicey called them. Fundamental law or the constitution is, therefore, the surest guarantee of the protection of civil liberty against the interference of the government.

Whatever be the nature of the constitutionl civil liberty will be at its greatest under two conditions. First, when the rights of private action are clearly defined in ample terms in order to cover the widest possible range of such action, and, secondly, when the defined rights are strictly enforced by definite remedies which can be applied as speedily and effectively as possible. In Britain, the definition of civil liberty is scanty or at any rate scattered, but the remedies for the enforcement of liberties are numerous and, above all, effective. The Constitution of the United States contains a Bill of Rights and it further provides that "no person shall be deprived of his life, liberty or property without the process of law." The Chapter on Fundamental Rights in the Indian Constitution is more elaborate as compared with the Bill of Rights contained in any other existing constitution of importance. Another important feature of Fundamental Rights in India is that there is a special constitutional provision for their enforcement (Article 32).

Liberty, according to Professor Laski, "is never real unless the government can be called to account; and it should always be called to account when it invades rights." In the United States any law or action of the national or State government can be challenged in a court of law, if it amounts to depriving a man of his civil liberty. There is no doctrine of the 'security of the State' in the United States and the legislatures cannot suspend or abridge an individual right on the ground of the security of the State. It is for the courts to decide and determine whether there is a "clear and present danger" to the existence of the social order so as to justify curtailment of civil liberty. The Constitution of India, on the other hand, imposes direct limitations on Fundamental Rights. Courts cannot question the propriety of legislation on the ground that it seeks to unduly restrict personal liberty, once it has been established that it is within the competence of the legislature to make such a law or in any way to modify its effect. The Forty-second amendment of the Constitution relegated Fundamental Rights to a position of inferiority bv establishing the primacy of the Directive Principles of State Policy, though the recent Judgement of the Supreme Court has nullified it.[5]

5. Minerva Mills case (1980).

In Britain, no court can challenge an Act of Parliament. Parliament may alter the Constitution; yet its action cannot be legally questioned. There is, thus, no constitutional guarantee of individual liberty in Britain in the sense in which it is found in the United States, India, and many other countries with a written Constitution. Rights in Britain are determined by customs and common law and protected by impartial and independent tribunals and the Rule of Law which involves absence of arbitrary power and privileges.

Civil liberty is not absolute. It is subject to limitations in order to secure or promote the greater interests of the community. The State may protect civil liberty through its laws against interference by other individuals, or through its constitutional system against interference by any single organ of government. But the State always possesses the power, through its legal machinery, to limit and abridge or even destroy civil liberty. Then, the real guarantees of civil liberty are not the many constitutional devices, but "what the people will stand," and what they will stand depends ultimately upon the outlook of the community. An intelligent community understands the social need of freedom. It does not fear healthy and honest criticism; in fact, it knows that if government is to be responsible it must thrive upon variety of opinions. Regimented opinion is no opinion and it cannot bring about the willing cooperation of all for proper articulation of the machinery of government. An intelligent and liberal community, in one word, "believes in freedom, and it assumes that in a free atmosphere men will, on the whole, use their freedom in a way which is not, in the long run, detrimental to the real interests of society — criticism being one of these. But beyond this it is difficult to go, nothing will make up for an illiberal public outlook and a judiciary that will yield to every pressure either of the government or of opinion."

Political Liberty. Political liberty is the liberty of free citizens to participate in the discussion and direction of the common affairs of the free State. Laski defines political liberty as the power to be active in the affairs of the State. It means that "I can let my mind play freely about the substance of public business. I must be able without let or hindrance to add my special experience to the general barriers in the way of access to positions of authority. I must be able to announce my opinion and to concert with others in the announcement of opinion."[6] Leacock calls political liberty "constitutional liberty" and means thereby, the right of the people to choose their government, which should be responsible to the general body of the people. Gilchrist takes political liberty as "practically synonymous with democracy" and gives the mass of the people not only a sphere of freedom, but also a share in authority.

Those who originally raised the slogan of liberty and fought for it, actually wanted the recognition of their civil rights. But it was soon realised that mere recognition of civil rights was not sufficient to protect them against the exercise of despotic authority. It, accordingly, came to be maintained that the people must also possess the power to compel the government to accept their point of view and ultimately to replace it, if it continued to act in violation of their will. This transfer of the ultimate authority of retaining or changing government into the hands of the people came to be known as their political liberty. Political liberty now, signifies:

6. Laski, H., *A Grammar of Politics,* p. 146.

1. The right of citizens to vote and to elect their representatives. But all citizens do not enjoy the right to vote. Political expediency demands that some proportion of the population of the State be denied this right. In general, aliens, lunatics, children, and in some countries even women, generally Islamics, are excluded from the right to vote, although the modern tendency is to extend this right to all adults, men and women;
2. The right to be elected. That is to say, every citizen who possesses the right to elect representatives, must also possess the right to get himself elected;
3. The right to hold any public office, provided a citizen possesses the requisite qualifications as prescribed by the laws of the State. The right to remain in office cannot, however, be held permanently or for an indefinite period of time. Representatives must be elected periodically, and so do the holders of offices in the government; and
4. The right of the citizens to be well-informed about all public matters and to freely discuss and criticise the policy of government. The citizens should be sufficiently vigilant about public affairs, as eternal vigilance is the price of liberty.

It will appear that political liberty is realised in countries which are democratically governed. It is another name for self-government and refers to political rights possessed by the people, that is, the share of governing authority which the State confers upon certain of its inhabitants. Political liberty is also the necessary complement of civil liberty. In the absence of political liberty, civil liberty is only an illusion.

Political liberty, according to Laski, "must not be regarded as something to be attained as an end in itself. It is to be attained for the higher moral end of the perfection of humanity, and as such its course must be marked by the gradual enlightenment of the citizens."[7] For political liberty to be real, Laski says, two conditions are essential. First, there should be adequate facilities for all and each one should have equal access to education. But the system of education which provides separate institutions for the children of the rich and the poor is to be highly deprecated, as it trains the former to habits of authority and the latter to habits of deference. Such a division of attitude amongst citizens can never produce political freedom. Those who are consciously trained as a privileged class will be imbued with the spirit of governing others who are trained to submit to their authority.[8]

The second condition of political liberty is the presence of an honest and free press. The press disseminates information and knowledge. For the enjoyment of political liberty it is essential that the news supplied by the press should be honest, straightforward, and unbiased, so that both the electors and the representatives may have truthful material to rely upon and decide issues. But this is not the real fact. Our press skilfully omits relevant facts and deliberately perverts news. When facts are deliberately perverted and reason is choked, our judgment will be unrelated to truth. A people deprived of reliable news are deprived of the very basis of freedom. "For, to exercise one's judgment in a miasma of distortion is ultimately to go disastrously astray."[9]

7. *Ibid,* p. 154.
8. *Ibid,* p. 147.
9. *Ibid* p. 148.

Economic Liberty. It has been justly said that economic liberty must precede political liberty. Liberty is meaningless when hunger, starvation, and destitution stare at a man at every step. Nor can there be any liberty, when there is a constant fear of unemployment and "insufficiency which, perhaps more than any other inadequacies, sap the whole strengh of personality."[10] The problem of the tummy and shelter is, undoubtedly, the foremost.

By economic freedom we mean "security and opportunity to find reasonable significance in the earning of one's daily bread." It is the freedom from want and freedom from fear. For liberty to be real, it is essential that every citizen should be free from the constant fear of unemployment and insufficiency. He must be safeguarded against the wants of tomorrow. Economic liberty aims at the creation of that structure of society wherein there is sufficiency for all before there is superfluity for the few. In such a society there is no class domination. The worker is not merely the seller of labour and recipient of orders, but a producer of services who finds in his work scope for the enrichment of his personality. "Without these freedoms, or, at least, access to them, men are hardly less truly slaves than when they were exposed for purchase and sale."[11]

Economic liberty implies democracy in industry. Democracy in industry means two things. In the first place, it means that workers possess certain economic rights. These rights consist in the individual's right to work, right to reasonable hours of work, and to a minimum wage, right to leisure by the regulation of hours of work, right to benefits against unemployment, sickness, accidents and old age, right to form unions and to fight for the redress of his grievances. Secondly, democracy in industry means that workers should have positive control in industry. In the absence of positive control, there is no spontaneity, initiative is frustrated and workers work mechanically. They subject themselves to the "routine" nature of work for fear of starvation. "A system built upon fear is always fatal to the release of the creative faculties, and it is, therefore, incompatible with liberty."[12]

National Liberty. The term liberty is applied to nations as well as individuals. A nation is said to be free when it is internally independent and subject to no foreign control. National liberty exists where the community is independent and sovereign. It is another name for national independence or national sovereignty. India did not enjoy national liberty before August 15, 1947. She is now an independent and sovereign Republic free to determine her own government and free from control on the part of any other State. Pakistan, too, is a free nation and enjoys national liberty. It is always a free nation which allows to its people real and maximum liberty. National liberty is, thus, the foundation of civil, political and economic liberty.

EQUALITY

Meaning of Equality. The popular meaning of the term equality is that all men are equal and all should be entitled to identity of treatment and income. Those who subscribe to

10. *Ibid*
11. *Ibid.*
12. *Ibid.*

this meaning of equality, assert that all men are born equal and nature has willed them to remain so. This natural equality of man was practically recognized in the Declaration of the Rights of Man (1789) issued by the National Assembly of France. It said: "Men are born, and always continue, free and equal in respect of their rights." A similar statement is found in the American Declaration of Independence: "We hold these truths to be self-evident, that all men are created equal." But nature has not created all men equal. Inequality is an inescapable, natural fact and it has to be accepted by society. Nature has endowed men with different capacities and so long as they differ in their wants, needs, and capacities in satisfying them, equality in its popular sense is inconceivable. Equality does not even imply identity of reward for effort. The statement, then, that all men are equal is as erroneous as that the surface of the earth is level.

Absolute equality is, in fact, an impossible ideal. Nature itself has created such vital differences between men that no power can make and keep them equal. No one with eyes in his head can or will deny the existence of these human differences. There are, however, certain elements of equality which must be secured and this needs a certain levelling process in the existing order of things. The principle of equality was, originally, a common man's protest against the gross inequalities created by the superior claims of the nobility in ancient societies. The idea of equality has, therefore, grown out of the idea of privileges. These inequalities and privileges persist even in our own times. Inequality, as such, refers to the conditions created in society by a limited number of privileged people who have always dominated the government of a country and used its power for their own purpose and advantage. This class of vested interests makes the fulfilment of their private desires the criterion of public good.

Equality means, first of all, that special privileges of all kinds should be abolished. All barriers of birth, wealth, sex, caste, creed and colour should be removed so that no one suffers from any kind of social or political disability. There should be, in short, no difference between man and man and whatever rights inhere in another by virtue of his being a citizen must inhere, and to the same extent, in me also. It means that I am entitled to the enjoyment of all those social and political privileges to which others are entitled. My vote in the election of the representatives is as valuable and potential as that of any other. I can also become the recipient of any office of the State for which I may be eligible. To refuse any man access to authority is a complete denial of his freedom, because, "unless I enjoy the same access to power as others, I live in an atmosphere of contingent frustration."[13] One who lives in an atmosphere of frustration has neither any inspiration in life nor any incentive for it. He accepts his place in society, which accident of birth has given him, as a permanent condition of his life. It is in this way that the faculty of creativeness is lost and men or a class of men become "animate tools", which Aristotle described as the characteristic of the natural slave. There can be no equality in a society where a few are masters and the rest are slaves. The principle of equality, accordingly, means that whatever conditions are guaranteed to me, in the form of rights, shall also, in the same measure, be guaranteed to others, and that whatever rights are given to others shall also be given to me. The chief characteristic of a right is its equalitarian basis.

13. *Ibid.*, p. 21.

Equality, like liberty, has a positive connotation as well. In this sense, it means provision of adequate opportunity. By adequate opportunities we do not mean equal opportunities. This is impossible. "In the modern world," says Laski, "broadly speaking, opportunity is a matter of parental circumstances."[14] All that is implied from the provision of adequate opportunities is that the State should provide suitable opportunities for all citizens without any discrimination for the full development of their intelligence. No one should be debarred from the realization of the ambition of his life, if he possesses the requisite ability. The principle of equality is satisfied when the State extends due opportunities to all for developing their abilities to their full stature.

Equality thus involves, first of all, absence of legal discrimination against any one individual, group, class or race. Secondly, equal claims to adequate opportunities for all, recognition of the fact that there can be no difference inherent in nature between claims of men to happiness, and especially, that no one person or group may be sacrificed to another. Finally, claims to a minimum of education, housing, food, and guarantees against economic insecurity.

Content of Equality. James Bryce makes mention of four kinds of equality: (1) civil equality: (2) political equality; (3) social equality; and (4) natural equality. Bryce's classification may be supplemented by (5) economic equality. Laski, however, takes note of only political equality and economic equality, whereas Barker adds two more, legal and social equality.

1. **Civil Equality.** Civil equality consists in the enjoyment by all citizens of the same civil rights and liberties. All should be subject to the law and equal before the law. There is no equality, if the law makes a distinction between men either according to their rank or wealth, their political opinions or their religious beliefs, or if laws are passed to benefit one class of people at the expense of another. Equality implies that all citizens should be treated alike in the matter of possession of rights. Its basis is equalitarian.

2. **Political Equality.** Political equality means that all citizens have the same political rights, an equal voice in government, and an equal access to all offices of authority, provided one possesses the necessary qualifications and requirements. This implies democracy and adult suffrage. But political equality is never real unless it is accompanied by economic equality. If there are glaring contrasts in the distribution of wealth, the political life of the country will be manned by those who have the means to foot the election expenses and get themselves elected. When wealth becomes the only criterion for the enjoyment of political rights, political equality is not possible. In such a society some are born to rule and others are born to be ruled. This is not a democratic ideal, because democracy rests upon the foundation of the equality of men, irrespective of their station in life. It accepts man as a man.

3. **Social Equality.** Social equality means that all citizens are equally tangible units of society and no one is entitled to special privileges. All have an equal opportunity to stand up and develop their personality. It implies no distinction in the social status of the people, because of differences in race, colour, sex, class or caste, that is, there exists no

14. *Ibid.*, p. 151.

unnecessary social restraint which retards the growth of an individual and the realization of his ambition of a good and happy life. In India, there is no social equality, as the society is rigidly divided into castes and free intercourse between different castes is a social taboo. The policy of racial discrimination followed in South Africa is negation of the principle of social equality. The division of society into different classes—the employers and the workers, the rich and the poor, the aristocratic and the plebian—is a prime feature of the capitalistic society and it is a great barrier to social equality. Social equality, however, cannot be forced upon people by the laws of the State, unless the sentiment of equality produces great changes in our social habits and social institutions. If the sentiment of social equality is wisely cultivated, it is sure to make a considerable addition to the realisation of social justice for which the world clamours now. But social equality is a difficult ideal to attain. It exists nowhere in the world, not even in the Soviet Russia despite the claims of its various Constitutions which were operative at different times of its history.

4. **Natural Equality.** We dealt with the concept of natural equality in the preceding pages of the chapter and emphasised that there is really nothing like natural equality. Nature has not willed that all men should be equal. Men differ obviously and profoundly in almost every respect beyond the mere equality of being human beings. "They are," as Cole points out, "radically unlike in strength and physical powers, in mental ability and creative quality, in both capacity and willingness to serve the community, and perhaps most radically of all in power of imagination."[15] It is, however, to be remembered that society can endure natural inequalities, but not unnatural, man-made inequalities. The cry of natural equality is made to free society from artificial inequalities created by man himself. What the doctrine of natural equality means is that none of those inequalities is to be recognised by law as creating inequalities in rights. The law must treat all alike, keep all doors open to all, admit of no official predominance due to anything else but the capacity shown by objective proofs which all may try to offer. It also means that law should work at reducing those inequalities, rather than perpetuating them, by providing those social and economic opportunities that equalise chances. Natural equality in this context may be to some extent an ideal rather than an immediate reality, but, the ideal must be taken as both desirable and realisable, as a guide for immediate practice.[16]

5. **Economic Equality.** There is nothing like absolute economic equality as Bryce interprets it. He said economic equality is "the attempt to expunge all differences in wealth, allotting to every man and woman an equal share in worldly goods." Such a concept of economic equality is beyond the bounds of practical politics. Not only do wants differ, but there is also a great difference in the capacity of men to satisfy their wants. Equality of wealth is, therefore, an unnatural conclusion, as there is no escape from these differences. But all men must eat, drink, and obtain shelter. These are the bare necessaries of life and they are equally urgent for all. Every man, accordingly, must have equal and easy access "up to the point where human urgencies are in question."[17] Beyond that point equality is not possible.

15. Cole, G.D.H., *A Guide to Modern Politics,* p. 488.
16. Solatu, R.H., *An Introduction to Politics,* p. 144.
17. Laski. H., *A Grammar of Politics,* p. 159.

Economic equality involves sufficiency for all to satisfy their primary needs. I have no right to eat cake, as Laski puts it, "if my neighhour, because of that right, is compelled to go without bread." Any social organisation which allows some to starve quietly and others to have abundance denies to man what enables him to be a man. It produces a society of social decrepits. Such a society of unequals, according to Mathew Arnold, "materializes our upper class, vulgarizes our middle class, brutalizes our lower." If we want a society of social equals, we can hope to build it only on a foundation of economic equality. The State should, accordingly, guarantee to all citizens access to the means of satisfying their primary needs. By assuring each man a minimum of sufficiency, the State guarantees to him all those things without which life is meaningless. This amounts to protecting the weak and limiting the power of the strong.

Economic equality, then, means equality to the margin of sufficiency. Beyond the margin of sufficiency inequality is justified, provided it is capable of explanation in terms of social good. "Once urgency is satisfied superfluity becomes a problem of so fixing the return to service that each man can perform his function with the maximum return to society as a whole."[18] Equality, thus, is a "problem of proportions." It implies a certain levelling process in order to reduce the excessive inequalities of existing fortunes, or to eliminate unnatural inequalities. In a society where every man has an opportunity to satisfy his primary needs, no one's personality suffers frustration to the private benefit of others. This is what justice means. Where there are great inequalities of fortune, there is always inequality of treatment and opportunity. It is not possible for men, says Cole, to be socially or politically equal as long as there exist among them differences of wealth and income so great as to divide them into distinct economic classes "with widely differing opportunities in childhood to become healthy, educated, travelled and used to regard the world as a place made to suit their convenience. The slum child is not so healthy as the child whose parents can afford to give him the privileges of good food and sunlight. In the schools, the children of the poorest classes lag behind those who come from better equipped homes. Secondly, education is still a privilege reserved for a minority selected mainly on economic grounds. And there is a wider difference, for the most part, between the few who are taught from childhood the arts of command and the many whose lessons are intended to inculcate rather the duties of obedience and respect for their betters."[19] The real roots of social and political inequality are mainly economic.[20] Economic equality, as explained above, is a panacea for our social and political ills. But can we obtain an equality of the communistic concept? It is hazardous to conjecture about it. It is not obtainable, as said earlier, even in Soviet Russia or in any other Communist country. In fact, the demise of Soviet Russia was essentially due to the economic disparities and invisible privileges enjoyed by the ruling elites.

Relationship between Liberty and Equality. Liberty, as we defined it, is moral freedom, and equality is essential to it, for without equality, the price of liberty for me might be the denial of liberty for you. Liberty and equality both go together in claims

18. *Ibid.,* p. 159.
19. Cole, G.D.H., *A Guide to Modern Politics,* pp. 488-90.
20. According to Barker the problem of economic equality are twofold. "It is partly a matter of status. It is partly a matter of property and income." Barker, E, *Principles of Social and Political Theory,* p. 155.

to fundamental rights. But the two have not always and everywhere been claimed with equal fervour. On the whole, the Anglo-Saxons have seemed to place more emphasis on liberty, while the French have always sought, first and foremost, to secure recognition of the principle of equality. This difference of emphasis may be explained as the result of different political evolutions or of different national characteristics. It is also possible to explain it by saying that, in reality, one or the other has to be chosen, because the two demands are really incompatible, that, as Lord Acton said, "the passion for equality makes vain the hope of freedom."

Whether equality is a condition of liberty or is in reality incompatible with it is a question which need clearly be answered, as it affects our whole conception of rights and duties. According to the Marxist thesis conditions of economic equality alone make possible the necessary conditions of liberty. Economic equality, it asserts, can only be achieved through revolution and dictatorship of the proletariat. The dictatorship of the proletariat uses all the power at its disposal to destroy Capitalism and to establish in its place Socialism, that is, to re-distribute material benefits which hitherto were enjoyed by some, the capitalist class, at the expense of others, the working class. For constructing a Socialist society the dictatorship of the proletariat may be invested with oppressive and autocratic powers. It may even regiment the faculties of men to a particular way of life. Once Socialism has been established, the State becomes superfluous and it must 'wither away'. The emerging society is a stateless and classless society where men will really be free. Equality is, therefore, an end to which men are led by a revolution.

But in a democratic State means cannot be divorced from the end, or to put it in simple language, "democracies assume that, in so far as it is humanly possible, they must not do evil that good may come." Freedom, therefore, is something that can be created by free men and the citizens themselves decide both what constitutes their freedom and also the means which they will employ to achieve their end. Good means must be adopted for a good end and for the attainment of liberty a considerable measure of equality is necessary. Unrestrained freedom for every individual to satisfy his appetite for wealth and power is not the condition of liberty. Whenever and wherever such a freedom has existed it resulted in the degeneration of the social order. Great inequalities make impossible the attainment of freedom for the less fortunate. Those who are wealthy and possess the means to control the government constitute a class of vested interests and they use their authority and privileges for perpetuating inequalities. This hampers the freedom of those who are deprived of the opportunities they need for their self-expression and self-development. Freedom means security and security demands the removal of those inequalities that place the weak at the mercy of the strong. Equality, which aims to end this glaring contrast, is, therefore, the true basis of liberty.

Without equality, liberty is a mere mockery. Civil liberty can only be ensured when all are equal in the eyes of law, the same law for all and no privileged classes or individuals exempt from its provisions. Political liberty provides equal status for all citizens and equal opportunities for their participation in the affairs of the State. It raises the common man on the pedestal of political glory. A society in which there exist gross inequalities in property can assure neither civil nor political liberty. Liberty consists in reciprocity, or, as Aristotle has said, friendship. There can be no friendship, that is, fellow-feeling, among people having unequal standards of living, education and culture. "If liberty means the power of expansion in human spirit, it is rarely presented save in a society of equals. Where there are rich and poor, educated and uneducated, we find always masters and servants." There can be no liberty for servants who are ever recipients of orders.

Inequalities of property also inevitably bring inequalities of treatment and right. There is no justice for the poor in a society of unequals. Equality in justice is a primary condition of justice. A magistrate who convicts a poor thief but acquits the one who is rich, ascribing the guilt of the latter to a nervous disease, does so because of differences in the economic status of the two, though the nature of offence in both the cases is the same. Such differences in the administration of law are dependent, not upon the law itself, but the social results of the inequality of wealth. Things seem wicked in the poor which are not wicked in the rich. Only a movement towards the equality of wealth can remove such injustices. All those countries which have moved towards the attainment of real liberty have, in fact, striven to remove economic inequalities. The Directive Principles of State Policy contained in the Indian Constitution declare the ideal of the Welfare State and emphasise that the regulatory State of the past has given place to the service State of today. Article 38 of the Constitution clearly prescribes that "the State shall strive to promote the welfare of the people by securing and protecting as effectively as it may, a social order in which justice, social, economic and political, shall inform all the institutions of the national life." The State shall, in particular, direct its policy so that wealth, its sources of production and its means of distribution shall not be concentrated in the hands of the few, but shall be distributed as to subserve common good. But nothing tangible has been achieved so far and the yawning disparities still plague the Indian Society. In the United States discrimination against blacks is longstanding and pervasive. The officials of the National Institute of Health told the Post Office and Civil Service Subcommittee on July 14, 1993, that the Institute had clustered black employees in low-paying jobs with little chance of advancement. Allegation of crimes against women had earlier been made against National Institute of Health by a consultant's report, but no one had ever been disciplined for racial bias.

Liberty and equality are, therefore, not incompatible. Equality is an aid to liberty. Tawney has aptly said that "a large measure of equality, so far being inimical to liberty, is essential to it."[21] Even Lord Acton did not find equality incompatible with liberty. What he found incompatible was "the passion for equality." And if the equalitarian communities, utopian or Communist, have been found unworkable and subjected to criticism, it is because equality is regarded as an end rather than a means to an end. If equality becomes a passion instead of an instrument, then liberty may be diminished by equalitarian measures as Marxism suggests.

SAFEGUARDS OF LIBERTY

It follows that liberty exists and thrives in a democratic State and the citizens of a democratic State are thinking human beings fully conscious of their rights and duties. A

21. Tawney, R.H., *Equality,* p. 245.

citizen of a democratic State makes an equal contribution towards the discovery of the best techniques of democratic government. Vigilance is the price of democracy and it is, as Laski says, "the proud spirit of citizens less than the letter of law, that is their most real safeguard"[22] against encroachment on the liberty of the people. Mere democratic institutions are not enough to safeguard liberty. The conferment of fundamental rights and existence of appropriate institutions to enforce and safeguard them constitute only half the battle. Victory comes only when citizens have the courage of conviction to maintain and uphold them, and protest, even resist, if any invasion is made on their freedoms either by any individual or the government. To express it in the memorable words of Thomas Jefferson: "What country can preserve its liberties, if its rulers are not warned from time to time that this people preserve the spirit of resistance."

Secondly, liberty can be best secured when there is mutual cooperation between the government and the people. In order to create a climate of trust and mutual cooperation, it is essential that the liberties of the people be incorporated and defined in the constitution of a country. If the government or any individual attempts to make encroachments on the liberties of the citizens, they can appeal to the written law and seek proper redress. The constitution of a country is the custodian of the liberties of the people and provides necessary safeguards against any possible encroachment.

In countries where the constitution is essentially unwritten and there is no Bill of Rights providing specific rights, the judiciary safeguards the liberties of the people. Britain is the classical example of such a constitution and judiciary in that country has proved to be the unfailing guardian of the rights of the people. It implies independence and impartiality of the judiciary and existence of the Rule of Law. If the people can secure speedy and impartial justice and all are equal before law and the same law is applicable to all and there is nothing which can be characterised as arbitrary action, their liberty is duly guaranteed. Montesquieu maintained, "It is principally by the nature and proportion of punishments imposed by law that liberty is established or destroyed."

Then, liberty can best flourish under a democratic form of government. In democracy political power rests with the people. The rulers are their nominees and they remain in office so long as the people wish them to continue. This is a useful safeguard of liberty. But democracy by itself is no automatic guarantee unless people possess the habit of tolerance and the majority party respects the liberty of the minorities. The majority party should not be prompted by sectional interests disregardful of the interests of the minorities. Nor should the minorities always suspect the intentions of the majority and be at perpetual political animosity with the latter. There must be, on both sides, moderation and the spirit of give and take, and agreement to differ, which is really a form of unity. "Our political machinery," once said Lord Balfour, "supposes a people so fundamentally at one that they can afford to bicker." The spirit of democracy is infinitely comprehensive, infinitely complementary and infinitely creative. It is in the integration of wills that the democratic character of majority rule consists.

Freedom, according to Laski, cannot be achieved for the mass of men in the presence of special privileges guaranteed to a small section of the community. Freedom for all to all places of authority is real liberty. Those who are denied the opportunity to authority

22. Laski H.J., *A Grammar of Politics*, p. 104.

assume the subordinate position of obedience and those who enjoy the privileged position of authority struggle to maintain their power and prestige and tend to justify their retention by the most specious and fallacious kinds of arguments. Whenever men become only recipients of orders they lose their individuality and the ability to realise their own good. They cannot appreciate the implications of liberty and the means to safeguard their rights. Moreover, there can be no liberty where the rights of some depend upon the pleasure of others. No person or group of persons should be in a position to encroach upon my liberty and the rights which belong to me as a citizen.

Montesquieu's doctrine of Separation of Powers is an important institutional check against the abuse of power by any authority of the government. His maxim was *le pouvoir arrete le pouvoir*, power halts power. If any branch of government exercised authority in excess of that permitted by law, it should be checked by the other in order to restrain its encroachments, he asserted. This balancing of power was necessary for safeguarding the liberty of the individuals and for avoiding tyranny. Montesquieu, accordingly, suggested, that the three branches of government— executive, legislative and judiciary — should be so organised that each should be entrusted to different personnel, and each branch should perform distinct functions within the sphere of powers assigned to it. There are two views, modern and traditional, about the analysis of the doctrine. Without going into the relative merits of the two, it can be safely said that the doctrine of Separation of Powers has become more important today than at any other time. The core of the modern problem of government is to find a synthesis between the need for the Welfare State and the need for freedom. The Welfare State means concentration of power and ascendancy of the executive over the legislative branch. This development is alarming unless controlling and balancing devices are properly developed. Separation of the organs of government and responsibility and responsiveness of the government coupled with an independent and impartial judiciary are the much needed checks to irresponsible exercise of power.

The party system is another safety-valve. In a parliamentary system of government the alteration of political parties is a great restraint on the vagaries of the government. The party in office is fully conscious that tomorrow is the day of election and they shall have to face the electorate and answer for their acts of omission and commission. Then, there is the party in Opposition to remind the government of vulnerability of its position and the weakness of its policies. Lapses of the government are the Opposition's opportunities and it is always on the lookout to fish loopholes in the transactions of the government to expose and plague it. Opposition of today is tomorrow's government. Then, there is the free press to ventilate grievances, offer views and comments and even bring to light hidden secrets of public importance. No government can afford to remain oblivious for long of the comments and views expressed in the editorials and views of well-meaning persons on the national scene appearing in the press, not even letters to the editor which find a good space in every newspaper. Responsible Opposition and free press are indeed the bulwark of liberty of the people. "A government", says Laski, "that is compelled to explain itself under cross-examination will do its best to avoid the grounds of complaint. Nothing makes responsible government so sure.[23]

23. Laski, H.J., *Parliamentary Government in England,* p. 149.

Finally, liberty can best be secured and preserved when the action of the State is unbiased. It means that the machinery of the State should move promptly and impartially neither to the advantage of some nor to the disadvantage of others. This ideal, however, is not always possible to be realised. But let it be, once again, repeated that the price of liberty is eternal vigilance and the secret of liberty is courage. If people are vigilant and jealous of their rights, they will not submit to any illegal interference and biased action of the State. If people have the courage to sacrifice and bear all consequences for the vindication of their rights, there will be the least violation of their liberty. The freedom loving spirit of the people, therefore, is the best safeguard of liberty, that is, liberty exists in the mind and soul of men, or not at all. "There are nations," wrote De Tocqueville, "which have tirelessly pursued freedom through every kind of peril and hardship. They loved it, not for its material benefits; they regarded freedom itself as a gift so precious and so necessary, that no other could console them for the loss of everything else. I attempt no analysis of that great emotion for those who cannot feel it. It enters of its own accord into the generous hearts God has prepared to receive it; it fills them, it inspires them; but to the meaner mind which has never felt it, it is past finding out." Various constitutional devices to safeguard liberty are only the external aspects of freedom. Love for liberty is its real safeguard. But the greatest of all tragedies is to suppress liberty under the weight of custom or convention, education or ignorance, poverty or riotous abundance.

SUGGESTED READINGS

Barker, E.: *Principles of Social and Political Theory,* pp. 130-67.
Barker, E.: *Reflections on Guvernment,* Chaps, I, II.
Bryce,J.: *Modern Democracies,* Vol. I, Chap. VI.
Burgess J.W.: *The Reconciliation of Government with Liberty.*
Bury, J.: *History of Freedom of Thought.*
Cole, G.D.H. and Margaret: *A Guide to Modern Politics,* pp. 478-95.
Deane, H.A.: *The Political Ideas of Harold J. Laski.*
Elton, Trueblod: *Declaration of Freedom.*
Gettell, R.G.: *Introduction to Political Science,* Chap. X.
Gilchrist, R.N.: *Principles of Political Science,* Chaps. VI, VII.
Hayek, F.A.: *The Constitution of Liberty.*
Lacy, G.: *Liberty and Law,* Chaps. II-IV.
Laski, H.J.: *A Grammar of Politics,* Chaps. II-IV.
Laski, H.J.: *Liberty in the Modern State.*
Laski, H.J.: *The Danger of Obedience and Other Essays,* pp. 207-337.
Leacock, S.: *Elements of Political Science,* Chap. V.
Lippmann, W.: *Public Opinion.*
Lord, A.N.: *Principles of Politics.*
Mackinnot, J.: *History of Modern Liberty.*
Martin, E.W.: *The Tyranny of the Majority.*
Mill, J.S.: *On Liberty.*
Seeley, J.R.: *Introduction to Political Science,* Lectures V, VI.
Shaw, Bernard: *Everybody's Political What's What,* Chaps. V, VIII.
Tawney, R.H.: *Equality.*

11 CHAPTER

Relation between the Individual and the State (Contd.)

LAW

Laws are the rules of life. No community can live without rules. Rules are necessary to ensure the minimum uniformity of conduct and behaviour in a desired manner, without which social life would be impossible. The rules which represent a pattern of social behaviour and are expressed in customs, traditions, precedents and usages are called social rules. The sanction behind them is the will of the community and they depend for their effectiveness on its support. Disobedience of social rules is followed by punishment either in the form of ridicule or social disapproval and even ostracism. There is no positive penalty attaching to social rules. It is the criterion of the law of the State. "The law of the State alone," says MacIver, "in a demarcated and advanced society is coercive."

We speak of the State as sovereign. Similarly, we speak of the State as law-giver, that is, it makes laws. And one may well define the State with Woodrow Wilson as "a people organised for law within a definite territory." The rules of behaviour which the State makes for its members are called laws, disregard of which meets with a penalty which is enforced by the State's machinery of power, that is, government, through which the State exercises its sovereign authority. A law, therefore, prescribes general conditions of human activity in the State. It is a law, because it is declared to be so by the State through the proper law-making organ, whether it be the will of the autocratic ruler, or an act of parliament. "It is not the issuing of law that makes the State a State; it is the force of the State that makes law," as Hocking puts it. What distinguishes a law from a social rule or a group rule is that the former is enforceable by the machinery of the State backed by the authority of its sovereign power. Whatever is not so enforceable is not law. Laws of the State are applicable to all without exception in identical circumstances. There can only be one body of law within the State.

We, then, come to the following conclusions. First, the general conditions of human activity which the State prescribes for its members are called laws. Secondly, a law is law, if it is enacted by a proper law-making authority. Thirdly, law is definite and precise, reference can be made to it, chapter and verse. Fourthly, there can be only one body of law within the State. Law is universal in scope and it is applicable to all without exception in identical circumstances. Finally, laws are enforced by the authority of the State and their violation is followed by penalties politically determined and applied. Once the law has definitely and finally spoken, there is no appeal except to force. A law is, therefore, known by its finality and manner of enforcement.

MODERN SCHOOLS OF JURISPRUDENCE

There has been a sharp cleavage between different schools of jurisprudence or the science of law. Each school looks at it from its own point of view and lays emphasis upon some sources of law and its enforcement. Among the most important modern schools of legal study arc thc following:

1. **The Analytical School.** John Austin may be regarded as the founder of the Analytical School, though he drew his inspiration from Hobbes, and Bentham, his teacher. To him law is a command given by a superior to an inferior and enforced by material sanctions. Every positive law is a creation of the sovereign power, which either established it directly or authorised some subordinate person or body to establish it, and penalties are incurred for its disobedience. The Analytical School, thus, emphasises that the sovereign is a determinate superior, what the sovereign commands is law, and disobedience of such commands is accompanied by punishment. Law is the expression of the absolute and unitary sovereignty of the State.

This conception of law has the attraction of simplicity and consistency. It also seems to accord with the citizen's everyday experience. Let us illustrate it. Under the authority of the Constitution, Parliament of India makes the law of income-tax and provides that disobedience to its commands shall be punished by the fine or imprisonment, or both. Under the authority given to it by the Municipal Act, the Municipal Committee, say, of Patiala, prohibits the parking of cars and other vehicles in certain congested areas and prescribes the punishment for violation of its bye-law. Both these cases answer the Austinian formula.

Austin's doctrine has been subjected to unsparing attacks. His critics ask, times out of number, how customs can be reconciled with the theory of command, and where we can find a supreme law-giver in primitive society. But both these objections do not affect the validity of Austin's position. Primitive society lies outside his domain. His sovereign is found in an independent political society, that is, the community which has achieved Statehood and which lives under a duly established and recognised government. To the pre-State custom, he gives the name of "positive morality." With respect to the common law of England, Austin contends that it is a judge-made law and that judges are agents of the sovereign power acting in its name and subject to any restraints it may impose. What the sovereign power does not forbid, Austin says, it accepts; what it accepts, it commands. Sir Henry Maine characterised Austin's method of assimilating the common law to a command as "a mere artifice of speech" and a "mere straining of language." But it is a fact that judges in Britain acted for the King in Norman and Plantagenet times and that their decisions were effective only as he enforced them.

The Analytical Theory of law can best be appreciated once it is recognised that Austin was a lawyer and his theory is a legal theory. He discovers in the State a person or body of persons which, in the last resort, has the *de jure* right to issue commands and fix punishment for violation of such commands. "But he does not claim that legal right is tantamount to actual power, that form and substance are the same." He is not oblivious that the electorate, when one exists, does impose limitations on the legal sovereign. In fact, he points out that "in any State, even when the government is autocratic, the sovereign is restrained by the opinions of the people and must defer to 'the principles and maxims' held by the bulk of them or by the most influential portion."[1] The main defect of Austin was, as Sait says, that "he erred in thinking of the influence of masses as negative rather than positive." Law must be the expression of the will of the people, if it can adequately serve its purpose. Moreover, the Analytical School makes law rigid. It is the letter of the law which must be followed and there is nothing to lubricate its application. It also breeds conservatism, as it does not cater to the needs of the people and the times. Nor does it run into the past to establish its natural evolution. Gettell has correctly said that "Analytical jurists tend to regard the law as static rather than progressive, and they are not interested in its historical evolution. As a result, they have sometimes reached absolute conclusions without examining an adequate material."[2]

2. **The Historical School.** The Historical School of jurisprudence found its origin in Germany at the beginning of the nineteenth century. Frederick Von Savigny was its most famous apostle, though not its founder. Sir Henry Maine was another eminent follower and supporter of this school.

The Historical School regards the people themselves as law-makers through the formation of habit and custom. Its sanction is not the coercive authority of the State, but a general sense of right of the society. People obey law as a matter of habit because, in their opinion, it conforms to their standard of right. Acceptance has, therefore, always been the theory and fact of law. "No rule of law was ever successful or even endured," says Zane, "unless it received practical general acceptance among the whole body of people, for the simple reason that universal human experience has demonstrated that a rule of law not accepted by any considerable portion of the people can never he enforced... Whatever the means by which law is recognised, whether it be the legislative enactments, by decisions of courts, by rescripts of rulers, law is in fact law only when it is cheerfully accepted and gladly obeyed by the great mass of the social body. Acceptance by the community is needed to breathe life into the edict of the harshest despot.... Government may superficially appear to make law as Hobbes and Austin mistakenly supposed, but it is the acceptance of the rules by society that makes laws and government."[3]

The advocates of the Historical School go to the primitive society in order to explain the nature and source of law. The conduct of the people in the primitive society, they assert, was governed by customary rules, which were rigidly obeyed by them notwithstanding the absence of any command of the sovereign. The customs so observed and followed scrupulously by the succeeding generations became the social habit and a pattern of social behaviour. What governed the conduct of men in primitive times has continued, and will continue, they say, to govern it at all times and under all conditions.

1. Coker, F.W., *Recent Political Thought*, p. 503.
2. Gettell, R. G., *Introduction to Political Science*, p. 179.
3. *The Story of Law*, p. 271.

"Human nature is not likely to undergo a radical change, and, therefore, that to which we give the name of law has been and still is and for ever continue to be custom." No legally constituted law-making authority, however absolute its power, can disregard the weight of customs and the pre-existing customs are the standard of laws.

Thus, law, according to the Historical School, is self-created and self-executed. It is not the deliberate creation of the law-maker, but the result of the slow development of society through centuries. The function of the State is not to create law, but to realise and enforce it. Legislation can be effective only when it is reinforced by customs supplementing and clarifying it and the punishments which it prescribes in case of disobedience are in conformity with the established habits of the people. No legislative authority, whatever be the extent of its legal power, can make or abrogate customary law. As Laski has said, "In law there was no part of the field of social fact he (Sultan of Turkey) could not alter: in practice he survived only by willing not to will those changes which might have proved him the sovereign of Austinian Jurisprudence."[4]

But the Historical School errs in reducing the element of command to a "metaphor." They insist that the rulers adjust their wills to the wills of the ruled and command only in name. Moreover, the adherents of this School tend to be conservative when they view law less as a matter of deliberate legislation than as an evolution within the social body. Their reverence for the past stresses legal history rather than the content of law and what law should really aim at.

3. **The Philosophical School.** The Philosophical School is not concerned with what the actual law of the past and the present is. Their effort is to develop the idea of justice as an ethical principle and consequently to create an ideal system of law. In the eighteenth century they put their faith in the law of nature which could be discovered by human reason. In the nineteenth century they engaged themselves in the metaphysical discussions of the existing law and in attempts to create a perfect system of law in codes and legislation. In the twentieth century they devoted themselves to social interests and ideals and to the formulation of theories of social justice. The jurists of the Philosophical School have always considered law as an abstraction and based it upon abstract ethical principles of justice. A law, as such, is removed from objectivity whereas it ought to be definite and precise, capable of universal application. Idealism must be blended with realism.

4. **The Comparative School.** Another school of jurisprudence, known as the Comparative School, is of modern origin. Its exponents adopt the method of examining and comparing the legal systems of the past and the present, and arrive at generalisations. They also draw upon other Social Sciences for their material for proper authentication and reliability. Although the programme of this school is ambitious and sufficient headway has been made in our knowledge of law, much still remains to be done. Comparisons are, no doubt, valuable aids and they bring us nearer to the truth. But if law is really to be the manifestation of the will of the people, it must be in conformity with the genius of the people concerned. No wholesale importation from outside can serve the desired purpose and fulfil the needs.

---

4. Laski, H.J., *A Grammar of Politics*, p. 51.

5. **The Sociological School**. The Sociological School, the most prominent representative of which are Duguit, Krabbe and Laski, describes the "orthodox" conception of law as a futile truth. They argue that law is not really made by an organised body of men. They admit that there are definite agencies in a society issuing commands or making decisions which are normally obeyed by the bulk of the community. But all such commands or decisions do not deserve to be regarded as laws. Some other quality is essential to give these rules the character of law. Law, according to Duguit, is the name for the rules of conduct which men observe while living in society. They obey these rules of conduct not because they are commands and are accompanied by punishment, but because they are the conditions of social living. Without obedience to these rules life would not be worth living. All of us are conscious of these rules of life which enable society to survive. Every man is, thus, impelled by self-interest to obey them. He knows instinctively or learns from experience what living together means. Consciousness of this fact accounts for social solidarity and it is the duty of the State to sustain such rules. Likewise, it is the duty of every individual to observe all such rules as help to realize social solidarity and abstain from all such acts as are detrimental to its growth. Laws, in brief "in the fundamental sense, are the rules of conduct which normal men know they must observe in order to preserve and promote the benefits derived from life in society." The sanction of law, Duguit asserts, is primarily psychological, "resting in each individual's awareness of the social approval or reprobation of his conduct according to its conformity or non-conformity to the fundamental social rules."

Krabbe explains law according to the source from which it springs. It is the sum total of all those rules, general or particular, written or unwritten, "which spring from men's feeling or sense of right." He holds that law is above and, in origin, independent of the State. He rejects the idea of State sovereignty and the only theory which he is willing to recognize is the sovereignty of law. Krabbe defines law as "the expression of one of the many judgments of value which we human beings make, by virtue of our disposition and nature." Law is, therefore, what is just and good from our standard of value and judgment. It is not a matter of external legal authority, but an internal human matter. It is obeyed, because it is just and good and not because of fear of punishment which its disobedience involves. The source of law, according to Laski, is the individual consenting mind. People obey it as it satisfies their desires. A good law, in his opinion, "is a law which has, as its results, the maximum possible satisfaction of desire; and no law save a good law is, except in a formal sense, entitled to obedience as such." He, thus, puts the source of law where it most truly belongs—in the individual consenting mind.

Jurists of the Sociological School hold divergent views on many points, but all believe that law is the product of social forces and should serve social needs. They do not concern themselves with the abstract theories, but judge the law by its results and find its sanction in the social needs that it serves. "The legal imperatives of any state", says Laski, "must always be conceived if they are to be capable of justification, in terms of the end it seeks to serve; they are, so to say, a permanent essay in the conditional mood."[5] Without any reservation, the Sociologists attack the idea of a sovereign State as

5. Laski, H.J., *Introduction to Politics*, p. 45.

the creator of law. It is possible, they point out, to conceive of a State in which there is law and no State, but it is not possible to conceive of a State in which there is no form of law. The purpose of law is to serve society and the purpose of the State is to enact and promulgate laws in order to achieve the socially desirable ends. Gettel has cogently summed up what the different Schools of Jurisprudence claim and explain. He says, "In contrast to the analytical jurist, who found the sanction of law in the command of the State, to the philosophical jurists, who found its sanction in its inherent justice, and to the historical jurist, who found its sanction in established habits and custom, the sociological jurist finds the sanction of law in the social needs and interests that it serves."[6]

6. **Marxian Concept of Law.** The Marxian concept of law is entirely opposed to the Schools of Jurisprudence hitherto considered. Law, according to Marx, is intimately associated with the nature of the State. He does not accept the view that law is the expression of the will of the people or reflection of the principles of social justice or the result of habits and customs or the social needs it serves. It is, on the contrary, merely an expression of the will of the State, the expression of the material form of life in that State, and in a class society it is the will of the ruling class. According to Vyshinsky, "Marxism-Leninism gives a clear definition (the only scientific definition) of the essence of law. It teaches that class relationship (and, consequently, law itself) is rooted in the material conditions of life, and that law is merely the will of the dominant class elevated into stature." In a Capitalist State, the law is only the tool of the State to maintain and safeguard the interests of the capitalist class, a dominant group in society. In a Socialist State the workers are the ruling class and, thus, law must be the safeguard of the proletarian State against the enemies of Socialism, and a tool for the construction of a Socialist Society.

There is an element of truth in what Marx says, but it is not the whole truth. The Marxian view of law does not accept other refinements connected with the State and law. Moreover, law for Marx is a vehicle for destroying Capitalism and constructing Socialism. As soon as it achieves its purpose the State "withers away." We do not accept this conclusion. For us, the State is the life-breath of human existence and whatever shape a government may take, the State shall ever endure. Its laws hold society together for the promotion and achievement of the all-round happiness of man.

Conclusion. Our conclusion regarding the nature of law is related to the rational needs of man in the State. No single theory adequately explains the concept of law. There is substantial truth in what each School of Jurisprudence advocates. Law is not entirely a command of the determinate human superior and based upon force. Nor can the sovereign command and enforce anything which is repugnant to the will of the community. It would be also wrong to say that all law finds its origin in the customary behaviour of the people and the sovereign can command and enforce nothing which is not acceptable to the masses. A customary law is stationary and it does not cater to the needs of the people and the realities of human life. Its source is the antiquated past and outmoded customs. If law is to really serve its purpose, it must be a progressive and expanding force and able

6. Gettel, R.G., *Introduction to Political Science,* p. 181.

to adjust itself according to the social, moral, religious and economic needs of the people The Jurists of all Schools now generally regard law as the instrument of human welfare. They consider not only what the laws are, but also what effects they have produced in the past, how they operate today, and how they may be improved by deliberate human effort. What a law may order and what it may prohibit is what appears to us just and unjust, good and bad. But if law is to be obeyed by all, there must be some compulsion behind it. Compulsion has two aspects, physical and ethical compulsion. The physical compulsion is to be found in the organised force of government. But the root of obedience to law is not coercion; it is the will to obey. It cannot, however, be denied that law takes the form of an imperative.[7] It is an imperative in the sense that it must be obeyed by all and in order that it must be obeyed by all, it should be accompanied by physical compulsion. Even the pluralists admit the compulsive nature of law, provided it coincides with the moral purposes of the State.

Two definitions of law, which are widely quoted, may be noted. The first is the one given by Holland. He says, "A law is a general rule of action taking cognisance only of external acts, enforced by a determinate authority, which authority is human and among human authorities is that which is paramount in a political society; or briefly, a law is a general rule of external action enforced by a sovereign political authority." This definition is a legal analysis of law, pure and simple. Woodrow Wilson's definition is more logical as it harmonises the analytical point of view of law with the historical point of view. "Law," according to Wilson, "is that portion of the established thought and habit which has gained distinct and formal recognition in the shape of uniform rules backed by the authority and power of government." According to MacIver, "The root of obedience to a law is not coercion but the will to obey; nevertheless, law takes the force of an imperative."[8]

THE SOURCES OF LAW

Law, like the State itself, is the product of history. In every country it has passed through various stages of development and several factors have contributed to its evolution. All these factors are described as the "sources" of law which may be outlined as follows:–

1. **Custom.** Custom is one of the earliest sources of law. In the primitive society all disputes were decided in accordance with the prevailing social customs. In the beginning, when the social organisation was simple, customs were based on the general usage of the family, clan or tribe. No one can say exactly when and how custom arose, "except that it was shaped by the cooperative action of the whole community and not by any kingly, or legislative command."[9] But one thing is clear, that customs are accepted and followed as a matter of habit. Their sanction is utility or the general desire of men for order and justice. Sometimes people choose to do a certain thing as a matter of convenience. When it is repeated, it becomes a habit and passes from one generation to another till its utility

7. MacIver, R.M., *The Modern State,* p. 21.
8. *Ibid*., p. 149.
9. Woodrow Wilson, *The State,* pp. 69-70.

is lost to the community. Sometimes a custom may grow accidentally and people begin following it.

The various schools of jurisprudence are in substantial agreement upon the importance of customs as a source of law. Customs are not laws in the political sense of the term. But when the State recognizes these customary rules as binding, they acquire the status of law. No State can afford to ignore the customs of the land, not even conquerors who impose new legal systems on defeated countries. If it does, the people who follow these customs will revolt against the authority of the State. "In the great book of law", says MacIver, "the State merely writes new sentences and here and there scratches out an old one. Much of the book was never written by the State at all, and by all of it the State itself is bound, save as it modifies the code from generation to generation. The State can no more reconstitute at any time the law as a whole than a man can remake his body."[10] The common law of England consists mainly of customs and the courts take due cognizance of it. Customary law is also an integral part of the legal framework in India.

2. **Religion.** In the primitive community custom was law and law was religion. Law and religion were so inextricably mixed up that the rules of life had a religious sanction. The institution of, first, the magician and, then, the priest-king, in the early stages of the development of the State, is a clear illustration of the relation between religion and politics. "Indeed," as Woodrow Wilson points out, "the early law of Rome was little more than a body of technical religious rules, a system of means for obtaining religious rights through the proper carrying out of certain religious formulas."[11] The most influential basis of the Hindu Law in India is the code of Manu. The Mohammedan Law derives itself from the Quran and the Shariat. Islamic law now forms the basis of the legal system of the Islamic Republic of Pakistan replacing the prevailing laws by those ordained by the Quran and Shariat and evolving an Islamic Jurisprudence. President Zia-ul-Haq, for instance, replaced the wealth tax and agriculture produce laws by *Zakat* and *Usur*. Religion, thus, is an important and in some the only source of law, as in the Arabian countries, Iran and Afghanistan.

3. **Judicial Decisions.** Gettel says that the State "arose not as the creator of law, but as the interpreter and enforcer of customs."[12] When men live in society disputes are sure to arise. In primitive society disputed points were referred to the wisest men in the community and their decisions were accepted and made precedents for similar cases. When social organisation became more complex and tribes intermixed either for the purpose of trade or matrimony, conflict of customs became more usual. At that time the necessity was felt to supplement custom by interpretation. Whenever custom failed to give a just solution or was obviously not suited to the case, the dispute was decided according to commonsense. Such decisions became judicial precedents. In the beginning they were oral and unwritten and passed from generation to generation by tradition. But in order to make them more definite they were later reduced to writing. In Britain, before

10. MacIver, R.M., *The Modern State,* p. 478.

11. Woodrow Wilson, *The State,* p. 71. "In early Rome, pontiff and judge were one and jurisprudence was *rerumedivinarun atque hamanarum notitia.* Religious observance was an integral part of that social order which it was incumbent on the state to maintain and defend." MacIver, R.M., *The Modern State,* p. 101.

12. Gettel, R.G., *Introduction to Political Science,* p. 171.

the rise of Parliament, judges went on circuit and were responsible for evolving uniformity in the law. By comparing decisions and by basing new decisions on preceding ones, they developed the Common Law.

This was not a characteristic only of early law. In our own times a judge, while applying the law, interprets it, and in doing so he modifies or explains it either subconsciously or deliberately. Customs, too, are to be fitted to dynamic conditions of society and their rigidity is lubricated by the progressive social forces. Even a written law requires filling in the gaps. This is done by judges, and Justice Holmes, of the United States Supreme Court, gave us a bare truth when he said that judges do and must make laws. Thus, law in its most characteristic form is the *case-law* or *judge-made* law.

4. **Scientific Commentaries.** Scientific discussions by eminent jurists also modify and develop law. In every country the greatest importance is attached by both judges and lawyers to the opinions of legal luminaries. The jurists collect and arrange in logical form past customs, decisions, and laws. They discuss and elaborate the existing law and make it clear where it is ambiguous. In this process they express their opinions as to what the law ought to be and its effect on society. On the basis of the past and the present law, they are able to arrive at general principles which may guide future legislation and indicate in broad lines the gaps that need filling in. The opinions of the commentators are not decisions. They are only arguments. When these arguments are repeatedly recognized, they amount to accepted decisions. To sum up: "The commentator, by collecting, comparing, and logically arranging principles, customs, decisions and laws, lays down guiding principles for possible cases. He shows the omissions and deduces principles to govern them."

5. **Equity.** The term equity means equality or fairness, The function of a judge is to administer justice. But law can never fit in every case. At many points it may be silent and at others it may be ambiguous. When the existing law does not provide any relief, principles of equity are applied and cases are decided according to commonsense or fairness. Moreover, positive law, with the lapse of time, becomes unsuitable for new and changed social conditions. To make it suitable, either the law should be changed by the law-making authority, or there should be some informal method of changing it. Equity is an informal method of making new law or altering old law, depending on intrinsic fairness or equality of treatment. Thus, equity is intended to provide relief where the existing law affords none. It aims at securing equality or justice and it is based on what earlier writers used to describe as the law of nature, that is, law guided by reason.

The interference of equity with law, according to Sir Henry Maine, is open and avowed.[13] Equity not only supplements law, but it also makes law flexible. It is an informal method of making new law and altering the old one. Equity, too, is a kind of judge-made law. But there is one important difference between the two. In *case-law*, the judge interprets the existing law. In equity, he adds to the law what is missing therein and creates a new one in order to make it suitable for the changed conditions. Equity, in brief, includes such principles as the following:–

13. Maine, H., *Ancient Law,* p. 28.

"Equity will not suffer a wrong to be without a remedy.
He who seeks equity must do equity.
Delay defeats equity.
Equality is equity.
Equity looks to the intent rather than to form."

6. **Legislation.** In addition to selecting customary usages for enforcement, Kings issued decrees concerning new matters. This practice was the source of legislation, which became the primary concern of the legislative assemblies with the emergence of a representative government. But the approval of the King or President is as much there now as it was in the past.

Legislation is, now, the most prolific and direct source of law. Law is regarded as the expression of the will of the people and the will of the people is expressed through legislative assemblies which are representative bodies. All other means of making laws have now been swallowed up by this modern method of legislation. Custom and equity are being replaced by definite legislative acts. The codification of law has limited the scope of judicial decisions, and scientific commentaries are used simply to discuss cases. Legislation has, thus, tended to supplant other sources of law. But we cannot ignore the practical utility of customs, equity, religious practices and judicial decisions. Though all these forces have not remained direct sources of law, yet they constantly influence its formulation.

Woodrow Wilson has beautifully expressed his views on the process of the development of law. He says, "Custom is the earliest fountain of law but religion is a contemporary, an equally prolific, and in the same stages of national development, an almost identical source. Adjudication comes almost as authority itself, and from a very antique time goes hand in hand with equity. Only legislation, the conscious and deliberate organisation of law, and scientific discussion, the development of its principles, await an advanced stage of its growth in the body-politic to assert their influence in law-making"

VARIOUS KINDS OF LAW

Broadly speaking, there are two distinct kinds of law – National Law, and International Law. National Law extends over the territory and people of the State. Within the sphere of the State there are two kinds of law. One, that which governs the State, and, the second, law by means of which the State governs its people. The former is called the *Constitutional Law* and the latter the *Ordinary Law*.

Constitutional Law. Constitutional Law is fundamentally distinct from Ordinary Law. According to Dicey, it includes "all rules which directly or indirectly affect the distribution or the exercise of power in the State", and which "are enforced by the courts." Constitutional Law defines the organisation of the State, determines the functions exercised by different departments of government, and establishes the relationship between the rulers and the ruled. Constitutional Law may be either written or unwritten. It may be the result of the deliberate effort of a body – like the Constituent Assembly especially convened for the purpose – or it may be the product of history and may consist largely in a mass of customs, usages, and judicial decisions, as in Britain. Since the whole of the Constitutional Law cannot be unwritten, a part of it may consist of laws passed by the Legislative Assembly of the country and enacted from time to time.

Ordinary Law. The State is both the child and the parent of law. The constitutional and the ordinary laws have different characters and have different sanctions. Ordinary law is made and enforced by the competent authorities of the State, and it determines the relations of the citizens to the State and to one another. The courts take cognizance of this law alone, apply it in deciding cases of dispute, and the government enforces obedience to their decisions.

Ordinary Law may, for proper comprehension, be divided into *Public Law* and *Private Law*:

1. Public Law regulates the relations of the individuals to the State. It is made by the State for and on behalf of the community. It determines, "within its range," as McIver says, "not so much the order of the State as the order of society." The State punishes the offender against it, using, if necessary, the force of its authority.

Public Law may further be sub-divided into *Administrative Law* and *General Law*. Administrative Law defines in detail the manner in which the government through its various organs exercises the powers that are conferred upon it by the Constitutional Law. In the narrower sense, it is that part of Public Law which fixes the organization and determines the competence of organs that administer the law, and indicates to the individual remedies for the violation of his rights.[14] There prevail two systems to deal with cases arising between private individuals and officers of the government acting in their official capacity. One is, what Dicey called, the Rule of Law, as it is obtainable in Britain, the United States of America, India and the other Commonwealth countries. The other is the Administrative Law administered in separate Administrative Courts and as prevailing in the Continental Countries of Europe, notable in France. We shall deal with both these systems in the Chapter on Judiciary.[15]

General Law determines the relation of private citizens to the State. It is necessary to distinguish between General Law made by the law-making authority, and decrees or orders issued in pursuance of the General Law. A General Law fixes some general and permanent rules of conduct, whereas a decree or order is the particular application of a General Law at a particular time. For example, a law will decide as to what the qualifications are for holding a certain position in the State; a decree or order will appoint a particular individual.

2. Private Law regulates the relations among individuals. It prescribes the conduct of man in society in his relation to others, and guarantees to each the enjoyment of his rights. In Private Law, sometimes termed civil law, the parties concerned are private persons and the State is the arbiter. The State, however, does not regulate all the relations among persons, but only those which in its opinion are of such social importance as to need legal regulation, for example, laws concerning property, contract, marriage, and torts. This is how Holland distinguishes Private Law from Public Law. "In Private Law,"

14. Gettel, R.G., *Introduction to Political Science*, pp. 184-85.

15. Chap. XX, *Infra.*

he says, "the parties concerned are private individuals above and between whom stands the State as an impartial arbiter. In Public Law also the State is present as an arbiter, although it is at the same time one of the parties interested."

Municipal Law is an ancient term which means the law of a particular State and Public Law and Private Law, combined together, are called Municipal Law, though we prefer to call it National Law. In contrast to the Municipal or National Law, there is also a body of rules which regulate relations between States and it is called International Law. We shall deal with this kind of law in the following Chapter.

The following table has been borrowed from MacIver. It shows the classification of the types of law:[16]

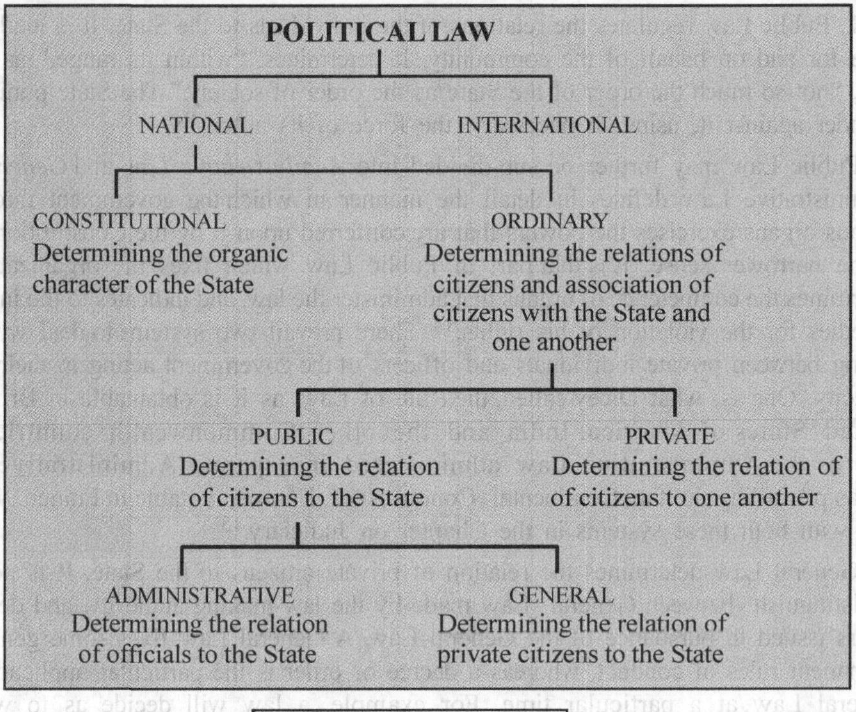

LAW AND MORALITY

Law is the subject of study in Political Science. Morality forms the subject-matter of Ethics. There is close affinity between Political Science and Ethics as both deal with man as a moral agent in society.[17] The end of the State is the promotion of general welfare and moral perfection of man in society. It exists for attaining those moral values which enable man to make the best of himself. In simple words, every State endeavours to promote those physical and social conditions which are necessary for the expression and development of a free moral personality. The actions of the State have, accordingly, an integral connection with the moral end of man and an ideal system of law would probably

16. MacIver, R.M., *The Modern State,* p. 290.
17. See Chapter II, *Supra.*

embody and enforce the highest ethical standards. So intimate is the connection between the two that ancient writers confused law with morality.

Distinction between Law and Morality. But a definite line of demarcation can be drawn between the two. Law and morality differ from one another in content, sanction and definiteness. Morality embraces the whole life of man, his thoughts and motives as well as his actions. Law is concerned only with the outward acts of man and has nothing to do with his thoughts and motives; it is objective whereas morality is subjective. Thoughts and motives, only when exhibited in actions, come within the purview of law. To tell a lie or to be angry are immoral acts, but unless I cheat someone by telling a lie, I am not guilty of doing anything illegal. Similarly, as long as I confine my anger to my own self, or simply express it in words, I do not do anything contrary to the laws of the State. But, if I inflict an injury on the person of someone in a fit of anger or abuse and defame him publicly, through spoken or written words, my action is against the law of the State and I can be punished for a breach of the law.

Law is enforced by the government and its disobedience is visited with punishment. Behind it is the sanction of force. The violation of a rule of morality, on the other hand, does not mean physical punishment, although it may mean social disapprobation, which may be severer in consequences than even physical punishment. Moral condemnation may socially damn a person, but it does not mean physical punishment. The sanction behind morality is that of public censure. Law is, thus, a matter of force and morality is the subject of conscience. A law remains a law, whether we like it or not. It is law even if it is immoral and we have to obey it.

Law is universal in character. There can only be one body of law within the State and applicable to all, without exception, in identical circumstances. Morality is individual and it differs from man to man. My morality differs from my son's; it is the imperative of the individual's heart or his conscience. The ethical appeal is always to the individual's own sense of what is right or wrong and, in the last resort, to his sense of what is good and evil. This sense of right or wrong may appear to be "the product of custom and social training, but as a principle of conduct it is the 'self-legislating' of a responsible person, choosing in the consciousness of his own liberty the means and ends of welfare."[18] Again, law is superior to morality in definiteness and consistency. Law is precise and certain, with chapter and verse given, because of its universality. Morality is characterised by a certain amount of vagueness and uncertainty because of its individuality; it may even differ from man to man.

Moral laws prescribe absolute standards of right or wrong, justice and injustice. But law follows standards of expediency. What a law prohibits may not be an immoral act. Driving on the right is a social danger and is prohibited by law. But it is not immoral, though it is illegal. There are many things which may be immoral and yet not illegal. To bet on the race-course or to play poker in a club may be immoral, but neither of the two is illegal. There is, thus, a legal conscience as well as a moral conscience, and they do not always coincide. The State makes some laws which are based upon expediency and convenience rather than on the standards of morality. Likewise, laws of the State may

18. MacIver, R.M., *The Modern State,* p. 55.

take no cognizance of moral rights. The State guarantees only the enjoyment of civil rights. It is my moral duty to support and serve my parents, since parents possess a moral right to demand this much consideration from their children. If I am not alive to my moral duty and prove an undutiful son, the laws of the State cannot force me to become dutiful. There is nothing to coerce me legally.

It will, thus, be clear that law does not and cannot cover all the ground of morality. "To turn all moral obligations into legal obligations would be to destroy morality."[19] Nor can the State dictate morality, for State-dictated morality is no morality. For example, a law may be enacted ordering every citizen to go either to a *gurdwara* or a *mosque* or a *mandir* every morning. If I disobey the law, I can be forced to obey it. But it does not mean that I become a moral man by going to a religious place. Morality is the subject of conscience and a matter of conviction. It cannot be forced upon anyone.

Affinity between Law and Morality. There are some glaring points of difference between law and morality. Nevertheless, there is a close connection between the two, as the State is founded on the minds of the citizens, who are moral agents.[20] A bad citizen means a bad State since its laws do not mould and shape him to be a good citizen. "The best State," according to Plato, "is that which is nearest in virtue to the individual. If any part of the body-politic suffers, the whole body suffers." This organic view of the State was the essence of Greek political philosophy. Modern political thought also believes that the individual and the State are inherently connected; both act and react upon each other. Man can be at his best only within the State, without the State he is nothing. It is a natural and rational institution. Its purposes are moral and the laws of the State set the standard of morality. As an Indian adage goes: 'as the King so are the subjects.'[21] Similarly, ideas of right and wrong, which represent the ethical standards of the people, affect the laws of the State, in their turn, and its actions.

The State, thus, performs a direct function in relation to morality and it takes two forms, positive and negative. The positive function of the State is to make laws which are conducive to the general happiness and are in accordance with the moral beliefs and sentiments of all sections of the community. For instance, untouchability is prohibited by the Constitution and in pursuance of this prohibition the Government of India has enacted legislation making its practice a penal offence. It is a moral sin to differentiate between man and man simply because of accident of birth. Similarly, it adds to the moral stature of men and society, if the laws of the State make drinking a penal offence. When the State repeals a bad law either by itself or as a result of public protest, it performs a negative function. Since our standards of right and wrong change, so laws too must change in conformity to such changes. *Suttee* and *Thugee* were declared illegal acts as they did not accord with our changed standards of virtues or values.

So close is the affinity between law and morality that "the margin between the illegal and the immoral is not always clear." The illegality of today may become the immorality of tomorrow and *vice versa.* "We regard the State," as MacIver has said, "as the condition

19. *Ibid.,* p. 157.
20. Gilchrist, R.N., *Principles of Political Science,* p. 172.
21. YATHA RAJA TATHA PRAJA.

of morality. The State and law continually affect both public opinion and actions; in its turn law reflects public opinion and thus acts as the index of moral progress."[22] Sometimes laws precede the public demand, and are made before their utility has been fully grasped. The Hindu Marriage Law in India was enacted at a time when public opinion in its favour was not well advanced. In fact, there was violent opposition to it, though its social value could not be denied. In the last analysis the sanction behind both law and morality is public opinion.

Law and Public Opinion. If law is to be the expression of the will of the people, it must conform to public opinion. If public opinion demands the repeal or enactment of any law, the Government and for that matter the legislature cannot afford to brush aside the demand for long. The representatives of the people, who make the legislature, know that they have ultimately to appeal to the electorate after the expiry of their legal term of office. If their actions are not approved by the electors at the general election, there is no chance of their re-election. A true representative government always ascertains the wishes of the people before attempting any kind of legislation. If it does not, the laws so enacted lose their appeal to the minds of the citizens and the foundation of loyalty is shaken. Hume has justly remarked that all governments, however bad, depend for their authority on public opinion. If there is a wide gulf between law and public opinion, it may lead either to widespread lawlessness or even to open rebellion.

But this is not the entire appraisal of the relationship between law and public opinion. If the relationship between the two is to be really organic, then, law should precede as well as succeed public opinion or, as Dr. P.S. Muhar puts it, "law should be not only firmly rooted in public opinion but should be a little ahead of it."[23] P.S. Muhar aptly cites the example of the law abolishing *suttee* in India and says, "If Lord William Bentinck had taken only public opinion for his guide when he abolished *suttee* in 1835, he would have had to wait much longer for his great social reform." Law must also be normative, if the State is to be the ideal of the aspirations of its people.

SUGGESTED READINGS

Allen, C.K.: *Law in the Making.*

Amos, S.: *Science of Politics,* Chap. XIL

Bodenheimer, E.: *Jurisprudence: The Philosophy and Method of Law.*

Brown, W.J.: *The Austinian Theory of Law.*

Bryce, J.: *Studies tn History and Jurisprudence,* Nos. II, XI-XVI.

Cohen, Morris: *Law and the Social Order.*

Dealey, J.Q.: *The State and Government,* Chaps. XVI-XVII.

Dicey, A.V.: *Law and Public Opinion,* Lecture I.

Duguit, L.: *Law in the Modern State.*

22. MacIver, R.M., *The Modern State,* pp. 153-54.
23. "Public Opinion : Its Nature, Limitations and Conditions for Expression." Bulletin of the Institute of Public Administration, Patna University, September 24, 1956.

Fieldmann W.G.: *Law in a Changing Society.*

Gilchrist, R.N.: *Principles of Political Science,* Chap. VIII.

Krabbe, H.: *The Modern Idea of the State.*

Lippman, W.: *Public Opinion.*

Lord, R.N.: *Principles of Politics,* Chap. VII.

MacIver, R.M.: *The Modern State,* Chap. VIII.

Maine, H.S.: *Ancient Law,* Chaps. 1, III, V.

Pound, R.: *Law and Morals.*

Seagle, William: *The Quest for Law.*

Sidgwick, H: *Elements of Politics,* Chap. XIII.

Willoughby, W: W.: *Fundamental Concepts of Public Law,* Chap. X.

Wilson, Woodrow: *The State,* Chap. V.

12 CHAPTER

Relations between States

External Aspect of the State. Political Science deals not only with the internal organisation of the State, but with its external relations as well. Every State is, in terms of law, an absolutely independent unit. It is subordinate to none and its sovereignty is unlimited over all persons and associations within its territorial limits. Nevertheless, no State can have an independent and secluded existence. All States are banded together in a variety of ways. Mutual intercourse between them is primarily due to certain natural causes. Nature has not willed man to be self-sufficient. Dependence is his very psychology. What is true of man is also true of States, for it is the people who make the State and the State exists for the people. If mutual intercourse between States is not recognised and established, society is bound to stagnate. Modern economic, scientific, social and cultural developments have further cemented the ties of mutual interests and common affinity. In fact, in the civilised world of today citizens of one country very largely share in the thought, the art, and the literature of the neighbouring communities. Mutual contact between States is strengthened if citizens of countries politically separate, for instance, India and Pakistan, speak a common language or "where a kindred descent enables them to look back to the same history and traditions in the past."[1]

The relations between States demand their regulation in the same way as man subjects himself to certain rules of conduct in his dealings with his fellow-citizens.[2] In the beginning, the rules of conduct between States were rudimentary and not uniform in character. Now there is an increasing tendency to conform them to a definite code of conduct. Uniformity and definiteness are necessitated by the greater economic and social interdependence of peoples or nations. Without such rules there would be confusion and chaos and all causes of disputes would have to be settled by the arbitrament of war.

International Law. The principles and rules which States observe in their dealings with one another are called International Law. International Law is defined as the system which orders the relations between States and governs their relations with one another. It binds them to mutually agreed and recognised principles and rules governing the rights of the States in relation to one another and prescribes a procedure by which those rights can be protected and, in the event of violation, redressed. Sovereign States are subject

1. Leacock, *Elements of Political Science,* p. 84.
2. MacIver, R.M., *The Modern State,* p. 282.

of International Law and its scope extends to the acquisition and meaning of Statehood, the rules and procedures of peaceful international intercourse, and the rules and procedure of war. The law of Statehood deals with the legal personality of the State and its rights, duties and privileges. The rules and procedures of peaceful international intercourse include the law of diplomacy, the law of treaties and the law of pacific settlement of international disputes. The law of war deals initially with the legal concepts of belligerency and neutrality. In addition, the law of war covers rules for the conduct of warfare relating to population, prisoners of war, prohibition of certain weapons, and similar matters.

But how far these principles, which constitute the content of International Law, are binding on the States and how do we reconcile such regulations with the sovereignty of the State are important questions to decide. German writers, for example, Hegel, Jellinek, and Trietschke, while admitting that States are bound in honour and good faith by the terms of international law and treaty obligations, maintain that they are not legal obligations. The States, they contend, voluntarily subject themselves to international obligations, and there is nothing to force their obedience. Trietschke upholds the right of every State to declare war and to repudiate its treaties. Hitler, too, declared unequivocally that treaties were nothing more than mere scraps of paper. The sanction of international law, they say, is auto-limitation which can be withdrawn at the will of the State "The subject of international law," says Trietschke, "being sovereign States subject to no legal superior, they are the Judges in the last analysis of their own rights and of their obligations to other States."

Legal Nature of International Law. It is a controversial issue whether the principles and rules governing the relations between States are merely a body of rules of international morality, without legal force, or whether International Law is in reality law, a branch of Jurisprudence proper. It was decided in *West Rand Central Gold Mining Company* v. *Rex* that no principle of International Law was enforceable in British Courts until it had been formally adopted into the body of the Municipal Law by an Act of Parliament. The Analytical School of Jurists, founded by Bentham and Austin, deny to International Law the status of law. They contend that law is a command issued by a determinate human superior to an inferior and its disobedience is accompanied by punishment. Law must also be precise and definite with regard to its origin and obligation. But in the community of nations, comprising sovereign States, there is no determinate superior political authority to issue commands and enforce sanctions and penalties. If it be presumed that there is one to command and others to obey, it establishes their subordinate status and with that they disappear as sovereign States. Nor are there courts with power to enforce International Law or impose penalties for disobedience. States, of course, refer matters of dispute arising between them to tribunals for arbitration, but the decisions of such tribunals are not binding on the sovereign States. It is for them to accept or reject such decisions and there is no authority competent and powerful to enforce and punish the recalcitrant States. The sanction of International Law is, therefore, customary. The law which rests on custom, consent and agreement cannot be law. It is only a sense of moral obligation that makes it binding and at the best it can be described as international morality. Lord Salisbury, while addressing the House of Lords, once said, "I think, my Lords, we are misled in this matter by the facility with which we use the phrase International Law.

International Law has not any existence in the sense in which the term law is usually understood. It depends generally on the prejudices of the writers of the textbooks. It can be enforced by no tribunal, and, therefore, to apply to it the phrase Law is to some extent misleading."[3] Similarly, Lord Coleridge observed in *The Queen* v. *Keyn* (1876) : "Strictly speaking, international law is an inexact expression, and it is apt to mislead if its inexactness is not kept in mind. Law implies a law-giver, and a tribunal capable of enforcing it and coercing its transgressors. But there is no common law-giver to sovereign States, and no tribunal has the power to bind them by decree or coerce them if they transgress."

But modern writers accept International Law as law in the real sense of the term. They regard Austin's theory of sovereignty in its international relations as "not only a legal fiction but a baneful and dangerous dogma which ought to be abandoned, and that notion should be expunged from the literature of international law." It is asserted that sovereignty of the State does not imply that the States cannot mutually agree to follow certain rules of conduct for common safety and well-being. Chief Justice Marshall, of the United States Supreme Court, recognized the absolute and exclusive authority of the State over all persons and things within its territory. But he admitted that considerations of mutual benefit and advantage in practice made necessary "a relaxation of that absolute and complete jurisdiction which sovereignty is said to confer."[4] Law is not always the command of a determinate human superior. There are various other sources of law too. No one can ignore the influence of customs and the common law. Common law does not emanate from the legislature. Nor do customs. Moreover, law must adjust itself to the social needs of the community. International Law is the result of the experience of ages, and its rules have been evolved and accepted as governing the conduct of States in times of war and peace.

People do not obey laws merely for fear of punishment. Even in the presence of the coercive authority of the State positive laws are disobeyed every day by scores of people. Violation of laws does not mean that they lose their significance as laws. The sanction of all laws goes back to public opinion. The sanction of International Law, too, has the same basis as the sanction of ordinary law. It is the force of the minds which made these rules and it is the force of the minds which impresses their practical utility and enjoins obedience. States are obviously ready for orderly behaviour and anticipate orderly behaviour by their fellow States. The society is never run by the law of jungle, nor even on what George Jellinek called "anarchic law." Men have a psychological preference for order over disorder, especially when the disorder involves war.

As regards the sanction behind International Law, it is now conceded by all that a world public opinion is rapidly growing to provide adequate sanctions. The United Nations crystallises world public opinion and it has means at its disposal to coerce a delinquent State by applying either political or economic sanctions, as it did in raising an army to fight against the aggression of China in Korea and in a number of other countries too. Sometimes individual States themselves apply these sanctions, as did Britain and France against Italy in 1935. The success of the United Nations in raising the Emergency Force

3. As quoted in Garner. J.W., *Political Science and Government,* p. 193.
4. *Schooner Exchange v. McFadaon* (1812).

in Egypt and the immediate withdrawal of British, French and Israeli forces from Egyptian territory, once again, demonstrated that the only support and sanction necessary for the effective operation of International Law is a broadbased public opinion. "Like individuals, States wish to enjoy the prestige of a good reputation. On material grounds, though not on these alone, they value the friendship of their fellows; above all, they realise that grossly illegal conduct may inflame foreign opinion and lead to the vicarious enforcement of their obligations." Even if it is admitted that absence of authority to enforce its orders is the weakest point in the nature of International Law, and States have very often flouted its prescriptions by their wilful actions, still, absence of sufficient authority to enforce the provisions of International Law or its deliberate violation by some States does not mean that it ceases to be law real and proper. As a matter of fact, even the ordinary statute law is obeyed chiefly because of social sanctions operating through public opinion and, where these are absent or weak, is honoured more in the breach rather than in the observance.

It is also untrue to say that there are no courts to decide international disputes and apply International Law. Arbitration or the settlement of differences between independent States has assumed considerable proportions since the establishment of the now-defunct League of Nations. The United Nations makes provision for the International Court of Justice. The purposes of the United Nations Charter include the adjustment or settlement of international disputes "in conformity with the principles of justice and international law." Legal forms are used in the International Court of Justice and in arbitral procedure, authorities and precedents are quoted as in courts of law. Finally, there are courts in every country which try prize cases in accordance with the provisions of International Law. Sir Henry Maine and others have shown that there have been systems of law which were enforced independently of the State or its courts of law.

World opinion is now veering round the point that the individual may be given an international status by accepting him as a subject of International Law and consequently make his rights enforceable against his own government. The United Nations Declaration of Human Rights may be considered the harbinger of such a move and if it succeeds, at no distant date an international bill of rights will take concrete shape. Lauterpacht says in this regard, "As a result of Charter of United Nations as well as other changes in International Law—the individual has acquired a status and a stature which has transformed him from an object of international compassion into a subject of international rights." This apart, the Nuremberg trial and punishment of Germans guilty of international crimes has given a new dimension to the nature and scope of International Law. International criminal law has now emerged as an effective instrument to punish those guilty of heinous international crimes.

The principles of International Law, it may be added, have been built up by legal reasoning and are applied in a legal manner. All civilised countries accept International Law as a part of their Municipal Law and their legislatures do not make legislation opposed to the provision of International Law. Piracy, for example, is prohibited by International Law and no State will pass legislation permitting piracy. Laws of no civilized States recognize slavery or permit its existence. The Weimar Constitution of the German Republic made a significant departure when it enacted that the rules of International Law, universally recognised, formed part of federal German law and as such had obligatory force.[5] Similarly, the Estonian Constitution adopted the generally accepted precepts of International Law as an inseparable part of her judicial order. So too, the Austrian Constitution.

It is, therefore, concluded that the principles of International Law are fundamentally the same as those of the Municipal Law. The former, like the latter, grows and develops in response to the spirit of each age and changing conditions of society. Order is the essence of human life, but order is precarious and hollow until International Law is assured. International Law may, thus, be defined as a body of those "rules of conduct which reason deduces as consonant with justice from the nature of the society existing among independent nations; with such definitions and modifications as may be established by general consent." It is law proper and is not a mere collection of moral rules. Its doctrines, as Hall says, "have been elaborated by a course of legal reasoning; in international controversies precedents are used in a strictly legal manner, the opinions of writers are quoted and relied upon for the same purposes as those for which the opinions of writers are invoked under a system of municipal law; the conduct of States is attacked, defended and judged within the range of international law by reference to legal considerations alone; and finally, it is recognised that there is an international morality distinct from law, violation of which gives no formal ground of complaint, however odious the action of the ill-doer may be."[6]

The only baffling point in this context is that although all civilised States have accepted rules of International Law as binding upon them, yet they are enforced by every State according to its own moral standard or convenience. And the moral standard of every State is influenced by the economic and political tendencies of the world as a whole and the expediency of the State concerned. Some States make a bid for world power and they enforce the principles of International Law according to their own convenience. If all the States were to pledge themselves scrupulously to the accepted principles of International Law and adhere to its ideals, much international hostility can be avoided and the controversy whether International Law is a law or not becomes futile.

HISTORY OF INTERNATIONAL RELATIONS

International Law is of recent origin, being only a little more than three hundred years old. Its fundamental principles, however, have their origin much earlier; some can be traced to have prevailed even in the post-Vedic period in India. Lawrence who has made a special study of its recent development divides it into three periods. The first embraces the period from the origin of the European civilisation till the beginning of the Roman Empire. The second period covers the period from the Roman Empire to the Reformation and the third extends from that date up to the present time. Though the history of international relations is divided into three periods, yet the earlier periods are really the basis of the later periods.

5. Article 4 of the Constitution.
6. *International Law,* p. 14.

First Period — To the Beginning of the Roman Empire. India knew much of International Law when the rest of the world was in a state of barbarism. In the post-Vedic period there existed a regular code according to which wars were declared and fought, treaties and alliances negotiated and concluded, and ambassadors accredited. In the European countries among the earliest peoples, about whom History gives us authentic information, there were no mutual claims and duties except between the communities which were bound to one another by bonds of common descent and common language. There was perpetual hostility between tribes alien to one another, and "war was declared without ceremony and carried on without mercy."[7] The Greeks even regarded their neighbours as "barbarians" to whom they owed no duties. The vanquished were rendered slaves and Aristotle too supported the institution of slavery. The real contribution of the Greeks was the Maritime Code, that is, rules governing inter-state commerce. They also, in a rudimentary way, recognised "the law of mankind", which established a vague system of the protection of envoys, obligations of alliances and sanctity of treaties. This contribution of the Greeks, though negligible, is regarded Law by Gilchrist as tangible, which helped the development of International Law.[8]

The Romans, too, before they became an Empire, occupied the same isolated position as the Greeks. But in the early period of Rome's Republican History there existed laws called *jus fetiale*. The *jus fetiale* contained precepts about war and peace and was enforced by a semi-religious college. But the real contribution of Rome in the development of International Law was the *jus gentium* or law of nations. The *jus gentium* was a code of regulations applied to the dealings of citizens belonging to different nations. It took its name, most probably, from the fact that its rules were presumed to consist of principles of conduct common to the laws of all nations.

Second Period — Roman Empire to the Reformation. With the spread of the World Roman Empire there was no development in international relations. The idea of a common superior supreme over all the political sub-divisions of the world was accepted. Even after the fall of the Roman Empire the theory of a common superior persisted till the Church presented itself as a rival power. With the emergence of the Church as a power "it became necessary in theory to divide universal dominion between the secular and the spiritual sovereigns whose conflicting pretensions helped to break down the conception of a single final authority." With the decay of the idea of single authority arose other influences which helped the development of international law. The feudal system brought in the concept of territorially independent States. The revival of commerce and the growth of practically independent cities led to the recognition of maritime codes regulating their dealings. The *Consolato del Mare*, formulated probably in the twelfth century and observed by all the Mediterranean powers, contained rules regarding peace and war, rights of neutral States, prize law, and navigation. Christianity had taught to the people humane methods of warfare. The savagery of the European wars helped to develop international law as a means of alleviating the horrors of war. For the first time jurisprudence was separated from theology and ethics in *De Juri Belli* (*The Laws of War*,

7. Lawrence, *op. cit.*, Chap. III.
8. Gilchrist, R.N., *Principles of Political Science*, p. 178.

1598) by Alberico Gentili, Professor of Civil Law at Oxford. In 1625, Hugo Grotius, the Dutch scholar, formulated the doctrine of International Law with clarity and attempted to analyse international practices in his famous book, *De Juri Belli et Pacis* (On the Law of War and Peace). Grotius did not claim any originality, but by combining natural concepts of reasons and justice with the natural practices of States throughout the period of human history revived the study of Roman Law, with the *jus gentium* as its basis.

Third Period — Reformation to the Present Day. With the emergence of independent national States organised on a territorial basis, new rules of mutual intercourse in peace and war were evolved and the inevitable outcome was the formulation of new international principles. Modern international law is essentially the product of this period and the result of the teachings of Hugo Grotius. Hugo Grotius emphasised two fundamental doctrines:—

(a) All States are equally sovereign and independent.

(b) The jurisdiction of the State is absolute over its entire area.

Here is the modern idea of the State, sovereign both in its external and internal aspects, and it is on this basis that modern International Law has developed. Grotius built his thesis on the universally accepted theory of the law of nature. In the Peace of Westphalia (1648), which created modern Europe, the leading principles of Grotius were recognised. Many writers subsequently contributed to its development and International Law is now accepted as a special branch of law. They furthered the work of Grotius by codifying the customs of nations and pointing out the differences between good and bad practices. The history of international relations from 1648 to our own time makes clear the increasing definiteness of International Law. It covers most of the problems of peacetime and defines the rights and duties of belligerents and neutrals during war-time.

SOURCES OF INTERNATIONAL LAW

The Statute establishing the International Court of Justice specified the following sources of International Law: international conventions; international customs; the general principles of law recognised by civilised nations; and judicial decisions and teachings of the most highly qualified publicists of the various nations, as subsidiary means for determination of rules of law. For purposes of clarity we consider them in the following order with an addition of a few more.

Roman Law. Roman law formed a complete and general code from which most of the Continental Countries in Europe derived their legal principles. It also provided a basis to cover the early relations of the States. The *jus gentium,* which was applied to the dealings of citizens belonging to different nations, was based upon justice, equity and commonsense. Besides, the *jus gentium* emphasised the idea of moral obligations which were equally binding on all the States. Finally, the Roman idea of equality of all citizens before law led to the idea of the equality of sovereign States in Intrnational Law.

Works of Eminent Writers. Works on history and biography provide useful information with respect to wars, diplomacy, treaties and alliances. But more important are the writings of eminent jurists who have reduced to a system the rules of conduct adopted by sovereign and independent States in their dealings with one another. These writers, by showing what rules nations actually do observe, by interpreting general opinion on given questions, and by giving definitions and modifications of previous rules based on general consent, provide a source of international law. The first and the most prominent among them was Hugo Grotius. His book, *On the Law of War and Peace*, exercised enormous influence on the external relations of all the States. Then follows a long list of able lawyers, like Byn Ker Shoek, Wolf, Vattel, Kent, Wheaton, Manning, Woolsey, Westlake, Lawrence and Hall who are usually recognised as authorities on International Law, and statesmen of all times have accepted their opinions as authorities. It may be noted that the mere opinion of one individual writer has, by itself, no binding force. Nevertheless, the opinions of eminent jurists carry a great force and it is customary to cite them as authorities. Kent says, "In cases where the principal jurists agree, the presumption will be very great in favour of the solidity of their maxims; and no civilised nation that does not arrogantly set all ordinary law and justice at defiance will venture to disregard the uniform sense of the established writers on International Law."

Treaties, Alliances and Conventions. Treaties, conventions and alliances, either for commercial or political purposes, form an important source of International Law. Treaties are compacts entered into by States, wherein the contracting States agree to observe given rules of conduct in their intercourse with one another. They are concluded either in accordance with the existing rules of International Law, or some new rules mutually agreed upon, modifying the previous ones. When most of the States become parties to such a treaty, convention or alliance, they tend to create an International Law. The most important treaties that form sources of International Law deal with questions of territory, like the treaties of Westphalia (1648), Utrecht (1713), Paris (1763), or the transfer of sovereign rights, as the treaties of Varsailles (1783), and Paris (1856), or conduct to be observed during war by both belligerent and neutral countries. The examples of the latter are the Geneva Convention (1864) and the Brussels Conference (1890).

Municipal Law. In the Municipal Law of every State may be found germs of International Law. The Municipal Law of every country regulates the questions of citizenship and naturalisation, neutrality, tariffs, extradition, diplomatic and consular services, etc. All these subjects are of international interest and the decisions on these questions are cited as precedents in international negotiations. Similarly, admiralty questions dealing with prize cases are based almost entirely on international usage. Some of the most important decisions of the Supreme Court of the United States relate to questions fundamentally international.

United Nations. Perhaps nothing has a greater impact on the development of International Law than the evolution of the United Nations. Broadly speaking, the United Nations has three main functions concerning law : it is an originator, an applier, and a developer of International Law. Of course these functions overlap each other to a very real extent. For example, it is often by 'applying' law that law is in fact developed. But these three threads are disentangled, for the relevance of law to the United Nations cannot be appreciated without having all these threads.

Decisions in International Cases. It is customary with the States to refer their disputes to international tribunals or courts of arbitration or conferences for adjudication. These decisions are accepted as precedents and become part of International Law.

Sometimes the cases of dispute are referred to international conferences. During modern times, The Hague, Washington and Lausanne conferences have made valuable contributions to International Law. The member-States of the League of Nations were pledged not to go to war till the matter in dispute had first been submitted to arbitration. The Covenant of the League of Nations provided the machinery by which peaceful settlements could be effected. The Council, the Assembly and the Permanent Court of International Justice all had jurisdiction to decide cases of dispute. The United Nations Charter also contains a similar provision. The pronouncements of the Court are treated by nations as authoritative, and are taken as correct interpretation of the present state of International Law. Though the Court does not regard itself as bound by precedent, in fact it considerably relies on its own prior judgments and opinions.

Reason. Another important source of International Law is reason. Cases often arise for which no precedent may exist, and for which there exists no established principle of tacit or explicit consent. In such cases, those who administer International Law must resort to determining by reason the principles of equality to be applied. By considering precedents, finding analogies, and expanding already accepted principles, they evolve a judicious principle to fit the cases under adjudication. Such decisions have come to constitute a body of precedents generally accepted as valid.

Customs. International Law is essentially customary. Certain usages and practices which particular States adopted have been accepted and followed so generally that they have come to constitute a definite body of rules. Many of the principles of conduct are based on analogies with principles regulating individual conduct. Here International Law resembles the English Common Law. It derives its authority from generally accepted principles of usage, and tests new cases by the application of precedents.

History of War and Diplomacy. The history of wars, of negotiations and conclusion of treaties are fruitful sources for the development of International Law. The declarations on policy, like the Atlantic Charter and the Potsdam Agreement, and manifestoes issued from time to time also help the growth of International Law.

Opinions of Diplomats and Statesmen. The correspondence between diplomats belonging to various States or between a government and its diplomatic agents accredited to other States is an important source of international usage. Often such opinions are regarded as confidential, but the United States, Britain and other countries with democratic governments publish a greater part of their foreign correspondence. Instructions issued by the States for the guidance of their foreign service representatives and to commanders of armed forces are also valuable in the growth of International Law. The French Marine Ordinance of 1861 formed the basis of Prize law. The Instructions for the Guidance of the Armed Forces of the United States in the Field (1863) exercised a great influence in adopting more humane methods of warfare.

SCOPE AND CONTENTS OF INTERNATIONAL LAW

Field of International Law. In contrast to natural persons who are subject to the law of the State, the subject of International Law are corporate bodies known as States. For purposes of International Law a State is defined as a permanently organised political society, occupying a definite demarcated territory and within that territory it is independent and free from control by any other State and, as such, it acts as an independent political agent in relation to other States. For the conduct of international relations, the actions of public officials designated by the State to represent it are distinctly acts of the State, for which the State is held responsible.

The area of State jurisdiction extends to the area in which the national laws of a State have effect and embraces its whole territory, except where it has extended immunity to diplomats of other countries. The State controls the seas, "territorial waters" for three miles off its coasts and all ships within those waters fall in its general province, save for crimes committed on board the ship. Foreign ships in ports have only limited immunity. Rivers flowing through or between more than one State, such as the St. Lawrence or Rhine, are not open to the ships of all States. Some of these international rivers, like the Danube, have been supervised by international commissions. Canals, irrespective of their location, are governed by the States owning them. On the high seas, that is, waters outside territorial waters, all States enjoy and exercise legal equality. States have complete jurisdiction over the air above their territory and the soil and resources beneath.

Here it is important to distinguish between International Law and International Private Law (conflict of laws). International Private Law is a branch of International Law, but whereas the former deals with individuals and affects their private rights, the latter is concerned with the State as an entity. International Private Law deals with the rights and obligations involved when individuals claim in one State rights acquired under the laws of another. These rules cover the validity of foreign marriages and divorces, wills, contracts, etc. But the Nuremberg trials of Germans, after World War II, in which individuals were held to account for actions of States, indicate that individuals are accountable to International Law.

The scope of International Law, therefore, extends to equal and sovereign States in no way subordinate to any other. All stand on a footing of equality so far as their status of statehood is concerned. "No principle of law is more universally acknowledged," said Chief Justice Marshall, of the United States Supreme Court, "than the perfect equality of nations. Russia and Geneva have equal rights. It results from this equality that no one can rightfully impose a rule on another." In outlining the scope and division of the relations among States, distinction should be made between the normal rights and obligations that exist in times of peace and the exceptional rights and obligations that exist in times of war. The first are called the laws of peace and the second the rules of war. The rules of war necessitate consideration of relations between actual belligerents, and the relations between the belligerents and neutrals. A more comprehensive division of the contents of International Law is:

1. Laws governing States in times of peace;
2. Laws governing States in times of war;
3. Laws governing States in the relation of neurality.

The laws of peace embrace the rights and obligations concerning the independence and equality of the States. They also include a discussion of the territorial limits of jurisdiction, the relation of a State to the adjacent waters of its coast and other allied problems. With this are connected the jurisdiction and responsibility of a State with reference to its citizens living within the State or abroad, rules governing aliens and principles of naturalisation. Finally, there are the rules of intercourse of States. These cover the rights and duties of officials attached to foreign offices; organization and procedures of International conferences; nature and method of treaty-making.

The larger part of International Law consists of the rules of war. Here we study the classification of wars; declaration of war; laws and customs of war on land, sea and air; effects of war; agents, instruments and methods of warfare; treatment of public and private property in war both on land and at sea, etc. Under the law of neutrality the scope of International law extends to the duties of belligerent States to neutral States, duties of neutral States to belligerent States, neutral commerce, contraband, blockade, etc.

International Relations. In history the bounds of cooperation have never coincided with political frontiers. Inter-State contacts and relationships are as old as the State itself. In the ancient past these contacts and relationships had been regional rather than world-wide, because communications were imperfect and the scramble for the inadequate and inelastic means of sustenance were keen. A new era opened with the progress of modern science and its application to industry and transport. The nineteenth century revolutionised the relations of peoples. It rapidly made of the world a single economic whole followed by international intellectual cooperation. International economic and intellectual interdependence and cooperation naturally brought about an extension of governmental co-operation. During the present century the process has, in spite of forebodings and setbacks, developed by leaps and bounds and now inter-State relations are at the core of the problem of international politics.

Hitherto international relations formed part of the study of Political Science and History. But recently a distinct discipline of international relations has emerged. International relations, despite international interdependence and cooperation and establishment of institutions of systematic international consultations and regulations, like love, had never run a smooth course. Successive wars are a reminder of the shifting behaviour and attitudes of the States toward one another. There is dualism in diplomacy based largely on parochialism, chauvinism and militarism. A very common line of thought is reflected by Horace Walpole who declared that no great country was ever saved by good men, because these would not go the length that might be necessary. Hobbouse notes that "in all relations with weaker people we move in an atmosphere vitiated by the insincere use of high sounding words. If men say equality, they mean oppression by forms of justice. If they say tutelage, they appear to mean the kind of tutelage extended to the fattened goose."[9] Those who preach peace, goodwill, mutual trust and cooperation in international relations and behaviour are the foremost to defy the rational demands of international amity.[10] If there had been no major war since World War II, there had been quite a good number of minor wars and tensions and conflicts are the order of the day making way for cold or hot war.

9. Hobhouse, L.T., *Liberalism*, pp. 43-44.
10. C.F. Dryden, "Art thou a statesman ? And canst not be a hypocrite ? Impossible." Also Alexander Pope, "Statesman, yet friend to truth."

Attempts have been made, from time to time, to evolve a scheme of an ideal society wherein should reign perfect inter-State harmony and chances of irritants, conflicts and war should not exist any more. But no one has ever suggested why should tension and conflicts take place and States go to war at all; what are the basic factors that determine the international behaviour and attitudes of the States, and why would they vary from time to time. These issues determine the foreign policy of a State and a band of intellectuals of international relations have made it a specialised area of their study and investigations. They have adopted scientific tools of analytical study to interpret the facts of international politics, examine and analyse the forces and pressures that shape the foreign policy of a State and changes it involves from time to time. Their approach is not utopian, as in the past, but objective and matter of fact. They deal with bare realities and not idealism and as Carr says, it is a "serious and critical analytical thought about international problems."[11]

INTERNATIONAL ORGANISATION AND INSTITUTIONS

Differences between independent and sovereign States are hound to arise. But they do not go to war always. History is full of examples when disputes between contending States had been settled by the mediation of a third party. During the mediaeval period and early modern times, when the theory of a common superior still persisted, disputes were very often referred to the Pope by the contesting parties for his arbitration. There was no international organisation which could provide machinery for an amicable settlement of international disputes. These conditions continued till the nineteenth century. By that time warfare had become highly mechanised and a costly venture. War also brought about untold misery not only for the belligerent States, but for the neutral countries as well. It meant dislocation of their economy, for the countries of the world had become, after the industrial revolution, interdependent financially and commercially. A strong premium, accordingly, was put on any method of settling quarrels without actual war. International arbitration began to be resorted to even when questions of great magnitude were involved. Between the United States and Great Britain arbitration was repeatedly employed especially for the rectification of boundary lines as in 1827 and 1846.[12] The most important arbitration was with respect to the Alabama case which ended in the award of a compensation of $15,500,000 to the United States. It is estimated that in the nineteenth century over a hundred important cases were decided through the medium of arbitration.

A further development in international relations can be seen in the attempt to constitute a permanent tribunal for the settlement of disputes and conclusion of treaties between various States, binding them to refer their disputes to this tribunal. A conference was convened at The Hague in 1899 and it was agreed to establish a permanent court of arbitration. Although it was not obligatory upon the signatory powers to refer their disputes to the Court of Arbitration, nevertheless the Court "offered standing facilities for

11. Carr. H., *The Twenty Years of Crisis*, 1919-1939, p. 9.
12. It was with regard to the north-east boundary lines in 1827 and to the boundaries on the Pacific Coast in 1846. The award made in 1827 by the King of the Netherlands was, however, rejected by the United States.

peaceful settlement very difficult to bring into being during the strained relations occasioned by the acute international controversy." Between 1899 and 1912 eleven States referred their disputes to the Court of Arbitration and its decisions were accepted by the parties concerned.

The Second Hague Conference met in 1907, and as many as 44 States participated in it. This conference considered the desirability of revising the system of arbitration adopted in 1899. But it primarily concerned itself with the consideration of the rules of war. The conference, led by Great Britain, attempted to create an International Prize Court of Appeal. A special conference consisting of the chief European powers and the United States and Japan met in London in 1909, and drew up the Declaration of London which contained provisions concerning blockade, contraband of war, the position of neutrals and compensation. The Declaration of London was withdrawn during World War I by the British Government.

The First Hague Conference was hailed as "the parliament of mankind" and was popularly designated as the Peace Conference. According to the International Peace Bureau of Berne, 133 treaties were concluded during the ten years following the first Peace Conference, the contracting parties having pledged to adopt settlement by arbitration whenever possible. These treaties, however, created delusive hopes about the prospect of permanent peace. The hope cherished during the opening years of the twentieth century, that war had become obsolete, was falsified by the events culminating in the Great War of 1914. But with the War also came the realization that some comprehensive organisation of States was needed if wars were to be prevented in the future. One of the most important tasks of the Peace Conference which followed the Great War was the creation of the League of Nations.

THE LEAGUE OF NATIONS

Aims and Objects. The League of Nations has been called the "Greatest event since Christ". When World War I ended, twenty-seven nations banded together and formed the League of Nations. Its objects were declared: "To promote international cooperation and to achieve international peace and security, by the acceptance of obligations not to resort to war; by the prescription of open, just and honourable relations between nations; by the firm establishment of the understanding of international law as the actual rule of conduct among governments; and by the maintenance of justice and scrupulous regard for all treaty obligations in the dealings of organised peoples with one another." The League of Nations was an association of States for the purpose of international cooperation, the settlement of disputes and the prevention of future wars. Its Covenant provided a number of agencies for the promotion of health, education and economic development as means to cement international cooperation and goodwill and thereby help prevention of future wars.

The avowed object of the League can best be expressed in the words of Manu. The Laws of Manu enjoined : "This is my countryman; this other is a stranger — so thinks the man of narrow mind and heart. The noble soul regards the whole world as his kin." The League of Nations was the development of an international movement to free nations from the demon of war. The World War had taken a toll of ten million dead and $386,000,000,000 of wasted wealth. It also brought in its wake famine, pestilence and hunger for millions of people. There was consequently a strong demand for some permanent international organisation for the promotion of peaceful international cooperation. But it was mainly due to President Woodrow Wilson's eloquent advocacy and insistent endeavour that the League came into being, although the United States of America could not join the League as it was feared that it would involve a departure from its traditional policy of non-involvement in non-American affairs.

There were other urgent problems, too, demanding the existence of a permanent international organisation. World War I was fought largely on the principle of nationality. Many nationalities became nations after the Treaty of Versailles. Some of them required guarantees against aggression and freedom for development. Finally, the management of the territories lost by the Central Powers accelerated the establishment of this world-wide organisation.

Organisation of the League of Nations. The League of Nations came into existence in 1920. Its original membership was restricted to 32 allied and associated powers, 13 neutral States, and the newly created States which had signed the Peace Treaty.[13] For new entrants to the League, it was provided that any sovereign State or Colony could become a member if the admission was agreed to by two-thirds of the members of the Assembly. No State could withdraw from the membership unless two years' notice to that effect had been given, and it had fulfilled all its international obligations under the Covenant.

There were four organs of the League. The Assembly was the supreme body and it consisted of the representatives of the various member-States including the Dominions of the British Commonwealth and India. Each State could send not more than three representatives, but it was entitled to only one vote. The functions of the Assembly embraced any matter within the sphere of action of the League or affecting the peace of the world. All decisions of the Assembly were to be unanimous. Unanimity was insisted on in order to prevent dissension among sovereign States who, it was apprehended, might act by commanding a bare majority in a way repugnant to some of them. The Assembly adopted the budget of the League, approved the work of the Council, Secretariat and other organs, and adopted draft conventions to be referred to the member-States for ratification.

To facilitate and expedite the work of the League, a smaller body, called the Council, was formed. Originally, it was to contain five permanent members from the United States, Great Britain, France, Italy and Japan, and four non-permanent members elected annually by the Assembly. Since the United States had not joined the League, it was not represented in the Council, which contained eight members in all, four permanent and four non-permanent.[14] The Council normally met three or four times in a year but could

13. USSR joined as late as 1934. Germany and the other States allied to it during the War were not allowed to be members at first, but most of them later became members.

14. In 1922, the membership of the Council was increased to ten, two extra seats being allotted to the smaller nations. In 1926, a permanent seat was given to Germany, when she was admitted to the League, this increased the permanent seats to five and the non-permanent seats were increased to nine. In 1933, a tenth non-permanent seat was created for three years. In 1936, it was continued for another three years and an eleventh seat was added for three years.

be summoned as often as necessary if emergency required. The Council was competent to deal with all matters concerning the sphere of action of the League or affecting the peace of the world. Its decisions, like those of the Assembly, were to be unanimous, except for a few minor matters expressly specified in the Covenant. The Council, thus, acted as a commission of inquiry and conciliation in any dispute referred to it, and to recommend action to enforce the obligations of the Covenant.

The Secretariat, headed by the Secretary-General, was the administrative organ of the League. The Secretary-General was appointed by the Council with the approval of the majority of the Assembly. The staff of the Secretariat was appointed by the Secretary-General and the Council. The expenses of the Secretariat were apportioned among the member-States of the League. Its functions were to keep all records of the proceedings of the League, to secure the necessary information required by the League, and to conduct correspondence on its behalf. All treaties concluded or international agreements entered into by the member-States were required to be published by the Secretary-General, otherwise they were not valid.

The main object of the League was to check all future possibilities of war and to evolve a scheme for thc settlement of international disputes. A permanent Court of International Justice was set up at The Hague. It consisted of nine Judges and four Deputy Judges elected for nine years by the Assembly and the Council respectively, and settled such disputes as were referred to it and required judicial settlement. It was also empowered to give opinions on matters referred to it either by the Assembly or by the Council.

The Covenant of the League of Nations included important clauses relating to future and existing treaties, and conditions of labour. An International Labour Organisation — an autonomous body within the League — was created in order to secure and maintain fair and humane conditions of labour throughout the world. The International Labour Organisation consisted of the International Labour Conference, a representative body of delegates of governments, employers and workers meeting at least once a year at Geneva. Besides this, there was the International Labour Office controlled by a governing body.

WORK OF THE LEAGUE

Settlement of Disputes. The three main functions of the League were settlement of international disputes, removal of the causes of war, and organisation of international cooperation. As regards settlement of disputes, the Covenant of the League provided for the territorial integrity and political independence of all its member-States. In case of any aggression or threat, or danger of aggression, the Council was empowered to advise the League on measures to be adopted for preserving the territorial integrity and independence of the member-States.[15] In case of war or threat of war, whether immediately affecting any of the member-States of the League or not, the League was empowered to take any action that was deemed wise and effectual to safeguard the peace of the nations.[16] Finally, in case of any dispute likely to lead to a rupture, the matter was required to be

15. Article 10.

16. Article 11.

submitted either to arbitration or to inquiry by the Council. In no case a resort to war was to be made until three months after the award by the arbitrators or the report by the Council.[17] In case a State went to war by violating its pledges, the other member-States were to break off diplomatic and other intercourse with it. There was just a vague provision for military sanctions.

The efforts of the League in this respect were commendable. It secured settlement in the Aaland Islands and Upper Silesia when all other means had failed. It saved Albania, in 1921, from piecemeal extinction. In 1925 Greco-Bulgarian clash was averted by the interference of the League and in the same year it succeeded in the mediation of Mosul oilfields dispute. The Permanent Court of International Justice at The Hague decided 27 cases and handed down the same number of advisory opinions. The reputation of the Court for impartiality was so great that its decisions were respectfully accepted by the contending States and, thus, the League, on many occasions, saved countries from international rupture.

Removal of the Causes of War. The members of the League recognized that the maintenance of peace required reduction of national armaments to the lower point consistent with national safety, and enforcement of common action on international obligations.[18] The Council of the League of Nations was empowered to formulate plans for the reduction of armaments for consideration and action by Governments of the member-States. It was, also, empowered to advise how the evil effects of the manufacture by private enterprise of munitions and weapons of war could be prevented. But the Disarmament Conferences, held from 1925 onwards, failed. Perhaps those who advocated disarmament were the first to arm themselves. Conquests of small States, the policy of Colonial expansion, and secret alliances, forbidden in the Covenant of the League, remained the avowed policy of all the major Powers. Specific blame could not be placed on any single country. It was the common action of all. The result was that every State, big or small, began pursuing the policy of war-preparedness. War-preparedness means increase in armaments and reckless increase in armaments creates a vicious circle, as it causes distrust and panic particularly in small States.

In graver matters the League, thus, failed miserably. Japan was the first to violate the sanctity of the solemn commitments by invading Manchuria in 1931. Till that time the authority of the League of Nations had been impressive. Mussolini was the next to follow Japan. The Duce pounced upon Ethiopia in 1935. In the meantime Hitler was militarising Rhineland and driving Germany forward on the road of conquest. After resigning from the membership of the League, Germany denounced the Locarno Treaty in 1936 and conquered Austria in 1937. The ineffectiveness of the League was further demonstrated by Germany's conquest of Czechoslovakia. Then came the subjugation of Poland both by Germany and Russia in September 1939.

Organisation of International Cooperation. The activities of the League in this sphere were really appreciable. The International Labour Organisation had become a recognized source of information about labour conditions. The League's financial section

17. Article 12.
18. Article 8.

presided over the successful rehabilitation of Austria, Hungary and Greece, administering large loans in each case. The League's world-wide fight against opium traffic was historic. Similarly, the work of the Transit and Communication Section of the League was admirable. Its work on intellectual cooperation could not be dismissed as negligible.

Causes of the League's Failure. On the whole, however, the League of Nations miserably failed in its mission. One of the main reasons for the League's failure was the international disequilibrium brought about by economic, political and social forces in the post-war period. Hunger for more land and craze for new markets became a mania with every country, particularly with Germany, Italy, and Japan. Economic nationalism and, thus, a plea, for self-sufficiency undermined the very basis of the League, that is, international goodwill and cooperation. In spite of its best efforts, the World Economic Conference, convened under the auspices of the League of Nations in 1927, could not solve the so-called insoluble problem of tariffs. It had its political repercussions, for economic retribution is always destructive in its results.

Immediately after World War I an unbridgeable gulf was created in the economic outlook of the States. This was due to the new political ideologies professed by them. Nationalism in its narrow sense did no longer remain the slogan of pseudo-politicians only, it had become the accepted policy of every State. Democracy gave way to concentration of authority; in every country, including the citadels of democracy—United States, United Kingdom and France. The economic depression of 1931 and the maldistribution of gold further aggravated the world problem and, consequently, there ensued an economic tug-of-war between the major countries. This created suspicions and distrust which ultimately culminated in war preparations, another major addition to the already existing vicious circle. The cumulative effect of all these forces was that the superstructure of international brotherhood, so cherishingly envisaged in the League of Nations, toppled down.

The prestige of the League of Nations waned. The deliberations of the Assembly and the Council became a mere farce. The promoters of war preached peace. "I cannot recall any time," said Sir Winston Churchill, "when the gap between the kind of words which statesmen used and what was actually happening in many countries was so great as it is now." The League could have succeeded in its object only if the representatives of the major member-States had genuinely striven for collective security. But events showed otherwise. "When the Covenant appeared to require action which might have entailed practical consequences for the mass of the people, successive governments preferred inaction."[19] It was, therefore, no surprise when the news of the War flashed across the world on September 3, 1939, tolling the death-knell of the League.

THE UNITED NATIONS

Atlantic Charter. From the very start of hostilities in 1939, the people had been persistently clamouring for a clear declaration of the War aims. On March 15, 1941, Franklin D. Roosevelt, in the course of a speech broadcast to the world, maintained: "We believe that

19. Carr. E.H., *The Twenty Years of Crisis—1919-39*. p. 184.

the rallying cry of the Dictators and their boasting about the master race will prove to be pure stuff and nonsense." He further declared that any nationality, no matter how small, had the inherent right of its own nationhood. Roosevelt, also, deprecated the idea of any one nation "which, because of its size and military might, asserts its right to goosestep to world power over other nations and other races." While justifying United States participation in World War II, President Roosevelt said, "Never in all our history, have Americans faced a job so well worthwhile. May it be said of us in the days to come that our children and our children's children will rise up and call us blessed."[20] President Roosevelt, again, reiterated the substance of these declarations in May 1941, when during a 'Fireside Chat' to the nation he pointed out the application of the four freedoms[21] to all the subject countries of the world.

Then came on August 15, 1941, the Eight-Point Joint Declaration, popularly called the Atlantic Charter. The Charter embodied the objectives for which the Allies had participated in World War II and enunciated the principles forming the basis of the future peace of the world. Roosevelt and Churchill guaranteed territorial integrity to all nations and the rights of man to all the peoples of the world. But Churchill denied the application of the Atlantic Charter to India. The wartime Prime Minister of Britain harked back to the seemingly logical, but really inconsistent and even hypocritical, plea that Britain could not "renounce the obligations arising from our long connection with India and our responsibilities to its many creeds, races and interests." The Atlantic Charter, thus, became a symbol of hypocrisy and so Pearl Buck rightly pointed out that World War II "is no longer a fight for human freedom, but only to save European civilisation."[22]

Dumbarton Oaks Proposals. World War II had, however, increased the necessity of some international organisation which should make the nations internationally minded and possess sufficient authority to enforce its decisions. Some suggested the idea of reviving the League of Nations by strengthening its powers and membership. But the United States devised a new plan which was submitted to the representatives of the United Kingdom, the Soviet Union, France and China, at a conference held at Dumbarton Oaks in the United States of America on October 7, 1944. The five powers agreed to submit the proposals for the structure of the future world organisation to all the United Nations Governments, and to the peoples of all countries for their study and discussion. The Dumbarton Oaks Plan contained two important proposals. The first was about the creation of an agency called the Security Council, consisting of eleven members, entrusted with the responsibility of preventing future war. Second, the member-States of the new organisation were required to place armed forces at the disposal of the Security Council in its task of preventing war and suppressing acts of aggression.

The plan was fully discussed by allied countries. Comments and constructive criticism came from several governments. The allied nations gave it wide publicity, particularly to the provision of placing armed forces at the disposal of the Security Council. Extensive

20. As cited in Anup Chand Kapur, *India and the Atlantic Charter*, p. 3.
21. Roosevelt defined the four freedoms as: (1) Freedom of speech and expression; (2) freedom of every person to worship his God in his own way; (3) freedom from want; and (4) freedom from fear.
22. As cited in Anup Chand Kapur, *India and the Atlantic Charter*, p. 44.

press and radio discussions were arranged so as to enable the people to judge for themselves the merits of the new plan. But the Dumbarton Oaks proposals had yet to decide about the voting procedure in the Security Council. This was done at Yalta, in the Crimea, where Roosevelt, Churchill and Stalin met in conference. On February 11, 1945, it was announced that a Conference of the United Nations would be called to meet at San Francisco in the United States on the 25th April 1945, to prepare the charter of an international organisation on the lines of the Dumbarton Oaks Plan.

San Francisco Conference. Delegates of fifty nations representing over eighty per cent of the world's population met on the scheduled date at San Francisco. They had before them the Dumbarton Oaks proposals, and working on this basis, they planned to set up an organisation which would preserve peace and help in building a better world. The Conference was divided into various Committees and Commissions each entrusted to the completion of a special task. There were only ten plenary meetings of all the delegates, but nearly 400 meetings of the Committees were held at which every line and comma was hammered out. On June 25, the delegates met in full session for the last meeting, when the United Nations Charter was passed unanimously. The next day, each delegate affixed his signature on the Charter. "The Charter of the United Nations which you have just signed," said President Truman, on this occasion, "is a solid structure upon which we can build a better world. History will honour you for it. Between the victory in Europe and the final victory, in this most destructive of all wars, you have won a victory against war itself... With this Charter the world can begin to look forward to the time when all worthy human beings may be permitted to live decently as free people."

Birth of the United Nations Organisation. The United Nations Organisation did not come into existence at the signing of the Charter. In many countries it had to be approved by their Parliaments. It was, accordingly, provided that the Charter would come into force when the Governments of China, France, Great Britain, the U.S.S.R. the United States of America, and a majority of the other signatory States had ratified it and deposited notifications to that effect with the State Department of the United States of America. On October 24, 1945, this condition was fulfilled and the United Nations Organisation came into being. Thus, "four years of planning and the hope of many years had materialized in an international organisation designed to end war and promote peace, justice and better living for all mankind."

United Nations Charter. The United Nations Charter contains 111 articles embodying the purposes and principles of the United Nations, and the organs through which its will is expressed and manifested. The Preamble expresses the inspiration and guiding spirit of the United Nations. It begins with: "We the people of the United Nations" — an unprecedented feature of an international document — and then sets forth the basic aims of the United Nations, which are:

1. To save succeeding generations from the scourge of war;
2. To reaffirm faith in fundamental human rights;
3. To establish justice and respect for international obligations; and
4. To promote social progress and better standards of life.

For the realisation of these ends, the Preamble enjoins on the peoples of the United

Nations to practise tolerance, to live in peace as good neighbours, to unite to maintain peace and security, to ensure that armed forces shall not be used, except in the common interest, and to employ international machinery for the social and economic betterment of all peoples.

Purposes and Principles of the United Nations. Obviously the urgent and fundamental needs of the peoples are freedom from war and from fear of war. The first purpose of the United Nations is defined as the maintenance of international peace and security. The organisation is to employ all peaceful means to prevent or remove threats to peace and suppress acts of aggression and other breaches of peace. It is required to adjust or settle in accordance with justice and international law, international disputes and situations which may lead to conflict. To achieve these results, the United Nations was required to take effective measures. The second aim of the United Nations is to adopt means to develop friendly relations among the peoples of all nations so as to cement the ties of international brotherhood. This friendship among nations should be based on respect for the principle of the equal rights of and equal self-determination by peoples.

The most fruitful cause of international conflicts is the economic rivalries between nations and other maladjustments. The United Nations aims to strive for cooperation among countries for solving international problems of an economic, social, cultural and humanitarian character. This is the third purpose of the United Nations. Closely connected with it is the object of promoting and encouraging basic human rights and freedoms for all peoples without distinction of race, sex, language or religion. Finally, the United Nations, as the principal world organisation, shall work as a centre for harmonising national action in order to achieve these common ends. This is described as the fourth purpose of the United Nations.

The above four purposes are the cause and object of the Charter to which the member-States collectively and severally subscribe. The Charter, then, defines the basic principles on which the United Nations Organisation is based. These principles are the seven general obligations which bind member-States and the United Nations Organisation as a whole. The seven obligations are:

1. The United Nations Organisation is based on the sovereign equality of all its members;
2. Each member-State shall fulfil its obligations under the Charter in good faith;
3. All member-States shall settle disputes by peaceful means and in such a manner that peace, security and justice are not endangered;
4. No member-State shall use force or the threat of force against the territory or independence of any State or in any manner not consistent with the purpose of the United Nations;
5. No member-State shall help any State against which the United Nations is taking enforcement actions, and every member-State shall support the Organisation in any action that it takes in accordance with the Charter.
6. The United Nations shall ensure that States which are not members act in accordance with these principles as far as it is necessary for the maintenance of peace and security; and
7. The United Nations shall not intervene in matters which are essentially within the domestic jurisdiction of any State, or compel any member-State to submit any matter

to settlement by the United Nations — a principle which will not apply when coercive measures are applied in order to deal with threats to the peace, breaches of the peace and acts of aggression.

Membership of the United Nations. All the fifty States which were signatories to the Charter at San Francisco were accepted as original members of the United Nations Organisation. The membership is open, vide Article 4 of the Charter, to all other peace-loving States who accept the obligations of the Charter, and in the judgment of the United Nations are able and willing to carry out these obligations. Admission is effected by the General Assembly on the recommendation of the Security Council. In 1946, the Security Council unanimously recommended the admission of Afghanistan, Iceland, Siam and Sweden, and on the approval of the General Assembly these States became accredited members of the United Nations. In the following year Pakistan and Yemen were admitted, and in 1948 Burma also became a member, bringing the membership to fifty-eight. But unfortunately there had been an unhealthy rivalry between the major powers of East and West on the issue of admission of new States in their bid "for maintaining the existing balance in the General Assembly between their respective supporters. The deadlock continued till 1956, when matters were eased by the "package deal" enabling thereby the admission of 17 States. The total membership of the United Nations was 80 on January 1, 1957. At the end of 1964, it was 115, including Indonesia, which withdrew its membership in January, 1965. On October 25, 1971, the General Assembly approved by 76 votes to 35, with 17 abstentions, the formal resolution tabled by Albania, Algeria and twenty other nations, admitting the Peoples' Republic of China to the United Nations. Simultaneously, Taiwan, which had till then represented China in the United Nations, was expelled. With the admission of a tiny principality of Monaco followed by the newly independent country of Eritrea in May 1993 the membership increased to 183. Another principality was granted admission in July 1993, thus, bringing the present total to 184 member-States. With the re-admission of South Africa the number comes to 185.

The Charter of the United Nations provides for the suspension and expulsion of members, but no provision has been made for withdrawal from membership. It has, however, been held that the absence of an express prohibition "must be deemed to have preserved the right to sever",[23] and Indonesia's withdrawal set the precedent. If a member-State persistently violates the principles of the Charter, it may be expelled from the Organization by the Assembly on the recommendation of the Security Council. Similarly, if the United Nations is taking preventive measures or enforcement action against a member-State, it may be suspended from exercising its rights and privileges by the General Assembly on the recommendation of the Security Council. The Security Council may, however, restore these rights whenever it deems necessary.

ORGANS OF THE UNITED NATIONS

The Charter establishes six organs of the United Nations. It is through these organs that the manifold work of the United Nations is carried out. The principal organs are: the General Assembly; the Security Council; the Economic and Social Council; the Trusteeship

23. Oppenheimer, *R. International Law,* Vol 1, p. 411.

Council; the International Court of Justice; and the Secretariat. The General Assembly, the Security Council and the Economic and Social Council are authorised to create subsidiary organs consistent with the provisions of the Charter.

The General Assembly. The General Assembly is the largest of all the organs of the United Nations. This is the great deliberative body of the Organisation which discusses every matter within the scope of the Charter. It consists of all the member-States. Though each member-State may send up to five representatives to participate in its deliberations, yet member-States have only one vote each. Important questions specified in the Charter — maintenance of peace and security, the election of members to other organs, the admission, suspension or expulsion of member-States, matters relating to trusteeship, and budgetary questions — are decided by two-thirds majority of the members present and voting. All other questions are decided by a simple majority of those voting. The Assembly itself, and voting by simple majority, may add new categories of questions which are to be decided by a two-thirds majority. Normally, the Assembly has to meet in regular session once every year, in September,[24] but special sessions may be convened at the request of the Security Council, or by a majority of the member-States. The President is elected by the General Assembly for each session. It also elects seven Vice-Presidents and appoints six Working Committees:-(1) Political and Security; (2) Economic and Financial; (3) Social, Humanitarian and Cultural; (4) Trusteeship; (5) Administrative and Budgetary; and (6) Legal — all appointed for the session. Besides, the Assembly also constitutes at every session two procedural, two standing and five special committees.

The Assembly elects, by a two-thirds majority of those present and voting, non-permanent members of the Security Council for two years. The Charter requires that in electing these members, the General Assembly shall pay due regard to the contribution that they may make to the maintenance of peace and security and to the other purposes of the United Nations, and also to equitable geographical distribution. It also chooses all the eighteen members of the Economic and Social Council, and members of the Trusteeship Council. By a complicated system of parallel voting, the Security Council and the General Assembly, independently of each other, elect the fifteen judges of the International Court of Justice, no two of whom may be the nationals of the same country. Finally, the Assembly appoints the Secretary-General who is the head of the UN Secretariat.

But the most important functions of the General Assembly are initiative, discussion, study and recommendation. It has the right to discuss all questions and matters within the scope of the Charter and within the activity of the United Nations. The Assembly is competent to take up and discuss any question bearing on the maintenance of peace and security submitted to it by any member-State, by the Security. Council or, in certain circumstances, by a non-member, and make its recommendations either to the. Security Council or to the member-States direct. But there is one limitation which the Charter places on the powers of the General Assembly. While the Security Council is dealing with any dispute or situation, the General Assembly may not take up that matter for consideration and make recommendations on the subject unless the Security Council requests it to do so. The Secretary-General informs the Assembly of any matters concerning peace and security which are being dealt with by the Security Council. As soon as the

24. The 1964 Session was held in December.

Security Council has ceased to deal with these matters, the Secretary-General informs the Assembly or the member-States, if the Assembly is not in session. The General Assembly has the right to call the attention of the Security Council to situations which are likely to endanger peace. Subject to the provision of not making a recommendation on a dispute or situation being dealt with by the Security Council, the General Assembly may recommend measures for the peaceful adjustment of any situation likely to impair the general welfare of friendly relations among nations. This includes violation of the purposes and principles of the United Nations as well. It is true that the recommendations of the Assembly are not legally binding, but they do serve as an important instrument for bringing the weight of public opinion in the world to bear upon the members of the United Nations. In particular, the right of discussion and accommodation comprises questions of cooperation in the maintenance of international peace and security, including disputes brought before the Assembly, as well as the principles governing disarmament and regulation of armaments. The Assembly may call the attention of the Security Council to situations likely to endanger international peace and security.

The Assembly may also discuss the powers and functions of other organs of the United Nations and establish subsidiary organs necessary for the performance of its functions. The General Assembly is given wide power to initiate studies for the purpose of promoting international cooperation in political, economic, social, cultural, educational and health matters. The studies so initiated should include the encouragement of the progressive development and codification of International Law and realization of human rights and fundamental freedoms for all, without distinction of race, sex, language or religion. It, also, has the power to consider principles governing disarmament and the regulation of armaments and make recommendations.

In promoting international cooperation in economic, social, cultural, educational and health matters, the General Assembly works mainly through the Economic and Social Council. The Council itself is the principal organ of the United Nations but it acts under the authority of the General Assembly. Finally, the General Assembly considers and approves the budget of the United Nations, and decides on the share of expenses to be borne by each member-State.

The Security Council. The member-States of the United Nations have delegated the primary responsibility for maintaining world peace and security to the Security Council. Every member-State is pledged to accept and carry out the decisions which the Security Council takes. The Security Council originally consisted of a total of eleven members, five permanent and six non-permanent members. The five permanent members are the representatives of China, the United Kingdom, France, Russia and the United States of America. But its membership has now been increased to 15, five permanent and ten non-permanent members. The expanded 15-member Security Council took office on January 1, 1966, in terms of the amendments to the United Nations Charter, which were approved by the General Assembly in 1963, and which became effective on September 1, 1965, after being ratified.[25] Under the terms of expansion five of the ten non-permanent seats

25. India took a leading part in securing the amendment to the Charter in 1963. For a number of years, the Afro-Asians, who during the past decade had become the majority of the U.N. membership, had been seeking expansion to provide greater representation for themselves, but were repeatedly baulked through various objections.

go to Afro-Asians (three Africans and two Asians), two to West Europe and others, and two to Latin America. The ten non-permanent members are elected by the General Assembly for a period of two years. The retiring member-State is not eligible for re-election immediately after the expiration of its term in order to enable other States to take their term at membership of the Security Council.

The Charter provides for a continuous session of the Security Council and every member-State, which is represented on the Council, is required to maintain a delegate at the Headquarters of the United Nations. The Council must meet at least once every two weeks or as often as is necessary. The Charter permits the Council to hold its meetings at any place other than the Headquarters if that would facilitate the work of the Council. Each member of the Council has one vote and on matters of a procedural nature, votes of nine members are now necessary for a decision. On substantive matters, too, the affirmative majority of the nine members, as against seven before 1 January, 1966, is required, but the affirmative majority of nine votes must include the concurring votes of all the permanent members. Any decision to impose sanctions, either economic or military, must be taken with the concurrence of the five permanent members even if one of them is a party to the dispute which is before the Council. It means that any permanent member, by disagreeing with the majority, can veto the proposition. This process of obtaining concurring votes of all permanent members is known as the unanimity of the "Big Five." There is, however, one exception to this rule. When the Security Council is considering peaceful settlement of a dispute, a member-State which is a party to the dispute abstains from voting.

Only the members participate and vote in the proceedings of the Security Council, but in certain circumstances countries not represented on the Council and even countries not members of the United Nations may participate in the proceedings without the right of voting. This may happen, first, whenever the Council considers that the interests of any particular member-State are specially affected in the discussion of any question. Secondly, if a member is a party to a dispute under consideration of the Security Council, it must be invited to participate in the discussion without a vote. Even States which are not members of the United Nations may be invited to participate in the discussion of any dispute to which they are a party on just conditions to be laid down by the Council. The Security Council elects its own President and that office rotates month by month among members.

The position and authority of the Security Council is the most important. The Charter confers on the Security Council the primary responsibility of maintaining international peace and security. It further lays down that if member-States are parties to a dispute which is likely to endanger peace, they must seek a solution by all possible peaceful means. If they fail to settle their disputes by negotiations, inquiries, mediation, consultation, judicial settlement or by other peaceful means, it is the duty of the Security Council to call upon the parties to settle their disputes. The Council is further empowered to investigate any situation which may cause international friction or dispute in order to determine whether the situation is likely to endanger peace and security of the world. Apart from the Security Council's own initiative, it is open to any one of the member-States to draw the attention of the Security Council or the General Assembly to such a situation or dispute. Even a non-member State of the United Nations can bring any dispute to which it is a party to the notice of the Security Council or the General Assembly, provided it accepts beforehand the obligation of a peaceful settlement under the terms of the Charter. The Secretary-General may likewise bring to the attention of the Security Council any matter which, in his opinion, threatens the maintenance of international peace or security.

If, in the opinion of the Security Council, continuance of such a dispute is detrimental to world peace, or peace has actually been broken, or an act of aggression has been committed, it may do any one of these things: (1) call upon the parties to settle their disputes by peaceful means; (2) recommend appropriate procedures and methods for ending the dispute; (3) propose the actual terms of settlement. If one or both the parties to the dispute fail to comply with the recommendations of the Security Council, the Council may ask other member-States of the United Nations to either break off diplomatic relations with the country or countries concerned, or to cut all rail, sea, air, postal, telegraphic, radio and other communications, or to break economic relations partially or completely with the offending State or States. Should the Security Council deem that such measures are inadequate or have proved inadequate, it is competent to take such military action as may be considered necessary to meet the situation. Every member-State is pledged, under Article 43, to supply to the Council on its call such military forces as are needed to meet the situation. The Security Council maintains a Military Staff Committee to assist and advise it on all its military requirements including the employment and command of the armed forces placed at the disposal of the Council and on the regulation of armaments and disarmaments. This Committee consists of the Chiefs of Staff (or their representatives) of the permanent members—China, France, the United Kingdom, Russia and the U.S.A.

In order to enable the United Nations to take urgent military measures, member-States are required to immediately make available their national air-force contingents for combined international action. The Security Council is required to make the plans for the application of armed forces with the assistance of the Military Staff Committee and the Charter requires the members of the United Nations to join in affording mutual assistance in carrying out the measures decided upon by the Security Council.

The other functions of the Security Council are: to recommend the admission of new members to the General Assembly; to recommend to the General Assembly the suspension of the rights and privileges of any member-State against whom it is taking preventive or enforcement action; to recommend to the General Assembly the expulsion from the U.N. of a member-State persistently violating the principles of the Charter; to convoke a special session of the General Assembly by a request to the Secretary-General; and to establish subsidiary organs for the due performance of its functions. All the functions of the United Nations with respect to Trust areas classified as "Strategic" are exercised by the Security Council. It votes simultaneously, but independently of the General Assembly in the election of the Judges of the International Court of Justice. When a party to a case fails to carry out a judgment of the Court, the Security Council may, on the appeal of the other party, make recommendations or decide upon measures to be taken to give effect to the judgment. The Atomic Energy Commission, set up in 1946, reports to the Security Council and receives directions from it on matters affecting the maintenance of peace and security. Finally, the Secretary-General is appointed by the General Assembly on the recommendation of the Security Council.

The Economic and Social Council (ECOSOC). The most striking feature of the Charter is the emphasis it lays on the constructive tasks of peace. But the authors of the Charter were also aware "that economic and social maladjustments are often the diseases of which war is the final symptom and they envisaged peace not merely as a period of non-shooting but as the zestful pursuit of the common good of all mankind." This purpose of the United Nations finds a prominent place in the Preamble of the Charter which proclaims that the peoples of the United Nations are determined "to promote social progress and better standards of life in larger freedom." Article 1 states that it is a primary purpose of the United Nations to achieve cooperation in solving international problems of economic, social, cultural or human rights and fundamental freedoms without distinction of race or sex, language or religion.

These purposes of the United Nations are realized through the Economic and Social Council, ECOSOC. The delegates at the San Francisco Conference described the Council as potentially the most important of the organs of the United Nations. It consisted of eighteen members prior to the amendment of the Charter and now since January 1, 1966, its membership has been twenty-seven, all elected by the General Assembly. Nine, as against six prior to January 1966 are elected each year and the normal term of office is three years, that is, one-third members retiring every year. Retiring members are eligible for re-election. Each country elected to the Council has one representative with one vote and all decisions are taken by a simple majority of those present and voting. The Council is required to invite any member of the United Nations to participate, without a vote, in its deliberations on any question which is of particular interest to that member. It may also make arrangements for representatives of international specialised agencies to participate, without a vote, in the activities of the Council and its discussions. The Council elects its own President for one year and meets at least three times in a year.

The Council (Article 45 of the Charter) is responsible for promoting:

(*a*) Higher standards of living, full employment, and conditions of economic and social progress and development;

(*b*) Solutions of international economic, social, health and related problems, and international cultural and educational cooperation;

(*c*) Universal respect for, and observance of, human rights and fundamental freedoms for all without distinction as to race sex, language and religion.

For the realization of its purposes the Economic and Social Council performs the following special functions:

1. It makes and initiates studies and reports on all matters within its scope either directly or through an expert commission.
2. After its investigations are complete, the Council makes its recommendations to the General Assembly or to the member-States or the specialised agencies.
3. The Council may also submit draft conventions to the General Assembly which are sent, after ratification, to the member-States for their acceptance and implementation.
4. The Council makes arrangements with the member-States to obtain their reports on

the steps taken to give effect to its recommendations, and to communicate its observations to the General Assembly.

5. The Council is entrusted with the duty of submitting information to the Security Council whenever demanded and assist in the discharge of its functions.

The Council works through several Commissions, Standing Committees, ad hoc Committees, and Special Bodies. The Commissions are of two types: functional and regional. Under the first come Economic and Employment, Transport and Communications, Statistical, Human Rights, Social Status of Women, Narcotic Drugs and Fiscal and Population problems. The Regional Commissions are : the Economic Commission for Europe, the Economic Commission for Asia and the Far East, the Economic Commission for Latin America, the Economic Commission for Africa, etc.

There are four Standing Committees and four special bodies: The Permanent Central Opium Board, the Supervisory Body, the International Children's Emergency Fund, and the United Nations Appeal for Children.

The Trusteeship Council. The Trusteeship Council provides for an international trusteeship system for the administration and supervision of:

1. the territories placed under it by means of trusteeship agreements submitted by the administering powers and approved by the United Nations;
2. the territories, held under the mandate system of the League of Nations, and territories detached from enemy States as a result of the Second World War; and
3. the territories voluntarily placed under the trusteeship system.

The aims of the trusteeship system are fourfold: (*i*) to further international peace and security; (*ii*) to promote advancement of the people and their development towards self-government or independence depending on the circumstances of each country, the freely expressed wishes of the people and the terms of each trusteeship agreement; (*iii*) to encourage respect for basic human rights and the recognition of the interdependence of the people of the world; and (*iv*) to ensure equal treatment for all members of the United Nations and equal treatment and justice for their nationals in social, economic and commercial matters so long as this does not conflict with the welfare of the inhabitants. The Trusteeship Council functions under the authority of the General Assembly.

The Council is composed of permanent members of the Security Council — China, France, Russia, United Kingdom, the United States —, member-States which administer trust territories, and, finally, other States elected by the General Assembly in order to maintain equality of numbers between members who administer trust territories and those who do not. The Trusteeship Council must meet at least twice a year and the President is elected at each regular session. Each member-State of the Council has one vote, and all decisions are taken by a majority of the members present and voting.

Supervision over the administration of the trust territories is exercised by the General Assembly, but in reality it is carried on by the Trusteeship Council. It receives reports from the administrations of trust territories, receives complaints and petitions from the peoples of the trust territories and examines them in consultation with the administering authority, makes annual inspections of the trust territories, and takes such actions as are in conformity with the terms of the trusteeship agreements. The Council is also charged with the formulation of a questionnaire on the political, economic, social and educational advancement of the inhabitants of each trust territory within the competence of the General Assembly and is required to make an annual report to the General Assembly upon the basis of such a questionnaire.

The International Court of Justice. One of the purposes of the United Nations is to adjust and settle international disputes in conformity with justice and International Law. It was, accordingly, deemed essential to establish a judicial organ of the United Nations and it is known as the International Court of Justice. Although the Charter describes the International Court of Justice as the principal judicial organ of the United Nations, yet it does not debar the member-States from referring their disputes to other tribunals for peaceful settlement. As all the members are sovereign States, it is not possible to summon any State against its will to submit to the jurisdiction of the Court. Moreover, the Court cannot proceed to adjudicate a dispute merely because one State files a case against another. The other party, too, must agree to the jurisdiction of the Court.

The jurisdiction of the International Court of Justice extends to cases which involve the interpretation of a treaty, questions of international law, the existence of any fact which, if established, would constitute breach of an international obligation, and the nature or extent of the reparation to be made for wrongs suffered by a State. Several nations have signed the so-called "Optional Clause" by which they have agreed that the Court may try all cases or cases relating to specified subjects, which may arise in future. But most countries have specified a limited number of subjects on which they will accept jurisdiction. Once a case has been brought before the Court, the parties to the dispute must abide by its decision. Should any party to a case before the Court fail to perform its obligation under a judgment of the Court, the other party may bring the matter before the Security Council. The Security Council is empowered by the Charter to make recommendations or decide upon measures to be taken to give effect to the judgment.

The Court consists of fifteen members elected independently by the General Assembly and the Security Council. The Judges should be persons of high moral character and possess qualifications required in their respective countries for the highest judicial offices or they should be *Juris Consults* of recognised ability in International Law. No two of the Judges may be nationals of the same State. The normal term of Judges is nine years, although, in the first election, five Judges were chosen for a term of three years, five for six years and the other five for the full nine-year term. The Judges elect from among themselves the President of the Court for a term of three years. The Court is permanently in session, except during judicial vacations. A quorum of nine Judges is necessary to hear a case and all decisions are by majority of the Judges present. If the votes are equal, the President has a casting vote. Where there is on the Court a Judge of the nationality of one party to a dispute and none of the other, the other party is permitted to choose a Judge for the hearing of that dispute.

In addition to deciding cases, the Court can be asked by the General Assembly and Security Council to give advisory opinions on any legal question. The other organs of the United Nations and the specialised agencies, subject to the approval of the General Assembly, may ask the Court for advisory opinion on matters within their competence.

The permanent seat of the Court is in the Netherlands at The Hague, but it can meet elsewhere when it thinks desirable.

The Secretariat. To carry out the administrative responsibilities of the United Nations, and to assist its organs in the due performance of their functions, the Charter established a Secretariat, consisting of a Secretary-General, and such staff as is required by the Organisation. The Secretary-General, who is the chief administrative officer of the United Nations, is appointed by the General Assembly on the recommendation of the Security Council for a five-year renewable term. The first Secretary-General was Trygve Lie. Dag Hammarskjold of Sweden, the second Secretary-General, became the Congo martyr. He was followed by U Thant who was succeeded by Kurt Waldheim. Waldheim, who remained in office for two terms, offered himself for the third term too, but he ultimately withdrew from the contest essentially due to the constant (fifteen times) use of Veto by China. The fifth Secretary-General was Javier Perez De Cuellar, who remained in office for two terms. The present incumbent is Dr. Boutros Boutros-Ghali of Egypt.

The Secretariat staff is appointed by the Secretary-General under regulations framed by the General Assembly. The main consideration in the selection of the personnel of the Secretariat and the conditions of service is the highest standard of efficiency, competence and integrity. But the Charter also provides that due regard shall be paid to the importance of recruiting the staff on as wide a geographical basis as possible. The Secretariat has nine departments, each under an Assistant Secretary-GeneraI. They are : Security Council Affairs; Economic Affairs; Social Affairs; Trusteeship and Information from Non-Self-Governing Territories; Public Information; Legal Problems; Conferences and General Services; Administrative and Financial Services; and Technical Assistance Administration.

On the Secretary-General devolve important functions in addition to the control and direction of the Secretariat. The Charter provides that he shall act in his capacity at all meetings of the General Assembly, Security Council, Economic and Social Council, and Trusteeship Council, and perform such other functions as are entrusted to him by these organs. He is required to submit an annual reporl to the General Assembly on the work of the United Nations. He is also empowered to bring to the notice of the Security Council any matter which, in his opinion, may threaten the maintenance of international peace and security. At the request of a majority of member-States or of the Security Council, the Secretary-General summons special sessions of the General Assembly. Every treaty and every international agreement entered into by any member-State must be registered with the Secretariat and published by it. Declarations by States, parties to the Statutes of the International Court of Justice, accepting the Court's compulsory jurisdiction, are to be deposited with the Secretary-General. In fact, the duties of the Secretary-General and his Secretariat are many and arduous. The immense amount of preparatory work-from the drafting of research documents surveying a problem to the arrangements for the convenience of the delegates — falls upon the Secretariat and when decisions have been taken, it is the duty of the Secretary-General and his staff to help implement those decisions by continuous administrative action. To sum up, it is the Secretariat that keeps the machinery of the United Nations going and on its efficiency depends a great deal of the effectiveness of the Organisation.

Specialised Agencies. Besides the six organs described above, there are fourteen specialised agencies of the United Nations which deal with specific international problems. Three were established before World War II: The International Telecommunication Union (ITU) and the Universal Postal Union (UPU) were originally founded in the latter part of the nineteenth century, whereas the International Labour Organization (ILO) developed with the League of Nations. The remaining 11 agencies, products of World War II and the United Nations, include: The International Bank for Reconstruction and Development (IBRD), The International Monetary Fund (IMF), The International Finance Corporation (IFC), The International Development Association (IDA), The Food and Agriculture Organization (FAO), The United Nations Educational, Scientific and Cultural Organization (UNESCO), The World Health Organization (WHO), The International Civil Aviation Organization (ICAO), The World Meteorological Organization (WMO), and The Inter-Governmental Maritime Consultative Organization (IGMCO). Since the International Trade Organization remains only a charter with insufficient adherents, the actual work of expediting international trade is done through the General Agreement on Tariffs and Trade (GATT), established in 1948.

A brief reference is made to the organization and activities of the most important of these fourteen specialised agencies.

International Labour Organization. The International Labour Organization was established in 1919 as an autonomous institution associated with the League of Nations. Its original constitution formed part of the Treaty of Versailles. In 1946, ILO became the first specialised agency associated with the United Nations. The ILO was founded to advance the cause of social justice and, in so doing, to contribute to the establishment of universal and lasting peace. The Declaration of Philadelphia, adopted by the International Labour Conference in 1944 and later annexed to the ILO Constitution, reaffirms the principles to which the organization is dedicated. It states that "all human beings, irrespective of race, creed or sex, have the right to pursue both their material well-being and their spiritual development in conditions of freedom and dignity, of economic security and equal opportunity." The ILO's motto is : "Poverty anywhere constitutes a danger to prosperity everywhere." Its aim, therefore, is to improve labour conditions in regard to wages, hours of work and conditions of work.

The ILO is a tripartite organization and includes representatives of the governments, employers and the employees. The International Labour Conference is the supreme deliberative body of the ILO. It meets only at ILO headquarters at Geneva and is attended by more than 1,000 delegates, technical advisers and observers. Each national delegation is composed of two government delegates, one employers' delegate and one workers' delegate. The conference elects the Governing Body of the International Labour Office, adopts the ILO budget, sets international labour standards, in the form of conventions and recommendations, and provides a world forum for the discussion of social and labour questions. The Governing Body (executive council) consists of twenty-four Government members, twelve employers' members and twelve workers' members. Ten of the Government members represent States of chief industrial importance–Canada, China, France, Germany, India, Italy, Japan, Russia, the United Kingdom, and the United States. The Governing Body normally meets three or four times a year at Geneva, elects the

Director-General of the International Labour Office, and approves the budget for the adoption of the confidence. It determines policy and work programmes, decides the conference agenda, in so far as this is not fixed by the conference itself, and supervises the work of the office of the various ILO Committees and other bodies.

Food and Agriculture Organization. The Food and Agriculture Organization came into being in October 1945, with a view to collecting, analysing, interpreting and disseminating information relating to nutrition, food and agriculture. The founder nations of FAO expressed the wish to raise levels of nutrition and standards of living, to improve production and distribution of agricultural products to secure improvements in the efficiency of the production and distribution of all food and agricultural products, to better the condition of rural population and to contribute towards an expanding world economy. In 1965, it was decided to add to the FAO's mission, at the instance of the then Director-General, Dr. B.R. Sen of India, the goal of ensuring humanity's freedom from hunger. To help members reach these goals, FAO provides an intelligence service, including not only facts and figures relating to nutrition, agriculture, forestry and fisheries, but also appraisals and forecasts of production, distribution and consumption in these fields; promotes national and international action to improve production, marketing, processing and distribution of the products of agriculture (including fisheries and forestry), conservation of natural resources, and credit and commodity arrangement policies; and furnishes, on request, technical assistance in any of the above fields.

FAO works through a Conference, a Council and a staff. The Conference is the policy-making body, in which each member-State has one vote. Associate members have the right to attend and to take part in the discussions, but without the right to vote. The Conference normally meets biennially. Between sessions of the Conference, the Council supervises the work of the FAO, reviews the world food and agricultural situation and makes recommendations to member-governments, and to international bodies, on measures to improve the situation. The Council consists of thirty-one member-governments elected by the Conference.

U.N. Educational, Scientific and Cultural Organization. The United Nations Educational, Scientific and Cultural Organization (UNESCO) grew out of the International Intellectual Cooperation Organization of the League of Nations. Its aims can best be described in the words of the Preamble to its own constitution, which declares that "since war begins in the minds of men, it is in the minds of men that the defences of peace must be constructed." And in the articles of its constitution it is provided that "the purpose of the organisation is to contribute to peace and security by promoting collaboration among the nations through education, science and culture in order to further universal respect for justice, for the rule of law, and for the human rights and fundamental freedoms which are affirmed for the people of the world without distinction of sex, language or religion by the Charter of the United Nations." The UNESCO, in brief, aims at promoting international peace and security through education, science and culture and thereby to further universal respect for justice, rule of law, human rights, and fundamental freedoms for all the peoples. It is not concerned with the task of solving any urgent political problems, as the Security Council and the General Assembly do, but it is to take positive steps to promote peace and international understanding through a sustained educational campaign of the new philosophy of humanism. It is, thus, dedicated to fostering an awareness of the intellectual and moral solidarity of mankind.

UNESCO's activities are so varied as to defy a brief description. It strives to increase international exchange of students and scholars, to conduct the study of social problems likely to create national and international tensions, and to provide technical assistance for the economic and political development of undeveloped areas. How significant it is, is evident from the fact that States are requesting more technical assistance from UNESCO than it has funds to supply. The habit on the part of many countries of turning to an international agency for help can hardly fail to develop international-mindedness.

UNESCO has also devised means to lessen illiteracy in the world and has liberally assisted in the rebuilding of educational systems in the developing countries. It has periodically arranged holding of seminars and conferences to standardize knowledge by pooling scholarship. It has also published illuminating reports of such deliberations and discussions, which add to a common understanding of the international problems in the field of education.

The organisation works through a Generaly Conference, which is held now once in two years, an Executive Board and a Secretariat. The General Conference, consisting of representatives from each member-State, convenes every two years to formulate policies and to approve the programme and budget for the next two years. The Executive Board, composed of 30 members, elected by the General Conference, is the body responsible for the execution of the programme, adopted by the Conference. The Secretariat is the pivotal organ which is responsible for the day-to-day administration and for implementing the programme adopted by the General Conference and endorsed by the Board. It is headed by a Director-General proposed by the Executive Board and appointed by the Conference.

National commissions, composed of representatives of the Government and non-governmental organization in each of the member-States, link UNESCO with the educational, scientific and cultural life in each country and assist in carrying out UNESCO's programme.

International Monetary Fund. The Fund was established to promote international cooperation on monetary problems through a permanent institution which provides the machinery for consultation and collaboration. Its main purposes are: to facilitate as primary objectives of economic policy, the expansion and balanced growth of international trade, contributing thereby to the promotion and maintenance of high levels of employment and real income and to the development of productive resources of all members; to promote exchange stability, to maintain orderly exchange arrangements among members and to avoid competitive exchange depreciation; and to give confidence to members by making the Fund's resources available to them under adequate safeguards.

The Fund works through a Board of Governors, a Board of Executive Directors, a Managing Director and a staff. All powers of the Fund are vested in the Board of Governors consisting of one Governor and one Alternate appointed by each member. The voting power of the Governors is related to the size of the quota of the member-nations they represent. The Board of Executive Governors is responsible for the conduct of general operations of the Fund and exercises the powers delegated to it by the Board of Governors. The Executive Directors appoint a Managing Director, who must not be a Governor or an Executive Director.

International Bank for Reconstruction and Development. The International Bank for Reconstruction and Development is an essential adjunct to the International Monetary Fund. The primary purpose of the Bank is as its title indicates to assist the reconstruction and development of member-States and this purpose is to be achieved by facilitating the investment of capital for productive purposes. It makes loans to member-governments and government agencies or private enterprises under governmental guarantee.

All powers of the Bank are vested in the Board of Governors, which meets annually and consists of one Governor and one Alternate appointed by each member. The Board has delegated most of its powers to twenty Executive Directors, who meet at least once a month. They function as a Board. The President of the Bank is selected by the Executive Directors and also serves as their Chairman. Subject to the general direction of the Executive Directors on questions of policy, he is responsible for conducting the business of the Bank.

World Health Organization. The World Health Organization came into existence on April 7, 1948. Its functions are to coordinate international health work; to eradicate epidemic, endemic and other diseases; to promote the improvement of nutrition, housing, sanitation, recreation, economic and working conditions and other aspects of hygiene; to develop, establish and promote international standards with respect to food and biological, pharmaceutical and similar products, and to standardize diagnostic procedure; and to foster activities in the field of mental health, especially those activities affecting the harmony of human relations. WHO runs a number of world-wide services, such as the notification of quarantinable diseases, assists member countries, on request, to improve their health services; and stimulates medical research in a variety of ways.

The main organs of WHO are the World Health Assembly, the Executive Board, six regional committees and the secretariat. The World Health Assembly is the supreme governing body. It meets each year and is composed of delegations of the organization's member-States. It determines the policies and programmes of the WHO and votes the budget. The Executive Board, a technical and non-political organ, is composed of twenty-four persons designated by as many member-States elected by World Health Assembly. It meets twice a year to prepare the work of the Assembly and to give effect to its decisions. WHO's headquarters are in Geneva, but the activities of the organization have been largely decentralized to six regional organizations, each having a regional committee composed of government representatives of the countries in the region and a regional office

THE U.N. AT WORK

We have described the structure and functions of the most comprehensive international organisation hitherto established. The United Nations can claim definite superiority, in some respects, over the old League of Nations. From the very beginning it has inspired greater international confidence, as it is representative of wide interests and a more comprehensive organization than the League of Nations. The Charter of the United Nations, as it emerged from the exhaustive discussions at San Francisco, is indicative of the efforts of fifty delegations, representing great powers and small, of their will to peace and security, and "better standards of life in larger freedom." It provides for the means whereby the representatives of sovereign States may speak as well as listen, and may, by free mutual discussion and patient negotiation, reconcile their viewpoints in the interests of world peace and progress. The inclusion of the United States of America and Soviet Russia gave the United Nations a more solid foundation. Its universality of membership now, numbering one hundred and eighty-five, inclusive of South Africa, member-States is expressive of the strength behind the organisation and the strong determination of the nations uniting together to achieve the basic aims of the United Nations. Moreover, the Charter of the United Nations, as one writer put it, is more realistic in so far as it places the responsibility for security where power lies. The Security Council is vested with the primary responsibility of maintaining world peace and security. The Charter clearly specifies how these powers are to be used and every member of the United Nations is pledged to accept and carry out the decisions of the Security Council. The decisions of the Security Council are not made to remain a mere threat. It may call upon the member-States to break off diplomatic relations with an offending State or declare a blockade or use economic sanctions against it. Should the Council consider that these measures are inadequate, it may take all military action required by the situation. Every member-State of the United Nations is pledged by Article 43 to supply it, on its call, with the armed forces, the assistance and the facilities it requires, including right of passage.

Then, the Security Council is in continuous session and each member-State is permanently represented at the Headquarters. Eternal vigilance is the price of peace. Eternal vigilance and prompt action may well mean the difference between security and disaster and, by the rules of procedure, the Security Council meets as often as is necessary, and at least once every two weeks. The Charter also permits the Council to hold its meetings at any place other than the Headquarters, if that would facilitate the Council's work. The Council is empowered to investigate, on its own initiative, any situation which may, in its opinion, cause international friction or dispute. The Charter also allows any party to a dispute, any other member-State or the Secretary-General, to bring to the attention of the Security Council any actual or potential breach of peace, for collective action by it. Furthermore, unlike the League of Nations, the Charter of the United Nations improved the prospects of collective action by requiring a 7-4 majority prior to January 1966, and 9-6 now, instead of a unanimous decision.

There is impressive evidence that in the implementation of its resolve to attack the causes of not only war but of all conflicts, the United Nations, during its career of more than four decades, has devoted almost equal attention to the keeping of peace, decolonization and stimulating economic cooperation between the rich and the poor nations. Particularly notable have been the achievements of the UN Agencies, such as ECOSOC, UNESCO, UNICEF, WHO, and FAO. Talari says that "before another decade is over, the growing generation in the developing countries will have been assured of at least a square meal a day, opportunities for growth and education and freedom from disease." If this is achieved, the United Nations really justifies its existence.

The United Nations has also admirably succeeded in its pursuit of decolonization and the rise of one Asian and African country after another to independence. The process of decolonization can be said to have begun after World War I when the Turkish and German Colonies were made mandates of the League of Nations. But except in the case of "A" class mandates there was no obligation placed on the mandatory powers to develop their charges with the eventual objective of making them fully independent. After the United Nations came into being, new trusteeship agreements were signed in 1945 and 1946 for the mandates that had survived World War II. By 1961, all the hitherto trust territories had achieved independent status and the work of the Trusteeship Council, which supervised their administration, had virtually been concluded. The principal exception is South-West Africa for which a special committee still exists. There is also a committee for information on non-self-governing territories. When the founding fathers signed the Charter, the United Nations consisted of 50 members, of whom only nine came from Asia and Africa. Today the United Nations consists of one hundred and eighty-five members, of whom the Afro-Asians command a comfortable majority. The Afro-Asian member-States have also succeeded in securing amendments to the Charter, for the expansion of the Security Council and the Economic and Social Council.

The record of the United Nations in keeping peace and avoiding conflicts, if not spectacular, is, no doubt, commendable. The United Nations interposed its physical presence between the Arabs and the Israelis in the Palestine conflict and contributed significantly to the liberation of Indonesia and to the ending of the Greek-Albanian conflict. It maintains a ceasefire in Kashmir despite heavy odds. The Tashkent Declaration, which enabled the USSR to persuade India and Pakistan to abide by the resolution of the Security Council, was a great step forward in dealing with a critical situation, which, but for the initiative of the United Nations, would have certainly led to a large-scale war. The United Nations can also claim to have brought about a cease-fire in the Arab-Israeli war in June 1967. It intervened effectively in the Suez crisis, prevented the collapse and disintegration of the Congo and calmed the civil strife in Cyprus for keeping peace between the Greek and the Turkish Cypriots. But the remarkable achievement of the United Nations is clarity of its role which the world body has lately recognised. The rapidity with which United Nations opinion solidified in favour of the view that issues as Farakka are best left to bilateral negotiations is indicative of the fact that the United Nations is now less exploitable as a means by which to whip up support from one case against another in a bilateral dispute.

A 10-year $25 billion African Development Initiative ceremoniously launched on March 15, 1996, by the UN Secretary-General, Boutros, Boutros-Ghali, aims at lifting the African Continent out of the economic and social crisis bedevilling it and by providing assistance to key areas to put it back on the path of development and good governance. What gives credibility to this ambitious project is that the World Bank has committed itself to find much of resources needed for implementing the venture about 85 per cent of the total cost involved. "At a time when conditions are improving for many people around the world, the socio-economic plight of Africans remains a matter of concern," said Boutros Boutros-Ghali, while explaining why the African Initiative had become so urgent. "The situation has reached a critical stage. Of the 47 Least Developed Countries in the world, 32 are in Africa. Today over 220 million Africans live in conditions of absolute poverty and Africa is the only region in the world where poverty is expected to increase during this decade." He said the initiative being launched now was both substantive and action-oriented.

In spite of this credit side, there are certain serious defects in the scheme of the United Nations. The attitude of the victors to the defeated powers was exactly the same as it had been after World War I. The smaller States and even the large ones, which are militarily and economically less advanced, still suspect the United Nations as a mere tool in the hands of the Big Powers. The United Nations is based on the sovereign equality of nations, but, as Field Marshal Smuts, one of the outstanding statesmen at the San Francisco Conference, observed, "equality of status does not mean equality of functions." The war-time allies and the promoters of the United Nations were, till disintegration of Soviet Russia in 1991, divided into two power blocs and engaged in a constant Cold War. Possession of atomic weapons by both blocks with a systematic race in stockpiling and other such developments, made the people at large to believe that it was a mockery of the United Nations. In his Tenth Annual Report of the United Nations, the then Secretary-General, Dag Hammarskjold, observed that the actual establishment of an agreed international system for the control and reduction of armaments and armed forces "can take place only in an atmosphere of confidence, trust and understanding among the nations, an atmosphere which has not yet come into being." The failure of the special UN session on disarmament, that crawled along for five weeks, was a telling commentary on the attitude of the big powers and world affairs. In the absence of any worthwhile agreement, the Assembly dispersed in the first week of July 1982 with a so-called consensus report which, even in terms of phraseology, marked a retrogression from the resolution earlier adopted in 1979. When vital questions remain unresolved, it is natural that the common man may think of the United Nations as an organisation of "Disunited Nations."

The United Nations Organization was really a combination of strange bed-fellows. There were old jealousies and ideological differences between the "Big Five" and these differences were glaringly witnessed by men at large every day in the proceedings of the General Assembly and the Security Council. Past, but not forgotten, differences persisted between the United Kingdom and the erstwhile Soviet Union. Disguised economic rivalries persisted between the United Kingdom and the United States of America and with the waning of United Kingdom's political and economic prestige the inward gulf between the two widened. The differences between the United States and the former Soviet Russia were irreconcilable, though fluctuating and unpredictable. With the open rupture between the former USSR and China the situation became intriguing. Then, there could not be any unanimity on the Japanese Peace Treaty, and the Peace Treaty itself was a mere show of power politics. The most regrettable part of the entire transaction has been that the settlement of peace terms with Germany remained in abeyance entailing the division of the country into two parts sharply divided amongst themselves. Though united now, but old memories still haunt them.

Five Great Powers — the United States, the United Kingdom, the former Soviet Union, France and China — were given permanent seats on the Security Council with the right of veto, because the authors of the United Nations Charter felt that all these States would be in a position to make an exceptional contribution to the maintenance of international peace and security. But it was justly maintained that the procedure of voting in the Security Council was designed to shield these "Big Five" powers against their own sins. On all substantive matters the affirmative majority of seven originally, and nine members now, was required. The majority must include then and now the concurring votes of all the five permanent members.[26] It means that one of the "Big Five" could and can even now vitiate the decisions and discussions of the Security Council at any stage. It also means that a friendly State to any of these "Big Five" can make the decisions of the Security Council ineffective. This indirect veto may be used and it has been used for expediency rather than justice. For example, the United States vetoed the UN motion criticising the action of Israel in annexing the Golan Heights in January 1982 when it had supported the December 1981 resolution of the Security Council declaring the annexation of the Golan Heights as null and void. The most blatant attempt by China to pressurize the United Nations by the persistent use (for fifteen times) of veto was witnessed in the third term election of the Secretary-General, Kurt Weldheim. Boutros Boutros-Ghali's second term appointment as Secretary-General was vetoed by the United States. President Bill Clinton openly declared his intention to veto the appointment, though Ghali's re-appointment was supported by the rest of the four permanent members.

There were heated discussions on the subject of veto at the San Francisco Conference. The non-Great powers, who called themselves "the Little Forty-Five", fought hard for the modification of the veto. The "Big Five", however, stood solidly together and resisted any material modification. Winston Churchill, the Prime Minister of the United Kingdom, called the veto "a shield for the strong and a mockery for the weak." The "Little Forty-Five" were ultimately reconciled to the veto without illusions. "When we, Little Powers, are fighting," said a Latin American delegate at the San Francisco Conference, "the Great Powers will stop us. But, if and when the Great Powers are at loggerheads, God help us."

In 1950, the General Assembly adopted, as a measure of abundant precaution, a resolution, known as "United Action for Peace Resolution", to safeguard against the power of veto vested in the permanent member-States. The Assembly resolved: "If the Security Council because of lack of unanimity of the permanent members fails to exercise its primary responsibility for the maintenance of international peace and security in any case, where there appears to be a threat to peace, breach of peace or act of aggression, the General Assembly shall consider the matter immediately with a view to making appropriate recommendations to members for collective measures, including, in case of breach of the peace or act of aggression, the use of armed forces when necessary to maintain or restore international peace and security."

The provision of coercive action against aggressive States was really intended to coerce the smaller States. The Big Powers may themselves disturb international peace and repudiate the principles which they enjoin and even force upon smaller States. On October 11, 1945, Lord Winster, intervening in the debate in the House of Lords. said: "This Organization (the United Nations) will be one for keeping small boys in order by prefects who themselves are exempt from the rules that they will administer." Events in Egypt, Hungary, Jordan, the Lebanon, Congo and Falkland prove it. Even without a Veto UN resolutions are openly flouted. Economic sanctions were recommended by UN resolutions against Rhodesia and South Africa as punitive measures against their racialist

26. Informally, it has now been agreed that when a permanent member fails to vote it is not tantamount to a veto.

policies. The sanctions did not work because the United States and the West in general were backing these regimes as they were anti-Soviets and anti-communist. The Secretary-General, Javier Perez de Cuellar, in his first annual report submitted in September 1982, warned of a "new international anarchy" and proposed an extraordinary top-level meeting of the Security Council to consider ways of bolstering the United Nations as the guardian of peace. Once again, in his 1985 report, the Secretary-General posed a choice for member-States to cooperate in building on the existing foundations of the United Nations as a useful, coherent, effective institution, or the alternative of each member-State taking their own short-sighted and self-interested course, He warned the General Assembly that if they made the latter choice, the promising foundations would "end up surmounted by a rambling, contentious slum, the breeding ground for endless new troubles and disasters."

In order to create this sense of awareness, it was decided to hold a special commemorative session of the General Assembly marking the 40th anniversary of the United Nations in October 1985. More than 80 heads of State or Government attended this session and the Secretary-General expressed the gratification at the response from the world leaders to his suggestion for participation. The world leaders assembled there recounted, once again, regional conflicts in different parts of the globe, national crisis and called for strengthening of the economic and social functions of the United Nations. All this proved to be a simple rhetoric. There could be no consensus on the declaration to be issued after the conclusion of a "summit of summits." As President of Botswana, Dr Quett K.J. Maisre, put it : "The UN had been a victim of the paralysis caused by the East-West ideological rivalry reflecting a competition for world hegemony in which the ideological power blocs were engaged. We play no part in that struggle."

Decline of the U.N. In more than four decades of its life, the United Nations should have come of age. The fact that in some respects it has not happened can be ascribed to its members' shortcomings. If the first two decades of its life were periods of foundation and growth, the third, which should have been the decade of consolidation, was in grave danger of becoming one of crisis. The responsibility for all this does not lie upon any one particular State or group of States, but on all of them though the promoters of this world organisation played the key role that created a big dent on its working. U Thant, the Secretary-General, believed that the ineffectiveness of the United Nations resulted from the "non-supportive attitudes and patterns of behaviour on the part of many national governments."[27] In his message to the United Nations Day 1970, he urged, "It is time for governments to make a fresh start and to lift themselves again to the same high level, if not a higher level, of vision and determination as that of the authors of the Charter. We must give the Charter a real chance at least. We must pass from words to deeds." Javier Perez de Cuellar dramatised his concern at the erosion of the United Nations peace-keeping ability by devoting almost all his 1982 report to that crucial issue instead of surveying the broad spectrum of UN activities. He wrote, "Certainly we have strayed far from the Charter in recent years. Governments that believe they can win an international objective by force are often quite ready to do so, and domestic opinion not infrequently applauds such a course." He said that there had been "alarming succession of international

27. Leon Gorden Ker (Ed.), *The United Nations in International Politics*, p. 186.

crises" during the past year and also referred to the "current tendency to resort to confrontation, violence and even war," in pursuit of what were seen as vital interests, claims or aspirations. "We are perilously near to an international anarchy." be deplored. "Such a trend must be reversed before once again we bring upon ourselves a global catastrophe and find ourselves without institutions effective enough to prevent it." He appealed to all nuclear-nations that something must be done, and urgently, to strengthen "our international institutions and to adopt new and imaginative approaches to the prevention and resolution of conflicts."[28]

The period between the late 1950s and 1960s was, in restrospect, the "golden age" in the annals of the United Nations. This was the time of institutional innovations and pioneering intellectual and political exercises in policy formulations and negotiations. Earnest and ceaseless efforts in the various forums of the United Nations culminated in the establishment of UN Conference on Trade and Development (UNCTAD), U.N. Industrial Development Organisation (UNIDO), Special Fund (later UNDP or UN Development Programme) and International Development Association (IDA).

The object was to accelerate the growth of developing countries and identify them on basis of priority. This effort of the United Nations was enthusiastically hailed all the world over and widely accepted. The various studies, analyses and researches undertaken during this period revealed "the glaring inequalities, injustices, exploitative character and the sheer anomalies of the manner in which the world economy functioned."

The 1970s were a period of disillusionment with the United Nations on the part of both developing and developed countries. The enthusiasm of developing countries waned as the hopes they had fondly entertained for the rapid growth of their economy failed to materialise. There was deliberate tardiness on the part of the developed countries to implement the policies agreed upon and duly planned for fulfilment within the given frame work of time. The developing countries also realised that the entire scheme of development envisaged in the policies agreed upon, just touched a fringe of their manifold problems. In 1974, they gave a call, which was endorsed by the General Assembly, for establishing a New International Economic Order (NIEO) with its objective, amongst others, of a vital change in international economic structures and institutions aiming to promote economic and social progress in the developing countries in the context of the expanding economy. But not to speak of the global issues of NIEO, NIO, etc., the United Nations failed even to find an answer to such issues as a code concerning restricted business practices of governments and multinationals on the transfer of technology. It is well known that when and if codes are evolved, ideological conflicts, which had plagued the working of the United Nations, would never allow them to become operative.

The North felt beleaguered by these collective demands and pressures of the NIEO. They found that the United Nations was being steered in a direction far removed from the original intentions in promoting this world body. They, therefore, resented the decisions of the past, forgetting that they themselves were parties to all such decisions. Attributing their past decisions to what they termed "unthinking and relentless operation of mechanical majority in the United Nations forums they began to distance themselves from these decisions as well as forums."

28. *U.N. Monthly Chronicle,* 7, 9 (October 1942).

After winning independence the Afro-Asian countries *en masse* joined the United Nations and after complaints of lopsided and bloc voting and arbitrary decisions in the various forums were voiced reflecting the fear that the majority among the member-States belonged to the Third World and by definition hostile to the West. But it was not so. Except on such issues as colonialism, racialism, nationalism or a fairer economic deal for the underdeveloped countries, the Third World did not and could not speak with one voice and it was not necessary that they should. New Delhi had always deprecated existence of blocs within the United Nations and outside it. However, this was not the same thing as excluding the right to canvass support for a point of view or an issue the representation of which could be of far reaching consequence.

The fact is that the major powers have no alternative but to adjust to an organisation with a majority of newly emergent States whose dominant interest is their rapid development and whose attitude is coloured accordingly. But the developed countries firmly believe that the way the United Nations is being carried away defeats the ideals and intentions of the founders of this world organisation. After the 1980s, the indifference of the developed countries, spearheaded by the United States of America, assumed open hostility towards the United Nations itself which is committed *inter alia* to promote social progress and better conditions of life. There was even an active and fairly successful effort to dismantle what had been achieved earlier and reshape the United Nations "after the image of their perceived interests and preference. In this, they fully exploited the complete vulnerability of developing countries brought about by the development and debt crisis of the 1980s."[29]

The United States' frustration over the manner of handling United Nations affairs was reflected in a law passed by Congress which limited the United States payments to the UN and its specialised agencies to 20 per cent of the budget unless the world body recognised in its budgetary system and provided for a voting strength proportionate to the size of the contribution. Another law required the total United States federal deficits to be progressively reduced to zero and where direct programme cuts were not possible pro-rata pruning on all federal programmes would become necessary.

Sometime later the United States left the International Labour Organization complaining its political biases, and in 1984 followed it by pulling out of the UNESCO accusing it of over-politicalisation, mismanagement and wastefulness. The United States was the largest donor to UNESCO which provided 25 per cent of organisation's total budget. Then came Britain to withdraw. Britain accused the UNESCO of bad management, persistent bias against the West through peace, information and human rights programmes, with one-sided Soviet bloc views. The Reagan Administration also decided to derecognise the International Court of Justice at The Hague, which automatically implied not to comply with the decisions of the world court. The reason given was that the Court's objectives were being "subverted by Nicaragua's effort to use the Court as a political weapon." The reference was to Managua's complaint before the International Court that the United States contributed and directed the Nicaragua rebels trying to overthrow the

29. Muchkund Dubey, "UN at the Cross Roads: Steady Erosion in its Global Role", *The Times of India,* New Delhi. June 22, 1992.

Government in violation of International Law. The decision of the Court had gone against the United States. Reagan himself admitted, a little before the expiry of his term of office, that he had secretly provided funds to the Nicaragua rebels.

Another target of Reagan Administration was the World Health Organisation (WHO). The international repercussions of withdrawals, withholding or sequencing of contributions to the various agencies were meant to render the world body financially paralysed and functionless. It is coercion pure and simple to force the recipients to bow to the dictates of the donor country.

At the 40th Commemorative General Assembly session, the Secretary-General, Javier Perez de Cullar, apprised this highest forum of the world body about the most serious crisis in the history of the United Nations and revealed that at the end of 1985-86 the UN was $242 million in debt and unless drastic steps were undertaken the shortfall for 1986-87 was expected to be over $245 million. The deficit, he explained, had been the result of the delinquent member-States. Some of them refused to pay part of the contributions because of the disagreement with certain programmes of the United Nations, and also because some other member-States had not been regular in their payments and that the United States was the latest to join the "arrear member-States". On November 21, 1987, the Secretary-General told the UN Staff at the Annual staff Day that the world body was almost "broke" without reserves and that it did not have enough money to pay December salaries. He also disclosed that the United States was the largest contributor and debtor and currently owed $342 million of the total unpaid assessment of $456.4 million. He further said that 93 of the 159 member-States (in 1987) owed $456 million in back dues, or about half the annual budget of almost $800 million. Before leaving his office in 1992 Perez de Cuellar said in anguish, "It is a great irony that the UN is on the brink of insolvency at the very time the world community has entrusted the organisation with new and unprecedented responsibilities." At the end of 1992, all the five permanent members of the Security Council were in arrears with Russia and the United States as being by far the most delinquent. The Secretary-General, Boutros Boutros-Ghali, warned the 184 member-States, on August 7, 1993, that if it did not receive the funds the world body would be forced to freeze its current missions and abstain from undertaking new ones. In his letters to the Heads of the State and government and foreign ministers of the member-States, Dr. Ghali, *inter alia*, emphasised that he was deeply preoccupied with the "unprecedented financial crisis confronting the United Nations." The official spokesman of the UN explained that out of the Security Council members only Britain, France and New Zealand had paid their contribution till July 15, 1993. The United States was the largest debtor with $836 million followed by Russia with $508 million. If the situation remained unchanged, the UN would not be in position to assume the responsibilities in the field of peace and international security. In a letter to the Washington Post, UN Under-Secretary of State, Joseph E. Connor, disclosed that by the end of 1995, the United States owed the United Nations a total of $1.6 billion, driving the World Organisation to the financial edge". Connor said prompt payment of dues is a treaty obligation as approved by the UN under the consensus system adopted at its instance 10 years ago. The UN "has no reserves and no capital. It is totally dependent on cash inflows (assessments) from member-states to provide liquidity. Unpaid assessments now exceed $ 3.2 billion." The

Under-Secretary further asserted that the UN bureaucracy is "far from blorated". In recent years, he added, the number of hight level posts has been cut by 30 per cent. The U.N. Secretariat wrote "years ago, the UN Secretariat staff numbered 12,000. In 1996, it began with 9,500."

It is a pity, pointed out Rakshat Puri, that the White House and Congressional leaders in the United States should have shot down almost without consideration UN Secretary-General Boutros Boutros-Ghali's suggestion for UN tax on foreign exchange transactions at the rate of 0.001 per cent which was likely to provide the World Organisation with some three billion dollars annually.

The difficulties between Secretary-General Boutros Boutros-Ghali and the Security Council after just six months of his assuming office are symptomatic of the great change which the UN organisation had undergone since the end of the Cold War. Prior to 1991, the "Big Five" had always to agree among themselves on a candidate for the post of the Secretary-General, a process in which the United States had a major say. But with the United States present ascendancy over the United Nations and the world, the future Secretary-General will be primarily an American candidate. An unwritten rule for the Secretary-General's job is that he must be a competent mediocrity and those who intend seeking enhanced powers for the post are, therefore, the least desired. Washington took long to recover from the shock of discovering in Dag Hammarskjold a Secretary-General "of originability and daring. The last thing Washington would desire is another Hammarskjold" says Surinder Nihal Singh.[30] Dr. Boutros Boutros-Ghali, the most attractive of the African candidates and Egypt's Foreign Minister, had not for many reasons enthused the United States and the most important reason being there was no guarantee that he would prove to be unduly paliant to Washington's wishes.

With the collapse of the Soviet Union and Moscow's pursuit of a non-ideological foreign policy, the United Nations became a different proposition for the United States. As the Security Council's conduct during the Gulf War proved, UN became "a new important instrument of American foreign policy." Indeed, in the "dramatically changed circumstances," as S. Nihal Singh says, there "is a longer medium-term American goal for the United Nations. With the countervailing power of the Soviet Union having vanished, the United States needs the UN more than it ever has in clothing its foreign policy goals in the garb of a collective world consensus."[31] And Washington knows that "it has the clout to get most of the other countries to toe its line in the UN".[32]

Since 1991, the General Assembly, the Secretary-General and the Third World have all lost their influence and prestige. Consensus in the Security Council means that other organs of the United Nations have lost their relevance. Under the provisions of the Charter, the General Assembly cannot discuss any matter of which the Security Council is seized. With the Security Council in continuous session and fully operational, the General Assembly gets nothing of importance to discuss and resolve. Russia was given the place of the former Soviet Union in the Security Council without reference to the

30. "UN at Crossroads", *The Hindustan Times,* New Delhi, September 24, 1991.

31. *Ibid.*

32. *Ibid.*

General Assembly. Important questions, such as, admission of a State in the UN, or suspension of a State from its memberships are to be decided on the recommendations of the Security Council by the General Assembly with a two-thirds majority of its members present and voting.

Sanctions were imposed against Libya demanding extradition and trial by American or British Courts of two Libyan nationals, suspected of involvement in the December 1988 Pan Am flight 103 bombing over Lockerbie, Scotland, that killed 270 people. Extradition is not automatic in International Law, but is governed by extradition treaty between the two countries. There was none between the United States or Britain and Libya. The United States Supreme Court had also ruled that in the absence of extradition treaty between Libya and the United States, the matter should be deemed closed. Libya had also moved the International Court of Justice at The Hague for the interpretation of the 1971 Montreal Convention or suppression of the unlawful acts against civil aviation and had agreed to place the two alleged suspects in the custody of a neutral country pending the verdict of the International Court of Justice. But the Security Council without waiting for the Court's verdict set an arbitrary deadline for compliance of handing over the alleged suspects otherwise sanctions would be imposed. On March 31, 1992, Resolution 748 imposing air embargo on Libya became operative. The Bush Administration, as Jaya Mehta says, "was obviously more interested in punishing Col. Gaddofi than in extraditing the two Libyans and the U.N. obliged."[33]

The embargo, originally imposed in March 1992, was renewable every 120 days. The Security Council renewed it for a fifth time on August 30, 1993, after reviewing Libya's compliance which was found once again, "in defiance of the will of the international community." As usual, there was no open meeting or vote in the Security Council. After the meeting the United States, Britain and France issued a statement saying that they would try to freeze Libya's financial assets and ban the purchase of oil equipment if Tripoli did not turn over two suspects in a terrorist bombing by October 1, 1993."[34] Libya eventually agreed to hand over the suspects but embargo still continues even after a period of 5 years (March 1996).

The world had also seen the "high-handed" manner in which Resolution No. 687 of the Security Council against Iraq was implemented. Whether President Saddam Hussain was justified or not in refusing entry of the United Nations inspection team to the Agricultural Ministry building at Baghdad is controversial. But it remains an undisputed fact that the American President, George Bush, did not consider it necessary and proper to formally place the matter before the Security Council. When the resolution of the Security Council is not implemented, it is the duty of the Secretary-General to devise means for its proper implementation. But the Bush Administration sidetracked both the Secretary-General and the Security Council by increasing its military strength in the Persian Gulf. The *modus operandi* of George Bush was quite clear and he had made no secret of it in his public utterances on various occasions. He was determined to humble Saddam Hussain and liquidate his regime in Iraq. When he failed in his mission, Bush

33. Jaya Mehta, "West Usurping U.N. Assembly," *The Times of India*, New Delhi, August 25, 1992.
34. *The Hindu*, New Delhi, August 15, 1993.

floated the bogey of violation of human rights against the Shias of South Iraq and repression of Kurds. This, too, misfired. But the issue of violation of human rights and repression of minorities remained alive. Bill Clinton, who succeeded George Bush, in his inaugural address on January 20, 1993, unequivocally declared his commitment to adhere to the foreign policy of his predecessor and to vigorously protect the minorities from repression of any kind. His Secretary of State, Warren Christopher, warned Saddam Hussain, who had earlier hailed Bill Clinton on his election to the Presidency, in blunt terms, on May 24, 1993, of the United States' "resolute retaliation" if Iraq staged an offensive against Kurds in an "autonomous enclave" in the north Iraq. He disclosed that the United States would be "watching very carefully" to see "if Iraq intended such an attack." He knows, the Secretary of State emphasised, "what he has to do if Saddam Hussain attempts it." The United States, he added, would enforce the sanction "with great resoluteness," and would be looking for "any change in that situation that might call for further action from the United States."[35] "Further action" could not possibly be anything else except the repetition of the Gulf War.

India, along with other Asian countries, expressed grave apprehensions over a proposal, by the United Nations Secretary-General Boutros Boutros-Ghali, for "preventing United Nations intervention in domestic conflicts." The Secretary-General stated that the time had come for preventive deployment of United Nations forces "either at the request of the government, or all parties concerned, or with their consensus." Various governments, including India, warned against this kind of preventive diplomacy as it might become a pretext for interference in the internal and domestic affairs of a sovereign country and asserted that the United nations should venture such an attempt only with the express consent of the host nation. Chinmoy Rajninath Gharekhan, Indian Ambassador to the United Nations, told the Special Committee on the Peace-keeping Operations, on May 9, 1991, that India supported the peace-keeping role of the world body, but he simultaneously stressed the "bedrock requirements" that such operations must be carried out with "due respect for sovereignty and territorial integrity of the country or countries concerned." This principle needs to be stressed, he added, "in view of recent world-wide events and the possibility of increasing United Nations commitments in the future."[36]

Later, the Indian Ambassador to the United Nations without naming any country told the UN Committee that it required to be ensured that a request by one State for preventive deployment on its territory did not become a cover for terrorist activities. In this context, he pointed out that the world had witnessed "perceptible" increase in State-sponsored terrorism which constituted a new threat to international peace. Referring to the suggestion for preventive deployment of UN forces in case of national crisis, Sreenivasan warned that this could embroil the United Nations in the political disputes and processes within the country opening the world body to the charges of partiality and intervention. "These are the very charges which would erode the fundamental ingredients of the United Nations functioning and its Charter," he stressed.

Addressing the working group of UN General Assembly on: "Agenda for Peace,"

35. *The Hindustan Times*, New Delhi, May 26, 1993.
36. *The Times of India*, New Delhi, May 11, 1991.

presented by the Secretary-General, Boutros Boutros-Ghali, Sreenivasan emphasised that any increase in the authority of the 15-member Security Council necessitated its democratisation. "An expansion of the Council is, therefore, essential before new responsibilities such as preventive deployment are entrusted to the Council."

On February 22, 1993, the Security Council adopted Resolution 808, by which it decided to establish an international ad hoc tribunal to prosecute people responsible for serious violations of humanitarian law in former Yugoslavia. In pursuance of this Resolution the Security Council unanimously decided, in May 1993, to set up an 11-Judge International Court at The Hague to try people accused of war crimes in former Yugoslavia, including murder, rape, ethnic cleansing, torture and other atrocities. The Security Council adopted a 34-Article Statute governing the functions of the Court, which would try cases involving grave breaches of the Geneva Conventions, violation of the 1948 Conventions against genocide and other crimes against humanity and the law of war. The Court was to consist of two trial Chambers with three judges each, and a five-judge appeal Chamber. The court was also to include a prosecutor and his staff, entrusted with the duty to investigate and prosecute the perpetrators.

It was to be the first international court of its kind since the main allied countries after World War II set up courts, at Nuremburg and Tokyo, to try leading axis powers' war criminals. It appeared that in the context of the world leadership role the United States has assumed and other major countries have acquiesced, the world is slowly inching towards a permanent international criminal court. Many developing countries and minor States are worried about this new development. At present, the violations of International Law are a legal concern of the international community but the enforcement of criminal sanction is left primarily with the nation-State.

Revamping the UN. The Tenth Summit of the Non-Aligned Movement (NAM) opened at Jakarta on September 1, 1992, with a call by the Indonesian President Suharto for establishment of a high-level working group to formulate proposals for restructuring of the United Nations. He said, "We believe that the United Nations in this new era would remain the major instrument of global governance and the centrepiece of any new international order. We must now more actively contribute to the revitalisation, restructuring and democratisation of its functions. For it is through the United Nations we can deal integrally with all aspects of international peace including, more urgently than before, its economic and social dimensions."

Despite the end of big powers', (United States and Soviet Russia) confrontation, Indonesian President said, the world was still faced with many problems and "still far from being a peaceful and secure place." There was need to ensure that the new world order did not turn out to be a "new version of the same old pattern of domination of the strong over the weak and the rich over the poor."

Although the main theme of the speeches delivered at the Plenary session of the Summit had been for reforming and restructuring the United Nations, but leaders of all the participating countries realised the near impossibility of achieving the desired objective as it called for a drastic revision of the Charter. UN Secretary-General, Boutros Boutros-Ghali, who was present at the session, made it clear that changing the UN Charter was an almost impossible task. "If you want to change the composition of the UN Security

Council, you have to deal with the version of the Charter and according to Article 109 there will be no such revision without the five permanent members." He afterwards told newsmen that the only way possible for a revision of the Charter was by persuading the five permanent members that it was important to do so. "But this is not my job," the Secretary-General remarked.

The 37th Commonwealth Parliamentary Conference, held in New Delhi in September 1991, called for the expansion of the Security Council by the inclusion of countries like India, Japan and Germany as permanent members to strengthen the authority of the world organisation and prevent it from being manipulated by any one State.

Speaking at the two-day inaugural session of the Rajiv Gandhi Foundation, in May 1993, the world leaders made a fervent plea for abolition of weapons of mass destruction and evolution of world order based on the principles of non-violence. The leaders also called for a restructuring of the United Nations system. The former Prime Minister of New Zealand, David Lange, affirmed that permanent members of the UN Security Council should not have the power to veto. The Canadian Nobel Laureate, Professor Douglas Rosch, favoured expansion of the permanent membership of the Security Council with India and Japan from Asia, Brazil from Latin America and Nigeria from Africa as permanent members. Commonwealth Secretary-General, Emeka Anyaoky, said that adherence by nation-States to certain universally accepted norms and principles of conduct, and not disarmament alone, could ensure durable peace and the advancement of human civilisation. Central to such value system must be a belief in common humanity.

Eduardo Faleiro, the Indian Minister for External Affairs, inaugurating a seminar on India's Foreign Policy at the Academy of Third World Studies of Jamia Millia University, Delhi, stressed the need for introducing functional and other reforms in the United Nations to make it a more effective instrument of international will and suggested the decision-making procedure of the Security Council and other important bodies of the United Nations should be made "more democratic and transparent." The practice of the permanent Security Council members "presenting their decisions to others for endorsement should be replaced by greater efforts to involve the developing countries in the decision-making process." The present composition of the Security Council "does not reflect either the vastly-expanded composition of the General Assembly or the current power configuration in the world." He pleaded that proposals submitted by India, Brazil and other countries in this regard should be examined.

Writing on "New World Order by reshaping the U.N.",[37] Ingvar Carlsson,[38] Julius Nyerere[39] and Willy Brandt[40] made a strong plea to the world leaders "to act now to build a new system for peace and security or the 1990s may become a decade of dangerous instability." The "new World Order, they affirmed, must be one founded on the vision of belonging to one global neighbourhood" and based on a sense of common responsibility,

37. *Los Angeles Times Syndicate* and reprinted in *The Hindustan Times,* New Delhi, May 16, 1991.

38. Ingvar Carlsson had been Prime Minister of Sweden.

39. Julius Nyerere, Africa's elder Statesman, was Tanzania's first President, a post he held from 1962-85.

40. Willy Brandt was Chancellor of the former West Germany from 1969 to 1974 and won the Nobel Peace Prize in 1971.

in which the notion of security is expanded to include economic and ecological, as well as military dimensions. This "new order," they believed, "will be far better suited to the interdependent realities of the next century than the old system of competitive and confrontational blocs." In order to cope with exigencies of any kind and other turbulences, including the recurrent famine and civil war in Africa, the international institutions, it was suggested, must be strengthened.

With these challenges in mind, more than 25 political leaders of the world[41] agreed to endorse the "Stockholm Initiative" as it had come to be known. They met at Geneva and outlined a programme of action aimed at strengthening the international security system in a spirit of cooperation and common responsibility. It was, accordingly, proposed that the United Nations should be modernized, taking on a broadened mandate at the Security Council level which formed the hub of the entire problem. With today's power structure and the new global interdependencies, the composition of the Security Council and the use of veto by permanent members should necessarily be reviewed. The present composition of the Council and veto right reflected the world balance of power at the end of World War II. Similarly, the method of appointing a Secretary-General must be reviewed. The Secretary-General should be given a stronger position and the means to exercise authority. He should have the power to act swiftly when international crises call for it–if need be without prior consent of the Security Council.

The United Nations must also have improved capabilities for anticipating and preventing conflicts. The Secretary-General is already authorised to bring to the attention of the Security Council any matter which in his opinion may threaten the maintenance of international peace and security. But the system needs a better monitoring apparatus.

The Secretary-General should be the first to know when a conflict may develop, and then be able to be the first to take preventive action. To this end, permanent political officers in key regions, military observer teams, fact-finding missions and military collective security forces could constitute a global emergency system. The emergency system would constitute a "trip-wire" for potential aggressors, "hopefully leading them to reconsider hostile action."

A global law enforcement role for the United Nations should be elaborated focussing on the role of sanctions and military enforcement measures. There must be a clear understanding of the enforcement measures, their sequencing and timing, that can be implemented by the international community when international law has been violated. As military measures may sometimes become necessary, the potential of the Military Staff Committee of the Security Council should be reviewed. This Committee, practically dormant during the years of Cold War, could have a significantly more important role to play.

The role of the UN peace-keeping forces should also be expanded. They should not only deal with monitoring cease-fires and other means of ending or containing conflicts, but could be used to ensure that countries are not destabilised across frontiers. The UN missions could be used to oversee elections, as was the case in Namibia, Nicaragua and

41. The world leaders included : Czech President Vaclauv Havel, former Prime Minister of Pakistan Benazir Bhutto, Norwegian Prime Minister Gro Herlem Brundtland, Organization of African Unity head Salim Salim, former U.S. President Jimmy Carter and former Soviet Union Foreign Minister Eduard Shevardnadze.

Combodia. Military units of the armed forces of all nations could be earmarked for the peace-keeping tasks.

The chronic financial crisis of the United Nations has debilitated the organisation. Withholding contributions have been destructive way for some to exercise influence. In strict accordance with the UN Charter, those who choose not to adhere to the financial rules should be deprived of the right to vote.

Besides reorganising the structure of the United Nations, the international community should concentrate on limiting of arms in areas of political conflict. In the aftermath of Gulf War, there is a particular danger of new spiral of arms transfers. Greater knowledge and open information would help limit arms trading that fuels conflict. The monitoring of world arms transfers should be strengthened, particularly by the United Nations, with the purpose of eventually agreeing on global norms for regulating such trade.

Proposals were also made for eradication of poverty, cooperative international development of the industrially backward nations, reduction of protectionism by nations, strategy for radically cutting debt overhang, control on global environments issues, etc., all measures aiming to meet the challenges developing countries are facing in the last decade of the outgoing century.

The reshaping of the United Nations is, therefore, deemed to be the harbinger of the New World Order and democratisation of the Security Council is the first and the foremost step in this direction. The Security Council, as pointed out earlier, is at present dominated by the five permanent members who belonged to the allied countries of World War II and who had arrogated to themselves the power to veto; the United States clearly leading the rest. With greater democratisation of the Security Council the United States would still remain a preponderant power, able to manipulate, but its margin for manoeuvre is sure to be substantially narrowed benefiting not only international security, but optimising United States power itself.

J.N. Dixit, Foreign Secretary in the Government of India's External Affairs Ministry, in the Krishna Menon lecture delivered in New Delhi in May, 1992, called for greater democratization of the UN organisation and recommended that the developing countries should articulate their interests even at the risk of clashing with the interests of the five permanent members of the Security Council. Indeed it may be asked what right does the Security Council have to demarcate the international border between Iraq and Kuwait, especially when it was a contentious issue? The Council had every right and duty to repel Iraq's aggression, which it did. "But it is time now to question whether the UN is not exceeding its authority by lending its prestige to an operation designed unmistakably to oust Saddam Hussain from power by prolonging sanctions against Iraq."

Syrian Vice-President Abdul Hamlim Khaddam said, during his talks with the visiting India's Minister of State for External Affairs, in Damascus on August 22, 1992, that the Security Council was not properly represented as Asia having half of the mankind had only one permanent member out of five. It was a long outstanding demand and it was, accordingly, necessary that the UN Charter was amended increasing the number of permanent members. Germany and Japan should be there. There should be an African member, probably Egypt or Nigeria, and a Latin American one, perhaps Brazil. This would enhance the dignity and perceived legitimacy of the Council. It would also somewhat diminish the inevitable predominance within it of the United States. All these countries, he said, would have no veto power.

There is an overwhelming support amongst the member-States of the United Nations for expanding the Security Council and making it more representative of the world. But the process of change, says Bhaskar Menon, "is likely to be slow and the prospect that developing countries, such as India, will benefit seems uncertain. This is evident from an analysis of responses to date from governments in a *Note Verbale* circulated by the Secretary-General." asking all the 183 (now 185) members to express their ideas by June 30, 1993.[42] The matter was scheduled to be discussed at the forthcoming General Assembly in September 1993.

In a step towards enlarging the Security Council, the General Assembly, on December 4, 1993, set up a working group to consider how this should be done. The working group was to be "open-ended," meaning all United Nations member-States would be eligible to participate in its deliberations and decision-making and the first meeting of the group was scheduled to be held in late January 1994. It was to be chaired by the Assembly President, Ambassador Samuel Insanally of Guyana, who said sub-groups might be appointed to study specific issues.

An informal paper along with the views of nearly 100 members of the United Nations was circulated among the members of the Assembly, which then consisted of 184 members, on January 21, 1994. The working group was required to send an interim report to the General Assembly's regular session starting in September 1994. The work involved was so complex with many interest groups to be satisfied that none could predict when the working group's final report would be made.

The informal working paper virtually favoured an increase in the membership of the Security Council, but views on the criteria for revising the Council's composition varied widely. Most States favoured the number to be between 15 and 25, although some favoured 31. Many States stipulated, however, that an increase in the membership should not diminish the Council's efficiency. Most States wanted to retain the existing categories of permanent and non-permanent members, although the new categories of membership were also suggested. Some States envisaged an increase of at least one, and as much as seven in the number of permanent members. However, others felt that there should be no additional permanent seats at all.

There is no definiteness among the permanent members also. The United States is the most forthright among them saying definitely that Germany and Japan should be made permanent members. It is also prepared to consider how the Council might be expanded to include a modest number of additional members. France and China acknowledge the need for expansion of the Council, but are not specific to their preferences. The United Kingdom and Russia are the only two States that do not acknowledge the need for change. Both have their opposition on what they see as the current effectiveness of the Security Council. United Kingdom affirms that the Security Council has been working with an unprecedented degree of consensus responding to challenges in Kuwait, Namibia,

42. Bhaskar Menon, "Members backed UN expansion," *The Times of India,* New Delhi, August 30, 1993.

Somalia, Cambodia, the former Yugoslavia and many other parts of the world. States are increasingly turning to the Security Council which remains able to respond rapidly and effectively. France favours enlargement, but suggests that the smaller the Security Council, the better the chances of reaching agreement on divisive issues.

There is, however, almost universal expectation among States who strongly support expansion that any new permanent members included into the Security Council would not have the veto. The views of the "Big Five" are crucial as for any change in the number of members of the Council requires amendment of the UN Charter and even a single veto can torpedo attempts to restructure the Security Council. Expansion did come finally in September 1996 resulting into the inclusion of Germany and Japan. But both are non-permanent members. India was not included and it caused a great disappointment in the country and other countries sympathetic to the claim of India and its contribution to the advancement of the Security Council and its other agencies.

SUGGESTED READINGS

Bentwich & Martin: *Charter of the United Nations.*

Brierly, J.L.: *The Law of Nations.* Chaps. I-II.

Burns. C.D.: *Political Ideals* (1929).

Cart. E.H.: *The Twenty Years of Crisis, 1919-1939.*

Chase. E.P.: *The United Nations in Action.*

Curtis. L.: *The Way to Peace.*

Dickinson. E.D.: *The Equality of States in International Law.*

Eichelberger. C.M.: *U.N.: The First Twenty Years.*

Evatt. H.V.: *The Task of Nations.*

Evatt. H.V.: *The United Nations.*

Fenwick. C.G.: *International Law.* Chaps. II-V.

Goodrich. L. & Hambro. E.: *The Charter of the United Nations.*

Harnam Singh (Ed.): *Studies in World Order.*

Haas. Ernst B.: *Collective Security and the Future International System.*

Kay. David A.: *The New Nations in the United Nations.*

Leon Gordenker (Ed.): *The United Nations in International Politics.*

Mattern. J.: *Concepts of State: Sovereignty and International Law.*

Miller. Linda B.: *World Order and Local Disorder.*

Morrison. H.S. and others: *The League and the Future of the Collective System.*

Naomi Rosenbaum (Ed.): *Readings on the International Politics.*

Oppenheim. L.: *International Law.* Vols. I, II.

Sidwick. H.: *Elements of Politics.* Chaps. XV-XVIII.

Schuman. F.L.: *International Politics.*

Sharp. W.R. and Kirk. G.: *Corntemporary International Politics.*

United Nations: *Handbook of the United Nations and Specialised Agencies.*

United Nations: *Year Book of the United Nations*

United Nations: *These Rights and Freedoms.*

Westlake. J.: *International Law.*

Willoughby. W.W.: *Fundamental Concepts of Public Law.* Chaps. XVI, XVII.

PART - II

The Organisation of the State

13

CHAPTER

Forms of Government

Forms of State and Government. Some writers on Political Science classify the forms of government as the forms of the State. But this is wrong. There can be no forms of the State. All States are alike in their nature and all combine the same essential elments—population, territory, organisation and unity or sovereignty. Differences in population and territory do not make any difference in their status of Statehood. A distinction is sometimes made between a City-State, a nation-State, and a world empire. But this distinction has no practical value in Political Science, for the classification of States on the basis of territory and population is a mere historical description, and a fallacy coming down from Aristotle's time when no distinc- tion was made between the State and government. To classify States on the basis of unity or sovereignty is also impossible. All States are sovereign and all sovereign States are equal. It is, therefore, illogical to classify equals.

But States do differ in their organisation. The organisation of the State is its government and it is through the instrument of the government that the State formulates, expresses, and realises its purposes, The purpose of every State is the same, the well-being of its people, and the form of government is the expression of the way in which the purpose of the State is to be realised. This involves the problem of determining: in whose hands is vested the legal authority of the State, to what extent is actual use made of it, what are the instrumentalities of organs employed in its use, and what rules and procedure are followed by such organs in performing their functions? These differences are wide from State to State and matter a good deal in differentiating the organisation of one State from another. The form of government is, therefore, the actual basis of division.

TRADITIONAL CLASSIFICATIONS

Aristotle's Classification. The traditional classifications of government follow the course set by Aristotle. Aristotle, however, was not original. He borrowed from Plato as Plato had borrowed from Socrates. Aristotle based his classification on two principles:

1. the number of persons who exercise supreme power, that is, the location of sovereignty within the State; and
2. the ends they seek to serve.

Applying the first, the numerical principle, Aristotle said, if sovereignty resided in one person, it is Monarchy; if it resided in a small minority of the population, it is

Aristocracy; and if it resides in a large proportion of the population, it is Polity. Having said so, Aristotle, then, proceeded to distinguish between the "*normal*" and "*perverted*" forms of the State, basing his conclusions on the ends which the rulers sought to serve. By a normal State, Aristotle meant one guided and ruled by law and justice. The ruler or the rulers in such a State always aim at the good of the community as a whole. By *perverted* State, he meant, one guided and ruled by the selfish and capricious, without law and without restraint. The ruler or the rulers in such a State were selfish and he or they exercised power vested in them for his or their own benefits rather than for the benefits of the community as a whole.

Monarchy, Aristocracy and Polity were, according to Aristotle, *normal* forms of the State. In their *peverted* from they became Tyranny, Oligarchy, and Democracy. Tyranny was the degenerated form of Monarchy, Oligarchy the degenerated form of Aristocracy and Democracy the degenerated form of Polity. For Aristotle, Monarchy was the best, and Tyranny the worst. Tyranny placed in the hands of the king, arbitrary control over the lives and fortunes of the citizens and all affairs of the State were directed to his own good. In Oligarchy, the wealthy few ruled for selfish ends and they used their powers and privileges for the oppression of the common people. Democracy meant rule of the mob and in a democratic State the interests of none were safe as there would be confusion all round.

Although Aristotle held that Monarchy, the rule of a true and good king, would be the best, yet, at the same time, he recognized certain practical difficulties in attaining the best. He, therefore, concluded that Polity was the best; a democratic form of government with constitutional guarantees, as a student of Political Science would now define it. Aristotle pointed out that if Polity were to disintegrate into its *perverted* form the result would not be so bad as the *perverted* forms of Monarchy and Aristocracy, namely, Tyranny and Oligarchy.

Aristotle's classification may be stated in the following tabular form:

	Normal	**Perverted**
Rule by one	Monarchy	Tyranny
Rule by Few	Aristocracy	Oligarchy
Rule by Many	Polity	Democracy

Two points about this classification deserve sattention. First, Aristotle draws a clear distinction between aristocracy and oligarchy, whereas modern usage does not differentiate between. the two and we often use them synonymously. Secondly, democracy for Aristotle had not the same meaning as it has for us. He regarded it as a *perverted* form, a mob rule, whereas we regard democracy as the best form of government. The *perverted* form of democracy, according to the modern use, is mobocracy or ochlocracy. Moreover, modern Sociologists have clearly shown that there is no government of the many. All governments are really governments of the few, or, in fact, oligarchies.[1] Nowhere in the world do the people or even a substantial number of them rule. In all States the exercise of government is left to a few hands, while the determination of policy is actually in the

1. MacIver, R.M., *The Web of Government,* p. 149.

hands of a yet smaller minority, the political leaders. The Cabinet in Britain is the supreme directing authority, "the magnet of policy", as Barker calls it, and it now consists of sixteen or eighteen members. The actual determination, control and direction of cabinet policy rests still in a few hands, the inner cabinet. The Executive power in the United States of America is vested in the President. He has his 'cabinet,' but the role of the 'cabinet' there is simply advisory. The policy flows from the President, though it may be influenced by the advice tendered by the 'cabinet'.

Cycle of Aristotle's Political Change. Like his teacher Plato, Aristotle, too, subjected his forms of the State to cyclic political changes. Aristotle did not merely classify the various forms of the State. He even marked out how in the course of history one form of the State had given place to another. Just as the wheels of a cycle revolve, so do the forms of the State. His cycle of political change starts from monarchy. The first State, he says, was monarchic and the king governed his people with love and justice, dedicating himself to heir service. In course of time, kings forgot their duty to the people. With the degeneration of the character and aims of the monarchs, it became Tyranny when government was no longer directed towards the public good. But a tyrannical government could not continue for long. The people ultimately revolted and succeeded in overthrowing the rule of the tyrant and replaced it by a governmere of the few talented persons, who were guided by the ideas of the common good. Aristocracy, a government of the few for the welfare of the people, took the place of monarchy. With the lapse of time, the best few also degenerated. The ideals of public spirit which inspired them in the beginning, disappeared. Aristocracy lapsed into Oligarchy. But the people could not for long tolerate a government the aim of which was the benefit of the ruling class alone. When the opportunity came, citizens as a whole made a successful revolt against such authority and established a Polity, the supreme power being vested in the hands of a large proportion of the population and it was used by them for the common good. When Polity became *perverted* it was substituted by Democracy.

Democrcy, according to Aristotle's terminology, was a rule by the mob which had always been an intolerable confusion. There was neither certainty nor stability. It was at this stage that some powerful warrior-statesman, imbued with the spirit of service for the common-weal, came to the forefront and took the reign of government in his own hands. Monarchy was, again, established and, thus, revolved Aristotle's cycle of political change. "The first governments," says Aristotle, "were kingships, probably for this reason, because of old, when cities were small, men of eminent virtue were few. They were made kings because they were benefactors, and benefits can only be bestowed by good men. But when many persons equal in merit arose, no longer enduring the preeminence of one, they desired to have a commonwealth and set up a constitution. The ruling class soon deteriorated and enriched themselves out of the public treasury; riches became the path to honour, and so obligarchies naturally grew up. These passed into tyrannies, and tyrannies into democracies for love of gain in the ruling classes was always tending to diminish their number, and so to strengthen the masses, who in the end set upon their number, and so to strengthen the masses, who in the end set upon their masters and established democracies."[2]

2. Aristotle, *Politics II,* Chap. XV.

Criticism of Aristotle's Classification. Such is Aristotle's classification. The cycle of political change given by him is fully corroborated by the history of the Greek City-States in the centuries preceding the Peloponesian war. Recent history, too, provides examples of a similar political progression. The last phase of political anarchy to be suppressed by a military autocracy is a common feature of our own times and it reminds us of various *coups d'etat*, the most recent being one led by General Naguib in Egypt, Brigadier Kassem in Iraq, General Ayub in Pakistan, Lt.General Ibrahim Abhoud in Sudan, General Daud in Afghanistan. General Zia-ul-Haq in Pakistan, General Ershad in Bangladesh, and many others. In fact, *coup de'etat* has become a normal feature in the African politics and no less in some parts of Asia too.

In spite of this pragmatic progression, Aristotle's classification has been subjected to severe criticism. It is argued that his classification is not based on any scientific principle, as it emphasises the quantitative rather than qualitative aspect; his division is mechanical and not spiritual in character. But this criticism does not hold good. Aristotle ignores the various stages in the development of the political consciousness of the people, but his test is, indeed, ethical and spiritual whether the form of government is Monarchy or Aristocracy or Polity. Aristotle might have differed in his political philosophy from his teacher, yet his, as it was with Plato, true test of a good government was knowledge, spiritual and ethical. The determining factor of his classification lies in the character of the one, or the few or the many. Burgess has rightly said that Aristotle's classification is organic or spiritual rather than numerical.

But Aristotle's classification does not include and explain modern forms of government like constitutional Monarchy, Unitary, and Federal governments of Parliamentary and Presidential types. The City-States of Aristotle, as Seeley says do not fit in with modern 'country-States.' Perhaps Aristotle could not conceive, at the time when he flourished, the various forms into which a government might develop. Nor do we use Democracy in the same sense in which Aristotle used it. Aristotle's classification into Monarchies, Aristocracies, and Polities is also not satisfactory according to our forms of division. If we accept his classification, are we to class Great Britain as a Monarchy or a Democracy and how is it to be differentiated from the government of the United States? Finally, Aristotle definitely distinguished between Aristocracy and democracy (polity). But the attempt to distinguish between the two is futile in our times, for it is not easy to find out where one ends and the other begins.

Other Classifications. In spite of these defects Aristotle's classification was accepted as fundamental till quite modern times. The modern writers dropped the ethical or qualitative basis and classified governments on the quantitative basis alone. Three-fold classification of governments—Monarchies, Aristocracies, and Democracies—became the generally accepted norm till the end of the World War I, when Democracy merged others, except for subject countries, colonies, dependencies or trust territories and others where dictatorships had been established.

Among the modern writers Montesquieu proposed a three-fold division: Republican, Monarchical and Despotic governments. The Republican government is that in which the people as a body or even a part of the people, possess the sovereign power. Under a Monarchical form of government there is rule by one single person, but he governs only by fixed and established laws. In a Despotic government, on the other hand, there is a single person who rules, but without any law, and he conducts everything according to his will and caprice. How long can a particular form of government last? Montesquieu's reply is that it depends upon the "persistence in given society of that particular spirit which is characteristic of the form."

Rousseau divided governments into Monarchies, Aristocracies, and Democracies. He subdivided Aristocracies, into three forms—natural, elective, and hereditary. He considered elective Aristocracy as the best and hereditary the worst. Rousseau was a great champion of direct Democracy. He also admitted the existence of mixed forms of government. Bluntschli gives us another classification. He accepted Aristotle's classification as fundamental, but added to it one form of his own. His division was: Monarchies, Aristocracies, Democracies and Theocracies. Theocracy is that form of government where the supreme power is attributed to God, or to a god, or to some other superhuman being, or to an Idea. The men who exercise authority are deputies or viceregents of God or a god, Theocracy, according to Bluntschli, is a normal form of government, but when it becomes perverted it is known as idolocracy. Such a classification, however, seems quite fallacious. The modern political scientist separates religion from politics and he does not bring God into his division of forms of government. His task is to locate sovereign power and it rests, for all intents and purposes, either in one person or a body of persons. But exceptions still there are as in the case of the Islamic Republic of Iran the Muslim Arab countries, Pakistan and Afghanistan. Revival of Muslim fundamentalism aims to establish a government governed by the laws of Islam strictly in conformity to the prescriptions of the Quran. Some traces of democratic institutions may seem to exist, but the structure is entirely theocratic.

There are other writers who classify States on a historical basis. Von Mohl, a German poblicist of the nineteenth century, is prominent out of this school. He distinguishes Patriarchal, Theocratic, Despotic, Classic, Feudal and Constitutional States. He gives other types of government as well and subdivides Classic States into Monarchy, Aristocracy and Democracy. Von Mohl's classification, even on a superficial examination, is forthwith rejected. It is based on no single principle and he does not distinguish between the State and government.

Marriot's Classification. J.A.R. Marriot, a political scientist of recent times, classifies Governments on a threc-fold basis. He accepts Aristotle's classification as fundamental, but regards it as inadequate for modern governments. Marriot's first basis of classification is the distribution of the powers of government. Governments are, accordingly, divided into *unitary* and *federal*. In a Unitary Government there is concentration of powers at the centre and the provincial governments enjoy only delegated powers as they are the the creation of the central government. In a Federal Government there are two sets of government and authority is divided between these two—central and state or provincial governments. Both the parts of government enjoy original powers granted to them by the constitution and each is autonomous in its own sphere of jurisdiction.

Marriot's next basis is that of a rigid and a flexible constitution. In the third place, his basis of classification is the relation between the executive and the legislature. When the executive is superior to the legislature, the form of government is Despotic. If the executive is coordinate in power with the legislature, the type of government is Presidential. If the executive is subordinate to the legislature, as in the United Kingdom, the form of government is Parliamentary or Cabinet.

Leacock's Classification. Stephen Leacock's classification is almost similiar to the one given by Marriot. He, however, does not attempt to include in his classification all the historical forms which have appeared in the evolution of the State. Leacock confines himself to actually existing types of government. His fundamental division is between despotic and democratic types. In a despotic government the sovereign-power is concentrated in the hands of one single person who rules according to his will. In a democracy the sovereign power resides in the people or a majority of them. Democratic governments are divided into a Limited Monarchy and a Republic. In a Limited Monarchy the head of government is the king, but his authority is limited, as in the United Kingdom, where the King reigns but does not rule. In a Republican government, the executive is elected by the people for a fixed term of office. Each of these types may assume one of the two forms, Unitary or Federal. A Unitary or a Federal government may either be Parliamentary or Presidential. In a Parliamentary government the real executive is responsible to the legislature. In a Non-Parliamentary or Presidential type the executive is not responsible to the legislature, as in the United States of America.

Leacock's classification can best be explained by the following table borrowed from him:[3]

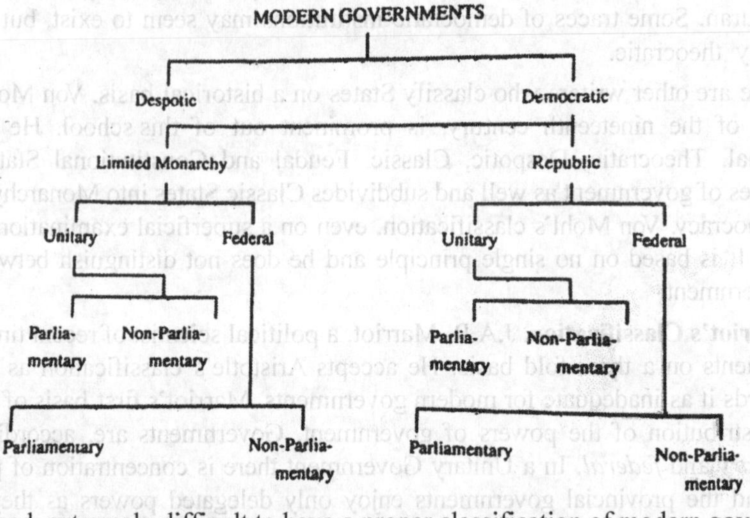

It is, indeed, extremely difficult to have a proper classification of modern governments. The form of government is the product of numerous factors, historical, geographical, social, economic, and psychological. Some of these factors are comparatively permanent and give a peculiar impress to the institutions in their evolution and functioning. Both Britain and France, for example, have in common a Parliamentary system of government. But the government of Britain is, in ultimate theory, an absolute Monarchy, in form a limited constitutional Monarchy, and in actual practice a Democratic Republic. Practice outruns theory in Britain. France, on the other hand, is a country with the form of a Republic, the institutions of a Monarchy, and the spirit of an Empire. There is, in general, a tendency for the French citizen to think of politics in intellectual rather than in practical terms, to attach more importance to symbols than to concrete achievements. The result is, as Siegfried says, "French politics are often both unrealistic and passionately ideological."

The United States of America and Canada, two neighbouring countries, are Federations. The United States is the classical example of a Federal polity, which brought into existence the union of hitherto sovereign States for purposes of national unity. The component units, of the federation called 'States,' enjoy juridicial status and corporate personality and are autonomous, except in a few enumerated subjects which are of common national interest. Subjects which concern the nation as a whole fall within the jurisdiction of the national or federal government. Residuary powers, those which neither belong to the federal government nor to the state governments, rest with the constituent states. The fathers of the Canadian Constitution were not wedded to the narrow ideas of a Federation. They adopted Federation as a device for bringing together diverse elements and to solve administrative and economic problems which confronted the country then. The Provinces were, accordingly, given certain enumerated powers, leaving the rest, together with some over-riding powers, for the Central Government. Lord Haldane would not describe Canada a Federation and Professor Wheare called it a "quasi-federal constitution." But in actual practice the unitary elements in Canada have now become obsolete or are being worked in a manner as to nullify the unitary effects. United States, on the other hand, has a federal constitution as well as a federal government, though the process of centralization there is now assuming alarming proportions.

The Indian Constitution is federal in form, but it sets up a highly centralised structure of government. The unitary tendencies found therein nullify to a great extent the broad features of federalism. And the founding Fathers deliberately did it. B.R. Ambedkar, the Law Minister and the principal architect of the Constitution, himself claimed in the Constituent Assembly that India was a Federation during times of peace, with a unitary system of government during times of war.

It follows, then, that no two forms can be absolutely identical any more than two human beings, whatever likeness there may be. And, like a human being, no government remains the same. Change is at work all the time and more so in this atomic age of ours. The needs of man and his environments have become so numerous and complex that no mechanism of government can claim perfection and consequently finality. The atomic age needs revolutionary changes and a dynamic mechanism of government to suit the purposes to be realised. Could anyone visualise a decade or so before that planning would become a democratic plea for the realisation of the well-being of men within the framework of a capitalistic structure of society?

Recent Classification. With the emergence of the Welfare State the distinction based on 'socialism' and 'private enterprise' is wearing pretty thin. This necessitates revision of the traditional methods of classification. Our approach should not be confined merely to outward forms as they give no clue to the real purpose of the State. Paine wrote 150 years ago: "When it shall be said my poor are happy, neither ignorance nor distress is

3. Leacock, S., *Elements of Political Science*, p. I 17.

to be found among them; my jails are empty of prisoners, my streets of beggars; the aged are not in want, the taxes are not oppressive,—when those things are said, then may that country boast of its government." The primary purpose of every State is the same and every government is charged by the community with the double task of maintaining what MacIver calls "an established code of living and of adjusting this order to new conditions and emergency needs." It does not matter what the head of the State is called. We shall assign to a particular government proper place and label by knowing what it actually does in realising the purpose entrusted to its charge: the well-being of the people. Well-being and well-feeding are not synonymous. Well-being means an expansion in the human spirit and, as such, it is a question of liberty in all its aspects. On the political front it implies responsiveness and responsibility of the government. How far government is responsive and consequently responsible for its actions depends upon the size of the electorate and the freedom they enjoy in influencing its laws. The Greek statesman Alcibiades remarked to his uncle Pericles that a law adopted by the popular assembly was nothing but an arbitrary act when the majority imposed it on the minority without persuading the latter.

Recently, politics have been classified into: Democracies, Authoritarian and Totalitarian political systems. Democratic political systems are divided into three sub-classes. The first of these has high sub-system autonomy such as British or the American. The second sub-class is characterised by limited sub-system autonomy and it includes France of the Third and Fourth Republics, Italy after World War II and Weimar Germany. The third class of democratic political systems is made up of those with low sub-system autonomy. Mexico provides an example of this type of democratic system. In Authoritarian systems liberty is restricted and parliamentary institutions are absent or meaningless, but they are not tyrannical regimes. The society is traditionally oriented and power is exercised by small groups such as military leaders, bureaucrats, or religious figures. Examples are Argentina under Peron, Spain under Franco, and Portugal under Salazar. Finally, there are Totalitarian political systems as pre-1990 Soviet Union, the Fascist regime in Italy and the Nazi system in Germany. The regime in a Totalitarian system is based on a dominant leader supported by a mass party acting on an aggressive ideology which explains and conditions political actions. A Totalitarian regime is differentiated from an Authoritarian system by its total control over and attempt to regulate in detail on behaviour and by the subordination of all organisations to the State.

MONARCHY

Absolute Monarchy. Monarchy represents that form of government where the source of all political authority is to be found in a supreme ruler. All the organs and officers of Government are agents of this ruler for the purpose of carrying out his will. All acts of Government are his acts and derive their validity from his sanction. All laws are his commands, though they may have been formulated by one of his agents. As the bearer of sovereignty, his authority is supreme, unlimited, and self-determined, both as regards the extent to, and the manner in which it shall in fact be exercised. Louis XIV of France expressed this idea in the famous phrase "*L'e'tat, c'est moi*," (I am the State), what he really meant was: "I am the Government and what I say goes." This is absolute Monarchy.

The institution of Monarchy is a product of history and it has grown as a part of the evolution of the State. In the early stages of the development of the State the Monarchical system was the most beneficial, for it was characterised by singleness of purpose, unity, vigour and strength. The Monarch combined in him the functions of the law-maker, the judge, the executive and the military commander. He was, thus, able to hold together by his own personal force a society which otherwise might have broken up into many elements.

In the beginning, the Monarch was elected and, then, the institution became hereditary and it is now the normal type, wherever it exists. The early Roman kings were elected. The mediaeval kings were both hereditary and elected.[4] — A king may be elected in our own times. Nadir Shah, the father of the last ruler of Afghanistan, Zahir Shah, was an elected king. But it is not a normal feature and all monarchies are now hereditary. A hereditary king enjoys a life-long tenure and the office passes to his heirs according to the law of primogeniture.

Absolute Monarchy has existed both in the East and in the West up to very recent times. In the East, the leading example of a government of this character was that of.Japan. In the eighties of the last century, Japan decided to abolish her old system of government and to establish in its place one corresponding to modern political ideas as represented by the existing governments of Europe and America. But even the new Constitution (1889) established a type of absolute monarchy. Article 1 of the Constitution clearly stated that "the Empire of Japan shall be reigned over and governed by a line of Emperors unbroken for ages eternal." Barton Ito, in his "Commentaries on the Constitution of the Empire of Japan", explained the meaning of the phrase "reigned over and governed" and commented: "it is meant that the Emperor on his throne combines in himself the sovereignty of the State and the government of the country and of his subjects." In the West, the two most important examples of governments resting on an absolute basis were those of Russia before the Revolution of 1917, and Germany immediately before the adoption of the Weimar Constitution of 1919.

The despotic king always claimed that he got his authority direct from God, that he was God's viceregent on earth, that he ruled by divine right, and that he was answerable to none except God. This belief in the divine right of the kings to rule prevailed in all countries. In China the Emperor was described as the "Son of Heaven" and he claimed to rule by virtue of the mandate that he had received from Heaven. Referring to Europe and Britain, Bryce says, "from the fifth to sixteenth century whoever asked what was the source of legal sovereignty and what the moral claim of the sovereign to obedience of subjects would have been answered that God has appointed certain powers to govern the world and that it would be a sin to resist His ordinance." The king was, accordingly, free from all human limitations. He was accountable to God alone and not to his subjects. Some kings, no doubt, took high view of their duties and governed well and yet they were subject to no restraints, except the law of God.

Merits of Absolute Monarchy. Perhaps, there could have been no better form of government than absolute Monarchy for disciplining the uncouth and uncivilised people

4. Sabine, *A History of Political Theory* pp. 210-11.

who had emerged out of barbarism. John Stuart Mill rightly said, "Despotism is a legitimate mode of government for dealing with barbarians, provided the end be their improvement and the means be justified by actually effecting that end." Absolute Monarchy possesses the merits of strength, vigour, energy of action, promptness of decision, unity of counsel, continuity and consistency of policy. Undivided counsel, promptness of decision and a consistent policy are the essential requisites of a good and efficient administration, particularly during periods of national crises and emergencies. Monarchy, therefore, comes as a beneficial antidote to chaos or a weak government. History is full of examples when the rule of one has been reimposed as a means of protecting the interests of the people at large from the rapacity of the few. The English supported their strong Tudor kings, "to be their protection against the lawlessness of the armed nobility."

As all the powers of government, executive, legislative, judicial and military; are concentrated in the Monarch, he is able to keep a greater uniformity of purpose in the State. A sagacious king having sturdy commonsense can easily secure the best advice and acts upon it with confidence. His policy is more stable and consistent than the shifting policy of the assembly in a democratic government. An assembly is usually guided by sentiments and is swayed by the arguments of the politicians. Moreover, a Monarch generally takes a very high view of his duties. He is free to select his officials according to his own pleasure and make them work according to his directions. As the officials can be held to strict accountability, they run the administration to the best of their ability and capacity. The absolute Monarchies of the seventeenth and eighteenth centuries, says Bryce, "saw many reforms in European countries, which no force less than that of a strong monarchy would have carried through."[5]

Defects of Absolute Monarchy. But no man is fit enough to exercise absolute power. A despot crushes his subjects to the earth and leaves them nothing they can call their own. Even a good despot teaches his subjects to mind their own private interests and to leave everything else to the government. Absolute government is a government by one single person and he administers according to his own good sense of what can be good and right for his subjects. And history tells us that the good of the subjects has really meant the interests of the ruler himself. He has never cherished the interests of the subjects. If he does, his absolutism disappears. Moreover, a good king, under a system of hereditary monarchy, is a sheer chance or accident. There is no guarantee that an able, capable and benevolent ruler must always succeed to the throne. History tells us that imbeciles and fools have been the rule whereas the statesmen and sage rulers have been the exceptions. "A hereditary ruler," says Leacock, "seems on the face of things as absurd as the hereditary mathematician or hereditary poet laureate."

Even if it be admitted that absolute Monarchy is a good form of government, we, who are brought up in the twentieth century, do not believe in good government unless it is self-government, for good government is no substitute for self-government. "No government which does not rest upon the affections of the people, which does not stimulate among them an interest in public affairs and create an active, intelligent, and alert citizenship, can be called ideal, and, certainly, no government from which the

5. Bryce, J., *Modern Democracies,* Vol. 11, p. 536.

participation of the people in some from is excluded will ever be able to produce such a body of citizens." An absolute monarch dare not allow liberty and rights to his subjects. He does not inspire in them a vigorous political vitality, patriotic loyalty and social solidarity. If he does, he invites his own demise as an absolute monarch. He will adopt all measures to firmly establish his authority and it remains unquestionable. To adopt measures that help to infuse in his subjects the spirit of awakening and allows them the enjoyment of rights and other freedoms will spell the destruction of his own authority and most probably his own annihilation.

Limited Monarchy. Limited Monarchy is that type of government in which the authority of the Monarch is limited either by the prescriptions of a written constitution or by certain fundamental conventions, as in Britain. Sometimes the constitution is promulgated by the ruler himself. Sometimes it has been forced upon him by a successful revolution. But whatever be the cause, limited Monarchy is a constitutional government, and it is, in principle, like the Republican form of government. The only difference between the two is that under a system of limited Monarchy the chief executive Head of the State is a hereditary king whereas in a Republic the chief executive, usually called President, as in the United States of America and India, is elected for a number of years and after the expiry of his term of office, if not re-elected, he joins the ranks of the ordinary citizens of the State. But both the constitutional king, under a limited Monarchy, and the President of a Republic, exercise authority as ordained by the Constitution or conventions as in Britain. They cannot go beyond it. In a limited Monarchy the authority of the king is nominal. The real functionaries are his ministers who are elected members of the legislature and belong to the majority party. They remain in office as long as they can command a majority in and retain the confidence of the legislature. They cannot be dismissed by the king at his pleasure. Nor can they be chosen at random. Britain is a typical example of a constitutional Monarchy where the King or Queen reigns but does not rule.

Uses of Limited Monarchy. The very fact that the authority of the Monarch is limited goes to show that in essence it is a democratic form of Government. The King or Queen in Britain, as Bagehot remarks, has the right to be consulted, the right to encourage, and the right to warn; beyond this he or she cannot go. He or she does not exercise any real authority. The actual government is carried on by ministers who represent the majority party in the legislature. The legislature renews its mandate after every four or five years when General Elections are held. Limited Monarchy, therefore, gives the people the real opportunity to actively participate in public affairs and elect administrators who rule the country according to their behest. It is the people who, in the last resort, are the ultimate sovereigns.

The chief merit of a limited Monarchy in Britain is the hereditary nature of the ruler. By virtue of a long and uninterrupted tenure of office the King or Queen gains mature administrative experience to guide his or her ministers who are generally amateurs in the art of administration. He or she exercises what Lowell calls the "unifying, dignifying and stabilising influence." Moreover, the Monarch belongs to no party whereas his or her ministers belong to one. The Monarch, as such, is an umpire in the midst of rival parties, whose main concern is to see that the game of politics is played according to rules.

The days of absolute Monarchy are over. Now even King Ibn Saud of Saudi Arabia, who was the solitary example of an absolute Monarch, was ultimately replaced by Prince Feisal as a result of the decision taken by the Council of Ministers and the Consultative Assembly. The powers of Kings, in all countries where Monarchy persists, have been limited either by the prescriptions of a written constitution or by fundamental conventions which form the basis of the Constitution. In Iran, Shah Mohammed Reza Pahlvi was the national symbol and powers vested in him were really exercised by his council of ministers. Constitutional monarchy is the only way now to maintain the hereditary principle and royal dignity. A limited Monarchy, according to Woodrow Wilson, "is one whose powers have been adapted to the interests of the people and to the maintenance of individual liberty ..... Roughly speaking constitutional government may be said to have had its rise at Runnymede when the barons of England exacted the Magna Carta from John." From a King arose, by slow and steady progress, the institution of Kingship and the Monarch now reigns; he or she does not rule. To put it in the legal form, the King or Queen can do no wrong.

ARISTOCRACY

Meaning of Aristocracy. Originally, Aristocracy meant that form of Government which was conducted by the best men of the community and was guided in the exercise of authority and functions by the most virtuous principles. Such a form of Government comes down to us from Aristotle. *Aristos*, in Greek, means the best and *Kratos* means power. Aristocracy according to Greek philosophers, was a form of government par excellence. Its principle was virtue: the moral and intellectual superiority of the ruling class and the virtuous qualities which they disseminated into those over whom they ruled. Aristocracy has, now, come to signify that form of Government. in which the political power rests in the hands of a small section of the community. But this is not the true test of Aristocracy. It is really Oligarchy, sometimes with implications of the corrupt few. The character of Aristocracy depends on the method of selection of the people who wield power, and the aims they keep in view, and not the smallness of the number.

The methods of selection are various and have been devised in accordance with certain leading ideas which had pervaded and still pervade society. First, there is the idea of the importance of birth. In primitive society, families most directly descending from a common ancestor constituted a class by itself, in which outsiders were not admitted, except perhaps by adoption. In modern society we do not speak of a common ancestor, but we still defer to the notion that some families are better than others and consequently they are best fitted to rule. In the second place, selection may be by merit, that is, persons of superior intellect and ability are chosen to govern others. This is Aristocracy of intellect. Selection by favour is another method. When a king confers high rank on those who serve him best, the method of selection is by favour. Again, there may be an Aristocracy of wealth, when the criterion of selection is only the possession of riches. The poor, whatever be their intellect or merit, have no chance to assume public offices and participate in public affairs. It means, some are born to rule, if they happen to inherit wealth or amass it themselves, whereas others to be ruled, if the accident of birth or circumstances do not make them so fortunate.

Jellinek has laid emphasis on the social aspect of aristocracy. He maintains that there is always some social class which wields the dominant power in the State. It may be the priestly class or military class or landed aristocracy. But whatever be the type, power will belong to that social class which is more powerful than the rest, and this class enjoys certain special privileges which are denied to other classes. Jellinek, accordingly, concludes that it is an error to define Aristocracy merely as a government by the few.

Kinds of Aristocracy. Aristocracy for Aristotle was a normal form of government. Its perverted form was oligarchy, government by the few, that is, by the rich for the rich. Rousseau divided aristocracies into natural, elective and hereditary. The general basis of classification had been: of wealth, of birth, of talent and intellect and of culture and education. Some writers have, during recent times, used the term "aristo-democracy" for aristocracy. Aristo-democracy means that only best types of men wield power. In a sense, a democratic government is more or less aristocratic in that a considerable proportion of population takes no part in government and the greater share of the governing power is concentrated in the hands of a comparatively small number (the Theory of Elite). Public opinion is influenced, moulded and shaped by the leadership of the few. The majority party forms the government and its leaders man the administration. The majority party, together with the minority in the legislature, enact laws. The masses simply elect their representatives and leave the rest to the actual administrators till they are called upon to elect the rulers again. The line between Aristocracy and Democracy is, therefore, difficult to draw. But it must be remembered that Aristocracy places no confidence in the ability of the masses. It is a government of the select few; may it be the "aristocracy of breeding", or "aristocracy of intellect", or "aristocracy of talent." Democracy has faith in the ability and capacity of man and its principle is equality. It accepts man as a man and provides equal opportunity to all to rise to the highest public office in the State. Thus all persons who are fit to perform the duties of a citizen can have a share in the direction of the affairs of the State.

Merits of Aristocracy. One of the great merits of Aristocracy is that it emphasises quality and not quantity. It assumes that some are better fitted to govern than others. They govern as they are the best and the criterion of their being best is the moral and intellectual superiority which they possess over others. "It is the overlasting privilege," says Carlyle, "of the foolish to be governed by the wise." Aristocracy, thus, gives to the community a ruling class which can be trusted to administer public affairs with complete integrity and honour, because they possess a great position independent of politics. These individuals have powers of perception usually denied to others. They can see an order in human affairs and they can discern major trends that are obscure to the generality of their fellow citizens. They rise above emotions and interests, and can see the meaning of justice and virtue in ways that others cannot. Aristocracy can also claim superiority over other forms of Government in respect of stability and efficiency, and, thus, can maintain a consistent and vigorous policy both in domestic and foreign relations. John Stuart Mill says that "the governments which have been remarkable in history for sustained ability and vigour in the conduct of affairs have generally been aristo-cracies." It is further argued that Aristocracy would refrain from an unwise and immoderate use of power. Burke believed that the elite in a society would be more realistic than the common people. The aristocrat, he further said, has more of a sense of shame because he must ask himself what posterity will think of his actions; the anonymous citizen in a popular majority has no such thoughts. Supporters of the "aristocracy of breeding" defend hereditary aristocracy on the ground that genetic inheritance produces superior qualities in certain family lines. Having roots in their national tradition and being able to take a large-range perspective on the future, their approach to politics is conservative in the best sense. Political training runs in their blood and they take naturally to the business of government more efficiently and diligently. They represent a standard of perfection, derived from heredity and environment, and set a model for others to imitate as well as revere. Since members of this aristocracy have material security, they enter political life out of sheer sense of duty. They can, thus, promote the broader interests of society and do not have to pander to the momentary whims of a capricious electorate.

Aristocracy, it is claimed, is pre-eminently conservative. Since admini-stration rests in the hands of the wise, talented and experienced administrators, who have inherited high traditions of public service, they would naturally avoid rash and radical political experiments Moreover, stability is one of the foremost requirements of a good government and stability demands "conservative innovation." Violent changes involving suppression of institutions, which become venerable with age, agitate popular feeling and, as such, endanger the stability of government. "It is, therefore, of the greatest importance in social and political progress that the principle of progress or liberalism should always be joined to the principle of stability or conservatism."[6] Aristocracy serves the desired purpose. It allows only slow change and there is no complete break with the past. Aristocracy is a reservoir which conserves experience and transmits wisdom to the present as well as to the future. Conservativeness and continuity are the two essential conditions of stability and Montesquieu said "moderation" is the chief principle of Aristocracy.

Cabinet Government is in essence Aristocracy. Those who constitute the Ministry are party leaders. According to Laski, the essential contribution of the Ministers to the Cabinet is "their commonsense, their ability to put before their colleagues that judgment about decisions which public opinion, and especially party opinion, will make after they have been published."[7] This is Aristocracy tinged with responsibility. Modern governments have preserved the element of aristocracy in the composition of the Upper Chambers of their legislatures. For instance, the British House of Lords consists primarily of hereditary peers. In countries where the Second Chambers are elected, the elections are usually so arranged as to make them representative of the best minds in the nation. The Council of States, the Second Chamber in India, consists of two hundred and fifty members, of whom twelve members are nominated by the President. The members nominated by the President are persons having special knowledge or practical experience in respect of such matters as literature, science, art and social service.[8] This system of representation is aristocratic in the best sense.

Weakness of Aristocracy. But the evil inherent in all kinds of Aristo-cracies is that

6. Garner, J.W., *Political Science and Government,* p. 231.
7. Laski, H., *Parliamentary Government in England,* p. 286.
8. Article 80, clauses (1), (2) and (3).

they form a separate interest which is almost certain to come into conflict with the interests of the community. No wise and just principle has so far been devised for the selection of the ruling class, and no safeguard has been suggested to ensure that the few will rule in the interests of all and not for their selfish advantage. The privileged persons, who are destined to rule, form a class of vested interests and they look on their privileges as a matter of right which ought to be transmitted unimpaired to their successors. Even Aristocracy of the best soon degenerates into a class rule. Flushed with power and authority, they become arrogant and proud, and display towards the classes excluded from a share in the government, a harshness and cruelty which have been the more intolerable because accompanied by contempt.

Even an aristocracy of intellect has no convincing appeal to make. High intelligence is not the exclusive property of any single group, and rational individuals are distributed at random up and down the social scale. Of course, a person from a wealthy background stands a better chance of having his intellectual potentialities developed, for he will receive encouragement from his parents and the benefits of higher education. However, experience has shown that many of our finest intellects have sprung from humble surroundings and many of them have all but educated themselves.

The rule of hereditary succession, "aristocracy of breeding", works evil as well as good. When it has prevailed for a long time, a considerable number of hereditary dignities descend to persons quite unfit to exercise power or to make a good use of social influence. Moreover, the division of people into classes provokes envy and opposition. The rulers become narrow, selfish and domineering causing widespread disaffection and eventually rebellion. It is not rational to maintain and to put faith in the myth that some are born to rule and others to be ruled. Such a government is unresponsive and irresponsible, for it excludes the masses from finding interest in government. They become only recipients of orders. Aristocracy, therefore, is exclusive. It does not offer the people political training or political consciousness, which is so essential for citizenship. It is a government for passive dumb-driven creatures and not for politically awakened and active citizens. Similarly, property, like birth, should not be the criterion for elevating a person to rule. Governing power cannot be wisely restricted to persons who, either by accident of birth, are born in rich families or to whom some freak of fortune has brought riches. Such fortunate persons, when in power, devise all means, sane or insane, to perpetuate their own interests, reducing the masses to a pitiable plight.

A great defect of aristocracy, says Bluntschli, is its excessive rigidity. A government which has reverence for long-established customs and traditions cannot have a dynamic outlook. A good government must keep pace with the economic and social requirements of society. Aristocracy will resist all such changes in order to preserve its power. It is not a dynamic mechanism of government for the fulfilment of the needs of a dynamic man. It cannot, therefore, serve the purpose of our times. It stands for backwardness. Finally, Aristocracy stands for pomp and splendour. All this grandeur and dignity entail huge expenditure and extravagance at the very high cost of public good.

DEMOCRACY

While conventional historical sources state that democracy began 2,500 years ago in some of the City-states of ancient Greece, it is important to know that democratic institutions existed in India as early as the Vedic period. Chanakya's *Arthshastra* and Shukracharya's *Nitisasra* tell us that in ancient India, an autonomous village community with a 'panchayat' at its head was the basic unit of local government. Accountability was built into the system — a member of the panchayat could be disqualified on account of moral turpitude or financial mismanagement. Importantly, women were enfranchised and had the right to candidature.

Representative parliaments, the product of the 19th and 20th centuries, became the central institutions of democratic governments. "Democratic ideas fuelled the revolts against colonialism and laid the foundation of the modern welfare state." Democracy, unlike Communism or Socialism, "has never become identified with a definite doctrinal source. A by-product of the entire development of post-Renaissance civilisation, it indicates both a set of ideals and a political system."[9]

Meaning of Democracy. The term democracy is derived from the Greek words, *demos* and *kratos*, the former meaning the people and the latter power. Democracy, thus, means power of the people. It is now regarded as a form of government in which the people rule themselves either directly, or indirectly through their representatives. Definitions of democracy, as a form of government, are various. But like many other definitions in Political Science, they differ in their content and application. The Greeks meant by it the Government by many and Aristotle considered it as a *perverted* form of government. Modern writers do not regard democracy as a *perverted* form of government. What Polity was for Aristotle democracy is for us. Nor do they employ the mere numerical consideration to designate it so. Their emphasis is that in democracy all persons, who are fit to perform the duties of citizens, should have a share in the direction of the State and their will should ultimately prevail. Seeley means by it a government in which every one has a share. Dicey defines democracy as that form of government in which the governing body is a comparatively large fraction of the entire nation. Bryce accepts the definition of Herodotus and says that democracy denotes that form of government in which the ruling power of the State is largely vested in the members of the community as a whole. He adds, "This means in communities which act by voting, that rule belongs to the majority, as no other method has been found for determining peaceably and legally what is to be declared the will of the community which is not unanimous."[10]

MacIver says, "Democracy is not a way of governing, whether by majority or otherwise, but primarily a way of determining who shall govern and broadly, to what ends.[11] This involves a freedom of choice in electing the rulers and the consent of the electors that those who receive the mandate should alone rule. It means that democracy has a popular base and it hinges upon the consent of the governed.

9. Arun Balasubramanian, *Times of India*, New Delhi, May 26, 1993.
10. Bryce, J., *Modern Democracies,* Vol. I, p. 20.
11. MacIver, R.M., *The Web of Government,* p. 298.

But the mere consent of the people is not enough to make a government democratic. The people ought to be, to use the words of Plato their own "watch-dogs." The consent of the people must be real, active and effective in order to make it a genuine democracy. Eternal vigilance is the very life of democracy, if democracy can really claim, in the words of President Abraham Lincoln, to be a government of the people, by the people, and for the people. Government is, of course, always of the people, but it need not be government by the people. Monarchies and Aristocracies are governments of the people but not by the people. A government by the people means that people either directly or through their representatives govern themselves, and their will remains supreme on all questions of social direction and policy of the government.

It is not correct to say, however, that democracy is a government by the representatives of all people. "The people" has been a varying term, as Bryce points out, and it has come to mean something vastly different from what it meant to Aristotle, or even to Lincoln.[12] It now means the majority of the people. Democracy, according to Bryce, is a form of government "in which the will of the majority of the qualified citizens rules, taking the qualified citizens to constitute the great bulk of the inhabitants ...."[13] It is obvious that democracy allows every qualified citizen to express an opinion on affairs of the State. But it cannot secure that every man's opinion shall influence the actions of the State. All citizens cannot be made to agree on all questions of importance. Moreover, all citizens cannot have a voice in determining the policy of the government. Even the most ardent democrat will not vote for lunatics, criminals or infants. Participation is always limited by age; and frequently by sex, as it is only recently that women have been given the franchise in many leading countries, and in many they have not yet received it. In many States the suffrage is restricted to those who possess a certain amount of property, and in most cases a certain minimum of literacy and education is required. Therefore, democracy does not mean participation by all the people. Whenever we speak of government by the people or the will of the people, we mean the will of the majority for the time being.

There are two reasons for the will of the majority to prevail. First, they are on the whole more likely to be right than the minority. The majority, when considered as a collectivity, possess a wisdom of their own that may be superior to that of any minority. For one thing, it has been pointed out that there may be several minority groups in the community, each of which claims to be superior to and profoundly wiser to the other. Quite frequcntly one minority may clash in a serious way with the other on what constitutes rational causes of action. By allowing the majority to govern, the problem of deciding which of various minorities is "really" superior is avoided. Secondly, a majority in most cases is physically stronger than a minority. Unless the majority grossly abuses its power, it is politic for the minority to submit to its will, lest the majority should resort to coercion. But it must be admitted that "the coercion of dissentient minority constitutes a special difficulty for a government founded on the principle of consent."[14] Democracy can be successful only when minorities feel that they are not subjected to oppression by

12. Bryce, J., *Modern Democracies,* p. viii.
13. *Ibid.,* p. 26.
14. Sidgwick, *The Elements of Politics* p. 611.

majority and that their case has been properly heard. When we admit that under a democratic government there is political equality, we mean thereby that opportunity is provided to all citizens "to pass judgment freely and frequently on the work of the political engineers whose decisions affect their lives."[15] It is then only that a government can be by the people. A democratic government cannot please everybody any more than a Monarchical or an Aristocratic government. But the former concedes to every citizen the rights of speech, publication and association. These rights are integral to democracy because they make possible free discussion and the continuous participation of the people in the government. A government by the people must, accordingly, mean a government by discussion and criticism—discussion of competing ideas, "leading to a compromise in which all the ideas are reconciled and which can be accepted by all because it bears the imprint of all."[16]

Rights of minority, as those of majority, are, thus, embedded in the basic democratic elements of freedom, equality, and rationality. When men deliberate collectively the goodness and rationality rise to their heights. For, in the course of discussion they exchange facts and ideas and also come to appreciate the interests and opinions of others. In this way the majority emerges with a sense of what its own needs are and, hopefully, what is best for society as a whole. It is, indeed, rare for a majority to impose its will harshly on minorities. Reasonable members of a majority will insist on justice and fair play as reasonable members of a minority will insist on submission and obedience, for today's minority may become tomorrow's majority. This makes democracy a government of restraints in which reciprocity prevails, that is, restraints on a majority as well as on a minority and both respecting restraints relating to each other.

The meaning of government for the people can best be explained in the words of Mazzini: "the progress of all through all under the leading of the best and wisest." The test of government is the welfare of the people, and that form of government is to be preferred which gives to human tendencies the fullest scope for development. The primary functions of a democratic government are similar to those of any other form of government. But, in addition to this, "democracy stimulates to self-education, for participation in governmental activities, opens wider horizons for the individual and leads to broadened interests."[17] The lessons of democracy are liberty, equality, fraternity and rationality. Its principle is that all persons who are fit to perform the duties of citizens should have a share in the direction of the State so that each man may have an identical oppurttmity to grow and expand to the best of his capacity, and there is no man or group of men who will exploit the weakness of others. Democracy does not differentiate between man and man. It raises the common man high on the pedestal of social and political glory and this is the meaning of a government for the people.

For a democratic government there must be a democratic society. A democratic government aims at justice and happiness. Justice, because no man or class or group will be strong enough to wrong others; happiness because each man judging best what is for

15. Appadorai, *The Substance of Politics*, p. 141.

16. Ernest Barker, *Reflections on Government.* p. 36.

17. *Dunning, op cit., Recent Times,* p. 63.

his good, will have every chance of pursuing it. "The principles of liberty and equality are. justified by the results they yield." Here liberty and equality have a reference to the well-known dictum of Kant : "So act as to treat humanity whether in your person or in that of another, in every case as an end, and never merely as a means." This is the requisite of a democratic society, for it instils the democratic ideal into the human mind. It is the worth and dignity of the human being as an individual which a democratic society recognises and it is, again, the worth and dignity of man which a democratic government provides maintains and guarantees. Both aim at what Bentham has reduced into a beautiful formula: Every one to count for one and no one for more than democratic one. A democratic government, therefore, can exist and thrive when the society is democratic.

Dunning has rightly remarked that our failure to understand democracy in its wider meaning, as a form of society, is the main reason for its being subjected to severe criticism. "Democracy", writes Sir Stafford Cripps, "is a system of government in which every adult citizen is equally free to express his views and desires upon all subjects in whatever way he wishes, and to influence the majority of his fellow-citizens to decide according to those views, and to influence those desires." It means that uniformity of belief or action is neither necessary nor desirable in democracy. Truth only comes by the clash of opinion with opinion and every citizen has something of value to contribute and he must not be hindered from bringing it forward. Democracy is, thus, rooted in equality and can be found in a democratic society in which all enjoy equal rights and privileges without any barriers of class distinctions.

"A democratic society," says Wolf, "is a society of free, equal, active and intelligent citizens, each man choosing his own way of life for himself and willing that others should choose theirs." The brotherhood of man is the basis of a democratic society and all its members stand equal in the common fraternity. Birth, wealth, caste, or creed do not determine the status of man. A society riddied with social and economic inequalities cannot be called a democratic society. Social and economic inequalities bring inequalities of treatment and right. Where a common man is not as good a factor of society as another, true citizenship cannot be secured and a democratic government cannot succeed in such an undemocratic society.

The Communists give a new meaning to democracy. They deny the need for a democratic government, but emphasise the necessity of a democratic State and a democratic State to them is only a socialist State with the dictatorship of the proletariat. They ridicule the western system of democracy with its economic and social inequalities and regard the toleration of minorities, which is the life-blood of democracy, as a show of hypocrisy, because for them the existence of minorities does not help the abolition of privileges. It is only in a socialist society which is classless, they assert, that there are no exploiters and no exploited. All the people are toilers and there exists no antagonism among them. But the Communists are really not democrats and theirs is not a democratic State. They permit the existence of only one party, the Communist, and difference of opinion with regard to the socialist structure of society is not allowed to prevail. All must be ideologically committed Communists and imbued with a socialist spirit. The dictatorship of the proletariat is a transitional phase in the evolution of socialism. When socialism is fully established, the State 'withers away' and gives place to a Communist society. This may be democracy, but not as we understand it. According to our conception, democracy is not hostile to the State. It is the best form of government and a permanent feature of the State in which equal opportunity is provided to every man, irrespective of the opinion he holds, to contribute his judgment to the determination of public policy. As a theory of society, democracy stands for that social order which recognises the inherent worth of every human being and has a never-ending faith in the common man. But such a recognition can only be ensured by the State and guaranteed by its laws.

Democracy is, therefore, difficult to define and Freeman correctly says that "it is commonly very hard to make out what modern writers mean by democracy." It is not a mere form of government. Dewey has aptly said that "to say that democracy is only a form of government is like saying that home is a more or less geometrical arrangement of bricks and mortar, or that church-is a building with pews, pulpit and spire." Democracy, according to Barker, is a mode of spirit, an attitude of mind of those who profess it, and only those who profess it can practise it. There is synchronisation of thoughts and actions and this is the essence of democracy.

DIRECT AND REPRESENTATIVE DEMOCRACY

As a form of government, there are two types of democracy—(1) pure or direct, and (2) representative or indirect.

Direct Democracy. When the people themselves directly express their will on public affairs, the type of government is called pure or direct democracy. The people formulate and express their will in a mass meeting and they assemble for this purpose as often as required. In the small City-States of ancient Greece and Rome all adult male citizens were expected to meet together in the Assembly—the *Ecclesia* of Athens, the *Commitia* of Rome. Pure democracy had not been confined to the ancient world. Its surviving relics are found today in the Swiss *landsgemeinde* or popular legislature. There were twenty-six *landsgemeinden* in the middle of the eighteenth century; today, there are only five, and one of them has been confined to elective functions. On a Sunday in April or May the adult male citizens in the Canton assemble to consider in full open-air meetings the governmental affairs of the Canton. At such meetings new laws are agreed upon and old laws changed, taxes levied, budgets adopted and officials chosen.

But pure or direct democracy can exist and function only in small States with a limited, homogeneous population where people can conveniently meet and deliberate together. In large and complex societies, when the number of the people is too large and the area of the State is too extensive, direct democracy is impracticable. Even the Swiss landsgemeinde is cantonal and nowhere is it associated with the national government. This institution has been commended by some writers with great enthusiasm, but a close acquaintance with its actual working produces a very different effect. "It would be naive," says Rappard, a Swiss scholar, "to believe that even a small community of a few thousand well-trained citizens could, under the complex conditions of the twentieth century, effectively govern itself by means of such an ephemeral legislative assembly. One might as well expect a football crowd, assembled for a few hours in a stadium, to make itself responsible for the establishment of an academic curriculum or for the drafting of a measure of social insurance."

Direct democracy now assumes the form of the referendum and the popular initiative, and they have long been familiar in Switzerland and the United States. After the First World War they made an appearance in Germany, Latvia, Estonia, Ireland and even in Soviet Russia. They were deleted from the Irish Constitution in 1928, and were lying dormant for thirteen years in Germany when Hitler struck down the Weimer Constitution. The 1936 Constitution of U.S.S.R. empowered the Presidium to submit, on its own initiative, legislative measures and other important matters to popular vote and hold a referendum. The 1977 Constitution abolished it, but substituted that referendum might be invoked as a last resort if both the Houses failed to reach agreement on a legislative measure for the second time after its reference to the Conciliation Committee. In U.S.A. direct legislation is obtainable only in eleven States, most of them in the west. Popular, or direct legislation, as Sait remarks, "is little more than a fad outside of Switzerland, where unique conditions prevail."[18] In Switzerland direct legislation has a natural growth or, as Bryce says, it is "racy of the soil. There are institutions which, like plants, flourish only on their hillside and under their own sunshine."[19]

Indirect or Representative Democracy. The prevailing system of democracy is indirect or representative. The will of the State is formulated and expressed not directly by the people themselves, but by their representatives to whom they delegate the power of discussion and decision making. They are referred to as representatives and this type of government as representative democracy. The representatives are periodically elected by the people. John Stuart Mill defines indirect or representative democracy as one in which "the whole people or some numerous portion of them, exercise the governing power through deputies periodically elected by themselves."

In a representative democracy the ultimate source of authority remains with the people. But it draws a distinction between the possession of authority which resides in the electorate and its exercise, which is by the elected representatives. Hobhouse says, "Democracy means or may mean, two things which, though allied in idea, are not necessarily found together in practice, viz., (*i*) direct participation of the mass of ordinary citizens in the public life of the community, (*ii*) ultimate popular sovereignty." The voters elect the representatives for a number of years and after the expiry of their term, they report back to their masters, the electors. The electors judge them by their deeds and determine whether or not they should repose their trust in them for the next term. If they prefer to discontinue with them, they would do so by electing new representatives. Representative democracy guarantees, in other terms, a general harmony of purpose between government and the governed by reconciling effective authority and political freedom.

It must, however, be noted that voters who have returned their representatives in a majority and placed them in office to make a policy and run the government, must not exert undue pressure, personal or regional, on them for the fulfilments of their own ends. To pressurize them for gaining personal and selfish advantages and benefits is a democratic

18. Sait, E.M., *Political Institutions,. A Preface,* p. 432.
19. Bryce, J., *Modern Democracies,* Vol. I, pp. 453-454.

sin which deserves no condonation for it demoralises the citizens and detracts democratic ideals. A degree of pressure is permissible to remind representatives of their constituents' sentiments, but it must not get out of hand. The law-makers and administrators have to be able to give reasoned consideration to policies and programmes, and they cannot be stampeded by regional or group clamour of the moment. Indeed, if superior men are selected for office, then they should be allowed to exercise their knowledge and intelligence in an atmosphere of calm and objectivity.

After World War I a good deal of dissatisfaction was expressed against the working of representative democracy, and devices of popular control, the *referendum*, the *initiative* and *recall*, were introduced by some of the States. These devices aimed at transferring from the representatives to the people themselves the right to have the final verdict over legislative and administrative matters and to recall from office those representatives who did not perform their duties diligently, honestly, or in accordance with the wishes of the people. But the dominant verdict has proved hostile to these direct devices of popular control and the representative institutions continue to be instruments of democracy.

REQUISITES OF DEMOCRACY

Democracy, in its broader sense means, faith in the common man and seeks to give assurance to all people inhabiting the State that all have equal opportunity to achieve their goals as they come to envisage them, and to provide positive means for this purpose. A genuine democracy is an active, growing, progressive force responsive to the will of the people and animated by the ideals of mutual service and public welfare. It involves the presence of a democratic idea among the people, and a democratic idea, according to Ivor Brown[20] means : —

An "action of will." The people should not only imbibe the will to have democracy, but the power to retain it as well. They should be fully conscious of their political rights and duties as vigilance is the price of democracy.The citizens should not be silent spectators, simply watching the game of politics. Nor does it mean mere submission or acquiescence on their part. Democracy demands from the common man rational conduct and active participation in the affairs of government. Democratic government is government by criticism. The people should have the courage to protest against and criticize the injustice and tyranny of the government. "To be articulate is its very life; to be dumb its demise." It is only the will of the people to action which can save them from the tyranny of the rulers. The rulers become masters when citizens are passive. They become their servants when citizens assert and uphold their right that they are the masters. The successful working of democracy depends upon the intelligence, interest, public spirit and civic sense of its citizens, the sense of 'public spirit' and social consciousness in brief.

Democracy involves fellowship, that is, a feeling of fraternity or what Giddings calls the 'consciousness of kind'. Fellow-feeling aims at realization of a common end—the welfare of humanity. Fellowship appeals to our sense of common humanity. Democracy

---

20. Burns, C.D., *The Meaning of Democracy,* Chap. XIII.

does not recognise class distinctions. Fellowship knows no limits created by religion, caste, birth or wealth. It is only in a society of equals that harmony can be secured. By equality we mean, of course, equality of opportunity—a fair and open field for all.[21] This kind of equality ensures social justice, which is the very life-breath of democracy. When there exist vast inequalities of wealth, social justice cannot be obtained. A wide gulf between the rich and the poor makes it impossible for the latter to live and exercise their political rights independently and freely. The rich become a class of vested interests and equality in all its meanings disappears. Where there is no equality, there can be neither liberty, nor fraternity nor rationality. Democracy is the product of. liberty, equality and fraternity and all these three make for rationality.

Democracy demands a spirit of tolerance. This is necessary, as democracy involves the rule of the majority and submission of the minority or minorities to the decisions of the majority. The majority should not be prompted in its public actions by sectional interests and ruthlessly disregard the interest of minorities and frustrate their aspirations. A rational majority is the prerequisite of tolerance and tolerance is the basis of democracy. Exactly, the same rational role the minority is expected to play. It must not act in an irresponsible manner and play a constructive role in opposing and proposing to the party in office. It must not always suspect the *bona fides* of the majority and remain at perpetual political animosity with it. There should prevail a sense of give and take; the habit of tolerance and spirit of compromise. The more there are cleavages and party squabbles in society the more difficult it is to make democracy operative and enthuse democratic spirit among citizens The differences in majority and minority opinion prove beneficial only when they are directed towards the common good and are free from partisan considerations. Each party should have full and fair opportunity to express its opinion and influence government's policy by reasoning and persuasion. But once the decision has been taken, it is the duty of the minority parties to abide by it and perform the well-recognised functions of a responsible Opposition. This is true resignation and true service; the real meaning of fellowship. A democratic system envisages alteration in government and both the victors and the vanquished should accept that at some future date their positions may be reversed and, as such, there should be wide agreement on the benefits of playing the game of politics according to rules.

There should be adequate provision of opportunities for the individual to develop his personality. This can be realised when everyone has free access to knowledge, security against unemployment, a minimum wage, fair conditions of work and leisure, and provision against sickness and old age. Democracy here invades the realm of industry. It has now become a common demand that economic democracy must precede political democracy. A society where wealth is most unevenly distributed and one class of people is out to exploit the rest, democracy cannot succeed. A democratic society is a partnership among equals. The democratic ideal, therefore, cannot be realised until industry is entirely democratized and inequalities in the distribution of national wealth are reduced to the minimum. To some this may mean socialism, but democracy, too, aims at social justice. Justice, as Barker says, is a joining or knitting together not only of persons, but also of

21. *See Ante,* Chap X.

principles. "It joins and knits together the claims of the principle of liberty with those of the principles of equality, and both with those of the principles of fraternity or cooperation. It adjusts them to one another in a right order of their relations."[22]

Democracy is participation. It means doing things in common with others, and taking your share of the responsibilities involved. "The democratic problem," says Lindsay, "is the control of the organisation of power by the common man." A citizen of a democratic State must be a thinking human being possessing independent opinion, which is the result of his considered judgment, and intelligent interest in public affairs. Widespread participation in politics is the *sine qua non* of a democratic government and its success essentially depends upon the ability, character and power of discrimination the common man possesses. Democracy becomes a show affair if he exhibits a sheep-like behaviour —a crowd mind in public affairs.

The active and intelligent participation of citizens in public affairs can be assured if : all of them are adequately educated. The government must, therefore, provide a system of free and compulsory education for all. Education produces thinking human beings who know, according to Rousseau, that they are both sovereign and subjects and they must fulfil their dual obligations. A citizen of a democratic polity is not merely to obey; he has also to see if his obedience is rational. Vigilance, wisdom, intellect, commonsense and honesty are the virtues which citizens must possess and all such qualities flow from the gift of education. President Lincoln said: "You can fool part of the people all the time, and all the people part of the time, but you can not fool all the people all the time." If citizens are educated and they have the courage to be critical of the government this befooling business becomes infinitely difficult. Those who follow Bentham's maxim: "While I will obey punctually, I will censure freely" are the true citizens of a democratic polity. They possess the powers of discrimination to obey and to criticize. They do not belong to an uncritical herd. This means that there should be a free and fearless mass media of communication which should serve as a popular forum of educating and shaping public opinion. The press, most importantly, should be a jealous guardian of the rights and liberties of the people, if democracy is to be a government of the people, for the people and by the people.

APPRAISAL OF DEMOCRACY

Defects of Democracy. But the assumptions of democracy are too idealistic and difficult to be realised in practical life. Democracy demands from the people a high degree of civic capacity which involves intelligence, self-control, and devotion to a common cause, and the capacity to subordinate private interests and desires to it. It relies on the spirit of give-and-take. It also demands time to share in common activities and to study the issues involved. The common man, the critics of democracy maintain, is indolent in politics. He is neither politically intelligent nor sufficiently educated. He does not possess the capacity to understand complex political problems and is incapable of intelligent action. "Democracy is suited," observed Beni Prasad, "to a state of society in which the

22. Barker, E., *Principles of Social and Political Theory,* p. 167.
23. Beni Prasad, *A.B.C. of Civics*, p. 95.

people want to exercise power, are capable of sinking minor differences and cooperating for the general good and have acquired knowledge and judgment enough to elect suitable representatives and to judge as to the propriety of general lines of policy."[23] But an average citizen has not the time, inclination and ability to inform himself on the affairs of the State. The apathy of the voters in most democratic politics is proverbial. A voter has to be cajoled and dragged out from his place of work in order to cast his vote. The obvious result is that power passess into the hands of a professional politician, a demagogue, who is ever ready to exploit the masses. Godkin explained democracy as "delegating sovereignty to the demagogue, the grafter and the boss." The ultimate sovereign, the people, for the most part have neither the will nor the power to find the best men to lead them.

It is further maintained that democracy is inefficient as a form of government. Democracy, it is urged, is based on the assumption that all men are equal and that one man is as good as another, whatever his real worth. He votes and is eligible for office on a level with them all. But, it is an irrational and impracticable dogma, the critics maintain. They assert that men are manifestly not equal. Physically and mentally they differ widely from one another. Votes are, then, counted and not weighed. Counting of votes determines a majority and the decisions will have to be those of the majority, no matter what the margin may be and howsoever superior wisdom and better judgment the minority may claim. Faguet considers democracy as a hopeless rule of ignorance. He makes democracy synonymous with incompetence, as it is a government by amateurs, or as another theorist has put it: "government by fools." Lecky characterised it as "the government of the poorest, the most ignorant, the most incapable who are necessarily the most numerous." The representatives assume the responsibility of governing the State not because they are able and possess specialized knowledge in administration, but only as they command a majority "A youth must pass" remarked Sir Sydney Low "an examination in Arithmetic before he can hold a second class clerkship in the Treasury but a Chancellor of the Exchequer may be a middle-aged man of the world who has forgotten what little he ever learnt about figures at Eton or Oxford and is innocently anxious to know the meaning of those little dots." The inefficiency of a democratic government is essentially reflected in its policies, especially those relating to defence and foreign relations, which are weak and vacillating. A government which depends for its existence upon the uncertain passions of unthinking people (as it happend in many States of India after the Fourth General Elections in 1967) and is never sure of its life cannot afford to undertake a sound and long-term policy. Nor can it ensure efficiency as it lives and thrives on nepotism. Offices are distributed by corrupting the representatives, who coquette with the electors to ensure their berth.

Nazi-ism and Fascism were the two serious critics of democracy before World War II. Those associated with these doctrines characterised democracy as incompetent and inefficient in dealing with serious economic problems. Hitler described it as "stupid, corrupt and slow-moving." It has also been maintained that a democratic government is not suited to the complexities which a Welfare State involves. It cannot cope with the gigantic tasks and new responsibilities confronting the modern State. "When a government does a few things, mistakes hardly matter, but when it does many things, failures are always serious and may be calamitous." It is pointed out that democracy might have proved its usefulness in a simple age, when political units were small or when *laissez faire* prevailed and the services provided by the government were few, but it is incompetent to solve the modern complex problems and to face situations which require immediate decision and concerted action. The very principle of compromise which stimulates a democratic system of government further militates against efficiency, consistency, and effective government. Sir Henry Maine was afraid that popular government would not only destroy the stability of government but also check progress and inaugurate an era of chronic stagnation. Sir James Fitz Stephen was convinced that universal suffrage tended to invest the true and natural relation between wisdom and folly.

Party system is indispensable for democracy. But the manner in which party system actually works in modern democracies deprives countries of the services of some of their best citizens. Political parties encourage hollowness and insecurity, create cleavages in the life of the nation, debase normal standards and distribute the "spoils."[24] Election propaganda misguides and miseducates people. Moral considerations are subordinated in order to secure the largest number of votes. People vote for the party and not for the candidate. The representative owes responsibility to the party on whose ticket he contested the election and he must say and do what he is told to do. Rigid party discipline makes representatives cowardly and subservient as they lose honesty, courage and independence. Under such a system of representation, popular control, which is the essence of indirect democracy, becomes illusory, Then, the system works mechanically. There is no option for the individual voter who intends to exercise his independent judgment. "He has to choose between two or more candidates who may be either knaves or fools and for none of whom he cares, and decides between two or three issues, none of which meets his approval."[25] When voting becomes so mechanical, democracy loses its educative and moral value. It is in this sense that democracy has sometimes been equated with the "Nemesis of Mediocrity."

Again, democracy is criticized, because it has encouraged the growth of class struggle. Candidates who offer themselves for election are generally moneyed men, who can foot election bills and contribute liberally to the party funds. This propertied oligarchy will make laws to the advantage of its own class rather than in the interest of the community as a whole. The obvious result will be the prosperity of the few at the cost of the many, creating a class of vested interests. Modern democracy is, accordingly, stigmatised as capitalistic, and a capitalist society is a society of unequals. Where inequality prevails democracy does not exist. Social and economic democracy must precede political democracy, if the latter is to succeed.

The most militant and systematic of the contemporary attacks upon the democratic system comes from the Marxists. Democracy, they hold, is the political system of a class society and it reflects the interests and wishes of the *bourgeois* or the dominant class, the propertied class who own productive property. So long as class society endures exploitation of the working class will continue unabated. Marxism concedes that capitalist democracy is a 'real' democracy for the rich, but is only a sham for the poor.

---

24. Bryce, J., *Modern Democracies,* Vol. l, Chap. XI.
25. Asirvatham, E., *Political Theory* , p. 478.

Then, it is said that democracy is a highly expensive form of government. Its governmental machinery is complex and its functions involve much waste of time and money. At many stages the process of administration is just duplication. Take, for instance, the system of bicameralism. Whatever be its political utility, bicameralism is a heavy toll on the exchequer. Elections, which are so frequent in democracy, have become inconceivably expensive. Even in a poor country like India, it may cost a candidate quite a couple of lakh rupees[26] and it is in fact, a conservative estimate. In the United States a Senator is reported to have spent half a million dollars on his election. This is surely a waste, not only of money, but also of time and is inconsistent with the spirit of democracy.

The ethical value of democracy is also seriously questioned. Its critics assert that it discounts honesty—honesty in the sense of reasoned conviction, refined habits and integrity of character. There is much falsification and vilification. Election campaigns and party meetings convened for purposes of nursing the constituency are very often mud-slinging campaigns where issues are "vulgarised and popularised" before they can make an appeal to the people. Questions are not discussed dispassionately. They are discussed in such a manner as to catch votes. And catching of votes is a nefarious device, because it strangulates thought and chokes reason. The voter is not given an opportunity to pause and think. A man who does not think is not serving the purpose of his creation. The result is that he is easily led astray. Most of the electors being uneducated, some indeed illiterate, as is the case with quite a sizable percentage in India, adult franchise is a farce. Many do not know for whom they are voting, others vote as they are told to do for considerations of religion, caste and regional affinities. Votes are purchased and even dead voters are resuscitated for the day of election. Few countries can deny that their practice and their theory do not fully coincide. It is, indeed, difficult, not to say impossible, to secure the complete elimination of bribery, of inefficiency, and of influence due to birth and wealth. James Bryce who devoted a separate Chapter[26a] to "Money Power in Politics" showed that electors, members of legislatures, administrative officials and even judicial officers frequently succumb to the lure of money.

Democracy has also been criticised for excessive interference in the technical details of government. It has insisted and it always insists "on specific mandates to legislators, on direct democratic control of administrative departments, or popular retrial of cases adjudged. Thus, members of parliament and congressmen are harassed and diverted from their proper work by constant instructions from local committees, petitions from constituents, protests from caucuses, demands for explanations from the disappointed, and incessant meddlings from all quarters. The result of this needless or excessive interference is a weak, inefficient and corrupt government. Paralysis seizes the State. The legislature becomes timid and time-serving; the executive feeble and afraid; the judiciary double-minded and unjust. The result is disaster." The critics also maintain that democracy perishes by disintegration. Those in authority cannot afford to displease their electors, as

26. The Chief Election Commissioner of India disclosed that one of the candidates for election to Parliament had spent rupees 5 crores to get him self-elected.

26a. Refer to Bryce, J., Modern Democracies, Chap. LXIX.

tomorrow is the day of election. The electors are generally seekers of favours and in pursuit of their self-interest pester the ministers always and everywhere. And the latter succumb to their demands whether they like it or not. The result is obvious. The ministers and others in authority can neither work with vigour nor can they do justice under the circumstances. There is also a tendency to insubordination when political pulls matter at all levels.

The territorial or geographical basis of election and representation is considered misrepresentative as it contradicts the spirit of democracy. A representative elected on a territorial basis, it is claimed, does not and cannot represent all the varied and diverse interests and occupations. He can represent at best the interests or the class of the people to which be belongs. People pursuing the same kind of work or functions have more things or ideas in common than people living in the same locality. It is, accordingly, suggested that the territorial system of representation should be replaced by functional representation which is the only true and democratic system.

James Bryce, a fervent exponent of democracy pointed out the following defects. His conclusions were based upon his personal observations of the six major democracies of the world.

1. "The power of money to pervert administration or legislation.
2. "The tendency to make politics a gainful profession.
3. "Extravagance in administration.
4. "The abuse of the doctrine of equality and failure to appreciate the value of administrative skill.
5. "The undue power of party organisation.
6. "The tendency of legislators and political officials to play for votes in the passing of laws and in tolerating breaches of order."[27]

Merits of Democracy. Bryce, nevertheless, points out that the first three defects are common to all forms of government and are not inherent only in democracy. The last three are associated more closely with democracy, but are not insurmountable evils. "Democracy," as Dunning says, "has closed some of the old channels of evil; it has opened some new ones, but it has not increased the stream."[28] Democracy must face self-interest and irresponsibility of power, both of which underlie its major problems. But it has two powerful weapons to fight against these evils : law and opinion. The latter cannot be realised in any other form of government except democracy. While admitting that democracy has defects, Herman Finer says, that the political, social and economic gifts of democracy endow mankind with vast riches. He observes that under a democratic government, "we have the assurance that the sphere of our private life—our family, our diversions, our worship, our work—will not be invaded except by due process of law in which we have an equal say with any. We rest tranquil that officials and judges will not abuse us and that they themselves will have to answer for discrimination and bias and unauthorised invasions of our private and public life to a public tribunal in which we, as of right, sit as judge and jury.[29]

27. *Ibid.,* Vol. II, p. 504.
28. Dunning, *op. citd., Recent Times* Vol. IV, p. 63. Refer to *Modern Democracies, op. citd.* Vol. II, p. 459.
29. Finer, H., *The Theory and Practice of Modern Government, op. citd.,* p. 952.

In spite of the unsparing attacks to which democracy has been subjected, it still tends to spread, conferring more and more power on the people. The Second World War was fought on the basis of democracy *vs*. dictatorship. It was a victory for democracy. With it, however, dictatorship did not vanish altogether. It did appear in some new countries other than those vanquished. But once the dictators received recognition and their *de jure* authority was duly established, they tempered their dictatorships with democratic processes and eventually became elected Presidents in their countries. Nasser in Egypt and Ayub in Pakistan. The United Arab Republic adopted a Republican Constitution in 1964. Even the Communists are so much enamoured of the appeal the term "democracy" has that they characterise the Dictatorship of the Proletariat as the best from of a democratic government.

It means that democracy has a great appeal for all people and they have not lost faith in it. It remains their beau-ideal. The problem of democracy centres on the one point: whether or not man is increasing in wisdom. The answer is in the affirmative, for while no other form of government gives so much to the citizen as democracy does, at the same time, no other form of government demands so much from him as does democracy. The rights which a democratic government confers on a citizen and the duties he owes as a result thereof, make him an active participant in the politics of his country and it is a widespread activity. He thinks over and tackles the problems facing him and his country as a rational man and rationality is one of the fundamental tenets of democracy. A corollary to this is that no one has a monopoly of reason. No one is the sole repository of wisdom. All men have something of value to contribute, however little it may be. The process of making this contribution is democracy. Democracy will, therefore, not perish as long as there is hope in the rationality of man, that is, as long as man is free to think and reason and solve his problems. Thinkers are doers and a citizen of a democratic State does not only think for himself, but he also thinks for the fraternity to which he belongs. Faguet feels that "it is necessary to know what a people thinks, what it feels, what it suffers, what it desires, and what it hopes, and all this can be learnt only from the people itself'."

Democracy, as said earlier, is more than a form of government. It is a form of society as well, even an ideal or a spirit, a doctrine of human optimism. Democracies, says Finer, "admit the pragmatic nature of their search for perfection, and recognise that of perfection there is no single exclusive principle. Yet they surmise that if such there should be, it is one yet to be discovered in a process of evolution, and if the unfolding is to arrive at unsoundness, it must be founded on the unfettered expression and interplay of all opinion." Democratic societies recognise and welcome change. They must evolve with the development of new points of view, new techniques, new possibilities for human life. With the extension of the concept of democracy old egalitarian doctrines have been discarded. By equality we do not now mean that all men are alike. There are physical, intellectual and moral differences between one man and another. Granting all these obvious variations, the term equality is interpreted to mean equality of opportunity. Democracy is that form of society in which every man has a chance and knows he has

30. Mill, J.S., *Representative Government*, p. 52.

it. Democracy, therefore, has the merit of ensuring the twin principles of liberty and equality. Under it there is no class of persons possessing special privileges. All are equal amongst equals under the umbrella of equality of opportunity and equality before the law. This is the highest attainment of man's life.

The test of a government is the welfare of the people, and that form of government is to be preferred which gives full scope to the development of human capacities. Democracy makes authority a trust. Those who exercise authority are chosen by their fellow-citizens for short terms of office and are responsible to them for the exercise of their trust. It implies a recognition of the duties of the government and the rights of the people. Democracy is superior to other forms of government, as John Stuart Mill points out,[30] for two reasons. First, the rights and interests of the individual can be safeguarded only when he is able to "stand up" for them himself. Secondly, there is a great degree of general prosperity which is more widely diffused as the energies and interests of all the people are stimulated and enlisted in its support. Indirect democracy does not mean actual rule by the people, "for the people rather determine the ends towards which their government shall aim, and watch over those into whose hands they have placed the actual power of administration."[31] In short, it is claimed that popular election, popular control, and popular responsibility are more likely to ensure a greater degree of efficiency and welfare than any other system of government.[32] There is, thus, no justification for the assertion of Sir Henry Maine that Aristocracy is the mother of all progress, that popular government "is charactcrised by great fragility, and that since its appearance, all forms of government have become more insecure than they were before."[33]

The critics of democracy contend that men are not rational as democracy accepts them to be and, as such, the complicated societies in which we live need the best men in government. They insist that democracy never picks the best and often the worst instead; votes are counted and not weighed is their familiar argument. No one denies that some men are not rational. Neither are men always rational. But neither can one assert that men are always irrational or that all men are irrational. Men are men, with all their frailities. This is true of all governments and democracy is no exception to it. But the simple question is what form of government can provide the scope for the use and flowering of rationality? It is democracy, because it is informative and is the only conduit for social forces that is at all adequate in modern times. It admits the will of all members into the determination of social policy, secures the representation of all views and feelings and is therefore more responsive to social and economic changes. It taps sources of political talent which lie beyond the purview of other systems of government. It is best qualified constantly to adjust the supply of control to social need and favours a wholesome social equilibrium. It deepens the sense of social obligation.

Similarly, the merit of democracy does not lie in its efficiency as a form of government. Nobody has ever defended democracy on grounds of efficiency. It is defended on the grounds that the denial of freedom involves the denial of certain personal values which are more important than efficiency. A good government, tested on the touchstone of

31. Dunning, *op. citd.,* Vol. IV, p. 63.

32. Garner, *Political Science and Government*, p. 390.

33. Maine, H., *Popular Government,* p. 20.

efficiency alone, is no substitute for self-government. Democracy is the most cherished goal of self-government. It is a government by the people for their welfare and, as such, it stimulates them to self-education. The supreme test of excellence in government is not the well feeding of the people nor is it to be found in the rigidity of order the State maintains. "It is the character a polity tends to create," as Lowell remarks, "in the citizens by whom it must be sustained. The best government in the long run is one that nurtures a people strong in moral fibre, in integrity, industry, self-reliance, and courage." Democracy elevates the character and develops the political intelligence of the masses. It is an active, growing, progressive force inspired by the ideal of service to mankind. Self-government is not a mere form of institution to be had when desired. It demands from an average man a certain degree of intelligence, honesty, public spirit and discipline. These virtues give a people, as Woodrow Wilson points out, "self-possession, self-mastery, the habit of order and peace and common counsel and reverence for law which will not fail when they themselves become the makers of law; the steadiness and self-control of political maturity." Democracy, therefore, develops the potential intellectual and spiritual qualities of man. It promotes a better and higher form of national character, because the citizens feel that they are a part and parcel of government.

Democracy is inseparable from a belief in the methods of peaceful persuasion, in the ultimate reasonableness of man, and his response to rational argument. A democratic society is not susceptible to revolutions. The people know and feel that they are both sovereign and subjects. If they have any grievances, the redress is easy and can be had by peaceful and constitutional means. The political life of the community is based on complete freedom of discussion out of which emerges public opinion which is the guiding source of political authority. "Since the law will be made and the administration be given momentum and controlled by us, voters," writes Finer, "and since our power can be successfully exerted by association and persuasion, the impulse of the system is to foster fellowship and a common conscience among all men"; the spirit of self-help, self-reliance, self-respect and cooperation and a sense of responsibility in the individual. Does any other form of government offer so much?

Future of Democracy. Democracy, no doubt, has its own defects, but "no form of government", as Lowell maintains, "is a panacea for all human ills." Democracy may not have created a sense of fellow-feeling; it may not have drafted the best trained mind to State service, or dignified and purified politics, but in comparison with governments of the past it has justified itself. Things may be bad today, but they were worse yesterday. The world tried unlimited monarchy, aristocracy and oligarchy at various times and there is no desire to go back to them. Burns has strikingly said, "no one denies that existing representative assemblies are defective; but even if an automobile does not work well, it is foolish to go back into a farm cart, however romantic."[34] We experimented with dictatorship lately and gave it up as a hopeless form of government, since dictatorship is the negation of individual liberty and initiative, and is antagonistic to the development of human personality.[35] It is, accordingly, mischievous to search for another form of government instead of improving what we have. The essence of democracy, in the words

34. Burns, C.D., *Democracy*, p. 80.
35. See Chap. *XV Intra.*

of Mazzini, is "the progress of all through all under the leading of the best and wisest." Its supreme value is ethical and educational. As a form of government democracy can flourish and decline in proportion to the moral and intellectual stature of man. As Robert MacIver pointed out, "there is only one way to keep it in being, and that is through the intelligent perception, permeating the people, of what it is and what makes it precious. We guard our spiritual treasures only by learning to appreciate them."[36] It is in the people alone to preserve it. It can neither be guaranteed by law nor protected by any police system. The future of democracy in the last analysis, depends upon man and how he accepts man, first as a fellow-citizen and then, as a member of that great fraternity of mankind. It is the recognition of this sense of brotherhood that helps to stabilise fellow-feelings and cement the bonds of comradeship. Democracy can only succeed, when democratic feelings synchronise with democratic actions at all levels.

But this is the ideal of a perfect democracy. Before such a fraternity is established the existing democratic institutions require immediate examination and readjustment. Political democracy is unthinkable without a social and economic programme and, as such, our democratic institutions must be progressive, adaptable, and flexible to meet the present aspirations of the people and provide a precious mould for the future. It is now agreed amongst all that capitalistic democracy is completely out of date as it does not provide an adequate answer to the present social needs. The demand of democracy is speedy responsiveness to public opinion and capitalistic democracy does not provide a proper atmosphere for the genuine public opinion to shape itself, for where it is tempted to be active in defence is just where democracy is tempted to be active in offence. The result is obvious. Our social, economic and political orders have become shaky and unless democracy, as a form of government, finds the means of equalizing opportunity and wipes out the existing wide economic disparities, its future appeal is doubtful. Political need arises for the sake of a happy and just life and if a democratic apparatus of government does not provide to man what his basic demands are, the clamour for its substitution by some other form of government, which can assure the same, is not a vain search. But that is groping in the dark with far distant hope even for the twilight. Democratic light is still there to illuminate the path of life. Clement Attlee correctly said that capitalistic democracy may not give freedom or equality of opportunity to the mass of the people owing to economic inequalities but democracy is the only method by which economic and social equality will ultimately be achieved.

Finally, democracy is really a question of relationship of rights to duties which have become so complex during the twentieth century. If a nineteenth century democrat could return to this earth and compare the present with the position of the citizens of a century ago, he would certainly not fail to note two striking changes. First, the modern citizen is much more dependent upon the State, not only for the essentials of civilised life but also for much of what goes to make up his standard of living. Secondly, as the minimum standard rises, as the citizens come to demand more and more from the State, obligations increase commensurately with rights. Moreover, our conceptions of what men require from the State in order to lead a full life have moved from the purely physical plane to

36. MacIver, R.M., *The Rambarts We Guard*, p. 4.

include the intellectual, the emotional and the psychological. The increase in the responsibilities of citizens demands from them to be articulate and creative to ensure their rights. The future of democracy will certainly depend upon the responsiveness of citizens to the new demands of democracy.

But a caution must be sounded, lest we seem to be concluding on an unrealistic optimistic note. We have said nothing about how long the process of modernizing and democratizing the developing nations of the world may take. Democratic forms of governments were most cherishingly adopted in the developing countries and experience shows that all, except a few, settled down either as authoritarian regimes or military dictatorship in one form or the other. Whatever be the reasons, this is the lesson of the twentieth century history. Even in countries which had been deemed as the citadels of democracy, the spirit of authoritarianism is much in evidence and the practice of democratic principles throughout the body politic is at much serious a discount. The democratic direction, *inter alia*, depends upon at least a nominal measure of international order and security. And the international situation today leaves an ominous question mark over the future of democracy—as it does over the future of the world. Neither established democracies nor the developing countries can maintain democratic institutions under conditions of international tension or something approaching what Lasswell calls the "garrison state."

SUGGESTED READINGS

Adams, H., *The Degradation of Democratic Dogma.*

Allen, C.K., *Democracy and the Individual.*

Almond, Gabriel, A; and Coleman, James, S.,: *The politics of Developing Areas.*

Barker, E., *Reflections on Government,* Chaps. III, VI.

Bryce, J., *Modern Democracies,* Vol. I, Part II: Vol. II, Part III.

Burns, C.D., *The Challenge to Democracy.*

Burns, C D., *Democracy; Its Defects and Advantages.*

Chambers, William N., and Salisbury Robert H., *Democracy in the Mid-Twentieth Century.*

Dealey, J.Q., *The State and Government,* Chaps. X-XI.

Faguet, E., *The Cult of Incompetence.*

Finer, H., *The Theory and Practice of Modern Government,* pp. 937-54.

Follet, M.P., *The New State,* Chaps. XVI, XXI.

Friedrich, Carl J., *Constitutional Government and Democracy*

Friedrich, Carl J; and Brezezinski, Z Bigniew K., *Totalitarian Dictatorship and Autocracy.*

Garner, J.W., Introduction to Political Science, Chaps. VI-VII.

Garner, J.W., *Political Science and Government,* Chaps. XIII-XVI.

Greaves, H.R.G., *The Foundations of Political Theory,* Chap. XI.

Hearnshaw, F.J.C., *Democracy at the Crossways.*

Lindsay, A.D., *Essentials of Democracy.*

Lindsay, A.D., *The Modern Democratic State.*

MacIver, R.M., *The Modern State,* Chaps. XI-XII.

MacPherson, C.B., *The Real World of Democracy.*

Maine, H., *Popular Government,* Chap. II (1885).

Maritian, Jacques., *Man and the State,* Chap. V.

Mayo, H.B., *An Introduction to Democratic Theory.*

Mill, J. S., *Representative Government (1890).*

Parkinson, N.C., *The Evolution of Political Thought,* Chaps. XIII-XIX.

Pink, M.A., *A Realist Looks at Democracy.*

Roche and Stedham., *The Dynamics of Democratic Government.*

Rossiter, C.L., *Constitutional Dictatorship: Crisis Government in Modern Democracies.*

Sait, E.M., *Democracy.*

Seley, J. R., *Introduction to Political Science, Lectures II, VI-VII.*

Sidgwick, H., *Elements of Politics,* Chaps. XXII, XXX.

Stamps, Norman L., *Why Democracies Fail?*

UNESCO: *Democracy in a World of Tension.*

Wallas, G., *Human Nature in Politics.*

Wells, H.G., *Democracy Under Revision.*

14
CHAPTER
Forms of Government (Contd.)

UNITARY AND FEDERAL GOVERNMENTS

The State is unity and a like quality attaches to its government as well. But the term government is also used for its various levels of administration and the contemporary use of the term extends to the internal "government" of various corporations, groups and associations and all these "governments", its innovators claim, operate in response to forces that it seems natural to call political. It would appear from such a use as if there could exist within the State a number of governments at the same time. But it is not so. It may be called a traditional approach, but in the real sense there can be no government within a government. What seem to be separate governments are in reality parts of one governmental system. They all form parts of one integrated governmental organisation. This point is important to grasp for proper appre-ciation of the distribution of powers among its different levels of administration and the character of the governmental system resulting therefrom. The conventional use of the term for all levels of administrations. however, is universally accepted and practised. All the same, its use for the internal management of corporations, associations and groups is likely to cause confusion and even ambiguity in properly understanding the operative part of the machinery of the State.

Though a State can have but one government, yet such is the extent of territory over which many modern States exercise jurisdiction and so numerous and varied are their functions that it is impossible for any single authority to do its work from one single centre. Then, it is not only the problem of doing the work. It must be done effectively and efficiently. It is, therefore, imperative that the sum total of governmental powers should be split up and distributed among different organs and authorities, and, together, they should all constitute one harmonious scheme for the administration of public affairs.

Territorial and Functional Division. There are two methods of dividing governmental powers, territorial and functional. The territorial division of powers seeks to divide the territory of the State into a number of distinct divisions and sub-divisions each of which is charged with the performance of certain governmental functions within its boundaries and is provided with a machinery of governance for that purpose. The result of such territorial divisions and sub-divisions is the existence of national government and a series of local authorities. The functional method is that where the distribution among particular organs or authorities is made in accordance with the character of the functions to be performed. These two are not alternate methods. Both are used in the organisation of all modern governments, but differently, this leads to different characters of the resulting govermental systems.

Division on Territorial Basis. The desirability of distribution of governmental powers among territorial units results not only from the extent of the territory of modern States, but also from the fact that many functions of government affect exclusively, or primarily, the interests of particular localities rather than the country as a whole. It does not, however, mean that one single central authority cannot perform these functions. But if it does, the burden of work and responsibility would be too heavy for effective and efficient administration. It would also result in intolerable expense and delay. Moreover, it is politic to entrust the smaller communities with the affairs that concern them alone, because of the presumption that the people belonging to a particular locality can best know and appreciate their needs. Besides, it gives to a larger number of persons an interest and share in political affairs. "We cannot realise the full benefit of democratic government," says Laski, "unless we begin by the admission that all problems are not central problems, and the results of problems not central in their incidence require decision at the place, and by the persons, where and by whom the incidence is most deeply felt."

The system of territorial sub-division is essentially similar in all modern States. First, for certain purposes which are vital to the life of the nation, the entire country is treated as one political unit and the organisation managing all such affairs is called the Central or National government. Next, the country is divided into a relatively small number of important divisions, variously designated as constituent States, Provinces, and Cantons, etc., with a complete governmental organisation of their own. These grand divisions are, in their turn, further sub-divided into smaller areas known as Districts, Countries, Townships, Communes, etc., each also having its political organisation. Further sub-divisions, if there are any, are usually of a purely administrative character. In addition, all States recognise that urban and rural areas present different problems of government and, consequently, grant to them distinct political organisations for the performance of the governmental duties specially affecting their peculiar interests.

Analysis of the Problem. But the real problem is that of determining how the sum total of governmental powers shall be distributed territorially. If we analyse this problem, it will be found that in it are involved four distinct questions: (1) What authority shall decide the distribution of powers ? (2) What shall be the geographical system of division into different political units? (3) What shall be the powers of the government of each territorial unit? (4) What shall be the type of governmental organization in each territorial unit?

For a student of Political Science the first of these four questions, viz., what authority has the legal right to determine the distribution of governmental power among the different territorial units, is much the most important, for its decision determines the character of the resulting governmental system.

Two Types of Government—Unitary and Federal. Two systems are found in modern States with two types of resulting governments, unitary and federal. A unitary government is a single integrated system of government for the exercise of all powers. The legal sovereign confers all the powers of government in the first instance upon a single central government. The central government may exercise all these powers by itself or create political sub-divisions and delegate to them such powers as it may deem wise to delegate. The central government is competent to change their boundaries as well as powers at its pleasure, by ordinary legislative enactment. A federal government, on the other hand, is a system of government in which powers are divided and distributed between the central government and governments of political divisions. Both sets of governments exercise powers granted to them by the Constitution and are, within a sphere, coordinate and independent, that is, both are free and autonomous within the spheres assigned to them by the Constitution and neither is helplessly dependent on the other for its existence and proper functioning. It means equality of status between the two sets of government; the one is not simply the creation of the other. Both, the national government and the regional governments, enjoy a juridical status and a corporate personality.

Unitary System. Britain, France, Italy, Belgium, Japan, Afghanistan, Iran, and many other countries have unitary governments. There is one integrated system of government and the supreme power belongs to the central. government. For administrative convenience and other considerations the country may be divided into political divisions of different categories, but all authority flows from the central government. These sub-divisions have no original existence of their own. They are the creation of the central government and may be altered at its will. The power exercised by them is only a delegated and subordinate authority which can be increased, diminished or withdrawn at the discretion of the central government. The sub-divisions are, therefore, the agents of the central government and whatever autonomy or governmental competence may have been conceded to them, exists by sufferance rather than by constitutional guarantee.

The real point to know is the authority by which such areas are established and their powers and governmental organisation determined. Britain allows maximum autonomy to her local areas, but they are the creatures of Parliament and all such powers are determined and derived from the Acts of Parliament and can be enlarged or restricted at the will of the government at London. Whitehall also exercises considerable administrative control over all such areas and, as Ogg sums up: "All told however, central control is both wide and deep; not only so, but it is steadily penetrating to new phases and levels."[1]

France is divided into administrative units called "Departments" which are divided into cantons, *arrondissements*, and communes, each having its organs for local administration. But general opinion is that it is almost misleading to talk about local government in France.[2] Centralization is the essence of French local government—"Centralization raised to a superlative degree. All authority converges inward and upward."[3] The local organs are merely agents of the central government. From the communes to the Ministry of Interior the administration is linked up in one chain. The Minister of the Interior just "presses a button—the prefects, sub-prefects and mayors do

1. Ogg, F.A., *English Government and Politics.* p. 366.
2. *Ibid.,* p. 583.
3. Munro, W.B., *The Governments of Europe,* p. 566.

the rest. All the wires run to Paris." Ogg and Zink give a matter of fact summing up of the nature of local government in France. They say, "Not only are there no constitutionally separate spheres of governmental authority, there is really one government, functioning equally through Ministers and Parliament at Paris and prefects and councils throughout the country at large. Local areas have only governing organs, local bodies only such powers as are given to them by national law. All of the threads are gathered ultimately in the hands of the central government at, Paris. More than this, the entire mechanism of departments, *arrondissements* and communes, heads up at a single ministry at the capital, i.e., Interior."[4]

The Government of India, too, was unitary in character under the Act of 1919. Although the Provinces were given a partial responsible government, called *dyarchy*, and the central and provincial subjects were demarcated, normally allowing the Provinces to legislate on provincial subjects, yet the Government of India was supreme in all affairs of Provincial governments, executive and legislative. The Act of 1919 had vested the superintendence, direction and control of the civil and military government of India in the Governor-General-in-Council who was required to give due obedience to all such orders as he might receive from the Secretary of State for India. The Governor-General had wide powers of assenting to, vetoing, or of reserving for the significance, of His Majesty the King-Emperor, and of returning for further consideration bills passed by the Central Legislature. He could exercise similar powers in relation to bills passed by the Provincial legislatures. The Indian Legislature was competent to make laws for all persons and all things within British India, except that the previous sanction of the Governor-General was necessary for the introduction of any measure regulating any provincial subjects as classified according to the Act of 1919. Similarly, the Central Legislature had the power to repeal or amend any law in force in any part of British India, except that the previous sanction of the Governor-General was necessary for introducing a bill, repealing or amending any Act of a Provincial legislature.

Merits of Unitary Government. The unitary type of government represents the most effective type of governmental organisation. The whole problem of the organisation of government is enormously simplified and the system possesses the merit of flexibility. One of the essential features of a good governmental system should be its ability to modify and adjust its organisation, and the manner in which its powers are exercised, as new needs and conditions demand such a change. In a unitary government territorial division of powers is a matter for the government itself to determine; it has, accordingly, full powers to modify its scheme of internal organisation and distribution of powers, as and when need arises.

The outstanding feature of the unitary government, as the name itself implies, is unity. All powers of government are concentrated in the hands of a single set of authorities and all organs of government constitute integral parts of one piece of administrative mechanism. There is uniformity of laws, policy, and administration. All the organs of government can thus be brought to bear directly upon the problems of administration to be solved. There can be no conflict of authority, no conflict or confusion regarding

4. Ogg, F.A. and Zink, H., *Modern Foreign Governments,* p. 583.

responsibility for work to be performed, no over-lapping of jurisdictions, no duplication of work, plant or organization which cannot be immediately adjusted. In the fields of foreign policy and national defence the strength of the centralised government is especially manifest. It exihibits promptness of decision and firmness of action. Unified administration checks centrifugal forces and saves the administration from disruption. The focus of loyalty is not divided; it concentrates at one single point. It, thus, injects a sense of single patriotism and vouches for the unity and integrity of the State. Finally, a unitary government, being simple in organisation, is less expensive. There is no duplication of political institutions.

Defects of Unitary Government. The one major defect which can be ascribed to a unitary government is that it tends to repress local initiative, discourages rather than stimulates interest in public affairs, impairs the vitality of local governments, and facilitates the development of centralised bureaucracy. The present-day central governments, it is maintained, have to tackle so many complex problems, national and international, that they have neither the initiative nor the time to devote to local affairs. Local areas cannot, accordingly, progress. But such a criticism will not hold valid once we distinguish between centralization of authority and centralization of the use of this authority. A really centralised government is one in which the central government, instead of making use of agencies to which large powers of discretion are granted, attempts itself directly to administer local affairs. It is in this sense that France, in comparison with other countries, has a highly centralized government, and not because it has adopted a unitary form of government. There is nothing in the unitary form of government which does not permit decetralization in the actual exercise of governmental powers, or the conferring of autonomy or powers of self-government upon political sub-divisions. All the same, unitary government is best suited for small countries which have a geographical unity and which are racially and culturally homogeneous. It does not suit a country with a large territory and huge population consisting of diverse races and cultures, as India and the United States of America. Only a federation can bring unity out of this diversity.

FEDERAL POLITY

Federal System. The term federation is derived from the Latin word *foedus* meaning treaty or agreement. A federal polity comes into existence either as a result of centripetal or centrifugal forces. When hitherto sovereign and independent States, either because they are too weak to resist foreign aggression individually, or because they remain economically backward by standing alone, voluntarily agree to unite, as in union there lies strength, they form a federal union. Such a union comes into existence as a result of centripetal forces. The instrument by which a federation is brought about is of the nature of a treaty or agreement between independent States and the new unit of government, national or central, which they agree to create. A new State is, thus, created to which the hitherto sovereign States surrender their sovereignty and agree to become its component parts, known by different names—*States* in the United States, Australia and India, *Provinces* in Canada and Pakistan, Cantons in Switzerland, Union *Republics* in the erstwhile Soviet Union, and the *Lands* (Lander) in the former German Federal Republic—in different federal States.

The central or national government, which comes into existence, as a result of such a union, and the resultant new State is entrusted with powers of general character, which concern the nation as a whole. Other subjects, which are of local interest, or in which variety of practice can be peemitted, are left within the jurisdiction of the regional government, States, Provinces or Cantons whatever be their name. The powers so distributed between the two sets of government, central and regional, are protected by the Constitution and neither of the two can encroach upon the jurisdiction of the other or destroy its existence by itself. Alterations can be made by amending the Constitution alone. Sovereignty lies neither in the central government nor in the regional governments. Neither can it be divided between the two, as many writers have held. It resides in the State alone and it is exercised by the authority which has the power to amend the Constitution. In a federation, therefore, separate States disappear, their sovereignty being destroyed; and their citizens having divested themselves of the old allegiance, create, on the basis of a national unity, a federal polity within a new State.

A federation may also come into existence when a unitary State with a large area, which needs unity out of its diversity, divides its power into two sets of government and grants constitutional autonomy to its units. The new apparatus of government comes to be like this: the central government retains only those subjects which are of national importance and transfers the rest to the jurisdiction of the units, each autonomous within the sphere assigned to it. In this case centrifugal forces operate and bring about a federal form of government. For example, the Government of India Act, 1935, envisaged a federation consisting of all the eleven Provinces, which then comprised British India and those Princely States which were to express their desire to accede to the federation after signing the Instrument of Accession.

Whatever be the method of its coming into existence and whatever be the system of division of powers, a federal polity is a dual government, in which powers are divided and distributed by the Constitution between a central government and regional governments. Unlike the unitary government, powers of the units in a federation are original and not derived. They are not the grant of the central government, but the gift of the Constitution and they are constitutionally protected. Both the central and regional governments are coordinate, independent authorities within their allotted spheres of jurisdiction. Neither can encroach upon the powers of the other. If any change is desired to be made in the distribution of powers, it cannot be made by any one of the two sets of government alone. It must be made by amending the Constitution as prescribed by law. This means equality of status and this is the essence of federalism, although equality of status does not necessarily imply absolute equality of powers. This is an impossible task and not within the reach of practical politics. The distribution of powers between the central government and regional governments depends upon various factors and every country has its own peculiar problems. Carl Friedrich observes, "It goes without saying that such divisions of the 'competencies', that is, the sphere within which each may operate, must and will vary according to time and space. Economic and social life, the military and geographical factors, all will play their role in determining the particular arrangement. From a political standpoint, no distinctive generalization or principle can be derived."[5] The balance of

5. Friedrich, C.J., *Constitutional Government and Democracy,* p. 204.

powers is, accordingly, differently tilted in different federations; in some it is in favour of the central government and in others it is in favour of regional governments. But it does not deprive the government of its federal character so long as the one is not rendered helplessly dependent on the other for its existence or proper functioning. By the federal principle, observes Wheare, "I mean the method of dividing powers so that the general and regional governments are each within a sphere, coordinate and independent."[6] The existence of a sphere of activities for either government central and regional—where they are coordinate and independent—is the essential attribute of federalism. Dicey defines federation as a "political contrivance intended to reconcile national unity with the maintenance of State rights", the desire for national unity and determination of each individual unit to maintain its identiy and independence.[7]

The basic features of a federation may, thus, be summarised:

1. A federation is born out of the desire for union rather than unity. Unity is the essence of a unitary system whereas union is the basis of a federation, Federation allows the federating units to preserve their identity by retaining their independent jurisdiction, save in matters that are of common national interest;
2. the States willing to federate lose their sovereign character as soon as a federation is formed. A new State emerges as a result of this union and it, accordingly, becomes sovereign;
3. the mechanism of a federal government consists of two parts, national or central government, and the regional governments called by various names, states and provinces usually;
4. the powers of government are divided and distributed into these two parts. The central government is given jurisdiction over subjects of a general nature, which are common to all and among others those promoting the union. The regional governments are given power over matters of local importance and utility, which do not require uniformity;
5. a federation is made, it does not grow. It is made deliberately with a view to having the benefits of union. And since the union establishes a system of dual government in which powers are divided and distributed, a written Constitution is the logical necessity of such a government;
6. it also involves rigidity of the Constitution so that neither the central government nor the regional governments may be in a position to deprive the other of its powers. If any change is desired to be brought about, it must be made by amending the Constitution wherein both parts of a federation are participants;
7. the process of constitutional amendment is prescribed in the Constitution. This establishes the supremacy of the Constitution. The supremacy of the Constitution is essential, if the government is to be federal;
8. federation is a permanent union in contrast to various other kinds of unions and alliances between States.

Federal and Unitary Governments. In a unitary government there is a single

6. Wheare, K.C., *Federal Government,* p. 11.
7. Dicey, A.V., *Law of the Constitution,* p. 157.

integrated authority and the entire territory of the State forms one single political unit. For administrative convenience, it may be divided into various subdivisions, but they are created, their powers defined and their forms of organisation determined by the central government. Federation is a device towards union and not unity. While making a union, the hitherto sovereign States still desire to retain their individuality, and for that matter, all issues involved are decided by common agreement and all this is incorporated in the Constitution of the newly established State. The Constitution clearly defines the jurisdiction of the two sets of government, national and regional, it establishes and any change desired to be made therein can be effected by amending the Constitution in accordance with the prescribed procedure.

It means equality of status between the two sets of government and this is one of the cardinal principles of a federal polity. In a unitary government, it is not so. The central government is supreme and its various political sub-divisions are subordinate to it. The central government can make and unmake them, enlarge or diminish their authority at will, as and when it deems necessary. In a federation, the Constitution is supreme.

All cases of conflict of jurisdiction between the central government and the units of a federation or between one unit and another are decided by an impartial judiciary, called the Supreme or the Federal Court. It is the guardian of the Constitution and it can declare any law, federal or that enacted by any of the units, or an executive order unconstitutional and, consequently, inoperative. A unitary government does not need such a process, because the powers of the various sub-divisions are not their original powers. They are delegated to them by the central government and what it delegates it can withdraw, diminish or increase. The authority of the central government in this respect is undisputed and unchallengeable.

In a federation there are two sets of laws as there are two sets of government, each government legislating on subjects assigned to its jurisdiction. A citizen of a federal State must obey the laws enacted by the national as well as local governments. It also envisages double citizenship. In a unitary system of government there is single citizenship and a uniform system of law prevails throughout, as in Britain and France. All this means that the loyalty of a citizen is divided and local jealousies and dissensions plague the federal system. A unitary system of government does not suffer from any of these drawbacks.

Federation and Confederation. Sometimes the terms federation and confederation are used interchangeably as if they are one and carry the same meaning and set up a similar form of government. For example, the Swiss Constitution of 1874 is entitled Swiss Confederation and the use of the term is continued in the Preamble and various Articles of the Constitution. Even a modern authority like Dicey uses the terms interchangeably in a single sentence.[8] A federation and a confederation resemble one another inasmuch as both the words come from the same root; otherwise there is a fundamental difference between the two. "A confederation," says Hall, "is a union strictly of independent States which consent to forego permanently a part of their liberty of action for certain specific objects, and they are not so combined under a common government that the latter appears to their exclusion as the international entity."

8. Dicey A.V., *Law of the Constitution,* p. 603.

A Confederation is an association of sovereign States formed for the purpose of promoting or achieving certain specific objects. They unite on a basis of equality and the most obvious motive for such a union is to gain security and strength in foreign relations and economic matters. A central organisation is set up, usually consisting of a congress of delegates, who represent the governments of the States composing the Confederation. The delegates usually vote by States and under instructions from the governments that they represent. The member-States retain their sovereignty and they do not create a new State. The instrument which creates a Confederation and defines the powers of the central organisation so created, is of the nature of a compact or treaty among sovereign States. It has certain powers, as defined in the treaty, over the member-States, but has nothing to do with the citizens of these States. Any member of a Confederation may withdraw therefrom. A confederacy, in the words of Oppenheim, consists of "a number of full sovereign States linked together for the maintenance of their external and internal independence by a recognised international treaty into a union with organs of its own, which are vested with a certain power over the member 'States', but not over the citizens of these States"[9]

Confederations have been numerous in the historical development of the State. More recent examples were the old German Confederation from 1815 to 1866, the Swiss Confederacy from 1815 to 1840, and the union of the Thirteen American States under the Articles of Confederation from 1781 to 1789.

A Confederation is similar to a Federation in two respects. Both in a Confederation and a Federation different States associate with one another for certain specific purposes, and in both cases a central authority is established for the realisation of common objects. Beyond this the similarity does not go and the differences between the two appear fundamental. The most important difference between the two is that the States entering a Confederacy preserve their full independence and sovereignty and that the States entering a Federation lose them. According to the expressive German term, the former is a *staatenbund* or league of States, and the latter is a *bundesstaat* or a united State. Through Federation one State appears in the place of several; through Confederation no such change occurs. A Confederation does not bring a new State into being; it only creates a new relationship between the existing States.

A Federation is created by a Constitution which is legally a law, and which depends upon the consent of the people. A Confederation, on the other hand, is created by an agreement or a compact which is of the nature of an international treaty concluded by the confederating States and, accordingly, it rests upon the consent of the member-States. A Federation is a permanent union and it is illegal for the units composing it to secede or withdraw therefrom. But the confederating States may withdraw from the union whenever they desire and when they do so, their action is not illegal, though it may be deemed a violation of international good faith. If there is armed conflict between the various units of a Federation, as there was once between the Northern and Southern States of America on the question of slavery, it is a civil war. If hostilities break out between two or more confederating units, then, it is an international war and not a civil war.

9. Oppenheim, M., *International Law*, Vol. I, p. 178.

The national or central government in a Federation is created by the Constitution and its powers are defined therein. The federating units can neither destroy the central government nor modify its powers on their own initiative, That can only be done by amending the Constitution and according to the prescribed method. But in a Confederation the member-States create the central authority, sometimes called even government, which they can destroy, or widen or narrow its powers. Control of such an authority or a government over the member-States in a Confederation may be of a shadowy sort. Under the Articles of Confederation, the Congress in the United States could requisition the States for soldiers and money upon a fixed system of quotas and make treaties with foreign countries. But while the States were bound by the agreement to honour the requisition and comply with the treaties, there were no means of compelling them to do so; the power of the Congress was only recommendatory and not mandatory. Finally, a Federation deals with the citizens of a federal State; in a Confederation the common organ of authority deals with governments of the member-States; it is a union of States and not of the people. A Confederation has no citizens or subjects to whom its commands can be directly addressed. To sum up:

1. A Federation makes a new State as a result of the union of hitherto sovereign States whereas a Confederation remains an agglomeration of independent and sovereign States.
2. A Federation creates a new one single sovereignty, but in a Confederation there are as many sovereignities as the number of sovereign States composing it.
3. A Federation creates a new nation. It is not so in a Confederation. There are as many nations as States composing a Confederation. Each State remains an international entity.
4. A Federation is a permanent union and is indissoluble. A Confederation is temporary and the member-States can withdraw therefrom at their will. Confederate authorities have no constitutional power to compel a dissatisfied member to remain within the Confederation.
5. In case of conflict between the various units of a Federation, it is a civil war. But war between the member-States of a Confederation would be an international war.
6. In a Federation there are two sets of government with powers divided between the two as prescribed by the Constitution. In a Confederation every member-State has its own system and machinery of government unrelated to others in any manner. Similarly, every State has its own laws and its own citizenship distinct from others.
7. The statutes and laws in a Federation are made by its legislative assemblies, both central and regional. The rules and regulations which govern a Confederation are the result of the conference of the member-States wherein their nominees participate.
8. A Federation is a union of the people. A Confederation is a union of the States. Both are in the nature of an alliance. But a Federation is a permanent Union whereas a Confederation is a temporary alliance.

Prerequisites of a Federal Polity. A federal polity envisages a dual government of divided powers. The division between the two sets of government rests upon the basic principle that there is a single independent authority for the whole country in respect of some matters that are of national importance and concern the interests of the community as a whole and that there are independent regional authorities for other matters of local importance, and each set of authorities is coordinate with and not subordinate to the other within its own prescribed sphere. Such a system of government demands the presence of certain conditions which should exist to pave the way for a federation to materialize. According to Dicey there should be, in the first place, a strong desire to have a union. The will to have a union and to be under a single independent government for some purposes is really the basis of a Federation. It means that the federating units must be inspired and bound together by a sense of oneness with a desire to objectify it politically. Unless they become a community of interests, sharing each other's weal and woe, their cohesion into a new State is extremely difficult. The second requisite condition is that the federating States must desire union rather than unity, that is, while there should be a desire on the part of the federating States for national unity and to be under a single independent government, they must desire, at the same time, to maintain their individuality and autonomous existence by establishing independent regional governments in some matters at least. The aim of federalism is to give effect to both these sentiments. It is in this context that Dicey defined a Federation as a political contrivance intended to reconcile national unity and power with the maintenance of State rights. Or to express it in the words of Wheare, the group of States or communities "must desire to be united, but not to be unitary."10

But this is not all.Something more is needed. There should not be the desire to have a Federation, but the power or ability to operate it as well as to maintain it. The States or communities desiring to have a Federation, explains Wheare, "must have the capacities to work the system they desire. Federal government is not appropriate unless the communities concerned have the capacity as well as the desire to form an independent general government and to form independent regional governments." The factors which determine their desire or aspirations as well as their capacities to make them operative ideals may be called the prerequisites of a federal polity. It may, however, be noted that it is unlikely that all these factors will be present among States desiring union, but it is necessary that most of them must be present if the federal system is to work smoothly and efficiently.

One of the main incentives to closer association is a feeling of homogeneity; what Mill calls mutual sympathies among the population. "The sympathies available for the purpose," he says, "are those of race, language, religion, and above all, of political institutions as conducing most to a feeling of identity of political interest."[11] In his earlier enumeration of the factors making for nationalism, Mill included geographical unity and common memories, that is, a common historical tradition. Obviously, both should appear here. Geographical unity and common historical traditions help to create a sense of oneness even if other factors do not exist. Mill observes that people may bind themselves together in resistance to oppression. The Swiss did so and they continued to cooperate in spite of the diversity of language and religion, at a time when religion was the grand source of irreconcilable political enmity throughout Europe. Exposed frontiers

10. Wheare, K.C., *Federal Government*, p. 36.
11. Mill, J.S., *Representative Government*, p. 36.

and the danger of aggression from avaricious neighbours dictate union for the purposes of defence. The greater the menace, the closer will be the union. In Canada the desire to union arose in spite of differences of language, religion and race. And the union of South Africa occurred in spite of similar differences between the Dutch and the English, who inhabited the country.

It will, thus, be clear that strong as the forces of language, race, religion and nationality are in producing a desire for union, such a desire can nonetheless be produced among people who differ in all these particulars, but possess a sentiment of union, that is, a common sentiment that in union lies strength and this strength can be achieved by a political cohesion. The sentiment of unity," says Gilchrist, "is the index of a common mind."[12] A great deal, therefore, depends upon the political leadership or statesmanship at the right time, which helps to combat the forees of racial, religious and linguistic differences and instil in the people instead a desire to unite itself. The desire for union in Canada was made effective by the leadership of men like John Macdonald, Alexander Galt and George Etienne. In America the people had a community of language, race and religion and similarity of political institutions, but these factors had failed to produce anything beyond a Confederation. It was under the leadership of Washington, Hamilton, Madison, Jay, Benjamin Franklin and James Wilson that the delegates at the Philadelphia Convention of 1787, "with a manly confidence" in their country, threw the Articles of Confederation aside and designed to bring unity into the diversity of the new nation." But it happened the other way in India. The Muslim League, under the inspiration of Mohammed Ali Jinnah, had all through relied upon the theory of a separate Muslim nation and the creation of a separate homeland for Muslims. If the separatist tendencies based upon race, religion and language had not been fostered so assiduously by the Muslim leadership, the result would have been a united Indian federation rather than the division of the country into two parts, India and Pakistan. "This factor of leadership, of skill in negotiation and propaganda, can make," observes Wheare, "all the difference between stagnation and an active desire for union."[13]

The areas having the desire to federate should be geographically contiguous, that is to say, the States desiring to federate, or to be brought within the fold of a federation as a result of centrifugal forces, should not be separated from one another by distant spaces of land and water. They must exist in the vicinity of one another, for neighbourhood makes them a community of interests and the desire for union is inspired by the needs of common defence, common economic advantages, and similarity of institutions. Geographical contiguity also helps to produce the capacity to work a federal union. A federal government demands of units to run their own administration as well as to participate in the federal government. "Distance leads to carelessness or callousness," says Gilchrist, "on the part of both central and local governments. National unity is difficult to attain where the people are too far apart."[14] The benefits of common defence and the economic advantages from union cannot be adequately secured. One of the

12. Gilchrist, R.N., *Principles of Political Science,* p. 359.
13. Wheare, K.C., *Federal Government*, p. 40.
14. Gilchrist, R.N., *Principles of Political Science,* p. 359.

causes of the success of federalism in America is the continguity of all the States. So are the Cantons of Switzerland, the Provinces of Canada and the States of Australia. The Indian Federation also commands contiguity of its component States. But there was no contiguity of area between the two parts of Pakistan. West Pakistan was separated from its eastern counterpart by a wide stretch of land. The erstwhile East Pakistan was land-locked by Indian territory and this separation was, *inter alia*, one of the causes of the secession of East Pakistan from West Pakistan and the establishment by the former of the new State of Bangladesh.

Of all the factors which produce the desire for union, similarity of social institutions and particularly political institutions is the one which is very important, because it produces best the capacity for union. Wheare remarks that the desire for union has practically never been aroused unless similarity of political institutions "was present actually or potentially among those who envisaged the union." Similarity of institutions creates conditions of common political structure which, in its turn, makes possible the development of a common political culture. It is essentially for this reason that the system of government established at the centre finds its replica in the federating units also. The Constitutions of the United States and Switzerland both require that their respective units must have a republican form of government. In Canada, Australia and India the parliamentary system of government has been explicitly established in all the units.

Not only is it desirable that there should be similarity of political institutions in the rederating units, but it is also essential that these institutions should not be autocratic or dictatorial. "For autocracy or dictatorship, either in the generall government or in the regional governments, seems certain, sooner or later, to destroy that equality of status and that independence which these governments must enjoy, each in its own sphere, if federal government is to exist at all."[15] Limited and free government is the most important feature of federalism and the system of government which it establishes must, therefore, ensure free elections and a party system and the existence of an Opposition. There can be no free elections where there is autocracy and the representatives in the government are the nominees of the autocrats in the regions. Dictatorship is a one party government and it does not permit existence of an Opposition. Elections are just a routine affair wherever dicatorship has existed. This is the negation of free elections and, as such, incompatible with the working of the federal principle. Carl Friedrich says that federalism is an integral part of modern constitutionalism. "A federal government structure," he explains, "provides a spatial or territorial, as distinguished from a functional division of powers. Such a division operates as a rather effective restraint upon the abuse of governmental powers by the central authorities."[16]

It would have been difficult to operate a union between the Provinces and Princely States as envisaged in the Government of India Act; 1935. The proposed federation would have been a combination of strange bed-fellows. The Provinces were given, under the Act of 1935, provincial autonomy with representative institutions and a responsible form of government whereas the States were to continue under the personal rule of the Princes. The representatives of the Indian States in the central legislature would have

15. Wheare, K.C., *Federal Government,* p. 47.
16. Friedrich, C.J., *Constitutional Government and Democracy,* p. 220.

been the nominees of their rulers and not elected representatives of the peoples of the States. The British Government, in the words of Sir Samuel Hoare, the then Secretary of State for India, had really intended to counterpoise democracy with aristocracy. Before inaugurating the new Constitution of India in 1950, which declares India a Union of States, all the Princely States were liquidated and homogeneous political institutions established in all the component States of the Union. The States Reorganisation Act, 1956, abolished the distinction between Part A, B and C States, which the Constitution had established in 1950. The States Reorganisation Commission aptly remarked that the "only rational approach to the problem, in our opinion, will be that the Indian Union should have primary constituent units having equal status and a uniform relationship with the centre, except where, for any strategic security or other compelling reasons, it is not practicable to integrate any small area with the territories of a full-fledged units."[17]

Similarly, there should be similarity of social institutions generally. It is true that the desire for union can be created in spite of dissimilarities of social institutions, as happened in the United States and Canada, "but such differences," says Wheare, "do make a government more difficult, and there is a limit to the degree of dissimilarity which can be permitted. The capacity to work together cannot survive in extreme divergence."[18] The capacity of States to form and work a federal union, he adds, "depends upon some agreement to differ but not to differ too much."[19] A stable federalism demands a considerable capacity to agree in practice upon what is a matter for unity and what is a matter for diversity. It is, accordingly essential that the nature of the diversity and of the unity be such that, in practice, views can be adjusted and the differences reconciled. There should be a common meeting ground upon national policy as well as upon the local liberties of the constituent units.

The capacity of States to work a federal union is also greatly influenced by their size. It is desirable that there should be, as far as possible, equality among the component parts of a Federation in their size and population. If there are wide differences in size and population, as in India where the States of Uttar Pradesh, Madhya Padesh, Bihar and Rajasthan are in no comparison with the small states of Punjab, Haryana, Sikkim, Goa and many others, the federating States are not equal partners in a union. Units larger in size and population and more powerful in resources than others may be too proud and domineering for smaller ones. They may even overrule the others and bend the will of the central government to themselves. The idea of dominance by some creates suspicion and lack of confidence in others. Confidence is the essence of the will to federate and the capacity to work the federal government. The essential prerequisite of a federation, says Mill, is that there "should not be any one State so much more powerful that the rest as to be capable of vying in strength with many of them combined. If there be such a one, and only one, it will insist on being master of the joint deliberations; if there be two, they will be irresistible when they agree and whenever they differ everything will be decided by a struggle for ascendency between the rivals."[20]

17. *Report of the States Reorganisation Commission,* para, 237.
18. Wheare, K.C., *Federal Government,* p. 48.
19. *Ibid,* p. 49.
20. Mills, J.S., *Representative Government,* pp. 367-8.

It is true that some divergence in size between the units must necessarily be present before a federal union is desired and this is an important factor in the making and maintenance of federal systems today. But "there must be" succinctly observes Wheare, "some sort of reasonable balance which will ensure that all the units can maintain their independence within the sphere allotted to them and that no one can dominate the others. It must be the task of those who frame and work a federal government to see that no unit shall be too large, and, equally important, none too small."[21] Equality of the federated units is a key to federal organization.

Finally, the federating States must possess adequate economic resources to support both an independent national government and independent regional governments. A federal government establishes a new national government and it must be given sufficient independent economic resources if it is to perform its duties efficiently and effectively. Likewise, it is also imperative that the regional governments must also be left with adequate economic resources to run their administrations and perform the functions assigned to them satisfactorily without being dependent on the doles of the national government. If the resources left are not sufficient to support an independent regional government, "then no matter how much states desire a federal union and no matter whether a federal constitution is drawn up, in practice federal government will not be possible. Soon the regional governments will be unable to perform their functions or they will be able to perform them only at the price of financial dependence upon the general government, that is, at the price of financial unification." One of the reasons for which the leaders in South Africa rejected a federal union was that the country would be unduly taxed if they were required to support both a central government as well as independent regional governments. A federation is an expensive mechanism and it should be adopted only when the constitutent units can pay the price of retaining their separate identity and independence of action in the sphere assigned to them.

American Federalism, the Start of an Invention. Federalism is of extreme modernity. Its theory and practice in the modern States are not older than the American federation, which came into existence in 1787. Prior to 1776, the thirteen Colonies were severally and separately bound to Britain. In no way were they connected together. The Declaration of Independence announced the Colonies States, each independent of the Crown and politically independent of each other. But to declare independence, to fight and win the war against British Imperialism, and to build a new nation, required union and the result was a Confederation, a "firm league of friendship" under the name of the United States. The declared purpose of the Confederation was to provide for the common defence of the States the security of their liberties, and their mutual and general welfare.

The war against the British ended and the Treaty of 1783 acknowledged the independence, freedom and sovereignty of the thirteen Colonies. But the Confederation became a league of disgruntled independents, which revealed the powerlessness of the Congress created under the Articles of Confederation. It lacked the authority to weld the States into a unity, to mitigate their commercial rivalries, to establish a sound currency, to remove the causes of domestic disorders, and to foster American interests abroad.

21. Wheare, K.C., *Federal Government*, p. 53.

Washington, Hamilton, Madison and many others, who had laboured to bring together the States in bonds of union, were convinced that the government of the Confederation must either be revised or superseded entirely by a new system. Washington wrote, "I do not conceive that we can exist long as a nation without having lodged somewhere a power which will pervade the whole nation in as energetic a manner as the authority of the State Governments extends over the several States." They all experienced the feeling that all America should be one, a feeling which cements the bonds of oneness, giving birth to a nation. "We are now a new nation," said Rush, ".... the more a man aims at serving America, the more be serves his colony. We have been too free with the word—independence; we are dependent on each other, not totally independent States ... when I entered that door I considered myself a citizen of America."

Here are the germs of a union which now carries the nomenclature of a federal government. The delegates to the Philadelphia Convention of 1787, who were sent by the States for the purpose of preparing a revision of the Articles of Confederation, went beyond their instructions and drafted a new constitution without knowing that they were devising an entirely novel and ingenious scheme of government, and that it would become a distinctive and influential contribution of America to the art of government. And here is the illustrious example of right leadership at the right moment.

The Founding Fathers sought to remove the two principal defects of the Articles of the Confederation: (1) to remove the predominance of the parts over the whole and to reconcile two different powers, the power of the States and the power of the central government; and (2) to remove the dependence of the government at the centre upon the governments of the States that acted as intermediaries between it and the individual. They adopted the principle that the functions and powers of the national government being new, general and inclusive, had to be carefully defined and stated, while all other functions and powers were to belong to the States. To make the powers of the central government real, they accepted the fact that it be empowered, among other things, to coin money, to regulate commerce, to declare war, to make peace, and to levy taxes. The central government was endowed with a Congress, to make laws on subjects assigned to its jurisdiction; an executive with adequate means of enforcement; and a judiciary with authority to preserve an equilibrium between the whole and parts and to uphold the supremacy of the Constitution. Above all, the national government was to derive its support and mandate from the people as voters and to carry its services directly to them as individuals.

Other Countries that Followed. Once the example of the United States had demonstrated that a federal union could work successfully, a precedent was established that others, whose situations were similar, could follow. The first to do so was Switzerland. In 1847, the Swiss Confederation was convulsed by an attempt of seven Catholic Cantons to secede. The Protestant majority crushed the secessionists, who had formed a separate league called the *Sounderbund.* The defeat of the seven Cotholic Cantons was, in fact, the triumph of the movement of national unity. Next year the Swiss Diet approved a new constitution which created a federal union closely patterned on that of the United States.

The next to adopt this system was Canada in 1867, although the Canadian federation was produced by a different combination of factors. The direct cause of the federal movement was the racial conflict between the British and French "national groups, two nations warring within the bosom of a single State" as the Durham Report had lamented, which rendered the unitary government unworkable. Economic problems also plagued a divided Canada. Nor was defence unimportant. In 1864, a coalition government took office, pledging unification. The final outcome was the North America Act, 1867, and the Dominion of Canada was established. The scheme of distribution of powers between the Centre and the Provinces was just the reverse of the American model and it was essentially due to the lessons of America's civil war of 1860. The Provinces were given exclusive legislative control over a list of enumerated subjects, reserving the rest for the Dominion. The Dominion government was also given the power to disallow any Act passed by a provincial legislature, to appoint the Lieutenant-Governor of a Province, and to instruct him to withhold his assent from provincial bills and to reserve them for consideration of the Governor-General, who might refuse assent to such reserved bills. Finally, appointments to all the important judicial posts were placed in the hands of the Dominion executive.

In the formation of the Australian federation the need for common defence was probably the strongest, though economic issues were also involved. The Commonwealth came into existence on January 1, 1901. The Constitution enumerated substantial powers for the federal government, the residue remaining in the hands of the States. The main taxation powers were given to the federal government with three-quarters of the revenues to be returned to the States during the first ten years.

The Soviet Union adopted the federal form of government as a concession to the various nationalities and tribes inhabiting Russia, with a view to building a strong and powerful State. Lenin characterised federalism as a step towards "the most solid unification of the different nationalities into a single, democratic, centralised Soviet State." The Constitution of 1936 gave certain specified powers to the Union government and left the residuary powers with the constituent Republics; and each Republic exercised its authority independently of the central government. The Constitution also gave to the constituent Republics the right to secede. The 1977 Constitution closely followed the federal pattern set by its predecessor Constitution.

When India became independent, the Government of India Act, 1935. provided a working machine in the Provinces, and, as Jenning correctly points out, "it was not possible to start afresh when Provinces became States." The scheme of federation under the Constitution of 1950 is fundamentally the same as that under the Act of 1935. There are three lists of subjects, the Union List, the State List and the Concurrent List, exhaustively enumerated in the Constitution, and the residuary powers rest in Parliament. The Constitution empowers the Union Governments to give directions to the States and failure to comply with such directions entitles the President of India to supersede a State government for the time being and thereby bring it under the unitary rule of the Union. State Governors are appointed by the President and a State government can be superseded on a report from the Governor. The Governor may reserve a bill passed by the State legislature for the consideration of the President. The Upper House of the Union Parliament may, by resolution passed by two-thirds majority, declare a particular subject or subjects in the State List to be of national importance and interest, empowering Parliament to make laws thereupon. Then, there are the Emergency Powers of the President. When the

Proclamation of Emergency is in operation, Parliament is empowered to make laws for the whole or any part of the territory of India with respect to any matter contained in the State List. Finally, the Union Parliament is also empowered to pass legislation implementing any treaty, agreement or convention with another country.

Methods of Distribution of Powers. These variations on the federal theme show that two methods have been adopted in the distribution of powers between the central government and the regional governments. The system of the United States, Switzerland and Australia are that their central govern-ments have been given enumerated powers whereas the residuary powers are left with their State governments. For the United States this point is covered by the Tenth Amendment which provides that "the powers not delegated to the United States by the Constitution nor prohibited by it to the States, are reserved to the States respectively, or to the people." The Swiss Constitution expressly declares that the Cantons "are sovereign in so far as their sovereignty is not limited by the Federal Constitution, and, as such they exercise all rights which are not transferred to the Federal power." The reasons for the adoption of this system are largely historical. The federal union was, in each case, formed by the union of previously independent sovereign States. At the time of the union, the latter desired to retain to themselves all governmental power except such as was plainly necessary to confer upon the central government in order that an effective union might be established.

In Canada the method adopted was just the reverse of that in the United States and Switzerland. Here, too, historical events determined the course. "All Constitutions," as Jennings remarks, "are the heirs of the past as well as the testators of the future." The presistent racial conflict between the British and the French and the failure of the unitary government, coupled with the cool relations with the United States, enforced the argument for unification and for a national authority. Federal government seemed the obvious solution. But the experience of the near-dissolution of the American Union in the Civil War led British and Canadian statesmen to the conclusion that the central government must possess more powers than those that belonged to its counterpart in the United States The Canadian Constitution—the British North America Act, 1867—accordingly divided the powers between the Provincial and Dominion governments in such a way that the Provinces had exclusive control over a list of enumerated subjects, and the Dominion had exclusive control over the rest, which "for greater clarity" were enumerated, though not exhaustively. The legislatures of Dominion and the Provinces are distinct from each other; neither has the power to alter the Constitution so far as the distribution of powers is concerned. In Canada, therefore, enumerated powers are given to the Provinces and residuary powers are left to the Dominion government.

The Constitution of India contains three lists of subjects, the Union List, the State List and the Concurrent List, and the residuary powers rest in Parliament. The total number of subjects exclusively given to the Central government are ninety-seven as compared with sixty-six which are under the actual exclusive control of the States. The Concurrent List contains forty-seven subjects upon which both Union and State legislatures make laws. Here is an enumeration more than anything attempted in any other federation. The provisions which deal with a conflict between the Union and State laws are interesting.[22] In general, they require that State laws on concurrent subjects must give

22. Article 254.

way to the laws of the Union government to the extent of their repugnancy to such laws. The Union legislature has also been empowered to legislate on any matter in the State List, if the Council of States (Rajya Sabha) passes a resolution by a two-thirds majority, declaring a particular subject or subjects of national imortance or interest.[23] When Emergency is in operation Parliament makes laws for the whole or any part of the territory of India with respect to any matter enumerated in th State List.[24] Article 253 further empowers Parliament to pass legislation implementing any treaty, agreement or convention with any other country. The last phrase is remarkably vague, as Jennings maintains, because under this provision the Union Parliament can acquire jurisdiction on any subject, as for example, even over university education "by the simple process of decision of the Inter-University Board of India which is an international body because it contains representatives of universities in Burma and Ceylon."[25]

B. R. Ambedkar, Law Minister, in the Government of India and the principal architect of the Constitution, admitted in the Constituent Assembly that "the constitution has not been set in a tight-mould of federalism." The federal principle has, indeed, been so much modified by unitary elements in the form of control by the Central government over the State governments and the intervention in the conduct of affairs of the State governments has become so proverbial[26] that the Indian Constitution, many critics maintain, cannot claim to establish a federal union. And the Constitution nowhere uses the word federation. The omission is deliberate and shows the intentions of the authors of the Constitution. It is true that the federal principle has been introduced into the terms of the Constitution to some extent and Wheare deems it "justifiable to describe it as a quasi-federal constitution,"[27] but a system of government in which one partner can unmake another cannot claim to have even the semblance of a federation. The Indian Constitution may have the form of a federation, but to have federal form does not make it a federation. A Federation is a partnership among equals; oneness of the State with the separateness of the units is its formula, although equality of status does not mean absolute equality of powers.

There are some students of federalism who hold that the federal principle consists in the division of powers in such a way that the powers to be exercised by the central government are enumerated in the Constitution and the residue is left to the regional governments. It is not enough for federalism, they assert, that the central and regional governments should each be independent in its own sphere That sphere must be marked in a particular way, that is, the residuary powers must lie with the regional governments. Applying this criterion, a government is not federal if the powers of the regional governments are specified and the residue is left to the central government. The Constitutions of the United States, Switzerland and Australia embody the federal principle, because they distinctly enumerate subjects over which their central legislatures exercise

23. Article 249.
24. Article 250.
25. *Same Charactertics of the Indian Constitution*, p. 66.
26. Refer to Anup Chand Kapur's Government of Indian Republic, Chap. IV.
27. Wheare, K.C., Federal Government, p. 28.

control and they further provide that powers not so given to the central governments remain with their states and Cantons.

But such a test of federalism, in the opinion of Wheare, concentrates on a relatively superficial characteristic. "The essential point," he says, "is not that the division of powers is made in such a way that the regional governments are the residuary legatees under the constitution, but that the division is made in such a way that, whoever has the residue, neither general nor regional government is subordinate to the other."[28] It is, no doubt, true that the question of residuary power is important as it affects the balance of power in a federation, but this factor itself does not make a government federal. The fundamental point in a federal principle is whether the powers of government are divided between coordinate, independent authorities or not. It is im-material what the system of distribution of powers is and where the residuary power rests. The circumstances of each country decide which method is adopted. Carl Friedrich points out, "The existence of residuary powers has ever been held to constitute the decisive test of 'statehood' for the component units. In reality, such residuary powers are an illusion, if the powers and functions delegated to the central government are practically all-embracing, as they were in Weimar Germany, broad delegated powers would mean more 'local government' in actual practice than such a residue of 'genuine' self-determination'. In either case, the only guaranty (guarantee) for whatever distribution of functions there is, delegated or residuary, is the constitution which determines the governmental structure as a whole."[29]

What distinguishes a federal from a unitary government is that the regional governments are not subordinate to the central government; the one is not simply the creation of the other. Both enjoy a juridical and corporate personality, no matter whether division of powers is made by enumerating the powers of the central government and leaving the rest for the regional governments, or the division is made by enumerating the powers of both the central and regional governments and leaving the residue to the former. What made the Canadian Constitution "quasi-federal" was the matters in which the Provincial Governments were subordinate to the Central Government, and not coordinate, with it. These matters were: the power of the Dominion executive to disallow any Act passed by a Provincial legislature even if it fell within its sphere of jurisdiction, the Dominion executive appointed the Lieutenant-Governor of a Province, and it could instruct a Lieutenant-Governor to withhold his assent form Provincial bills and to reserve them for consideration by the Dominion executive, and it might refuse assent to such reserved bills if it deemed fit.

These are all unitary elements in an otherwise strictly federal form of constitution. But the law of the constitution is one thing; the practice is another, thus, signifying the difference between a federal constitution and a federal government. Wheare places particular emphasis on this difference and says, "A country may have a federal constitution, but in practice it may work that constitution in such a way that its government is not federal. Or a country with a non-federal constitution may work it, in such a way that it provides the example of federal government." In actual practice the unitary elements

28. *Ibid* p. 13.

29. Carl, J. Friedrich., *Constitutional Government and Democracy* p. 204.

in Canada had either become obsolete or were being so worked as not to compromise with the federal principle. "If Canada, therefore," as Wheare says, "has not a federal constitution, it has a federal government." The United States, Switzerland and Australia have federal Constitutions as well as federal governments, though the process of centralisation in all these countries is assuming alarming proportions.

A concurrent jurisdiction is found in all modern federal governments and with it a provision that when the laws of the central government upon matters in the concurrent field conflict with the laws of the regional governments in that field, then, the regional laws must give way to the central laws to the extent of their repugnancy. The extent of the concurrent jurisdiction varies greatly. In Canada it consists of only two subjects whereas in the United States and Australia the concurrent field is extensive. In Switzerland it is smaller than in the United States and Australia, though wider than in Canada. In India, the concurrent list covers forty-seven subjects. Concurrent jurisdiction is not incompatible with the federal principle. There are, indeed, many good reasons for providing concurrent jurisdiction.[30] Wheare is of the opinion that "it is better always, if possible, to admit concurrent jurisdiction. if only perhaps, as a transitional measure. In most cases it will be unavoidable. But what is likely to work best is a short exclusive list and a rather longer concurrent list."[31]

Doctrine of Implied Powers. The Doctrine of Implied Powers has assumed a very great constitutional importance ever since it was propounded by the Supreme Court of the United States. The Constitution only enumerates the powers assigned to the Central government, leaving the rest to the State governments. But the concluding part of Article VIII, enumerating these powers, authorises Congress "To make all laws which shall be necessary and proper for carrying into execution the foregoing powers and all other powers vested by this Constitution in the Government of the United States, or in any Department or officer thereof." Chief Justice Marshall came to the conclusion that this provision authorised the Congress to make laws on subjects, though not specifically assigned, yet implied or latent in some other specified powers. This doctrine of Implied Powers "is imperceptibly pervading the decisions of Supreme Courts in almost all federations thus filling up a gap in the specification of powers" and thereby strengthening the Central government where it has been assigned certain specified powers. Referring to Article VIII of the American Constitution, Charles Beard remarks that it has really proved a Pandora's box of wonders.

ESSENTIALS OF FEDERAL GOVERNMENT

The division of powers between central and regional governments, involves three consequences. First, the arrangement must be embodied in a written constitution, secondly, the constitution must be rigid, and, finally, the presence of a federal Court.

1. A Written Constitution. For a federal government the Constitution must almost necessarily be a written Constitution which defines the relation between the Central

30. Report of Joint Select Committee on Indian Constitutional Reform, 1934, para, 51.
31. Wheare, K.C., *Federal Government*, p. 83.

government and the regional governments, marks out the sphere of each, and is paramount over the Constitutions of the regional governments, if each component part of the union has its own separate Constitution. "To base an arrangement of this kind", writes Dicey, "upon understandings or conventions would be certain to generate misunderstandings and disagreements."[32] The articles of the treaty, or in other words of the constitution, must, therefore, be reduced to writing; the constitution must be a written document for it is the "charter of rights and duties of the federal and state authorities."[33] Wheare says, that if the government is to be federal, its constitution must be supreme. By the supremacy of the constitution he means that "the terms of the agreement which establishes the general and regional governments and which distributes power between them must be binding upon the general and regional governments. This is a logical necessity from the definition of federal government itself."[34] If the Central government and the regional governments are to be coordinate with each other, neither must be in a position to override the provisions of the constitution regarding the powers and status which each is to enjoy. Definiteness of constitutional status and powers stimulates the will to federate and creates confidence in the federating units that the sanctity of their spheres of jurisdiction will be maintained. In case of invasion on their rights and encroachment on their constituent functions there are constitutional remedies to seek judicial redress. The power of judicial review is inherent in a federal polity.

2. A Rigid Constitution. The natural corollary of the supremacy of the constitution, and it being a written document, is that it should not be alterable either by the central legislature or by regional legislatures under their ordinary law-making procedure. "The law of the constitution," says Dicey, "must either be immutable, or else capable of being changed only by some authority above and beyond the ordinary legislative bodies, whether federal or state legislatures, existing under the constitution."[35] It is essential for a federal government, says Wheare, that the power of amending the constitution, "so far at least as concerns those provisions of the constitution which regulate the status and powers of the general and regional governments, should not be confined exclusively either to the general government or to the regional government."[36] If it is confined exclusively to one set of the government, it does not give equality of status to both and it is also probable that the one which possesses this power may in an ordinary process of legislation make an invasion on the powers of jurisdiction of the other.

It does not matter legally where the power of amending the constitution is placed, but "there can be no doubt," as Wheare suggests, "that practically it is wise to associate both the general government and the regions, either their governments or their peoples, in the process" of amending the constitution. In the United States amendments to the constitution may be proposed by a majority of two-thirds of both Houses of Congress or by a convention summoned by Congress on the application of the legislatures of two-thirds of States. The proposed amendments become effective when ratified by the legislatures of

32. Dicey. A.V., *Law of the Constitution,* p. 142.
33. Strong, C.F., *Modern Political Constitutions,* p. 101.
34. Wheare K C., *Federal Government,* p. 55.
35. Dicey, A.V., *Law of the Constitution,* 142.
36. Wheare, K.C., *Federal Government,* p. 57.

three-fourths of the States or by conventions in three-fourths of the States according to the one or the other method of ratification proposed by Congress. No alterations in the boundaries of the existing States, the constitution further prescribes, can be made without the consent of the legislatures of the States concerned as well as of Congress.[37] In Australia the constitution can be amended[38] on a proposal by an absolute majority of the two Houses of Parliament of the Commonwealth—or in certain circumstances one House—and its ratification at a referendum of the people. If at this referendum a majority of all the electors voting approve the proposed law, and if, in a majority of the states, a majority of the electors voting also approve the proposed amendment, then. it is submitted for the royal aassent. It is further provided, that amendments relating to changes in the representation of the states in either House of Parliament or any alterations in the boundaries of the states must be approved by a majority of the electors in the states concerned.

In Canada, the power of amending the North America Act, 1967, rested with the Parliament of Britain. No authority in Canada had power till 1982, alter the, division of powers between the Dominion and Provincial governments. The convention, as it existed, was that Parliament in Britain would amend the Canadian Constitution on a request from Canada. But there was no settled convention whether the request for amendment should come from the Dominion Parliament and government alone, or from the Provincial Legislatures and governments alone or through some sort of cooperation between the two. With the patriation, of the Canadian Constitution in 1982, the Consitution can now be amended by a resolution of the Senate and House of Commons of the federal government and seven Provinces representing 50 per cent population of the country. The amending formula gives for the first time a legal role to the Provinces in making constitutional changes.

The Constitution of India, like the Union of South Africa Act of 1909, makes no pretence of making a federation. Since Wheare says that the "new constitution of India . . . established, indeed, a system of government which is at most quasi-federal, almost devolutionary in character; a unitary state with subsidiary federal features rather than a federal state with unitary features."[39] It would be interesting to note the process of constitutional amendment. The Constitution prescribes three different methods of amending it. Some parts of the Constitution can be amended by a simple majority in both Houses of Parliament, for example, new States may be created or the existing States reconstituted,[40] and Upper Chambers created or abolished in the States.[41] Then, certain specified subjects, as amendments affecting the method of electing the President, the extent of the executive and legislative powers of the Union or the States, the provisions regarding the Supreme Court, the representation of the States in Parliament, and the method of amending the Constitution, require a majority of the total membership in each House of Parliament, a majority of two-thirds of the members present and voting in each House of Parliament and ratification by the legislatures of one-half of the States. Finally, for the remaining

37. Article IV, 3 (1).
38. Article 128.
39. *Ibid,* p. 60.
40. Article 4.
41. Article 169.

provisions there must be a majority of total membership in each House of Parliament and a majority of not less than two-thirds of the members persent and voting in each House of Parliament.

It follows that if the constitution of a country is to be a living document, responsive to the needs of the people and times, it must contain a provision for amending it, and every federal constitution contains such a provision. But the process of amending the constitution, which provides a federal polity, must be distinct, involving a different procedure, from the ordinary law-making procedure, and all interests and parties in the federation should be participants therein. The method of amending a federal constitution is, therefore, more difficult and complex than amending a unitary constitution and it is peculiarly rigid.

3. Presence of Federal Court. In a federation the necessity of a supreme or fedcral court with authority to interpret the constitution is an established fact. The federal judiciary performs two important functions: (1) it decides disputes of jurisdiction arising between the central government and the regional governments or between one regional government and another; and (2) it keeps different governments within their limits so that none may enroach upon the sphere of jurisdiction of the other. If the federal principle is to really work, it is necessary that there should be an umpire independent of both the central and regional governments which should ever be vigilant to prevent either set of government from disturbing the balance between the centrifugal and centripetal forces. Happy balancing between the two forces is the essence of federalism and there can be no other authority than an independent and impartial judiciary which can act as the guardian of the constitution and thereby protect the constitutional distribution of powers. The need for the federal judiciary has been expressed by Mill and his words have often been quoted or paraphrased. "It is evidently necessary," he says, "not only that the constitutional limits of authority of each (central and regional governments alike) should be precisely and clearly defined, but the power to decide between them in any case of dispute should not reside in either of the governments, or in any functionary subject to it, but in an umpire independent of both. There must be a Supreme Court of Justice, and a system of coordinate courts in every State of the Union, before whom such questions shall be carried, and whose judgment on them in the last stage or appeal, shall be final."[42] Sidgwick says that the more stability is given to the constitution by making the process of changing it difficult, the greater becomes the importance of this judicial function of interpreting its clauses.[43]

Every federal constitution, accordingly, provides for an independent and impartial judiciary entrusted with the work of deciding disputes between the several governments, to uphold the supremacy of the constitution and to interpret it. But while interpreting, the judges also expound the constitution by explaining its implications, as happened in the case of the Doctrine of Implied Powers propounded by the Supreme Court of the United States. The Supreme Court derives its authority directly from the constitution and the method of appointment of the judges, their removal and the pay and allowances they are

42. Mill, J.S., *Representative Government*, p. 370.
43. Sidgwick, H., *Elements of Politics*, p. 540.

entitled to are all prescribed by the constitution ensuring the independence and impartiality of the judiciary.

APPRAISAL OF FEDERALISM

Advantages of a Federal Government. Federalism is a device which has rendered immense service in the past and may still render in kniting together under a common government peoples whose political interests are alike. Many regard it as a panacea for so many economic and political ills from which the world suffers today and even envisage the scheme of a World Federation. Without going into the realm of political speculation regarding the feasibility of a World Federation, and accepting federalism as it is, it can be said that small independent States cannot exist in the midst of modern competing States and they find a good substitute in a federal system of government which brings them the advantages of union while retaining their political autonomy at the same time. Federalism offers a new hope to small nationalities claiming the right of self-determination. While acquiring local autonomy as constituent units of a federation, they save themselves from the risks of perpetual insecurity that haunts the smaller sovereign States in the present competing international politics.

In fine, in large countries federalism is calculated to afford scope for local development and administrative experimentation, to localise discord, to prevent "apoplexy at the Centre", and "anaemia at the circumference" and to checkmate the tendency of a metropolis to absorb all control. It saves national legislatures from being overweighted and overwhelmed with business. But the autonomy of the constituent units must now be of a somewhat different order from that which political theory and American experience have familiarised us.

Federalism, as a principle, is the combination of unity and diversity. Such a need exists particularly in countries with a large territorial expansion or deep-seated racial, cultural, religious, or linguistic differences. For the solution of such problems, a federal government is probably the only possible answer. It harmonises local autonomy with national unity and thereby provides an equilibrium between the centripetal and centrifugal forces. The central government is assigned functions which are of national importance and general concern. Problems of local interest that differ in different sections of the country are left to the people of those areas for solution. In this way, a federal government presents a happy blending of centralization and decentralization.

A federal government prevents the rise of a single despotism, checks the growth of bureaucratic authority and conserves the political liberty of the people. Abuse of power by the central authority is more easily checked by a vigorous federalism than by any other form of government. Federalism, observes Bryce, allows experiments in local legislation and administration that might be dangerous if applied to the entire country. Territorial division of functions also relieves congestion of legislative and administrative work at the centre. It adds to the efficiency of administration as well, because the division of powers is related to the actual needs of life.

Federal governments also afford excellent schools for political education, as they are found on the democratic principles of free election, free criticism, and representative institutions. Each citizen has a full-pledged miniature government relatively near the abode on which he can make his mark far more easily than on national administration. He is encouraged to take greater interest and initiative in public affairs. His needs and aspirations are also better satisfied.

Drawbacks of a Federal Government. It cannot, however, be denied that federalism has its disadvantages too. The constitution framing body of a federal government has to bear the burden not only of providing for two sets of government, but also of determining the manner in which the total governmental power shall be distributed among them. This is a task of such difficulty that a satisfactory performance of it at one time is impossible. What might formerly have been safely left to the separate units may, with the lapse of time and under changed conditions, demand a national regulation and decision. This leads to bitter contests regarding the jurisdiction of the two governments and the political history of the United States and other federal countries is marked by such controversies. "The proper adjustment of central to local governments thus becomes," says Gettell, "a constant source of difficulty and the danger of rebellion or the formation of sectional factions is always present."

Then, the prerequisite of a federal government is the supremacy of the constitution, which implies a written and rigid constitution. Supremacy of the constitution means that the terms of the agreement, which establish the central and regional governments and which distribute powers between them, must be binding upon them. If any change is desired to be brought about, it must be made by amending the constitution as prescribed by law and not by the unilateral action of any of the two sets of government. But the process of amending a federal constitution being difficult and circuitous, it is not possible to get the desired results as and when the needs of the people and the country demand. It is also possible that the capricious policy of a number of regional governments may create unnecessary difficulties in the passage of the amendment. All constitutional amendments in the United States require ratification by three-fourths of the States after having been passed by a two-thirds majority of Congress. There is no prescribed time-limit for ratification unless specifically determined by a resolution of Congress. The absence of such a prescription makes the issue a plaything of the states and indefinite delay takes away the purpose underlying the amendment. For example, the child labour amendment was proposed by Congress in 1924, without specifying the time-limit for ratification. So far only twenty-eight States have ratified it, the last one being Kansas in 1937. On one occasion Ohio ratified an amendment submitted eighty years earlier. Connecticut, Georgia and Massachusets voted in 1939 to ratify the first Ten Amendments one-hundred and fifty years after they had been submitted to them for ratification. The American system of amending the Constitution also makes possible for thirteen small states to pool together and hold up an overwhelming majority of the remaining states in their effort to make a much wanted constitutional change.

The powers in a federation are divided and the organs of government, instead of being parts of one highly integrated piece of administrative machinery, are parts of as many different administrative systems as there are federating units. Being coordinate in status a uniform policy for the common good can only be secured by voluntary agreement among all the units to cooperate. This is something which it is often difficult, if not impossible, to secure. The particular interests of all the component units of a federation are not always identical and each unit is likely to pursue a policy which seems to be conducive to its own interests over those of the State as a whole. More serious still, this divergence of interests may bring the several units into sharp conflict with one another or collectively into conflict with the central government. Even when there is no conflict of interest, great loss often results when a given job is not to be done under a single direction.

In the conduct of foreign affairs, the federal government exhibits inherent weakness and inconsistency. The experience of the United States in particular has shown that the individual members of the federal union, by virtue of their reserved powers over the rights of person and property, may embarrass the national government in enforcing its treaty obligations in respect to aliens residing in the United States. When internal differences are carried into foreign relations, the national government loses its international prestige. A fluctuating foreign policy leads to manifold troubles. Federation becomes a weak government both internally and externally. Similarly, in times of war the federal government may sometimes be found lacking in promptness of decision and firmness of action, due to the multiplicity of powers, which a national emergency of this kind demands. It was, perhaps, for this reason that Adolph Hitler altered Germany from a federal to a unitary State in 1934.

A federal government is financially expensive, since there is much duplication of administrative machinery and procedure. There are as many sets of legislatures, courts and administrative departments, with Ministers and Ministries, as the number of the units composing the federation plus the top-heavy identical institutions at the Centre. And all these function within the framework of a democratic machinery which is often cumbersome and usually expensive. Moreover, mechanics of federalism are wasteful of time and energy in that it much depends on negotiation, both at political and administrative levels, to secure uniformity of laws and proper administrative compliance.

Finally, though federation is an irrevocable union, yet the possibilities of secession are there. Regional loyalties seldom die and linguistic differences everremain uppermost. There is conflict of economic interests too. Then, there are racial prejudices. The American Civil War and collapse of the Soviet Union in 1991 are reminders of such tendencies. The United Arab Republic distintegrated with the separation of, Syria. There. is a ferment now in Canada. In May, 1964, the Quebec legislature set up a committee to report on all the implications of a breakaway from the federation. The French-Canadian grievance has been building up over the rival scope of the two languages and the two cultures in Canada. But more realistically the problem is economic. The development of the English-speaking Provinces is held to be at the expense of the French-speaking Quebec. Till recently, the separatist groups had not spelt out their separation in terms of outright secession. But Quebec's Premier Rene Levesque, who headed the separatist Parti Quebecois' (PQ), immediately after assuming office in December 1976 threatened secession. It was averted as the proposal was negatived at a referendum. But the separatist tendencies have not disappeard. It will be a sad development in the career of federalism if at all it ever happens. India is also torn asunder into twenty-five lingustic States with territorial, economic, and cultural disputes plaguing the solidarity of the nation. Recent events in the North-East region, particularly in Assam, Punjab and Jammu and Kashmir, show that Indian nationalism is fragile and the federal set up, although forty-four years old now, has not helped to dissipate separatist tendencies.

Tendency towards Centralization. But the theory and practice of federalism has undergone a radical change and the fact of the matter is that in all federal polities there has been a steady movement to counteract the disadvantages resulting from a constitutional distribution of powers by progressively increasing the powers of the Central government. In the United States it has been accomplished partially by constitutional amendments, but, chiefly by giving to the clauses of the Constitution defining the powers of the Central government a broadness of interpretation that certainly was not in the contemplation of the framers of the Constitution. The doctrines of implied powers, inherent powers, of the sanctity of contracts and many other decisions of the Supreme Court stand foremost in extending the influence or control of the national government over functions which formerly were considered to be within State jurisdiction. Likewise, in Australia a centralising process has been sanctioned by the High Court. "The Australian States," says W.K. Hancock, "have learned in bitterness that it is not always the residuary legatee who comes off best under a will. Sometimes the specific legatee takes the hulk of the estate and leaving him nothing but debt."[44]

In Switzerland four important factors have contributed to the process of centralisation: war, economic depression, the demand for ever increasing social services, and the mechanical and technological revolution in transport and industry. These factors are not peculiar to Switzerland. They are as much in the Swiss as in other federations. "Intensive government," says Sait, "is the reaction against intensive pressure and the pressure may be internal as well as external." War is always a great centraliser. It increases the control of the State over society, since protection and security become the nation's paramount concern and these are pre-eminently the primary functions of the State. War demands, in order to win it, a unified command, coordinated plans and prompt action. It also means mobilising the necessary activity and powers of all institutions of government, central and regional. The obvious result is that the constitutional limits which tend to check the jurisdiction of the various parts of government become unworkable. It is, of course, true of a world that is scared by past wars and scared of new ones. No country can afford to wait for defence until war is declared. It must always be prepared to ward off the probabilities of war and to win it, if it actually comes. It means the ability to man the industrial resources of the country and to apply the nation's scientific knowledge to the task of defence. Evervthing from the physics courses taught in the schools to the conservation of natural resources and the maintenance of economy, affects the war-making potential.

The New Deal legislation of President Roosevelt and the Supreme Court's attitude thereto is clearly indicative of the rapid development of centralisation. The New Deal was devised as the new means of combating a new national emergency, the depression. The world today is as much scared of depressions as it is scared of war and this emphasises the recognition of the need for the reallocation of powers in a new balance, not excluding

44. *Australia* (1930), p. 117.

strong local organs of governmerit. "Since the New Deal," says Lipson, "the situation has changed almost beyond recognition. Federal-State relations have become ampler and closer. Federal-local relations have been established. Federal-State local cooperation is now frequent."[45] Much of this is due to the more generous use of the device of the conditional grants-in-aid. A Committee of the Council of State Governments appointed in the United States, defined federal grants-in-aid as "payment made by the national governments to State and Local governments, subject to certain conditions for the support of activities administered by the States and their political sub-divisions." As these grants are conditional, it is a matter of common experience that one who gives money must see the fulfilment of those conditions. The conditions that the central government imposes are in respect of the principles and purposes of the service in question, the structure and procedure of administration, the recruitment and management of the personnel, the furnishing of reports, and submission to inspection. The grant-in-aid, accordingly, "offers a middle ground between direct federal assumption of certain state and local functions and their continuation under exclusive state and local financing, with haphazard coverage and diverse standards. It makes possible the achievement of national minimum standards, yet retains most of the benefits of administration close to the people."

The Indian Constitution makes a wider departure from the traditional theory of federalism. Since the Constitution became operative in 1950, the bias has increasingly been towards centralization. Even Ministers of the Union Government have from time to time given expression to their feelings decrying the tendency toward the increasing concentration of power, authority and functions. The charge of over-centralization making inroads on State authority is the logical consequence of a single party government both at the Centre and in the States for an uninterruplied period of seventeen years in the latter and thirty years in the former and the importance that national or economic development has assumed since the formation of the Planning Commission in 1950. The undefined position of the Planning Commission, an extra-constitutional body, and its wide terms of reference have gradually led to its growth as the "economic cabinet", not merely for the Union but also for the States.

All federal countries are moving towards a unified economic and social svstem coexistensive with its whole territory. No problem can be isolated and looked at exclusively from a single point of view. Nor can a local solution be found for all local problems. As population grows more dense and industry is highly developed, the mechanism of life becomes so complicated, its parts so closely entwined, and the activities in various areas so intimately bound together that local regulation will no longer suffice, If business corporations and trade unions become big, developing into nation-wide organisations and producing goods that will move across State lines, it is evident that labour relations can no longer remain within the exclusive jurisdiction of the states, the component units of a federal polity. If the vagaries of nature are to be counteracted by harnessing nature, then, agriculture can no longer remain a state subject. The authority that is wider and wealthier can only sponsor huge irrigational schemes, like the Damodar Valley, Bhakra-Nangal and Beas projects in India. Health and education, both state subjects in all

45. Lip Son, L., The Great issues of Politics p. 313.

federations, have likewise assumed national stature. Bad health conditions in one state have an impact on the nation as a whole and the poor educatioual system in one part of the country affects the prosperity of the country as a whole.

But the great centralising factor has been the contrast in the attitude of the people towards the central government and the governments of their states in former times and in our time. At the time of the making of the federations of the United States, of Switzerland, and of Canada there were differences of nationality, but as time went on, a common nationality came to impose itself upon the differences. The citizens of these federal States came to feel that their primary interests and allegiance was in and to the nation as a whole rather than to their particular states. Thus, there is not only the constantly increasing tendency to look to the central government for action in meeting their problems as they arise, but the growing conviction that only by the action of the central government can their problems be satisfactorily solved. A good part of President Roosevelt's New Deal policy sought to permanently regulate matters that had hitherto rested with the states. But many Americans justified this "usurpanon" on the ground that the pressure of economic and social problems could be borne effectively only by the Federal Government. The old school of states rights, therefore, is steadily losing its hold upon the people, and in its place is arising the tendency to look to the central government for the solution of the more important political, economic and social problems. A Welfare State cannot afford otherwise. This makes a fundamental change in the theory and practice of a federal government.

Future of Federalism. The result is obvious. There is one general tendency in all federal governments to concede that the central governments have increased in importance and strength at the expense of the regional governments. Some students of federalism have concluded from this tendency that federal government represents but an intermediary stage in the political development of the modern State. "States move forward," says Salt, "from alliance to confederacy, from confederacy to federation, from federation to complete union, that is, from lower to higher forms. These successive forms, therefore, may be regarded as a biological series."[46] W. F. Willoughby maintains, "This step taken (the formation of a federation), there immediately develops a steady growth of the spirit of nationalism and, in response to needs actually felt, a progressive development, both absolutely and relatively, of the powers of the central government as opposed to those of the states. So marked is this that it may almost be said that from the moment the system of multiple government is adopted, the tendency is for efforts to be mode to get away from the consequences of the decision that has been made."[47] To Lipson it seems an unavoidable conclusion that "older patterns of decentralizations—whether in the form of local autonomy under a unitary system or of states' rights in a federal union—were doomed to dissolve in the corrosive acids of twentieth century politics, economics and technology: Virtually all the great driving forces in modern society combine in a centralist direction."[48] The critics of federalism further assert that integrated economic planning and true federalism are incompatible. A planned economy is national in character and it

46. Sait, E.M., *Political Istitutions, A Preface,* p. 375.

47. Willoughby, F.W., *The Government of Modern States,* p. 185.

48. Lipson, L., *The Great Issues of Politics,* pp. 315 -16.

is an expression of unity, while federalism is based on division, diversity and limited powers.

Where does not accept the point of view that federal government is really no more than a stage towards unitary government. He says, "This is a prophecy, not an historical judgment, for so far, no federal government—as I define it—has become a unitary government."[49] He admits that war and economic depression are the enemies of federal government, and that if they occur frequently, they "will almost certainly turn federal governments into unitary governments." So far as the growth of social services is concerned, he says, that they, too, will tend towards the same end. But he also says that the growth in the powers of the central governments is only one tendency. "One other tendency at least must be noticed. It has not been the general governments alone which have grown in strength. The regional governments have also expanded. In all the federations the regions now perform functions which at the establishment of the federations, they performed either not at all or to a much less degree than now."[50] This is one element in a tendency, he adds, "which may be broadly stated by saying that there has been a great increase in the sense of importance, in the self-consciousness and self-assertiveness of the regional governments. This has gone on side by side with the growth in importance of the general governments and it has obviously been stimulated by it."[51] It has led to a sense of grievance in the regional governments that their position is being imperilled by this tendency towards centralisation. "And in some cases they have felt so unjustly treated by the general governments that they have talked of resigning from the federation. The secession movement in the State of Western Australia was one example."[52] Wheare's emphasis that the reason which originally prompted the independent States—oneness of the State with the separateness of the units—to form the federal union and not a unitary union, have not ceased to operate. True it is, he further says, that every region in a federal system does not feel the desire for independence to the same degree, "but in every federation a few regions feel it so intensely that no attempt could be made to impose uniformity without bringing into view the possibility of breaking the union in pieces."[53] Keeping these considerations in mind, Wheare concludes that "the prospect of federal government is not so short as is suggested by those who concentrate entirely on the tendency of the general government to increase at the expense of the regions. Federal government is still desired by some regions in all the federations. There is no conclusive evidence that federal government is to be no more than a stage in the process towards unitary government."[54] Referring to the United States, particularly where the centralized activities assumed new dimensions during and after the Second World War, Carl Friedrich says, "It would be a mistake, however, to declare federalism in the United States dead; in some areas the states have captured some of their power through more vigorous insistence upon their participation in the federal administration."[55]

49. Wheare, K.C., *Federal Government,* p. 253.
50. *Ibid.,* pp. 253 56.
51. *Ibid.,* p. 256.
52. *Ibid.*
53. *Ibid.,* p. 257.
54. *Ibid.*
55. Carl J. Friedrich, *Constitutional Government and Democracy,* p. 218.

Kennedy, who takes a more liberal view of the minimum requirements of a federal constitution, observes, "The real questions to decide, shorn of all theories are these: Are the national and provincial governments related to one another as principal and delegate? What is the real and precise nature of authority which they exercise within their spheres?..." The regional governments have "a juridical status and a corporate personality. They are clothed with plenary powers, legislative and executive. The provisions of the constitution relating to the scheme of distribution of powers cannot be unilaterally altered. Finally, in every federal country there is the provision of an independent tribunal in the form of the Supreme Court to give interpretations to the constitution with finality. This is the crux of the whole problem."

People and countries have not lost faith in federalism so far. While federal States have shown signs of closer unification, other States, especially those new born, are adopting federal constitutions and many writers predict a further union of States on federal basis. It happened very recently in the case of Egypt and Syria with the consequent emergence of a federation named the United Arab Republic, though Syria seceded subsequently. Nationalist leaders from many parts of Africa met from December 5 to 12, 1958 to attend the All-African People's Conference with a view to getting rid of the remaining Colonial regimes on their Continent, and to begin the first steps toward a federation of their existing States. Only weeks after the Maastricht treaty came into force, the Greek government on December 21, 1993, launched its plans for its turn at the helm of the European Union (new name adopted for the European Community), by suggesting that work on a real federal constitution for Europe should start in the next few months. Theodore Pangalos, the Deputy Prime Minister of Greece, suggested that a committee of personalities possessing political and scientific qualities spend the first few months of 1994 "designing a truly federal structure with a central government responsible to the European Parliament and national ministers reduced to acting as a Senate." Pangalos, who took over as Chairman of the European Union's Foreign Affairs Council on January 1, 1994, compared his suggestion, which had also been floated by MEPs and the French government in 1986. But it is highly doubtful if the proposal succeeds. Even Pangalos admitted that he had no idea whether his plan would gather the unanimous support it would need to go ahead. But the germs are there and it is also likely that the plan may become an accomplished fact at some distant date.

Federalism, in fact, has made an important contribution to the solution of the world's political problems. By reconciling the claims of local autonomy with those of national unity, federalism paves the way for the adjustment of inter-State disputes. Even a great admirer of unitary government, W.F. Willoughby, admits that we should not "close our eyes to the immense service which the development of the idea of multiple government has rendered in the past and may still render in knitting together under a common government peoples whose political interests are largely identical but which for sentimental reasons are unwilling wholly to surrender their political autonomy."[56] Federal government, as Wheare says, does not stand for multiplicity alone. "It stands for multiplicity in unity. It can provide unity where unity is needed, but it can ensure also that there is variety and

56. Willoughby, W.F., *The Government of Modern State*, p. 416.

independence in matters where unity and uniformity is not essential."[57] This exercise in self-governments, he further says, "is sufficiently valuable to be worth the cost it entails and federalism marches towards triumph."

The "New" Federalism. The traditional theory of federalism stands modified today to fit into the needs and demands of the present conditions. The emerging concept is that of "cooperative federalism." It is argued that no society, much less a developing society, can afford the luxury of a rigid division of powers which was possible in the social and economic conditions of the eighteenth century. In the contemporary world, marked by industrial technology as a foundation for effective power, uniformities on a broad geographic scale are necessary to viability in the effective use of modern techniques of production and distribution. Smaller units of government lack requisite power, geographic span of control, and knowledge of resources to cope with inescapable issues related to economic stability and development, and are unable to assume satisfaction of basic needs and broadening wants, not to be neglected in the age of the common man. Moreover, the world today, is as much scared of depressions, as it is scared of war, and this aspect of the problem emphasises the recognition of the need for the reallocation of powers in a new balance, not excluding strong local organs of government.

A. H. Birch has aptly said that a federal government is not limited to its own sphere when it passes a good deal of legislation in relation to welfare, and state governments are not in practice independent of the federal government when they derive a considerable proportion of their revenues from federal payments.[58] This is precisely the position in the United States, Canada, Australia and Switzerland and it is equally applicable in India too. The execution of welfare projects cannot succeed in isolated moulds, particularly when a State is constitutionally committed to a welfare ideal. The Constitutions of the United States and India are both committed in their Preambles to promote general welfare and to establish justice. The welfare content of the State can only be secured through the joint and cooperative efforts of the national and state governments. In India the cooperation is sought in different ways and the best example in this respect is the Zonal Councils. According to Morris-Jones, Zonal Councils have proved "a most useful device in the development of cooperative federalism." These Councils help to facilitate cooperation between the Centre and the states, and the states themselves. As regards the United States Carl Friedrich says, "there has grown up a wide area of effective cooperation between the states and the federal government which is mutually advantageous and not necessarily destructive of the broader constitutional division of powers. The federal government stands in need of the more intimate contacts with local problems in such fields as social security, while on the other hand the local authorities in the poorer sections of the country may require the financial aid of the national government. The forms which such cooperation between the federal and state governments may take are many. Grants-in-aid, federal tax credits, cooperative use of personnel, as well as agreements and formal compacts have been employed. "In recent years there has been an increasing amount of dovetailing of legislation, examples of which include making federal laws contingent on state activities,

57. Wheare, K.C., *Federal Government*, p. 260.
58. Birch, A., Federalism. Finance and social Legislation ,Canada, Australia and the United States, p. 290.

suggesting model statues, and protecting through federal legislation one state against the unfair competition of another."[59]

Economic planning on a unified basis has, indeed, the effect ot centralizing power, but this is consistent with those tendencies of cooperative federalism which have operated in the federal systems of the United States, Canada, Australia and Switzerland. In India, the preparation, defining the stages in the execution of the plan, allocation of resources and fulfilment of targets are decided by mutual consultation and understanding. "The plan", according to V.T. Krishnamachari, "is a joint national enterprise in which the Centre and the States are partners, united in a common purpose and working with agreed policies in different fields of national development."[60]

The dominant spirit of federalism is, therefore, not competitive, but cooperative exercise of authority by different governments. The traditional theory of federalism is a political anachronism and the concept of 'dual sovereignty' is untenable now, Birch defines federalism as a system of government ``in which there is a division of powers between one general and several regional authorities, each of which, in its own sphere, is coordinate with others, and each of which acts directly on the people through its own administrative agencies."[61] He eliminates from his definition the, term ``independent" within ``its own sphere,"[62] although he retains the ``coordinate" character of government at both levels. But M.J.C. Vile does not agree with Birch. He says that the coordinate status of the federal and regional governments is as difficult to sustain as that of their independence in the spheres assigned to them. Their status of equality, he asserts, ``may be defensible in legal terms, but it is very difficult to interpret in terms of power and influence."[63] The leadership of the central government is unchallengeable and all federal unions have moved alike in the same direction.

It does not, however, mean that the federal government should become so dominant that it should always dictate its decisions. What distinguishes a unitary system from a federal polity is that no level of government in a federation is wholly or continuously subordinate to the other. Federalism, with its division of powers between the central and regional authorities is, as Carl 'Friedrich says, ``a main stay of constitutional government."[64] But neither of the two is wholly dependent or independent of another. The functions of the State cannot be divided into water-tight compartments. Nor can they be construed as static. The purpose of the State can only be secured through the joint and cooperative efforts of both national and regional governments. Both act independently within the spheres assigned to them, but when the vital interests of the State intervene the decisions of the national government, as the bearer of national security and prosperity of the realm, should prevail, though they may concern matters outside its jurisdiction.

59. Carl J. Friedrich, *Constitutional Government and Democracy*, p. 217.

60. *Five-Year Plan* (India, Progress Report), 1953, p. 1.

61. Birch, A.H., *Federalism, Finance and Social Legislation in Canada, Australia and the United States*, p. 305.

62. Refer to K.C. Wheare's definition of federalism. *Federal Government*, p. 97.

63. Vile, M.J.C., *The Structure of American Federalism*, p. 199.

64. Carl J. Friedrich, *Constitutional Government and Democracy*, p. 216.

Vile, accordingly, defines federalism as ``a system of government in which central and regional authorities are linked in a mutually interdependent political relationship; in this system a balance is maintained such that neither level of government becomes dominant to the extent that it can dictate the decision of the other, but each can influence, bargain and persuade the other. Usually, but necessarily, this system will be related to a constitutional structure establishing an independent legal existence for both central and regional governments, and providing that neither shall be legally subordinate to the others. The functions of government will be distributed between these levels (exclusively, competitively or cooperatively), initially perhaps by a constitutional document, but thereafter by a political process, involving where appropriate, the judiciary; in this process, the political independence of the two levels of government is of the first importance in order to prevent one level from absorbing all effective decision-making power."[65]

What really matters in a federation is whether the centre and the States ordinarily enjoy autonomy within the spheres assigned to them. Such a constitutional division of powers, is, no doubt, a restraint which both the sets of government exercise upon each other, but it "should not, blind us to the fact," observes Carl Friedrich, "that all governmental units share in the common task of accomplishing the 'will of the people'." He rejects the argument advanced by Miss Jane P. Clark that "an emphasis on separateness or rivalry tends to forward the least desirable developments in American government today" and says that this remark "belittles the constitutional importance of divided powers." Federalism constitutes a device for preserving constitutionalism. Not all the accretion of power to the central government represents a net loss to the regional governments. The latter have been steadily gaining power, from two sources; from the development of new governmental functions, and by the transfer of functions from the local areas. The same forces that have made for centralization within the nation have also promoted the transfer of local power to the regional governments. This apart, the self-consciousness and self-assertiveness of regional governments deter even a strong centre from intervening without a convincing cause which it may be able to plead at the bar of public opinion. In a democratic set-up the actions of government are ever under scrutiny. No government forgets that tomorrow is the day of election. If the central government ventures to trespass the limits ordinarily assigned to it, it shall have to pay the penalty at the next election.

The conclusion is obvious. Consistently with the interests of the modern world there are certain subjects hitherto assigned to regional governments, such as, agriculture, industry, commerce, finance, education, sanitation or transport, that cannot be exclusively placed under regional management. The doctrine of state-rights cannot be pushed far in an age which is outgrowing national independence itself. So far as the major activities of the State are concerned, there is an imperative need of centralised normative legislation, leaving supplementary legislation and administration to federal units. They can have a free hand in minor affairs. In fact, there can be no minor affair in the context of planning and welfare activities. Yet, on the whole the range of co-operative activities is becoming so vast and the need of local adaptation, administrative decentralisation and all round-consultation so urgent that federal units may be expected to retain a large share in the

65. Vile, M.J.C., *The Structure of American Federalism,* p. 197.

transaction of public affairs. While they may lose in height, they are sure to gain in breadth. According to Richard H. Leach, a United States expert on federalism: "In operation federalism requires a willingness, both to cooperate across government lines, and to exercise restraint and forbearance in the interests of the entire nation."

Of late, a new concept of creative federalism has emerged in the United States. The advocates of creative federalism put emphasis on getting the job done without regard to who is in the pivotal role, the centre or the units of a federal polity. India has yet to learn the lessons of cooperative federalism and if she can imbibe the spirit of creative federalism, it will certainly be a movement for the regeneration of the country. India today is in the tight grip of separatist trends, if not always for secession, at least of particularism, that is, a recognition of the need for separate and special treatment to a particular region or state. At no stage after Independence the situation was so grim as it is today. Soaked in deep regionalism and diversity of various varieties the spirit of nationalism has not enthused the people with the consciousness of unity.

SUGGESTED READINGS

Acton, Lord: *Essays on Freedom and Power.*
Aiyar, S.P. and Usha Mehta (Ed.): *Essays on Indian Federalism.*
Anderson, W.: *The Nations and Slates, Rivals or Partners.*
Asok Chanda. *Federalism in India.*
Beard, C.: *American Government and Politics.*
Bannet, W.H.: *American Theories of Federalism.*
Benson. G.S.C.: *The New Centralization: A Study of Inter-governmental Relationships in the United States.*
Bowie, R.R., and Friedrich, C.J.: *Studies in Federalism.*
Bryce, J.: *The American Commonwealth,* Rev. ed. 2 Vols.
Corry, J.A.: *Democratic Government and Politics.*
Dicey, A.V.: *Introduction to the Study of the Law of the Constitution.*
Elazar, D.J.: *The American Partnership; Inter-.governmental Co-operation in the Nineteenth Century United States.*
Finer, H.: *The Theory and Practice of Modern Government,* Chaps. X, XI.
Friedrich, C.J.: *Constitutional Government and Democracy,* pp. 189-221.
Garner, J.W.: *Political Science and Government,* pp. 346-356, 412-422.
Goodnow, F.J.: *Social Reform and the Constitution.*
Kennedy, W.P.M.: *The Constitution of Canada.*
Lipson, L.: *The Great Issues of Politics.*
Lowell, A.L.: *Government of England,* Vol. II, Part III.
MacIver, R.M.: *The Modern State,* Chap. XII.
MacMahon, A.W.: *Federalism-Mature and Emergent.*
McWhinney: *Comparative Federalism.*
Mogi, S.: *The Problem of Federalism, 2* Vols.
Rockefeller, N.A.: *The Future of Federalism.*
Sait, E.M.: *Political Institutions, A Preface,* Chap. XVII.
Santhanam, K.: *Union State Relations in India.*
Sharma, B.M.: *Federal Policy.*
Sidgwick, H.: *Elements of Politics,* Chap. XXVI.
Walls, R.L. : *New Federations Experiments in the Commonwealth.*
Wheare, K.C.: *Federal Government.*
Willoughby, W.F.: *The Government of Modern States.* Chap. X.
Zurehev, Arnold, *Constitution and Constitutional Trends Since World War II.*

15

CHAPTER

Parliamentary, Presidential and Totalitarian Patterns

A modern democratic government may have a parliamentary or presidential pattern of government and the difference between the two hinges upon the principles governing the relations between the executive and legislative branches of government. If the executive and legislative branches are unified and coordinated under the control of the same persons, so that they must work in harmony, such a system is called parliamentary. If the executive and legislative branches are largely independent of one another, but each possessing checks on the powers of the other in order to make power limited, controlled and diffused, the system is presidential. Here the head of the executive is constitutionally independent of the legislature in the matter of duration of his tenure and is in no way responsible to it for his political policies and actions.

Parliamentary System. In a parliamentary system a clear distinction is made between the head of the State and the head of government, *a* executive and *the* executive. Here the head of the State, King or Queen in Britain or President in India, possesses nominal or titular authority whereas the real authority rests with the government of which Prime Minister is the head. The King/Queen or President has a *de jure* authority, no doubt, and legally he possesses all the powers and privileges which the constitution and laws may confer upon him, but in practice he exercises none. He is simply the bearer of authority. Constitutional conventions in Britain deprive the King or Queen of all his or her powers, privileges and prerogatives. In India the authority of the President was governed by Conventions inherited from Britain and deemed as the *sine qua non* of a parliamentary system of government. The Forty-second Constitution Amendment Act, 1976, gave the convention a constitutional sanction and provided that the advice of the Council of Ministers shall be binding on the President. The Forty-fourth Amendment (1978), however, gives discretion to the President to refer the advice tendered to him on a particular matter for the reconsideration of the Cabinet, if he felt hesitant to accept it in the first instance.

The government is constituted from the majority party or a combination of parties, if they had agreed on certain fundamentals for purposes of a coalition, in the legislature. The normal procedure is that the Chief Executive, monarch or President, summons the leader of the majority party or a coalition of parties to form the government. The person so summoned is the Prime Minister-designate who chooses his own team of ministers from among the members of his party, in the legislature, including a few from outside if deemed necessary, and in case there is no constitutional bar to such an inclusion. The Council of Ministers, thus, constituted functions under the leadership of the Prime Minister and is collectively responsible to the representative chamber of the legislature. Out of the Council of Ministers, the Prime Minister chooses some fifteen or more but generally not more than twenty, persons, who are the most influential and important, and they make a Cabinet. Cabinet is a wheel within a wheel and it is the pivot on which the whole political machinery revolves. It is the supreme directing authority; the magnet of policy, as Barker calls it, which coordinates and controls the whole of the executive government and integrates and guides the work of the legislature.

There is a sharp distinction between a Cabinet and a Ministry or the Council of Ministers. The Cabinet. wherever the parliamentary system exists, has an extra-constitutional growth and consists of about twenty or less Ministers, who are the most influential and the most important of the Council of Ministers or the Ministry. These members of the Cabinet meet collectively, under the chairmanship of the Prime Minister, generally once a week, decide upon policy and in general 'head up' the Government, whereas the Council of Ministers or the Ministry includes some fifty or more Ministers of different categories—Cabinet Ministers, Ministers of the Cabinet rank, Deputy Ministers and Parliamentary Secretaries. The Council of Ministers, or the Ministry has no collective functions. It never meets as a whole and it never deliberates on matters of policy. The duties of a Minister, unless he is a Cabinet Minister, are individual duties relating to the administrative Department or Departments of which he holds the charge or to which he is attached. The Cabinet is, thus, the motive power of all political action. Such a system of government is commonly known as the Cabinet government, because Cabinet is the master of the government.

The Council of Ministers is headed by the Prime Minister. He is the captain of the team which plays the game of politics in accordance with the mandate which the majority party in the legislature, of which the Prime Minister is the duly accredited leader, had received at the general elections. The Prime Minister performs four important functions: (1) he is the head of the Ministry, that is, the government of his country; (2) he is also leader of the legislature of the country—the one whose intervention in the debates has the greatest weight, who states and interprets government policy, who is responsible for obtaining the approval of the legislature for the policy of his government; (3) he is the person through whom the head of the State, King/Queen or President, normally communicates with the Cabinet, with the legislature, and ultimately, with the country; (4) he is head of the legislative wing of the party and responsible for maintaining harmony with its organisational wing. They are the two limbs of the party that had been returned by the electorate in majority and to form the government.

Mechanism of Parliamentary Pattern. The Council of Ministers is the hub of a parliamentary pattern of government. It may be made up either entirely of members of the same political faith, or of members of somewhat differing affiliations, yet able to agree on a programme of immediate action. In any case, the Ministry is formed by a person who seems to the head of the State best able to form a team in conformity with the existing parliamentary majority. Under the dual-party system the choice of the head of the State is obvious, and he summons the leader of the majority party to form the government.[1] He is the only possible Prime Minister and there is no discretion. But when the party has not elected its leader or when there is not one single party having a legislative majority, as it happens usually under the multiple-party system, the head of the State has, a real choice. The Ministers are, by law or by binding convention, members of the legislature. Sometimes a Minister may not be an elected member of the legislature, for example, Ramsay MacDonald and Malcolm. MacDonald were both members of the Cabinet in Britain, from November 1935 until early in 1936, though they were not members of Parliament. But the House of Commons is extremely critical of such exceptions and Ministers remain out of Parliament only while they are trying to find seats. If they cannot get in and are unwilling to be created peers, they resign their offices. The Constitution of India provides that a Minister may not be a member of either House of Parliament for a period of six consecutive months. But such a Minister ceases to be a Minister at the expiration of that period unless he is duly elected. In Britain no one may speak in either House of Parliament unless he belongs to that House. In India, a Minister enjoys the privilege of occupying a seat in either House of the Legislature, of being heard, and of participating in its deliberations, but with the right to vote in the House of which he is a member.

A parliamentary or Cabinet system works on the well-accepted principle that Ministers are responsible to the legislature for all their official acts and they remain in office as long as they retain its confidence. This is called ministerial responsibility and it is this responsibility that gives to the parliamentary system the name of a responsible government as well. In Britain, legally, Ministers hold office during the pleasure of the King/Queen. But a legal truth in Britain is a political untruth and the pleasure of the King/Queen means the pleasure of Parliament. The Constitution of India also provides that Ministers hold office during the pleasure of the President.[2] But the pleasure of the President vanishes when the Constitution simultaneously prescribes that the Council of Ministers is collectively responsible to the House of the People (Lok Sabha).[3] This means the individual and collective responsibility of Ministers to the House of the People. It also means that whereas the Council of Ministers is collectively responsible to the House of the People for its policies, a Minister can be removed from office for his individual indiscretion or for acts of omission and commission and the President exercises his pleasure on the advice of the Prime Minister. Without such an advice he cannot act, independently. Ministerial responsibility is the essence of parliamentary government. Responsibility to the legislature means that so long as the policies and official conduct of the ministers command the support of the majority of the members of the legislature, they continue to hold the reins of office and govern the country. But as soon as the majority is reduced into a minority and the Ministry loses the confidence of the

1. President Zail Singh exercised his discretion in selecting Rajiv Gandhi, after the assassination of Indira Gandhi on October 30, 1984, to become the Prime Minister, although he had not been elected the leader of the Congress (I) Parliamentary Party.
2. Article 75 (2).
3. Article 75 (3).

representative House, House of Commons in Britain, and House of the People (Lok Sabha) in India, it must resign from office and give an opportunity to the Opposition to assume office, or the legislature may be dissolved on the advice of the Prime Minister and new elections held in order to ascertain the opinion of the electorate. The party returned in majority to the legislature as a result of elections, then, forms the Ministry. The second alternative is more common and is generally resorted to. The legislature reveals its disapproval of the acts of the Ministry either by an adverse vote on an important measure, or by a specific vote of no-confidence.

The ministerial office, is not incompatible with legislative mandate.[4] It means that the executive and legislative functions are "inextricably co-mingled" and there is no such separation between the executive and legislative powers as that which forms the distinguishing mark of the American system of government. On the contrary, there is a close and intimate inter-dependence of both the executive and the lagislative departments. Dicey emphasised that the parliamentary system is founded on a fusion of the executive and legislative powers and, at the same time, upon the maintenance of harmonious relations between them. Bagehot defines cabinet as a "hyphen that joins, the buckle that binds the executive and legislative departments together." The members of the cabinet are members of the legislature as well as heads of the executive departments of the government. They are responsible for defining the broader lines of national policy, collectively constituting the government, and running the administration. They resolve, initiate and pilot in Parliament legislation which they deem essential for carrying out their policy. The Ministers must always be prepared to answer the questions put to them while the legislature is in session, impart all information which members consider necessary to elicit from the government, and defend their policies whenever questioned, critisized or called upon to give an account of their official conduct. The Ministry, therefore, is a committee of the legislature sharing in both the creation and the administration of law and responsible and subject to the control of the legislature. It cannot successfully function independently of the legislature.

Parliamentary system is a party government. The government comes into office as a unit and goes out of office as a unit. This means that the essence of the parliamentary government is its solidarity, a common front, and it becomes binding on every member of the Cabinet, and, of course, on every Minister outside the Cabinet, to pursue an agreed policy for which all accept responsibility and on which they stand and fall together. It is, therefore, important that Ministers must essentially belong to one single political party. Collective responsibility, which is the *sine qua non* of the stability of government, can be obtained only when Ministers come in office as a team and go out as a team.When a Ministry is composed of heterogeneous parliamentary groups, as under a multiple party system, it is most unstable, for compromise, which brings the various groups together, is sure to break down at the slightest pretext. In a composite cabinet there is no homogeneity in the ranks of Ministers and there is no team spirit which can ensure oneness of purpose, and, consequently, collective responsibility of the Ministry rarely exists.

Prerequisites of Parliamentary Government. Parliamentary system is the most

4. Garner, J.W., *Political Science and Government*, p. 324.

cherished and aspired for as it is based on the fact that the government is carried on in the name of the head of the State, King/Queen or President, by Ministers who are members of the majority party in Parliament and are responsible to Parliament for all their public acts, both individually and collectively. There are, however, certain prerequisites without which parliamentary system easily turns into something quite different.

The first prerequisite is the presence of a *titular* executive head of the State. The head of the State is not the directing and deciding factor responsible before the nation for the measures taken. The executive power of the government is exercised in his name by political men who belong to the majority party in Parliament. Legally, government is vested in the head of the State, and the officers of the State are appointed in his name and dismissed by him. The Ministers are his Ministers and they remain in office during his pleasure. He summons, dissolves and prorogues Parliament. Laws made by Parliament cannot be enforced without his assent and if he so wishes, he may withold his assent thereto. But all this remains in theory and the Chief Executive does nothing by doing everything. Herbert Asquith, Prime Minister of Great Britain, wrote in 1913 a Memorandum on the rights and obligations of the King. He said, the King "is entitled and bound to give his ministers all relavant information which comes to him; to point out objections which seem to him valid against the course they advise; to suggest (if he thinks fit) an alternative policy. Such intimations are always received by ministers with the utmost respect and considered with more respect and deference than if they proceeded from any other quarter." Beyond this he must not go. In the oft-quoted phrase of Bagehot, the King has three rights—the right to be consulted, the right to encourage, the right to warn. "A king of great sense and sagacity," he added, "would want no others." This is the classical exposition of the powers of the head of the State in a Parliamentary system of government.

It is necessary that there must be a clear and stable majority in Parliament. Cabinet government means party government. The party provides the machinery to secure a stable government under a unified command of politically homogeneous and disciplined leaders. The fall of the Ministry is the fall of the party and the strength of the party in the legislature determines the solidarity and stability of the government. This is best achieved when there is a two-party system, one in office, the other in Opposition. But fairly good results can also be obtained when there are fairly solid blocs, each consisting of parties who habitually work together and who have enough in common to permit them to evolve a definite political programme. The classical example of a two-party system is Britain. Britain hates a coalition government, because it contradicts the fundamental principle that the cabinet represents a party united in principle. Britain's example has been admirably followed in the Dominion countries, although in Australia and New Zealand the anti-Labourite groups formed a partnership in order to defeat their Labourite opponents in 1949. In France and other Continental countries the multiple-party system exists and coalition government was the only possibility before the Fifth Republic in the former came into being. The result was that the government was a combination of strange bed-follows who had nothing in common; no leader to follow, no definite programme to pursue, and no discipline to observe. All this led to a precarious tenure of the government. For example, during the twenty-three years irom the end of the First World War to the French collapse in the Second World War, France had forty-two governments, while

Britain had eleven, averaging six months, and twenty-five months respectively. When the life of government is precarious and short, it is hesitant and unable to take a long view of policy. Its work is largely limited to matters of daily administration and its chief purpose is to remain in office instead of really governing. Moreover, when no party can definitely be made responsible because of a coalition, the government can neither be responsive nor really representative. An irresponsible government coupled with an incoherent public opinion is always a sectional government, which encourages corruption, jobbery, neopotism, toadying, and various other accompanying evils. The final result is the failure of the Parliamentary system as it happened in France. The Constitution of the Fifth Republic cannot legitimately be called a Parliamentary government. It was deliberately designed to correct the imbalances of the preceding Constitutions.

Two results flow from the two-party system as it operates in a Parliamentary government. One is the accepted leadership of the Prime Minister and the other is the principle of ministerial responsibility. Both are correlated and upon these two important institutions hinge the success of the Parliamentary system. The Cabinet is a team that plays the game of politics under the captaincy of the Prime Minister. He is the undisputed leader of the Parlia- mentary majority party who brings about unity and close association between Ministers on the one hand, and the cabinet and the Parliamentary majority on the other. C.F. Strong has succinctly said, "It is the party system which gives the cabinet its homogeneity, it is the position of the prime minister which gives it its solidarity."[5]

The Ministers in a Parliamentary system are answerable to the legislature and they remain in office as long as they can individually and collectively retain its confidence. Each Minister directs the work of the department over which he presides, in accordance with the policy as determined and decided by the cabinet, and he is answerable to the legislature for its successful implementation. In addition to this individual responsibility, each Minister shares a collective responsibility with other members of the government, "for anything of high importance that is done in any other branch of public business besides his own." On matters of high policy the Ministry comes into office as a unit, remains in office as a unit, and goes out of office as a unit. Ministerial responsibility ensures cohesion and solidarity and accounts for the stability of the government. Moreover, responsibility and responsiveness go together and it is only in a Parliamentary system of government that both can be secured.

Another essential feature of a successful Parliamentary system is a certain degree of moderation among political parties. Cabinet system is a democratic mechanism and democracy is inseparable from a belief in the methods of peaceful persuasion, in the ultimate reasonableness of man, and his response to rational arguments. It is, accordingly, necessary that both the majority party and the Opposition should understand and observe the rules of the game. The public duty of the Opposition is to criticise and oppose the policy of the government; to attack the government and individual Ministers. The majority party, at its end, must govern openly and honestly and it should meet criticism not by suppressing Opposition, but by rational argument. It means that there should prevail a sense of give and take; the habit of tolerance and compromise. They must have a strong

5. Strong, C.F., *Modern Political Constitutions,* p. 221.

commitment to the democratic process itself. A simple rule of British politics is, "if you wish to govern, you must first show yourself fit to govern." This rule acts as a powerful and valuable stimulus both to the majority and minority, for the minority party is legally recognised in Britain as His or Her Majesty's Opposition. Just as the party in power must reconcile differences with the Opposition in order to ensure a stable government representing public opinion and to win approbation of the electorate, similarly, the Opposition must remain moderate and sensible, if they are to win approval as an alternative government. When political parties become intolerant of one another and virulent in opposition and attacks, orderly government cannot exit. "Every trick, every method of obstruction and filibuster, is used to effect a certain political result, and if everything else fails, force may eventually be applied ... when that occurs orderly government often comes to an end and emergency decree takes the place of legislative act. From there it is only a step to dictatorship." For the success of the Parlia- mentary system of government rational and responsible Opposition is as necessary as the rational and tolerant majority imbued with the sense of give-and-take.

Experience has shown that the right of dissolution is vital to the smooth working of a Parliamentary system. If judiciously used, it is the solution to any possible deadlock. If Cabinet and Parliament disagree, the electorate will decide between them. The appeal to the people, as the ultimate source of political authority, is the only logical manner of settling any serious dispute between rival agencies of the State. Lack of it means Parliamentary absolutism. Being safe from dissolution and confident that its tenure goes by calendar, the legislature can overthrow the cabinet with impunity. This is what happened in France in the Third and the Fourth Rpublics and it made infinitely worse the tendency towards cabinet instability already created by the multiple party system.

Finally, cabinet is a secret body which is collectively responsible for its decisions. It must deliberate in secret, if mature, rational and independent discussion is to shape the policy. Publicity reduces the independence of mind of Ministers in relation to each other and harmony of views becomes well-nigh impossible. When it becomes known that members of the Cabinet have differed amongst themselves the spontaniety of party support disappears, and gives a rude shock to party solidarity. It also gives an opportunity to the Opposition to plague the government for their dissensions.

Merits of Parliamentary System. Parliamentary system is the only form so far devised in any representative democracy, which ensures harmonious cooperation between the executive and legislative branches of government. Ministers are the heads of the various administrative departments, and, at the same time, they are members of the majority party in the legislature. In the latter capacity they lead the legislature and provide Parliament with the policy on the basis of which decisions are to be made. There is no working at cross purposes between the executive and the legislative departments, as may be found in the United States when the President belongs to one party and the majority in Congress to another. On the contrary, under Parliamentary system, "from first to last there is full and harmonious collaboration between the law-making and money-granting authorities, on the one hand, and the law-enforcing and money-spending authorities on the other." There are, thus, few chances of conflict of authority and jurisdiction. With authority thus concentrated, the full power of government can be promptly brought to bear upon any great emergency.

Bryce adds two more advantages of the presence of Ministers in the legislature: "(1) being in constant touch with the Opposition as well as in still closer contact with the members of their own Party, the Ministers can feel the pulse of the Assembly and through it the pulse of the public opinion and can thereby obtain useful criticism, in a friendly way, of their measures. The members of the legislature can also call to the attention of the Government any grievance felt by their constituents and secure quick redress." (2) The system secures "swiftness in decision and vigour in action, and enables the cabinet to press through such legislation as it thinks needed, and to conduct both domestic and foreign policy with the confidence that its majority will support it against the attacks of the opposition."[6]

Parliamentary system is the best example of representative democracy, for it recognizes the ultimate sovereignty of the people. Ministerial responsibility is immediately to the legislature, but no majority dare ride rough-shod over public opinion. The ultimate appeal rests with the people, and the government must remember those to whom it will have to account in the future. "Government with us," says Jennings, "is government by opinion, and that is the only kind of 'self-government' that is possible." The government is ever under scrutiny and the Parliamentary system provides for daily as well as periodic assessment of what the rulers do. It is kept on the *qui vive* (alert) by the constant probing and questioning of the Opposition and by the publicity given to governmental policies and actions by the more responsible segments of the press. Parliamentary democracy, thus, keeps more nearly in step with public opinion than the Presidential system.

Parliamentary system is in the real sense a government by criticism. The majority party forms the government. The minority constitutes the Opposition. The Opposition must oppose and criticize the government. There is a saying in Britain that the Prime Minister knows the leader of the Opposition more than he knows his own wife. It explains how far the Ministry is alive to the opinion of the Opposition and apprehensive of its criticism. A government which neglects the Opposition, does so at its peril. The lapses of the government are its opportunities and the Opposition uses them to appeal to the public opinion. "The House is its platform, the newspapers are its microphones, and the people is its audience." No other form of government can, therefore, meet the ideal of rationality and responsiveness better than parliamentary democracy. In his inaugural address to the 37th Commonwealth Parliamentary Conference at New Delhi, on September 23, 1991, the President of India, R. Venkataraman described the system of parliamentary democracy as "supe-rior to all other systems that human ingenuity has so far been able to devise" and emphasised that if worked properly and honestly, there was perhaps no better substitute than the representative parliamentary democracy.

Another merit claimed for the Parliamentary system is its flexibility and elasticity. Bagehot highly eulogised this aspect and pointed out that people can, under this system of government, "choose a ruler for the occasion" who may be especially qualified to successfully pilot the ship of the State through a national crisis. Churchill replaced

6. Bryce, J., *Modern Democracies,* Vol. II, pp. 510-511.

Chamberlain as Prime Minister, because national emergency demanded it and this change was brought about without any political upheaval in the country. But such a smooth change is not possible under a Presidential type of government. The office of the President goes by calendar. Come what may, Presidential elections must be held after every four years. "The American Government," says Bagehot, "calls itself a government of the supreme people; but at a quick crisis, the time when the sovereign power is most needed, you cannot find the supreme people ... all the arrangements are for stated times. There is no elastic element; everything is rigid, specified and stated. Come what may, you quicken nothing and can retard nothing. You have bespoken your government in advance and whether it suits you or not, whether it works well or works ill, whether it is what you want or not, by law you must keep it."[7] This is one way of expressing the flexibility of the Parliamentary system. Another is the ease with which it can meet the crisis in the social and political life of the people. The executive can explain to and impress upon the legislature its assessment of the situation and the methods proposed to meet the emerging situation. Even well established customs may be waived temporarily, as was done in Britain in 1931, when the Ministers "agreed to differ" as against the constitutional convention of collective responsibility, to meet the abnormal situations.

Moreover, Parliamentary system can claim a high educative value. It cannot function without well-organised political parties. The object of every political party is to win elections and to capture government. To win elections means that the party should be in a position to secure the majority of votes and the electorate should approve its programme. It is like placing one's cards on the table and acquainting the nation with the party's political programme. It is for the people to judge one party and the other on its merits. If an issue of national importance arises subsequently, on which the verdict of the people had not been obtained by the party in power, the legislature may be dissolved and an appeal made to the electorate. Dissolution also helps to remove deadlocks between the executive and the legislature and makes the electorate the policy-determining factor. According to K. Leoewenstein, "In the authentic form of parliamentary government, dissolution is the democratic fulcrum of the entire process of adjusting power conflicts by making the electorate the ultimate policydetermining factor."[8] Mareover, by-elections, which are so frequent during the life of Parliament, serve as a barometer of public opinion and the government corrects or adjusts its policies according to the results obtained from such elections. All this democratic process has immense educative value. It makes the people politically conscious of their rights and responsibilities, and vigilance is the true price of democracy.

Finally, Parliamentary system has succeeded in democratizing governmental machinery in all civilised countries, particularly where exists the institution of hereditary monarchy. If Britain is called the citadel of democracy, it is because there is constitutional monarchy and the King or Queen does not actively govern. He reigns but does not rule. The latter is the function of his responsible Ministers. Bryce has aptly explained this aspect. He says, "As the actual working Executive has necessarily a party character it is a merit of this system that the National Executive, be he King or President, should be outside party,

7. Bagehot, W., *The English Constitution,* Chap. 2, Sec. 9.
8. Zurcher, A.J., *Constittutions and Constitutional Trends Since World War II,* p. 208.

and represent that permanent machinery of administration which goes on steadily irrespective of party changes ... when a cabinet fails, the transfer of power to another is a comparatively short and simple affair."[9]

Drawbacks of the System. In spite of the many practical merits of the system some objections have been urged against it. It has been argued that Parliamentary system violates the theory of Separation of Powers and, accordingly, it cannot commend itself. Combination of executive and legislative functions in the same set of individuals leads to tyranny. Sidgwick, while admitting the undeniable gain of harmony between these two chief organs of government, maintains that it is "to be purchased by serious drawbacks."[10] Ministers, he says, "are liable to be distracted from their executive duties by the work of preparing legislative measures and carrying them through parliament while parliament is tempted away from legislative problems by interesting questions of current administration in which, especially in foreign affairs, it is liable to interfere to an excessive extent."[11] The advantages of the division of government into different departments are, thus, "lost in the fusion or confusion of legislative and executive functions." This criticism, however, does not seem to be valid. Practical experience tells us that collaboration between the executive and legislative powers is essential for the well-being of the States. These departments cannot be divided into water-tight compartments. The theory of the Separation of Powers, in its traditional and consequently rigid form, is inconceivable and inoperative. While the same men may be at once members of the legislature and the executive, their functions in the two roles are distinct.

It is further pointed out that the Parliamentary system is unstable The government has no fixed life. It remains in office only so long as it can retain parliamentary majority which is subject to the vagaries of the representatives, particularly "if dominant majority in the representative chamber is either small or wanting in cohesion; and in the latter case it is also liable to be upset by a new combination of parties in the chamber—aided perhaps by personal intrigues—if the opportunity for the combination is skilfully chosen so that the newly-formed majority is not reversed on an appeal to the country."[12] The uncertainty in the tenure of office, the critics maintain, provides no incentive to the party in power to adopt a farsighted and consistent policy. Nor does it venture to embark upon durable projects. A new Ministry which assumes office, is sure to reverse the policy of the defeated Ministry, for it comes in with its own definite policy and programme. It may, however, be said that much of the above criticism is true only in countries with multiple political parties where the lease of life of the cabinet is short and precarious. Countries, like Great Britain, having dual party system in practice, do not demonstrate such a state of affairs as dual party system is really the true basis of parliamentary democracy.

It is sometimes deplored that the Cabinet system divides the country into two antagonistic sets of men, those who strive their utmost to get things done and those who do their utmost to obstruct. The Oppositions under the Cabinet government, must oppose tooth and nail all measures sponsored by the government, irrespective of their practical

9. Bryce,James, *Modern Democracies,* Vol. II, pp. 511-12.
10. Sidgwick, H., *The Elements of Politics*, p. 444.
11. *Ibid.*
12. *Ibid*, p. 445.

utility. Sometimes governmental policy is subjected to such a scathing criticism, that it proves detrimental to national solidarity and prestige. When Opposition indiscriminately opposses what the government may say or propose, it retards the progress of the country and it, also, amounts to national wastage, both of money and time. The antagonism between the parties is not confined to the legislature alone. They keep the country in a spirit of commotion and turmoil. As Bryce puts it, "the system intensifies the spirit of party and keeps it always on the boil. Even if there are no important issues of policy before the nation there are always the offices to be fought for. One party holds them, the other desires them, and the conflict is unending, for immediately after a defeat the beaten party begins its campaign to dislodge the victors. It is like the incessant battle described as going on in the blood vessels between the red corpuscles and the invading microbes."[13]

But the fact is otherwise. The essential feature of Parliamentary democracy is a certain degree of moderation among the political parties, or what may be described as political forbearance. The minority agrees that the majority should govern and the majority agrees that the minority must criticise. The Opposition is the prospective government and it understands and observes the rules of the game, as the majority does. The government so arranges the parliamentary programme as to give due opportunity to the Opposition to discuss and criticise its actions. The government even becomes wiser by that criticism and arrives at a compromise. This is the essence of discussion and Parliamentary system succeeds *par excellence* in this respect. The situation of ruthless opposition prevails only when extremist and anti-democratic forces gain a substantial membership in the legislature which they proceed to terrorise and ridicule. But this is not the way of Parliamentary system. "Whatever be the form of government," says Guerin, "a regime is democratic when the will to social cooperation of its members is stronger and more spontaneous than its anarchical impulses." Parliamentary system recognises and welcomes differences and it provides the machinery for their expression. But these differences must not go so far as to make the work of government impossible. If such things are allowed to happen, as they do in some of the states India, it is the end of parliamentary democracy.

Again, Cabinet system is said to be inefficient because it is a government by amateurs. The headship of different departments of government is entrusted to persons who may not be familiar even with the rudiments of administration "A youth must pass," as quoted earlier, "an examination in Arithmetic before he can hold a second class clerkship in the Treasury; but a Chancellor of the Exchequer may be a middle-aged man of the world who has forgotten what little he ever learnt about figures at Eton or Oxford, and is innocently anxious to know the meaning of those little first dots when confronted with Treasury accounts worked out in decimals."[14] Disraeli, while forming a Ministry, offered the Board of Trade to a man who wanted instead the Local Government Board. "It does not matter," said Disraeli, "I suppose you know as much about trade as the first Lord of the Admiralty knows about ships." Dr. Baldev Prakash was the Finance Minister in the Punjab Government, but with everything to learn about public finance; for the whole of his life Dr. Prakash had belonged to the medical profession. The Prime Minister is not

13. Bryce, J., *Modern Democracies,* Vol. 11, p. 512.
14. Sidney Low, *Government of England*, pp. 201-202.

concerned in the choice of Ministers with their aptitudes and knowledge of the departments they have to preside over. His choice is seriously limited by political considerations, the foremost of which is the preservation of a stable parliamentary majority. Hence, the amateur who obtains office is not always a gifted amateur. "Weak men, incompetents, are sometimes appointed to office or to inappropriate departments, out of such consideration of popularity, sometimes gained or faded a decade or more ago, or through the personal esteem or friendship of the Prime Minister." And once in office, the major part of their time is devoted to Parliament and cabinet meetings, social and other political activities and in nursing their constituencies. Nor does the brief and precarious tenure of their office leave any stimulus for them to learn the departmental technicalities. The result is, as the critics say, that Cabinet government is a government by inefficients who are mere tools in the hands of their permanent civil servants.

But this is not a correct appreciation of the Parliamentary system. Its essence is the responsibility of Ministers to the legislature. It is, no doubt, preferable to appoint a Minister who is well informed about the working of the department over which he presides. But it does not mean that he should be an expert. The business of the Minister is not to do the work of the department. He is only to see that it works properly and consistently with the declared policy of the government. In fact, there are many advantages if the head of the department is an amateur. A layman sees the department as a whole and his appraisal of the problem requiring solution is entirely different from that of an expert. "The cabinet", according to Ramsay MacDonald, "is the bridge linking up the people with the expert, joining principle to practice. Its function is to transform the message sent along sensory nerves. It does not keep the departments going; it keeps them going in a certain direction."

Another serious difficulty of the Parliamentary system is the ever-growing size of the cabinet in every country. Cabinets have grown everywhere too large for prompt and effective discussion and decision. The huge amount of work to be done by the Cabinet and the tremendous burden on each Minister—departmentally, parliamentarily, electorally, and socially—leaves very little margin of time for serious thought on any subject beyond the immediate task. Then, participation in international conferences imposes on several Ministers, particularly on the Prime Minister, the Foreign Minister, and the Finance Minister, rather long occasional absences from current duties of administration at home. All taken together, the period of office of Ministers, as Herman Finer observes, "is a period of practical work, not of reconsideration and survey." The obvious result is, as the critics point out, a deep and continued reliance on the administrative services. Bureaucracy under the circumstances, according to Ramsay Muir, "thrives under the cloak of ministerial responsibility." Whatever be the justification of criticism, there is no denying the fact that the necessity of reducing the size of the cabinet is being felt in every country and in Britain it was reduced in 1947 to sixteen members only, and so was the size of Churchill's Cabinet in 1951. Anthony Eden continued the practice when he formed his government in May 1955 and Macmillan followed Eden after the latter's resignation. It is now the usual norm in Britain and India, too, has followed more or less the same pattern. Amery has suggested that no cabinet should exceed six or seven ministers. But this is not a practical number considering vast expansion in the activities of the State and other political compulsions to a parliamentary system of government.

Parliamentary system, its critics maintain, has degenerated into a party government in which political power is monopolised by the majority party. So long as parliamentary majority is assured, it assumes dictatorial powers. The minority party is completely left out of active participation in the government and the nation is deprived of the talented persons who might be belonging to the minority party. Public opinion has no sweep over the policies of the government. The critics, thus, very often allege that Great Britain practises a form of "plebiscitary democracy" in which people vote 'yes' or 'no' on the record of the government in general but are deprived of any share in the "formulation of the individual policies."[15] The charge of dictatorship of the Cabinet is not quite baseless. But there is a redeeming feature too. Lowell correctly says, "if the parliamentary system has made the Cabinet of the day autocratic, it is an autocracy exerted with the utomost publicity under a constant fire of criticism."[16] Cabinet government provides its own safeguards and accountability to the electorate is the primary constitutional safeguard.

It is argued that the pressure and complexity of the affairs of a modern government have led to certain changes in the manner of operation of cabinet government. The cabinet has been regarded as the centre of governmental coordination and of policy-making, and as being collectively responsible for all decisions on major issues and approver of all other decisions. But the seemingly great power of the cabinet and its control over all policy matters is qualified by three factors. The first is the existence of politically more powerful individuals within the cabinet who constitute an hierarchy of their own and try to overlord the cabinet and the various ministries and departments. The second is the development of a structure of cabinet committees. These cabinet committees are the real decision-making bodies within the spheres assigned to them. And above all is the ascendancy of the Prime Minister to unprecedented heights. He no longer remains *primus inter pares*. He generally formulates the policy of the government and often takes decisions without consulting the whole cabinet. Ramsay Muir has said that the dictatorship of cabinet in the last resort means the dictatorship of the Prime Minister. The Prime Minister makes and unmakes the government, shuffles his pack as and when he likes, may advise dissolution of Parliament and being leader of the party may take disciplinary action against the members of his party who flout the party whip and do not toe the line of the Prime Minister.

But it must not be forgotten that the Prime Minister's position is bound up with the party. His prestige, no doubt, is one of the elements that make for the success of the party. He is also responsible for party cohesion. But without his party the Prime Minister is nothing. Whatever he is and whatever he can claim to be, is due to what the party has made him. Once the party disowns him, he meets the fate of Ramsay MacDonald. Within the cabinet he cannot do all that he wishes to do. He must listen to and respect the opinions of his colleagues. It is essential for the Prime Minister to retain the loyalties of his political friends who owe him a personal as well as party allegiance. Laski explains, "The parliamentary system is conducted on the vital hypothesis that no man is indispensable; and its daily operation is a constant and salutary remainder to the Prime Minister that his fortune depends upon the recognition of this truth."

15. Carter, Herz and Ranney, *The Government of Great Britain,* p. 326.
16. Lowell, A.L., *The Government of England,* Vol. I, p. 326.

Finally, Cabinet government is charged with lack of promptness in deciding and taking immediate action in times of national crisis or emergency. In emergency promptness and vigour of initiative are essential for success. But a cabinet consists of a large number of Ministers, which need many minds to be consulted. A quick and decisive opinion cannot, accordingly, be secured. Moreover, a cabinet under the parliamentary system with its divided responsibility, open discussions, and shifting majorities can hardly be expected to take prompt, united and vigorous decisions. These objections are also not borne by facts. World War II had fully demonstrated how cabinet government withstood the test of time. In India, too, there is cabinet government, both at the Centre and in the states. How successfully the Central and the state governments grappled with the refugee and other post-partition problems is now a matter of contemporary history.

PRESIDENTIAL PATTERN

Nature of the Presidential system. Bagehot said, "The independence of the legislative and executive powers is the specific quality of Presidential Government just as *fusion* and *combination* is the principle of Cabinet Government." Both Cabinet and Presidential systems are representative in character, but responsibility of the executive to the legislature is the *sine qua non* of the former, whereas the latter is constitutionally independent of the legislature. Under the Presidential system the legislature and the executive are two distinct departments of government. There is more or less a separation between the two. The executive is neither the creature of the legislature, nor is it responsible to that body for its public acts or dependent on it for remaining in office. The head of the State, the President, is the real executive both as a matter of law and fact, and such power is the result of a direct grant from the constituent authority effected through express provisions of the constitution. The fact that the President is not merely *a* Chief Executive but also *the* Executive makes all 'ministers' or 'cabinet members' his assistants and, thus, denies them the more independent positions of ministers in a Parliamentary system.

It is a misnomer to describe as 'ministers' who constitute the Presidential 'cabinet'. Neither is there 'cabinet' in the Presidential system nor are there 'ministers'. Both are the product of the Parliamentary system. The members of the so-called cabinet in the Presidential system are not members of the legislature and they do not belong to the legislative majority party. They have no access to the legislature. They do not take part in the debates and have no *locus standi* to initiate and pilot legislation or to defend the policy of government or stand in need of seeking its confidence. Nor have they any power to advise dissolution of the legislature and appeal to the electorate, if the legislature does not approve their policy. They have, indeed, no policy of their own. The policy of the government is that of the *head* of the State, who appoints them and retains them in office as long as it pleases him. They are responsible to him alone and to no one else. The 'cabinet' under a Presidential system, in brief, is the tool of the head of the State. He can override the opinions of its members or he may not seek it or even if he does. it is for him to decide whether to consult them individually or collectively. And as for its members, a breath unmakes them as a breath had made.

The Chief Executive in a Presidential system has a status independent of, and coordinate with the legislature, and is not subject to the direction or control of the latter either for his continuance in office or in respect to the manner in which he exercises his powers. The duties of the Chief Executive and his administrative officers (members of the cabinet, by law designated Secretaries in the United States) lie wholly in the executive and administrative field and they have no responsiblity in respect of the legislative functions, except as it may be their duty to make known to the legislature the need for legislation in order that their executive and administrative functions may be more effectively performed.

Garner gives a matter of fact analysis of the Presidential system. He says, "What has been called 'residential' government as contra-distinguished from cabinet or parliamentary government, is that system in which the execntive (including both the head of the state and his ministers) is constitutionally independent of the legislature in respect to the duration of his or their tenure and irresponsible to it for his or their political policies."[17] The system is not Presidential because it has an elected President as the Chief Executive. It is Presidential because President is the real executive who does not owe his office to the legislature nor can he be removed from office. In a Parliamentary system real executive is the creature of the legislature and remains in office at its will.

Presidential System in the United States. The Presidential pattern of government has its origin in the United States and is now confined to certain countries which are exclusively in the Western Hemisphere as well as in some other countries. Pakistan too adopted this system under General Ayub Khan, but, again, reverted to the Parliamentary system in 1973. It shall be instructive to know the factors which contributed towards its emergence in the United States and the shape of the governmental machinery which it assumed. There were two factors which influenced the framers of the American Constitution against the Cabinet form of government. In the first place, Montesquieu's theory of the Separation of Powers had a great appeal for the Americans. The theory of limited government, which is the natural corollary of the doctrine of popular sovereignty, had convinced the framers of the Constitution of the necessity of separating the three branches of government as it prevented tyranny and absolutism. If liberty had to last, they argued, the political direction of authority should not concentrate in any one of the branches of government. Secondly, they knew that Cabinet government could function only when the life of the nation was divided into distinct political parties, each with its separate programme and platform. Political parties, the framers of the Constitution believed, weakened national solidarity by creating sharp cleavages whereas the need of the time then was unity out of diversity of the new nation. They, accordingly, created an executive department independent of and coordinate with the legislative department; an "energetic yet dignified" executive capable of enforcing national laws firmly and one which should lend a note of stability to the new government.

The Presidency of the United States is one of the greatest political offices in the world. Its occupant has become—with the exception of the Central European dictators—

17. Garner, J.W., *Political science and Government* pp. 311-12.

the most powerful head of a government known to our day. He is absolutely free with respect to the exercise of his powers and tenure of office, except that all appointments made and treaties concluded by him are ratified by the Senate. As his term of office goes by calendar, his responsibility to the electorate is unenforceable. He can only be impeached by the Senate. His conviction by the Senate cannot carry a greater penalty than removal from office and disqualification to hold and enjoy any office of honour, trust, or profit in the United States.

In the exereise of his executive duties, the President is assisted by his Secretaries who are heads of different departments and are now ten in number. The Secretaries of the President are merely his personal assistants. They are appointed by him and are responsible to him. None of them is a member of Congress nor is he responsible to it. Though popular usage collectively gives to these departmental heads the name of 'Cabinet', yet it is a misnomer to designate. them as such. The President cannot shift his responsibility to this body or any officer of it. He cannot make them individually or collectively accountable to the legislature or the country for the policies and actions of the federal government over which he presides. Their responsibility is to the President alone. 'Cabinet' in the United States is a mere creation of the President's will. It is an extra-statutory and extra-constitutional body. It exists only by custom and if the President desires to dispense with it, he can do so. The procedure, as it stands today, is that the 'cabinet' meets ordinarily once a week and the President places before it questions upon which he thinks he needs their advice, and the members bring to the cabinet such matters in their respective departments as they deem appropriate for 'cabinet' conference and general discussion. Votes are seldom taken as they are of no importance beyond securing a mere expression of opinion. And even if ever they are taken, they have no value. 'Cabinet' members have no corporate rights as in Britain. This is well illustrated by two anecdotes, one relating to America and the other to Britain. "Seven nays, one aye, the ayes have it," anounced President Lincoln, following a 'cabinet' consultation in which he found every member against him. This attitude is so often contrasted with Lord Melbourne's putting a question on corn laws to the vote in the cabinet saying, "it does not matter what we will say, as long an we all say the same thing." Cabinet, in the United States, has been aptly described as the President's family.

The executive in the United States has no initiative in legislation, except that the President may send messages from time to time to Congress, recommending the enactment of particular laws. It is true that Presidential messages are favourably received by Congress and greatly influence the course of legislation, yet the executive in America lacks all initiative and guidance which is so important rather basic, feature of the Parliamentary government. Nor has the President the right to summon (except for extraordinary session) congress and the dissolve it. Congress meets automatically on dates specified in the Constitution and its duration is fixed. No doubt, the President can veto laws passed by Congress, but it is only a suspensive veto. If the Bill vetoed by the President is again passed by both the Houses of congress, with a two-third majority in each House, it becomes law without the signatures of the President and is forthwith promulgated.

According to Herman Finer the American Presidency has six outstanding characteristics.[18]

"It is a 'made' executive but it has grown;
"It is a 'solitary' not a 'collective' executive;
"It is popularly elected, in practice directly;
"It is more than an executive;
"It is separated from Congress;
"It may be tinkered with, but cannot be reformed."

Merits of the Presidential System. The chief merit of the Presidential system is that without being responsible it retains a representative character. The President is an elected representative of the people, but his tenure does not depend upon the fluctuating will of the legislature. A fixed tenure of office accounts for greater continuity of policy and firmness in administration, and it can be successfully carried out without any fear of break. The principal virtue of Presidential system is the fact that it creates a stable executive within the framework of a democratic order. This means promptness, vigour and initiative in administration. All executive authority is vested at one-centre and the head of the State is *a* executive as well as *the* executive. He is, in a word, the generalissimo of administration and, as such, there can be no question of divided policy. His Secretaries or 'ministers' follow the policy initiated by him.

Unity of control, quickness in decision, and concerted policy, which emergency of any kind may demand, can best be obtained in the Presidential system. The head of the State is the chief foreign policy maker and the Commander-in-Chief of the armed forces of the country. As Commanderin-Chief, he may even take, in case of war, the command of military operations and effectively control matters of vital importance in domestic and foreign affairs, just as Woodrow Wilson and Franklin Roosevelt did in the United States in the two World Wars. What President Roosevelt did, during the economic crisis of the thirties of the present century and George Bush in the Gulf War in 1991, are matters of contemporary history. All this is not possible in a Cabinet system of government. Even Winston Churchill, who attained new heights of power and authority, had not the personal powers of the President of the United States. To illustrate the difference in the position and powers of the President of the United States and the Prime Minister of Britain, Jennings writes that "the President pledged the United States to the realization of the objectives of the Atlantic Charter while the War Cabinet, not the Prime Minister, pledged the United Kindgom."[19] The President is also head of the nation and is not merely a party leader. This gives him greater dignity, prestige and authority. The nation looks to him to steer the country through any kind of national emergency.

The Presidential system also makes possible the appointment of experts to head the various departments of the government without consideration of their party affiliations. President Cleveland, a Democrat, appointed Waliter G. Gresham as Secretary of State and he had been thought of as a Respublican candidate for the Presidency. Theodore Ronosevelt and Taft each appointed a Democrat Secretary of War and Hoover made a Democrat

18. Finer, H., *The Theory and Practice of Modern Government,* p. 669.
19. Jennings, I., *Cabinet Government,* p. 181.

Attorney-General. Roosevelt's choice of Henry L Stimsen as Secretary of War and of Franklin as Secretary of Navy in 1940, both prominent Republicans, are two more notable examples. A Prime Minister in a parliamentary system cannot normally do this. If the Cabinet is to work as a team, it must consist of persons who think alike and belong to the same party to act alike. Again, though a Prime Minister has a choice in selecting his colleagues, yet his party expects certain men to be in the Cabinet and the country, too, expects them to be there. Then, the allotment of various departments to Ministers is a matter of political consideration and expediency rather than of aptitude for the work they are expected to perform. There is no political expediency which may weigh with the President and there is no party crisis which he may be afraid of.

Since the President's Secretaries or 'Cabinet ministers' have no berth in the legislature, the congressional load of work with them is negligible. Nor have they any constituency to nurse or to look forward to the day of election. They have, thus, the time and energy to devote themselves exclusively to administrative work and pursue the policies of the government unaffected by political exigencies. There is another advantage too. Since the executive is not responsible to the legislature and its adverse vote does not bring about a crisis in the government, the tumult of the party spirit is less in evidence. It is also claimed that due to the presence of the system of checks and balances there prevails a greater sense of stability and the administrative machine works more efficiently and effectively.

The advocates of the Presidential form argue that such a system is best suited for countries inhabited by different communities with diverse interests. Homogeneous dual party system, which is so essential for the success of a Cabinet government, cannot be secured under these conditions. Multiple party system is the general outcome, when the people are divided both horizontally and vertically. But a government formed out of heterogeneous elements is a weak and unstable government. Under the Presidential system there is a "solidarity" executive. The President is the unmistakable focus of responsibility. Government, either for its creation or for existence, does not depend upon the complexion of the legislature. In the United States, however, two-party system is firmly rooted.

Drawbacks of the system. The critics of the Presidential system are numerous and they urge that it divides government into watertight compartments, as it is based on Separation of Powers. In actual practice there can be no rigid division between the executive and legislative departments and to divide them into independent and coordinate departments is to create friction between them which is highly injurious to good and efficient government. Much time is consumed in struggles among the various branches of government to determine the extent of their respective powers. Also, the very stability of the system verges on inflexibility. By establishing the Presidential system, Finer says, the Fathers of the American Constitution "separated the executive sources of knowledge from the legislative centre of their application; severed their connection between those who ask for supplies and those who have the power to grant them; introduced the continuous possibility of contest between two legislative branches; created in each the necessity for separate leadership in their separate business; and made this leadership independent of the existence and functions of the executive."[20] When powers are divided

20. Finer, H., *The Theory and Practice of Modern Government,* p. 101.

between the executive and legislative departments without any means of proper coordination, there is always inordinate delay to arrive at an agreement even on pressing matters which demand expeditious disposal. One branch of government may be operating on one policy whereas the other may be following quite a different one, particularly when the executive belongs to one party and the legislative majority to another. This condition may produce a stalemate which, in time of crisis, as during 1931-32, can be disastrous.

Lack of direct initiative in legislation on the part of the executive is really a very serious defect in the Presidential system. Legislation is the main function of the executive and here the legislature does not act under its instructions. There can, accordinly, be no cohesiveness and the party ties, which bind the executive and the legislature, are too flimsy for an integrated policy. The result is that the legislative procedure is different essentially from the one in a country having the parliamentary system; financial procedure is worlds apart; there is no coordination of political energy or responsibility; but each branch has its own derivation of authority and its morsel of responsibility. And in order to remove the possibilities of concentration of authority at one single end, a system of checks and balances may have to be introduced as in the American Constitution. The system of checks and balances is not only the negation of the theory of Separation of Powers, but it is also highly injurious to administrative efficiency. Somewhat ironically, Prof. Beard remarks, that the checks and balances in the United States "designed to promote over-all equilibrium, often operate rather to aggravate than to ameliorate the ill-effects of separation, as for example, in the case of the Presidential veto and senatorial assent to treaties."[21] If the system of checks and balances has prevented the likelihood of authoritarian government, it has also led at times to the weakening of effective government.

Moreover, the Presidential system is characterised to be "autocratic, irresponsible and dangerous." Once the President has been elected the nation must continue with him, whether they like and approve of his policy or not. He may become autocratic and even degenerate into a dictator, subject to the provisions of the Constitution. The legislature has no constitutional power to withdraw the mandate which the electorate gave him at the time of election. This has been well explained by Bagehot. He says, "You have bespoken your government in advance and whether it suits you or not, whether it works well or ill, whether it is what you want or not by law you must keep it." The Presidential system is also criticised for its rigidity, for the constitutional provisions must always be adhered to both in times of peace and war. During World War II Presidential elections in America were held twice, whereas general elections were postponed in the United Kingdom by an Act of Parlia- ment. In America there could not be any postponement without amending the Constitution which is a difficult and lengthy process. The rigidity of the Consti- tution does not take cognisance of the needs of the hour. It must take its own course, though it may, at times, prove harmful to the interests of the nation.

Finally, the Presidential system has frequently been criticised for being unequal to the task of conducting a vigorous foreign policy. It is asserted that the President's dependence on the cooperation of a frequently recalcitrant Congress makes United States'

21. Beard, C.A., *American Government and Politics*, p. 16.

foreign policy a slow moving and uncertain affair. No one, including friends and foes, can guess about the degree to which executive actions or commitments will be sustained or repudiated by Congress. Absence of dissolution in the Presidential system is responsible for less harmony and more tension than in the parliamentary system. The executive has no means to bring to book a refractory legislature.

Bryce maintains that "the parliamentary system has many advantages for countries of moderate size, the Presidential, constructed for safety rather than for promptitude in action, and not staking large issues on sudden decisions, is to be preferred for states of vast area and population such as are the United States and Germany." In the United States of America the Presidential system has worked vigorously well. Wherever basic unity was required in an exceptional crisis, statesmanship and patriotism has always provided it. By effective appeals to the voters through the spoken words, press, radio, and lately television, the Presidents have succeeded in dramatizing their programmes and compelling consideration of their views. But a system of government, which cannot be generally and easily applied to ordinary conditions, fails to command universal respect and approbation. In countries influenced by the model of the United States, the Presidential system has not been altogether successful. Latin American systems have tended to become dictatorships, and only in a few countries such as Paraguay, Costa Rica, Chile, Brazil and Peru have attempts been made to limit executive power.

CONSTITUTIONAL AND NON-CONSTITUTIONAL POLITICS

Constitutional democracies. The recent norm is to divide politics into constitutional and non-Constitutional regimes. This division has been necessitated by the confusion caused by the contemporary regimes when all describe themselves as democratic in some fashion or the other. The former USSR, the People's Republic of China, the German Democratic Republic, and quite a few more like these are Communist States, though all claim their governments to be essentially democratic. Many of the new, developing countries of Asia, which began their careers as democracies soon shifted to totalitarian regimes, but retained the symbols of democracies realising that outright tyrannies are rare in the world now. 'President Sukarno of Indonesia thought of his regime as "guided democracy" and President Ayub Khan of Pakistan established "basic democracies" from the village level up.

Constitutional democracies include those regimes which have essentially similar ethos to be classified in one group without reference to the nature of political executive available in one or the other. The common characteristics of constitutional regimes are the presence of effective restraints on the holders of power so that they act in a responsible manner and not arbitrarily. The society is pluralistic and no single group or element enjoys dominant position or plays a unique role. In such a society there prevails a spirit of tolerance, willingness to compromise and commitment to constitutionalism. Elections are free, unrestricted and uncontrolled. Freedom to dissent is the accepted political norm and consequently the presence of a strong and responsible Opposition is the *sine qua non* of a constitutional democracy. Both the majority and the minority have a strong commitment to the democratic process and, accordingly, the victors and the vanquished at the polls accept the positions they assume and believe that at some future date their positions may be reversed without any violent action. As there is wide agreement on the benefits of the present rules of the game, there prevails a sense of unity; a consensus binds the people together and gives them a concern for the welfare of the community as a whole. The Opposition and other interest groups exercise a tangible impact on the decisions and policies of the government.

Constitutional democracies have in common the traditions of civility, political neutrality of the army and the civil service and the existence of the rule of law. Rule of law is the crucial factor which ensures legal impartiality and absence or reduction to a minimum of arbitrarinness. There is only one kind of law and one set of courts to which those who make and enforce law are amenable together with the citizens. All governmental acts are according to the law and subject to control by appropriate authorities and effective remedies are available against the State, if ever it ventures to transgress the law. Constitutional democracies invariably ensure the presence of an independent and impartial judiciary which protects individual rights. There is only one commitment of the judiciary, to uphold the Constitution and the law. In polities of this kind government does not control, not even largely influence, the mass media of communication.

Constitutional democracies exist, with few exceptions, in the older and more developed countries where politics is obviously competitive and free and where ruling group is responsible and participation widespread. The influence is not concentrated nor are the avenues to influence closed. The dispersal of influcnce means that limits are set to what rulers may do and also to what is generally regarded as 'political.'

Democracy in its traditional Western form has not spread to the newer nations of the world. Even in contemporary Western Europe regimes, such as French and the Spanish have come into existence by non-legal action or pressure. Similarly, regimes in the first lap of industrialization can rarely afford the luxury of political democracy or constitutional restraint or power. Economic development, especially industrialization, tends to disrupt traditional social relationships and behaviour. Economic planning is the prerequisite of industrialization, but it is a process of standardization and concentration of authority which demands from the people acquiescence and submission.

"Constitutionalism, the allocation of a higher sanction to the basic laws than to the immediate wishes of a ruler," says Michael Curtis, "marks an important stage to a democratic regime."[22] Power in a constitutional regime is limited, diffused and competitive and a large number of the persons who wield it are directly and periodically accountable to the people from whom they ultimately derive power. There is a continuous public scrutiny of what the ruler does and he is subject to daily and periodic assessment. The problem for the tyrant, as Aristotle knew, is to find people who will tell him the truth. Constitutional regime rarely suffers from this disadvantage. The people to tell the truth are obvious, the *ultima ratio* in a democratic polity.

NON-CONSTITUTIONAL REGIMES

Non-Constitutional regimes. Non-constitutional democracies include regimes of different

22. Michael Curtis, *Comparative Government and Politices,* p. 52.

types, though all are dictatorial in different degrees and lack an organized political opposition and a free press. They may exist because the country has no tradition of a constitutional behaviour or cannot agree on fundamentals, or due to the inability of the executive to rule, as a result of the presence of multiplicity of parties which prevent the formation of a stable and coherent government, or from the attempt to implement an ideology as in the USSR, the People's Republic of China and other Communist countries. As a result of these variety of reasons non-constitutional regimes are divided into authoritarian and totalitarian.

Totalitarianism. Totalitarianism is another name for dictatorship, the term hitherto used. Dictatorship as a form of government is not new. It was a recognised institution in the republican Rome where normally the authority of government was vested in two presidents called Consuls. In times of emergency the Romans used to appoint a Director to supersede the Consuls, granting him supreme powers to meet the crisis. But Roman dictatorship was a temporary expedient to meet a crisis and was discarded when the crisis was past. Moreover, the dictator was selected by a legal process with the obligation to submit his use of power to the scrutiny of the permanent authority. The Roman dictatorship was, therefore, "a constitutional device under which the constitution was suspended during a grave crisis of the State.[23]

This description of dictatorship does not apply to the modern dictators of former Soviet Russia, Italy, Germany and some other countries. Modern dictators are not selected by a legal process for a limited period of time in order to steer the State through a national emergency. They come into power as a result of a *coup d'etat*. Force is the criterion of their political authority and they remain in power as long as force can retain them. They are responsible to no authority except to themselves. The whole authority of the State is vested in one individual person and he personifies the State. Some writers are of the opinion that the Russian dictatorship was the dictatorship of a party while in Germany and Italy it was the dictatorship of individuals. But Naziism in Germany and Fascism in Italy were also the rule of a party, though they remained all through overshadowed by a single personality just as Bolshevism was in the days of Lenin and Stalin. Till yesterday, Khrushchev's personality loomed large on the political horizon. In fact, no government, as MacIver has shown, is ever actually in the hands of a single individual. If there is a single seemingly supreme ruler, he inevitably rests his power on the active support of an associated class. He rules in its interests no less than with its cooperation. He nearly always has a council of advisers who represent that class. Hitler and Mussolini were leaders of the Nazi and Fascist parties. They selected their ministers from the ranks of their own parties in order to pursue the ends of their respective parties. There is, accordingly, no difference between the Russian type of dictatorship and that of Central European countries. If there was any, it was only one of degree rather than of kind,In USSR it was really a triple dictatorship—that of the Communist Party as regards the mass of citizens, that of the inner group as regards the rest of the Party, and that of the leader as regards inner group, party and the nation.

Modern Dictatorship. Modern dictatorship is the product of World War I. The War

23. MacIver, R.M., *The Web of Government*, p. 227.

was claimed to be a fight of democracy against autocracy and it was fought to make the world safe for democracy. The Treaty of Versailles was also formed on broad democratic principles. It recognised the principle of self-determination of nations and built new States on the ruins of earlier monarchies. The defeated Germany presented to the world the best specimen of a parliamentary government through the Weimar Constitution. It was hoped that the new States as well as the old would gradually come round to parliamentary democracy. But surprising as it may seem, in close wake of the War, nearly three-quarters of the people of Europe found democratic government either destroyed or in danger of destruction. Italy came under the heels of Mussolini and his Fascist Party in 1922, after his famous march on Rome. Primo di Rivero was declared the father of Spain in 1923. The Weimar Constitution of 1918 was replaced in government by a dictatorship under Hitler and his Nazi party. In Poland the lingering shadow of parliamentary government was lost in 1929, when Pilsudski sent a body of soldiers into the lobby of the Chamber to remind the representatives of their limitations. In Yugoslavia, King Alexander dismissed parliament and suspended the Constitution. In Rumania, King Carol made a similar attempt at royal dictatorship in 1931. Besides these countries, Bulgaria, Portugal, Hungary, Austria and Turkey also came under the sway of dictators. In Greece, John Metaxes established himself in power on August 4, 1939, and began to regiment the life of the country on the patterm of Germany and Italy. In every case dictatorship was born of dis- illusion and despair, military defeat, economic crisis, breakdown of old traditions and the existence of a man or a group of men with a definite programme of action. In countries where democracies had appeared, it had been a plant with no deep roots as it was alien to the soil. Conditions were therefore not favourable to the successful functioning of democratic institutions.

In all these countries it was a dictatorship of the Right. But in Russia it was a dictatorship of the Left. The former means the dictatorship of the capitalist and the latter is the dictatorship of the proletariat, which is a transitional phase between the destruction of the capitalist society and the emergence of the comnunistic society when the State "withers away." Both these brands of "dictatorship are fundamentally opposed to one another in their ideology, but they operate on roughly the same principles. Their common feature was that both ruled by a single group and do not tolerate the existence of any other party. They begin with the community, not with the individual, and consider that the claims of the State, as representing the community, must always have precedence. They deny that the power of the State should be limited by appeal either to individual rights or to fundamental laws; law is the will of the State and there is nothing higher than the State. They deny that any part or aspect of human life can be outside the normal and continuous control of the State; the State is charged with authority over the whole, the totality of what goes within its territories—political, economic, religious, and cultural. Government is identified with the State and it is not responsible to anything or anybody. The non-accountability of government is, in fact, one of the fundamental concepts of dictatorship. The dictatorship of all types has, therefore, in common the negation of the fundamental principles on which democracy rests.

Modern dictatorships, therefore, gave birth to a totalitarian State as opposed to a democratic State. The Greek City-State was also totalitarian in the sense that the Greeks did not differentiate between the State and society. The State and society were practically synonymous for them and the Greek City-State was omnicompetent; it was the church, the school, and the State all combined. But the modern dictator's totalitarian State is not one like the Greek City-State. It is total government with autocracy extending its interest and control into every facet of the people's lives. The State is everything and the individual amounts to nothing.

Two important principles of modern dictatorship are: (1) to make a sharp distinction between rulers and subjects; and (2) to blur the distinction between government and the State. In order that his authority may not be challenged, the ruler not only monopolises the actual power, but denies to others the right to power. An effective means to this end is to obliterate the difference between government and the State. The ruler becomes the State. The State and, for that matter, government becomes omnicompetent. There is no sphere of life which the modern dictator's State will not cover. For Hitler and Mussolini there was nothing above the State, nothing beyond it, and nothing beside it. The State embraced all activities of the individuals and subordinated them to national ends. It was an omnicompetent and infallible State. Mussolini's motto to the people of Italy was: "All within the State, none outside the State, none against the State." This was tantamount to the worship of the State and this worship of the State was cultivated in schools, on the playground, in clubs, associations and in fact everywhere. The life of every individual did not belong to him, but to the State and the State alone. Thus, narrow nationalism, chauvinism, aggressive warfare and imperialistic expansion were some of the essential features of Facism and Naziism. Russian Communism had also become nationalistic and militaristic, although it was not yet aggressively imperialistic, despite what Russia had done to Finland, the small Baltic States and in Afghanistan.

When the nation is glorified, the obvious result is war. Hitler and Mussolini openly preached war. Hitler extolled force and violence and he had all praise for the man of action. He believed in the power of the victorious sword. According to Mussolini, peace "is an act of cowardice in the face of sacrifice." Italy and Germany pursued a policy of colonial expansion for procuring raw materials, for the sale of their manufactured goods, and for the realisation of their will to power. Mussolini said, "Imperialism is the eternal and immutable law of life." Italy, he declared, "must expand or perish."

Dictatorship means one-man or one-party political rule and all totalitarian regimes, to right or left, have adopted essentially the same technique. The leader or dictator who stands at the head obviously cannot do everything by himself. He rules through an *elite* or selected ruling class and this class is the party which is the basis of the system. It is, therefore, the very antithesis of democracy. Democracy, according to the dictators and their apologists, is a decaying corpse because it is "stupid, corrupt and slow-moving." Parliaments, it was maintained, are mere talking shops, "incapable of accomplishing results; at times of emergency they are absolutely helpless." Since modern dictatorship is one-man or one-party rule, it permits no political opposition and is hostile to individual liberty. Individual liberty, according to Communism, is a *bourgeois* conception, and Fascism and Naziism both, regarded it as a fetish of the past. The individual, it is said, has no life apart from the State, and so he must be completely subordinated to it. The totalitarian State, thus, does not give to its subjects the right to speech, the right to press, the right to assembly and all those rights which characterise the individual's life in a democratic State. In the USSR where they were conceded, they were subordinated to the cause of socialism and a socialist society. The ideal of Naziism and Fascism was "one reich, one people, one leader." The Fascist oath read: "In the name of God and Italy, I swear to execute without discussion the orders of the Duce and to serve with all my strength and if necessary with my blood the cause of the Fascist revolution." Mussolini's motto to the youth organisation of Italy was "To believe, to obey, to fight." Hitler put it: duty, discipline and sacrifice. This is regimentation of human life, pure and simple. The whole nation must think in one way, talk in one way, and act in one way. Free discussion and criticism of government were ruthlessly suppressed.

Communist totalitarianism is distinct from Fasicst or Nazi totalitarianism in one important fact. The State, its machinery and everything else that happens in a Communist regime is meant to be merely a transitional stage on history's inexorable path toward a future depicted as one of complete human emancipation and freedom. The Dictatorship of the Proletariat is armed with the revolutionary task of destroying capitalism and building socialism. Every coercive measure it adopts is justified to attain the end. The Party, which is the vanguard of the socialist society, is entrusted with the duty of educating the "backward" public in their "social consciousness." The Party must, therefore, exercise control and accumulate powers. The holders of powers are the agents of the movement of socialism and they act "democratically" in a more profound way than do the people's representatives in a capitalist democracy. The Communist leaders are accordingly, performing the historic task of social and general reconstruction.

It is a basic characteristic of Communism that it makes social change a major objective and that it mobilizes all the instruments of the modern indu- strial State—technology, education, communication media—to accelerate this process. In doing so, it has two objectives. To move as rapidly as possible toward the transcendant goals which are formulated by the leaders, and to keep the society so mobile that non-party groups, which are permitted to exist, have little chance to stabilize and exercise effective influence on its character. In communist regimes, there is what is often called "permanent revolution."

The purge is another characteristic of Communist regimes. It promotes specific policies and, at the same time, it removes those who oppose them. It may eliminate the power of those against whom it is aimed. The purge, accordingly acts against those considered a danger to the elite either because they hold different social objectives (as was true of sizable groups in the early days of Communist regimes) or because they endorse different techniques for moving toward the common goal or because they threaten to establish predominant influence (as it has happened after Mao's death in China).

To sum up, totalitarian polities, like democratic ones, may be both civilian controlled and popular, but in totalitarian Communist systems there is an official ideology. The ideology is totalitarian in that the totality of social life is considered a legitimate matter for political control. In a totalitarian regime not only power is concentrated in the hands of an individual or groups, but also the regime eliminates all opposition parties, controls communication mass media, exercises control over the economy, makes deliberate use of terror through the secret police, and completely amoral use of force. The existence of a single official ideology and a single party accounts for concentration of political and economic power in the same group.

It is, however, argued whether it is logical to fit in the USSR, Germany and Italy in the same category. In the Soviet Union of 1970s collective leadership was replaced by rule of a single leader; the police state came to an end and there was little use of terror and physical force. Even more free opinion was tolerated though the official ideology remained unchanged. The third session of the National People's Congress, held in September 1980, represented a watershed in the history of Communist China. It takes the process of post-Mao change a big step further. These are: to separate party and government posts, and to end the concentration of too much power in individual leaders, to consolidate the concept of collective leadership, to induct comparatively younger men into responsible positions, and to end the practice of life-long political vocation for ageing leaders. On the economic side, the emphasis is on decentralisation and liberalisation in the economy, which is reflected in the 1982 constitution.

Authoritarian Regimes. After World War II dictatorship did not become extinct. It appeared in new forms in most of the countries in Asia and Africa which had become independent after the War. All these countries started their careers with democratic institutions, generally of the parlia- mentary type, but barring a few, all of them succumbed to some form or other of dictatorial rule. But Hitler lying dead and burning in his Berlin bunker and Mussolini's dead body strung upside down on a gibbet for the crowd's jeer had made these dictators wiser. They had realized that autocracy in its naked form and the myth of leadership as preached by the totalitarians, would no longer keep them in power for long. They tempered their autocracy with constitutional process. They ascribed their rise to power to inexorable circum-stances and promised to bring about conditions for the restoration of democracy which the earlier regimes had corrupted and demoralised. The present day dictators, therefore, made democracy an umbrella to shelter their authoritarian rule.

General Naguib's *coup d'etat* in Egypt forced King Farouk to abdicate. Naguib was soon replaced by Colonel Nasser. But when his authority was fully entrenched, he summoned a Constituent Assembly and entrusted it with the duty to formulate a republican constitution. Colonel Nasser was elected President under the new Constitution. Autocratic traditions, however, lingered on and they formed a conspicious feature of the new Constitution. In 1964, another Constitution came into being with democratic traditions. Nasser was the President of the United Arab Republic and was succeeded, after his demise, by Sadat without any diminution in the Presidential authority and there is none even now with Mubbarak in the Presidential Palace.

In Pakistan, General Ayub Khan with the help of Iskander Mirza, President of the Islamic Republic of Pakistan, captured power in October 1958, by a military *cout d'etat*. The Constitution was abrogated, Martial Law promulgated and political parties banned. The constitutional machinery, thus, totally disappeared. Having fully established himself in power, Ayub forced Iskander Mirza to quit his office and virtually banished him from the country. In January 1960, Ayub Khan decreed setting up of local bodies elected through the scheme of controlled elections. In February these local bodies elected General

Ayub Khan as the President of Pakistan. In 1961-62, the President devised the contrivance of "Basic Democracies", which in all its essentials was identical to his previous scheme of local bodies, except for the attractive name of 'democracy' and that too 'basic'. Through the process of restricted elections some 1,500,000 voters, out of Pakistan's total population of 100 million, elected near-about 80,000 members of the "Basic Democracies." The "Basic Democrats" elected General Ayub as the President and conferred upon him the rank of Field Marshal. The "Basic Democrats" also elected the National Assembly as well as the Provincial Assemblies of East and West Pakistan.

Pakistan adopted a Constitution of the Presidential type in 1963 and elections thereunder were held by the end of 1964. Pakistan was again in turmoil in 1969 and Ayub Khan declared Martial Law on March 25, abrogated the Constitution and appointed General Yahya Khan as the Chief Marshal Law Administrator. Yahya Khan partially restored the 1963 Constitution and assumed the powers of the President. He abdicated after the 1971 Indo-Pak conflict and Zulfiqar Ali Bhutto succeeded him as the President and Chief Martial Law Administrator, with a promise to restore democracy. The democratic Islamic Constitution of Pakistan became operative on August 14, 1973 with Zulfiqar Ali Bhutto as the first Prime Minister enjoying unprecendented powers unknown in the annals of parliamentary democracy. General Zia-ul-Haq's *coup* in 1977 again established the military regime in Pakistan. He did not abrogate the 1973 Constitution, but drastically altered it to enable the Martial Law Administration to act expeditiously and effectively. General Haq assumed the office of the President and combined unto himself the offices of the Chief of the Army Staff and the Chief Martial Law Administrator. He promised to restore civilian rule and democratic institutions soon after normalcy was restored. He fed the people with the same promise for full five years, ultimately switching on to the ideology of Islamic democracy. Political parties were banned, strict censorship of the press was enforced and powers and jurisdiction of the judiciary drastically curtailed by amending the 1973 Constitution through the medium of Presidential Ordinances.

President Soekarno of Indonesia introduced the myth of "guided" or "controlled" democracy. Immediately after the assumption of power Soekarno dissolved the National Assembly. He constituted his Council of Ministers drawn from all political parties, thereby giving it the complexion of a national government, but all the ministers were chosen at the President's will and they were responsible to him alone. They represented no one except the President, expressed his will and executed his policies. Any direct or indirect opposition was crushed with a heavy hand. Soekarno was deprived of his power and authority as President in March 1967. Subharto succeeded him, retaining the same political and administrative apparatus.

In almost all the States which had become independent during the past two decade or so, there are Party dictatorships with almost unrestricted powers within the framework of a democratic mechanism. Opposition has been ruthlessly suppressed in all these countries and in some of them, as in Ghana, parliamentary institutions have also been abrogated and even the powers of the judiciary considerably curtailed. The leaders heading the governments of all these countries are those who had led their countries and won independence for them. The justification for concentration of power and the reasons for suppressing the opposition are the same as advanced by the dictators in Egypt, Pakistan,

Indonesia, Iraq and other countries. Exercise of such a power, they plead, is necessary to protect their countries from all possibilities of revolution, to maintain the independence and integrity of the State, and to accelerate the pace of prosperity of the people. Algeria also saw military dictatorship brought about by the chief of the Army Staff, Colonel Hourai Boumedienne. Previously Algiers was a one-party dictatorship under President Ben Bella and Colonel Hourai Boumedienne was the greatest supporter of the President.

From this survey, it is clear that many developing countries are something short of dictatorships, military or totalitarian, and yet are short of democracies. The spectrum of immediate forms and styles of political organisation and operation is broad. Legislative assemblies, for instance, go through all the legislative processes and perform their normal functions, and may exercise some power, but it is largely window-dressing. Frequently the effective leadership in these countries "is consciousl making use of democratic forms to build the requisites of democracy to the point where substance may be added to the form of democracy."[24] Edward Shils has coined the term "tutelary democracy"[25] for these regimes. In them one party is dominant but other parties are tolerated. The dominant party is itself far from monolithic, containing numerous divergent elements. Top leaders of the dominant party tend to occupy the highest posts in government. Charismatic leadership is heavily relied upon. Such a regime may better be called authoritarian rather than "tutelary democracy."

A totalitarian regime is differentiated from an authoritarian system by its total control over and attempt to regulate behaviour, and by the subordination of all organizations to the State. In authoritarian regimes, as explained earlier, liberty is restricted and parliamentary institutions are absent or meaningless but the system is not tyrannical. The society is traditionally oriented, and power is exercised by small groups, such as military leaders, bureaucrats or religious figures. In a totalitarian regime not only power is concentrated in the hands of an individual or group, but also the regime does not tolerate opposition. The regime is totalitarian in that the totality of social life is considered a legitimate matter for political control. In practice, social control is not total but the scope of government is, nevertheless, very great compared with other political systems. The control that is exercised is by a relatively small group sustained by a single mass political party, a monopoly of the mass media of communication, and a subservient judiciary.

The constant dilemma for authoritarian systems is that rebellion or revolution is the only way to register disaffection. *Coup d' etat* is now the normal feature of authoritarian regimes and it is so frequent and widespread in Africa and some parts of Asia particularly that it seldom causes a flutter in international politics. In fact, recognition for the new regimes is as much a matter of routine as the *Coup* itself.

Merits of Dictatorship. There has been widespread praise for dictatorships. They have been claimed as regimes of "strong men who get things done." There seems to be some justification in this claim. In majority of the European countrire parliaments and politicians miserably failed to solve the post-war problems. Their unsettled economic and

24. J. Roland Pennock and David G. Smith, *Political Science, An Introduction,* p. 612.

25. Edward Shils, "Political Development in the New States," *Comparative Studies in Society and History*, pp. 389 ff. Shils uses also the category of "modernizing oligarchies."

political conditions and extreme economic distress demanded stable governments with vigour of will and action. But owing to the presence of multiple parties, divided and debased by their factiousness, they could not forge a united front. So the people were ready to yield to the authority of any power who could give them sufficient to eat and stable and efficient government respected at home and abroad. The dictators succeeded admirably in fostering national unity and established confidence in the people by demonstrating to them that they could act more promptly and vigorously and arrive at quicker decisions. Their firmness and determination stood in sharp contrast with the weak and vacillating policies of democratic rulers. When Hitler was asked about the programme of the Nazi party he replied that Germany had enough of programmes; she now needed action. Americans had praised particularly the Italian dictatorship, charactersing it as a system which they intended "to run, to function, to do, to accomplish."[26]

The dictator has either no one to consult or the persons whom he consults are his own men who always dutifully submit to his will. He can, therefore, be quick and prompt in his decisions and, consequently, able to meet emergencies efficiently. The recent history of Russia, Germany, Italy, Turkey and Spain is the history of marvels which a cletermined dictator can bring about in the national life of his country. Let us take the achievements of the Spanish dictator Rivera as a typical example. Jackson, in his book, *Europe Since the War*, writes: "For the first time in their history the Spanish trains ran punctually. New railways were laid down, and a system of fine motor roads took the place of traditional mule tracks of Spain. The commerce and industry prospered under the dictator ..... Agriculture flourished. Labour unrest was mitigated." Poverty and unemployment did no longer exist—indeed a remarkable achievement when it is remembered that the dictators began their careers at a time when the economic and political conditions of nearly all the Continental countries were in complete chaos. They began in an atmosphere of national revival, and placed the high ideals of patriotism, comradeship and sacrifice constantly before their countrymen, thus, infusing in them the virtue of service. A dictator alone can brush aside ruthlessly all elements of disorder and opposition in order to rehabilitate a nation's political, economic and social life.

Demerits of Dictatorship. Dictatorship may have given to the people well-feeding. But well-feeding is not the end of human life. To regiment human life and to subordinate it to the State is to dwarf intelligence and initiative. "At best a dictatorship is run as an elaborately organised house of correction, in which inmate is assigned his task and vigilantly inspected as to the manner in which he discharges it."[27] This is good enough for the delinquent and defective members of society, but not for normal men or men towering above others in character and ability. A centralised and coercive direction of public life destroys the possibility of development of human personality, learning, literature and art. According to Mussolini, the Fascist doctrine did, not recognise the individual except "in so far his interests coincide with those of the State." Totalitarianism, therefore, "has meant the crushing of individual liberty and the suppression of human personality, violence at home and unashamed aggression abroad, the brutalising of human nature and the militarisation of a whole people"[28] Moreover, the administrative efficiency, which

26. Coker, F.W., *Recent Political Thought*, p. 488.
27. *Ibid*., p. 490.

dictatorship secures, is suicidal to the very spirit of the people. The dictator dictates and every one else is expected to do his duty. It is tantamount to killing the initiative and enterprise of the individual.

Force and fear are natural foundations of authority for those who regard national power and glory as ends in themselves. But indiscriminate use of force involves dangers. The lessons of history are, says Benedetto Croce, "that .... regimes of force can survive only among decadent peoples; that they can figure only as temporary expedients in nations that are growing and in the ascendant; and that repressions only produce more violent explosions of the forces they would restrain."[29] What is created by force is destroyed by force. Force, is not the stabilising basis of the State. Consent of the governed is its real and enduring basis. As dictatorship does not derive its authority from the consenting people, the dictator can never be sure of his position. He adopts violence and coercive measures to suppress even the slightest opposition. Such a policy spells disaster for the future, for to eliminate all differences is to eliminate all that keeps the community mentally and spiritually alive.

Glorification of the national power fosters international intimidation. The ideal of totalitarian State is a national State "well-ordered internally but aggressive, and bent on expansion." It is opposed to international amity and is thus, the bankruptcy of human reason and intelligence. Can we, under the circumstances, regard dictatorship as a suitable alternative to democracy ? Dictactorship, according. to a modern writer, is a tyrant's paradise, "the totalitarian State is a prison and its subjects are closed in by walls, nonetheless real because they, are invisible." The dictatorial rule and its methods are repugnant to the finer feelings of man and are disastrous to the promotion of higher values in life.

Dictatorship versus Democracy. Whatever we may think of dictatorship ideally, empirically it cannot be denied that it has proved an effective form of government in solving the emergent social problems and mobilising the resources to accelerate the economic and technological progress. So far only war and defeat has brought dictatorship to an end: after eleven years in Germany and after twenty years in Italy. In the U.S.S.R. in more than seventy years of its career in the construction of the socialist society stupendous and incredible results were achieved and rightly the 1977 Constitution could claim that the goal of completely developed socialist society had been attained. In the international politics, too, the Soviet State enjoyed enviable position. The People's Republic of China and other Communist States might not have reached that much of stature, but their achievements in a comparatively shorter period of their careers were no less astonishing. And socialism despite, its recent decay, is not only spreading to other lands, but even capitalist countries are increasingly adopting socialistic policies to solve their problems. Hunger, poverty, unemployment and under-employment are the stark realities in all these countries, though their intensity may be lesser in the developed countries as compared with the underdeveloped.

The efficacy of democracy and democratic institutions in solving the sufferings of the

28. Asirvatham, E., *Political Theory*, p. 517.
29. Coker F.W., *Recent Political Thought*, p'. 488.

masses has of late been seriously questioned and opinion is tilting toward dictatorship as a substitute. Even ardent advocates of democracy have expressed their scepticism and James Bryce is one of them. He wrote, perhaps in anguish: "when the spiritual oxygen which has kept alive the attachment to liberty and self-government in the minds of the people becomes exhausted will not the flame burn low and perhaps flicker out."[30] But all have not lost faith in democracy and Laski is the foremost among them. He considers the democratic government "is doubtless a final form of political organisation in the sense that men who have once tested power will not, without conflict surrender it."[31] He had abiding faith in the permanence of democracy and firmly believed that it would continue.

In spite of its failings, which are many and some of them quite grave, democracy is, as a rule, the most appropriate form of government for modern times and it is the logical sequence of evolution. Its appeal is still great for the people as no better alternative is open to mankind. But democratic institutions shall have to be reformed in order to become progressive, adaptable and flexible vehicles responsive to the aspirations of the people. Our economic, social and political orders have been rendered shaky and unless democracy finds the means of equalising opportunity and wiping out the yawning economic disparities which have paralysed the social structure and destroyed the political fabric, its future is definitely bleak. After all democracy is an operative ideal and it is the skill and dexterity of its operators that can save it. MacIver has cogently said that there is "only one way to keep it in being, that is through the intelligent perception, permeating the people, of what it is and what makes it precious. We guard our spiritual treasures only by learning to appreciate it."[32] The traditional approach to democracy has proved a sheer sham. It requires to be substituted by reorienting our democratic values than substituting it by a totalitarian regime. Totalitarianism may present a fascinating balance-sheet of achievements-improvement in the condition of the masses by providing order and security, economic amelioration restoration of nationalistic self-respect, hopes and ambitions and national unity. But at what cost ? The cost is great and immeasurable. It is achieved by stifling the liberty of thoughts expression and association and dwarfing the stature of the people. What totalitarianism takes away from the people, democracy provides a climate for its preservation and growth. Clement Atlee had appropriately said that democracy is the only method by which economic and social equality would ultimately be achieved; not by regimentation of opinion and administration and ideological commitment but by persuasion and conviction that there lies the well-being of humanity.

30. Bryce, J. *Modern Democracies,* Vol. 1, p, 603.

31. Laski, H.J,, *A Grammar of Politics,* p. 17.

32. MacIver, R.M., *The Ramparts We Guard*, p. 4.

SUGGESTED READINGS

Almond, Gabriel A., and Coleman, James S. (Eds.),: *The Politics of the Developing Areas.*

Anupchand Kapur: *Two Constitutions.*

Arendt, H.: *The Origins of Totalitarianism.*

Asirvatham, E.: *Political Theory,* Chap. XV.

Babbit, I.: *Democracy and Leadership.*

Bagehot, W.: *The English Constitution,* Chap. II.

Barker, E. *Reflections on Government,* Chaps. VII-X

Beni Prasad: *The Democratic Process.*

Birach, A.H.: *Representative and Responsible Government.*

Brian Chapman: *British Government Observed.*

Brogan, D.W.: *The American Political System.*

Bryce, J.: *The American Commonwealth.*

Bryce, J.: *Modern Democracies,* Vol. I, Part II; Vol. II, Part III.

Cobban Alfred: *Dictatorship, Its History and Theory.*

Finer, H.: *Mussolini's Italy.*

Finer, H.: *The Theory and Practice of Modern Government,* Chaps. XXIII, XXVI, pp. 90-94, 951-54.

Ford, G.S.: *Dictatorship in the Modern World.*

Ford H.J.: *Representative Government,* Chap. XI.

Garner, J.W.: *Introduction to Political Science,* pp. 179-91,197-200.'

Garner, J.W.: *Political Science and Government,* pp. 332-44, 423-38.

Hoover, C.B.: *Dictatorship and Democracies.*

Hitler, A.: *Mein Kempf*

Jennings, W.I.: *Cabinet Government.*

Lsski, H.J.: *Parliamentary Government in England.*

Lowell, A.L.: *Government of England,* Vol I, Chaps. II III, XVII-XVIII.

Mussolini, B.: *The Political and Social Doctrines of Socialism.*

Parkinson, C.N.: *The Evolution of Political Thought.*

Rossiter, Cinton: *Constitutional Dictatorship.*

Row, E.F.: *How States are Governed?*

Sidgwick, H.: *Elements of Politics,* Chaps. XIX-XX.

Wilson, W.: *Congressional Government.*

16

CHAPTER

Separation of Powers

Distribution of Powers Functionally. In the preceding Chapter[1] we said that two methods may be employed for distributing governmental powers, the territorial and the functional. These two are not alternative methods. The territorial division relates to the splitting up of the territory of the State into political divisions and the distribution of governmental powers among such divisions. Each of the political divisions is provided with a governmental organisation through which it performs its functions. But the work of government is so wide and complex that it is imperative to establish special organs for the performance of the several kinds of work to be done. This is necessary for two obvious reasons: first that the benefits of specialisation may be secured and, secondly, responsibility may be more definitely located. When the work of government is distributed to political organs in accordance with the nature of function to be performed, it is the functional distribution powers. Carl J. Friedrich says that true constitutional government does not exist "unless procedural restraints are established and effectively operating. Such restraints involve some division of power; for evidently some considerable power must be vested in those who are expected to do the restraining. Such a division of governmental power under a constitution has largely taken two forms: the functional division—such as that into legislative, executive, and judicial, and the spatial (territorial) division of federalism."[2]

Based upon this principle of distribution, all the powers of government have long been conceived as falling within one or another of three great classes, according as they have to do with : (1) the enactment of making of laws, (2) the interpretation of these laws and (3) their enforcement. To these three classes have been given the names, legislative, judicial and executive. Structurally considered, government has been deemed to be made up of three branches having for their functions the enactment, the adjudication, and the enforcement of law, and the branches to which these functions belong are known as the Legislature, the Judiciary, and the Executive respectively.

This three-fold division of governmental powers had received such general recognition that it became a classical division. But recently it has been held by some writers that this division is unscientific. Willoughby, for example, says "that attempts to act upon it lead

1. Chapter XIV *ante.*
2. Carl J. Friedrich, *Constitutional Government and Democracy,* p. 173.

not only to confusion of thought but to serious difficulties in working out the practical problems of the distribution of governmental powers functionally."[3] He suggests that electorate and administration are distinct branches of government and it is important to recognise their distinct character in the practical work of organising and operating a government. In Sweden administrative power has been separated from the executive power and Carl Friedrich says, "without any theoretical recognition of the fact, the American federal government tends in the same direction of differentiating between strictly executive and purely administrative functions."[4] Gladden, however, does not support this point of view, and is of the opinion that administration "is subordinate to the main powers or branches of government." Gladden's opinion is convincing and we adhere, to the three-fold division. Nor can there be a divorce between the electorate and legislative functions. Political sovereign and legal sovereign are the two aspects of the sovereignty of the State. The will of the electors is the controlling power behind the legal sovereign and it is to their mandate that the legal sovereign must ultimately bow.

Theory of the Separation of Powers. Political liberty, we have emphasised, is possible only when the government is restrained and limited. The theory that the functions of government should be differentiated, and that they should be performed by distinct organs consisting of different bodies of persons so that each department should be limited to its own sphere of action without encroaching upon the others, and that it should be independent within that sphere, is called in its traditional form, the theory of the Separation of Powers. Montesquieu, the celebrated French scholar, wrote in his famous book, *The Spirit of the Laws*, that "constant experience shows us that every man invested with power is apt to abuse it, and to carry his authority until he is confronted with limits." Montesquieu poses the question clearly enough. He asserts that concentrated power is dangerous and leads to despotism. But how to avoid concentration of power? His answer is simple: by separating the functions of the executive, legislative and judicial departments of government so that one may operate as a balance against another and, thus, power should be a check on power. *Le pouvoir arrete le pouvoir*; power halts power. A constitution may be such that none "shall be compelled to do things to which be is not obliged by law, or not to do things which the law permits."[5] Montesquieu's thesis is the division of powers by functions and the theory emerging therefrom is known as that of the Separation of Powers. The exposition given by Montesquieu has now become classical.

The idea contained in the theory of the Separation of Powers was not entirely unknown before Montesquieu. Its origin can be traced back to Aristotle, if not indeed to earlier writers. In the *Politics* is found an analysis of three "parts", or branches of government—the deliberative, executive and judicial.[6] Aristotle did not go into details. He confined himself to a description of their personnel, organisation, and functions, without suggesting their separation. Various political philosophers, from Marsigilo of Padua in the fourteenth century, gave some attention to the theory of Separation of Powers, but it meant little to Political Science until the issue of political liberty became urgent. In the seventeenth

3. Willoughby, W.F., *The Government of Modern States,* p. 227.
4. Carl J. Friedrich, *Constitutional Government and Democracy,* p. 182.
5. *Esprit des Lois,* Book XI, Chap. 4.
6. Book IV, Chaps. 14-16.

century it "began to acquire meaning, and in the eighteenth, with critical times, it came to the forefront of discussion."

There are traces of the theory in John Locke's *Civil Government*. Locke distinguished between three powers that existed in every commonwealth. These he called legislative, executive and federative; the federative power related to the conduct of foreign affairs. The executive and federative powers, he pointed out "are always almost united", and to this union he expressed no objection. But he would not permit the union of the executive power with the legislative. The legislative power, he said, "in well-ordered commonwealth, where the good of the whole is so considered as it ought", is placed in the hands of an assembly that convenes at intervals. But since the administration and enforcement of law is a continuous task, a power distinct from the legislative must remain "always in being." In practice, "the legislative and executive powers come often to be separated." In principle, too, Locke argued that they should be separate, "because it may be too great temptation to human frailty, apt to grasp at power, for the same persons who have the power of making laws to have also in their hands the power to execute them."[7] This division of authority and the separation of executive and legislative power is justified and explained by Locke on the ground that it is necessary for the maintenance of liberty. Liberty suffers when the same human beings make the laws and apply them.

The Ideas of Montesquieu. Here were the threads for Montesquieu to gather, elaborate and expand, and then to formulate them in concrete terms. Montesquieu lived in the time of Louis XIV, the author of the famous dictum, "I am the State."[8] The monarch combined in his person all the three powers. His word was law and his authority was unquestionable. There was no liberty for the people under such an oppressive and despotic government. Montesquieu happened to visit Great Britain and was tremendously impressed by the spirit of freedom prevailing there. He tried to find, out the causes of the liberty of the British people. He compared the independence of the judges and the strength of Parliament there with the subordination of the judiciary to the French Monarchy and the virtual extinction of the Estates-General. Not foreseeing the rise of the Cabinet system of government in Britain and keenly desiring to substitute political liberty for royal absolutism in France, Montesquieu advocated the separation of powers as a device to make government safe for the governed. The division of powers that he envisaged was the same as that of Locke, except for renaming Locke's executive power and calling it the judicial power. The executive function, as described by Locke, had been to execute the laws in any case. He also changed Locke's terminology and named his federative power as the executive power. But in his insistence that they must be entrusted separately to different personnel he went considerably ahead of his predecessor. His most famous statement runs thus:

"When the legislative and executive powers are united in the same person, or in the same body of Magistrates, there can be no liberty; because apprehensions may arise, lest the same monarch or senate should enact tyrannical laws, and execute them in a tyrannical manner. Again, there is no liberty if the judicial power be not separated from the legislative and executive. Were it joined with the legislative, the life and liberty of the subject would

---

7. (Second) *Treatise of Civil Government,* Chap. 12, Secs. 143-148.

8. Refer to Carl Friedrich's *Constitutional Government and Democracy,* p, 177.

be exposed to arbitrary control, for the judge would then be legislator. Were it joined to the executive power, the judge might behave with violence and oppression. There would be an end of everything, were the same man or the same body... to exercise those three powers, that of enacting laws, that of executing the public resolutions, and of trying the cases of individuals."[9]

To explain briefly and in simple language, Montesquieu endeavoured to establish that whoever has unrestrained power, will abuse it. If the legislative and executive powers arc combined in the same person or body of persons, there can be no liberty, because the same agency becomes the maker and executor of laws. Similarly, if the legislative and judicial functions are combined the maker of laws is also their interpreter. If the executive powers are combined with the judicial, the same agency is the prosecutor as well as the judge. If all the three powers are concentrated in a single hand there would be an end of everything, as there will be tyrannical laws interpreted and enforced with the violence of an oppressor. Montesquieue's thesis is that concentration of legislative, executive and judicial functions, either in one single person or a body of persons, results in abuse of authority, and such an organisation is tyrannical. He urged that the three departments of government should be so organised that each should be entrusted to different personnel, and each dapartment should perform distinct functions within the sphere of powers assigned to it.

There has been some controversy among students of Political Science whether Montesquieu contemplated an absolute or only a limited separation of three powers. One school is of the opinion that Montesquieu desired absolute separation so that each department remained independent and supreme within its own sphere. Others believe that he never thought to separate the powers completely. He rather suggested modification of the concentration of powers. "Montesquieu was searching for means," as Herman Finer observes, "to limit the Crown; to make a constitution; to build canals through which, but not over which, power should stream; to create intermediary bodies; to check and balance probable despotism and yet he did not wish to fly to the extreme of democracy."[10] For Montesquieu, the executive convenes the legislature, fixes its duration, and votes legislation. The legislature has the right of impeachment. It may not arraign the chief of the State but, "as the person entrusted with the executive power cannot abuse it, without bad counsellors, and such as have the laws as ministers, though the laws protect them as subjects, these men may be examined and punished." His idea of impeachment is akin to that of political responsibility of ministers in our times. Loeke's analysis of the government structure, too, proves that the various powers of government were not to be separated into watertight compartments.He made them dependent on the supreme power of the people, the executive functioned in subordination to the legislature; and the judiciary worked as part and parcel of the executive.

The essence of Montesquieu's theory of Separation of Powers is that it imposes on each organ of government the obligation to explain itself and to see that it acted within law and not beyond it. If the authority exercised is in excess of that permitted by law,

9. *Spirit of the Laws,* Book VI, p. 6 ed. Franz Neumann, trans. Thomas Nugent (1949), pp. 151-52.
10. Finer, H., *The Theory and Practics of Modern Government*, p. 277.

it should be checked by the other in order to restrain its encroachments. And this is the correct meaning of *le pouvoir artere le pouvoir*—power halts power. There must be a separation of powers within the structure of government in order that one power may operate as a balance against another power. Such a check Montesquieu considered necessary for safeguarding the liberty of the individual and for avoiding tyranny. Montesquieu follows Locke, "but with more system and it is important to observe that he never thinks to separate the powers completely, but rather to modify the concentration of powers."[11]

Blackstone's View. A similar view was expressed by Backstone, the British jurist. In his : *Commentaries on the Laws of England*, Blackstone said, "Whenever" the right of making and enforcing the law is vested in the same man or one and the same body of men, there can be no public liberty. The Magistrate may enact tyrannical laws and execute them in a tyrannical manner since he is possessed, in his quality of dispenser of justice, with all the power which he as legislator thinks proper to give himself ... Where it (the judicial power) joined with the legislative, the life, liberty, and property of the subject would be in the hands of arbitrary judges whose decisions would be regulated by their opinions, and not by any fundamental principles of law which though legislators may depart from yet judges are bound to observe. Were it joined with the executive this union might be an over-balance of the legislative."

Practical Effects of Montesquieu's Theory. Montesquieu's theory of Separation of Powers had a great democratic appeal and it soon became a political dogma. The teachings of Montesquieu gave fillip to the French Revolution, and nearly all governments of the revolutionary period were organised on the principle of Separation of Powers. The famous Declaration of Rights, issued after the Revolution, laid down that "every society in which the separation of powers is not determined has no constitution." The Constitution of 1791 made the executive and the legislature independent of each other, and the judges elective and independent. For a short span of time, during the regime of Napoleon, it was defied, but the doctrine was constantly in the minds of the people. As a constitutional maxim it is jealously cherished even today.

In the United States, Montesquieu's theory found its best expression. "We shall never know," says Herman Finer, "whether the Fathers of the American Constitution established the separation of powers from the influence of the theory, or to accomplish the immediately practical task of safeguarding liberty and property."[12] But they definitely desired liberty in the sense enunciated by Montesquieu. They also desired limits upon despotism. Independence from British suzerainty had given them the first. A short experience with legislative supremacy, after the Declaration of Philadelphia, had convinced them that concentration of power in any one institution was fraught with abuse. While writing about the Constitution of Virginia, Jefferson wrote: "All the powers of government, legislative, executive, and judicial, result to the legislative body. The concentrating of these in the same hands is precisely the definition of despotic government. It will be no alleviation that these powers will be exercised by a plurality of hands, and not by a single one. One hundred and seventy-three despots would surely be as oppressive as one."[13]

11. *Ibid.*
12. *Ibid.*, p. 99.
13. As quoted in Lipson's *Great Issues of Politics,* p. 277.

The same point was elaborated by Madison while issuing a similar warning: "The legislative department is everywhere extending the sphere of its activity, and drawing all power into its impetuous vortex ... They (the founders of our republics) seem never to have recollected the danger from legislative usurpations, which by assembling all power in the same hands, must lead to the same tyranny as it had been threatened by executive usurpations."[14]

If concentration of power was the evil to be avoided, was there besides executive or legislative omnipotence some third possibility? The alternative was what has come to be called Separation of Powers. In fact, Separation of Powers became a political creed with the statesmen and those engaged in the framing of the national constitution at the Philadelphia Convention. They were not new to the theory. The governmental system of the Colonial period embodied a species of Separation of Powers. Prior to 1776, the executive branch, under the Governor, was distinct from the legislative, and controversies between them were rampant in the two decades that led up to the Independence. With the principle of judicial review, the statesmen of that day were also equally familiar as the constitutionality of Colonial Acts could be challenged before the Judicial Committee of the Privy Council in London. "History, therefore, joined hands with philosophy in writing a separation of powers into the federal constitution."[15] The influence of Montesquieu was, indeed, powerful and decisive. Madison unequivocally maintained that Montesquieu was "the oracle who is always consulted and cited on the subject."[16] Whatever be the respective weights of influence in the Philadelphia Convention, the American Constitution, as Finer observes, "was consciously and elaborately made an essay in the separation of powers and is today the most important polity in the world which operated upon that principle."[17]

But the American Constitution did not explicitly state that powers ought to be separate. It simply distributed the powers; legislative powers were vested in Congress, the executive powers in the President, and the judicial in the Courts. While apportioning the lion's share of powers to one department of government the Constitution gave smaller slices to each of other departments. This was done to avoid concentration and consequent abuse of power. The maxim with the Fathers of the Constitution was that power should be limited, controlled and diffused. "If power is not to be abused then it is necessary, in the nature of things, that power be made a check to power." In the field of legislation, for example, the bulk of the law-making power was placed in Congress, but the President received his share in the powers to recommend measures, to summon Congress in special session, and to veto bills. Similarly, the Senate shared with the President his power to make appointments, declare war, and ratify treaties. The Supreme Court, by exercising the power of judicial review, asserted its claim to a portion of the legislative function. Congress, too, acted in a judicial capacity in cases of impeachment where the House was empowered to prosecute and the Senate sat in judgment. The President could intervene in the business of the courts through his power of pardon for all offences except treason.

14. *The Federalist,* No. XLVII.

15. Lipson, L., *The Great Issue of Politics,* p. 280.

16. *The Federalist,* No. XLVII.

17. Finer, H., *The Theory and Practice of Modern Government*, p. 29.

As portions of each function were distributed among different agencies, the Separation of Powers was really intended to result in a system of checks and balances. The system of checks and balances had two obvious results. First, and ordinarily, unless the members of the three branches of government saw eye to eye and cooperated harmoniously, none of the principal functions of government could be adequately performed. Second and conversely, if any department or pair of departments ventured to exceed their constitutional authority, they "could be restrained by the refusal of a third to connive." In this way, the Fathers of the Constitution destroyed the concert of leadership in government which is so prominent a feature of our times. Finer, thus, sums up the theory of Separation of Powers as it has worked in the United States. He says, "Legislative procedure has come to differ essentially from that in Britain and France; financial procedure is worlds apart; there is no coordination of political energy or responsiblity; but each branch has its own derivation and its morsel of responsibility. All is designed to check the majority, and the end is achieved. At what cost?" The cost cannot be measured in terms of dollars. With powers divided between the executive and legislative departments without any means of proper coordination, there is always inordinate delay to arrive at an agreement even on pressing matters which demand expeditious disposal. One branch of governinent may be operating on one policy whereas the other may follow quite a different one, particularly, when the executive belongs to one party and the Congressional majority to another. Some Presidents have, no doubt, succeeded in bridging the gap separating them from the legislature. "But while an emergency may bring," says Zink, "temporary coordination and the use of patronage can usually be counted upon to pave the way to some action, the National government is still torn to parts by the provision which the framers made for separation of powers."[18]

EVALUATION OF THE THEORY

The Theory Restated. Much has been said about the theory of the Separation of Powers. But what kind of Separation of Powers is needed ? Here much of the clarity is obscured by the use of the ambiguous term "power". The government has certain functions to perform in order to serve the purpose of the State. If functions are taken as powers, then, the idea of service entirely disappears and the organs of government become invested with power. Wherever there is power there is force. A government having its foundation on power becomes an engine of force. The use of the term power is most unfortunate and, accordingly, the cause of so much confusion. The doctrine of Separation of Powers is itself a protest against power and its meaning can be better analysed and appreciated, if we drop the reference to 'powers' and substitute for it 'functions' of the organs or branches of government. "A branch is an organisation of agencies with their personnel. The services they undertake are their functions." The functions of the government are legislative (rule making), executive (rule application), and judicial (rule adjudication).

Accepting this as the criterion of our distinction, the doctrine of Separation of Powers can be restated in the following manner: The activities of government group themselves

18. *A Survey of American Government,* p. 12.

into three divisions. These divisions are not a matter of theory, but it is a practical fact associated with the character of the functions themselves. It is one thing to legislate, another to administer, and a third to judge. By assigning each of these functions to different branches of government composed of separate personnel and following their own mode of action, separation is obtained. Such a statement transfers the doctrine from the realm of theory to that of political fact.

Absolute Separation Impossible. But it does not mean absolute separation. Separation of Powers, according to Barker, "must certainly mean a distinct mode of action." Each organ of government has its own distinctive mode of action." The legislative mode is "deliberate and deliberative"; the judicial mode is critical rather than deliberative and the executive mode is a rapid determination of decisions and instructions in order to give effect to legislative and judicial modes. In a word, as Barker says, "we shall find three organs corresponding to the three different modes of action; but we may find one of the organs so absolutely specialised in its mode of action, or so entirely separate in its province, that it cannot also act in the mode and enter the province of others."[19] Madison correctly explained the doctrine of Separation of Powers when he said, "The powers properly belonging to one department ought not to be directly administered by either of the other departments. It is equally evident that neither of them ought to possess, directly or indirectly, an over-ruling influence over the other in the administration of their respective powers." The premise of *Federalist Paper* 47, which is essentially concerned with the political theory of federalism, is that any person or body of persons possessing power may be tempted to abuse it unless controlled, and that power can be checked by power. The Separation of Powers attempts to create a balance among the competing units.

The State is an organic unity and the various departments of its machinery are inter-connected. By the nature of their functions, they cannot be divided into water-tight compartments. The government must always be viewed as a whole, and its organs, though distinct, must work in unison in order to be useful and effective in serving the purposes for which they have been created. The real problem, according to MacIver, "is so to articulate these that responsibility shall not be divorced from efficiency." The functions of government are divided into different departments so that each department does its job to the best of its efficiency and with due regard to its responsibility. Efficiency demands expert knowledge of the problems which face a country and responsibility means the diversion of that knowledge towards those channels which are responsive to the needs of the people. This is the first principle of democracy. The Separation of Powers is, accordingly, needed for proper articulation and not for the division of organs of government into water-tight compartments. To put it in the language of Almond and Powell the theory of Separation of Powers is pre-eminently a functional theory. "Among its central concerns are the nature of legislative, executive and judicial power; the question of how best to maintain their separateness; the values resulting from such separation; and the problem of how best to mesh these separate institutions of government with the structure of society."[20]

19. Barker, E., *Principles of Social and Political Theory,* p. 261.

20. Almond, G.A., and Powell, G.B., *Comparative Politics.. A Developmental Approach,* pp. 10-11.

There cannot be any isolation or disharmony between the different departments of government. Isolation is not the essence of the doctrine and Montesquieu never suggested it. Each department performs some functions which actually do not belong to it. In fact, in all modern systems, institutions exercise overlapping functions of some kind or provision is made for some degree of cooperation between the different organs and branches to perform the work of government. The legislative department is not wholly and solely confined to the legislative mode of action, although it is primarily and mainly concerned with that mode. There is a judicial organ primarily and mainly concerned with the judicial mode of action, but not necessarily confined to that mode. There is, similarly, an executive organ which may be concerned with other modes of action besides the executive. A judge, for example, makes a new law when he gives a decision on a point covered by law or in which there does not exist a precedent. Here is a case in which the judicial and legislative functions combine as a result of natural process. Again, the executive everywhere possesses the power of issuing *ordinances* and proclamations. This is a device of practical utility, but it has to be admitted that *ordinances* and proclamations are a formidable substitute for legislation. The executive is a legislature in another sense too. It suggests and guides the process of law-making by the legislative organ. It does so under the American system of division of functions between the President and Congress; and it does so even more under Cabinet system such as the British and the Indian. The legislature, too, performs various executive functions. In a parliamentary government it creates the real executive, retains it in office and controls its functions. In the Presidential system, as obtainable in the United States, the Senate has a share in making appointments and ratifying treaties. Executive and legislative departments perform judicial functions too. The Chief Executive head of the State everywhere possesses the power of pardon. The House of Lords is the highest Court of Appeal in Britain. The Senate in the United States acts as a court of impeachment.

There is no Separation of Powers in Britain as Montesquieu is claimed to have understood. He had in his mind a longing for liberty against the autocratic powers of Kings and princes. Britain presented to him a sharp contrast with the conditions prevailing in his own country. Without forming a real idea of the actual working of a democratic government, more so a responsible, he concluded that liberty can be secured only by a mechanical check of one department over the other. For him this was above all else a practical recipe for political liberty. But Montesquieu wrote at a time when institutional cheeks appeared to be the only feasible ones. The value of the doctrine by dispersing functions among different political institutions is that it attempts to provide a limit to political power and a brake on action by constitutional devices. Power must be limited if liberty is to exist, for unchecked power is as dangerous as the unity of temporal and spiritual powers. This is precisely what Montesquieu enunciated.

All Departments not Coordinate. The traditional analysis of the doctrine of Separation of Powers takes for granted that the three wings of government are coordinate or equal. But this is not precisely so. With the growth of democracy the executive has been reduced to a subordinate position. The legislature is really the regulator of administration. By its control over the finances of the country, it limits and controls the executive, howsoever theoretically independent the executive may be. In a Cabinet system of government the subjection of the executive to the legislature at every step is undisputable. The judiciary, too, is obviously subordinate to the legislature, although its independence is the most coveted maxim of democracy.

It does not, however, mean that legislature is not subject to any kind of check. The bounds of the sovereign legislature are many and various. In the first place, legislature is bound by moral and ethical codes. All proposals for law are assayed on the touchstone of practical utility and moral considerations. No parliament can pass laws which are against the facts of nature or are against the established codes of public or private morality. Secondly, the legislature, like the whole of government, is limited both by the purpose it fulfils and the mode of action it follows. The most important limit on the legislature is the limit imposed by the development and activity of political parties. There is, what has been described as, a parliamentary forbearance. The minority agrees that the majority should govern, and the majority agrees that the minority must criticise and oppose. Opposition is an effective restraint on the vagaries of the majority party in the legislature. Both the party in office and the Opposition understand the rules of the game and know that at some future date their positions may be reversed. Thus, the concept of Separation of Powers, in its traditional analysis, has been impossible to realize in any complete way.

Totalitarian Objection. The totalitarians reject the doctrine of Separation of powers from beginning to the end. Separation of Powers is aimed at preventing despotism whereas totalitarianism believes in unity and oneness of power. One of the Commumst jurists wrote, "The Separation of Powers belongs to a political era in which political unity was reduced to a minimum in the interest of an autonomous *bourgeois* society. However, national and ethnic unity and oneness demand that all political powers be gathered in the hand of one leader. The Communists reject the doctrine outright as it is *bourgeois* principle." Vyshinsky wrote, "... From top to bottom the Soviet social order is penetrated by the single general spirit of the oneness of authority of the toilers. The programme of the All Union Communist Party rejects the *bourgeois* principle of Separation of Powers." Soviet writers argued that Montesquieu developed the theory as a means of limiting the absolute powers of the Kings of France. In the Soviet Union there was no class conflict and hence there was no need to limit one branch of government by another. All organs of government had to work in the same interest.

What the Doctrine Means Today. The modern democratic view does not accept the traditional analysis of the doctrine of Separation of Powers. It is explained that Montesquieu's views were the product of an era which looked upon government itself as something inherently dangerous and possibly despotic. That government was deemed best which governed least as it existed to protect and restrain, not to foster and promote. But today, even the most conservative person is unable to think of government in purely passive terms. The intensive integration and complexity of modern industrial society, and the accepted concept of a Welfare State demand more and more action and services from the government. All this needs planning the life and resources of the nation.

The Welfare State tends to concentrate power on the executive level and, consequently, it means ascendancy of the executive over the legislative branch. Locke had conceived of the relation between the three powers in terms of legislative supremacy. Montesquieu and Madison preferred to see an equilibrium between the three coordinate branches. But such a division now seems outmoded for all practical purposes as it is incapable of guaranteeing the services which the government is expected to render. Planning and active service cannot be the work of separate branches of government which cancel each other out. Planning must be unified. Fusion and not rigid separation of functions is required. Thus, "moulds are broken in which the thoughts of Locke, Montesquieu and Madison were cast and their contents have spilled together."

The ascendancy of the executive and the blurring of the traditional division of functions have been influenced by two other important tendencies. One is the organisation of the career civil service and the second is the emergence of political parties with their nationwide organisations. Political parties unite what one may try to separate. The development of the executive, therefore, into what may be called a multi-functioning organ, is one of the most notable features of a modern government. To put it in the words of Barker, "If the growth of the legislative organ, in consequence of the development of the cabinet system, was the notable feature of the eighteenth century, it may be said that the growth. of the executive organ in consequence of the extension of rights and the corresponding extension of services which mostly fall to the lot of the executive, is the notable feature of the twentieth."[21] Today, the executive is not only an executive, it is also, at the same time, a legislature; it exercises a judicial jurisdiction too. Administration and adjudication no longer seem as different as they had once appeared.[22]

The core of the modern problem of government is to find a synthesis combining the answer to two needs—the need for the Welfare State and the need for freedom. The Welfare State, as said before, means concentration of power on the executive level and, accordingly, the ascendancy of the executive over the legislative branch. This tendency seems to be an alarming development to many. It is, undoubtedly, alarming unless controlling and balancing devices are properly developed to keep pace with the ever-changing face of the executive power. The doctrine of Separation of Powers has become important today than perhaps at any other time.

One of the checks on the executive is the system of judicial review. Montesquieu himself was particularly interested in the judicial power as check over and arbiter between the other two branches. This concept is more clearly realized in the United States, India and some. Commonwealth countries. The idea of an independent and coequal judicial branch also spread to Germany (Bonn) and Austria. In France and Italy the supreme admistrative court, the Council of States in the former, applies the most effective check on the executive power, although it is nominally a part thereof.

The balance between executive and legislative branches is a legal question primarily in countries with the Presidential system of government. There the Constitution prescribes the rights of both as well as their limitations. The emergence of political parties in the

21. Barker, E., *Principles of Social and Political Theory.* p. 261.
22. Refer to the independent regulatory commissions such as the Inter-State Commerce Commission in the United States of which Justice Holmes of the U.S. Supreme Court said that it performed "legislative, judicial and executive acts only softened by a *quasi*." Also refer to administrative justice in Great Britain and other countries.

United States, it is suggested, has tended to redistribute the authority divided by the Constitution and have obliterated the doctrine of Separation of Powers to a considerable extent. Carl Friedrich, however, is of the view that emergence of the political parties "does not obliterate the Separation of Powers but it certainly softens it. At the same time .... the alteration of two parties itself constitutes a regularized restraint which consequently reduces the need for rigid separation."[23] But under a parliamentary system the principal check is the existence of political parties and the development of the constitutional custom of party alteration. There is also the impartial judiciary. Then, the elected representatives debate and "propose" in Harington's phrase, while the electorate resolves through general elections the party to form the government and the one to constitute the Opposition. By this process is effectively preserved the basic conception of balance and counterpoise.

Barker suggests another check. He accepts the bare truth of our times that the executive is a multi-functioning organ, but he emphasises that when the executive performs legislative and judicial functions let it employ the mode of action relevant to that department. For example, if the executive exercises judicial functions let it adopt the proper and peculiar mode of judicial action, i.e., it must accept the procedure of public hearing, summoning witnesses and recording of evidence according to the rules of evidence. It must publish its decisions and it must also admit, if it possibly can, the possibility of appeal.

The need is, therefore, for union as well as separation. Democratic government demands that a synthesis be found between the Separation of Powers, and the possibility of concerted government action. The first is obtained by continuing with the separate organs of government. It is intrinsically good to do so, for it sets a limit of jurisdiction over the functions of each organ. Each organ establishes its own distinctive mode of action with its own distinctive technique. But it does not mean that separation of functions prevents leadership. Too much separation destroys responsibility, immobilises action and ultimately destroys free government. Without leadership there would soon be a constitutional crisis and possibilities of the risc of dictatorship. But it is essential to temper leadership by imposing limitations upon it. The real limitations are those which make the government responsible to the people, that is, it must answer to the people for its policies and if its answers are not satisfactory to the people, they should have the means to replace it. It can be ensured further by the presence of an independent and impartial judiciary, the guardian of the rights of the people. Thus, the Separation of Powers is a living force in all democratic countries as a check to irresponsible power.

In the context of what has been said above the theory of Separation of Powers now rests upon broader grounds than suggested by the limited doctrine of Locke and Montesquieu. It reconciles theory with practice and thereby establishes harmony between division and concentration of powers to maintain the safety of the political order as a whole. It stands for an effective system of divided powers as contained in the classical doctrine and considers it sound, but holds that there is nothing sacrosanct about it. It appreciates the difficulties resulting from divided powers and considers them great, but it also realises that the consequences of concentrating power are really disastrous.

23. Friedrich, C.J., *Constitutional Government and Democracy* p. 185.

This has given rise to a new theory of divided powers; a scheme suitable, on the whole, to the needs of an industrial society. The advocates of this new theory point out that the classical doctrine of Separation of Powers "has an implicit double meaning. On the one hand it contains a generalization, theory or hypothesis; on the other hand it contains a practical suggestion, a proposal for the organization of government in the interest of individual liberty." The idea that there are three major types of governmental power seems to them a valid generalization and one in accord with the operations of the human mind. They agree with Immanuel Kant that this distinction of powers corresponds to the pattern of a practical syllogism, divided as syllogism into the major premise, the minor premise, and the consequent."[24] The resemblance of the distinctions underlying the separation of powers and the pattern of a syllogism is due to the fact that commands imply decisions, and decisions in turn imply judgments."[25]

Power means, *inter alia*, that a person or group possesses the ability to command and the ability to command involves the ability to decide, whenever there is a choice between several alternatives. Power, therefore, admits of commanding and deciding. Specific decisions and commands are the realm of executive power, general decisions and commands fall within the sphere of legislative power. The latter is for that reason often called the rule-making power. Similarly, the executive power may be called measure-taking or rule application. The judicial power apparently stands between the two, for it transforms a general into a specific decision. When a general command has been given, or a general decision made, that is, the rule has been established, there still remains the further decision involved in adjudicating the rule. The judicial power makes a specific decision by applying the rule. The decision made is not a command. It is for this reason that the pronouncements of the courts, while adjudicating, are described as decisions and the whole process as rule. That is, the specific decision is rendered while applying rules.

But the advocates of the new theory of divided powers contend that most of the time the government functionaries are their own judges. Whenever they decide to do or not to do something because the law demands or forbids it, they apply that law "by subsuming the particular situation with which we are confronted under the established legal rules."[26] Ordinarily, it is only the doubtful and controversial points of law which are brought before the courts. Majority of them are decided by various commissions and tribunals with which an industrial society is honeycombed today. The decisions of these commissions and tribunals are administrative in their nature and not in strict accord with the classical theory of the Separation of Powers. Those who criticise the new theory of divided powers seldom appreciate the practical aspect of the functions of government and the task which

24. Kant's statement of this analogy is,' "Every state contains three powers, i.e., the general and united will in three fold personification. The power to rule (sovereignty) in the person of the legislative, the executive power in the person of the governor (in accordance with law) and the law-interpreting power (attributive to each what is his according to law) in the person of the judge. [.....] Similar to the three propositions in practical syllogism: the major premise which contains the law of a will, the minor premise which contains the command to proceed according to that law, i.e., the principle ofsubsuming [.....] under the law, and the consequent which contains the sentence or judicial decision as to what is law in the particular case." Refer to CarI J. Friedrich, *Constitutional Government and Democracy,* p. 621.>

25. *Ibid.*, p. 183.

26. *Ibid.*, p. 184.

it has to undertake. Administrative tribunals and commissions have taken deep roots in almost all countries and, in some, such tribunals carry a constitutional sanctity, as in India. The only point which need be emphasised is that these commissions and tribunals should adopt the mode of judicial action as Barker suggested.

SUGGESTED READINGS

Black, H.C.: *The Relation of the Executive Power to Legislation.*

Barker, E.: *Principles of Social and Politcal Theory,* pp. 255-68.

Fairlie, J.A.: *The Separation of Powers.*

Finer, H.: *The Theory and Practice of Modern Government,* Chaps. VI, VII.

Carl J. Freidrich: *Constitutional Government and Democracy,* Chap. X.

Garner, J.W.: *Political Science and Government,* pp. 322-344, 423-428.

Garner, J.W.: *Introduction to Political Science,* Chap. XIII.

Hamilton, A. and Jay, J. and Madison, J.: *The Federalist,* Everyman's Library Dent.

Lipson, L.: *The Great Issues of Politics,* Chap. XI.

MacIver, R.M.: *The Modern State.*

MacIver, R.M.: *The Ramparts We Guard.*

Montesquieu, C.: *Spirit of the Laws.*

Sidgwick, H.: *Elements of Politics,* Chap. XIX-XX.

Webb, Sidney and Beatrice: *A Constitution of the Socialist Commonwealth of Great Britain.*

17

CHAPTER

The Framework of Government Constitution

Meaning and Definition of Constitution. Every State needs some kind of order, some system by which a reasonably orderly process of government may emerge. Without such an order there is anarchy. This *order* or *system*, in technical terms called *constitution*, must lay down certain rules which define the organs of government and how they originate, their mutual relationships, and the relationship between government and the people over whom its authority is exercised. A constitution is, therefore, the basic design of the structure and powers of the government and the rights and duties of its citizens. There can be no State without a constitution. Sometimes the constitution of a State is definitely formulated in a document or documents; sometimes it is found in an established body of rules, maxims, traditions and practices in accordance with which its government is organised and its powers are exercised.

The constitution need not be written. Nor does a written constitution represent the actual structure of the country and of its political institutions. Custom plays a considerable and often a preponderant role. "The attempt to embody the fundamental institutions of a State in a single document or small groups of documents," says Lowell, "is rarely, if ever, successful; and even if the constitution when framed covers all the main principles on which the government is based, it often happens that they become modified in practice, or that other principles arise, so that the constitution no longer corresponds fully with the actual government of the country."[1] What the constitution establishes is some sort of legal order which is enforced and which keeps the parts of the State together. Woolsey says that a constitution is the "collection of the principles according to which the powers of government and the rights of the governed and the relationship between the two are adjusted." Bryce defines it as "the aggregate of laws and customs under which the life of the State goes on"; "or the complex totality of laws embodying the principles and rules whereby the community is organised, governed, and held together"[2] Herman Finer says, "The State is a human grouping in which rules a certain power relationship between its individuals and associated constituents. This power relationship is embodied in political

1. Lowell, A.L., *The Government of England,* Vol. I, p. 1.
2. Bryce, .L, *Studies in Jurisprudence,* Vol. I, pp. 136 and 217.
3. Finer, H., *The Theory, and Practice of Modern Government,* p. 116.

institutions. The system of fundamental political institutions is the constitution .... the autobiography of a power relationship."[3] Wheare defines it as "that body of rules which regulates the ends for which and the organs through which governmental power is exercised."[4] Gilchrist writes that the constitution consists of "that body of rules or laws written or unwritten, which determine the organisation of government, the distribution of powers to the various organs of government, and the general principles on which these powers are to be exercised."[5]

Constitution and Constitutionalism. Contemporary political scientists give a distinct meaning to the term constitution and say that it is the process by which governmental action is effectively restrained. It is a "technique of effective regularized restraint upon governmental actions"[6] as Carl Friedrich puts it. "As a political process", he adds, "the constitution can be described as analogous to the rules of a game insuring fair play. This is the meaning of the word 'constitution' in its functional sense, as distinguished from its meaning in law, in history, and in medicine."[7] A constitution, therefore, defines and thereby limits public power. Its basis is belief in a limited government and consequently "genuine constitutions" determining effective limitations can exist only in non-totalitarian countries. In a totalitarian dictatorship the power exercised by its governing group is unlimited and unrestrained whereas the exercise of political authority in a democratic government is limited by a constitutional framework which protects certain areas of personal and group life from governmental interference and provides that governmental powers shall be exercised in accordance with the known procedures. Carter and Herz, accordingly, conclude that "Formal appearances notwithstanding, totalitarian regimes do not have" genuine constituions. At least such regimes may enjoy merely a self-limitation on the part of the ruling group. And in any case whatever rules exist "are forever provisional, changeable, revocable, they do not have the nature of generality, reliability and thus calculability which the rules of law elsewhere possesses."[8] Constitutions, according to Michael Curtis are "usually regarded as of higher validity than other rules thus bestowing legitimacy on those who claim to wield power according to constitutional rules. Constitutions reflect different aspects of the life and behaviour of the community."[9]

There is nothing like a 'constitution' and a 'genuine constitution'. The emphasis of the contemporary writers is on constitutionalism rather than on constitution. This is made clear by Carter and Herz themselves. They say, "Genuine constitutionalism is likewise absent when constitutions are forever made and remade, changed and abolished so as to fit the political needs of the respective holders..." When a constitution is in flux there may not be constitutionalism, but the constitution is there. India amended her constitution nineteen times in six years and the forty-second amendment alone covered 59 clauses of the existing Constitution and the forty-fourth amendment also did not lag behind. Article 31 has been amended and reamended five times in this process. Now there is a rapid

4. Wheare, K.C., *The Statute of Westminster,* p. 12.
5. Gilchrist, R.N., *Principles of Political Science,* p. 211.
6. Friedrich, C.J., *Constitutional Government and Democracy,* p. 26.
7. *Ibid.,* p. 121.
8. Carter, G.M., and Herz, G.H., *Government and Politics in the Twentieth Century,* p. 64.
9. Curtis, Michael, *Comparative Government and Politics,* p. 70.

succession of amendments; a total of 74 and many more are awaiting completion of the process.

All these definitions differ from one another in some way. But when we analyse them one point becomes clear, that the province of the constitution is government, not the State as a whole. It deals with the fundamental concerns of government and as there are different kinds of governments there are different kinds of constitutions. But every State, no matter what form of government it has, must have a constitution. It is impossible to contend that the State with an autocratic government exists without a constitution or that the framework of government is not a constitution unless "the community hath agreed to it", or unless it guarantees "rights" and "privileges" to the people. If the State with a democratic government has a constitution, so has the State with an autocratic government. There can be no State without a constitution, and every State that ever existed has had a constitution of some kind.

CLASSIFICATION OF CONSTITUTIONS

Evolved and Enacted Constitutions. While possessing a common characteristic in content, constitutions differ greatly in type. Some writers classify them into *cumulative* or *evolved*, and *conventional* or *enacted*. A *cumulative* or evolved constitution is the result of slowly working evolutionary changes; the product of accumulated material which has moulded and shaped the political institutions of a country. Such a constitution is not made, it grows with its roots in the primitive past. The edifice it presents is the accumulated wisdom of the past and the result of numerous customs, usages, traditions, principles, judicial decisions which have influenced its development. The *conventional* or *enacted* constitution, on the other hand, is the result of the deliberate efforts of man. It is consciously made and either may be the outcome of the deliberations of a Constituent Assembly specially convened for that purpose, or it may have been promulgated by the command of the sovereign authority, King or Parliament. The prescriptions of an enacted constitution are embodied in a document or a series of documents.

Costitutions are now divided, for brevity and definiteness; into written and unwritten; although the distinction between them is more or less the same as is between evolved and enacted constitutions.

Unwritten Constitution. Down to a century and a half ago, constitutions differed little from each other in form. The prevailing type was unwritten and flexible and what survives today, by way of exception in Britain, represents an earlier norm. An unwritten constitution is one which reflects the evolutionary or Darwinian conception which predicates the complex nature of institutions, their gradual development, and unpredictable change. Referring to the Constitution of Britain, Jennings says, "If the constitution consists of institutions and not of the paper that describes them, the British Constitution has not been made but has grown—and there is no paper."[10] The institutions necessary for carrying out the functions of government emerged as the need arose. "Formed to meet immediate requirements they were then adapted to exercise more extensive and sometimes

10. Jennings, I., *The Law and the Constitution*, p. 8.

different functions. From time to time political and economic circumstances have called for reforms. There has been a constant process of invention, reform and amended distribution of powers. The building has been constantly added to, patched, and partially recon-structed so that it has been renewed from century to century; but it has never been razed to the ground and rebuilt on new foundations."[11]

An unwritten constitution is, accordingly, the child of wisdom and chance; the product of history and the example of Sir James MacIntosh's dictum that constitution grow instead of being made. It is the result of a process in which many elements, like statutes, judicial decisions, precedents, usages and traditions have entered, piling themselves one upon the other from age to age and shaping the political institutions of the country according to the wants of the people and needs of various times. There is no single document or documents which *contain* it, though many sources may be found which *describe* it. There may be some enactments of a fundamental character which make the constitution, but this kind of written element is in a much smaller proportion than the unwritten element, and it does not, at the same time, bear one single date. These laws were made as and when they were needed. The most important part of an unwritten constitution is just what is kept out of the written law and given over to the sole guardianship of custom.

The best and the only example of an unwritten constitution, as said before, is that of Britain. The fundamental political institutions of that country, which are the basis of all governmental authority, are not set down in writing in any formally accepted document or documents. They are regulated by first, judicial decisions; sometimes founded on more or less vague "immemorial rights and liberties", and sometimes founded on agreements, resolutions and laws made by rebellious parliaments. Then, secondly, there are a number of statutes dealing with separate parts of government like the Act of Settlement, the Franchise Acts, the Parliament Act of 1911 as amended in 1949, and the Crown Proceedings Act of 1947. Thirdly the major part of what forms the soul of the British Constitution is regulated by simple customs or conventions. Britain is something more than the "mother of parliaments", and its growth was more or less spontaneous, slow and sometimes haphazard. It took eight centuries to transform parliament into a governing body resting on the suffrage of all adult persons in the country and the process has only been completed in our own times. The (Glorious) Revolution of 1688, settled once for all that Parliament had supreme power and it could control every aspect of national life. The powers of the King were limited and the constitutional result was the emergence of the cabinet. Conventions alone provide for the essential rules of Cabinet government. They demand that Ministers of the King must be members of Parliament, they should belong to the majority party in the House of Commons and function under the party leader, the Prime Minister. Convention further demands that the Cabinet is responsible to Parliament for all its acts and it remains in office so long as it retains the confidence of the House of Commons. That Parliament meets annually and that it consists of two Houses rest on custom. Then, there are many conventions regulating parliamentary procedure. The principle that no Peer other than a Law Lord sits when the House of Lords is acting as

11. *Ibid.*

a court of appeal is also customary. It will, thus, be clear that so firmly is the mechanism of government erected on the foundation of conventions that without them the constitution becomes maimed, if not absolutely unworkable.

It does not, however, mean that the written element in the British Constitution is negligible. Judicial decisions form a body of written constitutional law and the statutes certainly do. The utterances of Parliament on various supreme occasions list in the constitutional documents of the country and are "authentically existent." These taken together, are, Herman Finer says, as explict and usually more explicit than the "written constitutions" of other countries.[12] The conventions, he adds, are not so recorded by an institution with such authority as the courts of law or *Parliament*. "Nevertheless, they are understood with fair exactness, and have been recorded by ministers in their correspondence and political speeches, accepted with inappreciable dissent by politicians and scholars, and even written down in great detail by such authorities as Hearn, Bagehot, Dicey, May, Anson and Jennings."

Finer, accordingly, poses the question: where is the difference between the unwritten Constitution of Britain and the written Constitutions of other countries? He himself answers that the difference is two-fold. First, the major part of the British Constitution consists of conventions "which are taken for granted but not formulated, save occasionally by individuals. Second, and more important, is that no body of people was deliberately called together and entrusted with the establishment of a constitution, as in other countries."[13]

Written Constitution. This makes easy the meaning of a written constitution. A written constitution is a consciously planned system, a constitution formulated and adopted by a deliberate creation, a Constituent Assembly or a Convention. The Constitution of India was formulated and adopted by the Constituent Assembly of India. The Preamble of the Constitution begins with the words, "We the people of India having solemnly resolved to constitute India into a Sovereign Democratic Republic" and ends with the words, "In our Constituent Assembly this twenty-sixth day of November 1949, do hereby adopt, enact and give to ourselves this Constitution." The Constitution of the United States was drafted by a special Convention of delegates, presided over by George Washington and it met on May 14, 1787, in the Independence Hall at Philadelphia. The Constitution, as it emerged out of the Philadelphia Convention on September 17, 1787, was referred to the States for their ratification. The Preamble announces unequivocally that "we the people... do ordain and establish this Constitution."

A written constitution is, thus, a deliberate design of the institutions that it creates whereby government is conducted and all this is contained in a document generally bearing one single date. There are some examples of written constitutions contained in a series of documents bearing different dates. The French Constitution, under the Third Republic, was fragmentary and did not consist of one single document. It was composed of three constitutional laws passed on February 24, February 26 and July 26, 1875.

A written constitution is distinct in character and is held in special sanctity. It is the

12. Finer, H., *The Theory and Practice of Modern Government*, p.118

13. *Ibid.*, p. 119.

supremacy of the constitution. It means nothing may be done or enacted which conflicts with the provisions of the constitution and that the constitution must be amended or altered according to the procedure prescribed by the constitution. Here is a clear distinction between the constitutional or fundamental law and the statutory law. The constitutional law embodies the will of the sovereign and it should not be altered by the ordinary legislative process. If the statutory law conflicts with or is not in conformity to the constitutional law, it is *ultra vires* or unconstitutional and, *ipso facto*, it is void and inoperative. The. constitutional law is paramount, the statutory law is subordinate.

Michael Curtis assigns five major reasons for the existence of written constitutions:

1. They are the sign of successful internal revolution against the former rulers as in the Soviet Union; or revolt against external rulers as in the United States.
2. They signify the existence of a regime after the downfall of the previous regime in war or internal collapse. Examples are France of the Third and Fourth Republics or post-war Italy and Germany.
3. They illustrate concessions made by ruling groups or rising groups in the community, as in France in 1814 or in post-war Morocco, where democratic institutions were established while the authority of the monarchy was reinforced.
4. They mark the creation of a regime formed by a union of hitherto separate units, as in federal or confederal regimes.
5. They are signs of independence granted by a former colonial power or military victor as the British Commonwealth countries whose constitutions are formally statutes of the British Parliament."[14]

Not a Real Distinction. But the distinction between a written and unwritten constitution is not real. There is no constitution which is either wholly written or entirely unwritten. All written constitutions grow and expand if they are to endure and serve their purpose. The real constitution is a living body of general prescriptions carried into effect by living persons. No constitution can ever be a strait-jacket. Nor can it be ever in the mind of the constitutional fathers to work out in all details a complete and final scheme of government operative for generations to come. They always seek merely a starting point and consequently provide a skeleton to be clothed with flesh, by customs, exigencies, national emergencies, economic developments, and various other factors affecting the welfare. of the nation. Written constitutions, Bryce remarks, become "developed by interpretation, fringed with decisions, and enlarged by customs so that after a time the letter of their text no longer conveys their full effect." The constitution remains a printed document, no doubt, but explained by judicial decisions, precedents and practices and illuminated by understandings and aspirations.

This point may be illustrated by few examples taken from the United States which is represented as the best type of a written constitution. The most notable example is the extra-constitutional development of the political parties. The constitutional Fathers sought to provide a mechanism of government which would be free "from all violence of the faction", as Madison called it. But in the Presidential election of 1796, the third under the Union and the first in which Washington was not a candidate, there were two national

14. Curtis, Michael, *Comparative Government and Politics,* p. 73.

parties, one supporting John Adams and the other supporting Thomas Jefferson. By 1800, the party system had settled itself quite firmly in the government, even to the extent of necessitating the addition of the Twelfth Amendment so as to make the electoral college method workable. Since that time, party system forms the hub of the American national life. Then, there is no basis in the organization of the 'cabinet' which advises the President. President Washington found it uselul to have a small group of advisers to whom he could look for counsel. Other Presidents continued with it and, today, it is impossible to dispense entirely with such a body. 'Senatorial courtesy', 'presidential nominating conventions' and the 'residence' requirements in the election of Representatives are some of the other examples of constitutional usages. 'Legislative committees' are not authorised in the Constitution, but custom and usage has made then, as permanent as if they were a part of the Constitution.

In the oft-quoted observation made by Chief Justice Hughes, of the United States Supreme Court, lies the truth how the American constitutional system has developed through judicial interpretation. He said, "We are under the Constitution but the Constitution is what judges say it is." The judges have to interpret the constitution and to give a phrase a new interpretation is to give it a new meaning, and to give it a new meaning is to change it. The Supreme Court vested the power of dismissal in the President, excluding the Senate altogether, though the Constitution says nothing about it. The decisions of the Supreme Court interpreted means of communications to embrace telegraphic, telephonic and radio communications, and in the means of transport were included rail, roads and airways. The Constitution declares that "Congress shall have power... to regulate commeree." As to what is meant by the word "commerce", and what it includes, the Supreme Court has given varied meanings to suit new situations, and make it responsive to new problems. "It has been the work of the Supreme Court, through the power of judicial interpretation," says Munro, "to twist and torture the term 'commerce' so that it will keep steps with the procession."[15]

The British Constitution, the only example of an unwritten constitution, includes a considerable statutory element. Statutes regulate the succession to the throne, the executive departments, the suffrage, elections, the duration of Parliament, the relations between the two Houses, the judiciary, and much besides. Some of these matters have been subject to parliamentary action for centuries now. Others were formerly left to custom. It was the conflict over the budget of 1909, that led to the enactment of the Parliament Act, which gives the House of Commons exclusive control over Money Bills and a means of enacting legislative bills without the consent of the Lords. The Amending Act of 1949 further strengthened the supremacy of the House of Commons. The statutory element seems to be gaining in relative strength. The Ministers of the Crown Act now gives legal recognition to the Cabinet, the office of the Prime Minister, the political parties and even to His Majesty's Opposition.

The distinction between written and unwritten constitutions, therefore, is not only confusing, but unscientific. Professor Strong calls the division between written and unwritten constitutions false, misleading and illusory. The difference between them is

---

15. *The Government of the United States,* p. 70.

really one of degree rather than of kind. Bryce's conclusion is that the terms "written" and "unwritten" are not happily chosen, "although the distinction they aim at expressly is a real distinction."[16] Herman Finer, in his own characteristic way, says, "Comparatively, then, and not absolutely, the adjective 'unwritten' when applied to constitution ... means: (*i*) that all is not included in writing which might be, while somethings are altogether excluded which in other constitutions are included; and (*ii*) that it is not the result of deliberate establishment and adoption as a whole, with the result that no external sign marks of a constitutional from an ordinary law."[17] K.C. Wheare observes that the classification of constitutions into written and unwritten should be discarded and "the better distinction is between countries which have a written constitution and those which have no written constitu-tion..."[18] Michael Curtis makes a significant departure from all the reasons assigned so far. He says, "But the distinction between regimes with a 'writter' and those with an 'unwritten' constitution—formerly a means of comparing Britain and other systems—is not today of great political importance. Regimes possessing constitutions may be of any nature, democratic or dictatorial, liberal or conservative, communist, capitalist, or with a mixed economy. What is significant is that political actions adhere to an agreed pattern of behaviour or the generally understood principles of the political system."[19]

Flexible and Rigid Constitutions. Bryce suggests a new scheme of classification. Under this scheme constitutions are of two types flexible and rigid. The basis of this classification is the method of changing the constitution and its relation to the ordinary or statutory law.

The flexible constitution places constitutional law and ordinary law on the same level in the sense that both are enacted in the same way and both proceed from the same source. If the constitutional law can be amended, repealed or altered by the same procedure as the ordinary law, the constitution is flexible. It does not matter whether the constitution is primarily written or consists largely of conventions. What is essential to determine is, how the constitutional law and statutory law stand to one another. Do they stand at par with one another or is some sanctity, some superiority, attached to the constitutional law? And what is the procedure required for altering or amending the constitutional law? If the constitutional law and the ordinary law emanate from the same source and both go through the same procedure in passing and amending them, then, the constitution is flexible. It means that there is no difference between the constitution-making authority and the ordinary law-making authority. Parliament in Britain is sovereign and by sovereignty of Parliament Dicey means:

1. There is no law which Parliament cannot make;
2. There is no law which Parliament cannot unmake; and
3. There is under the English Constitution no marked or clear distinction between laws which are fundamental or constitutional and laws which are not.

16. Bryce J., *Studies in History and Jurisprudence*, Vol. 1, p. 127.
17. Finer, H, *The Theory and Practice of Modern Government*, p. 119.
18. Wheare, K.C., *Modern Constitutions*, pp. 20-21.
19. Curtis. Michael, *Comparative Government and Politics*, p. 72.

Constitutional changes in Britain can be made by Parliament in the same way as it may pass a law prohibiting drinking. A law aiming to effect constitutional changes and the ordinary law are both subject to the same legislative procedure, that is, a bill must be read three times in each House of Parliament and after having been approved by both Houses, it becomes law on being formally assented to by the King. The courts have no authority to nullify any enactment of Parliament. It means no special sanctity is attached to the constitutional law, and the constitutional and statutory laws stand at par with one another.

Flexible constitutions were almost the only kind known to the ancient world. The position is now reversed. The only surviving example of a flexible constitution and unwritten, too, is Britain. Austria-Hungary had also an unwritten and flexible constitution before World War I. The Constitution of Italy down to 1928 was flexible, though written. Similarly, the first constitution of the Irish Free State (1922-37) was written and it provided for two methods of amendment, but it "became, in practice, flexible."[20]

The rigid constitution possesses a special and higher status, standing above the ordinary law and alterable by a procedure different from the one used in the case of ordinary law, thus, making it difficult to change. The object is to emphasise that the constitutional law embodies the will of the sovereign and it should not be alterable by the ordinary, legislative process. A rigid con- stitution interposes a barrier to statutory encroachments. The powers of the legislature are limited by the constitution itself. If the statutory law conflicts with or is not in conformity to the constitutional law, it is *ultra vires* or unconstitutional and cannot become operative. But who shall say what a particular clause of the constitution means or whether this or that statute is consonant with it ? Legislatures cannot be entrusted with such a power, because the object is to devise means against legislative encroachments. The courts then become the guardians of the constitution. They fix its meauing, they set bounds to the competence of the legislature under it and annul what, in their opinion, goes beyond the constitution. This method of securing rigidity is called judicial control or judicial review.

The distinction between rigid and flexible constitution is a real one and it found its full expression when for eighteen years Congress of the United States found itself without power to levy income-tax, and when, by decisions of the Supreme Court, Roosevelt's New Deal was torn to pieces. Britain affords a sharp contrast. There ordinary statutes may override any decision of the highest court. And what Parliament has enacted, the courts interpret and apply unless parliament has otherwise provided.

Process of Amendment. The process of amendment varies a good deal between countries with rigid constitutions, especially as between unitary and federal States. In the unitary State amending power is entrusted to the legislature, which, for this purpose, acts under special rules of procedure. In federations, as one would naturally expect, some protection is given to the units of the union. In the United States the initiative is taken by Congress with a two-thirds vote in each House, and, then, it is required to be ratified or approved by the legislatures or conventions in three-fourths of the States. Australia makes use of the referendum. An amendment, when proposed by absolute majority in

20. Sait, E.M., *Political Institutions. A Preface,* p. 333.

both House of Representatives and Senate, is ratified by popular vote, but there must be a favourable majority not only in the Commonwealth but in a majority of the States too.

In Canada, Parliament and Provincial legislatures, both participate in the amending process. The method of amending the Indian Constitution is not so complicated, for it avoids the difficult process laid down by the American and Australian Constitutions. Some parts of the Constitution can be amended by a simple majority in both. Houses of Parliament; certain specified subjects require a majority of the total membership in each House of Parliament, a majority of not less than two-thirds of thc members present and voting in each House, and ratification by one-half of the States; the remaining provisions of the Constitution require a majority of the total membership in each House of Parliament and a majority of not less than two-thirds of the members present and voting in each House.

But the degree of rigidity depends upon two other factors beyond the language of the amendment. When the legislature is the judge of its own powers under the constitution, there is no legal barrier to its encroachments. When the courts determine the constitutionality or otherwise of the acts of the legislature, they prevent legislative unsurpation. Undoubtedly, judges respond to changing circumstances and public opinion, but they do so rather more slowly than the legislature. Secondly, it depends upon the content of the constitution. Some constitutions are short, others long; some limited to general provisions, others replete with details; some willing to leave civil liberty with the legislature, others the reverse. "What makes the Indian Constitution so rigid," says Jennings, "is that in addition to somewhat complicated process of amendment it is so detailed and covers so vast a field of law that the peroblem of constitutional validity must often arise."[21]

Appraisal of a Rigid Constitution. The safeguards which a rigid constitution provides are not negligible. A rigid constitution must necessarily be a written constitution and a written constitution would be a model of draftsmanship, of linguistic elegance, and of apparent clarity. The constitutional fathers pour into the document their wisdom as into a vessel so that it may inspire the confidence and command reverence of the generations to come. Since a constitution provides the first sedative for an over-excited state of mind; it is "an act of self preservation for a society", says Woolsey, "to make a constitution somewhat difficult to alter." A rigid constitution safeguards legislative encroachments and is a guarantee against hasty changes. Placing serious obstacles in the way of organic changes is absolutely essential for the safe working of democracy. "It may be added," says Laski, "that an age which, like our own, has seen the classic safeguards of representative government thwarted on every side needs to reinforce its conviction of their urgency."[22] A rigid constitution guarantees to minorities their rights. Where fundamental rights are concerned, minorties cannot be expected to agree to their rights being imperilled by a majority action. If the majority ventures it, the judges perform their function of guardianship most conscientiously. Justice Jackson of the Supreme Court of the United States declared in *West Virginia State Board of Education* v. *Barnette*, "The

21. Jennings, I., *Some Characteristics of the Indian Constitution,* pp. 9-10.
22. Laski, H., *A Grammar of Politics,* p. 335.

very purpose of a Bill of Rights was to withdraw certain subjects from the vicissitudes of political controversy, to place them beyond the reach of majorities and officials and establish them as legal principles to be applied by the courts."

A rigid constitution is conservative in the sense that it is free from dangers of temporary popular passion. It possesses the merits of permanence and stability and is sure to command the confidence of the people. The people weigh even ordinary legislation in terms of the provisions of the constitution. Finally, the facility of amendment sometimes carries a deleterious effect. Referring to the situation under the German Republic, Max Radin said, "The heaping up of constitutional changes by simple votes the *Reichstag* destroyed what Professor Lowenstein of Yale aptly calls the 'constitutional conscience' of the nation, and rendered far-reaching and revolutionary changes by ordinance and *coup d'etat* less shocking."[23]

But when rigidity and conservatism are carried beyond requisite necessity, they prove elements of weakness. The difficulty in amending the constitution very often proves detrimental to national interest. It causes unnecessary delay which may lead to revolution. Take, for example, the method of constitutional amendment in the United States of America. There is no prescribed time limit, unless specifically determined by a resolution of Congress, within which a constitutional amendment may be ratified by three-fourths of the States legislatures. It can be delayed indefinitely, thereby defeating the purpose of the amendment. Moreover, thirteen smaller States in America can veto the constitutional amendment, much to the detriment of national interests. According to Lord Macaulay, the most important cause of all revolutions is the fact that while nations move onward, constitutions stand still. A rigid constitution becomes stationary unless amendment is easy or its text is flexible. A good constitution is that which can be easily adjusted and adapted to the changing social, political and economic conditions of the country and keeps pace with the time. "Progress demands adaptability and flexibility and such adaptability and flexibility can only be secured in countries with rigid constitutions by a sufficiently easy method of amendment."[24]

A rigid constitution, which is necessarily written, having been made at a particular time, cannot foresee the distant future. The vision of its framers however far-sighted they might had been, must remain blurred; they cannot imagine the shape of things to come. "It (a rigid constitution) is like an attempt to fit a garment to an individual without taking into consideration his future growth and changes in size .... "[25] Moreover, a rigid constitution is without any regard to the past and without anticipation of the future, and is, therefore, conservative in outlook. It does not adequately admit growth and expansion.

Under a rigid constitution the main concern of the judiciary is to see whether the law conforms to the provisions of the constitution or not. Judges are generally conservative in their outlook and when they go to the letter of the law, they are disregardful of the new spirit to which the constitution needs to be adjusted. "To entrust the judge," says Laski, "with the power to override the will of the legislature is broadly to make him the

23. As cited in E.M. Sait, *Political Institutions, A Preface,* p. 339.
24. Gilchrit, R.N., *Principles of Political Science,* p. 213.
25. Garner, J.W., *Introduction to Political Science,* p. 394.

decisive factor in the State."[26] The judiciary becomes a super-legislature, but not in its representative capacity. Its decisions are political in nature and are, therefore, not impressive, impartial and worthy of any special respect as the decisions of the courts should generally command. The attitude of the judiciary, which lacks elasticity and adaptability, may accelerate the forces which upset the constitution itself.

Some writers hold that rigid constitutions are more valuable, because they are less subject to party feelings. But this is not correct. Rigid constitutions are the focus of national sentiment; they are centres of national discussion and, as such, are more subject to party forces than flexible constitutions.

Merits of a Flexible Constitution. The advantages of a flexible constitution lie in its remarkable elasticity and adaptability. A flexible constitution can be amended with the same ease and facility with which ordinary laws are altered. It makes possible the adjustment of the constitution to the new and the changing needs of society. It is the flexible character of the British Constitution which has saved Britain on so many occasions from the dangers of revolution. Moreover, a flexible constitution is particularly best adapted to the needs of a progressive State since it ensures legal and orderly growth. As it easily meets new emergencies, a flexible constitution either minimizes or prevents revolutions by meeting them half way. In the life of every man, as also in the life of every nation, there are occasions when inelasticity proves not only harmful, but even dangerous. The Constitution of the United States of America demands that Presidential election must be held after every four years, whether there is peace or war. If Roosevelt had been defeated by Dewey, it would have meant a new policy by the new government, though the primary object of Dewey, too, was sure to have been as that of Roosevelt, to win the war. General Elections during the period of war mean dislocation and distraction, but they cannot be avoided when the constitution is rigid. Such constitutional demands can be conveniently postponed under a flexible constitution. General Elections in Britain were postponed year after year during World War II without disturbing the administrative machinery of the country and at the same time preserving continuity in the government's policy. Immediately after the cessation of hostilities, Britain, once again, went to the polls, returning in majority the Labour Party and dislodging Churchill from power. Bryce has aptly remarked, "They (flexible constitutions) can be stretched or bent so as to meet emergencies without breaking their framework: and when the emergency has passed, they slip back into their old form like a tree whose outer branches have been pulled aside to let a vehicle pass."[27]

A rigid constitution, its critics assert, cannot justly claim to be representative of the needs and thoughts of the people. It is neither the result of natural historical growth, nor does it represent the experiences of the people, nor is it moulded by the conventions of national life. A flexible constitution, on the other hand, provides an excellent mirror of the national mind. It represents the historical continuity of the nation's life and incorporates within it the changes as and when the need arose. A flexible constitution can, thus, claim to feel the pulse of public opinion. Judge Cooley had said that "of all the constitutions

26. Laski, H., *A Grammar of Politics*, p. 304.

27. Bryce, J., *Studies in History and Jurisprudence*, Essays 3, "Flexible and Rigid Constitutions", p. 22.

which may come into existence for the government of the people, the most excellent is obviously that which is the natural outgrowth of the national life, and which having grown and expanded as the nation has matured, is likely at any particular time to express the prevailing sentiment regarding government and the accepted principles of civil and political liberty."

Weakness of a Flexible Constitution. A flexible constitution is characterised to be unstable and with no guarantee of performance. The process of amendment being simple, it is liable to be seriously affected by ever-changing popular passion and popular passion is devoid of reason as it depends upon emotion. Emotion chokes reason and strangulates thought and it offers a psychological opportunity to the demagogue to play upon it and gain his end. Again, the constitution may be changed not to meet the exigencies of the time, but to satisfy the whims of the political majority. As Sidgwick says, "Valuable rules and institutions may be abolished in a transient gust of unpopularity and lose the stability given by antiquity and unbroken customs." Flexible constitution therefore, is not suited to a country where the people have insufficient political training. It is suitable only for a people whose political training has been carried to a high degree of perfection. "In that training two elements would be of vital conseuquence to the safety of the system: first, an accurate understanding of their political rights and duties, general among the citizens; second, sleepless vigilance to detect violations of the constitution, and the utmost promptness and energy to resist and punish them." The rights of the people are liable to be encroached upon under a flexible constitution where the citizens are not vigilant.

A flexible constitution has also been criticised as the "plaything of judicial tribunals." Again, there is a popular belief that a flexible constitution vests wide powers and a greater discretion in public servants. Finally, it is argued that a flexible constitution is not suited to democracies. It has greater affinity for aristocratic societies. "The masses in a democracy are suspicious, if not hostile, to constitutional prescriptions which have not been formally enacted but which rest mainly upon custom and usage," and all these customs and usages had been set by the aristocracy of the past.

Conclusion. Whatever be the merits of a flexible constitution the modern tendency is towards a written and rigid constitution. The British Constitution now remains the only example of a flexible constitution and Gilchrist predicts "that in a few years not a single example of the flexible type will exist."[28] The United States was the first to devise a written and rigid constitution and other countries followed her. The future seems to be with rigid constitutions and many reasons can be enumerated in support of it. In the first place, the modern tendency is in favour of constitutional guarantee of rights which definitely restrains the powers of a government. In the second place, democracy finds its best expression in the ideal of self-government which is embodied in a written constitution. The powers of government divided and distributed between different political divisions should not be changed by the ordinary law-making process. Restraints are the core of constitutionalism and the constitution is, as Carl Friedrich says, an "effective regularized restraint."[29] Thirdly, whenever a new form of government is introduced in any country

28. Gilchrist, R.N. *Principles of Political Science,* p. 213.
29. Friedrich, C.J., *Constitutional Government and Democracy,* p. 123.

replacing the old, the tendency generally is to make the new form definite in a written constitution. Finally, the world is veering round to federalism and a federal form of government needs necessarily a written and a rigid constitution. But the process of amendment should not be so complicated or difficult as to prevent the organisation of the State from corresponding to the existing political conditions. The amending process should be neither so rigid as to prevent change nor so flexible as to encourage needless tampering with basic principles. This can be best expressed in the words of Jawaharlal Nehru. Speaking on the process of amendment provided in the Constitution of India, he said in the Consituent Assembly: "While we want this Constitution to be as solid and permanent as we can make it, there is no permanence in constitutions. There should be a certain flexibility. If you make anything rigid and permanent, you stop the nation's growth, the growth of a living, vital organic people. In any event, we could not make this Constitution so rigid that it cannot be adapted to changing conditions." Like the "safety valve of an engine", says Gettell, "the amending process should safeguard the governmental machine against too great speed and at the same time serve as an outlet against the danger of explosion." The process of amendment should, therefore, be intended, as Laski has said, "to avoid the unlimited authority of parliament, on the one hand, and the unique inaccessibility of the American Constitution to amendment on the other. A written constitution which may be amended by a two-thirds majority of the legislature supplies the adequate via-media."[30]

Origin of a Rigid Constitution. A rigid constitution may find its origin in two ways:

1. It may be made by a Constituent Assembly.
2. It may be granted by a superior government.

In the second type we include the Constitution of the British Dominions which were granted by the British Parliament, except the Constitution of the Eire (the Irish Free State). The British North America Act of 1867, which essentially determines the Constitution of Canada, was the first in this connection. At that time and till the passage of the Statute of Westminster the legislatures of all the Dominion countries were subordinate law-making bodies. Technically, they could not amend or alter their constitutions. But the Dominion legislatures have now practically full powers to change them. Similarly, the Government of India Acts, passed from time to time, were the grants of the British Parliament and the Indian Central or Provincial legislatures were incompetent, being subordinate law-making bodies, to make any amendment to them.

Theory of the Constituent Assembly. The theory of a special representative assembly to frame the constitution is the product of democratic revolutions of the seventeenth and eighteenth centuries. It originated during the English Revolution of the seventeenth century, when the Levellers placed before the Army Council, in 1648 and 1649, two Agreements embodying the proposals for a representative assembly which "should draw up foundations of just government."[31] While Britain set the precedent for modern, written and rigid constitutions, she had herself recovered her normal temper, and not adhered to the Revolutionary method. The practical application of the doctrine of a representative

30. Laski, H.J., *A Grammar of' Policies,* p. 305.
31. Kapur, Anup Chand, *Theory of the Constituent Assembly and its development in India.*

assembly to frame the constitution found its first expression in the Philadelphia Convention, when the delegates of the original Thirteen States met to frame a constitution for the United States of America. The concept of the Constituent Assembly is complementary to that of a written constitution, and both of them were a part of the technique designed to secure the liberty of the individual against the arbitrary exercise of power by government and to establish a mechanism of government based on the consent of the people. The French Revolution demonstrated the most complete development of the theory of the Constitutent Assembly, and the people placed such an abiding faith in its political utility that since then all the democratic countries of Europe, with the exception of pre-Mussolini Italy, were the creation of constituent assemblies.

The theory of the Constituent Assembly emphasises two important political lessons. These are the ideals of self-government and free government. Self government means a government by consent of the governed through their chosen representatives. Free government means limited government, a government which respects individual rights and guarantees certain fundamental liberties. Both self-government and free government can best be secured through the technique of a written constitution. But a written constitution should be one made by a specially convened representative body of the people. As the constitution is an instrument for the realisation of individual rights and public interests, it is of supreme importance that the task of constitution making should not be entrusted to any small group of self-selected men, however eminent they may be in public life. If it is true that what concerns all must be consented to by all in the ordinary matters of government, it logically follows that in the matter so important as to the future of their government the people should be consulted. This is possible only through the medium of a representative Constituent Assembly or Constitutional Convention, by whichever name we may call it.

Requisites of a Constitution. A good constitution must possess certain characteristics. In the first place, the constitution should be definite and precise. It should be expressed in as clear a language as possible, because even the slightest ambiguity or doubt may lead to conflicting interpretations. In this respect a written constitution is more satisfactory than an unwritten one. The provisions of a written constitution are embodied in an instrument prepared and formulated after careful and mature deliberations. It is obviously more definite and less uncertain than a constitution which primarily consists of customs and usages. The constitution must also be comprehensive. It should cover the whole field of governmental organisation and clearly enunciate the principles for the exercise of all political power. A good constitution should leave no gaps. It should not also go into rather needless details at some points and at others omit fundamentls. The French Constitution of 1875 contained no Bill of Rights, nor was there any express guarantee of civil liberty. It did not say how the ministers were to be elected, whether or not they were to be members of parliament and to which House of the legislature they were responsible. There was no provision for annual budgets and besides a clause authorizing the Senate "to be erected into a High Court", the judiciary went entirely unmentioned. Such fundamental ommissions in a constitution are likely to cause much ambiguity and necessitate filling in the gaps which may be twisted to meet certain purposes. Then, a good constitution should be precise. It must not be inundated with detailed clauses.

Details often lead to possibilities of disputes. Besides, a detailed constitution indicates distrust of government. Legislatures deteriorate and avoid responsibility, if matters of importance are removed from their authority and decided in the constitution. Moreover, a constitution which goes into details, very soon becomes overgrown. New social, political, and economic influences render many of the provisions obsolete necessitating frequent amendments. Frequent changes take away the sanctity of the constitution. Changes are, no doubt, necessary and inevitable, but it is better to have them emerge through casual and relatively spontaneous ways rather than through the formal procedure of constitutional amendment.

Finally, stability and flexibility are the two prime requisites of a good constitution. The system of government which the constitution establishes must have a high degree of stability and its desirability should be questioned by no one. The making of frequent changes, *inter alia*, tend to weaken that allegiance to, and respect for, the government which is such an important factor in securing an orderly conduct of political affairs. But, at the same time, the constitution of a modern State should be susceptible to progressive change or growth as errors of judgment in its framing are revealed by experience, as conditions change, and as the political aspirations and beliefs of people undergo alteration. The problem is, therefore, to adopt a policy and procedure in respect of amending the constitution that will represent a compromise between stability and flexibility: neither so rigid a constitution as to prevent change, nor so flexible as to encourage tampering with basic principles.

CONTENTS OF A WRITTEN CONSTITUTION

A written constitution generally contains three sets of provisions:—

1. A series of prescriptions setting forth the fundamental, civil and political rights.
2. A series of provisions outlining the organisation of government.
3. Provision for the amendment of the constitution.

These provisions are regarded as the three basic essentials of a constitution. Burgess calls the first group of provisions the constitution of liberty, the second, the constitution of government, and the last, the constitution of sovereignty.

Constitution of Liberty. The constitutional provision of fundamental rights is considered the *sine qua non* of liberty, for it imposes definite limitations on the powers of the government. Their inclusion in the constitution is a declaration of the fact that certain elementary rights of the individuals are inviolable under all conditions and the shifting majorities in the legislature of a country should not be able to tamper with them. The theory of funda- mental rights implies limited and free government. It aims at preventing the government and the legislature from becoming despotic and it is the duty of the courts to ensure their observance. Fundamental rights, are, accordingly, justiciable. In a Republican State it is given the name of "Bill of Rights" or "Declaration of Rights." The people of the United States of America attach great sanctity to these rights. The Constitution of India contains an elaborate declaration of these fights under the heading Fundamental Rights."[32] These declarations of fundamental fights surpass even the

32. Refer to Part III, pp. 5-18.

declarations of the Weimar Constitution which had been considered to be the best of all hitherto made.

But fundamental rights are not absolute. They are subject to limitations in order to secure or promote the greater interests of the community or the State. Freedom does not mean anarchy. Restrictions are a necessary part of the rights and many constitutions provide for such restrictions. When constitutions state the rights broadly and leave their interpretations to the courts, reasonable restrictions have been imposed in public interest.

Constitution of Government. The purpose of the constitution is to create and outline the powers of its various organs and prescribe the general manner in which these powers are to be exercised. In its widest sense the organisation of government includes the division of powers among the various departments, the organisation of the particular agencies through which State manifests itself, the extent and duration of their authority, the modes of appointment or election of public functionaries, and the constitution of the electorate. In some constitutions these provisions are fragmentary and very general in character. The French Constitution of 1875 provided only that the Deputies shall be elected by universal suffrage. It contained no provisions regarding the composition, the method of election, the term of office, organisation, or the powers of the Chamber of Deputies. It was absolutely silent on the organisation of the Judiciary. But the Constitution of the United States adequately provides for the distribution of powers among the executive, legislative and judicial departments and their organisation in a general way. It contains a brief and logical statement of their jurisdiction and powers. Then, there is a list of prohibitions both for the Central and the State governments. The Constitution of the United States also contains a few miscellaneous provisions. According to Bryc the Constitution of America "ranks above any other written constitution for the intrinsic excellence of its scheme, its adaptation to the circumstances of the people, the simplicity, brevity, and precision of its language and its judicious mixture of definiteness in principle with elasticity in details."[33] The Constitution of India, too, is a remarkable specimen of this excellence, though it is the bulkiest in the world and at many points goes into needless details. There are quite a number of provisions which do not need to be constitutionally protected.

Constitution of Sovereignty. A written constitution must definitely contain the method or procedure for amending the constitution and it is regarded as an essential part of every written constitution. It is upon the method of amendment that the guarantees of individual liberty and the adaptability of the constitution depend. No written constitution is complete without such a provision. "Human societies must grow and develop with the lapse of time, and unless provision is made for such constitutional readjustment as their internal development requires, they must stagnate or retrogress."[34] President Wilson had said that the constitution must of necessity be a vehicle of life and that its substance is the thought and habit of the nation. If the constitution can be amended easily, by a method that enables the political sovereign to express its will, there can be no conflict between actual conditions and legal organisation. But an easy method of amending the constitution leads

33. Bryce, J., *The American Commonwealth,* Vol. II, p. 28.

34. Garner, J.W., *Political Science and Government,* p. 537.

to instability, as a slight swing in popular opinion may change the fundamental form of the government. If, on the other hand, the constitution is difficult to amend or if the political sovereign does not possess the means to express its will, one of the two things may happen. First, there may grow up extra-legal institutions fully supported by public opinion. Take, for example, the election of the President in the United States. The constitution provides for an indirect election. It has now come to be a direct one, but without amending the constitution. Secondly, if the extra-legal institutions are not permitted to grow, the consequent result is an open revolution. Jennings says that a constitution has to work not only in the environment in which it was drafted but also centuries later. "It must therefore be capable of adaptation to new conditions as they arise." Carl Friedrich is, accordingly, of the opinion that a well-drawn constitution should "provide for its own amendment in such a way as to forestall, as far as humanly possible, revolutionary upheavals."[35]

It is not possible to consider all the modes of amendment as adopted in different countries. Three different methods are, however, generally followed:

1. The constitution may be amended by the ordinary legislature as in the case of Britain. The procedure is exactly the same as that for the enactment or amendment of ordinary statutory legislation. Sometimes while the ordinary legislature is empowered to effect amendments, it may, at the same time, be made subject to a special process. For example, the Constitution of India provides that an amendment of stated provisions of the Constitution may be initiated in either House of Parliament, and when the Bill is passed in each House by a majority of the total membership of that House and by a majority of not less than two-thirds of the members of that House present and voting, it shall be presented to the President for his assent and the Constitution will then stand amended. But if the amendment seeks to make any change in the Union List, Concurrent List, and State List, or the representation of States in Parliament, or the powers of the President, the Supreme Court, amendament of the Constituion, etc., the amendment shall also require to be ratified by the legislatures of not less than one-half of the States before the Bill is presented to the President for his assent.[36]

2. A special body may be created for the amendment of the constitution. The typical example is the United States of America. An amendment may be proposed by a two-thirds vote in both Houses of Congress and ratified, unless Congress specifies which method should be followed, either by legislatures in three-fourths of the States or conventions in three-fourths of the States. The second method is that on an application of the legislatures of two-thirds of the States, Congress may call a national constitutional convention for proposing amendments and it should be ratified by the legislatures of three-fourths of the States or by conventions in three-fourths of the States.

3. Popular referendum is another device and it aims at referring amendments to the people for their approval. This is regarded as the most democratic method. Popular referendum for amending the constitution obtains in Switzerland, Australia, France and in some of the States of the United States of America.

35. Friedrich, C.J., *Constitutional Government and Democracy,* p. 135.
36. Article 368.

It must again be emphasised that no constitution can be regarded as final or unchanging. A written constitution requires to be modified as a result of new political ideals. The provision for amendment should, therefore, neither be so rigid as to make the required changes practically impossible nor so flexible as to make possible frequent and unnecessary changes and lower the authority and respect of the constitution. The machinery of amendment should be like a safety valve, so devised as neither to operate the machine with too great facility nor to require, in order to set it in motion, an accumulation of force sufficient to explode it. While providing for the process of amendment the authors of a written constitution should keep these considerations in view: the requirements of growth, and the element of conservatism.

DEVELOPMENT AND EXPANSION OF CONSTITUTION

As previously stated, no constitution can be regarded as final. "Constitutions must grow," observed Lord Brougham, "if they are of any value; they have roots, they ripen, they endure." Written constitutions grow in four ways: by custom and usage, by judicial interpretation, by statutory development, and by amendment. The last mentioned method of growth is described as formal.

Custom and Usage. What habit is to the individual, usage is to the State; nations, like men, get into the habit of doing things in a given way. Habit then hardens into usage, which becomes difficult to change. The political customs and usages, which have their basis neither in laws nor in judicial decisions, are essential parts of the basic framework of the fundamental rules of the government in every country. They modernise, amend and democratise the otherwise rigid constitutions.

But there are two considerations in this respect. The first is that customs play an important part in the case of old rather than of new constitutions. Secondly, customs develop and thrive in countries where the inhabitants cherish respect for the past and a higher regard for precedents. In India, there is no set of established conventions. The reasons are obvious. The Indian Constitution had ever been in the melting pot, and her late masters (British) always gave a small dose of reforms whenever the patriotic movement gained momentum. The present Constitution though new yet it is prolific in amendments. It has been amended seventy-four times during a span of forty three years and many more are waiting in a row. Thus no opportunity has been given to customs to grow and get permanently established. In France, too, development of the constitution through usage and custom has been very small, because France has been the laboratory of constitutional experiments. Between 1789 and 1875, she adopted and then rejected nearly a dozen constitutions and all those constitutions were the result of revolutions rather than of evolutions.

But the Constitution of the United States of America has considerably developed and expanded through customs and usages. Does the Constitution authorize the President to have a 'Cabinet' and to consult its members as a collective body? The written Constitution is silent. President Washington found it useful to have a small group of advisers to whom be could look for counsel and other Presidents have continued with it, and, today, it is impossible to dispense entirely with such a body. The Constitution also provides for indirect election of the President. But the electoral system did not function as the framers of the Constitution had contemplated. The electors have now been reduced to mere dummies and the Presidential election has become direct. There are many more examples of customs and usages, like senatorial courtesy, legislative committees, and residential requirements in the case of the Representatives, which have supplemented the Constitution and without them it would be unworkable. The most revealing of these is the rise and organisation of political parties. The party system that grew and matured in the eighteenth century was antithetical to the ideals of the men who had drafted the Constitution. The system of government they set up did not anticipate the emergence of parties, but today it is impossible to work the institutions of the country without parties.

Development by Judicial Interpretation. The development of a written constitution as a result of judicial interpretation is now a well-established fact and it may be due to many causes. A written constitution, howsoever carefully framed, is likely to contain some ambiguities of language and deficiencies of expression. And words have meanings in the context of the time in which they are interpreted. When differences of opinion arise, a duty devolves upon the judiciary to ascertain not only the true meaning of that which is expressed in the Constitution, but also that which the framers intended to express. The judges, then, draw their own conclusions. The Constitution of the United States gives to the Centre, *inter alia*, power over the armed forces of the country and the means of communication and transport. The Supreme Court interpreted armed forces to mean the army, the navy and the air force. Similarly, the means of communication and transport as interpreted include rail, road, water, air, telegraphic, telephonic, television services, etc. There are innumerable other examples and almost every clause of the Constitution has been the subject of interpretation and construction. The Constitution of the United States of America, indeed, to a large extent consists of "addenda." The judge-made definitions have added essential portions to the foundation work of the Constitution. Justice Frankfurter put it rather bluntly that the "Supreme Court is the constitution." Chief Justice Marshall's decision in the famous case *Marbury* v. *Madison* (1803) vindicates Justice Frankfurter's assertion. Marshall declared that the judicial power conferred by the Constitution together with the oath to uphold the Constitution, which the Justices take on the assumption of office, requires that the Courts should declare when they so believe, that the Acts of Congress are in violation of the Constitution.

Since then the principle of judicial review has been embedded in the American system of government, although there is no direct provision in the Constitution which empowers the Supreme Court to declare the constitutionality or otherwise of State or Federal Acts. The *Marbury* case forms the basis of this important authority of judicial review exercised by the Supreme Court. It has brought about important changes in the United States Constitution and the Supreme Court is characterised as a "continuous consti-tutional convention", interpreting, developing and expanding the basic law.[37]

Development by Statutes. No constitution is complete by itself and nowhere has an attempt ever been made to reduce all details into writing.[38] The framers of a constitution

37. Ogg and Ray, *Introduction to American Government,* pp. 57-58.
38. Beard, C.A., *American Government and Politics,* p. 15.

always leave room for the system to grow. Chief Justice Marshall declared in *McCulloch* v. *Maryland* that a constitution is "intended to endure for ages to come, and consequently, to be adapted to the various crises of human affairs. To have prescribed the means to which government should, in all future time, execute its powers, would have been to change, entirely, the character of the instrument and give it the properties of a legal code. It would have been an unwise attempt to provide, by immutable rules, for exigencies which, if foreseen at all, must have been seen dimly, and which can best be provided for as they occur." The constitution, therefore, confers powers in general on the various agencies of government and leaves the details to be filled in by statutes enacted by the legislative assemblies in order to complete the framework of government. Article II of the United States Constitution assumes administrative departments, but it says almost nothing about them. The elaborate organization of the federal administration has been established by statutes, with federal departments created, reorganized, or given new functions by Congress. Similarly, Article III of the Constitution states only that there shall be one Supreme Court and such inferior courts as Congress may from time to time ordain and establish. The Judiciary Act of 1789 laid the foundation of the American judicial system, fixed the number of judges of the Supreme Court and their salaries, provided for the Court's organization, and set forth its jurisdiction. This Act has been amended from time to time. Several times Congress has passed laws changing the number of Justices of the Supreme Court. Still more, nowhere does the Constitution prescribe the precise way in which minor officers of the government are to be selected. Congress enacted a civil service law providing for their appointment by competitive examinations.

After enumerating various powers of Congress, the Constitution concludes with a sort of general grant empowering Congress to make all laws which it may deem necessary and proper for carrying into execution the jurisdiction assigned to it. This is sometimes called "the elastic clause" and many matters that Congress might not otherwise feel authorized to deal with have been covered under this provision. In the same way, by broadly interpreting the Constitution, Congress has established a huge defence establishment, created scores of administrative boards and bureaus, entered into the business of education, banking, insurance, etc., and found authority to regulate the economic and social life of a highly industrialized nation.

Development by Amendment. A written constitution clearly provides for the mode of amendment and this is the most definite source of constitutional expansion. Constitutions must grow and develop as the life of the nation changes. No constitution can be permanent unless it guarantees progress. "Living political constitutions must be Darwinian in structure and in practice." This aspect we have duly developed and discussed in the last section of the present Chapter.

Informal Method. A constitution also grows by a process called inforinal. The letter of law remains the same, unchanged and unaltered, but expediency and exigency give to the provisions of the constitution another meaning which is radically different from the original meaning given to them. Talking about the United States Constitution, Charles Beard said that "it is a printed document explained by judicial decisions, precedents and practices and illuminated by understanding and aspiration. In short, the real constitution is a living body of general prescriptions carried into effect by living persons."[39] The constitution is today not the written fundamental instrument of the Federal Government framed at Philadelphia together with its amendments. It also includes statutes enacted by Congress, executive orders and actions which enable the government to function efficiently, the monumental judicial decisions, and the innumerable political habits, govemmental usages and needs which chisel the constitution to achieve the dynamic political purposes. The constitution remains the same, but the political habits of the people and their attitude towards government and the solution of problems confronting the government change the spirit of the constitution.

The factors which prominently account for informal growth and expansion of a constitution are:

1. The process of centralization is the first and the most important in the count. Centralization is the shifting of governing authority from lower or member units to higher units, with a tendency for power to grow at the top. Federal centralization, a universal phenomenon now in all the federal governments, is the tendency for the national government to assume influence or control over functions which formerly were considered to be under State jurisdiction thereby disturbing the constitutional division of powers between the Central and State governments. War, economic crisis, the growth of social services and planning are the primary causes of the process of centralization. Moreover, the people of all countries, federal or unitary, at all stages of their development, had always looked to the national government for solving their problems. Their desire to make the country big and prosperous necessitates big business, big agriculture and big labour, and all add up to big government. All this means enhancement of the powers of the national government without making any amendment in the constitution. The acquiescence of the people in this process is spontaneous irrespective of the barriers which the constitution might have created. All this means a vital change in the spirit of the constitution.

2. The second factor is the party system. Political parties are indispensable for the working of a democratic government, yet no constitution provides for them, except in one-party States. Though it has an extra-constitutional growth, yet it forms the hub of the political life of the nation. Referring to the United States of America, Brogan says, "But for the appearance of a national party system the election of a President really enough. of a national figure to carry out his duties, might have been impossible. And it is certain that the greatest breakdown of American constitutional system, the Civil War, came only when the party system collapsed."[40] The President is chosen as a party man to head a government operated under a party system. He surrounds himself with advisers of his own political faith, consults usually with men belonging to his party in framing policy, and he uses his power as chief legislator to pursue the party's programme to a crowning victory. All this has meant a fundamental change in the spirit of the constitution.

3. The electoral system prevalent in a country also influences the working of the constitution. The method of voting, the qualifications of the electors, their behaviour at

39. Brogan, D.W., *An Introduction to American Politics,* p. 45.
40. *Ibid.*

the polls and the complexion of political parties all influence the operative part of the constitution. Uninterrupted one-party rule, absence of an effective Opposition, multiple-party system particularly based upon local loyalties and religion plague the working of a constitution. Defections are another bane of such politics as they pollute the political system whatever be the lofty ideals of the constitution. All constitutions plan for a stable government, but when the electorate determines an uncertain composition of the parties and the strength of the executive in the legislature, it creates conditions of uncertainty and the operative ideal envisaged in the constitution is rendered impracticable. The mass party system in the newer States is still more reprehensible. It chokes normal constitutional channels.

4. The attitude of the people toward their constitution also affects the machinery of the government it establishes. President George Washington succinctly explained this in his farewell address. He said, "Time and habit are at least as necessary to fix the true character of goveruments as of other institutions." In countries practising constitutionalism, people respect their constitutions to the point of veneration. For example, the people of the United States have so much abiding faith in the sagacity, moderation, and "sense of the possible" shown by the framers of the constitution that the original document is virtually worshipped. Although there is no document which contains the British Constitution, the constitutional structure essentially has remained the same through all these centuries. The institutions necessary for carrying out the functions of the State were established from time to time as the need arose. But as Jennings says, "Formed to meet immediate requirements they were then adapted to exercise more extensive and sometinies different functions. There has been a constant process of invention, reform and amended distribution of powers. The building has been constantly added to, patched and partly reconstructed, so that it has been renewed from century to century, but it has never been razed to the ground and rebuilt on new foundations."[41]

On the other hand, France had been the "laboratory" of constitutions. The constitutions in the developing States, both in Asia and Africa, are always in the melting pot. Pakistan is the most convincing example in this respect. The problem of emerging Asian and African States is still a social, more than a political one and if the constitutions are to grow and endure, the need is to build a strong sense of unity in the country so that criticism and diversity may not seem like treason. If this cannot be achieved, the only alternative is revolution. Soviet Russia was at the extreme, where the constitution was ordained as a transitory phase and it was to die its own death with the "withering" away of the State. Till very recently, the constitution was what the leadership of the Communist Party determined it to be. There was nothing sacrosanct about it and the constitution provided no effective restraints on governmental actions, which really meant actions of the Communist Party. The same pattern existed in other Communist countries.

41. Jennings, W.I., *The Law and the Constitution*, p. 8.

SUGGESTED READINGS

Boutmy, E.: *Studies in Constitutional Law.*

Bryce, J.: *Studies in History and Jurisprudence,* Essay III.

Dicey, A.V.: *The Law of the Constitution.*

Finer, H.: *Theory and Practices of Modern Government,* Chaps. VIII IX.

Friedrich, C.J.: *Constitutional Government and Democracy.*

Garner, J.W.: *Political Science and Government,* Chap. XVIII.

Hawgood,J. A.: *Modern Costitutions Since* 1817.

Kapur, A.C.: *Theory of the Constituent Assembly and its Development in India.*

Kelsen, H.: *General Theory of Law and State.*

Lowell, A.L.: *Government of England,* Vol. I, Chap. I.

Lipson, L.: *The Great Issues of Politics,* pp. 240-256.

McBain, L. and Rogers, L.: *New Constitutions of Europe.*

Mcllwain, C.H.: *Constitutionalism and the Changing World.*

Neumann, R.G.: *European and Comparative Governments,* Part V, Chap. II.

Roucek, Huzar and others: *Introduction to Political Science.*

Sidgwick, H.: *Elements of Politics,* Chap. XXVII.

Strong, C.F.: *Modern Political Constitutions,* Chaps. VI-VII.

Wheare, K.C.: *Modern Constitutions.*

Willoughby, W.F.: *Government of Modern States,* Chaps. VI-VII.

Wilson, Woodrow: *Congressional Government,* Chap. I.

Wormuth Francis D.: *The Origins of Modern Constitutionalism,*

18

CHAPTER

The Electorate and Representation

Democracy has two patterns—direct and indirect. Under a system of direct democracy the will of the State is formulated and expressed by the people themselves. They make their own laws without the intervention of any intermediary agency. But such a type of democracy is impossible to obtain in our times. The modern State is a huge State with enormous area and population. It is physically impossible for the people drawn from the length and breadth of the whole country to frequently assemble together and take a direct part in making laws. Modern democracy is indirect and representative. The voters elect their representatives and they become members of the legislative assemblies charged with duty of making laws and bringing harmony of purpose between the government and the governed.

Origin of Representation. But how did this practice of representation originate?[1] There is no conclusive proof to determine how and where the practice of representation really originated. The general belief is that it originated in the Middle Ages as a device used by certain monastic orders and was applied to bodies called by the king for consultation on questions of broad interest, especially taxation. Under various names—Parliament in Britain, Estates General in France, Cortes in Spain, and Diet in Germany—such bodies came into existence toward the end of the thirteenth and the beginning of the fourteenth centuries and were soon playing an important part in the national affairs of their respective countries. For example, in Britain Parliament acquired rights of taxation and consultation and it became an indispensable part of the government. But assemblies were in no country democratic in any sense. They only represented certain elements in the population; the aristocracy, landed gentry, the rich businessmen, and the higher clergy. But these elements, observes Soltau, "were probably fairly expressive of what may be called the politically conscious elements of the community; there is no reason to think that a larger electorate would have acted differently in any important issue."[2]

With the end of the Middle Ages and with the emergence of the nation-States, monarchy became more powerful and assemblies were either ignored altogether or they were reduced to mere formal bodies. This was, however, not the case with the British

1. There is an illuminating chapter on *Representation* in E.M. Sait's *Political Institutions, A Preface,* pp. 467-99.
2. Soltau, R.H.: *An Introduction to Politics,* p. 179.

Parliament. The struggle between Cromwell and Charles resulted in the victory of Parliament. The Revolution of 1688 established the sovereignty of Parliament by reducing monarchy to dependence upon it, but Parliament was still very far from being a democratic Parliament. Before 1832, there were only a few thousands of voters spread all over the country and parliamentary seats were in the grip of rich men and were bought and sold like shares on the stock exchange. The first change in the system of representation, fixed in the Middle Ages, was made in 1832 and yet it was a long way from being a people's parliament. At intervals after 1832 extending to 1928, there had been successive electoral reforms and now all adults over eighteen, men and women, in the country possess the right to vote and elect their representatives to the House of Commons. Parliament today is really the House of commons.

In other countries the champions of democracy ceaselessly advocated and strove for the creation of representative assemblies, which should be the centres of political authority. The struggle became so relentless and the demand became so popular that monarchies could survive only by making concessions to the general demand for parliamentary systems. Today, representative institutions have become the distinguishing feature of a democratic State and its indispensable instrument of government. In fact, so strongly is entrenched the idea of popular government that even dictatorial governments have deemed it advisable to establish assemblies which they claim to be representative of the popular will. Hitler and Mussolini had their parliaments. The erstwhile Soviet Union and other Communist States had their legislatures whose members were popularly elected, and were declared in their respective Constitutions as "the highest organs of State power."

The Electorate. But all the people living in the State do not elect their representatives. Those who exercise the power of voting and periodically elect their representatives are a comparatively small fraction of the whole population. No country gives the right of voting to minors, to persons of unsound mind or to aliens. Some States deny this right to women. Others impose property or educational qualifications. Citizens of the State enjoying the right of electing their representatives are voters and the entire body of such voters or electors is known as electorate. The electorate constitutes the whole population of the State minus those who, at any time, are denied the right to vote.

Theories of Franchise. What should be the true basis of franchise is one of the most difficult problems of democracy. Two schools of thought, however, have been prominent. During the eighteenth century, when the doctrines of natural rights, equality of men, and popular sovereignty were favourite themes of every political thinker, the demand was for universal franchise. It was held that sovereignty ultimately resided in the people and it was the right of every citizen to vote and participate in the determination of the policy of government. Democracy, it was further asserted, postulated equality of men and political equality could be assured only when all citizens were granted the right to vote. It was claimed that laws and policies of government concerned all people and what toucheth all should be decided by all. To grant suffrage to some meant the exclusion of others from representation. Unrepresented interests were likely to be neglected by the government. To safeguard the interests of all elements of population, it was essential that everyone must possess the right to have his opinion counted in the final decision of public affairs.

The second school was led by Bluntschli, Lecky, John Stuart Mill and Sir Henry Maine. They held that franchise was not an inherent right of a citizen. It was a right which was conferred by the State and it should not be granted to all. Moreover, franchise was a sacred right which required an informal exercise of judgment in the election of representatives. To extend it to the unenlightened and ignorant masses was to invite dark days for democracy. It was, accordingly, suggested that all citizens of the State should not possess the right to vote. This school of thought was against the idea of universal suffrage.

It is, however, now admitted that by universal suffrage its advocates meant universal adult suffrage. Minors had always been excluded from the right to vote. So were the lunatics and the aliens. Conviction for a crime has been regarded as a reasonable cause for disqualification. The modern view in regard to the nature of suffrage is that it is an office or function which is conferred by the State upon only such persons as are believed to be most capable of exercising it for the public good and not a natural right which belongs without distinction to all citizens of the State. But what ought to be the qualifications of persons believed to be most capable of exercising their vote for public good? Every State has its own electoral laws. Adult suffrage is the maxim of democracy, but at present electorates include a fractional part of the population, reaching as high as three-fifths in the more liberal States; and in several States, such as New Zealand, where adult suffrage is permitted, almost one-half of the population are voters. India, too, stands in this category.

Excluded Classes. All States exclude minors, aliens, and lunatics from the right to vote and by adult suffrage is meant every citizen, male and female, who is not a lunatic or criminal. France has fixed the adult age at twenty-one years. Britain, the United States, India and Russia consider eighteen years sufficient. In some cases the limit is as high as twenty-five. The underlying idea is that a certain maturity is essential for the proper exercise of judgment in electing representatives. Criminals in confinement, idiots and lunatics are invariably excluded, because they do not possess the requisite mental and moral qualifications deemed necessary for a voter. Some States disqualify, either temporarily or permanently, persons convicted of crime for the reason that they are not good citizens and lack civic sense. Aliens are nowhere permitted to vote as they are not citizens of the State in which they reside, but owe allegiance to another State.

Some States impose other limitations, which may either be the survival of earlier restrictions or may be necessitated by political reasons. One of these is that a voter must necessarily be an educated person with at least the ability to read and write. John Stuart Mill said: "I regard it as wholly inadmissible that any person should participate in the suffrage without being able to read and write ... and perform the common operations of arithmetics." He emphasised that universal teaching must precede universal enfranchisement. With the spread of universal desire for compulsory education majority of the advanced States now do not insist on this qualification to be prescribed in their electoral laws. Herman Finer, summing up the argument that formal education is not absolutely necessary as a qualification for voting, observes that "it is a fundamental fallacy to argue that political behaviour has depended, depends now, or must depend upon instruction. It depends upon will, upon the passions ... and men and women vote primarily for what they want and not from purely intellectual guidance." But in some States of America it is still being retained "chiefly to disfranchise the Negro." Here comes in political expediency. In India illiteracy is not a disqualification, if a citizen possesses another qualification such as the payment of land revenue, income-tax, municipal or district board rates. Literacy, of course, entitles a person to vote, irrespective of any other qualification.

The representative form of government was born on the ruins of feudalism and for long the exercise of suffrage was limited to property-holders alone. The theory underlying the property qualifications was that only those who own a certain amount of property may fairly be regarded as having a stake in the country. Another argument advanced in favour of the property qualification was that the right to vote should be conferred on those who paid taxes. John Stuart Mill was an ardent supporter of property qualification. He maintained: "It is important that the assembly which votes the taxes, either general or local, should be elected exclusively by those who pay something towards the taxes imposed. Those who pay no taxes, disposing by their votes of other people's money, have every motive to be lavish and none to economise as far as money matters are concerned, and any power of voting possessed by them is a violation of the fundamental principles, a severance of the powers of control from the interest in its beneficial exercise."

Ownership of property had been a very common qualification for the exercise of suffrage in every modern State, except Russia. But the old theory does not hold true any longer. Possession of property may be one of the necessary qualifications for the exercise of suffrage, but it cannot be regarded as the only essential qualification. Political right, if hedged by property qualification, is no right at all. It is tantamount to disfranchising and disqualifying a vast majority of the people, however worthy citizens of the State they may be. When property is the only qualification to elect representatives, the legislatures will be representative assemblies of only the propertied class and other sections and interests of the community would naturally remain unrepresented. Such a nature of representation is a mockery of democracy. The argument that those who pay taxes should possess the right to vote stands entirely on a different footing. It has nothing to do with possession of property. A tax is a contribution paid by individuals in a community for the services rendered by government. Taxation and representation go together and it is a much valued democratic argument of the theory of representation. Taxes are paid, directly or indirectly, by all citizens of the State and not only by the propertied class. Those who foot the bill of government must have the means to see how money is being spent, no matter whether they possess property or not.

Women Suffrage. Till very recently the franchise was confined to males only and women were not given the right to vote. In the United States full suffrage rights were extended to women in 1920. In Britain, the Representation of the People Act, 1918, allowed only a limited system of female suffrage. This Act was altered in 1928 and now there is equal franchise for men and women. Although the old prejudices against women suffrage are disappearing, yet some States still deny to their women the right to vote and the right to be elected to public office.

Female disfranchisement arose out of no rational consideration of women's need to participate in political activity, but out of the general social position of women, as determined by sexual role, family life and religious tenets. Those who opposed women's suffrage emphasised that woman was the ministering angel of home and maternity was her proper mission. The exactions of political life are inconsistent with the duties of child-bearing and the rearing of families. Nature had not intended her for political life. Her participation in politics was sure to destroy the integrity of the home. If husband and wife differed in political views and supported opposing candidates, it might mean discord in family life. Moreover, women would lose respect and honour which was naturally due to them, if they got themselves involved in the mud and mire of political controversies. Their participation in public affairs, in brief, would destroy their qualities as mothers and home-makers. The opponents of women suffrage further pointed out that women had shown general apathy in public affairs wherever they were granted franchise. They were unable, being physically weaker, to perform the arduous duties of citizenship and, as such, they had no right to demand the privilege of franchise. Besides, women would be guided by emotion rather than by reason in electing the representatives. And finally, their interest in public affairs would last only until the novelty wore off.

The demand for woman suffrage has worked simultaneously with the spread of democracy. Democracy, as a matter of principle, does not differentiate between man and man. Why should it then differentiate between sexes? Both on logical and rational grounds suffrage cannot be denied to women. The right of voting is based upon moral and rational grounds rather than on physical considerations. "I see no adequate reason," says Sidgwick, "for refusing the franchise to any self-supporting adult, otherwise eligible, on the score of sex alone: and there is a danger of material injustice resulting from such refusal so long as the State leaves unmarried women and widows to struggle for a livelihood in the general industrial competition without any special privileges or protection."[3]

The advocates of women's suffrage argued that as they were physically weaker, they were more dependent on law and society for protection. They must have their own say on the laws which affected their status. Moreover, men had, all through the ages, dominated womanhood, subjected their women to inhuman treatment and deprived them of their just rights and privileges. They could defend themselves against unjust class legislation only if they had the right to vote and their views got adequate representation. It was also wrong to say that their participation would deteriorate the domestic and political life. In fact, the admission of women in politics would introduce in political life a purifying, ennobling and refining influence that not only would tend to elevate the tone of public life and bring about more wholesome political conditions in society, but also would insure better government. To deny her the right of suffrage was to deprive womanhood of the instinct of good citizenship. Woman was the cradle of civilization and the future of every State depended upon her active participation in the affairs of government. If she was deprived of the civic sense, she had nothing to impart to her children. Finally, when women enjoyed all civil rights it was inconsistent and irrational not to give them political rights. Political rights must necessarily go with civil rights.

Democracy is a government of the people with the consent of the people. Both men and women living within a definite territory constitute the people of the State. If women

3. Sidgwick, H., *Elements of Politics,* p. 385.

are not given the opportunity to express their consent, it is a negation of democracy. The old prejudices must necessarily disappear and women should stand at par with men in political life. Women in no way lag behind. They have proved their worth in the social and political life of every country. Why then should they be denied the right to franchise?

The enfranchisement of women has been followed by their election to public offices. The Congress Party in India fixed an appreciable quota of women candidates amongst its list of candidates, both for the Central and State legislatures, in the elections of 1957, and this principle was followed in the subsequent elections too. In the course of legislative proceedings women members have everywhere shown special interest in health, housing, temperance, social security, education, international peace and other like problems. They have also presided over various departments of government, and a woman was Prime Minister of Sri Lanka and a woman occupied the same august office in India and in Britain both for a long period of more than a decade. Even in Pakistan and Bangladesh, two Islamic countries, Prime Ministers are currently Muslim women. Turkey, a secular Muslim country, has a woman Prime Minister. So was one in Israel. Herman Finer brings forward an interesting issue for deep consideration. It would be instructive to quote him in extenso. He says, "The wholesale entrance of women into politics must inevitably introduce complications, owing to the contact of different sexes. No one who has an experience of co-education and cooperation in industry can avoid the conclusion that the minds of men and women are often diverted from objective considerations and are seriously affected by considerations of courtesy and the personal beauty and desirability of one of the opposite sex whose fate or interest is involved. Boys and girls tell lies for each other, and turn in work in someone else's name; pugnacity is aroused in the presence of girls, and discipline is audaciously rejected because it is humiliating. Time is wasted in philandering, and the mind loses itself in idle fancies. In business women are often shielded from responsibility because of their sex; they are appointed because they are pleasing; they are dismissed and passed over in promotion because they are ugly. Women become extraordinarily devoted to their work because they are devoted to a particular manager, and work badly for others in the firm. We all know such facts, and they should not escape us in public life. And although the vast majority of people in a representative assembly, its committees, and the ancillary organizations may be married, and therefore presumably (but only presumably) less susceptible to the charms and wiles of the opposite sex, everyday experience teaches us to expect certain results."[4] Whatever Finer says may be the result of his minute study of sex relations prevailing in the Western countries, but it cannot be true of the East where womanhood is held in high religious esteem and sanctity of relations between the two sexes is the main basis of the social order.

Plural or Weighted Voting. The modern democratic principle, is that every adult man and every adult woman, if not otherwise disqualified by the electoral laws, should exercise the right of voting in the election of their representatives. This may be reduced to the maxim of one vote, one person. But in certain States prevails the system of plural or weighted voting which is also sometimes called differential voting. The system of

4. Finer, H., *The Theory and Practice of Modern Government,* p. 234.

plural voting means that certain persons have more than one vote. The idea behind the system of plural voting is that persons better qualified or those supposed to have greater interests at stake are given more votes than those less qualified or having smaller interests in the country. Belgium introduced this system as early as 1893 and it continued till very recently. Every citizen having attained the age of twenty-five years and having lived in the Commune for at least one year was allowed one vote. In addition to this, a supplementary vote was allowed to every man who had reached the age of thirty-five years, had a legitimate child and paid a tax of five francs to the State, and two supplementary votes to all male citizens of twenty-five years age who possessed a diploma from an institution of higher teaching or had held or held a public office. No one, however, had more than three votes. The_system of plural voting prevails in India as well. For example, graduates of universities have more than one vote in the State elections, where two chambers exist. In Britain, before 1918, voters had as many votes as positive qualifications. The Reform Act of 1918 permitted, at most, two votes per voter to be chosen among the qualification of residence, occupation, and university degree. In 1945 it was estimated that there were 200,000 qualified to cast a business vote and 175,000 a university vote. The Labour Government abolished the "plural vote" by the Representation of the People Act of 1948.

The opponents of universal suffrage were reluctant to entrust political power to the ignorant masses. They feared that a demagogue or a self-seeking politician would usurp the real power by misleading the ignorant and uninstructed people. The device of plural voting was invented as a "counterpoise to the numerical weight of the least educated." John Stuart Mill was a great apologist of this system. He maintained that it was a great political wrong to rate all votes as equal. Votes, he added, should not be counted; they should be weighed and those who have a greater stake in the country or who are better qualified to vote should be given greater weight. The poet lqbal also satirized democracy for the same reason:

جمہوریت اک طرزِ حکومت ہے کہ جس میں
ووٹوں کو گنا کرتے ہیں۔ تولا نہیں کرتے۔

(*Democracy is a form of government in which votes are counted not weighed*)

But the practical defect of plural voting is the difficulty in prescribing a just and equitable standard of weighing the votes. To put a premium on education or property is to attach arbitrary values to a certain category of votes. Thus, while a university graduate may receive a special vote, the Civil Engineer or Architect who is highly qualified in his particular branch of works, may justily complain that he has no extra vote. Property, too, is not a true criterion. Democracy cannot work when political rights are based upon wealth. Weighted voting for the wealth means a class government to perpetuate vested interests. Such a process is most undemocratic as it is inconsistent with the principle of political equality. Plural voting, therefore, is fast disappearing as it has disappeared in Britain. One vote, one person is the requirement of democracy.

Methods of Making Electoral Areas. Two methods are generally adopted in the forming of electoral areas. One is to parcel the total area into as many electoral districts, technically called *constituencies*, as there are representatives to be chosen, one member to be chosen from each constituency. All electoral districts, or constituencies, are equal or approximately equal in size. This method is known as the single district, or in French *scrutin d'arrondissement*, or the single-member constituency. The second method is the general ticket system or *scrutin de liste*, or the multiple-member constituency. Under this system, the country is not divided into as many electoral districts as the number of representatives to be elected. A smaller number of districts, or constituencies, are created from each of which several members are elected. The size of the district determines the number of representatives it will send and each elector has as many votes as there are members to be returned.

The advantages claimed for the single district system are that it establishes a more intimate relationship between representatives and their constituents and ensures that all parts of the State will be duly represented. The representative may also be known to the constituency, for very often he belongs to the district itself. The voters can, thus, intelligently exercise their votes and elect those persons who are deemed best and capable of discharging their responsibilities most conscientiously. The representatives, in their turn, being personally familiar with the needs of their constituents, can get their grievances removed.

To sum up, the single-member constituency method of electing representatives "increases the responsibility of the voter in choosing his representatives and, at the same time, perhaps, intensifies the interest of the representative in and his responsibility to his constituency."[5] The representative is keen to regularly nurse his constituency and acquaint his electors how he has justified the trust reposed in him. He cannot afford to remain oblivious of the fluctuations in public opinion and if he feels that the popularity of the party to which he belongs is receding, he becomes clamorous, because it means a fall in his electoral support. This system of election also provides adequate opportunities for the representation of minorities, and secures a reasonable balance of interests. The comparative smallness of a single-member district tends to reduce the expense and trouble of an election. The system is simple and intelligible, and it can be conveniently and advantageously applied in large States.

But the single-member district method is not free from defects. The first objection is that it narrows the choice in the selection of candidates which may lead to the election of not only inferior, but often corrupt representatives. The choice is still more restricted when the single-member constituency method is coupled with the locality rule. The representatives so chosen begin to entertain a very narrow idea of representation. They regard themselves as the representatives of local interests rather than the representatives of the nation as a whole. Such a political mentality is highly detrimental to national solidarity. "The custom which regards the legislator," says Garner, "as the representative of a particular locality is responsible for the election of men whose energies are likely to be engrossed with the pressure of petty local influences, and, therefore, often deprives

5. Garner, J.W., *Political Science and Government*, p. 633.

the State of the services of able statesmen who would be willing to serve in the legislature could they be freed from such influences."[6] Finally, as the single-member constituency method requires a constant revision of areas, the party in power resorts to the process of "gerrymandering", that is to say, the electoral areas are formed in such a way that the ruling party's majorities are spread over the largest number of constituencies possible and coop up the oppossing party with overwhelming majorities in a small number of districts.

The merits claimed for the general ticket method are that it ensures that the majority will prevail. Finer says that "the ideal system — that is to say, a system having exactness of representation as its only object — would be that in which the whole nation was taken as a single constituency, where lists of candidates for the whole number of members of the legislature could be presented and advocated by anybody. Such an arrangement, if it could be organised, would provide an exact reflection of majority and minority groups."[7] Then, the general ticket method allows greater freedom in selecting candidates and this permits the election of superior men. And when the members elected represent the whole State, instead of a single district, they will make their actions conform to the welfare of the State as a whole rather than to those of particular districts.

But the defects of this system "are not only serious", observes Finer, "they are actually destructive of the values most people want from representative government." The general ticket method leads to a mushroom growth of political parties with confusing programmes, baffling the judgment of voters. Then, the electoral area being the State as a whole or huge multi-membered districts, it will not be possible for the electors to have a personal assessment of the candidates. The result is centralised authority of the party machine to organise the issues and conduct the campaign. And it permits the least degree of local and personal adaptation of the candidates. There is, accordingly, complete divorce between the electors and their representatives. Neither it is possible for the representatives to nurse their constituencies nor does the system allow bye-elections. All this is against the elementary principles of a representative government.

Finally, it does not give adequate representation to minorities. Under the general ticket system, a party casting a majority of the votes can elect all the representatives with the result that minority parties, even though they constitute a very considerable part of the electorate, may be wholly without representation. Under the district system the minority parties, unless they are in a minority in all the districts taken independently, will secure some representation. It should be noted, however, that under the district system, it is possible for a party that is in a minority in the State as a whole, to secure a majority of the representatives. This happens when the bulk of the voting strength of the majority party is concentrated in a few districts while that of the minority party is widely spread over.

In spite of certain obvious drawbacks, the single district plan has been accepted as the most favoured electoral method. In fact, there is no plan of election which may be free from drawbacks. The general ticket plan, too, is making a rapid headway with the introduction of the system of proportional representation. The system of proportional

6. *Ibid.*, p. 635.

7. Finer, H., *The Theory and Practice of Modern Government,* p. 55.

representation possesse not only all the advantages of the general ticket method, but obviates its disadvantages by ensuring that minority parties will secure representation and that such representation will be proportionate to their relative strength.

METHODS OF ELECTION

Direct and Indirect Methods of Election. There are two methods of electing representatives. If the voters directly participate in election and elect their representatives, it is known as the direct method of election. The process of direct election is very simple. Every voter goes to the polling station and records his vote either in favour of one candidate or the other. A candidate securing the maximum number of votes is declared elected. This method of election is the most popular and is followed in all democratic countries for electing members of the representative or the people's chamber. The election of the House of Commons in Britain is direct. All members of the State Assemblies and the House of the People (Lok Sabha) in India are now directly elected, exeept for two nominated members from the Anglo-Indian community.

When voters do not directly participate in the election of their representatives, but choose only an intermediary body which alone will make the final choice, the method of election is called indirect. This intermediary body of electors is usually known as an electoral college. Indirect method of election involves double election. In the first instance, the general mass of voters elect from among themselves a small group of electors. These electors then elect the final representatives who become members of the legislature. The final choice of electing the representatives is, not that of the general mass of voters, but of the intermediary body of electors whom the general mass of voters had elected in the first instance. This system of election limits the power of the voters.

The indirect method of electing representatives is often used for the constitution of second, or what are popularly called upper chambers. In France, the Upper Chamber is indirectly elected. In former U.S.S.R. the Upper Chamber was called the Soviet of Nationalities. Deputies of the Soviet of Nationalities were voted for separately by the Councils of Union Republics, Autonomous Republics, Autonomous Regions and National Areas.[8] According to the Government of India Act, 1935, the Federal Assembly was to be indirectly elected by the members of the Provincial Legislative Assemblies. The Constitution of India provides for indirect election of the Upper Chamber at the Centre, the Council of States (Rajya Sabha).[9]

Direct election makes people conscious of their rights and duties and it is fully in keeping with democratic principles. A direct contact between the electors and their representatives stimulates interest in public affairs and develops the sense of public spirit. It also sharpens the political intelligence of the people. Democracy has an educative value and there is no better method of educating citizens than giving them the opportunity of directly participating in the election of their represenatives. The spirit of political vigilance so injected in the people enables them to see and judge if their representatives justify the trust reposed in them.

8. Karpinsky, *The Social and State Sructure of the U.S.S.R.*, pp. 186-87.
9. Article 80(1).

But the method of direct election has been vehemently opposed by some political thinkers. It is maintained that all voters are not the best judges to wisely exercise their political right. The average voter, it is argued, cannot always choose for himself the able man. His judgment, while casting a vote, is very often influenced by considerations other than political standards. Direct election means election campaigns and intensive political propaganda for and against different candidates. Both the press and the platform are geared up for this purpose. The demagogue plays with the emotions of the masses and the catchwords of the professional politicians mislead them. When voters are swept off their feet by gusts of popular passion, the natural result is the election of undesirable candidates. Election campaigns often assume ugly forms and candidates are vilified. Many citizens, who otherwise would have established their mark as legislators and administrators, avoid to contest an election. They are "election shy", as it is termed, and the nation suffers when deprived of their services.

Indirect election, its advocates claim, offers the only escape from the dangers of universal suffrage and the evils of mob rule. The ultimate chance of representatives rests with the body of selected persons constituting an electoral college. These electors possess superior intelligence and political knowledge. In the selection of representatives they are guided by a keener sense of responsibility than an average voter. Moreover, when representatives are indirectly elected, popular passion is avoided. There are neither election campaigns nor party propaganda. All this tends to reduce the evils of party system. Indirect election, it is further said, "introduces an element of delay in elections, and acts as a sort of sieve through which election fever passes."[10] Emotions subside, reason plays its part and the election of the representatives is according to certain norms of values. Finally, indirect election is best suited for those countries where the people are not sufficiently educated and experiment with a democratic government has just started. Those whose judgment should really count elect the representatives.

But the indirect method of election does not find much favour. It is held to be undemocratic and politically inexpedient. Nor has it any educative value. When voters have no direct participation in the election of their representatives, they take only a lukewarm interest in politics and eventually become negligent in public affairs. Moreover, the indirect method of election does not decrease the evils of party system. Actually it leads to more party commotion and in countries where political parties are well-organised, election by indirect method has become a sheer formality; the typical example is the Presidential election in the United States. Indirect elections, also, mean intervention of the middle-man in politics who has been regarded as a perpetual source of political mischief. Finally, it is feared that this system of election increases the chances of bribery and corruption. A handful of people can be easily tempted and they easily succumb to such temptations.

LENGTH OF OFFICE AND INSTRUCTED REPRESENTATION

Length of Office. If the legislature is to be the barometer of public opinion, it is essential that there should be periodical election of its members. A perpetual or a long term of

10. Gilchrist, R.N., *Principles of Political Science,* p. 280.

office is contrary to the principles of representative government. But what exactly ought to be the legislative tenure? There is no precise rule of universal application and the practices of the States vary widely. For example, members of the British House of Commons and the National Assembly in France are elected for a period of five years. The House of the People (Lok Sabha) in India was originally elected for five years. The Forty-second Constitution Amendment Act, 1976, raised its term to six years. The Constitution was again amended in 1978 to bring it back to five years. The life of the United States House of Representatives is only two years. The tenure of the Upper Chambers in every country is usually longer. The membership of the House of Lords is hereditary, except for the Law Lords and the Peers appointed for life. The French Senate, according to the Constitution of 1958, is elected for nine years. The life of the Council of States in India and the Senate in U.S.A. is six years.

Four or five years is now considered the most-favoured term for the popular assemblies although it is only one year in two of the States in America. At one time annual elections were widely accepted as a real test of knowing popular feeling. The supporters of annual elections even maintained that, "where annual elections end, tyranny begins." But this principle had to be given up, because of practical difficulties and obvious inconveniences which annual elections involved. One year is too short a term for the representatives to understand administrative technicalities and rules of legislative procedure. It also means a constant shifting in membership and the chambers in large parts are composed of new and inexperienced members who have everything to learn. Too short a tenure without any certainty of re-election makes representatives oblivious of their duties toward their constituents. The administration also becomes unresponsive and irresponsible as there is no continuity in policy. Fluctuating governments bring inefficiency, corruption, nepotism and deterioration in the moral tone of the governors and the governed.

Annual election also means perpetual agitation and excitement throughout the country, nourishing political factions and encouraging unnecessary restlessness. The frequency of elections, as Judge Story observed, favour "rash innovations in domestic legislation and public policy, and produce violent and sudden changes in the administration of public affairs founded upon temporary excitements and prejudices." The voters, too, become disinterested if there are elections every year. The best type of candidates always avoid such an ever-recurring strain and excitement. At the same time, annual elections are very expensive.

It is true that popular opinion changes, but it does not change so quickly as to justify elections every year. A representative government provides other means for the expression of public opinion and getting grievances redressed. Annual elections are, therefore, impracticable. If the legislatures can really be responsive and responsible to public opinion, it is imperative that their tenure should neither be so short as to defeat the true purpose of representation, nor should it be so long as to remove the representatives from the range of popular control. John Stuart Mill observed: "On the one hand, the member ought not to have so long a tenure of his seat as to make him forget his responsibility, take his duties easily, conduct them with a view to his own personal advantages, or neglect those full and public conferences with his constituents which, whether he agrees or differs with them, are one of the benefits of the representative government. On the other hand, he should have such a term of office to look forward to as will enable him to be judged not by a single act, but by his course of action."[11]

Types of Representatives. There are different concepts of what a representative should be and the duty which he owes to his electors. We divide them into four types: (1) The Mirror type; (2) The Chameleon type; (3) The Statesman type; and (4) The Party member type.[12]

The advocates of mirror type of representation explain that representatives should mirror or reflect the electorate they represent. They should be precisely like the people, rich and poor, farmers and industrialists, lawyers and merchants, teachers and medical men, landlords and tenants, in every representative assembly and exactly in proportion to the numerical strength of each class in the population of the State. For example, if two-thirds of the population is agricultural, then, the assembly should in that proportion consist of the farmers and others directly or indirectly engaged in agriculture. In short. members of the legislature should be as much like their constituents as possible. As Jennings has put it, there should "be Tom, Dick and Harry in every Parliament."[13] It is urged that common people representing other common people can best represent the will of the people and they are the best to tell the government what it cannot do and what the people will not stand. This is tantamount to what actually the body-politic could have done if they were to decide the problems themselves.

The Chameleon type is the representative who does what exactly his electors tell him to do, nothing more, nothing less. He should change his views as the chameleon changes his colour. This type of representation is also known as the telephone type of representation. According to this view, a representative is the deputy or agent of the people who elected him and he speaks as his masters desire it. He exercises little independent judgment except in the process of trying to discern what his constituents want. He is not expected to make any alteration or modification in the terms of his instructions without the express authority of his electors. In fact, he has no wishes or will of his own as a representative. This type of representation is also known as instructed representation and was generally the accepted theory of representation in the early stages. In a federation, members representing the constituent States in the Upper House of the federal legislature were deemed as ambassadors of the States they represented. It was, accordingly, the inherent right of the States to instruct them about the attitude and stand they were to take on different problems before the legislature and the manner in which they would vote on a particular issue.

But the modern theory of representation outright rejects the idea of instructed representation. Laski regards it as wholly false. Lieber considers it "unwarranted, inconsistent and unconstitutional." Intelligent instruction, it is maintained, is not available. It is altogether impossible to ascertain the real and genuine will of the electors. If it may be assumed that intelligent instruction can be made available, even then, it is impossible for the representatives to refer all the problems with which they are confronted to their

11. Mill, J. S., *Representative Government,* Ch. XI, p. 39.

12. Dillon, Conley H., and others, *Introduction to Political Science,* p. 62.

13. Jennings, I., The *British Constitution*, p. 80.

electors for instruction. Promptness in legislation is as necessary as deliberation itself. If representatives are required to consult their constituents item by item, the entire legislative activity of the State is sure to come to a standstill. Moreover, legislation is a difficult process as it involves many technicalities. Many things come to the knowledge of the representatives only on the floor of the House and they adjust their views there and then as the conditions or circumstances advisedly permit. It is, therefore, unwise to bind them in advance with instructions and pledges, or that they should change their views on the behest of their constituents as and when they want and as often as they desire. The electors have, undoubtedly, the right to get the fullest expression of the general attitude of their representatives. They are also entitled to know their views on all current problems. They may reasonably ask for their explanation on any question of their decision. But the representatives cannot and should not subordinate their judgment to the will of the electors. If a representative is to appeal to his electorate on every point in order to get their verdict, the representative ceases to have either morals or personality.[14] Nor can he keep abreast of events and the needs of his country when he knows that he may be thwarted at every step and with as many instructions as there are voters. The instructions given may not only be conflicting, but diametrically opposed to each other. This is not the purpose of representation and representative democracy. The legislative assembly consisting of the chameleon type of representatives has no coherent voice, no maturity and no stability and firmness in the transaction of the business before it. When all representatives speak in deference to the wishes of their own constituents, the legislature is not a forum of discussion. It is a babel of tongues.

The statesman type of representative finds its classic definition in the words of Edmund Burke. He said, nearly two centuries ago, "Your representative owes for not his industry only, but his judgment, and he betrays instead of serving you if he sacrifices it to your opinion."[15] The representative must respect the view of his constituents, he should endeavour to redress their grievances and feel their pulse and act accordingly. But he must not sacrifice his independence of judgment and narrow his horizon of approach to various problems. He should look at all problems from the national rather than from a local viewpoint. Burke also gave a true analysis of the relationship between the electors and their representatives. "The Parliament," he declared, "is not a Congress of ambassadors from different and hostile interests, which interests each must maintain as an agent and advocate against other agents and advocates. But parliament is a deliberative assembly of one nation, with one interest, that of the whole where not local purposes, not local prejudices, ought to guide, but the general good resulting from the general reason of the whole. You choose a member, indeed, but once you have chosen him, he is not a member of Bristol, but he is a member of parliament." A national assembly is an embodiment of national interests. Burke tried to emphasise: find the best man to represent you, a man in whom you would have full faith and confidence as your representative, but once you have elected him depend upon him to use his judgment about what is best.

The concept of statesman or uninstructed type of representation is based on two important facts. The first is that most people are not well enough informed about problems

14. Laski, H., *A Grammar of Politics,* p. 319.

15. The writings and speeches of Edmud Burke (Little Brown and Company, Boston, 1901), Vol. II, p. 95.

confronting the government to make decisions, and, secondly, that, even if they were, the process of decision making is so difficult and complex as to preclude the people as a whole from exercising a good judgment on isolated issues. If instruction is to be the basis of representation, able and conscientious men can hardly be expected to serve in legislatures where they are expected to say only what it pleases their electors. They will keep themselves away from such a farce of representative institution rather than to serve therein. The services of great, talented and experienced statesmen would, thus, be lost to the nation.

The fourth type of representative is the party-member type. Elections are now contested by political parties rather than individuals. The voters vote for a party and its programme. It is, accordingly, necessary that the representative should rigidly live up to his party label even if he is to surrender his independence of judgment as well as dependence upon the judgment of his constituents. The theory is that political party is the only real vehicle of representative democracy and for the accomplishment of political programme. It is the party that selects candidates to contest an election and campaigns to win it and, thus, constituting the majority to form the government and to implement its policies. If it is in Opposition, it must oppose the party in power, criticise its policies and expose it to the electorate in order to win their support and to win elections. In whatever role the party is, it is nothing without the unity, solidarity and disciplined duty of the representatives elected on the party ticket. They must swim and sink together. If a representative elected on the ticket of a particular party decides to change his party label, political morality demands that he should submit himself for re-election on the ticket of the party to which he now owes allegiance "Clearly, he is not entitled," as Laski has said, "to get elected as a free trader and to vote at once for a protective tariff."[16]

The consensus of opinion now is that there is much to be said in support of the party-member type of representative. A representative democracy is unthinkable without political parties. A reasonably fixed legislative tenure provides a sufficient guarantee to the constituents to judge the party by what it did for them. No political party can to any dangerous extent afford to misrepresent the feelings of its constituents. When the party is judged by the constituents at the general election and people vote for its programme, the unity of the party demands that members elected on its tickets must act in unison as disciplined adherents. Without such a code of conduct representative democracy cannot succeed.

QUALIFICATIONS OF REPRESENTATIVES

The responsibilities of representatives are many and difficult. The problems which they are required to tackle are various and complex. They should, therefore, be the pick of the nation chosen with due regard to their experience of public affairs and renowned for their honesty, integrity, broad outlook and selfless patriotism. Every State prescribes some qualifications for representatives in order that those seeking election may offer proof of a genuine interest in public affairs. "Absence of limitation," writes Laski, "may give us

16. Laski, H., *A Grammar of Politics*, p. 319.

a Younger Pitt, but it gives us also a large number of members who go to the legislative assembly merely for the prestige which membership confers."[17] These qualifications are not fixed. They differ from country to country, but all governments insist upon the following minimum qualifications :

Citizenship. A representative must be a citizen of the State either by birth or by naturalization, and in possession of full civil and political rights. An alien, who owes allegiance to another State and whose sympathies belong to a foreign country, should not be elected a representative and entrusted with the duty of law-making. If an alien is permitted to seek election and gets elected to the legislature, his aim would either be personal to gain his own interests, or to secure favourable legislation for his own financial interests, or to further the political interests of his own country. In all probability his interests would be antagonistic to the interests of the country of which he has been elected a representative. The propriety of excluding aliens from the legislative assemblies is now universally accepted.

Residence. Some States insist upon residence within the constituency as a necessary qualification. In the United States, so far as the House of Representatives is concerned, while there is no constitutional provision that members shall be residents of the districts by which they are chosen, it has nevertheless become a political practice that such conditions shall obtain. In the case of the State legislatures, this requirement is often one of constitutional or statutory character, and, when not, the practice is almost invariably followed. In Britain, India and many other countries the practice is for candidates to be selected regardless of their legal place of residence. The advantages of non-residence system are frankly acknowledged everywhere, including the United States, for it tends to encourage the entrance into public life of persons whom it is desirable to have in public service, and enables members to view their responsibilities from the national standpoint rather than from the interests of the particular locality.

Age. Practically all States require that a representative must have attained the age of majority. A higher age is insisted upon because for law-making experience and mature judgment are considered of vital importance. Twenty-one or twenty-five years is generally the age limit fixed for representatives in the legislative assemblies. For Second Chambers, however, a higher age is necessary, the idea being to check the radicalism of the popular chamber by maturer judgment and conservatism. In France, a Senator was required to be forty years of age. According to the Government of India Act, 1935, thirty years was the minimum age for Upper Houses and twenty-five for Lower Houses, both federal and provincial. The Constitution of India also prescribes the same age limits for the Council of States and the House of the People, respectively.

Property. Some States demand possession of property as a necessary qualification for representatives. It is maintained that representatives who own property have sufficient leisure to devote their time and attention to legislative work, and for nursing their constituencies. They have not to worry for a living. Moreover, they have more stake in the State and so they discharge their duties more diligently and without even remuneration.

But possession of property as a necessary qualification for purposes of election is

---

17. *Ibid.*, p. 34.

now rapidly disappearing. It is considered a political anachronism. Democracy is established on equality and enjoyment of equal rights by all citizens of the State. It does not differentiate between man and man because of the accident of birth or due to some misfortune over which he has no control. Likewise, there is no justification in the argument that only owners of property have the leisure to devote their time and energy to legislative work and that they are likely to be cautious in initiating legislative measures. Payment of remuneration to the legislators is now a common accepted practice of representative democracy and those who have no property get the wherewithal to devote their time exclusively to legislative work.

Office. In every State holders of certain offices are debarred from becoming members of the legislature. In the United States of America members of the executive cannot have seats in Congress. This is due to the rigid application of the theory of Separation of Powers. In countries with a parliamentary form of government, as in Great Britain and India, ministers, who are heads of the executive departments, are also members of the legislature, but the permanent officials are not. In India the law specifies that no one may be a member of the legislature if he holds any office of profit other than an office declared by Act not to disqualify the holder. The idea is that those who hold offices of profit, if allowed to become members of the legislature, would always secure legislation to further their own interests.

Election Malpractices. Every State prescribes rules for the fair conduct of elections and election campaigns. If any candidate infringes these rules, he renders himself liable to disqualification. So much evil has been wrought by corrupt customs and election malpractices that Acts have been passed in every country, prescribing rigorously what each candidate may spend, how he may spend it and the norms he should observe in his election campaign. For example, in India a candidate must not appeal for vote on religious, caste or other sectarian basis. If he does, it is a malpractice and he can be disqualified by the competent tribunal, if his election is challenged.

Religion. In some countries law may require that a person may believe or have faith in a particular religion in order to become a member of the legislature. In Great Britain, for example, ministers of the established churches and the clergy of the Roman Catholic Church cannot be elected to the House of Commons.

Experience. Professor Laski suggests that a representative must possess previous experience and adequate knowledge of the working of a local body. He is of the opinion that a representative should be compulsorily required to serve at least for three years on the local body in order to make himself eligible for a seat in Parliament. In this way, the representatives "would gain that 'feel' of institutions so necessary to success."

MINORITY REPRESENTATION

The Problem of Minority Representation. It is maintained that the existing system of representation does not represent the whole people. A candidate who secures a majority of votes is declared elected and he represents in the legislature the point of view of those electors only whose votes he was able to secure. Those who had supported an unsuccessful candidate remain unrepresented. The situation becomes still more confusing when the difference in votes secured by the successful and defeated candidates is almost negligible. Let us assume that from a particular constituency, two candidates, A and B, seek election. Let us, again, suppose that out of a total of 4,000 voters in that constituency 2,005 vote are cast in favour of A and 1,995 votes are cast in favour of B. Since A has secured the majority of votes, he is declared elected. It means that 2,005 voters only find representation and the remaining 1,995 voters remain unrepresented. The minority stands in danger of being disfranchised.

Such a system of representation, where mere majority election exists, cannot be the real basis of democracy. A democracy is a government of the people and the people constitute the whole mass of the people in a State. It is an essential principle of democracy that it must not deny to a considerable portion of people participation in the conduct of their political affairs. Democracy, if it can claim to be the government of the people, must be representative of all classes of opinion. Law, in order to be the manifestation of the will of the people, should be supported and approved by the representatives of the large majority of electors. But when minorities are not adequately represented and they have not the opportunity to express their opinion, laws made by a legislature cannot be said to have the widest consent of the people. In a country where large groups of people feel that their will does not find expression in the making of the laws, which they are called upon to obey, such laws cannot command a deferential and effective obedience. The unrepresented minorities fret and fume and ultimately they are compelled to revolt against the tyranny of majority rule as political malcontents of today are the revolutionaries of tomorrow. "In a really equal democracy," says John Stuart Mill, "every and any section would be represented, not disproportionately, but proportionately. A majority of the electors would always have a majority of the representatives; but a minority of the electors would always have a minority of representatives. Man for man they would be as fully represented as the majority. Unless they are, there is not equal government, but a government of inequality and privilege; one part of the people rules over the rest, there is a part whose fair and equal share of influence in the representation is withheld from them, contrary to all just government, but above all, contrary to the principle of democracy, which professes equality as its very root and foundation."

Adequate representation of minorities, therefore, is the most important question which confronts representative democracy. Minorities may be of many kinds — political, national, racial, linguistic or communal. It is unfortunate to have so many minorities and particularly those divided on racial, linguistic and religious grounds. Political minorities are the product of representative government. But the problem of minority representation is not so insoluble when the people are divided on political ideologies. It is all a question of giving to the minorities adequate representation. When minorities differ from the majority in race, religion and language, and every minority desires to have a distinct expression of its separate individuality in order to safeguard its religious, cultural and social institutions, it is, then, that the problem of minority representation assumes a vicious complexion. But this is not really the question of representation of minorities. It is a plea for appeasing such minorities and it is in this aspect that the problem becomes insoluble.

India is the only unfortunate country where people are divided both horizontally and vertically and communalism has always been the bane of her politics. In other countries people are essentially divided on their political or economic issues. All schemes of minority representation in these countries aim at adequate representation of the political minorities. It is this aspect of minority representation which has received universal support, especially at the hands of John Stuart Mill, Lecky, and others. Lecky declared, "The importance of providing some representation for minorities is extremely great. When two-thirds of a constituency vote for one party, and one-third for the other, it is obviously just that the majority should have two-thirds and the minority one-third of the representation." Mill admitted that in a democracy the majority must rule, but he insisted that the minority should be represented in proportion to its number. He emphasised that there could be no real democracy, but a false show if all minorities were not represented proportionately. If every or any section was disproportionately represented, there would be no equal government, but a government of inequality and privilege.

Proportional Representation. Mill was an ardent advocate of proportional representation. Proportional representation is that method whereby the percentage of seats in a legislative assembly captured by one party is proportionate to its share of the popular vote. The assumption is that if the Socialist Party polls 2 per cent of the votes, it should wind up with 2 per cent of the seats in the legislative assembly. The aim is to give representation to all sections of opinion and all interests in the State in proportion to the numerical strength of their votes, and that no vote should be lost.

There are many expedients and forms which are suggested and practised to secure representation for the minorities. But all such schemes are not the varieties of proportional representation. There are only two varieties of proportional representation: the Hare Scheme of Single Transferable Vote, and the List System. The idea underlying both these systems is to secure a representative assembly reflecting with more or less mathematical exactness the various divisions in the electorate. The rest are schemes of minority representation. The difference between proportional representation and minority representation is important. All schemes of minority representation aim at giving representation of some kind to minorities, but not in proportion to the number of their votes, whereas proportional representation gives representation to minorities in proportion to their voting strength. In both these cases, however, the existence of parties or groups is formally recognised, and each party or group is given special representation. It must, however, be noted that no scheme of proportional representation can work on the basis of a single-member constituency. It involves, firstly, a multi-member constituency, and, secondly, the candidate is not elected by securing a relative or absolute majority, but only if he reaches a quota of votes, that is, total number of votes cast divided by the total number of seats determines the quota of votes necessary to get elected. This is done to bring about mathematically exact representation of the electorate in the legislature.

SCHEMES OF PROPORTIONAL REPRESENTATION

The Hare System. The scheme most commonly connected with proportional representation is called the Hare system and it is associated with the name of Thomas Hare, who formulated it in 1857 and then elaborated it in his book, *The Machinery of Representation*. But Thomas Hare's scheme cannot claim to be the first exposition of the idea of proportional representation. The idea appeared in the French National Convention in

1793, "without leading to action." It was further elaborated by the mathematician Gergonne in 1820 and developed independently by Thomas Wright Hill in Britain. Hill's son took it to Australia in 1839. In 1842, the idea gained popularity in Switzerland and Victor Considerant proposed a proportional representation system to the Council of Geneva. Two years later Thomas Gilpin brought out another plan of proportional representation. Finally, twelve years later a Danish Minister of Finance, Carl Andrae, worked out a system resembling the Australian plan and the years following it came Thomas Hare's publication, "*The Machinery of Representation*."[18]

The Hare system is sometimes termed Single Transferable Vote System as the surplus of votes of the candidates who are declared elected are transferred to other candidates whom it can help. Others call it Preferential System, because of the preferences which a voter is required to give to different candidates on the list. With whatever name it may be called, this system of representation provides for the election of representatives by general ticket. The constituencies are multimember with at least three seats. No maximum is considered necessary, although Lord Courtney suggested a fifteen-member constituency as a reasonable limit.[19] Whatever be the number of the representatives to be returned from a constituency, each voter has only one effective vote. Every voter is, however, asked to indicate on the ballot paper his first preference or choice, second preference, third preference, and so on by marking the figures 1, 2, 3 against the names of the candidates. He can vote for as many candidates, by denoting his preference, as there are seats to be filled from that constituency. The candidate in order to be elected requires a certain quota of votes. Different methods are followed to determine the quota. The simplest is to divide the number of votes cast by the number of seats to be filled from the constituency, and the quotient is taken as the quota or the number of votes necessary to elect a candidate. For example, if the total votes cast are 8,000 and there are 8 members to be elected from that constituency, the quota necessary for election will be 1,000. But Droop suggested another method of determining the quota. He found that in constituencies of 3 to 8 members sometimes inaccurate results were achieved in the practical operation. He suggested to determine the quota by dividing the total number of votes cast by one more than the number of seats to be filled and then by adding one to the result $\left(\text{quota} = \frac{\text{Total number of votes}}{\text{Number of seats} + 1} + 1\right)$.

In counting the votes only the first preference or choices are counted first and a candidate securing the required quota is declared elected. His surplus votes, if any, are passed on to candidates not yet elected, in the order expressed in the preferences. The process of transferring surplus votes to the next preferences continues down the list until the necessary number of representatives have been elected. Not only surplus votes of successful candidates are transferred to later choices, but, if need be, of those candidates as well who have secured so few votes that they have no chance of being elected at all. The idea is that no vote is to be lost. The voter is, thus, assured that if the candidate of his first choice does not require his vote, his second or other choices will gain by it.

18. Refer to Carl J. Friedrich's *Constitutional Government and Democracy,* p. 277.
19. Gilchrist, R.N., *Principles of Political Science,* p. 275.

This method of proportional representation prevailed in Great Britain in the election of the members of the four University constituencies to the House of Commons. In South Africa it is used for Senatorial elections and in certain municipalities. In India, it has not been much in vogue. Members of the Council of States (Rajya Sabha) are elected by the members of the State Legislative Assemblies in accordance with the system of proportional representation by means of a single transferable vote. The same system is used for the Presidential election.

The obvious defects of the Hare System are that it is a complex scheme and is unintelligible to the ordinary voter. There is also the probability of mistakes to occur in counting and recounting the votes. As it conceives of multi-member constituencies, undue advantage would be taken by party knots, cliques and sectarian combinations. It, therefore, perpetuates sharp cleavages which undermine the unity of the nation.

List System. Another variant of proportional representation is the List System. According to this plan, all candidates are grouped in lists according to their party labels and every party offers a list of its candidates up to the number of seats to be filled for each constituency. The voter need only select the party of his choice and by voting for that party he automatically votes for the list submitted by that party and for the candidates thereon in the order in which the party has determined the list of candidates. It takes the form of "bound list" as differentiated from "free list", which has been introduced in some countries as an improvement. It means that the free-list system, unlike the bound list, gives the voter a choice to indicate his preferences among the candidates of a party for which he had decided to vote. The seats are divided among the parties in proportion to the number of votes each list had secured.

The number of votes required, the quota to secure a candidate's election, is determined, as in the Hare System, by dividing the total number of votes cast by the number of seats to be filled, or by dividing the total number of votes cast by one more than the number of seats to be filled, and then adding one to the result, as suggested by Droop. Then, the total number of votes polled by each party list is divided by the quota and the result is the number of representatives to which each party is entitled. If all the seats are not filled up, the party which has the largest fractional surplus gets the remaining seat. There is another device which may also be followed. The fractional surplus of votes secured by the party in the neighbouring constituency may be added to make up the deficiency in the quota. Let us suppose that the total number of votes cast is 50,000 and five representatives are to be elected from that constituency. Let us, again, suppose that there are three party lists : the Janata Dal, the Congress, and the Communist (Marxist) and each list has polled 21,500, 20,500 and 8,000 votes respectively. The quota of eligibility being 10,000 votes, two seats go to the Janata Dal and the Congress. None can go to the Communist (Marxist). One of the two things may happen. If the fractional surplus method in the constituency is followed, then, the fifth seat may go to the Janata Dal, because their fractional surplus is higher than that of the Congress. If constituency transferring fractional surplus of votes method is followed, then, the votes polled by the Communist (Marxist) party in the neighbouring constituency, say 2,500, are transferred to be added to the total of 8,000, thus, entitling the Communists to claim one seat. Similarly, the surplus of 1,500 votes secured by the Janata Dal may be added to the votes of the party in another constituency entitling it to an additional seat.

The List System is exceedingly simple, since the voter need only select the party he likes and by selecting it he votes for the entire list of candidates of the party he has selected. But all this amounts to undue importance of the party leaders. The electorate has nothing to choose and decide. The strict List System has, accordingly, been subjected to a great deal of criticism. Recently some modifications have been offered to it and in a number of countries the voters have been allowed to indicate their own preferences, thus, making a departure from the "bound list." This system is known as "free list." Such a system has recently been adopted in Italy and in certain parts of Australia. Switzerland had previously given considerable freedom to its voters, permitting them to substitute names on the lists. The Swiss system is another variant of the List System. It allows the voter to write on the list of candidates an additional name of his own choice.

Arguments For and Against Proportional Representation. The advocates of the proportional system praise it for its mathematical accuracy in reflecting popular opinion and consider it the most democratic and just method of election. It is a device which ensures representation to all parties, big or small, and that, too, in proportion to their voting strength. The parliament in this way becomes a mirror of the opinion of all the people. Lord Acton has observed that the method of proportional representation "is profoundly democratic, for it increases the influence of thousands who would otherwise have no voice in the government; and it brings men more near an equality by so contriving that no vote shall be wasted and that every voter shall contribute to bring into parliament a member of his own." It is here that democracy really works as a government of the people. Proportional representation gives to minority parties a sense of security and political contentment. The Hare System gives every elector a real representative for whose choice he alone is responsible. The representative is not a normal representative chosen by others. By giving him a first or second preference the elector has actually willed him to remain the custodian of his trust and while reposing that trust in him he might have paused and thought over the suitability of his choice. This political intelligence in the electors carries two advantageous results. In the first place, it develops civic interest, and, secondly, it helps to elevate the character of the legislature by securing the election of more enlightened and distinguished representatives. Moreover, proportional representation "recognises the nature of modern political parties as based, not altogether on sectional divisions but on social and economic problems of national scope." When all the shades of opinion are effectively represented, the social and economic problems confronting the country get a wider and really representative base for solution. Single-member constituencies return candidates submerged in local and regional affinities and interests and, accordingly, they offer no national solution of the problems.

Besides providing representation of important minorities representing diverse interests, proportional representation possesses the merit of getting rid of difficulties as to the size and structure of constituencies. "As long as the population shifts, periodic readjustments of the boundaries of electoral districts are necessary if gross injustices such as the rotten boroughs are to be avoided. In the United States that problem is a familiar one through the recurrent strruggle over reapportionment."[20] It must be conceded that single-member constituencies usually show considerable maladjustments in the size of the electoral districts. Worst of all, it lends itself to the practice of "gerrymandering,"[21] that is, the process by which the party in power may draw the boundaries of the electoral districts in such a way as to crowd large percentages of the opponents into a few constituencies, and then so divide the rest as to give your party a majority. Proportional representation also acts as a great check on bribery and extravagance. Keith offers two more arguments in favour of proportional representation. Voters under such a system of representation, he says, "will be able to vote for men of character and independence of judgment and they will not be forced to accept the policy of a particular party." This is, however, problematic. A really cogent argument offered by Keith is that the "margin of unattached votes, the swing of which usually decides the fortune of elections, shall diminish to insignificance."

But the political efficacy of proportional representation is seriously questioned wherever it has been tried. Laski is of the opinion that the difficulties of the modern State cannot be remedied by reform of electoral machinery. These difficulties are mainly moral in character and should be met "by the elevation of the popular standard of intelligence and the reform of the economic system rather than by making men choose in proportion to the neatly graded volume of opinion".[22] The system of proportional representation has, indeed, failed to improve the standard of public life, because it breeds small parties and groups which make it impossible to obtain coherent public opinion. Multiple-party system implies weak government, and weak government ultimately means irresponsible government. Irresponsible government coupled with incoherent public opinion is a sectional government which encourages corruption, jobbery, nepotism, toading, and all other evils inherent therein. Proportional representation has, in fact, been an effective agent of ministerial instability. It makes impossible the broad large majorities on which effective government is based, and turns every government into a precarious combination of group representatives liable at any time to be withdrawn by their patrons. Where every party is ensured representation, vested interests help in creating new parties. The mushroom growth of political parties with incoherent public opinion ultimately means the failure of the parliamentary system of government and shaking of the people's faith in democracy. The Republic of Ireland adopted the single transferable vote system of proportional representation which the British Proportional Society had so long been advocating. In the General Elections of 1948, no party received a majority and the choice was between a minority and a coalition government. The coalition government was formed, combining all groups, with 79 votes as against the largest party's 68. Some writers and statesmen hold proportional representation responsible for the collapse of the German Republic of 1919. At one time there were thirty political parties which contested the Reichstag election.

Dicey points out that the mathematical representation of all sorts of opinion is highly objectionable, for there may be an opinion which may be bad, foolish and even undesirable. Taking an extreme example, he asks, would it be desirable to have an advocate in parliament

20. Friedrich, C.J., *Constitutional Government and Democracy,* p. 282.
21. It is called after a former Governor of Massachusetts, United States, who perceived the potentialities of affecting the electoral result by "manipulating the geography of constituencies."
22. Laski, H., *A Grammar of Politics,* p. 315.

of those who have extreme hatred of the Jews? Dicey also holds that the more you make the system of election complicated and difficult, the more you throw the voters into the clutches of the party agents and wirepullers.[23] Sidgwick too said that proportional representation gives encouragement to demagogy and sectional legislation. But the worst side of proportional representation is that it destroys the national character of the legislature and makes it an arena of divergent sectional interests. All issues deliberated upon in the legislature are discussed not with reference to their bearing on the general well-being of the nation, but from the point of view of a particular group or interest. In this way, legislation is paralysed as group legislation inevitably tends to increase class legislation and class legislation jeopardises the life of the nation.

The areas for election, under all schemes of proportional representation, must be multiple-member constituencies. Multiple-member constituencies intensify the complexity of choice and increase the power of the parties, and particularly of the central councils of parties. Nominations, especially under the List System, may become the preserve of entrenched party elites or bosses, over which even the party "people" have very little influence. When the party leaders settle the lists of names, they can demand unconditional allegiance from the successful candidates. The result is that the attention of the representatives is directed to and concentrated always on the party machinery more than to the constituency. The intimate contact between the voter and his representative is eliminated. A good electoral system should enable the candidates to be known to the electors in a genuine way, and after elections the representatives must remain closely connected with their constituents so that a personal relation develops between them. But the system of proportional representation destroys any prospect of personal relations between the member and his constituents; he would simply become an item in a list, voted for almost entirely on party grounds. Further, the election campaign becomes less intensive, and more extensive, that is, "it does not occupy itself with the cultivation of the individual voter by personal appeals, but in the institution of monster demonstrations, like processions, in which the mechanical apparatus for making a noise or creating a diversion is predominant." Nor does the system provide for by-elections. A by-election is always the barometer of public opinion. If no opportunity is provided for the expression and realisation of changes in the public opinion, the legislature loses its representative character.

The system of proportional representation is sufficiently complicated and beyond the comprehension of an average voter. Under the Hare System counting and recounting of votes is a complex and tedious problem with the intricacies of preferences and transferring of votes. Moreover, it places voters at the mercy of the counting authorities. In the List System there is an additional danger of corruption. Prospective candidates are tempted to use unfair and corrupt methods to get their names included in the party list. It also helps to increase the influence of party bosses and encourages party manoeuvring. The group managers arrange the original lists in such a way as to secure a majority for their own nominees.

On these grounds the bulk of competent opinion is opposed to the introduction of

23. Dicey, A.V.; *Law of the Constitution,* pp. LXVII-LXXIII

proportional representation.[24] Laski says that its alleged better representation of national opinion is doubtful.[25] He does not agree with the opinion that in a single-member constituency the minority remains unrepresented while in the proportional system this danger is adequately met. Laski fully agrees with Herman Finer that the "horizon of a minority is not limited by the boundaries of a constituency." Political decisions are not made by an arithmetical process of counting votes. "More urgent is the weighing of influences that take place in the law-making process. And minority views may find adequate institutions therein for the expression of their opinions and desires."[26] The late Professor Esmine, an eminent French jurist, condemns outright the system of proportional representation. He says, "To establish the system of proportional representation is to convert the remedy supplied by the bicameral system into a veritable poison; it is to organise disorder, and emasculate the legislative power; it is to render cabinets unstable, destroy their homogeneity, make parliamentary government impossible."[27]

Humphreys, Ramsay Muir, and Keith have tried to meet the objections of the critics of the proportional representation. A realistic approach will, however, disclose that proportional representation is not pure vice as its critics would have us believe. Nor is it all virtue as its advocates seem to prove. The system has now been incorporated in some of the modern constitutions and it is a convincing proof that proportional representation does attempt to remedy some of the evils from which the body-politic suffers. Even in Britain, where the two-party system virtually exists, it has found due recognition. The Government there offered a proposal to parliament, in October 1940 and renewed it in October 1941, that "it will be the desire of His Majesty's Government when a General Election again becomes practicable to give sufficient notice for the creation of a new register, and this interval will also afford opportunity for parliament to consider, if it so desires, questions connected with changes in our electoral system." The proposal did not materialize, but the question of introducing the method of proportional representation is not off the cards. The Leader of the Liberal Party, after the General Election results in October 1964 as well as in 1974, declared that he would press for its introduction. That has not happened. But if Britain adopts the system of proportional representation, the Liberals, as they plead, would have many members in Parliament, for the Party's proportion of the total vote in the past three General Elections had been much higher than its proportion of MPs, Carl Friedrich, however, is of the opinion that homogeneity which parliamentary government needs is not only not created by proportional representation, but is actually destroyed. He concludes that the "prevalent English and American opinion against proportional representation is practically sound. There are special conditions which might mitigate this conclusion. But the proportional representation enthusiast, who would argue from the relative success of proportionalism in some small countries that we should try it in Great Britain and in the United States, goes wrong."[28]

24. Sidgwick, H., *Elements of Politics,* p. 396.
25. Laski, H., *A Grammar of Politics*, p. 316.
26. *Ibid.*, p. 317.
27. As quoted in J.W. Garner's *Political Science and Government,* p. 663.
28. Friedrich, C.J., *Constitutional Government and Democracy.* p. 294.

Some countries which adhere to the system of proportional representation have tried to eliminate its shortcomings through special devices. In West Germany,[29] for instance, a "5 per cent clause" denied any representation in the legislature to parties failing to poll a minimum of 5 per cent of the votes. This successfully prevented the formation of splinter groups. In fact, all but two or three parties had tended to disappear from the political arena and the voters rallied, as under the single-member constituency, to only the largest groups. But this device takes away the essence of proportional representation that minorities will be represented in proportion to their strength. In France, Belgium and Scandinavia the voter has been allowed to change the order of the candidates on the list, that is express a personal preference. But this, too, does not solve the problem.

OTHER SCHEMES OF MINORITY REPRESENTATION

There are some other schemes of minority representation. But none of them is a scheme of proportional representation. All these schemes allow some representation to minorities, but not necessarily in proportion to their numerical voting strength.

The Limited Vote Plan. Of the various schemes which have been adopted to ensure representation to minorities, one is the Limited Vote Plan. Under this system there are multi-member constituencies with at least three seats. Each voter is allowed to cast a smaller number of votes than there are seats to be filled. Moreover, he must not give more than one vote to any single candidate. His votes should be spread over to as many candidates as there are votes to cast. For example, in a five-member constituency each voter may be allowed to vote for four candidates or even less. In this way minority parties become reasonably certain of electing one or two members. This method had been used at various times by Britain, Italy and Japan for election to lower Houses, but it no longer prevails.

In practice the limited vote plan secures representation only for fairly large minorities. It does not work when there are many parties. Then, it does not allow proportional representation. It is a method intended to give only limited representation. The method can be employed only under an electoral system in which three or more members are to be chosen from each constituency. It cannot be applied under a system of single-member constituencies. Finally, it tightens the party machine, increases the power of the party bosses and does not permit independence to the members thus elected, of course, with no choice to the voter.

The Cumulative Vote System. The cumulative vote system allows the elector to cast as many votes as there are representatives to be chosen from a constituency. He is permitted either to cumulate all his votes on one single candidate, or distribute them among the different candidates as he pleases. If there are five members to be elected from a constituency, it is the option of the elector to give all his five votes to one member, or give one vote to each, or distribute them in any other way. The cumulative method is popularly known as "plumping."

The advantage of this method is that it enables even a small minority to elect at least

---

29. Germany is now unified.

one member by cumulating all votes on one candidate. But minorities must be well organised in order to ensure the election of their candidates. It also requires strict party discipline and careful instruction to the voters as to how they are to distribute their votes. All this entails rigidity of party control and the evils connected with it. It may even happen that where five members are chosen, the minority party elects two or three and the majority only one or two. The cumulative method also involves a waste of votes. The surplus of votes accruing to a popular candidate cannot help other candidates. It does not secure proportional representation. Finally, the constituencies should be large enough so that the members elected from each constituency should be more than three. If the constituencies are small, returning, say, only three members, the results of the Limited Vote Plan will be repeated.

The Second Ballot System. Another method of minority representation is the Second Ballot System. When there are only two candidates contesting election for a single seat, the one who secures a simple majority is declared elected. But when there are more than two candidates, it may happen that the candidate elected secures only a relative majority and not an absolute majority. For example, if in a constituency three candidates are contesting election, candidate A may secure 5,000 votes, candidate B 4,000 and candidate C 3,000 votes. A has secured a majority over B and C, but candidates B and C have more votes between them than those secured by A. That is to say, candidates B and C secured 2,000 more votes than candidate A. The representative elected under such an electoral system represents only a minority of votes. To avoid such an unjust nature of representation the system of Second Ballot is adopted.

The Second Ballot System makes a new vote for the second time necessary. But all the candidates do not contest this time. The candidate who secured the least number of votes is dropped out. The contest now remains between A and B only, the idea being that the voters who previously voted for C may now vote either for A or B and the candidate securing a majority of votes may be elected. If at the second poll a majority of votes go to candidate B, then B, and not A, would be elected. If the system of relative majority had prevailed, then, A would have been elected. "The second ballot (there might be a third or further ballot where there are many seats)," says Gilchrist, "secures a more just reflection of the opinion of the electorate where three or more candidates seek election." The Second Ballot System demands a single-member constituency, and it does not secure proportional representation.

The Alternative or Contingent Vote. The Second Ballot suffers from serious defects and to avoid its evils and shortcomings, the Alternative or Preferential or Contingent Vote method has been put forward. The system proposes only one election, but every voter is permitted to mark his preferences on the different candidates, thus, indicating his first, second or third choice. The candidate of the first preference is declared elected if he gets an absolute majority. If none of the candidates gets an absolute majority, then, the candidate who has got the least number of first preferences is dropped and his votes are distributed to other candidates according to the second choice of the voters. The candidate securing an absolute majority after the redistribution of votes is declared elected. If no candidate even now gets an absolute majority, the candidate at the bottom will again be dropped and his votes similarly transferred according to the third choice of the voters.

The candidate who secures an absolute majority will then be declared elected. This method, too, necessitates a single-member constituency system and it does not ensure proportional representation, although it is an improvement on single-member constituencies with a relative majority. Secondly, certain small minorities may still not be represented at all.

Communal Representation. A novel device for the representation of minorities found its origin in India during the British regime. This was representation on communal basis. Under this system of representation parties were not divided on political or economic issues, but on differences of religion, faith and creed. Every religious community secured a separate representation. This was done in two ways. First, by separate electorates where voters of each community voted separately for candidates of their own community, e.g., the Hindus voted for Hindu candidates, the Muslims for Muslims, the Sikhs for Sikh candidates, and so on. The second method was the reservation of seats under a system of joint electorate as in the case of the Scheduled Castes. Under such a system a voter may cast his vote in favour of a candidate other than his own community, but in deciding the result a candidate of the community, for which the seats are reserved, who gets the highest number of votes from amongst the candidates of his community will be declared elected even if a candidate belonging to another community might have secured the highest number of votes.

To divide the people on the basis of religion is to destroy root and branch of the national solidarity of a country. Such a system creates a new mentality among the leaders of various communities. They hug the system and agitate for its continuance and extension. A vicious circle is created. Communities which have not hitherto received separate recognition begin to agitate for their rights. National solidarity is torn asunder, threatening even the unity of the country. The system of communal representation has been abolished from the Indian Republic, but the separatist trends so systematically encouraged and nursed by the Britishers have left behind a trail of sinister forces which still appear in various forms; reservation being the most cherished.

FUNCTIONAL REPRESENTATION

Functional Representation. Functional or occupational representation is a protest against the system of territorial or geographical representation. In modern States the usual basis of representation is territorial. A district or constituency is demarcated and voters living within the terrtorial limits of that constituency elect a representative or representatives. This system of territorial or geographical representation is held to be inconsistent with the spirit of democracy. It is maintained that members elected from different constituencies are not representatives in the real sense of the term. It is a misrepresentative system rather than representative as a representative elected on the territorial basis cannot represent the varied and diverse interests living in a constituency. He can represent only his own interests which he has in common with others. People pursuing the same kind of work or functions have more things or ideas in common than people living in the same locality. It is, therefore, proposed to replace the traditional territorial system of representation by occupational representation in which various industrial or other occupational groups should be reflected.

In the beginning the demand for reform in the electoral system of territorial representation took the form of a demand for proportional representation. But it was soon realised that the system of proportional representation ensured representation only to minorities which were recognised as political parties. It gave no representation to other large and important groups, economic, social professional, and others which had special interests peculiar to each. All such interests, it was urged, required special representation in the legislature. Only a cobbler should represent cobblers and the really representative bodies are these which are related to the various functions which individuals performed.

Advocates of the Representation of Interests. The system of representation based upon classes, professions, occupations, or other groupings of society is not of recent origin. Mirabeau, at the time of the French Revolution, declared that a Legislative Assembly ought to be a mirror of all the interests of society. Sieyes, too, emphasized the need for special representation in the legislature of the great industries of society. In more recent times, however, the system of functional representation found an increasing number of advocates. Duguit maintains, "All the great forces of the national life ought to be represented — industry, property, commerce, manufacturing professions, and even science and religion."[30] But the theory of functional representation is primarily associated with the name of G.D.H. Cole. Cole says that in place of an omni-competent representative body there should be in society as many separately elected groups of representatives as there are distinct groups of functions to be performed.

There are two divergent groups who advocate occupational representation from different motives. The Communists support it, because it centres the voter's attention upon his work relationships and forces him to think in proletarian terms. The non-Communists, on the other hand, advocate it because of their disgust with the present system of electing legislators from single-member constituencies. Graham Wallas is of the opinion that while the lower chamber may be elected on the territorial basis. it is necessary that the second chamber be representative of various interests and functional groups. Sidney and Beatrice Webb advocated in 1920 a system in which there should be a "Political Chamber" and an "industrial Second Chamber."[31] In 1947, Christopher Holis, M.P., In his book, *Can Parliament Survive*' put forward proposals for a kind of Functional Third Chamber. Both these groups, however, believe that men are "much more intelligent and trustworthy, judges of the real qualities of those who work in the same industry than of those who live in the geographical district, while many also believe that the chief political issues are necessarily industrial issues which need to be decided by the representatives of the industries involved."

The system of functional representation is commonly known as the Soviet system. The geographical or territorial system of representation was replaced in Soviet Russia by a system based on the vocational principle, i.e., workers, farmers, professional men and other classes choose their own representatives without regard to territorial areas. A

30. Refer to Garner in his *Political Science and Government,* p. 599.
31. Sidney and Beatrice Webb, *A Constitution for the Socialist Commonwealth of Great Britain,* pp. 64-71.

representative in the Soviet Union did not represent the district from which he happened to elected. He represented a particular interest. Mussolini introduced the system of occupational representation in Italy and the Senate was, accordingly, reorganised. It consisted of various trades and professions, employees and trade unions recognised by the Fascist Government. The Weimar Constitution of Germany (1919) introduced an innovation by creating a National Economic Council representing the interests of labour, capital, and consumers.[32] The National Economic Council contained the elements of a third legislative chamber. The Council did not possess the power of legislation, but the Constitution provided that all drafts of important laws relating to social and economic matters should, before introduction in parliament, be submitted to the Council for its opinion. It could, also, through its own members initiate bills directly in parliament. In Great Britain the universities had till recently special representation in the legislature. Representation of interests prevails in India, both in the Central and State legislatures where seats have been reserved for several interests.

Criticism of Functional Representation. The principle of functional representation "has such serious weaknesses as to make it little, if any, better than territorial representation."[33] The late Professor Esmien stigmatised it as "an illusion and a false principle which would lead to struggle, confusion, and even anarchy." Herman Finer says that the principle of functional representation "does not proceed from the integration of the community, and then temper this with the representation of differences, but it proceeds at once from the postulate of disintegration into a large number of separate communities whose ultimate integration is thenceforward to be fabricated." Human affairs cannot be divided into watertight compartments, and it is disastrous when lines of division, which are in no sense marked, between one economic interest and another, are accentuated. Even Professor Laski is opposed to the system of functional representation. He says, "The territorial assembly built upon universal suffrage seems, therefore, the best method of making final decisions in the conflict of wills within the community." The legislature elected on territorial basis cannot act in an irresponsible fashion. It is the creature of electoral will. Laski maintains that various interests within the States will receive adequate representation, if the legislature is made "to consult the organised wills of the community before it acted upon them."[34]

Functional representation, it is further maintained, is inconsistent with the principle of national sovereignty. The legislative assemblies are chosen to represent the interests of the nation as a whole, and not the special interests of particular occupations or classes. The principle of vocational representation would force citizens to consider first of all their particular interests and ignore the national interests. It would promote a struggle between different interests and forces, accentuate the feeling of antagonism between them, and undermine the sound doctrine that a man's interest in the welfare of the group, class or profession to which he belongs, should be secondary to the interest in the welfare

32. Article 165.
33. Dunning, *op. cit.,* Vol. IV, p. 265.
34. Laski, H., *A Grammar of Politics,* p. 84.

of the whole society. It is suicidal to encourage class-consciousness, as it undermines the very basis of political organisation.[35] A man is a citizen first, worker or peasant afterwards. Moreover, an expert who is himself likely to be personally or professionally affected by contemplated legislation constitutes a vested interest. There is a danger that he will be an advocate rather than a trustee in the national interest, which is what a legislator is expected to be in democracy. Laski even questions the very basis of vocational representation. "Why," he writes, "a function, like that of medicine, for instance, is properly relevant to the purpose of a legislative assembly? There is not a medical view of foreign policy, of the nationalisation of mines, or of free trade." It is, again, incorrect to emphasize that the industrial interest is dominant with many. Perhaps, a majority of electors would desire to be represented in some other capacity than that of merely being workers in a given occupation.

Vocational representation, it is further argued, does not solve the problem of minority representation. Nor does it offer any protection to an independent voter who may not like to vote for a candidate put up by his profession or trade. Then, there is the practical difficulty involved in classifying a huge population on a vocational basis suitable for electoral purposes. There are sure to be enormous difficulties in determining to which group an individual may belong. It is not easy to arrive at any satisfactory system of classifying either industries or occupations. Finally, the system of vocational representation does not make an adequate provision for those who move from industry to industry.

The accepted opinion of the majority of political thinkers and statesmen is in favour of continuing with the system of territorial representation and political responsibility ought to remain where it is now; with the democratically elected representatives. "Weaver, miner, baker, teacher, each has his part to play in the commonwealth. But it would seem on the whole advisable that all these economic interests should combine to send to the Imperial Parliament a representative of the locality to which in common they belong, rather than by vocational representation to emphasize their class interests and exaggerate their economic antagonisms." Some political thinkers suggest that the system of proportional representation in the form of single transferable vote serves the purpose of vocational representation in essence. The merit of this system is that it permits men to be represented according to their occupational interests, if these interests are considered dominant over other interests. But it does not force the voters to be so represented if other interests are deemed paramount.

35. Corry says, "Function becomes so important that it obscures the individual. Also, too much preoccupation with the clear articulation and vindication of function weakens the sense of community, of belonging to some thing that contains but transcends the function. The deputies do not belong to the nation or even to the individual voters in the constituencies but only to their separate functions." Corry, J.A., *Democratic Government and Politics,* p. 290.

SUGGESTED READINGS

Bryce, J.: *Modern Democracies,* Vol. 1, Chap. VIII.

Cole, G.D.H.: *Guild Socialism Restated.*

Commons, J.R.: *Proportional Representation.*

Corry, J.A.: *Democratic Government and Politics.*

Dealey, J.Q.: *Development of the State,* Chap. X.

Dealey, J.Q.: *The State and Government,* Chap. XVII.

Friedrich, C.J.: *Constitutional Government and Democracy.*

Garner, J.W.: *Introduction to Political Science,* pp. 440-48 and 489-516.

Garner, J.W.: *Political Science and Government,* Chap. XIX.

Hoag, C.G. and Hallet, G.H.: *Proportional Representation.*

Humphreys, H: *Proportional Representation.*

Lakeman Enid, James, D.: *Voting in Democracies.*

Lowell. A.L.: *Public Opinion and Popular Government.*

Mill, J.S.: *Representative Government,* Chaps. VII-XII.

Ross, J.F.S.: *Parliamentary Representation.*

Seymour, C., and Frary, D. P.: *How the World Votes*

Shepard, W.1.: *Theory of the Nature of Suffrage.*

Sidgwick, H.: *Elements of Politics,* pp. 378-400.

Smith, T.E.: *Elections in Developing Countries.*

Willoughby, W.F.: *The Government of Modern States,* Chaps. XII, XVI, XVII.

19

CHAPTER

The Legislature

Three branches of government. Since the time of Aristotle it has been generally agreed that political power is divisible into three broad categories. There is, first, the legislative power which formulates and expresses the will of the State. Being a representative assembly, the Legislature in a democratic government enacts the general rules of society in the form of laws. The laws of the State prescribe the manner in which people are expected to live in a politically organised society. Secondly, there must be some power to see that the laws of the State are duly obeyed by all and there is no infringement. This is the work of the executive. There is, thirdly, the judicial power. The judges determine whether the law is applicable in a particular case or not. The judicial power determines "the manner in which the work of the executive has been fulfilled. It sees to it that the exercise of executive authority conforms to the general rules laid down by the legislateure."[1] If the executive acts in excess of the power vested in it by law, the judges may declare that the order issued by the executive is in excess of the authority given to it and, accordingly, *ultra vires* and inoperative.

But the legislature unquestionably occupies a superior place. The primary and the most important function of the State is legislative. The executive and the judicial departments cannot function until the legislature has functioned. Law must exist before a judgment can be given or the executive takes action. Every executive and judicial act involves primarily an enactment made by the legislature. Gilchrist compared the relation of the legislative, executive and judicial departments to the major and minor premises and conclusion of a syllogism. He says, "The legislative authority forms the major premises; the judiciary, the minor; and the executive, the conclusion... . As the major premise is more important than the minor and conclusion, so the legislature is more important than the executive or judiciary."[2] But the scales are reversed now. The all-round accepted concept of the Welfare State has blurred supremacy of the legislature. The Welfare State tends to concentrate power on the executive level and, consequently, its ascendancy over the legislative branch. This is the inescapable reality of the twentieth century.

1. Laski, H., *A Grammar of Politics,* p. 295.
2. Gilchrist, R.N.., *Principles of Political Science*, p. 293.

FUNCTIONS OF THE LEGISLATURE

Varying Extent of Functions. The functions of the legislature are not identical in every country. They entirely depend upon the form of government. If the pattern is unlimited monarchy, as it was in Czarist Russia, the legislature is merely a consultative body subordinate to the executive for all practical purposes. Under a bureaucratic type, as it existed in the Provinces of India before 1937, and persisted at the Centre till India became a sovereign State in August, 1947, the legislature is completely subservient to the executive. A dictator, like Hitler or Mussolini, pays scant attention to the existence of a legislature. Both Hitler and Mussolini suppressed the powers of the legislatures and ruled mainly by issuing decrees or ordinances. The German Parliament conferred upon the National Cabinet in 1933, in fact, upon Hitler himself, power for four years to make laws, conclude treaties, adopt budgets, and indeed to do, without check or restraint, "anything whatsoever, inside or outside of the constitution...".[3] But the power conferred on Hitler never came to an end during his lifetime. Even the Iron Chancellor Bismarck, who wielded enormous authority in his time, never approached the power placed in the hands of the Nazi chief.

But in a Parliamentary System, as it obtains in Britain and India, the legislature is superior to the executive in the sense that the latter is responsible to the legislature for all its acts and Ministers remain in office only so long as they can retain its confidence. Parliament in Britain is legally sovereign. It plays a double role and combines the constitutional and the legislative powers. It is competent to make and alter the constitution and, at the same time, make ordinary legislation. In the United States of America, on the other hand, the powers of the legislature are co-extensive with those of the executive.

The functions of the legislature, therefore, differ from State to State. There is no uniformity. The main functions of the legislature may, however, be classified as follows:

Legislative Functions. As stated earlier, law is now regarded as the expression of the will of the people. The will of the people is expressed through representative assemblies and all other means of making laws have been swallowed up by legislation. Legislation is the most prolific and direct source of law. Again, laws must be consistent with the changing conditions of society and in harmony with the new social environments. Old laws, which have become obsolete, are repealed and new ones substituted in their place. Under a parliamentary system the executive has a direct hand in the making of laws. Before a Bill begins its career in the legislature, the Cabinet discusses the proposal to introduce a Bill on the initiation of a Minister. If the Cabinet accepts the proposal, it is introduced in either House of the legislature and it is the duty of the Minister concerned to pilot the Bill through all stages of parliamentary procedure and see that it is finally passed and duly enacted. But under the Presidential system the executive is not in direct touch with legislature. It only exerts its influence either through Presidential messages or through members of Congress who belong to the President's party. The Government has no place in the legislature and all Bills, public or private, are introduced and defended by members of the legislature.

Deliberative Functions. Legislative functions consist of two kinds of work: law-

3. Ogg, *op. cit.*, p. 720.

making and deliberative. In fact, there can be no separation between the two. Both are parts of the legislative functions, although some writers, as John Stuart Mill did, treat them separately. They argue that the function of law-making, particularly drafting of a bill, is a skilled work which needs considerable experience, study and research. Mill said that a "numerous assembly is little fitted for the direct business of legislation."[4] The amateurs make a bad job out of it when entrusted with this specialised function. The making of law should, therefore, be entrusted to a small committee of experts while the actual work of deliberation should be the function of the whole parliament.

To make a law really the mirror of public opinion, it is necessary that it should not be made hurriedly. It needs proper thrashing so that its contents and ends may be considered from all points of view. For discussion two heads are better than one, and two hundred are better than two. In this respect a legislature is par excellence a deliberative body. The term parliament, which may be used for a legislature, is derived from the French word *parler*, which means to talk, and *parlement* which means a meeting for discussion. Legislature is a forum where thinking is done, as it consists of many persons representing numerous interests, various points of view, and different sections of the community. Deliberation, in fact, is at the heart of a democratic polity. It is the chief process by which policy is determined and laws are made.

Since deliberation is a continuous process of debate, it was long felt that political deliberation should be carefully institutionalized and that led to the development of the elaborate codes of parliamentary procedure and practices which pervade the British House of Commons, the Indian Parliament, Congress of the United States and, indeed, parliaments of all democratic countries. This procedure leads to better and fruitful discussion, for deliberation not only gives an opportunity to each participant to promote the views and interests of the political party or group he represents, but also permits him to adjust his own views and even to change his opinions by listening to others. For this reason there are, generally, three readings for every legislative bill before it is finally voted upon. The first reading comprises only introduction of the measure and generally, there is no debate or discussion. After the Bill has been introduced, it is printed and members get its copies to be ready for the second reading. On a day fixed in advance, the Bill is read for the second time. This is a crucial stage in the life of a Bill. The supporters and opponents of the Bill participate in discussion and stoutly present their respective points of view. There is a general discussion and no amendments to the Bill are moved. Upon the conclusion of the debate votes are taken. If the majority votes in its favour, the Bill goes to the next stage. If it is defeated, it lapses.

After the second reading, the Bill automatically goes to an appropriate committee of the House. The size of modern legislatures makes it impossible for full consideration to be given to all measures by all members. Therefore the committee system has evolved. Here the Bill is discussed, voted on clause by clause, and probably amended. The committee may even seek information from any source with respect to any point, invite experts from outside and summon anyone for evidence, both oral and documentary. After the committee stage, it is referred back to the whole House for further discussion. There are many other

4. Mill, J.S., *Representative Government,* Chap. V.

rules of procedure. The objects aimed at are orderly and efficient dispatch of business, the prevention, on the one hand, of precipitate and ill-considered action, and, on the other, fruitless prolixity of debate. Deliberation is, indeed, hammering legislation and chiselling it into a law.

Financial Functions. We are well aware of the conflict between the Stuarts and Parliament in Britain. It was all about financial matters and the principal means by which Parliament mounted to power was the power of the purse. The fact of representative democracy is the control and regulation of national finances by the legislature, and this is its most important function. It is a fundamental principle of public administration, and one which is nowadays generally recognised in all civilised countries, that no taxes shall be levied or expenditure authorized without the approval of the representatives of people. The theory 'no taxation without representation' recognises the supremacy of the legislature in raising revenues and incurring expenditure. In some countries, like the United States, war can be declared only with the consent of the legislature. This power is vested in the legislature obviously for the reason that war entails stupendous expenditure and the verdict of the representatives of the people must be taken regarding the justification of war and the expenditure which is to be incurred in fighting it out. In Britain, war may be declared by an executive act, but grants are made available by Parliament. The executive cannot sanction expenditure without parliamentary approval. In this way, the legislature controls the domestic and foreign policy of the State.

The principal financial function performed by a legislature from year to year is the presentation, consideration, and authorization of the budget. Viewed in simple outline, a budget is the nation's annual statement of accounts which shows, on the one hand, estimates of financial expenditure and, on the other, a calculation of anticipated revenues. The financial year generally begins on April first and the estimates of the coming financial year are presented to the representative chamber of the legislature in the second or third week of February. The estimates are discussed by the legislature and the number of days allotted for their consideration vary from two to three weeks or even more. The debate gives an opportunity to the government to explain and defend their proposals and to the Opposition an opportunity to air their grievances or to criticise the general policy of Government.

Administrative Functions. Nowhere in the world does a popular assembly actually participate in administration. Its proper jurisdiction is that of superintendence and control. But in countries where the parliamentary or Cabinet system prevails, the control of the legislature over the executive is direct and immediate. The latter is responsible to the former for all its actions. Questions and interpellations are asked to seek information from the government on matters of administration. If any act of government is resented by the public, their representatives may move a vote of censure and condemn that action. If the government abuse their trust or act in flagrant disregard of the public opinion, the legislature may pass a vote of no-confidence and expel them from office and appoint their successors. Strict control of the executive is enforced by the review of government's policies involved in discussions of the budget and the approval of proposed expenditure. If the government fails to get supplies, it must quit office and make room for others who can carry the legislature with them.

In the United States, the Upper Chamber of Congress, the Senate, is vested with certain specific administrative powers. The Senate shares with the President the power of making all federal appointments. Again, all treaties negotiated and concluded by the President are to be ratified by a two-thirds majority of the Senate. The Senate also possesses, by usage, the power of investigating into various administrative scandals and cases of corruption. The investigating committees so set up can summon witnesses, official and non-official, call for papers and documents, and seek any other kind of information which may be deemed necessary. In a Presidential type of government the investigating committees usefully serve the purpose of controlling the executive. The legislature's control over the executive, thus, keeps the government fully informed of what the country is thinking of, what it wants and especially of what it will not stand. Under a parliamentary system control and responsibility naturally go together. Since responsibility of government means its resignation from office whenever the policy of government proves fundamentally unacceptable to the popular assembly, an obligation rests on the house to exercise a day-to-day control over the Ministry in such a way that fundamental disagreement between the executive and the representatives of the people will be clear and manifest. If the actual and possible mistakes of the government were not apparent, the government might become irresponsible. So important is the function of controlling the executive that many statesmen would assign it to the legislature as its first and foremost duty. Bagehot placed legislation last among the functions he allocated to parliament. Taylor, on the other hand, considers it a bit odd suggestion. His opinion is that the very essence of parliament is its power to make laws. "Indeed much of the force of the criticisng power of the House," he says, "is derived from this fact: that it is a body which can, by means of passing laws, do anything it likes."[5] Laski does not support Taylor's opinion. To him the function of legislation is not the only function of parliament. "Its real function is to watch the process of administration to safeguard the liberties of private citizens."[6]

The obligation of controlling the Government is more urgent today than before. The functions of the Government are so extensive now that they touch the very bones of individual lives. "The government departments," aptly remarks Herman Finer, "are virtually great monopolies; they need a strong force outside them to shake them up." The Opposition in the legislature does this job on so many counts.

Judicial Functions. The legislature in every country, generally, consists of two Houses. One is known as the Upper House and the other as the Lower House. The Upper House, in most countries, performs certain judicial functions. In Britain, the House of Lords is the highest court of appeal. The Senate, in the United States, sits as a court of impeachment for the trial of the President and the Vice-President, while the charges of impeachment are preferred by the House of Representatives. Similarly, the Senate in France, according to the Constitution of 1875, was empowered to sit as a High Court of Justice for the trial of the President and the Ministers for high crimes. In India, either of the two Houses at the Centre can prefer a charge for the impeachment of the President. If the charge is

5. Taylor, E., *The House of Commons at Work,* p. 126.
6. Laski, H., *Parliamentary Government in England,* p. 167.

preferred by the House of the People (Lok Sabha), the Council of States (Rajya Sabha) investigates the charge. If the Council of States prefers the charge, then the House of the People investigates it. But instead of making the investigation itself, the House may delegate the work of investigation to any Court or tribunal appointed by the House for that purpose. The impeachment succeeds if the House investigating the charge passes a motion by a two-thirds majority of the total membership of the House that the charge has been sustained.

Constituent Functions. Legislatures have also constituent functions to perform. Parliament in Britain is both a legislative body and a constituent assembly. It can change or abrogate any law whatsoever and by the same procedure. Proposals to amend the United States' Constitution must be made by a two-thirds majority of the Congress or by a national Convention which Congress calls at the request of the legislatures of two-thirds of States. Bills to amend the Constitution of India may originate in either Chamber and be passed by each House of Parliament by a majority of its total membership as well as by a two-thirds majority of the members present and voting. Some specified provisions are, in addition, to be ratified by half the number of states of the Union.

Electoral Functions. Not only do legislatures usually elect their own officers, but they may also elect some executive officials. The elected members of both Houses of Parliament in India form a part of the electoral college for the election of the President. The United States Congress has electoral functions too. As a matter of routine, it meets in joint session every fourth year to count the electoral votes cast for the President and the Vice-President. If no candidate receives a majority of the electoral votes for President, the House of Representatives selects, each State voting as a unit, the President from among the candidates with three highest votes. When no candidate secures a majority of the electoral votes cast for the Vice-President, the Senate makes the choice from among the two candidates with the highest number of votes. The President of France was elected by the joint action of the two legislative chambers. The Swiss legislature elects the judiciary, members of the Federal Council, and the head of the civil service.

Miscellaneous Functions. Parliament in India has the power to move for the removal of judges of the Supreme Court and of the High Courts on the ground of proved misbehaviour and incapacity, and the address for such a removal must be passed by a two-thirds majority in each House. In Britain judges can be removed only by a joint address of both Houses of Parliament to the Crown. Judges in the United States can be removed by the process of impeachment and the procedure followed is exactly the same as in the case of the President, that is, the Senate sits as a court of trial.

Legislatures also work as organs of inquest or inquiries. They often appoint commissions of inquiry relating to agriculture and industry or to find out the causes of social unrest, or mob violence, etc. Such commissions of inquiry collect information, receive memoranda, hear evidence and make recommendations.

In order that the executive may not interfere in the legislative branch, a good number of constitutional safeguards are provided. It chooses its own Speaker and other officers and adopts its own rules of procedure and business. Its members may not be arrested while attending sessions or travelling to and from them for any reason except the commission of crimes. They may not be punished for anything they say in debate except by the House to which they belong.

ORGANISATION OF THE LEGISLATURE

Unicameral and Bicameral Organization. Law, according to Aristotle, should be "reason without passion." This statement involves two things. In the first place, it is essential that those who are entrusted with the duty of making laws should avoid the dangers of rash, hasty, and ill-considered legislation. A due amount of caution and reflection are the prerequisites of legislation. Passion is dangerous in law-making. Secondly, as laws are to affect all alike, it is necessary that the legislature should be a representative body of all the people representing numerous interests in order to secure the consent of all sections of opinion. Various means have been adopted to sccure these ends. One of them is the manner of the organisation of the legislature.

When there is only one legislative assembly, the system of organisation is called unicameral. When the legislature is organised into two Houses, it is called the bicameral system. It is almost a dogma of Political Science now that the legislature ought to consist of two chambers. Single-chamber government is considered the apotheosis of democratic rashness. Some writers characterise government by a single chamber as visionary, "if not corrupt and violent", which usually ends in depotism. Sir Henry Maine expressed the opinion that almost any kind of second chamber is better than none. He said what ought to be expected of the second chamber is not a "rival infallibility but an additional security."

Historical Development of the Bicameral System. The British Parliament is, in a very true sense, the mother of Parliaments. It constitutes the first successful example of a legislature in the modern sense and its most important feature is that it is bicameral in character. "It is safe to say," observes Willoughby, "that had it not assumed this form, there is little likelihood that this mode of organisation would now be so prevalent."[7] It is, thus, of prime importance to know how the system of bicameral legislature came into being in Britain.

In Britain nothing is arranged. It just grows and, like Parliament itself, the bicameral structure is also the child of chance and growth; the result of historical accident. As it was not a deliberate creation, no such thing as a deliberate weighing of the relative advantages of different types of organisation took place. When Edward I called his Model Parliament in 1295, all the different classes of people summoned to attend met in one single assembly. But afterwards they broke into three groups of "estates"—Nobles, Clergy and Commons—to hear separately the King's plea for money and "to make such response as they individually chose." Gradually, however, practical considerations led to a different arrangement. The greater barons and the greater clergy, who were feudal lords and land-holders too, had many interests in common and they began associating together in one body. The lesser clergy found attendance at Parliament very irksome. Moreover, they were jealous of their clerical privileges and preferred to make their money grants in their

7. Willoughby, W.F., *The Government of Modern States,* p. 335.

"Convocations." They soon ceased to attend Parliament altogether. Similarly, the knights, after a good deal of wavering, found their interests identical with the burgesses and finally united with them for all purposes. The result was the division of Parliament into two chambers; in one sat the peers, Temporal and Spiritual, in the other representative Knights of the Shire and the representative Townsmen. How and when exactly this arrangement came about, nobody knows. It was accidental and the result of social and economic circumstances. By the close of the reign of Edward III this bicameral organisation seems to have been fully established.[8] Thenceforward the distinction between the two Houses became political.

The next country to develop strong legislative bodies was the United States of America. Regarding the desirability of creating a national legislature consisting of two chambers, there was little difference of opinion among the members of the Philadelphia Convention. The foremost reason which prompted bicameralism was the spirit of great compromise without which, perhaps, the union would not have come into being. The hitherto sovereign and independent States would not agree to the new administrative set-up, unless their old status was preserved in one branch of the legislature and where they could be represented as constituent political units. On the other hand, the larger States would not agree to a plan of the new constitution unless they were given adequate representation in proportion to their numerical strength. There were economic reasons too. The North, the more populous part of the country, was commercial in interest, whereas the South, the sparsely populated part, was agricultural. The division of legislature into two Houses based on two different principles of representation was in part influenced by these considerations in order to balance and harmonise the two distinct economic interests in the national government.

To these considerations may be added yet another, and it is as important today as before. The Fathers of the Constitution had entertained the fear of majority rule, and they desired to set up a Senate as a conservative check on the turbulence of democracy. And if it could prove an effective check on the radicalism of the popular House, then, it should not be a mere duplication of the latter both in its composition and powers. The propertied class had found another reason for creation of the Senate. Their feeling was that the rule of the majority offered acute dangers, the chief of which was the possible "exploitation of the propertied classes by those less favourably situated." Although it was thought that these dangers could be met largely through the adoption of the representative type of government, still it was felt that certain additional safeguards were desirable. Such safeguards, it was believed, "should be secured by providing for a bicameral legislative system, one of whose chambers would be more directly representative of property interests and be, thus, in a position to protect such interests."[9]

But the historical circumstances which led to the adoption of bicameralism in the United States did not set a stage for its universal adoption. In fact, in the eighteenth and early part of the nineteenth centuries unicameralism was generally favoured. Benjamin Franklin was its enthusiastic advocate in the United States and it was largely under his

8. Adams, G.H., *Constitutional History of England,* pp. 194-95.
9. Willoughby, W.F., *The Government of Modern States,* p. 337.

influence that the legislature of Pennsylvania, under its first Constitution, was made unicameral. In Britain, at the same time, Bentham advocated a single-chamber legislature. In France, reckless belief in popular sovereignty overcame the theories of Montesquieu and Delolme, which suggested a bicameral system of commons and lords. The ideology of Rousseau was accepted and the Constituent Assembly conceded to the argument that sovereignty was indivisible and the nation was sovereign, and hence that its representative body could not but be one. A single-chamber legislature was provided in the Constitutions of 1791 and 1793.

Public opinion, however, soon went in favour of bicameralism and the countries which had previously adopted unicameralism abandoned it for the bicameral system. In Pennsylvania one chamber continued until 1800, when it was replaced by two chambers. In France, two chambers were created in 1795, which remained in existence until 1884, when France again reverted to unicameralism. But this was just for a brief interval. Other States, like Mexico, Spain, Portugal, Naples, and many others, all abandoned it after trial for the double-chamber system. In a few countries, for example, Norway and Israel, the legislature even now is organised as a unicameral body. Commonly, however, a legislature is composed of two Houses and it is a bicameral body.

Arguments in Favour of Bicameralism. It will be evident from the foregoing analysis that the bicameral system did not originate because of any reasoned belief in its superiority from a technical standpoint, as an instrument of legislation. In Britain, it was the result, in part of the historical development of Parliament and in part of the affinity of economic interests between the two distinct classes of the people, the landed aristocracy and the common people. In the United States, many historical factors intervened and bicameralism was found valuable for purposes of compromise between hitherto sovereign States, though here, too, the Senate was intended as the guardian of "property generally and especially of the landed interests, the Yeomanry of the State."[10] The same reasons prompted the German Empire. In France, the experience with a single-chamber legislature was not satisfactory and their proceedings "were marked by violence, instability and excess of the worst kind."[11] Other countries adopted it for giving expression to certain political principles that prevailed then. And for a long time it had become axiomatic that legislature should consist of two chambers.

During recent years a great change has been witnessed in the theory and practice of the bicameral system of legislature and this, too, began in Britain. While the struggle between the King and Parliament was continuing, there developed a struggle within Parliament as to which House should speak for Parliament in financial matters. The House of Lords never admitted the claim to sovereignty by House of Commons on financial matters, although by usage gradually the Lords acquiesced in the claims of the representatives of the people. But in 1860, the House of Lords began interfering in financial matters and in the beginning of the present century it made a bid to revive its powers by rejecting the proposals aiming to levy certain new taxes on landed property. The result was the passage of the Parliament Act of 1911, which not only confirmed the

10. Observations of Chief Justice Spencer made at a convention held in 1821 to revise the Constitution of the State of New York. It is cited by W.F. Willoughby in his *The Government of Modern States,* p. 338.
11. Garner, J.W., *Political Science and Government.*

sovereignty of the House of Commons in money matters, but made it omnipotent in matters of ordinary legislation too. The position, today, is that while Britain continues to have a legislature that is apparently composed of two Chambers, the existence of the House of Lords does not matter at all. If the House of Commons were to pass a law abolishing the House of Lords, there is nothing to obstruct it.

This action by Britain in radically diminishing the status of the Upper House as one of the coordinate branches of the legislature had a profound influence on those States which were compelled after World War I to adopt new political systems or to modify their existing systems. Many States discarded bicameral legislatures altogether, and those which adopted them followed the example of Britain, the mother of Parliaments. In the United States, too, the Seventeenth Amendment to the Constitution, adopted in 1913, largely nullified the prime consideration that had led to the original adoption of the bicameral system.

Unicameralism, however, could not persist for long and at present the bicameral system is almost of universal prevalence. But with the changes referred to above, the force of the arguments originally adduced in favour of the adoption of a bicameral system have been greatly weakened, if not entirely destroyed. To illustrate it, the first French Constituent Assembly in 1946 adopted the unicameral system. The second Constituent Assembly reverted to the system of bicameralism, but the powers given to the Council of the Republic were not even near to the weaker second chamber like the House of Lords. It was a Council for reflection, as one of the writers described it, and not a Council of action. There was nevertheless a strong body of opinion to the effect that the bicameral system has certain intrinsic merits. To some extent bicameralism is based on a distrust of popular opinion and its expression in the popular House. Following are the main arguments generally advanced in support of bicameralism.

John Stuart Mill pointed out that the concentration of power in one single Chamber makes it despotic. This means that all power has a tendency to degenerate, and if not checked by a rival chamber, it is likely to go beyond its limits. Lord Acton, accordingly, maintained that the second chamber is "the essential security of freedom." The necessity for two chambers was, thus, based, as Bryce said, on the belief that the innate tendency of an assembly to become hateful, tyrannical, and corrupt needs to be checked by another House.

Second chambers are defended on the ground that popularly elected representatives can be overhasty and they need checking by a less impulsive and more experienced body. "We need a mechanism that enables us to delay the first rough impulses of a body fresh from its contact with the electorate, and eager, in its inexperience, to experiment with every kind of novelty." A popular chamber elected on the basis of adult suffrage is usually radical in its outlook. Its members are comparatively young and they are a|ways keen to establish their mark by doing something radical and thereby ensuring their berth in the next general election. Upper Houses are usually for longer terms and elected under conditions which make for greater conservatism among their members. Conservatism, the advocates of bicameralism assert, is needed to check the radicalism of the popular chamber and it is a brake of considerable political advantage. Moreover, when radicalism is injected with conservatism, the result is reason without passion and that is what law really ought to be. The essence of the second chamber is that it should not be subject to the same impulses and the same pressures as the representative House. Bicameralism is, therefore, a necessary check upon hasty, rash and ill-considered legislation. It acts as a brake by revising the legislative activity of the popular House and there is a greater likelihood of temperate and deliberate discussion resulting in balanced, equitable and careful legislation.

Interposition of delay is needed to crystallise public opinion on all bills before they become laws. In fact, it is of considerable advantage that the decision of the popularly elected chamber should be given a second thought and that, too, under conditions of a calmer atmosphere in a chamber which is less susceptible to immediate popular pressure. Take, for example, the House of Lords. The Lords can afford to have full and free debates on issues which the Commons are too busy to discuss or which party leaders may consider too explosive to touch. By their debates the Lords prepare the public for the consideration of the important issues, educate public opinion, and make the government susceptible to public reaction. The House of Lords, thus, performs a useful function in influencing the people and the government. Reference of a measure to the second chamber, after having been passed by the first, provides a sufficient pause for reflection and deliberation. Second chambers, accordingly, ensure that opportunity will always be given for a sober second thought, thereby exercising a controlling, modifying, retarding, and steadying, influence on legislation. There is careful scrutiny of legislation by both the chambers. The length of time that elapses between introduction in one chamber and final passage in both reduces the chances of the tyranny of the majority, haste and carelessness attendant thereon, and ill-conceived legislation.

Moreover, this pause also enables the opinion of the nation to be adequately expressed on the proposed legislation. It would be especially needed as regards bills which affect the fundamentals of the constitution or introduce new principles of legislation or which raise issues whereon the opinion of the country may appear to be equally divided. "It is not," says Carl Friedrich, "really so much a matter of expression of opinion, as of crystallization. The cabinet governs in accordance with the general mandate of the majority, but there are issues upon which more than a majority may be desirable."[12]

The system of bicameral legislature is the correct barometer of public opinion. A single chamber may, before the expiry of its term of office, grow out of tune and not keep in harmony with popular opinion. It does not hold any verdict from the electorate on questions of public importance which the legislature may be required to decide after the representatives have been elected. But this defect can be conveniently remedied, if there are two chambers chosen at different times or for different terms. There will be a constant flow of fresh public opinions under a bicameral system as the legislature reflects the popular will at all times. The House of Representatives in the United States is elected for two years whereas the Senate is elected for six years, one-third of its members retiring after every two years. The House of the People (Lok Sabha) in India is elected for five years while the Council of States (Rajya Sabha) is elected for six years, one-third members retiring after every two years.

12. Friedrich, C.J., *Constitutional Government and Democracy*, p. 306.

The popular chamber in every democratic country is now flooded with work. Growth in the functions of the State has made legislation numerous, complex and specialised. Consequently, there is so much rush of work that one chamber cannot have sufficient time to devote and to fully deliberate upon all measures. Second chambers avoid congestion of business and relieve the popular chambers of many arduous tasks, enabling them to concentrate on important measures. Not only do non-controversial bills originate in the Upper Chamber and find an easier passage in the Lower Chamber after having been fully discussed and put into well-considered shape, but it also usefully does the examination and revision of bills after they have passed through all the stages in the Lower Chamber. This is now more needed since the time of the popular House is rationed and it is obliged almost on all bills to act under special rules limiting debates, thereby curtailing the possibilities of free and full discussion. Upper Chambers generally function under no such limitations. Their membership being reasonably limited and consisting of the best brains of the country, veteran statesmen and seasoned politicians with diverse experiences, there is intimate, practical and highly intelligent discussion and criticism.

Moreover, a finished Act of Parliament must be word perfect. For if mistakes are made, the government may be involved in administrative difficulties or confusion or it may place the community in grave difficulties as a result of legally correct but unexpected and disturbing decisions of courts. The second chamber is a valuable institution in this matter of spotting lack of clarity or doubtful matters of drafting.

Bicameralism provides a convenient means of giving representation to different classes and interests and assures representation of minorities and for professional and vocational interests. Then, there are some talented persons in every country who are election-shy. In a system of bicameral legislature, they, too, can find an easy berth in the Upper Chamber, Take, for example, the Upper Chambers in India both at the Centre and in the States. The President is empowered to nominate twelve members to the Council of States, who should be persons having special knowledge or practical experience in respect of such matters as literature, science, art and social services. Similar provision is made for nomination to the Legislative Councils, wherever they exist, in the constituent states.

Second chambers are indispensable for States with a federal form of government. The Lower Chamber in a federation is elected on the basis of population and is a representative chamber of the people as a whole. The Upper Chamber is representative of the constituent units. In several States units are given equal representation in the Upper Chamber. Equality of representation is claimed to prevent the domination of the legislature by the bigger and prosperous units. Bicameralism thereby secures the spirit of compromise among different interests, as it did in the United States, in the absence of which national unity would not have been possible.

The bicameral system protects individual freedom against legislative despotism. If there is no balancing of authority and all law-making were concentrated at a single centre, it is likely to become tyrannical in its transactions. It is a simple maxim of democracy that if liberty is to be real and lasting, political direction of authority should not concentrate at any one place. "In framing a government which is to be administered by men over men," wrote Madison, "the great difficulty lies in this: it must first enable the government to control the governed; and in the next place oblige it to control itself."

Bicameralism is a device to restrain and control the despotism of either one chamber or the other.

To sum up, bicameralism has been justified as a check on undivided power, rashness and irresponsibility, as a delaying and deliberative mechanism, as representing various interests in the community, as a reservoir of knowledge and wisdom, and as representing small and big states alike in a federation. It protects individual freedom against legislative despotism.

Unicameral System. As said earlier, a single, chamber legislature was quite fairly favoured towards the close of the eighteenth century and during the early years of the nineteenth. This was essentially the result of the theory of popular sovereignty which had then become the basis and watchword of democracy. It was believed that sovereignty rested with the people and it was indivisible and hence only a single chamber could represent their will. "The law," said Sieyes, "is the will of the people; the people cannot at the same time have two different wills on the same subject; therefore, the legislative body which represents the people ought to be essentially one."

But this could not last long and many countries, which had adopted single-chamber legislatures originally, abandoned them in favour of the bicameral system. It was generally held that single chambers "were characterised by instability, violence, and passion and that their actions were unbalanced and impulsive." It was consequently thought necessary to check this rash and unwise action by the more serene and balancing power of the second chamber. During recent years, again, the idea of a single chamber has been revived and it found favour with many political writers. It is maintained that unicameral system is simple and responsibility under this system can be definitely located. The bicameral system, in contrast with this, is complicated and responsibility is divided. When both the chambers are popularly elected and possess coequal powers, discord and division is inevitable. Division of responsibility means inaction, thereby paralysing the will of the people. When one House is a replica of the other, it has no utility, because "if the two assemblies agree", as Sieyes said, "the second chamber is unnecessary; if they disagree it is obnoxious." There is duplication of effort as both chambers seek independently to obtain the same information by debating the same questions with their elaborate rules of procedure. MacIver, too, points out that the Second Chamber "unless it is constituted on a broad representative principle, lacks the authority which derives from the support of public opinion; if it is so constituted it tends to be a duplicate of the first house and lacks a *raison d'etre*."[13] It is, therefore, suggested to co-opt specialists on the Select Committees of the popular chambers, which should examine the details of the provisions of the bill rather than to make legislatures bicameral.

A second chamber, it is asserted, "is a clumsy addition—a sort of fifth wheel on the coach", which prevents or delays the necessary and urgent transaction of business. In very many countries second chambers have proved citadels of reaction, retarding the forces of progress. Illustrating this point, Laski says that the House of Lords cannot fulfil the demands of democracy, because "where it is tempted to be active in defence is just where democracy is tempted to be active in offence." He argues for abolishing the House

13. MacIver, R.M., *The Modern States,* p. 383.

of Lords, and the critics of bicameralism unequivocally regard second chambers as destructive of national solidarity, creating deadlocks and frictions between the different sections and interests of the people.

It has been further maintained that there is no unanimity of opinion regarding the organisation of the second chambers. This disagreement is itself an argument against bicameralism. In countries which have two chambers there is much discussion about reconstituting them. The House of Lords has always been condemned to be out of tune since it represents no one, except the peers who form a class by themselves. The method of nomination of the members of the Canadian Senate has all through been subjected to serious objections. The utility of the second chamber in a federal State has also been questioned. It is maintained that the representatives of the constituent units of a federation now vote on party lines rather than as representatives of their respective regional governments. There is, as such, no use giving the constituent units separate representation through second chambers. And the minorities get better protection from constitutional safeguards than from doubtful representation through second chambers.

It is also argued that legislation passed by a single chamber is neither hasty nor ill-considered. Almost every measure that becomes law is the result of a long process of discussion and analysis. In fact, every modern legislature takes its cue, while making laws, from the opinions expressed in the press and on the platform. Such being the case, there is no need to give unnecessary duplication to deliberation and delay the much-needed legislation. Nor is there any truth in the assertion that bicameral system prevents legislative despotism. There are many other safeguards, like the suspensive veto of the executive, and a second vote in the same chamber after some interval, against the so-called despotism of a single chamber.

Finally, double-chamber system, its opponents maintain, duplicates work, leads to delay in action and is an unnecessary burden on the national exchequer. Laski and many other writers, therefore, conclude that a single-chamber assembly seems best to answer the needs of the modern State.

Here is a resume of the comparative advantages of unicameralism and bicameralism:

For Unicameralism A Single House:	**For Bicameralism Two Houses:**
1. Permits speedy action	1. Provide a check on hasty and ill-considered legislation.
2. Avoids obstruction of the will of the people.	2. Avoid despotism of a single chamber.
3. Permits clarity of responsibility of the Cabinet in a Parliamentary system of government.	3. Help public opinion to crystallise by interposing delay.
4. Reduces duplication and confusion of responsibility relating to legislation.	4. Reflect the popular will at all times and there is no time lag.
5. Adds to the quality and prestige of the legislators through absence of conflict.	5. Help divide the workload.

6. Is less expensive and ensures speedy transaction of business.	6. Do useful and careful revision of legislation. 7. Allow representation to different classes and groups. 8. Account for their necessity in a federation. 9. Protect individual freedom against legislative despotism.

Bicameralism is now the well established and essential feature of a representative democracy. There is no doubt that genuine bicameralism, if the Upper House does its proper job of being a House of review and reconsideration, slows down the legislative machinery and tends to render radical reforms and changes more difficult. Yet, bicameralism is based on an enduring principle that resolutions of government which have widespread results need a multitude of counsellors. Two Houses are more advantageous as deliberation and solemnity strengthen the prospect of obedience and acceptance. But if second chambers are to do their job, the two obviously must not be carbon copies of each other. They should differ in their composition, method of election, tenure and in powers. They should be so constituted as to make themselves felt through opportunities of organised co-operation with the other organs of government. They should suggest and criticise measures, deliberate on important affairs and assist in planning. But they should not be able to create deadlocks, to interpose long delays or to nullify the policy of the lower chamber. The upper chamber is intended to act as a brake, but not too tight a brake. Its necessary function is to resist and not to persist. The more popularly elected chamber must be the final determining authority.

STRUCTURE OF LEGISLATIVE BODIES

Composition of the Upper Houses. Granting the utility or a delaying authority and a desire for having a multitude of counsellors for discussion, criticism and argumentation, controversy centres round the composition of the two chambers, designated as upper and lower, as well as first and second chambers to distinguish the two Houses. These terms suggest that the upper or the first chamber is of greater significance than the lower or the second chamber. But this is not exactly correct. In the matter of constitutional powers the so-called upper or first House is in all cases, except the American Senate, the weaker of the two. Its functions are secondary and it is not always a representative chamber. It is only a historical legacy that the past name is retained and is called an upper or first House.

It must be at once said that a really satisfactory formula relating to the composition of the Upper Chamber is hard to find. The Upper Chambers in modern States exhibit considerable diversity in their structure and usually contain important survivals of historical development. "In qualification of their members and in the methods by which these members are chosen they often show traces of the class that preceded modern democracy, and on the basis of their representation, especially in federations, they indicate the historic units by whose combination the State was formed." The following are the most important methods by which members of Upper Houses are selected. Many States combine two or more of these methods.

The first is the hereditary principle, as it is obtainable in Britain. The House of Lords essentially consists of hereditary peers and they account for more than ninety per cent of the total membership of the whole House. How did it come about? It was a historical chance. There is no evidence to show that the Kings had ever a mind to create peerage of a hereditary character. It was, however, a custom that a King, whenever he summoned a Parliament, would send for the same peers who had sat in an earlier one, or if in the meantime they had died, for their eldest sons. In course of time custom became a right and a seat in the House of Lords descended from father to eldest son, just as the family estate under the law of primogeniture.

The remaining membership of the House of Lords is non-hereditary and includes the Lords Spiritual, the Law Lords appointed for life, Peers and women Peers appointed for life, and the Princes of the Royal blood. But the very idea of a hereditary chamber is repugnant to a democratic age, and it can be safely predicted that no civilised country will venture to deliberately bring it into being. If the British people were themselves to sit together to re-fashion the whole of their political machinery, the first to disappear would be the hereditary House of Lords. It is really to put democracy to shame that more than ninety per cent of the Peers should sit in their places because their forefathers had there sat before them. "The idea of hereditary legislators," wrote Thomas Paine, "is as inconsistent as that of hereditary judges or hereditary juries, and as absurd as a hereditary mathematician or a hereditary wise man, and as ridiculous as a hereditary poet laureate." Serious efforts have been made to abolish the hereditary character of the House of Lords, though without any tangible results. But even the Peers themselves are now agreed upon the imminence of some change in the composition of the House of Lords. The principle of appointment for life and the inclusion of women Peers are valuable indications of the desired change.

The second is the principle of nomination. The members are appointed to their office by the executive either for life or for a given period. The method of nomination has one advantage. The process of popular election does not always result in the selection of the ablest and most upright men. There are in every country many talented men who are reluctant to seek election because they cannot withstand its turmoils and put themselves in the full glare of publicity and criticism. The system of nomination enables such distinguished men to participate in public affairs without subjecting themselves to the rough and tumble of an electoral campaign. But a chamber composed of nominated members is not a representative chamber and, accordingly, it lacks the authority possessed by a popular House. Mereover, nomination does not always result in the selection of talent and ability. Favouritism and services rendered to the party in power are the main criteria of nomination. The power of nomination is, therefore, likely to be abused. The best example of a nominated chamber is the Canadian Senate. "Senatorship has been invariably regarded," writes Professor Dawson, "as the choicest plums in the patronage basket, and they have been used without compunction as rewards for faithful party service." The result is the low regard in which the Senate is popularly held. The Canadian

Senate hardly commands its own confidence. It is merely a recording body and it hardly disagrees with the Lower House or opposes any public bill. Sir George Foster, in the course of a debate, remarked: "Who on the street asks to know what is the opinion of the Senate upon this or that question? Who in the press really takes any trouble to know whether the Senate has any ideas, and if so, what they are upon any branch of legislative concern, or upon conditions which require the best and most united work of all in order to arrive at a successful conclusion." It is, therefore, difficult to see any solid value in a body of this kind.

Two methods may be adopted for the election of an Upper House: direct elections and indirect elections. Directly elected Upper House may be found in federal States like the United States of America and Australia. The U.S. Senate is composed of 100 members: two senators being returned by each one of the 50 States. The Australian Senate has 60 members, the six States of the Commonwealth returning ten members each on the general ticket system. The main difficulty in the case of directly elected upper chamber is that it becomes a mere duplication of the Lower House. Being a representative chamber, its members cannot afford to disregard the wishes of their constituents. Even the most courageous and honest must keep a weather eye on popular feeling. Moreover, when both the Houses are directly elected, one becomes a replica of the other and it leads to chronic constitutional deadlocks as both the chambers are of equal importance and stand on an equal footing.

The Council of States in India is indirectly elected. The French Council of the Republic, under the Fourth Republic, was also indirectly elected. The American Senate, too, before 1913, was an indirectly elected chamber. Laski, who is a supporter of unicameral legislature, is of the opinion that "of all methods of maximising corruption, indirect election is the worst".[14] He further says, "If such a chamber is, at the time of its selection, hostile to the government of the day, it is destructive of the quality of the work, while if it is favourable, it is probably superfluous."[15]

It is not, however, easy to suggest a satisfactory method of constituting Upper Chambers. Bluntschli said that distinction between the aristocratic and democratic elements in the State could not be ignored. To allow representation to only one of these elements was to do injustice to the other. John Stuart Mill proposed a second chamber constituted on the principle of political experience and training. If one is the people's chamber, the other should be a chamber of statesmen—a council composed of all living public men who have passed through important political offices or employments. Such a chamber, Mill added, "would be not merely a moderating body, or a simple check, but also an impelling force."

Another method proposed is one in vogue in Norway and advocated by Lees Smith. The second chamber, according to this plan, would be a small body elected by the Lower House and its sole function would be to postpone and to revise.[16] The best method is, perhaps, the one recommended by Sidgwick.[17] His ideal is the combination of nomination

14. Laski, H., *A Grammar of Politics,* p. 30.
15. *Ibid.,*
16. Lees Smith, *Second Chambers in Theory and Practice,* p. 249 f.
17. Sidgwick, H., *Elements of Politics,* p. 473 f.

and indirect election. Indirect election, he said, gives to the House a representative character to some extent and nomination provides an opportunity to bring talent and experience into the legislature whose discussions may wield great influence on the electorate. The composition of the Council of States (Rajya Sabha) in India fulfils both these conditions. The maximum strength of the Council is 250 and it consists of 238 members representing the states and the Union Territories. The representatives of the states are chosen by the elected members of their Assemblies in accordance with the system of proportional representation by means of the single transferable vote.. In the case of Union Territories members are chosen in such a manner as Parliament may by law determine. The method of election is, accordingly, indirect. The remaining twelve members are nominated by the President to represent literature, science, art and social service. Somewhat similar are the provisions of the Constitution of the Union of South Africa which empowers the Governor-General-in-Council to appoint eight Senators in addition to the thirty-two who are indirectly elected. The Italian Constitution makes all former Presidents of the Republic Senators for life and permits the President to appoint as Senators for life five other Italian citizens "who have brought renown to the country by merits of the highest order in the social, scientific, artistic or literary fields." In the United States, too, it has been suggested that all ex-Presidents be given a life-time seat in the Senate. The proposal emanates with a view to bringing Congressional-executive relations closer, but the underlying idea to make the Upper Chamber a reservoir of knowledge is also there.

Composition of the Lower House. The development of lower chambers has coincided with the development of popular representation. Since they usually do not have historical antecedents as old as those of the Upper Chambers, the Lower Houses are usually uniform in their basic structure. Qualifications of a relatively simple nature for the members, as compared with those required of members for many of the Upper Houses, are indicative of the popular nature of the Lower Houses. To this may be added the fact that members of these Houses are almost universally elected by a direct vote of the people who reside in different territorial constituencies. The membership of the Lower House is larger than the Upper House. All this accounts for the primacy of the Lower Houses and relegation of the Upper Houses to an insignificant position.

The British House of Commons has consisted of 635 members. The House of the People in India consists of not more than 525 members directly elected from the States and not more than 20 members to represent the Union Territories. Till recently, the membership of the United States' House of Representatives was "frozen" at 435. The entry of Alaska in 1958, as forty-ninth State, and Hawaii in 1959, as the fiftieth, made it at 437, but it dropped back to 435 in 1962 and remains there. The Swiss National Council consists of 200 members since 1963. The number, thus, varies from State to State. But what should be the advisable number? Viewed solely from the operative standpoint, a relatively small chamber has undoubted advantages over a large body. A small well-knit assembly attains coherence above all and helps to establish definite responsibility. But a small House cannot, from its very nature, have the same representative character as has the large House. If the basis of representation is population, the constituency electing a representative must be larger in the case of a small House than in the case of a large one. The bigger the number of the representatives the smaller need the district be, "This conduces to," says Finer, "heightened representativeness. For good law representativeness is of cardinal importance; all men get the sense that they are being duly heard in the uses of authority."[18] Finer would strongly favour the increase in size of the Lower House to eight hundred in all modern democratic States.

The length of term of members usually varies from three to five years. It is only two years for the United States House of Representatives. In the United States, as John Adams, and the author of the Federalist, tells us, there was a current maxim with the new States that "where annual elections end, tyranny begins." Connecticut and Rhode Island were half-yearly, and the rest, save South Carolina which was biannual, were annual. The House of Commons is elected for five years and the term of the House of the People is also the same. But both are subject to dissolution and, accordingly, the term of office may come to an end earlier. Dissolution involves new elections.

From the standpoint of representation, it is desirable that the term of legislators should be relatively short. From the standpoint of efficiency alone a longer term is advocated. But an efficient government is no substitute for self-government and it is claimed that the legislative term should neither be too long nor too short. If it is too long, the legislature cannot claim to be the mirror of public opinion. There will be time lag. If the term is too short, the legislators will not have the time and opportunity to gain the requisite knowledge and experience which their arduous and technical job requires. Nor shall they be in a position to develop a legislative policy, and establish legislative traditions to enable the chamber to function properly and efficiently. It will be a race with time.

The practice of various States is to fix the term at four or five years. The supporters of this desirable medium claim that it permits the legislator to become proficient and he can devote adequate attention to legislative problems. It also reduces the insecurity attending frequent elections with their demands on time and money. According to Laski, "the best period of power for a legislature seems to be not less than four, not more than five years."[19] Finer would rigidly fix it at four years. He says, "My judgment that a four years' term is a modern necessity is reinforced by reflection on the obvious mounting trend to national planning. A longer term than four years is inadvisable because the broader the activity of government, especially when it is (as much must be) still of an experimental nature, the more opportunities ought there to be for reference back to the citizens. The way back must be kept open. The more massive and complicated the administrative apparatus, the more ought it to be subjected to the periodical lashing waves of popular opinion."[20]

The Two Chambers Should Differ in Principle. Where the structural principle of both Houses of the legislature is the same, much of the value of the bicameral system is lost. If the two Houses are identical in constitution. the second is a mere duplication of the first, and the advantages of the additional chamber are questionable. "If the two Houses were elected for the same period and by the same electors," observes Lieber,

18. Finer, H., *The Theory and Practice of Modern Government,* p. 390.
19. Laski, H., *A Grammar of Politics*, p. 342.
20. Finer, H., *The Theory and Practice of Modern Government*, p. 390.

"they would amount in practice to little more than two committees of the same House; but we want two bona fide different Houses representing the impulse as well as the continuity, the progress and the conservation, the onward zeal and the retentive element, innovation and adhesion, which must ever form integral elements of all civilisation. One House, therefore, ought to be large; the other comparatively small, and elected and appointed for a longer time."[21] What is required in order to realise the true benefits of bicameral system is that the two chambers should be differently composed and should rest on dissimilar bases. The members of one House must enjoy a 1onger term of office, they should represent a larger constituency, they should be subject to higher membership qualifications, and they might well be chosen in a different manner and by a differently constituted electorate.

Powers of the Two Houses. In the process of law-making the theory is that the two Houses, in a system of bicameral legislature, are generally equal and coordinate. A bill may originate in either House and pass through the same legislative procedure in both the Houses before it is finally voted upon. No bill can become a law without the consent of both the Houses. Either House may propose amendments to a bill and they become valid by receiving the consent of the other. In the case of bills relating to the raising and spending of money, the powers of the two Houses are generally coordinate, but not co-equal. The Lower House possesses supreme control over the finances of the State, the maxim being that representation and taxation go together. The representatives of the people are the final arbiters over all matters of income and expenditure of the State. All financial bills, accordingly, originate in the Lower House and its power in this respect is decisive. The British House of Lords may not originate, amend or reject a money bill. In France the powers of the Senate, under the Constitution of 1875, were co-equal with those of the Chamber of Deputies, except that money bills originated in the latter. The Senate might amend or reject them. But in reality the Senate was invariably in a position of inequality and the supremacy of the Chamher of Deputies was an established fact. Under the Fourth Republic financial legislation was initiated in the Assembly alone and it was transmitted to the Council of the Republic for its opinion. But the Council was required to give its opinion within the same span of time as the Assembly had herself taken. Therefore two months span, which was required in the case of ordinary legislation for the opinion of the Council of the Republic, was not necessary with regard to financial bills. Under the Constitution of 1958, the Senate and the National Assembly have equal powers except that the budget originates in the National Assembly. In India money bills can only originate in the House of the People (Lok Sabha) and the Council of States (Rajya Sabha) must send its recommendations thereon within fourteen days of receipt. If it does not return the bill within fourteen days or returns it with recommendations which are not acceptable to the House of the People (Lok Sabha), the will of the House of the People (Lok Sabha) prevails. In Britain the House of Lords can delay a money bill for one month. In the United States, on the other hand, the Senate, though forbidden to originate bills for raising revenues, possesses the undisputed power to amend or reject them.

21. As cited by J.W. Garner in *Introduction to Political Science,* p. 439.

There must be a sharp distinction between the powers of both Houses of the legislature. The differences in powers will, of course, depend upon the mode and composition of the Upper House. If the Upper House is hereditary or nominated, as in Britain and Canada, its powers are considerably limited. But if it is an elected House, it stands on a footing of equality with the Lower House as far as the law of the constitution is concerned. The march of democracy, however, has decidedly made the Lower House a "predominant partner."[22] In the event of conflict between the two, the verdict of the House which is more representative of the people must ultimately prevail. The case of the American Senate, which was deliberately designed to enjoy greater powers than the House of Representatives, is quite exceptional. Wherever both the Houses possess co-equal powers, much of the value of bicameralism is lost. Identical powers mean sheer duplication and the advantages of such a system of legislature are questionable. The Upper House, for all intents and purposes, is a revising body. Being a chamber solely created for purposes of reflection and not action, it is intended to exercise a moderating influence on the radicalism of the Lower House. It may serve as a brake, but not too tight a brake, which may lead to open rupture between the two Houses. If public opinion supports the attitude taken by the Upper Chamber, the Lower House would automatically mend itself; otherwise the former should respectfully bow to the wishes of the wider representatives of the people. The function of the Upper House, in fine, is to *resist* but not to *persist.*

It has long been an almost universal practice to confer upon the Upper Chambers certain special powers which the Lower Houses do not possess. Nearly in every country Upper Chambers are vested with the exercise of judicial powers. The House of Lords is the highest court of appeal in Great Britain. In the United States, the Senate serves as a court for the trial of impeachment cases. The French Constitution of 1875 empowered the President of the Republic to dissolve the Chamber of Deputies with the consent of the Senate. In the United States the Senate exercises certain specific executive powers. All Presidential appointments must have the assent of the Senate, all treaties require its ratification.

DIRECT LEGISLATION

Need for Direct Legislation.[23] The representative democracy during recent years has been subjected to a great deal of criticism. This is primarily due to the popular belief that legislatures play excessive party politics and the welfare of the people as a whole is generally discounted. The whole machinery of the government is so geared as to serve the party ends and party politics are really the politics of the party bosses. It is their will and their decisions. Both the legislators and the administrators have nothing to decide and deterinine. In order to mitigate the vigours of the party discipline and the corrupting influence of the representative system, the direct participation of the people themselves in the affairs of the government is impressed. To express it in the words of Carl Friedrich, "Indeed, the ever-recurring problem of 'legitimacy,' that is, the question of how authority can be made to appear legitimate to those over whom it is wielded, seemed to many

22. Refer to the controversy between the House of the People and the Council of States in India.
23. Refer to Anup Chand Kapur's *The Government of Switzerland,* Ch. VII.

ardent democrats at the beginning of the twentieth century to call for an ever greater extension of personal participation of as many citizens as possible in as many decisions as possible."[24]

Even the totalitarian dictators of this century relied upon this device for "legitimatizing their unconstitutional and anti-constitutional regimes," as did Napoleon through the process of referenda or plebiscites.[25] But such direct popular approval is obtained under duress and is just a propaganda screen for the dictatorial *coup d'etat* and a device to suppress democratic opposition at home and a pretence abroad that the will of the people had been obtained in support of their regimes.

Rousseau was the great apostle of direct democracy and his classical dictum that "England is free only on the day of election" shows his mistrust of representative democracy. But direct participation of the people is the distinctive contribution of Swiss democracy, and it is as old there as Swiss history. It is still kept alive in some of the cantons, but in others it has been replaced by the referendum and the initiative as a substitute for personal attendance of the people at the annual meetings of the Cantonal assemblies. The referendum was generally used from an early period by states in the United States for the ratification of the new constitutions and subsequent constitutional amendments. Their use for legislative purposes spread to the United States in 1898. Now nearly all the states use some form of referendum, a good number of them permit the use of initiative and referendum on a local level; and more than half the states provide for statutory and constitutional initiative. The turn of the century brought direct legislation into several European States too. The Constitution of former U.S.S.R. provided for referendum if the differences between the two chambers of the Supreme Soviet on a legislative measure could not be reconciled for the second time after its reference to the Conciliation Commission.

The Referendum. Literally, the word referendum means "must be referred." As a concept of Political Science it means the process by which the verdict of the people is sought on a proposed law or constitutional amendment on which the legislature has already expressed its opinion. If it is ratified by the required majority of popular votes, it becomes law. If it is rejected, the measure is given up; the underlying idea is that a law must be the manifestation of the will of the people, and every law passed by the representative assembly should be submitted to the people for their final approval.

The referendum may be of two kinds: (1) facultative or optional, and (2) compulsory or obligatory.

When a law, after it has passed through the legislature, is submitted to the people for their acceptance or rejection on a petition from a specified number of citizens, it is known as the optional or facultative referendum. If the majority vote is in the affirmative, it becomes a law; otherwise the decision of the legislature stands reversed. In Switzerland a petition for facultative or optional referendum is required to be made by 50,000 citizens

24. Friedrich, C.J., *Constitutional Government and Democracy,* p. 546.
25. Napoleon sought the approval of the people at certain crucial moments in his career, such as his election to remain First Consul for life and his assumption of the position of Emperor. Napoleon III revived the practice of Napoleon Bonaparte in 1851 and sought the approval of the people on his *coup d'etat.*

or the legislatures of eight Cantons for ordinary law unless the Federal Assembly declares the matter urgent.

In the case of compulsory or obligatory referendum all laws of a specified type must necessarily be referred to the people for their acceptance or rejection before they can become laws. The obligatory form is obviously more democratic, for it requires expression of popular opinion on every law. In Switzerland and Australia, all constitutional amendments are subject to compulsory or obligatory referendum. In some of the Swiss Cantons even ordinary laws are compulsorily referred to the people for their opinion.

Arguments in Favour of Referendum. The principle of popular sovereign, it is maintained, finds its real expression in direct legislation. In a representative system genuine public opinion is unobtainable, for it is moulded and shaped by the partisan influences of the parties, the press, the platform and the propaganda. The referendum, on the other hand, is the surest method of discovering the real wishes of the people and is, therefore, an excellent barometer of public opinion. According to Carl Friedrich, direct popular action in its several forms serves to strengthen the democratic element. They "provide a modern constitution with an integrating device by which the dissensions of parties, pressure groups, and propagandas can from time to time be overcome."[26]

The advocates of direct legislation claim that a citizen knows better than his representatives what can serve him best and when he is required to express his opinion thereupon by approving or rejecting the legislation, it would enhance his interest in the public affairs. A law, which comes direct and straight from the people, carries with it fuller moral authority and commands unquestioning obedience than a law made for them by their representatives.

The referendum minimises the importance of political parties and discourages partisan spirit. It is a popular check on the vagaries of the legislature and the political machine. Frequent rejection by the people of measures passed by the legislature shows that the latter does not always know or give effect to what has proved to be the real will of the people. It ensures, at the same time, that laws opposed to the popular will have no chance of being enacted. The referendum, as a matter of fact, puts a veto in the hands of the people.

The referendum reduces the political high-handedness of the majority party. Under the representative system a law is usually what the majority party in the legislature wishes it to be. It seldom represents the will of the minority parties. If it is referred to the people before it can be finally enacted, the minorities do get an opportunity to adequately express their opinion and to muster strong their opposition and, if possible, to negative it. This is real democracy.

There is no time-lag in direct legislation. "Direct legislation", says Bryce, "helps the legislature to keep in touch with the people at other times than at General Election and in some respects a better touch, for it gives the voters an opportunity of declaring their views on serious issues apart from the destructive or distorting influence of party spirit."

When the people feel and realise that they are the real legislators, their patriotism and

26. Friedrich, C.J., *Constitutional Government and Democracy,* p. 571.

their sense of responsibility are fully stimulated. Direct legislation has more educative value than the representative system. When the people know that they themselves are to make and unmake laws, they are prompted with a keener and more active interest in public affairs. This is the true price of democracy.

The process of direct legislation is conservative in character. The people will seldom introduce radical changes when they themselves know that they are the arbiters on legislation. They know what laws, if need be, can be easily adjusted to their needs and requirements. They will, accordingly, refrain from making sweeping changes.

The referendum, it is maintained, is the best means of resolving deadlocks between the two Houses of the legislature. In the Australian Constitution direct legislation is recommended as a device for breaking a deadlock between the two chambers.

Finally, as Bryce says, "There must somewhere in every government be a power which can say the last word, can deliver a decision from which there is no appeal. In a democracy, it is only the people who can thus put an end to controversy."

Arguments against Referendum. Those who are against direct legislation assert that the working of referendum shows that its advantages have not been realised in countries where it has been experimented except in Switzerland. Bryce concluded that while the Swiss were well qualified by intelligence and knowledge of public affairs, it was, however, difficult to say that it had unqualified success in other countries as well. Finer thinks that direct legislation has done little good and its experience "would, perhaps, warn us not to accept direct legislation as a remedy for the defects of a parliamentary government. It improves nothing; neither the laws nor the people. It disturbs without providing solutions."[27]

Following arguments may be examined in this connection:

One of the chief objections against the referendum is that it has undermined the prestige of the legislative assemblies and has adversely reacted on the quality of membership. When representatives know that ultimately the result of their efforts may be reversed by the process of referendum, they will take little interest in the discharge of their legislative duties. If the measure succeeds at the popular vote, the credit for it goes to the people and not to the legislature. If it does not succeed, the blame goes to the legislature. The status and authority of a legislature must suffer with the result that the people become less deferential towards it. Bryce, in summing up the effects of direct legislation on the legislature, says: "Its sense of responsibility is reduced and it may be disposed to pass measures its judgment disapproves, counting on the people to reject them, or may fear to pass laws it thinks needed lest it should receive a buffet from the popular vote." The real difference between direct popular action and the action of the legislatures lies in the field of deliberations. The voters cannot assemble and discuss matter and consequently the opportunity to arrive at truth is lost. Truth emerges from the clash of opinions.

The man in the street is not adequately qualified to form and deliver an opinion upon many subjects of legislation, particularly when legislation has become so technical and

27. Finer, H., *Theory and Practice of Modern Government, op. cit.*, p. 568.

complicated. A simple 'yes' or 'no', as referendum requires, does not indicate the real will of the people. "The difficulty, in fact", as Laski points out, "which direct government involves is the final difficulty that it is by its nature too crude an instrument to find room for the nice distinctions inherent in the art of government."[28] The making of laws requires special training and experience which the people at large cannot possess. Nor can they have the knowledge necessary to enable them to precisely appreciate the implications involved in the proposed legislation. The interests of the people are really safer in the hands of the representatives chosen for their talent and maturer judgment than when submitted to the hazard of a popular vote. All legislative measures are minutely discussed and deliberated on the floor of the legislative assemblies. Amendments and alterations are made in the light of discussion and the knowledge of new facts. But "you cannot amend and alter when your legislative assembly consists of millions of members."[29] The people must accept or reject the bill, no amendments are possible. The vote must be given for the whole bill. "It is an appeal from a court which has the makings and some of the equipment of a wise legislature, to all the crudities of a majority vote."[30]

One of the criticisms against direct legislation, and really a cogent one, relates to the small size of the votes cast, at a referendum. It is maintained that the result of the ballot does not fairly represent popular opinion, because in most cases the opponents of the measures go to the polls in larger proportion than its supporters. The number of large abstentions at a referendum also proves that many a voter either cares little for his civic duties, or knows his unfitness to perform them. "The low percentage of voters," says Carl Friedrich, "participating in many of these decisions has raised the problem of the trustworthiness of the result. In the case of the compulsory referenda in the United States with their very low percentages, this trustworthiness has been widely questioned. Cases can readily be cited where the electorate reversed itself in short order."[31]

Moreover, when people are frequently asked to cast their votes, they develop "electoral fatigue" and psychologically abstain from voting. The result is that the decision arrived at is invariably that of a minority of the citizens and it becomes difficult to know whether there is any public opinion at all on the referendum.

The referendum sometimes involves unnecessary and harmful delay in passing many laws of vital national importance. All this takes away the educative value of the referendum. When citizens do not interest themselves in public affairs, direct legislation becomes a farce.

When people cast an affirmative vote and the law is ratified by a small majority vote, as it happened on the question of the Swiss Federal Penal Code, and of the Federal Economic Articles in 1938 and 1947, with a majority of only 53 per cent in both the cases, the moral authority behind the law may suffer more than would be the case had opinion been nearly equally divided in the Legislative Assembly. In countries, where direct legislation does not exist, a law passed by representative legislatures is accepted

28. Laski, H., *A Grammar of Politics,* p. 322.
29. *Ibid.*
30. Finer, H., *The Theory, and Practice of Modern Government,* p. 568.
31. Friedrich, C.J., *Constitutional Government and Democracy,* p. 555.

in a normal course and no one cares to enquire what was the majority that passed it. It comes in the regular way from the usual organ of the people's will and it is accepted by people in the usual way. But when it goes to the popular vote, everyone is keen to know the majority that passed it. Those who opposed it, carry on their opposition openly as they feel aggrieved to have been overridden by a negligible majority.

There is no justification to hold that direct legislation lessens the evils of party system. As a matter of fact, political parties become more active when frequent votes are to be taken. The referendum accentuates political rivalry and partisan spirit which, in a parliamentary government, may prove embarrassing to the party in power.

Finally, "the most comprehensive but also the vaguest argument", says Bryce, "adduced against the referendum is that it retards political, social and economic progress." Sir Henry Maine developed this point in his book, *The Popular Government*, in 1885, and it particularly impressed Englishmen who had always associated the masses with conservatism. But it is not supported by Swiss experience. It is true that prejudice or undue caution has in some cases delayed the progress of economic or social reforms which the Federal Assembly proposed, but no general harm has followed in Switzerland from that conservatism.

All told, one is disposed to agree with Professor Laski that direct legislation has not any special contribution to make to our problems. Herman Finer suggests that "we should all be better served if our concern were fixed upon the reform of the party system; we should strive, then, to make the parties more responsible-minded, more sensitive, more masters of the social sciences." Even the question of referendum, he concludes, is the question "of the quality of the country's political parties."[32] And if it has admirably succeeded in Switzerland, it is due to the tranquillizing influence of Swiss party system. Politics in Switzerland is conducted almost without regard to party leanings. There is no professionalism in politics and demagogues do not find favour with the Swiss people.[33]

The Initiative. The referendum aims at referring to the judgment of the people measures considered and passed by the legislature. But this device of direct legislation alone has not been considered sufficient to remove the defects of representative system. The advocates of direct legislation assert that it is the inherent right of the citizens to propose legislation and when ratified by the popular vote, it must become law, no matter even if it has been disapproved by the legislature. Such a device of popular legislation is called the *initiative*. By this process, it is claimed, a voter can make his influence felt in those cases where the legislature may not agree to adopt a constitutional amendment or a law.

The initiative is very often erroneously compared to a *petition*. But both essentially differ from one another. A petition is a mere popular submission made to the legislature suggesting the desirability of enacting a particular kind of legislation. The legislature may or may not act upon such a petition; it is not binding on it. But the initiative is the vindication of the inherent right of the people to propose legislation without regard to the opinion of the legislature, and even against its wishes. It is, accordingly, mandatory on

32. Finer, H., *The Theory and Practice of Modern Government,* p. 568.
33. *Ibid.*

the legislature to consider all popularly initiated legislative measures. If the legislature does not approve them, but the popular vote accepts them at a referendum, they become laws.

The initiative may also take two forms: *formulative* and in *general terms.* When the demand is couched in general terms, it is the obligation of the legislature to draft, consider and pass the law as desired by the constitutionally required number of citizens, subject to the ratification of people. If the proposal is *formulated* in the form of a bill complete in all respects, it is the duty of the legislature to consider the measure as it is.

The initiative obtains in Switzerland, federal and Cantonal. For constitutional amendment, the petition for initiative may be made by 100,000 citizens. There is no federal initiative for ordinary laws, and the result is that the constitutional initiative has been used to place all kinds of matters in the Federal Constitution. In the Cantons, the initiative applies to both constitutional and ordinary laws. In the United States of America, the initiative for constitutional amendment is allowed in fourteen states and for ordinary laws in nineteen states.

Arguments in Favour of Initiative. Arguments in favour of the referendum and the initiative are more or less identical. But as the conditions of the latter's application are different, it needs to be considered separately.

The initiative is claimed to be the necessary development of the idea of popular sovereign. The people cannot truly rule if they act through representatives. The individual will of the citizen really expresses itself by his own voice and vote. However politically moral and best intentioned the representatives may be, they must act in accordance with and in conformity to the policy of the party to which they belong and obey its whip and, thus, may misrepresent those whose representatives they claim to be. The referendum gives only the negative right to the people, whereas the initiative gives them the positive right of framing laws which they actually need. If the referendum protects "the people against the legislature's sins of commission so initiative is a remedy for their omission."

The legislatures, it is maintained, are very often apathetic to the needs of the people and the representatives lag behind public opinion. Moreover, they primarily concern themselves to push through party programmes. If this is the case, then it is argued, "why should a body of persons chosen by the people close the door against the people themselves allowing only such proposals as take fancy to pass through so that the people can deal with them?" A law initiated by the people carries with it the impress of public opinion and is, therefore, held in greater sanctity and, consequently, there is more ready and willing obedience to it. Such political behaviour on the part of the citizens adds to the stature and stability of the government and all-round reverence for the institutions of the country. Finally, the initiative minimizes the possibilities of political upheavals, because there is no indefinite postponement of legislation deemed essential by the people for their welfare; they hold it in their own hands. They act immediately and on their own initiative rather than to depend upon their representatives to feel their pulse and know what they actually want.

Arguments Against. But the initiative, like the referendum, reduces the authority and responsibility of the legislature. Making of laws, more especially drafting of bills, is a complicated and difficult task. It requires specialization which only experts connected with the work and members of the legislature acquire by long experience. An average man cannot be expected to know the technicalities required in drafting bills. The result is that popularly initiated bills are "very often crude in conception, unskillful in form, marred by obscurities and omissions." The language used in the initiated bills is very often seriously defective and liable to many interpretations. This process of direct legislation. therefore, transfers legislative initiative from knowledge to ignorance. In the Cantons of Switzerland, where the initiative has been much more freely used, it has not been the parent of any reforms which might not have been obtained through the legislature. The people, on the other hand, have sometimes placed unwise laws on the statute book. The much acclaimed advantages of initiative, therefore, are actually negatived by the practical results.

Qualities Necessary for the Success of Direct Legislation. Whatever be the degree of success of the referendum and the initiative in countries other than Switzerland, it cannot be denied that the mechanism of direct legislation is a difficult ideal and it demands certain qualities in the people to make it operative. The success which it has achieved in Switzerland is due to the historical antecedents of the Swiss people, to their long and continued practice of self-government in their small communities, to their social equality, and to their spirit of patriotism and sense of public duty. Similar success cannot be expected in countries where similar conditions are not obtainable. "It is racy of the soil," as Bryce says. "There are institutions which, like plants, flourish on their hillside and under their own sunshine."[34]

Independence of judgment is the first quality which citizens must possess and exhibit in deciding political issues, when left to their determination. Democracy, no doubt, is unthinkable without political parties, but party sentiments must not dominate the minds of the citizens. Each proposal should be dealt with on its merits, and voting of any kind must not closely follow party lines. This is, indeed, impossible under the existing conditions, but the Swiss voter, as Bryce says, "always independent, is most independent when he has to review the action of his legislature."[35]

The quality most important in a legislating nation is compounded of two things; absence of passion and presence of intelligence. Wherever these qualities are present, there is cool-headedness and, consequently, exercise of judicious judgment. The Swiss are the embodiment of this quality. They are neither an emotional nor a passionate people. They have the habit of voting in a calm spirit. They are cautious in their judgment and the great majority of the nation have always shown resolute hostility to the extreme demagogic spirit. Finally, compromise and tolerance are the two other elements. A people more given to absolutes or inclined to extremist debates over abstract principles would find the system of direct legislation unworkable. There are not "talkers and fighters" in Switzerland. Politics there is unadulterated and a game of veterans who play it in a sportsman spirit.

Future Prospects. What good has direct legislation done in the countries where it has been actually used? "The answer must surely be," writes Finer, "that these countries, save for the combating of the dishonest 'bosses' in the American states, are no better off and are probably worse off."[36] This is, he further adds, "certainly the opinion in America."

34. Bryce, J., *Modern Democracies,* Vol. I, pp. 453-54.
35. *Ibid.*, p. 433.
36. Finer, H., *The Theory and Practice of Modern Government,* p. 564.

In Switzerland the opinions, both of scholars and statesmen, on the value of direct legislation are most divergent. Some extol it as the most perfect institution, in theory and practice, so far devised. There are others who decry it on the ground that people are consulted on matters which they do not understand and assert that the actual working of the system has been bad. Some reformers resent the delays and checks inherent in the referendum and some voters complain of the excessive demand made on their spare time. And yet the people as a whole value the privilege. The institutions of the referendum and the initiative are the pivot upon which hinges the entire Swiss governmental system. If they are abolished, certainly the present relations among the executive, the legislature and the judiciary will have to be altered, and either the American or the British system of government adopted. This the Swiss are not prepared to do. The institution has become permanent in Switzerland. But Finer gives a stern warning not to accept direct legislation as a remedy for the defects of parliamentary government. "It improves nothing," he says, "neither the laws nor the people. It disturbs without providing solution. It is an appeal from a court which has the makings and some of the equipment of a wise legislature, to all the crudities of a majority vote. Its operations leave stark naked the physical power of numbers, surely not a desirable thing."[37] But Carl Friedrich does not take so gloomy a view. Referring to the operation of direct legislation in the American states, he says, "On the whole, the experience has been the same in Switzerland; neither the ardent hopes of its first expounders nor the dire apprehensions of its opponents have materialised. But referendum and initiative have become recognized parts of the American political machinery,"[38] with one difference. Whereas in Switzerland the referendum and the initiative have been developed extensively in national affairs, in the United States they have so far been used in the states.

SUGGESTED READINGS

Bryce, G.: *Modern Democracies,* Vol. I, Chap. XIX, Vol. II, Chap. LXIV-LXV.

Finer, H.: *Theory and Practice of Modern Government* (1954), Chaps. XVII-XVIII, pp. 560-68.

Friedrich, C.J.: *Constitutional Government and Democracy.*

Kapur, Anup Chand: *Government of Switzerland,* Chap. VII.

Laski, H.J.: *A Grammar of Politics,* pp. 308-40.

Lees-Smith, H.B.: *Second Chambers in Theory and Practice.*

Loewenstein, Karl: *Political Power and the Government Process.*

Lowell, A.L.: *Government of England,* Vol. I, Chaps. IX-XXIII.

Luce, R.: *Legislative Assemblies,*

Macridis, Roy C., and Brown, Bernard E.: *Comparative Politics: Notes and Readings.*

Marriot, J.A.R.: *Second Chambers* (1927).

Mill, J. S.: *Representative Government,* Chaps. IX-XIII.

Peaslee, Amos J.: *Constitutions of the Nations.*

Roche, John P., and Merry S. Stedman, Jr.: *The Dynamics of Democratic Government,* Chaps. VI-VIII.

Sidgwick, H.: *Elements of Politics,* Chaps. XXIII, XXVII.

Smith, T.V.: *Legislative Way of Life.*

Willoughby, W.F.: *Government of Modern States,* Chaps. XIX-XX.

Wilson, W.: *Congressional Government.*

37. *Ibid.,* p. 563.

38. Friedrich, G.J., *Constitutional Government and Democracy,* p. 554.

20

CHAPTER

The Executive

Meaning of the Term Executive. The second branch or organ of government is the executive. The term executive is used to designate all those officers of the government whose business it is to execute, or put into effect, the laws. It is the pivot around which the actual administration of the State revolves and includes all officials engaged in administration. Herman Finer says that "it is most useful to look upon the executive as the residuary legatee, for that explains the mixed nature of its functions and parts."[1] In early times, all power, of every kind, rested with one single person, the prince, and he exercised that power with his narrow circle of advisers. They not only executed policy but planned it and sat in judgment. As the movement for responsible government advanced, it caused "portions of the power to be taken over by other institutions, the remainder itself being subjected to certain norms of constitutional morality and controlled by the new organs." As thus understood, the executive embraces the whole governmental organisation with the exception of the legislative and judicial organs and includes all officials, high and low – the Head of the State, his principal advisers and ministers, as well as the whole body of subordinate officials through whom the laws are administered. In this wide sense the term executive is the aggregate or totality of all the functionaries or agencies which are concerned with the execution of the will of the State as that will has been formulated and expressed in terms of law.

But it is customary to use the term executive in its narrow sense which refers only to the Chief Executive Head of the State and his advisers and ministers. The executive in Britain in this context means Queen Elizabeth II and her Ministers with Prime Minister at the top. In India, it is President of the Union, plus all Ministers headed by The Prime Minister. In the United States of America the President and his Secretaries constitute the executive. The primary duty of this part of the executive is to formulate policy and to see that it is properly implemented. The policy implementation function is the job of the permanent civil service who actually run the various departments of the government and the field officers. Both, those who see that the laws are properly enforced and those who actually enforce them, are really integral parts of the same machinery and all collectively constitute the executive department of the government. The only difference between the two is that the former initiate the policy and supervise its implementation. If it cannot be carried out within the framework of the existing law, they propose new legislation in

1. *The Theory and Practice of Modern Government,* p. 575.

order to enable them to carry it through. The latter, members of the civil service, are not concerned with policy-making though at the top they considerably influence the policy-makers. Their primary function is policy execution or enforcement.

Nature of the Executive : Real and Nominal. In considering the nature of the executive we must further distinguish between the real executive and the nominal executive. The distinction is really between the head of the State and the head of government. Before the emergence of parliamentary system such a distinction did not exist; but it is important now. The distinction is relatively easily seen where the two roles are separated, say, the Queen and the Prime Minister in Britain or the President and the Prime Minister in India. In a parliamentary system the head of the State performs ceremonial duties. Normally the area of influence of ceremonial heads is very limited. The real functionaries are the political persons who make the government and are headed by the Prime Minister. There is, thus, a clear difference between *a* executive and *the* executive; the authority of the former is nominal or titular whereas of the latter it is real or actual. There is wide difference between theory and practice here. In terms of law the head of the State may be the source of authority, but his legal functions have become obsolete either as a result of binding conventions or as a result of Constitutional provisions.

When the same person plays both the roles of head of the State and head of the government, he combines unto himself the ceremonial as well as political responsibilities. There is a single identifiable head of the executive, the President of the United States, who will also be the head of the State. He is *a* executive as well as *the* executive. Under absolute monarchy and dictatorship the question of distinguishing the real from the nominal executive does not arise. Here all authority is concentrated in a single person or a group of persons.

Single and Plural Executive. Legislature is organised on the principle that two heads are better than one, or that in a multitude of councillors there is wisdom. The function of the executive is not to deliberate, but to enforce the will of the State as expressed by the legislature, and to carry out the decisions of the courts. The prime need for the efficient discharge of such functions is promptness of decision, singleness of purpose, energy of action and sometimes secrecy of procedure. It goes without saying that this is difficult to obtain when authority is equally distributed among a number of persons. Concentration of authority is the first requisite of the executive. A plural executive destroys responsibility, unnecessarily wastes time and is highly dangerous, particularly in times of emergencies. The advantages of a single chief, says Woolsey, "are obvious: he is able to bring unity and efficiency into the government, and being alone, he or his Ministry is responsible; whereas two Presidents would be apt to checkmate one another, if they were of different parties, and would be jealous and rivals if they were of the same party."

The executive, in brief, is organised on the theory that one bad general is better than two good ones. The executive organised on the plural principle is incompatible with force, energy, unity of purpose and independence. It is, therefore, politically expedient that there should be some one person who can, in the last resort, exercise a decisive and final authority. Absolute monarchy and dictatorship are typical examples of a single executive, Under a Parliamentary system the real executive is the cabinet, plural, no doubt, but the cabinet, headed by the Prime Minister, is a unit which provides political leadership. It comes into office as a unit, it functions as a unit and goes out of office as a unit, and collective responsibility is the method by which this unity is secured and enforced. The Cabinet is a policy-formulating body and its members preside over the administrative departments of government. Both for policy and administration, they are responsible to Parliament and they all act under the leadership of the Prime Minister. "The Prime Minister is," according to Lord Morley, "the keystone of the Cabinet," and occupies a position of exceptional and peculiar authority. "The Government", as Greaves puts it, "is the master of the country, and he is the master of the Government." He forms it, he can alter or destroy it. He is the Chairman of the Cabinet, which formulates policy, and is the chief coordinator of the policies of several Ministers and Ministries. He is also the leader of the chamber to which the cabinet owes responsibility and that chamber looks to him as the fountain of policy. He is also recognised to have an immediate authority to correct what he may consider the errors of omission and commission of his colleagues in the government. Their identity is unknown without the Prime Minister. The Cabinet is, thus, a unity in collectivity and the question of divided responsibility does not arise. In the United States, the President is the real executive and his 'cabinet' works under his direction and guidance. They are his subordinates. His 'cabinet members' may make speeches in support of the general policy of the administration and may even initiate a line of policy, which having been approved by the President, may be described as their own contribution, but the ultimate source of policy remains the President. Laski remarks, "But, in general, the American Cabinet Minister lives and moves and has his being in the context of Presidential thought. However able and distinguished, he is bound to be eclipsed by the major significance of his chief."[2]

States in the past had tried the experiment of a plural executive. In ancient Athens the executive power was divided among a number of officials, each independent of the others. Sparta, in early times, had two kings and the Republican Rome had two Consuls, both invested with the executive power, and each could veto the action of his colleague. France, too, after the revolution, established plural executive under several different constitutions. Till recently, Switzerland, Russia, Yugoslavia and other Communist countries of Eastern Europe presented systems of plural executives. The executive authority of the Swiss federation is exercised by a commission of seven men known as the *Bundesrat* or the Federal Council. The Federal Council is chosen after every four years by the Federal Assembly and one of its members is annually elected to serve its Chairman and is designated as President. The office of President rotates among the members of the Federal Council according to seniority. The President is in no sense the chief executive, although he holds an office of some dignity and enjoys some precedence over his colleagues. Nor is he the chief administrator. He has no more power than his colleagues and is not more responsible for the exercise of executive authority than other Councillors are. All decisions emanate from the Federal Council as a single authority. The President is simply chairman of the Federal Council and he presides over its meetings. As chairman he only exercises

2. Laski, H., *The American Presidency,* pp. 79-80.

a casting vote and that, too, in case of a tie. Such official authority as he may exercise comes to him as a member of the Council and as head of one of the seven administrative departments.

In the U.S.S.R. there was no formal presidency. The Presidium, a body consisting of thirty-nine members and elected for a term of four years by the Supreme Soviet, performed functions executive in character, which were the prerogatives of the chief executive head of the State in other countries with a single executive. The Presidium had its chairman, designated President officially though not constitutionally but he had neither any special privileges nor any individual authority. Stalin called the Presidium a "collegiate President." The Constitution described the Council of Ministers as the highest executive and administrative organ of State power. But under a system of one-party government the policy determining and directing force was the inner circle of the Communist Party. The Presidium was, however, a unique institution indigenous to the Soviet system and without a parallel anywhere else. The People's Republic of China, Yugoslavia and other Communist States patterned their executives on the Soviet model.

Many advantages have been claimed for a plural executive. An executive organised on the collegial principle, it is claimed, does not afford temptations and opportunities for abuse of power. To vest the supreme authority of the State in a single person is a relic of absolutism and is, consequently, opposed to the spirit of republicanism. A plural executive, its admirers argue, may lack the advantage of unity and energy, which characterise a single executive, but a group of men are likely to possess more ability and wisdom than can be found in any single individual. The executive functions involve not merely the ministerial function of executing legislative command but also the formulation of policy. This onerous task can best be performed by a board consisting of the wisest and the talented. Finally, plural executive renders more difficult executive encroachments on the legislative power and on the liberties of the people.

The experience of plural executive has, however, demonstrated its inherent weakness. The practical working of the plural executive in Switzerland has been really admirable. But one single exception does not set a precedent. Its success there is mainly due to certain habits and traditions of the Swiss people. And then the executive in Switzerland is not a separate and independent organ of the government. It is subordinate to the National Assembly, which is sovereign and functions on its behalf. In the USSR the directing force remained the Politburo, the inner circle, of the Communist Party and those who directed the Party had their due place in the Presidium of the Supreme Soviet. Here, too, the Presidium functioned on behalf of the Supreme Soviet. Modern political opinion is almost unanimous in favour of unity in the organisation of the executive. Plural executive lacks force, energy, unity of purpose and independence. It destroys responsibility, delays action by the necessity of consultation and hence establishes feeble government. Feeble government is another name for bad government. "Energy in the executive," Hamilton said, "is a leading characteristic of a good government."

MODE OF CHOICE OF THE EXECUTIVE

Five different methods of choosing the head of the State have been followed in practice: the hereditary principle; direct election by the people; indirect election by a body of electors chosen for that purpose; election by the legislature; and nomination.

Hereditary Principle. The hereditary principle is associated with monarchical governments. The term of office is for life and succession goes from father to son governed by the law of primogeniture. Hereditary monarchy is the result of historical conditions rather than of deliberate choice and it now survives in a handful of old countries. It is true that a hereditary executive carries with it certain manifest advantages, but the idea of monarchical government is so distasteful in this age that it now assumes only an academic interest. Its ultimate disappearance will doubtless follow in the course of political evolution in the future. Even in Britain survival of monarchy is being widely discussed.

Direct Popular Election. The choice of the Chief Executive by the direct vote of the people is the opposite principle of the hereditary method. This method is the vindication of the principle of popular sovereignty. It grants the people the right to elect their Chief Executive who should represent their will and enjoy their confidence. But, in spite of its popular appeal, the method of direct election has been sparingly adopted in practice. The framers of the American Constitution ruled it out for various considerations. They desired to establish a method which would, as Hamilton put it, "afford as little opportunity as possible to tumult and disorder", and did not "convulse the community with any extraordinary and violent movements." They, accordingly, adopted a plan of indirect election. But, in point of fact, this intention on the part of the framers has been completely defeated, since the system created has been so worked in practice as to establish what is in effect election by popular vote. France adopted direct election at the establishment of the Second Republic in 1848, but abandoned it when the Third Republic was established. In the recent past, France under the Fifth Republic, some of the Latin American States and the former Democratic German Republic deliberately adopted it. But the method is in frequent use in the selection of the "Chief Magistrates" of the territorial divisions of modern States as, for example, the Governors of the constituent states of the United States of America, and of the local executives of the Swiss Cantons.

Many advantages are claimed for the direct mode of electing the Chief Executive. The method of popular election, it is maintained, is more distinctly in accord with the modern ideas of popular government, as it secures the responsibility of the executive directly to the people. When the people themselves have to determine who the Chief Executive should be, they minutely evaluate the merits and virtuous qualities of each candidate seeking election and the final choice falls on a man in whose ability and integrity they have faith. Such a system stimulates interest in public affairs, affords a means of the political education of the masses and presents the example of a government by the people.

But there are some serious objections to this mode of popular choice. The masses are incompetent judges for electing so high a personage as the head of the State. The electors can easily be influenced by the demagogue, who always tries to play with their emotions, and the popular choice may not be the best. Moreover, periodical elections of the Chief Executive of the State create political tension and excitement in the country. Political rivalry, factious intrigues and often corrupt methods employed by the party machines account for general demoralisation. "As soon as one candidate is elected, those who aspire to succeed him proceed to canvas the people. Party feeling is perpetuated and at election time it often becomes very bitter; it may even lead to foreign intrigue."[3] Hamilton feared that direct election would "convulse the community with extraordinary and violent movements and lead to heats and ferments" that would disturb public tranquillity. Popular election of the Chief Executive under the parliamentary system produces a radical change in the character of public life. The Chief Executive becomes the standard bearer of a party or a combination of parties. He could hardly be expected to maintain, under these circumstances, the mediating role as head of the nation. If he is popular and commands the respect of the people, he may use his position and authority to the detriment of the party in power in case of disagreement between the two and even make a bid to become a hero. If ever it happens, even perchance. it shall be destructive of parliamentary democracy.

Indirect Election. Indirect election is more common. It involves election by an electoral college elected by the people. In theory, the President of the United States of America is elected by an electoral college in which every State has as many representatives as it has in both the Houses of Congress. The method of indirect election claims the advantage of avoiding the heats, tumults and convulsions of direct election. The choice of electing the executive head is left in the hands of persons who are better qualified to judge than the masses. When the final choice rests with a small body of representatives, the selection is likely to be intelligent. "It was desirable," maintained Hamilton, "that the immediate election should be made by men most capable of analysing the qualities adapted to the station. A small number of persons selected by their fellow-citizens from the general mass will be most likely to possess the information and discernment requisite to so complicated an investigation."[4]

But all this is a mere theory. The elections are indirect only in name. The immediate representatives, who constitute an electoral college, give little evidence of independence of character and judgment. In almost every country, where political parties are highly organised, the electors are chosen on party pledges to vote for the party's candidate. They hold a definite mandate and are mere party agents with no discretion to exercise their votes. The election of the President in the United States has not only become direct in practice, but it has now assumed the form of an important national pageant. "It is an operation of the first magnitude putting at stake the ambition of individuals, the interest of classes, and the fortunes of the entire country." Nearly everybody in America, from the President in the White House to the man in the street, interests himself in it. It is a momentous event which involves nationwide propaganda and entails an expenditure of millions of dollars on publications, meetings, "rounding up delegates" and "seeing that the goods are delivered." Thus, what was intended to be a scheme of indirect election of the Chief Executive has become in reality a system of direct election.

Election by the Legislature. Election by the legislature is another type of indirect election. The Constitution of India provides that the President of the Republic shall be

3. Gilchrist, R.N., *Principles of Political Science,* p. 307.
4. *The Federalist,* No. 68.

elected by an electoral college consisting of the members of both Houses of Parliament and the elected members of the legislatures of the states. The President of France, according to the Constitution of 1875, was elected by the National Assembly consisting of two Houses of the legislature—the Senate and the Chamber of Deputies—sitting in a joint session at Versailles. Under the Fourth Republic, too, the President was chosen at a joint meeting of both Houses. In Switzerland, the Federal Executive Council is elected by the Federal Legislature.

The idea underlying this method of election is that selection should be made by those who are best qualified to exercise their judgment in public affairs. The members of the legislature are sure to make a wiser selection than the general mass of voters or intermediate electors constituting an electoral college. Being actively concerned with public affairs and intimately acquainted with the public careers of the statesmen, the members of the legislative assemblies are, of all the persons, more qualified to choose the best man for this august office. This method ensures greater harmony and cooperation between the legislative and executive departments, thereby avoiding all possibilities of friction between the two.

But election of the Executive Head by the legislature is a negation of the theory of the Separation of Powers. When the Executive Head is elected by the legislature, he becomes its nominee, and this may lead to political bargains, intrigues and jobbery. "It would be in the power of an ambitious candidate," observed Judge Story, "by holding reward of office, or other sources of patronage and honour silently but irresistibly to influence a majority of voters and thus by his own hold and unprincipled conduct to secure choice, to the exclusion of the highest and purest and most enlightened men in the country." Such a method of election is sure to impair the independence of the Chief Executive and make him subservient to the will of the legislature. It, also, seriously interferes with the normal functions of the legislature, particularly at times of great and exciting contests. This may not only lead to unnecessary waste of parliamentary time and energy, but also gives "a party colouring to the consideration of many measures which are in reality non-partisan in character."

There is, however, no doubt that the system of election of the Chief Executive by the legislature has given excellent results wherever it has been experimented with. In all these countries the election of the President takes place with little or no popular disturbance. The modern tendency is, accordingly, in favour of election by a legislature.

Nominated Executive. Nominated executive, for the most part, exists in dependencies of some great powers. The Governor-General, during the British rule in India, was a nominated executive. Similarly, the Governor-General of Korea was appointed by the Emperor of Japan and the Imperial Diet. The choice of the incumbent of the office is made on the basis of his qualifications and special fitness for the job which he is called upon to supervise. The Governor-General of Canada as well as that of Australia were appointed by Her Majesty the Queen on the recommendations of the Governments of their respective States from amongst Englishmen in public life, or the nationals of their own countries. These countries had preferred such a method of appointment themselves and it did not make them subordinate to Britain. Both Canada and Australia are sovereign States.

Term of Office. Opinions differ as to the length of the term for which the Chief Executive should be elected. In practice, the executive tenure ranges from two years, which is the rule in many states in the United States, to seven years. which is the term of the President of the French Republic, The President of India holds office for a term of five years, whereas it is only four years in the case of the President of the United States. The term of the Swiss Federal Council is four years and the office of its President rotates every year among its members. The nominated Governors-General of Canada and Australia were appointed for a term of five years.

The argument in favour of short tenures for the executive is that the shorter the period of office, the greater the security against abuse of power. There had prevailed a strong belief in the democratic countries that executives with long tenures are always exposed to a temptation to transform their offices by means of a *coup d'etat* into monarchy tenure, as Napoleon did when he converted his Consulship of ten years into one for life and then into an imperial office. Whatever be the verdict of history, there is no denying the fact that too short a term of office, like one or two years, is politically inexpedient. A short term makes the executive timid, weak, lacking in independence, and without a policy. There is neither any inducement nor any incentive to initiate either a new policy or a programme. The most that can be expected of the majority of men, under such circumstances, will be "the negative merits of not doing harm instead of the positive merit of doing good."

Popularly elected Executives are generally amateurs in the art of administration. By the time they acquire some familiarity with their duties and responsibilities, their brief term of office expires and they quit. The result is that another amateur comes in who is as much inexperienced as his predecessor was. Continuity of executive policy and stability of administration are impossible under such circumstances. Moreover, short tenures mean frequent elections accompanied by the inevitable popular excitement and commotion.

The term of office for the executive head should neither be too short nor too long. A very short term of office bears no fruit and a very long term may lead to abuse of power. A four to five years' term has much more to commend it. It is long enough to constitute energy, stability and efficiency in administration. It can also ensure responsibility of the executive to public opinion. It is a period, observed Chancellor Kent, reasonably long enough to make the executive "feel firm and independent in the discharge of his trust and to give stability and some degree of maturity to his system of administration." A six-year or seven-year term is not favoured. It is considered to be an unduly long term. A responsibility which cannot be enforced at shorter intervals than once in six or seven years manifestly loses much of its effectiveness.

Re-eligibility for Office. A long term of office obviates the necessity of re-eligibility. But when the tenure is short, the desirability of re-eligibility of the executive head becomes an obvious necessity. There is, however, a variety of practice. In some Latin American States the Constitution forbids re-election. In Argentine, Brazil and Chile a second term election is permitted after the lapse of a specified intervening period. The Constitution of the United States, till the Twenty-second Amendment became effective in 1951, was silent over the re-election of the President. It simply provided that the President would be elected for a term of four years. President George Washington set a precedent, limiting it to two terms. This was scrupulously followed till President Franklin D. Roosevelt broke it and offered himself for the third and fourth terms and was re-elected. The Constitution now limits it to two-term election. The Irish Constitution permits one term re-election. The Burmese Constitution, too, was limited to one term re-election. The Constitution of India does not impose any express limitation to the number of terms for which the President may be re-elected. When the first President Rajendra Prasad was elected for the second term, a non-official Bill was sponsored in the House of People in 1957, favouring restriction to two consecutive terms. The Bill was withdrawn after the Law Minister expressed the view that such matters should be left to convention and not decided by statute. Dr. Prasad did not offer himself for election for a third term, and thus, a two-term precedent was set.

Many advantages are claimed for a single term. Ineligibility to a second term, it is maintained, tends to secure independence in the executive, and it serves as a check upon the personal ambitions of the head of the State. A man who knows that he is not eligible for re-election will not pander to the people. In all his public acts he will maintain independence of character and judgment, When re-election is permitted, he will undertake nothing new and a large portion of the latter part of his term of office will be occupied in matters relating to his election and to the neglect of his official duties.

But the consensus of opinion is in favour of re-eligibility of Executive Heads elected for short terms. The advantages of re-eligibility were nicely summed up by Hamilton in *The Federalist*. He asserted that re-election of the executive was necessary "to enable the people, when they see reason to approve of his conduct to continue him in the station in order to prolong the utility of his talents and virtues, and to secure to the government the advantage of permanency in a wise system of government." The system of re-eligibility enables the State to retain the services of experienced and talented men who command public approbation and confidence. To forbid re-eligibility is to deprive the State of the services of a wise and experienced statesman. "What could be more strange," maintained Judge Story, "than to declare at the moment when wisdom was acquired that the possessor of it should no longer be enabled to use it for the very purpose for which it was acquired." A man who is assured of re-election can best harmonise his interests with duty. Re-eligibility helps him to rise high in the service of the nation. "The desire of reward and fame," to quote Hamilton again, "is one of the strongest incentives of human conduct; and the best security for the fidelity of mankind is to make their interest coincide with their duty." The rule of ineligibility, on the other hand, creates in the Executive Head a tendency to make the best use of the opportunity in order to promote personal ends. He "might not scruple to resort to the most corrupt expedients to make the harvest as abundant as it was transitory." Finally, re-eligibility ensures stability in administration. If re-eligibility is not permitted, administration would drift along without plan or policy.

The expediency of re-eligibility, however, depends upon the length of the term of office and the extent of power which the executive head actually exercises. One elected for six or seven years can manifestly be made ineligible for a second term but the executive head elected for, say, four or five years should obviously be made eligible for the second term to increase his responsibility.

FUNCTIONS OF THE EXECUTIVE

The most fundamental executive functions are those which relate to essential activities of government. The modern State is a complex structure, and it has to cater for the satisfaction of innumerable human needs. The province of the State has, consequently, considerably increased and modern governments have become more socialistic in their outlook. We do not agree with the old theory of Individualism that the State is a necessary evil and its only function is to preserve internal peace and external security. Our political outlook is entirely changed. The State is now regarded as a means for achieving the welfare of man. It must provide for that atmosphere in which welfare can best be realised. If this is the *raison d'etre* of the State, then, no rigid line of demarcation can be drawn to define its functions. There is, however, no uniformity between the executive functions of one State and those of the other. Broadly speaking, the essential functions may be enumerated as:

Internal Administration. Every State is a politically organised society. The purpose of the State cannot be realised, unless there is internal peace and order. It is the foremost duty of every executive to devise ways and means in order to ensure the maintenance of peace within the country. The department which is responsible for the maintenance of internal peace and order is called the Home Department, or the Department of the Interior—the nomenclature varies from State to State.

Then, it is the duty of the executive to implement policies and direct the execution of laws. It entails the division of the work of government into different departments and agencies and their organization in such a manner as to ensure efficient and effective administration. It also coordinates the business of government. Various departments of government do not function in watertight compartments. They act and react upon one another.

The political executive appoints secretaries and other top officials to head the various administrative departments. In the United States, Secretaries are appointed by the President with the consent of the Senate. In Britain, India and other countries with a parliamentary government, they are appointed, in terms of law, by the Chief Executive of the State, but, in actual practice, the Cabinet does so and, to be more precise, they are really the choice of the Prime Minister. They hold office at the pleasure of the head of the State, though their removal is governed, according to the provisions of the Constitution and laws enacted by Parliament. In the United States the power of the President is unqualified. The Supreme Court has ruled that the consent of the Senate is not necessary in case of removal, as it is in the case of appointments.

External Administration. All States are sovereign and independent. But no State can lead an isolated life or exclusive independence. All States exist under conditions of mutual dependence. To ensure mutual peace and security and to avoid all acts of aggression against one another, States adjust their differences, if any, through diplomatic negotiations. In order to further international goodwill and amity treaties are concluded and representatives are appointed in foreign countries. The department of government which conducts foreign relations is called the Department of Foreign or External Affairs. The conduct of foreign relations includes the reception and dispatch of diplomatic agents and recognition or non-recognition of the independence or legitimacy of new States and governments. It negotiates and concludes, through its representatives, treaties and agreements. In some States the treaty-making power of the executive is subject to approval and ratification of one or both the Houses of its legislature. In the United States the Senate ratifies all treaties. Although the legislature, generally, controls the foreign policy of a country, yet it rarely interferes in the actual administration of the foreign department, as the conduct of foreign affairs requires high technical skill, secrecy of information and personal tact.

Defence and War. It is the essential function of the executive to secure territorial integrity of the State and to protect the country from external aggression, and when necessary, to wage war. The problem of common defence today is entirely different from what it was a century or so before. No country can afford to wait for defence until war is declared. It must always be prepared to ward off the probabilities of war and to win, if it actually comes. The department, which is concerned with the defence of the country and controls its military operations, is called the Defence and War Department. This department may be bifurcated into two—internal defence, and war-department when a country is in the midst of hostilities. The Defence and War Department determines the strength and organisation of the armed forces of the country, Army, Navy and Air Force, and appoints the general and other commanders. In Great Britain, the Executive has the power to declare war independently of the legislature. In the United States war can be declared by Congress and in India it is declared by Parliament. But in every country the powers of the executive during the period of war increase immediately and immensely. Usually the legislature expressly confers powers on the executive to control production and transportation, to establish rationing, to institute censorship, and to suspend the operation of certain guarantees of rights and civil liberties. Even when such powers are not conferred, the executive may take any action necessary to safeguard the safety of the State and ensure the successful prosecution of war.

Financial Functions. All governments spend huge sums of money every year to perform their multifarious functions. When money is to be spent, it must be obtained by some means. Governments meet their expenditure by taxing the people and by tapping other sources of income. This is an executive function and the department which makes provision of ways and means is called the Finance Department or the Treasury. This department is the most powerful, because it not only allocates money to the different departments but also regulates and controls their expenditure through audit.

Legislative Functions. The legislative functions of the executive vary with the form of government that prevails in the State. It is everywhere the right of the executive to summon, adjourn and prorogue the sessions of its Parliament. In countries where there is a parliamentary government, the executive dissolves the popular House and orders fresh elections. It can also convene special sessions of the legislature whenever necessary. The executive furnishes necessary information to the legislature regarding the needs of the country, either at the beginning of the session, or from time to time, during the continuance of the session. The Speech from the Throne, at the opening of Parliament in Britain, or the Presidential Address, on the opening day of the session of Parliament in india, is, generally, the exposition of the policy which the government desires to pursue and the legislation in pursuance of that policy which it intends to enact. In the United States the President has the right to send messages to Congress, embodying the various legislative actions considered expedient, including the budget.

In a parliamentary government the real executive, that is the Ministry, is part of the legislature; it controls the time schedule of the legislature and, thus, provides the much needed element of leadership to the legislature. It is the function of the executive to initiate and pilot all public bills and see them through in the legislature. All bills passed by the legislature must receive the assent of the executive head in order to become laws. He can also veto or refuse his assent thereto. The veto power has, however, fallen into disuse in most of the countries with parliamentary government; in others it is only a suspensive veto. For example, in India the President can withhold his assent to a bill. But when he does so, he must send the Bill to Parliament for reconsideration along with his message. If Parliament again passes it either with or without amendments, the President must give his assent thereto. In Britain, legally the King may refuse assent to anv bill passed by Parliament. But this power of the King has now become obsolete; it has never been exercised since 1707. In a non-parliamentary or presidential government the power of vetoing a bill by the Chief Executive is an effective control over the legislature, although it may not be an absolute veto, as in Britain. The President's veto in America can be negatived on reconsideration of the Bill by a two-thirds majority vote in each House of Congress. Nevertheless, it is a potent instrument in his hands, because two-thirds majority in each House is difficult to secure. The President also exercises what has come to be known as a "pocket veto," and it is absolute. If the President fails to sign a Bill within the specified period of ten days and if Congress adjourns within that period the Bill lapses and is automatically killed. A considerable number of last-minute Bills, to which the President may be opposed or for which he does not want to take responsibility, are not assented to and, thus, fail to become law. The Presidents have generously used this device. President Jimmy Carter killed in a single day, November 11, 1980, three Bills he considered inflationary. The veto power vested in the executive is, therefore, valuable as a means of preventing hasty and ill-considered legislation and gives the executive a means of defence against encroachments on its powers and prerogatives.

In every country the executive is armed with the power of issuing Ordinances. It is a sort of subsidiary power of legislation which takes the form of decrees. Frequently, this power is expressly conferred on the Chief Executive by the Constitution. The Constitution of India empowers the President to issue at any time, except when both Houses of Parliament are in session, Ordinances, which will have the same effect as Acts of Parliament. Every such Ordinance must be laid before both Houses of Parliament and it ceases to operate at the expiry of six weeks from the reassembly of Parliament or if before the expiry of that period resolutions disapproving it are passed by both Houses. In the absence of an express authority in the Constitution, it is deemed to be an inherent power of the Chief Executive to issue Ordinances. In countries with a monarchical form of government, the Ordinance issuing power is considered a part of the royal prerogative, unless there is a constitutional or statutory limitation to it. This device of legislation has still more enhanced the legislative powers of the executive.

The increased range of activities of the State has forced Parliaments, during recent years, to delegate wide legislative powers to the executive. The legislative delegation of authority may be effected in various ways. For example, in Britain Parliament may legislate in general terms on some question and leave one of the departments to work out the detailed regulations necessary to give effect to the statute. It may also merely empower a department to make rules with regard to a specified matter. Rules, Regulations, and Orders so made are known as delegated or subordinate legislation and have the force of law. They are declared unconstitutional only if they offend against the parent law.

Delegated legislation is quite inescapable in the context of a modern State and it has significantly added to the powers of the executive. It is also an ideal arrangement for an emergency as it arms the executive with power to take immediate action. The Committee on Ministers' Powers in Britain, while dealing with this aspect, reported: "In a modern State there are many occasions where there is a sudden need for legislative action. For many such needs delegated legislation is the only convenient or even possible remedy." Moreover, delegated legislation enables the Executive to provide for all the unforeseen contingencies arising out of reform without having to return to Parliament for amending acts or for additional powers. Delegated legislation also relieves the pressure on parliamentary time by removing details of administration from Acts of Parliament.

Judicial Functions. The right of pardon or clemency is, by common consent, regarded as a natural and necessary part of executive function. This is a semi-judicial function and is justified for various reasons. In the first place, it is intended to correct an error of judgment of the judiciary which cannot be rectified otherwise. Moreover, a judge decides the case on its merits and not on grounds of political expediency. Many persons may be convicted of political offences, but with the lapse of time their detention may become inexpedient. By vesting the executive with the power of pardon, the release of such persons can be ensured.

A very important result of delegated legislation is the emergence of administrative adjudication empowering the executive agencies designated by statutes to hear cases involving particular fields of administrative activity. Finer maintains that "wherever there is administration and law, there is administrative law." The great majority of legislation passed by Parliament of every country and Regulations made thereunder relate to matters of public administration and vest judicial power in the executive to administer the law. Delegated legislation has naturally made the executive more powerful than before. This has evinced a stout protest and Lord Hewart in England reflected the attitude of alarmed jurists in his book, *The New Despotism*, and called to the attention of the public the dangers that he believed to be attendant on this development.

Other Functions. The functions enumerated above are usually regarded as essential functions of the executive. But, as stated above, we cannot circumscribe the functions of a modern government. No government can afford to ignore subjects like commerce, education, agriculture, transport, communications, etc. These are beneficient departments and without their proper development it is impossible to promote that atmosphere which helps to advance the welfare of man. Similarly, most of the governments now actually run certain public utility services, and impose statutory restrictions on the production and sale of various commodities. These changes in the province of the State have been introduced as a result of conscious attempts to bring the economic organisation in conformity to the moral and political ideas. Much has been done to moralise our economic system and "coordination, regulation and control, initiative and encouragement, in many cases ownership, are regarded as essential in these fields; and the departments concerned are little less important in the eyes of the public than the so-called essential or major departments."[5] The scope of the modern State has, in fine, increased enormously and with it have expanded the functions of the executive. Finer has given a matter-of-fact summing up of the enormity of its task. He says that the scope of the State today "hardly fails to envisage any branch of the moral or material sides of human endeavour. The record is written on the roads, the gutters and the buildings and spells what the State has done in order that society may have a modicum of wisdom, protection of persons against criminals and mechanically propelled vehicles, and environmental and personal defence against deadly bacteria. The annual thousands of Rules and Orders, the detailed and present plan of activity of all modern States, reveal how the State concentrates upon each individual and weaves his very impulse into the myriad threaded warp of its existence....The State is everywhere, it leaves hardly a gap."[6]

Executive Leadership. The development of the executive into what may be called a multi-functioning organ is one of the notable features of the modern government. To quote Ernest Barker, "If the growth of the legislative organ, in consequence of the development of the cabinet system, was the notable feature of the eighteenth century, it may be said that the growth of the executive organ, in consequence of the extension of rights and the corresponding extension of services which mostly fall to the lot of the executive, is the most notable feature of the twentieth." For a brief era between the decline of absolute monarchies and the twentieth century, parliamentary supremacy was proclaimed, the functions of the government were limited, and the power of the executive seemed to give way before the "omnipresent hand of Adam Smith which brought economic and political equilibrium." But the normal situation is that the executive leadership is concerned, as Chester Bernard argued in *Functions of the Executive*, with the determination of objectives, the initiation of policy, the manipulation of the means, control over the instruments of action, and stimulation of coordinated action.

The core of political power in modern systems, both developed and developing, lies in the executive organ of government and the administration it serves. Its legislative leadership is unchallengeable both in Parliamentary and Presidential patterns. It initiates, guides and pilots legislation in a Parliamentary government. When Cabinet has determined on a policy, the appropriate ministry or department carries it out either by administrative action within the framework of the existing law or submits a new bill to Parliament so as to change the law for the effective implementation of the new policy. Legislation is the handmaid of administration and Cabinet is the instrument which directs Parliament to action in a certain way and so long as it can command a majority in Parliament it gets the necessary approval. We cannot make a vivid distinction between legislation and administration. "In modern State," writes Jennings, "most legislation is directed towards

5. Gilchrist, R.N., *Principles of Political Science,* p. 316.
6. Finer, H., *The Theory and Practice of Modern Government.* p. 1165.

the creation and modification of administrative powers." The Cabinet plans the legislative programme at the beginning of each session of Parliament. Public bills are introduced and piloted in Parliament usually by a Cabinet Minister or by some other Minister acting on Cabinet's approval. Cabinet is, therefore, the legislative leader and, truly speaking, it legislates with the advice and consent of Parliament. Even the Opposition expects the government to lead the legislature, as the Opposition of today is the government of tomorrow. Summing up the leadership of the executive, Ogg maintains that the Cabinet "formulate policies, make decisions, and draft bills on all significant matters which in their judgment require legislative attention, asking of Parliament only that it gives effect to such decisions and policies by considering them and taking the necessary votes."

In the Presidential system, the President is not merely *a* chief executive, but he is also *the* executive. In the presence of checks and balances the legislature considers itself as equal to the executive. But really it is not. The status and position of the President is exalted. He has been justly described as a party leader, chief legislator, and general mobilizer of public opinion. The role played by outstanding Presidents of the present century, such as Wilson and Roosevelt, is an accurate description of leadership both in the legislative and executive branches. The President has a direct access into the legislative field through his constitutional powers to send messages, to recommend measures, to summon special sessions, and to veto bills. In addition, he has many other means to supplement his political strategy. By the use of patronage, "Jobs could be traded for votes. By effective appeals to the voters through the spoken word, press, radio, and lately television, chief executives have been able to dramatize their programmes and compel consideration of their views" and get them accepted even if the legislature is hostile. The issue of executive leadership is projected in the comparative analysis Harold Laski made about the President. He said that the President of the United States is "both more and less than a king; both more and less than a prime minister."

The executive, apart from and in addition to its work of suggesting and guiding the process of law-making through the legislative assemblies, also acts as a legislature when it issues Decrees, Ordinances, Rules, Regulations and Orders. The power of issuing rules and regulations is exercised in virtue of delegation of a legislative power authorised by the legislature itself. It has now become a normal practice with all legislatures to pass laws in general terms, leaving discretionary authority with the executive to fill in the gaps, and this is tantamount to legislating in fact. In 1931, the Gold Standard (Amendment) Act empowered the Treasury in Britain to legislate for the control of the Exchange. The National Economy Act empowered the King-in-Council to effect reductions, including cuts in salaries, in certain public services. The National Recovery Act, 1933, authorised the President of the United States to organise and regulate the industries, to create new agencies, to make regulations for them, to delegate functions for subordinates, and to do other things deemed necessary to bring about economic prosperity. The Trade Agreement of 1934 empowered the President to make trade agreements with foreign nations and lower the existing tariff rates by 50 per cent.

The extension of services, particularly social services, which has largely caused the growth of executive legislation, has also caused the growth of judicial jurisdiction of the executive. This aspect is rather more serious than is the growth of executive legislation.

When the legislature confers "a measure of legislative power upon the executive, it takes something away from itself; but when it confers upon the executive a measure of judicial power, it is diminishing not itself, but an organ other than itself." Administrative adjudication, as it is called, is the latest addition in the armoury of executive powers. It may be defined as the process by which administrative agencies settle issues arising in the course of their work when legal rights are in question. According to Leonard White, "Administrative adjudication means the investigation and settling of a dispute involving a private property on the basis of law and facts by an administrative agency."[7]

The exact role of the modern executive is reflected in the increased activities of the State. Planning and active service, the essence of a Welfare State, need unified action, that is, anticipating problems and finding solutions for them. This may include gearing the entire life of the nation to maximise production and equalise the channels of distribution embracing controls over prices and wages to check inflation or restore a favourable balance of payment account. It may involve the stimulation of economic growth, development of public works programmes, ownership or sponsorship of industry, reduction of unemployment to the lowest manageable level. It implies control over taxation and banking loans, over public expenditure and the total volume of expenditure in the community.[8] The State has become increasingly concerned with the extension of education, in all fields of knowledge, not only because this is desirable in itself; but also to provide the supply of competent, well-equipped and specialised man-power to man the complex structure of administration and the various fields of industry and commerce. The "concert of leadership", as Herman Finer names it, is now provided by the executive.

Emergencies call for quick action in order to maintain the safety of the nation from external attack. Legislatures are not appropriate forums for the discussion of military tactics and strategy. Some decisions must be taken on the basis of confidential information concerning the might and military capability of the enemy and it is usually not considered expedient to give too many hints to the other side concerning one's own intentions. The instability of international relations in the modern era had led inexorably to enhanced importance of the military, and consequently also of the branch of government best able to direct the military. Power accumulated in this area has added to the executive's powers in all other regards.

The growth of political parties, with rigid organizational discipline, the need for rational action in the interest of the public, and the urgency of despatch in military and foreign affairs, in brief, have resulted in the shift of leadership in all modern democracies. Executive leadership has, in fact, at all times been essential to the success of government. But "constitutionalism and constitutional democracy," observes Carl Friedrich, "have been confronted with a most delicate task: how to discover institutional patterns which would provide vigorous and effective action, without allowing those who are called upon to take such action to turn into irresponsible despots."[9]

Limits on Executive Leadership. Formal checks on executive power result from

7. White, L., *Introduction to Public Administration,* p. 553.
8. Michael Curtis, *Comparative Government and Politics,* p. 203.
9. Friedrich, C.J., *Constitutional Government and Demacracy,* p. 385.

constitutional limitations. Restraints are the core of constitutionalism and hence some system of restraints is central to the constitution of any regime that aspires to constitutional government. Simply by establishing the framework of government, any constitution in a measure acts as a restraint on power. Provision of specific ways and means for governmental action by implication forbids others. But constitutions go further and specifically limit powers by stating the bounds of governmental authority and by establishing fixed and fair procedures for governmental action. The rules are guaranteed against arbitrary action by governors, that is, men are to be governed only by law.

The rule of law is probably the deepest and strongest tradition of constitutionalism and it has been the central aim of constitutional reform in all lands. Rule of law is nothing more nor less than the principle that public authorities hold and derive their powers and exercise those on the basis of specific provisions of the constitution or the laws made thereunder, and that every act of every person occupying elective or appointive office is done under the authority of law. All such acts are subject to judgment and control by appropriate legal authority as to whether they were in fact justified by law. Where the action of any public authority infringes or abridges his fundamental rights, that legal authority must be a court of law. As a corollary of this principle, those who act on behalf of the government are personally answerable for any illegal act and are liable to trial or civil action for any wrong they may do. No servant of the State can claim special privileges or immunities.

But the most meaningful check on the behaviour of the executive results from the glare of publicity shone by free press and from the presence of an organized Opposition. A free press presents news, expresses opinion, disseminates knowledge, and helps in moulding and shaping public opinion. Political executive in a constitutional democracy is accountable for what it does and there is a periodical and daily assessment of its policies and programmes. The Opposition criticises and exposes the government, press gives it wide publicity and the electorate takes them to task at the next general election. For a constitutional regime responsible Opposition is indispensable. It is not only a restraining factor on governmental behaviour but also an expression of loyal discontent. It possesses a real chance to become the government in the future. Diligent and responsible Opposition is, therefore, the major check which a democratic regime provides upon corruption, defective administration and abuse of authority. Jennings has aptly said that dictators who have to appeal to the country at frequent intervals are the servants of the people and not their masters.

Even in democratic regimes references are often made to President or Prime Ministerial dictatorship. Whatever be the extent of the powers of the President of the United States or the Prime Ministers of the United Kingdom and India, all leaders, as Michael Curtis says, "must have known that it is wiser to use honey than vinegar." The leader cannot use coercion, in any form, too frequently. Nor should he expect his orders to be agreed to and executed automatically. A Prime Minister must always strive to maintain cabinet unity, to accommodate the more extreme supporters to the House, which makes ministerial responsibility and to carry his party with him as also the electorate when time requires that he shall meet it. Similarly, General De Gaulle, with his substantial powers, had to carry the country with him to the extent of avoiding the loss of majority support in the

National Assembly or defeat of his supporters in parliamentary elections. Even a dictatorial executive may find it beneficial to appear limited. It may, for example, issue laws and orders in the name of the assembly, or cabinet, or similar bodies with more revolutionary sounding names, but in practice there may all be agencies to legitimatize the executive, not to check it.

CIVIL SERVICE

As stated earlier, the term executive, in its broadest sense, includes not only the head of the State, but also the entire body of administrative officials, high and low. The real work of administration is done by the permanent members of the government. In fact, the work of government would never be done, if there were only the Ministers. It is true that each department of administration is headed by a Minister, but it is not his business to run the department. His business is to see that the department pursues a definite policy and runs in a certain direction. Those who *actually* run the department and implement the policies of the government are known as members of the permanent Civil or Administrative Service. They have a permanent status and tenure and are selected for their administrative capacity alone. They have no interest in party politics and do not go out of office when a Ministry changes. Permanency of tenure gives to the Administrative Services security of service, and specialisation in their field of work. Permanent civil servants are the reservoir of experience and knowledge. They furnish to Ministers and legislature all information necessary for shaping and enacting policies on a multitude of subjects. Laski says, "Every State is enormously dependent upon the quality of its public officials."[10]

The term Civil Service, therefore, covers the large number of officials necessary to run the machinery of government. This enormous mass, that goes into hundreds of thousands in a large State, is divided into various ministries or departments, together with a multitude of field officers. At the top is a Minister, an amateur and a political head of the department, and immediately below him are the departmental Secretries and Deputy Secretaries, who share with him the direct framing and execution of departmental policy. Then, there are persons of different categories, at the bottom the most junior clerks, employed in the carrying out of ministerial orders and doing all routine work connected therewith. These orders are implemented by officials of the relevant department spread throughout the country.

Method of Appointment. Such being the importance of the Administrative Services in the framework of the government, it is necessary that public servants must be persons endowed with ability, efficiency and a high calibre. "The civil service," writes Sir William Beveridge, "is a profession, and I should like it to become and realise itself as a learned profession." It is, accordingly, essential that recruitment should be based on merit rather than on favouritism. According to Laski, the Administrative Services "must live under the aegis of two rules." In the first place, the executive should possess the least control over the appointment of public officials. When appointments are left to the exclusive control of the political executive, it is a prolific source of corruption in public life. This is clear

10. Laski, H.J. *A Grammar of Politics* p. 89.

from the experience of every modern State. The notorious spoils system in the United States led to administrative dislocation and a public scandal.[11] Before the Haileybury experiment, Civil Service in Britain had little to commend itself.[12] Unless the public service is beyond the reach of the political executive, it is inevitable that the mind of the minister should be devoted not only to the problems of his office, but to the need of rewarding his followers. Public servants recruited under these circumstances "will use the posts they fill not for the importance of their duties, but for lining their own pockets at the public expense." It will deplete the public service of experience, ability, and expertness which are so essential for the efficient conduct of public administration.

Appointment of public servants, therefore, should be made under rules which may reduce to a minimum the chance of personal favouritism. The principle of open competition for recruitment is the only satisfactory method which can commend itself. This means that for all, except purely technical posts, admission to the Administrative Services must be on the sole basis of being able to satisfy suitable tests for the type of appointment vacant. The Trevelan Committee in Britain recommended that "as an indispensable means of attracting able young men into the service, admission should be placed on basis of competitive examinations open to all administered by an independent Central Board." Experience has shown that the competitive examination system has proved the more satisfactory method of selection for the civil service. Another important principle for the recruitment is that entrance to the public service should normally be at the age, when, in a similar position in ordinary life, a young man or woman expects to earn a living.

It means adoption of Civil Service as a permanent career or professionalisation of Civil Service. According to Professor Milton Mandell, it is a system "predicated on recruiting young men and women with capacity to learning and growth, training them in order to develop and utilise their aptitudes, and offering them opportunities for advancement in responsibility and remuneration."[13] Willoughby defines the term Government Services Career as "a system that offers equal opportunities to all citizens to enter the government service, equal pay to all employees doing work requiring the same degree of intelligence and capacity, equal opportunities for advancement, equally favourable conditions and equal participation in retirement allowances, and makes equal demands upon the employees." Prospective candidates are recruited in service at an early age, during their formative period, and are, then, systematically trained in the technique of administration with a view also that they should possess the intrinsic qualities which a civil servant should possess. The theory is that civil service has a distinct character of its own. "It is different," as Finer says, "from business, from an art, from teaching, from other professions. Its objectives are individual, its spirit and methods are special."[14] The young people,

11. Cf. J. Bryce: "Artemus Ward's description of Abraham Lincoln swept along from room to room in the White House by a rising tide of office-seekers is hardly an exaggeration. From 4 March when Mr. Garfield came into power, till he was shot in July following, he was engaged almost incessantly in questions of patronage." American *Commonwealth*, Vol.-I, p. 64.
12. In their evidence before a commission high officials confessed that their departments were full of idle, incapable, aye, illiterate nominees. A select committee in 1853 declared that the Civil Service had become the dumping ground of the unambitious, the indolent and the worthless.
13. M. Marx (Ed), *Elements of Public Administration,* pp. 558-59.
14. Finer, H., *Principles of Public Administration,* p. 206.

therefore, should enter the government service at an age "when their minds are open to influence by the individual character of government activity."[15] By making civil service a career, the government guarantees to its employees permanence of tenure of office, the fullest freedom of advancement and promotion and a comfortable pension on retirement.

It also entails the systematic classification of government jobs. When the employees of a government cover such a large number of people performing diverse jobs and representing almost every vocation, occupation and profession, it is necessary to standardise and classify their positions in order to integrate them into a pyramidal structure. It should really be the *sine qua non* and, indeed, the starting point of public employment. Such a classification and standardisation help to settle the questions of pay, line of promotion, requirements of transfer and other day-to-day matters concerning the service.

How the Government Operates. Government operates through its secretariat. The secretariat is divided into Ministries or Departments among which various subjects of government activity are distributed according to administrative convenience. Each Department or Ministry, under a parliamentary system, is presided over by a Minister. In most of the Departments or Ministries there is at least one junior Minister whose task is to assist the Minister in his administrative and parliamentary duties. Besides the political heads of various Departments are a number of permanent officials and the clerical staff. At the head of each Department is the Secretary who occupies a position of very high responsibility and importance. The Secretary is the key-man in the Department who helps his political chief so that the Department works efficiently and in conformity with the policy of the government. The Secretaries have, in most cases, been so long attached to their respective Departments that they acquire complete grasp of affairs within their own spheres and provide a permanent brains trust to the Ministers, who are amateurs in the art of administration. Then, there are in the Department, possibly a Joint Secretary, a Deputy Secretary, and an Under-Secretary, Assistant Secretaries, Superintendents, and many others who do merely secretarial work of a purely routine character and transmit the orders and instructions to field offices for implementation. The civil servants, in brief, keep the wheels of the governmental machine going and act as agents for the fulfilment of the policy of the party in office. Their rigid neutrality and rigorous impartiality in the political issues is the first code of their official conduct and they serve with equal fidelity, whatever be the complexion of the government. All civil servants owe a temporary allegiance to the party in power and its programme, no matter what their bias or personal conviction. "The first thing," observes Viscount Attlee, "a Minister finds on entering office is that he can depend absolutely on the loyalty of its staff and, on leaving office, he will seldom be able to say what the private political views are even of those with whom he has worked most closely."[16]

Functions of a Department. The functions of a Ministry or a Department may broadly be said to be four. First, a Department must answer for its administration to the people. Since it translates policy into practice, the Department must be capable of

15. Finer, H., *Theory and Practice of Modern Government,* p. 786.
16. *Indian Journal of Public Administration*, April-June, 1955, p. 96.

explaining itself. It means the accountability of administration to both the legislature and the public. The Department must, accordingly, provide to its political chief all relevant information so that he may be able to defend the actions of his Department on the floor of the legislature and on the public platform. It involves that the work of the Department should be so conducted and its policy so framed that it should be capable of "articulate rational defence."

The second function of a Department is the drawing up of its policy. Policy is, in fact, formulated by the cabinet. But all details for the working out of policy so formulated and all routine business connected therewith are left to various departments of the government. Very often the Department may itself devise proposals within the framework of the policy of the government. Such proposals may either be the outcome of the Department's own administrative experience or may be the result of the directions given to it by the political chief. Whatever be their origin, the Department prepares the draft of the scheme, works out its details, and consults the interests likely to be affected by it. If the scheme of the policy cannot be carried out within the framework of the existing law, then, it passes into the stage of proposals for a bill. After it has been approved by the cabinet, it is drafted as a bill to be laid before the legislature. The bill is sponsored and piloted by the Minister in charge of the Department to which it relates and it is his responsibility to see it through. The members of the Civil Service have to remain in attendance in the legislature to assist the Minister with information and advice, whenever he is under fire in the House.

Most modern statutes are "Skeleton" legislations. Legislatures legislate in general terms, empowering the Departments to work out the detailed regulations necessary to give effect to the statutes. The Department will, probably, concurrently with its preparation of the bill, work out regulations and subordinate acts of legislation and shortly after the bill becomes law, will issue them as drafted by the Law Department. In the application of the rules and regulations to specific cases the Minister or a member of the Civil Service may assume a quasi-judicial role and decide disputes accordingly. This is the third function of a Department.

Finally, the function of the Department is to implement policy. When policy has been determined, presented and sanctioned, it becomes the duty of permanent officials of the Department to see that it is faithfully carried out by the field officers appointed at different levels. The Department directs, instructs, supervises and controls, whereas the field officers obey, implement, and report, if necessary, accompanied by suggestions. It is for the Department to accept those suggestions or not. The actual authority flows from the Department, and the actual impact of the officials of the Department is always considerable.

Public Service Commissions. It is a cardinal principle of Civil Service recruitment that the selections should be made by a specially constituted agency, called a Public Service Commission. A Public Service Commission, as a rule, has statutory existence and powers, the object being to ensure the integrity and independence of its members. The members of a Public Service Commission are appointed under special term of tenure, and they can be removed from office under circumstances similar to those of the judges.

The functions of the Public Service Commission are best described in the Constitution of India.[17] It prescribes:

1. The Union and the State Public Service Commissions shall conduct examinations for appointments to the Union and State Services respectively;
2. To give advice;
   (*i*) On any matter referred to them relating to methods of recruitment to civil services and for civil posts;
   (*ii*) On principles to be followed in making appointments, and in making promotions and transfers from one service to another;
   (*iii*) On all disciplinary matters including petitions on such matters;
   (*iv*) On the claim made by any person that the costs of defending legal proceedings against him for acts done or purporting to be done in the execution of his duty should be borne by the Government;
   (*v*) On any claim for the award of a pension in respect of injuries sustained by a person while serving under the government in a civil capacity and any question as to the amount of any such award.
3. Any other functions as respects service conferred by Parliament in the case of the Union Commission and by the State legislature in the case of State Commission.

Administrative Services Evaluated. The Administrative Service embraces all the permanent officials in the State, high and low, that is, a multitude engaged in clerical jobs of a routine nature and those actually concerned with administration, including the highest departmental adviser to the political chief of a great Department of the government. The welfare of the State depends normally far more on the former than the latter. With their expert knowledge they help their political chief to see that the Department works efficiently and in a particular direction. Lord Balfour has given a true picture of the position which civil servants occupy in Britain: "They do not control policy; they are not responsible for it. Belonging to no party, they are for that very reason an invaluable element in Party Government. It is through them, especially through their higher branches, that the transference of responsibility from one party or one minister to another involves no destructive shock to the administrative machine. There may be change of direction, but the curve is smooth."

The higher branches of Administrative Service make a significant contribution even in the determination of policy. The determination of policy is, no doubt, the work of the cabinet or, for that matter, of a Minister, but the preparatory work is the task of the department and in great part the result of the influence exerted by the members of the Civil Service at the top. When the policy has been determined and finally sanctioned by Parliament, it becomes the duty of the permanent officials of the department to see that it is faithfully carried out. The men at the top, again, decide and instruct how best the practical fulfilment of the policy can be realised. The orders are made and given at the pinnacle. Then follows the chain of those who act on those orders and instructions and accomplish the results.

17. Article 320.

In short, these experts functioning at all points of political control and in hierarchies, embody knowledge and experience, exercise the profoundest influence on responsible ministers and chiefly determine the execution, if not also the inception, of policy. The departments supply the details of statutes, many of which must necessarily be of the nature of skeletons, and by virtue of them perform not merely legislative but also quasi-judicial functions, often without publicity, without recognised rules of procedure and without further appeal.

The Administrative Service has been lavishly praised for its efficiency and exceptionally high rating. But it does not mean that it is perfect. There is evidence to prove that merit, in every country, has often been discounted and the evils of political patronage have not been quite so completely eradicated. The nature of examinations conducted by the Public Service Commissions is too academical and the entrants are recruits with no knowledge of the department in which they are to be posted. Administrative Services carry with them all the defects of bureaucracy. Officialism and red-tapism are the rule and not the exception. A certain amount of exactness is, of course, essential in the observance of regulations, but excess in this direction means multiplicity of forms and files and endorsements and records so that the transaction of business is impeded rather than eased. Another danger inherent in bureaucracy is that of "departmentalism"—the danger of splitting up the work of government into different isolated and self-dependent sections each pursuing its own ends.[18] This compartmentalisation results in departmental friction, as every Department plans only for its own betterment without any regard to efficient coordination with others. There is also evinced a tendency of self-aggrandisement and self-importance, because of the professional or expert knowledge of the civil servants. It breeds a narrow outlook.

"The exaggeration of the hierarchical principle makes one fear to do anything at all, when it is possible to shift the responsibility to someone above." Such an attitude of mind produces a flood of paper work, unnecessary noting and a cloud of irresponsibility. Centralisation also means that thinking can only be done by the head of the department, "the Commander-in-Chief." This clearly shows that there must always be "anemia at the extremities and apoplexy or congestion at the brain."

But it cannot be denied that there is almost a uniformly high quality of men and women who are attracted to the Administrative Service in every country. Ogg, while giving a description of the British Civil Service, remarks that amongst the members of this service "some are impelled by a sense of civic duty; some are drawn by the prospect of a career in a field in which the way is open for talent and industry irrespective of family connections; some no doubt are appealed to by a profession which promises a steady and assured income, without much risk."

18. Commenting on a classic case, Marquess Curzon, Governor-General of India, remarked that "departmentalism is not a moral delinquency. It is an intellectual hiatus—the complete absence of thought or apprehension of anything outside the purely departmental aspects of the matter under discussion. For fourteen months it never occurred to a single human being in the departments to mention the matter, or to suggest that it should be mentioned. Round and round, like the diurnal revolution of the earth, went the file, stately, solemn, sure and slow; and now, in due season, it has completed its orbit, and I am invited to register the concluding stager. How can I bring home to those who are responsible the gravity of the blunder or the absurdity of the situation ?"

The defects of bureaucracy — officialism, narrowness of conception and departmentalism — have been counter-balanced by ministerial responsibility in countries with Cabinet form of government. The Civil Service in these countries is very responsive to public opinion and its members adjust themselves to the changes of policy. Then. there is an excellent *esprit de corps* which the service has always displayed and a commendable interest that it has exhibited for its own improvement. The schools of Public Administration and societies of Civil Servants, which exist in every country, aim at maintaining the high ideals and traditions of which Civil Servants everywhere are justly proud. But it must be remembered that bureaucracy is like fire, which is invaluable as a servant but ruinous when it becomes the master. Bureaucracy must be organised on a sound basis and control by Parliament must be proper and effective, if it is to remain a servant. Thus, the administration, and particularly the higher bureaucracy, must be constantly alert both about the purposes of the political leaders of the country and the needs as well as desires of the public. This has become more necessary with the trend of policy making to pass to the executive branch. The emergence of executives as more influential than legislatures, as policy-makers than executors of the laws, has substantially increased the importance of the high-level administrators.

SUGGESTED READINGS

Barker, E.: *Reflections on Government,* Chaps. III, X.

Brown, B.E.: *New Directions in Comparative Politics,* Chap. III.

Bryce, J.: *Modern Democracies,* Vol. II, Chap. LX.

Blunt, E.: *The I.C.S.*

Champman, Brain: *The Profession of Government: The Public Service in Europe.*

Dealey, J.Q.: *The State and Government,* Chaps. XII, XIII.

Finer, H.: *The British Civil Service.*

Finer, H.: *The Theory and Practice of Modern Government,* Chaps. XXII, XXVI.

Garner, J.W.: *Political Science and Government,* Chap. XXII.

Jennings, W. Ivor: *Cabinet Government.*

Lapalombara, Joseph: *Bureaucracy and Political Development.*

Laski, H.J.: *A Grammar of Politics,* pp. 356-410.

Laski, H.J.: *Parliamentary Government in England,* pp. 262-301, and Chap: VI.

Mill, J.S.: *Representative Government,* Chap. XIV.

Ricker, William H.: *Democracy in the United States.*

Sidgwick, H.: *Elements of Politics,* Chap. XXI.

White, Leonard D.: *Introduction to the Study of Public Administration,* Chaps. XXII, XXIII, XXIX, XXX.

Willoughby, W.F.: *Government of Modern States,* Chaps. XIV, XVI.

Willoughby, W.F., and Rogers, L.: *Introduction to the Problems of Government,* Chap. X.

Wilson, Woodrow: *Constitutional Government in the United States,* Chap. III.

21

CHAPTER

Consultative and Advisory Bodies

Need for Consultation. The leadership of the executive, which we discussed in the preceding Chapter, is a clear recognition of the fact that legislative and administrative initiative lies with the executive. This is essentially due to the advance in the functions of the State from protection and order to justice and welfare. The concept of welfare is a broad one. It embraces economic prosperity, moral well-being and the whole system of values that compose the goal of a good life. The result is that the field of government activities has immensely increased and the State has reached from its starting point of man's need for protection to the terminus of an ethical ideal.

If the government is to wisely perform its many functions and advantageous results are to be obtained therefrom, it imperatively calls for alterations in the techniques of doing a job. A government committed to planning and control must proceed on democratic lines and enlist the cooperation of those affected by its policy. There is also another point in it. Planning and control require exercise of wide discretion and judgment which may involve invasion on the sanctities of private life. If welfare is to be real and a matter of substance, it, then, necessitates that those whose liberties are to be limited and even narrowly restricted must be consulted before they come into operation. "The proper use of advisory bodies," maintained Sir Arthur Salter, "is the right answer of representative democracy to the challenge of corporate States." It is, thus, essential that committees composed of well-informed persons equipped with necessary talent and commanding the confidence of the people and the interests concerned should be created for consultation and guidance. Such committees may be intended to serve the cabinet as a whole, and through it parliament as well, or they may function simply in relation to a particular department or office. The government, in short, should be surrounded by organised committees which it must consult in all its transactions. It means prior consultation of all interests which are likely to be affected by the proposed policy or undertaking of the government.

Consultation should be Representative. But consultation must be representative and not selective. If the government appoints people of its own choice, it is no consultation. Selective consultation is a biased expression of opinion which a government can always secure. Real consultation means eliciting opinions from representatives nominated by the interests concerned. In almost every aspect of social life, with which government is likely to be concerned, there are representative organisations which have come into being for the purpose of protecting specialised interests. In the field of industrial relations there are trade unions and employers' federations. The chambers of commerce in almost all civilised countries have a public status. In local government there are associations of different types and the local authorities themselves are representative bodies. There are similarly associations concerned with the welfare of children or of animals, with social services, with scientific and cultural matters and with numberless other activities embracing the life of man. Sometimes, however, there are rival associations, each claiming to represent the same interests. In some cases there are associations representing opposed interests. Government must be certain that if they take consultation at all, it must be representative of all shades of opinion so that it should be comprehensive, otherwise they will be accused of partisan consultation and, therefore, of partiality. If, for example, the Government of India decides to remove protection from the sugar industry, it must consult all the interests involved in the manufacture of sugar the representatives of the manufacturers, cane growers, workers, both skilled and unskilled, chambers of commerce, distributors, and consumers. They should be really the representatives of all interests concerned and not those nominated by government, whose views are already known and coincide with proposed policy of the government. Modern researches in Social Psychology have convincingly proved that no public activity can succeed unless "it functions as an arm of the people." Mere consent means the approval of the ideas and actions of those who put them up for consent. But genuine agreement is the integration of the activities of many who have reason to participate in those activities and own them to be their own.

Purposes of Consultation. The purposes of consultation may be various. A government may genuinely seek information or advice when, for instance, it is not clear how great a demand there is for some reform, or in what shape a reform is wanted. In such a position it might proceed by way of *ad hoc* enquiry through a commission, such as the States Reorganisation Commission appointed by the Government of India, or a Parliamentary Select Committee or a Departmental Committee. The interested associations would then be represented by witnesses who would be summoned along with other witnesses chosen for their expert knowledge or practical experience of the matter under enquiry. Such witnesses, or the associations they represent might, also, be invited to submit or might themselves volunteer to submit memoranda containing statements of their points of view. "A government," says Professor Laski, "which embarks on a policy must offer the means of judging that policy. The opinion it has elicited by organised inquiry is fundamental to that end. The evidence it has collected, the facts at its disposal, can never be refused to its subjects if it is to build its opinion in the reasoned judgment of its citizens."[1]

Then, consultation might be undertaken, and this would apply especially when government has some legislation definitely in mind, in order to test the reaction to its proposals. Such consultation, which helps to shape a bill before it is introduced, enables a government to forestall parliamentary criticism and to take the wind out of the sails of the Opposition. Consultation for this purpose is also sought by departments of the government which have been given power of making rules and regulations under the

1. Laski, H., *A Grammar of Politics,* p. 133.

authority of a statute. In this way, the department is sometimes enabled to make adjustments in the proposed rules, avoiding the unpopularity which it would have incurred otherwise. Finally, a further purpose of consultation may be to keep in touch with public opinion about the administration for which the department is responsible. That is, the department must be capable of explaining itself and defending its actions. Consultative Committees and advisory bodies provide a means of "articulate rational defence." Administration does not operate in a vacuum.

Advantages of Consultation. The advantages of such a method of consultation are obvious. It provides, in the first place, the means of access to the government of all the interests involved in the decision. They get adequate opportunity to give an authoritative and representative exposition to their opinions and, at the same time, get an opportunity to learn and appreciate the point of view of the government. They can, accordingly, oppose or support the policy and decisions of the government more effectively and their appeal to public opinion is direct and based upon actual knowledge and established facts. It is a well balanced judgment capable of organising true public opinion. Secondly, the representatives of the interests concerned can supply to the government authentic and valuable information on which details of the measure may be constructed. They can even suggest the probable results of the working of such measures. "They form, in brief, a deposit of expertise upon the different aspects of policy which, effectively used, creates an atmosphere of responsibility about governmental acts. If the Minister acts upon their opinion, he is at least building upon a foundation of experience; if he rejects them, the creation of an opposition and, as a consequence, of the discussion that is the life-blood of democratic governance, is adequately assured."[2] Moreover, those who stand outside the machinery of government can only be made responsible when they are associated with it. "The only way to do thing for people," emphasises Laski, "is to make them do things for themselves."[3] Such a step is really a democratic step, because by making the people responsible we make their will effective and increase their inventiveness. The people feel that it is their government. This is the essence of democracy. The policy formulated and decisions taken by the Ministers may not always be for the public welfare. The Ministers are essentially swayed in their decisions by two important considerations: the solidarity of the government and the unity of the party which they represent. They have always to keep in mind that the resignation of a powerful colleague, if he happens to disagree with the official policy, must be prevented. Even a compromise may be arrived at which may not be coincident with the public welfare. But such an eventuality is not likely to happen if there are proper and representative channels of consultation. Here the discussion "is rooted in the principles of its subjects; personal considerations are, *a priori*, out of place. The Minister is dealing directly with minds and only indirectly with votes. He is being driven to counter reason with reason. He is being trained in responsibility to choose whose desires must shape his will."[4] Consultation brings the whole hierarchy of services into organic association with public opinion, let in a continuous stream of ideas and suggestions and perform the equally necessary function of educating

2. *Ibid.*, pp. 80-81.
3. *Ibid.*, p. 268.
4. *Ibid.*, p. 82.

public opinion. The officials and experts would thus become advisers of one another and of the public. The cross-fertilization would largely change the spirit of administration. Finally, these thought-organisations would counteract the tendency of legislatures and cabinets to function primarily as will-organisation[5] and of the services to turn into soulless machines. "They would establish an organic relationship between government, knowledge and experience of life, and bring the administration into line with democratic requirements. Thus will political democracy become creative."[6]

Advisory Committees. Laski, therefore, rightly maintains that "the first great need of the modern State is adequately to organise institutions of consultation." The democratic and scientific technique of administration demands the presence of permanent and continuous organs of consultation before decisions are reached by the government. In a sense the cabinet system is a method of government by consultation, because a Minister can, and he does, in the administration of his department, seek the advice of either his colleagues or the Prime Minister. In fact, all vital decisions are made by the cabinet and inter-departmental problems are closely deliberated upon by the ministers concerned and decisions are taken as a result of this consultation. The same is true of the Senate in the United States. The original object for creating the Senate, apart from its legislative functions, was to serve as an advisory council to the President. Although this object could not be realised, yet its various committees are a powerful check on and aid to the powers of the President. The Standing Committees in the Continental countries of Europe not only advise, but also control the administrative departments of government. The Commissions in France, which were originally intended to be simple organs of criticism and suggestion, had, before the Fifth Republic, become the engines of control of the executive. They went even so far as to dominate the administrative departments of the government, and the vigour and independence of the great Commissions were, indeed, the main reasons for the weak parliamentary position occupied by the cabinet in France.

But all such committees in France are constitutional instruments. The combination of executive work and advice, however, can best be done extra-constitutionally by executive action. The best illustration of such committees are the Committee of Defence and the Economic Advisory Council in Britain. The former, originally known as committee of Imperial Defence, is charged with investigation, reporting and recommending on all questions of defence. The Economic Council is charged with the duty of studying and

5. In the will-organisation of modern government the inadequacy of thinking has long been realised. In 1878 Gladstone confessed that protracted experience of public affairs had convinced him that. "Of the more difficult descriptions of the public business, apart from simple routine, it is only a small part that is transacted with the requisite knowledge, care, and thoroughness." In 1879 Lord Roseberry wrote of cabinet meetings, "The collection of heads of departments at sparse intervals to discuss hurriedly topics for which they are often unprepared."
6. Beni Prasad, *A Democratic Process,* pp. 263-64. Miss Follet wrote: "Democracy is not worked out at the polling booths; it is the bringing forth of a genuine collective will, one to which every single being must contribute the whole of his complex life, as one which every single being must express the whole of at one point. Thus the essence of democracy is creating." She further added, "The fallacy and self-and-others fades away and there is only self-in-and-through-others, only others so firmly rooted in the self and so fruitfully growing there that sundering is impossible." Follet, M.P., *The New State,* pp. 6-7.

reporting to the cabinet on commercial, industrial, and other economic problems of general interest.

Equally important is the rise of advisory committees attached to particular departments. The right of the departmental heads to consult informally individuals or groups outside the public service had existed in Britain for generations past. As far back as 1899, provision for departmental advisory committees composed of non-governmental heads began to be made, for example, Board of Education and Board of Trade. During World War I a large number of such committees were provided by executive orders. The Machinery of Government Committee warmly endorsed the advisory committee plan so long as the advisory bodies were not permitted to impair the responsibility of Ministers to Parliament. The general testimony is that departmental advisory committees are rendering valuable service not only by bringing to the departments information and advice based on first-hand knowledge, but also "by inspiring greater public confidence in administrative authorities as being guided by such information and advice rather than by sheer theory of bureaucratic Presupposition."[7] The Advisory Committees in Britain and India have no power to direct or control administrative work or to dictate policy. The ultimate decision is entirely that of the departmental head. But he always decides after he has taken the responsible experts into confidence and heard their point of view. The business of the committees is solely to discuss and advise.

The Government of India, in pursuance of the Cabinet decision of July 1954, constituted a number of informal consultative committees of members of Parliament. They have been formed to enable members to have a glimpse into the working of government departments or Ministries. Each Committee consists of about thirty members. These informal committees do not have any statutory functions or responsibilities. Nothing will be referred to them for decision. It would be for the Minister concerned to determine what to discuss in these committees and what to divulge to them. Quite a sizable number of Advisory Committees were attached to the machinery of the Central Government in 1962, and since then some new committees have been set up, the more important being: Board of Trade, Advisory Committee on Economic Policy, National Advisory Council, National Defence Council, and Citizen's Central Council.[8] The number and nomenclature of some of the Committees have since changed as a result of organization and reorganization of the Ministries. The five Zonal Councils are also advisory bodies intended to bring about better cooperation and coordination between the States included in each Zone.

Functions of the Advisory Committees. No one can deny the utility of the advisory bodies. "We think," reported Lord Haldane's Committee on the Machinery of Government in Britain, "that the more they are regarded as an integral part of the normal organisation of a department, the more will ministers be enabled to command the confidence of Parliament and the public in their administration of the services which seem likely in an increasing degree to affect the lives of large sections of the community." A government which summons Advisory Committees, places before them the policy which it intends to

7. Ogg, *op. cit.*, p. 111.
8. Shriram Maheshwari, "Committees in the Central Government (India)", Supplement to *Indian Journal of Public Administration,* Vol. IX, No. 3, July-September 1963, pp. 186-200.

pursue, and listens to the criticism of the interests concerned, is, undoubtedly, very different from a government which secures the support of its policy as a result of party allegiance.

But what should be the functions of such committees? It must be emphasised, again, that Advisory Committees have no executive function. They are extra-constitutional institutions and the ultimate decision is that of the government. Even if they have a statutory existence, they are to advise, as their name suggests, about administration; they are neither to direct nor to control it. Nor are they to prepare any policy. It is the sole concern of the Minister concerned or the Cabinet. Generally, the functions of the Advisory Committees may be reduced to four. First, the committee has the right to be consulted on all proposed bills before they are initiated in the legislature. The department should submit all proposed bills to the committee for criticism. A free and frank discussion should be organised at a conference between the Minister and his permanent officials on the one side, and the departmental Advisory Committee on the other. The bills should be explained and examined threadbare. The committee might offer its suggestions, leaving the Minister free to reject or accept them.

Secondly, the committees should be consulted upon general administrative policy. It would, of course, depend upon the discretion and choice of the Minister to decide about the matters that he should refer to the committee of consultation. The Minister may not refer any matter at all to the committee and act without consultation. It would, however, be advisable if it is made possible for each member to suggest matters for discussion and entitling him, "in the event of ministerial objection, to an explanation of the hostile attitude."[9]

The committees, in the third place, should be given the widest scope to make suggestions. Here, indeed, the Advisory Committees can make useful contribution and prove their real utility. The members chosen on the committees for their expert knowledge and representing special interests are in the best position to suggest ideas and it is highly beneficial for a government to explore them. In the opinion of Laski, "It is one of the few ways open to us to correct the dangers of professional conservatism. A Committee of Ministry of Justice, for example, upon which the lay mind as well as the legal mind found place, could indicate a score of places in the law where the need for revision and experiment is essential."[10]

We have already discussed how the legislatures of today are flooded with work, and with the increase in the area of State activity the major portion of detailed and exhaustive statutes has been replaced by skeleton acts the details of which are, in various ways, filled in by the departments concerned. This growth in the power and discretion of the departments, which also amounts to increase in the powers of the permanent Civil Servants, needs to be checked and the advisory committees are the best instruments to serve this purpose.[11] Laski makes a very concrete proposal in this connection. He says, "No

9. Laski, H.J., *A Grammar of Politics,* pp. 380-93.
10. *Ibid.,* p. 381.
11. *Ibid.,* p. 382.

department shall issue orders under its delegated powers without having first consulted the appropriate consultative committee; and that in the event of objection from the latter the order shall not be issued without the specific approval of the Legislative Assembly."[12] This is a negative function and the fourth in enumeration.

Committees to advise may, thus, be consulted at any stage in the process of administration—in the formulation of policy, in its application or administration or in the review of policy and its application, and finally, on orders, rules and regulations which the department will issue under its delegated powers. In practice, as Professor Wheare says, "it is at the stage of application or administration that committees to advise are most widely used, while the committee to inquire is more usually found either at the stage of formulation or at the stage of the review of policy."[13] Professor Wheare has arranged committees into six types: (1) committees to advise; (2) committees to inquire; (3) committees to negotiate; (4) committees to legislate; (5) committees to administer; and (6) committees to scrutinize and control. And "the principle upon which arrangement has been made is that of the function of process," he says, "which the committee carries out rather than of the institution of which it forms a part or with which it is connected."[14]

All these functions are merely consultative and advisory. Consultation does not imply shifting of responsibility to the consultative bodies. The responsibility of the Ministers, to repeat, must remain unimpaired. Laski says that the method of seeking consultation is not intended "to divide power in order to make it responsible; what is essential is to make coherent the organs of reference to which the power must defer."[15] There is inherent in the notion of committee an idea of a derived status; it lacks original jurisdiction.

Composition of the Advisory Bodies. What judgment can we make upon the value of the committees to advise? In determining the usefulness of a committee to advise its size is, undoubtedly, important. Prof. Wheare says, "It may be said, with a little dogmatism perhaps, that if a committee to advise is so large that its members have to stand up and address each other, it is unlikely to be effective."[16] The departments bring advisory committees into existence because they feel the need of obtaining knowledge either from experts or from interested parties. Where discussion proceeds by way of conversation rather than of set debate and the members sit round the table, the discussion is effective, difficulties are removed, misunderstanding eliminated, objections brought to light, compromises suggested and finally a *modus vivendi* reached. This is the real purpose of consultation. If the size of the committees is small, there is give and take of discussion round the table and appreciation of each other's point of view. Professor Wheare, accordingly, suggests that where an advisory body is large, it can be effective only if it breaks itself into sub-committees, and meets as a full committee to discuss the reports of

12. *Ibid.,* p. 383.
13. Wheare, K. C., *Government by Committees,* p. 45.
14. *Ibid.,* p. 2.
15. Laski, H., *A Grammar of Politics,* p. 382.
16. Wheare, K.C., *Government by Committees,* p. 63.

these sub-committees, or to discuss certain questions of general principle. "In fact most advisory committees," as Professor Wheare says, "are small, and where they are large they break up into panels or sub-committees. If they do not do so it is difficult to escape the conclusion either that they do not mean business or that they are intended to do business." Fifteen or nearabout is an effective number.

"It is wise to guard against advisory committees being too big," further says Professor Wheare, "it is wise also to guard against the members themselves being too big." There is a general tendency to appoint to some committees, particularly at the national level, eminent and distinguished persons "who are found in practice so eminent and so busy and so remote from the day-to-day work of the organisation they represent, that they are in fact not of much use as advisers." They "circulate" from one advisory committee to another, seldom knowing about the business of any one committee. They are so much preoccupied in other matters that they have neither the time nor the initiative to master a subject and contribute to the discussion which is the purpose of the advisory committees. Professor Wheare, accordingly, suggests that advisory committees composed of less eminent people can really do valuable work. "The best advice is often to be obtained," he says, "from persons of less eminence, still so little in demand that they are able to master fully one branch of knowledge or activity." Shriram Maheshwari, in his paper on the "Advisory Committees in the Central Government (India), suggests that "while appointing persons on these committees, the primary consideration should be their qualifications, experience and probity." He further suggests that since committee work is in addition to a man's principal avocation, "he should be required to submit his occupation workload and other preoccupations, and the Government should evolve suitable yardsticks to ascertain objectively whether he may spare time adequate enough for the work of the committee."[17]

Then, the consultative committees must necessarily be representative of two kinds of members: (a) majority of the total membership should be chosen representatives of the interests concerned with and affected by the decisions of the department; and (b) a small minority nominated by the Minister to represent technical knowledge and experience, and special interests indirectly affected by the policies of the department.

Laski suggests nomination for a period of three years subject to the renewal of the terms, depending upon the absolute discretion of the appointing body. As regards the election of the members, he says, they "should preferably be elected by the Councils of their nominating bodies, miners by the executive of the Miners' Federation, teachers by the Council of the National Union of Teachers, and so forth. They should also be paid for their services sufficiently to compensate for lost time, but not enough to make their election sought after on grounds of income."[18]

The emphasis on representative element is of recent origin. It is the result both of the maturity of the representative principle in the modern world "and of the recognition that

17. Supplement to the *Indian Journal of Public Administration*, Vol. IX, No. 3, July-September, 1963, pp. 196-197.
18. Laski, H., *A Grammar of Politics*, p. 330.

though legislatures may have the plentitude of authority, they have not the plentitude of wisdom."[19]

Economic Councils. In addition to the advisory committees, there has been in one country after another, a movement in recent years, to set up central economic councils and to confer on these bodies advisory functions. It is a way of integrating the economic life of the nation and the government takes the initiative of securing the cooperation of associations of labourers, professional men, farmers, manufacturers, traders, bankers, in fact, all major interests concerned in the act of production, and consults them in formulating policies of legislation or administration. Economic councils, therefore, aim to achieve the ideal of national industrial planning within the framework of the capitalist society.

A capitalist economy is the very negation of planned economy. It permits and emphasises economic freedom and the economic activities are the result of independent decisions arrived at by a multitude of persons. There is no coordination and the owners of land, labour, capital and organising ability are free to use their factors of production as they please and dispose of their earnings as they wish. This incoherent pursuit of economic activities is responsible for many economic and political ills and the device of economic councils aims to remove that incoherency in order to maximise the interests of the society as a whole.

The mechanism of modern roundabout production is highly complex and delicate. The producers in one industry are consumers of other industries. The separate trades are one another's customers. So intimately related are the many units in productive machinery that a boom or depression in one tends always to produce a boom or depression in others. This is supplemented by another fact. The workers in one industry are the consumers of the products of their fellow workers engaged in another industry. Distress and depression in one industry consequently creates a vicious circle and there is depression all-round. Just as depression in one industry tends to spread to others, so also prosperity in one industry spurs others to greater efforts. There is, therefore, synchronism of depression or prosperity, because bad times and good times in various industries synchronise or occur approximately at the same time.

No factor of production can, thus, act in isolation. So the urgent need is to coordinate and regulate different and independent economic activities by setting up national economic councils jointly representing labour organisations, associations of industrial employers, chambers of commerce, professional associations, agricultural, banking and insurance groups and consumers' societies. The object of these councils is to assist the Ministry in planning economic legislation and to help Parliament in its consideration of such measures as the council may deem necessary and advantageous for the interests of the nation. It may, accordingly, sponsor a large number of comprehensive investigations in problems like unemployment, housing, industrial organisation, labour relations, international trade and so on and these investigations may become the basis for subsequent legislation. Economic councils are, in every country, now regarded as a valuable aid in the formulation of national policy in economic matters. It must, however, be remembered that their

19. Finer, H., *The Theory and Practice of Modern Government,* p. 454.

functions are essentially investigatory and advisory. They have no legislative functions and no power to make laws. They simply provide "the regular political authorities with vocational representative bodies whose research work and counsel can be of considerable value."[20]

In Germany, the Weimar Constitution of 1919 provided for the setting up of a national economic council and it came into being in 1920. It had a membership of 326 persons arranged in 10 occupational groups. These groups were represented according to their respective economic and social importance. The council did not possess the power of legislation, but the Constitution required that important social and economic measures proposed by the Ministry should be submitted to it for its opinion before being introduced in Parliament. The council was also empowered to introduce such measures on its own initiative and to have its proposals and views presented to the Reichstag, whether or not the Ministry assented to them.

Composed as it was of the representatives of important classes and interests of society, who were experts in their respective spheres, the National Economic Council of Germany was sufficiently capable of furnishing the legislature with expert advice and keeping it informed of the legislative needs of the various interests which it represented.[21] In the first ten years of its existence, the Council "rendered useful service in considering proposed economic and social legislation, initiating occupational measures for parliamentary consideration, and giving the legislative authorities the benefit of its presumably expert advice."[22]

In several other States economic councils have been set up or provided by the Constitution. The Constitutions of Yugoslavia, Poland and Danzig, all provided for the establishment of such councils to assist their legislatures in making laws in respect of economic and social problems. More or less similar councils were also established in Italy, Spain and Portugal. In France, too, a national council was set up by decree in 1925. In 1936, the council was enlarged and given a permanent statutory basis. Its general assembly consisted of over a hundred members representing the consumers, the labouring classes, the agriculture, the commerce, employers' associations, the educationists, the bankers, a small group of expert economists, etc. The Prime Minister was the ex-officio President of the Council. The statutory functions of this body were to investigate national economic problems, and to advise the government thereon. All bills of an economic character, when introduced in Parliament, were to be forthwith submitted by the Ministry of the National Economic Council. All decrees, if they had economic implications, were to be submitted to it. "In addition, the ministry may submit any economic question to it for study, and the same may be done by any parliamentary committee. Or the council may take up any economic problem and submit recommendations on its own initiative."[23] Any Plan, or any bill dealing with a Plan, of an economic and social character was submitted

20. Munro, *The Government of Europe,* p. 455.
21. Garner, J.W., *Political Science.and Government,* p. 664.
22. Ogg., *op. cit.,* pp. 650-51.
23. Munro, *op. cit.,* p. 454.

to it for its advice. The recommendations of the council were made to the Prime Minister, but its reports were to be laid before Parliament.

The British Economic Council consists of twenty persons. The Prime Minister is the *ex-officio* Chairman. The Chancellor of the Exchequer and three other Ministers are its *ex-officio* members. It also includes such other Ministers as the Prime Minister may name and varying representatives of business, cooperative, trade union, scientific and other interests. "On the whole," says Ogg, "the council's usefulness has not yet been demonstrated convincingly."[24]

Recently, a further consultative device has been operated by the Board of Trade in the shape of "working parties." The functions of these bodies are to examine the organisation of the main consumer's goods industries and their methods of production and distribution, and to make recommendations for increasing efficiency. In each "working party" one-third of the members belong to the employers, one-third go to the Trade Unions, and one-third are independent members nominated by the President of the Board of Trade. The President of the Board has also nominated an independent chairman.

"It has become plainer and plainer," says G.D.H. Cole, "to those who have watched the operation of the economic councils in Germany and other countries that bodies which are based on the balancing of forces between the representatives of employers and workers are incapable of any real constructive achievement."[25] The interests of the employers and the employees are essentially conflicting, and there is very little hope to reconcile them under the existing economic structure of society. The result is that economic councils in all the countries where they exist, have shown no sign of any independent initiative leading towards a reconstruction of the industrial system. The powers of these councils are merely investigatory and advisory. They have been given far too little authority to achieve any considerable result. Moreover, in most cases their membership has not been such as to stimulate confidence and hope that they are likely to develop into satisfactory planning bodies. "They have been constituted by too little of experts and too much of representatives of conflicting industrial interests, and their members have been, for the most part, far more intent on preserving the structure of the capitalism and preventing the growth of Socialist enterprise than on developing any coherent national industrial plan."[26] But Cole's plea is for vocational representation which has hardly found favour in any country.

Referring to the National Economic Council of Germany, Laski had said that its power of initiating measures in parliament "tends to lead it to multiply suggestions for legislation without having the responsibility to carry them into effect."[27] It entailed upon Ministers a serious burden of extra labour. "The need to appear and speak before it, the knowledge that its activity is always encroaching upon the margin of the Reichstag's

24. *Op. cit.*, p. 110, note.
25. *Intelligent Man's Guide Through World Chaos*, p. 593.
26. *Ibid.*
27. *A Grammar of Politics*, p. 88.

competence, the satisfaction of its immeasurable appetite for documents and information, are rather a hindrance than a help to the channels of administration proper."[28]

SUGGESTED READINGS

Cole, G.D.H.: *A Guide to Modern Politics,* pp. 411-14.

Cole, G.D.H.: *The Intelligent Man's Guide Through World Chaos* pp. 591-95.

Finer, H.: *The Theory and Practice of Modern Government,* pp. 452-58.

Laski, H.J.: *A Grammar of Politics,* pp. 80-85, 266-70, 375-87.

Ogg, F.A.: *European Governments and Politics,* pp. 110-12, 650-54.

Shriram Maheshwari: "Advisory Committees in the, Central Government (India). Supplement to the Indian Journal of Public Administration. Vol. IX, No. 3, July-September, 1963, pp. 186-200.

Verson, R.V., and Mansergh, N.: *Advisory Bodies, A Study of Their Uses in Relation to Central Government,* 1919-1939.

Wheare, K.C.: *Government by Committees.*

28. *Ibid.*

22 CHAPTER

The Judiciary

Importance of Judiciary. The administration of justice, the chief task of the judiciary, comprises the third organ of the governmental machinery. The welfare of citizens greatly depends upon speedy and impartial justice. James Bryce has aptly remarked that there is no better test of the excellence of a government than the efficiency of its judicial system. The judiciary is the guardian of the rights of man and it protects these rights from all possibilities of individual and public encroachments. The feeling in an average citizen that he can rely on the certain and prompt administration of justice maximizes his liberty. If there is no adequate provision for the administration of justice, the liberty of the people is jeopardized, for there is no definite means which should ascertain and decide rights, punish crimes, and protect the innocent from injury and usurpation. "If the law be dishonestly administered," says Bryce, "the salt has lost its flavour; if it be weakly and fitfully enforced, the guarantees or order fail, for it is more by the certainty than by the severity of punishment that offenders are repressed. If the lamp of justice goes out in darkness, how great is that darkness."[1]

In ancient polity the executive and the judicial functions were combined. The early monarch was the fountain of justice. But it afterwards came to be realized that justice could not be secured if the judicial and executive functions were combined in one person. Historically, the concentration of power to interpret and administer in the same hands has always been associated with tyranny.[2] Every citizen needs the amplest protection against the danger of a capricious interpretation of law. The modern State is, accordingly, inconceivable without a separate judicial organ functioning independently and impartially.

Principles of modern justice. Such being the importance of the judiciary, it is necessary to know some basic principles of almost universal application on which modern justice rests. The first, of course, is that there is in every State one judicial system, and one law, both the creation of the State, and administered by judges and other officials appointed for that purpose. Every member of the community is subject to that law, and is entitled to its protection. It means that law must apply to all men as men and equal protection of life for everyone under the law, and equal penalties for everyone violating it. Justice must, therefore, be administered strictly according to law and no one may be

1. Bryce, J., *Modern Democracies*, Vol. II, p. 284.
2. Laski, H.J., *A Grammar of Politics*, p. 129.

punished for any offence, which the law does not consider an offence. Punishment must only be what the law prescribes for a particular offence and it must always remain the same for the same kind of offence. The object of punishment is not vengeance, but the protection of society from the criminal and those who may imitate him. Also independence of the judiciary is practically a universally accepted principle of modern justice. It is a crime for the judges to receive "a bribe or for anybody to offer them one, or to threaten them, or bring any kind of pressure to bear on them. It is also wrong for the government to interfere, by trying to secure condemnation or acquittals; verdicts must be given in accordance with the facts and with the law governing the case, and not to suit the desires of politicians or other influential persons."[3] This means that in modern civilised life the character, means and methods of justice raise or debase a nation in the estimation of other people. Laski expresses the same idea rather emphatically when he says, "When we know how a nation-State dispenses justice, we know with some exactness the moral character to which it can pretend." Sidgwick, too, had said that "in determining a nation's rank in political civilisation, no test is more decisive than the degree in which justice, as defined by law, is actually realised in its judicial administration, both as between one private citizen and another, and as between private citizens and members of the government."[4]

Functions of the Judiciary. Administration of justice is, thus, the chief function of the judiciary. Courts are agencies for the decision of disputes between individuals, and between them and the State, and for the trial of persons accused of crime. But while deciding disputes and punishing criminals, courts do a number of important things beyond the settlement of controversies. The first thing that the courts do is to investigate and determine facts. In the greater majority of cases coming before courts, whether civil or criminal, the law involved is clear and no legal issue is presented. The function of courts in all such cases is simply to determine facts according to the recognised procedure. The procedure is that the parties involved in the case produce evidence. Evidence consists of oral or written statements of witnesses. With the facts determined, the next step is to apply the existing law to such facts and render decisions. To a judge it is a matter of no importance whether, in his opinion, the law is good or bad, just or unjust. He is to accept the law as it is and apply it to the ascertained facts. A judge is, therefore, the interpreter of law.

But it may happen, as it does frequently, that the existing law may be ambiguous and it may be so worded that it is difficult to determine its exact meaning, or that with constantly changing conditions, issues are presented which were not considered when the laws were made or the existing laws may be inconsistent with each other and doubt may exist in respect of which two provisions or which of two laws, should govern in a particular case. It is here that the courts have the very important function of determining what law is, what is its scope and meaning, and when there is an apparent conflict between different laws, which shall prevail. Judges weigh the merits of the case and are guided in their decisions by the principles of justice, equity and commonsense. And in doing so, they set precedents to be applied and followed by others in similar or analogous

3. *Ibid.*, p. 542.
4. Sidgwick, H., *Elements of Politics*, p. 431.

cases. Under the doctrine of what is known as *stare decisis* (the matter has been decided), a legal principle enunciated in a decision made by a court, is deemed to be of a controlling force in similar or analogous cases thereafter arising. Dicey observed, "The adhesion by our judges to precedent, that is their habit of deciding one case in accordance with the principle, or supposed principle, which governed a former case, lends inevitably to the gradual formation by the courts of fixed rules for decision, which are in effect laws."[5] Apart from removing ambiguities in the law and filling in the gaps, the judges adopt and recognise customs, and give them the decisive support of the public power. Here the judges act in a quasi-legislative capacity and judge-made law is an important feature of the judicial system in Britain, the United States, India, and many other countries. The judges are, thus, interpreters of law as well as law-makers and a large volume of law is made up of 'judge-made' laws.

There is yet another way in which the courts can, and to a certain extent do, participate in the determination of law. This consists in the duty, which the constitution may impose upon judges of the Supreme Court of a country, to give advisory opinions. The Constitution of India confers on the President the power to refer to the Supreme Court any question of law or fact which, in his opinion, is of public importance. He may refer such a question not only where it has actually arisen, but also where it appears to the President that it is likely to arise. The President can refer to the Supreme Court whether a proposed bill will be *intra vires* of the legislature or not. Similarly, the Canadian Supreme Court Act, 1906, authorises the Governor-General to refer important questions of law and fact and obtain the opinion of the Supreme Court. Some of the American States impose a duty upon Justices of their Supreme Courts to give advisory opinions on legislative proposals, whenever the legislatures may feel grave doubts concerning their constitutionality. In all such cases the judges participate in the determination of law, as the advice asked from the courts may have considerable influence in the creation of law. In some countries a more formal pronouncement of a court, known as a declaratory judgment, may become a device of lawmaking. Here the chief purpose is to secure a clarification of the law and the courts set forth what the law requires, when parties solicit such opinions, without compelling them to go to the expense of litigation. The opinion rendered is binding, not advisory. Declaratory judgments have been used increasingly since 1900 by British Courts and in the United States since 1920.

Another function performed by courts is that of preventing infractions of law and the violation of rights. Originally, courts had no such function. But gradually courts in Britain and the United States took the position that it was not necessary that private parties should wait until their rights had been actually violated before they could appeal to the courts for protection. If such persons had sufficient reasons to believe that attempts would be made to violate their rights, they could appeal to the courts and the courts would issue orders prohibiting such attempts or at least restraining their commission until the rights of the parties were determined. The orders so issued are known as "restraining orders" or "injunctions." If the authority to which such orders are issued disobeyed them, the courts have the power to punish for contempt. In the beginning courts exercised this

5. Dicey, A.V., *Law of the Constitution,* p. 60.

power rather arbitrarily and it had been the cause of a good deal of criticism. Now legislation determining the power of courts to issue injunctions and for punishment for contempt has been enacted in most countries.

The judiciary is also the guardian of a federal constitution. In a federation, the constitution delimits the jurisdiction of the various branches of government. Neither the Central Government nor the federating units can pass legislation which is contrary to the prescriptions of the constitution. This necessitates the presence of an agency entrusted with the function of deciding whether the oridinary legislature has transgressed the provisions of the constitution and it is *prima facie* a strictly judicial function. In some countries their constitutions specifically provide for such a court competent to declare a law passed by the legislature as *ultra vires*. In States where such a constitutional provision is not made, it is assumed that it is inherent in or incidental to the judicial power to question the validity of any law duly made by the legislature. The Constitution of India empowers the Supreme Court to interpret the Constitution (Article 132/147), declare the law (Article 141), and enforce the limitations of the rule of distribution of legislative powers between Parliament and the state legislatures, and other constitutional limitations, for instance, prohibition against enactment of laws in derogation of the Fundamental Rights as enshrined in Part III of the Constitution. This was amplified to the clearest extent in *A.K. Gopalan* v. *The State of Madras*.

There is no direct authority in the Constitution which empowers the United States Supreme Court to declare the constitutionality or otherwise of federal or states acts. Chief Justice Marshall decided in *Marbury* v. *Madison* (1803) that the courts had the inherent right to declare the actions of Congress and the executive invalid. In 1810 the case of *Fletcher* v. *Peck* extended the power of judicial review to the acts of state legislatures, and in 1819 the *Dartmouth College* case put contracts anywhere in the country under federal protection. Since then judicial review has been the prerogative of all courts from the highest to the lowest. Even a Justice of the Peace may exercise this authority in proper cases, although his decision will be certainly appealed against.

Judicial review is, therefore, a term to describe the power of courts to declare acts of legislature or executive of no effect and consequently, invalid if they are found to be in conflict with the Constitution. Summing up this power of the courts, Harold R. Bruce says, "Judicial review is 'a rights protecting service' rendered by the courts—to protect personal rights against legislative and executive action, states' rights against national action, national rights against state action, and the respective rights of executive and legislative bodies—as these various rights are held to exist under the national constitution. It is a virtual necessity in governments having a written constitution, federal division of powers, agencies of limited powers, and guaranteed personal rights."

The power of judicial review has been subjected to serious criticism. The critics maintain that the courts have expanded their authority by this process to such an extent that they have become non-elective superlegislatures. Carl Friedrich says that "The institution of judicial review substitutes the judgment of judges for the judgment of elective representatives of the people whenever doubts exist regarding the full meaning of a constitutional provision." The judges while giving decisions, and in whatever legal dress such decisions are clothed, it is contended, render political decisions. They do not confine themselves to such legal questions as the limits of the federal or state jurisdiction, or the carrying out of legal regulations which are essential to make due process of law (in the United States), but they discuss the advisability of legislation and its conformity to the law of reason. The law of reason and essential justice are what the temperaments, characteristic attitudes and views of the judges are. It is further maintained that all such decisions had come forth with five to four majority in the United States and six to five hitherto in India. The Forty-second Amendment to the Constitution of India fixed the minimum number of seven Judges of the Supreme Court for determining any question of constitutional validity of Central and state laws. No law could be declared invalid unless two-thirds of such Judges held it to be constitutionally invalid (nullified by the Forty-third Amendment). There is much truth in the claim of Chief Justice Hughes of the Supreme Court of the United States that "we are under the Constitution but the Constitution is what the judges say it is." Justice Frankfurter expressed it rather bluntly when he said that "The Supreme Court is the Constitution."

Despite such a severe criticism, judicial review is the "balancing wheel" of the constitution. Judicial interpretation neutralises and rationalises and, thus, balances the various interests and groups in the community. This is a wholesome sign of the strengthening of constitutionalism. No other "constitutional jury than such a judiciary will be sufficiently neutral and detached to exercise effectively the function of the guardian of the constitution." Justice Holmes of the United States made a beautiful statement of the deeper insight into the function of courts and judicial interpretation. He wrote in his famous treatise on the *Common Law*: "The life of law has not been logic; it has been experience. They felt necessities of the time, the prevalent moral and political theories, intuitions of public policy, avowed or unconscious, even the prejudices which judges share with their fellowmen, have had a good deal more to do than the syllogism in determining the rules by which men should be governed. The law embodies the story of a nation's development through many centuries, and it cannot be dealt with as if it contained only the axioms and corollaries of a book of mathematics. In order to know what it is, we must know what it has been and what it tends to become."

But with the emergence of the Welfare State the role of the judiciary has become arduous. Human liberty and human progress function not in isolation or antithesis but in synthesis and the law has to reconcile the two concepts. Individual rights must, accordingly, be defined in the context of public purpose, social utility and personal and social development. At times property rights are given precedence over the public good. The letter of the law may ordain so, but it may be flagrant violation of the spirit of the constitution. Chief Justice Gajendragadkar, of the Supreme Court of India, while delivering the Feroze Gandhi Memorial Lecture in New Delhi (1964), observed: "If the judicature is the custodian of the Fundamental Rights of the citizens, it is also the interpreter of socio-economic philosophy underlying the welfare laws."[6] The judges must realise that the constitution is a living document meant for the welfare of living human beings. Its words, therefore, must not be interpreted in a static manner or in the strict dictionary sense, if the constitution is to endure long.

6. *The Indian Express*, New Delhi, September 10, 1964.

Judges may be called upon to conduct a judicial enquiry into some serious incidents resulting from the alleged errors of commission or omission on the part of some public servants or agents of the government. A Committee or a Commission, presided over by a Judge, may also be appointed to enquire into some important and complicated matters which require thorough investigation. The Commission may even consist of a single judge as in the case of the Life Insurance Corporation of India, or the Commission, known as Das Commission, to enquire into the allegations made to the President against the Punjab Chief Minister, Pratap Singh Kairon. A similar enquiry was held against the former Chief Minister of Jammu and Kashmir, Bakshi Ghulam Mohammad. The Sarkaria Commission enquired into the alleged charges of corruption against the former Tamil Nadu Chief Minister M. Karunanidhi and some of his other colleagues in the Government. The demand for judicial commissions of enquiry is much too frequent in India and the people are so vocal as to make the demand even on a minor affair or even when there exists no cause for it.

The judiciary may also perform a variety of miscellaneous functions. Strictly speaking, these functions are not essentially judicial in character, but have been assigned to the courts as a matter of economy and convenience. In many cases where the ownership, use or rights, in property are in dispute, courts will take over the administration of such property pending the final settlement. This occurs in the settlement of the estates of deceased persons, and where corporations have failed to live up to their financial obligations. In these cases the court appoints a receiver or administrator to take over the property and administer it subject to its orders. In the case of minors, the court appoints guardians and trustees.

In a number of other ways courts at times perform functions of an administrative character, for example, granting of licences, naturalization of aliens, performance of marriage ceremonies and appointing certain officials.

INDEPENDENCE OF THE JUDICIARY

Need for Independent Judiciary. Justice is considered to be one of the divine attributes and a judge is described as a blindfolded person who holds the scales of justice, which he administers even-handed. In ancient times the function of the judge was vested in the priest. Though in the modern States religion has nothing to do with the machinery of government, except for Islamic countries, yet the sanctity attached to the office of a judge remains unchanged. The functions of a judge are multifarious and arduous. Howsoever just and sound the laws be, unless they are applied by an upright, honest and impartial authority, citizens cannot secure justice. The judges should, accordingly, be men of keen intellect, high legal acumen, integrity, dignity, and independence of judgment. If they lack wisdom, probity, and freedom of decision, the high purposes for which the judiciary is established cannot be secured. Bacon had succinctly said that there was no worse torture than the torture of laws. The torture of law can only be removed or mitigated when judges who apply and interpret the law are independent and impartial. Impartiality and independence go together. By the independence of the judiciary we mean that judges should exercise unfettered discretion in the interpretation of laws and administration of justice, and they should remain uninfluenced in the discharge of their duties. The maintenance of the independence and impartiality of the judiciary both in letter and spirit is the basic condition of the Rule of Law and, as such, that of the liberty of the people, and human progress.

An independent judiciary is as much the need of a popular government as it is that of governments of an autocratic character. In the latter, it is essential to protect the people against the arbitrary interference and oppression of one single person, and in the former it is essential to protect the minorities against the tyranny of the majority and uphold the rights of the people. Truly speaking, no tyranny is so great as that of a majority and a people establishing a popular government had never been oblivious of this. They devised means to avoid this danger and entrusted to the courts the duty of seeing that no branch of government exceeded its powers and that no temporary majority shall infringe the rights of the minority. This point was most cogently explained by President Taft of the United States in his address on the "Judiciary and Progress." He said, "But the judiciary are not representative in any such sense, whether appointed or elected. The moment they assume their duties they must enforce the law as they find it. They must not only interpret or enforce valid enactments of the legislature according to its intention, but when the legislature in its enactments has transgressed the limitations set upon its powers in the constitution the judicial branch of government must enforce the fundamental and higher law by annulling and declaring invalid the offending legislative enactment. Then, the judges are to decide between individuals on principles of right and justice. The great body of the law is unwritten, determined by precedent, and founded on the eternal principles of right and morality. This the courts have to declare and enforce. As between the individual and the State, as between the majority and the minority, as between the powerful and the weak, financially, politically, or socially, courts must hold an even hand and give judgment without fear or favour. In so doing they are performing a governmental function, but it is a complete misunderstanding of our form of government or any kind of government that exalts justice and righteousness to assume. that judges are bound to follow the will of the majority of an electorate in respect of the issue of their decision."[7] The judges must, accordingly, do everything possible to create confidence among the people in the purity, fairness and impartiality of the administration of justice.

The need for independence of the judiciary has acquired an added dimension. Under modern conditions of the Welfare State the more modern government interferes, administers, and regulates, the more urgent is the need to preserve a check on the way these activities affect individuals and groups. The helplessness of the individual in the absence of such control is all too obvious in systems where the judiciary is either dependent or powerless. The courts must, therefore, be separate, independent agencies, bound by their own rules of procedure and determining cases according to publicly known law.

The factors which ensure independence of the judiciary and enable judges to fearlessly discharge their duties are the following:

Mode of Appointment of Judges. Since judicial decisions demand mature judgment,

7. As cited in W.F. Willoughby's *The Government of Modern States,* pp. 433-34.

knowledge of contemporary social and economic conditions, thorough knowledge of law, and the highest personal integrity with ability to be impartial and non-partisan, it is prerequisite that judges should be selected by some method which will emphasise these qualities and minimize political considerations. There is a wide variation of opinion as to the method by which a merited selection can be made.

Three methods of appointing judges are followed in practice: (a) election by the legislature; (b) election by the people; and (c) appointment by the executive. Election by the legislature is not a common and accredited method of appointing judges, because this system is a violation of the principle of the Separation of Powers. But more importantly, it makes the judiciary subservient to the legislature. Moreover, election by the legislature means election of party candidates. When party affinities intervene in the selection of judges, merit is discounted and independence of the judiciary disappears. Such party election encourages a type of judge far removed from the ideal of fairness and reasonableness which judicial decisions demand.

The system of popular election of judges was first introduced in France in conformity to the theories of popular sovereignty and the Separation of Powers. It now prevails in some of the Cantons of Switzerland, and in a few states of the United States of America. But popular election of judges is even more objectionable than election by the legislature. "Of all the methods of appointment," says Laski, "that of election by the people at large is without exception the worst."[8] Popularly elected judges can never be impartial, honest, independent and dignified. Popular election means party election and judges so chosen become subject to popular passion and prejudice. It tends to lower the character of the judiciary. The position becomes still worse when judges are elected for short periods. The desire to court popularity is a temptation few will be able to resist when their re-election is dependent on their popularity. This would create a strong temptation in judges to tailor their judicial decisions and, indeed, their whole judicial conduct in such a way as to meet the approval of those to whom they have to look for re-election. The voters, too, are not in a position to equitably weigh the qualities which a judge should necessarily possess. Moreover, candidates for judicial offices make frequently poor candidates. They cannot possibly put before the electorate either a programme or a personal plea concerning their judicial conduct. The result is that a politician becomes a judge whose entire outlook is partisan, and there can be no independence of the judiciary.

The appointment of judges by the executive is the most common and the best available method of choice, and it is in practice in nearly all countries of the world. It is claimed that the executive is the most appropriate agency to judge the qualities necessary for a judicial office. Judges chosen by the executive are likely to be independent of popular influence and political or sectional considerations. The opponents of this method contend that personal favouritism and political consideration may determine the appointments and instances are cited from Britain, the United States and India. It is maintained that often the appointees are those who had an active political career than a judicial one before their appointment as was the case with Chief Justice Warren, former Governor of California. Laski did not consider simple nomination by the executive as an adequate system. He

8. Laski, H, *J., A Grammar of Politics,* p. 545.

suggested that all judicial appointments should be made "on the recommendation of the Minister of Justice, with the consent of a standing committee of the judges, which would represent all sides of their work."[9] This method, no doubt, represents the best guarantee we could have that appointments are made consistent with the qualities essential in a judicial officer. In Britain, and many countries in the Commonwealth of Nations, the judiciary is generally selected from among practising lawyers. On the Continent of Europe, where court systems are unified under the Ministry of Justice, the judiciary is a career. The entrants are selected as a result of competitive examination and are promoted from court to court. In India, too, recruitment to the subordinate courts is through a competitive examination whereas in the case of courts above, it is according to the method as prescribed in the Constitution, but the appointing authority is the executive.

Judicial Tenure. The judicial tenure is as important as the method of appointment in securing the independence and impartiality of judges. The most common judicial tenure is during good behaviour, with compulsory retirement at a definite age. In most of the Swiss Cantons and some of the States of America, where judges are popularly elected, there are short terms of tenure subject to re-election. But popular election of judges and their short tenures are not politic as they tend to rob the judge of their independence. Freedom and independence are best secured by long tenures. Judges appointed for short terms are likely to abuse their position. They would make the best of their short term disregarding all canons of justice and even the principles of decency. Good behaviour till the age of retirement is, therefore, the method which is the best and is now generally recommended and followed. "The standard of good behaviour for the continuance in office of the judicial magistracy," said Hamilton, "is certainly one of the most valuable of the modern improvements in the practice of government. In a monarchy, it is an excellent barrier to the despotism of the prince; in a republic, it is no less excellent barrier to the encroachments and oppressions of the representative body. And it is the best expedient which can be devised in any government to secure a steady, upright and impartial administration of the laws."[10] Finally, a good-behaviour tenure is necessary to secure full minute and mature knowledge of law and judicial precedents which constitute one of the most important sources of strength in the judicial office. In the course of a long and uninterrupted judicial career, a judge can and does acquire a complete knowledge of precedents, the nature and operation of laws as in other countries, of the psychology that determines human conduct and the social and economic changes which characterise a dynamic society. To understand man and the principles on which law is built is as important as to know the law itself. This obviously cannot be gained by one whose tenure is brief and precarious.

Removal of Judges. Good-behaviour tenure involves the question of removal of judges from office. In all States a provision is made for the removal of corrupt and inefficient judges. But it must be a difficult process so as to obviate the abuse of power and its capricious operation. If the tenure of a judge is to depend upon the pleasure of a particular person or agency, neither independence nor impartiality can be ensured,

9. *Ibid.*, p. 548.

10. As quoted in J.W. Garner's *Political Science and Government*, p. 800.

because the slightest ill-will incurred by a judge may result in the termination of his services. It is, therefore, deemed desirable that the process of removal of a judge from his office should involve much consideration and should pass through the hands of more than one person or agencies. In Great Britain, a Judge can be removed by the King on a joint address by Parliament indicting him for corruption or moral turpitude. In the United States, the Judges of the Supreme Court are removed by impeachment. The process of impeachment is that the House of Representatives prefers the charges and the trial is held by the Senate. In India, judges held office, before 1947, during the pleasure of the Crown. Judges of the Federal Court and of High Courts were removed from office by the Crown for misbehaviour or infirmity, on a report of the Judicial Committee of the Privy Council. The Constitution of India (1950) provides that a judge of the Supreme Court and of a High Court shall be removed from office by an order of the President after an address by each House of Parliament supported by a majority of the total membersbip of that House and by a majority of not less than two-thirds of the members of that House present and voting has been presented to the President in the same session for such removal on the ground of proved misbehaviour or incapacity.[11] A difficult method of removal, where more than one agencies intervene, ensures security of office and it is one of the most important factors responsible for the impartiality of the majority party. But in countries where the system of recall exists, the independence and dignity of the judiciary has considerably deteriorated..Judges become plaything of the people and their vagaries. This method is also opposed for the same reasons for which popular election of Judges is deemed unwise.

Salaries of Judges. Next to permanency of office nothing contributes more to the independence of the judiciary than a fixed and adequate salary. It was judiciously remarked by Hamilton that "in general course of human nature a power over a man's subsistence amounts to a power over his will." To give to Judges courage and firmness in the dispensation of justice, it is necessary that they should be confident of the security and adequacy of their salaries. The salary must be paid regularly and it should be sufficient enough to befit the status of a Judge. Low-paid Judges are very often ill-behaved and susceptible to corruption and bribery. Finally, the salaries should not be alterable during their tenure of office. When in 1931, a special law was passed in Britain to enable the salaries of all government servants, from the Prime Minister downwards, to be reduced as an economy measure, the Judges protested against their inclusion as involving an encroachment upon their absolute independence. The salaries of the Judges of the Supreme Court and High Courts in India are specified in the Constitution. But the President has the power to reduce their salaries during the continuance of the Proclamation of Financial Emergency under Article 360(4) (b).

Apart from the adequacy of salary, it is equally essential that the conditions of service of the Judges should be such as to ensure their independence and impartiality. and are consistent with the dignity of the office that they hold. They should be in receipt of handsome allowances as permissible under rules and be in the enjoyment of other amenities. Their allowances and other privileges should not be altered to their disadvantage during

11. Article 124 (4).

the tenure of their office. Their postings and transfers must not be subject to the vagaries of the executive, if they are to perform their duties with dignity, integrity and efficiency. And above all, the fear of tomorrow must not haunt them. There should exist a specific provision for payment of adequate pension after retirement or retirement compensation. Rules framed regarding termination of their services and removal from office should be such as to protect them against any kind of arbitrary action.

Qualifications of Judges. "The importance of the judiciary in political construction," to quote Sidgwick again, "is rather profound than prominent... in determining a nation's rank in political civilisation, no test is more decisive than the degree in which justice, as defined by the law, is actually realised in its judicial administration...."[12] The men who are to make justice in the courts must be legal luminaries, learned and skilled in their profession. An incompetent judge, not fully conversant with legal niceties and technicalities, is sure to taint the eminence of the judiciary. It is, again, essential that a judge must be reputed for his impartiality and independent views and he scrupulously avoids straying in politics. The strength of the administration of justice depends upon gaining the confidence of the public in general and the litigant public in particular. All these qualifications can best be secured if Judges are selected from the bar; those who have spent their life in the legal profession and have specially prepared themselves for the difficult task of knowing and interpreting law.

Separation of Judicial Functions. It is highly desirable that the judicial and executive functions should be distinct and separate from each other. The same person should not be a prosecutor as well as a judge. If both these functions are combined in the same person, there cannot be justice worth its name. If the prosecutor sits also as a judge there is abuse of judicial authority and capricious administration of justice. The most familiar example in this respect was that of the Deputy Commissioner-cum-District Magistrate in pre-Independent India, who combined the executive and the judicial functions. It is a well recognised complaint that there can be neither independence nor impartiality of the judiciary under such a system. The subordinate magistrates could not go against the wishes of the District Magistrate who was also the executive authority in the district. They decided cases, very often, as the District Magistrate expected them to do. Sir Harvey Adamson, at one time Home Member of the Government of India, pointed out that "the exercise of executive control over the subordinate Magistrates by whom the great bulk of criminal cases are tried is the point where the present system is defective. If the control is exercised by the officer who is responsible for the peace of the district there is the constant danger that the subordinate Magistracy may be unconsciously guided by other than purely judicial consideration." Many States in India have now separated judicial and executive functions but there still remains much to be achieved. The Directive Principles of State Policy, as embodied in the Constitution, enjoin the separation of both these organs of government in order to ensure justice and as a safeguard against encroachments on the rights and liberties of the people.

Committed Judiciary. Judiciary in the former USSR was an arm of the administration and not an independent branch of the government. The Courts there functioned as part

12. Sidgwick, H., *Elements of Politics,* p. 481.

of the political machinery "for guidance, and it has to be ensured", as Polyansky wrote, "by appropriate means that they are truly instruments of the policy of the Communist Party and the Soviet Government...The Party's decisions have absolute binding force for all the State officials, and, therefore, for the judiciary also." In 1967 a clamour was heard in India for a committed judiciary; the type obtainable in the erstwhile USSR and other countries having the same political system. The advocates of committed judiciary wanted from the Judges conformity with the political philosophy of the party in power, if not with their policies and programmes. This meant to appoint persons as Judges who would interpret law in the light of the ideology of the ruling party, and it was only a short step from asking the Judges to decide cases according to the wishes of that political party.

The object of the Constitution framers of India was to keep the politicians off the Bench and to ensure the independence of the judiciary and to enable the Judges to discharge their duties impartially necessary safeguards were provided into the document. But the concept of committed judiciary wanted politicians to reach the Bench. It is difficult to imagine a more dangerous trend in a democratic set-up. It is fraught with the gravest danger to individual liberty and society, if the Judges cloud their judgment with the ideology of the political party in office. A Judge must dispense justice unaffected by the political changes in the moods of the people. The pattern and conception of justice cannot change every time a government changes. Tinkering with judiciary by appointing committed Judges, on political basis, would mean the end of the Rule of Law and the democratic way of life.

ORGANISATION OF THE JUDICIARY

Regardless of their differences in the system of law and courts, States recognise certain well-accepted and uniform principles of judicial organisation. It is essential that the executive should not attempt to influence or control the procedure and judgment of the courts. It is equally essential that the legislature should grant them powers and funds adequate for the efficient performance of their functions. It is also imperatively necessary that the courts should be independent agencies rendering decisions according to publicly known laws and not as instruments of the regime in carrying out its political and general purposes. For example, the Soviet Law of August 1938 prescribed that it was the duty of the Soviet Courts "to educate the citizens in a spirit of devotion to the fatherland and to the cause of socialism, in the spirit of an exact and unfaltering performance of Soviet laws, careful attitude towards Socialist property, labour discipline, honest fulfilment of State and public duties, respect towards the rules of the Commonwealth." The primary function of the Soviet Courts was the protection of the social and State system of the USSR. The Soviet judges, too, had never claimed to be independent of the policy of the government. Really, they took pride in the fact that the courts participated directly in the historic venture of the construction of the communist society. This aspect sharply distinguishes the Soviet judiciary from that of other democratic countries which are wedded to the principles of the independence and impartiality of the judiciary and the Rule of Law.

Courts of Appeal. The organisation of the judiciary is not similar to either the legislative or the executive department. Courts all over the world are organised on an ascending scale, one above another, with a right to appeal from the lower to the higher courts. At the apex there is a final or Supreme Court with powers of revision or cessation, that is, annulling the decision of a court or judicial tribunal. The function of the court of appeal is to make sure that the law is being interpreted in substantially the same fashion in all the different parts of the judicial structure and to reverse decisions which seem to be based upon an erroneous interpretation of the law. In performing their functions courts of appeal must have in mind primarily the general principles that seem to be involved in any case which reaches them, rather than the concrete merits of the immediate controversy. Technical rules governing appeals generally are adjusted to this conception. The cases which reach the highest courts are normally argued there solely on the basis of certain specific dubious points of legal interpretation. In some countries, the highest court of appeal is also vested with an original jurisdiction and such specified cases are tried there.

A court of appeal consists of several judges generally sitting together in a bench and reaching their decisions by a majority vote. Usually, the court gives an opinion explaining the legal grounds for its decision. Sometimes, individual judges give separate opinions, including those judges who disagree with the majority decision and whose opinions are consequently called "dissenting opinions." The judicial opinions of the higher courts are regularly published and these opinions constitute a major authoritative source of law in countries following Anglo-Saxon jurisprudence.

Trial Courts. Trial Courts primarily or exclusively conduct the initial trial of cases. In a trial court both facts and law must be considered. The plaintiff, or prosecution in a criminal case, submits evidence to support his contentions as to the facts of the case. In civil cases much of the evidence, particularly in countries following Roman law jurisprudence, may be in the form of "depositions" sworn to by witnesses outside of the actual trial. In common law countries the evidence in criminal cases must in general be submitted orally in court by the witnesses in person. The testimony submitted orally by witnesses for the plaintiff or prosecution is subject to "cross-examination" by the defence. After the evidence for both the parties has been concluded, arguments are submitted by their respective lawyers and, then, the court renders decision.

In all countries there are special trial courts for petty cases involving small civil claims or minor infractions of criminal law. A single judge usually presides and makes the decision in such courts, and proceedings are likely to be highly informal. Other courts handle the trial of more serious cases, and judges of these courts occupy a relatively high rank. Sometimes an intermediate sets of courts is provided for the trial of offences or of civil claims of an intermediate grade: of seriousness. In most jurisdictions some trial courts with highly specialised jurisdiction exist alongside those which handle the more ordinary cases, for example, courts dealing with the probate and administration of the estate of deceased persons, juvenile delinquency, and claims for compensation for actions of the governmental services.

In countries with federal polity there are usually two sets of Courts: Federal and state or provincial or cantonal courts. The Federal Courts exercise the national or general jurisdiction of the national or Central Government and the state, provincial or cantonal courts exercise the local jurisdiction in each federating unit. In the United States of America the federal government has its own judicial organisation consisting of the Supreme Court, Federal Courts of Appeal, and the District Courts. There is at least one District Court in each state. If the state is sufficiently large with a hefty population there may be many such courts in that state, each having a specified territory under its jurisdiction. Then, each state has its own judicial organisation, and its own law and procedure applicable to the civil and criminal jurisdiction of the state. In India, too, there is the federal judicial organ, the Supreme Court, that stands alone, and the state judiciary. The jurisdiction of these courts differs. But the Supreme Court of India, unlike the one in the United States, has appellate, civil and criminal jurisdiction throughout India, and it performs advisory funcrions also.[13] Moreover, it has no organisation of its own in the states.

In spite of these common features there is, however, considerable variety of judicial organisation in modern States. In the Common Law countries, as in continental Countries, all courts, except those of the justices of peace, are "collegial", that is to say, they consist of a bench of judges, and no judgment is valid unless rendered by at least three judges. "Plurality of Judges," it is believed, "afford a safeguard against arbitrariness and enables the court in criminal cases to resist more effectively the influence of the public prosecutor." There is a proverb in France, *juge unique juge inique* (a single judge is an iniquitous judge), which gives expression to French antipathy to judgment rendered by a single judge. In the trial of serious crimes it is usual to empanel a jury of impartial citizens to determine the guilt or innocence of the accused under instruction as to the relevant legal rules by the presiding judge or judges. In Common Law countries a similar use of a jury is traditional, but now it is less common in practice in serious civil cases as well. Secondly, in France, and other Continental countries, there is unity of civil and criminal justice, which means that civil actions and criminal cases are for the most part handled by the same courts and not by separate courts as in Britain and in the United States. In the third place, in the Anglo-American countries judges go on "circuit", holding courts in different places for the convenience of litigants, that is, the courts go to the litigants. On the Continent of Europe the courts are "sedentary" or localised, that is, courts commonly sit only at one specified place and the litigants take their cases to have them decided.

In Britain, the United States and India, there is the Rule of Law. This means that all citizens—private individuals and public officials—are equal before the law and they are amenable to the same court, the same law and the procedure prescribed under the law. In France, and the rest of the Continental countries, there are two sets of judicial organisation: ordinary courts and administrative courts. Administrative courts deal with the controversies of public officials in their relations both with private individuals and between themselves. The Administrative Law, which is applied in the Administrative Courts, is quite distinct from the ordinary law which the ordinary courts apply. In the Anglo-American countries precedents or 'judge-made' law constitutes an integral part of the judicial process and are applied by courts to identical cases. Continental countries discourage judge-made law or judicial precedents. Finally, in the United States and India,

13. Articles 132 to 134.

judiciary is the guardian of the Constitution and it can declare any law *ultra vires*. In countries like Britain courts must accept and apply law as it emanates from the legislature. They have no jurisdiction to declare it constitutional or unconstitutional.

JUDICIARY IN RELATION TO EXECUTIVE AND LEGISLATURE

Relation of the Judiciary to the Executive. In spite of the emphasis on the separation of the judiciary, as the basis of the independence and impartiality of the judges, the executive exercises a certain control over the judiciary inasmuch as judicial decisions can only be enforced by the executive supported by the force at its command. Should the executive fail to take necessary steps to enforce a decision, the judiciary would have no means of compelling such action, except the *writ of mandamus*,[14] which in those circumstances might be disregarded. Besides, the appointment of judges is made by the executive and although it does not exercise any control after appointments have been made, yet the complexion of the judiciary may be influenced by the party in power responsible for making such appointments. In English speaking countries a lawyer who maintains professional reputation and, at the same time, attains some prominence in politics, may normally expect his elevation to the Bench. In the United States, the President appoints federal judges subject to approval by the Senate. As a result of "Senatorial Courtesy" it is customary that the selection of the District Court Judges is made by the Senators from the state where the vacancy occurs if they are members of the same political party to which the President belongs. In countries where tenure of office during good behaviour is the rule, the character of the appointment of judges may determine the course of government for years to come. For example, the appointment, to the United States Supreme Court, of John Marshall who believed in judicial supremacy, ensured a long line of decisions upholding the right of the federal government to control various matters, even after those who favoured the right of the several states to larger autonomy had gained control of the legislative and executive branches.

In Continental countries there exists what may be called the "career service." In such countries the judicial service constitutes a branch of the general civil service and is usually entered only at its lowest levels by persons who have just completed their legal training. All the higher positions are normally filled by promotions from the lower ranks. This means judges are subject to a certain control of the political authorities who decide and determine promotions. But more important are the judicial powers that are still exercised directly by the executive department, for example, the Court Martial and the enforcement of Administrative Law. The right of granting pardon still belongs to the executive and it is the direct survival of its original judicial function.

The Judiciary, too, in its turn has considerable powers of administration and control over the executive. In all democratic countries the executive is amenable to the jurisdiction of the courts. Its actions can be challenged and appropriate remedies sought by means of an appropriate writ, and if the exercise of authority is deemed in excess of the powers

14. Judicial orders commanding government officials to perform the duties required by law.

vested in it by law such an action may be nullified. The rights of courts to uphold their dignity by instituting contempt of court proceedings and punishing offenders is a great check exercised by the judiciary on the executive. Finally, the judiciary has to perform a number of functions which are, strictly speaking, executive in character, for example, granting of licences, issuing of permits, appointing of guardians and trustees, official receivers etc.

Relation of Judiciary to Legislature. The legislature makes law and the courts interpret and apply it. This is the most obvious relation between the judiciary and the legislature. The legislature sanctions all appropriations necessary for the maintenance of the judicial department. In this way the legislature controls the judiciary. Except in the United States and India, where the federal judiciary is provided and its tenure fixed by their Constitutions, judicial departments are created by legislative statute and may be modified or abolished by legislative enactments. Even in the United States and India Congress and Parliament respectively prescribe the number of judges, fix their salaries, and create new courts. In many States certain judicial powers have been retained by the Upper Houses of their legislatures. In Britain, the House of Lords is the highest court of appeal, although this function is actually performed by the Law Lords. The framers of the American Constitution, influenced by the theory of the Separation of Powers, limited the judicial powers of the Senate, except that it can try cases of impeachment against high executive officials. Finally, judges in certain States are appointed by the legislature. In the United States the Senate ratifies all judicial appointments made by the President.

The judiciary may exercise considerable control over legislation, wherever it has the right, either by precedent or by express grant, to review laws in order to determine their constitutionality. The power of judicial review seems to have reached its greatest height in the United States, despite the fact that there is no express provision in the Constitution which empowers the Supreme Court to declare the constitutionality or otherwise of federal or state Acts. The principle on which it is based was set forth by John Marshall in the famous case of *Marbury* vs. *Madison* (1803). Justice Marshall reasoned that the Constitution is the Supreme Law of the land and the judges are bound by oath to give effect to it. When the court is called upon to give effect to a statute passed by Congress which is clearly in conflict with the supreme law of the Constitution, it must give preference to the latter and hold the former void and of no effect. In India, there is no express provision declaring the Constitution to be the Supreme law. But the power of judicial review by the Supreme Court is subject to no controversy, although its scope is not as extensive as that of the Supreme Court of the United States.

In Britain, sovereignty of Parliament is admitted and no court will declare an Act of Parliament unconstitutional. But enactments of minor legislative bodies may be declared illegal. British courts have also refused to enforce executive orders deemed to have been issued without sufficient legislative authority. They may also declare void rules and regulations which offend the parent law.

The interrelation of the judiciary and the legislature can best be found in case-law or judge-made law. Judges not only interpret law, but they also make it. Whenever a case before a court for decision is not covered by law, it is the duty of judges not to determine what the legislature meant, but "to guess what it would have intended on a point not present, if the point had been present." In this way, judges legislate to fill up the *casus omisus* or the cases of omission. Judges also create a law for the particular case in determining the exact meaning of law, expanding its details and applying the general principles of justice or morality. In Britain, India and the United States, judicial decisions are cited as precedents and are considered binding in subsequent cases on the principle of *stare decisis.* Judge-made law, thus, forms a large part of the system of jurisprudence. In countries where codes based on Roman Law are used, as in France, precedents are not considered binding.

THE RULE OF LAW

Meaning of the Rule of Law. The "rule of law" is recognised as one of the very important characteristics of the British Constitution. It means that in Britain the ordinary law should be everywhere supreme, and every person is subject to the ordinary law courts. There is nothing which may be characterised as arbitrary power. Every action of the government must be authorised by law, either by law passed by Parliament, or by the ancient principles of Common Law which have been recognised for many hundred years. The test is that all actions of government can be appealed against in the ordinary law courts. This remains the general rule, though in recent years there have been encroachments upon it and they have excited some alarm.

The "rule of law" is the product of centuries of struggle of the people for the recognition of their inherent rights. In Britain the Constitution does not confer specific rights on the citizens. Nor is there any Parliamentary Act which lays down the Fundamental Rights. Yet, the people enjoy maximum liberty and judiciary is their unfailing guardian, because there exists "the rule of law." The government have power only to carry out the law, not to do whatever they think fit. The Latin tag *salus populi suprema lex*—the welfare of the people is the supreme law—cannot be used by the government as an excuse for pursuing its own idea of the public interest without regard to legality. Anything done by government officials either beyond law or in excess of law is subject to control by courts. The ordinary law of the land is of universal application and there are no divisions of separate systems of law, for instance, one for officials and another for ordinary citizens. The maxim carries with it the rule that the remedies of the ordinary law will be sufficient for the effective protection of the rights of the citizens. Rule of Law, in brief, ensures liberty and security to all individuals alike and is, therefore, antithetic to arbitrariness and discrimination of any kind. It accepts all men as alike before law and the same law is applicable to all irrespective of their station in life. Rule of Law is really the essence of democracy. Democary subsists where Rule of Law prevails.

Dicey's Analysis. The conception of the "rule of law" was given classical formulation about a century ago by A.V. Dicey. The "rule of law", according to Dicey, has three meanings:

1. "It means, in the first place, the absolute supremacy or predominance of regular law as opposed to the influence of arbitrary power, and excludes the existence of arbitrariness, of prerogative, or even of wide discretionary authority on the part of government. Englishmen are ruled by the law and by the law alone; a man may, with us,

be punished for a breach of the law, but he can be punished for nothing else." It means that the executive has no arbitrary powers over the individual; no powers that had not been sanctioned either by Parliament or by the Common Law. It is the paramountcy of law and its sanction is the consent of the people.

This principle implies that no person may be arbitrarily deprived of life, liberty, or property; no one may be arrested or detained except for a definite breach of law which must be proved in a duly constituted court of law. Trial must be held in an open court with a free access to the public. The accused person has the right of being represented and defended by a counsel and in all serious criminal cases he should be tried by a jury. Judgment is rendered in an open court with a right to appeal to High Court. The presence of these rights reduces to the minimum the possibilities of executive arbitrariness and oppression.

2. "It means, again, equality before the law, or the equal subjection of all classes to the ordinary law of the land administered by the ordinary law courts." It means that everyone is subject to the ordinary law of the realm and can have his rights determined in the ordinary courts.

There are two implications in it. First, equality of every citizen, irrespective of his official or social status, before law. Secondly, there is one kind of law to which all citizens are amenable. All public officials, high or low, are under the same responsibility for every act done by them. If public officials do any wrong to an individual or exceed the power vested in them by law, they can be sued in the ordinary courts and tried in the ordinary manner, and are subject to the provisions of ordinary law. The equality of all in the eyes of law minimises the tyranny and irresponsibility of the executive. Dicey, while elaborating the equality of all before the law says, "With us every official, from the Prime Minister to a constable or a collector of taxes, is under the same responsibility for every act done without legal justification as any other citizen." The general legal theory holds that an executive official is privately liable whenever he oversteps the precise authority which the law assigns him.

3. "The 'rule of law', lastly, may be used as a formula for expressing the fact that with us the law of the constitution, the rules which in foreign countries naturally form part of the constitutional code, are not the sources, but the consequences of the rights of individuals, as defined and enforced by the courts,....It means the main principles of the constitution, such as the right of personal liberty or of public meeting, have been set up on the foundation of the old common law and not as thing derived from any general constitutional theory." Rights in Britain do not flow from the constitution, but from judicial decisions, as in the famous Wilkes' case.

Limitations on the Rule of Law. But the "rule of law", as enunciated by Dicey, is now subject to serious limitations. The great increase in the activities of the State during the past sixty years or so has limited the "rule of law" far more seriously. It is difficult for Parliament to find time to discuss the details of bills which must necessarily contain a long string of highly technical clauses. And in many matters those technical clauses require frequent modifications to meet a changing situation. Therefore, the practice has grown up of enacting skeleton legislation the details of which are to be filled in by the appropriate government department and are to have the force of law. These departmental regulations and orders once made are immune from criticism by courts, unless they conflict with the provisions of the parent law, because they have been given the force of law beforehand. As long ago as 1909, in a case in which the Board of Agriculture authorised the compulsory sale of a farm, Justice Darling found the Board to be "no more impeachable than Parliament itself."

Moreover, whenever there is delegated legislation there is discretionary authority. If discretionary authority is in violation of the rule of law, then the rule of law is inapplicable in any modern State. When Dicey, in 1885, wrote the first edition of his *Law of the Constitution*, the primary functions of the State were the preservation of law and order, defence and foreign relations. Today, the functions of the State are more positive and they regulate the national life in multifarious ways. Discretionary authority is, thus, in every detail inevitable. What is essential to emphasise here is that discretionary power should not mean arbitrary power, i.e., power exercised by an agent responsible to none and subject to no control.

A still more serious innovation is the practice of authorising officials by statute to decide disputes between their departments and private citizens. Acts of Parliament, such as Acts dealing with factory, trade boards, with public health, or with town and country planning, are examples of the kind of enactments that bestow judicial powers upon administrative agencies. Such decisions are usually final, and there is no appeal from them to the ordinary law courts. This means that the Minister for the department or any other officer, whoever has been authorised by statute, has the right to decide questions which affect the right and interests of the private citizens. The officer who actually makes the decision remains unknown to the public. His decisions are made privately, and he is not bound, as the ordinary courts are, by rules of procedure and evidence. Evidence may be excluded at will and interested parties are seldom interviewed. Government departments are not courts in Dicey's sense and they do not follow the judicial mode. And yet they decide cases involving their own actions. The old theory, therefore, that the executive in Britain is strictly accountable to the courts for the legality of all its acts has acquired now a somewhat formal character.

The second meaning given by Dicey to the rule of law requires some qualifications under the existing conditions. In the first place, there remain, even alter the operation of the Crown Proceedings Act, 1947, certain privileges and immunities which are open to public authorities and their officers. Among these may be noted the Public Authorities Protection Act, 1893, which, as amended by Section 21 of the Limitation Act, 1939, "imposes a severe time limit upon actions brought against public authorities and their officers in respect of acts or omissions occurring in the course of official duty."[15] These provisions make it necessary that proceedings against public officials for the excess, neglect, or default of the public authority must be started within six months of the Act, otherwise they lapse. A heavy penalty by way of costs is to be paid if a citizen's suit against public authority fails. Judges are not liable for anything said or done in the exercise of their judicial functions, even if they exceed their jurisdiction, unless the judge ought to have known the facts ousting his jurisdiction.

15. Wade, E.C.S. and Philips, *Constitutional Law*, p. 55.

Then, in common with other civilized countries, Britain, too, gives immunities to the persons and property of other States, their rulers and diplomatic agents, in the form of exemption from process in the courts, but not from legal liability as such.[16] There are even instances where internal political expediency has required the conferment of special immunities. For instance, Trade Disputes Act, 1906,[17] prohibits the bringing of any action against a trade union in respect of a tort.

This apart, two other points may be noted which significantly restrict the operative part of the rule of law. So long as wide social and economic gaps continue to exist between the different segments of society, legal equality does not in fact exist. Litigation today is very cumbersome and expensive and it is beyond the reach of an ordinary man to seek appropriate redress. It also breeds discrimination because those who have the wherewithal have the due protection of law whereas it is inaccessible to those who suffer from the accident of birth and are born in poor families. Moreover, the public officials enjoy certain characteristic rights as compared with private citizens. As Jennings points out, "The Home Secretary can compel me to make up a census return, though my neighbour cannot. A sheriff can summon me to serve on a jury, though my friends cannot."[18]

In spite of these qualifications the rule of law still remains a cardinal principle of the British Constitution and of every democratic government. It is true that delegated legislation and administrative jurisdiction are both the worst enemies of the rule of law. The development of delegated legislation and administrative justice, however, are not only inevitable but, also, with porper modifications and safeguards, desirable. The motive at work is not that of a despot as Lord Hewart asserted in his book, *The New Despotism*. British officials retain a respect for the tradition of the rule of law in which they have been bred. "Their object is usually to avoid, not parliamentary control, but parliamentary delays; not the authority of the law, but the obstructiveness of wealthy litigants."[19] Moreover, the question whether a department is acting *ultra vires* can always be brought before the ordinary courts. In this way, Ministers and officials can at least be prevented from exceeding their statutory powers.

What the rule of law precisely involves is the absence of arbitrary power, "effective control of and proper publicity for delegated legislation, particularly when it imposes penalties; that when discretionary power is granted the manner in which it is to be exercised should as far as practicable be defined; that every man should be responsible to the ordinary law whether he be private or public officer; that private rights should be determined by impartial and independent tribunals; and fundamental private rights are safeguarded by the ordinary law of the land ."[20]

---

16. *Dickenson, v. Del Solar* (1963), I.K.B., 376.
17. Section 4(d).
18. Jennings, W.I., *The Law of the Constitution,* p. 312.
19. Derry, K., *British Institutions of Today,* p. 83.
20. Wade and Philips, *Constitutional Law,* p. 58.

ADMINISTRATIVE LAW AND COURTS

Ordinary and Administrative Courts. In France and other Continental European countries there are two systems of courts. One of these is a system of ordinary courts; the other is a system of administrative courts. The ordinary law and the regular courts are concerned with the administration of justice as between man and man while administrative law is concerned with the adjudication of rights as between a citizen and his government. If a citizen finds that he has been wronged by an official of the State, or the action of that official is the result of bad judgment, or is arbitrary in nature, he can seek redress, but he must seek it from special tribunals which are maintained for that purpose and which apply Administrative Law as distinguished from ordinary law. Continental jurisprudence is largely based upon the Roman Law. It regarded the State as an end itself, the individual only as a means to the perfection of the great body-politic. From this, it naturally followed that those who served the State in an official capacity were entitled to special consideration and for their official acts they could not be made amenable to ordinary law and ordinary courts.

Origin of the Administrative Law and Courts. The Administrative Law and Administrative Courts first found their origin in France as a result of historical circumstances and the political beliefs of the time. Before the French Revolution there was a general aversion to the control which the judiciary exercised over the administrative authorities. The persons actively concerned with the Revolutionary movement felt that if judges were allowed to decide controversies between the State and its administrative authorities, on the one hand, and private individuals, on the other, it would result in judicial interference with the operations of the government and impair the efficiency of the administration. Montesquieu's theory of Separation of Powers had also a great ideological appeal. The result was that in the period immediately following the Revolution, many laws were enacted preventing the judiciary from interfering in the work of administration. Even punishment of judges, who should encroach on administrative functions, was provided in the Penal Code.

The imposition of absolute prohibition on the judiciary resulted in an unsatisfactory situation. Administrative authorities were freed from all judicial control, and for the private individual there were no other means for the relief from administrative excesses except an appeal to their political representatives. According to Revolutionary ideas this was sufficient guarantee against the abuse of authority. But it was otherwise as "the administration possessed a dominant position, and it practised domination." An inevitable reaction to this was many developments which finally helped to improve the position of the individual in his relationship to the administration. The first step was taken by Napoleon Bonaparte by establishing councils of juris consults. At the national level, the Council of State was set up, and in the departments the Prefectorial Councils. Out of these developed the present system of Administrative Courts spreading to other lands as well.

Administrative Law is Case-Law. Administrative Law, or *droit administratif*, in France may, thus, be defined "as a system of jurisprudence which, on the one hand, relieves public officials from amenability to the ordinary courts for acts performed in their official capacity, and, on the other hand, sets up a special jurisdiction to hold them accountable." It determines:

(*i*) the position and liabilities of all public officials;

(*ii*) the rights and liabilities of private citizens in their dealings with public officials as representatives of the State; and

(*iii*) the procedure by which these rights and liabilities are enforced.

But Administrative Law is not codified. Some of the rules have been established by the decrees issued from time to time, while the most important and, by far, the largest part of it depends upon the decisions of Administrative Courts. In this respect Administrative Law somewhat resembles the common law which has been slowly built up in the regular courts by one decision after another. It is essentially a case-law.

Justification of the System. "The French system of administrative law, and the very principles on which it rests," observed Dicey, "are quite unknown to English and American judges and lawyers." This might have been true when Dicey wrote the first edition of his book, *The Law of the Constitution*, but it is not so today. Even at that time Dicey did not give to Admimistrative law its real meaning. Legal relationships are a significant part of the administrative function in the execution of policy. Every administrator is, in effect, a law-enforcement officer. He may rightly or wrongly enforce the law. He may also determine a dispute between parties, which arises under the law and the rules and regulations made thereunder. Certainly the administrator is frequently called upon to apply an interpretation of the law to a peculiar set of circumstances. At times, in some countries, he may be a participant in a legal battle in special or regular courts to defend or ensure his position. Some critics maintain that these statements are broader than are necessary to illustrate the scope of administrative law, but as Finer says, "In short, administrative law is no more mysterious or sinister than simply the law relating to public administration."[21] Wherever there is administration, there is administrative law, though there may not be separate courts for administrative adjudication. In the nature of things there are generally such courts and are named as tribunals. The inevitableness of the growth and existence of Administrative Law and Administrative Tribunals and their place in modern administration is fully established.

Similarly, Dicey was utterly wrong in contending that the system of Administrative Law and courts is antithetic to the Rule of Law and is, therefore, the embodiment of arbitrary or irresponsible power. He pointed out that justice could not be expected from the administrative courts, because the officials constituting the courts would be naturally favourably inclined towards their fellow officials. Nor can the instruments of government, themselves concerned in influencing the policy of the government, be expected to administer justice and adversely affect the policy of the government. Impartiality and independence cannot be secured under such circumstances and individual rights are always liable to be sacrificed when administration is both the offender and judge of the offence.

But in the light of the French experience, it is not true to say that there can be no liberty under a system of Administrative Law and Administrative Courts. On the contrary, Frenchmen have always considered it the cornerstone of their liberties. According to Carl Friedrich, the development of Administrative Law in France and elsewhere "is a definite

21. Finer, H., *The Theory and Practice of Modern Government,* p. 924.

achievement of the constitutional era. For it does not signify the supremacy of administrative officials over the law, but its exact opposite, namely, the standardization for all administrative conduct in terms of legal rules. The central concern of administrative law has been the legal limitation of administrative discretion."[22]

There is also no justification for suspecting Administrative Courts of partiality in favour of public officials. The French Council of State (*conseil d'etat*), as the highest administrative tribunal, has established admirable traditions of impartiality. Duguit affirmed that the great body of case-law worked out by the Council of State, which enjoys considerable prestige as the chief arbiter of the claims of citizens against alleged misuse of power of administrative officials, affords the individual "almost perfect protection against arbitrary administrative action." A private citizen in France gets more real redress from the Administrative Courts than an Englishman gets from the ordinary courts. Administrative Courts are constituted of expert administrative officials and their judgments are bound to have the nature of expert decisions. There are many administrative technicalities and departmental problems which a judge presiding over an ordinary court of law may not be able to understand. As a layman, he is liable to give a wrong judgment. Then, the access to Administrative Courts is so easy and inexpensive. The procedure is so simple and the decisions are speedy.

There is virtue in the Administrative Law being not codified. It is primarily a case-law and a case-law is flexible and adaptable. A law built up in this way covers a wide range. To sum up, as Garner says, "there is no other country in which the rights of the private individuals are so well protected against administrative abuses and the people so sure of receiving reparation for injuries sustained for such abuses" as in France.

SUGGESTED READINGS

Blachlay, F.F.: *Administrative Legislation and Administration.*
Bryce, J.: *Modern Democracies,* Vol. II, Chap. LXII.
Cardozo, B.N.: *The Nature of the Juridical Process.*
Carr, R.K.: *The Supreme Court and Judicial Review.*
Corwin, E.S.: *The Doctrine of Judicial Review.*
Dicey, A.V.: *The Law of the Constitution,* Chap. XII.
Finer, H.: *The Theory and Practice of Modern Government,* Chap. XXXVI.
Frank Jerome: *Courts on Trial.*
Friedrich, C.J.: *Constitutional Government and Democracy.*
Garner, J.W.: *Political Science and Government,* Chap. XXIV.
Goodnow, F.J.: *Principles of Constitutional Government,* Chaps. XVIII-XIX.
Goodnow, F.J.: *The Law and the Constitution,* Chaps. VI, VII, and Appendix II.
Haines, C.G.: *The American Doctrine of Judicial Supremacy.*
Laski, H.J.: *A Grammar of Politics,* Chap. X.
Lowell, A.L.: *Government of England,* Vol. II, Chaps. LIX-LXII.
Marriot, J.A.R.: *Mechanism of the Modern State,* Vol. II, Chaps. XXI-XXXIV.
Robson, W.A.: *Justice and Administrative Law.*
Roche, John P., and Steadman, Murrays: *The Dynamics of Democratic Government,* pp. 309-15.
Sait, E.M.: *Government and Politics of France,* Chaps. XI-XII,
Sidgwick, H.: *Elements of Politics,* Chap. XXIV.
Willoughby,W.F.: *Government of Modern States,* Chap. XV.
Willoughby, W.F.: *Principles of Judicial Administrations.*

22. Friedrich, C.J., *Constitutional Government and Democracy*, p. 113.

23 CHAPTER

The Party System

Definition of a Political Party. Political parties serve as the motive force in crystallizing public opinion, and as the unifying agency which makes democracy workable. They are the indispensable links between the people and the representative machinery of government. They are the vehicles through which individuals and groups work to secure political power and, if successful, to exercise that power. They make people politically conscious, that is, aware of their role as citizens. This role cannot be performed simply by voting, but must be a continuous one if government is to be kept responsive to public interest. Thus, political parties are responsible for maintaining a continuous connection between the people and those who represent them either in the government or in the Opposition.

By a political party, then, we mean an organised group of citizens who hold common views on public questions and acting as a political unit seek to obtain control of the government with a view to further the programme and the policy which they profess. MacIver defines a political party "as an association organised in support of some principle or policy which by constitutional means it endeavours to make the determinant of government."[1] Leacock compares it to a joint-stock company to which each member contributes his share of political power.[2] Every political party is based upon two fundamental aspects of human nature. The first is, that men differ in their opinions, but, at the same time, they are gregarious by nature. If they are to live in society they must adjust their differences with others and agree on fundamentals of certain opinions. Secondly, they combine with persons holding similar views in order to put forward those views in an organised manner, and to support the principles or policy which they jointly favour and support. Five conditions are, accordingly, necessary to constitute a political party:

1. That there must be a certain measure of agreement on fundamental principles which can bind the people together as a political unit. They may differ on details, but there should be no difference of opinion on principles they stand for. If there is no agreement on fundamentals, they cannot cooperate with one another and achieve their political ends; the desire to attain political power.

2. That the men and women holding similar views must be duly organised. Without proper organisation the people make just a disorganised crowd and it is impossible to

1. MacIver, R.M., *The Modern State*, p. 390.
2. Leacock, S., *Elements of Political Science.* p. 311.

conform to the common principles on which they agree. It is their organisation into a permanently cohesive body that enables them to acquire strength so as to act in concert.

3. That the men so banded and organized should formulate a clear and specific programme which they should place before the electorate to win their support and devise all possible means to maintain it. They can only succeed in their mission if all solidly stand for that programme and present a united front. Even the slightest deviation is sure to plague the party.

4. That a political party should seek to carry out its policy by constitutional means. It is the ballot box which should decide the fate of a political party and its claim to form the government. Any organisation that aims at employing unconstitutional methods, that is, to seize power by violence and suppress all other parties, is not a party in the sense we view a political party.

5. That all political parties must endeavour to promote national interests as distinguished from sectarian or communal interests. Burke defines a political party as "a body of men united, for promoting by their joint endeavours the national interests upon some particular principle in which they are all agreed."[3] When a political party directs its activities in furthering sectional interests and selfish ends, it degenerates into a faction. A faction is a loosely united group of men who unite to achieve sectional interests as opposed to national interests.

It will, thus, be clear that a political party without a well-knit organization is nothing. It has neither the means to present nor to promote its programme. It has no national appeal to make and no possibility to succeed in its political mission in winning elections and forming the government. The old conception that a political party is a group of men professing the same political doctrine is not the entire truth now. The einphasis has shifted from ideology to organization and this has been necessitated by the extension in the franchise and consequently the nationwide appeal a political party should have for its programme. Roucek Huszar has said that a political party "is held together, primarily by its ideology and organisation."[4] Carl Friedrich defines a political party as "a group of human beings, stably organized with the objective of securing or maintaining for its leaders the control of a government, and with the further objective of giving to members of the party, through such control, ideal benefits and advantages."[5]

Importance of Political Parties. Political parties are indispensable for the working of a democratic government. They supply the motive-power which keeps the wheels of administration moving. Without political parties, says MacIver, "there can be no unified statement of principle, no orderly evolution of policy, no regular resort to the constitutional device of parliamentary elections, nor of course any of the recognised institutions by means of which a party seeks to gain or to maintain power."[6] Those who deplore the existence and influence of political parties, perhaps, do not understand the working of the

3. Edmund Burke, "Thoughts on the Cause of Present Discontents" in *The Works of Edmund Burke,* Vol. I, p. 530.
4. Roucek Huszar and others, *Principles of Political Science,* p. 447.
5. Friedrich, C.J., *Constitutional Government and Democracy,* p. 419.
6. MacIver, R.M., *The Modern State,* p. 396.

machinery of democracy. As Lowell says, "The conception of government by the whole people in any large nation is, of course, a chimera; for wherever the suffrage is wide parties are certain to exist and the control must really be in the hands of the party that comprises a majority or a rough approximation to a majority of the people." Without party organisation there may be factions and cabals, people appealing and petitioning to government for the redress of personal and sectional grievances. A faction lacks a stable organization and it is a group with a scattered leadership in pursuit of sectional interests. Whereas stable organisation is a distinguishing feature of a political party and it pursues "desirable objectives for the corporate body as a whole" and it functions under recognised leadership. Political parties, thus, seek to make government. They are permanent organizations and their primary business is to influence the electorate to support their programmes, to win election, and to form a government in order to pursue the programme endorsed by the electorate at the General Elections. And for that matter political parties need to be continually operative if a democratic system is to work effectively.

Political parties, therefore, perform a necessary service; they are inevitable like the tides of the ocean. "Their essential functions," says Lowell, "and the true reason for their existence, is bringing public opinion to a focus and framing issues for a public verdict."[7] They are the instruments for carrying on popular government by concentrating public opinion. Their function is to make candidates and programmes known to the public and attract them to those programmes, so that they can speak with a united voice, instead of uttering an unintelligible babel of sound. If the millions went to the polls without any sort of thought and agreement, they would scatter their votes among so many candidates possessing and professing so many divergent views and policies, thus, creating chaos, pure and simple. Political parties make the scheme of representative government workable and in advance of the election help to bring together large numbers of men in acceptance of a common basis of action. The importance of political parties may be summed up in the words of Bryce. He says, "In popular governments, however, parties have a wider extension if not a more strenuous life, for everywhere a citizen has a vote, with the duty to use it at elections, each of the parties which strive for mastery must try to bring the largest possible number of voters into the ranks, organise them locally, appeal to them by the spoken and printed words, bring them up to the polls. Ballots having replaced bullets in political life, every voter is supposed to belong to one of the partisan hosts to render more or less obedience to its leaders."[8]

Party System an Extra-legal Growth. An institution of such vital importance as the party system is an extra-legal growth in every democratic country. Though it exists outside the legal framework of the State and it is not referred to in the constitution of any country, it has become as indispensable as the law itself. The Constitution of the United States of America does not presume the existence of political parties. The makers of the Constitution shared the common opinion that political parties were highly detrimental to national solidarity as they encouraged strife, division, chicanery, and personal manipulation. Yet, within a few years of the career of the Union party divisions and party

7. Lowell, A.L., *Public Opinion and Popular Government*, p. 70.
8. Bryce, J., *Modern Democracies*, Vol. I, p. 125.

spirit were sufficiently evident. In the Presidential election of 1796, there were two national parties, one supporting John Adams and the other supporting Thomas Jefferson. By 1800, the party system had settled itself quite firmly in the government, even to the extent of necessitating the addition of the Twelfth Amendment so as to make the electoral college method workable. Since then political parties have played a very vigorous role and today this extra-constitutional growth forms the hub of the political life of the nation. "But for the appearance of a national party system," as Professor Brogan realistically points out, "the election of a President really enough of a national figure to carry out his duties, might have been impossible. And it is certain that the greatest breakdown of the American constitutional system, the civil war, came only when the party system collapsed."[9] Gilchrist is of the opinion that the "party system is really the method whereby the too great rigidity of the American Constitution has been broken down." What the framers of the Constitution had divided into three departments, all put asunder, the party has reunited.

It is, again, a curious fact that in Britain, where the party system first began, political parties are still unknown to law. But without the political parties the whole nature of the British Constitution would be changed and many of the conventions would become unworkable. His Majesty's Government is a party government and the Prime Minister is the leader of the majority party in the House of Commons. The party in Opposition is His Majesty's Opposition and it is recognised as a necessary and vital element in the working of the British Constitution. The functions of the Opposition are to criticise and to vote against the policy of the government, the party in office, with a view to overthrowing it and taking its place, one party to give place to another party. Jennings has, therefore, aptly said that "a realistic survey of the British Constitution today must begin and end with parties and discuss them at length in the middle."[10] Similarly, political parties in India are extra-constitutional, but they are life-blood of the system of government established at the Centre and in the States.

Even the government of the U.S.S.R. was a party government, although it was a misnomer to call it a party government in the original sense of the word. In Russia there was only one party and only one set of social and political ideas. So long as one general line was demanded, one ideology was prescribed, and one party alone was permitted by the Constitution to exist, the necessary conditions of a democratic State were necessarily absent. Democracy is a government by discussion and involves differences of opinion. Opposition is the hub of a democratic government and upon its strength depends the success or failure of democracy. Totalitarianism does not tolerate differences of opinion on any issue, big or small. Discipline, duty and sacrifice are its three cardinal principles. In dictatorship, therefore, there is no place for the Opposition and it cannot be permitted to exist as it may mean the demise of the dictatorship itself.

THE ORIGIN OF PARTIES

A genuine party system, that is, one which contains two or more parties is a major step in the attainment of political maturity and it was only a century and a half back that

9. Brogan, D.W., *An Introduction to American Politics,* p. 45.
10. Jennings, W.I., *The British Constitution,* p. 31.

political parties in the real sense came into being. MacIver has correctly said, "It was only when the logic of parliamentary government brought it about that a dispute between the ministry and the representatives was decided by an appeal to the country, involving the retirement of the ministry if defeated (the first clear case being that of Peel in 1835) or when an unpopular government found it expedient to resign, that the importance of parties emerged and they began to assume a new status."[11] Before that "there were trends of opinion, popular clubs, philosophical societies, and parliamentary groups, but no real parties."[12] Today, parties function in most countries of the world, and in others there is an attempt to imitate them.

Historically, the emergence of political parties has accompanied the growth of the modern electorate. Indeed, it was the latter that made the former. The more the right to vote became extended and multiplied, the more it became necessary for party organisations, which previously had been based upon legislative cliques, to organise the electors in order to make the candidates known and to canalize the votes in their direction. Parties, thus, acquired their new character. They became mass organisations, linking together a large body of citizens with their representatives in the legislative assemblies. They developed institutions of their own and with a view to fighting and winning elections, they collected financial contributions. In this way the parties responded to the real need. Without them the millions of voters who composed the new electorate would have become a disorganised crowd unable to formulate their aims or debate the important and many issues they confronted. "By means of parties, the voters obtained a medium that, to state it in no stronger terms, afforded a chance of rational and coherent action."

The Theory of Human Nature. In 1882, W.S. Gilbert wrote:

> "How nature does always contrive
> That every boy and every gal
> That's born into this world alive
> Is either a little liberal
> or else a little conservative."

One main explanation of party divisions is that it is based on human nature. According to this theory some people are instinctively conservative and want to leave things as they are; others are instinctively progressive and want to make changes. These inborn temperamental differences incline an individual towards one party or another. To these two natural or psychological party divisions are given the names of parties of the Left and Right. These names take their origin from the custom followed in the legislatures of European Continental countries where the progressive members sit on the left of the President, and their opponents on the right—this custom dates as far back as the French National Assembly of 1789.

These innate temperamental differences are often modified by age as well as by circumstances. Advancing years are always accompanied by the cautious conservatism of

11. MacIver, R.M., *The Modern State,* pp. 397-98.
12. Duverger, M., *Political Parties,* XXIII. Introduction.

age. Conservatism is the product of mature intellectual judgment whereas youth is radical. Emotionalism and impulsiveness are regarded as the special attributes of youth. Young men are, as a rule, radical in their thoughts and actions and aim at introducing drastic and revolutionary changes in the existing social order. There is, therefore, much truth in the saying of a King of Sweden: "A young man, my dear Minister, who has not been a Socialist before he is five and twenty shows that he has no heart. But if he continues to be one after five and twenty he shows that he has no head," the implication being that there is a tendency for political opinion to grow less progressive with age.

In the concluding Chapter of his *Public Opinion in War and Peace*, Lawrence Lowell presents a theory of political dispositions. Discarding an old classification of people into those desiring liberty and progress on one side and defence of the established order on the other, he suggests that people be divided into the contented and the discontented, and into those who are sanguine or not about possible changes. By combining any of these two traits, one finds four groups of people: those who are discontented with present conditions and sanguine about improvement, the radicals; those who are contented and sanguine, the liberals; those who are contented, but not hopeful of improvement, the conservatives; and, finally, those who are not contented with existing conditions and at the same time see no prospects of better things to come, reactionaries. Then, in considering the change from one of these dispositions to another, Lowell, following Rohmer, speaks of the tendency of men to run the cycle from radical to reactionary as they grow old. He also points out "the rarity of persons changing from one disposition to another diagonally opposed, the reason being that two basic changes would be involved, that from content to discontent and from sanguinity to despondence, a combination which is not very likely to occur at the same time."[13]

Conflict of Economic Interests. But the more realistic basis of division into parties is the conflict of economic interests. Arthur Halcombe has correctly said that "national parties cannot be maintained by transitory impulses or temporary needs. They must be founded upon permanent sectional interests, above all upon those of an economic character."[14] Differences in possessions, economic outlook of the people and economic conditions are the vital forces behind the formation of political parties. Men of property are invariably inclined to caution, distrusting and dreading change because it threatens their economic security. Others, having no possessions, thrive upon the hope that change will improve their lot but is not likely to make it substantially worse. Conflict of economic interests is such an important factor in the division of parties that even Lord Macaulay so linked together diversities of temper and diversities of interest as if they were of the same order. Some people are repelled by the suggestion that human conduct is shaped by economic motives. There may be some force in their argument that politics is not all economics, but certainly without economics, politics is an utter mystery.

Environmental Effect. It is often claimed that men inherit their politics and religion. Membership in a party, as in a church, is less a matter of man's conviction and decision. It is the pressure of his environments and particularly of the goups to which he belongs,

13. Friedrich, C.J., *Constitutional Government and Democracy,* pp. 421-22.
14. Halcombe A., *Political Parties of Today,* p. 41.

the family group exerting a potent influence. The young man joins a particular party, because his father belonged to it. Party allegiance, like property, is often transmitted from generation to generation. In the vast majority of cases the son enters politics on the same side as his father. Sometimes, also, there may be settled political traditions in a wider group. This may combine with the influence of group interests, but it may be largely independent of that. In the United States, for instance, it used to be said that the people of Irish descent would traditionally incline to the Democrats and people of German descent to the Republicans. In Britain sometimes, though less than formerly, certain districts or regions have a traditional attachment to one particular party.

Religious and Communal Sentiments. Political parties may also be based on religious affinities. In the Western countries religious and communal passions are excluded from the conduct of government. But in India political parties were unfortunately divided by her past rulers on religious grounds in order to defeat the nationalist forces and to strengthen their hold on the country. Today, India is a secular State, yet communal parties like the Bharatiya Janata Party, the Akalis, the Muslim League Party of India and many others still exist with their own communal labels. Political parties with communal colouring are bound to militate against the development of national spirit and the successful working of Parliamentary government. For the building up of national unity secularization of politics and pursuit of a vigorous social and economic programme are absolutely necessary. "The wisest of leaders in all denominations," says Beard, "have deplored the introduction of religious disputes into political discussions and campaigns."[15]

Four Types of Parties. We, thus, find men generally divided into four types of parties. First, there are men who move with the times and desire to bring about changes by gradual reform in the existing institutions. They are called Liberals, There are others who will continue with the old order and want to maintain *status quo*. They are called Conservatives. There are still others who will like to replace the present institutions by those which existed in the past. Past is a golden age to them and they advocate return to the methods, customs and institutions of the ancients. Such a class of people are called Reactionaries. Lastly, are the Radicals. They would not go slow, but advocate revolutionary changes even if such changes could be brought about by a revolution. They have no faith in the existing institutions, and will abolish or uproot them altogether and establish new ones in conformity to their ideals.

But this is really a simple analysis of the party division. A party is a synthesis of various interests. It is as much the result of mental traits of men as they are of the interests near to their heart, of the conditions and surroundings in which they live and of the social structure of which they are the members. Bryce beautifully sums up when he says that "though the professed reason for the existence of a party is the position of a particular set of doctrines, it has a concrete side as well as a set of abstract doctrines. It is abstract in so far as it represents the adhesion of many minds to the same opinions. It is concrete as consisting of a number of men who act together in respect of their holding or professing to hold such opinions."[16]

15. Beard, C.A., *American Government and Politics*, p. 55.
16. Bryce, J., *Modern Democracies*, Vol. I. p. 126.

FUNCTIONS OF PARTIES

Political parties are the indispensable links between the people and the representative machinery of government. Their role is more obvious when election is in prospect, but they need to be continually operative if a democratic system is to work effectively. It is the political parties that organize the vastly diversified people by nominating candidates for office, and by popularizing the ideas around which governmental programmes are built. They are vehicles through which individuals and groups work to secure political power and, if successful, to exercise that power. If there were no political parties, politics would be a sheer babel of tongues. A disorganised mass of people can neither formulate principles nor agree on a policy.

Political parties, therefore, bring order out of chaos by putting before a multitude of people their programmes and securing their approval on vital issues of policy. They plan and contest elections and endeavour to win by taking up positions on policy matters and presenting them as choices between parties. By raising issues, selecting from them, taking sides and generating political heat they educate the public and clarify opinion. As a consequence of this ordering of competing men and measures political parties create and keep open lines of communication between governors and governed, through which government may work more effectively. Opposition opposes and the public reacts. In this way, political parties are responsible for maintaining a continuous link between the public and those who represent them either in the government or in the Opposition.

The first role of the political parties is to sort out the issues for the electorate. They select candidates for election, plan and execute the election campaign and present them with alternatives to the people between which they may choose. Parties are alternatives and the programmes which they put before the electorate, represent a selection made by each party out of the numerous possible issues of the moment. Herman Finer remarks that without parties "an electorate would be either impotent or destructive by embarking on impossible policies that would only wreck the political machine."

The second role of the parties is to supply the majorities without which government cannot remain in power. If there were no parties, if members of legislatures were completely disorganised and formed only a mass of men voting one way today and another way tomorrow, the government could not be sure how long it could stay in power. It would, consequently, have no stability and no power to plan a coherent policy, national or international. In fact, it would be difficult to form a government under such chaotic conditions. Parties hold the representatives together subjecting them to the party whip and party discipline. The legislatures cannot work smoothly without party whip and party whip is necessary for party solidarity and for carrying out a coherent policy or programme.

Parties provide alternative teams to run the government. They prevent the same people remaining in power too long and looking on an office as a matter of right. A party system guarantees to the electorate that change in government can be effected if they wish it. It is always wholesome to know that no one is indispensable in politics and you can be replaced tomorrow. A party system always reminds the rulers that the ultimate appeal rests with the people, and they must remember those to whom they will have to account in the future as well as those who entrusted them with power. Under a representative government you hold your job on good behaviour only. Finally, where considerable separation and division of powers exist, as under the Presidential system, political parties serve as the necessary unifying agency. In the United States political parties have united what the Constitution had put asunder.

ORGANISATION OF PARTIES

Party Organisation. If the primary function of a party is to consolidate public opinion in advance of the election, permanency and organisation are, then, the prerequisites of a party system. If the parties are not duly organised, they will remain vague, shapeless, mere tendencies to similar views but not units capable of doing their real work: controlling the government. But parties can only be organised if they are permanent. Short-lived parties are just transitory phases of political developments over passing issues or temporary problems. They are not parties, but groups without any unified programme and policy and without any definite influence on the electorate. And since the life of the groups is short and precarious, they rarely develop lasting traditions and loyalties. Nor do they dominate the government and instead become an instrument in the hand of a clever politician.

"An organised party is almost like a small state within a big one." It has its active membership and its passive adherents, its local branches or constituencies, with their branches of propaganda, fund collecting and recruiting, its election to the party councils, responsible for its choice of leaders and officials, and the adoption of the party policy. "By degrees which to the ordinary citizen were imperceptible," says Finer, "these nation-wide fellowships have come into being and organised themselves with a gigantic and complex apparatus. They possess buildings and newspapers, printing presses and advertising experts, songs and slogans, heroes and martyrs, money and speakers, officials and prophets, feast days and fast days; like all religions they disrupt families and produce heretics, and among their agencies of discipline and subordination are the novitiate and penance."[17]

Party organisation, thus, operates incessantly and the permanence of organisation and activity differentiate the parties of the present from the parties of a century ago. Before the middle of the last century political parties were loosely organised and remained inactive before elections. They would mobilise their men and resources just before the election and demobilise after the polling day. Today, the parties operate throughout and all through, partly because victory in parliamentary elections is otherwise impossible, but also because in the modern State there are many local elective offices to fill. Local elections are the index of public opinion and they give the shape of things to come. The trends of opinion expressed at local elections indicate the electoral support the party is likely to secure at the General Elections.

Every party must, therefore, keep itself abreast of the public opinion. In fact, the local party branch plays a most important part in the party organisation. "The party branch," says Soltau, "is a local unit of the army, provides the recruits, and is also a

17. Finer, H., *The Theory and Practice of Modern Government,* p. 363.

centre of intelligence as to what is going on within the party and in the country in general." It is here that the citizen expresses his views freely and easily and makes his mark in the party policies. The local influence, which he exercises, paves a way for him to enter the arena of national policies. A local branch of the party is, in fact, a school of democracy, and public life. It is also the nerve centre of information as to what is being thought and said of the party and its politics.

Political parties are organized along different lines in every State. Generally speaking, in European States all political parties have annual meetings of party leaders to decide policy and plan programme. The debates and discussions at such meetings are of immense value both to the leaders and the rank and file members in promoting and understanding of the issues and evaluating the competence of the total leadership in the party. Once the party policy and programme have been decided, members at all levels of the party are required to strictly follow it. Any deviation therefrom may make the member subject to party discipline. In Britain party discipline is particularly strict.

The two major political parties in the United States are formally organized on a hierarchical basis with a national committee, a state committee, a county committee, and city, town, borough, village, parish and other committees. The control of this complex organization does not flow from the top to the bottom. The units at the local level are the most important. The county executive committee is also an extremely important part of the party structure. It has the deciding voice in matters of policy and of local patronage. The party members, it is significant to note, are not subject to any discipline. Nor is there any machinery to enforce it. The obligations of members are voluntary. The result is that the members of the Republican and Democratic parties in Congress do not hesitate to cross party lines to support legislation "more in keeping with their own predilections or those of their narrow and localized constituencies." The American political system, therefore, makes little provision for the real and responsible leadership such as the Cabinet system requires.

Ideal and Material Objectives. Political parties, in order to live and function, says Carl Friedrich, "must be compounded of ideal and material purposes or objectives."[18] He does not accept the distinction between "patronage parties" and "parties of principles." There is "no such thing as a party", he maintains, "which lacks either of these elements," and concludes that a "realistic political science can state with some confidence that all parties strive for a combination of ideal and material objectives."[19] The working of government actually proves that the ideal objectives are forced upon parties by their struggle for gaining control of the government. "It is a platitude of practical politics," asserts Friedrich, "that the outs are invariably more emphatic in their advocacy of principles than the ins."[20]

The party organization operates incessantly and throughout to disseminate its ideas and in order to achieve its purposes, it must secure power. With the securing of power follow the material objectives in the form of patronage and the rest. In fact, patronage

18. Friedrich, C.J., *Constitutional Government and Democracy,* p. 414.
19. *Ibid.*, p. 415.
20. *Ibid.*

is a concomitant of the entire process of the party machine. The vehicles of patronage are the sole monopoly of the party in power and it uses them for its own cohesiveness and solidarity. Since the party in Opposition is denied the privileges of patronage, it advocates the principles for which the party stands by highlighting the lapses of the party in power and its deviation from the principles which constitute its ideal objectives; the ideas of the party on law and government and the shape which the political apparatus should take ultimately.

It will be instructive to refer here to Hatschek's law. The preponderance of material objectives in a large party organisation led Julius Hatschek to suggest a rule regarding the development of political parties in Great Britain. He says that the development follows a definite course and "may have more general significance." First, a party with a distinct and coherent programme incorporating the ideal objectives comes into power. With the lapse of time the party loses its appeal, as it fails to realize the ideal objectives which it had set forth as its goal. Some parts of its programme may even be impossible to realize at all. There ensues differences of opinion verging upon antagonism amongst the members of the party itself. The factious spirit, thus created, leads to the disintegration of the party and a new party is born on the ruins of the old party. This party, thriving upon its own ideal objectives, gains ascendancy. After some time this party, too, disintegrates as a result of the same process. "This means that once party organizations have come into existence, the existence of a realizable program (programme) is no longer necessary. A party can not only continue to live, but may be able to displace the other party in the government, merely because its organization under a powerful leader is more effective than is that of the other party. The party lives by the strength of its organization, and therefore the organization is the main thing, the programme a side issue."[21]

It follows, then, that the older the party, the more pronounced its concern with material interests. Hatschek deduced this law from the development of the parties in Great Britain and characterised it as a peculiarity of British political life. Friedrich, however, is of the opinion that had he considered American parties, "he would unquestionably have concluded that the situation was much the same here. A similar trend occurs in other countries and under very different conditions of party life."[22] Three times split in the Indian National Congress Party, first in 1969, the second in 1978 and the third in 1995 is a pertinent example to vindicate Hatschek's analysis.

WEAKNESS AND STRENGTH OF THE PARTY SYSTEM

Merits of the Party System. The advocates of party system emphasise that it is in accord with human nature and the innate qualities automatically divide the populace into parties. As a political contrivance, the party system makes democracy workable. It enables people scattered all over the country to agree upon some common principles and to work together in support of those principles. In the absence of organised political parties there would be conflicting groups of opinion without anything common to harmonise them into

21. *Ibid.*, p. 417.
22. *Ibid.*

an effective working mechanism. The success of a representative government largely depends upon the energy, efficiency, and enterprise of the party system.

"Without the party system," says MacIver, "the State has no elasticity, no true self-determination."[23] Irresponsive and irresponsible government is based upon force rather than on the will of the people. The only method of securing a change of government, under these circumstances, is *coup d'etat* or revolution. But a party government lives and thrives on public opinion. Force is replaced by appeal. It regards "persuasion as more desirable than compulsion, and the conflict of ideas more creative than the clash of arms."[24] The party system ensures sober and healthy criticism of government both inside and outside the legislature. Since it is a government by criticism, Opposition acts as a check on hasty, ill-considered, and class legislation. The party in power is amenable to the opinions of the Opposition and it is always eager to accept its reasonable suggestions, for the indispensable conditions of majority rule are forbearance, moderation and generosity. Both the majority and the Opposition accept the principle of "live and let live" in the knowledge that the system of representative democracy allows to each in turn and in time its fair share of power.

The party system was in particular the mechanism by which the class-State was transformed into the nation-State. All States at one stage of their development were class-States. Their government was controlled by and in the interests of the dominant classes. "The decisive distinction is between the classes and the masses, the classes in this significance being generally two, the nobility and the clergy." The authority of the nobility rested upon the ownership of land, the leadership in war and the prestige of birth and station. The authority of the priesthood rested on the prestige of culture and spiritual dominance. Government under these conditions of class rule was not amenable to public opinion. The masses had nothing to do with the policy of the government. They led a life of suppression, frustration and desperation. But party-rule is the antithesis of class-rule. Party, in fact, begins as a protest against the vested interests and inviolable rights of the class in power. Party-rule "implies the alteration of power, a system of succession which gives each its opportunity." If the policy of the party in power is not approved by the people, it must necessarily give place to the party or parties in Opposition. Thus, party system has furthered the ends of democratic government by organising and directing public opinion. Political parties "make articulate the inarticulate desires of the masses." They act, in the words of Lowell, as the brokers of ideas.

Furthermore, the party system promotes legislative excellence and makes elections easy by nominating candidates much in advance of the actual polling. It has two advantages. In the first place, the electorate comes to know the candidates and their labels. They, accordingly, get sufficient time to consider their comparative worth as representatives and evaluate the policies of their respective parties. Secondly, political parties help candidates to secure election through their collective strength. Party funds and party organisation help the election of poor and also able politicians who otherwise would have no chance of being elected. Political parties also bring harmony between the two wings

23. MacIver, R.M., *The Modern State*, p. 399.
24. *Ibid.*

of government, the Executive and the Legislative. Under the Parliamentary system of government the party commanding a majority in the legislature forms the government and is answerable to it for all their public acts. In the oft-quoted words of Bagehot, Cabinet is a hyphen that joins, a buckle that binds the Executive and Legislative departments together. The Fathers of the American Constitution put asunder the Executive and Legislative departments by rigidly adhering to the doctrine of the Separation of Powers and consequently established the Presidential system of government. But the political parties now join what the Fathers had scattered. A President, according to Theodore Roosevelt, combines in his person the two offices of King and Prime Minister. The President is chosen as a party man to lead a government operated under a party system. He surrounds himself with advisers of his own faith, consults usually with men belonging to his party in Congress for appointments, confers with his own men in the party in formulating policy, and he uses his power as chief legislator to push through the party's programme to a crowning victory.

Then, by their election campaigns political parties arouse public spirit and influence the masses to take active interest in public affairs. In this way, they inculcate civic enthusiasm and help in the realization of the democratic spirit, that vigilance is the price of democracy. Political parties help the people to feel that they are the masters of their own destiny. They determine for themselves the kind of government they wish to have. Bryce has cogently said, "Party strife is a sort of education for those willing to receive instruction, and something soaks through even into the less interested or thoughtful electors. The parties keep a nation's mind alive, as the rise and fall of the sweeping tide freshens the water of long ocean inlets."[25] Moreover, political parties gather up the whole nation into fellowship and "they lead," as Herman Finer says, "in the sense of bringing to the individual citizen a vision of the whole nation, otherwise distant in history, territory and futurity."[26] The party system, thus, broadens the horizon of voters and representatives alike by breaking sectional barriers and discounting local interests. The political parties are really nationalising agencies. Finally, the party system involves discipline. It not only brings order out of the chaos of a multitude of voters, it trains the members themselves in loyalty and consistency. Loyalty and allegiance are its watchwords, and obedience its rigid demand. Without this no party can exist and more so succeed in its political objective.

Demerits of Party System. The critics of party system condemn it categorically and characterize it as the most unnatural political phenomenon. They maintain that party divisions are not the result of human nature and, as such, set up a peculiarly artificial agreement among people who profess to have identical political views. Similarly, the disagreement with their opponents is equally artificial. "Each side," thus, "remains in a state of wilful inconvincibility, with individual judgment frozen tight in the shape of the party mould."[27] This artificial agreement and disagreement divides the people into hostile groups at regular and perpetual strife with one another. Such a bitterness is highly detrimental to national solidarity and the integrity of the State.

25. Bryce, J., *Modern Democracies* Vol. 1, p. 134.
26. Finer, H., *The Theory and Practice of Modern Government,* p. 275.
27. Leacock, S., *Elements of Political Science,* p. 312.

A party, like a broker, "tries to simulate a larger amount of agreement than actually exists." Such a nature of political ties encourages hollowness and insincerity. The party system, therefore, demoralises politics and makes it sordid. It crushes the individuality of the party members and reduces them almost to the position of camp followers. No one can rise high in politics except through the regular channels of some party. An independent citizen, who does not tag himself to some party, is looked upon as a "crank" or a "goody-goody." But a party member must bow to party dictates otherwise the party discipline coerces him. Thus, by insisting on slavish obedience to party behest, independence and individuality are destroyed. This is contrary to the spirit of democracy.

It is further maintained that party system makes the political life of a country machine-like.[28] The Opposition party is always hostile to the party in power. Opposition is a party principle and it has nothing to do with utility or logic of the policy or a law. All laws proposed by the government must be opposed tooth and nail, no matter how useful and urgent they may be for the country. It must censure the government on all matters of policy no matter what the question may be. This is not the way of government by discussion. There are three axioms which must be accepted and obeyed if government by discussion is to work successfully—the axiom of agreement to differ, the axiom of the rule of majority, and the axiom of compromise. In the din of party politics and the hostility that is engendered these axioms of practical utility are forgotten. Another evil of the party system is that it gives an opportunity to self-seeking political adventurers to exploit the masses for their own personal interest. If there does not exist any political party, a political adventurer will endeavour to create one. Just as every cock likes to have his own dunghill to stand upon and crow, so does this political opportunist to ensure his berth for furthering his own selfish ends. The mushroom growth of such parties complicates the political problems of a country, India being a glaring example of the evil. Again, party government means excessive pandering to the people. This results in popular legislation, not for the good of the country but to catch votes. The party system, therefore, debases public morals and gives rise to the 'spoils' system. There is a regular race in job hunting and patronage of the worst type. Merit is ignored and persons are dumped upon party members and their supporters. The tone of administration, under these circumstances, severely deteriorates and disaffection and dissatisfaction grips the whole community. It means total paralysis of the normal political life.

The party system, its opponents maintain, lowers the moral tone of society by preaching falsehood and suppressing truth. The methods employed to ensnare the voters and thereby capture their votes are sometimes obnoxious. The language used in the meetings of the party campaigns is very often scandalous. Parties try to impress on the electorate "the truth of their views and the falsity of those of others. In this way parties are often guilty of the sins of *suppressio veri* and *suggestio falsi*."[29] Perverted party propaganda chokes reason and strangulates thought. It helps the flaring up of emotions. Swayed by emotions and deprived of reasoning power, the masses blindly follow what they are told to do by their leaders. It is the triumph of demagoguism and emergence of this kind of herd

28. Gilchrist, R.N., *Principles of Political Science,* p. 337.

29. *Ibid.,* p. 338.

psychology is the death of democracy. A citizen of democracy is not merely to obey, he has also to see if his obedience is rational.

The party elects the leader and once he has been elected the party men do not only obey him, but prostrate themselves before him. Carl Friedrich points out that parties "try to secure power for their leader or leaders, rather than for themselves. For only through such leaders can the body of the party membership hope to secure the material and ideal gains which they seek."[30] The purpose of democracy, for the attainment of which parties are indispensable, is, thus, defeated. The party system, it is further contended, keeps many good citizens aloof from public life. The nation thereby is deprived of the intellect, knowledge, and experience of the talented persons who are either election-shy or refuse to be bound by the rigidity of the party whip and the party discipline. There is another aspect of it too. Under a parliamentary system only the majority party forms the government and for that purpose talent is to be searched within the party itself. The water-tight party antagonism narrows choice and the majority party runs administration with men of inferior ability. Inefficiency of the ministers is the heaven for bureaucracy.

The party system narrows the vision of the people. Members of the party place the party before the nation. They behave as partisans rather than citizens working for the common good. Goldsmith wrote on Burke:

> "Who born for the universe narrowed his mind
> And to party gave up what was meant for mankind."

This is correct to a great extent. When party loyalty is carried too far and allegiance to the excess, claims of patriotism are obscured and the higher call of country is ignored. Such an attitude is disastrous especially in times of national emergency.

The party system adversely affects local life. Local elections are made the arena of party politics. Local considerations are, thus, brushed aside and candidates are nominated and elected on the basis of national issues and general party differences. The election campaign assumes the same pitch and intensity as the general elections and a scene of warring armies is presented. It is, finally, asserted that party system has created double governments. "The real governing power is without legal responsibility and is practically free from statutory and legal restrictions." Hence, it makes a mockery of responsibility in a democratic government.

The Way Out. Some of the defects of the party system, listed above, are real. The political history of every country, where party government has prevailed, is a record of party strife, factional spirit and sectional legislation. Party spoils are indiscriminately distributed among party men for personal services rather than for national patriotism. Though the extent of these defects may not be the same everywhere, yet there appears to be some truth in Alexander Pope's definition of party as "the madness of the many for the gain of the few." Rousseau declared that any community in which parties existed was incapable of a true common will. Even James Bryce was of the view that political parties encroached upon and undermined the democratic process. In the ideal democracy, he argued, each citizen is intelligent and impartial. The soundest arguments and best candidates

30. Friedrich, C.J., *Constitutional Government and Democracy,* p. 418.

will win out. But politicians discover that the citizen is neither informed nor interested—nor perhaps even intelligent. Hence, the politicians endeavour to organize voters instead of persuading them. "Organization and discipline," warned Bryce, "mean the growth of a party spirit which is in itself irrational, impelling men to vote from considerations which have little to do with a love of truth or a sense of justice." Similarly, Robert Michels argued, in his study of the German Social Democratic Party, that party organization becomes an end in itself. Organization means oligarchy which governs. According to Duverger, "The leadership of parties tends naturally to assume oligarchic form. A veritable 'ruling class' comes into being that is more or less closed; it is an 'inner circle' into which it is difficult to penetrate."[31] This is negation of democracy and the democratic spirit.

The emergence of one-party system after World War I, particularly those created in Germany, Italy and USSR, made a sharp change in the view that parties were destructive of democracy. It began to be universally viewed that parties were indispensable for the operation of democratic institutions. It was contended that democracy is bound up with the existence of at least two or more political parties. In their absence there would be no check on the egoism of the rulers. Duverger even maintained that "liberty and party coincide."

But there was another swing. In the last decade or so political parties have fallen, once again, in disrepute, especially in the developing countries. Eminent and respected leaders of many countries in Asia and Africa have categorically denounced political parties and regard them as "worms upon the body-politic." In many countries, as in Burma, South Korea, Pakistan and Egypt, the army seized power professedly in order to rescue the State from the corrupting influences of the political parties and the moral degradation to which they reduced the citizens. In other countries, notably India, a non-party democracy was envisaged as the only means of improving public morality and making government really representative of the people's will. The party system in India is also in complete paralysis. When the statesmen and politicians defect[32] from one party to another not once but many times, and that, too, in a bid to get offices in the government, the plea for a partyless democracy has a profound appeal.

But partyless democracy is an impossible political expedient. It is, in fact, utopian to think of it. It is literally impossible to imagine how democracy could work in the absence of political parties. They are the most effective agency in educating the public and enabling the electorate to determine for themselves the rulers whom they would like to entrust the government for the time being. Again, they are the main institutions through which the responsibility of the rulers is enforced. If political parties fail in performing this function, other institutions likewise vital to democracy will, *ipso facto*, fail. There are certain glaring defects, no doubt, in the party system, but they are not so serious as to necessitate the total abolition of parties. Abuses of party system can diminish only, if improvements are made in the standards of public morality and sound public opinion is

31. Duverger, M., *Political Parties,* p. 151.
32. The Constitution (Fifty-second Amendment) Act, 1985, provides for disqualification on ground of defection as provided in the Tenth Schedule.

developed. A public opinion must fulfil two conditions. It should, in the first place, be an opinion which is widely held, and secondly, it should be of a public nature. Loyalty to the nation should precede loyalty to the party. Parties organized on the basis of race, region or religion should not find place in the body-politic. They promote sectional interests and parochialism. Sectarian loyalties debase public life and corrupt political morals.

For the purification of the party system, it is essential that there should be more active participation of upright and public-spirited citizens in party politics. This can only be possible when party control is diffused and members at all levels are sure that they have a say in the working of the party and the determination of its policy. All party members must feel that they are integral parts of the organization to which they belong and not merely its show-boys. Their voice counts as much as that of any other member and they have the opportunity to assert themselves. Such a democratization of the party structure and its working precludes the emergence of a small clique of party bosses or a powerful person who dominates the party and concentrates all power unto himself. If democracy needs political parties, political parties need a democratic spirit and democratic processes. Without them, it is dictatorship with all the evils inherent therein.

The right type of political education of the masses and the presence of an impartial and free press greatly contribute in mitigating the evils of the party system. An unattached and fearless press helps to increase the general level of education and intelligence of the citizens by presenting to them untwisted facts and honest comments. Two important factors help the growth of such conditions. In the first place, it involves the education of the masses and the reorientation in the prevalent system of education. The object of education should be to produce rational human beings dedicated to a common cause. Here comes in the second involvement and it is the right type of leadership. A leader should inspire the people by his dynamic personality, virtuous qualities and devotion. He should enlighten public opinion by his selflessness and dispassionate views on all problems and lead the various opinion forming groups and their instruments. It is only then that politics can be moralised. The future of democracy, therefore, depends upon the ability, character and devotion which education can instil into the people and the capacity of the leaders to lead them.

Sidgwick has suggested certain practical remedies for removing or mitigating the disadvantages of the party system.[33] He says that all these remedies are partly political and partly moral, the former naturally varying according to the form of government. He suggests, in the first place, that the influence of the party on government will be greatly reduced if under a Presidential form of government the President is elected by the legislature and the subordinate executive officers hold office independent of party ties. Secondly, in a parliamentary executive certain matters of legislation and administration may be withdrawn from the control of the party system. For example, the preparation of legislation may be entrusted to parliamentary committees other than the cabinet; certain heads of departments, who possess trained skill and specialized knowledge, should not retire with the cabinet, and if necessary, they may even be appointed from outside the

33. Sidgwick, H., *The Elements of Politics,* pp. 600-03.

party. Thirdly, a custom may be established that Ministers need not resign from office, because the legislative measures proposed by them have been defeated. They should resign only when a formal vote of want of confidence is carried against them in the representative chamber of the legislature. Finally, the process of referendum, even to a limited extent, will at any rate reduce the dangers of the party system. But all these changes essentially entail revision of the principles governing the functioning of parliamentary system of government and the factors governing the solidarity of the cabinet. They do not aim to purify and ennoble politics.

TWO-PARTY vs. MULTIPLE-PARTY SYSTEM

Two-Party System. In a State there may be two or more political parties. When the parties are only two in number, it is called a dual or two-party system. When there are more than two parties, it is known as the multiple-party system. The two-party system prevails in Britain, the United States, Canada, Australia, New Zealand and South Africa. The multiple-party system is obtainable in the Continental Europe and India. Most of the traditional two-party systems also include one or more smaller parties, as Britain, for example, includes the Liberal Party; the United States, the Communist Party, the Socialist Party and the Prohibition Party; Canada, the New Democratic Party and the Social Credit Party; South Africa, the Liberal, and since 1959, the Progressive Party. But the essential contest is between two parties only. The third, or the third and fourth parties, may secure a limited number of seats, but not enough to become the official Opposition. In 1906, the Liberal Party had 376 seats in the British House of Commons. In 1943, it had 20 seats and that was the beginning in its decline with only 14 seats in 1981. In April 1981 came to an end the cycle of two-party system when the Social Democratic Party was formed as a result of split in the Labour Party. Social Democrats and Liberals became allies and contested elections together, but it did not make a significant dent on the two major parties. The main contestants are the Conservative and the Labour Parties. The British Constitution has grown and evolved under the two-party system and its working tends to maintain and perpetuate it. Consequently, the party system as worked in Britain and in those countries that have borrowed her pattern of government implies, strictly speaking, the existence of two parties only.

The essence of party government, as practised in Britain and other countries with two-party system and cabinet government, is that the party enjoying majority in the Lower Chamber forms the government and its leader becomes the Prime Minister. The Ministers are responsible to Parliament and they remain in office so long as they retain the confidence of the Lower House. On losing its confidence, they are obliged, by a constitutional usage, to resign. One of the two things may happen then. Either the Opposition party assumes office, if it can command a majority in the Lower House, or, more commonly, the Prime Minister may ask for dissolution of Parliament, when a general election takes place and verdict of the electorate is obtained. The party returned in majority in the Lower House, then, forms the government.

A two-party system, therefore, can be said to exist when:

1. There are only two parties sufficiently strong to share the major part of the

electoral vote and to exercise political control, though other parties may exist and obtain some seats in the representative assembly.

2. The major parties alternate in the exercise of power. If this condition is not present as in West Germany where the Socialist Party did not exercise power at the federal level until the 1967 coalition, Japan, where the Liberal Democratic Party dominated post-war politics, till July 1993 elections, although it still commanded the highest number of seats in the House of Representatives, the lower chamber of the Diet, or in some parts of the United States of America where one party traditionally wins, the regime cannot exactly be termed a two-party system. "Perhaps," says Michael Curtis, "the term 'one and a half' party system might be applicable in such circumstances."

Multiple-Party System. In most countries of Continental Europe, notably in France, there are multiple parties, sometimes numbering from 17 to 20 and even 30. India, too, is a close second to France. The multiple-party system is really intriguing. Where there are numerous parties, it is a misnomer to call them "parties." They are, as a matter of fact, political "groups." Moreover, multiplicity often encourages further fragmentation. Dissident elements tend to split off. To a certain extent, this tendency is the reflection of a body-politic in which political tolerance is low and the various shades of opinion are held with uncompromising vigour by their various partisans. Once such a system becomes operative with the virtual impossibility of any party aspiring to command a majority, it encourages its own perpetuation.

But the difference is not in name alone. There are fundamental differences in the working of a two-party and a multiple-party system. When there are a number of groups, say as many as nineteen or twenty, there can be no well-defined single majority party able to form a stable government. Majority can be obtained only by a combination of groups called a *bloc*. An outstanding leader is selected from the various party groups and he sets about to make the ministry. The prospective Prime Minister negotiates with such leaders of other groups as can gather working majority. This is a matter of bargaining and compromise. Every ministry under the multiple-party system is a coalition ministry. A ministry which is the result of compromise between heterogeneous groups is sure to break down at the slightest pretext. Nor are the ministers subject to parliamentary loyalty and discipline. There is no common party leader who can bind them together into a team to play the game of politics under his captaincy. Every minister is a prospective Prime Minister. Cabinets formed by this method are notoriously weak and unstable. M. Briand remarked on one occasion that the day on which a French Prime Minister takes office is the day upon which one at least of his colleagues begins to prepare his downfall.

Case For and Against Two-Party System. The chief merit of the two-party system is that it ensures more permanent and stable cabinets than those formed under the multiple-party system. All ministers are taken from one single party which is returned to the legislature in a majority. The political homogeneity makes them well-organised and responsible team workers who play the game of politics with singleness of purpose under the captaincy of their accredited leader, whose undisputed authority they all accept and respect. They rise and fall in unison and are individually and collectively responsible for the policy which the cabinet initiates and they carry out. Their strength is like that of an iron rod. Practically, every ministry, under a multiple-party system, is a coalition ministry, a combination of heterogeneous political elements with nothing common in them by way of principle. Even if the combining parties of a multiple-party system may differ slightly in their views, their differences are often insisted upon with a vigour and intransigence unknown to most countries where the two-party system prevails.

As no one party under a multiple-party system is sufficiently representative of the nation as a whole to form a government without drawing upon other sections of opinion and influence, the leaders of such groups simply compromise to come to a working agreement. Such a ministry is uncertain of its existence from day to day. They continue to work together so long as they can be made to agree. Their strength is like that of an iron chain with many links. As soon as one link loosens the whole chain disintegrates. Similarly, when one combining group falls out, the government falls. In France, for example, between 1870 and 1934, there were a total of 88 Ministries, with an average life of less than nine months. During the same period Britain had 18 Ministries, lasting an average of three and a half years. The natural result is that "government in France is little more than a succession of starts and stops, of rapid, sudden and bewildering shifts of policy with no end of confusion and waste."[34] When the life of the government is uncertain, short and precarious coherent policy becomes more difficult to obtain, and political responsibility remains more ambiguous than a two-party regime in which strong responsible government is obtainable. Nor is there any possibility of venturing an ambitious plan. But a multi-party system does not necessarily lead to governmental instability. A number of countries have shown governmental stability for the most part as Switzerland, the Scandinavian countries, the Netherlands, Israel and Germany. France and Italy provide the best examples and warnings of governmental instability.

Dual-party system secures a representative government in the real sense. It provides the only method by which the electors, at the time of election, directly choose the government. Both the parties have their well-defined programmes and a direct appeal is made to the electorate on that basis. The electors choose between the programmes and decide about the party which is to come to power. Two parties, thus, bring the electorate to a point where they are faced by a simple alternative. One of the two parties will win a majority and become responsible for the enactment of policies; the other will be the Opposition; both homogeneous with their clearly defined policies which they had put before the electorate at the time of the General Election and which they sustain while nursing their constituencies. The multiple groups have no party organisation. Sometimes they have no organisation outside the legislature, and they have no programme to lay before the electors. The electors vote for personalities and not for programmes. They do not even know who will form the government.

Government formed by a single majority party, on the other hand; is a government by consent and criticism, and it truly reflects the spirit of political democracy. It is the consent of the people which returned the majority enabling it to form the government and hold the reins of power. The party in minority forms the Opposition of which the majority is always conscious. This consciousness makes the Opposition most orderly and responsible in its relations to the party in power. The criticism of the government is more sober than

34. Laski, H., *Democracy in Crisis*, p. 96.

it is under the group system. The leaders of both the parties are accommodating and they try to adjust on crucial issues. One of the writers has said that the Prime Minister in Britain knows the leader of the Opposition better than his wife. It is an organised Opposition whose function is to criticize and vote against the ministerial party with a view to ousting it from office. When there are many groups, there is no organised Opposition. It is all a question of manipulation; even members of the cabinet are actuated by various more or less opportunistic motives. "Even if they were personally minded to hang firmly together, the groups behind them are full of dissentients who make dependable support impossible, and indeed may shift position or even dissolve completely almost overnight."[35] Laski, while summing up the advantages of the two-party system, says: "It is the only method by which the people can at the electoral period directly choose its government. It enables the government to drive its policy to the statute book. It makes known and intelligible the results of its failure. It brings an alternative government into immediate being."[36]

Arguments in Favour of Multiple-Party System. The two-party system has, however, recently come in for serious criticism.[37] The late Professor Ramsay Muir, for instance, denounced it in his works in unmeasured terms. He says that the two-party system has been the cause of the gravest defects in the British system of government. Bi-party system, according to Ramsay Muir, has destroyed the prestige of the legislature and has given rise to the dictatorship of the cabinet. The dictatorship of the cabinet is really the dictatorship of the majority and so long as a government has a real majority, it can be reasonably certain of maintaining itself in power for the full life of Parliament. This almost mechanical source of power enables government not only to propose, but to dispose whatever they wish to dispose. It might even violate the solemn pledges which it made at the time of general elections. True democracy, it is maintained, consists in free expression of opinion and every kind of opinion should get due representation. Under a two-party system the choice of the electors is reduced to a simple acceptance or rejection of the whole political programme of one of the parties. There is no other alternative. The modern State, it is contended, is a complex structure with diversity of economic interests. It is, accordingly, essential that all these interests should be duly represented. By dividing the political life of the country into two parties, we deny representation to many interests. A multiple-party system provides greater elasticity and mobility and gives an opportunity to various opinion groups to organise themselves. "It does not divide the nation into irreconcilable groups. People can associate and organise without a serious compromise on principles." The two-party system, its critics further assert, "substitutes blind devotion for intelligent appreciation and choice in both the followers and leaders." It creates strong vested interests and party prejudices. Extreme rigidity and discipline discount free expression of opinion and encourage spoils system.

Conclusion. Whatever be the merits of the multiple-party system and howsoever it may reflect more accurately the way in which the popular mind is actually divided, it is

35. *Ibid,* p. 469.

36. Laski, H., *A Grammar of Politics,* p. 314.

37. Muir, R., *How Britain is Governed: The Future for Democracy.*

impracticable as an operative ideal. The essential need in administration is the absence of uncertainty. An executive must be able to plan its way continuously to an ordered scheme of policy. This involves a stable majority in order to have a strong government. "A legislature, otherwise, is so much the master of the executive that the latter is unable to attempt great measures, and the time which should be spent upon them is devoted to manoeuvring for positions which are lost almost as soon as they are occupied."[38] Under a multiple-party system there is trading of votes and sacrificing of principles in a bid to form the government. And yet no one knows from one day to another how much longer the government will be able to carry on. Professor Sait, thus, poses a question: "Who can be held responsible for the numerous and secret shifts or for the achievements and derelictions of the chamber throughout the session?" His answer is, "Such being the case, the practical convenience of two parties must be preferred to the logical appropriateness of many."[39] Finer, in his own characteristic way, concludes that the two parties "are better for the happiness and duty of nations than many parties, and two parties contesting seats everywhere. For then lies and error may be in all places challenged, while destruction of will and disintegration of outlook are reduced."[40]

In spite of these obvious advantages of the two-party system, the existence of the two-party system or the multiple-party system is not really something on which a deliberate decision can be made by the people of any State. A country does not weigh consciously advantages and disadvantages in order to choose one system over the other. Political parties are extraordinarily complex social institutions whose character inevitably is determined by the historical traditions of the society in which they grow. There are five large parties in Finland, Norway, and Denmark and four in Sweden and Iceland, yet all Scandinavian countries are noted for the dynamism and relative stability of their governments. The question, therefore, whether two parties or many parties are more compatible with the success of a democratic government assumes an academic interest. Nevertheless the question is a real one in so far as it relates to tendencies to greater or lesser party divisions, rather than to change-over from one major type of party-system to another. The basic problem, then, involved is the weighing of the merits of simple against complex divisions. It must also be noted that long established divisions of caste, creed, class, and section are not magically dissolved by the agency of a political party. They persist and when combined with regional pride and loyalty, they seriously hinder the emergence of two stable parties.

SINGLE-PARTY SYSTEM

What a Single-Party System Means. Dictatorships also find the political party an indispensable instrument, but they use it in a very different way. Parties are the necessary means of democracy. In dictatorships they become the end. This happens when electorate, parliaments and cabinets are all, in their different ways, subordinated to the exigencies and brought under the control of the party. In the same way and by the same process the

38. Laski, H., *A Grammar of Politics,* pp. 314-15.
39. Sait, E.M., *Political Institutions, A Preface.* p. 520.
40. Finer, H., *Theory and Practice of Modern Government.* p. 360.

party which is a part may become the whole by the exclusion of other parties. It may happen in two ways. First, both in Germany and Italy the Nazi and Fascist parties respectively were given by law a special status regarding their property and the dignity and physical safety of their membership. Simultaneous to the promulgation of this law there was sweeping liquidation and prohibition of other parties. And Mussolini could write in 1932 for the *Italian Encyclopaedia*, "A party which entirely governs a nation is a fact entirely new to history, there are no possible references or parallels."

But Mussolini did not state the truth. He owed a debt to Lenin and Stalin for establishing a single-party government in Soviet Russia long before Mussolini could claim that in Italy. The Communist government did not liquidate the political parties as a consequence of the positive law. Before assuming *de facto* control of government all opponents of the Communist Party leadership had been forcibly liquidated. In the Soviet Russia "anti-national" associations were not permitted, and since political parties are associations, the domination of the Communist Party was assured. The Preamble of the Party charter, as amended by the Eighteenth Congress in March 1939, *inter alia* reads, "....The Party is the leading nucleus of all organisations of toilers, both social and State, and ensures the successful construction of Communist Society." Article 126 of the Stalin Constitution provided that "the most active and politically conscious citizens in the rank of the working class and other sections of the working people unite in the Communist Party of the Soviet Union, which was the vanguard of the working people in their struggle to strengthen and develop the socialist system and the leading core of all organisations of the working people, both public and State."[41] The Communist Party was also the only political organisation listed in Article 141 as having the right to participate in Soviet elections. Both these constitutional provisions gave the Communist Party a ruling position in the Soviet Government and positive leadership in all other organisations. The 1977 Constitution ordained that the leading and guiding force of Soviet Society and the nucleus of political system of all organisations was the Communist Party of the Soviet Union.

A single-party, thus, has become a whole, and has assumed what is nowadays called a 'total' or 'totalitarian' in character. It is in its nature a supersession of parliament and the general system of parliamentary democracy. It does not expressly abolish parliamentary institutions, it simply makes them functionless. Both Hitler and Mussolini were in the beginning champions of popular sovereignty and advocated freedom of speech and expression, and rigid limitations of the powers of the executive. But both denied to their people on coming to power the right to rule themselves through democratic institutions and suppressed ruthlessly every manifestation of anti-Fascist or anti-Nazi thought or action and exalted the executive authority. On one pretext or the other all the parties were liquidated and public opinions regimented. "The political parties," proudly declared Hitler on July 9, 1933, "have now been finally abolished. This is an historical event of which the importance and far-reaching effects have in many cases not yet been realized by all. We must now get rid of the last remains of democracy, especially of the method of voting and of the decision by majority....The (National Socialist) Party has now become the

41. Article 6.

State." In the November election of the same year an unopposed Nazi list of candidates for the Reichstag was put before the country and all were duly elected. The climax was reached when one month later "the new all Nazi Reichstag held a seven-and-one-half-minute session and for the sole purpose of electing officers. 659 Brown Shirts rose and sat down in unison when the government's list was put to vote, and then went obediently about their own business."[42] In Russia Communist Party was a united fighting organisation bound by conscious iron proletarian discipline. It was strong through its unity, "its singleness of will and a singleness of action incompatible with deviation from the programme, with breach of party discipline, or with the formation of factions inside the Party." There could not be any conflict of authority or opinion between the Communist Party and the government because both were indissolubly joined by reason of their membership especially at the higher levels. One might go a step further and say that so rigid was the control of the Party over the administration that all higher officials and the astounding majority of lower officials in the government were at the same time disciplined members of the Party. The Party, therefore, was the ultimate source of power. All important decisions on governmental policy were made at Party Conventions, Committees and Bureaus, especially the Politburo or the Political Bureau, of the Central Committee. The government only ratified and government officials, as loyal and disciplined members of the Party, religiously carried them out.

A single-party government is, therefore, totalitarian. All the authority of government is concentrated in a single integrated political party. It even absorbs the State instead of merely acting on its behalf. The only redeeming feature of one-party dictatorships is that they have a democratic flavour about them and by adopting some democratic forms had taken up some of the ideas and programmes which had grown up under democratic auspices. But any single authority is by its nature total. It has no other authority at its side with which it must divide the exercise of power. The authority of a single-party government embraces all aspects of human life and every form and phase of the activity of community's life. The Fascists did so in the name of national unity and the Communists did it in the name of social unity. The African countries, with their newly won independence, do so in the name of national unity. Whatever name may be given to it, single-party government is autocracy pure and simple and it is the autocracy of the leader of the party who is also the head of the government.

Single vs. Plural-Party System. There is nothing in common between a single-party system and a plural-party system except the name. In democracies the party is a very different thing from the one in a totalitarian State. In the former, the distinction between society and the State remains, though "they are kept in connection and interaction". In the latter, the distinction between the two is blurred or confused by the party, which controls them both alike.

In democracies there is a distinction within the State, and the different organs of government are allotted their own spheres of jurisdiction and powers. Democratic parties are an extra-constitutional growth and they are informal and non-governmental organizations. The political party in a dictatorship is the body of the faithfuls dedicated

42. Ogg, *op. cit.*, p. 722

to the maintaining of one truth which its leader avows. It permeates every governmental as well as non-governmental activity and is virtually a part of the administration it dominates. Then, in democracies there "is compensation and balance" between the party in power and the Opposition party. In a totalitarian State there is no distinction in any of the forms. Opposition is not permitted to exist and it is only one party that rules supreme. In democracies toleration, discussion and compromise are involved by the presence of plurality of associations and consequently with many currents of opinion. In a totalitarian State there is a compulsory uniform society, regimentation of opinion, and the electorate is simply an instrument of opinion.

One of the great advantages of the party system, as we know it from the democratic point of view, is that it always provides a possible alternative government and gives the electorate a choice between them. Under the one-party system there is no alternative government and no genuine choice before the electors, so that the influence of the people on political decisions is reduced to a minimum.

Democratic parties are open to all whereas parties in dictatorship are closed to all except the selected. The former Communist Party of Russia probably had no more than 20 million members and the Fascist Party had something like three million members. The Nazi Party, too, had nearly three million members. The membership is intentionally restricted and with various objects, the foremost being to maintain the militancy of the organisation. With excessive members there arises a chance of internal dissent. "Also, closeness of organisation, discipline, a feeling of community are attained with smaller numbers." At the same time, it is desired to maintain a sense, both in the public at large and among the members of the organisation itself, that the members of the party are an *elite*, selected for their superior quality as compared with the rest of the population. It also means that admission to the party is a privilege and a reward and the members owe a debt of gratitude to the leaders who have been so gracious as to permit their membership. Finally, it implies that membership of the party demands proper performance of duties and sacrifice in the task of government and leadership.

This brings into prominence the principle of leadership. So much importance is assigned to the factor of leadership in the constitution of the party and thereby in the constitution of the State that the leader becomes the repository of faith. For Nazi-ism, the National Socialist Party was Hitler and Hitler was the Party. The Party organisation book contained the oath of loyalty to the *Fuehrer*, which ran: "I pledge allegiance to my *Fuehrer*, Adolph Hitler; I promise at all times to respect and obey him and the leaders whom he appoints over me." "Believe, obey and fight" was the motto prescribed by Mussolini for his countrymen. "In the name of God and of Italy I swear that I will obey the order of the Leader without questioning." This was part of the oath taken upon admission to the Fascist Party. Obedience to the leader was, therefore, deemed a religious duty in Italy and Germany and it was rigidly enforced by the arts of discipline and propaganda. Stalin was the Lenin of his own time. During his life-time Stalin was elevated to a superman possessing supernatural characteristics. "Such a man," said Khrushchev in his speech at the Twentieth Congress, "supposedly knows everything, sees everything, thinks for everyone, can do everything, is infallible in behaviour." He further added, "Such a belief about a man, and specifically about Stalin was cultivated among us for many years." And what did Stalin do? Khrushchev gave the answer. He said, "We have to consider seriously and analyse correctly this matter in order that we may preclude any possibility of a repetition in any form whatever of what took place during the life of Stalin, who absolutely did not tolerate collegiality in leadership and in work, and who practised brutal violence, not only towards everything which opposed him, but also towards that which seemed to his capricious and despotic character, contrary to his concepts." Khrushchev himself became Stalin and met the same fate at the hands of the new leadership.

Finally, the leader of the Party is the head of the government, and the head of the government dominates every power and every sphere of the action of the State. Throughout Mussolini's autobiography are his assertions of "my command", "my guidance", "my sense of balance and judgment", "my irresistible domination". II Duce spoke the first and the last word for party and government. "Dictatorial parties are not parties," concludes Finer, "but doctrinal despotism; they do not spread and encourage leadership but monopolise it."[43] To quote Lipson, "...a party is by definition a part of the whole and therefore implies the presence of an alternative and an opposition. To speak of the 'one-party State' is to employ a contradiction in terms. Such a State whether it is Fascist or Communist, whether its capital is Moscow or Madrid, Bucharest or Lisbon, exhibits a tyrannical monopoly of power. Its proper name is dictatorship."[44] Democracies anticipate an alternation of leaders and provide the public with a choice of candidates for office. Whereas democracies use the fervour and slogans of an electoral campaign to publicize the differences between programmes of the parties, the party in a dictatorship carries on continual propaganda campaigns in support of the government's objectives and is the chief means by which conformity is maintained throughout the society.

INTEREST AND PRESSURE GROUPS

Interest Groups. Modern pluralistic society consists of large numbers of economic, occupational, religious, possibly ethnic, and other groups in support of educational and cultural activities, inevitably confronts the problem of relation between these "interests" and those of government and politics. In an open society, interest groups will be permitted freely to organise themselves. They will not only engage in an interplay of forces *vis-a-vis* each other, but will also tend to bring their influence to bear on the machinery, the institutions and process of government. They would formulate demands, press for concrete specific interests or material advantages demanded by their members, oppose intended action which they deem objectionable, express or articulate the views of some part of public opinion on public issues, or campaign for new policies or even a new society. Of course, not all groups have any direct political mission and some even have little indirect significance. But quite a number of them play an important part and sometimes an indispensable part in political activity.

A division may be made into 'self-interested' and 'other-interested' groups, although

43. Finer, H., *The Theory and Practice of Modern Government,* p. 332.
44. Lipson, L., *The Great Issues of Politics,* p. 278.

allocation to a category is a matter of degree for pure examples are rare. A trade union is concerned to promote the interests of its members and while it may not promote them without regard to the effect on others, it is essentially concerned with its own interests. The Prisoners' Aid Society, on the other hand, is not concerned to reform in order that its members shall be better cared for if and when they are imprisoned, but with the welfare of others whose ranks the members do not expect to join. The Automobile Association is a group primarily concerned to look after its members, the motorists, while the Society for the Prevention of Cruelty to Animals has no animal paying subscriptions to it. The distinction is sometimes described as one between interest groups, which protect shared sectional interests, and attitude groups, which promote cause. Appreciation of the two-fold distinction is more important than the terminology. Taken together, they are here referred to as interest groups.

Although groups do cooperate from time, to time their activities are essentially competitive—they compete to pass, repeal or prevent laws and regulations, and in doing so they may find themselves directly opposed by other interests. Competition is usually indirect, but direct opposition often arises from a group specifically formed as a countervailing force to one already in existence. Out of this competition and participation of political parties and governments public policy emerges. The national, or public, interest may not be served as a consequence—for what is it? "Certainly not the view of one interest, nor of a government without regard to interests, not a party of few interests. In the absence of a known general interest, policy based on publicized competition of interests with government as the 'Great Arbiter', may be the best available."[45]

Pressure Groups. When interest groups exercise pressure upon government in order to obtain laws and administrative decisions compatible with their special interests, they turn into pressure groups. Pressures on rulers is as old as a political system and have always taken a variety of forms, from riots, acts of organised violence and rebellions, social movements and political parties to the peaceful presentation of petitions seeking the redress of grievances or the ability to influence decisions. "What is distinctive in modern times," says Michael Curtis, "is the sustained nature of group activity and the prominent role played by groups in obtaining or preventing action, and in influencing decisions and policy."[46]

Pressure Groups and Political Parties. Pressure groups differ from political parties. What differentiates political parties from pressure groups is the breadth and variety of their followings and the orientation of their programmes. Political parties embrace the whole nation and their followings know no fetters of territory, region, class, occupation or section. They join the people from the entire length and breadth of the country and knit all those who think alike and subscribe to the programmes which embrace the interests of the nation and concern the issues that confront the country from within and without. Pressure groups, on the other hand, tend to emphasise special areas of interest, giving them sharper and more detailed expression than can be done by political parties. The interests of pressure groups are sectional or localised while the emphasis of political

45. Eric Rowe, *Modern Politics,* p. 77.

46. Michael Curtis, *Comparative Government and Politics,* p. 124.

parties is upon achieving the organisation of opinion on all public issues, internal and external. A party is a generalist in the organisation of opinion, whereas a pressure group is a specialist rather than generalist. A pressure group performs the function of interest articulation while a party is an aggregation of interests. Because awakening interest in the broader questions of national importance is a more difficult task than stimulating interest in matters that obviously affect the business, occupation or caste, parties must make people politically conscious, that is, aware of their role as citizens. Pressure groups are seldom imbued with such ideals.

Political parties contest elections and campaign to win. They put up candidates, present their programmes before the electorate, mobilize the party workers and appeal the voters and the public at large to support their programmes. The party that wins capitalizes on its success. Pressure groups do not contest elections and have no programmes to offer. They are oriented towards affecting policies, especially on the issues that touch them closely. They lend their support to the parties that espouse their cause, but they do not permanently associate with or support one party. In reality they reward their friends and punish their enemies by working against those which have no sympathy for their cause. Thus, a pressure group usually declares itself to be a "non-partisan organisation of persons united for the achievement of certain principles and for the protection or promotion of material activities and of ideal causes deemed vital to the group's existence or survival."

Pressure Groups and Lobbies. Pressure groups and lobbies are not synonymous. There is a distinct difference between the two. Pressure groups tend to influence the legislators, the administrators and public opinion. Lobbies, on the other hand, confine their activities essentially to the legislature while it is in session and are concerned with the passage or defeat of a bill. Thus, the extent of the activities of pressure groups is wider than those of the lobbies. Most pressure groups maintain their lobbies, in addition to their attempts to influence legislation indirectly by affecting public opinion. As Key says, "The political interests of agriculture, for example, may be advanced through lobbying and propaganda activities of pressure groups such as American Farm Bureau Federation"[47] Pressure groups in the United States appoint their agents to establish personal contacts with the legislators of the States and Congressmen and influence their votes either in favour or against a particular bill. They also issue pamphlets and books portraying their cause and even use the radio, where the media is not state owned or controlled to influence public opinion.

Appraisal of Pressure Groups. Pressure groups have been variously viewed. It has often been argued that the expression of group interests is undesirable in itself and may be contrary to the public interest. Rousseau was of the opinion that there should be "no partial societies within the State", because they were a danger to social and political unity. Hobbes considered that corporations were "worms in the entrails of national man". Carl Friedrich points out that pressure groups "were viewed with moral indignation and alarm by the last generation. They were held up to scorn both by muckrakers and by sane students of politics. They were the sinister force growing at the foundations of modern democracy, of representative government,. and the word 'lobby' supposedly comprehended

47. Key, V.O.. *Politics: Parties and Pressure Groups,* p. 130.

a whole congeries of abuses, corruption, fraud and the like."[48] Friedrich believes that there "was and is more than a kernel of truth in these assertions." Interest and pressure groups are the living "public" behind the political parties and the activities of these interests have weakened the belief in popular government. They seek to arrogate to themselves power without corresponding responsibility and undermine faith in the united people by exalting the interests of small segments of the people disregarding the interests of all or a substantial segment of the people.

Woodrow Wilson's attack upon Congressional government, and its committee system, was based upon allegations relating to powers which interest groups arrogated unto themselves. He wrote, "It is in committee rooms that legislation not desired by the interests dies. It is in the committee rooms that legislation desired by the interests is framed and brought forth."[49] James Bryce devoted a searching appendix to the "lobbies" in his book, *American Commonwealth*.[50] Key writes, "The use of the term pressure conjures up a picture of a wicked lobbyist attempting to coerce a righteous legislator to deviate from his disposition to follow the public interest. By and large the relations between organized interests and legislators must be described in other terms, although on occasions the crudest pressures are invoked for indefensible purposes."[51] According to Karl Deutsch, the political progress, in one sense, is the result of bargaining among different groups and the politics of bargaining furnishes the basis of Robert Dahl's model of a Western system.[52] "In such a pluralistic society," he says, "any number can play. Each special interest can set up its own group, its own office, its own organization; each can hire secretaries, each can buy mimeograph machines and begin to churn out releases, each can retain lobbyists in Washington to provide legislators with ample, although one-sided, information and to take legislators to lunch or find more substantial inducements for legislators to vote the way the interest group desires."[53]

But in a society, as the United States, where almost every substantial interest group is organized, two serious problems, according to Deutsch, arise. First, if most interest groups are organized, "heaven help the residual groups that are not—the tenants in the slums, the poor and some of the ethnic minorities." Since they had no organization and consequently lacked the bargaining power, they got the worst out of political bargaining. They did not get support from any of the older interest groups. Secondly, when almost everybody is organized, "society reached a point where almost nothing can be done. Groups with limited power usually find it easier to veto someone else's proposal than to push through any positive policy of their own. When this happens, politics becomes negative, and interest groups run into veto groups." Even when positive policies are possible, all major proposals must be agreed to by every relevant interest group. And the larger the number of organized groups, there is more consultation and consequently more delay with the result that it becomes harder "to turn any idea into action."[54]

48. Friedrich. C.J., *Constitutional Government and Democracy,* p. 460.
49. Wilson, W., *The New Freedom,* p. 125.
50. Bryce, J., *American Commonwealth,* Vol. 1, pp. 691-92.
51. Key, V.O., *Politics: Parties and Pressure Groups,* pp. 158-59.
52. Dahl, R.A., *Modern Political Analysis,* p. 43.
53. Karl, W. Deutsch, *Politics and Government,* p. 53.
54. *Ibid.,* pp. 53-54.

Deutsch concludes from this analysis that "Pluralistic organization can lend, therefore, to creeping immobility. The society becomes harder and harder to move, and attempting reform and innovation becomes as frustrating as swimming in a sea of molasses. Eventually, it becomes so difficult to get things done that some device must be found for breaking the deadlock." The device is the *emergency*, which does not require consultation with all the interest groups as rapidity is the *sine qua non* of emergency. "If there is a real emergency, we greet it with relief. If there is none, we are tempted to invent one. Thus, the politics of a highly pluralistic, highly organised society, a *polyarchy* (rule by many) as Dahl would call it,[55] becomes a cycle of alternating states or immobility and emergency."[56]

But this is not exactly a correct appraisal. The feeling that pressure groups are necessarily harmful, because they seek to exalt the interests of the small, though possibly wealthy or highly organised segments of the population, disregarding the interests of all or a substantial segment of the people is not the entire truth. It all depends upon the extent of influence the pressure groups exercise and the consideration that they receive at the hands of the appropriate authorities. If all the interest groups and not only the powerful and better organised, get a fair deal and if the internal organisations of all such groups function in such a way that their entire membership rather than their entrenched oligarchies determine their policies, their utility in the political structure of a country cannot be lightly brushed aside. In other words, it means "how much democracy, in the sense of responsibleness, there is in the internal structure of these groups, as well as in their relation to government and society at large."

It should be one of the objectives of a democratic system to reveal to the public the pressure of influence groups so that their services and impact can be evaluated by the general public. Democracy lives on responsibility and, consequently, it requires sufficient openness about how political and administrative decisions are reached, so that the public may spot out undue influence and in case of any lapse it is corrected. One of the short-comings of the non-democratic regimes is that pressures, which do exist in the Communist and Nationalist systems, are kept secret and the public does not know who is responsible for making a decision and what the decision actually is.

Where they work in the open, pressure groups fulfil a necessary and potentially wholesome function. As a matter of fact, lobbying can claim two essentially democratic procedures: the right to participate in the formulation of policy, and the right to seek redress of grievances. They provide a useful link between the people and the government and can, thus, help the administrators or legislators to secure information on facts and attitudes. Any democratic government will like to assess the reactions of its intended policy or programme, particularly those likely to be concerned with it. The widespread attitude of *laissez faire* towards interest groups, says Eric Rowe, "is due to the dependence on them by governments of modern complex countries. Government leaders are assisted by the groups in the provision of teachnical information, in the execution of policies and in the defence of policies against attack by others." The assistance provided by interest

55. Dahl, R.A., *Modern Political Analysis,* p. 73.
56. Karl W. Deutsch, *Politics and Government,* p. 54.

groups in these and other ways has led to groups being represented in the formal structure of government on various councils, committees and other advisory bodies. The functions of these councils and bodies are advisory indeed, but they provide a meeting ground of different interests where details can be discussed and ideas thrashed and hammered. The purpose of bringing advisory bodies early in the policy-making process is to know and assess the general commitment at an early stage. The policy emerging from such consultation is the agreed policy which shields the government against subsequent criticism and allow it to avoid amendments likely to inhibit the process of government.

Interest groups, quite apart from making more effective by the provision of information and advice, are beneficial in involving more individuals in the process of policy-making and emphasise diversity in a society which national party allegiances tend to blur. They also provide a continuous and open channel of communication between rulers and ruled and encourage both regard for the claims of others and protection against the claims of others which might otherwise proceed unchecked. In a representative system whereas responsibility of a party for the execution of a mandate is periodic, it becomes a continuous process when supplemented by a network of interest groups. There is a continuous policy debate, diversified influence and government by conciliation and occasionally consensus.

But the problem created by the pressure groups is that they very often force their will upon legislators or administrators and thereby they not only lower standards of public morality, but also distort to their own advantage policy which is or should be designed to the public interest, or at least should constitute a fair compromise of conflicting interests or opposing groups. But how far pressure groups can rig the political market depends upon the strength or weakness of the political decision-making process. The type of the political system, too, has a good deal to do with the way in which pressures operate. In a parliamentary system basic decisions are made at the top level of the executive rather than the legislature. The pressure lobbyist would, therefore, pressurize the executive rather than the members of the legislature. In a Presidential system the executive and the legislature are two separate branches of government and pressures are likely to affect both the branches equally. Likewise, the way in which political parties represent or reflect particular interests has a bearing on the chances and methods of pressures. Much also depends upon the type and attitude of leadership and upon the social origin of the political elite.

SUGGESTED READINGS

Barker, E.: *Reflections on Government,* Chap. X.

Brown, B.E.: *New Directions in Comparative Politics,* Chap. II.

Chandrasekharan, C.V.: *Political Parties.*

Castles, F.G.: *Pressure Groups and Political Culture.*

Duverger, M.: *Political Parties.*

Ehrmann, H.: *Interest Groups on Four Continents.*

Field, G.C.: *Political Theory,* Chap. XI.

Finer, H.: *Theory and Practice of Modern Government,* Chaps. XIV, XV, XVI.

Gilchrisi, R.N.: *Principles of Political Science,* Chap. XV.
Holcombe, A.N.: *Political Parties of Today.*
Holcombe, A.N.: The *New Party Politics.*
Holtzman, A.: *Interest Groups and Lobbying.*
Kapur, A.C.: *Government of the U.S.S.R.,* Chap, XII.
Key, V.O., Jr.: *Politics, Parties and Pressure Groups.*
Leacock, S.: *Elements of Political Science,* Chap. VIII.
Leiserson, A.: *Parties and Politics.*
Lowell, A.L.: *Government and Parties in Continental Europe,* Vol. I, Chaps. XXIX-XXV, Vol. II, Chaps XXXI-XXXVII.
MacIver, R.M.: *The Modern State*, Chap. XIII.
Maine, H.: *Popular Government.*
McKenzie, R.T.: *British Political Parties.*
Michels, R.: *Political Parties.*
Munro, W.B.: *Personality in Politics.*
NeuMann, S. (ed.): *Modern Political Parties.' Approaches to Comparative Politics.*
Ostrogorski, M. I.: *Democracy and the Party System in the United States.*
Ostrogorski M.I.: *Democracy and Organization of Political Parties.*
Potter, A.M.: *Organized Group in British National Politics.*
Ray, P.O.: *Introduction to Political Parties and Practical Politics.*
Rossiter, Clinton: *Parties and Politics in America.*
Sait, E.M.: *American Parties and Electrons.*
Sait, E.M.: *Political Institutions — A Prefce,* Chap. XXI.
Schapiro, Leonard: *The Communist Party of Soviet Russia.*
Schattschneider, E.E.: *Party Government.*
Sidgwick, H.: *Elements of Politics,* Chap. XXIX.
Truman, David: *The Governmental Process.*
Wilson, F.G.: *The Elements of Modern Politics,* Chap. XIII.
Wilson, F.G.: *"Independent Voting" Encyclopaedia of Social Sciences,* Vol. VII.

24

CHAPTER

Public Opinion

Meaning and Nature of Public Opinion. All cooperation and regulation rest on opinion whatever be the nature and character of government. David Hume says, "It is ... on opinion only that government is founded and this maxim extends to the most despotic and most military governments as well as to the most free and most popular."[1] Public opinion is an organization of separate individual judgements, a "cooperative product of communication and reciprocal influence,"[2] as Cooley observes. But there is a difference in the nature of opinion as obtainable in democratic and non-democratic polities. In a non-democratic polity opinion is mere acquiescence, a quiet consent or submission due to either respect for authority, habit of obedience or fear of tyranny. It is neither spontaneous nor the expression of individual's free and considered judgement. In authoritarian regimes it is tailor-made, regimented and ideological. A free expression of opinion emerging from the clash of opinions and representing the will of the people directed towards the welfare of the community is essentially a democratic process. It assumes the role of popular opinion and as MacIver says, "This incessant activity of popular opinion is the dynamic of democracy."[3]

It cannot be said with precision how did the concept of public opinion originate, although the idea behind it had existed always and it commanded great prestige. The Greeks held that there was divinity in the voice of the people and the Romans used the term *consensus populi*, consent of the people, though they applied it only in the juridical sense. During the Middle Ages the dictum *Vox populi, Vox dei*, the voice of the people was the voice of god, was the common belief and formed the norm of political behaviour. Niccolo Machiavel, in the *Discourses*, compared the voice of the people with the voice of god.

But it took a tangible shape and political content at the hands of Jean Jacquess Rousseau on the eve of the French Revolution. He distinguished his doctrine of the general will from the will of all and declared that the former must be disinterested and concern the general welfare. The general will being the compound of the best wills of all citizens willing the best interests of the community and its lasting welfare, it must

1. David Hume, *The First Principles of Government.*
2. Cooley, C.H., *Social Organisation,* p. 121.
3. MacIver, R.M., *The Ramparts We Guard,* p. 28.

always be followed. Here are the germs of public opinion for what it stands in essence today.

The idea underlying the concept of public opinion matured after the French Revolution and it became a democratic process and a working measure of common agreement and a driving force of governmental actions and policies. During recent times the concept of public opinion has acquired a fresh significance at the hands of some eminent intellectuals who have made it an area of specialised study. They question the validity of the assumptions on which the concept of public opinion was based and call it a traditional approach which is devoid of realities of life.

Traditional Concept. Rousseau is the apostle of democracy and the exponent of its direct form. He regarded representative government as a specious form of slavery. For Rousseau, law is not the will of a class, but the will of the whole nation. "This will," he says, "is to be discovered simply by asking the nation to meet together and declare it. Only when I actively assist in legislation am I really a citizen and genuinely free, and since the fewer the citizens are, the more weight my voice has amongst them." He, thus, firmly believed in direct government by citizens, who should themselves, in public meetings, make laws, without being betrayed by the elected representatives. He declared that England is free only on the day of election.

But Rousseau's disdain of representative government did not deter its growth and evolution. A small State became a political anachronism with the birth of the nation-State. Since then, the march of indirect democracy was slow but discernible even in the heyday of absolute monarchies. When the people demanded their rights and privileges and protested against the absolute authority of the monarchs, they succeeded in snatching from them some concessions which had the rudiments of self-government. The process started in England during the reign of King John and steadily extended its impact to other lands. Each step taken was the natural consequence of some earlier step and the final shape to emerge was representative government with which we are familiar and accept it as synonymous with democracy.

When the system of representative government had generally taken firm roots, public opinion came to rest on the premise that when a multitude of people arrived at a consensus on any public issue, it was representative of the opinion of the community and, accordingly, formed the basis of public decisions. This analysis of public opinion accepted the notion of political man as a rational being; a thinking man who discriminated between right and wrong and was guided by the honesty of purpose in arriving at decision on public matters. Such an enlightened opinion was expressed freely and ultimately consensus reached on the issues involved and it represented the will of the community. The will of the community reflected a single soul aiming at the good of all. This homogeneous opinion was free from all taints of factional and sectional interests.

Critics of the Traditional Concept. But such a homogeneity is rare to achieve. Politics is based on disagreement and if there were virtually no disagreement politics is seriously curtailed, if not destroyed, and that is the end of democracy. A public is composed of a multitude of individuals and they differ in their views, interests and characteristics and it is impossible in any grouping to agree unanimously or even to arrive at consensus to represent a homogeneous opinion. There are the infirmities of human nature and social disharmonies that inhibit, pervert and distort public opinion. Man in politics is not so rational as it had been assumed by the traditionalists. Opinion is very often manipulated by those who have the power to wield influence or the religious or caste enchantment to attract and dictate. Public opinion is, therefore, not the result of the considered judgment, of the rational man and his appraisal of the issues involved. It is a manufactured pattern of opinions and there are as many opinions as there are groups of men. Opinions are of publics and for political purposes. There can be no single opinion.

James Bryce was the first to revolt against the traditional concept of public opinion. "The term (public opinion)," he maintained, "is commonly used to denote the aggregates of the views men hold regarding matters that affect or interest the community. Thus understood, it is a congeries of all sorts of discrepant notions, beliefs, fancies, prejudices, aspirations. It is confused, incoherent, amorphous, varying from day to day and week to week. But in the midst of this diversity and confusion every question as it rises into importance is subjected to a process of consolidation and clarification until there emerge and take definite shape certain views, or set of disconnected views, each held and advocated in common by bodies of citizens. It is to the power exerted by any such view, or set of views, when held by an apparent majority of citizens, that we refer when we talk of public opinion as approving or disapproving a certain doctrine or proposal, and thereby becoming a guiding or ruling power. Or we may think of the opinion of the whole nation as made up of different currents of sentiment, each embodying or supporting a view or a doctrine or a practical proposal. Some currents develop more strength than others because they have behind them larger numbers or more intensity of conviction, and when one is evidently the strongest it begins to be called public opinion *par excellence*, being taken to embody the views supposed to be held by the bulk of the people."[4]

Bryce made an empirical study by moving among the unbiased persons in order to find out their views on public questions. He came to the conclusion, as a result of his investigation, that not all persons are interested in politics. Nor have they any knowledge and capacity to judge and form views on matters that affect the interest of the community. It is only a small section of society, educated, intellectually alive and well-informed, who evince keen interest on the problems of the nation, go deep into the issues involved, sort out the complexities bristling such problems and suggest ways and means to solve them. This small segment of society comprising different groups do not think alike on the same problems. They differ in their approach and analysis in accordance with their own way of thinking and offer solutions in conformity to the views they form on the subject. They present their views to the public at large either by pen or word. A comparatively larger section of the society, who are passive in politics but understand the intricacies of the issues involved, listen and read what the elite has to say, and present their own views and suggestions through various channels of communication. The elite think and judge the views so expressed and correct and modify their own, if the critics are sufficiently articulate and their arguments are well-meaning. In this process definiteness is achieved and opinion is crystallised. If the majority of the people are convinced that the opinion

4. Bryce, J., *Modern Democracies,* Vol. I, p. 173.

that had taken a final shape is for the good of the community or the intensity of the opinion, even if it is a minority opinion, is so great that there is no way out but to accept it, it becomes public opinion. But the criterion of such an opinion must be the general welfare of the community.

Alfred Lowell and Walter Lippmann were two other notable critics of the traditional concept of public opinion and both together paved the way for the development of the contemporary view about the meaning and nature of public opinion. Lowell argued that public opinion can never be unanimous. It is always divided and different opinions are held by different groups of people on the same problem or problems. When a particular opinion is accepted by a huge majority of the people and the minority is convinced, after full and thorough discussion of its pros and cons, that it aims at public good, it is a public opinion. Lowell explained that if the minority does not give free and full support or gives it grudgingly or unwillingly, it cannot be called public, though majority may be at the back of the prevailing opinion.[5]

Walter Lippmann introduced the concept of 'Stereotypes' in his analysis of public opinion.[6] He investigated into the inter-connection between man and his environments in the opinion forming process. He pointed out that our world being beyond the reach, the sight, and the mind of the ordinary "shut in man" has to be explored, reported and imagined, and that he really responds not to facts, but to pseudo-environments, a most inadequate picture of the "great society." Generally speaking, he argued, man's political ideas are moulded by the surroundings in which he lives and the information he gathers from such environments. It is not based on facts of which he may himself be the author through the evidence collected or seen by him. His source of information is secondary coming to him from the people living in his vicinity or emanating from various channels of communication, like the newspapers and the radio. He, thus, sees the world largely through the eyes of others and relies upon the information communicated to him and this, too, may be distorted and very often it is. The result is that he forms "a picture in his head" which it is not possible to efface. This fixed pattern of thought Lippmann calls "Stereotypes," that is, thought process in formation of opinion which is not the result of individual's own perception and judgement and lacks objectivity.

The notion of rationality of man has also been questioned on the ground of inequality of men in their intellectual capacity to understand the complexities of politics, national and international. Then, there are day-to-day compulsions of life in which men are so inextricably enmeshed that they have no time for politics even if they are inclined to find interest. From those two disabilities from which men generally suffer Lippmann concludes that the general public is as it were "led by the nose" by a small minority of those individuals who have the intellectual capacity to know and understand the political problems and offer their solutions. The trend of opinion is created by this small segment of society and public is drugged with the opinions of this elite divided into different groups of opinion. They accept one opinion or the other which is the conscious creation of a handful of opinion-creating individuals.

5. Lowell, A.L, *Public Opinion and Popular Government,* Chs I & II.
6. Lippmann, Walter, *Public Opinion,* pp. 15, 25, 29, 48, 50.

Contemporary View. The contemporary view outright rejects the dogma of homogeneity of opinion which Lippmann, thus, explained : "All mankind was within hearing that all mankind when it heard would respond homogeneously because it had a single soul."[7] The contemporary view is that there is no single opinion but multiplicity of opinions held by different groups and there are as many opinions as there are politically articulate groups each commanding its own public support of that opinion. A particular type of public is distinguished from others in its aims and objects and it offers its own solution of political problems confronting the country strictly in accordance with its ideological approach. The aims and objects of a trade union are different from those of the employers association. There may be even geographical groups with a rural or urban identification. India is a cluster of religious, regional and caste groups. Religious groups, exclusively having members of their own community, as Muslims and Sikhs, play a significant role in the politics of the country because religion for them is inseparable from politics. Then, there are political parties, some national and others regional, with different labels and ideologies. A group becomes politically significant when, either singly or in coalition with other groups, it is returned to power after receiving the electoral mandate and such a majority embodies public opinion.

Criteria of Public Opinion. A public opinion must be public rather individual or sectional. Individual or sectional opinion is neither public nor opinion as its aim is not the good of the people as a whole or at least a majority of them. And it must really be an opinion firmly and convincingly held. A mere wind or gust of popular opinion cannot be an opinion of a public nature. It must have stabilising effect because public opinion does not suffer from telescopic defects. Its horizon is vast and it takes due cognisance of the necessities of today and the exigencies of tomorrow. A public opinion must be stable and enduring. Secondly, it should be an opinion as widely held as possible. Opinion cannot be regarded as public unless it is substantially shared by the dominant portion of the community. This does not, however, mean that it should be an opinion of the majority. Nor is unanimity required, although the more generally an opinion is held the more public it can be said to be. In fact, progress begins with the minority and it is completed, as George William Curtis says, "by persuading the majority, by showing reason and the advantage of the step forward, and that is accomplished by appealing to the intelligence of the majority." History has sufficient examples to prove that no reform in any country met with popular favour at the outset. In most cases a few persons took up a cause arousing very great opposition in the beginning. Their persistent efforts, however, enabled them to enlist popular opinion in their favour. Willoughby says, "In any community of men that what has assumed the character of public opinion is the result not of the opinion of all its members but only of those persons, few or many, who are led to think and to form judgements regarding matters of general interest." A true public opinion is, therefore, one which is promoted by due regard to public welfare. It rests on weighing the facts and is not the result of a prejudice or an impression. It is an enduring opinion of the people.

The true worth of public opinion is that while the minority may not share the majority opinion, but they must feel by conviction, not by fear or coercion, to accept it as it aims

7. Lippmann, Walter, *The Phantom Public,* pp. 168-69.

at the good of all and no sectional interests are involved. If the majority promotes its own interests disregardful of the interests of the community as a whole, it is not a genuine public opinion. On the other hand, if the majority opinion is inspired by the ideals of the good of the community, it is a genuine public opinion. It means that in a representative government where the majority party holds the reins of administration and decisions are taken by majority of votes, the majority party should so conduct itself that the opinion held by it is *par excellence* and the legislation it enacts has the spontaneity of acceptance by all sections of the people otherwise there shall be neither peace nor contentment nor obedience to laws nor loyal devotion to the State. If the criterion of law is that it should be the expression of the will of the people, it is a condition precedent that it must be representative of the popular opinion.

Public Opinion and Democracy. It is a truism that democracy means government by public opinion. It represents at once a working measure of common agreement and a driving force in working the governmental machinery. It has always commanded great prestige and has now and then been invested almost with superhuman dignity. It is true that opinion has often been perverted and distorted by social disharmonies and it has split into sectional opinions, yet despite its imperfections, it is an active and propelling factor in a democratic State. The people at regular intervals are called upon to elect their representatives and the electors express their opinion in favour or against certain programmes and policies put before them by different political parties. If the majority vote goes in favour of a party it gives a mandate to that particular party or coalition of parties, who had agreed on some basic principles prior to the election, to form government. The mandate is withdrawn at the next election if the confidence reposed in them had been betrayed. In fact, no party, whether in power or Opposition, can afford to forget that to-morrow is the day of election. The ultimate appeal rests with the people, and the party in office must remember those who entrusted them with power. Responsibility and responsiveness to the people keeps the government alert and removes possibilities of arbitrary exercise of authority. It, thus, ensures a certain measure of fairplay to minorities.

Public opinion has also played an invaluable role in the working of political institutions and serves as the most potent agency of coordination. In the presidential system, it smooths the functioning of the executive and legislative departments and brings harmony between the two without the one being responsible to the other. What the framers of the Constitution had put apart public opinion tries to bring together for mutual action. It also prevents or solves deadlocks between coordinate legislative chambers. In Britain, the House of Lords, though a secondary chamber, has always respected the electoral mandate. The Conservative majority, immediately following Labour victory in 1945, approved bills embracing such measures as nationalisation on the ground that the Labour Party had received a mandate from the electorate.

Democracy generates freedom and guarantees expressions of views to influence public policy. By giving to citizens an opportunity to have their say, democracy binds them with a sort of vital tissue to government. There are, thus, not only outgoing currents of commands and ordinances issued from the central seat of authority, but also incoming currents in the form of suggestions, desires and grievances of people. Democracy is best qualified constantly to adjust the supply of control to social need and favours a wholesale social equilibrium. It deepens the sense of social obligation. Public opinion enables democratization of political institutions and keeps them true to the constructive role and offset the shortcomings of *expertise*. The governing class is particularly sensitive to its obligations and the majority party in office is alive to the fact that one class rules by sufferance of the whole nation as trustees of the public. This makes them exceedingly careful not to ride roughshod over public opinion and violate the decencies of their public conduct. It, thus, keeps all agencies of control and service up to certain standards of behaviour. It throws outworn laws into desuetude and influences judicial pronouncements, bringing the administration of justice abreast of the times.

Democracy lives and thrives on public opinion, provided it is honest, forceful and vigilant. It has no place for Lippmann's "stereotypes." A citizen of a democratic State must necessarily be a thinking human being who actively participates in the affairs of the State and responds to real facts with fulness of human sympathy. A common man cannot be expected to form an opinion on the details of all public questions, but he should be able to discern whether the ruling party keeps to the standards of public decency by observing rules of the game and, thus, be able to discover whether the party which he had supported before and intends to support now is generally seeking to promote the welfare of the community. This he can do by judging the broad principles of rival policies.

OPINION FORMATION AGENCIES

Opinion Formation. But in every society, whatever be the desideratum, Lippmann's "Stereotypes" constitute a vast majority. This category of people are more or less indifferent to politics, read little and think less. They generally adopt whatever view that prevails in the social class or the industrial milieu to which they belong. It is only a small minority of the intellectual elite-statesmen, legislators, politicians, journalists, administrators and eminent intellectuals specialised in various aspects of public affairs that formulate public opinion. They have the capacity to judge and form views on matters that interest and affect the community. They marshall the facts, formulate specific views and argue them out through different channels of communication for consideration of the public. As a vast majority of the people have neither the time nor the inclination to know the complexities of public affairs, it is only for the comparatively passive segment of society who listen and read, consider and weigh and form judgments on the facts and arguments presented to them by the formulators of public opinion. Channels of communication aside, there are various other agencies of moulding and shaping opinion. Some of them disseminate knowledge and sharpen the intellect to form an intelligent judgment and their impact is enduring. Others influence views and are the creators of opinion, especially for the "stereotypes."

Press. An extraordinarily powerful agency of communication is periodical literature and the most potent of such literature is the daily press. Lippmann attached so much importance to the daily press in educating the people and forming opinion that he called it the "bible of democracy." The rapid spread of mass education, the phenomenal development in the means of transport, the latest innovations in the printing process have tremendously increased circulations of the newspapers and are available even in the remotest corner of a country at a price that is within the reach of an average man. Their arrival is anxiously awaited and with almost all the educated people reading of the newspapers is the first priority of the day. For the urbanites it is mostly a bed-tea necessity.

The daily press reports national and international news, proceedings of the legislative discussions and debates, if in session announcements of government statements including policy statements, and publishes views of statesmen, eminent persons, scholars, partymen and columnists on various issues of public importance. Presentation of facts is not the only function of the dailies. Facts are systematised and interpreted and highlighted and commented in the editorial columns. The manner in which the news are splashed and given the slant, the tone in which they are presented and the comments offered in the editorials depend largely on the policy of the managing agency of the daily, the intellectual calibre, the tastes, and predilections of those to whom they are addressed. Every reader is deeply attached to one newspaper or the other that caters to his tastes and leanings. The news and views projected in the daily of his choice generally form the basis of the opinion of the people indifferent to public affairs and the 'stereotypes' of Lippmann's conception. Even those who interest themselves in politics sift information supplied by newspapers to select that which will buttress an existing commitment.

The newspapers also provide a forum for the expression of the views and opinions of the people on matters of public importance, policies of the government, and ventilation of grievances. Almost all the dailies reserve a few columns on the editorial page for the expression of such views and ventilation of grievances. "Letters to the Editor" is the familar name under which they are published. A government by publicity, as a democratic government is, cannot remain oblivious of people's reactions to its policies and the grievances they seek to be redressed. If it does, it does so on its own peril. All democratic governments maintain their highly organised Public Relations Departments to keep liaison between the people and the government and bring all such matters containing suggestions and grievances, comments of the press and views of statesmen to the notice of the government for appropriate action. Here newspapers play a vital role in the crystallisation of public opinion.

A free and impartial press is indispensable for the successful functioning of a democratic government. It acts as a jealous guardian of the rights and liberties of citizens and is a forum for the discussion of public policies enabling the government to feel the pulse of the people. But as the conditions prevail, press manipulates opinion by suppressing facts and distorting news. News is purveyed as fact, comment as news and common occurrences are made specially dramatic in pursuit of gain by the managing agencies and the columnists. The newspapers change their opinions rapidly to catch every passing breeze of popular sentiment or the whims of the powers-that-be. Too often the press has been converted into an agency of official propaganda in consideration of patronage through lucrative advertisements. A good number of the dailies essentially depend upon advertisements for their existence and it is not uncommon, particularly in India, for ministers to ring up editors in the evening to give the keynote of morrow. If some newspapers incur the displeasure of government, they turn to other selfish interests to compensate for their loss. In times of excitement and agitation, governments have been known to control the access to facts and to strike at the roots of independent opinion.

Even more sinister than government control is the influence of wealth.[8] Big business has been capturing the press and treating it as a commercial enterprise and not a vehicle of dissemination of information, knowledge and expression of opinion. The stupendous costs of production and dependence on advertisements have rendered a large section of the press an appendage of capitalism in many countries. "Newspapers have been syndicated and sold like mechanical plants to the highest bidders. The changing whims and caprices of press magnates have sometimes been reflected with such fidelity in the daily press as to make it a laughing-stock."[9]

To sum up, the low standards of the reading public, control by government, influence of wealth, pandering to the interests of advertisers and the readers to increase circulation by manipulating facts in order to cater to their tastes have served to bring the press into discredit. The result is as Herman Finer points out, "The amount of objectively true information and balanced opinion is, on the whole, small, and the press has acquired an extraordinary dominance over opinion, aggravating rather than correcting its defects."[10] This poses a serious threat to democracy as genuine public opinion becomes impossible to obtain. Lippmann has suggested the institution of fact-finding bodies to counteract the "stereotypes" of opinion. But lasting improvement depends on enlightened public itself and through journalistic standards and professional decencies.

Mass Media. Radio, television and cinema are effective instruments of educating the people in public affairs and help to shape their opinions. Newspapers are within the reach of the educated class of society only. In developing and underdeveloped countries, where percentage of illiteracy is fairly high, audio-visual media fill in the gap to a great extent. But cinema has remained almost exclusively a means of entertainment than a source of education, knowledge and information. As the industry is in private sector, its promoters are entirely guided in their enterprise by commercial interests. Documentaries and other educational films are seldom ventured, although their educational value can hardly be denied.

Radio and television are the popular mass media of communication. They have multiplied audiences to millions and opinion leaders have access to almost every home. Consequently, man sees the world through the eyes of others and forms opinion as the image opinion leaders create on his disinterested and unthinking mind. Where this mass media are a monopoly controlled by the State, as in India, public opinion is clearly largely what it is made to be. The task of the controllers is not only to entertain and inform the listeners but to unite the community behind the rulers and their policies. Nor do opportunities exist for equal participation and expression of independent views by other parties and sections of the opinion. The manuscripts of talks and discussions are submitted to the controllers much in advance of the scheduled broadcasts, vetted and even pruned, if the subject matter is not in accordance with the norms fixed by the

8. CF. Bryce J., *Modern Democracies,* Vol. II, p. 533. Democracy may say, as Dante said, when he reached in his journey through hell dwelling of the god of riches. "Here we found wealth, the great enemy".
9. Beni Prasad, *A Democratic Process,* pp. 274-75.
10. Finer, H., *The State in Theory and Practice*, p. 385.

government. In countries, where there is competition, it is not likely to be great because the initial capital required to launch a medium is prohibitive, except for exceptionally rich individuals or organisations. Even in countries where competition exists, there is some control by public bodies and everywhere, with or without official support, the media are used to control or manipulate as well as to inform and entertain. Where all organs speak with their master's voice "the falsehood and twisted logic are more easily hidden." But Finer believes that "on the whole, no country—whether, as in England, broadcasting is under government control, or as in the United States, maintained by private enterprise — is really exploiting the educative potentialities of the radio on the grand scale which is possible."[11]

Platform. Among the most cherished rights of man are freedom of association and freedom of speech and both the freedoms are at the core of the formation of public opinion. Opinion leaders representing different views and labels organise meetings, seminars and conferences to place their opinions before the people, listen and weigh what they have to say, watch their reactions and finally correct and modify their opinions in response to the cogency of their points of views in order to elicit maximum support. But generally the audience is recipient of opinion rather critics, and men accept it as it comes either due to the charismatic personality of the opinion leader or the worthwhileness of the group to which loyalty is owed, or the superiority of leaders to whom a person defers. Facts are seldom discussed and realities rarely explained. The platform is generally used as an opportunity to impress the truth of one's own point of view and the falsity of those of others. The oratorical skill with which perverted and distorted facts are presented flare up emotions and choke thought and reason to consider the issues dispassionately. Swayed by emotions the mass of people follow like meek sheep the leader who shepherds the flock to a predetermined destination, the conscious creation of opinion by others.

Despite these imperfections of the platform, it may be admitted that opinion leaders set the process of public thinking on issues of political importance and it brings the masses in direct contact with the formulators of public opinion. The whistle-stop tours in the United States and the wide travels of many Indian leaders, Jawaharlal Nehru, Indira Gandhi and to some extent Morarji Desai, even between elections is evidence of the importance still attached to this contact.

Propaganda. The right to propagate one's views and to convert others to his point of view is concomitant to the freedoms of speech and association. In a plural society every organised group has its own publicity and propaganda cell and its main function is to popularise its platform through the medium of pamphlets and periodical literature and disseminate information and group's approach to the various political problems and convince the masess that the solutions it offers are in the best interests of the community. It is a subtle method of persuasion to influence opinion formation. Lippmann considers it as the most significant revolution of the modern times that is taking place in "the art of creating consent among the governed. Within the life of the new generation now in control of affairs, persuasion has become a conscious art and a regular organ of popular government."[12] A popular government must conduct its operations in full publicity. It is

11. *Ibid.*, p. 272.

12. Lippmann, Walter, *Public Opinion*, p. 422.

subject to close scrutiny and criticism, both within and outside the legislature, and sometimes the criticism is devastating. It is the duty of the government to diligently combat criticism and convincingly put forward its own case, supported by rational facts and arguments, publicise its achievements and the policies it intends to pursue. This is done through periodical literature issued by the publicity wing of the government and the public statements made by ministers and spokesmen of the ministries concerned to allay the doubts and fears created in the public mind. This is the "art of creating consent among the government," as Lippmann suggested.

The canvas of propaganda by publicity is vast. It embraces national and international problems that concern the nation and their international impact. The new international world order presupposes an alert world public opinion that closely watches and scrutinises the policies of every international entity and its impact on the international community. It is the constant endeavour of every government to win support even for its national policies on the international level in order to command respect in the eyes of the world opinion. International stature of every State is as much coveted now as its national respectability and esteem.

In the United States publicity and propaganda "with temptation too great" and "with weapons too efficient "assumed so vast dimensions that Siegfried, way back in 1927, predicted its dangers to the political system and commented that the "methods of organising it, crystallising it, and inflamming it to the point of hysteria are so well understood and the technique is so perfect that, given the malleability of the people, there appears to be no limit beyond which they cannot be led."[13] His obvious reference was to the manufactured pattern of opinion with which the people are confronted leaving no option for them to form their own independent opinions based upon rational judgement. Sait, however, does not agree with this conclusion. He believed that there is always a limit beyond which the people cannot be led. "Propaganda cannot succeed beyond the moment unless it runs along with some pre-existing disposition of the popular mind or with sympathetic social tendencies and it cannot succeed for the moment if it conflicts seriously with some pre-existing disposition or tendency."[14] Man may be irrational in his political behaviour and conduct or he may be emotionally swayed by his commitment to the group to which he owes loyalty or the superiority of the leader to whom a person defers, all the same, it cannot be denied that man is a thinking human being and it is his innate quality. He cannot be, always and beyond a certain limit, led by nose, not even the inmates of a lunatic asylum because there is method even in the madness of man. There is much truth in Abraham Lincoln's classical statement that "You can fool part of the people all the time, and all the people part of the time, but you cannot fool all the people all the time." Man does make a choice and he has also certain preferences to make. It is the common way of life and this attitude and behaviour transcends to his political activity as much as to his other aspects of life. The real problem of public opinion is man's ability to judge the broad principles of rival policies before him and make a choice between them by discovering that to what an extent the programme offered by a party or a group of his choice promotes general welfare.

13. Siegfried, Andre, *America Comes of Age,* pp. 245-46.
14. Sait. E.M., *Democracy,* p. 511.

Political Parties. The role of political parties in the formation of public opinion and consequently their inseparability from a democratic system was discussed in the preceding Chapter.[15] Political parties sift issues, select candidates and present them to the electorate to make their choice, offer programmes and policies for their consideration and seek their mandate. If the electorate favours the programme and policy of a particular party it is an electoral mandate for that party to form the government. It is expressive of public opinion and a choice between alternatives. Parties, whether in office or in Opposition, have forced many reforms to the statute while their interaction has in many cases gone a long way to harmonise progress with order. But political parties have also accentuated differences and sharpened cleavages, thus dividing the people in warring camps. Parties look on citizens primarily as voters to be caught than convinced. Bryce correctly said that party platform is "neither to define nor to convince, but rather to attract and confuse." It, thus, reduces politics to a branch of the science and art of advertisement, and government by opinion is nothing but mockery, he added.[16] Astute observers of the party system point out that party managers are now using psychology to manutacture spurious consent. Graham Wallas, Lippmann and many others have demonstrated how the chief appeal made by parties comes through symbols and shibboleths calculated to rouse emotional response, for example, Gandhi's and Nehru's names, charkha and the plough as party symbols. Graham Wallas describes this empirical art of politics as "the creation of opinion by the deliberate exploitation of subconscious, non-rational inference."

Despite these imperfections and infirmities the importance of the party system in crystallising public opinion and as the unifying agency that makes democracy workable can neither be ignored nor depreciated. Lowell correctly observed that parties "bring public opinion to a focus and framing issues for a public verdict."[17] The evils of the party system can be mitigated to a great extent if the general body of citizens are enlightened, public spirited and vigilant. An independent and impartial press importantly contributes in politically educating the people and also keeps the parties alert as they show no malice to any and bring into prominence the actual run of events supported by authentic data.

Education. The tone of public opinion depends largely on the general character of social institutions and relationships, on the adjustment of loyalties to the family, to associations, to the nation and humanity. It is moulded by education, periodical literature and the press, the operations of the party system, and the opportunities of contact between the average citizen and the administration. The more complex the environment, the greater is the need of education-development and sharpening of intellectual capacity, power of discrimination and acquiring social habits to accept man as man and to view the world as a society of human beings possessing common innate feelings, desires and aspirations. Plato and Aristotle recognized the importance of education in the body-politic and regarded it as one of the fundamental problems of politics. Rousseau, too, had-perceived its importance and sought to reorganize education, "Never was its reorganisation and diffusion more urgent," Beni Prasad explained, "than in an age

15. Chapter 23 *ante*.
16. Bryce, J., *The American Commonwealth,* p. 334.
17. Lowell, A.L., *Public Opinion and Popular Government,* p. 70.

which is called upon to entrust problems of unprecedented magnitude and complexity to the average man."[18]

Ignorance in motion, said Goethe, is the most terrible force in nature. The human mind "refuses to be satisfied with negatives, longs for positive opinions and, in the absence of knowledge and trained judgement, clutches at prejudices, dogmas and catchwords."[19] Education prevents the paralysis of mind, ignites thoughts and probity, chisels ideas, banishes emotions, strengthens the will and power of conviction and improves the quality of leadership. A rational man in a rational society, purified and ennobled by education, has the capacity to express without fear or favour his opinion, to own right and eschew falsehood. Such a climate enhances the quality of expectations and behaviour of the people and their leaders. That is the gift of education and Plato, Aristotle and Rousseau had this virtue of education in view when they emphasised its importance in politics.

Education is, therefore, not a mere preparation for a vocation and transmission of culture. It is a vision of the meaning of life, the starting point of a spiritual venture. The right attitude of mind can be inculcated in primary and secondery schools by the teacher, who is more important than anything else at the school stage. Colleges and universities are its temples and they should be able to turn out men and women to whom it will be natural to think on a large scale to see life steadily and as a whole, to take the whole world as the orbit to their minds. Education is, therefore, an exercise in intellectual expansion and not a training into any conformity with the beliefs or dogmas whether religious, political or nationalistic. It should be permeated by the scientific spirit of detachment and liberated from imposition of views on young minds by teachers regarded as propagandists of any kind.[20] A teacher should not succumb to any temptation of taking undue advantage of the plasticity of young and inculcate mere intimation of the mental patterns of adults. He should think, plan and decide independently for himself and by himself.

But this type of instruction is not the order of the day. Nor is a teacher so dedicated to his profession. He does not pulsate with a sense of duty to instil in his students the noble ideals of education that it is a quest for knowledge and a search for truth. He is a mercenary and his main concern is to impart instruction that may equip students for a vocation. At the higher centres of education, most of the teachers are committed to one ideology or the other and their mode of instruction and approach toward students is in

18. Beni Prasad, *A Democratic Process,* p. 269.
19. *Ibid.*
20. The Committee on Studies and Textbooks of the public schools of New York City (consisting of principals and teachers) laid down in the course of their report dated 27 March 1922: "The textbook must contain no Statement of derogation or disparagement of American heroes. It must not question the sincerity of the aims and purposes of the founders of the Republic or of those who have guided its destinies .... (In discussing the American Revolution) everything essential is accomplished when it is made plain to the pupils, that the Colonists had just grievances; that they rebelled because they could obtain no redress; that they were inspired by a fierce love of liberty; that they counted neither the cost nor the odds against them; that the dominating spirit of the Revolution is found in the words of Nathan Hale: 'I regret that I have but one life to lose for my country," Hayes, C. *Essays on Nationalism,* p. 114, quoting the *Historical Outlook,* vol xiii October 1922, pp. 250-55.

conformity to their own leanings or commitments. When students get out from these seats of learning the orbit of their minds is overshadowed by the ideas their teachers had designed to instil in them. They do not see the world with an open mind and the colour of their vision determines their social and political attitude and behaviour. Democracy is tampered with such ideas and so do they effect public opinion. Herman Finer deplores this tendency and correctly observes, "If the teaching policy in schools and colleges assumed important dimensions and a character of indoctrination, they could not possibly resist invasion in various ways by the managers, bosses and officials of political parties. A narrow path must be trodden that of education, not party propaganda—and a high temperature will stimulate the attack of political disease germs from the outside upon the bodies academic."[21]

Legislative Assemblies. Legislatures are the barometers of public opinion and are the forums where thinking is done by the representatives of the people on public affairs. The term parliament is derived from the French word *parlet* which means to talk and *parlement* a meeting for discussion. Parliament is, thus, essentially a deliberative body where public affairs of high importance are debated and final decisions arrived at including the laws of the State. Legislatures are numerous bodies representing different shades of opinion and different interests representing various sections of the community. If law is to be the mirror of public opinion, it is necessary that it should be considered threadbare, its contents and ends examined and thrashed to the minutest detail. In this respect legislature is *par excellence* a deliberative body.

Legislatures reflect public opinion than mould or shape it. But they crystallise opinion on all public measures before they finally become laws. Interposition of delay is a necessary condition of parliamentary procedure and a bill is read three times, sieving through different stages, including the legislative committees and may even be referred to the people for eliciting their opinion. After it is passed in one chamber it is transmitted to the other chamber to undergo the same procedure before it becomes a duly enacted law. The institution of bicameral legislature is a democratic necessity against hasty and ill-considered legislation and a check on the rashness and vagaries of a single chamber, an additional security, as Sir Henry Maine said, for freedom. It is a delaying mechanism and provides an opportunity to the people to examine the merits of the measure, propose suggestions through views expressed in the newspapers and conveyed to the government by submitting petitions and other channels of representation. A strong and responsible opposition may force the government to amend and modify the original provisions or even to drop the bill itself as a result of stout and persistent opposition by the public fanned by Opposition. The floor of the legislative chamber is Opposition's platform, the newspapers are its microphone and the people are its audience. A government that loses popular support will ultimately lose its majority and it means government's political demise.

But the Opposition must be responsible and it should play the game of politics according to rules. It is a prospective government and the ruling party recognises its duty to govern openly and honestly by meeting criticism not by coercion or suppressing the

21. Finer, Herman, *The Theory and Practice of Modern Government,* p. 271.

Opposition, but by rational arguments that may command approbation of the people at large. A like duty is a clear obligation of the Opposition too. If the Opposition behaves irresponsibly, frustrates the channels of discussion and debate and chokes all other reasonable outlets of opinion, it not only makes mockery of responsible government but eliminates the chances of public opinion to crystallise. Such a climate or irresponsibility offers an opportunity to the government to act arbitrarily and even make a point for resort to emergency. India and many other Asiatic countries are monuments of this gloomy picture of government. Sometimes, the behaviour of members of a legislature, belonging to the ruling as well as Opposition parties, is shameful. To take a single example, shouts, shrieks and din lasting 40 minutes during 'Zero Hour' in the Rajya Sabha (the Council of States), upper chamber of Parliament of India, on 7 August, 1980, forced an exasperated Chairman, who was also the Vice-President of India, to observe that he would like the proceedings to be televised "for the whole country to see" what the custodians of public do and how they actually behave in Parliament where decisions are taken on vital issues of public importance.

How to Ascertain Public Opinion. No perfect method has so far been discovered to ascertain public opinion. The press, the pulpit and propaganda, the potential instruments for the dissemination of knowledge, formation, and expression of public opinion, remotely serve the purpose of ascertaining public opinion. The press is no guide as its impartiality is questionable. Almost every newspaper has a 'tendency and dogma' and the interests to safeguard. "The newspaper proprietor like the candidate for political office," says Sait "must employ the arts that captivate the crowd. Journalism and politics reflect the public taste. The newspaper gives its readers what they want and what they deserve."[22] Similarly, the platform is no sure index. Venues of meetings are packed to capacity by a skilled party organiser either by persuasion or cajolery. Audience may even be hired to swell the number. And they are the most vociferous in applauding and shouting slogans in favour of the party leaders. This is an understandable *quid pro quo* between the organisers and those who had been hired. The vehicles of publicity and propaganda manipulate opinion rather than deal with truth. The facts are suppressed and falsehood is preached. The result is that the masses do not possess adequate and factual knowledge on issues which demand their opinion.

Bryce suggested an empirical method of ascertaining public opinion. He pointed out that the best method for the investigator was to go about and freely mingle with the people to assess their views on public questions. Majority of opinion alone was not enough for Bryce to make it a public. Nor should it be sectarian and sectional. A public opinion must, for all intents and purposes, be for the good of the community. But here, too, the basic question, how to ascertain public opinion, remains unanswered. Rationality and intensity of opinion that go together to make it public cannot be quantitatively measured and the qualitative measurement is as elusive as the quantitative.

During recent times statistical or quantitative method has been used in ascertaining the flow and extent of public opinion. Statistical analysis is as old as Plato, but as a field of scientific investigation it is only a generation old. In some Western countries 'public opinion polls' or 'Gallup Polls' are held to assess the opinion of the people on the performance and policies of the government and the holders of office and on matters of

22. Sait, E.M., *Democracy*, p. 517.

public importance. Even a slight drift in public opinion is investigated and its repercussions on the opinion and behaviour of the people are examined and the likely results anticipated. But the success of the statistical method importantly depends upon the sampling technique adopted by the investigator, the nature of questions asked, the manner of conducting the interview and total detachment of the person who makes the enquiry. Lowell has correctly said that statistics, like real pies are good if you know the person who made them, and are sure of the ingredients as "by themselves they are strangely likely to mislead, because unless the subject is understood in all its bearings some element can easily be left out of account which wholly falsifiics the result."[23]

If precision in ascertaining public opinion is lacking, its pulse can, no doubt, be felt accurately. By-elections are the barometer of public opinion as they indicate the drift and the extent to which a party has risen or fallen in popular esteem and the support it is likely to receive from the electorate at the following general election. All parties trim their political sails to every wind of popular opinion and adjust their policies accordingly. The party in power, particularly, keeps a 'weather eye' on popular reactions on the measures it adopts and the policies it pursues. A clear drift of electoral opinion from its support may even sow a spirit of rebellion before which even a government with vast majority is impotent. Nor the party in power is insensitive to the reactions of its followers. A legislator tenderly nurses his constituency and keeps himself abreast of the direction in which opinion of his constituents moves. If he feels that the popularity of the ruling party is receding, he becomes clamorous, because it means a fall in his electoral support and dim chances of his re-election. Thus, a democratic government works against a background of constant outside appraisal which also finds its echo in the lobbies of the legislature and it is the primary function of party whips to keep informed on trends of opinion both in and outside, the legislature and to warn party managers of the reasons of its unpopularity and drift.

Disagreement is a necessary condition of politics and if politics is not to disappear in chaos there needs to be both recognised limits to disagreement and the measure of agreement to ensure orderly conduct of society. As a result, from clash of opinion with opinion emerges the spirit of tolerance, a sense of give and take to demarcate the area of agreement. Thus, emerges consensus or adjustment of various opinions on certain fundamentals. The consensus so reached brings satisfaction to all the segments of opinion, because their views and interests had been considered and given due weight in the formulation of public policy. A consensus-oriented policy is representative of different shades of opinion which are politically articulate. Anderson points out, "The agencies wielding political power respond to all politically oriented influences. Opinions expressed by well-organized, competently led segment of the public will always be carefully weighed in the scales with other such petitions. The result of this compromise of influence will be reflected in public policy,"[24] and that epitomises the meaning of public opinion.

---

23. Lowell, A.L., "The Philosophy of Politics", *American Political Science Review,* Vol. IV, p. 10.
24. Anderson, T.J., *Principles of Political Science,* p. 391.

SUGGESTED READINGS

Angell, Norman : *The Public Mind*

Beni Prasad : *A Democratic Process*

Bryce, J. : *The American Commonwealth*

Bryce, J. : *Modern Democracies*

Cooley, C.H. : *Social Organisation*

Corry, J.A. : *Democratic Government and Politics*

Dicey, A.V. : *Law and Public Opinion*

Finer, H. : *The Theory and Practice of Modern Government*

Lippmann, Walter : *The Phantom Public Opinion*

Lippmann, Walter : *Public Opinion*

Lowell, A.L. : *Public Opinion and Popular Government*

Lowell, A.L. : *Public Opinion in War and Peace*

MacIver, R.M. : *The Modern State*

MacIver, R.M. : *The Ramparts We Guard*

MacIver, R.M. : *The Web of Government*

Sait, E.M. : *Political Institutions: A Preface*

Willoughby, W.W. : *The Nature of the State.*

25 CHAPTER

Local Government

In the Chapters immediately preceding, we have considered the problem of distribution of governmental powers territorially from the standpoint of the manner in which these powers may be distributed as between the Central Government and the various political units into which all countries of considerable size are divided. And we brought out in that consideration two distinct types of government, the unitary and the federal. In the former, the territorial units, generally called provinces, are created, their powers defined and their form of organisation determined by the central government. They remain, for all intents and purposes, integral parts of that government. In a federation, the constituent units enjoy a juridical status and a corporate personality. Their powers are the grant of the constitution which can neither be altered nor amended by the central government. It needs amendment of the constitution if any change is desired to be made therein and all this means equality of status between the two sets of government; the one is not simply the creation of the other.

The major territorial divisions of both unitary and federal governments are further divided into smaller areas. But the problem here, too, is whether the smaller territorial areas should be governed from the seats of government of the major territorial divisions or they should be entrusted with certain specific powers which they may exercise locally. The answer to this question constitutes what is known as the problem of local government.

Need for Decentralisation. The government of the provinces of a unitary State and the constituent states of a federation within their jurisdictions is unitary. This is an important point. The work of the government is concentrated in the "capital" or "seat" of the government and all important decisions of policy are taken at this place. It is here that the legislature meets and laws are passed, the High Court decides all points in the interpretation of laws, and rules and regulations are framed by the superior officials in the executive departments. The whole governmental life of a province or a state, in brief, is centralised at one place. The position is similar to one which necessitates the territorial division of the country into major political divisions and distribution of governmental powers between the central government and the provincial or state governments. Such are the amount and variety of work to be done that it is impossible for a single authority directly to undertake the performance of all those duties adequately, effectively and efficiently. In fact, the provincial government has neither the time nor the requisite knowledge of all the diverse problems which are peculiar to different areas. "We cannot realise the full benefit of democratic government," says Laski, "unless we begin by the admission that all problems are not central problems, and that the result of problems in their incidence require decision at the place, and by the persons, where and by whom the incidence is most deeply felt."[1] This constitutes the real problem of local government and from this problem emerges the need for decentralisation. Decentralisation means distribution of governmental powers and responsibilities between the Centre and the local areas in which the country, if it is small in size like Britain, or the provinces of a big unitary State, or the states of a federation, are divided for administrative convenience. The provincial or state government is the central government for all local areas within its jurisdiction. Decentralisation is, thus, a centrifugal movement which aims at entrusting local organs created in local areas with powers local in character, the presumption being that people belonging to the locality can know best and appreciate their own problems and needs and can solve them best. The entire problem of local government is the problem of personal touch with the affairs concerning the locality and their solution. If the local people are denied association with local life, they would not only stultify their talent, energy, initiative and enterprise, but they lose all sense of responsibility.

Meaning of Local Government. Local government, therefore, refers to the operations of corporations, municipalities, district boards, panchayats in India and other bodies which are entrusted with the execution of functions relating to and concerning the residents of a given area or locality. These functions do not concern the community as a whole, but embrace only a portion of the total population and territorial area of the State. The essence of all such functions is that they are purely local in character and need local solution in deference to the requirements of the people inhabiting that locality. The extent of the territory covered and the number of persons ruled over do not make any difference in the nature of local government. The Corporation of Calcutta or Mumbai (formerly Bombay) exercises its authority over a vastly greater number of people and considerably more extensive area than the Municipal Committee of Patiala or Kapurthala or a village Panchayat. And yet all are the units of local government performing more or less identical functions and occupying the same constitutional position.

Sidgwick says that the term local government in a unitary State means organs, which though completely subordinate to the central legislature,[2] are independent of the central executive in appointment and to some extent in their decisions, and exercise a partially independent control over certain parts of public finance. As regards the constitutional relationship between the central government and local government, the latter derives its powers from the former and is subordinate to the authority that created it. But though a subordinate body, yet it has certain independence of action within the sphere assigned to it. It can make its own rules and regulations, or by-laws, to perform its functions and to control its finances.[3]

This brings into prominence the question of the functions of local bodies. According to MacIver the State seeks to fulfil three types of functions. In the first place, there are

1. Laski, H., *A Grammar of Politics,* p. 411.
2. Sidgwick had the example of Britain in his mind.
3. Sidgwick, H., *Elements of Politics,* p. 511.

some functions which concern and affect the whole community and are of national importance. All such functions must belong to the national or central government. There are other functions which are of a universal character, but which for their efficient fulfilment, or on other grounds, may be assigned to the provincial governments. Lastly, there are functions which are of peculiar concern of the locality, for example, water supply, sanitation, maintenance of hospitals and libraries, running of public utility services, like supply of electric energy, tramway or omnibus transport. These services have reference to the local needs and it seems reasonable that the locality should have direct and fairly complete control over them. The efficient performance of all these functions requires local experience and knowledge of local details. As Laski put it, "Local Self-Government offers the best opportunity to the people to bring local knowledge, interest and enthusiasm to bear on the solution of their own local problems."

It is not, however, possible to rigidly separate the functions of local bodies. "Local interests," as MacIver says, "merge into national interests in variant degrees,"[4] particularly with the emergence of the Welfare State there are hardly any matters of local concern that are not matters of national concern. Subjects like education and health, for example, are local in character and require local solution, but they are really of national importance and the central government cannot remain unconcerned about them. The control of local government over subjects which vitally concern the locality can never be absolute in this era of conscious, consistent and sustained process of economic and social planning. The problem of local government is, therefore, not to draw sharp lines between the functions of central and local governments. The real problem, as MacIver says, "is to assure at once the reality and responsibility of local government."[5] So long as the local body does not exceed its powers or is not found guilty of some flagrant piece of negligence, the central government should not interfere in its performance. Professor Jenks rightly remarked that "So long as the local authority does its best and keeps within the law, however mistaken that may be, the central government has no right to interfere, even on the request of the persons suffering the consequences of the mistake."[6]

Functions of Local Government. The functions of local bodies, broadly speaking, fall under two heads: direct services to the public, and indirect functions. Under the latter the local bodies are required to conduct election of their members, to provide legal advice and action, to assess property for taxation, to plan, to control and audit local finances. The functions performed under the heading direct services are important in the interests of public welfare and are sub-divided into three groups:

1. **Functions Relating to Cultural Developments.** In this category are included functions of providing instruction, control of environments by planning the town or the city, maintaining and supporting of art galleries, museums, zoos, libraries and other places of public recreation such as parks and gardens and centres for games and sports.

2. **Social and Physical Functions.** The local bodies look after sanitation, provide a proper system of sanitary drainage, conservancy arrangements and other conditions

4. MacIver, R.M., *The Modern State,* p. 393.
5. *Ibid.*
6. *English Local Government,* p. 15.

necessary for preserving public health. Closely connected with it is the provision for medical relief and other arrangements for checking the spread of diseases and epidemics. Then, come services like construction, maintenance and repairs of roads, lighting of streets and thoroughfare, promotion of local safety against fire and other accidents and regulation of structures and traffic.

3. Under the third category come functions of providing and regulating water supply, heat, light, public transport, collection and disposal of waste and regulation of food supplies through healthy markets.

Some major local bodies render certain public utility services such as provision of water supply, gas, electric light, bus or tram and local train services. There has been a remarkable expansion in the activities of local bodies in Britain and the United States. But the scope of these functions is somewhat limited in India. In the undertaking of ambitious civic schemes desired to inculcate aesthetic, cultural and economic activities, the Acts creating local bodies do not offer sufficient scope, though an appreciable change has been made in the case of panchayats.

Assessment of Local Government. The institution of local government is at its best in countries which are governed on democratic lines. It is the experience of many countries that all matters of a local concern are ultimately best administered by a properly organised system of local government. Local government means the regulation and administration of local affairs by the people inhabiting the locality through representative bodies composed mainly of elected representatives. These local assemblies of citizens, says De Tocqueville, "constitute the strength of free nations. Town meetings are to liberty what primary schools are to science; they bring it within the people's reach; they teach men how to use and how to enjoy it. A nation may establish a system of free government, but without the spirit of municipal institutions it cannot have the spirit of liberty." This foundation aspect of local government is described as "grass-roots" democracy, a phrase which has become popular. Local bodies serve as a training ground in the art of self-government and the experience and knowledge acquired in local governance can best be utilised for the wider affairs of central government. Laski says that the institution of local government is educative in perhaps a higher degree than any other part of government.[7] It cultivates a sense of civic duties and responsibilities and inculcates among citizens a corporate spirit of common administration of common interests. "Whoever learns to be public spirited, active and upright in the affairs of the villege," says Bryce, "has learnt the first lesson of the duty incumbent on a citizen of a great country." Local institutions train men not only to work for others but also work effectively with others. The citizens develop common sense, reasonableness, judgment and sociability, the qualities of moderation, accommodation and social dependence, which are so essential for the success of democracy. It is a process of political socialization. De Tocqueville especially argued that local government was valuable because it associated citizens with each other and with the government. It fosters in the citizen "a sober love of the laws of which he is himself the author."

When all problems of administration are not central problems the obvious inference

7. Laski, H., *A Grammar of Politics,* p. 411.

is that those functions of government which affect mainly or solely the inhabitants of a limited portion of a country should be placed under the special control of this section of the community. Local knowledge brings about a closer adaptation of administrative activity, for there is a consciousness of common purposes and common needs. "Neighbourhood," says Laski, "makes us automatically aware of interests which impinge upon us more directly than upon others."[8] The central government is very often indifferent to these interests, and if it interests itself in them at all, its transactions are subject to red-tapism which unnecessarily delay the plans requiring immediate execution. Moreover, an administration which is not local is unresponsive to local opinion. It is, thus, "bound in the nature of things, to miss shades and expression of thought and sentiment the perception of which is in a real degree urgent to the success of administration."[9] The central government, in other words, cannot grasp the genius of the place. Being government from without, it fails to evoke either interest or responsibility from the people it seeks to control. It may well evoke indignation, but it does not succeed in eliciting the creative support of citizens. It is a matter of common knowledge that what is done by our common counsel in the solution of our common problems gives us a degree of satisfaction which is unobtainable when it is done for us by others from outside.

Both John Stuart Mill and De Tocqueville argued that local institutions of government promote virtue in their citizens. The small unit of government, which they hold, fosteres civic morality by linking the exercise of political power with the consequence flowing therefrom. A citizen of a locality feels that he is a trustee of the public good. He delegates his authority of governing himself to his fellow citizens and assesses whether they are deserving or unworthy of that trust. If they betray the trust reposed in them the confidence is withdrawn and others who are deemed worthy of the job are entrusted with it. It is a continuous process of responsibility and vigilance which is the essence of a democratic arrangement.

Moreover, central government inevitably aims at uniformity and not variety. Local problems need variety, because they are peculiar to the needs of a particular area. Uniformity is usually cheaper, "because it is almost always easier to make a single solution and apply it wholesale than to make a variety of solutions and have them piecemeal."[10] But uniformity is only a mechanical solution of all problems. Problems peculiar to a particular locality are not standardised in character. They must be individually solved with reference to the conditions which demand their solution.

Local government aims at division of governmental functions and it lightens the burden of the central government. If the central government is overloaded with work, it becomes incompetent and it would do things tardily, expensively, and above all inefficiently. At the same time, centralisation means the presence and functioning of a strong bureaucracy. Bureaucracy may create and provide for conditions of an effective and efficient government which is, no doubt, the nature of a good government, but a good government is no substitute for self-government. Unless local bodies are entrusted with

8. *Ibid.*
9. *Ibid.*, p. 412.
10. *Ibid.*, p. 413.

active powers, the central authority will not merely stifle all local initiative, but destroy also that well-spring of local knowledge and local interest without which it cannot possibly exercise its functions. Local government, therefore, is necessary for efficiency and responsibility. Inaugurating the first Local Self-Government Ministers' Conference (India) in 1948, the Prime Minister, Jawaharlal Nehru, observed: "Local Self-Government is and must be the basis of any true system of democracy. We have got rather into the habit of thinking of democracy at the top and not so much below. Democracy at the top may not be a success unless you build on this foundation from below." It is only through local government that self-government becomes real. To put it in the words of Bryce, "The best school of democracy and the best guarantee for its success is the practice of self-government."

Economy is secured by local government. Local functions are performed by local authorities out of funds raised locally. Equity demands that services rendered exclusively or mainly to a limited population, who live within a certain area, should pay for them. The incidence of such services should not be shifted to others who expect no gain therefrom. As the inhabitants of the area have to pay for the local services, it is natural for them to demand proper control over those services. It has three results. In the first place, participation in the work of local bodies tends to develop among the people a sense of mutual interest in their common affairs and trains them to work for others honestly and efficiently. Secondly, the people entrusted with the management of local affairs will manage them more efficiently in order to keep their bill of costs as low as possible. Finally, by making responsibility widespread the institution of local government encourages a spirit of self-help and self-dependence. The institution of local government is, as such, a great advancement in the realization of true citizenship. Burke has cogently said, "To be attached to the sub-division; to love the little platoon we belong to in society, is the first principle, the germ as it were of public affections. It is the first link in the series by which we proceed towards a love to our country and mankind."

The vigorous development of local government is the only means of realizing the welfare purpose of every progressive State. Welfare services require a flexible technique to cater for individual cases. The local bodies, on account of their nearness to the people, their wider representative character, their natural familiarity with the details of the situation, and their intimate knowledge of the means and wants of the inhabitants are eminently suited to evolve such a technique. The State has really found in them its most effective instrument for social amelioration.

Soviet Russia was the home of socialism, both national and local. The town Soviets, which were the Russian prototypes of Indian Municipal Committees, besides exercising the usual municipal functions, regulated also the entire political and economic life of the local community. Commerce, industries, retail trade, cooperation, housing, land partition, criminal justice, recruitment and mobilization, protection of the revolutionary regime, supervision and application of the national progress, etc., all came under its jurisdiction. The Soviets also supervised and controlled all the organs and institutions of government functioning within their area, and would voice the dissatisfaction of the local community with any of them when necessary. They acted in the dual capacity of agents of the central government and the representative bodies of the local community.

Compared with local bodies of advanced countries, the functions of municipalities in India are less extensive principally in three directions, namely, police, trading enterprises, and the big group of social services comprising health, housing, sickness and unemployment insurance. Some of these functions are not even legally permitted to the municipalities. Apart from the legal restrictions, the main difference between Indian municipalities and their foreign prototypes is that in respect of legally permitted functions, like education or water supply, the actual standard of development here is very low. Then, the government of the local bodies in India is neither local nor is it self-government. They have not the means to extend their activities even if permitted by law. Their own resources are not sufficient. They have to depend to a large extent on the financial help of the State governments through grants-in-aid, loans, etc. The authority that pays must also control and direct. The autonomy of the local bodies, accordingly, vanishes under all encroaching control and direction of the Deputy Commissioner. The Control of the State government is ubiquitous and a minor lapse may mean supersession of a local body. The action may even be politically motivated.

Critics of local government assert that local home rule narrows the outlook of the people and breeds local patriotism. Such an attitude stifles the life of the community. What is political virtue in the local context becomes parochialism on the national stage. The good local citizen of nineteenth and twentieth century France or Germany was often the bad national citizen. It is further pointed out that devolution of authority to local bodies not only multiplies administrators, but also results in divided responsibility. The obvious result is inefficiency, delinquency, waste and incompetence. The officers of local bodies succumb to all sorts of local influences as they are "locally selected and locally directed and locally controlled." Devolution of authority also deprives local bodies of central direction and advice. With scanty resources at their disposal, and a meagre source of information and knowledge at their command, local bodies cannot perform their functions adequately and effectively, and if they do, they do it tardily and inefficiently.

What the critics of local government say is true to a great extent, particularly in a country like India where the vision of the people is blurred by the barriers of localism, regionalism, caste and religion. To love one's home and locality is the natural instinct of man and there is nothing wrong in it provided it does not inhibit men in performing their higher duties towards their country and its people as a whole. It is our membership of the State which bestows upon us the benefits of devolution of authority and the privileges of working for others with others living in our neighbourhood. Once this becomes the norm of the political behaviour of man, local government fulfils the purpose of common consciousness of common good. It binds the people living in different areas in a community of feelings and interests and in these feelings narrow localism finds no place.

Willoughby suggests a concrete reform. He says that local officers should be appointed by the State or provincial Government, but a local advisory council in each area, consisting of the eminent and trustworthy citizens, may be associated with them. The advisory council should be given the responsibility and duty of advising local officers with local problems, to bring to the attention of their superior officers all cases of lapses on their part and failures to perform their duties properly and diligently, to suggest to such authorities proposals which they deem advisable, and to protest against the action of the government where they believe that their areas are not receiving equitable treatment. But this is not the real solution of the problem. Nor does it advance the cause of local government which aims to inculcate the spirit of intelligent and creative citizenship.

Whatever be the defects of local government, "grass-roots" democracy forms a vital element of democracy for the modern State. The absence of healthy local political roots is a disaster. Robson has cogently said, "Democracy on the national scale can function in a healthy manner only if it is supported and nourished by democratic local government."[11] De Tocqueville relevantly argued that local institutions have a special role to play in the preservation of liberty and independence and decentralization of political power is the necessary component of democracy. Local democracy gives many people a voice in matters touching them most immediately. It associates citizens with one another, with the process of government, and with the rules of government of which they are in part the authors. Access to the government broadens popular participation and fosters public virtue in the participants and energy in the people. "Popular government," as Carl Friedrich says, "includes the right of the people, through their majority, to commit mistakes."[12] The decisions, which local people make, may seem unwise from the standpoint of experts and technicians, but the citizens "will discover it in time and they may learn a vital lesson in self-government." Local government is the best school of citizenship. Such homilies as "democracy stops beyond the parish pump" and "charity begins at home" indicate that "grass-roots" democracy "holds a special place in American folklore and they are accustomed to thinking of dispersed power as more democratic and more conducive to liberty than concentrated."[13]

Relation between Local and Central Governments. The powers, functions and constitution of local bodies are determined by statute. Within the limits fixed by law creating local bodies, they are independent subject to such powers of direction, control and advice which have been specifically retained by the central government. But how far is control by the central government desirable? This is, of course, one of the most baffling problems of local administration. There is no uniform practice followed even by the most advanced democratic countries. In France, local government is highly centralised and from the Commune right up to the Ministry of the Interior the whole administration is linked up with one chain. This centralisation and uniformity in France is a sharp contrast to the decentralised character of local government in Britain. The principle accepted and followed in Britain is that a local area has the inherent right to conduct its affairs in its own way, and consistent with its requirements without the interposition of the central authority, unless supervision is clearly demanded in the interests of the public. But in Britain, too, the centralising tendency, during recent years, has assumed alarming proportions.

The position in the United States is rather appreciable and there is complete local autonomy. Every township is a local democracy, a republic within a republic. The authority of the superior officials of state government over the affairs of the local bodies has been

11. Robson, A., *The Government and Misgovernment of London,* p. 349.
12. Carl Friedrich, *Constitutional Government and Democracy,* p. 238.
13. *Ibid.*

constitutionally reduced to the minimum. If local authorities exceed the powers vested in them by law or abuse their authority, there is the usual method of judicial redress through courts. In India, the recent Panchayat Acts passed by the state legislatures have revolutionised the nature of local government.

It may generally be said that matters assigned to independent local organs should be those in which local separation of interests is clearly marked, local knowledge most important, the need of uniformity least evident, and the cooperation of private and governmental agencies likely to tell most. Where the interests concerned are clearly common to all parts of the State or where the advantages of uniformity are overwhelming control over the administration should be national and not local. But a rigid separation of local interests is rarely complete. A carefully adjusted cooperation of local and central organs is often required to obtain the best results Experience has shown that the central government should exercise some control over local bodies, because, as Sidgwick points out, "the central government has greater enlightenment derived from greater general knowledge, wider experience and more highly trained intellects." But such a control should be exercised with a view to the efficient discharge of local duties and responsibilities. Undue interference and direction is bound to destroy local initiative and local responsibility. Excessive central control may also encourage favouritism in the local services, thus, vitiating the very idea of local government. Whenever party spoils intervene, efficiency disappears and development at all levels is severely retarded.

While we do not discount the practical utility of central control over local bodies, it may, however, be emphasised that the degree of control should vary in proportion to the efficiency of a local body. Were all local bodies of the same standard of efficiency, the problem of supervision and apportionment of functions would have been easier. But this is not so. Everywhere the central government is continually faced with the difficulty that all local bodies are not equally efficient. This may be essentially due to the differences in the size of local areas and resources of local bodies. The smaller municipalities, howsoever noble the ideal of public spirit of the citizens may be, cannot be expected to maintain the same services as the larger bodies. They have to depend on the doles of the central government which necessitate more rigid control on their activities. Moreover, the traditional view that local functions are the concern of the locality itself has lost its validity. There are no local functions in that sense now. The making and maintenance of local roads, lighting, drainage, cleansing, etc., have, under modern scientific analysis, been found to involve important national aspects as well. Under these conditions there can no longer be any clear-cut demarcation of spheres of influence between central and local governments. They must collaborate, consistent with the requirements of the Welfare State, over the entire field of governmental activity. This means a close integrated partnership between central and local authorities for high achievements in municipal administration. It is, however, essential to avoid reducing local authorities to the position of mere agents of the central government if they are to continue to make their indispensable contribution to the democratic way of life.

SUGGESTED READINGS

Clarke, J.J.: *Outlines of Local Government.*

Cole, G.D.H.: *Local and Regional Government.*

De Tocqueville, A.: *Democracy in America,* Vol. I, Chaps. 14 and 16.

Finer, H.: *English Local Government.*

Gilchrist, R.N.: *Principles of Political Science,* Chap. XVII.

Jackson, R.M.: *The Machinery of Local Government.*

Jenks, E.: *English Local Government.*

Laski, H.J.: *A Grammar of Politics,* pp. 410-29.

MacIver, R.M.: *The Modern State,* pp. 390-95.

Mill, J.S.: *Considerations on Representative Government,* Chap. 15.

Robson, A.: *The Development of Local Government.*

Sidgwick, H.: *Elements of Politics,* Chap. XXV.

26

CHAPTER

The Finances of the State

Public Finance. The mechanism of government entails stupendous expenditure for its proper functioning. This expenditure must be obtained from the community which is expected to benefit from the many and various activities of the State. The subject of study which considers and investigates the ways in which government taps different sources to raise money and the manner in which it is to be expended for the common welfare is called public finance. Public finance, according to Bastable, "deals with expenditure and income of the public authorities of the State and their mutual relation as also with financial administration and control."

Today, the study of public finance has become more important than what it was in the past. The modern State no longer remains only a police State entrusted with the bare functions of maintaining peace and order within the country and protecting it against any contingency of foreign aggression. The province of the State has increased very considerably necessitating a corresponding growth in public expenditure and in public revenue. This is due to many reasons. In the first place, the great increase in population has itself entailed an extension in the functions of the States. Secondly, the modern State is vitally concerned in catering services which help to create that atmosphere where the individual can rise to the full stature of his personality. This involves huge expenditure on running the beneficent departments, like education and public health. Thirdly, as society has progressed and wealth has increased, State enterprise, too, has increased. It does not only regulate industries but actually undertakes many economic activities, such as the public utility services. Furthermore, the State must provide for the poor, the sick, the unemployed and the economically weak. Finally, must be mentioned the enormous increase in the expenditure of the modern State in order to provide for the adequate defence and security of the community. In the nuclear age, in which we live, the expenditure on defence and security has increased beyond all conceivable proportions. In fact, there is a mad race between countries for war-preparedness. All this makes the functions of the State many, complex and difficult, and so public finance assumes an important role in public administration.

Public and Private Finance. The State and the individual both are concerned how to manage their respective incomes and expenditures. Although fundamentally all forms of finance must be governed by the same economic principles, there are, however, certain considerations which distinguish the practice of public and private finance:

(*i*) The relationship of expenditure to income. In private finance the expenditure is naturally limited by the amount of income. In other words, it is the income that determines expenditure. One must cut his coat according to the cloth he has. In public finance the government first determines what expenditure is to be incurred and then proceeds to find out funds so as to bring the necessary revenue. A government, we may say, arranges for cloth according to the length of the coat it proposes to have.

(*ii*) For earning his income the individual must work. He cannot order or compel others to contribute towards his income. The State, on the other hand, issues an imperative and thereby compels persons to pay taxes. The State works only when it undertakes an economic enterprise. If an individual's income is not sufficient to meet his necessary expenditure, he may resort to borrowing. So does the State. But there is a difference between private borrowing and public borrowing. The borrowing power of a private person is limited by the credit he can command and the resources at his disposal. The credit of the State is far superior to that of an individual and its field more extensive as it can borrow from within and without the country.

(*iii*) In private finance an individual tries to save something to meet various exigencies and future liabilities. This is not true of public finance. Surplus is not the deliberate aim of public finance, except in the case of revenue-bearing services, like the railways, the post and telegraph service, where a profit may be deliberately aimed at. Generally, every State devises means to have a balanced budget, that is, the total revenues must equal the total expenditures. But balanced budgets are difficult to obtain and they are no guarantee of sound financial policy. Sometimes it is a surplus budget and at another time the budget is deficit. Some statesmen are of the opinion that it is advisable to have surplus budgets in order to meet deficits in bad times.

(*iv*) The public and the private expenditures are governed by the same principle of maximum satisfaction. In actual practice, governments seldom follow the principle of maximum social welfare. Party politics and other political considerations influence public expenditure in a modern democratic State.

(*v*) Finally, the State should not, and usually it does not, discount the future at as high a rate as an individual. Individual expenditure is generally governed by immediate and not by far distant considerations. The long-period factor is especially important in the services rendered by the State. It may even undertake schemes and incur expenditure which are to benefit only future generations.

THE BUDGET

We said that every State performs functions and howsoever broad or limited the functions it undertakes, it must tackle the two-fold problem of obtaining funds to pay for the services it renders, and to manage the expenditure to be incurred thereon. Public funds are raised primarily through taxation, although there are also other sources of revenues. Generally, expenditure is controlled through a detailed financial plan known as the Budget. The Budget is a detailed financial statement, drawn in advance of the fiscal year to which it applies, which lists. in detail, all anticipated expenditures and revenues, in a balanced accountant's statement. The fiscal year in most of the countries begins on April 1, and ends on March 31, of the following year.

No State ever had a financial system entirely planless, but until comparatively modern times, well-coordinated schemes were the exception rather than the rule. Toward the end of the eighteenth century, Britain, recognizing the necessity for reviewing fiscal policy as a whole, introduced what may be considered the earliest modern budget. The use of the word budget in public finance originated in the expression "The Chancellor of the Exchequer opened his Budget," which was applied in Parliament to the annual speech of the Chancellor of the Exchequer explaining his proposals for the balancing of revenue and expenditure.

By definition, a budget must present a complete picture of the Government's finances. Long-term financing of major public schemes constitutes the capital outlay budget, and should show in detail the cost of the capital schemes and the methods by which the cost is to be met. The expenditure for the current year, for ordinary running expenditures of the Government, and for such extraordinary expenditures such as is necessitated or likely to be required as relief, etc., constitute the current budget. This must likewise show the means of raising funds to meet the expenses, whether by taxation, miscellaneous revenues or otherwise.

The budget must also give a clear picture of the public debt. Although a complete statement of the total debt need not be included, if sound financing is to be effected, a condensed statement of it should be made, with statement of the obligations to mature during the financial year.

Preparation and Passage of the Budget. Well in advance of the time at which the Budget is to be presented to the legislature, Heads of the various Ministries or Departments submit their estimates of the funds needed for the fiscal year to the Finance Ministry or Department. In the United States these are submitted to the Director of the Bureau of the Budget. The Finance Ministry examines the estimates in its relevant branch and determines the reasonableness of the demands. It is the work of the Finance Ministry to prepare a coordinated statement of the needs, itemized by various Ministries or Departments, and a statement of funds required to meet them. Often the Finance Department has wide discretionary power to change the requests submitted to it.

In the United States, the President transmits the Budget to Congress with his message outlining his financial scheme. The Constitution establishes the supremacy of Congress by specifying that "no money shall be drawn from the Treasury but in consequence of appropriation made by law." The Constitution also provides that all bills for raising revenue shall originate in the House of Representatives. Usage has added to it that the appropriation bills are also initiated there. The Senate possesses co-equal powers with the House of Representatives in accepting or rejecting financial bills.

In Britain, presentation of the Budget by the Chancellor of the Exchequer, when he delivers his budget speech, is the main occasion in the year for reviewing the finances of the government and the economic state of the nation. The formal action by Parliament that renders legal the expenditure of public money takes the form of an Act of Parliament. Such an Act authorises the payment of money out of the Consolidated Fund. Consolidated

Fund is a great reservoir into which all the revenues of the kingdom are poured and out of which all the money required for public expenditure is drawn. The Act of Parliament which authorizes the Government to draw money from the Consolidated Fund is known as the Annual Appropriation Act. The Consolidated Fund is replenished through moneys paid into it by authority of the Act of Parliament which gives legal validity to the raising of revenues. The principal Act in this respect is the Annual Finance Act.

The Indian Constitution has adopted the fundamental principles governing the British financial system, that is, parliamentary control over the receipt and expenditure of public money. The procedure of the passage of the budget is also more or less identical.

EXPENDITURE OF THE STATE

What functions the State should legitimately perform is a subject of great controversy. At one time the theory of Individualism or *laissez faire* was prevalent. It was maintained that the very existence of the State implied the association of its members for defence against external enemies and for the maintenance of internal peace and order. It was also conceded that the effective discharge of these *protective* and *primary* functions necessarily involved the *secondary* activities of taxation, and legislation. Beyond these activities the State was to do nothing and every individual should be left alone with the maximum of economic freedom. It was asserted that the State was a necessary evil and it should perform only negative functions.

But it soon became apparent that the policy of non-interference or *laissez faire* led to the widespread evils of the factory system, to the sordid exploitation of the workers, and to the terrible oppression of the poor. The negative role of the State was severely criticised and it was emphasised that the State had duties other than the provision of army, navy and police, and that a defence of quite a different kind was necessary. The community, as a whole, must unite to enforce right against might, to protect the economically weak against the economically strong, to prevent the exploitation of the poor by the rich and to restrict the growth of poverty and disease. It came to be acknowledged that certain services of public utility could not be left to private enterprise. The State, in brief, has positive functions to perform.

This viewpoint was actively supported by the Socialists who advocated nationalisation of the factors of production. Former Soviet Russia, China and a few other countries were the only countries which had socialised structure of society. Other countries of the world are capitalist and recognise *laissez faire* to be the basis of society. But it is not Individualism of the old pattern. The modern individualist State has emerged as a guardian of the rights of man and community. Its end is to uplift man from the political, economic and social degradation. The functions of the State, therefore, are not only political, they are economic and social as well. It means considerable expansion in the province of the State and, thus, it brings into prominence the nature of public expenditure.

Analysis of the Objects of Public Expenditure. The general principle of public expenditure in the modern State is: that the government is for the good of the governed and the best criterion of State interference and State expenditure in any form is the benefit which will accrue, directly or indirectly, to the community as a whole. "Any

State, then, which directly or indirectly develops the natural or human resources of the nation or leads to their more economical use may be expected to increase national prosperity by increasing the national wealth and may thus be expected ultimately to 'pay for itself' given the important qualification that the gain due to the increased expenditure is not less than the loss caused by the heavier taxation."[1]

Following is an analysis of the general objects of public expenditure:

1. The first object of the public expenditure is the provision of services yielding indivisible benefit. In this category are included maintenance of law and order, defence, safeguards against spread of diseases and epidemics, etc.
2. The provision of collective benefits or services that cannot, even if it were desirable, be undertaken by private enterprise, for example, construction and maintenance of roads.
3. The provision for the sick, destitute and unemployed.
4. All such functions in the field of industry where the primary object is to secure great efficiency and output, for example, public utility services, as railways, posts and telegraphs, airways, supply of gas and electricity.
5. Functions in the field of income and social standards where the chief aim is to safeguard the interests of citizens and mitigate tile effects of unequal distribution of income These functions include control and regulation of currency, exchange and credit, social insurance, factory legislation, fixing of minimum national wages, protective tariff, mechanism of rationing and price control, etc.

Principle of Maximum Social Advantage. If public finance is to be treated as a scientific branch of public administration, the principle of general welfare must be at its root. The principle of general welfare, to which Dalton gives the name of Maximum Social Advantage, aims at securing the great social good for the community by judiciously regulating the expenditure and the revenue of the State. According to Dalton, the two main conditions of an increase in the welfare of the community are: (1) improvement in the productive power, and (2) improvement in the distribution of what is produced. Public taxation and public expenditure should, accordingly, be conducted in such a way that the productive efficiency of a country may be increased, so that "a larger product per head of the population shall be obtained with smaller effort." This implies (*i*) a better method of taxation, (*ii*) reduction in the inequalities of income, and (*iii*) the nature and composition of public expenditure.

Public Expenditure in Relation to Production and Distribution. The nature and composition of public expenditure is of immense importance, because the manner in which public money is spent exercises considerable influence on the production and distribution of wealth. Defence of the country and maintenance of law and order are, of course, necessary for the well-being of the community, but this expenditure should be and must be reduced to the minimum level without endangering the safety of the State. The money saved from this kind of unproductive expenditure can usefully be employed for promoting and developing productive and beneficent departments. A greater figure of

1. Robinson, M.E., *Public Finance*, p. 7.

expenditure devoted to the nation-building schemes, like education and health, adds to the mental and physical efficiency of the people as a whole and contributes to greater production of national wealth. The State must necessarily be vigilant about the proper development of industries and the workers employed therein. It is also necessary that the State should provide for the organisation and conduct of researches in different spheres of economic, political and social activities. Similarly, due proportion of expenditure of the State should be divided toward such undertakings as the public utility services and those industries where private enterprise is not likely to come forward.

From this brief survey, it will be clear that a well regulated public expenditure greatly contributes to the growth of the national wealth and yields the maximum social advantage. It tends to remove inequalities in the distribution of national wealth by taxing the rich and benefiting the poor classes of the community by the provision of goods, services and amenities which help to better their lot. If the State adopts a progressive policy of taxation and imposes high death duties, and spends a big portion of the money realised in providing the poor with better means of employment, better conditions of work, national minimum wages, better and more sanitary houses, free and advanced educational facilities, free and highly developed facilities and medical aid, it produces better fed and more contented citizens who are a real asset to the nation. But this can be possible only when the guiding principle of public expenditure is the attainment of maximum social advantage. According to Dalton, "The two chief conditions of an increase in the economic welfare are, first, improvement in productive powers, and, secondly, improvements in the distribution of what is produced."

PUBLIC REVENUE

The provision of adequate revenue to meet the ever-increasing expenditure of the modern State is obviously a matter of considerable difficulty and intricacy. In normal times every progressive community endeavours to meet its annual expenditure out of its annual income. The State obtains its income chiefly by taxing its citizens. It may also include smaller revenues not of the nature of taxes. Following are the permanent sources of the revenues of the State:

1. **Regular Revenues.** (*i*) Revenues from State-ownership of (*a*) land and buildings, (*b*) productive undertakings, for example, incomes from postal services, State-owned railways and other public utility services.

(*ii*) Revenues from private income, including taxation in all its forms.

2. **Irregular Revenues.** These are miscellaneous sources, casual and irregular in nature such as fines, penalties, gifts, forfeitures, etc.

The Nature of Taxation. Taxes are levied practically upon all persons in the community to cover the cost of the services rendered by the State. A tax is a compulsory contribution which the citizens are required to pay for the services rendered by a public authority. The essence of a tax, as distinguished from other charges of government, is the absence of a direct *quid pro quo* between the taxpayer and the public authority. While levying a tax, it is not the intention of the government to render a service to the tax payer equivalent to the amount of the tax paid by him. In other words, you cannot refuse to pay a tax on the plea that you do not use a service.

Taxes are usually classified into direct or indirect, although these classifications are sometimes overlapping and are not always mutually exclusive. Direct taxes are those paid by the individual directly on the basis of his possession or receipt of property. They may be based on real or personal property, tangible or intangible, owned at a specified time, or received during a specified period. Indirect taxes are those which are levied on particular articles, or transactions, and which may be borne by others than those from whom the tax collector receives payment.

As to the nature of taxation in general several theories have, at different times, been advanced.

(*i*) One of the earlier theories was that the contribution made by every citizen to meet the expenditure of the State should be proportionate to the benefits received by him from the State. A tax was, accordingly, regarded as a payment made by each individual in return for benefits received from government. There was, as such, a direct *quid pro quo* in a tax.

The benefit theory is held to be unjust and impracticable. It is obviously inconceivable that the weakest members of the society, who may be assured to benefit most from the services of the State, should be made to pay the heaviest contribution. But as Bastable points out, "If security is to be sold like an ordinary commodity, there ought, on the strictest commercial principles, to be some allowance made to the purchaser of a large quantity."[2]

(*ii*) The exponents of the Financial Theory are not concerned with equity. They aim exclusively at obtaining the necessary revenues as expeditiously and as cheaply as possible. The aim of the public finance is, thus, to raise the largest sum of money with the least trouble. Accordingly, each person should pay in proportion to his income, of course, the rich paying more than the poor.

Closely connected with it is the "cynical" theory of taxation. The advocates of this theory attempt to secure the needed revenue in such a way as to encounter the maximum taxation with least opposition. It is maintained that any tax is good which yields a large income with comparatively little protest. This policy of taxation is consistent with the maxim attributed to the French Minister Colbert: "Pluck the goose with as little squealing as possible."

(*iii*) According to the Social-political theory a tax is regarded as an instrument for attaining an economic or social end, such as reduction in the inequalities of income, or fostering of certain industries.

The advocates of this theory deliberately use the fiscal machine to reduce the gap between high and low incomes, or would employ tariffs and such other measures as a means of stimulating production.

(*iv*) Taxation is frequently advocated to restrict the consumption of luxuries or of

2. *Op. cit.*, p. 299.

noxious articles and, as such, sumptuary theory explains the nature of taxation. The object in such a kind of taxation is moral.

It is impossible to devise a system of taxation which may satisfy different points of view as to the nature of taxation. Nor is it possible to devise a single system of taxation which would be regarded as satisfactory from the point of view of both the tax-payer and the State exchequer. All modern States adopt a mixed system of taxation including both direct and indirect taxes, spread over property, income and consumption, the whole system conforming, as far as possible, to the various canons of taxation discussed hereafter. It is true that the enormous expenditure of modern governments necessitates that the system of taxation should be productive from the point of view of the government. But the principle of equity cannot be disregarded. A tax should not be devised in a manner which affects adversely the productivity of the tax-payer. Nor should it entail a heavier burden on the poor and a lighter one for the rich. It must be consistent with the principle of the ability to pay, which naturally means that the people with higher incomes should be called upon to pay higher taxes. "Justice between the various classes is essential so far as it can be attained, and taxation which conforms to the general principle of equity is to be favoured even though it may not yield the maximum economic benefit." Nevertheless, it is impossible to devise a system of taxation which will satisfy classes and individuals in the multitude of different circumstances which may exist in modern society. There are always some cases in which conditions make the burden of taxation press more heavily than it would in other circumstances. It is, however, more politic and satisfactory to adopt certain general principles to meet each individual case. This will mean less inconvenience and fewer hardships. The best tax systems are based on one principle; they are usually a compromise between a number of systems, and have been devised as the result of long experience and careful consideration of the peculiar needs of the community concerned.

Canons of Taxation. No discussion on the principles of taxation can be complete without a reference to the canons of taxation laid down by Adam Smith.[3]. Although the theory and practice of taxation has been considerably extended since his days, yet his propositions are still fundamentally true and they remain the starting point of sound public finance:

(*i*) "The subjects of every State ought to contribute towards the support of the government, as nearly as possible in proportion to their respective ability; that is in proportion to the revenue which they respectively enjoy under the protection of the State. In the observation and neglect of this maxim consists what is called the equality or inequality of taxation."

Equality here involves equality of sacrifice, and not equality of the amount paid. The poor and the rich both should pay what they can pay and equality and justice demand that no one should pay more than what he is able to pay.

(*ii*) "The tax which each individual is bound to pay, ought to be certain, and not arbitrary. The time of payment, manner of payment, the quantity to be paid, ought all to be clear and plain to the contributor, and to every other person."

A tax should not be arbitrary. Everyone must know well in advance what he has to

3. *Wealth af Nations*, Book V, Chap. II, Vol. II.

pay, when he has to pay, and where he has to pay. When he knows all this, a tax-payer can adjust his expenditure with the least inconvenience. The government, too, becomes certain, as far as possible, of its receipts.

(*iii*) "Every tax ought to be levied at the time or in a manner, in which it is most likely to be convenient for the contributor to pay it."

A tax should be collected at the time when the tax-payer has the means to pay. If public authorities demand payment when it is not convenient for the tax-payer, it becomes burdensome and there is probability that it may not be paid at all. A convenient tax is justified on the grounds of productivity and good government, and also from the point of the tax-payer, particularly when he belongs to the poor class in the community. The greater the convenience the less waste of time and of resources involved in collection and payment.

(*iv*) "Every tax ought to be so contrived as both to take out and keep out of the pockets of the people as little as possible over and above what it brings into the public treasury of the State."

The machinery required for collecting taxes should be simple and economical so that the cost of collection and the loss to the individual and the community should be small in proportion to the proceeds. It is, therefore, necessary that an able Finance Minister should always see that the cost of collection does not exhaust the major portion of the receipts. Similarly, a sound system of taxation should scrupulously avoid all taxes which discourage saving and hamper the growth of capital.

Following are a few more principles for a good system of taxation which may be added to Adam Smith's canons enumerated above:

(*v*) From the point of view of the government a tax should be productive of revenue. But no tax should be imposed which may tend to diminish the economic resources of the community. A tax may be immediately productive of a large revenue, yet under certain conditions it may ultimately result in a reduction in the nation's income.

(*vi*) It is better to have a few productive taxes than many less productive ones. It is always cheaper to collect a few remunerative taxes than a large number of smaller amounts spread over a wide field.

(*vii*) The tax should permit of an automatic growth as wealth and population increase.

(*viii*) The tax should be elastic and it should be responsive. The system of taxation should contain at least some taxes which permit of an increase in the rate and yield in order to meet emergencies without necessitating an increase in expenditure on administration or collection.

(*ix*) The system of taxation should be as simple and intelligible as possible. If it is complex and difficult to understand, it may create doubt and friction between the government and the tax-payer. A simple and intelligible system of taxation creates confidence, a better appreciation of the needs of government and, at the same time, it injects political consciousness into a citizen.

PART - III

The Functions of the State

27

CHAPTER

The Limits of Political Control

Having studied the origin and machinery of the State, we now ask the question: what is all that machinery for? What is it to do? In other words, what are the proper functions of the State? The answer to this question is the real issue of Political Science and, yet, this issue has not so far found a satisfactory solution. It is no answer to say that the State must act for the general welfare or common interest. There is no activity of the State and no action of government, down to the most ruthless and tyrannical, which has not been defended on the ground of general welfare. Can we, then, lay down any general principles by which to test the activities of the State and say with definiteness that the claim of general welfare is justified by the results? Here we return to the same old question with which we began our study of the State: what is the purpose of the State? The purpose of the State can best be understood if we clearly understand the relationship between the State and society.

The State in Relation to Society. It may be well to remind ourselves of what we said in an earlier Chapter, namely, to "identify the social with the political is to be guilty of the grossest of all confusions which completely bars any understanding of either society or State."[1] To equate the State with society is to justify State interference in all aspects of human life. The Greek City-State was an omnicompetent State, because among the Greeks there was no difference between the State and society. The State was to them all in all and it embraced their entire life. The citizen was nothing except as a member of the State and his whole existence depended on and was subject to the State. Plato's Communism was based on the conception that the State was the supreme entity for which the individual must sacrifice all that he had, even his hearth and home. To Aristotle the State was prior to the individual and it continued in existence for the sake of good life. The nineteenth century German theory, represented in its highest development in the writings of Hegel, regarded the State as the highest creation of reason and morality. The individual is moral because he is a member of the State. He should, accordingly, render complete submission to the State. It is, in fact, the moral duty of the individual to obey the State in whatever commands it may issue. There is no limit to its functions. A dictator, too, will pay scant attention to the distinction between the State and society. There is no sphere of life which his State will not cover. To Hitler and Mussolini there

1. MacIver, R.M., *The Modern State*, p. 5.

was nothing above the State, nothing beyond it, nothing besides it. The same were the demands of Soviet Russia and other Communist States of her pattern.

The State exists within a Society. Their geographical areas may be the same and their membership may also be identical. But they are distinct in origins, aims and functions. Society is natural and instinctive; the State is the creation of will and reason. "The organization of the State is not *all* social organization," as MacIver says, "the ends for which the State stands are not *all* ends which humanity seeks, and quite obviously the ways in which the State pursues its objects are only *some* of the ways in which, within society, men strive for the objects of their desire." The State is, thus, not co-equal and co-extensive with society. Its functions do not embrace the whole range of human activity. It exists for one single purpose whereas society exists for a number of purposes, "some great and some small", as Barker puts it, "but all in their aggregate deep as well as broad."[2]

Though we do not equate the State with society, yet the State provides the framework of the social order. The State, as Laski says, is a way of regulating human conduct and it prescribes rules of behaviour by which men must regulate their lives.[3] The State, as such, represents the highest form of social organization. It exists to regulate and cement social relations. It binds people together and enjoins upon them certain uniform rules of behaviour without which a well-ordered social life is not possible. Society, in brief, is held together by the State. But the State is an agent of society and as an agent of society, it has certain rights. Like all other rights, the rights of the State, too, are relative to its functions. The State is, accordingly, not exempt from the imperative : "Thus far and no further", to which all agencies of society are subject.

The distinction between the State and society is all the more necessary to understand, because the will of the State is in actual operation the will of government. The sovereignty of the people is, no doubt, a dogma of democracy and it is the basis of all political decisions, but in actual practice it is nothing more than an indication in a vague manner of the general direction in which the sovereign people wish to see events move. The effective source of State action is the small number of men who constitute the government and whose decisions are legally binding upon the community. If the State and society were to be identical, all human relations and social activities will ultimately be at the mercy of the few men who constitute the government and act on behalf of the State. In the name of the general welfare and common interest the government may prescribe anything. Its interference in the social order may become all-comprehensive, and instead of acting as an agent of society for the maintenance of rights of man, it may begin creating rights "as the lordly dispenser of gifts."

The Purpose of the State. The government, says Laski, "are the trustees and governors and it is their business to glean the needs of society and to translate those needs into terms of effective statutes. The purpose of the State finds its personification in them." The purpose of the State is the ultimate aim for which it exists and it is two-fold: the promotion of individual welfare and the realisation of the collective ends of society. It

2. Barker, E., *Principles of Social and Political Theory,* p. 42.
3. Laski, H., *An Introduction to Politics,* p. 15.

is a means to an end and not an end in itself and being a means, it has to perfom certain functions. But moral means must be adopted to achieve desirable ends. Every act is in pursuance of an end and the end is merely the result of a series of acts that are undertaken as means. The functions of the State, which are the means, must be justified in relation to its primary end. The end of the State is to create conditions of the freest possible development and creative self-expression of its members. Whatever functions the State undertakes and whatever action the government takes in consequence thereof, it must be proved that it enables men to realise the best that is in themselves and it helps ultimately the promotion of their happiness and spiritual uplift. This is the first criterion by which the activities of the State should be tested.

There have been sharp differences between the Individualists, the Idealists and the Socialists over the question whether the State is a means to an end or an end in itself, and whether the State helps or hinders the development of the individual. It is now universally accepted that the purpose of the State is the organisation of justice and happiness and it seeks to create conditions, consistent with the interests of society as a whole, under which the individual leads a fuller life and may complete the fulfilment of his personality. The Idealists give to the State a separate, mystic personality, "a march of God on earth" and the individual depends for his existence upon it. He owes it a debt of gratitude for granting him all those moral conditions which enrich his personality and develop his faculties to their full stature. The State, they regard, an end in itself and the individual a means in the realization of the highest expression of social morality, which the State represents. But this is not true. It is the people which make the State. Without the people there can be no State and to submerge the individual in the State is to destroy his individuality. The ultimate purpose or end of the State is to enable the individual to achieve his best self. Social good, in the final analysis, means the good of the individuals who make up the social whole. Without them neither there is society nor the State; parts make the whole.

Graham Wilson gives a matter-of-fact answer to the question whether the State is an end or a means. He says, "For those who stress consent, the State is clearly the means; for those who believe in the moral or the force theory, the State becomes an end in itself whether good or bad." The political thinkers belonging to the latter school exalt the State to mystic heights and make the exercise of power as its characteristic expression and estimate unending "achievement to be won by domination and regarding coercion as the primary condition of social order."[4] But this extolling of the State, one way or the other, is morally wrong and politically dangerous. The argument of force is might and coercion and it is only the clumsy and stupid, as MacIver says, who seek to attain their ends by force. Force holds nothing together and when it is made the basis of the State, it crushes the personality of men and destroys the very social order which the State is supposed to build and sustain. By its very existence the State performs a service and, as such, it orders and commands. But "it commands only because it serves, it owns only because it owes." The State owes to its members a duty to build and sustain that universal framework of social order within which their lives may seek out the ways of their fullest development.

4. MacIver, R.M., *The Modern State*, p. 420.

The State is an organisation of force to the extent that it performs its functions adequately and efficiently in creating an atmosphere in which human purpose can be realised without undue interference or disruption. The mere fact that the State retains force and reserves to itself its use deters individuals and groups to use force in the attainment of their ends. It is, therefore, a potential instrument and the State should not use it unduly. Let force remain subservient to the common welfare and common will. If it becomes master, it will destroy not only "material goods but also the cultural gains, the spirit of truth, the work of the mind, the fertility of thought."[5] Hitler's Germany and Mussolini's Italy are its glaring examples.

When we subordinate force to the common welfare and common will, we accept the State as an organisation of cooperative citizenship, a fellowship of men aiming at the enrichment of common life. Its moral character is not different from any other association and it exacts loyalty from us "upon the same grim conditions that a man exacts loyalty from his friends."[6] We always judge a friend by his deeds and owe him loyalty accordingly. We also judge the State by what it does. The State is, therefore, "subject to a moral test of adequacy."[7] If in order to protect and promote the well-being of its citizens, the State is compelled to use force, then, force should be justified by its value to the society. The State, in brief, does not possess force without conditions. As an agent of society, its purpose is service and those who serve strive for results rather than exalt for power.

FUNCTIONS OF THE STATE

Toward *laissez faire*. We have said that the State is subject to the imperative 'thus far and no further', that is to say, what the State should do and what it should not do. Men's views on this problem have varied widely at different periods of history and from one country to another. In the Europe of Middle Ages, life was essentially ruled by customs and traditions, whose control was no less rigid than that of the State. But there was no State in the real sense of the term at that point of time. The State and the Church both ruled together, the former in the temporal and the latter in the moral sphere. The functions of the State were to maintain law and order, to dispense justice and to conduct dealings with foreign States. There were no good roads and the only method of transport being the horse, the average individual lived in a small and isolated community, in which he was far more conscious of the impact on his life of his employer, the lord of the manor and the priest, than he was of the State.

With the growth of industry and commerce in the sixteenth and seventeenth centuries, the rigid mediaeval system of control, based on custom and tradition, gave way to systems of private enterprise. These were encouraged by governments themselves as increased production increased the national resources and so did the national power and prestige. Industrialization, however, had its own problems. It changed the social and economic structure of society and brought into existence the new relationship between the employer and the worker replacing the mediaeval relationship. The pace was accelerated

5. *Ibid.*, p. 423.
6. Laski, H. J., *A Grammar of Politics*, p. 37.
7. *Ibid*, p. 28.

in Britain which was the first to establish a national State. In France, the rhythm of change was different and feudal relationships persisted right up to the Revolution of 1789. Russia was on the other extreme and here pre-industrial civilisation persisted up to the revolution of 1917. The process of transformation to modern industrial capitalism in the nineteenth century so radically changed the nature of Britain's civilisation that enlightened public opinion demanded from the Government enactment of labour regulations which should create hygienic labour conditions in the factories and save the industrial labour from the spread of disease.

Nevertheless, in Britain of the nineteenth century, politicians and economists believed that the State should interfere only in so far as intervention was necessary to prevent flagrant abuses of humanitarian principles and to safeguard public health. The modern concept of the Welfare State, with the duty of protecting the individual against natural inequalities and misfortunes, was still unborn. The State was expected to leave the individual alone, *laissez faire*, to determine his own destiny and the fullest and free development of his own capacities and interests. The principle of *laissez faire* meant the free play of competition which was the law of nature. Most people felt that it was natural and inevitable for some to be rich and privileged and others to be poor and miserable, and that the State ought not to interfere, except to ensure conformity with some rudimentary rules of social life.

From *laissez faire* to Welfare. When Marx published the first volume of his Das Kapital or Capital in 1867, the picture of society was not fundamentally different. He concluded that the State was using its authority exclusively in the interest of the economically dominant class. He argued that poverty was unnecessary and it was the result of special economic and political conditions. It could be got rid of by changing those conditions, but the economically dominant class, which was also the ruling class and used the machinery of the State to prepetuate its own interest, would never attempt any change to remove poverty and misery of the masses. Hence, there must be a revolution.

There were social reformers in the nineteenth century, however, who saw the State as a potential instrument by which a more just society could be created, without the upheaval of a revolution. They pleaded that it was the duty of the State to step in and to interfere in what had been hitherto the citizen's private affairs, with the object of removing injustices of the capitalist system. They protested against the social and economic anarchy which the capitalist system had produced and proposed that land and capital be placed under social ownership in order to ensure a more equitable distribution of the means and appliances of happiness. From the economic point of view they argued that the industry would be more efficient when it was socialized, and from the moral point of view it would ensure justice. With the social legislation of the nineteenth century, there was born a concept of positive State interference which was to develop during the following century into the social service State, with its comprehensive system of social security from the cradle to the grave.

Since then the province of the State has extensively increased. Governments in all countries have now fully realized that chronic want among their people is an economic liability and a political danger to the State, for the economy and the general system of government stand in integral relations to each other and the contours of one will inevitably be shaped by the outlines of the other. But all governments do not perform identical functions. They vary with the degree of social and economic development of the people and adjust themselves as their needs and requirements demand. No government can for long remain unresponsive. It must ultimately undertake tasks which are dictated by changing conditions, though one government may be more alert in sensing the needs of time or demands of the people. But whatever the government does must be explained and justified in relation to the primary end of the State, the common good. Common good cannot be divorced from the individual good. Common good really means the all-round perfection—physical, mental, moral, religious, economic—of all individual members of the State, and even the rest of humanity. No living individual or group of individuals should be positively excluded from the benefits of the State, and if they are excluded the State must justify that such an exclusion is for their own all-round perfection. This means that the conception of the 'police State' has been finally abandoned and with it the old classification of the functions of the State. Today the State is accepted as a 'Welfare' or 'Social State' with new significance of functions it is required to perform. These are divided into three main categories: Protective or Police, Welfare or Ministrant, Economic and Regulatory.

1. **Protective or Police Functions.** Protective or Police functions are those indispensable and essential activities of the State upon which its existence depends, such as the preservation of external security and the maintenance of internal peace and order. If the State is to exist as an independent sovereign State, its first duty is to secure universal order within its frontiers and to safeguard itself from all probabilities of foreign aggression. For this purpose, the State must be equipped with military forces of all kinds and in possession of modern weapons. Defence of the State also necessitates manning the industrial resources of the country and applying nation's scientific knowledge to the task of defence. As long as we live in a world where war is an ever present possibility, the defence activities of the government will be many and varied and they will, as such, impinge on all aspects of the lives of citizens.

If defence of the country is the primary function of the State, so is the maintenance of internal peace and security. To ensure organized community life, the State must keep adequate police force and make laws universal in application with a view to regulate the conduct of its citizens. The offenders should be punished and the crime repressed. The government, accordingly, administers civil and criminal justice, and protects citizens in the enjoyment of their life, liberty and property and other civil and political rights. The State, today, also exercises control over certain aspects of the family life of the individual such as prescribing conditions for marriage, divorce, inheritance, adoption and care of children, provision for the maintenance of wife, etc. These are essential conditions of a happy family. The State is a system of relationships between individuals and family is the basic and moral system of such relationships.

Another function closely connected with the maintenance of internal peace and external security is the development and management of the major agencies of transportation and communication. Well developed means of communication and transport make the State a viable unit, knit the people in fraternal bonds of togetherness, and enable them to share one another's weal and woe. They are, in brief, the nerve centre of the country's social, economic and political life. They contribute to the process of modernization.

There are other essential functions that all except the very simplest governments undertake. They include the establishment and maintenance of certain standards with which all subjects of the State must comply in their dealing with their fellow citizens. This function may extend to the regulation of markets, the control of weights and measures, minting and coining of money, the control of prices, etc. These functions are so primary that they found their due place in the Athenian list of State functions.

2. **Welfare Function—Order and Protection.** But these are mere police functions and no State can afford to remain simply this. Being an organ of society, it is the primary duty of the State to serve the purpose for which it came into existence. It must create those conditions and provide for an atmosphere in which every man gets an opportunity for the development of his faculties so that he may grow and expand to the best of his capacity and ability. This is the real essence of order, which the State is charged to maintain. Order should not be merely for order's sake. It should serve to ensure justice and happiness for all by regulating the dealings of citizens with one another, by checking disorder and high-handedness of one class of people over others, and by maintaining all those righls which are fundamental to the existence and spiritual uplift of man. When the government does so, the order which it maintains becomes a part of the larger task of the State, or to put it in the words of MacIver, "it is not order for the sake of order but, order for the sake of *protection* and of *conservation* and *development*."

To protect the weak against the strong is the modern interpretation of the maintenance of order and, consequently, it is an essential function of the State. It means that the policies of the government should be so determined and its laws so formulated that equal opportunity is provided to all to grow and expand and no one is denied the basic necessities of health and decent living simply because of the accident of birth or misfortune which is beyond man's control. To express it in the words of President Roosevelt, the State should strive to establish a social order which should ensure "freedom from want" and "freedom from fear" for all. These are welfare functions and a government which claims to be responsive to the needs of the people cannot afford to ignore them. "This expansion" in the functions of the State, MacIver remarks, "has done much to change the very conception of the State, so that from being, in the eyes of those subject to it, mainly an instrument of power it has become, so far as its internal activities are concerned, in large measure an agency of service." The State has a collective life and the attainment of common purpose depends upon the welfare of every individual.

The welfare of the people involves, in the first place, their physical welfare. It is now generally admitted that the State has a definite responsibility for the physical welfare of its members, because the happiness and prosperity of a nation are directly dependent upon their physical fitness and vitality. The public health schemes, on which every State today spends hefty sums of money, are both preventive and curative. The idea of prevention is largely of the twentieth century origin. Diseases must be fought and checked, hygiene developed and the medical aid guaranteed. In industry, hours of work must be limited, conditions of work in shops and factories must be fixed, and security against sickness and disability, underemployment and unemployment ensured. It is impossible to make a complete list of those departments of collective life which may either be regulated or controlled by the State in order to maintain the health of its members. Good health is both a prerequisite for the success of the personality of the individual and a necessary condition for the enjoyment and exploitation of success of the individual himself as well as that of the State itself. Healthy citizens are the health of the State; the sinews of its prosperity, prestige and respect.

Development of human capacities is another aspect of welfare, and education ranks the foremost of all. There are few States now that do not feel responsible "for the procuring and dissemination of knowledge," as Lindsay calls it. Popular education is necessary for the preservation of those conditions of freedom, political and social, which are essential to free individual development and creative self-expression. Education not only equips the citizen with the accomplishments of citizenship, but it also provides him the means of access to adequate knowledge and opportunities. It is the key-stone of the arch of good life. There can be no other agency than government which can undertake obligations so universal of character in providing mass education. It should be the first charge on every exchequer. Nor should any community be satisfied with a gradual progress of education. Education produces its best effect not when it trickles slowly but when it is rapidly universalised.

National State-controlled systems of education, from infant school to university, now exist in almost every country and this came about, mainly in the last hundred to hundred and fifty years, from two absolutely different causes. France and Prussia were the pioneers of State education on the ground that the State could not leave the making of citizens to private hands. "It must mould the young to the proper shape, give them the right point of view, exclude dangerous ideas and risky experiments." It was, therefore, not a concept of the Welfare State and the plea for the development of human capacities which induced France and Prussia to adopt the system of State education.

In other countries, especially the Anglo-Saxon, State education came from the inadequacy of private enterprise. There was no pressure of political uniformity. Popular education was deemed a social necessity, because without it the citizen had no chance of mental development. Denominational institutions had neither the resources nor the means to provide for universal compulsory education. It was, thus, the need of educational opportunities in the name of freedom which brought education in these countries within the ambit of State functions. But the difference of approach has resulted in wide differences of educational policy, uniformity being the aim of one, variety and experimentation of the other. All the same, public education has a great task to accomplish in enabling the young to enjoy the best of their lives by driving from the treasures not only of their own country but of the world the worth and wonder of human achievement. It is a road of intellectual expansion and adventure and every progressive State makes for the organisation of a comprehensive system of education, basic and higher, general and technical for all citizens. Education should neither be standardized nor tailored to cater to any ideology. It should be free and liberal with the object of acquiring knowledge in order to reveal what is universal. Education would thus be socially renovating, facilitating change and development in traditions which otherwise engulf the average man. Its aim is to kindle light and solve the riddles of humanity.

But the most important function of the Welfare State is the creation of conditions which assure social justice by removing social iniquities created by capitalism. Poverty and unemployment have been problems in all except the most primitive society. These problems did not become less acute with the advance of civilization; on the contrary, industrialization involved profound changes in society and brought with it many new problems. Intervention of money economy created the wage-system and urbanization, and labour mobility weakened the communal ties, leaving the worker to rely primarily upon himself and his ability to earn. For the great majority, therefore, constant employment became a necessity and the unproductivity of old age a grim prospect. Then, there were the rigours of underemployment, uncertainty of employment, permanent or temporary disability involved through accidents and sickness and the horrors of the wage-system.

It was, under the circumstances, thought that only a system based on socialist doctrines could assure social justice. But European governments, determined to retain the capitalist system, asserted that social security laws could operate harmoniously within such a system and stabilise it by mitigating the effects of business cycles. Britain was the first to insure workers against the hazards of unemployment. A national compulsory unemployment insurance plan was introduced there in 1911, and during the following quarter century, most of the major European countries passed similar laws. The Beveridge Plan in Britain attempted to provide what has been called "the cradle-to-grave security" and in pursuance of that Old Age Pension, Unemployment and Sickness Insurance, Maternity and Accident benefits to workers were put into operation. The Labour Government devised a scheme of National Health. In the United States there are Old Age, Survivors and Disability Insurance, and a Plan for Public Assistance for needy old persons who could not benefit under the insurance system, children who had been deprived of support and care because of the parent's death, disability, or absence, and needy blind persons. The Social Security Law of 1935 provided for unemployment insurance financed by employers' contributions. Workmen's Compensation Laws provide for adequate compensation to the workers injured on the job, or in the event of fatal injury their survivors receive death benefits. Next, there are provisions for Sickness or Temporary Disability Insurance, The Guaranteed Annual Wage in the principal Automobile, Steel, Rubber and Aluminium manufacturing industries, etc.

Thus, the functions relating to social security provide a high degree of protection against the misfortunes and hazards of life. All schemes of social security signify that man can no longer be regarded simply as a 'unit of labour power' and that the modern State accepts obligations "meeting certain dependent needs of the individual and the family."[8] But perhaps most important characteristic of the Welfare State, next to the provision of cradle-to-the-grave security and the provision of adequate housing, is its acceptance of responsibility for the greatest economic hazard of them all, the maintenance of high employment of men and machines and of a high level of productivity. This

8. Titmuss, Richard M., Essays on " *The Welfare State*", p. 54.

obligation involves the regulation of labour-management relations, in the effort to prevent or settle strikes, and in the gigantic tasks of alleviating the ups and downs of the business cycles.

3. **The Economic and Regulatory Functions.** The functions which we discussed and enumerated above are such that they could in principle be undertaken by any type of government, in any stage of the development of the State, although the extent and manner of operation would of necessity vary with the changing conditions. Directed to the betterment of the conditions of living for the members of the State, they do not imply any particular order. What they seek to establish is the national minimum of decent and effective living for all citizens. But the modern State committed to the service of the community and having for its purpose to make it more truly a community must have newer range of functions including a part in the running of the economic system. The State must, therefore, help all those forces that work away from it or against it. So long as the activity of the State has relation to the common life and it promotes the welfare of the people by securing and protecting as effectively as it may a social order in which justice, social, economic and political, informs all the institutions of the national life, it is a relevant activity of the State and it must undertake.

It means that the State should be a direct agent of the economic life of the community. It should endeavour to improve or to doctor the existing economic order and if need be to substitute the economic order itself. The State should so direct its policy that wealth, its sources of production, and its means of distribution shall not be concentrated in the hands of the few, but shall be so distributed as to subserve the common good. It is not necessarily the Socialist State, but, in fact, the modern State which has become a direct sharer in the economic activities. The old self-regulating, self-restoring mechanism has completely failed necessitating the positive intervention of the State in order to restore by whatever measures the social equilibrium.

The intervention of the State manifests itself in many ways. It adjusts its tariff policy to assist nascent, indigenous industries and renders help to those industries in various forms, such as subsidies, loans and technical assistance. To gear up the productive forces, cordial relations are devised to be maintained between employers and workers and with a view to improving the health and efficiency of the latter, working of the factories is regulated, hours of work are fixed, conditions of work are prescribed, and the employment of women and children in certain trades and occupations is prohibited. In some of the progressive States minimum wages for the workers have been fixed. Machinery for the settlement of industrial disputes exists in most of the States and working of the trade unions, strikes, lock-outs, etc., have been determined by law. Similarly, States intervene and protect the tenants and agricultural labour against exploitation of any kind. It is, now, also conceded that land, the free gift of nature and limited in quantity, should not be left in the absolute control of a small fraction of landlords. The curse of absentee landlordism has compelled some of the States, like India, to fix by law ceilings on the ownership of land and have given the rights of fixity of tenure to the actual tillers of the soil. Likewise ceiling on urban property has been enacted with a view to providing shelter to all and eliminate the bane of pavement dwellers.

The States also undertake the regulation of trade, commerce, money market and credit agencies. Laws are enacted to prevent adulteration of foodstuffs and the sale of harmful drugs. India is experimenting with the policy of prohibition in some parts of the country. In some cases the State has appeared as a competitor to private enterprise and in others it excludes private enterprise. It owns and runs various social services as the railways, canals, postal, telegraph and telephone systems, electricity, water, transport and even industrial undertakings.

The Problem of Nationalization. There are two views of reforming the economic system and they inspire opposite programmes for governmental action. The first are those who see no solution of the prevailing economic problem except through the socialization or nationalization of the whole machinery of production. The second are those who believe that governmental action requires a positive intervention of a somewhat drastic character to restore the equilibrium which the capitalist society has grossly disturbed. *Laissez faire* has many items to its credit and from the material standpoint it has contributed enormously to the human well-being. But, at the same time, *laissez faire* has greatly disturbed the orderly run of society, by creating conflicts of interests, by reducing the personal creative activity of workers to mere mechanical occupations, by wasting much of society's resources in unprofitable expenditure and production of little social values, and by producing glaring contrasts between extreme wealth and extreme poverty, where conditions are such that two-thirds of the wealth are owned by an insignificant percentage of the population and the ownership of property is regarded as the badge of a class. This class, which becomes a class of vested interests, mans the political power and directs the whole machinery of government in furthering the interests of its own class alone. The result is social and political instability, and nearly twenty-four centuries ago Aristotle attributed revolution to "the disproportional increase in any part of the State. When the rich grow numerous, or properties increase, the form of government changes to oligarchy or government of families."

The modern capitalist State is confronted with two other problems of vital importance which characterise the prevailing system of production. The first is the hugeness of the scale of production which involves the hugeness of productive machine in men and equipment, and the extreme complexity and delicacy of the financial organisation on which it rests. Hugeness of the mechanism of production entails rationalization of industry and the emergence of monopolistic organizations. The whole process of this hugeness is pregnant with dangerous results. Hunger for foreign markets necessitates resort to imperialistic policies leading to international hostility and wars. Within the country it means displacement of'capital and labour, manipulation of prices to the disadvantage of the consumer, speculation and over-capitalization and social evils and illegal practices to kill competition.

The second problem is the blindness with which and in which private enterprise works. The capitalist production is largely unorganized, unrelated and purposeless, because private enterprise is haphazard and is inspired by selfish aims and immediate benefits. Each producer works on his own and from his own point of view. What the individual producer does, so does every industry. No industry cares to relate its production to other industries and the total needs of the country as a whole. Each works for its own individual profits and maximisation of profits. Such an uncoordinated production results into periodical breakdowns and widespread disorganisation which paralyse the economic life of the nation, causing widespread unemployment and distress.

Just as a man's livelihood is the basic factor of his existence, so the basic factor in any society is, as Tawney puts it, "the way it earns its living." Political activities rest on a foundation of economic activities. They go a long way in determining the nature of the State, by what class of men it will be governed, and in whose interests politics will be run. No State can now afford to remain oblivious of the forces which industrialism has released and the capitalist system has established. The old system of political control has become absolutely irrelevant. The social control of economic forces is the essential need of the modern State. If it does not do its duty, these forces would become so dominant as to destroy the basic unity of society. "Hence, the need for new integrations, in which men will feel they are employed in worthwhile occupations and will be able to relate their lives to understood and accepted ways of life."

One way of the new integration is the nationalisation of production on which certain States have entered. By nationalisation is meant the taking over by the State not only the public utility services, like postal, telegraph, telephone, and railway services, but the department of production, hitherto the field of the activities of competing and combining individuals and their establishments. The deliberate intention in nationalisation is to destroy competition and the profit motive, which is the *raison d'etre* of private enterprise and on which the industry had been built. In Soviet Russia, all land, its natural deposits and principal means of production were till recently owned by the State and operated by the people on behalf of the State. There was absence of exploitation and oppression and, thus, new social relations were established, not on individual interests but on cooperation and mutual assistance. All were workers and everyone worked for himself and for a society composed of workers. There are a few more countries which had followed the Soviet pattern. Others, which had not followed Soviet Russia in completely nationalising the whole productive and distributive process, have made a start with some of the key industries with an expanding programme. In these countries in which nationalisation is only partial and exists side by side with free enterprise in other industries, distribution remains free, sometimes within the limits of rationing and price control. The essential feature of such a system is that the State controls the whole output of certain commodities, decides how much shall be produced and of what quality, even fixes the price including the support price and determines the scale of consumption. In this way, the State substitutes its decision for the forces of demand and supply.

The policy of nationalisation resorted to by many States within the framework of the capitalist system has been the subject of active political controversy and in many cases the opposition parties are pledged to the reversal of nationalisation. Their main plea is that every extension of State activity means limitation on the freedom of its citizens. This is true. But when the activity of the State is directed to the furtherance of the cause of the economically and socially weak, it really enhances the freedom of the members of the State as a whole. When the State ventures an enterprise with a view to minimising inequalities in distribution of wealth and frees society from the parasitic control of absentee capitalism it does not restrict the freedom of its citizens, but, on the other hand, secures for each citizen those material conditions which will give him the fullest opportunity possible of a full life. When the State does not tolerate an economic system in which men are mere tools sacrificed to profit, it must devise means for a change, and when the community cannot benefit by such a system, it becomes the moral duty of the State, as an organ of society, to substitute it by a system which is more equitable, more just and more stable to promote and foster social unity.

The advocates of private enterprise ignore the important fact that the State with its command of resources and its universal reach can build for the future "in ways that no partial organisation can exert." The State does not discount the future and it suffers from no telescopic defects. It does not exploit the natural resources, limited in quantity and the free gifts of nature, for the gain of the immediate and of the few to the detriment of the future and the many. It can, thus, venture upon many constructive schemes and projects whose benefits will be shared by the future generations and all alike. It really means planning the resources of the nation and planning their utilisation for the wider interest of society.

Opposed to nationalisation is ***laissez faire.*** We have already said that there is little room left for the last stand of *laissez faire.* In fact, every modern State undertakes important functions of economic control, and the tendency, stimulated by technological developments and by the enormous growth of economic organizations of every kind, is constantly toward the enlargement and consolidation of these functions. Whenever government exercises control in any direction, may it be with a view to the stabilization of prices or for the conservation of the natural resources and for the development of the economic prosperity of the people, it inevitably affects the whole economy at important points and this necessitates economic planning. The primary resources of the country cannot be safeguarded without a long-term programme and the economic prosperity of the people depends on the proper utilization of the natural resources. The welfare service, therefore, turns into some kind of economic planning. Then, the real issue lies between those who stand for economic planning within the framework of a capitalist society and those who regard this task as impossible under capitalist system and aim to abolish it and substitute by a socialistic order.

Need for Planning. Whatever be the system of society no country can afford to do without planning. The necessity for planning is to be found in the inability of a non-planned economy to meet the needs of the modern world. Soviet Russia was the first to experiment with Five-Year Plans and by 1932, the world witnessed a phenomenally rapid industrialization under a most extensive programme of construction and exploitation of natural resources. By the time the Stalin Constitution could become operative in 1936, crises, poverty, unemployment and destitution had disappeared from the Soviet land and Stalin could proudly claim, "it is pleasant and joyful to know that the blood our people shed so plentifully was not shed in vain, that it has produced results." The Constitution guaranteed to the people full economic security. During the same period capitalist countries with unplanned economies were undergoing a paralysis or, at the least, a temporary breakdown of their systems, with proliferation of social diseases, falling prices, unemployment and stagnation both in the economic and political life. In a word, the capitalist countries suffered the bitterest consequences of destitution in plenty. Then, all economies, planned and unplanned alike, experienced War with its insatiable demand for materials and men, and the consequent pressure to conserve and plan. After the War, all had to plan for reconstruction and Russia did it admirably well. In others, the inequalities of wealth and unemployment deepened. In fact, they became intolerable in a professedly democratic society. Security of employment is the dominant demand of our times, and if for no other reason at least for that, there is no escape from some degree or form of planning.

The result is that few countries are without plans today. At one extreme was the Plan of the U.S.S.R. which controlled the use of virtually all resources and labour in the country and determined the distribution of resources for different purposes. At the other is the United States which has a plan for achieving and maintaining high levels of employment with minimum government interference. In between are various kinds of planned and semi-planned economies and the Five-Year Plans of India occupy a place of precedence in this category.

What is Planning ? Planning has no place under pure capitalism, for it does not allow much room for the capitalist trinity—sovereignty of the consumer, the tyranny of the price system, and the quest for profits. In a planned economy, the economic architects, who are the government authorities, generally determine what use is to be made of the limited resources and thereby impair the sovereignty of' the consumer, the basic element of capitalist economy. Their targets are determined according to an objective decided and planned by the government and, thus, price and income movements do not regulate the productive process. And since what is to be produced and the quantity and quality of the produce are determined by a board in accordance with the policy of the government, the planned economy supplants the entrepreneur, who is the human magnet in the capitalist machine.

It has been suggested that democratic planning is the only alternative to Communism which is one hundred per cent planning as it gears the whole life of man to planned regimentation and permits no phase of private sector. All decisions about planning were really made by one body, the Politburo of the Central Committee of the Communist Party in the U.S.S.R., and executed by the authority of the Government. The "Gosplan" or the State Planning Commission applied the decisions of the Politburo and filled in the details in order to prevent disproportions in economic development. The plans were not subject to public scrutiny. Only the results achieved and the targets attained were discussed in the Supreme Soviet. It was the Politburo which determined the failures and ordered removal of persons from Government who were held responsible for such failures, as in the case of Khrushchev. Democratic planning, on the other hand, as Sir Stafford Cripps defined it in the House of Commons in November, 1946, is "the layout of all national resources in the national interest to a nationally desirable end, and the organisation of the necessary methods, by the use of all the means that the people in a democratic society are prepared to give to the government." It includes, he went on to say, "six principal elements: choice of what is to be produced, the supply of the necessary labour, the supply of materials, the supply of capacity, the supply of the best location, and the supply of finance." If we add to this definition, "the five stages of planning", which Herbert Morrison stated in the British House of Commons, the definition of democratic planning would be complete. The five stages, he outlined, are: making up one's mind to plan, getting the necessary facts, devising alternative plans, choosing between these and deciding what is to be planned and what is to be left unplanned, and, finally, carrying out the plans, and adjusting and devising so that things happen in the right way and at the right place and at the right time. It is the very essence of democratic process to permit the questioning of any end at any time. Carl Friedrich has significantly said that democratic planning, "dedicated as it must be to achieving the greatest satisfaction for as many as possible, cannot neglect the reactions of all those whom a given policy affects."[9]

Planning and Freedom. The most serious doubts concerning the planned economy revolve round the issue of liberty. Is it compatible with freedom ? The U.S.S.R. did not succeed to prove that its planned society could co-exist with the other fundamental liberties. The Soviet Constitution granted the right to its citizens the fundamental freedoms of speech, press and assembly and other civil rights, they were to be consistent and in accordance with the socialist way of life. Vyshinksy made this point clear. He said, "In our State naturally, there is and can be no place for freedom of speech, press and so on for the foes of socialism." Writers of the eminence of Friedrich A. Hayck,[10] and Walter Lippmann[11] have vehemently criticised planning. They plead that it restricts the liberty of the individual and introduces statism. Lippmann points out, "Not only it is impossible for the people to control the plan, but what is more, the planners must control the people. They must be despots who tolerate no effective challenge to their authority."

In his discussion in *Full Employment*, Lord Beveridge, on the other hand, stressed the compatibility of a planned society and the retention of fundamental freedoms. "Britain," said Herbert Morrison in October, 1946, "is the first great nation to attempt to combine large-scale economic and social planning with a full measure of individual rights and liberty." Planning is not incompatible with freedom. The true background of freedom has always been conformity rather than chaos. But in our search for freedom we rely upon the traditional conformity which the liberal age had inherited from the old community culture of the Middle Ages. Such a concept of freedom is untenable now. Our search for freedom involves a search for a new conformity. And it is "identification with other members of the society, collective responsibility and the necessity for possessing a common background for our attitude and behaviour." This can be achieved within the framework of free parliamentary institutions.

The discussion on planning and freedom can best be summed up in the words of Professor Mannheim. He says, "While planlessness is anarchy and chaos, yet planning must not do violence to the spontaneous forces in society." Free parliamentary institutions provide a fuller scope for the expression of these spontaneous forces. But just as man must learn to live in peace with members of other States if he wants to survive, "so he

9. Friedrich, C.J., *Constitutional Government and Democracy,* p. 491.
10. *The Road to Serfdom.*
11. *The Good Society.*

must learn to reconcile the essentials of his freedom with life in a planned society." The welfare of each is involved in the welfare of all. Freedom must be responsive to the social needs and there must be a careful balancing of social and individual interests.

Our conclusions are now definite. There is no State which pursues the path of pure capitalism. Many of the policies adopted and pursued by the capitalist States are collectivists in their nature and extent. Such policies are not antagonistic to a democratic way of life, for democracy accepts man as man and this humane approach rests on the trinity of liberty, equality and fraternity. We have enough experience to know that important sectors of the economy can be nationalised without causing any injury to the democratic process. There is also little reason to doubt that collectivism could be introduced into new areas without endangering the democratic system if it secures freedom from want and freedom from fear, the two basic principles of social justice. The measures required to carry such a programme may give to the government important powers over the private sector. But there is no justification to regard them as a dangerous advance on "the road to serfdom" so long as they are responsive to the needs of the community. "The government of the new liberal society," Wilson says, "will be economically and culturally creative." Here democracy joins hands with pragmatic collectivism. Ernest Barker says, "Individualism and collectivism are not the banners of two separate armies, composed of two separate bodies of men. All of us fly them both, and we all serve under both."[12]. Planning should, therefore, be adequate to the scale and complexities of modern life. It should be flexible, continuous, in short, dynamic. The guiding motive ought to be the expansion and liberation of human personality in proportion to the available resources. Planning does not postulate complete socialisation of the means of production. It does, however, presuppose an extension of social control of economic activities. It is the correct selection of ends which should be the characteristic psychological element in the social process. Such a planning would represent a concerted effort to accelerate the democratic process.

What the State Should Not Do. Having conceded that democracy is compatible with some amount of collectivism and that the welfare service turns into some kind of planning and planning is a democratic process responsive to the changing needs or desires of the community, there are certain tasks which the State should not do. If the State does, "it only," as MacIver says, "ruins the material."

Public Opinion. Our first obvious conclusion will be that if there is one department of life from which government is automatically debarred, it is the formation and expression of opinion. In the days of class-bound oligarchies governments did not deign to explain their policies to the people as a whole nor did they generally need to prepare the way for the reception of these policies. Democracy, on the other hand, is built upon the belief that truth comes out by clash of opinion with opinion, and that every citizen has something of value to contribute and he must not be hindered in bringing it out. "Men who are prevented from thinking as their experience teaches them," says Laski, "will soon cease to think at all. Men who cease to think cease also to be in any genuine sense citizens. The instrument which makes them able to make effective their experience. rusts into obsolescence by disuse."[13] Community, no less than the individual concerned, suffers

12. Barker, E., *Principles of Social and Political Theory,* p. 273.
13. Laski, H., *A Grammar of Politics,* p. 120.

from any attempt on the part of the government to restrict the liberty of the formation and expression of opinion, for without freely thinking persons there is no community. The State, therefore, as MacIver bluntly says, "should not seek to control opinion, no matter what the opinion may be."[14]

Moreover, the programmes of legislation in the Welfare State are highly elaborate and technical which involve readjustments. If the government can claim to be a government by consent, it must conduct its operations in full publicity, make itself liable to criticism, and adequately organise institutions of consultation. Such a process provides access to all interests involved to reach the government. The acceptance of governmental policy, even when it issues from the democratic process, often demands psychological preparation of the public to receive it. It is, accordingly, not only vital that the government should value public opinion, but also provide adequate facilities to organise it and remain amenable to it. The pulpit, the press and propaganda are the vehicles for the expression of public opinion and their proper organisation is the source of maintaining effective authority. "To maintain the effectiveness of any authority," remarks MacIver, "it is necessary under these conditions that government should utilize modern methods of feeling the pulse of the public, should sense the currents of opinion and adapt their presentation of policy accordingly, should acquire knowledge of the differential impact of new measures on the diverse groups of the community and of the influences and motivations that operate with them."[15] A government, which chokes public opinion, cannot be a government for the sake of the governed. Regimentation of opinion strangulates thought and chokes reason, and the people are just like a herd doing what they are directed to do. It means government for the sake of the governors and such a government is not concerned with public welfare.

But the expression of opinion is not an unbridled democratic right. If the liberty to form and express opinion disturbs social order and is prejudicial to peace and tranquillity, it becomes a duty of the State to restrain it. Orderly conduct of society is the primary function of the State and the problem of liberty is the reconciliation of individual freedom with the just laws of the State. Liberty is never absolute; it must be under law. Laski has aptly said, "The State must, because its business is the preservation of order, concern itself to see that the peace is maintained. It is, therefore, entitled to say that any utterance which directly incites to immediate disorder is subject to penalty."[16]

Religion. Nor should the government interfere in or prescribe religion. Anything of the soul and of the mind derives its value exclusively from the reason which prompts the action. The religious and ethical appeal is always to the individual's own sense of what is right and what is wrong. Compulsory religion is a contradiction in terms. The State should, therefore, refrain from imposing any religious conditions of citizenship or any religious obligations on its citizens, should not grant special establishments, immunities, privileges, or favours to the members of any particular creed, and should not interfere on any religious grounds with the practices of any group of citizens. Barker has correctly said, "The standards of religion can only be applied in the area of voluntary life which

14. MacIver, R.M., *The Modern State,* p. 250.
15. *Ibid.,* p. 153.
16. Laski, H., *An Introduction to Politics,* p. 35.

lies outside the State; and the quality of behaviour which they involve can only be achieved if it is sought freely and without any shadow of legal compulsion. If the State attempts to draw religious standards, and the quality of behaviour which they involve, into the area of the legal association, and to enforce them as the prescriptions and by the sanctions of law, it simply fails."[17] But the practice of religion is subject to moral considerations. No State can tolerate the preaching and observance of immoral practices in the name of religion or to permit religion to pervert human beings or to corrupt social life. Similarly, no State can permit religious fanaticism to arouse communal passions to such a frenzy that it may result in the commission of heinous crimes against the adherents of other faiths.

Morality. Similarly, it is no more the function of government to impose a moral code than to impose a religious code. The legal code can never be identified with the moral code, as State dictated morality is no morality. T.H. Green stated the truth when he said that "the only acts which the State ought to enjoin or forbid are those of which the doing or not doing, from whatever motive, is necessary to the moral end of society." The moral end of society is the formation of free creative personalities. Morality is an expression of personality, as it conceives itself to other personalities.A moral rule is a rule that a man obeys from his heart, in the light of his system of values. State-prescribed morality, instead of making men moral, leads to evasion, hypocrisy, and corruption. "The major thesis is," as MacIver points out, "that law can no more be a substitute for morality than the hand can be a substitute for the eye." It must also be remembered that the moral codes of different groups are inevitably different. In the modern multi-group society State-prescribed morality may embitter one group against another which may ultimately lead to disruption of national unity.

Customs. The limits of the State action are again revealed when we turn to customs. What habit is to the individual custom is to the community. Communities, like men, get into the habits of doing things in a given way. Customs grow spontaneously, entrench themselves in the minds of the people and pass on from generation to generation. The State has neither the power to make customs nor the power to destroy them, though it may indirectly influence them by changing the conditions out of which they spring. It had long been recognised as a rule of empire that a conquering State must not interfere and seek to change the customs prevailing among a subject people. In democracies, the possibilities are generally there to abrogate the customs practised by minority groups. But experience shows that whenever and wherever such an attempt had been made, the minorities have stubbornly resisted the coercion of law, creating very often disorderly conditions difficult for the government to control and steer through. "Custom, when attacked," sums up MacIver, "attacks law in turn, attacks not only the particular law which opposes it, but, what is more vital, the spirit of law-abidingness, the unity of the general will."[18] To quote MacIver, again, "the main body of social customs is beyond the range of law, and is neither made nor unmade by the state."

Cultural Homogeneity. Similarly, the State should not provide for cultural

17. Barker, E., *Principles of Social and Political Theory,* p. 105.
18. MacIver, R.M., *The Modern State,* p. 161.

homogeneity and perform functions connected therewith as Plato proposed. The cultural heterogeneity of the modern State, the diversity of creeds, opinions and schools of thought professed and practised by its citizens, every State must endeavour to maintain. It should really be the function of the State to guarantee and to safeguard the cultural liberty of its diverse groups. This is essential on intrinsic and political grounds. There should be unity in diversity and any effort made to destroy it may even imperil the national unity which homogeneity may aim to establish. The State reflects the culture, "but does not create it. Culture is the work of community, sustained by inner forces far more potent than political law."[19]

Fashions. Nor should the State prescribe fashions. A King may set a fashion for others to follow, but not by prescribing it. "A people will eagerly follow the dictates of fashion proclaimed by some unknown coterie in Paris or London or New York, but were the State to decree changes in themselves so insignificant, it would be regarded as monstrous tyranny—it might even lead to tyranny."[20] Fashion is a matter of personal choice and preference. It is not a matter of imposition. But when fashion, such as scantiness of dress, offends the accepted norms of social decency and injures the susceptibilities of the people, the State may intervene in the interest of public morality and purity of social life.

SUGGESTED READINGS

Allen, C.K.: *Democracy and the Individual.*

Childs, H.L.: *Public Opinion, Nature, Formation and Role.*

Coker, F.W.: *Recent Political Thought,* Chapter XIV.

Ehrmann, H.W.: *Democracy in a Changing Society.*

Garner, J.W.: *Political Science and Government,* Ch. XVII.

Getell, R.G.: *Political Science,* Chap. XXI.

Lane, R.E., and Spears, D.O.: *Public Opinion.*

Laski, H.J.: *A Grammar of Politics,* pp. 25-43.

Laski, H.J.: *Liberty in the Modern State.*

MacIver, R.M.: *The Modern State,* Chaps. V, IX, XV, XVI.

Paul, W.: *The State in Origin and Function.*

Roche, John P., and Murray, S. Stedman, J.: *The Dynamics of Democratic Government,* Chap. 12.

Sidgwick, H.: *The Elements of Politics,* Chaps. III-IV.

Soltau, R.H.: *An Introduction to Politics,* Chap. XIII.

Titmuss, Richard, M.: *The Economic Functions of the State.*

Warbasse, J.P.: *Cooperative Democracy.*

Willoughby, W.W.: *The Ethical Basis of Political Authority.*

19. *Ibid.*, p. 191.
20. *Ibid.*, p. 162.

28
CHAPTER
Theories of the Sphere of State Activity

Theories — Old and New. We discussed in the last Chapter the limits of political control and demarcated the functions which the State should and should not do. The sphere of State activity all through the ages has been influenced by many factors including the environmental conditions and circumstances, social, economic and political needs of the people and their attitude towards the State. In this and in the following Chapters we discuss some of the important theories, old and new, regarding the sphere of State activity. All these theories tell us about the relation of the State to the individual, and the extent to which it should restrict the freedom of individual action in order to promote general welfare. On the one extreme is the Idealist or the Absolutist theory of the State. There is no sphere of human activity including man's thought and conscience, where the State, according to the advocates of this theory, does not step in. On the other end is the theory of Anarchism which seeks to establish a Stateless society. There are various other theories which aim at reconstructing the existing social order, but all of them are the product of socialistic ideas and emphasise the importance of economic interests in the State. Some of these theories minimise the role of the State and advocate decentralisation, while others magnify the State and make it a highly centralised unity of control.

IDEALISM

The Idealist Theory of the State, variously known as the philosophical, metaphysical or the absolute theory, forms an integral part of the traditional philosophical idealism which, until quite recently, exercised a dominating influence in the German and British political thought. It is 'Metaphysical' because the State is more of an idea than the actual State in the ordinary sense of the word. A better description of it is the absolute theory. The doctrines underlying the theory or what purport to be its doctrines have been said to provide the foundation of many totalitarian or reactionary systems of government. Originally, the theory is the product of the teachings of Plato and Aristotle, but in its modern typical form it was expounded by the German philosopher, Hegel. In Britain, the Idealist theory was made popular by T.H. Green, who drew his inspiration from Kant and Hegel as well as from Plato and Aristotle. Its most complete statement, however, is found in Dr. Bosanquet's book, *The Philosophical Theory of the State*.

Origin of the Absolutist Theory. The Idealist theory of the State is derived from two different sources which find a prominent place in Greek thought. Plato and Aristotle, in the first place, never differentiated between the State and society. They regarded the State as a self-sufficing entity identical with the whole of society existing for itself and by itself. The only relation which subsisted between one State and another was of indifference or hostility. As the State represented and contained within itself all the individual's aspirations and fulfilled all his social needs, it was an ethical institution. The true State was a "partnership in a life of virtue." Secondly, Plato and Aristotle started with the premise that man is by nature a social animal. He cannot live a life of isolation unless, of course, he is a god or a beast. It is only by living in society that a man can develop his personality and realise all that is best in him. Apart from society he is nothing and has no significance. Society alone provides him with all what he needs and consequently makes him happy and virtuous; in the proverbial words of Aristotle, "The State comes into being for the sake of life, and it continues to exist for the sake of good life."[1] The State is, thus, an unavoidable necessity, for it raises man's moral stature and accounts for his happiness.

Statement of the Theory. From this bare truth about human nature and the sound doctrine that the end of the State is social morality, modern Idealists developed a philosophy which magnified the State into a self-sufficing entity. They considered the State an organic unity and held it as the highest expression of social morality. Since the State is a moral organism, every individual is its inseparable part and he depends for his existence upon it. In addition to the obvious benefits of security against violence and redress against injustice that the individual receives from the State, he owes it a debt of gratitude for granting him all those moral conditions which enrich his personality and develop his faculties to their full stature. In sum, the State exists to create and maintain those conditions in which free and moral life is possible. It is "the reality", as Hegel says, "of the ethical spirit." It is the divine idea that exists on earth, the march of God on earth. By this conception the State is able to convert into duties to itself whatever rights may seem to belong to individuals. "This substantive unity (of the State) is its own motive and absolute end. This end has the highest right over the individual, whose highest duty is in turn to be a member of the State." The orders of the State have a moral sanction as they come from a moral leviathan. To put it all this in the words of C.E.M. Joad, "Since the state is regarded as representing and containing with itself all the individual's social aspirations, and at the same time fulfilling all his social needs, whatever claims the state may make upon the individual are held to be based upon an absolute authority."[2] The State is, thus, made omnipotent, infallible, omniscient, just and the guardian of morality. Its claims on citizens are, therefore, prior.

In this way, the modern Idealists idolize the State and glorify it to the point of edification. They regard the State as a vehicle of all individual development and progress. The individual apart from society has no meaning. He has no natural rights. Rights flow to him because he is a creature of society and the State is the creator and guarantor of

1. Aristotle defined the State as "the union of families and villages, having for an end a perfect and self-sufficing life."
2. Joad, C.E.M., *Guide to the Philosophy of Morals and Politics,* p. 585.

those rights. It guarantees rights by creating conditions necessary for the full moral development of individual's personality. The State is, thus, made the source as well as the guardian of the social good. Its authority is unlimited and its competence unrestricted. The Idealists, as such, place the State "upon a pedestal at the foot of which its members are expected to bow down and worship it." They teach that the State can do no wrong and its laws can never be unjust. Its authority must be obeyed without demur and resistance to its commands or revolt against its authority, however oppressive, is wicked and iniquitous. The German political philosophers carried to the extreme the claims of the State and asserted that the State is power, "therefore fall down and worship it." War, they said, is necessary to increase the power of the State and there is nothing which should limit its expansion.

Hegel's Philosophy. In developing his theory, Hegel, the renowned Professor of Philosophy in Germany, whom many have hailed as the outstanding philosopher of the nineteenth century, starts from Rousseau's conception of real freedom. In his view men enjoy as members of society a freedom which is more real than that which they abandoned in the hypothetical lawless state of nature to enter society. Hegel differed from Kant's idea that freedom is subjective and it resides in the individual's conscience and intention, and that it is negative as it manifests itself in duty alone. He held that freedom must be positive and objective or outwardly expressed. "This freedom, which became possible only in society, is an externalization or objectification of all that is highest in the conception of freedom in the individual's heart, a conception which but for society would remain unrealized."[3] In the State man has fully raised his outward self to the level of his inward self of thought. This real freedom which exists in, and is a product of society, is active and developing. It expresses itself in a series of outward manifestations—first in law, secondly, in the rules of inward morality, and, finally, in the whole system of social institutions and influences that make for the development of personality. The State, according to Hegel, makes possible the conditions for freedom and men enjoy real freedom only by living in it; without it they are completely in subjection. Freedom, he adds, is the outstanding characteristic of the modern State. He criticised the Greeks because they did not recognise that the State must rest on respect for personality. Their acceptance of slavery was a proof of their failure here.

What does Hegel mean by freedom? The development of the spirit, according to Hegel, is the development of freedom and the history of mankind is the history of freedom. History culminates in the State in which the spirit finds its final embodiment; "nothing short of the State is the actualization of freedom." Man, thus, finds his freedom within the State and by reason of his identity with it. It is only the State that can command the individual to do the rational thing constituting his true freedom. The State transcends the individual and absorbs his moral being, but this is only in order that the individual's freedom shall be rational. In brief, the State is man in his fulness and perfection of development. Hegel gives to the State, in this way, a real personality and a real will and the will of the State he names the General Will.

Hegel's general will is not the sum total of individual wills. The State is an entity

3. Joad, C.E.M., *Introduction to Modern Political Theory*, p. 12.

above and apart from the people who compose it. It is a new personality and "it is in the General Will and in the personality of the State that the will and personality of each individual are made to transcend themselves." It follows, then, that the actions of the State in so far as they proceed from the general will cannot be wrong and unjust. There is no higher rationality than the State. No one may disobey its commands. The commands of the State give man his only opportunity to find freedom and when he obeys the dictates of the State he really obeys his own real will.

The State, Hegel said, "must be comprehended as an organism." It is a natural growth and, thus, a whole. The whole is greater than the parts, because parts are intrinsically related to the whole and have meaning only in so far as the whole gives them meaning. It is an end in itself. "In this end," he says, "freedom attains its highest right. This end has the highest right over the individual, whose highest duty in turn is to be a member of the State." So the State is "the march of God in the world; its ground or cause is the power of reason realizing itself as will. When thinking of the idea of the State, we must not have in mind any particular State, or particular institution, but must rather contemplate the Idea, this actual God, by itself."

Hegel's State is, therefore, supreme and sovereign. It has the right of absolute decision and no one can question such a decision. Hegel allowed no place for individual freedom against the State. In his system the inalienable rights of man as an individual "were utterly obliterated." Since man finds his freedom within the State and by reason of his identity with it, social freedom, freedom through the State was Hegel's ideal. Men do not, he insisted, value individual freedom as highly as has been supposed. What they actually want is real freedom and this they can have only through the State. "The State restrains and represses, but in so doing it enlarges the freedom of society as a whole and, thus, enlarges the liberty of the individual." The State must, accordingly, be regarded "as the ethical whole and the actualization of freedom."

Hegel's conclusions complete the whole doctrine of the Absolutist theory of the State. The State, to Hegel, in the words of Garner, "is a 'God State', incapable of doing wrong, infallible, omnipotent, and entitled to every sacrifice which its interests may require of the individual. By virtue of its transcendent character and of the sacrifice and devotion which it has a right to demand, it elevates and ennobles the individual, whose tendency is to become selfish and self-centred and carries him back into the life of the universal substance."[4] He exalted the State to a mystical height and at all times, particularly during war, the State may lawfully exercise complete authority over its citizens. In an emergency, it may do what it pleases to choose; and as to what constitutes an emergency it is for the State to decide. It may even ask its citizens to place their lives at its disposal. The Absolutist theory of the State finds its complete expression in the omnipotence of the State in time of war. Hegel himself says that "the state of war shows the omnipotence of the State in its individuality."

But Hegel regards war as an evil, though not an absolute evil. He justifies war, because it illustrates the "movement of God in history" and the way in which supreme power passes from one nation to another. His justification of war is due to his deep

4. Garner, J.W., *Introduction to Political Science,* p. 232.

veneration for the nation-State. He does not believe in the brotherhood of nations because, in his opinion, the essential principle of the nation-State is struggle. Hegel, thus, paved the way for his recent disciples Hitler and Mussolini in Germany and Italy to preach and practise militarism and even brutalism.

Hegel's idea of the nature of the State may be summed up thus:

1. The State is the divine idea as it exists on earth; it is the march of God in the world.
2. The State is an end in itself. It is not only the highest expression to which the spirit has yet attained, it is "the final embodiment of spirit on earth." There can be no spiritual evaluation beyond the State.
3. The State is an organism. It is a whole which is far greater than the parts which compose it, and have significance only in it. Individuals must, therefore, be completely subordinated to the State.
4. The individuals derive their rights from the State. They have no right against the State. In case of conflict between the two, the rights of the State must prevail over the rights of the individuals.
5. The State is unchecked by any moral law. It is itself the creator of morality.
6. Whatever the State does is right. It can never be wrong and unjust. It is only in the State that man can find his freedom. When the individual obeys the commands of the State, he actually obeys himself.
7. The State being omnipotent and absolute, the will of the State cannot be bound by international law. Its own welfare is the highest law.
8. War is an evil, but not an absolute evil. He justified war as a virtuous activity since it preserved the ethical health of the people in their indifference to the stabilisation of infinite institutions.
9. As the State is the march of God on earth, to obey the State is to obey God. And as the authority of God is unlimited, unrestricted and absolute, so is that of the State.

Green's Philosophy. In England, T.H. Green developed his political philosophy after 1870. Although his name is intimately associated with the Absolutist theory of the State, yet he departs from Hegel's view in many respects. Green believed in international morality which Hegel too readily dismissed. He taught that the power of the State was limited within and without the country and that the life of the nation has no real existence except as the life of the individuals composing the nation. He said that war was the attribute of the imperfect State and it could at most be relatively right and never absolutely right. The State, for Green, is the product of reason which tells man of moral freedom as his essential quality. Human consciousness postulates liberty, liberty involves rights and rights demand the State. Thus, the State is meant to create those opportunities which are so necessary to the full moral development of individuals. The sovereign power which maintains rights is not based on mere force. Will, not force, is the basis of the State, for behind the actual sovereign is the common conviction of a common good, the General Will. Green's General Will is very much different from Hegel's General Will. He calls it "the common consciousness of a common good"; "a sense of possessing common interests, a desire for common interests on the part of the people." It will be obvious that Green's General Will, as Wayper says, "is the will for the State, not the will of the State."

It, therefore, leaves no margin for the rulers to preach and practise militarism and brutalism in the name of the will of the State as Hegel's disciples preached and practised.

Rights, according to Green, are the outer conditions necessary for man's inner development. The supreme right of every rational person is the right to become what a man should be. Natural rights have no other significance for Green than that they help a man to become a moral and ideal human being dedicated to himself and the society of which he is a member. Having said so much Green becomes Hegelian in his conclusions. Green believed that without the State man is not man at all. It is only in the State that he can fully express himself, and his nature can develop to its full capacity. Hence he must look to the State not as a necessary evil which is the result of his viciousness, but as a natural and ethical necessity which is the result of his own inherent virtue. The political life of a man, Green concludes, "is a revelation of the Divine Idea."

There was a realisation in Green of the majesty and might of the State. Rights, according to Green, exist because of society, and of a society in which some common good is recognized. Every right is, thus, derived from some social relation. Though the State does not create rights, yet it may still be true to say that the members of the State derive their rights from the State. "The State is the complex of social relations out of which rights arise, so far as those rights have come to be regulated and harmonized according to a general law." Green concedes the right of resistance to the authority of the State and here he essentially differs from Hegel, but he makes the path of resistance so difficult that ultimately it may be considered a denial of the right. He is emphatic that resistance can never be justified merely because legislation runs against personal inclinations. He warns men that in resisting the authority of the State they must not forget that they will probably be wrong and the State almost certainly right, for "the State will be speaking with the wisdom of the ages, and men." He repeatedly reminds the resisters that they must not forget that resistance may lead to disastrous results, "since it may tempt men to unleash the bonds of that mighty demon anarchy." He commands them, whatever constitutional system of government exists, to put up with the undesired laws until they are repealed by constitutional means. Where the constitutional government does not exist, men should feel justified to resist the authority of the State when certain conditions obtain. But it still requires serious thought and consideration before it is resorted to. "We must not sacrifice," says Green, "what is almost the whole for the sake of a part; we must not risk social chaos, and the disturbance of the existing system of rights, for the sake of adding a new element of the system."

Like Hegel, Green is very much concerned with the problem of freedom. Freedom, Green says, does not consist in being left alone to do what one likes. It all depends on what one likes to do. Man is free only when he is following his "true" good and his "true" good is also "social" good, because individual good can only be achieved when the good of others is also realised. Freedom, then, Green says, "is a positive power or capacity of doing or enjoying something worth doing or enjoying and that, too, something we do or enjoy in common with others." Freedom is, therefore, positive and it is of doing something worth doing, and that, too, in common with others. Freedom for Green was not unlimited. The conclusion is obvious. True liberty, according to Green, can only be realised in the State. For both, Hegel and Green, man is most free when he identifies himself with the State. Hegel emphasises the individual's complete identification with "Divine Spirit" and the "Divine Spirit" finds its embodiment in the State. For Green, the State is a natural and ethical necessity which is the result of man's own inherent virtue.

But Green never regards the State as an end itself. It is a means to an end, and the end is the full moral development of the individuals who compose it. He emphasises the importance and worth of every man and stands for the maintenance of his dignity and will, consequently, forbid his exploitation for any purpose whatever. "The life of the nation," he so very often repeats, "has no real existence except as the life of the individuals composing it." He unequivocally adds, "To speak of any progress or improvement or development of a nation or society or mankind except as relative to some great worth of persons is to use words without meaning." Green, thus, does not make the State absolute and omnipotent. It is limited, both from within and without. The State and its laws deal only with the external actions of man. They have nothing to do with his intentions and motives. The State cannot make men moral; it is to remove the obstacles which prevent men from becoming moral. Morality consists, according to Green, in "the disinterested performance of self-imposed duties." The functions of the State are, accordingly, negative and not positive. Here Green talks as an Individualist would do.

At the same time, Green is not completely an Individualist, for in order to remove obstacles the functions of the State become positive in content. For example, Green holds the State responsible to see that mental and physical malnutrition are removed. Hence, it should make education compulsory, do away with chances of intemperance by checking the growth of liquor shops, and forbid reckless beggary by providing certain pursuits which people may take up. "To uphold the sanctity of contract," he says, "is doubtless a prime business of government, but it is no less its business to provide against contracts being made which from the helplessness of one of the parties to them, instead of being security for freedom, become an instrument of disguised oppression." Paradoxical as it is, Green justifies the existence of capital, but he is against the continuance of the institution of landed property. Green stands for the happiness of man so that everyone should contribute something to the common good and to attain the both, he justifies the intervention of the State. Here the functions of the State become positive. He considers that the punishment for those who violated laws should be proportionate and reformatory in order to create conditions which make moral life possible.

Green's State is a community of communities and its supremacy over all is unquestioned. He resembles Hegel, but there is a significant difference between them. For Green associations are important, because they are prior to the State and they have their own system of rights which arises from their very nature. The State must be supreme over them, because it must coordinate and adjust them. But it must also preserve them. "A State," he says, "presupposes other forms of community, with the rights that arise out of them, and only exists as sustaining, securing and competing them." The difference between Hegel and Green with regard to the supremacy of the State over associations has been accurately explained by Wayper. He says, "Thus, while for Hegel if associations do not result in the State, they are no true associations; for Green if the State does not preserve associations, it is no true State. In both Hegel and Green the fact of the State's supremacy is unquestioned. But in the one the exercise of the supremacy of the State is unlimited because of its own nature and the nature of associations. In the other the exercise of the State's supremacy is limited by its own nature and the nature of associations."

If Green's State must preserve the rights of the various associations within it, it must respect the rights of the community of humanity outside it. Unlike Hegel, but like Kant, Green believes in a universal brotherhood of men. An international code, he believes, is the obvious extension of ethical system accepted within the State. "Both spring from a common source—man's desire as a moral being to fulfil himself." He condemns war as it violates the right of man to a free life. It may be justified only as a "cruel necessity"—one wrong to correct another previous wrong.

Green, it will appear, is more near Kant than Hegel. In his views on individual freedom, war and international morality, he is more Kantian than Hegelian. According to Green, the State is neither absolute nor omnipotent. He is Hegelian in as much as he emphasises the moral value of the majesty of the State.

Bernard Bosanquet (1848-1823). Bernard Bosanquet held the chair of Moral Philosophy at the St. Andrews University of Scotland. While at Oxford, Bosanquet came under the influence of Green and Jowett. Hobhouse described him as the most modern and the most faithful exponent of Hegel. This is no exaggeration. But it would be more apt to say that Bosanquet began in the ways of Rousseau and Green and ended almost in those of Hegel. His *Philosophical Theory of the State* is, in a sense, regarded as a definitive statement of Hegelianism for English-speaking people.

Bosanquet is a strong defender of the general-will theory. He starts with the conception of a free moral will as expounded by Rousseau and comes to the Hegelian thesis that the part finds significance through the whole; and that the finite is necessarily only a part of the absolute. He adopts the Hegelian view of the State as the sublimation of all virtue and authority, arguing that the "State may legitimately do whatever is required for the preservation and improvement of the organised life of the community, and is the sole judge of what is so required." The individual, Bosanquet holds, is related to the State as the idea in a man's mind is related to that mind.

There are three stages in the exposition of Bosanquet's doctrine of will: distinction between the actual will of the individual and his real will; distinction between the real will of the individual and the general will of society; and the State as the supreme expression of the general will. Actual will, he says, is the constant will of man, that is, his will when he acts from moment to moment as a conscious individual. But this will is created and amended by the considerations of what he wants at all other moments and adjusts to the will of others, it becomes the real will. The real will of the individual is bound up with the wills of other individuals with whom he lives in society and it becomes the general will. Man alone is nothing and his fulfilment cannot be achieved apart from the general will. The State is the perfect embodiment of the general will, because for the common life society depends upon the relationships which the State maintains. "By the State, then, we mean," writes Bosanquet, "society as a unit recognised as rightly exercising control over its membcrs through absolute physical power ...."

But the State as a political organisation using force, is the narrow sense in which

Bosanquet defines the State. His State is the supreme community, the guardian of morality and, consequently, the supreme ethical institution. It is synonymous with society and represents the synthesis of life. "The National State ...," says Bosanquet, "is the widest organisation which has the common experience necessary to found a common life." The State promotes common life which is a moral life and what it directs is always moral. But Bosanquet is near to Green regarding the nature and the sphere of State action. Both believe that the State is an ethical institution and both agree that the State cannot be used directly to promote morality. "Art, philosophy and religion," says Bosanquet, "though in a sense the very life blood of society, are not and could not be directly fashioned to meet the needs and uses of the multitude, and their aim is not in that sense social." Having said so, Bosanquet further says, "It (the State) has no determinate function in a larger community, but is itself the supreme community. the guardian of a whole moral world, but not a factor within an organised moral world. Moral relations presuppose an organized life; but such a life is only within the State, not in relation between the State and other communities." The immoral acts of an agent of the State, therefore, cannot be ascribed to the State. But the distinction between the acts of the State and the acts of its agents is unreal. Government is, no doubt, the agency of the State, but the State is abstract whereas government is concrete; a reality. The acts of government are really the acts of the State. Ernest Barker logically sums up the whole issue when he says, "If a citizen can treat his own State as legally responsible for damages, it is difficult to see why a State, which can undergo legal responsibility, should not also undergo moral responsibility, if there is anybody of moral opinion to affix responsibility." Bosanquet's State not responsible for the acts of its agents could be irresponsible and tyrannical particularly when he does not differentiate between the State and society. And more so, Bosanquet does not permit the individual the right of rebellion against the authority of the State.

Evaluation of the Idealist Theory. Idealism, as opposed to realism, stands for the political theory which deals with the relation of the individual and the State as it ought to be and not as it is. But the Idealists idealised the real. The present to them came to be equal to the future and the existing nature of the State and society they accepted as what it ought to be. The result was that instead of becoming a source of reform or radicalism, idealism became a conservative creed standing for the *status quo* in civilisation. For example, Aristotle idealises slavery; Hegel glorifies war; and Green reconciles private ownership of capital with his plea for nationalisation of land. Hobson describes Idealism as "the tactics of conservatism", because "it preached the divine right of things as they are."

The assumption of the identity of the State and society on which the Idealist theory is based is obviously false. We neatly distinguish the State from society. Once this distinction is realised the Hegelian concept of the State is rejected. Similarly, the contention that the State is above the principles of morality and that it is the State which prescribes morality is untrue. Morality is a subject of conscience and MacIver states a bare truth when he says that State-dictated morality is no morality. No moral prescriptions of the State have any effect upon conscience unless they appeal to man himself. Even if it be conceded that the State contains within itself and represents the social morality of all its citizens, it is difficult to understand why it should be disowned as a guiding principle in inter-State relations.

The Idealist theory attributes to the State a personality of its own which transcends the personalities of those who compose it. This doctrine has been rejected as absurd. Duguit and MacIver consider it fanciful as it preaches the omnipotence, absolutism, and divinity of the State. It sacrifices freedom of the individual by subordinating him to the all-embracing power of the State. Unlimited power of the State dwarfs the personality of the individual and makes him and society the poorer for it. It is true that man can develop his personality only while living in the State, but admission of this fact does not necessarily mean the omnipotence of the State. The State being an agent of society is a means to an end and not an end in itself. It exists for the welfare of man; man does not exist for it and its glorification. Nor is there any truth in the distinction of the real will and the unreal will. "It is only a device for giving an appearance of justice and democracy to what must otherwise appear purely arbitrary and tyrannical acts of sovereign State." Referring to the Hegelian glorification of the State, Hobhouse says, "The State is a great organisation. Its well-being is something of larger and more permanent import than that of any single citizen. Its scope is vast. Its service calls for the extreme of loyalty and self-sacrifice. All this is true. Yet when the State is set up as an entity superior and indifferent to component individuals, it becomes a false god, and its worship the abomination or desolation, as seen at Ypres or on the Somme."

The Idealist theory, as such, has been "denounced as unsound in theory, untrue to fact, and liable to extend a dangerous sanction to the more unscrupulous actions of existing States in the sphere of foreign policy." Hitler and Mussolini blindly followed Hegel with disastrous consequence to humanity. And the Absolutist theory produced such a bias against the State that in many quarters even its necessity was questioned, or indeed of any equivalent repository for sovereignty in the community.

UTILITARIANISM

Origin of Utilitarianism. In England the early part of the nineteenth century is marked by the growing ascendancy of that type of thought to which Hegel had been violently opposed. Its theoretical basis is the psychological individualism of the previous age and it is essentially associated with Jeremy Bentham. But it would be hardly consistent with facts to say that it began with Bentham. The founder of Utilitarianism was David Hume and it was professed by Priestley, Hutcheson and Poley, though its origin was from Helvetius and Baccaira. Hume opposed the rationalistic school and their philosophy based on the conception of the law of nature. Morality, he asserted, was based on expediency and utility was the touchstone of all institutions. Reason, he thought, was an inert principle and passions, arising from a sense of pleasure, motivate the actions of men. With this spring of knowledge, Hutcheson, for the first time, used the formula of the greatest happiness of the greatest number, upon which Bentham's utilitarianism hinges. Bentham also borrowed some of his ideas from Joseph Priestley. But to Bentham goes the credit for giving a systematic exposition of Utilitarianism and made widely known and admired the conceptions which are its characteristics.

Utilitarianism Explained. Utilitarianism is not a cult based on the abstract principles of Idealism of the eighteenth century. For an absolute idealism it sought to substitute an absolute empiricism. It is based on the realities of human life and is essentially practical judging everything from its practical utility. It aims to use the ascertained facts of life in such a way as to promote the progress and advancement of society and make life really worth living. It joins and blends the happiness of the individual with the happiness of others with whom he leads a life of togetherness. It does not separate the individual from society and the individual good from the social good. Utilitarianism, accordingly, discards the *laissez faire* theory of State action. It stands for promoting the happiness of the people, both individual and social, in order to obtain the greatest good of the greatest number. It enjoins on the legislators to devise and pass such laws that increase the pleasure of the people and lessen their sorrows and pains. The State, for the Utilitarians, is a human necessity for the promotion of general welfare.

Utilitarianism is hedonistic. Hedonism is the doctrine which establishes that every man seeks pleasure and avoids pain. This doctrine of pleasure versus pain goes back to the Greek times and finds its expression in the teachings of Epicurus. But there is a difference between the Greek Hedonism and the Utilitarian Hedonism. The former is egoistic, self-conceited, whereas the latter is altruistic, regardful of others. The Epicureans made happiness the sole aim of life and told the people to judge everything from the standpoint of their happiness alone. Utilitarianism seeks the happiness of the individual by securing the greatest happiness of he greatest number. Both accept pleasure as the ultimate end of the individual, but to the Utilitarians pleasure must add to his moral stature and the actions of the State should be so directed as to keep that end in view. Utilitarianisin has, thus, an ethical appeal.

The individual's happiness cannot be isolated from the happiness of others with whom he lives in society. While living along with others two impulses influence his conduct: *self-regarding* and *other-regarding* impulses. "If the emotional satisfaction of impulses is a powerful factor in human conduct, so is reason which compels a man to be other-regarding." Reason, therefore, is the basic factor in the life of togetherness and it is reason which helps man to reconcile his self-regarding with his other-regarding impulses. This reconciliation creates bonds of affinity which are the bonds of altruism and welds them with the sense of human affection. This philosophy of Utilitarianism is also described as the philosophy of "enlightened benevolence." The light of reason creates the spirit of benevolence joining the self with others producing the conditions of the greatest happiness of the greatest number.

The Utilitarians were the opponents of tyranny and injustice and the champions of individual freedom and happiness. They attached no sanctity to the existing political institutions if they failed to realize them. Their criterion of every action of the State was utility and, to a Utilitarian, it meant the greatest happiness of the greatest number. Utility was welfare and it embraced all that determined and constituted man's happiness. It was the only standard of right or wrong, good or bad. "Political institutions and public policies," as Maxey observes, "were not to be rated as good or bad relative to some visionary, and always arbitrary, conjecture of human rights and obligations, but more or less beneficial according to some fixed standard of utility in human affairs. By their fruits, not by their ideality, should they be judged." The standard of utility was the happiness and satisfaction which the individual enjoyed from the exercise of public authority. Such a happiness and satisfaction of the individual produced results of general welfare and it meant the greatest happiness of the greatest number. The Utilitarians rejected the dogma of natural rights. Bentham regarded natural rights as "simple nonsense, natural and imprescriptible rights, rhetorical nonsense upon stilts."

Jeremy Bentham (1748-1832). Jeremy Bentham was the founder of the Utilitarian school of thought. Though he had been characterised as "one of the oddest figures in the history of political thought", yet he was held in high esteem and regarded as the "foremost apostle of the practical," and his ideas tremendously influenced the policies of the governments. He was essentially a reformer who was out to reform English law along more rational lines. But experience had made it clear to him that before this had much chance of being accomplished, he should first undertake the task of reforming the existing political institutions and get rid of the "sinister interests", which stood out against reform and were hostile to general welfare. He had no respect for antiquities, and he had no reliance on the age-long institutions. The law and the institutions, he maintained, must represent the needs of the day and be judged from the point of view of their present utility.

According to Bentham, pleasure or the avoidance of pain is the sole end of man and the sole content of human good. This is how he explains: "Nature has placed man under the government of two sovereign masters, pain and pleasure. It is for them alone to point out what we ought to do, as well as to determine what we shall do .... They govern us in all we do, in all we say, in all we think .... We owe to them all our ideas, we refer to them all our judgments, and all the determinations of our life." Bentham gives a list of fourteen pleasures and twelve simple pains. From his concept of pleasure and pain, he propounds the principle of *utility* like this: "By this principle of utility is meant that principle which approves and disapproves of every action whatsoever, according to the tendency it appears to have to augment or diminish the happiness of the party whose interest is in question or, what is the same thing in other words, to promote or to oppose that happiness. I say of every action whatsoever, and, therefore, not only of every action of a private individual, but of every measure of government."

With this principle he comes to the conclusion that an action is right or wrong, sound or unsound as it brings pleasure or pain and it is from this standard that values and laws are to be determined. The greatest happiness of the greatest number is, thus, the social test of what is morally defensible in conduct, and the true method of evaluating is a "felicific calculus." According to Bentham, pleasure or pain could be arithmetically calculated by taking into account the seven factors of: intensity; duration; certainty or uncertainty; propinquity or remoteness; fecundity (the chance of its being followed by sensation of the same kind); purity and extent. The value of a pleasure could be found either by multiplying or adding to various factors. The task of the legislator was simply to "sum up all the values of all the pleasures on the one side, and those of all the pains on the other. The balance, if it be on the side of pleasure, will give the *good* tendency of the act upon the whole, with respect to the interest of that individual person; if on the side of pain, the *bad* tendency of it upon the whole ...." One of the seven factors for the measurement of pleasure or pain was "extent", that is, the number of persons affected. The value of a thing was more or less according to the number of persons taking part in a pleasure or pain.

Bentham had no faith in the Social Contract theory of the State. Political society and rights and duties of the State, he believed, did not flow from the consent of the people, as the Contractualists had professed. The ultimate reason for men submitting to political authority, he asserted, was the present utility. "The business of government," he affirmed, "is to promote the happiness of the society, by punishing and rewarding." It had no other justification for existence. The test of a good government is how it rewards and punishes. If the government does not employ effective means to promote happiness of society, "it nullifies its very title to authority." People obey law because it aims at four ends: security; substance; abundance; and equality. It is the general habit to obedience, born of utility, that gives a law its permanence and makes it effective, thereby promoting the greatest happiness of the greatest number. Bentham believed neither in natural law nor natural rights. Rights, he asserted, are created by law.

The very basis of utility implies limits upon the power of government. Government has the authority to act to produce the greatest happiness of the greatest number; it may legitimately do nothing else. Moreover, in many instances the action of individuals may voluntarily be directed to this end, and here government ought not to interfere. Bentham also said in the *Fragment on Government* that men should be informed by government with respect to what is being done and why. They have a right to know and a right to protest and oppose. In addition, government ought to be responsible, and the only way to see that it exercises responsibility is to have a system that facilitates the "frequent and easy" interchange of position of governors and governed. Bentham was, thus, out to remove the distinction between the governors and the governed and this he would do by investing sovereignty in the people themselves. A pure democracy in modern times, he considered, is impossible. But by letting people choose their representatives, and then by binding their representatives so closely as to give them no opportunity to betray their masters, an approximate identity of interest can be secured. The political idea of the Utilitarians, therefore, lay, first in the direction of extending suffrage, and then in originating devices that should subject representatives as strictly as possible to popular control.

John Stuart Mill (1806-1873). Bentham had a long list of prominent disciples and the foremost of them was John Stuart Mill. John Mill, in fact, is the most influential philosopher belonging to the middle period of the nineteenth century. He is very often described as the last of the Utilitarians and the foremost of the Individualists. This is true to a great extent, because he considerably modified Bentham's thesis of pleasure *versus* pain by admitting and emphasising a qualitative aspect of pleasure, and became an ardent defender of liberty. He agrees with Bentham that the happiness, or the greatest good of the greatest number, is the highest good and the criterion of morality, but Mill's calculus of pain and pleasure is different. Mill teaches that pleasures also differ in quality, that those which go with the exercise of intellectual capacities are higher, better than sensuous pleasures, and that persons who have experienced both prefer the higher pleasures. "No intelligent person would consent to be a fool; no instructed person would be an ignoramus." No person of feeling or conscience, he asserted, would exchange his lot for that of a fool, dunce or rascal, even if he was convinced that a fool, dunce or rascal is better satisfied with his lot than a man of conscience with his. "It is better to be a human being, dissatisfied," says Mill, "than a pig satisfied; better to be Socrates dissatisfied than a fool satisfied."

Bentham and Mill also agree that we ought to strive for the greatest happiness of the greatest number. But Bentham justifies it on the ground of self-interest, while Mill bases it on the social feelings on mankind; the desire for unity with our fellow creatures. He tells us that Utilitarianism requires a man to be as strictly impartial between his own happiness and that of others as if he were a disinterested and benevolent spectator. "In the golden rule of Jesus of Nazareth, we read the complete spirit of the ethics of utility. To do as one would be done by and to love one's neighbour as oneself, constitute the ideal perfection of Utilitarian morality." Indeed, the greatest happiness principle is meaningless and without rational significance, unless one person's happiness is of exactly as much importance as another's. "Bentham's principle of utility," observes Maxey, "in a society of wolves would exalt wolfishness; in a society of saints it would exalt saintliness. Mill was determined that saintliness should be the criterion of utility in any society whatsoever."

Mill regarded social well-being as inevitably bound up with individual well-being. He pointed out "the importance, to man and society, of a large variety in types of character, and of giving full freedom to human nature to expand itself in innumerable and conflicting directions." He rejected the doctrine of expediency as the paramount factor in determining the proper course of the action for the State. He insisted that there were various kinds and gradations of utility and among them "certain social utilities" were more important and absolutely imperative. And liberty, he considered, was one of this kind. The older Utilitarians had not ranked liberty so high in their scale of values.

Mill regarded individual liberty as the supreme possession of man and would permit governmental interference to the mininium. He would allow the individual to develop himself on his own lines and liberty, for him, included the freedom of thought and expression, freedom of conscience and association. But he would impose two limitations on individual liberty: (1) the individual was not free to do harm to others, and (2) he must share labours and sacrifices to secure the society and individuals against harm. Accordingly, he laid down a concise test of the functions of the State. His general proposition was that the State should not interfere with those acts which affected the individual alone, but the State may act in the interest of the general welfare when the acts of the individual affect others as well as himself.

He had an unflinching faith in the representative form of government, for it is the best schooling in citizenship. The first element of a good government, according to John Mill, is "the promotion of the virtue and intelligence of the people." And the government which promotes and fosters moral and intellectual qualities is, to him, the best. To make the government really representative, he vigorously advocated for proportional representation and women suffrage.

Utilitarianism Examined. Utilitarianism has been variously and scathingly criticised. It has been characterised as entirely materialistic which degrades human beings. Pleasure in itself is not the highest end of life. According to Sabine, there is no logical connection between the happiness of the greatest number and the greatest happiness. Moreover, the Utilitarians have proved that human beings are merely selfish. This is not the true estimation of the human nature. Nor is Hedonism universalistic. Pleasure is always individual. What is my pleasure may not be yours. Pleasure being personal, it is difficult to conceive of a thing like general pleasure.

All the same, it cannot be denied that Utilitarianism demolished the theories of natural rights and Social Contract and the mystic Idealism of the German philosophers. It brought political theory to the practical realm of life and, according to Green, "whatever the errors arising from its Hedonistic psychology, no other theory has been available for the social political reforms containing so much truth with such ready applicability." It rescued the individual from his absorption by the State and had been the harbinger of important reforms in Britain for the greater part of the nineteenth century. Bentham placed the individual before the State. He was convinced that individual initiative and freedom were the essentials of happiness, and that State interference must be jealously watched. In the same way, he asserted the necessity of men as equals. While rejecting the claim to equality on the grounds of a "Natural Right", he showed that equality was a political "good", because it was the only practical way of dealing with large number of people.

The Bentham criterion of utility also served to simplify the problem of sovereignty. The legislature and the executive existed, he said, not by right of any contract or divine right, but simply to create or to maintain general happiness. The law was certainly to be a command, but it was at the same time to be useful, otherwise the individual has a moral right of rebellion. The State, to Bentham, was, for all practical purposes, a service State.

Utilitarianism, thus, only means the gospel of utility, and, as Ivor Brown says, "if we give to utility a broad and generous content, if we recognise that a wild uncultivated moorland is just as 'useful' to humanity as a forty acre field with wire fences and motor-plough complete, then Utilitarianism becomes a doctrine and policy which needs comparison." For the Utilitarians the basic idea is simply that all actions must be judged by their results, that is, by their fruitfulness in pleasure. The Utilitarians carried forward their principles step by step, each great thinker adding something of permanent value. Progress was their watchword, and their enthusiasm for liberty and public good supplies the driving power. That is what the present time inherits from them.

INDIVIDUALISM: TRADITIONAL

Nineteenth-century Individualism. *Laissez faire,* the alternative name by which the traditional theory of Individualism is known, recognises the individual as the centre of all social life and aims to establish that the State should leave him alone to determine his own destiny and the fullest and free development of his capacities and interests. The advocates of Individualism maintain that it is for him and by him that the whole social structure exists and derives its being. Individualism, in brief, exalts the individual to the position of reality in life.

As society itself is nothing but the totality of individuals themselves, the State exists to protect and restrain, not to foster and promote. The State is a necessary evil and it continues to exist so long as man does not attain perfection. Its functions are, accordingly, negatively regulative or protective, which include: protection from foreign aggression, protection of individuals against each other, that is, from physical injury, slander, personal restraint, protection of property from robbery and damage, and protection of individuals against false contracts or breaches of contracts. Some theories extend the functions of the State to include the protection of the weak and imbecile as also the prevention of epidemics, but others, as Herbert Spencer, who subscribed to the doctrine of the 'survival of the fittest' opposed it vigorously.

Development of the Theory. Towards the end of the eighteenth century the prevailing doctrine of Mercantilism, which advocated a policy of active governmental regulation and protection of industry and commerce, received a final blow from the Physiocrats. The Physiocrats, the French School of Economists headed by Quesnay, maintained that the production of national wealth, like individual enterprise, should go its own way, unhampered and unhindered by legislative interference. They regarded private property and freedom of contract as the most obvious and essential phenomena of an ordered society. Their policy was that of "let alone", and of natural liberty, summed up in the famous phrase *laissez faire*, *laissez passer*. Accordingly, the Physiocratic doctrine considered a governmental policy good to the extent that it respected private property, permitted free competition everywhere, and recognised an absolute equality of all individuals before the law.

The new doctrine obtained a firm hold in France and from that country it spread all over Europe. But the creed of *laissez faire* became a more authoritative and accepted doctrine as a result of the teachings of Adam Smith and other English classical economists. Adam Smith has to his credit the achievement of taking the raw material supplied by others, of adding to it from his own genius, and of moulding it into such a form that without losing any of its scientific value, his book, *Inquiry into the Nature and Causes of the Wealth of Nations*, published in 1776, achieved immense popularity and was widely read. Adam Smith and his followers advocated that natural economic principles, fixed private property, and free competition were the essential features of a rational economic system. This doctrine was in accord with the then prevailing Utilitarian ethics and its authors tried to show how the natural economic and ethical principle should work normally in a capitalist system.

But Individualism as a social and political theory is a product of the nineteenth century and is essentially associated with the teachings of John Stuart Mill and Herbert Spencer, though its germs are found in the Social Contract Theory. The Contractualists, Hobbes, Locke and Rousseau, accepted the individual as a separate entity who strived for the maintenance of his natural rights and the State came into being to protect the same. But Hobbes ends in an absolutism of the worst type by upholding the claims of the State as against the individual. Locke remains throughout an Individualist. He starts from the Individualism of the state of nature and ends also in Individualism. Rousseau began in the methods of Locke and ended in those of Hobbes. Even if it be conceded that the exponents of the Social Contract Theory made the individual the only political reality, their Individualism, as Lords says, was "Abstract Individualism." It was in no way a systematic theory of the rights of the individual or a movement. Mill and Spencer regarded "individuality" as the only basis of social well-being and stated in clear and precise manner a full doctrine of the individual's rights against the possible claims of the State, and determined the province of its activity.

Adam Smith. It goes to the credit of Adam Smith to influence the economic ideas of Mill and even Spencer. To Adam Smith enlightened self-interest was the rule with every individual as it ultimately led to the good of the community itself. Every man, he asserted, would do that work for which he had an aptitude and was personally interested if he was left to himself. If every individual, he argued, was allowed to follow his pursuit as and what he deemed best, he would be a greater gainer and that would ultimately result in the good and prosperity of the community as a whole. Adam Smith based his arguments on the concepts of 'division of labour' and 'free competitive forces' and concluded that even if a few amassed wealth because of their superior ability, greater energy and enterprising spirit, still it would not be baneful as on the whole the wealth of the community had increased and civilisation advanced.

J.S. Mill. John Stuart Mill was certainly a great individualist and, in fact, the high priest of Individualism. His essay on "Liberty" is an eloquent enunciation of the principles he preached and a matter-of-fact analysis of his reasoned conviction. The object of his essay on Liberty, writes Mill, "is to assert one very simple principle, as entitled to govern absolutely the dealings of society with the individual in the way of compulsion and control, whether the means used by physical force is in the form of legal penalties, or the moral coercion of public opinion. That principle is, that the sole end of which mankind are warranted, individually or collectively, interfering with the liberty of action of any of their members, is self-protection. That the only purpose for which power can be rightfully exercised over any member of a civilised community, against his will, is to prevent harm to others. His own good, either physical or moral, is not a sufficient warrant. He cannot rightfully be compelled to do or forbear because it will be better for him to do so, because it will make him happier, because in the opinion of others, to do so would be wise, or even right. These are good reasons for remonstrating with him or reasoning with him, or persuading him or entreating him but not for compelling him, or visiting him with any evil in case he do otherwise. To justify that, the conduct from which it is desired to deter him must be calculated to produce evil to someone else. The only part of the conduct of anyone, for which he is amenable to society, is that which concerns others. In the part which merely concerns himself, his independence is, of right, absolute. Over himself, over his own body and mind, the individual is sovereign."

It is a lengthy quotation, but it epitomises the whole truth about the political philosophy of Mill's Individualism. Mill definitely and very clearly sets limits to the interference of the State with the liberty of the individual. The only justification to him for the interference of the State arises when self-protection demands it or when the individual's action jeopardises the liberty of other individuals or adversely affects them. Beyond this the State must not govern, even though it may be in the interest of the individual himself. "The only freedom which deserves the name," Mill maintains, "is that of pursuing our own good in our own way, so long as we do not attempt to deprive others of theirs, or impede their efforts to obtain it. Each is the proper guardian of his own health whether bodily or mental and spiritual. Mankind are greater gainers by suffering each other to live as seems good to themselves, than by compelling each to live as seems good to the rest."

Mill objects to the interference of the State on three grounds. Firstly, things are better done by individuals than by the government. A person specially interested in a particular business or industry and having an aptitude for that kind of work can do it better than "the hired servants of the government." Secondly, even if the individuals may not do the particular thing so well, on the average, as the officers of government, it is nevertheless desirable that it should be done by them rather than by the government as a "means to their own mental education ... a mode of strengthening their active faculties, exercising their judgment and giving them a fair knowledge of the subjects with which they are thus left to deal." Thirdly, leaving things to government means the great evil of unnecessarily adding to its power. "Every function superadded to those already exercised by the government causes its influence over hopes and fears to be more widely diffused, and converts, more and more, the active and ambitious part of the public into hangers-on of the government. If the roads, the railways, the banks, the insurance offices, the great joint stock companies, the universities, and the public charities, were all of them branches of the government, if in addition, the municipal corporations and local boards, with all that now devolves on them, became departments of the central administration; if the employees of all these different enterprises were appointed and paid by the government, and looked to government for every rise in life, not all the freedom of the press, and popular constitution of the legislature would make this or any other country free oherwise than in name."

Mill regarded the State as a necessary evil. He does not desire its abolition, but he wants to have as little of it as possible. He emphasises that the individual must be allowed the maximum of liberty to determine his own affairs, as every restraint is an evil and every extension in the power of the State is antagonistic to the individual's liberty. He says, "The mischief begins when, instead of informing, advising and upon occasions denouncing, it makes them work in fetters, or bids them stand aside and does their work instead of them." To Mill worth of the State in the long run is the worth of the individuals composing it. If it does not provide them an opportunity to develop and expand their mental faculties, it is neither good for the individuals nor for the government. But Mill, during his own lifetime, recognized the need of some sort of State regulation. This change in his ideas was necessitated by the socio-political conditions then prevalent in Britain.

Herbert Spencer. Spencer's contribution to individualism is also outstanding. His philosophy is characterised as "an incongruous mixture of natural rights and physiological metaphors" but out of the complexities he creates by using analogies from Biology and Physics, Spencer emerges, paradoxical as it is, an Individualist. He divided the stages of the development of society into those of status and contract, the former being the military stage with its characteristic of compulsory cooperation and the latter industrial with its characteristic of voluntary cooperation. He shows that in the movement of society towards progress there was "less of integration and more of individuation", and, as such, the functions of the State and its interference would lessen as society progresses till there would come a period when there prevails "the blessedness of final anarchy." Spencer would, therefore, assign to the State only negative functions embracing police, army and justice, and the maintenance of contracts. He asserted that the essential functions of the State were the enactment and enforcement of law, the administration of justice, the maintenance of order, the protection of life and property, and the prevention of invasion by foreign powers. The assumption of any other functions by the State, said Spencer, was an invasion on private rights.

According to Herbert Spencer, the individual has but one right, the right of equal freedom with everybody else, and the State but one duty, the duty of protecting that right against violence and fraud. He, accordingly, protested against all legislation for the regulation of commerce and trade; against sanitary legislation, such as, quarantine, vaccination and registration laws; against public education; against poor relief by the State; and even against State-managed post offices and currency issued by the State. Spencer, in fact, condemned what he called the worship of the legislature and asserted that as the "great political superstition of the past was the divine right of the kings, that of the present is the divine right of Parliaments." The State has, in brief, "no business to interfere with the wise severity of nature's discipline, which makes us better when we do things for ourselves and—what is more—makes the things which we do for ourselves, better done than those which the State does for us." Herbert Spencer admires and advocates the law of the survival of the fittest, according to which the State should allow the poor, the weak and imbecile, the insane, the ignorant and the inefficient to go to the wall.

Case For and Against Individualism. Following is the summary of arguments in support of and against individualism of the nineteenth century.

The ethical argument in defence of Individualism has been put forward by Kant, Fichte, Humboldt, and John Stuart Mill. Humboldt says, "The aim of the State should be the development of the powers of all its single citizens in their perfect individuality that it must, therefore, pursue no other object than that which they cannot pursue of themselves, viz., security." State interference with the individual's liberty of action destroys his initiative and self-reliance. It weakens his sense of responsibility, saps his energies and cripples his character. The individual can develop his personality only in an atmosphere of perfect freedom of action. The policy of *laissez faire* means the free play of the forces of competition, which is the law of nature. "Nature submits to him who most energetically and resolutely assails her. She grants her reward to the fittest, therefore, without regard to other considerations of any kind." Free competition develops in the individual the highest possibilities, sharpens and strengthens his powers of initiative, and increases his sense of self-reliance. Civilization and national progress depend on individual's faculties of self-help and self-reliance. The highest civilization "has been developed under individualism, a system which has produced more material and educational progress than could ever have been produced under paternalism."[5] Self-interest is a universal principle in human nature and each individual knows his own interests best. The considerations of justice, therefore, demand that man should have a natural right to be left alone. Morality consists in the performance of the self-imposed imperatives of duty. Spontaneity and

5. Garner, J. W., *Political Science and Government,* p. 461.

freedom are the essence of the moral development of man. An excess of government, says Mill, "starves the development of some portion of the bodily or mental faculties, when it deprives one from doing what one is inclined to do or from acting to one's judgment of what is desirable."[6] The ethical argument, in brief, rivets on the ideal to develop personality to such an extent that government becomes superfluous and each man becomes a law unto himself. Summing up the results of Government's interference and fostering policies, Lecky said that they lend to "the weakening of private enterprise and philanthropy; a lowered sense of individual responsibility; a diminished love of freedom; the creation of an increasing army of officials ..., the formation of a state of society in which vast multitudes depend for their subsistence on the bounty of the State. All this cannot take place without impairing the springs of self-reliance, independence, resolution, without gradually enfeebling both the judgement and character." The individual should, therefore, be left alone.

It has been contended that the principle of Individualism is in accord with the law of organic evolution. Herbert Spencer, with his biological analogy, proved that as in animal life so in the social order, the individual should struggle for himself and survive or perish, because the fittest will, and ought alone to survive, the weak and incompetent must go to the wall. Survival of the fittest is the law of nature and progress of society depends upon the elimination of the weak by the strong. Any attempt by government to interfere in the eternal struggle for existence is an attempt to modify nature. "The essential end of government is to support nature, to maintain as far as possible a condition under which each adult receives the good results and suffers the evil results of his own nature and conduct." Spencer says compulsory and public education, poor relief and social legislation are futile attempts to change natural conditions. The attempt to perpetuate the weak and put them on the same plane as the strong, is to preserve the unfit at the expense of the fit. "Government should let poverty and unsanitary houses alone, so that weaker types may sooner die out; it should let industrial competition alone, however intense, for by such competition the best individuals come to the top," and, thus, the good of society is promoted.

Besides the ethical and scientific arguments of Mill and Spencer, Individualism has been advocated on economic principles. Adam Smith is credited for influencing the economic ideas of Mill and Spencer. To Adam Smith enlightened self-interest was the guiding principle with every individual and each would do well the work in which he was personally interested, if he were left to himself. This would ultimateley lead to the good of society as a whole. Trade and industry, Adam Smith maintained, flourish best if left to private enterprise. In an open competitive market all factors of production adjust themselves to the forces of demand and supply. Free competition stimulates production, regulates price and encourages free flow of capital and labour. The freedom of each to do as he pleases with his land, labour, capital and organisation is in the general interests of all and consistent with Bentham's doctrine of the greatest happiness of the greatest number. Hence, from the economic standpoint it was urged that a policy of *laissez faire*

6. Mill, J.S., *Political Economy,* Vol. II, p. 561.

would be in the highest interests of society, and artificial restriction imposed by government would put out of gear the entire economic structure.

The supporters of *laissez faire* appealed to history to establish the wisdom of non-interference. It was maintained that whenever the State had tried to control and regulate the social or economic life of the community, it had miserably failed in its attempts. All props and supports of the State to industry, like bounties and subsidies, prohibition, protection, etc., were mischievous and destructive of the end which they were intended to secure. Referring to those who were responsible for this sort of legislation, Buckle observed that "they went blundering along in the old track believing that no commerce could flourish without their interference, hampering that commerce by repeated and harassing regulations, and taking for granted that it was the duty of every government to benefit the trade of its own people by injuring the trade of others."[7]

Finally, the exponents of Individualism argue that if the State is to interfere in the economic life of the nation, its omnicompetence may lead to incompetence. As an entrepreneur, government is bound to be an utter failure, for it is a simple principle of business that those who bear the risk conduct the business more efficiently and economically than the officials of the State who have nothing at stake. State management, moreover, means routine, red-tapism, unnecessary delay, bad economy and corruption. In short, State management of industry is artended with all the evils of bureaucratic administration.

The theory of *laissez faire* was warmly advocated in the nineteenth century and it practically became the political creed of every civilised government. But soon its defects became obvious and there was a great reaction against Individualism. Its critics argued that:

The assumption of the Individualist theory that the State is a necessary evil is essentially wrong. It is preposterous to suppose that the State came into existence for the sole purpose of keeping in check the selfish and evil propensities of man. The State, as a matter of fact, originated in the bare needs of human life, and it continues in existence for the sake of good life. It is the necessary medium of individual progress and, as Burke put it, the State is "a partnership in all science, partnership in all art, a partnership in all virtue and in all perfection." The functions of the State in a complex and highly integrated society like ours, cannot be merely repressive and "negatively regulative." It has a higher task of protecting, encouraging, and fostering the common welfare. The Individualists err in maintaining that 'civilization increases by leaving man alone to manage his own affairs. On the contrary, advancing civilization demands increasing State regulation. "The higher the state of civilization," observed Huxley, "the more completely do the actions of one member of the social body influence all the rest; and the less possible is it for any one man to do a wrong without interfering more or less with the freedom of all his fellow-citizens, so that even upon the narrowest view of the functions of the State, it must be admitted to have wider power than the advocates of the *laissez faire* theory are disposed to admit." The Individualism of Spencer is wholly inadmissible under the

7. As cited in J.W. Garner's *Political Science and Government,* p. 463.

conditions of modern society. His arguments have, indeed, contributed much to discredit the traditional Individualism.

Similarly, the advocates of Individualism wrongly assumed that extension in the activities of the State is antagonistic to liberty. As previously pointed out, liberty without restraint cannot exist. Unrestrained and unrestricted liberty is a licence. True liberty means the power to choose and do the right. If there is no opportunity for all to realise equally their rights, there is no liberty. The laws of the State do not curtail liberty, but promote and maintain it. Liberty involves certain restraints and in this sense law is the condition of liberty. Liberty is destroyed only when such restraints are arbitrary and unjust. Mill's contention, therefore, that every increase in the power of the State is a corresponding decrease of individual choice and spontaneity is too sweeping.

In the same way, it is a mistaken view of the Individualists that the intervention of the State in the interests of common good always involves a curtailment of individual freedom. One fails to understand how a pure food Act, a factory Act, compulsory vaccination or a quarantine regulation infringes the liberty of the individual. In fact, the good of all is enhanced and their freedom secured by necessary restrictions. It is somewhat like pruning a fruit tree or trimming a vineyard; it means a loss of some fruit, but better fruit is produced so that all are gainers in the end.

The argument that man is the best judge of his own interests is true only to a very limited extent. Society is a better judge of the intellectual, moral, and even physical needs of the individual than he himself can be. The Individualists placed too much reliance on the individual and expected too much from everyone. They assumed that every individual was "equally far-sighted" and possessed "equal capacity" to know and do what was really in his interests. They also assumed that every individual had an "equal power" and an "equal freedom" of choice to satisfy his needs. But all these assumptions ignore the differences in intelligence, capacity, determination and resolution of different men coupled with the complexities of one's social position. Self-interest is, undoubtedly, the motive of every man, but his interests and motives cannot be separated from the interests of society. Being a social animal, he adjusts his interests in such a way as they may not conflict with the interests of his fellow-beings. Man is born in society and he lives and dies as its member; he cannot, therefore, be so self-interested as to be altogether oblivious of his social obligations. If he is, the State, as the guardian of the rights of all, has the right to regulate individual activities. And, then, all governmental regulations may not have a prejudicial effect on the development of individual character. Past experience, on the other hand, tells us that the State provides and maintains those conditions which help man to be the best of himself.

The main thesis of *laissez faire* rests upon the forces of free competition. Competition may be good for those who are economically strong, but for the weak it is a positive handicap. Workers are the worst sufferers and their misery, starvation, ill-health and inefficiency are the direct results of the so-called free competition. There can be no competition in a society in which there exist glaring and galling inequalities. Moreover, the competitive methods of production involve the use of machinery, division of labour, localisation of industry and demarcation of functions. Free competition leads to the formation of combinations, pools, trusts and cartels. All these methods of capitalistic production really retard competition, create condition of over-production, and bring about disequilibrium between demand and supply. The producers produce heedlessly and without any reference to the social values of the commodities. The opponents of Individualism, accordingly, maintain that all this waste and maladjustment can be avoided if there is planned production. Proper planning also secures for every one equality of opportunity and equality of reward. The argument that government is least competent to undertake economic enterprise is disproved by facts. The State has now stepped in to fight against individual selfishness, apathy, and inefficiency which Individualism has produced.

Finally, the individualistic argument of the survival of the fittest is as misleading as it is inhuman. The law of the survival of the fittest cannot be applied to human beings. It is not the physically fittest, but the normally best who survive. If the law of the survival of the fittest is to be accepted as the natural law, it is just to glorify brutal forces and perpetuate barbarity. We must, therefore, say good-bye to such a kind of Individualism.

Economic and Political Consequences of Individualism. Some of the most notable changes which Individualism has brought about are those that have occurred in the field of production. Never before in history had mankind come within the reach of plenty, actual or potential, as in the nineteenth century. The technique of mass production is unprecedented, and it has made available to the consumer such a variety and volume of commodities hitherto unknown. Developments in the means of communication and transport, and freeing of domestic and international trade have resulted in great extensions of markets defying all barriers of distance and space. Mass production, standardization of goods, rationalisation and integration of industries, extensive markets, and competition have all contributed to reduction of prices to such an extent that in many instances what once were luxuries for the few have now become necessaries for the many. In general, all this has spelled itself out in a series of changes that from the material standpoint have contributed enormously to human well-being, and in various countries, among which the United States is the pre-eminent example, have made possible the highest standard of living in the world.

But every rose has a thorn and in the case of the *laissez faire* doctrine, it has proved to be a thistle. Whenever and wherever it has pricked, it has made the individual and the society bleed profusely. When millions of individuals take independent decisions in the act of production on the basis of their own calculations and individual judgement, the result is ruinous. A typical example is that of periodical depressions which put the entire economy of the country out of gear and shake the political stability of the country too. Economics and politics go together and if not all, most of governmental problems have far-reaching economic implications.

Then, the application of *laissez faire*, particularly to an economy in the course of change from a mainly agrarian to a mainly industrial base, has unhinged the entire social structure of society. "For industrialism alters the physical environment in which men move, reshapes their everyday habits of living and working, and produces effects that are drastic, the less there is of planning and regulation." Expansion and localisation of industries bring into existence huge congested cities where masses of human beings are overcrowded, overworked, underpaid and underfed. Competition has its own destructive results. A few become richer, and the more powerful and the baneful argument of the survival of the fittest paves the way for a privileged class to grow and society definitely comes to be divided into two classes—'haves' and 'have-nots'; the very rich and the very poor. The State does not move. "The central concept of *laissez faire* that upheld State inaction as a virtue formed an umbrella beneath whose shelter economic organisations could luxuriate and thrive."

But economics is politics too. Those who amass wealth begin to man the State as well. They divert the machinery of the State to their own advantage. Political democracy becomes an absolute farce. Hence, the net result of Individualism was to employ the powers of the State what business deemed its interest. The functions of government were deliberately limited and as Karl Marx observed, capitalism contained in itself the seeds of its own destruction.

To sum up, Individualism is not a tenable creed, because it rests upon false assumptions and pure Individualism in the conduct of government is not possible. "As a matter of political justice it rests on a mechanical attempt to divorce individual and social rights completely. On an economic basis it overlooks the plain advantages of cooperation and regulated efforts. As a scientific law it will not stand." The truth of this statement is manifest and, today, we do not find any State which is simply a police State and follows in entirety the practices dictated by Individualism.

MODERN INDIVIDUALISM

Factors Promoting the Growth of Modern Individualism. The reaction against Individualism of the nineteenth century was fully witnessed by 1880, when its authority began to wane, and by the end of the century it had been largely superseded by the Absolutist and Collectivist theories of the State. And when the Absolutist and Collectivist theories of the State were taken to the extremes there was again a reaction in favour of Individualism, though in a modified form. C.E.M. Joad correctly says, "But the reaction against Individualism has produced a reaction in its turn. The wheel has turned full circle, and the present dissatisfaction with the State has promoted a revival of individualist thinking akin in spirit, though not in form, to the Individualism of the nineteenth century."[8] Modern Individualism is a name given to certain modern tendencies which exhibit a reaction against the nature and characteristics of the State as attributed to it by the Idealists and the Collectivists. It represents a revolt against the intellectualism of the Hegelian philosophy and the omnicompetence of the State. It is, also, a protest against the despotism of the bureaucratic governments of World War I. Finally, modern Individualism is a deep reaction against the rule of the majority in a parliamentary system of government which is characterised as tyrannical and a complete defiance of the interests of the minorities. The fundamental difference between old and new Individualism is that the former emphasises the importance of the individual and raises him on the pedestal of political glory whereas in the latter the emphasis is on groups and associations which honeycomb the life of man. The individual, it is claimed, is nothing without group life. The modern Individualists even attack the concept of the sovereign State. They regard the State as one like various other associations and would not give it a status higher to that.

8. Joad, C.E.M., *Introduction to Modern Political Theory*, p. 32.

The most important factor promoting the growth of modern Individualism is the progressive growth of associations of all kinds embracing the whole life of man and thereby eliminating the State from his private life. These associations are, it is maintained, the expression of the plurality of the wants of man and the channels which satisfy those wants and account for his welfare. Wthout them man cannot be what he wishes to be. The associations are consequently as natural to man as his nature compels him to live in the State. Both are spontaneous and independent of one another in their origins. The State, therefore, cannot claim a special prerogative of superiority over other associations. They are equal and coordinate to one another. The State is only one among other forms of associations and it has no superior claim to the individual allegiance. The only difference between the State as an association and other associations is that the membership of the State is only a matter of necessity and, as such, compulsory, while the membership of other associations is a matter of choice and, accordingly, optional. But both serve the same purpose and strive to attain the same objects.

The second factor is the sense of frustration created by the conditions of World War I. The belligerent States made exacting calls on the people and their resources in an all-round effort to win the War. In the name of the State, its independence, sovereignty, and integrity, extreme sacrifices were demanded from the people and they gave a willing and enthusiastic response to all such calls in the beginning. But the heavy toll of life which the prolonged War had taken, together with the uncertainty of the results of War, produced a feeling of hostility against the State and government which had brought so much incessant misery, sorrow, affliction, devastation, destruction and destitution to mankind. The people even began questioning the utility of the State and familiar with the teachings of Hegel and their own experiences with the demands of Governments, they could see what this "march of God on earth" could contribute to the uplift of man and society.

They, thus, resented the enormity of the powers which the State had assumed for itself. The enormous extension of governmental activity and the consequent curtailment of the liberty of the individuals meant increase in the number of officials and in the scope of their authority. It began to be believed that it was the growth of a new despotism which need be curbed, and, hence, public resentment against the State and its authority. Even the foundation of traditional political obligation was shaken.

The people had also lost faith in the Parliamentary system of government. The War and war-time psychology gave rise to a quickened apprehension of the majority rule. The mechanical way in which the majority party supported the government, the irresponsible way in which the majority behaved towards the minorities, and the mob psychology displayed in the legislature, in the press and on the platform all created strong feelings of a serious threat to the individual's freedom of mind. The people felt that the representative system of government had in practice degenerated into a tyranny of the majority rule. It was, accordingly, realised that the transfer of legal sovereignty to "the majority of the moment under the name of the State was no guarantee of universal happiness." The way out was suggested in decentralising the powers and functions of the State over as wide an area as possible.

Philosophy Underlying Modern Individualism. The State, according to modern

Individualists, is little more than a federation of groups, a union of Guilds, or a "community of communities." They deny the proposition that the State came into existence in response to any peculiar need of man. The State is viewed as merely a piece of administrative machinery useful for coordinating activities and adjusting claims between conflicting groups and associations. They challenge the supreme moral position which is attributed to the State by the Idealists. It is maintained that the State is just one of the many associations and it cannot claim, on any moral grounds, any better allegiance of the people. The State does not and cannot possess a real personality and a real will over and above the personalities and wills of the individuals who compose the State. All groups possess, equally with the State, personality. Loyalty of the people to the groups sometimes outweighs the loyalty which they owe to the State. Laski maintains, "The only state to which I owe allegiance is the state in which I discover moral adequacy" and adds, if the individual's "church conflicts with the state, he chooses and he alone can choose, where his allegiance should go."[9] Viewed, as such, modern Individualists do not consider the State as indispensable; it can be scrapped off the moment a suitable machinery to replace it is devised.

Modern Individualism finds its expression in the teachings of recent political thinkers. Though there is a good deal of difference in their methods of approach, yet they exhibit a common endeavour to provide the basis for such a theory. The first is Norman Angell, the apostle of internationalism. Internationalism denies the identity of the State with society, and it strengthens the pluralist view of the State. Internationalism, like pluralism, aims at discrediting the monistic theory of the sovereignty of the State and emphasises the multiplicity of relations outside the State.

Norman Angell in his book, *The Great Illusion*, contends that men are united by a community of feelings based on economic interests, since they always do what pays them best. But they are led to take a wrong view of what pays them as the competing States baffle them misrepresenting the issues and fostering national feelings. Once they begin realizing that it pays them better to think and feel as members of the universal economic society, whose attribute is peace, they would discard the division of society based upon territorial boundaries whose attribute is war. Angell asserts, "People who act wisely as individuals act like fools as citizens, and the world suffers in consequence." He regards the State as merely a piece of administrative mechanism which can be superseded whenever a suitable machinery is evolved. Angell, therefore, looks forward to a time when the national State is merged in an international order of society based on an economic class basis. The Guild Socialists accept all that is good in Angell's but differ from him in defining the nature of society.

Graham Wallas is another exponent of modern Individualism. Wallas, in his book, *Great Society*, shows a similar "distrust of the power of the over-developed State." But he devotes himself mainly to the problem of representative government. He says that the modern centralised State, with Parliament as its chief organ, is hardly an effective instrument for the expression of the popular will. He regards the present system of representation as very much defective, because the electorate is hypnotized by the popular

9. Laski, H., *An Introduction to Politics,* p. 30.

press and drugged by the demagogue. Wallas, accordingly, proproses, in the first place, that representation should be both on vocational and geographical basis, the former for a second chamber and the latter for a lower chamber. Secondly, he suggests certain safeguards against the majority oppression.

The Guild Socialists also subscribe to the idea of a democratic society consisting of a network of functional bodies. They hold society as a federation consisting of two kinds of groups, the producers and the consumers. They attack the political basis of the modern State and emphasise democratisation of society by the functioning of autonomous Guilds.

Miss Follett, in her book, *The New State*, gives a new meaning to modern Individualism, and the sub-title of the book, "Group Organisation, the Solution of Popular Government" is significant of this meaning. Miss Follett agrees with the pluralists and others who contribute to the theory of modern Individualism on the importance of the groups. But she does not accept "the group as the unit of politics." The pluralists glorify the group whereas Miss Follett emphasises "the group in relation" as the object of our study "if that study is to be fruitful for politics." The individual, the group, and the State all play their respective parts. In the introduction of her book, Miss Follet says, ".... But the individual, the group, the State—they are all there to be reckoned with—we cannot ignore or minimise any one." She, therefore, does not agree with those pluralists who either intend to lose the individual in the group or those who abandon the State for the group. "No government," in her considered opinion, "will be successful, no government will endure, which does not rest on the individual, and no government has yet found the individual." And the individual of Miss Follett's dreams does not believe in the old and fallacious idea of "self-and-others" as the basis of his social existence. He seeks "self-in-and-through-others" for the expression of his personality. The true man is found only through group organisation, because "the potentialities of the individual remain potentialities until they are released by group life. Man discovers his true nature, gains his true freedom only through the group. Group organisation must be the new method of politics because the modes by which the individual can be brought forth and made effective are the modes of practical politics."

As regards the State, it is, according to Miss Follett, not made by external acts, "but by the continuous thought and action on the people who live its life. The life of the State is moral ordering and the power of the State is a moral power accumulated through the spiritual activity of its citizens. The spiritual activity of the citizens can be achieved through the creative power of man as brought into visibility and actuality through his group life." The State, thus, unifies the manifold interests of the individual. It is the "ordering of his infinite series into their right relations that the greatest possible welfare of the total may be worked out." This is the function of the State and it is morality in its essence and completeness.

Difference between Old and Modern Individualism. Modern Individualism differs from the old Individualism in certain fundamental aspects. The former regards the group and not the individual as its unit for political purposes. This is essentially due to the fact that Individualism of the nineteenth century failed to provide necessary protection to the individual against exploitation and oppression by the power of privately owned economic interests, and public opinion expressing itself in the rule of the majority.[10] The group is organised for two purposes: in the first place, to protect the individual against the oppression of the majority, and secondly, to promote certain interests and ideas which its members have in common. The enormous size of the State prevents a fuller expression of the common will and the development of individual personality. The smallness of a group, on the other hand, adequately provides such opportunities. The group is, therefore, considered as the best medium for the development of real personality of the individual and the only effective guarantee of that personal liberty, concern for which forms the most valuable element of the old Individualism as expounded by Mill.

FASCISM

Fascism Analysed. Fascism, too, is the product of the First Great War. It is a tragedy of human life that "two diametrically opposite babies be born of the same parents. On the one hand, the Pluralistic theory initiated an era of iconoclasm against the Absolutist State; on the other hand, sowed the seeds of a totalitarian State which was to be far more autocratic than any State we had so far seen."[11] As Ebenstein observes, "Stripped to its essentials, fascism is the totalitarian organisation of government and society by a single-party dictatorship, intensely nationalist, racialist, militarist, and imperialist."[12] Fascism presents a complete repudiation of the assumptions, ideals and methods of democracy, Liberalism, and Socialism. Liberalism and democracy look to the interests of the individual, Socialism looks to the interests of an economic class, for Fascism, society is the end, individuals the means and its whole life consists in using individuals as instruments for its ends. The ideology of Fascism is dominated by the dogmas of a State and an irresistible government, which has the right to interfere in all spheres of the individual's life, whether economic, moral or religious. Civil life, according to the Fascist creed, begins with the State and all are in the State and no one outside the State. It commands all and it is essence of the State to govern. A citizen's obligations to the State are more important than his rights. Fascism proclaims the rights of the State, pre-eminence of its authority, and the superiority of its ends. No aspect of social life escapes the discipline of Fascism. It repudiates pacifism and glorifies war. "War," said Mussolini, "alone brings up to its highest tension all human energy and puts the stamp of nobility upon the peoples who have the courage to meet it .... Thus, a doctrine which is founded upon this harmful postulate of peace is hostile of Fascism."

Rise of Fascism. Fascism first emerged in Italy in the critical period immediately after the Great War of 1914-18. Italy at that time experienced the worst characteristic features of post-war economic disorganisation. There were gross profiteering, inconceivable inflation, soaring prices, strikes for higher wages to meet the rising cost of living, deficit budgets and unemployment of the war-weary soldiers. Italy, though victorious in the War, was diplomatically defeated. Her gains from the spoils of the War were not commensurate with her sacrifices, and Italy had consequently to withdraw her delegation from the Paris

10. Joad. C.E.M., *Introduction to Modern Political Theory,* p. 38.
11. Coker, F.W., *Recent Political Thought,* p. 475.
12. Ebenstein, W., *Today's Isms,* p. 95.

Peace Conference. It was in these critical times that Mussolini, with his Fascist creed, stepped in to rescue Italy from collapse. It is beyond question that Fascism changed Italy. In 1929, seven years later, Mussolini, as head of the Fascist government, boastfully spoke of the "immense panorama of material and moral transformations which we have accomplished." Fascism gave to Italy a strong and centralised government which exacted disciplined obedience from her people and established her international reputation as a first-rate power. It ended the war between labour and capital which, before the rise of Mussolini to power, had threatened to plunge Italy into chaos. There was a phenomenal development of Italy's industrial and, especially, agricultural resources. Finally, Fascism taught the meaning of nationalism to Italians and inspired them with a new faith in new ideas.

The Structure and Policy of the Fascist State. After the famous "March on Rome" Mussolini accepted the allegiance of the King and became the Premier. For a brief period, he made some attempts to preserve the institutions and practices of Parliamentary government. But, Mussolini made it clear from the very beginning that he would ignore Parliament, if it withheld from him the extraordinary powers which he demanded to run the government. Meanwhile, opposition outside the legislature was being crushed by repressive governmental measures, and by the violent acts of the Fascist armed squads. In January 1925, Mussolini broke away from the constitutional system and governed Italy by decrees which gave legal forms to the Fascist policies and in achieving complete political centralization and absolutism. In November, 1926, all "opposition parties were dissolved and prison sentences were provided for those who tried to revive the parties or who carried on propaganda for their doctrines."[13] By other decrees the responsibility of the Ministry to Parliament was abrogated. The King formally remained the constitutional head of the State, but the real head of government was the Premier with full authority to issue decrees having the force of law. The Ministers were not colleagues, but his subordinates. They were appointed by the Prime Minister and were individually and collectively responsible to him. Italy, thus, like Russia, became a one-party State and the National Fascist Party, like the Russian Communist Party, was a closed corporation, hierarchically organised. Members were admitted to the party only after tests as to their Fascist character and loyalty. They were to take an oath to follow without question the orders of the Duce. "Having created the Fascist Party," wrote Mussolini, "I always dominated it."[14] The party and the government had given to Mussolini, in brief, a *carte blanche*. It was his party and his government. Throughout Mussolini's autobiography there are assertions of "my command", "my guidance", "my sense of balance and judgment", "my irresistible domination."[15]

The Fascist policy may be summarised as: the restoration of the power of the Italian nation externally, and the establishment of vigour in the domestic administration of economic and civil affairs. Mussolini and his counsellors had always believed "that the prestige and influence of the State require an assertive foreign policy and a rigidly

13. Coker, F.W., *Recent Political Thought,* p. 49.
14. Benito Mussolini, *My Autobiography,* p. 296.
15. *Ibid.,* pp. 144, 162, etc.

hierarchic organisation of domestic government." For the realisation of these aims the Fascists recognised no individual liberties as sacred. They instead relied upon the methods of moral intimidation, physical compulsion, and official propaganda. Both in their activities before seizure of formal power and in their subsequent government policy, the Fascists dealt summarily and malevolently with their opponents.[16] Unprecedented repressive methods were explicitly adopted and embodied in the laws and decrees of 1925 and 1926. It was a punishable crime to criticize government, to conduct propaganda for the doctrines and parties dissolved by government, and to spread "false" or "exaggerated" news abroad concerning internal conditions of the country. There was a rigid control of all published opinions. The law required "every newspaper or other periodical to be operated under the control of a Director approved by the government and limited the contributors to persons registered by the Government-controlled syndicates of journalists. The Government had vigorously prosecuted and suppressed socialist and liberal periodicals and had 'fascitized' the more mildly critical journals, forcing the replacement of independent managers and editors by persons who will applaud, without serious qualifications, the Fascist rule."[17]

Fascist Doctrine. Fascism had no political theory. It was wholly empirical and practical. Mussolini had a disdain for theory and very often he repeated, "My programme is action, not talk." He exalted Fascism by contrasting its reality and definiteness to the sterile theories of other movements. "Fascism," Mussolini said, "is based on reality; Bolshevism is based on theory ... we want to be definite and real. We want to come out of the cloud of discussion and theory." Despite this emphasis on realism, Fascism has certain theoretical assumptions which formulated its general social ideals. Its aim was a fundamental reorganisation and invigoration of Italian life and, to that end, a restoration of the strength and prestige of Italian governmental authority. In the fulfilment of these aims Fascism displayed a striking combination of realism and mysticism. Its clarion call was action first, theory afterwards. The methods which it adopted, in the pursuit of its ends, were not fixed, as they were not based on any reasoning. They were highly flexible and could easily be adjusted and made workable in attaining its objects; so, naturally, they could not be consistent with one another.

The State or nation, according to the Fascist assumption, is an independent entity with a real will of its own. This real will of the State is quite distinct from the popular will which democracy owns. The Fascists deemed popular sovereignty a fictitious creation of democracy; and democracy they denounced because it gave power to the masses to decide innumerable issues about which they had no knowledge to exercise a sound judgment. The democratic notion of the equality of men was held to be wrong, for it was a mechanical process of "levelling human beings to one plane," thereby denying to them the "noble training" of nature. Here it seems that Mussolini emphasized the law of the survival of the fittest. Fascism, in brief, not only accepts the fact of human inequality, but goes further and affirms inequality as an ideal.

By society the Fascists meant a nation and a nation to them was the State. A nation,

16. Coker, F.W., *Recent Political Thought,* p. 470.

17. *Ibid.*, p. 471.

they explained, was based on "biological" similarities. It had a life more continuous, permanent and important than the lives of its members. The State was the organic structure of the nation. The State was, thus, the primary expression of the fact of nationality and it stood for absolute sovereignty, both moral and legal. The interests of the nation must take precedence over the individual interests and those of other groups. "A war for the preservation, expansion, or exaltation of a nation may be supremely justifiable, even though it may frustrate the special interests of every lesser group and destroy the lives of the nation's most worthwhile citizens." Thus, Fascism did not concede to the people liberty, equality and other rights; it rather scorned them. The individual had rights only in so far as the State conferred these on him. His will counted when it coincided with the will of the State. Liberty was not understood as a right, but as a duty. The State and its laws were the supreme manifestations of liberty. The citizen gained true personality and liberty by merging himself in the State. The Fascists, accordingly, substituted for liberty, equality and fraternity, three words of a higher and more noble significance: duty, discipline and sacrifice, which "encourage a man to employ all his faculties in an efficacious participation in national life."

These basic ideals of Fascism, viz., the nation is more important than any or all its members, and the interests of the nation must always precede and predominate over any sort of private interests, determine the Fascist principles of governmental structure and policy. Political authority, it was advocated, must be aristocratic because "only a minority of the nation has the capacity to perceive and give effect to national interest." It should, at the same time, be autocratic, if it was to inspire respect and exact obedience. Sovereignty was not vested in the people, but in the nation-State and only the few selected had the right to speak for the nation. These selected few possessed the ability to sacrifice private interests to the national welfare, and they were capable of pursuing the right way to that end by virtue of their inherited character and cultural training. They were, therefore, supreme guardians of the destiny of the nation. To reduce it to a simple formula, Fascism claimed that only the few could rule; only the few could make decisions, when there was leadership, there was virility. Government by the *elite* is a principle of Fascism and the concept of leadership expressed the extreme form of the *elite* principle.

The Fascists had always been explicit in defence of violence as a means of achieving political aims. Fascism is totalitarian in its means and it uses any form of coercion, from verbal threats to mass murders, for obtaining its ends. Mussolini defended the destruction of property and maiming and killing of people as practically and morally necessary. Following the suppression of the general strike in August 1922, he said, "After having made use of it (violence) systematically for forty-eight hours, we got results which we should not have obtained in forty-eight years of sermons and propaganda. When, therefore, violence removes a gangrene of this sort, it is morally sacred and necessary." This violence, employed during the period of revolution, remained the essence of Mussolini's policy both at home and abroad. His creed was that a man who was unwilling or unable to be a ruthless despot was not fit to be the head of the State. Force must be used to whatever extent a ruler found it necessary in guaranteeing the prestige and stability of his government and "maintaining orderly and efficient action in the economic life of the nation."

Fascism was an enemy of internationalism. "International peace," it claimed, "is coward's dream," and imperialism, according to Mussolini, "is the eternal and immutable law of life." Italian expansion, he said time and again, was a matter of life and death. "We are forty millions squeezed in our narrow but adorable peninsula .... Italy must expand or perish." This is tantamount to preaching war. "We are charged," said Mussolini in 1925, "with having imposed upon our nation a war discipline. I admit it, and I glory in it." He said on another occasion, "War alone brings up to their highest tension all human energies and puts the stamp of nobility upon the people who have the courage to meet it."

The Fascists considered all economic questions from the standpoint of national utility. The production and distribution of wealth were primarily matters of national, not individual concern, because the nation must be economically and politically consolidated. "The productive energies of the nation must be maintained at their highest possible point in order to supply the means for maintaining virile citizens and preserving the national strength." The Fascists, therefore, managed and regulated the economic life of the country while maintaining individual responsibility and freedom of enterprise. Fascism rejected both *laissez faire* and State ownership. Private ownership of property was allowed, because economic self-interest was considered to be the most powerful incentive to productive activity. But this interest must be held in constant subordination to the national interest. The Fascist government was within its right to intervene at any time and in any way whenever it appeared to them that private initiative had failed in serving the national security and prosperity.

Corporativism. Originally, the Fascist party was favourably inclined to Syndicalism and it had advocated the right of each syndicate, or trade union, or workers to take over and manage production within the particular field of its own activity. But from 1926 onwards, or even earlier, it turned its original syndicalism into the new form of corporativism. It proclaimed the doctrine that in each branch or category of production a corporation should be established. There were two features of this corporation. In the first place, it was to be composed of syndicate (or trade union) of workers and the syndicate (or association) of employers concerned with that branch of production. In the second place, the corporation was not to take over and manage production, within its branch, to the exclusion of private property and private enterprise. It would simply "regulate" the working of private property and the conduct of private enterprise, "under the aegis of the State."

Corporativism was essentially based upon the Fascist creed of "organicity"; completeness of the life of the nation in its totality. Since the nation must work as a totality and not a series of conflicting group interests, corporativism defied both Liberalism and Socialism. The former made the individual an end himself whereas the latter attempted to place the allegiance of the worker with all other workers throughout the world. Fascism insisted that the allegiance of both employers and workers must be to Italy first, and the class conception of solidarity was resolutely denied. "No worker in the name of class loyalty can impair the general productive power of the State; no employer can injure the workers and consuming population in the interests of a profit that is pernicious from a national point of view; the government as the symbol of organic unity of all must insist that the objective national allegiance is preserved."

Various laws were passed from time to time for organization of the corporarive State. By 1934, the structure was complete. The corporations were vested with legislative powers that fell directly within their competence. Each corporation was headed by a cabinet minister and it provided a basis for coordination in national economic activities. In 1936, Mussolini announced the end of the Chamber of Deputies. From 1928 to 1939, the corporations provided a list of parliamentary candidates, which after revision by the Grand Council of the Fascist Party was submitted to the vote of the national electorate. After 1939, the corporations themselves served as electorate and elected the members. In this way, the corporations directly provided the great majority of the members in the new Chamber of Fascist. The Fascist Party, thus, enunciated the doctrine that the corporation was the proper basis for any system of national representation. "This was the answer," as Barker says, "to the Democrat, who thus saw his cherished system of quantitative representation on a territorial basis displaced by a new so-called 'qualitative' system which professed to elicit the last elements of the nation through the sieve of a vocation method of choice."[18]

Claims made for the Italian System of Corporativism. The Italian system of corporativism has been lavishly praised. It is claimed that it provided a new conception of the functions of the State. It is superior to the *laissez faire* and Socialism as it reconciled the State and the individual to one another by reconciling them both to the corporation. In the corporation the producers and the workers find their expression and conciliate their differences, the State standing by them and aiding them in their task. Secondly, corporativism is, or can be, distinct from any political regime. A totalitarian State is not only its climate, although it is the Italian product. Finally, corporativism is the democratic device of the twentieth century. By reconciling the differences of all factors of production in the field of economics, it brings them on a common pedestal and introduces a new system of representation which does not depend on geographical constituencies and ever hostile political parties, "but on the essential national cadres and their complementary interests."

But the claim made, particularly by the British admirers of Italian corporativism, that it is not essentially connected with a totalitarian State, and that it can be independent of a political regime is not tenable. Even the Italian theorists and statesmen had never made such a claim, except once by Mussolini when he had said that corporativism was a part of the general development of the world's economy. But Mussolini had also maintained that genuine corporativism required the system of the single party and the State ruled by the *elite*. Authoritarianism is the long Italian tradition of government and the Fascist State was totalitarian. Corporativism was an organ of the administration of the State.

Nor does the third claim hold good. The corporations were not based on a firm foundation of the freedom of the trade unions. The corporation was determined and controlled by the State. Persons suspected of non-fascist tendencies were rigidly kept out and corporations were dissolved even on the slightest suspicion of anti-national activities. The system was, therefore, not a source of popular representation. It was neither a pattern

18. Barker, E., *Reflections on Government,* p. 331.

of industrial democracy nor an alternative to Parliamentary democracy and, as such, there is no justification in characterizing it as a new style and form of democracy.

NAZI-ISM

Rise of Nazi-ism. World War I was claimed to be a fight of democracy against autocracy. It was hoped that after the cessation of hostilities the world would emerge safer for the growth of democratic institutions. But soon after the Treaty of Versailles nearly three-quarters of the people of Europe found democratic governments either destroyed or in danger of destruction. Italy was the first to experiment with a totalitarian State after Mussolini's famous march on Rome in 1922, Primo di Rivero was declared father of Spain in 1923. Then, followed the defeated Germany which had presented to the world the best specimen of a Parliamentary government through the Weimar Constitution.

The unsettled economic and political conditions in Germany did not provide a satisfactory climate for parliamentary institutions. Nor had she any democratic traditions. She was groaning under the humiliating terms of the Treaty of Versailles. Deprived of her colonies, committed to a programme of heavy disarmament, officially forbidden by the treaty to raise a German air force for years to come, and huge reparations which she had not the means to pay, Germany had become a third rate international power. Within Germany itself there was complete economic collapse. The flight of gold from Germany and the reckless policy of inflation resulted in inconceivable depreciation in the value of the Mark and unprecedented rise in prices. There was widespread unemployment, the number in 1932 reaching the peak figure of six million.

Germany, under the circumstances, could not be content with a sheer democratic Constitution. She was in need of an indomitable leader, no matter liberal or reactionary, who could steer the ship of the State out of the moorings of economic and political chaos. Then, there was a restless nationalistic fervour throughout the country. It was at this psychological moment that Adolf Hitler appeared on the scene. He was skilful in playing with the emotions of the people and promised to destroy the much resented Versailles Treaty, secure military equality for Germany, repudiate reparations, expel the Jews who throve on the misery of the Germans both during the War and after, suppress radical labour movements, provide employment for all, and take vigorous steps to pave down inequalities in the possession of wealth. Hitler's appeal was for all classes of population. Hungry people wanted employment and food. Labour needed work and security of employment. Landowners and the industrialists were in search of someone who could guarantee them their wealth in face of the spreading communistic ideologies and methods.

Hitler's movement to start with was known as the German Workers' Party. Next year, it was named the National Socialist German Workers' Party and later the National Socialist Party. The change in the party name was relevant to the needs of the time and psychology of the people. The National Socialist label was sufficient to enamour both the socialists and the nationalists. The Nazis, as they came to be known, rose to power partly by means of the violent acts of their "storm troops" and partly through an adroit propaganda. Hitler was called upon by President Von Hindenburg to form a coalition government in November 1932, but this he refused. The invitation was again extended to him in January 1933, which he accepted. Hitler was appointed Chancellor with a cabinet of Nazis and members of the centre and old nationalist groups. But he secured the dissolution of *Reichstag* and elections were proclaimed to be held on March 5. A few days before the date of the elections a mysterious and disastrous fire had consumed the *Reichstag* building. This was held to be the work of the Communists who, it was alleged, had flashed the signal for a general rising. It exasperated Hitler and his Nazi party. In opening the election campaign Hitler denounced the "crime of 1918", and unequivocally promised to destroy Marxism, Communism, and class warfare. He was an avowed opponent of parliamentary democracy as well and, accordingly, committed himself to end it and "find the way of reorganising the new unity of the German nation." He, also, pledged "to reawaken a popular veneration for the great traditions and to educate the Youth in reverence for the old imperial army as the emblem of the nation's greatest achievement."

In the confusion caused after the *Reichstag* fire, President Hindenburg, on February 28, suspended many fundamental rights of the citizens guaranteed by the Weimar Constitution, viz., articles prohibiting arbitrary arrest and imprisonment and guaranteeing private property, the sanctity of the home, the secrecy of private correspondence and freedom of speech, assembly, and association. It was in this atmosphere that the March 1933 elections were held which the Nazis and their Nationalist allies won by a slight majority of two per cent votes.

The Structure and Policy of the Nazi State. When the new *Reichstag* met on March 28, it gave blanket powers to the Nazi cabinet under Hitler, for a period of four years. It is from this date that the typical Nazi programme was put into operation. The accession to power of the Nazis was widely acclaimed by Italian newspapers "as a sign of the collapse of another democracy and as a vindication of the Fascist creed of strong and autocratic action." And the Nazis, too, had in aims and tactics approached nearly the Italian model. The government soon dissolved the Communist, the Socialist and other Opposition parties. A law was made making the National Socialist Party or the Nazi Party the only legal party in the country. Opposition newspapers were suppressed and the press, the radio, the theatre, and the cinema were placed under the control of Dr. Goebbels, Minister of Enlightenment and Propaganda. Thousands of political suspects were imprisoned or driven into exile and the Jews excluded from public life of the party and the government. The ideal of Nazi-ism, one *Reich*, one people, one leader, was achieved.

Thus, in rapid strokes the Nazis achieved a totalitarian State. The story, however, was completed by the November 1933 general elections of the *Reichstag*. The Nazis secured 92 per cent of the total votes cast and on first December the National Socialist Party was incorporated into the machinery of the State. Soon after the federal system of government was abolished and each unit of *Reich* was placed under the charge of Hitler's personal representatives vested with virtual dictatorial powers. Then, the Upper Chamber of the legislature at the centre, *Reichsrat*, was abolished. On President Hindenburg's death in 1934, Hitler became the President and the Chancellor combining into his person the supreme executive and legislative powers. The *Reichstag* was summoned occasionally and that, too, for registering the decisions of Hitler. One single instance illustrates it. After the November 1933 elections, "the new all-Nazi *Reichstag* held a seven-and-one-half-minute session for the sole purpose of electing officers. 659 Brown Shirts rose and sat down in unison when the Government's list was put to a vote, and, then, went obediently about their own business." This was the climax. Hitler, the Chancellor and Fuehrer, became the undisputed ruler of Germany. The Fuehrer spoke the first and the last word for the party and the government.

Nazi Doctrine. Nazi-ism had no well-defined doctrine. It was not either a philosophy of the theory of the State or government. It was just a movement which responded to a restless nationalistic fervour aroused by resentment over the terms of the Treaty of Versailles, although its appeal was in conformity with the political heritage of the Germans and their psychology. Hitler was an imperfectly educated man with no flare for philosophy and political theorising. He had probably never read in their original the writings of Hegel or Houston Chamberlain, yet "endowed with great native gifts" and trained in the methods of playing with the sentiments and emotions, he preached valiant action and popularized veneration for the great national tradition.

When the nation is glorified and the characteristic feature of the State is vigour and force, the obvious result is war. Hitler and his followers openly preached war. They extolled force and violence and had all praise for the man of action. "He who would live," said Hitler, "must fight. He who does not wish to fight in this world has not the right to exist. Such a saying may sound harsh, but that is how the matter stands." The task of the universities was not to teach objective science, "but the militant, the war-like, the heroic." Nazi-ism, therefore, preached and practised the gospel of the victorious sword and the principle of might as right. Hitler's theory of Vigour and Force was fully demonstrated in militarising Rhineland, by denouncing the Locarno Treaty and ultimately by conquering Czechoslovakia in 1938. Then, came subjugation of Poland by Germany and Russia in September 1939.

Hitler's Germany was an exclusive State. It meant two things. In the first place, it advocated the purity of race, the purity of language and the purity of literature. According to the teachings of Nazi-ism, "there are to be no more human beings in Germany, but only Germans."[19] With this extreme nationalism of the Nazis may be connected an intense devotion to German paganism in religion and the theory that the German woman was considered valuable only as a breeder of pure Nordic children and the preserver of the Nordic race.

The exclusiveness of the State, in the second place, meant achievement of economic self-sufficiency. The Nazis emphasised economic self-sufficiency in the name of national unity and solidarity. Nazi economic policy was neither pure capitalism, nor socialism, because both the creeds divided the nation into hostile camps. General welfare was placed above private interests. The capitalists and the workers were controlled in the name of the State. Big and heavy industries were allowed to continue under private enterprise, but the scale and nature of production was determined by the State. The leader of the party decided what to produce, where to produce, how to produce, and when to produce. Private determination and choice had nothing to do with it. Both the producers

19. Hitler first chose the Jews as the targets of German aggression; "once given a direction for their savagery, the Germans were not satisfied until they had sent six million Jews from Central and Eastern Europe to the gas chambers." Ebenstein, W., *Today's Isms*, p. 103.

and consumers had neither any choice nor any preference. There was no separate organisation of the labour, and strikes and lockouts were strictly prohibited by law. Wages and prices were fixed. Commodities were controlled and rationed. Imports and exports were permitted with the government permission.

The Nazis did not glorify the State to the same degree as the Fascists. Hitler rejected Mussolini's idea that the State is "a spiritual and moral fact in itself." The State was not regarded as an end but as a means and its highest purpose was to preserve and promote racial unity, racial purity and racial development. The Nazis transmuted in the *volk* or nation what they had denied to the State. They agreed to the dictum of Kant and Fichte that the individual possesses no rights but duties and the true freedom of the individual, they claimed, consisted in subordinating himself to the *volk* and working for its welfare. Nazi writers frequently spoke of the *volk* as a sort of metaphysical supernatural entity having a spiritual reality apart from the existence of its members. Hitler always said that the individual is nothing; *das volk* is everything. He ordained for the Germans three simple rules of conduct: duty, discipline and sacrifice. When the individual has no rights, no freedom of choice and no private initiative, it matters not whether the exaltation is that of the State or the volk. The results are the same. Hitler was the head of German nation as well as of the State.

Nazi-ism is the antithesis of democracy. Democracy according to Hitler was a decaying corpse as it was "stupid, corrupt and slow-moving." Parliaments were talking shops incapable of accomplishing results and at times of emergency they were absolutely helpless. Nazi-ism, accordingly, did not tolerate political opposition and was hostile to individual liberty. Individual liberty was regarded as a fetish of the past. "The political parties," proudly declared Hitler in July 1933, "have now been fully abolished. This is an historical event of which the importance, and far-reaching effects have in many cases not yet been realized by all. We must now get rid of the last remains of democracy, especially of the method of voting and of the decision by majority .... The (National Socialist) Party has now become the State." This is exactly what Mussolini had said and done.

The Party, according to Nazi teachings, was the authorised agent of the dictatorship and the State. Both in Itlay and Germany the principle of leadership from above was an established fact. It was the core not only of the constitution of the National Socialist Party, but also of its doctrines. Hitler was the head of the Party, head of the State, head of the government, and, most important of all, head of the German nation considered as a racial community. Obedience to the leader was declared a sacred duty and it was rigidly enforced by the arts of discipline and propaganda. The ideal of "one Reich, one people, one leader" did not involve any question of how and why. Hitler definitely put it: Duty, discipline and sacrifice to be the watchwords of German citizens. Religion became worship of the Fuehrer. Professor Ernest Bergman wrote: "We of the German religion today turn to the ancient Nordic, Indo-Germanic Light-Hero figure and get rid of a false and diseased Christ picture created by the Christian Pope and Church to the hurt of humanity. The high priest of the new German paganism is Hitler himself. He is the real Holy Ghost. Hitler is lonely. So is God. Hitler is like God. Hitler is a new, greater, and a powerful Jesus Christ."

The worship of Hitler was preached from the pulpit and at school, the stage, the cinema, the radio and the press. "When the child returned home from school for lunch the parents greeted him With 'Heil Hitler', a phrase which the Germans used from 50 to 150 times a day." A Nazi school text-book, which every German child was required to use, contained the following precious sentiment:

> "Our Leader, Adolf Hitler,
> We love you
> We pray for you
> We like to hear you
> We work for you, Heil"

Leadership was, thus, far more in Nazi Germany than just a matter of authority from above. "It was the instrumentality through which nationality, State, and all political processes were fused into one. The national leader was hailed as the supreme embodiment of spirit and will of the people and hence the infallible head of their political system. Totalitarianism, therefore, acquired a sanctity in Germany that was never attained in Italy."

Nazi-ism, Fascism and Communism. It will be instructive to have a comparative study of Nazi-ism and to know what makes it akin to Fascism and Communism and, at the same time, what are the main points of difference between them. It is true that the general conclusion and the general philosophy presented by National Socialism is something unique in Europe, but it has the element of the single party in common with the former Communist Russia and with Fascist Italy. Then, it has some elements of social economic policy common with Fascism. Nazi-ism, like Fascism, is based upon the executive eminence of power and responsibility, legislature having been reduced to a subordinate position just to register the will of the executive.

But, as said earlier, National Socialism is fundamentally unique. It is devoted to the ideal of a "closed" society, which is based on a peculiar and individual genius and stock. "It issues in a peculiar polity, expressive of that peculiar genius: it issues in a peculiar land self-contained economy which is similarly expressive." It was restoration of the old heritage of the directing leader and the old idea of a united *volk*. In its origin, the Nazi party mixed an old Nationalism with a non-proletarian Socialism. So far as it was National, it drew its followers from all, of whatever rank and station, who desired national renaissance. So far as it was Socialist, it appealed particularly to the peasantry, the small shopkeeper, and the lower middle class. Then, the party had a particular appeal to the young who had seen war service, and wished to preserve the best they had learnt in the war by cultivating the virtues of fellowship and heroism. From its beginning "the Party called itself German (the German Workers' Party); and whatever elements it gathered—youth or aged, the lower middle class or the great industries—it remained essentially and fundamentally German." National Socialism was, thus, wedded to the people and the community. From this it proceeded to drive out foreign elements and concluded by conceiving German community as a native and natural race, which must above all things "preserve its racial purity, enhance its racial vigour and expand to its racial limits." This was the climax of racial unity and racial exclusiveness. The National Socialist Party made Germans a "closed" society when it preached that only the pure race could possess and transmit the true spirit. These teachings, in fact, set the old conceptions on a firmer and deeper foundation.

This aspect of National Socialism differentiates it not only from the democratic pattern of society, but also from the Communists and the Fascists. The democratic pattern, in spite of national differences, "has a common thread and design." Communism, too, is based upon a few common ideas. It emphasises the common interest of the workers in all countries and aims at the international revolution of the proletariat. Even Italy could claim that the Fascist doctrine, and in particular its doctrine and practice of corporativism, had a general appeal which could be advocated to others and adopted by them. "in a word, both Communism and Fascism are general alternatives; they are presented to the world at large; and if in the Italian view Fascism is an alternative produced by the Italian genius and peculiarly connected with Italy, it is nonetheless an alternative presented to the common choice."[20]

What Germany presents to others is simply Germany by itself and in itself; incorporated in two central principles of the Nazi creed described by Carl Schmitt as the principle of Leadership (*Fuhrung*) and the principle of Identity of kind (*Atgleichheit*). Both these principles have roots in the soil of Germany and are peculiar to the genius and traditions of the people. There is, therefore, nothing in Nazi-ism which presents an alternative to other countries for their own internal choice. In the international sphere it preaches exclusiveness and does not offer any solution for the troubles of the world. In fact, Nazi-ism perpetuated international animosity and aggressive warfare.

SUGGESTED READINGS

Asirvatham, E.: *Political Theory,* Chap. XIII, pp. 447-72.

Barker, E.: *Political Thought in England from 1848-1914,* Chaps. I, III.

Barker, E: *Reflections on Government,* Chaps. XII, XIII.

Barnes, J.S.: *Fascism.*

Baurnont, M., and others: *The Third Reich.*

Bradley, F.H.: *Ethical Studies, My Station and its Duties.*

Brown, I.: *English Political Theory,* Chap. XI.

Coker, F.W.: *Readings in Political Philosophy.*

Coker, F.W.: *Recent Political Thought,* Chaps. XV, XVIII.

Cole, G.D.H.: *A Guide Through World Chaos.*

Cranston, Maurice *(Ed.): Western Political Philosophers,* pp. 91-98.

Davidson, W.: *Political Thought in England from Bentham to J. S. Mill.*

Dunning, W.A.: *Political Theories from Rousseau to Spencer.*

Ebenstein, W.: *Fascist Italy.*

Ebenstein, W.: *Today's Isms.*

Finer, H.: *Mussolini's Italy.*

Florinsky, M.T.: *Fascism and National Socialism.*

Follet, M.P.: *The New State.*

20. Barker, E., *Reflections on Government,* p. 391.

Friedrich, C.J. and Brzezinsk : *Totalitarian Dictatorships and Autocracy.*

Garner, J.W.: *Introduction to Political Science,* pp. 273-98.

Goad, H.E.: *The Working of a Corporative State.*

Green, T.H.: *Lectures on the Principles of Political Obligation.*

Harmon, Judd M.: *Political Thought from Plato to Present,* Chaps. XVII, XVIII, XXI.

Hitler, A.: *Mein Kampf.*

Hitler, A.: *My Battle,* tr. from the German (New York, 1933).

Joad, C.E.M.: *Introduction to Modern Political Theory,* Chaps. I, II.

Laski, H.J.: *Authority in the Modern State.*

Laski, H.J.: *Political Thought in England from Locke to Bentham.*

Laski, H.J.: "The Rise of Liberalism", Encyclopedia of the Social Sciences. Vol. I.

Lloyd, Christopher : *Democracy and Its Rivals;* Parts II, III.

Lord, A.R.: *Principles of Politics,* Chap. XI.

Merriam, C.E., H.E. Barnes, and others: *Political Theories; Recent Times,* Chaps. VI, VII.

Mill, J.S.: *Essays on Government.*

Mill, J.S.: *Representative Government.*

Mill, J.S.: *On Liberty.*

Mussolini, B.: *My Autobiography.*

Mussolini, B.: *The Political and Social Doctrine of Fascism.*

Parkinaon, C.N.: *The Evolution of Political Thought,* Chaps. XIX-XXII.

Rockow, L.: *Contemporary Political Thought in England,* Chaps 11. 111, IV, X.

Sabine, G.H. : *A History of Political Theory,* Chaps. XXX, XXXI.

Schuman, F.L : *The Nazi Dictatorship.*

Shirer, W.L.: . *The Rise and Fall of the Third Reich.*

Stephen, Lo : *The English Utilitarians.*

Vereker, Charles; *The Development of Political Theory.*

Villari, L.: *The Fascist Experiment.*

29

CHAPTER

Theories of the Sphere of State Activity (Contd.)

SOCIALISM

Meaning of Socialism. The word socialism appears to have been first used in the *Poor Man's Guardian* in 1833. In 1835, a society, which received the name of the Association of all Classes of all Nations, was founded under the auspices of Robert Owen (1771-1858), a successful capitalist who had made a fortune by the age of forty, and the words *socialists* and *socialism* became current during the discussions which arose there. The term was soon afterwards borrowed from England by a distinguished French writer, Reybaud, in his well-known work, the *Reformateur moderne*, in which he discussed the theories of Saint Simon, Fourier and Owen. Through Reybaud it gained wide currency on the Continent and is now the accepted name for one of the most remarkable movements of the nineteenth century.

Socialism is the legitimate child of two great revolutions, the Industrial Revolution which had established itself in England towards the end of the eighteenth century and of the parallel revolution in thought which, about the same time, found most prominent expression in France. Robert Owen had grown up in the midst of the industrial revolution and he was deeply conscious of the enormous abuses of the factory system, which he witnessed in his own industrial enterprises. He also knew the wonderful services that might be rendered by new technical improvements if only it were made subordinate to human well-being. Owen, thus, sought to bring the mechanism of the industrial system under the direction of the nobler principle, in which the good of all should be the great and sole aim. He advocated the organisation of producers' cooperatives in order to establish a new social order. He sank much of his fortune in producers' cooperatives in England, and he also spent several years and the better part of his wealth in a cooperative venture in the United States. The impracticability of Owen's scheme of cooperatives was obviously clear, yet no one denied the nobility of his purpose. His dream was to release the individual from the repressions and perversions of a competitive society and the creation of a society that would make an end of crime, poverty and injustice, a society in which the good in human nature could flower in full perfection and beauty.

If Owen had before his eyes the evils of industrialization, Saint Simon had before him the history of the hoary abuses of an idle and privileged feudalism. Revolution had, no doubt, fearfully shaken feudalism in France, but it was still strong in Europe, and in

France, as elsewhere, it powerfully revived during the period after Waterloo. Saint Simon saw that a new world, an industrial world, resting on labour had arisen while the old feudal and clergy classes steeped in ignorance and parasitic on society still ruled. Saint Simon sought to remove all this array of parasites through the industrial and scientific leaders as the real working heads of the people. What he exactly desired was an industrialist State. The men who were best fitted to organise society for productive labour should rule in it; his aim was the substitution of the feudal aristocracy by a working aristocracy of merit.

The contrast between labour and capital, so much emphasised by later socialism, is not present in Saint Simon, but he assumed that in the organised society the industrial chiefs would not exploit the labour of others but would rule in the interest of society. Later on, the cause of the poor received greater attention and in his book, the *New Christianity*, it became the central point of Saint Simon's teachings. "The whole of society," he wrote, "ought to strive towards the amelioration of the moral and physical existence of the poorest class. Society ought to organise itself in the way best adapted for attaining this end."

During the next stage in the development of Socialism, we see the influence of chiefly German and also Russian thinkers. Marx used the term *Communism* to denote his own theories in contradiction to the term *Socialism*. Marx and Engels gave expression to their doctrines in their celebrated *Communist Manifesto* (1848) and criticised the socialism hitherto preached and advocated. Later, the socialism of Owen and Saint Simon school came to be known as *Utopian Socialism* or *Utopianism* and the one which drew its inspiration from Marx as *Scientific Socialism* or merely *Socialism*. The term *Communism* denoted a distinct scheme of social reorganisation.

The term Socialism is derived from the word *socious* which means society. Socialism is concerned with society and it is the injustice of the capitalist system that has inspired it. It is a reaction against the social and economic anarchy which the capitalist system had produced. It is a revolt against the exploitation of man by man and of child, in field, factory, mine and workshop. It is a protest against the building of an economic and social system on the incentive of profit, not service. It is a challenge to competition which had degraded the working man and his family, starved many to keep a few in luxury, separated society into two classes—haves and have-nots—and dragged mankind into perpetual conflicts and war.

The socialist challenge to the existing order is primarily moral, though its basis is economic. It is the assertion of the rights of the producing class which had never obtained a fair deal anywhere during aII stages of social evolution. At one time this class was chiefly made up of slaves, then, of half-free or nominally free agricultural labourers, and, finally, of industrial workers. This class had always been excluded from the possession of land and capital, deprived of its share of the product of labour, denied the opportunities for effective participation in the affairs of the community, for political power without its economic counterpart is only a delusion and a snare. No reform or change can be of any use, they argued, as long as there is no change in the system by which the few owned and controlled the capital, and the whole productive and distributive machine. The Socialists, therefore, proposed that land and capital, which are the requisites of labour and the sources of all wealth, should be placed under social ownership in order to secure a more equitable distribution of the means and appliances of happiness. There should be Socialism or there will be social ruin, they concluded.

So far all the Socialists are agreed. But on the most important points of detail they differ very greatly. They differ as to the form society will take in carrying out the Socialist programme, as to the relation of regional and local governments to the central government, and whether there is to be any central government or any government at all. They are also sharply divided on the methods of achieving Socialism. Some expect it to come suddenly and completely with a catastrophic revolution, while others expect it to come slowly and gradually through the existing parliamentary institutions. The result is that there have emerged many schools of Socialism and each school has its own distinct philosophy, carries a separate name, and advocates its own point of view. And as the advocates of Socialism are numerous and the literature on the subject is enormous, varying according to the time and circumstances in which it appeared, it is difficult to approve or condemn the movement of Socialism *en bloc*. Joad had rightly said that "socialism is like a hat that has lost its shape because everybody wears it"[1] But the ideal of the Socialists is, whatever their variety, to remove poverty and privileges, vice and crime and other social evils from which society suffers today and to establish a new social and economic order where there will exist equal opportunity for all to flower to their best. As Spargo says, no definition of Socialism can be complete which does not consider it as: (i) a criticism of existing society; (ii) a philosophy of social evolution; (iii) a social forecast or ideal; and (iv) the attainment of the ideal. The description of the Socialist ideal is provided by G.D.H. Cole. He says, "Socialism means four closely connected things—a human fellowship which denies and expels distinctions of class; a social system in which no one is so much rich and poorer than his neighbours as to be unable to mix with them on equal terms; the common ownership and use of all the vital instruments of production; and an obligation upon all citizens to serve one another according to their capacities." Socialism is, thus, an economic doctrine related especially to the economic ills of the industrial revolution. Its aim is to establish social justice.

Marx's Contribution. The greatest and most influential name in the history of Socialism is unquestionably Karl Marx. He and his celebrated companion Friedrich Engels are the acknowledged heads of the "scientific and revolutionary" school of Socialism, and to them is due the credit for the formulation of a coherent body of Socialist doctrine and the formation of the International Socialist Movement which has continued to grow and spread throughout the world till very recently. They categorically condemned the capitalistic society and enunciated the philosophy of Socialism for a working man's movement.

Karl Marx's thesis on Socialism is found in the *Communist Manifesto*, published early in 1848, and in the three volumes of *Das Kapital* or "Capital", known as the "gospel" or "Bible" of the *Socialists*. The *Communist Manifesto* is the most widely read of all the Socialist documents and has been translated into almost every civilised language of today. It contains the clearest and most compact statement of Marx's conceptions of

1. Joad, C.E.M., *Modern Political Theory*, p. 40.

the past struggles between economic classes, the modern bourgeois-proletarian conflict, the inevitable present-day movements of its own destruction, and the programme of action working men adopt in order to fit in their efforts with the actual march of events.

The most essential of Marx's doctrines may be reduced to three: (1) the materialistic conception of history, (2) the law of the concentration of capital, and (3) the class war. *Das Kapital* or "Capital", the first and the most important volume of which appeared in 1867, and the other two volumes, edited by Engels published posthumously in 1885 and 1894, adds a wealth of factual detail to the thesis of the *Communist Manifesto*. It contributed the theory of *Surplus Value* which explains the actual mechanism of capitalist exploitation. The theory of *surplus value*, according to Bertrand Russel, can hardly be defended as a contribution to pure theory. "It is rather to be viewed," he says, "as a translation into abstract terms of the hatred with which Marx regarded the system that coins wealth out of human lives, and it is in this spirit rather than in that of disinterested analysis, that it has been read by its admirers."[2]

Marx's principal doctrines were not new. But he greatly amplified and systematized older ideas. He combined the scattered threads of all those ideas and gave them a logical, scientific, and effective exposition. His originality, however, is to be found partly in his appeal to the proletarian class, and partly in his call for organised action by the workers against their employers. His contribution, also, lies in his attempt to relate history with economic events and to trace the consequences of the evolutionary and revolutionary phases of socialistic action. He attempted to prove that a social programme must be based upon a systematic interpretation of social evolution and a critical analysis of the existing system of production and exchange. "More specifically his design was to show how a socialist community is to be built upon capitalist foundation."[3] Although Marx professed to be proceeding in his discussions objectively and inductively, yet it must be confessed that all his writings were dominated by a clearly preconceived purpose of attacking the existing system of economic and political order.

The Theory of Surplus Value. The central point in Marx's thesis is his theory of *Surplus Value*. Here he derives his inspiration from the classical labour theory of value, primarily associated with the name of David Ricardo. Marx held that labour was the sole source of value. He agreed with the classical economists that the market value of a commodity depends on demand and supply, but in the long run the value of anything is determined by the labour and time spent on its production. Karl Marx defined commodities as congelation of labour and regarded value as "crystallised labour." The inclusion of labour in the commodity gives it value. But the labour must be "socially necessary." This means two things. In the first place, labour must use instruments without which it cannot work. These instruments are factories, machinery, electric and steam power, etc. Secondly, the goods must be produced in such quantities that they can be easily marketed. If the market refuses to buy all the goods produced, the labour expended in the production of such goods is wasted.

Labour, says Karl Marx, is a commodity and its value, too, is determined like any

2. Bertrand Russel, *Roads to Freedom* p. 38.
3. Coker F.W., *Recent Political Thought,* p. 41.

other commodity. That is to say, its value in exchange is fixed by the labour needed to produce and maintain it, or, in other words, it amounts to the commodities needed to support the labourer. The worker must get wages sufficient enough to cover his expenses of maintaining himself and his family. But actually this does not happen in a capitalist society and labourers get wages much below their subsistence level. The reason is obvious. In the existing structure of society the instruments of production—machinery, tools and materials upon which labour can be performed—are owned by a relatively small class, called the capitalist class, who are the employers. Labourers merely own their ability to work, which they sell to the capitalist and for which they receive wages. But the wages paid to them bear no proportion to the price which the commodity fetches in the market. The capitalist class knows that labour is a highly perishable commodity and it suffers from many other disabilities. Labour's disabilities are the employer's advantages, because what is honey for him is vinegar for the worker. By paying him less wages, which he accepts because his labour is highly perishable, the employer increases his profits. The difference between the exchange value of a commodity and the wage paid to the worker, Karl Marx calls, *Surplus Value*. The Surplus Value which ought to have gone to labour is appropriated by the capitalist. It is, in fact, the product of unpaid labour and Marx characterises it as pure and simple exploitation. In the *Communist Manifesto* Marx says, "For exploitation, veiled by religious and political illusions, it (bourgeoisie) has substituted naked, shameless, direct brutal exploitation."

It was this exploitation of labour which Karl Marx sought to remove. The modern State, in his opinion, is a tool in the hands of the capitalist class and they use it to protect and perpetuate their vested interests. The only way to put an end to these conditions, according to Marx, is to destroy all opportunity for private enterprise and free competition. This can be achieved only under a Socialist society, where collective capital will replace private capital, both capitalists and wage-earners disappear, and all persons become cooperating producers.

The Materialistic Conception of History. Marx, then, proceeds to enquire how society came to be organised in such a way that a small privileged class has ever appropriated and continues to appropriate the surplus value created by the labour of workers with the full authority of law. He finds his explanation in history and gives to his doctrine the name of the Materialistic Conception of History. According to this doctrine all the phenomena of human society have their origin in material conditions of life. "Legal relations as well as forms of State," said Marx, "could neither be understood by themselves, nor explained by the so-called general progress of the human mind, but they are rooted in the material conditions of life... The mode of production in material life determines the general character of the social, political and spiritual process of life. It is not the consciousness of men that determines their existence, but on the contrary their social existence determines their consciousness." The political institutions of every country, its social structure, trade and industry, art and philosophy, and the customs, manners, traditions, law, religion and morality, all are influenced and shaped, according to Marx, by the material conditions of life. By material conditions of life, he means environment, production, distribution and exchange; production being the most important of all. "Thus to each stage of economic production there corresponds an appropriate political form and an appropriate class structure." Marx's philosophy, therefore, is a theory of history setting forth the natural phase of evolution.

He applies his doctrine in particular to two revolutions, one in the past, the other in the future. The revolution in the past was that of bourgeoisie against feudalism and it found its expression, according to Marx, in the French Revolution. The one in the future, is the revolution which Marx predicts, the revolution of the wage-earners or proletariat against the bourgeoisie in their bid to establish the Socialist Commonwealth. "The weapons with which the bourgeoisie felled feudalism to the ground are now turned against the bourgeoisie itself. But not only has the bourgeoisie forged the weapons that bring death to itself, it has called into existence the men who are to wield those weapons—the modern working class, the proletarian."

The Industrial Revolution brought into existence two distinct classes: a small privileged class, the owners of the means of production, and a large propertyless proletariat. There had been employers and workers before and even small-scale capitalist but the peculiar features of the modern capitalist society are the dominance of the capitalists as a class, the organisation of the State in such a way as to give expression to this dominance, and a constant and never-ending conflict between the capitalist and the proletariat. The capitalist class controls the machinery of the State and occupies all key positions in the government. The laws of the State are so made and the policies of the Government are so formulated as to safeguard and promote their interests. In fact, the whole machinery of government functions to the advantage of the capitalists as a class and they use it to fortify their liberty of ruthless exploitation. Karl Marx, thus, bluntly concludes: "Does it require deep intuition to comprehend that man's ideas, views, and conceptions, in one word, man's consciousness, changes within his social life, every change in the conditions of his material existence, in his social relations, and in his social life?"

The Law of the Concentration of Capital. Marx, then, proceeds to show how capital becomes concentrated into the hands of a handful of people. Marx pointed out that capitalist undertakings tend to expand. He foresaw the substitution of trusts and cartels for free competition, and predicted that the number of capitalist enterprises must diminish as the magnitude of a single enterprise grows through, what we call, rationalization of industry. With the diminution in the number of businesses as a result of monopolisation, the number of the capitalists, too, diminishes and capital comes to be concentrated in the hands of few capitalists. Marx, indeed, usually spoke as though each business were owned by a single man. The capitalists thrown out of their business, as a result of this process of concentration and monopolisation, would naturally join the ranks of the proletariat. "Our epoch, the epoch of bourgeoisie," says Karl Marx, "has simplified the class antagonisms. Society as a whole is more and more splitting up into two great hostile camps, into two great classes directly facing each other: Bourgeoisie and Proletariat." When the capitalists grow numerically weaker, less in number, that heralds their destruction. "All previous historical movements," according to Marx, "were movements of minorities. The proletarian movement is the self-conscious, independent movement of the immense majority; in the interests of the immense majority."

Marx applied the principle of the law of the concentration of capital not only to industry but also to agriculture. He predicted the landowners to become fewer in number while their estates grew larger and larger. This process would make more glaring the evils and injustices of the capitalist system and consequently strengthen the ranks of the opposition.

The Class War. In every age, Marx maintained, the differing modes of acquiring means of subsistence divide men into separate groups and create within each group special group consciousness. This group consciousness created by the affinity of economic interest makes them a community of interests, the bonds of which are more enduring and give rise to class struggles. The existence of a class war is, therefore, nothing new. "The history of all hitherto existing society is the history of class struggles." For a historian, history is warfare between nations, but for Marx it is a revolutionary struggle between classes. In these struggles the fight "each time ended either in a revolutionary reconstitution of society at large, or in the common ruin of the contending classes." All social changes appeared to Marx to have been determined chiefly by economic class struggle and the history of humanity was the history of class conflict. Every system of production, he says, has given rise to two opposing economic classes—the exploiters and the exploited, the owners and the toilers. "Free man and slave, partician and plebian, baron and serf, guildmaster and journeyman, in one word, oppressor and oppressed, standing constantly in opposition to each other carried on an uninterrupted warfare, now open, now concealed."

Society is dynamic; it changes and evolves. The capitalist society must, as a result of this evolution, ultimately pass away and be succeeded by another. The capitalist and the system of capitalism generate seeds of their own destruction. For some time the proletariat would continue toiling, fretting and fuming till ultimately they become desperate and unite to overthrow the capitalist class. Revolution follows, as a result of which the proletariat seizes power. This sequence is inevitable and invariable and can end in no other way. The dictatorship of the proletariat is bound to come and when it comes, it takes complete control over the economic functions of society by expropriating the private capitalist and by appropriating the means of production. Society, thus, passes into the socialistic stage through a revolution determined by the natural laws of evolution.

Socialism is a result determined by the inherent laws of social evolution, independent of the will and purpose of individual men. "All that the most powerful and clearsighted intellect can do is to learn to divine the laws of the great movement of society and to shorten and alleviate the birth pangs of the new era. The efforts of reactionaries to turn the wheel of history backwards are in vain."

The Socialist society which emerges from the proletarian revolution will be a classless society. All land and capital shall be owned in common, exploitation will cease, the tyranny of the owners of wealth will no longer be possible, and all men will be free. The *Communist Manifesto* ends with an appeal to the wage-earners to rise on behalf of Communism. "The Communists disdain to conceal their views and aims. They openly declare that their end can be attained only by the forcible overthrow of all existing social conditions. Let the ruling classes tremble at a Communist revolution. The proletarians have nothing to lose but their chains. They have a world to win. Working men of all countries unite."

But here emerges the great difference. Are the class war and the consequent rise of the proletariat inevitable? Can the desired social transformation be brought about by violent and catastrophic changes or will it come into being by the slow process of natural growth? Two different answers to these questions have given rise to the schools of revolutionary and evolutionary socialism. The latter is essentially the product of Great Britain.

The evolutionary school of socialism emphasises the biological aspect of Marx's thesis. Society, they argue, is the product of and is subject to evolution. It is an organism, a living structure and, like any other living structure, may grow or decay. Growth and decay are slow processes; "they may be detected by human intelligence and even assisted and accelerated by human effort, but they cannot be reversed or brought to a standstill, nor can they be speeded up into abrupt and catastrophic changes."[4] The path of progress consists, therefore, "in a series of reforms designed to assist the gradual movement of society towards the next transformation, a transformation which will consist rather in the sum total of these reforms than in any abrupt change of structure consequent upon them."[5] This school of evolutionary socialism is known also as collectivists or State Socialists.

COLLECTIVISM

What is Collectivism. Collectivism or State Socialism is one of the varieties of Socialism. It is a reaction against the extreme Individualism of the nineteenth century and refers to that school of thought which regards the State as a positive good and holds that its mission is to promote the common economic, moral and intellectual interests of the people as a whole. The central idea underlying Collectivism is that if the mass of the people are to rise above the level of wage slaves, they will have to be protected against the evils of free competition by a greater measure of interference with and regulation of industry by government as a representative of the community with a view that ultimately all means of production and distribution are collectively owned. "A socialist," Professor Ely says, "is one who looks to society organised in the state for aid in bringing about a more perfect distribution of economic goods and an elevation of humanity."

Collectivism Analysed. According to the Collectivists, the existing political organisation discloses several defects. It assures the happiness and comfort of the few and suffering of the many. The fate of the masses is their poverty in plenty. "It is always tragic," remarks Mrs. Barbara Wootan, "to starve and to be desperately poor or to have nothing to do. But to starve in the midst of plenty is ridiculous as well as tragic and to starve because of plenty is more ridiculous still. Equally it is ridiculous to have nothing to do when there are things which evidently require to be done and when plants and materials necessary for doing them are waiting to be used." And, then, it secures apparently political freedom for all. Without securing to them economic freedom. Without economic freedom the submerged masses remain just as submerged as before. They are held in bondage by sacred individual rights, because, as Maxey says, "economic overlords

4. Joad, C.E.M., *Modern Political Theory*, p. 45.
5. *Ibid.*, p. 46.

displayed an odious ability to gain control of political authority and use it to fortify their liberty of ruthless exploitation."

It is this order of society which the Collectivists are out to reverse. They demand that the power and authority of the State should be used to limit the free exercise of the sacred right of contract, the sacred right of property, and other hallowed concepts of the eighteenth century. For them the body-politic is an organism and the State is the best medium through which exploitation, degradation and starvation of the masses can be removed and equality of opportunity provided to all. "In any society," Lindsey says, "political organisation is necessary because common action is necessary to repair the disorganization caused by the fact that men act independently and yet affect one another by such action." The Collectivists, thus, believe in the necessity of the State and regard it as a supreme and positive good, an instrument which provides conditions of social welfare ensuring social justice.

The new social order which the Collectivists envisage is not to be brought about by catastrophic or revolutionary methods. The transformation of society is to be slow, gradual and peaceful. Society, they urge, should be permeated with socialistic ideas through education and propaganda. Those who subscribe to the creed of Socialism should be returned to the legislatures and public opinion should urge the adoption of legislative and administrative measures embodying socialistic objectives. When majority of the socialists is secured in the representative assemblies, then, they would be able to establish the control by the community of the instruments of production and distribution. The Socialists believe in the ultimate readiness of the possessing class, the capitalists, to yield, both because of the justice of the workers' claim and because of their inability to resist with any hope of success the overwhelming predominance of numbers.

The Collectivists would achieve their objective:

1. by abolishing private ownership of the means of production and consequently to bring important industries and services under public ownership and control;
2. industry to be carried on for the purpose of ministering to the needs of the community, and not with the object of making profits for individuals. The quality and quantity of the commodities produced is to be determined by considerations of social need; and
3. the motive of social service to be substituted for incentive of private profit.

There is, thus, a sharp difference between the Collectivists or State Socialists and the Scientific Socialists, the disciples of Karl Marx, or the Communists. The State Socialists are opposed to revolution as a means of attaining social democracy whereas Marx had advocated it as the only alternative for overthrowing capitalism. They also view with alarm the Dictatorship of the Proletariat because force is its *raison d'etre*. It is to be invested with oppressive and autocratic powers in order to destroy capitalism and construct socialism. When force becomes the criterion of political authority, it makes no difference whether it is the dictatorship of the proletariat or dictatorship of the individual. Collectivism appeals to reason and its instruments are education and propaganda. It aims at a slow, gradual and peaceful transformation of society. While the State Socialists have confidence in the State as a matter of principle, the Scientific Socialists accept it only as a transitory phase which will "wither away" when capitalism is destroyed completely. Finally, the State Socialists do not subscribe to the theory of worldwide revolution. They believe that it is by constitutional means that the ultimate goal of social democracy can be attained in all lands.

Arguments in Favour of Collectivist Control. The Collectivists argue that nationalisation of industry is the only effective method of replacing the capitalist system. It ends competition, the primary source of all economic and social evils. Surplus value is the beginning, middle, and end of capitalism. It is the surplus value which the capitalist appropriates and it is the keynote of the social tyranny. Socialisation of industries enables the State to appropriate surplus value and socially created values and consequently bring the downfall of capitalism.

The Collectivists deny the individual's right to the ownership of the free gifts of nature, like land and mines. These are limited in supply and if they are left to the individual he would exploit them for self-interest sacrificing national interests and for his immediate gain jeopardising the future social interests. It is not even distributive justice, the Collectivists urge, that the few should appropriate the free gifts of nature to the detriment of the predominating majority. Justice demands that they should be owned by the State on behalf of the community and exploited for the benefit of the community.

State management of industries, the Collectivists maintain, makes available to society those goods and services which are socially needed, but for which there does not exist sufficient demand. Moreover, Socialism aims at substituting the motive of social service for the motive of private profit. In a capitalist society, they assert, every individual is a competitor inspired by his own self-interest without any regard to the interest of others. This mad competitive race degenerates man and demoralises society. But the elimination of competition and private ownership of the means of production would bring about a psychological change in the outlook of the people. Their incentive will be social service and social welfare. A Socialist government will, accordingly, be incorruptible. There will be no temptation to enrich an individual self. The finer side of human nature is stimulated and the best self of man guides the individual and society.

Socialism, the Collectivists urge, is the complement of democracy. Democracy, they emphasise, is a sham if there is no equality in the distribution of wealth and opportunity. More than three-quarters of a century ago Matthew Arnold wrote, "The one insuperable objection to inequality is the same as the one insuperable objection to absolutism: namely, that inequality, like absolutism, thwarts a vital instinct and being thus against nature is against humanization. On the one side inequality harms by pampering; on the other by vulgarizing and depressing. A system founded on it is against nature, and in the long run breaks down." The demand for equality is the basis of Socialism. It holds that liberty is not worth having without the security equality provides. Socialists, accordingly, argue that economic democracy must precede political democracy. The Collectivists stand to realize this social transformation through the agency of a democratic State.

Not merely is capitalism accused of being unjust in its distribution of rewards for work, not only does it fail to give that security which is the distinguishing mark of an efficient economic system, but it is callous in its disregard of human happiness. It produces ugly articles under ugly conditions. A sudden unprecedented decline in arts coincided with the introduction of machinery, division of labour, standardization and mass production. All these factors stifled the instincts of the craftsmen to take pride in their work. When a worker has nothing to do but to turn a handle as the needle points in a certain direction, he cannot be expected to take an interest in what he produces. And when he is condemned to live in a slum for his pains, or to stand at a street corner for weeks on end because his labour is not needed, no wonder he feels frustrated and revolts against the existing order. Under the conditions of modern industry the workman ceases to be a human being, he becomes a mere cog in the machine. It is this danger of creating a society in which "wealth accumulates and men decay", that the Collectivists are determined to reverse and substitute in its place a social order in which shall prevail justice and happiness.

FABIANISM

Origin and Meaning of Fabianism. The principles of the Fabian Society form the basis of British Socialism. In January, 1884, a band of young reformers in Britain (prominent among them were Sidney Webb, George Bernard Shaw, Sydney Oliver, Graham Wallas, Mrs. Annie Besant, Headlam, Pease and, for a short time, H.G. Wells) founded the Fabian Society with a view to spreading Socialism and to persuade the national and local governments of Britain to put the doctrine gradually into practical operation. The Society adopted the name Fabian after Fabius (nicknamed Cuncta or delayer), the Roman General, whose tactics they defined: "For the right moment you must wait, as Fabius did patiently when warring against Hannibal, though many censured his delays: but when the time comes you must strike hard, as Fabius did, or your waiting will be in vain, and fruitless."

The Fabians in Britain were to adopt the methods of the Roman General for the achievement of their goal of Socialism. The Fabian Society did not direct its appeal to any particular class, but to men and women of all classes who saw the evils of capitalist society and desired their removal. It endeavoured to rouse social compunction by making the public conscious of the evil condition of society under the capitalist system. The Fabians were not revolutionary Socialists and they did not outright condemn capitalism or identified it with "exploitation." They were empirical in their outlook and their methods aimed to change the social structure by a slow and gradual process through the agency of a democratic State and by constitutional means. "The Fabians," Bernard Shaw said, "agreed to give up the delightful ease of revolutionary theories and to take to the hard work of practical reform on ordinary parliamentary lines."

Programme of the Fabians. The Fabians are not the followers of Karl Marx and they reject his doctrines of materialistic conception of history and of economic determinism. Nor do they believe in the inevitable, automatic and scientific process by which a social revolution would come of its own accord. They were influenced particularly by the doctrines of Henry George, the various British interpretations of Karl Marx, the developing of Collectivism in John Stuart Mill's exposition of his individualist doctrines, and the implications in the philosophy of T.H. Green. They were struck with the obvious fact of the existence of poverty among the masses and the concentration of land and industry in the hands of a few landowners and industrialists deriving huge fortunes without any effort on their part. In a manifesto, prepared by Shaw and adopted by the Fabian Society in September, 1884, is contained its policy and programme. The manifesto said:

1. "It therefore aims at the reorganisation of society by the emancipation of land and industrial capital from individual and class ownership, and the vesting of them in the community for the general benefit. In this way only the natural and acquired advantages of the country be equitably shared by the whole people."

2. "The society accordingly works for the extinction of private property in land and of the consequent individual appropriation, in the form of rent, of the price paid for permission to use the earth, as well as for the advantages of the superior soils and sites." The Fabians argued that the rent for the "unearned increment in the value of land is no right of the landlord. It is society's need of land which has made it valuable and consequently increased its rent. This, to begin with, should be transferred from the landlord to the community. The possessors of the more fertile land or land in a superior location derive huge incomes solely by virtue of possession and not by virtue of service."

3. "The society, further, works for the transfer to the community of the administration of such industrial capital as can conveniently be managed socially. For, owing to the monopoly of the means of production in the past, industrial inventions and the transformation of surplus income into capital have mainly enriched the proprietary class, the worker being now dependent on that class for leave to earn a living."

4. "If these measures be carried out, without compensation (though not without such relief to expropriated individuals as may seem fit to the community), rent and interest will be added to the reward of labour, the idle class now living on the labour of others will necessarily disappear, and practical equality of opportunity will be maintained by spontaneous action of economic forces with much less interference with personal liberty than the present system entails."

5. "For the attainment of these ends the Fabian Society looks to the spread of socialist opinion, and the social and political changes consequent thereon, including the establishment of equal citizenship for men and women. It seeks to achieve these ends by the general dissemination of knowledge as to the relation between the individual and society in its economic, ethical, and political aspects."

Fabianism is, thus, based upon the actual experience of the pitiable plight of the masses and the degrading lot to which they are subjected rather than on any well defined theory of Socialism. It is concerned with a more just distribution of income and the reconstitution of society in such a manner as to secure the general welfare and happiness. The Fabians reject the thesis of Marx that there is a perpetual conflict or class war between those who work for wages and those who employ wage-workers. Ramsay MacDonald declared in 1893, "The watchword of Socialism is not class-consciousness, but community-consciousness." The conflict is between the community, on the one hand, and those who grow rich through investments, on the other. "The individuals or class who possess social power have at all times, consciously or unconsciously, made use of that power in such a way as to leave the great majority of the fellows practically nothing beyond the means of subsistence according to the current living standard. The additional product, determined by the relative differences in productive efficiency of the different sites, soils, capitals, and forms of skill above the margin of cultivation, has gone to those exercising control over these valuable but scarce factors. This struggle to secure surplus of 'economic rent' is the key to the confused history of European progress and the underlying unconscious motive of all revolutions."[6]

The object of Socialism, as the Fabians thought, is to obtain for all members of the society the values which society creates. This object is to be achieved by gradually transferring land and industrial capital to the community. But such a transformation does not involve a violent change. A catastrophic change is foreign to the Fabian creed. Any kind of violent change, even if necessitated by the stress of circumstances, would fail to achieve the desired results, the Fabians assert. Barker convincingly sums up the object of Fabianism: "Resolved to permeate all classes it has not preached class antagonism .... Resolved gradually to permeate it has not been revolutionary, it has relied on the slow growth of opinion."[7]

For the Fabians the State must be fully representative of the community, if it could be "trusted with the rent of the country, and finally with the land, the capital and the organisation of the national industry." They regard the State, with a perfected machinery, the representative and trustee of the people, "their guardian, their men of business, their manager, their Secretary, even their stock-holder." They believe that the existing State could be made without radical transformation "if not absolutely perfect, at least trust-worthy." And to make it so the immediate reforms the Fabians advocated were: broadening of the suffrage, a better trained civil service, and provision for equal educational opportunities for all. They also advocated democratization of the source of power and consequently decentralization of authority and making local bodies the vital centres of governmental activities. It was, as such, proposed that the House of Commons might deal with national problems alone, leaving local questions to the jurisdiction of the municipalities so that the House became "merely the organ of federated municipalities." Decentralization, therefore, was with the Fabians, a prerequisite of Socialism. Bernard Shaw beautifully stated: "A democratic state cannot be a social democratic state unless it has in every centre of the population a local governing body as thoroughly democratic in constitution as the central parliament." [8]

The object of the Fabians was to persuade the British nation to make their political constitution thoroughly democratic, and to socialise their industries so as to make the livelihood of the people entirely independent of capitalism. The Fabian society enjoined upon its members that, instead of keeping aloof from other bodies, they should join them and premeate them with Fabian ideas. "Almost all organisations," according to their belief, "contained elements making for socialism." The Fabian Society, to sum up, was constitutional in its attitude, and its methods were the same familar and usual methods of political life in Britain. It stood for democracy, which meant simply the control of administration by freely elected representatives of the people. Socialism, as understood by the Fabians, meant the organisation and conduct of the necessary industries of the

6. "English Progress Towards Social Democracy ", *Fabian Tract* as quoted in Coker, *op cit.* p.150.
7. Barker, E., *Political Thought in England* (*1848 - 1914*), p. 194.
8. Shaw, B., *Essay in Fabian Socialism,* p. 47.

country, and appropriation of all forms of economic rent of land and capital by the nation as a whole, through the most suitable public authorities, parochial, municipal, provincial or central.

The great merit of Fabianism lies in the concrete plans wbich it devised "for diffusing more equitably the advantages of modern industrial civilisation by raising the economic and civic status of wage-earners and paring down the fortunes of property-owners." They worked out definite and attractive schemes for immediate application like: (1) "Social Legislation" embracing shorter hours of work, security against unemployment, minimum national wages, minimum standards for health and safety, improved educational facilities, etc., (2) public ownership, national or municipal, of public utilities and natural monopolies; and (3) taxation of inheritances, ground rents and investment incomes.

There had been a deep affinity between the Fabian Society and the Labour Party in Britain since World War I. In fact, the Fabian Society was the intellectual backbone of the Labour Party. Five members of the society, including two authors—Sidney Webb (later Lord Passifield) and Sydney Oliver—of the original Fabian Essays, were members of the first British Labour Government in 1924. Webb was also Secretary of State for the Dominions and for Colonies in the second Labour Government in 1928. The society is extinct now.

SYNDICALISM

Syndicalism Explained. Two schools of Socialists, the Syndicalists and the Guild Socialists, directed their attack upon the Collectivist State, the former in the late nineteenth century and the latter in the first decade of the twentieth century. Syndicalism, which originated in France, is, according to Sorel, "revisionism of the left" whereas Guild Socialism is in origin a purely English theory. The word Syndicalism is derived from *syndicat*, the ordinary French term for a labour union. It may be defined "as that form of social theory which regards the Trade Union organisations as at once the foundation of the new society and the instrument whereby it is brought into being." The important exponents of Syndicalism are Georges Sorel and Fernand Pelloutier.

The Syndicalists accept the general Marxian thesis that society is divided into two opposing classes, the employers and the employees, whose interests are conflicting. The modern State, they hold, is a class State dominated by the capitalists. They also accept the doctrine of class struggle as a fundamental characteristic of the capitalist society and regard the institution of private property as the root cause of all social evils. The State, the Syndicalists maintain, prepetuates the interests of capitalists and it should be eradicated forthwith. But they reject the Marxian idea that the workers could use the State, through the dictatorship of the proletariat, to accomplish their purpose. The Syndicalists, in fact, had a deep antagonism for the State in any of its form and rejected it outright. In its place, they proposed a society organised into trade unions or *syndicats*. They suggested that most problems could be solved by local *syndicats*, and that a national system of *syndicat* affiliations could administer affairs which transcended the local level. Syndicalism, thus, aimed to abolish private ownership of capital and to substitute it by collective capital owned by the community. It was to be a producers' commonwealth in which industries governed themselves. Instead of a political State there was to be a coordinating body elected out of the *syndicats*. To achieve their end the Syndicalists advocated a programme of direct action, including the use of violence.

Syndicalism is genuinely a working class movement guided and controlled by the workers themselves through the trade unions. The Syndicalists have a deep distrust of the middle class Socialism. They claim to be the "only school of Socialist doctrine which is the product of the workers themselves; all other forms of Socialism have emanated from the brains of clever middle-class theorists, and betray their origin. They show a tendency to regiment the workers in conformity with some pre-arranged system of society which was deemed good to a clique of intellectuals," who are out of touch with the workers and their needs. It is the workers alone, they assert, who can really and adequately express their needs. "The importance of keeping alive an intense class consciousness further forbids any *rapprochement* between the workers and the intellectuals of the middle-class, even when the latter are favourably disposed, as inimical to revolutionary ardour."

Socialism, they further urge, involves nationalisation, which would preserve, and, indeed, add to the hierarchy of officials who control and manage business or industry, and the real emancipation of the wage-earner would be as far off as ever. Moreover, in order to achieve nationalisation or even to work towards that end, the Socialist forces have been obliged to organise themselves into a political party. Any political party, the Syndicalists maintain, which participates in parliamentary action is bound to make compromises and follow the principle of give and take, thereby softening down the rigour of its revolutionary principles. A political party, they further argue, is a much less efficient instrument of action than a "class." The cause of the workers can best be served, if they organise themselves into independent, self-governing unions of producers, keep alive class-consciousness in its keenest and most uncompromising forms and bring the battle to its triumphant goal, the General Strike. The General Strike is not to bring some concessions. It is to be a proletarian general strike led by the workers for the revolutionary end of the reconstruction of society. "The task of revolution," as Pelloutier said, "is to free mankind not only from all authority but also from every institution which has not for its essential the development of production." All authority in the economic and industrial sphere will flow to the workers in a stateless society established after the revolution.

Hostility against the State. The Syndicalists regard the State as essentially a bourgeois or middle-class institution whose main task is to defend and safeguard the interests of this class. They endorse the Marxian condemnation of the State as an instrument of capitalist exploitation. The State will retain its character, the Syndicalists argue, whatever be the form of the social organisation in which it exists. Just as a leopard cannot change his spots, so the State cannot change its bourgeois character. It is asserted that service under the State makes men bureaucratic and unsympathetic to the needs and aspirations of the workers, who are engaged in the actual work of production. A governmental organisation with its concentrated authority promotes uniformity and routine, breeds narrowness, saps imagination, and distrusts local development and enterprise. Even a benevolent State, the Syndicalists maintain, would, if left in control of industry, be inimical to progress. For it cannot know, nor does it care to know, what exactly the needs and aspirations of the workers are. It is only the workers themselves and they alone who know what they actually need and how their needs may be precisely met.

Moreover, the State represents the consumers of labour only and not the producers of value. The authority and power of the State is the power of the consumers of labour, the employers. The State which safeguards the interests of the consumers cannot and would not be the guardian of the producers. By abolishing the State, the Syndicalists aim at installing labour in the position of authority. They demand the organisation of each industry under the workers of that industry. Finally, the Syndicalists attack the very basis of the State as it embodies an impossible ideal of social unity. Society, they argue, is essentially pluralistic and no political constitution can make it otherwise. In this way the doctrines of Syndicalism have been drawn from Marxian Socialism, Anarchism and Pluralism.

Syndicalist Structure of Society. Regarding the structure of the Syndicalist Society there is vagueness. The Syndicalists are more concerned with the methods of getting rid of the existing structure of society than with the ways of social affairs after the success of their movement. They do not, indeed, consider it worth their while to work out the future organisation of society. Their widespread belief is that the new social organisation will develop automatically when workers assume control of the factors of production and private capital is replaced by the collective capital. Sorel and Berth have maintained that "any attempt to depict the details to the future order would dispel those visionary institutions in which lay the chief power of Syndicalism." Syndicalism offers, therefore, a policy of revolution not of administration.

The only attempt to set forth fully the organisation of the future syndicalist society is found in the book of Pataud and Pouget, *Syndicalism and Cooperative Commonwealth: How We Shall Bring About the Revolution*. According to the "somewhat romantic prophecy" of the joint authors of this book, the Syndicalist revolution will be followed by the permanent, constructive tasks of Syndicalism. For these tasks the existmg syndical associations, for the most part, be sufficient. Ordinary functions of management will rest with the local industrial unions. These unions will have possession of buildings, machinery, and equipment in the several industries and will exercise immediate direction of production and execution of policy. The national services, like post offices, railways, highways, etc., will be assigned to the national federations of workers. There will be other national federations to supply technical information and expert advice to the local bodies. Finally, there will be a national body, like the existing C.G.T. (*Confederation Generale du Travail*), entrusted with the function of deciding matters that demand uniform treatment all over, such as, the determination of wages, the length of normal hours of work, the care of children, the old, and sick.[9]

The authors of the scheme recognise the necessity of certain disciplinary sanctions against the anti-human and anti-social acts of the members of the Syndicalist society. But these sanctions will be of a distinctive kind as compared with the coercive authority of the State. Each union will pass judgment upon any of its offending members. It may decree a moral punishment, like the boycott or in extreme cases the guilty person may

9. Coker, F.W., *Recent Political Thought,* p. 243.

be remanded to a general meeting of the unions where a sentence of banishment may be imposed. More heinous "offences will be spontaneously dealt with through acts of summary justice inflicted by eye-witnesses. Prisons and court-houses will, however, be abolished, for crimes will decrease in number because there will no longer be any occasions for anti-social acts caused by misery, inequality, or the evil deeds of capitalism; and the better social environment will tend to eliminate the offences that result from physiological defects and mental disease."[10]

The necessity of proper defence against any contingency of foreign aggression is duly admitted. Syndicslist policy, they explain, is not "the resignation and non-resistance preached by Tolstoy."[11] But the defence arrangements will differ fundamentally from those existing in the modern States. There will neither be any paid army nor offensive armaments. In each union of the Syndicalist society there will be an armed militia equipped with purely defensive arms."[12]

As already said, most Syndicalist writers regard any comprehensive picture of the future organisation of society as futile and an untimely attempt. But it will be a Stateless society with its characteristic feature of extreme decentralization. Local workers will form syndicates according to their trades and these syndicates would perform local police and judicial services. National federations of syndicates would collectively own the capital of society.

A pertinent question arises here. Are the syndicates competent by themselves to take over the organisation and control of so elaborate a concern as is a modern industry? It is really utopian to expect that a catastrophic revolution, following a successful General Strike, would find the syndicate fit to assume the great responsibilities which would be placed upon them. But Lagardelle makes the prophecy that "all the noble feelings which patriotism calls forth—heroism, self-sacrifice and unflinching obedience—the qualities which form the eternal foundations of life—will not cease to exist but, on the contrary, will continue to grow in the soul of the workers who are filled with the revolutionary spirit."

Methods of Syndicalism. The Syndicalists advocate direct methods of action to rouse the revolutionary spirit in the workers in order to bring about the desired changes in society. They are distrustful of constitutional methods, because of their bias against the State. For success in achieving their mission, they insist on the intensification of class consciousness till the time of General Strike when the "halt" of the capitalistic system will come. This is to be done through trade unions. The Syndicalists believe that workmen are imbued with a greater sense of solidarity in the industrial sphere than their cohesion as exhibited in political life. They deprecate political parties. A political party "is a poor revolutionary weapon; it is dispersed, it meets rarely, and it is apt to be too large to afford a direct expression of the common will."[13]

10. *Ibid.*, p. 244.
11. Joad, C.E.M., *Introduction to Modern Political Theory*, p. 69.
12. *Ibid.*
13. *Ibid.*

The Syndicalists would establish a network of efficient organisation of the trade unions by crafts and industries and charged with the duty of pursuing programme of continued agitation for better wages and shorter hours of work. Such an agitation makes the workers conscious of their exploitation. The workers would also be required to go on occasional strikes to keep up enthusiasm and discipline in their ranks and infuse in them a sense of solidarity. Any kind of strike, it is maintained, whether local or national, successful or partially successful, is important and vital in preparing the workers to be ready for the General Strike. Strikes are, the Syndicalists emphasise, a part of the general revolutionary movement, daily acts of revolutionary practice, and from them will evolve in time a complete Revolution. "Every strike", as Cole remarks, "is more or less general, and the same conception embraces them all: from the petty strike in a single workshop to the local, regional, national and international general strikes, all are touched with something of the glamour which attaches to the one great 'Social General Strike', in which is envisaged the complete overthrow of capitalist society."

The General Strike may not be a strike of all the workers in a country. By General Strike the Syndicalists mean a strike on the part of the sufficiently large number of workers employed in the key industries which may paralyse the whole economic life of the country and bring the capitalist system to an end. To be ready for the General Strike, it is essential that the workers must carry out a policy of perpetual offence by adopting methods of sabotage, boycott, the label and *ca'canny* practices. Through all such methods of direct action the proletariat expresses its will to conquer. The Syndicalists, thus, believe in the principles of violence in policies and Georges Sorel was one of the leading exponents.

Difference between Syndicalism and Socialism. The chief difference between Syndicalism and Socialism lies in the insistence of the former on entrusting the control of industry to the producers, *i.e.*, workers. The Socialists, on the other hand, will vest this control in the State which is the repository of the interests of the producers as well as the consumers. Secondly, Syndicalists hold that the workers, as producers, should exercise control not only in the industrial sphere bat also, in the political sphere. Their object is to create a stateless society. The functions of the State are to be taken over by *syndicats* of producers organised on a vocational basis. The Socialists will continue with the State, as they deem it a positive good and "the representative and trustee of the people." Thirdly, Socialism aims to end capitalism, because the institution of private property and the policy of *laissez faire* are detrimental to the good of society as a whole. Its object is not the good of a particular class, but the happiness of all. Syndicalism champions the cause of a particular class, the producers of values, that is, workers. In this respect, Syndicalism certainly tries to do what Socialism tries to avoid. The workers will dominate the Syndicalist Society. Max Nordau remarks, "that though Syndicalism may be said to arise out of Socialism, Syndicalism is the very antithesis of Socialism."[14] Fourthly, Socialism begins with its own philosophy and ideas and develops the socialistic organisation in the light of those ideas. Syndicalism, on the contrary, begins with the existing organisation of trade unions and develops ideas appropriate to it. Fifthly, Socialism

14. Quoted in *Socialism, Its Promise and Failure, op. cit.*, p. 4.

has an appeal to general public opinion, but Syndicalism has an appeal to the opinion of the workers only. Finally, the methods of Socialism are constitutional. The methods of Syndicalism are direct and revolutionary. It endeavours to paralyse administration both politically and industrially. Bertrand Russel calls Syndicalism as "Organized Anarchy."

To sum up, the Syndicalist movement is pre-eminently revolutionary; the socialist movement is reformist. Syndicalism puts itself deliberately outside the present system of society in order to get hold of it firmly and to shake it to its very foundation, whereas Socialism works within the present order of society with the view of gradually changing it. The Syndicalist knows of no compromise; class warfare, relentless and continual, is its supreme means. Sorel firmly believed that revolutionary energy is created by a conception of the supreme conflict. Thus, Syndicalism is the very antithesis of Socialism.

Criticism of Syndicalism. The idea of the Syndicalist society has been left vague and hazy. There is a reason behind it. But no political movement can appeal vigorously unless its goal is definitely defined. Syndicalism aims at entrusting the industrial and political control to the workers as producers. Then, how to safeguard the interests of the consumers? There is no guarantee that the producers of value, once saddled with power and authority, may not abuse their authority in the same manner as the consumers have abused it.

Serious objection may also be taken of the methods of direct action advocated by the Syndicalists. Strike, sabotage and *ca'canny* methods disturb the orderly character of society and create a vicious social and moral effect. It has been rightly said that "a general strike is unnecessary, because a general election is never far off." Constitutional methods which bear the impress of public opinion are more eduring, with stablising effects, than revolutionary methods intended to topsy-turvy the existing order of society, and with no certain result. Advocates of sabotage justify it as a part of class war against the capitalist, but in its more violent forms "it is cruel and probably inexpedient, while even in its milder form it must tend to encourage slovenly habits of work, which might easily persist under the new regime that the Syndicalists wish to introduce."[15] Habits seldom die with the people. Doubts are also entertained on the efficacy of strikes. Unsuccessful strikes demoralise the workers instead of intensifying class consciousness. Moreover, in the strike the working class, which has no surplus to rely upon during the period of the strike, are likely to starve before achieving their object. Many orthodox Marxians attack Syndicalism as being in essence anarchical. And so it is.

The "New Syndicalism" in France. World War I and post-war conditions produced a radical change in the character and policy of organised Syndicalism in France. Soon after the War began, a majority of the members of the General Confederation of Labour abandoned anti-militarism and anti-statism, joined the Socialists in entering into a truce with the government and cooperated actively in the various economic arrangements for furthering the successful conduct of the War. The post-War economic and social troubles in the country created further cleavages between the moderate nationalistic majority and the militant minority in the Confederation. The differences became so pronounced that

15. Bertrand Russel, *Roads of Freedom*, p. 79.

the two groups finally separated in 1922, and the militant minority formed a new organisation: The General Confederation of United Labour (the C.G.T.U.—*Confederation Generale du Travail Unitaire*). This new organisation adopted the revolutionary doctrines of the Communist International, while the older organisation—G.G.T.—renounced all its revolutionary tactics.

The policies and methods of the new Syndicalism have been well elaborated in various articles and addresses by Jouhaux, Perrot and others. A comprehensive exposition of the philosophy of the new movement comes from Maxime Leroy. The workers are enjoined to abandon their narrow conception of class war and concentrate upon all those processes of inter-group collaboration that proved effective in war time. "Workers can now safely admit that production is not simply a matter of hand labour, that the whole process involves administration, invention, research, artistic craftsmanship, distribution, and even use and consumption. The production of any basic commodity or service demands a coordination among manual labourers, technicians, managers, artists, scientists, carriers, purveyors, users—all vitally concerned in the quality, quantity and price of that utility."[16] The new Syndicalism is, accordingly, a philosophy of coordination and cooperation of all interests concerned directly and indirectly in the act of production and the consumers within the framework of the State. The presence of the State will be necessary for the supervision and cooperation of the activities of the different unions. The State will, according to Leroy, become "through all its laws and in all its services, an impulse to initiative, invention and economic heresy, with the same zeal with which the traditional state restrains spontaneity and innovation. It will endeavour to guide rather than restrain; its legislation will become more and more a means of enlightenment rather than dictation."[17]

The new Syndicalists will also need the State to maintain military defence and conduct foreign intercourse. The coercive power of the State will be, of course, reduced to the minimum with the modification in its functions. The new Syndicalists, adhering to a positive and comprehensive programme, condemn violence of any kind. There is, they say, "nothing proletarian about violence, it has been the weapon of malcontents of all ages and was inherited by proletarians from the bourgeois insurrectionary parties of the eighteenth and nineteenth centuries."[18] The new syndicalism is, thus, in some respects a return to the ideas of Waldeck-Rousseau and his associates some eight decades ago.

GUILD SOCIALISM

Rise of Guild Socialism. Guild Socialism, which had its birth in Britain, is described as "the intellectual child of English Fabianism and French Syndicalism"[19] Fabianism, which embodied the principles of Collectivism, failed to have appeal for many Englishmen. They maintained that Collectivism did not remove the evils of capitalism, but merely replaced the capitalist bureaucracy by the centralised bureaucracy of the State. Nor did

16. As cited in F.W. Coker's *Recent Political Thought,* p. 253.
17. *Ibid.*
18. *Ibid* p. 254.
19. Rockow, *Contemporary Political Thought in England,* p. 150.

it give the worker the power to determine his own conditions of work. Syndicalism, though a working-men movement, did not suit the British temperament. It was too revolutionary and anarchical. The ideas of a catastrophic change and a stateless society were foreign to the mentality of the British citizens trained in the machinery of democratic politics. The British Socialists, who did not believe with the Fabians, adopted a via media between traditional Collectivism and traditional Syndicalism. Something was taken from the Collectivists and with the fundamentals of Syndicalism a new doctrine was evolved known as Guild Socialism. To the Guild Socialists the trade unions represented the germs of the future organisation of industry. The trade union, they argued, should do for modern industry what the Guild did for the medieval arts and crafts. Guild Socialism, accordingly, aims at placing authority in the hands of democracies of producers and democracies of consumers within the framework of the State.

In its original form the doctrine of Guild Socialism was first expounded by British intellectuals in the first and second decades of the present century. Its basic ideas appeared in a book, *The Restoration of the Guild System* by A.J. Penty, published in 1906. In this book Penty advocated a return to the medieval "principle of self-government in industry, whereby craftsman who was a member of an autonomous Guild owned the instruments with which he worked, and determined the nature and extent of his production." Penty's arguments were based partly on sentimental, partly on aesthetic grounds and were actuated throughout by hostility against the modern methods of large-scale production and trading. His proposals of organising industry on the basis of the independent craftsman, however, did not seem practical and were characterised as "the Utopian phase of Guild Socialist propaganda.

The movement soon became popular and its adherents swelled. Guild Socialism assumed a more practical form at the hands of S.G. Hobson and A.R. Orage. They, too, advocated the revival of the medieval Guild system, but at the same time, they realised that modern conditions required some fundamental modifications in order to fit the doctrine with the system of large-scale production. They asserted that the Guild idea should be adopted to modern conditions on the basis of the existing Trade Union organization. Their plea was for self-government in industry by the workers concerned in the industry, grouped together in a system of industrial Guilds, of which the existing Trade Unions would form the germ. G.D.H. Cole was the chief active philosophic apostle of this new movement.

Cole was originally a Fabian and was actively associated with the organisation of the Society's Research Department. All through his stay in the Society, Cole had been persuading his fellow members that they should abandon their affiliations with the political labourites and the liberals. But he failed. Then, the War came. The enormous increase in the powers of the State gave him a rude shock. He came to the conclusion that the omnipotence of the State could not be the road to the Millennium. By this time he had become a sympathetic student of French Syndicalism. It had a considerable appeal for him and accepting William Morris as his patron saint, he began to advocate the restoration of the medieval society of societies. He favoured a federal structure for the State and emphasized that the State does not embody within it the whole society. In a more than dozen books and pamphelts, Cole amplified the critical and constructive ideas of

Guild Socialism and, thus, became "the best known and most influential figure in the movement."

Guild Socialism Analysed. The Guild Socialists opposed, as had Marx, the dehumanizing work involved in large-scale production with its division of labour. They accepted the labour theory of value and the theory of surplus value, although in modified form, and they maintained that property was justified only when it rendered a service to society. They did not object to political democracy; but they argued that a government by representatives elected on a territorial basis was incapable of understanding and solving the complex problems of an industrial society. The Guild Socialists maintained that a system of functional representation based upon industrial unions would be best suited to a modern community. They advocated the retention of the State, but thought that its functions could be greatly restricted, when the unions, or guilds, assumed responsibility for government in matters primarily related to the economy. The Guild Socialists were as opposed to revolution as were the Fabians.

According to the Fabians capitalism entailed the poverty of the masses whereas according to the Guild Socialists capitalism entailed the slavery of the masses and this they attributed to two causes: (i) the wage system, and (ii) the method of representation The Guild Socialists aimed to free the masses from the shackles of slavery by making work better paid and by making it in itself more interesting and more democratic in organisation.

The Guild Socialists condemned the wage system and pleaded emphatically for its abolition. Here they agreed with Marxian theory of surplus value and advanced the argument that surplus value was the legitimate share of the worker. But it was not only the surplus value accruing to the employer which the Guild Socialists condemned. In the capitalist society, the workers in return for wages were expected and asked to surrender all control over production to their employers. They were regarded as mere "hands" in the act of production. These characteristics of the wage system were marks of labour's degraded status and the Guild Socialists were out to reverse this order. They aimed at restoring to labour the positive control of industry so that the worker would become "a man among men, with rights and responsibilities with a human soul and a desire for self-expression, self-government and personal freedom." If democracy, they asserted, was really to be a success, the principles of democracy should be applied to industry as well as to politics. The Guild Socialists, accordingly, proposed to place the control of industry in the hands of guilds of producers who would, in their turn, cooperate with a democratised State representing the people as consumers. Each industry would be reconstituted as a public service under the control of those who actually worked in it, whether with hand or brain. In order to avoid the dangers of bureaucracy and of inefficiency, the Guild Socialists proposed to establish complete industrial government through an elaborate system of committees. It was claimed that the interests of consumers would be adequately safeguarded by vesting final rights of ownership of each industry in the State.[20] For Guild Socialists the main economic problem was to find "a way of restoring the spirit of craft, to devise a system that develops in workers not merely skill but also pride in

20. Cole, G.D.H., *Self-Government in Industry*, p. 154.

their work and an interest not primarily in the amount they earn but in the form and quality of what they make."

The Guild Socialists roundly condemned the existing political structure of society. They held the prevailing system of representatjon as 'misrepresentative and undemocratic' for "we choose, for a large number of desperate purposes, men who are qualified to represent us in reference to only a limited number of those purposes." A representative elected from a territorial constituency became the representative of all different interests residing in that area. But he really represented his own interests which he had in common with others. A cobbler only represented his fellow cobblers as they constituted a community of interests. Similarly, a worker belonging to a particular industry could be a true representative of his own industry and no one else. If a lawyer represented cobblers, workers, and a host of other interests, it was a sheer abuse of the principle of representation. The real representation, the Guild Socialists urged, must proceed on a functional and not on a geographical basis. A complete democratic society demanded that there should be "as many separately elected groups of representatives as there are distinct and essential groups of functions to be performed .... Man should have as many distinctly and separately exercised votes as he has distinct social purpose or interests."[21]

But the Guild Socialists did not intend to scrap altogether the system of territorial representation. There were various interests, apart from the vocational interests, which men, who were members of the same country, had common with others. Problems like internal peace and security, defence, education, currency and credit, etc., were national problems and were the same for all whatever the occupation of the people. Representation of national interests, it was proposed to be left to the existing system of territorial representation. A true representative character, according to the Guild Socialists, was a combination of the functional and geographical representation reflected in two legislative assemblies, a political parliament and a functional or economic parliament.

Local problems, like the provision of gas, water, electricity and other public utility services, the Guild Socialist would entrust to a local regional Guild. Finally, there would be Consumers' Councils. The functions of these Councils would be to determine, together with the workshop and factory committees of producers, the scale of production, costs and the prices of articles produced.

Thus, the principle of functional democracy occupied an important place in the theory of Guild Socialism. It was applied to the solution of questions both of industrial and political organisation. Joad has aptly remarked that the theory of functional democracy "reacting vigorously from the idea of a centralised and all-embracing State, advocates devolution of powers and functions to a number of different bodies which will, it is hoped, adequately express all the varied interests of man in the complex of modern society."[22]

The authors of Guild Socialism found room for the State as well as the Guild; and this they did by a "separation of powers." To the State they assigned all matters that concerned the national life, "for the guild they would vindicate all matters that concern

21. *Ibid.*, pp. 33-34.

22. Joad, C.E.M., *Introduction to Modern Political Theory*, p. 78.

the national income." In this way, two democracies—the economic and the political—could be realised in the State. For, unless there be economic democracy—the control by the workers themselves of their work—political democracy was all in vain. The factory, the Guild Socialists further urged, formed the necessary training school for active self-government, and unless democracy can be successfully established in the industrial sphere, it would never work as a real democracy in politics, however widely the franchise was to be extended. "For the conditions under which men work, exert powerful influence upon their minds and attitudes; and they cannot easily learn to control the wider issues that arise in politics unless they are given the opportunity of controlling the more immediate concerns which affect them in their daily lives. Of course, this doctrine involves not only self-government in industry, but also a widespread system of functional democracy extending over every field of collective activity."[23] The goal of Guild Socialism was the attainment of democracy in economic as well as in political life.

The Guild Socialists do retain the State, but with far less confidence in it than the Collectivists. They insisted on the need of plurality of organizations to express the plurality of interests of the individuals and society was a honeycomb of such associations; the State being one of them. The State, or the Commune, as the Guild Socialists described it, had just the care of residual interests left over after the guilds had effectively organized the primary interests of the workers. As a worker, a man was a member of the guild, but as a neighbour he was a member of the State or a Commune. The Guild Socialists not only recognised and safeguarded the interest of workers but of the consumers too by means of the consumers' cooperatives. It was, therefore, the people's movement.

Methods of Guild Socialism. The Trade Unions were the key to the methods of Guild Socialism. There was no satisfaction for Guild Socialists in the constitutional methods to gain their ends. The State, in its organisation and technique, was not a fit instrument, argued the Guild socialists, for making the changes they desired. Fundamental economic transformation could be secured only through economic means. This could best be done by enlarging and developing the existing trade union movement and, then, the workers should pursue a policy of "encroaching control." By encroaching control they meant "wresting bit by bit from the hand of the possessing classes the economic power which they now exercise, by a steady transference of functions and rights from their nominees to representatives of working class." It took two forms. In the first place, the workers should assume to themselves the right to appoint and dismiss the foreman of the factory. Secondly, the workers would enter into a "collective contract" with their employers by virtue of which the workers' organization would guarantee a special output and receive in return an agreed lump sum amount of money in lieu of the wages to be distributed among the workers in accordance with the principles of the workers' organization. Such an evolution of the workers' control of the industry would eventually, it was contended, lead to the end of capitalist control, and of capitalism too. The Guild Socialists, thus, intended to achieve their goal through evolution, "a natural and gradual, though consciously guided and expedited, development of the existing industrial situation." Here they basically differed from the Syndicalists who believed in, and advocated, revolutionary methods.

23. Cole, G.D.H., *A Guide to Modern Politics,* pp. 406-07.

Appraisal. Guild Socialism had apparently a great appeal both for the worker and the consumer. The Guild Socialist state was intended to be a decentralised State with separate autonomous units. Opinions, however, differed on the status of the State. Hobson, for example, says that the State will be supreme over all Guilds, local and national, and other associations as it shall be the deciding authority on all disputes arising between diverse economic and political units. Cole, on the other hand, regarded the State as an association like various other associations and not a dominating association over others as Hobson suggested. Barker has correctly said, "Any doctrine of separation of powers, such as Guild Socialism advocates, is bound to collapse before the simple fact of the vital interdependence of all the activities of the 'great society' of today."[24]

But Guild Socialism is now dead as a separate doctrine. Even Cole himself admitted that Guild Socialism "has since declined and virtually disappeared as a separate movement largely on account of the weakening of Trade Unions through industrial depression, of 1930, but also because the changes in the political situation have forced to the front the issue of seizing political power, and have, therefore, pushed into background the question of the forms of organisation to be adopted for the exercise of power when it has been won."[25] The Guild Socialists demanded too much of human nature. If selfish instinct in man could be taken out, then, Guild Socialism failed in its goal. Similarly, the scheme of functional democracy did not seem to be a workable plan. If functional representation destroyed social unity, functional democracy in industry presented its own insoluble problems. From where shall capital come and who bears the risk, are two pertinent questions which need proper answers.

SUGGESTED READINGS

Attlee, Clement: *As It Happened.*

Beer, M.: *A History of British Socialism.*

Bober, M.M.: *Karl Marx's Theory of the State.*

Chang, H.M.: *The Marxian Theory of the State.*

Cole, G.D.H.: *A History of Socialist Thought,* 5 vols.

Cole, G.D.H.: *Fabian Socialism.*

Cole, G.D.H.: *Guild Socialism Restated.*

Cole, G.D.H.: *Social Theory.*

Coker, F.W.: *Recent Political Thought,* Chaps II, IV.

Crosland, C.A.R.: *The Future of Socialism.*

Dewey, John: *Individualism, New and Old.*

Durbin, F.F.M.: *The Politics of Democratic Socialism.*

Ebenstein, W.: *Modern Political Thought.*

Ebenstein, W.: *Today's Isms.*

Hayek, F.: *J S. Mill and Harriet Taylor.*

Hayek, F.: *The Constitution of Liberty.*

24. Barker, E., *Political Thought in England, 1848-1914*, p. 208.
25. Cole, G.D.H., *A Guide to Modern Politics,* pp. 404-05.

Hayek, F.: *A Road to Serfdom.*

Hilton, J.: *Rich Man, Poor Man.*

Joad, C.E.M.: *Introduction to Modern Political Theory,* Chaps. III, IV.

Keynes, J.N.: *The End of Laissez Faire.*

Kirkup, T.: *A History of Socialism.*

MacDonald, J.R.: *Socialism, Critical and Constructive Capital.* Abridged popular edition by S. L. Trask.

Merriam, C.E., Barnes, H.E. and Others: *Political Theories; Recent Times.*

Rockow, L.: *Contemporary Political Thought in England,* Chaps. V, VII.

Roll, E.: *A History of Economic Thought.*

Russel. B.: *Roads to Freedom,* Chaps. I-III.

Sabine, G.H.: *A History of Political Theory,* Chap. 32.

Tawney, R.H.: *The Acquisitive Society.*

Ulam, Adam B.: *Philosophical Foundations of English Socialism.*

Wayper, C.L.: *Political Thought,* Chap. IV.

30 CHAPTER

Theories of the Sphere of State Activity (Contd.)

COMMUNISM

Meaning of Communism. Communism is used to express many different meanings. Sometimes it is used for a theory of society such as that of the early Christians, where nothing belonged to you and me but all property was held in common. Some people use it synonymously with Socialism, which, in reality, it is not. For, while all Communists are Socialists, all Socialists are not Communists. A man in the street is very often given to understand that Communism refers to that system of society under which food, clothing, shelter, education, medical aid, and other necessaries of life are freely administered according to want. But the fact of the matter is that Communism has none of these meanings. It is the philosophy of society as constructed by Karl Marx and the Communists are those who claim to be the inheritors of the true teachings of Karl Marx. The true Marxist use of the word Communism may be seen in the following quotation from Lenin, wherein he speaks of the transition from Capitalism to Communism: "What is generally called socialism was termed by Marx the 'first' or lower phase of Communist society. In so far as the means of production become common property, the word 'communism' is also applicable here, provided we do not forget that it is not complete communism." Communism is, thus, a theory of method which seeks to lay down the principles upon which the transition from capitalism to socialism is to be accomplished, and its two essential doctrines are the class war and the revolution, that is, the forcible transference of power to the proletariat

When Karl Marx and Engels promulgated the *Communist Manifesto* in 1848, they advocated the doctrine of 'Scientific Socialism', but in order to distinguish themselves from the petty bourgeois, reformers and utopian socialists, they took the name 'Communist'. With the lapse of time, however, the name 'Socialist' gradually came back and the followers of Marx were identified with it. At the close of the First World War Lenin went back to the original name of 'Communist' in order to make the position of the Russian Bolsheviks stand out in distinction to the German and French "perverters" of Marx.

Marxian Communism. To Marx we must return, then, if we are to grasp the meaning and the foundation of Communism. The leading features of Marx's thesis have already been briefly discussed.[1] It is, however, necessary to recapitulate and expand what has been said in order to formulate the principle upon which Communism is based. Marx saw all historical movements, whether religious or cultural or political, in terms of material conditions of life. "It is not the consciousness of man," he said, "that determines his existence, but quite the reverse, it is his social existence that determines his consciousness." Since the emergence of private property society has always been divided into two hostile classes: "Just as in the ancient world the interest of slave owners was opposed to that of the slaves, and in the medieval Europe the interest of the Feudal Lords was opposed to that of the serfs, so in our times the interest of the capital class, which derives its income from the ownership of property, is antagonistic to the interest of the proletariat class, which depends for its livelihood chiefly upon the sale of its labour power." The capitalist class appropriates the entire surplus value produced by the proletariat class which, according to Marx, is the latter's legitimate due. With the growing complexity of industrial technique the control of industry becomes monopolised and concentrated in the hands of fewer capitalists, while the conditions of the workers grow more precarious.

It is at this stage that capitalism generates the seeds of its own destruction. The instruments which capitalists use "to enlarge their profits and rents are the instruments which, when perfected, fall inevitably into the hands of the workers to be used by them to demolish the whole capitalist system." Marx develops this prognosis in concrete detail. In the first place, the tendency under capitalist production is towards large-scale production, increasing specialisation of functions, standardisation of goods and then monopolisation. As a result of this tendency large-scale producers succeed in throwing small-scale producers out of the market. The small-scale producers, thus, become exploited and they join the ranks of the exploited proletariat class, swelling their number and strength. When the ranks of the proletariat swell, those of the capitalists shrink. Secondly, the tendency is towards localisation and integration of industries. The former means the birth and growth of industries in such areas as offer the greatest relative advantages. The tendency towards integration means the cooperation and coordination under one management of all the processes involved in the production of an article, from the raw material to the final stage. All this brings about the concentration of thousands of workers together. These constant mutual contacts make workers conscious of their disabilities and hardships, which cement their group consciousness. Thirdly, large-scale production means two things. In the home market it results in unemployment, because of the extended use of machinery and other labour-saving devices in order to reduce costs of production. Unemployment means loss in the purchasing power and, consequently, the demand in the home market contracts. The producers hunt for new markets in foreign countries. Large-scale production also means extensive markets. Extensive markets can be possible only under conditions of highly developed means of communication and transport. This development breaks barriers of distance between different countries facilitating inter-communication among workers spread throughout the industrial world, thereby strengthening the common cause of the workers and bringing in them the consciousness of their universal disabilities.

Fourthly, a common feature of capitalist production is the occurrence of periodic

1. *See ante,* Chap. 28.

economic crisis. Crisis may be due either to over-capitalisation or competition. The workers receive too small a proportion of the product of industry. Consequently, in prosperous periods much of the surplus value created by producers passes into the form of fixed capital held by the capitalists. The purchasing power of the workers having diminished they consume less goods. Markets are glutted with the surplus of the goods produced and a period of failure and stagnation ensues. Finally, the constant endeavours of the capitalists to reduce costs of production result in the creation of a vicious circle. Unemployment in one industry means unemployment in other industries. This swells the number of workless workers and of all 'malcontents' the workless is the most discontented and hostile. Coker gives a matter-of-fact summing of the whole process: "... the capitalist system enlarges the number of workers, brings them together into compact groups, makes them class conscious, supplies them with means of inter-communication and cooperation on a world-wide scale, reduces their purchasing power, and by increasingly exploiting them arouses them to organised resistance. Capitalists, acting persistently in pursuit of their own natural needs and in vindication of a system dependent upon the maintenance of profits, are all the time creating conditions which stimulate and strengthen the natural efforts of workers in preparing for a system that will fit the needs of a working man's society."[2]

Marx and Lenin, in contrast to Hegel, who contended that the State alone provides a just balance between the contending interests in a society, maintained that the State is primarily an organ of class domination. The chief function of the State, they asserted, is the creation of an "order" which legalizes and perpetuates the oppression of one or more classes by another. The coercive dominance of the ruling class is achieved not only within the domestic, but also within colonial territories. Imperialism, Marx declared, is the ultimate form of State power under capitalism. This phase of Marxian theory was worked out more fully by Lenin. He believed that capitalism has entered its final "Imperialistic stage", in which its contradictions have become fully manifest. In his famous book, *Imperialism: The Highest Stage of Capitalism*, Lenin analysed the rise and development of capitalistic monopolies, and the correlative increase in the power and scope of "finance capital." He said, "Industrial and finance capital are being united under a single directorate, and are working in a close cooperation with the State. These changes usher in an era of tariffs, bounties and quotas, and restrictive trade agreements, in consequence of which the expanding productive forces come into ever intenser conflict with the forms of capitalistic concentration." In an attempt to find a way out of this impasse, the monopolists make frantic efforts to find out and employ cheap labour and tap new markets to get cheap raw materials and to sell their commodities. It means a fierce imperialistic struggle between the States controlled by capitalistic interests for a division and re-division of areas to exploit. The conflict inevitably culminates in world war, which deepens the crisis and prepares the way for open revolution.

The eventual result is open revolution overthrowing the capitalist society when the proletariat expropriates the private capitalist and appropriates the means of production. The capitalist methods of production are the cause of their own decay. Marx said, "Along

2. Coker, F.W., *Recent Political Thought*, p. 52.

with the constantly diminishing number of the magnates of capital grows the mass of misery, oppression, slavery, degradation, exploitation; but with this too grows the revolt of the working class, a class always increasing in numbers and disciplined, united, organized by the very mechanism of the process of capitalist production itself. Centralization of the means of production and socialization of labour at last reach a point where they become incompatible with their capitalist integument. This integument is burst asunder. The knell of capitalist private property sounds. The expropriators are expropriated." Marx maintained that the victory of the working class carries with it the emancipation of humanity. "Though the revolution itself is carried out on a class basis, the state of society which follows the revolution will be based on the abolition of classes." The Communists claim that their battle against capitalism, though outwardly waged on behalf of a dispossessed class, is really the battle of the whole mankind; and "it is this conviction, embraced with the intensity born of a disinterested ideal, which generates the power of self-sacrifice and self-devotion underlying a superficially somewhat arid and doctrinaire programme."[3]

Though the ultimate goal of the Communists is the emancipation of humanity by creating a classless and stateless society, yet its realization will take some time. The revolution of the proletariat paves the way, but it does not miraculously bring it into being. The revolutionary progress has been divided into two distinct stages: (1) a transitional revolutionary stage when the State dominated by the proletariat will continue functioning; and (2) a Communistic classless stage in which the State as a repository of authority will disappear.

The Revolutionary Stage. Although Capitalism proceeds naturally to its own destruction, yet it does not create Communism. Deliberate, intelligent, and informed action, according to Karl Marx, is needed for its achievement. A transition period must, therefore, occur during which preparations are made for the perfect Communist community to come into being. A few remaining elements of capitalism must be swept away. The minds of men must be purged of the remnants of the capitalist mentality with which they are infected. All these preparations require force, which means that the State and governmental machinery must be employed. The government will be a "dictatorship of the proletariat." The Communists have no faith in the ordinary constitutional methods of working a political democracy. "In order to break down the resistance of the *bourgeoisie*," says Marx, "the workers invest the State with a revolutionary spirit." It follows that the State during the transitional stage will be invested with oppressive and autocratic powers. "Since the State," says Engels, "is only a temporary institution which is to be made use of in the revolution in order to forcibly suppress the opponents, it is perfectly absurd to talk about a free popular State: so long as the proletariat needs the State, it needs it not in the interests of freedom, but in order to suppress its opponents; and when it becomes possible to speak of freedom, the State as such ceases to exist." The Communists apprehend that the *bourgeoisie*, though dispossessed by a sudden revolutionary *coup*, would still make frantic efforts to regain their lost political and economic power. "In any and every serious revolution," says Lenin, "a long, obstinate, desperate resistance of the exploiters

3. Joad, C.E.M., *Introduction to Modern Political Theory*, p. 90.

who for many years will yet enjoy great advantages over the exploited, constitutes the rule. Never... will the exploiters submit to the decision of the exploited majority without making use of their advantages in a last desperate battle or in a series of battles" He, therefore, asserts that "the transition from capitalism to communism forms a whole historical epoch."

The first stage in the realisation of Communism will be what Lenin calls a "*quasi state*" of the workers or proletarian dictatorship. All governments, Marx contends, are dictatorial. The proletarian dictatorship differs from the previous dictatorships in that it provides, for the first time in history, majority control. It is, Marx says, far more democratic than other governments have been, including the *bourgeois democracy* of capitalism. And while the proletariat operates for a time as an exploiting class, its purpose is not to perpetuate its own power but to eliminate oppression for ever. The proletarian dictatorship will take up the work of both construction and destruction; construction of Socialism and destruction of Capitalism. As destruction of Capitalism cannot be accomplished in one comprehensive stroke, the transfer from Capitalism to Socialism is to be made by degrees, "...that the first step in the revolution by the working class, is to raise the proletariat to the position of ruling class, to win the battle of democracy. The proletariat will use its political supremacy to wrest, by degrees, all capital from the *bourgeoisie*, to centralize all instruments of production in the hands of the State, *i.e.*, of the proletariat organised as the ruling class; and to increase the total of productive forces as rapidly as possible." The immediate measures to be adopted, according to the *Communist Manifesto*, are: abolition of private ownership of land, nationalisation of the means of communication and transport, taking over by the State of credit and banking, regulation of commerce, abrogation of the rights of inheritance, imposition of heavily progressive taxation, prohibition of child labour in factories, and an enforcement of equal liability of all to work, thus, breaking all privileges. These measures are to be followed by a gradual extension of public ownership in other fields of production. The destruction of Capitalism is the construction of Socialism and ultimately advent of the communistic society.

The Post-Revolutionary Stage. Once the *bourgeoisie* has been suppressed and all the defects and remnants of the capitalist system have been removed, the necessity of the State ceases to exist. It becomes superfluous and must "wither away." When the whole society comes down to one level everyone will be able to contribute his best to the social whole, and freely satisfy his needs. The State will give place to a free society of voluntary associations formed for the transaction of public business. It is this society whose advent bears witness to the fact that the revolutionary era has terminated. This "brave new world", as Marx names it, will be in effect the state of complete freedom; a society without antagonism, without exploitation, in which, as Lenin says, "people will become gradually accustomed to the observance of the elementary rules of social life ... without compulsion, without subordination, without the special apparatus for compulsion which is called the State."

This is the climax of Marx's Socialism. When Socialism is achieved, mankind will make the ascent, according to Engels, "from the kingdom of necessity to the kingdom of freedom." Marx's ultimate interest was in the liberated and cultivated individuals with time and opportunity for free development, intellectual and social. Marx's Socialism, therefore, like the goal of most other political creeds, radical or conservative, aims to bring about a social structure "in which the free and full development of every individual forms the ruling principle."

Critics of Marxian Theory. The Marxist theory has been severely criticised for its sweeping generalisations, inconsistencies, and contradictions. Werner Sombart has denied the entire historical-economic thesis of Marxism. He maintains that non-economic interests, such as religious and political, have on the whole held the primacy in history. Max Weber and Ernest Troeltsch also assert that the influence of religion had been original and profound. Georges Sorel insisted that myths, ideals and heroic attitudes often play a more important role than economic processes. Max Lerner believes that "Marxists have not been sufficiently aware of the irrational elements in human motivation: folk traditions, nationalistic sentiments, racial prejudices, group neuroses, subconscious or semi-conscious impulses. History is the product of the interaction of numerous forces and ideas, but Marx denies "pluralism in historical causation." He gave the economic factor a pivotal role in the causation of historical changes.

Communists' methods of overthrowing Capitalism and constructing Socialism through the revolutionary dictatorship of the proletariat require deep consideration. Wholesale violence and rcpressive methods are not the desirable means to gain the end, howsoever noble the end may be. Moral means must be adopted to achieve good results. It is difficult to believe that end justifies the means. Means and ends are convertible terms. To put it in the words of Gandhi, means may be likened "to a seed, the end to a tree; and there is just the same inviolable connection between the means and the end as there is between the seed and the tree." The dictatorship of the proletariat is invested with revolutionary spirit which sternly exercises repression to destroy all traces of Capitalism. Devotion to the party line or to face a purge was the simple truth of the dictates of Communism and it was the rule of common behaviour as practised in the former U.S.S.R. and other countries which had gone red. Beatrice and Sidney Webb deplore this "disease of orthodoxy" of Marxism. The violence of the dictatorship of the proletariat perverts and infects the goal of a peaceful cooperative Commonwealth, which Communism aims to establish. Violence and repressive policy stifles the democratic aspirations and creative spontaneity of the people who are told to march ahead for a classless and stateless society, which is to be without compulsion and without subordination.

Moreover, the course of Capitalist development has been quite unlike that foreseen by Marx, who assumed that Capitalism was in his time already on the verge of collapse. It is true that Capitalism which has persisted is considerably different from the system with which Marx was familiar, "but the transition from the exploitative capitalism of the early and middle nineteenth century to the moderate capitalism of the mid-twentieth century occurred as a result of actions which Marx had deemed impossible." The Fabians correctly regarded the transition to Socialism as the peacelul culmination of democratic and evolutionary processes. The regulation of hours of work, wages and working conditions, the prohibition of child labour, the establishment of unemployment insurance and workmen's compensation, and many more developments have resulted from legislative enactments and have created an entirely different situation for working people. Likewise, many Social Democrats have rejected the Marxian concept of class struggle and favour collaboration with all progressive forces. Even Stalin favoured such broad cooperation in achieving victory over the Axis Powers in the Second World War and in organising the peace. The Twentieth Congress of the former Russian Communist Party owned and emphasised such a collaboration with the progressive forces and it constituted the new Party thesis. Parliamentary collaboration with Social Democrats and other progressive forces was permissible to defeat the reactionary forces opposed to the popular interest. The long resolution adopted at the Twentieth Congress admitted that Socialism would not come to all the States in the same way and that "each State will make its own particular contribution to the one or the other form of democracy, to the one or the other type of dictatorship of the proletariat, to this or that tempo of socialist transformation in various aspects of the life of the society." The Congress expressed the view that "the establishment of the new socialist system in this or that country is an internal affair of the people in each country." Moreover, the rise of organised labour to a position of political power has also been contrary to Marx's theory. Marx had contended that the owners of the instruments of production always monopolised government and the legislative process in order to hold the labour class in subjection. But the Labour Party in Britain has been alternating with the Conservative Party in forming the Government since 1924. Similarly, the great influence on government of organised labour in the United States from 1932 to 1952 could hardly give credence to this fundamental aspect of the Marxian theory.

Marx believed that no society could supplant another until that other had developed fully all the potential that was in it. When feudalism had fully run its course it was replaced by Capitalism and Capitalism in its turn is subject to the same course of evolution. "No social order even disappears," he maintained, "before all productive forces for which there is room in it have been developed." But this had not happened in erstwhile Russia, China and other countries which had gone red. Taking the example of former Russia and China, neither of the two had anything like a complete industrial development. Both of them were primarily agrarian and nearly feudalistic societies prior to their leap into Socialism.

Whatever may be your and mine reaction to Marx's thesis, it cannot be denied that his influence on human thought and action has been profound. No social philosopher, ancient or modern, has exercised a vaster influence than Marx and Marxism had been till today the official ideology of millions. True, it was imposed by force upon most of them, but many had embraced it without compulsion because they had been convinced of its essential rightness. Convinced Marxists extol the truth of their doctrine with a zeal akin to that found in dedicated promulgators of a faith. And Marxism has an appeal to democrats because only a Communist society promises liberty as liberty is not worth having without equality. Equality can really exist in a classless society and Marx aimed to create such a society. In a society where equality can be secured there prevails fraternity. A Communist society, therefore, makes possible the realization of the true democratic ideals of liberty, equality and fraternity. Even the staunch advocates of capitalism today believe that political democracy is of little value unless supplemented by an economic system which provides a sufficient measure of security to all men.

Finally, there is also a psychological appeal in Marxist thought. "It offers an answer to men's problems. It tells the depressed that they are not themselves to blame for their inferior status; they are victims of a system and need only to change the system to be able to live on a plane of equality with all men." Marx's Socialism was scientific. His conclusions are fortified with historical facts and statistics. "To those who lack knowledge of the fields Marx dealt with such a display can be convincing. Those who are attracted to the goals of Marxism take satisfaction in knowing that their cause is scientifically proved"[4]

BOLSHEVISM

Lenin's Doctrine—"Leninism". Vladimir Lenin (1870-1924) was the most ardent follower of Karl Marx and the most famous of the revolutionaries who carried the banner of Marxian Socialism to its successful achievement in Russia and strived for the proletarian revolution. Lenin was not himself a workman, but a member of the middle-class intelligentsia who had become interested in the revolutionary movement and Marxism when still very young. The execution of his elder brother for his part in the attempt to assassinate Alexander III in 1887 affected Lenin deeply. The ostracism of his family after the execution accentuated his hatred of the society that supported privileges and submitted to the activities of the few privileged people. He found solace in the writings of Marx and Engels and, soon after, organised a Marxist group that called for revolution.

The Tsarist Government realised the danger ahead in the activities of Lenin, arrested him in 1895, and exiled him to Siberia in 1897. While Lenin was in exile his colleagues formed organisations, called the Leagues of Struggle for the emancipation of the working class, in all the key cities with a principal organisation at St.Petersburg. A meeting of the representatives of the various Leagues of Struggle was convened in the city of Minsk in 1898. The meeting proclaimed the organisation of the Russian Social Democratic Labour Party and issued a manifesto urging a fight against Capitalism until the victory of Socialism. Before the Party could come into being, all the members of the Minsk meeting were arrested. But it proved to be a spark and the organisation that had been announced came into existence in 1903.

Lenin returned in 1900, and plunged himself immediately into the organisation of the proposed Russian Social Democratic Party. But he soon found that there existed considerable differences of opinion even amongst his enthusiastic supporters. The liberal members of the intelligentsia were drifting towards the Socialist Revolutionary Party, formed from the remains of the Narodnik groups, and which had concentrated its work on the peasants. Plekhanov and Lenin's many other friends were of the opinion that the liberals could be helpful in furthering the cause of revolution and should be encouraged to join the proposed Social Democratic Party. Lenin, taking a position to which he adhered up to his death, answered that "liberals were generally half-hearted, cowardly, and ready to compromise with Tsarism." The group led by Plekhanov thought it unnecessary for the new party to become a single highly centralised organisation of trained revolutionaries. Another group, known as the "economists", preferred an organisation of mass character that would progress with the workmen as they developed a political and

4. Hermon, Judd M., *Political Thought from Plato to the Present*, p. 406.

social consciousness. In 1902, Lenin wrote a pamphlet, *What is to be Done*, calling for a vigorous, closely knit party of professional revolutionaries to lead the proletariat as its vanguard.

In the midst of these differences on plans and programmes the "First Congress" of the Russian Social Democratic Labour Party was called at Brussels on July 30, 1903. The Congress shortly moved to London, because of the police surveillance and there established itself as the Second Congress of the party. There was a good deal of opposition to Lenin's ideals about the revolution and the dictatorship of the proletariat. Leon Bronstein, known in the party and later to the world as Leon Trotsky, argued that the dictatorship of the proletariat could be accomplished only when the working class had become the majority of the population and had joined the party almost in its entirety. Lenin's views ultimately prevailed. But he lost on the rules regarding membership of the party. Lenin held the firm conviction that the party should be "a militant, disciplined, centralised organisation", and it should be limited to "a disciplined small group of schooled revolutionaries." Sympathisers, he believed, should have no place in the party. Trotsky and many others, who won on the rules, secured the vote of the Congress that anyone who accepted the programme of the party and promised to render all possible aid in the realisation of that programme, could become a member. This created a definite cleavage between the two groups and some of the moderates, who had helped to carry the vote over Lenin's group on the issue of membership, walked out of the Congress. This left Lenin's group in majority and the two factions in the party earned the names the *Bolsheviks* and *Mensheviks*, the former meaning majority and the latter minority.

The differences between the two factions became wide and the Mensheviks did not participate in the Third Congress of the Party. The Bolsheviks took this as an opportunity and annulled the rules of membership adopted in 1903. The new rules permitted membership to a small group of revolutionaries only, dropping out the sympathisers. A plan was also adopted for an armed uprising, and the political strikes in the country were to be used as the springboard of the uprising. It was decided that the leadership of the planned uprising should be in the hands of a provisional revolutionary group. The Bolsheviks, thus, took an active and direct part in the barricade fighting later known as the Revolution of 1905. The Revolution did not succeed and from its failure Lenin drew the conclusion that "the offensive against the enemy must be most energetic; attack and not defence must be the slogan of the masses."

There was no guide book for the revolution; Marxism provided only an ideological guidance. Lenin attempted to provide one while awaiting his opportunity to lead it. But hardly had he finished the first part of the celebrated volume, *The State and the Revolution*, which did not even cover an analysis of the events of 1905, when he ran back to Russia from exile to lead the revolution. Lenin was determined to act quickly, no matter at what cost. He caused the Bolsheviks to break with the Mensheviks and to form a separate party. This enabled the Bolsheviks to gain control of the Petrograd Soviet and with the new slogan "All power to the Soviets", the rest followed in rapid succession, and the first Socialist State came into being. Lenin, thus, adopted Marxism to Russia. The philosophy of Marx could not be applied to Russia, as he had anticipated that the proletarian revolution would take place in an advanced industrial country, like Germany or the United Kingdom.

Russia was an agriculturist country. But Lenin applied Marxian principles with an instinctive understanding of the Russian realities.

While Karl Marx put too much emphasis on the development of class-consciousness among the workers, Lenin's emphasis was on the party organisation. Without a strong and vigorous party organisation, he could not conceive of a revolution. "The Proletariat has no weapon," he said, "in the struggle for power except organisation. Constantly pushed out of depths of complete poverty, the proletariat can and will inevitably become an unconquerable force only as a result of this: that its ideological union by means of the principles of Marxism is strengthened by the material union of an organisation holding together millions of toilers in the army of the working class." At the same time, Lenin did not concede to members of the party the right to criticise the party policy and its programme. Party, for him, was a single, unified and centralised structure and in it only one will, one direction must prevail. It demanded of its members unanimity of views, the strictest of discipline, and all its decisions must be carried out unconditionally, precisely and punctually. "We are marching," said Lenin, "in a compact group along a precipitous and difficult path, firmly holding each other by the hand, we are surrounded on all sides by enormous forces, and are under their almost constant fire. We have combined voluntarily, especially for the purpose of fighting the enemy and not to retreat into the adjacent march. And now several in our crowd begin to cry out—let us go into this March." At another place he said, "Opportunity for open fighting. Opinions expressed. Tendencies revealed. Groups defined. Hands raised. A decision taken. A stage passed through, Forward. 'That's what I like.' 'That is life.' It is something different from the endless, weary intellectual discussions, which finish, not because people have solved the problem, but simply because they have got tired of talking."

Within the party itself Lenin attempted to combine a measure of democracy with one of discipline through the formulation of the principle of "democratic centralism." This principle requires that party members elect their own officials at all levels and they are accountable to those who elect them. It demands, however, strict party discipline and insists that once decisions have been taken these must be obeyed without demur. The decisions of the higher bodies are unconditionally binding on the lower ones. "Democratic centralism", accordingly, implies a combination between the principle of mass participation at the bottom and the concentration of leadership at the top.

The great achievement of Lenin, therefore, was the reconstruction of the Communist Party which became the vanguard of the Soviet people in their struggle to strengthen and develop the socialist system. In a formal sense, the Party and the State were separate institutions, but in actual reality they were hardly distinguishable. "The workers themselves," maintained Lenin, "do not know as yet how to rule and would have first to go through years of schooling. Hence in order to rule, an army of revolutionary Communists hardened in battle is necessary. We have such, it is Party."

The Marxian assumption was that the growing class consciousness of the proletariat would weaken and break the nationalist sentiment that tied the workers to their country. Patriotism, it was contended, was a fetish of the bourgeoisie to control the exploited and oppressed class. The proletariat would, Marx believed, eventually come to realize the strategy of the bourgeoisie and defeat this effort by giving their loyalty to their fellow workers irrespective of the national boundaries. Marxism was, thus, an international movement. But it was appalling to Lenin and his followers to see the patriotic fervour and deep sense of nationalism displayed by the members of the working class at the outbreak of World War I. The majority of the Socialists, too, though they paid respects to the views of Marx, supported their "*bourgeois*" government. Lenin was so deeply disgusted that he openly hoped for the defeat of Russia, because he believed that it would hasten the advent of revolution and wreck the Tsarist regime.

Lenin, then, wrote a book, *Imperialism, the Highest Stage of Capitalism*, wherein he attempted an explanation of the phenomenon described above, that is, that the proletariat appeared to be growing less, rather than more revolutionary. He attributed their apathy to certain operations of the Capitalist system which had extended its period of growth beyond that anticipated by Marx. Marx, Lenin said, had been unable to foresee the developmental potential of Capitalism. He gave an account of the evolution of Capitalism from the time of Marx's death to the beginning of World War I. He characterised this period by two important tendencies: (1) the export of finance capital and the control of the banks over industry, and (2) the growth of gigantic monopolies. The "inevitable" economic forces, Lenin maintained, would throw these monopolies in a savage struggle to find new markets culminating in war between the imperialist countries. Such a war, according to Lenin, is a war between trusts in which workers have no stake. Lenin admitted that certain parts of the proletariat, especially the skilled workers, profit from this imperialistic development. But, he believed that World War I was the beginning of the end for Capitalism. It will be followed, he said, by other wars, all of which will be fought for the same purpose. These wars will make the proletariat increasingly revolutionary and will speed the historical process to the final stage of world revolution. He appealed to the workers to seize the opportunity by turning the imperialist wars into civil wars. Class loyalty, Lenin contended, must be above national loyalty. As for himself, "he would sacrifice Russia rather than the revolution if the alternative should ever arise."[5]

Lenin had the deepest contempt for utopias in general and for the utopian socialists in particular. He would seldom venture to forecast future developments except in the broadest terms. But with regard to the process of the "withering away" of the State, he was unusually precise and concrete and it caused considerable embarrassment to his successors. He maintained that "the toilers need a State merely for the suppression of the resistance of the exploiters" and since the latter formed a small minority, the breaking down of their resistance appeared to him a matter "relatively easy, simple and natural." The proletarian State once established would immediately, he believed, begin to "wither away" as in society free from class contradictions the State was both unnecessary and impossible. There will be two stages of the Communist society, Lenin says. The first is the phase of socialism. Hence the means of production are publicly owned, classes still exist but are in the process of disappearing; so, too, is the State. A kind of equality exists in the sense that in this phase of development each contributes "according to his ability" and receives "according to his work," that is, according to his productive contribution. Since the State, too, in the first stage is in the process of 'withering away', Lenin outlined

5. Bertrand Russell, *The Practice and Theory of Bolshevism*., p. 31.

a number of steps which will accelerate this disappearing of the State. The first step was the abolition of the army and its replacement by an armed people, a popular militia. Then, he would abolish bureaucracy forthwith. Bureaucracy, Lenin regarded as a dangerous inheritance from the bourgeois regime and the victorious proletariat, he asserted, must not only be content to take over the machinery of government but it should be broken and destroyed altogether to get rid of all bureaucratic elements. Lenin, indeed, favoured the immediate introduction of a system under which "all should fulfil the functions of control and supervision, all should be 'bureaucrats' for a time and, therefore, none could be a bureaucrat." In the second stage, as envisaged by Lenin, classes and the State disappear. It becomes a classless and stateless society. Production is vastly expanded, and human behaviour achieves a degree of sociability that enables men to live together without state-imposed authority. The final stage is that in which men can live according to the principle, "From each according to his ability; to each according to his needs."

Finally, Lenin would retain the elective representative institutions in the new set-up of the socialist government, but he would forthwith scrap "parliamentarianism" as a system. By "parliamentarianism", Lenin meant the doctrine of the separation of the legislative from the executive power. Referring to the doctrine of the separation of powers, Vyshinsky writes, "... . From top to bottom the Soviet social order is penetrated by the single general spirit of the oneness of authority of the toilers." The proletarian representative assemblies, according to Lenin, must be places for work, not for idle talk. He characterised parliaments of bourgeois democracies as "talking shops" and advocated the abolishing of the immunities of the deputies. In fact, Lenin insisted that the Revolution necessarily demanded a complete shattering of the bourgeois State apparatus, and that a new Soviet State, based upon workers' councils ("soviets"), and directed by a single vanguard party of disciplined members, must take its place. And he was in a position to carry his ideals into execution.

Lenin combined political expediency and strategy with the Marxian ideology, though it meant a departure and even modification of Marxism. Lenin was pragmatic in his approach and he made Marxism adaptable to the conditions prevailing in Russia and in conformity to the genius of the people. Lenin's Russia was a land brimming with innumerable complexities and he had to weld the diverse elements, sharply differing from one another, into a unified nation within the fold of the new Soviet State. Naturally, Marx's thesis was to be balanced with the realities and it set the model for the generations to come.

What Bolshevism promised to the people of Russia under the inspiration of Lenin may best be described in the words of Bertrand Russell. It is a lengthy quotation, yet it is very instructive. He writes, "Bolshevism has supplied the new religion. It promises glorious things: an end of the injustice of rich and poor, an end of economic slavery, an end of war. It promises an end of the disunion of classes which poisons political life and threatens our industrial system with destruction. It promises an end to commercialism, that subtle falsehood that leads men to appraise everything by its money value, and to determine money value often merely by the caprices of idle plutocrats. It promises a world where all men and women shall be kept sane by work, and where all work shall be of value to the community, not only to a few wealthy vampires. It is to sweep away listlessness and pessimism and weariness and all the complicated miseries of those whose circumstances allow idleness and whose energies are not sufficient to force activity. In place of palaces and hovels, futile voice and misery, there is to be wholesome work, enough but not too much, all of it useful, performed by men and women who have no time for pessimism and no occasion for despair."[6] How far Bolshevism succeeded in fulfilling its mission after Lenin's death is revealed in the story of Stalin and his successors.

Joseph Stalin—Stalinism. Stalin was the successor to Lenin. But Lenin's death in January 1924, was followed by a bitter struggle within the Communist Party and it centred round the issue of world revolution. Trotsky, along with others who held similar views during the lifetime of Lenin, considered the promotion of world revolution not only the chief but the sole object of the Soviet Union. He believed that the construction of Socialism and the consolidation of the Dictatorship of the Proletariat were impossible in Russia without the direct support of the proletariat of Europe. Stalin, who had held similar views as lately as April 1924, suddenly reversed himself and championed the principle of "Socialism in a single country", provided the country concerned had a large territory, a large population and abundant natural resources. The Fourteenth Congress, in December 1925, endorsed Stalin's doctrine and the decision that the country was able to build Socialism even though surrounded by capitalist countries became the official creed of the Communist Party. The ideal of world revolution was not given up, but it ceased to be an active factor in Soviet policies both national and international. In its international relations the USSR sought the cooperation of capitalist States, and at home it embarked on vast schemes of economic reconstruction embodied in the Five-Year Plans. Stalin attached so much importance to his doctrine that in his report to the Fifteenth Congress in 1926, as well as on different other occasions, he unequivocally declared that without full assurance that Socialism could be built within the Soviet Union the industrial programme would be futile. At the Seventeenth Congress in 1937, he hailed the effort to complete the construction of "Socialism in a single country" as successful. And those who opposed his concept met the fate of Trotsky.

The doctrine of "Socialism in a single country" was a distinct departure from the Marxian theory and consequently it entailed a revision in the theory of the State. According to the official view, the State, having its origin and justification in class struggle, can exist only so long as there are classes. With the elimination of private ownership of the means of production class distinctions disappear and simultaneously the State should begin to "wither away". But Stalin held that the withering of the State can be accomplished not through the weakening of the State power, but through the maximum increase of its strength. In his report to the Eighteenth Congress Stalin explained the reasons why Soviet Communism differed from the norm set by Marx and Lenin. He said that the contradiction between the Communist Commonwealth envisaged by Marx and Lenin and the Soviet Union as it existed was due to the capitalist environment and especially due to the activities of "foreign spies, assassins and wreckers" sent to Russia by foreign intelligence services. Stalin pointed out that Engels never discussed the position of a single Socialist State encircled by hostile capitalist nations. He was either concerned with the inner

6. *Ibid.*, p. 19.

process of development of the future Socialist State, irrespective of the international situation, or proceeded on the assumption that Socialism would be victorious in all or in a majority of the countries. "But it follows from this," Stalin said, "that Engels' general formula about the destiny of the socialist state in general cannot be extended to the partial and specific case of the victory of socialism in one country alone. A country, which is surrounded by capitalist world and subject to the menace of the foreign military attack cannot, therefore, abstract itself from the international situation, and must have at its disposal a well-trained army, well-organised punitive organs, and a strong intelligence service—consequently must have its own state strong enough to defend the conquests of Socialism from foreign attacks." It is important to repeat here the views of Lenin. Lenin had said, "In a society free from class contradictions the State is both unnecessary and impossible." Disappearace of the army and elimination of bureaucracy were the principal ramifications, according to Lenin, of the withering of the State.

Stalin divided the history of Soviet Russia into stages. The first stage lasted from the advent of the Bolsheviks to power to the liquidation of the exploiting classes. During this period the State performed two principal functions: suppression of the exploiters at home, and defence of the Soviet Union from foreign aggression. The second stage was the period from the liquidation of the capitalist elements to the construction of Socialism and consequently the adoption of the Constitution in 1936, which registered and gave legislative embodiment to what had been actually achieved. The Socialist State, as Russia had in the second stage, Stalin maintained, was entirely novel and it differed considerably both in form and functions from the Socialist State of the period. USSR was moving towards Communism. Stalin, then, posed a question, "Shall we maintain the State under Communism?" He replied, "Yes, it will be maintained unless the capitalist environment has been liquidated, unless the danger of military aggression from the outside is removed. It is evident that, the forms of our State will be altered again according to the modification of the domestic and foreign policy." "No, it will not be maintained and will wither away, if the capitalist environment has been removed, if its place has been taken by a socialist environment."

In brief, the State, according to Stalin, will not "wither away" unless the capitalist environment has been liquidated; and a prerequisite of the withering away of the State is the existence of socialist environment. So long as the Soviet State is encircled by capitalist countries, it should be strong enough to consolidate socialist economy and to combat international aggression. Here Stalin differed both from Marx and Lenin.

While Stalin's dictatorship of the proletariat was building socialism in a single country, his nationalism also found expression in the creation of a new type of multinational State, and the Constitution of 1936 was a perfect mirror of the same. According to his definition, "a nation is an historically evolved, stable community of language, territory, economic life and psychological make-up manifested in a community of culture."[7] Upon this definition he distinguished various national areas within the USSR and permitted wide autonomy to all these regions. In pursuance of this ideal, the Soviet Government encouraged a remarkable diversity of language and culture. The changes introduced in the Constitution

7. Stalin, J., *Marxism and the National Question*, p. 12.

in 1944, granting to each constituent Republic the right to enter into direct relations with foreign States, to conclude agreements and exchange diplomatic and consular representatives with them, and to maintain troops, represented a further expression of the multinational policy of the Soviet Union.

The Stalin Cult. Stalin not only controlled the government, but also the Party machine. If under Lenin the party became the "vanguard of the proletariat," under Stalin the dictator became the vanguard of the party. Power, thus, accumulated in the hands of one single person and Stalin destroyed those who challenged his supremacy. The obvious result was Stalin's worship. No other public figure had been driven, during his lifetime, to such incredible lengths of adulation as Stalin was. He was described as "the greatest genius on earth": greatest architect of communism"; "wise teacher and leader": "inspirer of our glorious victories"; and "foremost authority on science, literature, linguistics, music, etc." And Stalin, as Khrushchev observed at the Twentieth Congress, acted not through persuasion, explanation and patient cooperation with people, but by imposing his concepts and demanding absolute submission to his opinion. Whoever opposed his concept or tried to prove his viewpoint and the correctness of his position was doomed to removal from the leading collective and to subsequent moral and physical annihilation." Even Lenin was cited by Khrushchcv, in his speech at the Twentieth Congress, to have described Stalin as "excessively rude" who did not have a proper attitude towards his comrades, and that he was capricious and had abused his power. Khrushchev further observed, "We have to consider seriously and analyse correctly this matter in order that we may preclude any possibility of a repetition in any form whatever of what took place during the life of Stalin, who absolutely did not tolerate collegiality in leadership and in work, and who practised brutal violence towards everything which opposed him, but also towards that which seemed to him capricious and despotic in character contrary to his concepts."

Stalin, in brief, was shown at the Twentieth Congress as a man of colossal conceit, unbounded ambition and ruthless nature; who did not hesitate to send thousands of persons to the gallows in order to maintain himself in power, and "the cult of the individual acquired", in Khrushchev's words, "such monstrous size chiefly because Stalin himself, using all conceivable methods, supported the glorification of his own person." This is supported by numerous facts. One of the most characteristic examples of Stalin's self-glorification and the lack of even elementary modesty is the edition of his Short Biography which was published in 1948. This book is the expression of most dissolute flattery, an example of making a man into a "godhead, of transforming into an infallible sage, the greatest leader, sublime strategist of all time and nations.

Stalin's contributions to the theory of Socialism consist mainly in his interpretation of Lenin's writings and are found principally in two books, *Foundations of Leninism*, and *Problems of Leninism*, both published in 1924, shortly after Lenin's death. In the *Foundations of Leninism*, Stalin reiterated and defended Lenin's theory of revolution and described the technique to advance the cause of world revolution. The Soviet Union should become a base, Stalin said, from which the revolutionary cause should be advanced. Stalin also outlined the plan for the world revolution more clearly than Lenin had done. Here he combined Trotsky's theory of permanent revolution with Lenin's theory of imperialism and proposed that the attention of the revolutionaries be directed to the

Colonies rather than to the advanced Capitalist countries. Stalin wrote, "The front of capital will not necessarily be pierced where industry is most developed, and so forth; it will be broken where the chain of imperialism is weakest, for the proletarian revolution is the result of the breaking of the chain of the imperialist world front at its weakest point. It is possible, therefore, that the country which begins the revolution, which makes a breach in the capitalist front may prove to be less developed from the capitalist point of view than others which are more developed but have remained, nevertheless, within the framework of capitalism."[8]

In his book, *Problems of Leninism*, Stalin warned of the dangers of imperialist capitalism in support of his argument for Socialism in a single country. Communism and Capitalism, he maintained, "cannot long exist side by side and the country must be prepared for a conflict." In this way, capitalist environments would disappear paving the way for international revolution and overthrowing of Capitalism.

New Thesis of the Communist Party. The cult of personality was resolutely opposed at the Twentieth Congress as alien to the spirit of Marxism and Leninism. The cult of personality, the Congress further held, turns one or another leader into a miracle-performing hero and at the same time minimises the role of the Party and the popular masses. Khrushchev said in his speech, "After Stalin's death the central committee of the party began to implement a policy of explaining concisely and consistently that it is impermissible and foreign to the spirit of Marxism-Leninism to elevate one person, to transform him into a superman possessing supernatural characteristics akin to those of a god. Such a man supposedly knows everything, sees everything, thinks for everyone, can do anything, is infallible in his behaviour."

The long resolution adopted on domestic and foreign policies by the Twentieth Congress marks a spectacular development in the policy of the Communist Party and the methods it would advocate for the realization of a socialist society ultimately leading to a Communist Commonwealth. The old thesis about the contradictions of Capitalism and inevitability of war had not been discarded, but it made a number of significant admissions and consequently modifications therein, particulary in relation to the transitional stage from Capitalism to Socialism. While admitting the non-inevitability of war, the Congress asserted that the Communists did not necessarily stand for the violent overthrow of the capitalist order. Socialism, it was maintained, would not come to all States in the same way. And that "each State will make its own particular contribution to the one or the other form of democracy, to the one or the other type of dictatorship of the proletariat, to this or that tempo of socialist transformation in various aspects of the life of the society." The Congress expressed the view that "the establishment of the new socialist system in this or that country is an internal affair of the people in each country."

The modifications of doctrine presented at the Twentieth Congress were thus:

(*i*) the non-inevitability of war;

(*ii*) the sanctioning of different paths to Socialism;

8. Stalin, J., *Foundations of Leninism*, rev. trans., International Publishers Company Inc., New York, 1932, pp. 33-34.

(*iii*) the acceptance of the possibility of Socialism coming to power by parliamentary means; and

(*iv*) the possibility of cooperation with the Social Democrats.

The Congress claimed that its resolution embodying the means of realising a Socialist society represented merely a return to Leninism. Whether it was a return to Leninism or it represented a new approach to the problem of Socialist transformation is debatable. But no one can deny that the resolution of the Twentieth Congress threw overboard the concepts of the inevitability of war between Capital and Communist States, class conflict, and the identification of democratic Socialism with Capitalism. Khrushchev summed up the new directive for the Communist parties abroad in these words: " .... The present situation offers the working class in a number of capitalist countries a real opportunity to unite the overwhelming majority of the people under its leadership and secure the transfer of the basic means of production into the hands of the people .... The working class, by rallying around itself the toiling peasantry, the intelligentsia, all patriotic forces ... is in a position to defeat the reactionary forces opposed to the popular interest, to capture a stable majority in Parliament, and to transform the latter from an organ of bourgeois democracy into a genuine instrument of the people's Will ...." It means that parliaments, which, according to Lenin, were to be utilised for the express purpose of their eventful destruction, were recognised as organs of genuine democracy for the working people and that parliamentary collaboration with Social Democrats and other progressive parties was permissible to defeat the reactionary forces opposed to the popular interest. The formation of the first Communist Ministry in the State of Kerala in India within the framework of the Constitution was the immediate implementation of the new directive of the Twentieth Congress for the Communist parties abroad. The Communist Party in the State of Kerala had also directed its best efforts to collaborate with the Praja Socialist Party in order to capture a stable majority and form a coalition with them, although the P.S.P. did not accept the Communist invitation. But it was indicative of a genuine desire of the Communist programme to seek the cooperation of the Social Democrats. Another aspect of the implementation of this programme was the series of visits by prominent socialists of all the countries of the world to Moscow on the invitation of the Soviet Government and the visits of top Soviet leaders, including Bulganin and Khrushchev, abroad.

The New Programme for Constructing a Communist Society. The Twentieth Congress instructed the Central Committee to draft a new programme of the Communist Party. The programme, called the Third Programme aiming to build the Communist society in the Soviet Union within the next twenty years, was adopted by the Twenty-second Congress held in October 1961. Khrushchev explained the reasons for setting the time limit and said, "When the draft programme was being discussed, some comrades wondered whether the time allocated to the task was not too long. No, comrades. To prepare society for the principles of Communism we have to develop productive forces enormously and create an abundance of material and spiritual values. And that takes a certain amount of time. The bowl of Communism is a bowl of abundance that must always be full. Everyone must contribute his bit to it, and everyone must take from it." Khrushchev further said that it would be a fatal error to decree the introduction of

Communism before all the necessary conditions for it had been fulfilled. In the economic sphere it meant to create powerful productive forces in the country and the development of the Soviet Union into the world's leading industrial power in order to ensure the world's highest standard. In the sphere of social relations, the still existing distinctions between classes may be eliminated. This meant, all classes hitherto existing in the Soviet Union and the distinctions prevailing between town and country and between physical and mental labour be eradicated and all such classes should fuse into a classless society of Communist working people. When this had been done there will be greater economic and ideological community "and the features of the man of the Communist society will develop, harmoniously combining ideological integrity, broad education, moral purity and physical perfection". Finally, in the political sphere all citizens would participate in the administration of public affairs, and society would prepare itself for the full implementation of the principles of communal self-government through a most extensive development of social democracy.

Shape of the Communist Society. The draft programme defined Communism and this definition gave a picture of the Communist society to come after twenty years. "Communism is a classless social system with one single form of public ownership of the means of production and full social equality of all members of society; under it, the all-round development of people will be accompanied by the growth of the productive forces through continuous progress in science and technology; all sources of public wealth will gush forth abundantly, and the great principle 'From each according to his ability, to each according to his needs' will be implemented. Communism is a highly organised society of free, socially conscious people in which public self-government will be established, a society in which labour for the good of society will become the prime vital requirement of everyone, a necessity recognised by one and all and the ability of each person will be employed to the greatest benefit of the people." Here are the salient features of Communism so defined and the stages through which it is to evolve:—

1. Communism was a classless social system. Overthrowing the rule of the exploiting classes, the landlords and the capitalists, and abolishing private ownership of the means of production was carried through as a result of October Revolution (1917). In the second phase individual small-scale commodity production was converted into a large-scale, completing the construction of a single socialist economic system, and abolishing the last of the exploiting classes, the class of the *Kulaks*. The third phase covers the new programme and it aims to remove class distinctions between workers and peasants, the essential distinctions between town and country, and creating conditions for an organic fusion of physical and mental labour.

2. This task was to be accomplished through a high degree of Communist consciousness. Industry, discipline, and devotion to the public interest were qualities typifying the man of the Communist society and this was bound up, above all, with a rapid growth of the productive forces. It was precisely a high level of the productive forces and socialist relations of production that actuated the gradual process of the distinctions between the classes of the working people.

3. The elimination of distinction between classes made for greater homogeneity of society. All people would have equal status in society, would stand in the same relation

to the means of production, would enjoy equal conditions of work and distribution, and would actively participate in the management of public affairs. Harmonious relations would be established between the individual and society on the basis of the unity of public and personal interests. Classless Communist society would, thus, constitute the highest form of organization of the human community. For all their diversity, the requirements of people would express the sound reasonable requirements of the fully developed person.

4. The purpose of Communist production was to ensure uninterrupted progress of society and to provide all its members material and cultural benefits according to their growing needs, their individual requirements and tastes. People's requirements would be satisfied from public sources. Articles of personal use would be in the full ownership of each member of society and would be at his disposal.

5. Communist society, which was based on highly organised production and ideology, would alter the character of work, but it did not release the members of society from work. It would by no means be a society of anarchy, idleness and inactivity. Every able-bodied person would participate in social labour and thereby ensure the steady growth of the material and spiritual wealth of society.

6. Communist production demanded high standards of organisation, precision and discipline, which were ensured not by compulsion, but through an understanding of public duty. Communism represented the highest form of organisation of public life. All production units and self-governing associations would be harmoniously united in a common planned economy and a uniform rhythm of social labour.

7. The dictatorship of the proletariat had fulfilled its historic mission and ceased to be indispensable in the USSR from the point of view of the tasks of internal development. The working class had transformed the state of proletarian dictatorship into a state of the whole people.

8. But it did not mean the disappearance of the State. The State would be retained. The process of its 'withering away' would be a very long one. "For some time, features of state administration and public self-government will intermingle. In this process the domestic functions of the state will develop and change, and gradually lose their political character. It is only after a developed Communist society had been built in the USSR and provided socialism wins and consolidates in the international arena, that there will no longer be any need for the State, and it will wither away."

9. The fact that the dictatorship of the proletariat was no longer necessary did not in any way imply any relaxation of public order and legality. The rights, freedom, honour and dignity of the citizens would be closely protected by society and by the State.

10. The principle of the co-existence of States with different social systems remained the general principle of the foreign policy of the Soviet State. In terms of internal conditions, the Soviet Union needed no army. But since the danger of war coming from the imperialist camps persisted, it was necessary to strengthen the armed forces and the defence potential of the Soviet Union. Defence of the country, and service in the State Armed Forces, it was enjoined, was the lofty and honourable duty of Soviet citizens.

Khrushchev's Exit. Khrushchev dominated the Soviet political scene for eleven years as Party Secretary and since 1958 to mid-October 1964, he simultaneously held the two posts of Secretary and Prime Minister. His exit was sudden and unexpected, ostensibly for reasons of health and age, but the Soviet people and the outside world were accustomed to such dramatic changes at the top. The strange aspect of Khrushchev's exit was that the Russians who wept for Stalin shed no tears for the more generous and affable Khrushchev. One possible explanation was that the former died in office before his crimes were exposed while the latter only lost his job when his "indiscretions" had sufficiently exasperated his colleagues and disgruntled a small army of officials.

But if Khrushchev and his methods had gone, much of his policy remained. Kosygin, the successor Premier, in his report to the Supreme Soviet, indicated some changes in emphasis in Russian policy. But there were few indications of striking new lines of policy, national or international. Peaceful co-existence was to continue to ensure peaceful conditions for the building of Communism and similarly reduction in the military budget, continuation of talks with Western Powers with special reference to developing relations with the West. In Kosygin's report there was a bare reference to the "serious mistakes" in agriculture, such as insufficient material incentives to collective farmers and the endless reorganizations. The new leadership hoped to overcome the lag in agricultural production within the next few years. All this confirmed the beliefs that the new leaders were opposed to Khrushchev's personal methods of conducting Soviet affairs, which resulted in his brinkmanship in Cuba, intense hostility to Peking and overtures to Bonn, for all of which the rest of the leadership was obviously unprepared. They accused him for ignoring the collective leadership, one of the familiar Khrushchev's charges against Stalin.

Khrushchev was one of the master-builders of the Soviet Union and his political eclipse in no way altered this fact. The eleven years of the Khrushchev era were years of radical and hopeful changes. Stalin had transformed USSR economically and made her a military power second only to the United States. Khrushchev inherited a cruel legacy and it required, indeed, a courage on his part to demolish the Stalin cult and to present a new thesis for achieving Communism as endorsed by the Twentieth Congress. Khrushchev's commitment to co-existence was sincere and both in his efforts to achieve a detente with the West and in his unflinching appreciation of the role of the non-aligned Powers in strengthening the peace, he showed strong determination and supreme statesmanship, without a peer in the Soviet history. But his policy was not pure Marxism-Leninism. Khrushchev's policy was one of liberalisation on all fronts.

Soviet Socialist democracy. Soviet Russia claimed to have established socialist democracy the basic principles of which were formulated by Marx and Engels and incorporated into the theory of scientific communism, forming a part of the doctrine of the socialist State. Lenin developed this doctrine and the Soviet Communist Party followed unswervingly the Leninist line of promoting Soviet socialist democracy in every way. This approach was clearly expressed in the Party Programme. The question of democracy was extensively dealt with at the 25th Party Congress held in February-March 1976 and reaffirmed with an unflinching faith.

For the first time in human history, Soviet socialist democracy, it was asserted, affirmed real people's power, the equality of peoples and nations, and freedom of the individual. This was a democracy of working people free from all exploitation and oppression, who were the sole masters of the State and society and were united by common political. social, and economic interests, and common goals — the building of socialism and communism. Such a democracy was effected under the leadership of the working class and its Communist Party in the interests of all working people of the Soviet State which was a state of the entire people. In his speech at the Conference of the Communist and Workers' Parties of Europe, held in Berlin in the summer of 1976. Leonid Brezhnev noted: "We have built a society free from monopolist oligarchy domination, free from the fear of crises, unemployment, free from social catastrophies. We have built a society of people who are equal to the broadest sense of the word, people who know neither class, property, race nor any other such privileges, a society which not only proclaims human rights, but guarantees the conditions under which they can be exercised. We have built up a stable, dynamic and united society."

As to the success of the social development of the Soviet society, Brezhnev added. it is "possible only as a result of the people's free and conscious creative work, of their increasingly active participation in shaping all aspects of public life. Therefore, our further advance in building communism will inevitably mean the further advance of socialist democracy." A responsible attitude on the part of every citizen to his duties, to the people's interest creates a reliable foundation for the fullest embodiment of the principles of socialist democracy and real freedom for the people. Everything that served the people's interests and the interests of communist construction was "morally sound and democratic" and must, accordingly, be followed vigorously and rigidly.

The Soviet State of the entire people was the next and higher stage of development of the dictatorship of the proletariat and the most effective political organisation of the masses in conditions of developed socialism. The leading role in regulating economic, social and political relations under socialism belonged to the Soviet State of the entire people. For carrying out its economic, organisational, cultural, educational, defence and other functions the State possessed such agencies and organisations as an economic and planning apparatus, the judiciary, the Procurator's office, the Army, and cultural and other associations. The Soviet State organised the building of the material and technical basis of Communism promoted the development of socialist relations into Communist relations, exercised control over the rate of production and consumption, took measures to increase the people's well-being, protected the rights and freedoms of its citizens, enforced socialist legality, educated people in the spirit of conscious discipline and Communist attitude to work, provided for the country's defences and safeguarded its security, developed cooperation with the socialist countries, and promoted the cause of peace.

A State representing the entire people was characterised by a higher level of relationships between the individual and society than any other type of State. This was manifest in the fact that the socialist State more fully guaranteed the political, economic and other rights and interests of its citizens, and in the correct understanding most citizens had of their obligations to the State. As Brezhnev said in the report to the 25th Congress: "We see the improvement of socialist democracy as consisting above all in a steady effort to ensure ever fuller participation of the working people in running all affairs of society, in developing the democratic principles of our State system. and creating conditions for an all-round flourishing of the individual."

True democracy, it was maintained, was inconceivable without socialism, just as socialism was inconceivable without a constant development of democracy. Socialism was a dynamically developing society and, accordingly, the work done during the past decades to improve the society's political system was reflected in the new Constitution of the USSR which replaced the older 1936 Constitution. It also reflected the great achievements of socialism and formalised the general principles of the socialist system, the basic features of the developed socialist society and also its political organisation. Also reflected in the Constitution were the principles of economic management relating to the building of the material and technical basis of communism, the role of the state in the intellectual and cultural life of society. The Constitution, in brief, established a State which set itself the goal of building Communism in the interests of every working man and the people as a whole, and further consolidation and development of socialist democracy.

The outstanding feature of this process of development was the emergence of the next higher stage in the path of socialism. The dictatorship of the proletariat had completed its transitory and revolutionary role and had given place to the Soviet State of the entire people. It was a democratic State which affirmed the real people's power, the equality of peoples and nations and freedom of individuals. It was a democracy of the working people. As democracy and socialism were indispensable for one another, the development of the future stage would depend upon the people's free and creative work under the leadership of the working class and its Communist Party. A new Constitution embodying the achievements and aspirations of the people was given to the people, with an apparatus of organisation, to reach the common goal—the building of Socialism and Communism. Withering away of the State was still not yet in sight.

EURO-COMMUNISM

Deviation from Marxism. Way back in 1899, Eduard Brenstein, the famous German socialist, rebutted Marx's analysis of the Capitalist society. In his *Evolutionary Socialism*, he argued that Marx was mistaken in his analysis that concentration of capital in the hands of few capitalist would accentuate class antagonism between the two great hostile classes, employers and workers, openly facing each other resulting eventually into the inevitable collapse of Capitalism and on its ruins would be built a classless socialist society. He pointed out that Marx could not visualise some important developments in the post-Marxist period, such as, the growth of the joint stock company with widely diffused shareholders, the emergence of a larger and more significant middle class, contrary to his prognosis, the rapid advancement of political democracy and stabilisation of democratic institutions, emergence of protective legislation and the phenomenal growth of trade unions and their recognition by all democratic governments. These developments, Brenstein pointed out, could not be overlooked and they actually carved out a path for the establishment of socialist society by an evolutionary process.

Brenstein candidly admitted that there were vital differences between his views and those of Marx and they were, he confessed, not short of 'revisionism'. He declared that the socialist movement was everything and that there was no need to set a final aim of socialism as the march of events in the post-Marxist phase had proved that any such aim was unpredictable. The socialist efforts, he explained, should be vigorously directed to secure important reforms, within the existing constitutional framework, ultimately leading to the establishment of real democracy. He outright rejected the doctrine of dictatorship of the proletariat armed with powers to suppress Capitalism and vigorously construct socialism, that is, to invest the State a transitional phase on the path of a socialist society with a revolutionary spirit.

Brenstein, thus, laid the basis for Euro-Communist movement in West Europe in the mid-seventies of the present century. Bolshevism, too, had made significant modifications in the Marxian analysis and the resolution of the Twentieth Soviet Congress was not only a deviation from the Communist theory but also a departure from Leninism. But being the first country to bring Marx's dream of revolution an accomplished fact, Russia became the epicentre of the International Communist movement and inspired the peoples of distant lands with the teachings of Marxim-Leninism and all those countries joining the family of the Communists looked to their mentors in Moscow for guidance and initiative. But Soviet Russia lost its leadership not long after. Yugoslavia's break with the Soviet Union, the Sino-Soviet split and Soviet intervention in Czechoslovakia were landmarks in the Communists' disillusionment with the Soviet concept of Communism. At the same time, it had come manifest to many Western European Communists that the Soviet type of Communism in their countries would not bring them near power in a millennium and, accordingly, some way should be found to get out of this impasse.

Euro-Communism. Euro-Communism, a product of West Europe, was the most important revolt against Soviet Russia's hegemony and it inflicted a real damage to Marxism. It was born out of the evolution of ideas and changing conditions in West Europe as well as the desire of the Communist parties in these countries to assume office and achieve power which otherwise was a far distant cry, if not absolutely impossible. What distinguished Euro-Communists from their more orthodox comrades was the repudiation of the Soviet system in total. They in clear terms accepted the existence of a plural society, were committed to multi-party democracy, and pledged to surrender power in the event of electoral defeat and, consequently, their faith in alternation of government. They owned and adhered to liberal or, in Marxian terminology, *bourgeois* freedoms, rejected the exclusive and pivotal role of the Communist Party in the body-politic, the doctrine of dictatorship of the proletariat, the classical Marxist economic theory and of Moscow as the only model for all the Communist societies. Santiago Carrillo, the Spanish Communist Party leader, summed it up neatly when he declared , "Moscow is not our Rome and October (l917 Revolution) is not our Christmas."

The disenchantment of the Euro-Communists with the Soviet Union was the consequence of their realization that there existed a wide gulf between what they professed and practised as reflected in the foreign policy and the treatment accorded to their comrade allies. They also became aware of the distinction between German Marxism and Russian Communism. The evolution of this important development was nurtured by important Marxist theories like Gramci's theory of hegemony, Togliatti's polycentrism, Marchais's enunciation of socialist democracy of universal validity, Carrillo's insistence that Marxist theory emerged from a "concrete analysis of concrete reality" and Berlinguer's "historic compromise." Thus, Euro-Communism crystallised in the process of a long term theorising and practice which had important roots in West Europe itself. The end result was the doctrine of Euro-Communism: that each Communist party to choose its own road and should be free to follow its own policy in order to achieve power without remaining the apron-string of Moscow. Euro-Communism, thus, did not only depart from the Marxian path of establishing a socialist society, but was visibly distinct from Leninist formulations.

Euro-Communism was coined as a word in 1975 by the Italo-Yugoslav' journalist, F. Barbiery. By late 1976, it had become a label for the largest Communist parties in Western Europe — Italy, Spain and France. Its major ideological exposition was given by Santiago Carillo of Spain in his book, *Euro-Communism and the State.* Over a decade or so Euro-Communism held its sway and the Spanish, the Italians and the French Communist parties emerged as its key-partners in West Europe. In 1975, Enrico Berlinguer and Georges Marchais, leaders of the Italian and French Communist parties, signed a joint statement in Rome committing the two parties "for the plurality of the political parties, for the right of existence and activity of the opposition parties, and for democratic alternative between the majority and the minority." The eventual building of a socialist order in Italy and France, the statement added, would be characterised by a "continued democratization of economic, social and political life" and the existing "*bourgeois*" liberties would be "guaranteed and developed". Spain later joined the Euro-Communist family.

The November 1975 statement constituted the manifesto of Euro-Communism—a new communism with commitment to a plural society and democratic freedoms. Realising that there was a remote possibility of revolution, as envisaged by Marx, in Western Europe, the Euro-Communists placed added emphasis on electoralism, on seeking popular support through calls for gradual reforms, on winning the cooperation of other left-wing parties even at the cost of doctrinal and political concessions and on the building of party's image as a progressive and responsible organisation functioning within the existing political system whose creed was not to overthrow the prevailing social and political structure but to preserve and transform it.

Failure of Euro-Communism. The movement of Euro-Communism repudiating the leadership of Soviet Russia and its deviation from Marxism-Leninism shook the orthodox Communist family and it alarmed Russia particularly for its possible repercussions on East Europe. The United States also did not take to it kindly, although President Carter's approach was more ambivalent and U.S. officials had meetings with French and Italian Communist functionaries. But the demise of Euro-Communism came much earlier than it could be anticipated. On the level of practical politics it did not happen the way the Euro-Communists had expected. The trouble began when the French Communists who had formed an alliance with the French Socialists in a bid for left unity ended in fiasco amidst mutual bickerings. As a consequence, in the 1978 general election the Communists lost heavily as compared with Socialists. The fate of the Italian Communists was not a whit less better. In their search for Berlinguer's "historic compromise" they came to truce with the Christian Democrats, their traditional rivals, and eroded their social base when they enjoyed unparalleled popular support from a wide cross-section of the Italian society. They were not in the government, but had to share the blame for its failures whereas all credit went to the Christian Democrats if the government achieved success in any direction. They were attacked by the trade unions and the radical left and had to pay heavily in the following regional and local elections. Italians, again, rebuffed them in the 1979 general election. With one seat less than their number in 1976, the Christian Democrats remained virtually as they were while the electoral support of the Communist Party dipped by as much as four per cent.

In Spain conditions were not as bad as in France and Italy. In the 1977 election, the first to be held since Franco's death, Communists secured 9.22 per cent of the votes, a significant achievement, inspite of bans for the preceding forty years or so. But the main problem facing Carrillo in his campaigns was the Socialist Party's moves to woo the electorate with almost identical policies and programmes. Consequently, the Communists hesitated to come to terms with the Socialists, on the French and Italian model, lest their own image as a separate party may altogether be blurred. This attitude also explained why they had not suffered electoral reverses, unlike their French and Italian counterparts. But the Communist Party fared disastrously in 1982 general election getting 8.8 per cent of the votes and only six seats, compared to the earlier 23.

These practical difficulties aside, the more fundamental reason was that Euro-Communism was an ill-defined and a nebulous concept. It combined the two incompatibles, bourgeois democracy with Communism. It accepted Marxist premises but did not relish what they led to in practice. It owned class conflict but outright rejected the dictatorship of the proletariat, an indispensable instrument to usher a classless society. It believed in revolution but wanted to be achieved through constitutional democracy. Euro-Communism believed in gradualism and progressive transformation through constitutional processes. As a matter of fact, there was so deep public distrust prevailing in West Europe against Communism that none believed in what the Euro-Communist claimed to profess. They saw their commitment to parliamentary democracy as nothing more than a tactical move to lull the electorate into voting them to power. Nor had the Euro-Communists a recognisable identity like the Social Democrats with their unambiguous and ideological commitment to constitutional democracy and an open system. Euro-Communism, "like the unicorn, was a mythical beast" and the contradictions in which it was wrapped hastened its death.

'Euro-Left'. With the demise of Euro-Communism for all effective purposes, a serious and widening cleavage separated the three major partners, the Spanish and the Italians on one side and the French on the other. In place of Euro-Communism, the Spanish find the Italian Communist parties, particularly the Italians, pursued a strategy similar to their previous parent body, but gave to their new find a new label. They referred to it as a search for the Euro-left, that is, offering to the electorate a wholly left alternative, comprising communists and socialists, to the centre-right alliance that had, sometimes with the support of centre-leaning socialists, held the reins of power in the post-war period.

Euro-left is not actually very different from Euro-Communism. Both these brands of Communism lay stress on independence from the stronghold of Moscow and agree on power-seeking and power-sharing strategy with non-Communist parties. Both profess and proclaim to retain the liberal or "*bourgeois*" freedoms in a socialist system. But they differ in two respects. First, as its name makes clear, Euro-left "plays down the ideological connections that Euro-Communism expressly emphasised because the communist parties feel that this will make them much more widely acceptable, especially in conjunction with the ideologically more moderate socialists, than Euro-Communism was able to do." Secondly, unlike Euro-Communism, as the "historic compromise" illustrated, Euro-left is purely an affair with the left spectrum and has nothing at all to do with the non-left parties.

The French Communists opted out of the Euro-left front and drifted back to Moscow for guidance and initiative. The failure of Euro-Communism convinced them not to dilute their ideological appeal. The French Communists, along with their Polish counterparts, sponsored the disarmament conference of East and West European Communists in Paris on 27 April 1980. Italy, Spain and Yugoslavia declined to participate and accused Georges Marchais, the French Communist Party leader, of allowing himself to be used by Moscow, in efforts to re-establish its leadership of the Communist movement.

The search for Euro-left did not rekindle any more hope than it was expected of Euro-Communism. The Communists were facing an uphill task in convincingly explaining the reasons for massive ideological shifts and the bloody conflicts for power and hegemony by and among Communist regimes. The horrors of Pol Pot's Cambodia, the Vietnamese invasion of Kampuchea and the Chinese attack on Vietnam, the Vietnamese-Soviet bid for hegemony in Indo-China, the *embourgeoisement* of Deng's China, the succession of bloody, shortlived regimes in Communist Afghanistan culminating in the virtual Soviet occupation over there, collectively "dimmed the lustre of Communism in many West European eyes".

No less significant was the role of the young, brilliant and imaginative leadership among West European Socialists. Since they held the middle path between the extremes of right and left, their platform seemed more attractive to the vast majority of the people of West Europe and the less orthodox Communists. This explained the growing influence the youthful socialist leaders like Michel Recard in France and Felipe Gonzalez in Spain, commanded not only within their own parties but in their countries at large. Gonzalez's brand of socialism was even more moderate than that of his counterparts, Papandreou in Greece and Miller in France. He long ago broke his Party's historic links with the Marxist ideology. The steep decline in the 1982 general election in Communist influence indicated that many former members of the Communist Party (PCE) approved of this break. The Socialists got 45.7 per cent of the votes polled for the lower house of Parliament, giving them absolute majority of 194 out of 350 seats. In France, too, Mitterrand headed the Socialist Government.

Then, there was the inescapable fact that the working classes in Western Europe neither wanted revolution nor were they enamoured of the socialist order of the Communist model which lay all around them in Eastern Europe. C.H. Cart explained in an interview to the *New Left Review* that European proletariat "has never been as little revolutionary as now. It has built up strong unions, but unions are not channels for building a revolutionary consciousness. Quite the contrary. They exist to get their members a large share of the capitalist cake and have, by large, accomplished this goal." European workers today are more prosperous with high standards of living and socially mobile, more healthy, better educated, enjoy greater personal freedoms and more individualism than they know any existing socialist set-up offers its own people and can hope to provide them. Faced with this fact, Professor Carr noted that the workers in West European countries are essentially concerned for a larger share for them of the capitalist cake, not the overthrow of the existing order by which they are doing extremely well.

All these factors impelled the Euro-Communists to adopt a more flexible and realistic attitude. But it did not work. What was the alternative then ? Professor Carr's answer was that if Euro-Communism failed, "... there are two alternatives.... The first is to remain Communists, and to remain an educational propagandist group divorced from political action.... The second is to go into current politics, become social democrats, frankly recognise and accept the capitalist system.... and work for those compromises between employers and workers and serve to maintain it."

This was a grim set of choices that Professor Carr suggested. But realities had to be faced squarely. If the Italian-Spanish analysis proved correct in floating the strategy of the Euro-Left and they were able, in alliance with the left groups, to muster sufficient support to form the government and come to power the prospects for them seemed to be encouraging. But the chances of their survival were as dim as they were for the Euro-Communists and the same factors that accounted for the demise of the latter repeated in the case of the Euro-Left too. The Communists did not support them for compromising on ideological essentials without gaining fresh adherents as Communists were suspects in the eyes of West European countries. No extent of argument could convince them that the Euro-Left communists meant business and they vehemently eschewed revolution, a closed society, dictatorship of the proletariat and subordination of personal freedoms to the socialist order. For them Communist was a Communist. Just as a leopard cannot change his spots so would a Communist not change his ideological base and his commitment to it. Euro-Left for them was another name for Communism and all what the latter stood for.

A New Image of Socialism. The tide of public sentiment against Communism was a phenomenon not peculiar to West Europe alone. Its canvas was wide. The shifts in the ideological base in Soviet Russia, China and Poland was a clear concession to the rising tide of these political sentiments. China's policy of *embourgeoisement* was nothing short of revisionism of the orthodox Marxian Theory. Soviet Russia swore by Marxism-Leninism, but the Party stalwarts there too were not immune from the impact of this new trend. The *Soviet Land*, under the caption, "Why has not Marxism-Leninism become obsolete ?", reported, "To dogmatists, to all those who would like to rest on their laurels, who interpret Marxist-Leninist theory as a set of immutable truths, as a complete collection of ready-made formulas and recipes to meet every contingency, genuine Marxists-Leninists, who creatively interpret this theory, have always said and will continue to say : that Marxism-Leninism is an ever-living and constantly developing teaching".[9] The concept of creatively interpreting Marxist-Leninist theory was unknown in the socialist annals of Soviet Russia, not even a decade back. The tide of public sentiment had admittedly changed the direction. Socialism (the first phase of Communism) thenceforward assumed a new image.

9. *The Soviet Land*, New Delhi, December 1979.

Thus, a wave of renewal was sweeping the Socialist part of the world. Although it had not yet embraced all the countries, there was more or less a conviction, to which even the orthodox Communists were no exception, that deep revolutionary changes were inevitable. At their roots was the crisis of the Stalinist and neo-Stalinist model of society, the crisis which had been aggravating over the decades before it became clear that this model had no prospects for the future.

Some East European countries, who had developed according to the Soviet model that was imposed upon or uncritically copied by them in the post-Second World War period, undertook reforms and renovation but these were accompanied by negative phenomena "and halted" and did not bring about the desired changes. However, they were precursor of future reforms. In the Soviet Union the CPSU initiated the elaboration of the theoretical foundation for a new image of Socialism. Its main features were defined at the 19th Conference of the CPSU (1988). Perestroika, restructuring the socialist society, was found the conducive answer of improving step by step, the conditions needed for the people's actual participation in governing the State, managing the affairs of Soviet society and for the implementation of Lenin's idea of self-government. Since the East European countries were facing problems similar to Soviet Russia, they also opted for Perestroika, without anticipating the shape of developments that would overtake these countries.

Perestroika and Glasnost. Since the mid-80s, when Mikhail Gorbachev took over as the Soviet Leader, the wind of radical change altered the tenor of life in the U.S.S.R. Though unique in scale and hitherto unknown to the theory and practice of Socialism (the first phase of Communism), these changes were imminently necessitated by internal causes and as a result of lessons drawn from errors and miscalculations of the recent past. Mikhail Gorbachev, General Secretary of the Communist Party of the Soviet Union (CPSU), said in early 1986: "We have resolutely taken the course of acceleration of the socio-economic development and renewal of our country, getting rid of everything that prevents the socialist system effectively using its mighty economic and social potential... we simply must make socialism stronger, more dynamically developing, successfully competing with capitalist society in all spheres."

The policies of Perestroika (restructuring) and *glasnost* (openness) and the "new thinking" underlying them—started emerging in the top-echelon meetings of the CPSU as early as April 1985; just a month after the assumption of the General Secretaryship of the Party by Gorbachev. They were put into operation following their approval by the 27th CPSU Congress in February-March 1986. The Central Committee plenary meeting of the Party on May 23, 1988, adopted ten theses or working points which were approved by the 19th All-Union Conference[10] held at Moscow in June-July 1988. It was an assembly of 5,000-odd delegates; one representing 3,780 Party members and elected by secret

10. The All-Union Party Conference was held after 47 years and was convened to endorse the theses adopted at the CPSU Congress. The next session of the Congress would have taken place in 1991, after 5 years, and it was deemed inexpedient to delay the reforms so long. The last Party Conference was held during Stalin's regime in 1941. It was the character of representation that distinguished a Party Congress from a Conference. Delegates to the Congress were elected practically by all party members, whereas to the Conference they were elected by the local committees of the Party.

ballot. The essence of the ten theses endorsed by the Conference was that Perestroika could only move ahead through the creation of a socialist civil society in which each citizen played a part in the decision-making instead of the existing command administrative structure which had been acting as a brake on the ideals of the Leninist revolution. It meant that the atmosphere of the new socialist civil society demanded the activity of its members, their participation in both nation-wide and local questions. The "human factor" was a new term added to the Soviet political vocabulary and the entire mechanism hinged upon this concept.

The meaning and content of Perestroika had never been defined in its totality, though it was conceived and put into operation in 1986. Indeed, Mikhail Gorbachev, its author, had been at pains all those years to tell his domestic and foreign questioners that it was an ongoing process whose scope was likely to widen as time passed. Of necessity, he said, it would consist of several "waves." extending over several years. "Of course, it will be much more than two or three years we should be ready for serious strenuous and tedious work to ensure that our country reaches new heights by the end of the twentieth century."

Even so as Gorbachev himself put it in his book, *Perestroika and New Thinking for Our Country and the Whole World,* "it means overcoming the stagnation process... and effective acceleration of social and economic progress... It means mass initiative... more glasnost, criticism and self-criticism in all spheres of our society and utmost respect for the individual and for personal dignity. Perestroika is the all-round intensification of the Soviet economy...the renunciation of management by injunction and administrative methods and the overall encouragement of innovation of social enterprise. Perestroika means a resolute shift to scientific methods...the combination of scientific and technological revolution with a planned economy. It means the priority development of the social sphere aimed at ever better satisfaction of the Soviet people's requirements for good living and working conditions...the elimination, from society, of the distinction of socialist ethics, and implementation of the principles of social justice." At another place Gorbachev said that "the essence" of Perestroika consisted in "its genuine revolutionary spirit and its all-embracing scope."

The above analysis of Perestroika involved three concepts which were important in the glossary of scientific socialism. The first was the strategy of acceleration. It had the aim of attaining a qualitatively new state of Soviet society when it made the most of the advantages inherent in socialism in all spheres. Acceleration meant not only and not so much higher economic growth rates as a new quality of growth: intensification of production on the basis of scientific and technological progress, structural reorganization of the economy, more effective forms of managing, organizing and stimulating labour.

The strategy of acceleration also implied the pursuit of an active social policy and consistent affirmation of the principle of social justice, improvement of social relations, renovation of the forms and methods of activity practised by political and ideological institutions, deepening of socialist democracy, resolute combating sluggishness, stagnation, conservatism — all that inhibited social progress.

The success of the strategic line of acceleration depended to no small extent on increasing the role played by the human factor, on promoting the creative work of the masses. To convince broad sections of working people in the process of acceleration, it was deemed significantly important to make them interested morally and materially and remould their mentality. The better the discipline and organization and the higher the responsibility of each for his work and its results, the more rapid the advance of the country, it was emphasised.

The problem of social justice was another important ingredient of Perestroika and it was thoroughly discussed and elaborated in the documents of the 27th CPSU Congress and other Party and Government documents. They also made the point that the substance of socialist social justice was embodied in the fundamental principle of socialism: "From each according to his ability, to each according to his work." Thus, under socialism social justice meant a struggle against unearned incomes and unjustified privileges, and on the other hand, improvement of moral and material incentives.

Social justice was not confined to the sphere of distribution alone. It pervaded all aspects of socialist social relations. It was to be seen in the real rule by the people, the equality of citizens before the law, the actual equality of nations, respect for the individual and creation of conditions for his all-round development, as well as social guarantees: full employment, accessibility of education and culture, the medical service and housing, care for the aged mother and child welfare.

Even fuller implementation of the principle of social justice in all spheres of social relations was held to be one of the basic tasks of restructuring socialism and, accordingly, an important condition for the unity of the people, political stability of society, and its dynamic development.

Before perestroika became operative, the economic basis of a Socialist Society was the state ownership of the means of production and the political apparatus was designed accordingly. Although it was dressed in democratic roles, power was actually concentrated at the top of the government pyramid, while democratic institutions and procedures were reduced to the mere formality of the political organisation of society. But it proved indisputably that such a political set-up inhibited initiative, marred the growth of personality of man and left no scope for the introduction of scientific progress and technological achievements.

When Mikhail Gorbachev embarked upon perestroika, the entire attention was concentrated on "economic tasks." But he soon realised the lacuna in his scheme of reforms. He found that the key solution of the economic reforms and task of social development "lies in democratizing all state and public life by creating all possible opportunities for the people's initiative and creative activity." At the same time, he made it clear that by advancing the goal of combining socialism with democracy and on this basis bringing out the entire potential of "our social system, we have no right to forget even for one minute that socialist democracy, like any other democracy, has nothing in common with a lack of discipline, wilfulness and anarchy." On the contrary, he emphasised that freeing people from excessive regimentation, providing them with all opportunities for free self-expression in production and creative work for active participation in tackling public affairs "call for greater personal responsibility of each and everyone for the situation in the country for its present and future." Perestroika, democratization and glasnost were inseparable for the consolidation of the State and public discipline "and the resolute struggle against all negative phenomena that make themselves felt in our life," he urged.

To ensure an effective functioning of the new economic model reflecting the new image of socialism, it was necessary to carry out a broad democratization of the whole system of State administrative government and also the "inner life" of the political institutions of society. This implied a sharp reduction of the role of the apparatus in administration. suppression of bureaucratic tendencies in its work, the transfer of many of its functions to lower echelons of government and economic management, a broad utilizaton of elements of self-government and pluralism in economic, social and political activity, he explained.

Such society's political life would give scope to the operation of self-regulating and self-adjusting economic mechanisms and the uninhibited operation of economic laws ensured by a law governed State which it was determined and firmly decided to build. One of the major functions of a law governed State is to strictly regulate political interference in the economy by defining its permissible forms and limit. On the political level a law governed State values the Rule of Law and it governs all the transactions of the government. It is a State where Rule of Law prevails and enjoys primacy.

It was, accordingly, deemed politic to bring about a radical change in the development of all the institutions of the Soviet statehood and the restoration and comprehensive application of their democratic potential. This was declared "most bluntly" at the 27th CPSU Congress (1986) and the Central Committee plenary meetings. A "lever was clearly and concretely defined which would render the restructuring irreversible." Gorbachev said in his address at the 19th Party Conference at Moscow : "One has to have the courage to admit today that if the political system remains immobile, unchanged, we shall not cope with the task of *Perestroika.* (Hence) the country's political system has to be overhauled."

In the main, the new political proposals provided for:(*i*) the creation of the post of the President of the Supreme Soviet of the USSR who "shall be elected and recalled through secret ballot by the Congress of the People's Deputies and be fully responsible and accountable to it (and not to the Communist Party hierarchy); (*ii*) the grant of greater powers to elective, constitutional bodies by laying down that "everything that the Supreme Soviet and the USSR Council of Ministers should be done by them"; (*iii*) there should be plurality of candidates contesting elections at various levels; (*iv*) a maximum of two five-year terms (not for life as heretofore) for all office-bearers; (*v*) the separation of the Party and the State, assigning to the former the leading guiding role, with the proviso that it should refrain from interfering in the day-to-day administration; (*vi*) the abandonment or "precluding of the practice when Party Committees adopt resolution containing directives to State and economic bodies and political organizations", so that (instead of the Party controlling the elected representative bodies) "the Party bodies should be controlled by the masses" or their representative bodies; (*vii*) "the creation of a socialist law-based state... where the main thing is the supremacy of law;" (*viii*) changes in the judiciary in the interest of equity and regarding the people's right to access to information; and (ix) an all-round enrichment of human rights and increased social activity and emphasis on the political rights of individuals."

At the behest of Gorbachev the Moscow Party Conference also approved two proposals which "seem to fly in the face of the above reforms." One was the institution of an elected executive Presidency on the pattern of the American Presidency, but in contrast armed with enhanced powers including emergency powers (Chapter 15 of the 1977 Constitution), and a relatively small Parliament being in almost continuous session. The second proposal was to make Communist Party heads in regions or districts, after their election by secret ballots, the chiefs of the "Soviets", the key instrument of social and economic change and decentralization.

One can assume that Mikhail Gorbachev believed that the task of implementing the proposed changes was so formidable that only in his ability to combine the twin roles of the new President of the USSR State and Secretary-General of the Communist Party can they have any chance of success. He would, thus, be in a sound position to ensure that Government business was not to be hindered by Party interference. During the process of election of delegates to the 19th Conference complaints were made that too many conservatives had found their way and they might eventually endanger the implementation of perestroika. In suggesting that the President of the USSR and the Party Secretary-General should be the same person, Gorbachev tried to achieve his objective of easing out of the veterans. as President Andrei Gromyko, who had served during the Stalin-Brezhnev periods and who would have been unable to adjust to the radical changes enbodied in perestroika.

The thrust of Gorbachev's proposals for endorsement by the Moscow 19th Party Conference in June-July 1988 is, thus, clear and unmistakable. In the economic and industrial sphere, he was keen on modernizing Soviet industry and economy so as to catch up with the most industrially and scientifically advanced nations like the United States of America, the then West Germany (West and East Germany are now unified into one Germany and a single nation) and Japan. And in the civil-political realm, he aspired for establishing a modern, rule of law-based democracy where through the flowering of personal creativity and initiative, the citizens of the Soviet Union should be able to give out their best to the Soviet nation. In this context Gorbachev's frequent references to "spiritual" and "moral" values and rights carried a special significance in a society or system overlaid with regimentation and the oligarchic domination of the Communist Party. With this background and the, presence of the vested interests of the 'old guard' and other entrenched elements in the Party, Harvard Sovietologist Marshall Goldman remarked that Gorbachev was "playing with fire" and gave him "no more than four years" in office.

There was no denying the fact that USSR was, indeed, in turmoil and in the winter of discontent Gorbachev's mechanism of perestroika and glasnost were in jeopardy. The impact of the acute economic crisis in the Soviet Union was being actually felt and the people were sceptical about the better days to come. The other problem facing the country was the nationalities question, which was assuming threatening proportions.

Since the ideology was being de-emphasised and the all too palpable element of fear that kept the constituent units together had largely disappeared, there was turmoil fuelled by local and regional nationalism. And it is well to remember that there were more than one hundred nationalities in the Soviet Union. The glasnost phase had given each of them the opportunity to express their historical resentments, including the shifting of populations under Stalin. According to preliminary results of "referendum" held on February 9, 1991, over 90 per cent of the Lithuanians voted for the Republic's independence from the Soviet Union.[11] President Gorbachev had denounced the poll as illegal but Lithuanians went ahead with their schedule of the poll defying the Presidential directive.

The Death of Soviet Communism. Marshall Goldman's prediction did not carry conviction at that point of time. Yet, it proved true and it was the cumulative effect of the deep and hiddent discontent of the Soviet people. The people had lost faith in any Scheme of reforms that aimed to purify the political and economic fabric of the country. The impact of acute economic crisis in the Soviet Union was clearly visible in declining growth rates, increasing scarcity of exploitable resources and most important, the worsening imbalance between military production and that of the general economy, especially consumer goods. In the consumer sector a very large portion of the capital stock was not only unproductive but was also simply at the limit of its physical capacity. Yet it was not being replenished. In the 10 years before perestroika began, according to Russian Prime Minister Ivan Silayev, only 15 per cent of investment in Russian Republics went to consumer industries. Military industries, on the other hand, were continuously supplied with new technologies without any constraint of capital supply.

Along with it went the deeds of the Soviet bureaucracies at all levels, including the Communist Party apparatus. They shifted from the limited autonomy of the Stalinist era toward a more corporate system. They increasingly neglected their goal of service to the State and society in favour of self-aggrandisement. Political and economic corruption which had existed throughout Soviet history increased systematically in the years before Gorbachev came to power. The size of the "second" or illegal "shadow" economy eventually accounted for 25 to 30 per cent of the market and became essential to the functioning of the economy as a whole. The Party apparatus had previously been less involved in illegal enrichment, but by the end of Brezhnev era it too became as bad as the administrative bureaucracy. Boris Yeltsin, in his book *Against the Grain*, has presented a shocking picture of this so called egalitarian society. He revealed that the "politbureau of the Communist Party enjoyed a luxurious lifestyle including marble dachas, an array of domestic help to satisfy their every whim and access to special stores, tailor shops and health clinics." Thus, the corruption of the bureaucracies and the Party elite only separated them further from the people they were supposedly in place to serve. The actual depoliticalisation of the people themselves "went so far that cynicism, hopelessness and passivity developed as a shield against the authorities. It, thus, became increasingly difficult to mobilise the population in almost any sphere of life.

The quality of the Soviet leadership was deteriorating as well, not only at the top,

11. The poll was boycotted by most of the non-indigenous population, mostly Russian speaking, which made up 20 per cent of the republic', total population of 3.6 million.

but also in the middle. This was true not only in terms of intelligence and organizational talent, let alone commitment, but also in a physical sense. Members of the Politbureau and the Central Committee of the Communist Party of the USSR were aged, dogmatic and lacked spark. The respect and fear they once generated were rapidly declining in an increasingly young and educated country ideologically committed. Yet the Party elites loved Brezhnev. Nikita Khrushchev may have given them security from threats to their lives, but Brezhnev gave them "security in officc, the good life, the blessing of domestic tranquillity and toleranceunless, of course, they crossed him personally." There were nevertheless many younger provincial Party Secretaries as well as officials of the central apparatus who were growing impatient for promotion for lack of emerging vacancies under the existing dispensation.

The weakness of political dissent within the Soviet Union was also important to the crisis. Under Khrushchev and in the early Brezhnev years political dissent grew rapidly and had "great importance beyond its actual influence inside the Soviet Union. It planted seeds of anti-totalitarianism and anti-Communism in the native soil, especially among the young intelligentsia, and showed the West that the spirit of freedom was not dead in Russia." But by early 1970s and early 1980s the most important dissenters were either silenced or they were obliged to settle abroad. Sympathy for their ideas was growing, but the political potential for active dissent inside the Soviet Union seemed to have sunk to a low. Dissent could have become immensely important to a process of renewal, if only internal conditions for its development would have changed.

Finally, the nationalities question in the Soviet Union—relations between non-Russian, nations and ethnic groups and the Russian Centre—was no less important. "It was potentially the most lethal yet insoluble crisis in the system, because both modernization and backwardness worked against Moscow. To the extent that non-Russian ethnic regions remained underdeveloped, peasant cultures, the depth of their attachment to traditional national culture and its religious context remained extraordinarily strong. These regions therefore were able to resist with surprising force subordination to Russian culture or submersion in the supra-national conception of the Soviet State." Alternately, "to the extent that non-Russian regions were swept up by the tide of modernization, they developed an intensely urban-centred orientation." The newly educated classes and the creative and managerial intelligentsia became the main carriers of this kind of ethnic identity. Thus lack of development led to cultivation of old ethnic identities, while the process of modernization "only created new strains."

Even by the time perestroika began, Communism had not been able to create a Soviet "nation." It was a multinational state comprising 109 nationalities plus 11 small national groups bound together in a federal polity. Since the Soviet Union was a conglomeration of many nationalities and ethnic groups, the 15 Republics of the federation were given unprecedented rights under the Constitution; the right to secede from the USSR, to maintain direct relations with foreign States even to the extent of concluding treaties and agreements and exchanging diplomatic and consular representatives. They could have their military formations too.

Not only the 15 constituent Republics of the Soviet Union, but even 20 autonomous republics within them had their own supreme bodies of state authority, their own constitutions, capitals, emblems and flags. Apart from Republics and autonomous republics, there were places inhabited by nationalities so small in size and population that they could not qualify to be autonomous republics and, therefore, to accommodate them, autonomous regions and autonomous areas were constituted. There were eight autonomous regions and ten autonomous areas. The Russian Republic was the largest and most populous Republic with immense natural resources and wealth. It was called the Russian Soviet Federative Socialist Republic (RSFSR) being composed of 16 autonomous republics, 5 autonomous regions, all 10 autonomous areas, 6 territories and 46 regions.

The Soviet Union was constitutionally a federation but in reality it was a unitary State ruled by the all powerful political apparatus of the Communist Party of the Soviet Union (CPSU). Various legislative bodies at the centre and in the Republics had hardly any effective power to take a decision independently and contrary to the ordains of the Communist Party which in practice meant its politbureau. But with the introduction of perestroika, glasnost and democratization in 1985, the political map in the country changed dramatically. While the conservative leadership of the Party was opposing the new policy of restructuring and openness, Mikhail Gorbachev went ahead with his policy to curtail the power of the ruling Communist Party and transferred the power it exercised in the domain of administration to the elected representatives of the Union and the Republics. Desperate conservative leaders made on to stage a *coup* against the Government in August 1991, but failed to achieve their objective. But the abortive *coup* hastened the demise of Communism and disintegration of the Soviet Union.

In fact, the federal structure had begun to crack in 1987, when the Nagorno Karabakh Autonomous Region witnessed sharp differences between the republics of Azerbaijan and Armenia. Nagorno Karabakh has a population of majority Armenian-christians but is an autonomous enclave in Azerbaijan, a Muslim republic. There had been a long running guerrilla war between the two republics and the fighting had, till August 1992, taken more than 2,000 lives. It was the worst ethnic dispute in the former Soviet Union. When Parliament of Azerbaijan moved to take an effective control of the autonomous region, citizens of that region voted at a referendum to declare it an independent State.

As the federal structure of the country began to crack, various republics of the Union that had been aspiring for independence declared themselves as sovereign states. Lithuania was the first to declare its sovereign status in March 1990 and was soon followed by two other Baltic States and then all republics seceded from the Soviet Union and declared their independence. The abortive *coup* was staged a day before the scheduled signing of the Union treaty, in Gorbachev's bid to save disintegration of the Soviet Union, by a few republics on August 1991. But the *coup* completely shattered the plan.

In an extraordinary interview conducted by America's ABC TV's network on September 5, 1991, from Kremlin, Mikhail Gorbachev and Boris Yeltsin expressed the view that Communism had failed. Gorbachev said that the historical experience of the USSR and Communism "has allowed us to say in a decisive fashion that model has failed which was brought about in our country, and I believe this is a lesson not only for our people but for all people." Boris Yeltsin, President of the Russian Federation suggested that Communism was a "beautiful idea" that would never work. "This experiment conducted on our soil was a tragedy for our people," he added. "It should have been better if this experiment had been conducted in some small country." Yeltsin also remarked that gradually the failure of Communism "will be understood by other countries where support for the idea of Communism still exists." Gorbachev, who intends to run in June 1996 for the Russian Presidential elections and run post-Communist Russia, blamed himself for leading the Soviet Union into oblivion. The lower House of Russian Parliament (Duma) denounced the C.I.S. Pact of 1991 and passed the resolution restoring U.S.S.R. Speaking at a press meet, Seleznyov said that personally he was in favour of denunciation of the U.S.S.R. Treaty by the presidents of Russia, Ukraine and Belarus, but the resolution of the Duma has no legal consequences neither for the Russian federation nor for other former Soviet Republics.

Contribution of George Bush, the American President, was no less important in the death of Soviet Communism and in Eastern Europe. Speaking at the acceptance of his second term nomination for Presidency at Houston on the closing session of the Republican Party Convention on August 21, 1992, he claimed the credit for the fall of Communism in the Soviet Union, in Eastern Europe and in Nicaragua in the northern hemisphere. He declared that his next target was Cuba and looked forward "to being the first President (of the United States of America) to visit a free, democratic Cuba."

ANARCHISM

Anarchism Explained. Anarchism is the doctrine that political authority, in any of its forms, is unnecessary and undesirable. The State is regarded as the embodiment of force employed in the government of the community. Liberty is supreme in the Anarchist creed, but it is sought by abolishing the State and all its institutions exercising forcible control over the individuals. "The liberty of man." Bakunin says. "consists solely in this, that he obeys the laws of Nature, because he has himself recognised them as such, and not because they have been imposed upon him externally by any foreign will whatsoever, human or divine, collective or individual." The Anarchists will, therefore. like to get rid of the State and all its instruments which are the symbols of force.

Anarchism in this sense is no new doctrine. Some of the stoics of ancient Greece questioned the moral and social legitimacy of State authority and held that good life could be obtained only "in a social condition in which men are able to act freely in response to natural instincts of sociability and justice." Restrictions imposed by the State were also resented by various religious sects during the Middle Ages. It was maintained that religion itself was a sufficient guarantee for a just and orderly civil life and men united in their Christian faith should be permitted to live under the control of their faith alone without any impositions from the government. Many poets and philosophers in all lands and climes and at all times talked contemptuously of the coercive power of the State and yearned for that free atmosphere of liberty wherein a just, happy and free social life was the desideratum. Disparagement of the political authority was more common in the seventeenth and eighteenth centuries when man's quest for freedom and equality brought him into clash with the despotic authority of the rulers. Individualism, too, in the nineteenth century condemned the State by regarding it as a necessary evil and advocating for the minimum exercise of political authority in order to secure maximum liberty for the individual.

The Socialists headed by Karl Marx regarded the existing State and its machinery an instrument of exploitation, because a part of the community had succeeded in defrauding their fellows of the just reward of their labour. The theory of Socialism is a revolt against the State and the capitalistic structure of society which it breeds. The modern Anarchism, too, is an indictment of Capitalism on economic and moral grounds and is, in an important aspect, akin to Socialism. Originally, the Anarchists were the followers of Karl Marx and they worked together with him for overthrowing the capitalist society and transferring the ownership of land and capital to the community. But Karl Marx and Michael Bakunin sharply differed on the methods by which a classless and stateless society could be reached. Karl Marx, and his English and German followers, considered the continuance of the State as an important phase of the revolutionary stage when capitalism had been overthrown. Marx had no love for the State. But true to his belief in evolution, he wished the proletariat to gain political power, and turn the *bourgeois* into the proletariat State, which, in its turn, would "wither away" after all classes had been abolished. Marx, thus, held that a dictatorship of the proletariat would have to precede the establishment of a Communist society. But Bakunin rejected Marx's programme of political action. Bakunin expressed horror of the State in any form whether proletariat or otherwise. His view was that man had already been prepared, by a long and arduous evolutionary development, to live a life free from governmental authority, and that it was only necessary to stage a revolution that would destroy the existing State to achieve a free, independent and idyllic existence, "The state," he held, "will always be an institution of domination and of exploitation a permanent source of slavery and misery." He further maintained that Marx was leading the International to a dangerous path, where exploitation and misery would increase rather than diminish. The proletariat State of Marx's conception, he asserted, "will be the sole capitalistic, the banker, the money-lender, the organiser, the director of all the national work, and the distributors of all its products." In brief, Bakunin had no use for the State in any form and at any stage in the development of free associations. Marx regarded Bakunin's view "as arrant nonsense of the radical and utopian kind which had long damaged the socialist cause." It was, he thought, a far cry from his own "scientific, practical, and hard-headed proposals."[12]

There was no meeting ground between the two and both Marx and Bakunin tried to eclipse each other. Bakunin commanded a substantial measure of support and the Basle conference in 1869 of the International was a victory for him. Marx tried to reverse the situation. Hc succeeded in securing the removal of the headquarters of the International to New York in 1872, and subsequently managed the expulsion of Bakunin and his associates from the organisation. Bakunin, then, gave a definite shape to his ideas, and established a distinct school of thought known as Anarchism.

Pierre-Joseph Proudhon (1809-1865). Proudhon is generally called the father of anarchism, although he called himself a socialist. He had wide differences with Karl Marx. He regarded Communism as utopian. "I am opposed to Communism," he wrote,

12. Harmon, Judd, *Political Thought from Plato to the Present*, p. 409.

"and if I am now considered as being the less advanced of the socialists, it is because I have left utopia, whilst the socialists are still in it." Communism, he said, resulted in a caricature of property. In fact, Proudhon was so much vehement in his criticism of Communism that he regarded it not science but the annihilation of science. "It is incapable of finding a formula," he said, "of distribution and of organisation. It is eclectic, unintelligent—it is the religion of misery. It neither thinks nor does it reason. It does not know how to organise, produce and distribute; it suspects labour and is afraid of justice. It borrows its ideas from the most ancient, mystic, obsolete, vague and undefinable tradition. Communism means privation everywhere and always."

Proudhon was against the State, since it had evolved out of the system of private property and had also supported the inequities in society. And what a paradox, Proudhon was not against the institution of private property itself. He even favoured the inheritance of property. He condemned it, because it brought social injustice and consequently privileges and authority. And since the State supported those inequities it was the vehicle of oppression. "Government of man by man in every form is oppression. The highest perfection of any society is found in the union and anarchy." Proudhon was the author of the term anarchy and his followers tended towards a theory of anarchy.

Liberty, Proudhon held, was not the daughter but mother of order. A society of his conception would consist of individuals and voluntary associations and in this society would prevail liberty and freedom, for all without restramt. The individuals and associations would engage themselves in productive enterprises with the aid of gratuitous credit supplied by cooperative banking associations. Karl Marx condemned Proudhon as a petit-bourgeois.

Count Michael Bakunin (l814-l876). In the same sense in which Marx is regarded as the founder of scientific Socialism, Bakunin is also regarded as the founder of scientific Anarchism. Bakunin, however, unlike Karl Marx, does not give us a coherent and systematic body of doctrine. It was left to his follower Kropotkin (1842-1921) to give refinement to the theory of Anarchism and present it in a logical manner. Both Bakunin and Kropotkin were Russians and the theory of Anarchism owes its fuller development chiefly to Russian thinkers.

The whole evolution of man, according to Bakunin, is from a condition in which animal impulses and physical restraints control the conduct of man towards conditions in which perfect liberty and ideal happiness prevail. Political authority, in any form, private property and religion are the conditions relating to the lower stage of man's development, because all of them are associated, in one way or another, with physical desires and fears; private property cultivates man's interest in material goods; the State supports private property through its physical compulsions; religion sustains both State and property, and also appeals to man's desire for physical comfort and to his fear of physical suffering after death. These institutions—private property, the State, and religion—which are the characteristic expressions of the primitive nature must ultimately disappear as a result of the operation of the natural laws of human evolution.

Bakunin's attitude towards the State is explicit and uncompromising. In his book, *God and the State*, he says: "The State is not society, it is only an historical form of it, as brutal as it is abstract. It was born historically in all countries of the marriages of violence, rapine, pillage, in a world war and conquest, with the gods successively created by the theological fantasy of nations. It has been from its origin, and it remains still at present, the divine sanction of brutal force and triumphant inequality." Despotism, he holds, is the essence of the State whatever be its form. Democracy and democratic devices are sheer cloak to hide the hypocrisy of the State oppression. The economically powerful class moulds and shapes the machinery of the government to their advantage by employing the economically weak classes as pawns on the chessboard of political intrigue. The system of private property is "both the ground of existence and the consequence of the State. To the millions of workers it brings economic dependence, laborious toil, ignorance, and social and spiritual immobility; for the few wealthy, it provides superfluous luxury and special opportunity for physical and artistic and intellectual enjoyment."

Apart from the perpetuation of an oppressive economic condition, the essential vice of the State is that it debases man morally and intellectually. A typical passage from Bakunin's *God and the State* is illustrative of this. He says: "The State is authority; it is force; it is the ostentation and infatuation of force. It does not insinuate itself; it does not seek to convert .... Even when it commands what is good, it hinders and spoils it, just because it commands it, and because ever, command provokes and excites the legitimate revolt of liberty; and because the good, from the moment that it is commanded, becomes evil from the point of view of true morality, of human morality (doubtless not of divine), from the point of view of human respect and liberty. Liberty, morality and the human dignity of men consist precisely in this that does good, not because it is commanded, but because he conceives it, wills it and loves it." Political authority also demoralises and degrades those who are entrusted with the power to exercise it. Power is intoxicating and corrupts even the best intentioned natures, and once in power, they would endeavour to retain it at all costs and by all means. They become flushed with an attitude of superiority. "Among those who exercise the power; natural sentiments of cooperation and fraternity are supplemented by tradition of prerogative, class differentiation, and sacrifice of individual welfare to the interests of public office. Thus the State makes tyrants or egoists out of the few and servants or dependents out of the many."

Bakunin regarded religion as an evil, because it permits evil institutions, and it is, also, incompatible with man's better nature. Religion, he held, is used as a cloak by the possessors of economic and political privileges to perpetuate their vested interests and to sanctify their unnatural superiority. "It diverts man's interest and effort from important affairs in the actual world of humanity; develops his fancy, superstition, and credulity; and aborts his reason and insight." Bakunin, as such, pleads that religious faith should be displaced by science and knowledge—"The fiction of future divine justice by the actuality of present human justice."

It follows that Bakunin will not admit of any privileged position or class, for "it is the peculiarity of privilege and of every privileged position to kill the intellect and heart of man. The privileged man, whether he be privileged politically or economically, is a man deprived in intellect and heart." Here is the summing up which Bakunin himself gives. He says, "In a word, we object to all legislation, all authority, and all influence, privileged, patented, official and legal even when it has proceeded from universal suffrage, convinced that it must always turn to the profit of a dominating and exploiting minority, against the interests of the immense majority enslaved."

Bakunin's methods of realising his programme are revolutionary. He makes all haste to sweep away the political and social institutions that prevent the realisation of his plans for the future. He advocates violence, pure and simple, with conspiracies, systematic assassinations and the like. "Our task is," Bakunin unequivocally asserted, "terrible, total, inexorable and universal destruction." The revolutionist of Bakunin's conception is a consecrated man, who will allow no private interests or feelings, and scruples of religion, patriotism or morality to turn him aside from his mission the aim of which is by all available means to overturn the existing State and society. And the emerging society will be a free federation of free associations wherein authority of any kind does not prevail.

Peter Kropotkin (1842-1931). Peter Kropotkin is the scientific interpreter of new Anarchism and he sought to give evolutionary and historical bases to his doctrines. The laws of evolution, he holds, apply alike to animals and their groupings and to men and human society. Kropotkin places clear emphasis upon two phases of natural evolution. The first is that in the normal course of the life of an individual vital forces operate in an orderly manner. But when these are interfered with, it may cause friction. In the beginning, the interference may accumulate; eventually, however, it leads to resistance of inconceivable strength. This resistance is justified as a necessary means of bringing natural processes back into their normal course. In the social life, too, there is slow and steady progress and the course of natural evolution runs its way smooth. But the normal course of social evolution may be obstructed by "misinformed or interested opposition" for gaining selfish interests. "On such occasions there is the need for great events that break the immediate course of history and draw mankind out of old ruts into new roads, but still on the main highway."

The second and more important principle of Kropotkin's evolutionary theory is the predominant part played in evolution by the cooperative, as distinguished from the competitive, natural of animals and men. The law of organic evolution is primarily a law of mutual aid, not of conflict. Kropotkin argued that the law of mutual aid manifests itself in social life, in the principle of equality, justice and social solidarity. It includes the spirit of: Do to others as you would have it done to you in like case. This golden rule of social conduct is the necessary condition for the attainment of the goal of social evolution.

Then, what are the hindrances to the progress of human society? Kropotkin catalogues three hindrances: the State, the property, and religion.

The State, Kropotkin holds, is without any natural or any historical justification. It is of recent origin. The State and its law came into existence only when society became divided into hostile and opposing economic classes, one of them seeking to exploit the other. It now exists to safeguard the interests of the minority of property-owners who control the government and obedience to its laws is obtained by the coercive power exercised by that ruling minority. The State, by its very nature, is opposed to man's natural cooperative instincts. He grows and develops only in a free atmosphere and by the spontaneous performance of his faculties and not by the spoon-feeding or the State. Restriction and restraint, if at all they are needed, must be self-imposed acts. "The people, acting spontaneously, can defend themselves against domestic brigands and foreign aggressors; history shows that standing armies have always been defeated by citizen armies and that invasion is more effectively thwarted by popular uprisings. Nor is government successful in protecting us against ill-disposed persons at home; prisons are more effective in spreading vice than in checking it; the cultural and benevolent activities of government are superfluous; when men are released from their economic and political dependence, voluntary activity will supply all that is needed for both education and charity."

In the same strain Kropotkin condemns private property. He says that production is the result of collective cooperative efforts of all the individuals engaged in the act of production, either directly or indirectly. Moreover, the existing stage in the advancement of industry is the cumulative result of the discoveries, inventions, and labours of many past centuries plus the present activities of varied and scattered groups of men. "Science and industry, knowledge and application, discovery and practical realization leading to new discoveries, working of brain and of hand, toil of mind and music—all together. Each discovery, each advance, each increase in the sum of human riches, owes its being to the physical and mental travail of the past and present. By what right, then, can any one whatever appropriate the least morsel of this immense whole and say—This is mine, not yours." It is, therefore, a heinous sin against justice that a small minority of the people retain the major benefit of the combined wealth produced by the collective efforts of the multitudes of men of both present and past generations. Kropotkin, then, proceeded to show the results of private property. Among the masses, he revealed, is "want and misery, millions unemployed, children of retarded growth, constant debts for the farmers; among the wealthy few—prodigality, ostentation, idleness, leading to the pursuit of the coarsest pleasures, debasing the press, and inciting war." What a real and matter-of-fact picture. This misery for the many and plenty for the few, Kropotkin associates with the political system which functions to protect private property.

Like Bakunin, Kropotkin rejects religion both on scientific and moral grounds. Religion, he said, is either a primitive myth and a rude attempt at explaining nature, or "it is an ethical system which, through its appeals to the ignorance and superstition of the masses, cultivates among them a tolerance of the injustices they suffer under the existing political and economic arrangements." According to Kropotkin religion is nothing but social morality that spontaneously develops among the people who live together. Such a natural religion, he believed, is essential to any society, in the sense that no "society can exist without certain moral habits and rules that evolve unconsciously and as a consequence of which men respect one another's interests and rely upon one another's words." This kind of morality, he said, is anterior and independent of formal religious creeds, and it is true religion, because it endures whereas traditional religions and systems of philosophy pass away.

Main Features of Anarchism. We, thus, find the following main features of Anarchism:

1. The social, economic and moral evils from which society suffers are intolerable. They can neither be cured nor alleviated by any action of the State which is always an instrument of personal or class domination.

2. Human nature is essentially good, but is corrupted by evil institutions. the State, private property and religion.
3. The division of labour and other forms of economic cooperation should always be on a voluntary basis for mutual benefit and advantages rather than contrived for the benefit of the propertied minority.
4. The new society can only result from a revolutionary change in the individual, his institutional environment, or both. It means destruction of the State and all other institutions connected therewith which aim to protect private property and perpetuate the hyprocrisy of religion.

Methods of Anarchism. The goal of Anarchism, according to Bakunin and Kropotkin, is to be attained both through evolution and revolution. The inevitable trend of social evolution is towards the anarchist goal. But this is not sufficient. The evolution, Kropotkin said, must culminate in revolution. A revolution in one country will grow into a general European revolution, probably lasting from three to five years. The revolution in its first phase will be destructive and violent. It means the destruction of all that is commonly understood in the sense of public order; existing governors removed from the seats of their political authority, prisons and forts demolished, armies disbanded and police liquidated, courts and offices removed. "A frightful storm is needed to sweep away all this rottenness, to vivify torpid souls with breath, and to restore to humanity the devotion, self-denial, and heroism, without which society becomes senile and decrepit, and crumbles away." Bakunin justifies bloodshed as a result of "the stupidity of those who will attempt to resist and of the natural feelings of revenge which many, in the first moments of their uprising, will feel towards their first oppressors."

After the political authority has been dissolved, the people will proceed to expropriate private property: peasants expelling land-owners, workers driving out factory owners, those having inadequate homes moving into dwellings that contain surplus. This having been secured, the work of a constructive reshaping of society will begin through a purely voluntary procedure. Establishment of any kind of government, may it be in the form of a transitional dictatorship, will, according to Kropotkin, mean the death of the revolution. "If the dissolution of the State is once started, if once the machinery of oppression begins to weaken, free associations will be formed automatically. When cooperation is not forced by government, natural wants will bring about a voluntary cooperation. Overthrow of the State and a free society will rise on its ruins."

Organisation of the Anarchist Society. We do not find in Bakunin's works a clear picture of the society at which he aimed. Kropotkin, on the other hand, explains in vivid terms the organisation of the Anarchist society. When the State disappears, a free society without distinction of race, colour, nationality or belief will be established in its place. Men living together in such a society will no longer be held together by the authority of the government. Every individual in this society will be permitted to labour and enjoy the fruits of his labour on equal terms. Individuals prosecuting the same end will combine into groups and these groups will form larger associations. "A complex interweaving of associations with order everywhere and compulsion nowhere, forms the stuff of which an Anarchist society will be made." These associations and groups will be for various purposes according to the actual needs and desires and all associations will be formed through voluntary contracts. Local associations may unite into larger territorial combinations, provided that at every stage there will be no compulsion about it. With each group disputes will be settled by voluntarily established courts of arbitration. The Anarchists really believe that there will be no incitement to anti-social acts as the new social order is based upon principles of freedom and justice. When and where individuals act anti-socially, "moral influence and sympathetic intervention will normally suffice to suppress them; in the rare cases where this is ineffective, fear of expulsion from the various fellowships, or of forcible intervention, either by individuals or by unorganised mass action will supply the necessary corrective."

As regards the economic organisation of the Anarchist society, there will be complete Communism. Society will own the land and all materials and instruments of production. Kropotkin regarded as fallacious and impracticable the doctrine that productive goods—machinery, factories, land, raw materials, means of transport—should be the ownership of the community, while finished goods—houses, clothing, provisions—should be privately owned. "The house," he says, "that shelters us, the clothing that covers us, the coal and gas we burn, the food we eat, the books from which we draw instruction, are just as necessary and useful for production as are machines, factories, and raw materials."

Land and other instruments of production will be taken into possession by those persons, acting individually or in freely formed associations, who are willing to use them productively. Every individual will then be permitted to share freely in the enjoyment of the products to the extent of the need, subject to the condition that he has put in his earnest and best productive efforts. The product will thus be shared only by those who work, and the distribution will be on the basis, not of service, but of need. Every labourer will be freely allowed to satisfy his need for all that is abundant. Scarce goods will be allotted according to individual needs, with preference for children, the aged, the infirm, and the weak. Under such a system of production and distribution, there will be contentment and sufficiency for all to live in comfort. When people are properly educated in the methods of cooperative life, when there is no inequality between rich and poor to provoke discontent, and no State protection of monopolies to inflame it, interests will rarely conflict, and occasions of disharmony will be few.

SUGGESTED READINGS

Almond, G.A.: *The Appeals of Communism.*

Beer, M.: *A History of British Socialism.*

Bobber, M.M.: *Karl Marx's Interpretation of History.*

Brameld, T.B.H.: *A Philosophical Approach to Communism.*

Chang, H.M.: *The Marxian Theory of the State.*

Coker, F.W.: *Recent Political Thought,* Chaps. I-IX.

Cole, G.D.H.: *Socialist Thought, Marxism and Anarchism, 1850-90.*

Cole, G.D.H.: *What Marx Really Meant.*

Cornu, Auguste: *The Origins of Marxian Thought.*

Crankshaw, E.: *Khrushchev's Russia.*

Ebenstein, W.: *Great Political Thinkers.*

Ebenstein, W.: *Modern Political Thought.*
Ebenstein, W.: *Today's Isms.*
Hallowel, J.H.: *Main Currents in Modern Political Thought.*
Harmon, Judd M.: *Political Thought from Plato to the Present,* Chaps. 19-20.
Hook, Sidney: *Marx and Marxists.*
Hook, Sidney: *Towards the Understanding of Karl Marx: A Revolutionary Interpretation.*
Laski, H.J.: *Communism.*
Lenin, V.: *Imperialism: The Highest Stage of Capitalism.*
Lenin, *V.: Marx-Engels—Marxism.*
Lenin, V.:*The Proletarian Revolution.*
Lenin, V.: *The State and Revolution.*
Low, A.: *Lenin on the Question of Nationality.*
Marx, Karl: *Capital.*
Mayo, H.B.: *Democracy and Marxism.*
Mayo, H.B.: *Introduction to Marxist Theory.*
Mayer, A.G.: *Leninism.*
Page, S.W.: *Lenin and World Revolution.*
Plamentz, J.: *German Marxism and Russian Communism.*
Russell, B.: *The Practice and Theory of Bolshevism.*
Sabine, G.H.: *A History of Political Theory,* Chaps. 33, 34.
Salter, F.R.: *Karl Marx and Modern Socialism.*
Seton-Watson, H.: *From Lenin to Khrushchev* : *The History of World Communism.*
Stalin, J.: *Foundations of Leninism.*
Stalin, J.: *Problems of Leninism.*
Trotsky, Leon: *The History of Russian Revolution,* tr. from the Russian, 3 Vols.
Wayper, C.L.: *Political Thought,* Chap. IV.
Webb, Sidney and Beatrice: *Soviet Communism, A New Civilisation?* 2 Vols.
Wells, H.G.: *Experiment in Autobiography.*
Wetter, G.A.: *Dialectical Materialism.*
Wolfe, B.D.: *Three Who Made a Revolution.*

31 CHAPTER

Gandhian Way of Life

Gandhiism and the Gandhian Way. Gandhi was not an inspired political philosopher destined to propound a new political philosophy and contemplate the world in the light of his creative vision. He was a common man whom the accident of circumstances had brought into the political field. But once he drifted to the field of politics, he made his mission sublime through his truthful nature, his sincerity, his tenacity, his industry, and his shrewd practical ability. Through his force of will and vital energy he grew by an evolutionary process to be a superman and was universally acclaimed: the Knower, the Doer, and the Sayer. He practised old philosophies and adhering to certain fundamental principles based upon truth, he led men to the realization of a better order of society than the destructive and cruel chaos in which mankind had hitherto existed. His mission was to purify politics, to rekindle love in the human breast, to rehabilitate the freedom of man, and to restore and teach the dignity of human labour.

Gandhiism is, thus, "not a set of doctrine or dogmas, rules or regulations, injunctions or inhibitions, but it is a way of life. It indicates a new attitude or restates an old one towards life's issues and offers ancient solution for modern problems."[1] There is no *ism* in Gandhi. *Ism* means a distinctive doctrine. Gandhi never claimed finality for his opinions. He was always experimenting with truth. He styled his activities as search for, or experiments with, truth.[2] Consistency, Gandhi said, "is a hobgoblin." No theory guided his thoughts and actions. He always strove to keep his mind open and he very often differed with himself. There was no rigidity with him and his life was an unending experiment. Gandhi himself had told the members of the Gandhi Sangh at Saoli in March 1936: "There is no such thing as 'Gandhiism' and I do not want to leave any sect after me. I do not claim to have originated any new principle or doctrine. I have simply tried in my own way to apply the eternal truths to our daily life and problems. The opinions I have formed and conclusions I have tried at are not final. I may change them tomorrow .... I have nothing to teach to the world. Truth and non-violence are as old as the hills. All I have done is to try experiments in both on as vast scale as I could do. In doing so I have sometimes erred and learnt by my error....Well, all my philosophy, if it may be called by that pretentious name, is contained in what I have said. You will not call it 'Gandhiism'; there is no *ism* about it."

1. Sitaramayya, P., *Gandhi and Gandhiism,* Vol. 1, p. 35.
2. Kripalani, J.B., *The Gandhian Way,* p. 159.

There is, therefore, no such thing as Gandhiism. It is only the Gandhian way and outlook[3] which is neither rigid nor formal nor final. The things he said had been said before, the truth he uttered, or even the principles he claimed, had been said and practised in earlier days also. He held these cardinal principles—truth and non-violence—religiously and based all his transactions on these principles. Gandhi's originality lies in the application of these principles on a mass scale covering the whole of life, individual and social, moral and material. No one before him had ever done so. The principles of truth and non-violence had been previously applied on individual scale to mould personal life and acts. But for Gandhi to separate the individual from society was to do violence to both. The individual and society, in his opinion, act and react upon each other and have to be raised simultaneously.

A casual reference may be made to the statement which Gandhi made at a public meeting at Karachi soon alter the Gandhi-Irwin Pact had been concluded, and just before the Karachi Session of the Congress. Gandhi is reported to have declared that "Gandhi may die but Gandhiism may live for ever."[4] "Apparently," says Dr. Sitaramayya, "he then and there coined the term *Gandhiism* as an expression which succinctly but comprehensively summarises the philosophy that underlies his cult of truth and non-violence."[5] The Gandhi-Irwin Pact, or the Delhi Pact, as the biographer of Lord Irwin calls it, was a triumph of truth and non-violence. It was tribute to his power of *satyagraha*, because the Pact, according to Gandhi, had established the basis of equality in principle, between India and Britain.[6] It was a new basis of relationship between the two countries, though the Pact neither promised independence nor Dominion Status. The success of the Pact depended upon the behaviour of the British Government and the outcome of the Round Table Conference. And Gandhi was doubtful of the good results. "There is every chance of my returning empty-handed," he said on going aboard the *Rajputana* which took him to London to participate in the Second Round Table Conference as the sole delegate of the Congress.

It will be too much to assert that Gandhi had claimed to establish a distinctive doctrine of his own when he said "Gandhiism may live for ever." The only logical meaning which can be given to it is that he desired to keep the torch of truth and non-violence burning for ever and glowing the path of true *satyagrahis* in reaching the goal of independence, and establishing a non-violent society or *Ram Rajya*. Perhaps, Gandhi was in a mood to remind his listeners at the Karachi meeting of the ordeals ahead of them, because the moment the Pact was signed, complaints of its non-fulfilment were levelled against the Government and Gandhi was again negotiating with the Viceroy, this time the new Viceroy, Lord Willingdon, well-known in India for his professions and deeds.

It would, therefore, be presumptuous to give the statement a meaning other than the

3. Refer to *Gandhian Outlook and Technique*—A Verbatim Report of proceedings of the Seminar on the contribution of Gandhian outlook and techniques held in New Delhi under the auspices of U.N.E.S.C.O. in January 1953.
4. Sitaramayya, B.P., *Gandhi and Gandhiism,* Vol. 1, p. 37.
5. *Ibid.*
6. Louis Fisher, *The Life of Mahatma Gandhi*, Vol. I, p. 34.

natural explanation in the context of the circumstances. There was no *Gandhiism* with Gandhi. Being a growing and evolving personality there could be no finally fixed modes of thought and action for him. As regards the two cardinal principles of *truth* and *non-violence*, there was no rigidity for him in their application. Even his closest associates could not make any positive forecast of how he would act under a particular set of circumstances. Gandhi himself freely admitted that *Ahimsa* might be applied differently in differing circumstances and situations. In fact, all *isms*, as Acharya Kripalani rightly says, "come into existence, not at the initiative of those in whose names they are preached and pormulgated, but as the result of limitations imposed upon the original ideas by the followers. Lacking the creative genius, the followers systematise and organise. In so doing they make the original doctrines rigid, inelastic, one-sided and fanatical depriving them of their original freshness and flexibility, which are the signs of youth."[7] Gandhi simply indicated the direction without trying to fill in the details finally or for all times to come. It was only a Gandhian way and outlook. When his impatient followers fill in the details making his ideas and technique rigid, it becomes Gandhiism. Then, the principles he preached and the modes he practised become rigid and extreme. Gandhi had always condemned extremism. "If only these *isms* (as Babu Bhagvandas puts it) would shed their extremism and taken instead, a little genuine spiritual religion and a few psychological principles," Gandhi said, "they would be at once shaking hands with each other or even running into each other's arms. All these ideologies and *isms* have great things to their credit, all have great crimes to their debit too." Gandhi's views are equally applicable to all varieties of *isms*, religious, economic, and political.

Background of Gandhian Outlook. The *Gita* ranks foremost in moulding Gandhi's outlook. Since 1889, when he first read it in Sir Edwin Arnold's translation, the *Gita* had always been his spiritual reference book, in fact, his daily and never-failing guide. "When doubts haunt me, when disappointments stare me in the face," declared Gandhi, "and I see not one ray of light on the horizon, I turn to the *Bhagavad Gita*, and find a verse to comfort me; and I immediately begin to smile in the midst of overwhelming sorrow. My life has been full of external tragedies and if they have not left any visible effect on me, I owe it to the teachings of *Bhagavad Gita*." Gandhi was pre-eminently a man of action. The *Gita* made him one. He remained twenty years fighting the battle of Indian rights in South Africa. He won it. The rest of his life is a continuous struggle against iniquity and injustice, social, economic, and political. He won for India political independence and brought about a new outlook in the country in the solution of her social and economic problems. He was a *Karma yogi*, a practical man of action who struggled without the desire for results. His was selflessness in action consistent with the teachings of the *Gita* and he held to them steadfastly. The message of the *Gita* is:

> *"Act thou, O Dhananjaya (Arjuna), without attachment, steadfast in yoga, with even-mindedness in success and failure, even-mindedness in yoga."*

Even-mindedness or a balanced state of mind can be obtained only by killing all passions and by renouncing desires than objects. Renunciation gives one the inner peace,

7. Kripalani, J.B., *The Gandhian Way,* p. 158.

the spiritual poise, to achieve results. Gandhi did not agree that warfare could be consistent with renunciation. "Let it be granted," he wrote in 1929, in an introduction to the Gujarati translation of the *Gita*, "that according to the letter of the *Gita* it is possible to say that warfare is consistent with renunciation of fruit. But after forty years' unremitting endeavour fully to enforce the teaching of the *Gita* in my own life, I have, in all humility, felt that perfect renunciation is impossible without perfect observance of *Ahimsa* in every shape and form." Then, comes the revolutionary Gandhi who declared that his loyalty to the *Gita* entitled him to amend such a notion. He very often refused to be bound by uncongenial texts, concepts and situations.

Gandhi's faith in *Ahimsa* was both hereditary and environmental. In no other part of India was the hold of Jainism on the life of the people greater than in Gujarat where Gandhi was born and brought up. His father, though a *Vaishnava*, freely associated with Jain monks. The ,Jain monks, Becharji Swami, helped Gandhi to go to England for his studies. Before he left for London, Becharji Swami administered an oath to Mohandas who then solemnly took three vows: not to touch wine, woman or meat.[8] Jainism, therefore, had perceptibly coloured Gandhi's thoughts and shaped his actions. The influence of Buddhism, too, was in no way less. It was, under these circumstances, natural that Gandhi should have a firm conviction that the practice of *Ahimsa* was essential for the state of non-attachment. And he had been striving to become a *Karma yogi* soon after reading the *Gita* and especially during his stay in South Africa. He fought the battle of *Ahimsa* in that country and the success he achieved there left an indelible impression on him about its efficacy.

Gandhi perfected the science and art of *Ahimsa*, extended its scope to all activities in life, and himself attained the status of *sthitaprajna*, the ideal man of the *Gita*; and the ideal man of the *Gita* is one who has abandoned desire and freed his mind from all worry, who receives pleasures and pains alike and is no longer subject to the passion of fear, anger and hatred, who is completely detached and is unconcerned with good or bad results.

John Ruskin's *Unto This Last* had also been one of the transforming influences which shaped Gandhi's views. This book was given to Gandhi by Henry S.L. Polak, an Assistant Editor of the *Transvaal Critic*. "This book," he said in 1946, "marked the turning point in my life." He immediately decided to change his "life in accordance with the ideals of the book." Gandhi learnt three lessons from it:

1. That economy is good which conduces to the good of all.
2. That a lawyer's work has the same value as the barber's, inasmuch as all have the same right of earning their livelihood by their work.
3. That the life of labour, that is, the life of the tiller of the soil and the handicraftsman, is the life worth living.

While in Volksrust prison in October 1908, Gandhi read Henry David Thoreau's famous essay on Civil Disobedience. It has often been said that Gandhi borrowed the idea of *satyagraha* from Thoreau. But he denied it in his letter, dated September 10, 1935, addressed to P. Kodanda Rao of the Servants of India Society. Gandhi wrote, "The

8. Gandhi, M.K., *The Story of My Experiments With Truth,* Vol. II, pp. 107-08.

statement that I have derived my idea of Civil Disobedience from the writing of Thoreau is wrong. The resistance to authority in South Africa was well advanced before I got the essay of Thoreau on Civil Disobedience."[9] He, however, regarded it as "masterly treatise" and admitted that "it left a deep impression" on him.

The Rev. J.J. Doke calls Gandhi a disciple of Tolstoy. Gandhi also considered himself "a devoted admirer who owes much in life to him." In his letter written to Tolstoy on April 4, 1910, Gandhi described himself an "humble follower of yours."[10] He read Tolstoy's *The Kingdom of God is Within You* at a time when he was passing through a crisis of scepticism. He had not by then completely surrendered himself to non-violence and accepted it as a creed in the solution of all problems in life. But "its reading," says Gandhi, "cured me of my scepticism and made me a firm believer in *Ahimsa*."

Tolstoy's philosophy is called Christian Anarchism. It is the application of the teaching of the *Sermon on the Mount* to the solution of the modern social, economic and political problems. The essence of Christ's teaching and the one adequate solution for human problem is, according to Tolstoy, love. "A Christian enters into no dispute with his neighbour, he neither attacks nor uses violence; on the contrary, he suffers himself, without resistance, and by his very attitude towards evil not only sets himself free, but helps to free the world at large from all outward authority." The Christian Anarchist, Tolstoy, makes love as the basis of his principle of non-resistance.

The *Gita* and the *Sermon on the Mount* had led Gandhi to the same conclusion. "Next to the late Raychandra,"[11] wrote Gandhi, "Tolstoy is one of the three moderners who have exerted the greatest spiritual influence on my life, the third being Ruskin."[12] Tolstoy preached peaceful, painful refusal to serve or obey evil governments. Gandhi also preached the same. In his letter to Gandhi dated April 25 (May 8), 1910, Tolstoy wrote, "I just received your letter and your book, *Indian Home Rule*. I read your book with great interest because of the things and questions you treat in it; passive resistance is a question of the greatest importance, not only for India, but for the whole of humanity."

Religion and Politics. Gandhi's religion made him political and his politics was religious. This is in essence the Gandhian outlook. "There are no politics," said Gandhi, "devoid of religion. Politics bereft of religion are a death trap because they kill the soul." To him, religion and politics were not apart from each other than body and soul. Religion was the very breath of Gandhi's being. He says, "At the back of every word that I have uttered since I have known what public life is, and of every act that I have done, there has been a religious consciousness and a downright religious motive."

By religion, Gandhi did not mean any particular creed. He believed in an all-pervading God. His God was Truth. His Truth was knowledge and where there was true knowledge there was bliss. He did not merely say that "God is truth", but also said that "Truth is

9. M.K. Gandhi, *An Indian Patriot,* p. 3.
10. *Young India,* Vol. I. p. 652.
11. Raychandrabhai was the poet-jeweller and a distinguished reformer of Bombay. Gandhi came in intimate contact with him after his return from England. He not only influenced Gandhi by his moral earnestness and deep religious nature, but helped him in the study of Hindu religion.
12. *Young India,* p. 652.

God." Gandhi was, accordingly, a seeker after truth and his God manifested Himself in *Truth* and *Love*. Love and *Ahimsa* were synonymous for him. Without *Ahimsa*, he said, it was not possible to seek and find truth. Both are the obverse and reverse of the same coin-one is the means, the other is the end. Whoever acts on these principles was for him a religious and spiritual person whether he believed in God or not, whether he was a Jew or a gentile, a heathen or a Christian, a Muslim or a Kafir. Gandhi's God and religion was, thus, a thing of the heart. It resided in every human heart and it must be evolved by each out of himself as it is always within us. "The ultimate definition of religion," he concluded, "may be said to be obedience to the Law of God. God and His Law are synonymous terms. Therefore, God signifies an unchanging and living being. No one has ever really found him. But *Avtars* and prophets have, by means of their *tapasya*, given to mankind a faint glimpse of the eternal law and assigned to each one amongst us the work of the moral scavenger—so as to clean and purify our hearts and get them ready;" ready for action and service of mankind in removing iniquity and injustice.

Gandhi's religion, in short, means, "belief in the ordered moral government of the universe".[13] It is identical with morality.[14] It is practical and universal and provides a basis for all the activities of man. He explained to the Christian pilgrims, who met him at Wardha, the motive of his work. Gandhi said, "My motive has been purely religious. I could not be leading a religious life unless I identified myself with the whole of mankind; and this I could not do unless I took part in politics. The full gamut of man's activities today constitutes an indivisible whole. You cannot divide social, political and religious work into watertight compartments. I do not know any religion apart from human activity. It provides a moral basis to all other activities which if they would otherwise lack reduce life to a thing of sound and fury signifying nothing.[15]

Gandhi's mission was to moralise man and society. But a moral man and a moral society could only be obtained when truth stood arrayed against all tyranny whether that tyranny was of the State or society or of the individual. Politics was, accordingly, an unavoidable evil for him.[16] If "I take part in politics," he said, "it is only because politics today encircles us like the coils of the snake from which one cannot get out no matter how one tries. I wish to wrestle with the snake .... I am trying to introduce religion into politics." Political freedom, he thought, was essential for the emergence of a non-violent State and a non-violent society, "He who does not know what patriotism or feeling for one's country is, does not know his true duty or religion and those who say that religion has nothing to do with politics, do not know what religion means."[17]

Gandhian Outlook Explained. Gandhi was a political engineer whose domain was action, first in South Africa and later in India. He was not a philosopher or thinker in the sense that he thought out a philosophy of life and chalked out a programme of action which he left to others to study and implement. He worked and experimented, identifying

13. *Harijan,* 10 February, 1940.
14. *My Experiment With Truth, op. cit.,* Vol. I, p. 5. Also refer to M.K. Gandhi's *Ethical Religion*, pp. 23-24.
15. *Harijan,* December 24, 1933, p. 393.
16. *Ibid.*
17. *My Experiments With Truth, op. cit.,* Vol. II, p. 591.

himself always and completely with the people. He was one of them and at one with them, devising means for their social, economic and political emancipation. All through his public life his was a relentless war against evil, evil in all aspects and there was no department of life, particularly embracing the life of Indians, which he did not touch, which he did not influence and in which he did not make his own contribution. P. Sitaramayya gives a graphic description of Gandhi. He says, "Gandhi lives for others. Society is Gandhi's temple, service is his sole form of worship, humanity is his single passion. Truth is his one God and non-violence is his only means of attaining it. His appeal is to the universal of which local forms an integral factor."[18] Gandhi was, thus, an embodiment of virtue and being a man of action and a firm believer in *nishkama karma*, action without the desire for the result, his mission in life was to strive for justice for all men; freedom for all nations to develop their own resources according to their own genius; freedom for individuals within nations, that is, complete freedom, no matter what colour, creed, what religion or political views they have; freedom from disease, hunger and poverty; in a word complete freedom for all so that each individual could attain his highest innate capacity for physical, psychological, and cultural development.

In his attempt to realise a better ordering of human society, Gandhi devised a new moral strategy; the method of regulating along non-violent lines, group life in its political, economic, national and international aspects. He condemned the methods hitherto employed to solve the group problems, because modern group life has degraded both individual and social morality. The individual is asked to play a dual and contradictory role and two different and conflicting moral standards regulate his conduct. As a citizen, he is enjoined to act as a good neighbour and to regulate his social conduct on the basis of natural trust, cooperation, truth and non-violence. As a member of a group and a nation, he is enjoined to consider other groups and nations as actual or potential enemies and his conduct is marked by selfishness, distrust, fraud, violence and war. These differing moral standards create conflicting loyalties and when "loyalties cannot be harmonised, they create internal and external conflicts." In the individual "they create a split personality. Conflicting moral standards produce social, economic and political contradictions and maladjustments and cause violence, revolution and war."[19]

Gandhi's solution for the present state of confusion is the necessity to moralise group and political life, which under the complexity of modern conditions encompasses the whole of our existence. There cannot be two consciences of man, one individual and social and another political. The same code of morality should be observed in all spheres of human activity. It must be considered as wrong and immoral to lie, cheat, exploit or kill fellow beings for political, economic and ideological as for any other reasons. "We have to make truth and non-violence," said Gandhi, "matters not merely for individual practice but, for practice by groups, communities and nations That at any rate is my dream."[20]

18. *Gandhi and Gandhiism, op. cit.*, Vol. I, p. 35.
19. Acharya J.B. Kripalani, A Paper submitted to the U.N.E.S.C.O., Seminar on the contribution of Gandhian Outlook and Techniques, *op. cit.*, Appendix B, p. 352.
20. *Harijan,* March, 1940.

In order to work out a synthesis between the individual and group, between social and economic and political life, Gandhi began with the individual, whose moral regeneration he deemed as the first requisite. Gandhi's *Swaraj* was concerned with the individual's inner freedom as well as his external freedom in society. His was a simultaneous reform of the individual and society. True morality must manifest itself in every action of the individual as individual and also as a member of society. The individual and society both act and react upon each other. "I do not believe," said Gandhi, "that the spiritual law works in a field of its own. On the contrary, it expresses itself through the ordinary activities of life; it thus affects the economic, social and political fields."[21] Gandhian outlook may be reduced to a simple formula: If you have to reform yourself you must do so while reforming society. There cannot be a divorce between the two.

Gandhian Technique. With a view to moralismg the individual and society, Gandhi prescribed certain principles or norms to which human conduct must conform. These principles are: truth, non-violence, and scrupulous regard for means. All these principles are inter-connected and, accordingly, supplementary and complementary to one another.

Truth is the first thing to be sought for, because there is no God higher than truth. But truth and non-violence are inseparable and presuppose each other. He who believes in non-violence believes in a living God and the living God for Gandhi is truth. Wherever there is truth there is love, and wherever there is violence there is untruth. One who holds to truth is not out to injure or destroy the opponent, but to convert him into an ally. Violence gains nothing. On the contrary, it aggravates the moral disease. It does not lead to the correction of the person on whom violence is perpetrated. Violence, in fact, is likely to kill the initiative of the person concerned and "to destroy" the very possibility of "change of heart" which is the essence of moral regeneration. Use of violence, Gandhi further asserted, not only lowers the victim, but also the user of violent means, because "non-violence is the law of our species as violence is the law of the brute."[22] The evil-doer should be weaned from error by patience and sympathy, that is, self-suffering. Pursuit of truth means realization of spiritual unity through love and service of all, and love and service of all is non-violence. The use of violence, in any form, Gandhi maintained, offends "the greatest truth, the unity and sacredness of all Beings."[23]

Gandhi did not distinguish between ends and means. He regarded the two as a continuous process. He rejected the maxim that the end justifies the means. Every act, he said, is in pursuance of an end. The end is merely the result of a series of acts that are undertaken as means. If each action has its appropriate result, then, a good action creates a good result and a bad action a bad result. Moral means must, therefore, be adopted to achieve desirable results. He likened means "to a seed, the end to a tree; and there is just the same inviolable connection between the means and the end as there is between the seed and the tree."[24] Means are, to him, everything. He believed that "if one takes care of the means, the end will take care of itself."[25] Gandhi so often maintained,

21. *Young India,* September 9, 1925.
22. *My Experiments With Truth, op. cit.,* Vol. II, pp. 53-54.
23. *Young India,* August 11, 1920.
24. *Hind Swaraj, op. cit.,* p. 60.
25. *Harijan,* February, 1939.

"the attempt made to win *Swaraj* is *Swaraj* itself."[26]

Gandhi evolved a way of resisting evil through the organisation of truth and non-violence or *satyagraha*; holding on to truth. The technique of satyagraha is Gandhi's unique and distinctive contribution not only to the armoury of political weapons, and the technique of revolution, but to the store of human knowledge and thought as well. It is a new science or a philosophy in action. It was tried and found successful in limited fields and it has the possibilities of being applied in new and wider fields, particularly in the explosive situation of the present-day world affairs. *Satyagraha* is the technique of resisting all that is evil, unjust, impure and untrue and resolving all maladjustments in human relations by love, voluntary suffering and self-purification by an appeal "to the divine spark in the opponent's soul." It is an expression of purest *Ahimsa* or non-violence and it precludes hatred, deception or untruth. To explain it in the words of Gandhi: *Satyagraha* "is a vindication of truth by bearing witness to it through self-suffering, in other words, love."[27] It is the opposite of coercion and is not even akin to passive resistance. It is the weapon of the strongest and the bravest; the true man of God who seeks to conquer evil by truth and to resist physical force by taking suffering on himself instead of inflicting it upon the opponent, that is, by love. The *satyagrahi* establishes his spiritual identity with the opponent and awakens in him a feeling that he cannot hurt him without hurting his own personality. The action of *satyagraha*, in the last analysis, proceeds through the technique of "identification" and "involvement." All differences and conflicts between man and man, between group and group, "are sought to be resolved by the mighty weapon of *satyagraha* by lifting these from the gross physical plane to the elevated spiritual and moral plane where they can be adjusted by the union of souls, by the deep calling unto the deep."

Satyagraha or Soul force or Love force, as Gandhi calls it, is like a coin on whose face you read love and on the reverse you read truth. "And as a *satyagrahi* never injures his opponents and always appeals either to his reason by gentle argument, or his heart by the sacrifice of self, *satyagraha* is twice blessed; it blesses him who practises it, and against whom it is practised." It has very often been maintained that the organisation of non-violent resistance or *satyagraha* of Gandhi's conception can be practised by only a select few. Gandhi did not agree to it. He said, "My experience proves the contrary. Once its simple principles—adherence to truth and insistence upon it by self-suffering—are understood, anybody can practise it. It is as difficult or as easy as any other virtue."

Satyagraha, as a method of redressing group and political wrongs, was first experimented by Gandhi in South Africa with a commendable success. It was again tried on an extended scale and covering many phases in India to achieve national independence. India won the non-violent battle of her independence. It stands unparalleled in history. No revolution for national independence had been as bloodless as the Indian revolution for independence and both the rulers and the ruled parted company in comparative friendliness.

Satyagraha, then, is resistance based on moral force as opposed to brute force. It is

26. *Speeches and Writings of M. K. Gandhi*, p. 720, Madras, 1922.
27. U.N.E.S.C.O. Seminar, *op. cit.*, p. 382.

not passive, but active non-violent resistance. "With *Satya* (truth) combined with *ahimsa* (non-violence)", said Gandhi, "you can bring the world to your feet. *Satyagraha* in essence is nothing but the introduction of truth and gentleness in the political, that is, the national life." He further observed that "it is totally untrue to say that it is a force to be used only by the weak so long as they are not capable of meeting by violence .... This force is to violence, and therefore to all tyranny, all injustice, what light is to darkness. In politics its use is based on the immutable maxim that government of the people is possible only so long as they consent either consciously or unconsciously to be governed."

The Technique of *Satyagraha*. The technique of *satyagraha* as corporate action may take the following forms:

1. **Non-Cooperation.** Oppression and exploitation, Gandhi argued, are made possible by cooperation, willing or forced, of the oppressed in their own exploitation or oppression through cupidity, ignorance or fear. If all people ceased completely to cooperate with an unjust or tyrannous system, it must ultimately collapse. "Even the most despotic government," Gandhi maintained, "cannot stand except with the consent of the governed, which consent is often forcibly procured by the despot. Immediately the subject ceases to fear the despotic force, his power is gone." What is true of governments also applies to other exploiting groups and organisations. Non-cooperation with evil takes the form of self-purification in the *satyagrahi* himself and the withdrawal on his part of cooperation from the unrighteous and unrepented institution which embodies the evil. Non-cooperation, thus, stresses the purity of means and the purity of ends as well as the purity of motives and intentions.

The non-violent methods which satyagrahis may employ to develop the non-cooperation movement are: hartal, social ostracism, and picketing.

(*i*) **Hartal.** *Hartal* means cessation of business as a measure of protest. Its object is to strike the imagination of the people .and the government or the institution involved. Two things are necessary here. In the first place, the *hartals* should not be frequent, otherwise they would cease to be effective; and, secondly, they should be strictly voluntary, the result of persuasion and other non-violent methods of propaganda.

(*ii*) **Social Ostracism.** This is tantamount to social boycott against blacklegs who defy public opinion and do not resort to non-cooperation. Gandhi felt that "in social life it is impossible to avoid ostracism to a certain extent, but it should not be used, except in a very limited sense." It does not mean depriving a person of indispensable social services or to make his life unbearable "by insults, innuendoes and abuse." All this would amount to coercion and violence.

(*iii*) **Picketing.** Picketing must necessarily be persuasive and not coercive. Gandhi had always condemned picketing in the sense of sitting *dharna* and described it as a barbarity and a species of violence. Similarly, he did not approve of picketing in the sense "of formation of a living wall of picket" in order to prevent the entry of persons into the picketed place. "The object of peaceful picketing is not to block the path of a person wanting to do a particular thing, but to rely on the force of public opprobrium and to warn and even shame the blacklegs. Picketing should avoid coercion, intimidation, discourtesy, burning or burying of effigies, and hunger-strikes."

2. **Civil Disobedience.** Civil disobedience is the last stage and the most drastic form of non-cooperation. Garndhi called it "a complete, effective and bloodless substitute of armed revolt." He defined civil disobedience as the "breach of unmoral statutory enactment." It signifies "the resister's outlawry in a civil, i.e., non-violent manner." Gandhi put greater emphasis on the word *civil* than on disobedience so that the movement might not become uncivil and violent. "Disobedience to be civil," he said, "must be sincere, respectful, restrained, never defiant, must be based upon some well understood principle, must not be capricious and must have no ill will or hatred behind it." And as it is an effective and more drastic remedy, it should be employed with the greatest caution and most sparingly. "....Its use must be guarded by all conceivable restrictions. Every possible provision should be made against an outbreak of violence or general lawlessness. Its area as well as scope should also be limited to the barest necessity of the case." Gandhi even recommended its practice by a select few "in the first instance at any rate." Quality, according to him, should be the prime consideration and the selection of the laws to be broken should be made not by each *satyagrahi* himself, but by the leader or some centrally constituted body of expert *satyagrahis*.

3. **Hijrat.** *Hijrat* means voluntary exile from the permanent place of residence. Gandhi recommended *Hijrat* to those "who feel oppressed, cannot live without loss of self-respect in a particular place and lack the strength that comes from true non-violence or the capacity to defend themselves violently."[28] He advised *Hijrat* to the *satyagrahis* of Bardoli in 1928, and of Limbdi, Junagadh and Vithalgadh in 1939. In 1935, he advised the Harijans of Kaitha to migrate as the caste-Hindus were regularly terrorising them and this had caused extreme despondency among the Harijans.[29]

4. **Fasting.** The most potent form of *satyagraha* is fasting. Gandhi called it a fiery weapon,[30] and claimed to have reduced it to a science.[31] At the same time, he characterised it to be the most dangerous technique, because it could so easily be misapplied. Fasting may be for penance and self-purification, or it may be a means of resisting injustice and converting the evil-doer. But whatever be its purpose, it must be resorted to on rare occasions by one skilled in the art of fasting or under expert guidance.[32] Fasting, according to Gandhi, presupposes that the person who launches on a fast possesses spiritual fitness and a clear vision. It is not the physical act of fasting, but the spiritual content of the fast that gives it potency. Then, it requires a high degree of purity, self-discipline, humility and faith on the part of the faster.[33] When it is properly organised, it stirs up as nothing else "sluggish conscience and fires loving hearts to action .... Those who have to bring about radical changes in human conditions and surroundings cannot do it except by raising ferment in society. There are only two methods of doing this—violence and non-violence. Non-violent pressure exerted through self-suffering by fasting ... touches and strengthens the moral fibre of those against whom it is directed."

28. *Harijan,* February 3, 1940.
29. *Harijan,* October 5, 1935.
30. *Harijan,* October 13, 1940.
31. His statement to the press, September 21, 1932.
32. *Harijan,* March 11, 1939.
33. *Harijan,* October 13, 1940.

5. **Strike.** Strike is the weapon of the labour for the redress of their legitimate grievances. Gandhi desired to make his concept of strike entirely distinct from its prototype in the West. He did not accept the proposition that the capitalist class should be eliminated and substituted by a labour 'capitalist' class. He envisaged all industry as a joint enterprise of labour and capital wherein both act as mutual 'trustees'. With the trusteeship basis of industrial control, Gandhi inculcated in the labour the attitude that they must regard the industry as a whole as their own and, accordingly, direct their attack against corruption, injustice, inefficiency and shortsighted greed of the owners. Strikes, he said, should be directed for achieving this end rather than in a bid to seize power of owning and controlling industry. The *satyagrahi* strike must be non-violent in spirit as well as in method. "It is voluntary, purificatory suffering undertaken to convert the erring opponent." Moreover, the demands of the strikers must be clear, feasible and just. Further, to ensure non-violence on the part of the strikers, Gandhi emphasised that they must acquire some manual craft so that they might not have to depend upon the strike fund to maintain themselves and their families during a prolonged strike.[34]

The Technique of Satyagraha to Meet Foreign Aggression. Gandhi indicated a plan of action in case of a foreign armed aggression, though he had not any opportunity to test it out. "A non-violent man or society," said Gandhi, "does not anticipate or provide for attacks from without." On the contrary, such a person or society firmly believes that nobody is going to disturb them. If the worst happens, there are two ways open to meet violence; to yield possession, but non-cooperate with the aggressor. Thus, supposing that a modern edition of Nero descended upon India, the representatives of the State will let him in, but tell him that he will get no assistance from the people. They will prefer death to submission. The second way will be non-violent resistance by a people who have been trained in the non-violent methods. They would offer themselves unarmed as fodder for the aggressor's canons. The underlying belief in either case is that even a Nero is not devoid of a heart. "The unexpected spectacle of endless rows upon rows of men and women," asserted Gandhi, "simply dying rather than surrender to the will of an aggressor must ultimately melt him and his solidery".[35]

Gandhi, therefore, offered two solutions to meet foreign aggression. During the invasion the technique would consist in offering non-violent resistance up to death to the last man to the invader, and complete non-cooperation with him in all forms of non-violent *satyagraha* to which reference has been made above. The advice given by Gandhi to the Abyssinians, the Czechs, the Poles, the British and other victims of aggression are typical examples of his technique. To the Chinese he advised, "If the Chinese had non-violence of my conception, there would be no use left for the latest machinery of destruction which Japan possesses. The Chinese would say to Japan, 'Bring all your machinery, we present half of our population to you. But the remaining two hundred million won't bend their knees to you.' If the Chinese did that, Japan would become China's slave."[36]

Gandhi, likewise, rejected the 'scorched earth' technique to check the advance of the

34. *My Experiments With Truth, op. cit.,* Vol. II, pp. 412-13.
35. *Harijan*, April 13, 1940.
36. *Harijan,* December 24. 1938.

aggressive forces. He did not accept it as consistent with the technique of non-violent resistance. "There is no bravery," he asserted, "in my poisoning my well or filling it in so that my brother who is at war with me may not use the water .... Nor is there sacrifice in it, for it does not purify me, and sacrifice, as its root meaning implies, presupposes purity."[37] Gandhi even suggested that the people of an invaded country should not miss any opportunity of rendering human service to the individual members of the invading army in their personal capacity whenever they might be in distress.

Attitude towards the State. Gandhi did not directly make any suggestion as the nature of a non-violent State. He was more concerned with the immediate present than the future. His immediate concern was to free India from the subjection of the British through the technique of non-violent *satyagraha*. And the science of *satyagraha* was yet in the making. He was still experimenting with it. He even admitted that the experiment had not reached an advanced stage of development.[38] Moreover, he thought it desirable that the details of a non-violent State should be determined by the people according to their moral level and their preferences. It, accordingly, appeared to him premature and unscientific to deal in details with the governmental shape of things to come. "I have purposely refrained from dealing with the nature of Government in a society based on non-violence .... When society is deliberately constructed in accordance with the law of non-violence, its structure will be different in the particulars from what it is today. But I cannot say in advance what the Government based wholly on non-violence will be like."[39]

Gandhi's technique of *satyagraha* embraced both the constructive and destructive phases. On the one hand, it was a non-violent 'war' for the settlement of political and group disputes; on the other hand, it was a constructive programme of minimising, if not altogether eliminating, internal conflicts and contradictions. His constructive aspect of non-violent direct action, therefore, gives us sufficient clue to the nature of a non-violent society which Gandhi would wish to have. His *Hind Swaraj*, and many stray passages in his speeches and statements also provide some material about the social order of his conception.

Gandhi has often been described as a "philosophic anarchist." He rejected the State outright and in any of its forms. The State, he maintained, commands and whatever is commanded cannot carry with it the moral value of the individual's action. An action is moral only when it is voluntary and "No action which is not voluntary can be called moral... So long as we act like machines, there can be no question of morality. If we want to call an action moral, it should have been done consciously, and as a matter of duty."[40] Moreover, the authority of the State rests on violence. Wherever there is violence there is exploitation, whatever be the democratic nature of the State. "The State represents," he said. "violence in a concentrated and organised form. The individual has a soul, but the State is a soulless machine, it can never be weaned from violence to which it owes

37. *Harijan.* March 22, 1949.
38. *Harijan*, May 27, 1939.
39. *Harijan,* February 11,1938.
40. *Ethical Religion, op. cit.,* p. 40.

its very existence."[41] Gandhi, accordingly, desired to establish a society wherein truth and non-violence would prevail and spontaneity and purity of actions flowed from its inhabitants. There will be no exploitation in such a society as people have an abiding faith in God. This makes them to steadfastly hold to truth, love and service and all their actions, as such, will be based on cooperation. When the people cooperate voluntarily, there is no need of political power and the emerging result is a *stateless* society. As Gandhi points out, "In the final state, therefore, there is no political power, because there is no state."[42] A stateless society is exactly what the Anarchists envisage.

His ideal democracy, a *stateless* and *classless* society, will consist of a number of self-contained and self-regulated village communities. Every village will be a republic of a *panchayat* having full powers even to meet foreign aggression, of course, in a non-violent way. The self-sufficient villages shall be bound together in a voluntary federation. But this federation will have its units the individuals, and not the states or provinces. In a federation of Gandhi's conception there will be no centralization of authority of any kind as it was inconsistent "with the non-violent structure of society." Centralization, according to him, connoted force and anything based on force was opposed to freedom and morality. Voluntary cooperation of the individuals is the condition of dignified and peaceful existence[43] and this is the essence of Gandhi's non-violent society. In such a society everyone is his own ruler, but he rules himself in such a way that he is never a hindrance to his neighbours.

But the idea of a *stateless* and *classless* non-violent society, Gandhi admitted, was unrealizable as "a Government cannot succeed in becoming entirely non-violent, because it represents all the people. I do not today conceive of such a golden age. But I do believe in the possibility of a predominantly non-violent society. And I am working for it."[44] The attainable middle ideal, he conceived, was a predominantly non-violent State. What will this predominantly non-violent State be like? Gandhi said that the character of the State would entirely depend upon how the political power was won. If political power is won through the non-violence of the weak, then, the emerging State will be democratic, but exploitation will still continue, as the non-violence of the weak permits the use of violence. If the political power is won by the non-violence of the brave, which is the essence of Gandhi's technique of *Satyagraha*, the resulting State will be a genuine democracy wherein exploitation and coercion exist to the minimum.

The State, for Gandhi, is not an end in itself, "but one of the means of enabling people to better their condition in every department of life." Being one of the means, the State is like various other associations which promote human welfare. It cannot claim any superior status and the individual owes to the State only limited and relative loyalty. He upheld the cause of the sovereignty of the people based on moral authority and conceded to the individual the right to resist the authority of the State through non-violent means, if its policies and actions did not appeal to his moral conscience. "*Swarajya* for me,"

41. *Modern Review,* October 1935. An Interview with Mahatma Gandhi by N.K. Bose.
42. *Young India,* July 2, 1931.
43. *Harijan,* January 13, 1940.
44. *Harijan,* March 9, 1940.

Gandhi said, "means freedom for the meanest of our countrymen." Applying his concept of *Swarajya*, he added, "Real *Swarajya* will not come by the acquisition of authority by a few but the acquisition of capacity by all to resist authority when abused." Gandhi, in fact, sought to develop in the people the capacity to resist the laws of the State, if they were repugnant to the individual's moral conviction, and such a resistance, he believed, was the only adequate safeguard against abuse of authority. It has been suggested that Gandhi's teachings involved a perpetual danger of anarchy. But resistance to political authority, according to the Gandhian way, must strictly be non-violent, the path of a true *satyagrahi* and Gandhi himself, as a true *satyagrahi* had resisted the tyranny of the State and society throughout his life.

Gandhi would entrust to the State minimum functions. He had a horror of the growing power of the State. By self-government, he meant a continuous effort to be independent of government control. "I admit," he said, "there are certain things which cannot be done without political power, but there are numerous other things which do not at all depend upon political power. That is why a thinker like Thoreau said that 'that government is best which governs the least'. This means that when people come into possession of political power, the interference with the freedom of the people is reduced to the minimum. In other words, a nation that runs its affairs smoothly and effectively without much State interference is truly democratic. Where such condition is absent the form of government is democratic in name."[45] His maxim was the less the authority of the State, the greater the moral freedom of the individual and that is the real *swarajya* for him.

Gandhi advocated a return to the system of rural communities more or less self-sufficient in the matter of their basic needs. These communities composed of simple, manageable units would be cooperatively knit together. They will be autonomous for all purposes, including the administration of justice, and keeping peace in the locality as far as consistent with the utility of the State. This was for Gandhi real *swarajya*, because in this way people get their moral freedom in their own environments, which they understand and can effectively control according to their genius. The *panchayats* would run the village administration. The villages in their turn would elect their district administration, each village within the jurisdiction of a district exercising one vote. The district administration would elect the provincial administration and the provincial administrations a parliament or President who was to serve as the chief executive. Gandhi was, thus, against direct election. Direct elections, he believed, led to many evils like corruption, bribery, impersonation, etc.

Gandhi was exactingly rigid in prescribing qualifications for the candidates seeking election. He prescribed that a candidate must be selfless, able and incorruptible. He should not hanker after office, must avoid self-advertisement and must not indulge in running down his opponent and exploit the voters. Gandhi would not even permit canvassing for the votes. His ideal was let service of the people be the criterion for securing votes and voters should be left to themselves to judge who has really served them the best. Gandhi would give to all citizens, men and women, the right to vote. The only qualification he would prescribe for a voter is manual work. "The qualifications for

45. *Hartjan,* January 11, 1936.

franchise should be," he said more than once, "neither property nor position but manual work....Literacy or property test has proved to be elusive. Manual work gives an opportunity to all who wish to take part in the government and the well-being of the State." Work, he further said, "will not be the antithesis of life, but the means of realizing the full content of life."

Such a State will be, according to Gandhi, a predominantly non-violent State, internally free and externally equal to other States. Freedom will exist and flourish, because the State is subject to no one else, and all its people, without barriers of caste, creed, religion, colour and sex, participate in its governance. And "if independence is born non-violently," Gandhi concluded, "all the component parts" of the State "will be voluntarily interdependent working in perfect harmony under a representative central authority which will derive its sanction from the confidence reposed in it by the component parts." But it does not mean that there will be no need for the police. There may be found even in a non-violent State some anti-social individuals who may resort to violence and break laws. Such people need to be reformed and the police will be needed for this purpose. But the police of Gandhi's conception will be entirely different as compared with the police which now maintains law and order and protects us from the undesired social elements. The ranks of the police, according to Gandhi, "will be composed of believers in non-violence. They will be servants, not masters, of the people. The people will instinctively render them any help, and through mutual cooperation they will easily deal with the ever decreasing disturbances. The police force will have some kind of arms but they will be rarely used, if at all. In fact the policemen will be reformers. Their police work will be confined to robbers and dacoits. Quarrels between labour and capital and strikes will be few and far between in a non-violent State, because the influence of the non-violent majority will be so great as to command the respect of the principal elements in society. Similarly, there will be no room for communal disturbances ...."[46] There will be no need for an army to save the country from any kind of external aggression. The State of Gandhi's dream will have an army consisting of the entire non-violent populace, who meet the aggressors in offering non-violent resistance up to death and to the last man like true *satyagrahis*.

The democratic State envisaged by Gandhi will have specific fundamental rights. These rights were contained in a resolution moved by Gandhi himself at the 1931 Karachi session of the Indian National Congress. The resolution read: "This Congress is of the opinion that to enable the masses to appreciate what *swarajya* as conceived by the Congress will mean to them, it is desirable to state the position of the Congress in a manner easily understood by them. In order to end the exploitation of the masses, political freedom must include real economic freedom of the starving millions. The Congress, therefore, declares that any constitution which may be agreed to on its behalf should provide or enable the *Swarajya* Government to provide for the following:

1. Fundamental rights of the people including :

   (*i*) Freedom of association and combination.

   (*ii*) Freedom of the speech and the press.

46. *Harijan,* September 1, 1940.

(*iii*) Freedom of conscience and free profession and practice of religion subject to public order and morality.

(*iv*) Practice of the culture, language and script of the minorities.

(*v*) Equal rights and obligations of all citizens without any bar on account of sex.

(*vi*) No disability to attach to any citizen by reason of his or her religion, caste, creed or sex in regard to public employment, office of power or honour and the exercise of any trade or calling.

(*vii*) Equal rights to all citizens in regard to public roads, wells, schools and other places of public resort.

(*viii*) Right to keep and bear arms in accordance with regulations and reservations made in that behalf.

(*ix*) No person shall be deprived of his liberty, nor shall his dwelling or property be entered, sequestered or confiscated, save in accordance with law.

2. Religious neutrality on the part of the State.
3. Adult suffrage.
4. Free primary education.
5. A living wage for industrial workers, limited hours of labour, healthy conditions of work, protection against the economic consequences of old age, sickness, and unemployment.
6. Labour to be free from serfdom or from the conditions bordering on serfdom.
7. Protection of women workers, and adequate provision for leave during the maternity period.
8. Provision against employment of children of school going age in the factories.
9. Right of labour to form unions to protect their interests with suitable machinery for settlement of disputes by arbitration.
10. Substantial reduction in agricultural rent or revenues paid by the peasantry and in case of uneconomic holding exemption from rent for such period as may be necessary, relief being given to small zamindars wherever necessary by reason of such reduction.
11. Imposition of a progressive tax on agricultural income above a fixed maximum.
12. A gradual inheritance tax.
13. Expenditure and salaries in civil departments to be largely reduced. And no servant of the State, other than the specially employed experts and the like, to be paid above a certain fixed figure which should not ordinarily exceed Rs. 500 per month.
14. Protection of indigenous cloth by exclusion of all foreign cloth and foreign yarn from the country.
15. Prohibition of intoxicating drinks and drugs.
16. No duty on salt manufactured in India.
17. Control over exchange and currency policy so as to help Indian industries and bring relief to the masses.
18. Control by the State of key industries and ownership of mineral resources.
19. Control of usury."

Gandhi was an egalitarian through and through. He did not believe that the ideal of non-violence could be realised in society so long as the wide gulf between the rich and the hungry millions remained. But by economic equality he did not mean absolute equality. His idea was approximate equality. "Economic equality must never be supposed to mean possession of an equal amount of worldly goods by everyone. It does mean however that everyone will have a proper house to live in, sufficient and balanced food to eat, and sufficient *khadi* with which to cover himself. It also means that the cruel inequality that obtains today will be removed by purely non-violent means."[47] This Gandhi intended to bring about by the institution of trusteeship both on land and in industry.

Property and Trusteeship. From the perusal of the Fundamental Rights, which Gandhi had wished that the Swarajya Constitution of India should contain, flows the concept of "Trusteeship" and his views on property. His ideal of trusteeship aims at transforming the character of the rich. Every man, he claimed, has a right to have a "balanced diet, a decent house to live in, facilities for the education of one's children and adequate medical relief."[48] Any possession over and above, he regarded as superfluous. But the superfluous wealth must be held by those who possessed it as trustees of the people to be used for ameliorating their condition. He further said that "Everything belonged to God and was from God. Therefore, it was for His people as a whole not for a particular individual. When the individual had more than his proportionate portion, he became a trustee of that portion for God's people." As far back as 1928, he warned the capitalist class in India that unless they "help to avert that tragedy by becoming trustees of the welfare of the masses and by devoting their talents not to amassing wealth for themselves but to the services of masses in an altruistic spirit, they will end either by destroying the masses or being destroyed by them."[49]

Gandhi did not contemplate any scheme of expropriating the capitalist and the landlord, if they changed their mentality and worked as trustees of the workers and the peasants. On the other hand, they should "supply brain to them and remove the present terrible inequality between them" and the workers and peasants. Gandhi's scheme did not envisage class antagonism. He aimed at "class collaboration and class coordination as the first step towards the classless democracy in which everyone will perform same form of productive physical labour and there will be no exploiters." As trustees, the capitalists and the landlords would use their talent and the bulk of their earnings not for themselves, but as a trust for the good of society. They would be entitled to a reasonable rate of earnings determined by themselves in consultation with society. But the rate of payment "would not matter so long as they agreed to surrender their existing titles based on absolute ownership for a trusteeship basis." If the capitalists and the zainindars (landlords) do not rise to the occasion and accept the new basis of ownership, the weapon of non-co-operation, Gandhi proposed, should be employed in order to make it impossible for the landlords and the capitalists to exploit. He warned the capitalist class to read the signs of the times, "revise their notions of God-given right of all they possess," and if this is done, "in an incredibly short space of time the seven hundred thousand dung-heaps which

47. *Harijan,* August 18, 1840.
48. *Harijan,* March 31, 1946.
49. *Young India,* December 20, 1928.

today pass mostly as villages can be turned into abodes of peace, health and comfort. There is no other choice than between voluntary surrender on the part of the capitalist of superfluities and consequent acquisition of the real happiness of all on the one hand, and on the other the impending chaos into which, if the capitalist does not wake up betimes, awakened but ignorant, famishing millions will plunge the country and which not even the armed force that a powerful Government can bring into play can avert."[50]

Here is the summing up of the scheme of Trusteeship as given by Pyarelal, a very close associate of Gandhi.[51]

"1. Trusteeship provides a means of transforming the present capitalist order of society into an egalitarian one; it gives no quarter to capitalism but gives the present owning class a chance of reforming itself. It is based on the faith that human nature is never beyond redemption.

2. It does not recognise any right of private ownership of property except in as much as it may be permitted by society for its own welfare.

3. It does not exclude legislative regulation of the ownership.

4. Under State-regulated trusteeship, an individual will not be free to hold or use his wealth for selfish satisfaction or in disregard of the interest of society.

5. Just as it is proposed to fix a living minimum wage, even so a limit should be fixed for the maximum income that could be allowed to any person in society. The difference between such minimum and maximum incomes should be reasonable and equitable and variable from time to time so much so that the tendency would be towards obliteration of differences.

6. Under the Gandhian economic order the character of production. will be determined by social necessity and not by personal whim or greed."

Gandhi favoured State-ownership of industries, if capital and labour did not work as mutual trustees and trustees of consumers. But the nationalised State-owned industries "ought only to be working under the most attractive and ideal conditions, not for profit, but for the benefit of humanity." He would concede to the workers the right to elect their representatives, who should share in the management of those industries. He was, however, against centralization and mass production. Centralization and mass production, according to Gandhi, vitiated democracy. Concentration of political and economic power, he further maintained, was the negation of fundamental rights and civil liberties and against the individual's moral freedom. Non-violence and centralised industries, whether under individual capitalism or State ownership, he held incompatible. Gandhi preferred individual violence to State violence, because the former was the lesser of the two evils. "If the State suppressed capitalism by violence it would be caught in the coils of violence itself....and fail to develop non-violence at any time. The State represents violence in a concentrated and organised form. The individual has a soul but the State is a soulless machine .... Hence I prefer the doctrine of trusteeship."

Estimate of the Gandhian Outlook. Gandhi was a saint and a revolutionary. He

50. *Young India,* December 5, 1929.

51. U.N.E.S.C.O. Seminar, *op. cit.*, A Paper submitted by Pyarelal. Appendix E, p. 391.

revolutionised the course of politics by moralising it and devised a new strategy, based upon the twin principles of truth and non-violence, for the solution of individual and group problems. The basis of the teachings of Gandhi is one of mutual adjustment, the feeling of contentment, and the desire to see others as happy as ourselves—a desire born of the spirit of live and let live and in essence that of cooperation. By developing this attitude one could not only lift oneself and enjoy true happiness, but also establish peace and happiness all around. This fact was amply demonstrated by Gandhi in his life-time by experiments on individual, social, national as well as international scale and he won for India the battle of her freedom. It is true that there were certain contributory factors that hastened the end of British rule, but the one most powerful factor was great non-violent struggle which the country launched under the leadership of Gandhi. In fact, he had believed that the future of non-violence depended upon its successful fruition in India and, as such, "it was India's historic mission to deliver to mankind the message of non-violence."

The unique contribution of Gandhi lies not in the fact that he has discovered new truths, but that he has applied old and eternal truths for the solution of modern problems. He is the greatest exponent of the theory and practice of non-violence. There is some scepticism about the efficacy of non-violence as a solution of our problems, particularly in the international field. Yet, the present-day world standing on the brink of an abysmal cataclysm does find solace in the Gandhian outlook and his peaceful technique. If the world peace had hitherto remained elusive like a will-o'-the-wisp in spite of the fact that no country professedly wanted war, it had been so because the world had not paid sufficient attention to the principles of peace and non-violence as preached by Gandhi. Now the war-scared and bewildered nations of the West do not find these methods the only way to have a real peace, but the very methods upon which depend human peace, freedom and culture, in fact, their survival. To put it a little more bluntly, the world today must choose between the Gandhian way of life and the atom or hydrogen bomb and other nuclear weapons. Perhaps, the bellicose nature of man may be curbed by the real nature of man and the ultimate choice may be with 'Gandhi'. If such a revolution comes about in the dealings of mankind who can, then, say that the Gandhian way of life is not revolutionary?

Gandhi had faith in human nature and its capacity, through a gradual process, to minimise evil. He realised that even the tallest among men have imperfections. But even the most depressed, he believed, cannot shake himself from the self-conscious impulse "to realise God who dwells in us." Accordingly, it was his conviction that it is more natural for man to be good than evil, "though apparently descent may seem easier than ascent." Gandhi is, thus, a realist who believes in 'Futurism' and inevitability of progress. But he is not oblivious of the means. He forthwith rejects the maxim that end justifies the means. His maxim is as the means so the end and good means must be adopted for the realization of good ends. Good means and a good end constitute a single whole pattern for him.

But in the realism of Gandhi there is an occasional touch of the celestial prophet and the ethereal mystic in him. This touch sometimes carries him high in the realm of idealism divorced from the realities of earthly life. His socio-economic structure of the non-violent democracy is inconceivable in the form in which he conceives it. He advocated a return to simplicity and nature. He opposed large-scale industrialism and mechanization. Later on he becomes somewhat realistic, at least in the context of the future Indian society, and advocates a reconciliation of large-scale and small-scale industries, the rationalisation of key industries, and the organisation of "urban centres not as lopsided outgrowths but functioning as catering to the interests of the village where the real soul of India lay." He would even allow the electrification of the rural areas. By conceding all this, he brings forward his concept of trusteeship. It is true that Gandhi's scheme did not envisage class antagonism. But is it humanly possible to reconcile the two antagonistic classes to a scheme of class collaboration and class coordination? It may be divinely possible. If labour and capital did not work as mutual trustees of consumers, he would favour State ownership of industries. At the same time, he had a horror of the State concentrating political and economic power, because it was the negation of fundamental rights and liberties, and against the individual's moral freedom.

In a sense, Gandhi was an anarchist. He considered the State as an organisation of violence and force. He postulated that in the ideal State of his conception, *Ramrajya,* there will be the sovereignty of the moral authority of the people and the State would disappear. But he would not get rid of the State immediately, because of the imperfections of man. His immediate concern was to transform the present-day sovereign State, with its coercive authority, into a non-violent State through a non-violent society. Gandhi does not outline the structure of a non-violent State as its character would entirely depend upon how the political power was won. That is, the quality of non-violence through which freedom is won. If it is won through the non-violence of the weak, the emerging State will be democratic but exploitation will continue. If the political power is won through the non-violence of the brave, the resulting State will be a genuine democracy wherein exploitation and coercion exist to the minimum. The non-violent State of Gandhi's dream will be internally free and externally equal to other States. Its aims would be to promote the greatest good of all and with a view to achieving this end it will govern the least leaving to individual initiative the largest part of the functions of the State. The State would meet foreign aggression and internal disturbances, as far as possible, non-violently; the police and the military will be least in evidence. In this way, the State will prepare for its own demise to be replaced by voluntary associations.

Is there any possibility of such a non-violent State to come into being? Does the Sovereign and Independent Republic of India fulfil the conditions of Gandhi's non-violent State? Is the socialistic pattern of society or the socialistic society, which the Congress Party intended to establish, in conformity with the ideals of Gandhi? Are the representatives of the people the embodiment of Gandhi's ideal; selfless, able, and incorruptible who have no craze for office and they do not indulge in self-advertisement and exploit the voters? Does the spirit of service dominate their lives and is that their merit which makes them representatives? Will the State, as today constituted in India, prepare the way for its own demise to be replaced by voluntary associations? These are some of the very pertinent questions which often agitate the minds of the students of Gandhian way of life. If Gandhi had been alive, perhaps, he would have either modified his views about the State or would have deplored the State emerging out of his labour and sacrifices. Yet, the one redeeming feature is that his teachings remain the beacon light and inspiration to the people. But "his ideal", as Bodh Raj Sharma succinctly observed, "so far as a poor mortal may foresee, will ever remain an ideal to be discussed in seminars and papers until God wills otherwise."[52]

SARVODAYA

The followers of Gandhi. If the teachings of Gandhi failed to mould and shape the policies and transactions of the Central and State Governments in India, several of his disciples, acclaimed as the true followers of the Mahatma and his real successors, were still dedicated to the realization of that ideal social order wherein the moral man would live in a moral society. These followers of Gandhi were his closest associates, the inmates of his *ashram*, and are distinguishable from his political followers who held and are holding the reins of the government of the country and have twisted its destinies for more than four decades now. In his paper, "Second Thoughts on Gandhism," Devarat N. Pathak makes a sharp distinction between the *personal* and *political* followers of Gandhi and maintains that, "Now it may be easily conceded that Gandhiism never received a whole-hearted support even during Gandhi's lifetime. Congress, which owed not a little of its success to Gandhi, often vehemently differed from him taking to a different path of action and policy, leaving Gandhi alone."[53] It was left to a few of his devotees to strictly adhere to his way of life.[54] "To his close followers," adds Professor Pathak, "Gandhi was a hard taskmaster, uncompromising and insistent on the minutest details of his programme". This inner ring of people followed Gandhi scrupulously and lived as small images of the master. Beyond this circle stood a large and more influential group of his followers like Sardar Patel, Nehru, Rajendra Prasad, Kripalani, Azad, Rajajee and others. "They all followed Gandhi's lead but they did not adopt Gandhiism in its entirety .... If the *Gandhiites* were the personal followers of Gandhi, the latter accepted him as their political leader. The former shunned politics and lived as Gandhi's inmates in the *ashram*. The latter group figured in political life and gained fame and popularity through their political career."[55]

Gandhi did not rejoice over the way India had won her Independence. In fact, he was afflicted, for it was the annihilation of his principles of truth and non-violence. He refused to give a message for the people on the historic day of the transfer of power. When the officer of the Information and Broadcasting Department, Government of India, who had come for a message, told Gandhi that if he did not give any message, it would not be good, he replied: "There is no message at all. If it is bad, let it be so."[56] The distressing developments inside the Congress after Independence and the moral degradation

52. *Gandhian Concept of State,* p. 150.
53. *The Indian Journal of Political Science,* Conference Number, 1960, pp. 33-34.
54. Refer to series of Articles 1 to 18 under the caption *"The Spirit's Pilgrimage"* by Mira Ben in the *Illustrated Weekly of India,* Bombay, 1960.
55. *The Indian Journal of Political Science,* Conference Number, 1960, p. 34.
56. Tendulkar, D.G., *Mahatma, Life of Mohandas Karamchand Gandhi,* Vol. VIII

of the men in the Congress further agonised Gandhi[57] and he gave serious thought to the future of the Congress. In the draft constitution of the reorganised Congress, which he prepared in the last days of his life, Gandhi had unequivocally stated that "... the Congress, in its present shape and form, as a propaganda vehicle and parliamentary machine, has outlived its use. India has still to attain social, moral and economic independence in terms of India's seven hundred thousand villages, as distinguished from cities and towns. The struggle for the ascendancy of civil over military power is bound to take place in India's progress towards its democratic goal. The Congress must be kept out of unhealthy competition with the political parties and communal bodies. For these and other similar reasons, the All India Congress Committee resolves to disband the existing Congress organisation and flower into a Lok Sevak Sangh under the following rules with the power to alter these as occasion may demand."[58]

Origin of the Sarvodaya Plan. But the political followers of Gandhi were in no mood to liquidate the existing Congress. Gandhi, then, turned to his true and disciplined soldiers, his constructive workers, for the reconstruction of the social order in the context of the changed conditions of the country. It was decided to hold a small conference at Wardha some time in February 1948. But Gandhi was assassinated on January 30, 1948, and the proposed conference could not be held. Subsequently, a Sarvodaya Economic Conference was held on December 22 and 23 next year with Kaka Kalelkar as President and it adopted a plan "to attain social, moral and economic independence" as envisaged by Gandhi. The plan was published on January 20, 1950. It aimed to establish a Sarvodaya Society and Acharya Vinoba Bhave, a loyal and devoted follower of Gandhi, became its chief exponent. Jayaprakash Narayan later on joined Vinoba and since then Sarvodaya workers had been busy in spreading the gospel of Sarvodaya adopting innumerable means to give it a practical shape.

In a Sarvodaya society "there will be freedom for all and utmost equality; there will be no class and castes; no exploitation nor injustice; and equal opportunity for each for fullest development. Man will be the centre of such a society, but self-interest will not be the basis of social organisation. Life in such a society will be integrated and whole, so that work, art and play will form a unified pattern making possible the growth of an integrated human personality." Thus, Sarvodaya society will be an ideal social order in which no one is downtrodden. It will be a society where "love is to reign and cooperation to prevail." A moral man in a moral society is the ultimate aim of Sarvodaya. Such a synthesis can be brought about by placing unflinching faith in man's dignity and growth, in human goodness and kindness and in the eternal instinct of mutual aid and cooperation. Gandhi had always believed in the eternal goodness of human nature and insisted on truth and non-violence as a means of changing hearts, and fighting against tyranny of all kinds. For him democracy was the basis of a non-violent and Sarvodaya society, which could be achieved by a decentralised socio-economic order based on cottage industrialism and

57. Refer to a Note written by Gandhi entitled *"A Tragic Phenomenon ;* Tendulkar D.G., *Mahatma. Life of Mohandas Karamchand Gandhi,* Vol VII.. p 186.
58. *Ibid.* Vol. VIII, p. 342.
59. See *ante.* Also refer to the Draft Constitution of the Congress, Tendulkar, D.G., *Mahatma, Life of Mohandas Karamchand Gandhi,* Vol. VIII, pp. 342-344.

village community life, self-governing and self-sufficient.[59] Gandhi was, thus, able to project in the name of Sarvodaya, the welfare of all, a theory deemed superior to what democracy or socialism offers.

Sarvodaya Society. Acharya Vinoba Bhave outlined the three characteristics of a Sarvodaya Society and explained that wheresoever and wherever these essential conditions are fuifilled such a society possesses the virtues of a Sarvodaya social order. But all these three characteristics are fundamental and they must be present and operate simultaneously. These principles are :

1. "No power should be dominant in society; there should only be a discipline of good thought;
2. All faculties of the individual to be dedicated to society which must provide the individual for growth and development; and
3. The moral, social and economic values of all the callings performed honestly should be the same."

The *Sarvodayavadis* aim at the creation of a social order free from every form of authority, stateless society where "the ruler and the ruled will be merged in the individual." They reject the State and its government no matter what its form, because both are coercive institutions and force is the ultimate sanction behind them. Even the Welfare State does not offer them any satisfaction. "The Welfare State," says Jayaprakash Narayan, "in the name of welfare threatens as much to enslave man to the State as in totalitarian State. The people must cry halt to this creeping paralysis." The human society must, therefore, be free from all coercive institutions. It does not, however, mean disappearance of the State all at once. "What we seek," Vinoba Bhave says, "is to grow out of the state of affairs where there is no government into one where there is good government and from that condition to one where people are free of government altogether." His progression is from "no government," that is, the condition of anarchy where exploitation and oppression prevail, to "good government," where no power is dominant and justice prevails, to a social order absolutely "free of government."

The *Sarvodayavadis*, thus, do not exclude some form of government in the intervening stage of a Sarvodaya society. But they will eschew a representative democracy—political parties, periodic elections and the rule of the majority are the indispensable parts of a representative government. The *Sarvodayites* condemn political parties and regard them as conspiracies against the people to divide them into warring camps. Parties create differences where there were none originally and they always take a narrow and partisan view of all matters. People become power crazy and there is a scramble for party tickets which are manoeuvred through by all corrupt practices. The propertied class and the professional politicians control the party organisation and the party line and they employ all corrupt practices to get their nominees elected. Votes are even purchased. thus, debasing and demoralising the body-politic. The result is obvious: "Suffrage for the rich and sufferance for the poor."

The *Sarvodayites* bewail the tyranny of majority rule or the tyranny of the numbers, as it is described. "Political Science," Acharya Vinoba Bhave says, "lays down that everything should be decided by majority. It started counting votes. If there are fifty-one votes in favour and forty-none votes in opposition, then the former must have an overriding voice." Similarly, Jayaprakash Narayan maintained, "Because fifty-one people out of a hundred decide to do a certain thing in a certain manner, why should the forty-nine people, who do not agree with that, be forced to accept that decision? What kind of democracy is this ? The laws passed in this way by the majority vote are not only oppressive to the minority, but also violate the principle of human unity and dignity as they consider "the individual as one of the many rather than as a unique individual possessing a personality. It thus tends to dehumanise humanity."

The mechanism of administration which a representative democracy sets up concentrates power at the centre and fortifies the power of bureaucracy. Such a society with a centralized, complex and top-heavy administrative machinery, according to Jayaprakash Narayan, "cannot but be heaven for bureaucrats, managers, technocrats and statists. It cannot be a home for brothers to live together as brothers."[60] As for the services themselves, Acharya Vinoba Bhave says,"The highly expensive administration and other departments of the government are known as 'services,' etc. And there are services galore: civil service, medical service, educational service, etc. The officials of the civil services are paid four-figure salaries, while their masters, the poor of the country whom they profess to serve, have to live on a pittance of fifty paise a day. It is a tragic paradox that those who earn lakhs are called servants while those who produce food for the nation are regarded as self-seekers who work to further their own interest. What is one to say of these services? If words are not to be deprived of their meaning then this is nothing but cant and hypocrisy."[61]

Sarvodaya society will be self-regulated and self-managed in small communities, rural or urban. Life in such a society will be a life of mutual aid and sharing, and of freedom. Freedom can be enjoyed fully and democarcy practised directly and intelligently only when small communities are able to manage and regulate their affairs. Coercion will not be the basis of such a society. In fact, coercion of any kind will not exist there. If at all there will be coercion, it can be called coercion of love.

Individual and the Society. Men composing the *Sarvodaya* society will be bound together in love and by love, every individual living for others and all others living for every individual. To Gandhi, society is just like a family and the relation between the individual and society is one of close inter-dependence. He rejects the theory of *laissez faire*, let the individual be left alone, and that he is not bound by social obligations. He also rejects the other extreme view that the individual is nothing without society and whatever he is it is because of society. Gandhi says, "I value individual freedom but you must not forget that man is essentially a social being. He has risen to the present status by learning to adjust his individualism to the requirement of social progress. Unrestricted individualism is the law of the beast of the jungle. We have learnt to strike the mean between individual freedom and social restraint. Willing submission to social restraint for the sake of the well-being of the whole society enriches both the individual and the society of which one is a member." Gandhi stood for the ideal of the "greatest good of all" and throughout his life he strove for that. The individual comes first and foremost

60. Jayaprakash Narayan, *Towards a New Society,* p. 35.

61. Vinoba Bhave, *Vinoba and His Mission*, p.275.

in the Gandhian outlook and in any scheme of social progress the first step always lies with the individual. But Gandhi's *Swarajya* was concerned with the individual's inner freedom as well as his external freedom in society. Individual and society must march ahead together. All faculties of the individual be dedicated to society which provides him with opportunities for free growth and development. In this way, Sarvodaya has been defined "as a synthesis of individualism and socialism, directed at the good of all."

Moral, Social and Economic Values. The moral, social and economic value of the callings pursued honestly must be the same. Gandhi drew his inspiration for *Sarvodaya*, of the ideal social order, immediately from a reading of Ruskin's *Unto This Last* and he acknowledged it in his Autobiography. Gandhi wrote that "a lawyer's work has the same value as the barber's in as much as all have the same right of earning their livelihood." It means that labour is the joy of life and labour must not be discriminated against labour." Elaborating it, Vinoba Bhave says, "It is futile to try and draw up a scale of the values of mental or manual services. How shall we pay in money the person who nurses a sick man and sits up with him in the night? What should be a judge's price for his impartial judgement? How shall we apply the rule of three in order to know how much is due to the man who pulls out of the water or saves us from the raging fire? These are infinitely precious services, in other words, they are priceless. It is, therefore, right that, giving up calculation, everyone should devote himself to the service of all with all he has, while society does its duty by providing for his keep."

Thus, in a *Sarvodaya* society there will exist no difference between mental and manual labour. Both stand at par and both will command equal utility and respect. Love is to reign supreme in such a society and all its members use their abilities and capacities to their best with a selfless purpose for the greatest good of all. In *Sarvodaya* thinking, physical labour and non-possession are the twin principles of true life and they fulfil the ideals of the principle of Communism : "From each according to his work, to each according to his needs." In the *Sarvodaya* society all wealth, including land, will be a common property to be used for the good of each and all. There will be no class distinctions, the capitalists and the workers, and, as such, profit, rent and interest will lose their meaning and disappear. Everyone will work for society according to his capacity and receive from society according to needs and in consonance with the needs of his fellowmen. Production in such a society will not be for commerce, but for consumption and mutual sharing. And "There will be no accumulation of wealth because all wealth will belong to society and each will receive only according to his needs and in consonance with the needs of fellowmen. Even social accumulations will be limited, remaining only as a safeguard against unforeseen needs."

Transformation of Society. A stateless and classless *Sarvodaya* society cannot come into existence immediately and all at once. Society must be transformed to the *Sarvodaya* ideal. It is, therefore, necessary to continue with the existing institutions, but modifying and purifying them with the nobler and virtuous ideals of *Sarvodaya* till the people are ready and worthy to be free of the State and government. Gandhi had also said, "A Government cannot succeed in becoming entirely non-violent, because it represents all the people. I do not today conceive of such a golden age. But I do believe in the possibility of a predominantly non-violent society. And I am working for it." According to Acharya Vinoba Bhave : "Our first step will be to get Gram Raj (Government by the village). The law suits and disputes will be judged and settled within the village. Then it will be Ram Raj (Kingdom of God) : then there will no longer be any law suits or disputes and we shall live as one family."

The first stage in the transformation of a *Sarvodaya* society is *Gram Raj* and it is analogous to Gandhi's *Panchayat Raj* or *Village Swarajya*. *Gram Raj* means the organisation of society based upon small administrative units with a population not exceeding three to four thousand people, self-sufficient for economic purposes and serving as ideal convenient units for representative democracy. In *Gram Raj* individual ownership gives way to community ownership. There is no individual possession of land, labour and wealth. "Each owns everything. Each will offer his all to the community and the community will take care of him."

In a *Gram Raj* State does not disappear. But it transforms its nature and the character of government "in consonance with a non-violent social order." Such a non-violent State possesses the following attributes which could in themselves be considered important characteristics of *Gram Raj* :

1. It is a secular State and all persons are free to profess and practise any religion or belief, so long as it does not interfere with the similar rights of others.

2. There will be decentralization or what Acharya Vinoba Bhave calls *Shasan Vibhajan*, that is, every village is "a complete and a thorough state in miniature." According to Vinoba, "The very term Swaraj or self-government implies decentralisation of authority. The principle has, therefore, to be applied to every practicable limit to all fields of life, social, economic and political."

3. The State represents the sovereignty of the people "based on pure moral authority." That is, the will of the governed is to be the basis of the authority of State and its functions.

4. The State whose essence is service, governs the least. Gandhi says, "I look upon an increase in the power of the State with the greatest fear, because although while apparently doing good by minimising exploitation, it does the greatest harm to mankind by destroying individuality which lies at the root of all progress." But the conception of the least government as given by Gandhi should not be taken as identical with the police functions of the State as believed by the Individualists. Being a service State based upon principles of non-violence, it strives to promote the "greatest good of all" by the free and willing cooperation of all the people.

5. Service to the community must be the criterion and aim of all those functionaries entrusted with the performance of the duties of government. In the draft constitution for the Congress sketched by Gandhi, he held that "... this body of servants derive their authority and power from service ungrudgingly and wisely done to their master, the whole of India."[62]

6. The policies of government should be framed on the basis of *Lok Niti* in place of *Raj Niti*. It means partyless government which has the public good as its aim.

62. Tendulkar, D.G., *Mahatma, Life of Mohandas Karamchand Gandhi*, Vol. VIII, p. 343.

In a State possessing these characteristics, Acharya Vinoba Bhave says, (*i*) the able will devote and concentrate their activities to the service of the people; (*ii*) individuals will be fully self-dependent and help each other; (*iii*) non-violence will be the basis of their continual cooperation or occasional non-cooperation or resistance; and (*iv*) every kind of honest work, moral and monetary, will have equal value. Such a State, with good government, paves the way for a *Sarvodaya* society, a new social order of government; *Ram Raj* or Kingdom of God.

Evaluation. There is something in common in *Sarvodaya* and Communism. Acharya Vinoba Bhave ways, "There is no permanent conflict between the two ideologies—Marxism and Sarvodaya."[63] Both strive for and aim at the State to disappear, abolition of exploitation and the principle : from each according to his capacity to his needs. But there are two significant differences between the two. According to Dr. Kumarappa, in *Sarvodaya*, "its essentially spiritual basis is the very antithesis of Communism which is avowedly materialistic, although in regard to its goal Sarvodaya is similar to Communism."[64] The late K.G. Mashruwala observed that "the difference between Communism and Sarvodaya is not in the ends but in the means." But it cannot be denied that there is much of the Platonic in Acharya Vinoba Bhave's conception of a *Sarvodaya* soceity. *Sarvodaya* "especially in its political aspect," rightly observes Usha Mehta, "is more of an idea which has not as yet taken a practical shape. This is mainly because the utopia of the Sarvodayites flounders on the rock of human nature as it fails to take account of the 'lower' and 'baser' elements of human nature in its over-enthusiasm to emphasise the 'higher' and the 'better'." She further adds, "What is needed is not renunciation either of faith in human goodness or of politics but realising that it will take a millennium before the whole of humanity is transformed to divinity and raising the standard of political understanding and action; the remedy is not less of democracy but more of it."[65]

Whatever be the practical aspect of *Sarvodaya*, the personal followers of Gandhi have purified and ennobled politics, raising it to the faith of humanity. It is that eternal quest for freedom, happiness and social justice for which unceasing efforts have ever been made and shall always be made in all states of social development. "From time to time," says James Bryce, "hope is revived by the appearance of a group of disinterested reformers, whose zeal rouses a nation to sweep away abuses and leave things better than it found them."[66] The *Sarvodayites* are at least a reminder to the political followers of Gandhi of his ideals. Gandhi's influence is not particularly manifest in Indian life today, although spokesmen of nearly all political parties and ideologies frequently refer to him and pay at least lip service to his teachings. Vinoba Bhave, who professed to have no interest in politics, was nevertheless one of the strongest forces in India and the techniques of this itinerant leader had a magic effect on people in all the walks of life.

---

63. *Communism and Sarvodaya,* reprinted in *New Age*, Oct., 1957, p. 41.

64. Editor's Note to Sarvodaya by M.K. Gandhi, p.iv.

65. *"Sarvodaya and Democracy", The Indian Journal of Political Science*, Conference Number, October-December 1959, p.374.

66. *Modern Democracies*, Vol. I, p. 56.

SUGGESTED READINGS

Dhawan, G.N. : *The Political Philosophy of Mahatma Gandhi.*

Dhawan, G.N. : "The Political Philosophy of Mahatma Gandhi", *The Indian Journal of Political Science.* January-March 1948, pp. 1-7.

Gandhi, M. K. : *Hind Swaraj or Indian Home Rule.*

Gandhi, M. K. : *My Non-Violence.*

Gandhi, M. K. : *Non-Violence in Peace and War.*

Ghosal, A.L. : "Gandhian Philosophy", *The Indian Journal of Political Science,* January-March, 1949, April-June 1949, pp. 22-31.

The Indian Journal of Political Science, Conference Number, Oct.-Dec., 1959.

The Indian Journal of Political Science, Conference Number, 1960.

Kripalani. J.B. : *The Gandhian Way.*

Majumdar, B.B. (Ed.) : *Gandhian Concept of State.*

Munshi, K.M. : *Gandhi, The Master.*

Munshi, K.M. : *I Follow the Mahatma.*

Namboodiripad, E.M.S. : *The Mahatma and the Ism.*

Narayan, Jayaprakash : *Towards a New Society.*

Paul F. Power : *Gandhi on World Affairs.*

Pyarelal, *Mahatma Gandhi : The Last Phase,* 2 Vols.

Radhakrishnan, S. (Ed.) : *Mahatma Gandhi : Essays and Reflections of His Life and Work.*

Sitaramayya, B.P. : *Gandhi and Gandhism,* Vol. I, II.

Tendulkar, D.G : *Mahatma, Life of Mohandas Karamchand Gandhi,* 8 Vols.

UNESCO, Seminar on *Gandhian Outlook and Technique,* Ministry of Education, Government of India.

Varma, V.P. : "Gandhi and Marx", *The Indian Journal of Political Science*, April-June 1954, pp. 115-33.

Vinoba Bhave : *Vinoba and His Mission.*

INDEX

M

N

O

P

R

S

T

U

V

W

Z